WILEY

IFRS

2009

Interpretation and
Application of
**International
Financial Reporting
Standards**

BECOME A SUBSCRIBER!

Did you purchase this product from a bookstore?

If you did, it's important for you to become a subscriber. John Wiley & Sons, Inc. may publish, on a periodic basis, supplements and new editions to reflect the latest changes in the subject matter that you *need to know* in order stay competitive in this ever-changing industry. By contacting the Wiley office nearest you, you'll receive any current update at no additional charge. In addition, you'll receive future updates and revised or related volumes on a 30-day examination review.

If you purchased this product directly from John Wiley & Sons, Inc., we have already recorded your subscription for this update service.

To become a subscriber, please call **1-877-762-2974** or send your name, company name (if applicable), address, and the title of the product to:

mailing address:
Supplement Department
John Wiley & Sons, Inc.
One Wiley Drive
Somerset, NJ 08875

e-mail: **subscriber@wiley.com**
fax: **1-732-302-2300**
online: **www.wiley.com**

For customers outside the United States, please contact the Wiley office nearest you:

Professional & Reference Division
John Wiley & Sons Canada, Ltd.
22 Worcester Road
Etobicoke, Ontario M9W 1L1
CANADA
Phone: 416-236-4433
Phone: 1-800-567-4797
Fax: 416-236-4447
E-mail: canada@wiley.com

John Wiley & Sons Australia, Ltd.
33 Park Road
P.O. Box 1226
Milton, Queensland 4064
AUSTRALIA
Phone: 61-7-3859-9755
Fax: 61-7-3859-9715
E-mail: brisbane@johnwiley.com.au

John Wiley & Sons, Ltd.
The Atrium
Southern Gate, Chichester
West Sussex, PO19 8SQ
ENGLAND
Phone: 44-1243-779777
Fax: 44-1243-775878
E-mail: customer@wiley.co.uk

John Wiley & Sons (Asia) Pte. Ltd.
2 Clementi Loop #02-01
SINGAPORE 129809
Phone: 65-64632400
Fax: 65-64634604/5/6
Customer Service: 65-64604280
E-mail: enquiry@wiley.com.sg

WILEY

IFRS

2009

Interpretation and Application of International Financial Reporting Standards

Barry J. Epstein   Eva K. Jermakowicz

WILEY

JOHN WILEY & SONS, INC.

CONTENTS

PREFACE

IFRS: Interpretation and Application of International Financial Reporting Standards provides analytical explanations and copious illustrations of all current accounting principles promulgated by the IASB (and its predecessor, the IASC). The book integrates the accounting principles promulgated by the Board—international financial reporting standards (IFRS), together with the earlier, still applicable international accounting standards (IAS)—and by the Board's body for responding to more narrowly focused issues—the International Financial Reporting Interpretations Committee (IFRIC), which succeeded the IASC's Standing Interpretations Committee (SIC). These materials have been synthesized into a user-oriented topical format, eliminating the need for readers to first be knowledgeable about the names or numbers of the salient professional standards.

IFRS have been adopted or adapted by over one hundred nations for mandatory or optional financial reporting by public and private entities, with many more adoptions scheduled to occur over the next very few years. A key event in the growing recognition of the primacy of IFRS was the US Securities and Exchange Commission's 2007 waiving of the former reconciliation to US GAAP requirement for foreign registrants preparing fully IFRS-compliant financial reports. Another important event, having worldwide implications, occurred in 2008 when the SEC granted permission for qualified "early adopters" to file financial reports for 2009 based on IFRS, with a concomitant promise to decide in 2011 whether to entirely phase out US GAAP in favor of IFRS. Universal adoption of IRFS appears to now be a virtual certainty, probably within a very few years.

The primary objective of this book is to assist the practitioner to navigate the myriad practical problems faced in applying IFRS. Accordingly, the paramount goal has been to incorporate meaningful, real-world-type examples in guiding users in the application of IFRS to complex fact situations that must be dealt with in the actual practice of accounting. In addition to this emphasis, a major strength of this book is that it does explain the theory of IFRS in sufficient detail to serve as a valuable adjunct to, or substitute for, accounting textbooks. Not merely a reiteration of currently promulgated IFRS, it provides the user with an understanding of the underlying conceptual basis for the rules, to enable the reasoning by analogy that is so necessary in dealing with a complex, fast-changing world of commercial arrangements and structures. It is based on the authors' belief that proper application of IFRS demands an understanding of the logical underpinnings of its technical requirements. This is perhaps more true of IFRS than of various national GAAP sets of standards, since IFRS is by design more "principles based" and hence less prescriptive, leaving practitioners with a proportionately greater challenge in actually applying the rules.

Each chapter of this book, or major section thereof, provides an overview discussion of the perspective and key issues associated with the topics covered; a listing of the professional pronouncements that guide practice; and a detailed discussion of the concepts and accompanying examples. A comprehensive checklist following the main text offers practical guidance to preparing financial statement disclosures in accordance with IFRS. Also included is an up-to-date, detailed, tabular comparison between IFRS and US GAAP, keyed to the chapters of this book. The book features copious examples of actual informative disclosures made by companies currently reporting under IFRS.

The 2009 edition of *Wiley IFRS* benefits from the helpful insights provided by Homiyar Wykes, B.Com, ACA (India), the Group Financial Controller for Stolt-Nielsen SA, a publicly listed (Oslo Stock Exchange) company and one of the world's leading providers of transportation services for bulk liquid chemicals, edible oils and acids through the parcel tanker, tank container, terminal, rail and barge services.

Mr. Wykes, who led the IFRS transition project for Stolt-Nielsen from US GAAP to IFRS, provided the case study based on this experience, which in included in Chapter 1. His prior accounting and auditing experience—with accounting firms Andersen and KPMG, and ArcelorMittal, the steel producer—includes postings in Bombay, Dubai, and London, and involvement in SEC filings and other challenging assignments. The authors express their gratitude for his many useful comments on this book.

The authors' wish is that this book will serve practitioners, faculty, and students as a reliable reference tool, to facilitate their understanding of, and ability to apply, the complexities of the authoritative literature. Comments from readers, both as to errors and omissions and as to proposed improvements for future editions, should be addressed to Barry J. Epstein, c/o John Wiley & Sons, Inc., 155 N. 3rd Street, Suite 502, DeKalb, Illinois 60115, prior to May 15, 2009, for consideration for the 2010 edition.

Barry J. Epstein
Eva K. Jermakowicz
December 2008

ABOUT THE AUTHORS

Barry J. Epstein, PhD, CPA, a partner in the firm Russell Novak & Company, LLP, has forty-two years' experience in the public accounting profession, as auditor, technical director/partner for several national and local firms, and as a consulting and testifying financial reporting and auditing expert on over one-hundred and twenty litigation matters to date. His current practice is concentrated on providing technical consultations to CPA firms and corporations on US GAAP and IFRS accounting and financial reporting matters; on US and international auditing standards; matters involving financial analysis; forensic accounting investigations; and on corporate governance matters. He regularly serves as an accounting, auditing, financial reporting, and financial analysis expert in litigation matters, including assignments for both the private sector entities and governmental agencies.

Dr. Epstein is a widely published authority on accounting and auditing. His current publications include *Wiley GAAP*, now in its 25th edition, for which he is the lead coauthor. He has also appeared on over a dozen national radio and television programs discussing the crises in corporate financial reporting and corporate governance, has presented hundreds of educational programs to professional and corporate groups in the US and internationally, and has had dozens of articles published in professional journals. He previously chaired the Audit Committee of the AICPA's Board of Examiners, responsible for the Uniform CPA Examination, and has served on other professional panels at state and national levels.

Dr Epstein holds degrees from DePaul University (Chicago—BSC, accounting and finance, 1967) University of Chicago (MBA, economics and industrial relations, 1969), and University of Pittsburgh (PhD, information systems and finance, 1979). He is a member of American Institute of Certified Public Accountants, Illinois CPA Society, and American Accounting Association

Eva K. Jermakowicz, PhD, CPA, has taught accounting for over twenty-five years and has served as a consultant to international organizations and businesses. She is currently a Professor of Accounting and Chair of the Accounting and Business Law Department at Tennessee State University. Her previous positions were on the faculties of the University of Southern Indiana and Warsaw Tech University in Poland, and she has taught accounting courses in several additional countries. Dr. Jermakowicz was a Fulbright scholar under the European Union Affairs Research Program in Brussels, Belgium, for the academic year 2003-2004, where her project was "Convergence of National Accounting Standards with International Financial Reporting Standards." She was also a Fulbright scholar in Poland in 1997. Dr. Jermakowicz has consulted on international projects under the auspices of the World Bank, the United Nations, and Nicom Consulting, Ltd. Her primary areas of interest are international accounting and finance.

Dr. Jermakowicz has had numerous articles published in academic journals and proceedings, including *Abacus, Journal of International Accounting, Auditing & Taxation, Journal of International Financial Management & Accounting, Multinational Finance Journal, Journal of Accounting and Finance Research, Bank Accounting & Finance, Financial Executive, Strategic Finance, CPA Journal,* and *Butterworths Journal of International Banking and Financial Law.* She is a member of many professional organizations, including the American Accounting Association, European Accounting Association, American Institute of Certified Public Accountants, the Tennessee Society of CPAs, and the Institute of Management Accountants.

1 INTRODUCTION TO INTERNATIONAL FINANCIAL REPORTING STANDARDS

The year 2005 marked the start of a new era in global conduct of business, and the fulfillment of a thirty-year effort to create the financial reporting rules for a worldwide capital market. For during that year's financial reporting cycle, as many as 7,000 listed companies in the 25 European Union member states, plus many others in countries such as Australia, New Zealand, Russia, and South Africa were expected (in the EU, required) to produce annual financial statements in compliance with a single set of international rules—International Financial Reporting Standards (IFRS). Many other business entities, while not publicly held and not currently required to comply with IFRS, will also do so, either immediately or over time, in order to conform to what is clearly becoming the new worldwide standard. Since there are about 15,000 SEC-registered companies in the USA that prepare financial statements in accordance with US GAAP (plus countless nonpublicly held companies also reporting under GAAP), the vast majority of the world's large businesses are now reporting under one or the other of these two comprehensive systems of accounting and financial reporting rules.

Most other national GAAP standards have been reduced in importance or are being phased out as nations all over the worlds are now embracing IFRS. For example, Canada announced that Canadian GAAP (which was very similar to US GAAP) will be eliminated and replaced by IFRS in 2011. More immediately, China has required that listed companies employ IFRS beginning with 2007 financial reporting. Both 2007 and 2008 (to date) have proven to be watershed years for the growing acceptability of IFRS, as well. In 2007 the SEC dropped the former reconciliation requirement (to US GAAP) that had long applied to foreign private registrants reporting under fully compliant IFRS. This easing of US registration requirements for foreign companies seeking to enjoy the benefits of listings in the US led, quite naturally, to a call for permitting domestic companies to freely choose between financial reporting under US GAAP and IFRS. As of late 2008, the SEC has begun the process of acquiescence, first for the largest companies in those industries having (world-wide) the preponderance of IFRS adopters, and later for all publicly held companies. None-theless, it is highly probable that only US GAAP will for the foreseeable future remain as the set of financial reporting standards of choice by the vast majority of US businesses, which are privately held and not subject to SEC requirements.

The impetus to convergence of presently disparate financial reporting standards has been, in the main, to facilitate the free flow of capital so that, for example, investors in the United States will be willing to finance business in, say, China or the Czech Republic. Hav-ing access to financial statements that are written in the same "language" would eliminate what has historically been a major impediment to engendering investor confidence. Addi-tionally, the ability to list a company's securities on a stock exchange has generally required filings with national regulatory authorities that have insisted on either conformity with local GAAP or formal reconciliation to local GAAP. Since either of these procedures was tedious and time-consuming, and the human resources and technical knowledge to do so were in short supply, many otherwise anxious would-be registrants forwent the opportunity to broad-en their investor bases and potentially lower their cost of capital.

These difficulties are probably soon coming to an end, however. The historic 2002 Nor-walk Agreement between the US standard setter, FASB, and the IASB called for "conver-gence" of the two sets of standards, and indeed a number of revisions of either US GAAP or IFRS have already taken place to implement this commitment, with more changes expected in the immediate future. More recently, as noted, the US Securities and Exchange Commis-sion waived the longstanding requirement that foreign private issuers (i.e., registrants) filing financial statements prepared in accordance with full IFRS (i.e., *not* European or other na-tional versions of IFRS) reconcile those financial statements to US GAAP. It has made a rule change that will permit US domestic registrants to choose between compliance with US GAAP and IFRS. These current and prospective changes, coupled with ongoing conver-gence efforts, seemingly portend a greatly expanded usage of IFRS in world commerce.

It thus is expected that, by the early to midportion of the next decade, all or virtually all distinctions between US GAAP and IFRS will be eliminated, if US GAAP remains an im-portant force at all, although there remain challenging issues to be resolved. For one exam-ple, while IFRS bans the use of LIFO costing for inventories, it remains a popular financial reporting method under US GAAP because of a "conformity rule" that permits entities to use the method for tax reporting only if it is also used for general-purpose external financial re-porting. In times of increasing costs, LIFO almost inevitably results in tax deferrals and is thus widely employed.

Origins and Early History of the IASB

Financial reporting in the developed world evolved from two broad models, whose ob-jectives were somewhat different. The earliest systematized form of accounting regulation developed in continental Europe, starting in France in 1673. Here a requirement for an an-nual fair value statement of financial position was introduced by the government as a means of protecting the economy from bankruptcies. This form of accounting at the initiative of the state to control economic actors was copied by other states and later incorporated in the 1807 Napoleonic Commercial Code. This method of regulating the economy expanded rapidly throughout continental Europe, partly through Napoleon's efforts and partly through a wil-lingness on the part of European regulators to borrow ideas from each other. This "code law" family of reporting practices was much developed by Germany after its 1870 unification, with the emphasis moving away from market values to historical cost and systematic depreciation. It was used later by governments as the basis of tax assessment when taxes on profits started to be introduced, mostly in the early twentieth century.

This model of accounting serves primarily as a means of moderating relationships between the individual company and the state. It serves for tax assessment, and to limit dividend payments, and it is also a means of protecting the running of the economy by sanctioning individual businesses that are not financially sound or were run imprudently. While the model has been adapted for stock market reporting and group (consolidated) structures, this is not its main focus.

The other model did not appear until the nineteenth century and arose as a consequence of the industrial revolution. Industrialization created the need for large concentrations of capital to undertake industrial projects (initially, canals and railways) and to spread risks between many investors. In this model the financial report provided a means of monitoring the activities of large businesses in order to inform their (nonmanagement) shareholders. Financial reporting for capital markets purposes developed initially in the UK, in a common-law environment where the state legislated as little as possible and left a large degree of interpretation to practice and for the sanction of the courts. This approach was rapidly adopted by the US as it, too, became industrialized. As the US developed the idea of groups of companies controlled from a single head office (towards the end of the nineteenth century), this philosophy of financial reporting began to become focused on consolidated accounts and the group, rather than the individual company. For different reasons, neither the UK nor the US governments saw this reporting framework as appropriate for income tax purposes, and in this tradition, while the financial reports inform the assessment process, taxation retains a separate stream of law, which has had little influence on financial reporting.

The second model of financial reporting, generally regarded as the Anglo-Saxon financial reporting approach, can be characterized as focusing on the relationship between the business and the investor, and on the flow of information to the capital markets. Government still uses reporting as a means of regulating economic activity (e.g., the SEC's mission is to protect the investor and ensure that the securities markets run efficiently), but the financial report is aimed at the investor, not the government.

Neither of the two above-described approaches to financial reporting is particularly useful in an agricultural economy, or to one that consists entirely of microbusinesses, in the opinion of many observers. Nonetheless, as countries have developed economically (or as they were colonized by industrialized nations) they have adopted variants of one or the other of these two models.

IFRS are an example of the second, capital market-oriented, systems of financial reporting rules. The original international standard setter, the International Accounting Standards Committee (IASC), was formed in 1973, during a period of considerable change in accounting regulation. In the US the Financial Accounting Standards Board (FASB) had just been created, in the UK the first national standard setter had recently been organized, the EU was working on the main plank of its own accounting harmonization plan (the Fourth Directive), and both the UN and the OECD were shortly to create their own accounting committees. The IASC was launched in the wake of the 1972 World Accounting Congress (a five-yearly get-together of the international profession) after an informal meeting between representatives of the British profession (Institute of Chartered Accountants in England and Wales—ICAEW) and the American profession (American Institute of Certified Public Accountants—AICPA).

A rapid set of negotiations resulted in the professional bodies of Canada, Australia, Mexico, Japan, France, Germany, the Netherlands, and New Zealand being invited to join with the US and UK to form the international body. Due to pressure (coupled with a financial subsidy) from the UK, the IASC was established in London, where its successor, the IASB, remains today.

The actual reasons for the IASC's creation are unclear. A need for a common language of business was felt, to deal with a growing volume of international business, but other more political motives abounded also. For example, some believe that the major motivation was that the British wanted to create an international standard setter to trump the regional initiatives within the EU, which leaned heavily to the Code model of reporting, in contrast to what was the norm in the UK and almost all English-speaking nations.

In the first phase of its existence, the IASC had mixed fortunes. Once the International Federation of Accountants (IFAC) was formed in 1977 (at the next World Congress of Accountants), the IASC had to fight off attempts to become a part of IFAC. It managed to resist, coming to a compromise where IASC remained independent but all IFAC members were automatically members of IASC, and IFAC was able to nominate the membership of the standard-setting Board.

Both the UN and OECD were active in international rule making in the 1970s but the IASC successfully persuaded them that they should leave recognition and measurement rules to the IASC. However, having established itself as the unique international rule maker, IASC had great difficulty in persuading anyone to use its rules. Although member professional bodies were theoretically committed to pushing for the use of IFRS at the national level, in practice few national bodies were influential in standard setting in their respective countries, and others (including the US and UK) preferred their national standards to whatever IASC might propose. In Europe, IFRS were used by some reporting entities in Italy and Switzerland, and national standard setters in some countries such as Malaysia began to use IFRS as an input to their national rules, while not necessarily adopting them as written by the IASC or giving explicit recognition to the fact that IFRS were being adopted in part as national GAAP.

IASC's efforts entered a new phase in 1987, which led directly to its 2001 reorganization, when the then-Secretary General, David Cairns, encouraged by the US SEC, negotiated an agreement with the International Organization of Securities Commissions (IOSCO). IOSCO was interested in identifying a common international "passport" whereby companies could be accepted for secondary listing in the jurisdiction of any IOSCO member. The concept was that, whatever the listing rules in a company's primary stock exchange, there would be a common minimum package which all stock exchanges would accept from foreign companies seeking a secondary listing. IOSCO was prepared to endorse IFRS as the financial reporting basis for this passport, provided that the international standards could be brought up to a quality and comprehensiveness level that IOSCO stipulated.

Historically, a major criticism of IFRS had been that it essentially endorsed all the accounting methods then in wide use, effectively becoming a "lowest common denominator" set of standards. The trend in national GAAP had been to narrow the range of acceptable alternatives, although uniformity in accounting had not been anticipated as a near-term result. The IOSCO agreement energized IASC to improve the existing standards by removing the many alternative treatments that were then permitted under the standards, thereby improving comparability across reporting entities. The IASC launched its *Comparability and Improvements Project* with the goal of developing a "core set of standards" that would satisfy IOSCO. These were complete by 1993, not without difficulties and spirited disagreements among the members, but then—to the great frustration of the IASC—these were not accepted by IOSCO. Rather than endorsing the standard-setting process of IASC, as was hoped for, IOSCO seemingly wanted to cherry-pick individual standards. Such a process could not realistically result in near-term endorsement of IFRS for cross-border securities registrations.

Ultimately, the collaboration was relaunched in 1995, with IASC under new leadership, and this began a further period of frenetic activities, where existing standards were again reviewed and revised, and new standards were created to fill perceived gaps in IFRS. This time the set of standards included, among others, IAS 39, on recognition and measurement of financial instruments, which was endorsed, at the very last moment and with great difficulty, as a compromise, purportedly interim standard.

At the same time, the IASC had undertaken an effort to consider its future structure. In part, this was the result of pressure exerted by the US SEC and also by the US private sector standard setter, the FASB, which were seemingly concerned that IFRS were not being developed by "due process." While the various parties may have had their own agendas, in fact the IFRS were in need of strengthening, particularly as to reducing the range of diverse but accepted alternatives for similar transactions and events. The challenges presented to IASB ultimately would serve to make IFRS stronger.

If IASC was to be the standard setter endorsed by the world's stock exchange regulators, it would need a structure that reflected that level of responsibility. The historical Anglo-Saxon standard-setting model—where professional accountants set the rules for themselves—had largely been abandoned in the twenty-five years since the IASC was formed, and standards were mostly being set by dedicated and independent national boards such as the FASB, and not by profession-dominated bodies like the AICPA. The choice, as restructuring became inevitable, was between a large, representative approach—much like the existing IASC structure, but possibly where national standard setters appointed representatives—or a small, professional body of experienced standard setters which worked independently of national interests.

The end of this phase of the international standard setting, and the resolution of these issues, came about within a short period in 2000. In May of that year, IOSCO members voted to endorse IASC standards, albeit subject to a number of reservations (see discussion later in this chapter). This was a considerable step forward for the IASC, which itself was quickly exceeded by an announcement in June 2000 that the European Commission intended to adopt IFRS as the requirement for primary listings in all member states. This planned full endorsement by the EU eclipsed the lukewarm IOSCO approval, and since then the EU has appeared to be the more influential body insofar as gaining acceptance for IFRS has been concerned. Indeed, the once-important IOSCO endorsement has become of little importance given subsequent developments, including the EU mandate and convergence efforts among several standard-setting bodies.

In July 2000, IASC members voted to abandon the organization's former structure, which was based on professional bodies, and adopt a new structure: beginning in 2001, standards would be set by a professional board, financed by voluntary contributions raised by a new oversight body.

The Current Structure

The formal structure put in place in 2000 has the IASC Foundation, a Delaware corporation, as its keystone. The Trustees of the IASC Foundation have both the responsibility to raise the $19 million a year currently needed to finance standard setting, and the responsibility of appointing members to the International Accounting Standards Board (IASB), the International Financial Reporting Interpretations Committee (IFRIC) and the Standards Advisory Council (SAC).

The Standards Advisory Council (SAC) meets with the IASB three times a year, generally for two days. The SAC consists of about 50 members, nominated in their personal (not organizational) capacity, but are usually supported by organizations that have an interest in international reporting. Members currently include analysts, corporate executives, auditors, standard setters, and stock exchange regulators. The members are supposed to serve as a channel for communication between the IASB and its wider group of constituents, to suggest topics for the IASB's agenda, and to discuss IASB proposals.

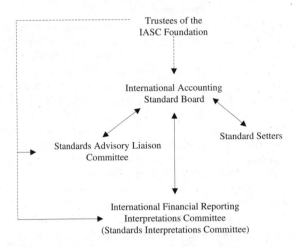

The International Financial Reporting Interpretations Committee (IFRIC) is a committee comprised mostly of technical partners in audit firms but also includes preparers and users. It succeeded the Standards Interpretations Committee (SIC), which had been created by the IASC. IFRIC's function is to answer technical queries from constituents about how to interpret IFRS—in effect, filling in the cracks between different rules. In recent times it has also proposed modifications to standards to the IASB, in response to perceived operational difficulties or need to improve consistency. IFRIC liaises with the US Emerging Issues Task Force and similar bodies liaison as standard setters, to try at preserve convergence at the level of interpretation. It is also establishing relations with stock exchange regulators, who may be involved in making decisions about the acceptability of accounting practices, which will have the effect of interpreting IFRS.

The liaison standard setters are national bodies from Australia, Canada, France, Germany, UK, USA, and Japan. Each of these bodies has a special relationship with a Board member, who normally maintains an office with the national standard setter and is responsible for liaison between the international body and the national body. This, together with the SAC, was the solution arrived at by the old IASC in an attempt to preserve some degree of geographical representation. However, this has been somewhat overtaken by events: as far as the EU is concerned, its interaction with the IASB is through EFRAG (see below), which has no formal liaison member of the Board. The IASB Deputy Chairman has performed this function, but while France, Germany and the UK individually have liaison, EFRAG and the European Commission are, so far, outside this structure.

Furthermore, there are many national standard setters, particularly from developing countries, that have no seat on the SAC, and therefore have no direct link with the IASB, despite the fact that many of them seek to reflect IASB standards in their national standards. At the 2002 World Congress in Hong Kong, the IASB held an open meeting for national standard setters, which was met with enthusiasm. As a result, IASB began to provide time concurrent with formal liaison standard setters' meetings for any other interested standard setters to attend. While this practice was not enshrined in either the Constitution or the

IASB's operating procedures, both are under review at the moment, and any changes made will be in place by the end of 2009.

Process of IFRS Standard Setting

The IASB has a formal due process which is set out in the *Preface to IFRS*, revised in 2001. At a minimum, a proposed standard should be exposed for comment, and these comments should be reviewed before issuance of a final standard, with debates open to the public. However, this formal process is rounded out in practice, with wider consultation taking place on an informal basis.

The IASB's agenda is determined in various ways. Suggestions are made by the Trustees, the SAC, liaison standard setters, the international audit firms and others. These are debated by IASB and tentative conclusions are discussed with the various consultative bodies. The IASB also has a joint agenda committee with the FASB. Long-range projects are first put on the research agenda, which means that preliminary work is being done on collecting information about the problem and potential solutions. Projects can also arrive on the current agenda outside that route.

The agenda was largely dominated in the years after 2001 by the need to round out the legacy standards, to ensure that there would be a full range of standards for European companies moving to IFRS in 2005. Also, it was recognized that there was an urgent need to effect modifications to many standards in the name of convergence (e.g., acquisition accounting and goodwill) and to make needed improvements to other existing standards. These needs were largely met by mid-2004.

Once a project reaches the current agenda, the formal process is that the staff (a group of about 20 technical staff permanently employed by the IASB) drafts papers which are then discussed by IASB in open meetings. Following that debate, the staff rewrites the paper, or writes a new paper which is debated at a subsequent meeting. In theory there is an internal process where the staff proposes solutions, and IASB either accepts or rejects them. In practice the process is more involved: sometimes (especially for projects like financial instruments) specific Board members are allocated a special responsibility for the project, and they discuss the problems regularly with the relevant staff, helping to build the papers that come to the Board. Equally, Board members may write or speak directly to the staff outside of the formal meeting process to indicate concerns about one thing or another.

The process usually involves: (1) discussion of a paper outlining the principal issues; (2) preparation of an Exposure Draft that incorporates the tentative decisions taken by the Board—during which process many of these are redebated, sometimes several times; (3) publication of the Exposure Draft; (4) analysis of comments received on the Exposure Draft; (5) debate and issue of the final standard, accompanied by application guidance and a document setting out the *Basis for Conclusions* (the reasons why IASB rejected some solutions and preferred others). Final ballots on the Exposure Draft and the final standard are carried out in secret, but otherwise the process is quite open, with outsiders able to consult project summaries on the IASB Web site and attend Board meetings if they wish. Of course, the informal exchanges between staff and Board on a day-to-day basis are not visible to the public, nor are the meetings where IASB takes strategic and administrative decisions.

The basic due process can be modified in different circumstances. If the project is controversial or particularly difficult, IASB may issue a discussion paper before proceeding to Exposure Draft stage. It reissued a discussion paper on stock options before proceeding to IFRS 2, *Share-Based Payment*. It is also following this pattern with its financial statement presentation project and its project on standards for small and medium-sized entities. Such a discussion paper may just set out what the staff considers to be the issues, or it may do that as well as indicate the Board's preliminary views.

IASB may also hold some form of public consultation during the process. For example, when revising IAS 39, *Financial Instruments: Recognition and Measurement,* in 2003, IASB held round table discussions. Respondents to the Exposure Draft were invited to participate in small groups with Board members where they could put forward their views and engage in debate.

Apart from these formal consultative processes, IASB also carries out field trials of some standards (as it recently did on performance reporting and insurance), where volunteer preparers apply proposed new standards. The international audit firms receive IASB papers as a result of their membership on IFRIC and are also invited to comment informally at various stages of standard development.

Constraints

The debate within IASB demonstrates the existence of certain pervasive constraints that will influence the decisions taken by it. A prime concern has, heretofore, been achieving *convergence*. In October 2002, the IASB signed an agreement with the FASB (the so-called Norwalk Agreement) stating that the two boards would seek to remove differences and converge on high-quality standards. This agreement set in motion short-term adjustments and both standard setters subsequently issued a number of Exposure Drafts and final standards changing their respective standards in order to converge with the other on certain issues. The agreement also involved a commitment to the long-term development of joint projects (business combinations, performance reporting, revenue recognition, etc.).

The desire for convergence was driven to a great extent by the perception that international investment is made riskier by the use of multiple reporting frameworks, and that the global capital market would benefit from the imposition of a single global reporting basis— but also specifically by the knowledge that European companies that wished to be listed in the US needed to provide reconciliations of their equity and earnings to US GAAP when they did this. Foreign companies registered with the SEC are required to prepare an annual filing on Form 20-F that, until late 2007—if the entity did not prepare its financial statements under US GAAP—required a reconciliation between the entity's IFRS or national GAAP and US GAAP for earnings and equity. This reconciliation was said to be costly to prepare, and resulted in companies reporting, in effect, two different operating results for the year, which was not always understood or appreciated by the capital markets. As of year-end 2007, this requirement was eliminated, provided that the foreign private issuers (i.e., SEC registrants) complied fully with IFRS. Note that IFRS as adopted by the European Union contains departures from IFRS as promulgated by the IASB, and thus reconciliation has not been (thus far, at least) waived.

A major concern for financial reporting is that of *consistency*, but this is a complex matter, since IASB has something of a hierarchy of consistency. As a paramount consideration, IASB would want a new standard to be consistent with its *Conceptual Framework* (discussed below). Thereafter, there may be conflicts both between being consistent with US GAAP and being consistent with preexisting IFRS. However, there is little or no desire to maintain consistency with standards marked for extinction or in clear need of major revision. For example, IASB believes that a number of extant standards are inconsistent with the *Framework* (e.g., IAS 20 on government grants), and need to be changed, or are ineffective or obsolete (e.g., IAS 17 on leases), so there is little purpose in seeking to make a new standard consistent with them. Equally, since it aims to converge with US GAAP, it seems illogical to adopt a solution that is deliberately at variance with US GAAP, which will then have to be reconsidered as part of the convergence program. (Note that the convergence effort is expected, at least in the near term, to continue, notwithstanding the elimination of the SEC's reconciliation requirement and the prospective replacement of US GAAP for public company financial reporting by IFRS.)

Those members of IASB who have worked in North America are concerned that standards avoid creating abuse opportunities. Experience has sadly shown that there may well be attempts by preparers to evade the intended result of accounting standards, using so-called "financial engineering," in order to be able to achieve the earnings or presentations in the statement of financial position that are desired, particularly in the short term (e.g., quarterly earnings). This concern is sometimes manifested as a desire to impose uniform and inflexible standards, allowing few or no exceptions. There is a justifiable perception that many standards become very complicated because they contain too many exceptions to a simple and basic rule (for example: eliminate complex lease accounting requirements and simply report the property rights and debt obligations implicit in all lease arrangements).

IASB also manifests some concerns about the practicality of the solutions it mandates. While some preparers might think that it is not sympathetic enough in this regard, it actually has limited the extent to which it requires restatements of previous years' reported results when the rules change, particularly in IFRS 1, *First-Time Adoption*. The *Framework* does include a cost/benefit constraint—that the costs of the financial reporting should not be greater than the benefits to be gained from the information—which is often invoked during debates over proposed standards, although IASB considers that preparers are not the best ones to measure the benefits of disclosure.

There is also a procedural constraint that IASB has to manage, which is the relationship between the Exposure Draft and the final standard. IASB's due process requires that there should be nothing introduced in the final standard that was not exposed at the Exposure Draft stage, as otherwise there must be reexposure of the material. This means that where there are several solutions possible, or where a line can be drawn in several places, IASB may tend towards the most extreme position in the Exposure Draft, so as not to narrow its choices when further deliberating the proposal in the light of constituents' comments.

Conceptual Framework for Financial Reporting

The IASB inherited the IASC's *Framework for the Preparation and Presentation of Financial Statements* (the *Framework*). Like the other current conceptual frameworks among Anglo-Saxon standard setters, this derives from the US conceptual framework, or at least those parts of it completed in the 1970s. The *Framework* states that "the objective of financial statements is to provide information about the financial position, performance and changes in financial position of an entity that is useful to a wide range of users in making economic decisions." The information needs of investors are deemed to be of paramount concern, but if financial statements meet their needs, other users' needs would generally also be satisfied.

The *Framework* holds that users need to evaluate the ability of the entity to generate cash and the timing and certainty of its generation. The financial position is affected by the economic resources controlled by the entity, its financial structure, its liquidity and solvency, and its capacity to adapt to changes in the environment in which it operates.

The qualitative characteristics of financial statements are understandability, relevance, reliability and comparability. Reliability comprises representational faithfulness, substance over form, completeness, neutrality and prudence. It suggests that these are subject to a cost/benefit constraint and that in practice there will often be a trade-off between characteristics. The *Framework* does not specifically include a "true and fair" requirement, but says that application of the specified qualitative characteristics should result in statements that present fairly or are true and fair. IAS 1, *Presentation of Financial Statements*, as revised in 2007, states that financial statements are "a structured representation of the financial position and financial performance of an entity...(whose) objective...is to provide information about the financial position, financial performance and cash flows of an entity that is useful to a wide range of users in making economic decisions." It further states that "fair presentation requires faithful representation of the effects of transactions, other events and conditions in accordance with the definitions and recognition criteria...set out in the *Framework*....The application of IFRS, with additional disclosure when necessary, is presumed to result in financial statements that achieve a fair presentation."

Of great importance are the definitions of assets and liabilities. According to IASB, "an asset is a resource controlled by the entity as a result of past events and from which future economic benefits are expected to flow to the entity." A liability is a "present obligation of the entity arising from past events, the settlement of which is expected to result in an outflow from the entity of resources embodying future benefits." Equity is simply a residual arrived at by deducting the liabilities from assets. Neither asset nor liability are recognized in the financial statements unless they have a cost or value that can be measured reliably—which, as the *Framework* acknowledges, means that some assets and liabilities may remain unrecognized.

The asset and liability definitions have, in the past, not been central to financial reporting standards, many of which were instead guided by a "performance" view of the financial statements. For example, IAS 20 on government grants has been severely criticized and targeted for either revision or elimination, in part because it allows government grants to be treated as a deferred credit and amortized to earnings, while a deferred credit does not meet the *Framework* definition of a liability. Similarly, IFRS 3 requires that where a bargain purchase is identified in a business combination, a gain on a bargain purchase (negative goodwill) should be released to profit or loss immediately—IAS 22 treated it as a deferred credit, which however did not actually meet the defined criteria for recognition as a liability.

Accounting standards are now largely driven by statement of financial position considerations. Both FASB and IASB now intend to analyze solutions to reporting issues in terms of whether they cause any changes in assets or liabilities. The revenue recognition project that both bodies are pursuing is perhaps the ultimate example of this new and rigorous perspective. This project has tentatively embraced the view that where an entity receives an order and has a legally enforceable contract to supply goods or services, the entity has both an asset (the right to receive future revenue) and a liability (the obligation to fulfill the order) and it follows that, depending upon the measurement of the asset and the liability, some earnings could be recognized at that point. This would be a sharp departure from existing GAAP, under which executory contracts (i.e., contracts upon which neither party has yet performed) are almost never formally recognized, and never create earnings.

The IASB *Framework* is relatively silent on measurement issues. The three paragraphs that address this matter merely mention that several different measurement bases are available and that historical cost is the most common. Revaluation of tangible fixed assets is, for example, perfectly acceptable under IFRS for the moment. In practice IFRS have a mixed attribute model, based mainly in historical cost, but using value in use (the present value of expected future cash flows from the use of the asset within the entity) for impairment and fair value (market value) for some financial instruments, biological assets, business combinations and investment properties.

FASB and IASB have been, since 2005, revisiting their respective conceptual frameworks, the objective of which is to build on them by refining and updating them and developing them into a common framework that both can use in developing accounting standards.

With concurrent IASB and FASB deliberations and a single integrated staff team, this is truly an international project. IASB believes that it has made good progress on the first phase of the project. Most of the debate for the first year or so focused on the objectives of financial reporting and the qualitative characteristics of decision-useful financial reporting information, and a joint Discussion Paper on these matters was issued in late 2006. This was followed, in May 2008, by Exposure Drafts of the first two (of eight) chapters for the proposed new conceptual framework. The first two chapters deal with, respectively, the objective of financial reporting and the qualitative characteristics of decision-useful financial reporting information.

Regarding the objective of financial reporting, the Exposure Draft proposes the following definition:

> *The objective of general purpose financial reporting is to provide financial information about the reporting entity that is useful to present and potential equity investors, lenders and other creditors in making decisions in their capacity as capital providers. Capital providers are the primary users of financial reporting. To accomplish the objective, financial reports should communicate information about an entity's economic resources, claims on those resources, and the transactions and other events and circumstances that change them. The degree to which that financial information is useful will depend on its qualitative characteristics.*

As with the existing FASB Conceptual Framework, this definition of the objective for financial reporting has a wider scope than financial statements, *per se*. It actually sets forth the objective of financial reporting in general, including a range of possible narrative and other presentations that would accompany and amplify the financial statements.

Financial reporting is aimed primarily at capital providers. That does not mean that others, such as management, will not find financial reports useful, but rather that, in deciding on the principles for recognition, measurement, presentation, and disclosure, the information needs of capital providers are to be given paramount consideration.

The draft holds that *decision usefulness* to capital providers is the overriding purpose of financial reporting. Providing information about *management stewardship* of the assets entrusted to it is an important part of that objective, however. The language of the Exposure Draft cites *present and potential* investors as its means of acknowledging that general purpose financial reports are used both for future investment decisions as well as assessing the stewardship of resources already committed to the entity.

The draft identifies equity investors, lenders and other creditors (including suppliers, employees and customers) as *capital providers*, which are those whose information needs are to be met through general purpose financial reports. Governments, their agencies, regulatory bodies, and members of the public are identified as groups that may find the information in general purpose financial reports useful, but these are not defined as being primary users.

The Exposure Draft continues with the current philosophy that financial reporting should provide information that enables capital providers to assess the entity's ability to generate net cash inflows, coupled with an ability to assess management's ability to protect and enhance the capital providers' investments.

The *stewardship responsibilities of management* are addressed explicitly by the draft document, which notes that management "is accountable to the entity's capital providers for the custody and safekeeping of the entity's economic resources and for their efficient and profitable use" and that the entity complies with applicable laws, regulations and contractual requirements. The ability of management to discharge these responsibilities effectively has an obvious impact on the entity's ability to generate future net cash inflows, suggesting that potential investors are also assessing management performance as they make their investment decisions.

IASB and FASB both note that users of financial reports should be aware of the limitations of the information included in financial reports—specifically because the information is heavily based on estimates, rather than exact measures, and thus involve the application of judgment. Also, users are cautioned to recognize that financial reports are only one source, of potentially many, of information needed by those making investment, credit and similar resource allocation decisions. Thus, other sources of relevant information must also be consulted, for insights about general economic conditions, political events and industry outlooks, among possibly many other topics.

The draft holds that information about the effects of transactions and other events that change assets and liabilities is also essential. Financial reporting must also include management's explanations (an example being the *management discussion and analysis* required under SEC filings in the US), since management knows more about the entity than could any external users. Such explanations, properly constructed and communicated, should provide insight into significant estimates and assumptions used by management.

Chapter two of the proposed new conceptual framework document, which has also been exposed for comment, addresses the qualitative characteristics and constraints of decision-useful financial reporting information. IASB and FASB have refined the approach first seen in the earlier (2006) Discussion Paper, such that there are now two fundamental qualitative characteristics:

- Relevance, and
- Faithful representation.

In addition, there are certain characteristics that are said to enhance the decision-usefulness of financial information. These are complementary to the fundamental qualitative characteristics and are: comparability (including consistency), verifiability, timeliness and understandability. These are defined as follows by the Exposure Draft:

Relevant information is that which has predictive value, confirmatory value or both; in other words it is capable of influencing the decisions of capital providers. The users do not need to use such information, but merely have to be given access to it.

Faithful representation implies that decision-useful financial information represents faithfully the economic phenomenon (those affecting financial position and results of operations) that it purports to represent.

The enhancing qualitative characteristics are said to help users to distinguish more useful information from less useful information.

Timeliness means that the information is provided when it is still highly useful for decision-making purposes.

Comparability refers to the ability to identify similarities in—and differences between—two sets of economic phenomena. It is not to be confused with uniformity, which still does not exist under either US GAAP or IFRS (although the range of alternatives has narrowed over recent decades). *Consistency* (the use of the same accounting policies and procedures within an entity from period to period, or in a single period across entities) aids comparability.

Verifiability helps to assure users that information represents faithfully the economic phenomena that it purports to represent. It implies that knowledgeable and independent observers could reach a general consensus (but not necessarily absolute agreement) that the information does represent faithfully the economic phenomena it purports to represent without material error or bias, or that an appropriate recognition or measurement method has been applied without material error or bias. It means that independent observations would yield essentially the same measure or conclusions.

Understandability enables users who have a reasonable knowledge of business and economic and financial activities and financial reporting, and who apply reasonable diligence to comprehend the information, to gain insights into the reporting entity's financial position and results of operations, as intended. Understandability is enhanced when the information is classified, characterized and presented clearly and concisely. The draft asserts that relevant information should not be excluded solely because it may be too complex or difficult for some users to understand.

The Basis for Conclusions accompanying the Exposure Draft lists additional candidate attributes that were considered by the Boards, but not included in the proposals. These include *transparency* (which was concluded was subsumed within faithful representation and understandability); *true and fair view* (deemed to be equivalent to faithful representation); *credibility* (which is implied by verifiability); and *high quality* (which generally is achieved by adherence to the objective and qualitative characteristics of financial reporting). One other candidate, *internal consistency*, was rejected because IASB and FASB concluded that this, while desirable and a goal of both bodies, could impede the evolution of financial reporting standards.

Two pervasive constraints may also limit the information provided in useful financial reports:

- Materiality, and
- Cost

Regarding *materiality*, which has long been invoked but often not defined in terms precise enough for users and preparers, information is to be deemed material if its omission or misstatement could influence the decisions that users make on the basis of an entity's financial information. Materiality is not a matter to be considered by standard-setters but by preparers and their auditors. That is, financial reporting requirements will be promulgated without regard to materiality criteria, but actual adherence to such rules may be omitted when the effect of doing so would not be material to the users.

As concerns the *cost-benefit* criterion, it has been stated that the benefits of providing financial reporting information should justify the costs of providing that information. Presumably this will constrain the imposition of certain new requirements, although this is a relative concept, and as information technology continues to evolve and the cost of preparing and distributing financial and other information declines, this constraint conceivably will be relaxed as well.

Discussion has since moved on to the elements of financial statements, in particular the definitions of an asset, a liability, and equity, and on what constitutes the reporting entity, and a Discussion Paper on reporting entity in May 2008. An Exposure Draft on this segment of the conceptual framework is promised for the latter part of 2009.

Other components of the conceptual framework project, which will address elements and recognition, presentation and disclosure, purpose and status, and application to not-for-profit entities, will follow, but the timing is uncertain. Elements and presentation and disclosure are the most active projects and may result in Discussion Papers, at a minimum before year-end 2009.

Hierarchy of Standards

The *Framework* is used by IASB members and staff in their debate, and they expect that those commenting on Exposure Drafts will articulate their arguments in terms of the *Framework*. However, the *Framework* is not intended normally to be used directly by preparers and auditors in determining their accounting methods. In its 2003 revision of IAS 8, IASB introduced a hierarchy of accounting rules that should be followed by preparers in seeking solutions to accounting problems. This hierarchy says that the most authoritative guidance is IFRS, and the preparer should seek guidance as follows:

1. IAS/IFRS and SIC/IFRIC Interpretations, when these specifically apply to a transaction or condition.

2. In the absence of such a directly applicable standard, judgment is to be used to develop and apply an accounting policy that is relevant to the economic decision-making needs of the users, and is reliable in that the financial statements: represent faithfully the financial position, financial performance and cash flows of the reporting entity; reflect the economic substance of transactions, events and conditions, rather than merely the legal forms thereof; are neutral; are prudent; and are complete in all material respects.

3. If this is not possible, the preparer should then look to recent pronouncements of other standard setters which use a similar conceptual framework to develop its standards, as well as other accounting literature and industry practices that do not conflict with higher level guidance.

4. Only if that also fails should the preparer look to the IASB *Framework* directly.

In effect, therefore, if existing IFRS do not address an accounting issue, the preparer should look to analogous national GAAP, and the most obvious choice is US GAAP, partly because that is the most complete set of standards, and partly because in the global capital market, US GAAP is the alternative best understood. In any event, given the professed intention of IFRS and US GAAP to converge, it would make little sense to seek guidance in any other set of standards, unless US GAAP were also silent on the matter needing clarification.

The IASB and the US

Although IASC and FASB were created almost contemporaneously, FASB largely ignored IASB until the 1990s. It was only at the beginning of the 1990s that FASB started to become interested in IASC. This was the period when IASC was starting to work with IOSCO, a body in which the SEC has always had a powerful voice. In effect, both the SEC and FASB were starting to consider the international financial reporting area, and IASC was also starting to take initiatives to encourage standard setters to meet together occasionally to debate technical issues of common interest.

IOSCO's efforts to create a single passport for secondary listings, and IASC's role as its standard setter, while intended to operate worldwide, would have the greatest practical significance for foreign issuers in terms of the US market. It was understood that if the SEC were to accept IFRS in place of US GAAP, there would be no need for a Form 20-F reconciliation, and access to the US markets would be greatly facilitated. The SEC has therefore been a key factor in the later evolution of IASC. It encouraged IASC to build a relationship with IOSCO in 1987. It also observed that there were too many options under IAS, and that it would be more favorably inclined to consider acceptance of IAS (now IFRS) if such alternatives were reduced. When IASC restarted its IOSCO work in 1995, the SEC issued a statement (April 1996) saying that, to be acceptable, IFRS would need to satisfy three criteria.

1. They must include a core set of standards that constituted a comprehensive basis of accounting;

2. The standards must be high quality, and enable investors to analyze performance meaningfully both across time periods and between companies; and

3. The standards must be rigorously interpreted and applied, because otherwise comparability and transparency would not be achieved.

The plan was predicated on the completion of a core set of standards, then handing these over to IOSCO, which in turn would ask its members to evaluate them, and finally IOSCO would issue its verdict. It was in this context that the SEC issued a "concept release" in 2000, in which it asked for comments on the acceptability of the core set of standards, but crucially on whether there was a sufficient compliance and enforcement mechanism to ensure that standards were consistently and rigorously applied by preparers, that auditors would ensure this and stock exchange regulators would check compliance.

This latter element is something which remains beyond the control of IASB, which is the domain of national bodies or professional organizations in each jurisdiction. The Standards Interpretations Committee was formed to help ensure uniform interpretation, and IFRIC has taken a number of initiatives to build liaison channels with stock exchange regulators and national interpretations bodies, but the rest is in the hands of the auditors, the audit oversight bodies, and the stock exchange oversight bodies. The SEC concepts release resulted in many comment letters, which can be viewed on the SEC Web site (www.sec.gov), but in the five years since its issue, the SEC has taken no definitive position.

The SEC's stance at the time was that it genuinely wanted to see IFRS used by foreign registrants, but that it preferred convergence (so that no reconciliation would be necessary) to acceptance without reconciliation of the IFRS as they were in 2000. In the years since, the SEC in its public pronouncements regularly supports convergence and has strongly implied that reconciliations might be waived as soon as 2008 if convergence progress continues to be made. Thus, for example, the SEC welcomed publicly the changes to US standards proposed by the FASB in December 2003, made to converge with IFRS.

Relations between FASB and IASB have grown warmer since IASB was restructured, perhaps influenced by the growing awareness that IASB would assume a commanding position in the financial reporting standard-setting domain. The FASB joined the IASB for informal meetings in the early 1990s, and this led to the creation of the G4+1 group of Anglo-Saxon standard setters (US, UK, Canada, Australia and New Zealand, with the IASC as an observer) in which FASB was an active participant. IASB and FASB signed the Norwalk Agreement in October 2002, which set out a program of convergence, and their staffs now work together on a number of projects, including business combinations and revenue recognition. Video links are used to enable staff to observe and participate in board meetings. The two boards have a joint agenda committee whose aim is to harmonize the timing with which the boards discuss the same subjects. The boards are also committed to meeting twice a year in joint session.

However, there remain problems, largely of the structural variety. FASB works in a specific national legal framework, while IASB does not. Equally, both have what they term "inherited" GAAP (i.e., differences in approach that have a long history and are not easily removed). FASB also has a tradition of issuing very detailed, prescriptive ("rules-based") standards that give bright line audit guidance, which are intended to make compliance control easier and remove uncertainties. In the post-Enron world, after it became clear that such prescriptive rules had been abused, there was a flurry of interest in standards that supposedly express an objective and then explain how to reach it ("principles-based" standards), without attempting to prescribe responses to every conceivable fact pattern. However, as the SEC study (mandated under the Sarbanes-Oxley Act of 2002) into principles-based standards observed, use of principles alone, without detailed guidance, reduces comparability. The litigation environment in the US also makes companies and auditors reluctant to step into areas where judgments have to be taken in uncertain conditions.

Events in the mid- to late-2000s have served to accelerate the pressure for full convergence between US GAAP and IFRS. In fact, the US SEC's decision in late 2007 to waive reconciliation requirements for foreign registrants complying with "full IFRS" was a clear indicator that the outright adoption of IFRS in the US is on the horizon, and that the convergence process may be made almost irrelevant. The SEC has since granted selected US registrants the limited right to begin reporting under IFRS in 2009, after which (in 2011) it will determine the future path of full-scale abandonment of US GAAP in favor of IFRS. As of late 2008, the SEC was expected to announce its so-called "roadmap" toward IFRS adoption at any moment. While at first this will promote or require IFRS adoption by multinational and other larger business entities, and then by all publicly held companies, in the longer run, even medium- and smaller-sized entities will probably opt for IFRS-based financial reporting, because some involvement in international trade is increasingly a characteristic of all business operations, and because the notion of reporting under "second-class GAAP" rather than under the standards employed by larger competitors will likely prove to be unappealing.

The IASB and Europe

While France, Germany, the Netherlands and the UK were founding members of IASC and have remained heavily involved, the European Commission as such has generally had a difficult relationship with the international standard setter. The EC did not participate in any way until 1990, when it finally became an observer at Board meetings. It had had its own regional program of harmonization since the 1960s and in effect only officially abandoned this in 1995, when, in a policy paper, it recommended to member states that they seek to align their rules for consolidated financial statements on IFRS. Notwithstanding this, the Commission gave IASB a great boost when it announced in June 2000 that it wanted to require all listed companies throughout the EU to use IFRS beginning in 2005 as part of its initiative to build a single European financial market. This intention was made concrete with the approval of the IFRS Regulation in June 2002 by the European Council of Ministers (the supreme EU decision-making authority).

The EU decision was all the more impressive in that, to be effective in legal terms, IFRS have to become enshrined in EU statute law, creating a situation where the EU is in effect rubber-stamping laws created by a small, self-appointed, private sector body. This proved to be a delicate situation, which proved within a very short time that it contained the seeds of unending disagreements: politicians were being asked in effect to endorse something over which they have no control, and were soon being lobbied by corporate interests that had failed to influence IASB directly to achieve their objectives. The EU endorsement of IFRS turns out to have the cost of exposing IASB to political pressures in the same way that FASB has at times been the focus of congressional manipulations in the US (e.g., over stock-based compensation accounting rules).

The EU created an elaborate machinery to mediate its relations with IASB. It preferred to work with another private sector body, created for the purpose, as the formal conduit for EU inputs to IASB. The European Financial Reporting Advisory Group (EFRAG) was formed in 2001 by a collection of European representative organizations (for details see www.efrag.org), including the European Accounting Federation (FEE) and European employer organization (UNICE). This in turn formed a small Technical Expert Group (TEG) which does the detailed work on IASB proposals. EFRAG consults widely within the EU, and particularly with national standard setters and the European Commission to canvass views on IASB proposals, and provides inputs to IASB. It responds formally to all discussion papers and Exposure Drafts.

At a second stage, when a final standard is issued, EFRAG is asked by the Commission to provide a report on the standard. This report should state whether the standard has the required qualities and is in conformity with the European company law directives. The European Commission then asks a new committee, the Accounting Regulation Committee (ARC), whether it wishes to endorse the standard. ARC consists of permanent representatives of the EU member state governments. It should normally only fail to endorse IFRS if it believes they are not in conformity with the overall framework of EU law; it should not take a strategic or policy view. However, the European Parliament also has the right to comment, if it wishes. If ARC fails to endorse a standard, the European Commission may still ask the Council of Ministers to override that decision.

Experience has shown that the system suffers from a number of problems. First, although EFRAG is intended to enhance EU inputs to IASB, it may in fact isolate people from IASB, or at least increase the costs of making representations. For example, when IASB revealed its intentions of issuing a standard on stock options, it received nearly a hundred comment letters from US companies (who report under US GAAP, not IFRS), but only one from EFRAG, which represented about 90% of IASB's constituents in the early 2000s. It is easy to feel in this context that EFRAG is seen at IASB as a single respondent, so people who have made the effort to work through EFRAG feel underrepresented. In addition, EFRAG is bound to present a distillation of views, so it is already filtering respondents' views before they even reach IASB. The only recourse is for respondents to make representations not only to EFRAG but also directly to IASB.

However, resistance to the financial instruments standards, IAS 32 and IAS 39, put the system under specific strain. These standards were already in existence when the European Commission announced its decision to adopt IFRS for European listed companies, and had been exhaustively debated before enactment. European adoption again exposed these particular standards to strenuous debate.

The first task of EFRAG and ARC was to endorse the existing standards of IASB. They did this—but excluded IAS 32 and 39 on the grounds that they were being extensively revised as part of IASB's then-ongoing *Improvements Project.*

During the exposure period of the improvements proposals—which exceptionally included round table meetings with constituents—the European Banking Federation, under particular pressure from French banks, lobbied IASB to modify the standard to permit special accounting for macrohedging. The IASB agreed to do this, even though that meant the issuance of a new Exposure Draft and a further amendment to IAS 39 (which was finally issued in March 2004). The bankers did not like the terms of the amendment, and while it was still under discussion, they appealed to the French president and persuaded him to intervene. He wrote to the European Commission in July 2003, saying that the financial instruments standards were likely to make banks' figures volatile, would destabilize the European economy, and should not be approved. He also said that the Commission did not have a sufficient input to the standard-setting process.

This desire to alter the requirements of IAS 39 was further compounded when the European Central Bank complained in February 2004 that the "fair value option," introduced to IAS 39 as an improvement in final form in December 2003, could be used by banks to manipulate their prudential ratios, and asked IASB to limit the circumstances in which the option could be used. IASB agreed to do this, although again this meant issuing an Exposure Draft and a further amendment to IAS 39 which was not finalized until mid-2005. IASB, when it debated the issue, took a pragmatic line that no compromise of principle was involved, and that the principal bank regulator of the Board's largest constituent by far should be accommodated. The fact that the European Central Bank had not raised these issues at the original Exposure Draft stage was not discussed, nor was the legitimacy of a constituent deciding unilaterally it wanted to change a rule that had just been approved. The Accounting Standards Board of Japan lodged a formal protest and many other constituents have not been delighted.

Ultimately, ARC approved IAS 32 and IAS 39, but a "carve out" from IAS 39 was prescribed. Clearly the EU's involvement with IFRS is proving to be a mixed blessing for IASB, both exposing it to political pressures that are properly an issue for the Commission, not IASB, and putting its due process under stress. Some commentators consider that the EU might abandon IFRS, but this is not a realistic possibility, given that the EU has already tried and rejected the regional standard-setting route. What is more probable is that we are enduring a period of adjustment, with both regulators and lobbyists uncertain as to how exactly the system works, testing its limits, but with some *modus vivendi* evolving over time. However, it is severe distraction for IASB that financial instruments, arguably the controversy of the 1990s, is still causing trouble, when it has on its agenda more radical ideas in the areas of revenue recognition, performance reporting and insurance contracts.

The "carve-outs" have most recently had the result that the US SEC's historic decision to eliminate reconciliation to US GAAP for foreign private issuers has been restricted to those registrants that file financial statements that comply with "full IFRS" (i.e., those using "Euro-IFRS" and other national adaptations of IFRS as promulgated by the IASB will not be eligible for this deletion). Registrants using any derivation of IFRS, and those using any national GAAP, will continue to be required to present a reconciliation to US GAAP. Over time, it can be assumed that this will add to the pressure to report under "full IFRS."

The Future Agenda for IFRS

The matter of performance reporting (now renamed financial statement presentation) is a priority project for IASB. The project was bifurcated, and the first part, dealing with what financial statements are to be presented, led to a mid-2006 Exposure Draft and the late 2007 promulgation of revised IAS 1 (discussed in greater detail later in this chapter). The second phase, which addresses presentation on the faces of the financial statements, has culminated with the issuance of a joint IASB-FASB Discussion Paper in October 2008. The announced intent is to promulgate revisions to IAS 1 based on this exposure document by 2010.

IASB is also pursuing a revenue recognition project. The purpose of this undertaking is to revisit revenue recognition through an analysis of assets and liabilities, instead of the existing approach which focuses on completed transactions and realized revenue. Such an approach has major implications for the timing of earnings recognition—it would potentially lead to revenue recognition in stages throughout the transaction cycle. It is unlikely that this project will lead to short-term changes, given the fundamental nature of the issues involved. IASB is projecting that a discussion document will be produced in late 2008, but that an Exposure Draft will not be released until 2010, with the goal being to promulgate a final standard in 2011.

Linked to these projects, which are revisions and extensions of the conceptual framework, is a joint project with the Canadian Accounting Standards Board on initial measurement and impairment, and a catch-up project with FASB on accounting for, and distinguishing between, liabilities and equity, which has eluded definitive resolution for well over a decade.

The very important topic of accounting for business combinations has been pursued in coordination with FASB over several years. In 2008, both Boards completed Phase II of their respective projects, resulting in the issuance of revised IFRS 3 and the release of FAS 141(R) and FAS 160 for US GAAP. Among the important changes to prior practice are the imposition of acquisition accounting, the requirement that minority interests be included in group equity, and the optional procedure for the inclusion of goodwill calculated with reference to 100% of the shareholders, rather than for just the holdings of the controlling group. Additionally, contingent assets and liabilities acquired in a combination will be recognized at fair value at the date of the transaction. Full details of IFRS 3 as revised are set forth in Chapter 11.

IASB is also working on revisions to the criteria for consolidation (IAS 27) which it hopes to develop to deal more effectively with issues such as latent control and special-purpose entities. As of late 2008, this remains under active development.

IASB is currently working on its own in the area of what had been known as SME accounting (tailored standards for small and medium-sized entities) and is now referred to as IFRS for private entities (PE). Broadly, the intention of this project (which was the subject of an IASB Discussion Paper in 2004) is to produce a single accounting standard for PE, to consist of simplified versions of the existing IFRS, in a manner analogous to what was achieved in the UK some years ago (financial reporting standards for smaller enterprises, or FRSSE, since revised several times). IASB was initially reluctant to involve itself in this area, but was persuaded by a number of institutions, including the UN and the European Commission, that this was an urgent need. The crucial issue of what is a PE is couched in conceptual terms, as being an entity in which there is no public interest, but precise size terms are left to individual jurisdictions to determine. The definition excludes entities with listed equity or debt or that have certain defined types of public accountability, such as financial institutions.

IASB issued a draft standard in early 2006, which, if adopted, will serve as an optional "all in one" standard for entities that have no public accountability (i.e., privately held entities with no fiduciary obligations to nonowners). A final standard has been promised for 2009. This proposal is discussed in detail later in this chapter.

While IFRS 4, issued in March 2004, provides a first standard on accounting for insurance contracts, this is only an interim standard issued to meet the needs of 2005 adopters, and it permits the retention of many existing national practices. IASB is committed to a full standard, an exposure document for which is now projected to be released in 2009. The project should now enter full development. Analysis thus far, based on an asset and liability approach, would potentially allow recognition of some gain on the signing of a long-term contract. This will undoubtedly cause insurance regulators some concerns. IASB is also using fair value as a working measurement assumption, which has aroused opposition from insurers, many of whom have long used an approach which smoothed earnings over long periods and ignored the current market values of insurance assets and liabilities. They claim that fair value will introduce volatility, which is likely true: IASB members have observed that the volatility is in the marketplace, and that the insurers' accounts just do not reflect economic reality.

A project addressing IAS 30 disclosure requirements came to fruition in mid-2005 with the issuance of IFRS 7. This standard eliminated IAS 30, which had set forth disclosures for banks, and merges them with requirements formerly presented in IAS 39. Because of issues arising during the "credit crises" of 2008, IASB quickly considered certain amend-ments to IFRS 7, and by late 2008 had issued an Exposure Draft, *IFRS 7: Disclosures.* If adopted, these changes would become effective mid-2009. The revised disclosures would closely parallel those mandated by US GAAP standard FAS 157, imposing a hierarchy of fair value measures that would drive the structuring of disclosures.

In mid-2005 IASB issued an Exposure Draft of an amendment to IAS 37. This evolved as part of the ongoing efforts to converge IFRS with US GAAP. In particular, it is responsive to the differences between IAS 37 (on provisions) and FAS 146, addressing certain disposal and exit activities and the costs properly accrued in connection with them. FAS 146 was promulgated by FASB, in part, to curtail certain abuses commonly called providing "cookie jar reserves" during periods of corporate downsizing, when too-generous estimates were often made of future related costs, which in some instances served to absorb costs that would properly have been chargeable to future periods. In other cases, excess reserves (provisions) were used for later release into income, thereby overstating operating results of one or more later periods. FAS 146 applies strict criteria so that reserves that do not meet the definition of liabilities at the end of the reporting period cannot be recorded, since they do not represent present obligations of the reporting entity. The proposal to revise IAS 37 also hews more closely to US GAAP's approach to guarantees, which distinguish between the unconditional element—the promise to provide a service for some defined duration of time— and the conditional element, which is contingent on the future events, such as terminations, occurring.

If adopted, the amended IAS 37 (discussed in great detail in Chapter 12) would eliminate the terms *contingent liability* and *contingent asset,* and would restrict the meaning of constructive obligations so that these would be recognized as liabilities only if the reporting entity's actions result in other parties having a valid expectation on which they can reasonably rely that the entity will perform. Furthermore, the probability criterion would be deleted, so that only if a liability is not subject to reasonable measurement would it be justifiable to not record it. Certain changes are also made to IAS 19 by this draft. As of late 2008, these proposed revisions to IAS 37 remain under discussion by the IASB.

IASB also has expressed its intent to replace IAS 20, and an Exposure Draft had been promised for late 2005 but has yet to appear. It now appears that this project will not be addressed for perhaps several more years, since the first conceptualized approach, using the model in IAS 41, has now been judged inadequate. (See discussion in Chapter 26.) One change to IAS 20 was made, however, as part of the 2007 Annual Improvements project; this required explicit recognition (as grant income) of the benefit conferred by below-market interest on loans made to an entity.

Yet another short-term convergence project has resulted in the elimination from IAS 23 of the former option of expensing borrowing costs associated with long-term asset construction efforts. IAS 23, as revised in 2007, thus converged to the parallel US GAAP standard (FAS 34), which requires capitalization of interest under defined circumstances.

Income taxes and segment disclosures were two additional subject areas where IASB expected to converge to the US GAAP positions. As to income taxes, both IFRS and US GAAP have long embraced comprehensive interperiod allocation using the liability method, but certain exceptions are permitted, and these are expected to be narrowed or eliminated by revisions still under consideration. Also to be conformed is the computation of deferred tax assets and liabilities, and the treatment of uncertain tax positions (US GAAP has recently been revised to address this, while IFRS has yet to do so). An exposure document is promised for late 2008, with a final standard expected for 2010.

Regarding segment disclosures, IFRS now replicates US GAAP, thanks to the promulgation of IFRS 8. This is expected to ease the current challenge of developing segment data under IFRS.

Other convergence projects still under development on discussion include those addressing derecognition criteria (exposure document expected early 2009), accounting for noncurrent assets held for sale (Exposure Draft issued late 2008, final standard due by mid-2009), revisions to earnings per share computations (Exposure Draft issued mid-2008, final standard anticipated for late 2009), refinement to IFRS 1 regarding transition to IFRS (expected late 2009), and amendments to the requirements for related-party disclosures (late 2009). A joint project with FASB to revise lease accounting requirements is not expected to reach the exposure document stage until 2010.

Finally, accounting requirements for joint ventures will likely be changed to delete the currently available option of applying the proportionate consolidation method, thus permitting only the equity method, as is the case under US GAAP. (Note that there are a few instances where US GAAP does permit proportionate consolidation, and IFRS may preserve limited options as well.) An Exposure Draft was published in late 2007, and a final standard is anticipated for early to mid-2009.

Europe 2008 Update

The IASB's long effort to gain acceptance for IFRS began to bear fruit several years ago, when the EU briefly considered and then, significantly, abandoned a quest to develop Euro-GAAP, and when IOSCO endorsed, with some qualifications, the "core set of standards" following major revisions to most of the then-extant IFRS. A significant impediment was removed with the recent (late 2007) decision by the US Securities and Exchange Commission to eliminate the longstanding requirement for reconciliation of major items to US GAAP. However, since "Euro-IFRS" contains several "carve-outs" from the standards promulgated by IASB, this waiver will not apply to European publicly held entities. This may serve as an impetus for changes in the EU rules previously adopted.

Beginning January 1, 2005, all European Union (EU) companies having securities listed on an EU exchange have been required to prepare consolidated (group) accounts in conformity with IFRS. It is estimated that this requirement has affected approximately 7,000 companies, of which some 3,000 are in the United Kingdom. Companies traded both in the EU and on a regulated market outside the EU that were already in 2005 applying another set of internationally accepted standards (for example US Generally Accepted Accounting Principles (GAAP), and companies that have issued debt instruments but not equity instruments could be temporarily exempted by the member states and not required to comply with IFRS until January 1, 2007. Consequently, those companies which took advantage of this exemption were required to implement IFRS in 2007 (for example Deutsche Bank).

On November 15, 2007, the US Securities and Exchange Commission (SEC) eliminated the requirement for foreign registrants to reconcile their financial statements to US GAAP, if the financial statements fully adhere to IFRS as published by the IASB. This regulation helped EU companies, such as Deutsche Bank, in their financial reporting requirements for listing in the US. SEC thus acknowledged that IFRS has the potential to become the global set of high-quality reporting standards, and that investors, issuers, and markets would benefit from the improved comparability of financial reporting across national borders.

It is thought to be quite possible that, within some reasonable interval of time, all the EU states will at least *permit* IFRS in the consolidated accounts of nonlisted companies, although this permission, in some states, might not extend to certain types of companies such as small entities or charities. Additionally, it is possible that most of the EU states will permit IFRS in the annual (i.e., not consolidated, so-called statutory) accounts of all companies, again possibly subject to some exceptions. Furthermore, some EU states, such as the UK, have already begun to converge their national accounting rules with IFRS.

Privately held EU companies may, if permitted to do so, choose to utilize IFRS for many sound reasons (e.g., for comparability purposes), in anticipation of eventual convergence of national standards with IFRS, and at the specific request of stakeholders such as the entities' credit and investment constituencies.

The remaining impediment to full IFRS conformity among the affected EU companies pertains to the financial instruments standard, IAS 39 which has proved to be extraordinarily controversial, at least among some reporting entities, particularly financial institutions in some, but not all, European countries. Originally, as noted above, all IAS/IFRS standards were endorsed, *except* IAS 32 and IAS 39, as to which endorsement was postponed, nominally because of expected further amendments coming from IASB, but actually due to the philosophical or political dispute over use of fair value accounting for financial instruments and hedging provisions. The single most important of the concerns pertained to accounting for "core deposits" of banks, which drew objections from five of the six dissenting votes on the EFRAG (European Financial Reporting Advisory Group) Technical Expert Group

(TEG). In fact, the dissents were a majority of the eleven-member TEG, but since it takes a two-thirds vote to refuse endorsement, the tepid support would be sufficient.

Notwithstanding that IASB had promised a "stable platform" of rules (i.e., no changes or new standards to be issued during the massive transition to IFRS in Europe, so that preparers could be spared the frustration of a moving target as they attempted to prepare, usually, January 1, 2004 restated statements of financial position and 2004 and 2005 financial statements under IFRS), the controversy over IAS 39 resulted in a number of amendments being made in 2005, mostly in order to mollify EU member states. Thus, IAS 39 was (separately) amended to deal with macrohedging, cash flow hedges of forecast intragroup transactions, the "fair value option," and financial guarantee contracts. (These changes are all addressed in this publication.)

Notwithstanding these efforts to satisfy EU member state concerns about specific aspects of IAS 39, the final EU approval was still qualified, with an additional "carve out" identified. Thus, there is the specter of partial compliance with IFRS, and independent auditors were forced to grapple with this when financial statements prepared in accordance with Euro-IFRS were first prepared for issuance in early 2006. At this point in time, the representation that financial statements are "in accordance with IFRS" can be invoked only when the reporting entity fully complies with IFRS, as the standards have been promulgated (and amended, when relevant), but without any deviations permitted in the EU legislation. Auditor references to IFRS have therefore been tempered by citing IFRS as endorsed by the EU as the basis of accounting.

Impact of IFRS Adoption by EU Companies

The effect of the change to IFRS has varied from country to country and from company to company. National GAAP of many European countries were developed to serve or facilitate tax and other regulatory purposes, so principles differed from state to state. The case study of a Belgian company, included in an appendix to this chapter, reveals the nature of many of the differences between IFRS and national GAAP reporting.

Complexity usually means additional cost. One survey of 1,000 European companies indicated that the average compliance cost across UK companies will be about £360,000. This figure rises to £446,000 for a top-500 company; £625,000 for companies with a market capitalization value between £1bn-£2bn; and over £1m for companies valued at more than £2bn.

Implementation, however, is not the only difficulty, and possibly not even the most significant one. Changes in principles can mean significant changes in statements of comprehensive income or statements of financial position. In a 2002 survey of EU companies, two-thirds of respondents indicated that the adoption of IFRS would have a medium to high impact on their businesses.

One of the most important effects of the change to IFRS-basis financial reporting will reverberate throughout companies' legal relationships. Obviously, companies must make appropriate disclosure to their stakeholders in order to properly explain the changes and their impact. Additionally, accountants and lawyers will also have to review the significantly expanded footnote disclosures required by IFRS in financial statements.

In addition to appropriate stakeholder disclosure, companies must reexamine legal relationships which are keyed to accounting reports. Changed accounting principles can undermine carefully crafted financial covenants in shareholder agreements, financing contracts and other transactional documents.

Drafters must examine the use of "material adverse change" triggers in the context of businesses whose earnings may be subject to accounting volatility. Debt, equity and lease financing arrangements may require restructuring due to unanticipated changes in reported results arising from the use of IFRS.

For example, IFRS may require a reclassification of certain financial instruments previously shown as equity on a company's statement of financial position into their equity and debt components. Additionally, IFRS permits companies to adjust the carrying values of investment property (real estate) to fair market values with any gains being reflected in profit or loss for the period.

Executives may be concerned about compensation systems tied to earnings increases between measurement dates when earnings can be so volatile, or they may simply be concerned that compensation arrangements are keyed to results which are no longer realistic.

Few companies want to entertain dated or "frozen" GAAP for document purposes because of the costs involved in maintaining two separate systems of accounting or an extensive set of "off-line" adjustments. As a result, companies, their lawyers and accountants will have to reexamine agreements in light of the anticipated effect of IFRS on companies' financial statements.

APPENDIX A

CURRENT INTERNATIONAL FINANCIAL REPORTING STANDARDS (IAS/IFRS) AND INTERPRETATIONS (SIC/IFRIC)

(Recent revisions noted parenthetically)

IAS 1   Presentation of Financial Statements (revised 2007, effective 2009)

IAS 2   Inventories (revised 2003, effective 2005)

IAS 7   Statement of Cash Flows

IAS 8   Accounting Policies, Changes in Accounting Estimates and Errors (revised 2003, effective 2005)

IAS 10   Events After the Reporting Period (revised 2003, effective 2005)

IAS 11   Construction Contracts

IAS 12   Income Taxes

IAS 14   Reporting Financial Information by Segment (superseded, effective 2009, by IFRS 8)

IAS 16   Property, Plant, and Equipment (revised 2003, effective 2005)

IAS 17   Accounting for Leases (revised 2003, effective 2005)

IAS 18   Revenue

IAS 19   Employee Benefits (revised 2004)

IAS 20   Accounting for Government Grants and Disclosure of Government Assistance

IAS 21   The Effects of Changes in Foreign Exchange Rates (revised 2003, effective 2005; minor further amendment 2005)

IAS 23   Borrowing Costs (revised 2007, effective 2009)

IAS 24   Related-Party Disclosures (revised 2003, effective 2005)

IAS 26   Accounting and Reporting by Retirement Benefit Plans

IAS 27   Consolidated and Separate Financial Statements (revised 2008, effective 2009)

IAS 28   Accounting for Investments in Associates (revised 2003, effective 2005)

IAS 29   Financial Reporting in Hyperinflationary Economies

IAS 31   Financial Reporting of Interests in Joint Ventures (revised 2003, effective 2005)

IAS 32   Financial Instruments: Presentation (revised 2003, effective 2005; disclosure requirements removed to IFRS 7 effective 2007)

IAS 33   Earnings Per Share (revised 2003, effective 2005)

IAS 34   Interim Financial Reporting

IAS 36   Impairments of Assets (revised 2004)

IAS 37   Provisions, Contingent Liabilities, and Contingent Assets

IAS 38   Intangible Assets (revised 2004)

IAS 39   Financial Instruments: Recognition and Measurement (amended 2005)

IAS 40   Investment Property (revised 2003, effective 2005)

IAS 41   Agriculture

IFRS 1	First-Time Adoption of IFRS (minor amendment 2005)
IFRS 2	Share-Based Payment
IFRS 3	Business Combinations (revised 2008, effective 2009)
IFRS 4	Insurance Contracts
IFRS 5	Noncurrent Assets Held for Sale and Discontinued Operations
IFRS 6	Exploration for and Evaluation of Mineral Resources
IFRS 7	Financial Instruments: Disclosures
IFRS 8	Operating Segments
SIC 7	Introduction of the Euro
SIC 10	Government Assistance—No Specific Relation to Operating Activities
SIC 12	Consolidation—Special-Purpose Entities
SIC 13	Jointly Controlled Entities—Nonmonetary Contributions by Venturers
SIC 15	Operating Leases—Incentives
SIC 21	Income Taxes—Recovery of Revalued Nondepreciable Assets
SIC 25	Income Taxes—Changes in the Tax Status of an Enterprise or Its Shareholders
SIC 27	Evaluating the Substance of Transactions Involving the Legal Form of a Lease
SIC 29	Disclosure—Service Concession Arrangements
SIC 31	Revenue—Barter Transactions Involving Advertising Services
SIC 32	Intangible Assets—Web Site Costs
IFRIC 1	Changes in Existing Decommissioning, Restoration and Similar Liabilities
IFRIC 2	Members' Shares in Cooperative Entities and Similar Instruments
IFRIC 4	Determining Whether an Arrangement Contains a Lease
IFRIC 5	Rights to Interests Arising from Decommissioning, Restoration and Environmental Rehabilitation Funds
IFRIC 6	Liabilities Arising from Participating in a Specific Market—Waste Electrical and Electronic Equipment
IFRIC 7	Applying the Restatement Approach under IAS 29, *Financial Reporting in Hyperinflationary Economies*
IFRIC 8	Scope of IFRS 2
IFRIC 9	Reassessment of Embedded Derivatives
IFRIC 10	Interim Financial Reporting and Impairment
IFRIC 11	IFRS 2: Group and Treasury Share Transactions
IFRIC 12	Service Concession Arrangements
IFRIC 13	Customer Loyalty Programs
IFRIC 14	IAS 19—The Limit on a Defined Benefit Asset, Minimum Funding Requirements, and Their Interaction
IFRIC 15	Agreements for the Construction of Real Estate
IFRIC 16	Hedges of a Net Investment in a Foreign Operation

APPENDIX B: REVISED IAS 1,

PRESENTATION OF FINANCIAL STATEMENTS

As noted in the body of the chapter, IASB has been pursuing a multiphase project dealing with financial statement presentation. The issuance of revised IAS 1, *Presentation of Financial Statements*, represented the culmination of the first stage of this undertaking. Later phases will address more fundamental issues for presenting information on the face of the financial statements, including: consistent principles for aggregating information in each financial statement; the totals and subtotals that should be reported in each financial statement; whether components of other recognized income and expense should be reclassified to profit and loss; and whether the direct or the indirect method of presenting operating cash flows provides more useful information. The IASB and FASB have decided that financial statements should present information in a manner that reflects a cohesive financial picture of an entity and which separates an entity's financing activities from its business and other activities as well as from its transactions with owners. Additionally, financing activities should be separated into transactions with owners and all other financing activities. Yet another phase of the project will deal with interim financial reporting.

The revised IAS 1 is largely into line with the corresponding US GAAP standard—FAS 130, *Reporting Comprehensive Income*. The FASB decided that it would not publish a separate Exposure Draft on this phase of the project but will expose issues pertinent to this and the next phase together in the future.

Revised IAS 1 is effective for annual periods beginning on or after January 1, 2009, with early application permitted.

Objective of revised IAS 1. IAS 1 prescribes the basis for presentation of general-purpose financial statements to ensure comparability both with the entity's financial statements of previous periods and with the financial statements of other entities. It sets out overall requirements for the presentation of financial statements, guidelines for their structure, and minimum requirements for their content. In revising IAS 1, IASB's main objective was to aggregate information in the financial statements on the basis of shared characteristics. Other sources of guidance on the financial statement presentation can be found in IAS 7, 8, 10, 12, 18, 24, 27, 34, and IFRS 5.

Scope of IAS 1. IAS 1 applies to all entities, including profit-oriented and not-for-profit entities. Non-for-profit entities in both the private and public sectors can apply this standard, however they may need to change the descriptions used for particular line items within their financial statements and for the financial statements themselves. This standard applies to those entities that present consolidated financial statements and those that present financial statements as defined in IAS 27, *Consolidated and Separate Financial Statements*. It does not apply to the structure and content of condensed interim financial statements prepared in accordance with IAS 34, *Interim Financial Reporting*.

Purpose of financial statements. IAS 1, which previously had been substantially revised in 2003, and which received further amendments in 2005 and 2007, refers to financial statements as "a structured representation of the financial position and financial performance of an entity" and elaborates that the objective of financial statements is to provide information about an entity's financial position, its financial performance, and its cash flows, which is then utilized by a wide spectrum of end users in making economic decisions. In addition, financial statements also show the results of the management's stewardship of the resources entrusted to it. All this information is communicated through a complete set of financial statements.

Presentation of financial statements. IAS 1 defines a complete set of financial statements to be comprised of the following:

1.   A statement of financial position as at the end of the period:

    a.   The previous version of IAS 1 used the title "balance sheet." The revised standard uses the title "statement of financial position."

2.   A statement of comprehensive income for the period:

    a.   Components of profit or loss may be presented either as part of a single statement of comprehensive income or in a separate income statement.
    b.   When an income statement is presented, it becomes part of a complete set of financial statements.
    c.   The income statement should be displayed immediately before the statement of comprehensive income.

3.   A statement of changes in equity for the period;
4.   A statement of cash flows for the period;

    a.   The previous version of IAS 1 used the title "cash flow statement." The revised standard uses the title "statement of cash flows."

5.   Notes, comprising a summary of significant accounting policies and other explanatory information; and
6.   A statement of financial position as at the beginning of the earliest comparative period when an entity applies an accounting policy retrospectively or makes a retrospective restatement of items in its financial statements, or when it reclassifies items in its financial statements.

    a.   This requirement is part of the revised IAS 1.

Financial statements, except for cash flow information, are to be prepared using accrual basis of accounting.

Fairness exception under IAS 1. There is a subtle difference between US GAAP and what was required by many European countries regarding the use of an override to assure a fair presentation of the company's financial position and results of operations. US auditing standards require a *fair presentation in accordance with GAAP,* while the European Fourth Directive requires that statements offer a *true and fair view* of the company's financial situation. If following the literal financial reporting requirements does not provide this result, then the entity should first consider the salutary effects of providing supplementary disclosures. However, if that is not seen as being sufficient to achieve a true and fair view, the entity may conclude that it must override (that is, ignore or contravene) the applicable accounting standard. US standards contain a rarely invoked exception that permits departure from GAAP if compliance would not result in financial reporting that was deemed appropriate to communicate financial position and results of operations.

IAS 1 has a similar approach. It states the expectation that the use of IFRS will result, *in virtually all circumstances,* in financial statements that achieve a fair presentation. However, in extremely rare circumstances where management concludes that compliance with a requirement in an IFRS would be so misleading that it would conflict with the objective of financial statements set out in the *Framework,* the entity can depart from that requirement if the relevant regulatory framework requires, or otherwise does not prohibit, such a departure, and the entity discloses all of the following:

1. Management has concluded that the financial statements present fairly the entity's financial position, financial performance, and cash flows;
2. The entity has complied with all applicable IFRS, except that it has departed from a particular requirement to achieve a fair presentation;
3. The title of the IFRS from which the entity has departed, the nature of the departure, including the treatment that the IFRS would require, the reason why that treatment would be so misleading in the circumstances that it would conflict with the objective of financial statements set out in the *Framework*, and the treatment adopted; and
4. For each period presented, the financial effect of the departure on each item in the financial statements that would have been reported in complying with the requirement.

When an entity has departed from a requirement of an IFRS in a prior period, and that departure affects the amounts recognized in the current period, it shall make the disclosures as in 3. and 4. above.

The standard notes that deliberately departing from IFRS might not be permissible in some jurisdictions, in which case the entity should comply with the standard in question and disclose in the notes that it believes this to be misleading, and show the adjustments that would be necessary to avoid this distorted result. In extremely rare circumstances where management concludes that compliance with a requirement in an IFRS would be so misleading that it would conflict with the objective of financial statements set out in the *Framework*, but the relevant regulatory framework prohibits departure from the requirement, to the maximum extent possible, the entity is required to reduce the perceived misleading aspects of compliance by disclosing all of the following:

1. The title of the IFRS in question, the nature of the requirement, and the reason why management has concluded that complying with that requirement is so misleading in the circumstances that it conflicts with the objective of financial statements set out in the *Framework*, and
2. For each period presented, the adjustments to each item in the financial statements that management has concluded would be necessary to achieve a fair presentation.

When assessing whether complying with a specific requirement in an IFRS would be so misleading that it would conflict with the objective of financial statements set out in the *Framework*, management should consider the following:

1. Why the objective of financial statements is not achieved in the particular circumstances; and
2. How the entity's circumstances differ from those of other entities that comply with the requirement.

    a. If other entities in similar circumstances comply with the requirement, there is a rebuttable presumption that the entity's compliance with the requirement would not be so misleading that it would conflict with the objective of financial statements set out in the *Framework*.

Going concern. When preparing financial statements, management makes an assessment regarding the entity's ability to continue as a going concern. If the result of the assessment casts significant doubt upon the entity's ability to continue as a going concern, management is required to disclose that fact, together with the basis on which it prepared the financial statements and the reason why the entity is not regarded as a going concern.

Accrual basis of accounting. Financial statements, except for cash flow information, are to be prepared using accrual basis of accounting.

Materiality and aggregation. An entity should present separately each material class of similar items as well as present separately material items of dissimilar nature or function. If a line item is not individually material, it is aggregated with other items either in those statements or in the notes. It is not necessary for an entity to provide a specific disclosure required by an IFRS if the information is not material.

Offsetting. Assets and liabilities, or income and expenses, may not be offset against each other, unless required or permitted by an IFRS. However, the reduction of accounts receivable by the allowance for doubtful accounts, or of property, plant, and equipment by the accumulated depreciation, are acts that reduce these assets by the appropriate valuation accounts and are not considered to be offsetting assets and liabilities.

Frequency of reporting. An entity should present a complete set of financial statements (including comparative information) at least annually. If the reporting period changes such that the financial statements are for a period longer or shorter than one year, the entity should disclose the reason for the longer or shorter period and the fact that the amounts presented are not entirely comparable.

Comparative information. An entity is required to include a statement of financial position as at the beginning of the earliest comparative period whenever and entity retrospectively applies an accounting policy, or makes a retrospective restatement of items in its financial statements, or when it reclassifies items in its financial statements. In those limited circumstances, an entity is required to present, as a minimum, three statements of financial position and related notes, as at

1. The end of the current period;
2. The end of the previous period (which is the same as the beginning of the current period); and
3. The beginning of the earliest comparative period.

When the entity changes the presentation or classification of items in its financial statements, the entity should reclassify the comparative amounts, unless reclassification is impractical. In reclassifying comparative amounts, the required disclosure includes (1) the nature of the reclassification; (2) the amount of each item or class of items that is reclassified; and (3) the reason for the reclassification. In situations where it is impracticable to reclassify comparative amounts, an entity should disclose (1) the reason for not reclassifying the amounts and (2) the nature of the adjustments that would have been made if the amounts had been reclassified.

Consistency of presentation. The presentation and classification of items in the financial statements should be consistent from one period to the next. A change in presentation and classification of items in the financial statements may be required when there is a significant change in the nature of the entity's operations, another presentation or classification is more appropriate (having considered the criteria of IAS 8, *Accounting Policies, Changes in Accounting Estimates and Errors*), or when an IFRS requires a change in presentation. When making such changes in presentation, an entity should reclassify its comparative information and present adequate disclosures (see comparable information above).

The revised IAS 1 is effective for annual periods beginning on or after January 1, 2009, with early application permitted.

APPENDIX C: CASE STUDY

GOING PRIVATE AND IMPLEMENTING IFRS

Background

Stolt-Nielsen S.A. (SNSA or the "Company") is one of the world's leading providers of transportation services for bulk liquid chemicals, edible oils, acids, and other specialty liquids. The Company, through the parcel tanker, tank container, terminal, rail and barge services of its wholly-owned subsidiary Stolt Tankers & Terminals and Stolt Tank Containers, provides integrated transportation solutions for its customers. Stolt Sea Farm, wholly owned by the Company, produces and markets high-quality turbot, sole, sturgeon, and caviar. SNSA is currently listed on the Oslo Stock Exchange under the ticker SNI, and was previously also traded in the US on NASDAQ.

On April 19, 2007, the Company announced its intention to voluntarily delist from the NASDAQ Global Select Market and this was effected from May 21, 2007, and it is no longer subject to the registration and reporting obligations under the Securities Exchange Act. The Company has maintained its listing in Norway on the Oslo Børs. Accordingly, the Company is required to present its financial statements under International Financial Reporting Standards ("IFRS") for the financial year ending November 30, 2008, and thereafter.

Legal Structure and Impact on IFRS Transition

SNSA, a Luxembourg registered company, will have a "primary" listing on the Oslo Børs following its delisting from NASDAQ and deregistration from the SEC. Since its flotation on the NASDAQ in 1987, SNSA had been preparing its financial statements in accordance with generally accepted accounting principles in the United States ("US GAAP").

European Union Directive 1606/2002 required all listed companies in the European Union[1] to apply IFRS for accounting periods beginning on or after January 1, 2005, along with comparatives for 2004, for annual consolidated financial statements. Article 9 of the Directive provides an exemption to defer preparation of IFRS financial statements for periods beginning on or after January 1, 2007, for companies that prepare financial statements under US GAAP. Luxembourg incorporated this exemption in its commercial legislation. Accordingly, SNSA was required to publish its first audited IFRS financial statements for the year ending November 30, 2008, with prior year comparatives under IFRS for the year ending November 30, 2007. In addition, quarterly financial statements under IFRS will be required for each quarter of the years ending November 30, 2007 and 2008. Based on this discussion, the implementation timeline is summarized below.

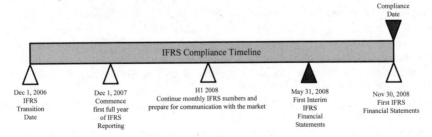

<hr />

[1]   At the time of the issue of this Directive, the European Union comprised 15 nations, which has since grown to 27 nations as of 1 January 2007.

Key Dates

IFRS 1 defines specific milestones in the preparation of the first financial statements of a company. The important areas to note while considering the transition date are discussed in the following paragraphs.

Most stock exchanges around the world, including the Oslo Børs, require that the interim or quarterly financial information released to the market should conform to the same accounting standards applied in the presentation of the annual financial statements. For SNSA, this meant that though the first audited IFRS financial statements were only due for the year ending November 30, 2008, the first interim unaudited financial information to be released under IFRS was for the quarter ended February 29, 2008! In effect, this is nine months less than what would appear required under IFRS 1. Of course, this also means that the comparative quarterly financial statements for February 28, 2007 must also be prepared in accordance with IFRS.

Another important aspect to bear in mind is that IFRS should be applied in full to the financial statements for all the periods presented.

The key dates in accordance with IFRS for SNSA were as follows:

Dec 1, 2006	Opening IFRS balance sheet (date of transition) ❖ Select policies ❖ Recognize and measure all items using IFRS ❖ Not published
May 31, 2007	First unaudited Interim Financial Statements ❖ Only balance sheet and income statement ❖ Required for comparative information for 2008
Nov 30, 2007	IFRS comparatives ❖ For 2008 full year audited IFRS financial
Nov 30, 2008	First IFRS Reporting Date ❖ Use Standards in force at this date ❖ First full audited IFRS financial statements published along with 2007 comparatives

Project Structure and Implementation Approach

One of the key determinants of the success of the implementation was tight project management and a project structure that ensured clear reporting lines and accountability for each step. The project team structure is summarized below.

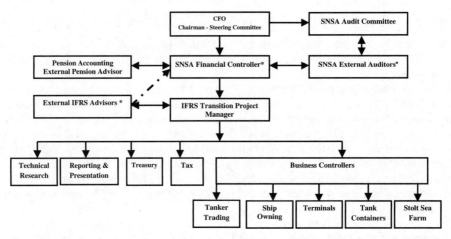

Overall, the implementation approach involved a mixed team of external advisors, external auditors and a strong in-house team at the Corporate Office to provide project management support and technical accounting support. In addition, the implementation approach involved each of the business controllers along with an external firm to provide hands-on support and technical expertise, both locally and at Corporate, to support the transition process. This ensured that the ultimate ownership of an IFRS issue would rest with the business unit, but with strong support from the Corporate Team. The business controllers were required to provide resource, input and accept responsibility for the IFRS financial statements but were given extensive support both from the Corporate Team and involvement from the external firm. SNSA did not have sufficient resources in the business to implement a project of this scale, complexity, and risk. Further, a number of steps in the transition were "one-off" in nature, and support from an external firm enabled the company to meet its objectives.

To project manage this effectively, a detailed project plan was developed, with week-by-week targets for achievement and responsibilities assigned for deliverables. While there were slippages, no issue was allowed to remain open for over two weeks. The project plan and the implementation were monitored through weekly conference calls of the core team members, including auditors and advisors.

External Auditor Involvement

SNSA's external auditors were integrally involved with the transition project to confirm technical accounting issues and agree treatment upfront. There are a number of areas where the external audit firm was able to assist management as an advisor in the IFRS Transition project. However, in order to maintain the requisite independence as auditors, the auditors would not assist management with preparation of financial statements and detailed accounting advice. This independence requirement, while understandable, did make it more difficult for both external auditors and management to achieve the key tasks within the IFRS transition project.

Training

Management conducted five IFRS Transition Training Workshops, including one for the Audit Committee, where the CEO was present. This was critical to establish buy-in and commitment from the top at the early stage of the project. Each of the workshops was targeted a different audience so there was a significant amount of customization to the training program. The importance of this phase cannot be overemphasized: it is vitally important to plan this in advance. In addition to the training there were a significant element of change management issues surrounding knowledge transfer and the ability of accounting staff to come to a new understanding of the building blocks (or DNA) of SNSA's financial statements.

So Where Did SNSA's IFRS Project Team Start?

After SNSA launched the IFRS Transition Project as noted above, its first step was to understand how different the then-current US GAAP accounting treatments were when compared to IFRS. This was again a critical success factor in our transition. A detailed comparison of IFRS and US GAAP was prepared, with assistance from both external advisors and external auditors. This list of similarities and differences was then applied to each of SNSA's four different businesses.

When IFRS implementation commences, a frequent lament may be heard – "IFRS is similar but not the same." The devil of the differences was in the detailed comparison of IFRS and US GAAP. The insight gained was this: the better and more detailed the comparison diagnostic, the better and smoother will be the IFRS transition. In most cases, SNSA's transition team continued with the US GAAP accounting treatment, albeit with some enhanced disclosures being added. Where IFRS offered an accounting treatment similar to US GAAP, SNSA adopted that method. This minimized the final list of differences when transitioning to IFRS to the following:

1. Areas of significant impact under IFRS 1:

    - Business combinations;
    - Actuarial gains and losses;
    - Reset of cumulative translation adjustment.
    - Significant differences from US GAAP which may impact SNSA's financial statements:
    - Property, Plant, and Equipment—component accounting, residual values;
    - Lease accounting;
    - Consolidation of entities;
    - Equity Accounting and FIN 46[R] compared to SIC 12;
    - Fair valuation of inventories of biological assets at Stolt Sea Farm;

2. Other possible areas which could result in a difference from US GAAP on implementation:

    - Impairment—two-step impairment evaluation process under US GAAP and only a single-step discounted cash flow process under IFRS.
    - Provisions—midpoint of an estimate under IFRS not the "best estimate" under US GAAP.
    - Probabilistic evaluation of provisions—higher threshold of "probable" under US GAAP than under IFRS.
    - Business Combinations.
    - Employee Benefits—Defined benefit pension schemes.
    - Financial instruments, including onerous disclosure requirements under IFRS 7.
    - Deferred Tax assets—classification and measurement.
    - Stock options—under IFRS, graded vesting of options must be accounted for using the accelerated attribution method not straight-line method.

When each and every accounting policy, treatment or disclosure is carefully considered as the transition to IFRS progresses, there will still be some risk that there may have been errors in the implementation of IFRS.

SNSA also ran the comparative diagnostic on its equity method investees and joint ventures. One significant change from US GAAP noted during transition was that the equity method investees and joint ventures not only had to comply with IFRS, but had to have IFRS accounting policies which were consistent with those of the rest of the company. In addition, the accounting period had to be coterminous to the year-end of the parent. This also raised a number of IFRS 1 issues in relation to when a subsidiary adopts IFRS and how the change to IFRS could affect the dividend distribution ability of that subsidiary. This matter is particularly important if there is a local legal requirement to have sufficient distributable reserves, which under IFRS could be lower than under current local accounting standards.

After completing the comparison diagnostic, we identified four additional areas to consider when transitioning to IFRS.

- Corporate Finance—if key numbers on which certain debt covenants are based change due to the transition to IFRS then early discussion and negotiation with the banks is critical.
- Tax—involvement of the tax team at the early stages so that they are aware of the transition differences and the impact on tax.
- Human Resources—impact of transition to IFRS on key metrics and incentive plans.
- Technology—changes required in the consolidation systems and in the general ledger accounting systems.
- Internal controls—IFRS requires a higher level of judgement and estimation than US GAAP. This means the controls and process surrounding accounting judgements and estimate must be robust since it will be challenged by the internal controls testing process.
- Investor Relations—it is never to early to start thinking about how the message of transitioning to IFRS will be communicated to the market. There are a number of excellent examples of European Companies that made detailed presentations to investors in 2005 and 2006 to show how they moved from their local GAAP to IFRS.

Materiality

When the GAAP comparison diagnostic is completed, it is extremely important to consider those areas where the measurement differences between US GAAP and IFRS might be "not material." The difficulty with ignoring some differences on the grounds of "materiality" is that the external audit firms will continue to collect these differences on their schedule of passed audit adjustments. Such "not material" differences could become material under the guidance of SAB 99 and SAB 108.

Treatment of Significant Accounting Differences on Transition Opening Balance Sheet under IFRS

An IFRS Transition generally has two kinds of difference—the first one is the difference only on transition and then does not occur each year. The second difference is the one that is a recurring difference. Both these differences need to be recorded in the accounting ledgers in the respective entities.

SNSA's reconciliation of shareholders' equity from US GAAP to IFRS at each of its key transition dates is summarized below.

In millions		Dec. 1, 2006	May 31, 2007	Nov. 30, 2007
Consolidated US GAAP equity		**$1,172.6**	**$1,295.2**	**$1,354.5**
IAS 37 – Record provision in accordance with IFRS	(a)	(1.9)	--	--
IFRS 1/IAS 19 – Pension and Other Postretirement Employee Benefits ("OPEB") adjustment	(b)	(19.3)	(14.4)	(0.7)
IAS 41 – Fair value of biological assets	(c)	22.9	10.8	12.4
IAS 16 – Componentization of Tankers' ships	(d)	(8.1)	(8.2)	(8.4)
IAS 16 – Adjustment to residual value of tank containers	(e)	5.6	6.0	6.7
Reclassification of minority interest to equity		0.3	2.3	10.9
Other items		(0.8)	(0.2)	(5.6)
Net changes		**(1.3)**	**(3.7)**	**15.3**
Consolidated equity under IFRS		**$1,171.3**	**$1,291.5**	**$1,369.8**

* *Full year financial statements under IFRS for the year ended November 30, 2008 had not been published at the time of the publication of this book.*

(a) Measurement of Provisions in accordance with IFRS

Under US GAAP, if a range of estimates is present and no amount in the range is more likely than any other amount in the range, the provision should be measured at the minimum of the range. However, in these circumstances, IAS 37, *Provisions, Contingent Liabilities and Contingent Assets*, requires the midpoint in the range to be used if all outcomes are equally likely. At December 1, 2006, SNSA had entered into negotiations with certain customers with regard to their claims in which the lower range of possible settlements was recognized under US GAAP. The use of the mid-point in the range had resulted in a $1.9 million reduction in retained earnings under IFRS at December 1, 2006 and an increase in revenue of the same amount for the year ended November 30, 2007, as this amount was recognized in the quarters ended February 28, 2007 and May 31, 2007 under US GAAP.

(b) Recognition of Previously Unrecognized Actuarial Losses on Pension and Other Postretirement Employee Benefits

Under US GAAP, the SNSA applied the "corridor" method in relation to the recognition of actuarial gains and losses through the profit and loss. Under this approach, only actuarial gains and losses that fall outside 10% of the projected benefit obligation or, if greater, pension assets are recognized through the profit and loss over the expected average remaining working lives of employees participating in the plan. In accordance with IFRS 1, SNSA recognized all cumulative actuarial gains and losses at December 1, 2006, resulting in a reduction of $23.3 million to retained earnings.

In addition, US GAAP allows the amortization of prior service costs over the expected service life of the employees involved, while IFRS requires prior service costs to be recognized immediately, if they are already vested. IFRS also requires that all plans have the same measurement date as the SNSA's year-end, which resulted in a change in the present value of the funded obligations for one plan. Both of these items have resulted in a $4.0 million credit to retained earnings at December 1, 2006. SNSA had adopted FAS 158, *Employers' Accounting for Defined Benefit Pension and Other Postretirement Plans* for the year ended November 30, 2007. FAS 158 requires an employer to recognize the funded status of a defined benefit plan, measured as the difference between plan assets and the projected benefit obligation, in its consolidated balance sheet.

For this reason, the net change between the numbers previously reported under US GAAP and those reported under IFRS was only about $0.7 million at November 30, 2007, and $0.8 million for the six months ended May 31, 2007.

(c) Fair Value of Biological Assets

Under US GAAP, SNSA reported its biological assets at cost and classified them as part of inventories. Under IAS 41, *Agriculture*, biological assets are required to be recorded at fair value and separately disclosed on the balance sheet. This resulted in an increase in current assets of $17.2 million and $13.0 million (with a deferred tax effect of $5.0 million and $4.5 million) at November 30, 2007, and December 1, 2006, respectively. For the six months ended May 31, 2007, this resulted in a $13.7 million decrease in net profit. Similarly, there was a $14.4 million increase to Investment in and Loans to Marine Harvest at December 1, 2006. This represents SNSA's 25% share of the fair value of biological assets in respect of Marine Harvest. This adjustment also reduced the gain recorded under IFRS on sale of investment in discontinued operations for the year ended November 30, 2007, from $21.8 million to $7.4 million.

(d) Componentization of Ships

Under IAS 16, *Property, Plant, and Equipment*, each component of an asset that has an expected useful life that is significantly different in relation to the total cost of the asset must be depreciated separately, while US GAAP does not explicitly require this treatment (although widely practiced). Following this policy for Tankers' ship components (including ships held by unconsolidated joint ventures) resulted in a decrease in retained earnings of $8.1 million at December 1, 2006. The effect of this adjustment for the six months ended May 31, 2007, was an increase in depreciation expense of approximately $0.1 million.

(e) Residual Value of Tank Containers

Under US GAAP, estimates of residual value of assets are reviewed only when events or changes in circumstances indicate that the current estimates are no longer appropriate, while IFRS requires that estimates of residual values are reviewed at least at each annual reporting date. Applying this policy and assessing the current expected residual value of the SNSA's tank containers at December 1, 2006, resulted in an increase in retained earnings of $5.6 million at transition date, $6.0 million at May 31, 2007, and $6.7 million at November 30, 2007. The effect for the six months ended May 31, 2007, of this adjustment is approximately $0.5 million decrease in depreciation expense.

Reconciliations of the consolidated balance sheets as of December 1, 2006, and November 30, 2007, and consolidated income statements for the four quarters and year ended November 30, 2007, from US GAAP to IFRS are included at the Company's Web site (www.stolt-nielsen.com/Investor-Relations/Accounting-Policies.aspx).

(f) Application of IFRS 1 Exemption to Adjust Currency Translation Reserve to Zero

Under US GAAP, on consolidation, assets and liabilities of subsidiaries are translated into US dollars from their functional currencies at the exchange rates in effect at the balance sheet date while revenues and expenses are translated at the average rate prevailing during the year. The resulting translation adjustments are recorded in a separate component of "Accumulated Other Comprehensive Income (Loss), net." While this is not different from IFRS, the Company has utilized an exemption in IFRS 1, which allows the cumulative translation reserve to be set to zero at the date of transition for all its foreign operations. Consequently, subsequent to the date of transition, amounts previously recognized in net income under US GAAP as a result of the sale of foreign operations of $3.1 million, have been reversed under IFRS.

Other significant accounting differences on transition.

Additional share option expense in relation to stock options with graded vesting features.

The Company grants several share options to its employees that contain graded vesting conditions. Graded vesting conditions exist whereby options granted vest in equal annual installments over a specified period, equal installments of 25% of the options granted each year over a four-year period.

Under US GAAP, the compensation cost of stock options with graded vesting features is amortized on a straight-line basis over the longest vesting period for the entire share option grant.

Under IFRS 2, each of the installments must be treated as a separate option grant and the compensation cost is recognized as the options vest for each installment. Therefore, the IFRS approach accelerates the compensation cost amortization to earlier periods in the overall vesting period. As a result, an adjustment has been recorded to retained earnings as of December 1, 2006, for $3.6 million of additional stock option compensation costs for options granted since 2000, and a further $1.0 million expense recorded for the year-end November 30, 2007.

Impairment of goodwill. Under US GAAP, goodwill is tested for impairment at the reporting unit level, which is an operating segment or one step below while under IAS 36, *Impairment of Assets*, goodwill is tested at the cash generating unit level that represents the lowest level at which goodwill is monitored by management. The use of the cash generating unit level has resulted in the full impairment of goodwill for one cash-generating unit at the date of transition.

Adjustment to equity investment for gain on ship sale. Under US GAAP, when a company sells an asset and immediately leases it back under an operating lease, a proportion of the gain is deferred on the balance sheet when certain conditions are met. The deferred amount is amortized in proportion to the method through which the related gross rental is charged to expense over the lease life.

Under IFRS, if the asset was sold at fair value, any gain or loss is recognized immediately. In the fourth quarter of 2007, the Company's 50% owned joint venture, NYK Stolt Tankers S.A. ("NST"), sold the Stolt Alliance at fair value and immediately leased it back. This resulted in a $5.8 million gain of which $3.8 million was deferred on the balance sheet under US GAAP.

Under IFRS, this amount, $3.8 million, of which the Company's share is $1.9 million, has been recognized in Other Income.

Severance accrual. Under US GAAP, if employees are required to render services beyond a minimum period until they are terminated in order to receive a termination payment, a liability for terminated benefits is measured initially at the date of communication to the relevant employees, based on the fair value of the liability as of the termination date. The liability is then recognized ratably over the future service period. Under IFRS, the liability is recorded immediately. Adoption of this policy resulted in a decrease in retained earnings at November 30, 2007, of $0.8 million and a decrease in net profit for 2007 of $0.7 million.

Balance sheet and income statement reclassifications. The following represents additional balance sheet and income statement reclassifications required by IFRS.

Deconsolidation of Lingang Terminal. The Company has a 65% ownership in Tianjin Stolthaven Lingang Terminal Co. ("Lingang Terminal") which is a development stage entity and in the process of building a terminal facility. Under US GAAP, the Company is required to consolidate this entity as it was considered to be a variable interest entity under FIN 46(R), *Consolidation of Variable Interest Entities*, and the Company was the primary beneficiary.

However, under IFRS the Lingang Terminal meets the definition of a joint venture as there is joint control over the entity, and so the entity has been accounted for under equity accounting.

Reclassification of minority interest to equity. Under US GAAP, minority interest is displayed as a long-term liability. IAS 1, *Presentation of Financial Statements*, and IAS 27, *Consolidated and Separate Financial Statements*, require minority interests to be presented within equity.

Reclassification of software to intangible assets. Under US GAAP, computer software is included in property, plant and equipment. In accordance with IAS 38, *Intangible Assets*, when the software is not an integral part of the related hardware, computer software should be classified as an intangible asset. Accordingly, $3.3 million and $3.1 million of computer software that is not integral to any associated hardware were reclassified from property, plant and equipment to intangible assets on transition to IFRS at November 30, 2007 and December 1, 2006, respectively.

Reclassification of drydocking asset to property, plant, and equipment. Capitalized costs related to the drydocking of ships are treated as a separate component of tankers under IAS 16, Property, Plant and Equipment. Accordingly they are classified as property, plant and equipment under IFRS while they are recorded as an Other Long-Term Asset under US GAAP.

Reclassification of short-term deferred tax assets and liabilities. Under US GAAP, deferred tax assets and liabilities are classified as either current or noncurrent based upon the classification of the related asset or liability.

A deferred tax liability or asset that is not related to an asset or liability recognised in the balance sheet such as losses carryforwards, is classified according to the expected reversal date of the temporary difference. Under IAS 12, *Income Taxes*, all deferred tax assets and liabilities are classified as noncurrent regardless of the classification of the related asset or liability and regardless of the expected timing of reversal of the temporary difference.

Reclassification of debt issuance costs against current portion of long-term debt and long-term debt. Under IAS 39, Financial Instruments: Recognition and Measurement, transaction costs directly attributable to a debt are recorded against the debt on initial recognition. Under US GAAP, debt issuance costs are recognized as Other Assets. This has required a reclassification of $5.1 million and $6.1 million from Other Assets to both the Current Portion of Long-Term Debt and to Long-Term Debt at November 30, 2007, and December 1, 2006, respectively.

Transfer of minimum pension liability adjustments to retained earnings. Under US GAAP, if the accumulated benefit obligation is greater than the value of the plan assets, a minimum liability must be recognized in the balance sheet for the unfunded accumulated pension liability. In cases where an additional minimum liability is required, a portion is recognized as a component of other comprehensive income.

There is no concept of an additional minimum pension liability under IAS 19, *Employee Benefits*. Therefore, amounts recognized in other comprehensive income under US GAAP have been reclassified to retained earnings on adoption of IFRS.

More detailed information on SNSA's IFRS Transition, including accounting policies, reconciliations of the consolidated balance sheets as of December 1, 2006, and November 30, 2007, and consolidated income statements for the four quarters and year ended November 30, 2007, from US GAAP to IFRS are included in the Company's Web site: http://www.stolt-nielsen.com/Investor-Relations/Accounting-Policies.aspx.

APPENDIX D

US GAAP RECONCILIATION AND RESTATEMENT—CASE STUDY

While the US SEC has now ended the requirement that foreign private issuers filing in the US reconcile their non-US GAAP financial statements to US GAAP, this waiver is applicable only if "full IFRS" is employed by the registrant in preparing its financial statements. Those preparing financial statements under non-US GAAP, including any national or other variations of IFRS (including "Euro-IFRS"), will not be permitted to enjoy this exception to SEC rules. To illustrate the process of reconciliation to US GAAP, the example of Finnish company Nokia Oy's 2005 filing with the SEC is hereby presented.

Nokia Oy prepares its financial statement in accordance with IFRS but also files in the US, where is must reconcile certain financial statement captions to the US GAAP basis. The following is taken from Nokia's 2005 financial statements.

	2001 (EUR)	2002 (EUR)	2003* (EUR)	2004* (EUR)	2005 (EUR)	2005 (EUR)
	Year ended December 31,					
			(In millions, except per share data)			
Profit and Loss Account Data						
Amounts in accordance with IFRS						
Net sales	31,191	30,016	29,533	29,371	34,191	40,489
Operating profit	3,362	4,780	4,960	4,326	4,639	5,494
Profit before tax	3,475	4,917	5,294	4,705	4,971	5,887
Profit attributable to equity holders of the parent	2,200	3,381	3,543	3,192	3,616	4,282
Earnings per share (for profit attributable to equity holders of the parent)						
Basic earnings per share	0.47	0.71	0.74	0.69	0.83	0.98
Diluted earnings per share	0.46	0.71	0.74	0.69	0.83	0.98
Cash dividends per share [(1)]	0.27	0.28	0.30	0.33	0.37	0.44
Average number of shares (millions of shares)						
Basic	4,703	4,751	4,761	4,593	4,366	4,366
Diluted	4,787	4,788	4,761	4,600	4,371	4,371
Amounts in accordance with US GAAP						
Net income	1,903	3,603	4,097	3,343	3,582	4,242
Earnings per share (net income)						
Basic earnings per share	0.40	0.76	0.86	0.73	0.82	0.97
Diluted earnings per share	0.40	0.75	0.86	0.73	0.82	0.97
Statement of Financial Position Data						
Amounts in accordance with IFRS						
Fixed assets and other noncurrent assets	6,912	5,742	3,837	3,161	3,347	3,964
Cash and other liquid assets [(2)]	6,125	9,351	11,296	11,542	9,910	11,735
Other current assets	9,390	8,234	8,787	7,966	9,041	10,706
Total assets	22,427	23,327	23,920	22,669	22,298	26,405
Capital and reserves attributable to equity holders of the parent	12,205	14,281	15,148	14,231	12,155	14,394
Minority interests	196	173	164	168	205	243
Long-term interest-bearing liabilities	207	187	20	19	21	25
Other long term liabilities	253	274	308	275	247	292
Borrowing due within one year	831	377	471	215	377	446
Other current liabilities	8,735	8,035	7,809	7,761	9,293	11,005
Total shareholders' equity and liabilities	22,427	23,327	23,920	22,669	22,298	26,405
Net interest-bearing debt [(3)]	(5,087)	(8,787)	(10,805)	(11,308)	(9,512)	(11,264)
Share capital	284	287	288	280	266	315

	2001 (EUR)	2002 (EUR)	2003* (EUR)	2004* (EUR)	2005 (EUR)	2005 (EUR)
				Year ended December 31,		
			(In millions, except per share data)			
Amounts in accordance with US GAAP						
Total assets	22,038	22,977	24,045	22,921	22,661	26,835
Shareholders' equity	12,021	14,150	15,437	14,576	12,558	14,871

* *2003 and 2004 financial accounts reflect the retrospective implementations of IFRS 2 and IAS 39(R). 2001 and 2002 data has not been adjusted from that reported in prior years, and therefore is not always comparable with data for years 2003 to 2005.*

(1) *The cash dividend for 2005 is what the Board of Directors will propose for approval at the Annual General Meeting convening on March 30, 2006.*

(2) *Cash and other liquid assets consist of the following captions from our consolidated statements of financial position: (1) bank and cash, (2) available-for-sale investments, cash equivalents and (3) available-for-sale investments, liquid assets.*

(3) *Net interest-bearing debt consists of borrowings due within one year and long-term interest-bearing liabilities, less cash and other liquid assets.*

APPENDIX E

USE OF PRESENT VALUE IN ACCOUNTING

Present value is a pervasive concept that has many applications in accounting. Most significantly, present value of future cash flows is widely recognized and accepted as one approach to the assessment of fair value, which is commonly invoked in various accounting standards. Currently, IFRS does not provide specific guidance to this subject matter, but in recognition of its importance, guidance drawn from US GAAP's Concepts Statement 7 (CON 7) is summarized on the following pages.

CON 7 provides a framework for using estimates of future cash flows as the basis for accounting measurements either at initial recognition or when assets are subsequently remeasured at fair value (fresh-start measurements). It also provides a framework for using the interest method of amortization. It provides the principles that govern measurement using present value, especially when the amount of future cash flows, their timing, or both are uncertain. However, it does not address recognition questions, such as which transactions and events should be valued using present value measures or when fresh-start measurements are appropriate.

Fair value is the objective for most measurements at initial recognition and for fresh-start measurements in subsequent periods. At initial recognition, the cash paid or received (historical cost or proceeds) is usually assumed to be fair value, absent evidence to the contrary. For fresh-start measurements, a price that is observed in the marketplace for an essentially similar asset or liability is fair value. If purchase prices and market prices are available, there is no need to use alternative measurement techniques to approximate fair value. However, if alternative measurement techniques must be used for initial recognition and for fresh-start measurements, those techniques should attempt to capture the elements that when taken together would comprise a market price if one existed. The objective is to estimate the price likely to exist in the marketplace if there were a marketplace—fair value.

CON 7 states that the only objective of using present value in accounting measurements is fair value. It is necessary to capture, to the extent possible, the economic differences in the marketplace between sets of estimated future cash flows. A present value measurement that fully captures those differences must include the following elements:

1. An estimate of the future cash flow, or in more complex cases, series of future cash flows at different times
2. Expectations about possible variations in the amount or timing of those cash flows
3. The time value of money, represented by the risk-free rate of interest
4. The risk premium—the price for bearing the uncertainty inherent in the asset or liability
5. Other factors, including illiquidity and market imperfections

How CON 7 measures differ from previously utilized present value techniques. Previously employed present value techniques typically used a single set of estimated cash flows and a single discount (interest) rate. In applying those techniques, adjustments for factors 2. through 5. described in the previous paragraph are incorporated in the selection of the discount rate. In the CON 7 approach, only the third factor listed (the time value of money) is included in the discount rate; the other factors cause adjustments in arriving at risk-adjusted expected cash flows. CON 7 introduces the probability-weighted, expected cash flow approach, which focuses on the range of possible estimated cash flows and estimates of their respective probabilities of occurrence.

Previous techniques used to compute present value used estimates of the cash flows most likely to occur. CON 7 refines and enhances the precision of this model by weighting different cash flow scenarios (regarding the amounts and timing of cash flows) by their estimated probabilities of occurrence and factoring these scenarios into the ultimate determination of fair value. The difference is that values are assigned to the cash flows other than the most likely one. To illustrate, a cash flow might be €100, €200, or €300 with probabilities of 10%, 50% and 40%, respectively. The most likely cash flow is the one with 50% probability, or €200. The expected cash flow is €230 (= €100 × .1) + (€200 × .5) + (€300 × .4).

The CON 7 method, unlike previous present value techniques, can also accommodate uncertainty in the timing of cash flows. For example, a cash flow of €10,000 may be received in one year, two years, or three years with probabilities of 15%, 60%, and 25%, respectively. Traditional present value techniques would compute the present value using the most likely timing of the payment—two years. The example below shows the computation of present value using the CON 7 method. Again, the expected present value of €9,030 differs from the traditional notion of a best estimate of €9,070 (the 60% probability) in this example.

Present value of €10,000 in one year discounted at 5%	€9,523	
Multiplied by 15% probability		€1,428
Present value of €10,000 in two years discounted at 5%	9,070	
Multiplied by 60% probability		5,442
Present value of €10,000 in three years discounted at 5%	8,638	
Multiplied by 25% probability		2,160
Probability weighted expected present value		€9,030

Measuring liabilities. The measurement of liabilities involves different problems from the measurement of assets; however, the underlying objective is the same. When using present value techniques to estimate the fair value of a liability, the objective is to estimate the value of the assets required currently to (1) settle the liability with the holder or (2) transfer the liability to an entity of comparable credit standing. To estimate the fair value of an entity's notes or bonds payable, accountants look to the price at which other entities are willing to hold the entity's liabilities as assets. For example, the proceeds of a loan are the price that a lender paid to hold the borrower's promise of future cash flows as an asset.

The most relevant measurement of an entity's liabilities should always reflect the credit standing of the entity. An entity with a good credit standing will receive more cash for its promise to pay than an entity with a poor credit standing. For example, if two entities both promise to pay €750 in three years with no stated interest payable in the interim, Entity A, with a good credit standing, might receive about €630 (a 6% interest rate). Entity B, with a poor credit standing, might receive about €533 (a 12% interest rate). Each entity initially records its respective liability at fair value, which is the amount of proceeds received—an amount that incorporates that entity's credit standing.

Present value techniques can also be used to value a guarantee of a liability. Assume that Entity B in the above example owes Entity C. If Entity A were to assume the debt, it would want to be compensated €630—the amount that it could get in the marketplace for its promise to pay €750 in three years. The difference between what Entity A would want to take the place of Entity B (€630) and the amount that Entity B receives (€533) is the value of the guarantee (€97).

Interest method of allocation. CON 7 describes the factors that suggest that an interest method of allocation should be used. It states that the interest method of allocation is more relevant than other methods of cost allocation when it is applied to assets and liabilities that exhibit one or more of the following characteristics:

1. The transaction is, in substance, a borrowing and lending transaction.
2. Period-to-period allocation of similar assets or liabilities employs an interest method.
3. A particular set of estimated future cash flows is closely associated with the asset or liability.
4. The measurement at initial recognition was based on present value.

Accounting for changes in expected cash flows. If the timing or amount of estimated cash flows changes and the asset or liability is not remeasured at a fresh-start measure, the interest method of allocation should be altered by a catch-up approach. That approach adjusts the carrying amount to the present value of the revised estimated future cash flows, discounted at the original effective interest rate.

Application of present value tables and formulas.

Present value of a single future amount. To take the present value of a single amount that will be paid in the future, apply the following formula; where *PV* is the present value of €1 paid in the future, *r* is the interest rate per period, and *n* is the number of periods between the current date and the future date when the amount will be realized.

$$PV = \frac{1}{(1+r)^n}$$

In many cases the results of this formula are summarized in a present value factor table.

(n) Periods	*2%*	*3%*	*4%*	*5%*	*6%*	*7%*	*8%*	*9%*	*10%*
1	0.9804	0.9709	0.9615	0.9524	0.9434	0.9346	0.9259	0.9174	0.9091
2	0.9612	0.9426	0.9246	0.9070	0.8900	0.8734	0.8573	0.8417	0.8265
3	0.9423	0.9151	0.8890	0.8638	0.8396	0.8163	0.7938	0.7722	0.7513
4	0.9239	0.8885	0.8548	0.8227	0.7921	0.7629	0.7350	0.7084	0.6830
5	0.9057	0.8626	0.8219	0.7835	0.7473	0.7130	0.6806	0.6499	0.6209

Example

Suppose one wishes to determine how much would need to be invested today to have €10,000 in five years if the sum invested would earn 8%. Looking across the row with n = 5 and finding the present value factor for the r = 8% column, the factor of 0.6806 would be identified. Multiplying €10,000 by 0.6806 results in €6,806, the amount that would need to be invested today to have €10,000 at the end of five years. Alternatively, using a calculator and applying the present value of a single sum formula, one could multiply €10,000 by $1/(1 + .08)^5$, which would also give the same answer—€6,806.

Present value of a series of equal payments (an annuity). Many times in business situations a series of equal payments paid at equal time intervals is required. Examples of these include payments of semiannual bond interest and principal or lease payments. The present value of each of these payments could be added up to find the present value of this annuity, or alternatively a much simpler approach is available. The formula for calculating the present value of an annuity of €1 payments over *n* periodic payments, at a periodic interest rate of *r* is

$$PV\ Annuity = \left(1 - \frac{1}{(1+r)^n} \right)$$

The results of this formula are summarized in an annuity present value factor table.

(n) Periods	2%	3%	4%	5%	6%	7%	8%	9%	10%
1	0.9804	0.9709	0.9615	0.9524	0.9434	0.9346	0.9259	0.9174	0.9091
2	1.9416	1.9135	1.8861	1.8594	1.8334	1.8080	1.7833	1.7591	1.7355
3	2.8839	2.8286	2.7751	2.7233	2.6730	2.6243	2.5771	2.5313	2.4869
4	3.8077	3.7171	3.6299	3.5460	3.4651	3.3872	3.3121	3.2397	3.1699
5	4.7135	4.5797	4.4518	4.3295	4.2124	4.1002	3.9927	3.8897	3.7908

Example

Suppose four annual payments of €1,000 will be needed to satisfy an agreement with a supplier. What would be the amount of the liability today if the interest rate the supplier is charging is 6% per year? Using the table to get the present value factor, then n = 4 periods row, and the 6% column, gives you a factor of 3.4651. Multiply this by €1,000 and you get a liability of €3,465.10 that should be recorded. Using the formula would also give you the same answer with r = 6% and n = 4.

Caution must be exercised when payments are not to be made on an annual basis. If payments are on a semiannual basis n = 8, but *r* is now 3%. This is because *r* is the periodic interest rate, and the semiannual rate would not be 6%, but half of the 6% annual rate. Note that this is somewhat simplified, since due to the effect of compound interest 3% semiannually is slightly more than a 6% annual rate.

Example of the relevance of present values

A measurement based on the present value of estimated future cash flows provides more relevant information than a measurement based on the undiscounted sum of those cash flows. For example, consider the following four future cash flows, all of which have an undiscounted value of €100,000:

1. Asset A has a fixed contractual cash flow of €100,000 due tomorrow. The cash flow is certain of receipt.
2. Asset B has a fixed contractual cash flow of €100,000 due in twenty years. The cash flow is certain of receipt.
3. Asset C has a fixed contractual cash flow of €100,000 due in twenty years. The amount that ultimately will be received is uncertain. There is an 80% probability that the entire €100,000 will be received. There is a 20% probability that €80,000 will be received.
4. Asset D has an *expected* cash flow of €100,000 due in twenty years. The amount that ultimately will be received is uncertain. There is a 25% probability that €120,000 will be received. There is a 50% probability that €100,000 will be received. There is a 25% probability that €80,000 will be received.

Assuming a 5% risk-free rate of return, the present values of the assets are

1. Asset A has a present value of €99,986. The time value of money assigned to the one-day period is €14 (€100,000 × .05/365 days).
2. Asset B has a present value of €37,689 [€100,000/$(1 + .05)^{20}$].
3. Asset C has a present value of €36,181 [(€100,000 × .8 + 80,000 × .2)/$(1 + .05)^{20}$].
4. Asset D has a present value of €37,689 [€120,000 × .25 + 100,000 × .5 + 80,000 × .25)/$(1 + .05)^{20}$].

Although each of these assets has the same undiscounted cash flows, few would argue that they are economically the same or that a rational investor would pay the same price for each. Investors require compensation for the time value of money. They also require a risk premium. That is, given a choice between Asset B with expected cash flows that are certain and Asset D with cash flows of the same expected amount that are uncertain, investors will place a higher value on Asset B, even though they have the same expected present value. CON 7 says that the risk premium should be subtracted from the expected cash flows before applying the discount rate.

Thus, if the risk premium for Asset D was €500, the risk-adjusted present values would be €37,500 {[(€120,000 × .25 + 100,000 × .5 + 80,000 × .25) − 500]/(1 + .05)^{20}}.

Practical matters. Like any accounting measurement, the application of an expected cash flow approach is subject to a cost-benefit constraint. The cost of obtaining additional information must be weighed against the additional reliability that information will bring to the measurement. As a practical matter, an entity that uses present value measurements often has little or no information about some or all of the assumptions that investors would use in assessing the fair value of an asset or a liability. Instead, the entity must use the information that is available to it without undue cost and effort when it develops cash flow estimates. The entity's own assumptions about future cash flows can be used to estimate fair value using present value techniques, as long as there are no contrary data indicating that investors would use different assumptions. However, if contrary data exist, the entity must adjust its assumptions to incorporate that market information.

APPENDIX F

USE OF FAIR VALUE IN ACCOUNTING MEASUREMENTS

The use of fair value measurements, sometimes also called *market values* or *fair market values,* has expanded in financial reporting over the decades, for two major reasons. First, it has become ever more obvious to preparers and users alike that fair value measures provide the most relevant information for use by decision makers, particularly when compared to the traditional alternative measure, amortized historical cost. And second, the availability of valid, relevant fair value data has greatly increased as information technology has provided most preparers, auditors, and users with access that previous generations could not even imagine.

The use of fair value (or equivalent) measures for financial reporting purposes is hardly a new development. During certain periods in the past (e.g., when inflation caused historical cost data to become particularly obsolete over short time horizons) a number of experiments have been pursued to make financial reporting more relevant by using current cost, replacement cost, fair market value, or other surrogates for pure fair value. Many accounting standards, under various national GAAP regimes as well as IFRS, have always made use of fair values as the appropriate measurement for financial statement representations. Common examples include net realizable value for accounts receivable, lower of cost or market (or realizable value) for inventories, and amortized cost less impairments for many categories of long-lived assets. While the goal of fair value reporting was only partially met by using such surrogates, given the limitations of information availability and the unease many accountants have felt when departing from the absolute verifiability of historical cost measures, these were reasonable and reasonably successful efforts.

During the great inflationary period of the late 1960s to the early mid-1980s, there was a particular concern with developing income measurement strategies that at least partially obviated the inflation effect of matching older, lower costs for goods sold and depreciation charges against more recent product prices, the impact of which was to overstate economic earnings and, inadvertently, encourage such destructive practices as paying excessive dividends, granting excessive wage increases, and failing to post selling price increases to the extent the market would allow them. The illusion of profits caused by the mismatching of costs and revenues led many managers to take actions that thus left the entities unable to maintain their physical capital (e.g., not being able to replace inventory sold at a nominal profit because the replacement cost thereof exceeded the proceeds of the goods already sold).

In reaction, a number of nations, including the US and the UK, implemented supplementary financial reporting requirements (using the very similar but not identical current values, current costs, or replacement costs) to more meaningfully measure results of operations. These were, at best, partial efforts, focusing only on key cost components (cost of goods sold and depreciation, in general), in an attempt to ease the burdens and make the extra effort palatable. Once inflation was generally brought under control by the mid-1980s, interest in these supplementary reporting methodologies largely waned and most requirements were revoked.

Subsequently, however, new attention was directed at the use of fair value measures for monetary assets and liabilities. Compared to the concerns of the 1970s and early 1980s, which were directed exclusively toward the current value measurement of nonmonetary assets (inventory and long-lived assets, primarily), the move to address fair value reporting of monetary items has been greatly facilitated by the fact that information is much more readily available. For many monetary assets, such as marketable securities, data is easily obtained from (previously) daily newspapers and (now) online quotation services. Thus, at least superficially, the practicality issue has been rendered moot.

Market values for only a limited class of assets are immediately obtainable and highly reliable, however. For many of the assets and liabilities for which fair value measurement has been increasingly mandated over recent decades, it is necessary to analogize from market values for similar, but not identical, assets; and for a fraction of these, no close analogies exist at all, a situation which then necessitates the use of "models" to approximate a fair value measurement. During the period of expanded, large-scale financial reporting frauds in the late 1990s and early 2000s, the use of certain variants on the fair value theme (notably, Enron's "mark to model" approach to energy futures contract valuation) contributed to catastrophic corporate abuses and bankruptcies. While the abusive practices were never GAAP-compliant and implicated audit failures, perhaps more than poor GAP standards, the popular perception was that these failures, in part, sprang from such liberalizations as the move away from eminently verifiable historical costs.

After at most a brief pause, the trend to wider use of fair value measures continued, notwithstanding these experiences. A watershed event occurred when the US standard setter, FASB, issued FAS 157, *Fair Value Measurements*, in 2006. This standard—which did not mandate any wider use of fair value measures than already existed—established a three-level hierarchy of methodologies, coupled with expanded disclosure requirement. By late 2006, IASB had issued a Discussion Paper addressing the same topic, and in fact essentially "wrapped around" FAS 157 some additional considerations. If an Exposure Draft of a final standard is released (promised for mid-2009), ultimately to be followed by a final standard (now anticipated for sometime in 2010), based on this Discussion Paper, the standard will closely parallel FAS 157 and may even fully replicate it.

While FAS 157 and the international financial reporting standard that will eventually address the same issues are intended to guide users attempting to apply fair value measurements, without dictating broader application of fair value, both FASB and IASB have also made clear their respective intentions to expand the use of fair value measures in financial reporting. Thus far, these intentions have been limited to financial instruments and other monetary items, with fair value reporting of monetary liabilities being among the more prominently noted expansion targets. The "fair value option" rules propounded under IFRS, at first (via an amendment to IAS 39), and later under US GAAP (FAS 159), have been the most notable of these efforts thus far.

A detour of sorts on the road to expanded use of fair values has recently occurred, as a by-product of the worldwide financial institutions crisis precipitated by the sudden deflation in residential real estate values, followed by concerns about poor credit quality (the so-called subprime lending issue), a growing reluctance to lend by banks and thrifts, and the resultant economy-wide credit crunch that now (as of late 2008) threatens a major and protracted recession, and which has triggered the most far-reaching restructurings of the financial institution segments of major world economies seen since the 1930s, at least. Fair value accounting has become, oddly enough, the scapegoat of choice by bankers, politicians and others seeking an explanation other than the obvious collapse of the housing bubble that had been widely observed and forecast for over a decade.

The coincidence of expanded fair value reporting and the real estate collapse has facilitated this particular spate of blame-shifting. While it is certainly true that fair value-based reporting may result in greater volatility in reported earnings, this only occurs if and when the underlying economic performances of the reporting entities are indeed volatile. An entity enjoying stable performance will report stable earnings, absent such extraneous actions and events as the holding of large, passive investment portfolios which become buffeted by market forces unrelated to the reporting entity's central business activities (and few companies have the luxury of being able to hold large investment portfolios, other than financial institutions, for which such portfolios are a central aspect of their operations).

As with all generalizations, however, there is a large kernel of truth in the observation that fair value accounting has contributed to the near-panic situation that developed by mid-2008, with the collapse of venerable banks and investment banks and the near-elimination of an entire industry segment (the large, formerly private but more recently publicly held investment banks, of which all the only surviving independent US members have sought the shelter of commercial bank charters). With the collapse of the subprime mortgage lending business, resulting from rapidly growing defaults by debtors willing to walk away from "underwater" properties, entities (not limited to banks, although these have been among the major victims) were required to recognize "mark-to-market" adjustments and huge losses which decimated many banks' capital, prompting seizures by regulatory authorities, forced mergers with healthier institutions, and some outright failures. As some institutions failed, the ripple effect on others holding debt or other instruments of those banks, or holding the same or other similar investments as were held by failing institutions, grew apace.

All dramatic declines in value lend themselves to exaggerated claims and explanations, and the current one is no exception. In the present situation, the claim being made is that banks and other (mostly regulated) institutions, faced with holdings of mortgage-backed and other debt securities that suddenly have become "illiquid" due to temporary market anomalies and the so-called "flight to safety" previously also experienced during, for example, the Asian credit crisis of the late 1990s, have been forced to essentially write-down all such holdings to zero, under the fair value accounting rules that, arguably, offer no alternatives when markets seize up at the end of the reporting period. A closer look at the fair value hierarchy under FAS 157 (the best guidance presently extant, even for those reporting under IFRS), however, reveals a greater degree of flexibility than is being publicly acknowledged. This will be further explained later in this appendix.

The increasingly widely held view by late 2008 was that, absent the twin evils of (1) the need to "mark-to-market" these investments at all, and (2) the dramatic declines in fair values caused by the downward price spiral precipitated by declining residential property values and its follow-on effects (loan defaults, foreclosures, the market-dampening effects of the surfeit of for-sale foreclosed and other properties, etc.), which triggered round after round of write-downs and further failures, this crisis would not have occurred. Many interested groups, including preparers and users of financial statements, have begun to agitate for suspension, relaxation or outright repeal of "mark-to-market" accounting by banks and other financial institutions, and possible revision or rescission of the fair value hierarchy established by FAS 157 and in the process of being developed or mimicked by IASB. While leaders including the chairs of both FASB and IASB have publicly identified the fallacies of placing responsibility for the residential real estate and subprime lending bubble burst on the fair value accounting rules, the ultimate outcome cannot be forecast at this early date.

One feature distinguishes the current standard-setting and standard-revising concerns in the US from what may take place under IFRS. US GAAP more generously allowed the use of "off-statement of financial position" vehicles, much (but not all) of which was designed to facilitate the securitization of debt obligations so that the ultimate investors in the debt (which had been divided into so-called *tranches* having varying credit qualities and cash flow properties) were far removed from the actual credit granting process and often had little idea of the actual underlying composition of the investments they held. These vehicles, originally known as SPEs (special-purposes entities), and later as SPVs (special-purpose vehicles) and QSPEs (qualified special-purpose entities), and most recently as VIEs (variable interest entities), were designed to accomplish specific financial objectives, for example, making diversified pools of underlying loans available for investments by investors of only modest means; providing a more liquid secondary market for previously rather illiquid investments (e.g., residential mortgages) and specific financial reporting objectives (removing assets and related debt obligations from the reporting entities' statements of financial position, thereby improving the entities' apparent debt/equity ratios and making further lending activities more feasible). Largely in reaction to certain abuses and the fallout from the residential real estate market declines and subsequent epidemic of loan defaults, FASB is deliberating rule changes that would likely put back on sponsors' statements of financial position some or all of the previously derecognized assets and liabilities.

The IFRS requirements have always been less accommodating, however, with fewer opportunities available for reporting entities to remove assets and liabilities from their statements of financial position. In contrast to the corresponding requirements under US GAAP, which makes use of complex determinations of primary beneficiaries of variable interest entities established by reporting entities, the IFRS approach has been to effectively require consolidation of most such financing structures. Utilizing a much simpler concept of *control*, IFRS require consolidation (and hence, no derecognition) of QSPE-like entities. While there can be very important reasons for employing such structures (most importantly, to isolate certain financial assets so that less risk attaches to the cash flows associated with them, which facilitates using these assets as collateral for further borrowings), the *accounting* result of derecognition will not necessarily follow.

The remainder of this Appendix will explain the IASB's discussion paper on *Fair Value Measurements*, as well as FASB's FAS 157, *Fair Value Measurements*. The authors believe that the move toward greater application of fair value measurements will continue (possible after another brief pause), particularly for financial instruments and other monetary items such as receivables and payables, and that this guidance will be necessary and useful.

The IASB Discussion Paper on Fair Value Measurements

The November 2006 IASB Discussion Paper, *Fair Value Measurements*, essentially wrapped a series of questions around the FASB's then-new standard, FAS 157 (discussed below). It challenges users to consider whether IASB should issue guidance identical or very similar to that standard, which would then provide the sole source for authoritative guidance on this topic. In soliciting these observations, the DP notes the many differences (both substantive and terminological) between US GAAP and IFRS, and invites comments relative to how these differences would, or would not, demand an alternative approach to the hierarchy of fair value measurements set forth by FAS 157. For example, FAS 157 adopts an "exit price" definition of fair value, which was a notable departure from much existing guidance under US GAAP, and would likewise be a deviation from at least certain of the current requirements of IFRS. This issue is particularly acute with regard to the fair value measurement of liabilities.

As of late 2008, IASB is anticipating that an Exposure Draft will be issued in the first half of 2009, and that a final standard will appear the following year. If IASB decides to essentially embrace FAS 157 in its totality, this project can move forward as planned. However, if IASB (based on constituent feedback received by the April 2007 deadline, as well as input from an Expert Advisory Panel appointed in June, 2008) determines that it must create a unique standard to provide for the needs of IFRS users, then even this leisurely pace may be further extended.

FASB FAS 157, *Fair Value Measurements*—The Mixed Attribute Model

Under longstanding US GAAP, mirrored to a greater or lesser extent by other national GAAP and IFRS, assets, liabilities, and equity have been measured and presented in a reporting entity's statement of financial position by applying a disjointed, inconsistent assortment of accounting methods. This is sometimes characterized as the "mixed attribute model." The following table summarizes the current state of the mixed-attribute model as exhibited by US GAAP and the effects of FAS 157 and FAS 159 (if any) on specified assets and liabilities of reporting entities that are not financial institutions, investment companies, or insurance companies.

Assets			**Liabilities and Equity**		
Key*	*Caption*	*Customary measurement attribute*	*Key**	*Caption*	*Customary measurement attribute*
A	Cash and cash equivalents	Cost, approximating fair value	E	Notes and bonds payable	Unpaid principal adjusted for accrued interest, unamortized premium or discount, unamortized debt issue costs
E	Accounts receivable (with terms not exceeding one year)	Estimated net realizable value	A	Accounts payable	Contractual price agreed upon by the parties; depending on the contractual terms, often will approximate fair value
E	Notes, loans and accounts receivable with terms exceeding one year	Unamortized principal due less allowance for credit losses; also subject to evaluation for impairment when holder considers it probable that it will be unable to collect all amounts due in accordance with the contractual terms	A	Payroll taxes withheld and accrued; sales taxes payable	Amounts due to taxing authorities; due to short periods during which these amounts are outstanding, they usually approximate fair value without being discounted to their present value
N	Inventory	Lower of cost or market using FIFO, LIFO, average cost, or specific identification	N	Income tax liabilities currently payable	Amounts due to taxing authorities based on positions claimed on income tax returns filed or to be filed
N	Deposits	Cost less portion applied by the holder or for which no future benefits are expected	N	Unrecognized income tax positions	Amounts due to taxing authorities for income tax positions claimed or to be claimed on tax returns that exceed the maximum amount that is more than 50% probable of being sustained upon audit
E	Investments in debt and marketable equity securities including those held by a not-for-profit organization	Trading and available-for-sale securities at fair value; held-to-maturity securities at amortized cost subject to evaluation for other-than-temporary impairment	N	Deferred income taxes	Future taxable temporary differences multiplied by the effective tax rate expected to apply upon their future reversal

Assets   **Liabilities and Equity**

Key*	Caption	Customary measurement attribute	Key*	Caption	Customary measurement attribute
E	Investments, cost method	Historical cost less dividends received by the investor in excess of the investee's net accumulated earnings since the date of acquisition by the investor, and subject to evaluation for other-than-temporary impairment	N	Accrued expenses	Expenses incurred or allocated to operations that have not yet been invoiced by the supplier or provider and are not yet currently payable
E	Investments, equity method	Historical cost adjusted to recognize the investor's share of investee income and losses, dividend distributions, and amortization of difference between investor cost and underlying net assets of the investee ("equity method goodwill"); subject to evaluation for other-than-temporary impairment	E	Warranty obligations	Estimated costs expected to be incurred over the warranty period
A	Derivatives	Fair value (depending on the measurement, the derivative can be an asset in one period and a liability in another period)	N	Deferred compensation arrangements, pensions, other postemployment benefits	Subject to highly complex GAAP that, in general, accrues the cost of the benefits to be provided in the future in a manner that results in compensation cost being recognized in the periods benefiting from the services provided, including factors for the time value of money, various actuarial assumptions relevant to the measurement, and when the arrangement is funded and based on assumptions regarding future investment returns
N	Prepaid expenses	Cost less amounts consumed in operations or allocated to operations based on the passage of time	E	Guarantee liabilities	Initially recognized at fair value; reduced during the life of the guarantee as the guarantor is discharged from the obligation to stand ready to perform
N	Deferred income taxes	Future deductible temporary differences and carryforwards multiplied by the effective tax rate expected to apply upon their future reversal and less a valuation allowance for the portion, if any, that is not more than 50% probable of being realized.	N	Asset retirement obligations	Initially recognized as the expected present value of the future cost associated with a legal obligation to retire an asset or group of assets; generally increased in subsequent periods for accretion of interest on the obligation

Assets

Key*	Caption	Customary measurement attribute
N	Property and equipment held and used	Cost less accumulated depreciation subject to evaluation for impairment upon the occurrence of certain events and circumstances
N	Property and equipment held for sale	Fair value less cost to sell
N	Cash surrender value of life insurance	Amount realizable under the contract at the end of the reporting period net of outstanding policy loans
N	Goodwill	Arises in business combinations: FAS 141: The excess of the purchase price over the fair values of identifiable tangible and intangible net assets acquired; subject to annual impairment tests; FAS 141(R): The excess of the consideration transferred plus the fair value of any noncontrolling interest in the acquiree at the acquisition date over the fair values of the identifiable net assets acquired; In both cases, goodwill is subject to annual impairment testing
N	Other intangible assets	Fair value at initial recognition; subject to considerations as to whether the intangible is amortizable and whether impaired; Under FAS 141(R) this category includes in-process research and development assets acquired in a business combination

Liabilities and Equity

Key*	Caption	Customary measurement attribute
N	Contingencies	If probable that a liability has been incurred and amount is reasonably estimable, the estimated settlement amount

*ABBREVIATION KEY:

E—Generally eligible for fair value election under FAS 159
A—Already stated at fair value or an amount that approximates fair value
N—Not eligible for fair value election or to be measured at fair value on a recurring basis

Further complicating this state of affairs under US GAAP is the current state of specialized industry accounting rules. A commercial bank holding a debt instrument is subject to FAS 115, *Accounting for Certain Investments in Debt and Equity Securities*, and thus would consider whether the debt instrument is held for trading purposes, is available for sale, or is expected to be held to maturity. Depending on how the instrument is classified, the bank would report the security at either fair value or at amortized cost. Furthermore, if the instrument is classified as available-for-sale or held-to-maturity, changes in fair value will not be recognized in the statement of comprehensive income while the bank holds the instrument, unless it becomes impaired and that impairment is considered "other-than-temporary."

An investment banking entity, however, that holds the same security would measure the security at fair value and recognize all changes in fair value, whether increases or decreases, in net income in the period they occur.

Objectives of FAS 157. Since the late 1980s, FASB has pursued a stated goal that would require all financial instruments and many other assets and liabilities to be stated at the end of each reporting period at fair value, with changes from period to period recognized as gains or losses in profit or loss. The pursuit of this goal has resulted in a succession of standards that increased the number of fair value measurements required and, to provide more transparency to users, increased the scope and complexity of the related disclosures required.

In December 1991, with the issuance of FAS 107, *Disclosures about Fair Value of Financial Instruments,* the term "fair value" was coined to replace the previously popular term "market value" (for which the term "fair market value" was sometimes substituted). This change was made to emphasize the fact that, even in the absence of active primary markets for an asset or liability, assets and liabilities could be valued by reference to prices and rates from secondary markets discounted. Over time, this concept was expanded further to include the application of various fair value estimation models, such as the probability-weighted expected cash flow model first introduced by FASB Concepts Statement 7 (CON 7).

As these broader fair value concepts were evolving, the preexisting "market-based" literature had not been revised. Further, the concepts and definitions of fair value were not consistently understood or applied in similar situations by similar reporting entities. The need for comprehensive guidance to identifying and applying valid fair value measurement strategies became ever more evident as time progressed.

FAS 157 was issued in September 2006 in order to

- Establish a single, consistent GAAP definition of fair value
- Provide uniform, consistent guidance on how to measure fair value including the establishment of a hierarchical fair value measurement framework that classifies measurement inputs based on their level of market observability
- Expand the information required to be provided to financial statement users about fair value measurements

FAS 157 did not mandate new fair value measurements, but rather only provided "clarification" regarding the application of these measurements in the existing literature. While technically accurate, this understates the major impact that FAS 157 would be destined to have.

Definition of fair value. Fair value is defined in FAS 157 as the *price that would be received to sell an asset or paid to transfer a liability in an orderly transaction between market participants at the measurement date.* An "orderly transaction" is explained as being a hypothetical transaction assumed to take place on the measurement date with the item being valued having been exposed to the market for the usual and customary period of time for transactions involving such assets or liabilities in order to provide sufficient time for marketing activities. Further, an orderly transaction is not a sale where the seller is under duress (e.g., a forced liquidation or distress sale).

Fair value measurements are to be considered from the perspective of a market participant that holds the asset or owes the liability. Thus, the objective of measuring fair value is to determine an exit price: the price that would be received to sell an asset or the price that would be paid to transfer the liability. This concept will be explained and illustrated later in this appendix.

Scope of the standard. In pursuing an incremental approach, FAS 157 contained scope exceptions for certain, highly complex specialized applications.

1. Share-based payments (FAS 123 [R])
2. Measurement models that are based on vendor-specific objective evidence (VSOE) such as

   a. Multiple-deliverable arrangements
   b. Software revenue recognition
   c. Software stored on another entity's hardware

3. Market value of inventory for the purposes of applying the lower of cost or market model to measure inventory realizability.

In addition to the scope exceptions listed above, FAS 157 retains the exceptions included in GAAP that tacitly acknowledge that it is sometimes not practical to estimate fair value without "undue cost or effort." When this is the case, however, management is required to inform the users of the financial statements that it has invoked this exception, as well as the reasons that it believes making fair value measurements would be impractical.

This exception applies to certain measurements made in connection with matters such as advertising barter transactions; asset retirement obligations; business combinations; contributions made and received; exit and disposal activities; financial instrument disclosures; guarantees; nonmonetary transactions; not-for-profit organizations; pensions; postemployment benefits other than pensions; puttable marketable securities; and transfers of financial assets.

Measurement principles and methodologies under FAS 157. It is helpful to break down the measurement process under FAS 157 into a series of discrete steps. Although not necessarily performed in a linear manner, the following procedures and decisions need to be applied and made, in order to value an asset or liability at fair value under FAS 157. Each of the steps will be discussed in greater detail in the following pages.

1. *Identify the item to be valued and the unit of account.* Specifically identify the asset or liability, including the unit of account to be used for the measurement.
2. *Determine the principal or most advantageous market and the relevant market participants.* From the reporting entity's perspective, determine the principal market in which it would sell the asset or transfer the liability. In the absence of a principal market, consider the most advantageous market for the asset or the liability. Once the principal or most advantageous market is identified, determine the characteristics of the market participants. It is not necessary that specifically named individuals or entities be identified for this purpose.
3. *Select the valuation premise to be used for asset measurements.* If the item being measured is an asset, determine the valuation premise to be used by evaluating whether marketplace participants would judge the highest and best use of the asset utilizing an "in-use" valuation premise or an "in-exchange" valuation premise.
4. *Consider the risk assumptions applicable to liability measurements.* If the item being measured is a liability, identify the key assumptions that market participants would make regarding nonperformance risk including, but not limited to, the reporting entity's own credit risk (credit standing).
5. *Identify available inputs.* Identify the key assumptions that market participants would use in pricing the asset or liability, including assumptions about risk. In identifying these assumptions, referred to as "inputs" by FAS 157, maximize the inputs that are observable (i.e., that are based on market data available from sources independent of the reporting entity). In so doing, assess the availability of relevant, reliable market data for each input that significantly affects the valuation, and identify the level of the new fair value input hierarchy in which it is to be categorized.

6. *Select the appropriate valuation technique(s).* Based on the nature of the asset or liability being valued, and the types and reliability of inputs available, determine the appropriate valuation technique or combination of techniques to use in valuing the asset or liability. The three broad categories of techniques are the market approach, the income approach, and the cost approach.

7. *Make the measurement.* Measure the asset or liability.

8. *Determine amounts to be recognized and information to be disclosed.* Determine the amounts and information to be recorded, classified, and disclosed in interim and annual financial statements

Item identification and unit of account. In general, the same unit of account at which the asset or liability is aggregated or disaggregated by applying other applicable US GAAP pronouncements is to be used for fair value measurement purposes. FAS 157 prohibits adjustment to the valuation for a "blockage factor," which is an adjustment made to a valuation that takes into account the fact that the investor holds a large quantity (block) of shares relative to the market trading volume in those shares. The prohibition applies even if the quantity held by the reporting entity exceeds the market's normal trading volume—and that, if the reporting entity were, hypothetically, to place an order to sell its entire position in a single transaction, that transaction could affect the quoted price.

Principal or most advantageous market and market participants. FAS 157 requires those performing valuations to maximize the use of assumptions (inputs) that are observable from market data obtained from sources independent of the reporting entity. In making a fair value measurement, management is to assume that the asset or liability is exchanged in a hypothetical, orderly transaction between market participants at the measurement date. To characterize the exchange as orderly, it is assumed that the asset or liability will have been exposed to the market for a sufficient period of time prior to the measurement date to enable marketing activities to occur that are usual and customary with respect to transactions involving such assets or liabilities. It is also to be assumed that the transaction is not a forced transaction (e.g., a forced liquidation or distress sale).

FASB had tentatively concluded that fair value should be measured by reference to the most advantageous market for the asset or liability being measured. For practical reasons, however, it concluded that if there is a principal market for an asset or liability, the measure of fair value is to be the price in that market (whether directly observable or determined indirectly using a valuation technique), even if the price in a different market is potentially more advantageous at the measurement date.

Management is to identify the *principal market* for the asset or liability, if such a market exists. If the entity has access to more than one market, the principal market is the market in which the reporting entity would sell the asset or transfer the liability that has the greatest volume and activity level for the asset or liability. The greater volume of activity ensures that the measurement is based on multiple transactions potentially between multiple counterparties, and is thus more representative of fair value than if the measurement were based on less extensive data.

Note that the determination of the principal market is made from the perspective of the reporting entity. Thus, different reporting entities engaging in different specialized industries, or with access to different markets, might not have the same principal market for an identical asset or liability. Inputs from the principal market are to be used irrespective of whether the price is directly observable or determined through the use of a valuation technique.

If there is no principal market for an asset or liability from the perspective of the reporting entity, then management is to use the most advantageous market for the measurement.

The most advantageous market is the market that the reporting entity has the ability to access at the measurement date, in which it would maximize the price it receives from the sale of an asset or would minimize the price it pays to transfer a liability. In determining the most advantageous market, management considers transaction costs. However, once the most advantageous market had been identified, transaction costs are *not* used to adjust the market price used for the purposes of the fair value measurement.

FAS 157 provides a typology of markets that potentially exist for assets or liabilities.

1. *Active exchange market.* A market in which closing prices are readily available and that generally represent fair value (e.g., NYSE Euronext, Toronto Stock Exchange, London Stock Exchange, Hong Kong Stock Exchange).

2. *Dealer market.* A market in which parties (dealers referred to as market makers) stand ready to buy or sell a particular investment for their own account at bid and ask prices that they quote. The bid price is the price the dealer is willing to pay to purchase the investment and the ask price is the price at which the dealer is willing to sell the investment. In these markets, these bid and ask prices are typically more readily available than closing prices characteristic of active exchange markets. By using their own capital to finance and hold an inventory of the items for which they "make a market," these dealers provide the market with liquidity. Examples of dealer markets in the US are "over-the-counter" markets that publicly report prices through the National Association of Securities Dealers Automated Quotations Systems (NASDAQ) or Pink Sheets LLC, and the market for US Treasury securities. Dealer markets also exist for various financial and nonfinancial assets and liabilities, including commodities and used equipment.

3. *Brokered market.* These markets use "brokers" or intermediaries to match buyers with sellers. Brokers do not trade for their own account and do not hold an inventory in the security. The broker knows the bid and asked prices of the potential counterparties to the transaction but the counterparties are unaware of each other's price requirements. Prices of consummated transactions are sometimes available privately or as a matter of public record. Brokered markets include electronic communication networks that match buy and sell orders, as well as commercial and residential real estate markets. In some cases, each of the counterparties is aware of the other's identity, while in other cases, their identities are not disclosed by the broker.

4. *Principal-to-principal market.* A market in which the counterparties negotiate directly and independently without an intermediary. Because no intermediary or exchange is involved, little if any information about these transactions is released to the public.

Market participants in the principal or most advantageous market are buyers and sellers that

1. Are unrelated third parties
2. Have the ability to enter into a transaction for the asset or liability
3. Have the motivation to voluntarily enter into a transaction for the asset or liability without being forced to do so under duress
4. Are knowledgeable about the asset or liability since they would possess a reasonable understanding of the asset or liability and the terms of the transaction based on all available information including information obtainable through the performance of usual and customary due diligence procedures

Those determining the measurement are not required to identify specific individuals or entities that would potentially be market participants. Instead, it is important to identify the distinguishing characteristics of participants in the particular market by considering factors specific to the asset or liability being measured, the market identified, and the participants in that market with whom the reporting entity would enter into a transaction for the asset or liability.

Measurement considerations when markets become illiquid or less liquid. At the time many entities were in the process of implementing FAS 157, those same entities were experiencing the effects of a tumultuous credit market in the US and abroad. The previously active markets for certain types of securities became illiquid or less liquid. Questions arose regarding whether transactions occurring in less liquid markets with less frequent trades might cause those market transactions to be considered forced or distress sales, thus rendering valuations made using those prices not indicative of the actual fair value of the securities. In order to respond to these concerns, the Center for Audit Quality (CAQ), a nonprofit group based in Washington, DC, closely affiliated with the AICPA, issued a white paper on October 3, 2007, entitled, "Measurements of Fair Value in Illiquid (or Less Liquid) Markets."[2]

The white paper indicates that an imbalance between supply and demand can occur when there are more sellers than buyers for a particular instrument and that imbalance can result in "forcing prices down." Transactions in markets affected by this situation—where there is a lack of equilibrium between buyers and sellers—are not considered to be forced or distressed transactions as contemplated by FAS 157 (or, for that matter, by the standards that preceded FAS 157). The white paper cites a 2004 SEC Accounting and Auditing Enforcement Release[3] in which the Commission imposed a cease-and-desist order on a registrant because the registrant departed from using established market-based valuation methods when it believed that supply and demand were not "in reasonable balance." For obvious reasons, granting financial statement preparers *carte blanche* to define markets as disorderly to avoid having to use market prices would be a dangerous precedent.

One of the practices covered by the cease-and-desist order involved the valuation of bonds, primarily in the telecommunications industry, that were contained in a high-yield bond portfolio near the end of 2000 when the telecommunications industry was experiencing significant turmoil (liquidations, reorganizations, and bankruptcy filings resulting from factors such as overexpansion of capacity in anticipation of business growth that never materialized). The registrant, a financial services firm, believed that market conditions rendered third-party price quotations unreliable and, rather than use such quotations in its fair value measurements, decided to take a "longer view of the market" and use management's own subjective opinion regarding the value of the bonds.

According to the SEC, the registrant in effect, "valued its positions at the price at which it thought a willing buyer and seller *should* enter into an exchange, rather than at the price at which a willing buyer and a willing seller *would* enter into a current exchange." (Emphasis added.) The situation cited in the release was exacerbated by the fact that the registrant had valued some of the same high-yield bonds held in the portfolios of its own mutual funds using a lower valuation.

Under FAS 157, orderly transactions are occurring in the marketplace for an asset or liability when knowledgeable buyers and sellers independent of the reporting entity are willing and able to transact, and are motivated to transact without being forced to do so. If orderly transactions are occurring in a manner that is usual and customary for the asset or liability, then the transactions are not to be characterized as forced or distress sales. Just because

---

[2] *http://www.aicpa.org/caq/download/WP_Measurements_of_FV_in_Illiquid_Markets.pdf*

[3] *AAER No. 2132; US Securities and Exchange Commission; November 4, 2004;*
    http://sec.gov/litigation/admin/34-50632.htm

transaction volume in a market drops significantly from prior periods does not necessarily mean that the market is no longer active. The white paper asserts that persuasive evidence would be required to establish that an observable transaction is a forced or distressed transaction and, furthermore, it is inappropriate to assume that all transactions in a relatively illiquid market are forced or distressed transactions.

Selection of the valuation premise for asset measurements. The measurement of the fair value of an asset is to assume the *highest and best use* of that asset by market participants. Generally, the highest and best use is the way that market participants would be expected to deploy the asset (or a group of assets within which they would use the asset) that would maximize the value of the asset (or group). This highest and best use assumption might differ from the way that the reporting entity is currently using the asset or group of assets or its future plans for using it (them).

At the measurement date, the highest and best use must be physically possible, legally permissible, and financially feasible. Determination of the highest and best use of the asset will establish which of the two valuation premises to use in measuring the asset's fair value, the in-use valuation premise, or the in-exchange valuation premise.

Strategic buyers and financial buyers. FAS 157 differentiates between two broad categories of market participants that would potentially buy an asset or group of assets.

1. *Strategic buyers* are market participants whose acquisition objectives are to use the asset or group of assets (the "target") to enhance the performance of their existing business by achieving benefits such as additional capacity, improved technology, managerial, marketing, or technical expertise, access to new markets, improved market share, or enhanced market positioning. Thus, a strategic buyer views the purchase as a component of a broader business plan and, as a result, a strategic buyer may be willing to pay a premium to consummate the acquisition and may, in fact, be the only type of buyer available with an interest in acquiring the target. Ideally, from the standpoint of the seller, more than one strategic buyer would be interested in the acquisition, which would create a bidding situation that further increases the selling price.

2. *Financial buyers* are market participants who seek to acquire the target based on its merits as a stand-alone investment. A financial buyer is interested in a return on its investment over a shorter time horizon, often three to five years, after which time their objective would typically be to sell the target. An attractive target is one that offers high growth potential in a short period of time resulting in a selling price substantially higher than the original acquisition price. Therefore, even at acquisition, a financial buyer is concerned with a viable exit strategy. A financial buyer, unlike a strategic buyer, typically does not possess a high level of industry or managerial expertise in the target's industry. Transactions involving financial buyers are often highly leveraged when the economic environment is such that the cost of debt is lower than the cost of equity.

The in-use valuation premise. This premise assumes that the maximum fair value to market participants is the price that would be received by the reporting entity (seller) assuming the asset would be used by the buyer with other assets as a group and further, that the other assets in the group would be available to potential buyers. The target might continue to be used as presently installed or may be configured in a different manner by the buyer. The assumptions regarding the level of aggregation (or disaggregation) of the asset and other associated assets may be different than the level used in applying other accounting pronouncements. Thus, in considering highest and best use and the resulting level of aggregation, the evaluator is not constrained by how the asset may be assigned by the reporting entity to a reportable or operating segment under FAS 131, a business under EITF 98-3,[4] a reporting unit under FAS 142, or an asset or disposal group under FAS 144. The assumptions regarding the highest and best use of the target should normally be consistent for all of the assets included in the group within which it would be used. Generally, the market participants whose highest and best use of an asset or group of assets would be "in-use" are characterized as strategic buyers, as previously described.

The in-exchange valuation premise. This premise assumes that the maximum fair value to market participants is the price that would be received by the reporting entity (seller) assuming the asset would be sold principally on a stand-alone basis. Generally, the market participants whose highest and best use of an asset or group of assets would be "in-use" are characterized as strategic buyers, as previously described.

Risk assumptions when valuing a liability. Many accountants, analysts, and others find the concept of computing fair value of liabilities and recognizing changes in fair value as they occur to be counterintuitive. Consider the case when a reporting entity's own credit standing declines (a "bad thing"). A fair value measurement that incorporates the effect of this decline in credit rating would result in a decline in the fair value of the liability and a resultant increase in stockholders' equity (a "good thing"). The justification provided in FAS 157 (and by quoting from CON 7) is that

> *A change in credit standing represents a change in the relative positions of the two classes of claimants (shareholders and creditors) to an entity's assets. If the credit standing diminishes, the fair value of creditors' claims diminishes. The amount of shareholders' residual claims to the entity's assets may appear to increase but that increase is probably offset by losses that may have occasioned the decline in credit standing. Because shareholders usually cannot be called on to pay a corporation's liabilities, the amount of their residual claims approaches, and is limited by zero. Thus a change in the position of borrowers necessarily alters the position of shareholders, and vice versa.*

As FAS 157 was originally drafted and issued, fair value measurements of liabilities assume that a hypothetical transfer to a market participant occurs on the measurement date. In measuring the fair value of a liability, the evaluator is to assume that the reporting entity's obligation to its creditor (i.e., the counterparty to the obligation) will continue at and after the measurement date (i.e., the obligation will not be repaid or settled prior to its contractual maturity). This being the case, this hypothetical transfer price would most likely represent the price that the current creditor (holder of the debt instrument) could obtain from a marketplace participant willing to purchase the debt instrument in a transaction involving the original creditor assigning its rights to the purchaser. In effect, the hypothetical market participant that purchased the instrument would be in the same position as the current creditor with respect to expected future cash flows (or expected future performance, if the liability is not settleable in cash) from the reporting entity.

The evaluator is to further assume that the nonperformance risk related to the obligation would be the same before and after the hypothetical transfer occurs. *Nonperformance risk* is the risk that the obligation will not be fulfilled. It is an all-encompassing concept that includes the reporting entity's own credit standing but also includes other risks associated with the nonfulfillment of the obligation. For example, a liability to deliver goods and/or perform services may bear nonperformance risk associated with the ability of the debtor to fulfill the obligation in accordance with the timing and specifications of the contract. Further, nonper-

---

[4] *EITF 98-3 was nullified by FAS 141(R) effective at the beginning of the first annual reporting period beginning on or after December 15, 2008. FAS 141(R) simplified the definition of a business, which will result in more asset acquisitions being characterized as business combinations, including entities that are in the development stage.*

formance risk increases or decreases as a result of changes in the fair value of credit enhancements associated with the liability (e.g., collateral, credit insurance, and/or guarantees).

Reporting entities have reported to the FASB staff that they have experienced various operational difficulties in applying FAS 157 to fair value measurements of liabilities. Many businesses do not issue bonds in public debt markets and are not privy to the amounts that would be realized by their creditors for transferring or securitizing their debt to other market participants. It has been asserted that the price that one investor pays another investor to purchase a debt instrument held as an asset would not be indicative of an exit price that the debtor would be required to pay to induce another party to assume the debt in a hypothetical exit transaction.

To respond to these concerns, the FASB staff issued Proposed FSP FAS 157-c, *Measuring Liabilities under FASB Statement No. 157,* on January 18, 2008. As of late October 2008, this has not been finalized. Based on the results of the redeliberations to date, the following tentative conclusions were reached:

1. The best measurement of fair value for an entity's liability is the price at which that liability is traded as an asset. Thus, a quoted, unadjusted price for the identical liability (and the identical unit of account) in an active market is the best evidence of fair value for that liability; this measurement would be equally valid for both the obligor of the liability and the asset holder.

2. In the absence of a quoted price for the identical liability in an active market, management of the reporting entity may measure the fair value of a liability at the price it would receive if it were to issue that liability at the measurement date.

    It is important for the reader to note that this valuation concept is not the same as the concept of the incremental borrowing rate used in accounting for leases. The incremental borrowing rate assumes that the borrower is incurring debt in addition to its existing debt. The valuation concept that would be used in the proposed FSP assumes that the borrower either did not owe the liability being measured as of the measurement date or refinanced it with the same repayment terms and remaining number of payments.

Example of measuring a liability absent a quoted market price (based on proposed FSP)

Gladwell Development Inc. (GDI) owed a commercial bank $2,679,824 at December 31, 2009 (the measurement date). When the loan was originated on December 31, 2006, it bore a fixed rate of 9.25% which, at the time, represented the lender's prime rate plus 2%. The original principal amount was $3,000,000 and the loan was to be repaid over a 15-year term with monthly payments of $30,876 of principal and interest.

In order to disclose the fair value of its financial instruments in accordance with FAS 107, it needs to measure the fair value of this debt.

As is usually the case in private lending transactions, there is no available market information at December 31, 2009, the measurement date, regarding the amount that GDI would be required to pay an unrelated counterparty with similar credit standing to assume its debt.

Alternatively, GDI's management contacts local lending institutions and inquires about the availability of terms to refinance its existing debt based on current interest rates and its current credit standing. GDI's management determines (and contemporaneously documents) that based on an improvement in its credit standing, it could obtain $2.7 million of replacement financing at 6% on the measurement date, which represents the lender's prime rate of 5% plus an additional 1%.

Management calculates the fair value of the loan at December 31, 2009, by solving for the present value of 144 remaining payments of $30,876, discounted at 6%, which yields $3,164,010. The logic behind this result from the standpoint of GDI is that, due to a favorable change in interest rates and in its own credit standing, the fair value of its debt has increased. It would be more attractive for a counterparty to purchase the existing debt from the originating lender since the yield on the loan exceeds yields based on December 31, 2009 interest rates for investments with similar risk characteristics.

The FASB Staff proposed that the FSP be applied prospectively effective on the later of (1) the beginning of the first reporting period ending after the issuance date of the FSP or (2) the beginning of the period in which an entity initially applies FAS 157. Earlier application would not be permitted. The effect of initial application would be included as a change in fair value in the period of adoption. The authors recommend that readers/researchers monitor the status of this project on the FASB Web site (www.fasb.org) as it progresses to ensure that any effect a final FSP might have on the application of fair value measurement principles to liabilities is fully considered in applying the guidance we provide in this and other affected chapters.

Inputs. For the purpose of fair value measurements, inputs are the assumptions that market participants would use in pricing an asset or liability, including assumptions regarding risk. An input is either observable or unobservable. Observable inputs are either directly observable or indirectly observable. FAS 157 requires the evaluator to maximize the use of observable inputs and minimize the use of unobservable inputs.

An *observable input* is based on market data obtainable from sources independent of the reporting entity. An *unobservable input* reflects assumptions made by management of the reporting entity with respect to assumptions it believes market participants would use to price an asset or liability based on the best information available under the circumstances.

FAS 157 provides a fair value input hierarchy (see diagram below) to serve as a framework for classifying inputs based on the extent to which they are based on observable data.

Hierarchy of Fair Value Inputs

Level 3 Inputs
Unobservable

Inputs that are unobservable; that reflect management's own assumptions about the assumptions market participants would make.

Level 2 Inputs
Indirectly Observable

Directly or indirectly observable prices in active markets for similar assets or liabilities; quoted prices for identical or similar items in markets that are not active; inputs other than quoted prices (e.g., interest rates, yield curves, credit risks, volatilities); or "market corroborated inputs."

Level 1 Inputs
Directly Observable

Quoted prices in active markets for identical assets or liabilities that the reporting entity has the ability to access at the measurement date. Such prices are not adjusted for the effects, if any, of the reporting entity holding a large block relative to the overall trading volume (referred to as a "blockage" factor).

Level 1 inputs. Level 1 inputs are considered the most reliable evidence of fair value and are to be used whenever they are available. These inputs consist of quoted prices in active markets for *identical* assets or liabilities. The active market must be one in which the reporting entity has the ability to access the quoted price at the measurement date. To be considered an active market, transactions for the asset or liability being measured must occur frequently enough and in sufficient volume to provide pricing information on an ongoing basis.

If a market price at the exact measurement date is not readily available, or is available but not representative of fair value because the market is not active or because events occurring after the last available quoted price would have affected fair value at the measurement date,[5] the quoted price is to be adjusted to more accurately reflect fair value. As discussed previously, in order for a market to be considered active, it must have a sufficient volume of transactions to provide quoted market prices that are the most reliable measure of fair value. Markets experiencing reduced transaction volumes are still considered active if transactions are occurring frequently enough on an ongoing basis to provide reliable pricing information. FAS 157 requires that quoted prices from active markets (Level 1 inputs) be used whenever they are available. The use of Level 2 or Level 3 inputs is generally prohibited when Level 1 inputs are available.

Although not fully contemplated when FAS 157 was being drafted, recent (2008) market developments will challenge management to support assertions that market transactions are not valid Level 1 inputs. As discussed above, the burden of proof will be on those making such an assertion, even if market volatility and the virtual collapse of orderly trading of certain classes of securities (such as CDOs of subprime bank debt or mortgages) makes it somewhat suggestive that current market quotes are not truly indicative of underlying values.

Importantly, even if management were to conclude that a reduction in transaction volume in a particular market rendered that market inactive (i.e., the market is unable to provide reliable pricing information) the observable transactions that were occurring in that market would still be considered Level 2 inputs which need to be taken into account by management in its measurements of fair value. Management is required to establish and consistently apply a policy for identifying events that potentially affect its fair value measurements.

If the reporting entity holds a large number of similar assets and liabilities (such as a pool of debt securities), and quoted prices are not accessible with respect to each individual asset and/or liability in a cost-effective manner to enable timely financial reporting, management may choose to substitute, as a practical expedient, an alternative pricing model that does not rely exclusively on quoted prices such as using a matrix pricing model for debt securities. The use of a pricing model as an alternative to directly pricing each asset or liability in the group will require management to characterize the measurement in its entirety as being a level lower than Level 1 in the hierarchy.

Under no circumstances, however, is management to adjust the quoted price for blockage factors. Blockage adjustments arise when an entity holds a position in a single financial instrument that is traded on an active market that is relatively large in relation to the market's daily trading volume. While there is no common agreement as to how large a position would constitute a "block" of a particular instrument, FASB unconditionally prohibits any adjustment as a result of blockage, even if the market's normal daily trading volume is insufficient to absorb the quantity held by the reporting entity and irrespective of whether the placing of an order to sell the position in a single transaction might affect the quoted price.

Level 2 inputs. Level 2 inputs are quoted prices for the asset or liability (other than those included in Level 1) that are either directly or indirectly observable. Level 2 inputs are to be considered when quoted prices for the identical asset or liability are not available. If the asset or liability being measured has a contractual term, a Level 2 input must be observable for substantially the entire term. These inputs include

---

[5] *Examples of such events that could occur after the close of a market but prior to the measurement date would include the existence of principal-to-principal transactions or brokered trades about which the evaluator has access to reliable information, or announcements made in press conferences, shareholders meetings, or in regulatory filings.*

1. Quoted prices for *similar* assets or liabilities in active markets
2. Quoted prices for identical or similar assets or liabilities in markets that are *not active*. As discussed in the previous section, these markets may not be considered active because

    a. They have an insufficient volume or frequency of transactions for the asset or liability
    b. Prices are not current
    c. Quotations vary substantially over time
    d. Quotations vary substantially among market makers (e.g., in some brokered markets)
    e. Insufficient information is released publicly (e.g., a principal-to-principal market)

3. Inputs other than quoted prices that are observable for the asset or liability (e.g., interest rates and yield curves observable at commonly quoted intervals; volatilities; prepayment speeds; loss severities; credit risks; and default rates)
4. Inputs that are derived principally from or corroborated by observable market data that, through correlation or other means, are determined to be relevant to the asset or liability being measured (market-corroborated inputs)

Adjustments made to Level 2 inputs necessary to reflect fair value, if any, will vary depending on an analysis of specific factors associated with the asset or liability being measured. These factors include

1. Condition
2. Location
3. Extent to which the inputs relate to items comparable to the asset or liability
4. Volume and level of activity in the markets in which the inputs are observed

Depending on the level of the fair value input hierarchy in which the inputs used to measure the adjustment are classified, an adjustment that is significant to the fair value measurement in its entirety could render the measurement a Level 3 measurement.

During the turmoil experienced in credit markets beginning in early 2008, a holder of collateralized mortgage obligations (CMOs) backed by a pool of subprime mortgages might determine that no active market exists for the CMOs. Management might use an appropriate ABX credit default swap index for subprime mortgage bonds[6] to provide a Level 2 fair value measurement input in measuring the fair value of the CMOs.

Level 3 inputs. Level 3 inputs are unobservable inputs. These are necessary when little, if any, market activity occurs for the asset or liability. Level 3 inputs are to reflect management's own assumptions regarding an exit price that a market participant holding the asset or owing the liability would make, including assumptions about risk. The best information available in the circumstances is to be used to develop the Level 3 inputs. This information might include internal data of the reporting entity. Cost-benefit considerations apply in that management is not required to "undertake all possible efforts" to obtain information about the assumptions that would be made by market participants. Attention is to be paid, however, to information available to management without undue cost and effort and, consequently, management's internal assumptions used to develop unobservable inputs are to be adjusted if such information contradicts those assumptions.

---

[6] *ABX indices are disseminated by Markit Group Limited, a London-based consortium of 16 large banks and four hedge funds that provides credit derivative pricing data, valuations, and trade processing services.*

Inputs based on bid and ask prices. Quoted bid prices represent the maximum price at which market participants are willing to buy an asset; quoted ask prices represent the minimum price at which market participants are willing to sell an asset. If available market prices are expressed in terms of bid and ask prices, management is to use the price within the bid-ask spread (the range of values between bid and ask prices) that is most representative of fair value irrespective of where in the fair value hierarchy the input would be classified. FAS 157 permits the use of pricing conventions such as midmarket pricing as a practical alternative for determining fair value measurements within a bid-ask spread.

Classifying inputs. Classification of inputs as to the level of the hierarchy in which they fall serves two purposes. First, it provides the evaluator with a means of prioritizing assumptions used as to their level of objectivity and verifiability in the marketplace. Second, as discussed later in this chapter, the hierarchy provides a framework to provide informative disclosures that enable readers to assess the reliability and market observability of the fair value estimates embedded in the financial statements.

In making a particular measurement of fair value, the inputs used may be classifiable in more than one of the levels of the hierarchy. When this is the case, the inputs used in the fair value measurement in its entirety are to be classified in the level of the hierarchy in which the lowest level input that is significant to the measurement is classified.

It is important to assess available inputs and their relative classification in the hierarchy prior to selecting the valuation technique or techniques to be applied to measure fair value for a particular asset or liability. The objective, in selecting from among alternative calculation techniques, would be to select the technique or combination of techniques that maximizes the use of observable inputs. Note that the intended use of the hierarchy is to prioritize the inputs themselves, not the valuation techniques in which they are used.

Valuation techniques. In measuring fair value, management is to employ one or more valuation techniques consistent with the market approach, the income approach, and/or the cost approach. As previously discussed, the selection of a particular technique (or techniques) to measure fair value is to be based on its appropriateness to the asset or liability being measured as well as the sufficiency and observability of inputs available.

In certain situations, such as when using Level 1 inputs, use of a single valuation technique will be sufficient. In other situations, such as when valuing a reporting unit, management may need to use multiple valuation techniques. When doing so, the results yielded by applying the various techniques are to be evaluated and appropriately weighted based on judgment as to the reasonableness of the range of results. The objective of the weighting is to determine the point within the range that is most representative of fair value.

Management is required to consistently apply the valuation techniques it elects to use to measure fair value. It would be appropriate to change valuation techniques or how they are applied if the change results in fair value measurements that are equally or more representative of fair value. Situations that might give rise to such a change would be when new markets develop, new information becomes available, previously available information ceases to be available, or improved techniques are developed. Revisions that result from either a change in valuation technique or a change in the application of a valuation technique are to be accounted for as changes in accounting estimate, although an exemption was granted for the disclosures that apply to other changes in accounting estimate.

Market approaches. Market approaches to valuation use information generated by actual market transactions for identical or comparable assets or liabilities (including a business in its entirety). Market approach techniques often will use market multiples derived from a set of comparable transactions for the asset or liability or similar items. The evaluator will need to consider both qualitative and quantitative factors in determining the point within the range that is most representative of fair value. An example of a market approach is matrix pricing. This is a mathematical technique used primarily for the purpose of valuing debt securities without relying solely on quoted prices for the specific securities. Matrix pricing uses factors such as the stated interest rate, maturity, credit rating, and quoted prices of similar issues to develop the issue's current market yield.

Income approaches. Techniques classified as income approaches measure fair value based on current market expectations about future amounts (such as cash flows or net income) and discount them to an amount in measurement date dollars. Valuation techniques that follow an income approach include the Black-Scholes-Merton model (a closed-form model) and binomial or lattice models (an open-form model), which use present value techniques, as well as the multiperiod excess earnings method that is used in fair value measurements of certain intangible assets such as in-process research and development.

Cost approaches. Cost approaches are based on quantifying the amount required to replace an asset's remaining service capacity (i.e., the asset's current replacement cost). A valuation technique classified as a cost approach would measure the cost to a market participant (buyer) to acquire or construct a substitute asset of comparable utility, adjusted for obsolescence. Obsolescence adjustments include factors for physical wear and tear, improvements to technology, and economic (external) obsolescence. Thus, obsolescence is a broader concept than financial statement depreciation which simply represents a cost allocation convention and is not intended to be used as a valuation technique.

Measurement considerations.

Initial recognition. When the reporting entity first acquires an asset or incurs (or assumes) a liability in an exchange transaction, the transaction price represents an entry price—the price paid to acquire the asset and the price received to assume the liability. Fair value measurements are based not on entry prices, but rather on exit prices; the price that would be received to sell the asset or paid to transfer the liability. While entry and exit prices differ conceptually, in many cases they may be identical and can be considered to represent fair value of the asset or liability at initial recognition. This is not always the case, however, and in assessing fair value at initial recognition, management is to consider transaction-specific factors and factors specific to the assets and/or liabilities that are being initially recognized. Examples of situations where transaction price is not representative of fair value at initial recognition include

1. Related-party transactions
2. Transactions occurring under duress such as a forced or liquidation transaction
3. The exchange transaction occurs in a market different from the principal or most advantageous market in which the reporting entity would sell the asset or transfer the liability. An example of this situation is when the reporting entity is a securities dealer that enters into transactions in different markets depending on whether the counterparty is a retail customer or another securities dealer.
4. Different units of account that apply to the transaction price and the assets/liabilities being measured. This can occur, for example, where the transaction price includes other elements besides the assets/liabilities that are being measured such as unstated rights and privileges that are subject to separate measurement or when the transaction price includes transaction costs (see discussion below).

Transaction costs. Transaction costs are the incremental direct costs that would be incurred to sell an asset or transfer a liability. While, as previously discussed, transaction costs are considered in determining the market that is most advantageous, they are not used to adjust the fair value measurement of the asset or liability being measured. FASB excluded them from the measurement because they do not represent an attribute of the asset or liability being measured.

Transportation costs. If an attribute of the asset or liability being measured is its location, the price determined in the principal or most advantageous market is to be adjusted for the costs that would be incurred by the reporting entity to transport it to or from that market.

Fair value disclosures mandated by FAS 157. Substantial disclosures regarding fair value are required by many different pronouncements that comprise authoritative US GAAP literature. In the preparation of the financial statements, these disclosures are often placed in different informative notes including descriptions of the entity's accounting policies, financial instruments, impairment, derivatives, pensions, revenue recognition, share-based compensation, risks and uncertainties, certain significant estimates, etc. FAS 157 requires additional quantitative and qualitative disclosures. FAS 157 encourages, but does not require management to combine its fair value disclosures with other required disclosures. In addition, FAS 157 encourages disclosure of information about other similar measurements that are not intended to represent fair value such as inventories measured at the lower of cost or market. FAS 157 uses a hybrid principles-based approach and rules-based approach to detailing the fair value disclosures it requires. It provides the following high-level disclosure objectives:

1. For assets and liabilities measured at fair value on a recurring basis subsequent to their initial recognition, management is to provide information that will enable financial statement users to assess the inputs used to develop those measurements and, further, for measurements using significant unobservable (Level 3) inputs, the effect of those measurements on earnings for the period.
2. For assets and liabilities measured at fair value on a nonrecurring basis subsequent to their initial recognition, management is to provide information that will enable financial statement users to assess the inputs used to develop those measurements.

To operationalize these objectives, FAS 157 provides the following required disclosures. The quantitative disclosures are required to be presented in a tabular format. Unless otherwise specified, the disclosures are required to be made in each interim and annual period.

Disclosures required to be made with respect to assets and liabilities measured at fair value on a recurring basis in periods subsequent to initial recognition. Disclose separately for each major category of assets and liabilities

1. The amount of the fair value measurements at the reporting date
2. The level within the fair value hierarchy in which the fair value measurements fall in their entirety; separately disclosing the amounts of fair value measurements that use quoted prices in active markets for identical assets or liabilities (Level 1), significant other observable inputs (Level 2), and significant unobservable inputs (Level 3)
3. For those fair value measurements using significant unobservable (Level 3) inputs, a reconciliation of the beginning and ending balances, separately stating changes during the period attributable to

    a. Total realized and unrealized gains or losses for the period segregating those gains or losses included in income (or changes in net assets of a not-for-profit organization) and a description of where those gains or losses are reported in the statement of income (or statement of activities of a not-for-profit organization)

       (1) The unrealized gains or losses included in this disclosure that relate to assets and liabilities still held at the end of the reporting period and

       (2) A description of where, in the statement of income, those unrealized gains or losses are reported

  b. Purchases, sales, issuances, and settlements (net)

  c. Transfers in and/or out of Level 3 (e.g., due to changes in the observability of significant inputs)

Note that, for the purposes of this reconciliation, derivative assets and liabilities are permitted to be presented net.

4. In the first interim period of the fiscal year of adoption and subsequently in annual financial statements, the valuation techniques used to measure fair value and a discussion of changes in valuation techniques, if any, during the period

Disclosures required to be made with respect to assets and liabilities measured at fair value on a nonrecurring basis in periods subsequent to initial recognition (such as impaired assets). Disclose separately for each major category of assets and liabilities

1. Fair value measurements recorded during the period and the reasons for the measurements

2. The level within the fair value hierarchy in which the fair value measurements fall in their entirety; separately disclosing the amounts of fair value measurements that use quoted prices in active markets for identical assets or liabilities (Level 1), significant other observable inputs (Level 2), and significant unobservable inputs (Level 3)

3. For fair value measurements using significant unobservable (Level 3) inputs, a description of the inputs and the information used to develop them

4. In the first interim period of the fiscal year of adoption and subsequently in annual financial statements, the valuation techniques used to measure fair value and discussion of changes in valuation techniques used to measure similar assets and/or liabilities in prior periods

APPENDIX G

IFRS FOR PRIVATE ENTITIES

A long-running debate, which had gathered considerable momentum over the past several years, may be headed for a resolution over the near term. This pertains to the movement to either develop a unique set of financial reporting standards for what many refer to as smaller and medium-sized entities (SMEs), or to extract from existing IFRS a slimmed-down set of requirements to be referenced by such reporting entities as their primary source of guidance. An antecedent for this can be found in UK GAAP, which in late 1997 developed as FRSSE (Financial Reporting Standards for Smaller Entities) a single standard containing excerpts from many, but not all, existing UK GAAP standards. (Revisions have been made to FRSSE, essentially updating the original pronouncement for certain new standards promulgated since its most recent full revision.) The argument took on added urgency when the "principles-based vs. rules-based" debate erupted, stimulated by the flurry of financial reporting frauds in the US in the late 1990s and early 2000s, which some IFRS enthusiasts cited as evidence for the proposition that detailed guidance based on a plethora of mechanical rules actually offered more, not less, opportunity for financial reporting shenanigans. The US standard-setting bodies, FASB and AICPA, subsequently undertook a SME project, as well.

The stimulus for this undertaking seems to center on the perceived complexity of modern financial accounting requirements, which some believe exceed the abilities of financial statement preparers and auditors to fully comprehend, and which arguably serve to make financial statements and accompanying footnote disclosures incomprehensible to both entity management and other, external users. In the authors' view, this is a highly debatable proposition, since it is not the unilateral actions by accounting rule makers but rather the ever-increasing complexity of business transactions that have, for the most part, necessitated the creation of newer and admittedly complex requirements. For one obvious example, the growing use, even by smaller businesses, of "engineered financial instruments" such as forwards and options (e.g., currency forwards used by importers of products to protect against currency fluctuations when purchase obligations are denominated in foreign currencies) has resulted in necessarily complex standards on hedging transactions. (Note that adoption of comprehensive fair value accounting would obviate the need for special hedge accounting, but post–Enron this once widely-stated goal seems to have become less attainable, politically.)

Other complex accounting standards have been the (some would say, unfortunate) result of standard setters' accession to preparers' demands for deferrals and various other smoothing techniques. A prime example: accounting for defined benefit pension and other post-retirement benefit programs. Were market-driven fluctuations in the values of investments, changes in interest rates, and revisions to actuarially determined amounts such as life expectancies fully and immediately reflected, pension accounting would be radically simplified, albeit still subject to estimations that are certain to change over time. The willingness of FASB, IASB and various other national standard setters to countenance various smoothing strategies has resulted in many complex standards—and, not coincidentally, late-blooming recriminations about the broader societal impacts such departures from reporting economic reality have caused or contributed to.

Nonetheless, a popular demand has arisen for "simplified" financial reporting, which often cites the fact that the vast majority of all reporting entities are not large or publicly held companies, suggesting that since most users of financial statements will be management and other "insiders" having access to such details as they may optionally desire to obtain, a stripped-down set of financial reporting rules should suffice, easing the task of preparing and auditing such financial reports. Similar efforts in past decades, often labeled as the debate between "Big GAAP" and "Little GAAP," have (with the exception of the FRSSE standard under UK GAAP) not been successful, since even advocates of differential standards have largely conceded that *recognition* and *measurement* standards cannot vary, if all preparers' financial statements are to be found "fairly presented." The differential disclosures that have been identified even by proponents of "Little GAAP" have been very few, indeed. In short, once it is acknowledged (as it seems destined to have to be) that recognition and measurement cannot logically vary based merely on the entity's size or its status as a private or public company, the effort largely devolves to a debate over the extent of required informative disclosures.

Before addressing the specifics of IASB's Private Entities (PE, formerly SME) project, there are a few final observations to make regarding the wisdom of differentiating accounting standards based upon some criterion concerning the preparers' size or the extent to which it is "publicly accountable" (i.e., reports to outsiders lacking the ability to obtain further information directly from management). In the authors' opinion, the only rational basis for differentiation of GAAP or IFRS is based on the economic transactions and activities engaged in by the reporting entities themselves.

If a reporting entity engages, say, in hedging activities, then the promulgated standards directing how such transactions are to be accounted for need to apply, whether the entity happens to have outside shareholders or not. Leaving aside the question of whether, say, IAS 39 is too complicated, or based on unsound principles (which matters should be addressed directly by revising or amending the standard), it may well be true, and appropriate, that a large, publicly held entity that does not engage in hedging activities could present less complex financial statements than a small, private company that does engage in such activities.

There should be one single set of high-quality global financial reporting standards, and companies should not be permitted choices in selecting their financial reporting standards. The primary objective of the IASB, as set out in its *Constitution* and in the *Preface to International Financial Reporting Standards*, is "to develop, in the public interest, a single set of high quality, understandable and enforceable global accounting standards..." The word "single" implies that the IASB's proposal on PEs conflicts with its constitution. An unfortunate consequence of this approach is that some IASB constitutions may defend the need for another accounting treatment in their particular circumstances, as occurred with European banking interests with regard to IAS 39. If, in addition, PEs are permitted to choose to follow PE standards or IFRS or a combination of the two, this may result in PE financial statements that are not comparable to those of non-PEs and possibly not even comparable to other PEs, potentially impairing the usefulness of financial information.

Furthermore, the parallel existence of what will be widely viewed as two sets of financial reporting standards will contribute to the creation of a two-tiered accounting profession, with some practitioners seen as being qualified for PEs but not for "real" IFRS. This could even have impacts on the educational system, perhaps with an abbreviated course of study for those who will become qualified for the PE level of work, versus a longer program for those aspiring to be expert at "full" IFRS. The problem with this is that it will artificially isolate some, probably smaller, practitioners, who may come to find their credibility (say, with bankers) has become attenuated as a result.

The possibly most deleterious consequence, although likely the least obvious one, will be the higher cost of capital to be borne by smaller entities—those using "second class" IFRS and being audited or reviewed by "second tier" accountants. Cost of capital (bank loans, trade credit, equity infusions) reflects the perceived riskiness of the investment, which in turn is directly impacted by the quality of information made available to investors and creditors.

The poorer or more incomplete such information is, the higher the perceived risk and hence the higher the cost of capital, which diminishes the expected residual return to the owners. In short, the capital markets will punish companies that opt for less than "full" IFRS, even as (according to the standard setters' survey data) they support the abstract idea of "simplified GAAP."

In the authors' view, this is an unnecessary and ill-advised risk. To the extent that promulgated IFRS (or national GAAP) is wrong, fix it. To the extent that preparers struggle with complex rules, independent accountants should help them gain the needed understanding. If lenders and other users of the financial statements cannot cope with the increasing profusion of complex standards, then perhaps the education system is inadequate to the task, or a more rigorous set of requirements for the continuing education of practicing professionals needs imposition. None of these symptoms, however, necessarily imply that certain standards are inappropriate for *certain* classes of preparers.

With this background in mind, and with the authors' view clearly stated, however, note that standard setters (both in the US and the IASB) seem determined, this time, to produce a stand-alone standard (or compendium of rules) that would appease advocates for simplified GAAP or IFRS. The goal appears to be to at least eliminate some, perhaps much, of the verbiage now found in the full text of existing standards, perhaps also dropping examples and other less essential guidance, so that at least the aura of responsiveness to a perceived public demand can be created. This may be as much a "political" undertaking as a technical one, but given the precarious position of the private-sector standard setters—particularly in the US, where the quasi-official but nominally private Public Company Accounting Oversight Board (PCAOB), established under mandate of the Sarbanes-Oxley Act (which itself was a response to the shocking epidemic of financial reporting frauds largely, but not entirely, committed by US-based publicly held companies) could expand its mandate to set accounting, as well as auditing, standards—it is understandable.

It seems that there is significant support by accounting standard setters and preparers of financial statements around the world for a separate set of internationally accepted accounting standards for PEs, giving consideration to the different needs of users and costs of compliance faced by these entities. This support stems from the fact that in most countries in the world, unlike the US, all or most companies are legally required to prepare financial statements that conform to accounting principles that are generally accepted in their home country (national GAAP), and the vast majority of those companies are PEs. For instance, the Accounting Law and *plan compatible* in France apply to financial statements of all legal entities, including PEs. We note that significant differences exist in the regulation of financial reporting in the US and in IASB countries. In the US, market forces influence private company financial reporting in response to user needs and cost-benefit trade-offs. Since in several IASB countries market forces are restricted, a separate set of IASB Standards may appear to be justified.

On a more positive note, in the EU, IASB Standards are now required for consolidated financial statements of approximately 7,000 listed companies, while more than 7,000,000 unlisted PEs will most likely continue to follow diverse national standards, based on the EU's directives, at least for the near term. Thus, there may not be a satisfactory level of comparability across national boundaries, or even within a country. Within the EU, PEs have considerable economic significance. Thus a set of global standards for PEs could ease the transition to a full set of financial reporting requirements for entities that are growing and wish to enter the public capital markets as well as play an important role with respect to developing countries, in helping them attract foreign investment. These countries, often with limited accountancy resources, have numerous PEs and special difficulty in applying the full set of IFRS. Consequently, this PE project may prove to be important politically for the acceptance of IASB around the world.

The IASB PE effort actually began as early as 2001. As de facto standard setter for many developing nations, some of which have fewer cadres of trained accountants and thus, perhaps, greater challenges in implementing the more complex standards, it was sensitive to charges that its rules were more responsive to needs of the more industrialized and developed nations, which (before the recent surge of interest in *converging* national GAAP with IFRS) in fact were not the major users of IFRS. Following the lead of the UK standard setter, the initial, albeit short-lived, stated objective was to develop standards for small and medium-sized entities. Currently, the objectives of the PE project, as stated by the IASB, include the development of high-quality, understandable and enforceable accounting standards suitable for PEs globally, to reduce the financial reporting burden on PEs that want to use global standards, and meet the needs of users of PE financial statements. As early as 2003, the IASB agreed to a four-step plan to

1. Extract from all existing IFRS and Interpretations the *basic principles* in those standards. Given the then-practice of setting forth major principles in "black letter" (i.e., bold-face) text, with explanatory materials in "grey letter" (nonbold) text, it would have been rather simple to thus excerpt the principles in the "black letter" paragraphs of those standards, plus key elements of the *Framework*, plus some principles in IASB and IFRIC EDs that were not yet finalized.
2. Reorganize those excerpts topically (perhaps in financial statement order) if it was concluded that this would make the presentation of the principles more user friendly.
3. Review those for principles or guidance that had been omitted in the original extraction but that, on review, might be deemed to be essential to operationalize the standards for PEs, and add those to the principles already extracted.
4. Review the results with a view to identifying helpful simplifications for PEs, and then present those potential simplifications to an Advisory Group and the IASB for deliberation.

This action plan quickly ran up against the reality of the fact that even a superficially simple goal of assisting "small" businesses would have to address the difficulty of defining "small" and "medium"—and that even if this could be done, it could not be presumed that such entities were not engaging in relatively complex economic transactions. It short order, IASB concluded that a size-based test was not advisable, and that another threshold criterion would be preferable. The fact of "public accountability" by the reporting entity was seen as being a more meaningful distinction, where public accountability soon was defined, subject to determinations ultimately to be made by national regulatory authorities, in terms such as public stock ownership and plans to "go public" in the near term. It was also concluded in 2003 that no changes would be made to recognition or measurement concepts established by the full set of IFRS.

As work progressed, it soon evolved that the ultimate PE version of IFRS would incorporate some, but not all, of the fundamental requirements of IFRS, with a prescription that financial statement preparers using the new standard would, in the absence of complete guidance in the new PE standard, be required to look to standard ("full") IFRS for direction. In other words, the PE version of IFRS would hopefully contain enough guidance for many, perhaps most, of the reporting entities meeting the to-be-developed qualifications for its use (i.e., those not having "public accountability"), but if such preparers were engaged in economic activities of greater complexity, they would have to refer to the original standards and be bound to comply with them. The PE guidance could thus be seen as providing a handy compendium, but not as a distinct set of financial reporting rules.

IASB later expanded on the concept of "public accountability" as follows:

The "public accountability" principle implies that an entity is publicly accountable if

1. There is a high degree of outside interest in the entity, from investors or other stakeholders;
2. The entity may have a social responsibility because of the nature of its operations; and
3. The substantial majority of stakeholders depend on external financial reporting, as they have no other way of obtaining financial information about the entity.

IASB also agreed to adopt presumptive indicators of public accountability. A business entity would be regarded as having public accountability if it meets any one of the following criteria:

1. It has filed, or it is in the process of filing, its financial statements with a securities commission or other regulatory organization for the purpose of issuing any class of instruments in a public market.
2. It holds assets in a fiduciary capacity for a broad group of outsiders, such as a bank, insurance company, securities brokerage, pension fund, mutual fund, or investment banking entity.
3. It is a public utility or similar entity that provides an essential public service.
4. It is of economic significance in the jurisdiction in which it is domiciled.
5. One or more of its owners has expressed objection to the entity's decision to use PE standards rather than full IFRSs (all owners, including those not otherwise entitled to vote, having been informed of that decision).

It is interesting to note that IASB discussed a number of possible situations where PE requirements could have been "simplified" versus full IFRS. For example, it considered the alternative classification of expenses permitted in the statement of comprehensive income, the optional use of classified or nonclassified statements of financial position, and the provision of illustrative examples, all found in the original IFRS, and determined that all these attributes were to be preserved in the PE version. IASB was apparently discovering, as had others before it, that actual differentiation of PE from full-blown standards is more difficult to achieve than is apparent when first embracing the concept of "slimmed down" guidance.

In 2004 IASB published a Discussion Paper on the Board's Preliminary Views on Accounting Standards for Small and Medium-Sized Entities. The Discussion Paper focused on issues relating to IASB's approach to the project, but did not include proposals for specific financial reporting standards for PEs, which were promised for a later discussion document. Among other basic concepts this document set forth, it stated that a subsidiary, joint venture, or associate of a publicly accountable entity should use full IFRS in any stand-alone financial reporting it engaged in, as well.

Subsequently, IASB addressed the possible PE versions of a number of standards, and it was clearly established that these would exclude many details, and that users would be directed back to the underlying standards for further guidance, should they encounter the need for such. For example, the PE version of IAS 16 was to exclude discussion of the revaluation model, which would, nevertheless, be available to PE adherents, who would have to refer to IAS 16 itself for instructions. Likewise, the PE version of IAS 23 would permit either interest capitalization (where warranted) or immediate expensing, but would only discuss expensing, with readers directed to the parent standard for guidance on capitalization. (This has probably been rendered moot by the 2007 revision to IAS 23, which made capitalization of borrowing costs, under defined circumstances, mandatory.)

Despite earlier rejection of differential recognition or measurement, in April 2005, IASB published a staff questionnaire on possible modifications of the recognition and measurement principles in IFRS for use in IASB standards for small and medium-sized entities. To date, however, the idea of differentiating recognition or measurement has not gained traction, and almost all attention has been directed at disclosures and, especially, at the level of detail to be included in a compendium of standards for PEs.

IASB claims there is wide support for it to issue global PE standards, and indeed wide support for simplifications apart from those affecting recognition and measurement (e.g., eliminating difficult options, scope exceptions that require calculations or complex judgments, and eliminating guidance not relevant to PEs). IASB has also found wide support for recognition and measurement simplifications, but posing difficulties is the fact that different constituents support different recognition and measurements simplifications, for a variety of different reasons. These likely are irreconcilable and, in any event, of dubious validity.

On February 15, 2006, the International Accounting Standards Board (IASB) issued for public comment the Exposure Draft of its International Financial Reporting Standard (IFRS) for Small and Medium-Sized Entities (SME, now renamed Private Entities, or PE). The stated aim of the proposed standard is to provide a simplified, self-contained set of accounting principles derived from the full IFRS to be used by smaller, nonlisted companies. If this proposal is adopted, as appears quite likely as of late 2008, the full IFRS would become primarily of interest for listed companies, although PEs could make reference to the more expansive set of standards as necessary or desirable.

The perceived need for a stand-alone set of simplified standards has become increasingly manifest in recent years, and FASB is also weighing development of such a streamlined group of financial reporting requirements. This latest development follows by about a decade a similar undertaking in the United Kingdom, where Financial Reporting Standards for Smaller Entities (FRSSE) have been successfully implemented. The IASB changed the name of the standard to IFRS for Private Entities in May 2008 as part of its redeliberations replacing "small and medium-sized entities" with "private entities" in order to more accurately describe the target preparers.

The support for the IASB's project from national accounting standards setters throughout the world stems mostly from the widely perceived complexity of the full IFRS, and from the different statutory requirements for financial reporting in many countries, compared to the United States. The complexity of the full IFRS (or, for that matter, full US GAAP) imposes a high cost of implementing and applying these standards. In addition, in most countries, in contrast with the United States, PEs are legally required to file statutory financial statements prepared in accordance with national GAAP, and to make them available to all users. For example, in the European Union about 7,000 listed companies were implementing the IFRS in 2005, but more than 5 million PEs have to prepare their financial statements in accordance with national GAAP (resulting in a lack of comparability). Additionally, many believe that the IFRS for PEs would allow companies as well as countries an easier transition to the full IFRS.

Some commentators do not support the approach taken in the development of the IFRS for PEs. They argue that, rather than simply streamlining existing standards, the IASB should have taken a user-based, more conceptual approach in creating "differential accounting" for PEs. They insist that fundamental differences exist between the objectives of financial reporting for PEs (being primarily focused on the role of stewardship) and those of reporting by large public companies, and that these differences should be incorporated into the conceptual framework. The ultimate success of the IFRS for PEs will depend on the extent to which users, preparers, and their auditors believe the standards meet their needs.

Opponents of a separate set of standards for PEs believe that all entities should follow the same basic accounting principles for the preparation of general-purpose financial statements, whether the IFRS or US GAAP. Some have noted that complexity in accounting is merely a symptom—the inevitable result of the ever-increasing complexity of transactional structures, such as the widespread use of "engineered" financial products. Based on observations of the difficulties faced by companies implementing and applying the full IFRS, others have concluded that the problem is not that PEs need simpler accounting, but that all entities need reporting requirements that are less complex and more principles-based. In addition, some opponents note that PE standards would adversely affect accounting education, by shifting the focus from preparing professionals to choose the best means of reporting the economic effects of any given transaction or event, to merely following what the "single solution" rulebook says. A worst-case scenario result would be a two-tiered accounting profession, wherein some practitioners would be seen as capable of handling only "little GAAP" assignments. Because the IASB lacks the power to require any company to use its standards, the adoption of the IFRS for PEs will be a matter for each country to decide; that is, a country's government legislators and regulators, an independent standards setter, or a professional accountancy body. Each country will have to set criteria to determine eligibility.

Definition of PEs. After debate over the appropriate threshold criteria, the IASB determined that the proposed standard should be intended for entities that do not have public accountability. An entity has public accountability—and therefore should use the full IFRS—if it meets the following conditions:

1. It has issued debt or equity securities in a public market; or
2. It holds assets in a fiduciary capacity for a broad group of outsiders.

The latter category of entity would include banks, insurance companies, securities broker/dealers, pension funds, mutual funds, and investment banks. The proposed standard does not impose a size test in defining PEs, notwithstanding the nomenclature used.

Modifications of full IFRS. Compared to the full IFRS, the length of this proposed standard has been reduced by more than 85%. This was achieved by eliminating topics deemed to be not generally relevant to PEs, by eliminating certain choices of accounting treatments, and by simplifying methods for recognition and measurement. These three sets of modifications to the content of the full IFRS, discussed below, respond to both the needs of users of PEs' financial statements and to cost-benefit concerns. According to the IASB, the set of standards in the proposed IFRS for PEs would be suitable for a typical entity having fifty employees, but would also be valid for so-called microentities having only a single employee or a few employees.

Omitted topics. Certain topics covered in the full IFRS were viewed as not relevant to typical PEs (e.g., pertaining to transactions thought unlikely to occur in an PE context), and have been omitted in the Exposure Draft. Because PEs would have the option of applying a cross-reference to the relevant IFRS if needed, PEs would not be precluded from applying any of the financial reporting standards and methods currently found in the IFRS. In other words, use of the IFRS for PEs would effectively be optional.

Topics addressed in the full IFRS that are omitted from the proposed IFRS for PEs, with cross-references to the full IFRSs if needed, are as follows:

- General price-level-adjusted reporting in hyperinflationary environment;
- Equity-settled share-based payment;
- Determining the fair value of agricultural assets;

- Extractive industries;
- Interim reporting;
- Lessor accounting finance leases (finance lessors are likely to be financial institutions, which would be ineligible to use the IFRS for PEs);
- Recoverable amount of goodwill (PEs would test goodwill for impairment much less frequently, but if a PE is required to perform such a test it must follow IAS 38, *Intangible Assets*); and
- Earnings per share, segment reporting, and insurance contracts (insurers would not be eligible to use the IFRS for PEs, because they hold assets in a fiduciary capacity for a broad group of outsiders).

Inclusion of only the simpler option.   Where the full IFRS provides an accounting policy choice, only the simpler option is included in the IFRS for PEs.   PEs would be permitted to use the other options, obtaining needed guidance by cross-reference to the relevant IFRS.   Because most of the underlying principles incorporated into the full IFRS would be retained, the same interpretation and application issues are likely to arise when applying these standards.

The simpler options selected for inclusion in the IFRS for PEs are as follows:

- The cost-depreciation model for investment property (fair value through profit or loss is permitted by reference to IAS 40, *Investment Property*).
- The cost-amortization-impairment model for property, plant, equipment, and intangibles (the revaluation model is allowed by references to IAS 16, *Property, Plant and Equipment;* and IAS 38, *Intangible Assets*).
- Expensing of borrowing costs (capitalization allowed by reference to IAS 23, *Borrowing Costs*).   Note that this may have been made inapplicable by the late 2007 revision to IAS 23, making capitalization of qualifying borrowing costs mandatory.
- The indirect method for reporting operating cash flows (the direct method permitted via reference to IAS 7, *Statement of Cash Flows*).
- One method (based on that set forth under IAS 41) of accounting for all government grants (the use any of the alternatives in IAS 20, *Accounting for Government Grants and Disclosure of Government Assistance,* is allowed).

Note that, even if this draft standard is adopted, it would remain up to each jurisdiction to mandate what financial reporting methods would be permitted.   Thus, in adopting the IFRS for PEs, an individual jurisdiction could decide to proscribe an option that is cross-referenced in the full IFRS.

Recognition and measurement simplifications.   The IASB proposed significant simplifications to the recognition and measurement principles included in the full IFRS.   This area is perhaps the most controversial aspect of the proposal, because earlier attempts at simplification (e.g., omitting earnings per share and segment data for private reporting entities under both the IASB and FASB standards) have been directed only at differential disclosures.

Examples of the proposed simplifications to the recognition and measurement principles found in the IFRS are as follows:

- Financial instruments.
- Classification of financial instruments.   Only two categories of financial assets are provided, rather than the four found in the full IFRS.   Because available-for-sale and held-to-maturity classifications under IAS 39 would not be available, there would be no need to deal with all of the "intent-driven" held-to-maturity rules or related "taint-

ing" concerns, and no need for an available-for-sale option, among other simplifications.

- Derecognition. In general, the principle to be applied would be that, if the transferor has any significant continuing involvement, derecognition would not be permitted. The IASB believes that the complex "pass-through testing" and "control retention testing" of IAS 39, *Financial Instruments: Recognition and Measurement,* relate to transactions in which PEs are typically not engaged, and thus can be omitted.
- Simplified hedge accounting. The Exposure Draft includes simplified hedge accounting and less strict requirements for periodic recognition and measurement of hedge effectiveness than IAS 39.
- Goodwill impairment. An indicator approach would supersede the mandatory annual impairment calculations in IFRS 3, *Business Combinations.*
- R&D. All research and development costs would be expensed as incurred. IAS 38 requires capitalization after commercial viability has been assessed.
- Joint ventures. The cost method of accounting for associates and joint ventures would be used, rather than the equity method or proportionate consolidation.
- Simplified accounting for deferred taxes. The "temporary difference approach" for recognition of deferred taxes under IAS 12, *Income Taxes,* is proposed.
- Agriculture. The Exposure Draft would not require the use of fair value for agriculture unless it were readily determinable without undue cost or effort.
- Defined benefit plans. Only one option of the four available under IAS 19, *Employee Benefits,* would be used: the recognition of actuarial gains and losses in full in the profit and loss statement when they occur. The complex "corridor approach" would be omitted.
- Share-based payment. The intrinsic value method is prescribed.
- Finance leases. Simplified measurement of a lessee's rights and obligations.
- First-time adoption. Less prior-period data would have to be restated than under the IFRS 1, *First-Time Adoption of International Financial Reporting Standards.*

Because under the IFRS for PEs draft, the proposed default accounting treatment for financial instruments would be fair value through the statement of income, some users of PE standards might actually be required to apply more fair-value measurements than those reporting under the full IFRS.

Other issues. In addition to the explanations of PE reporting requirements in the body of the Exposure Draft, disclosure requirements have been comprehensively set forth in the Draft Implementation Guidance: Illustrative Financial Statements and Disclosure Checklist.

PEs have expressed concerns not only over the complexity of the IFRS, but also about the frequency of changes to standards. To respond to these issues, the IASB intends to update the IFRS for PEs approximately once every two years via an omnibus standard. Users are thus being assured of having a moderately stable platform of requirements.

The ED posed 12 questions and invited comments to be submitted to the IASB in writing. During the exposure period, the IASB conducted roundtable meetings with PEs and small firms of auditors to discuss the proposals. It also conducted field tests and field visits on the proposals in the Exposure Draft. Enactment of the standard is now expected in early or mid-2009.

Implications of IFRS for PEs. The Exposure Draft of IFRS for PEs is a significant development that may have a real impact on the future accounting and auditing standards issued by organizations participating in the standards-setting process.

In early 2007, FASB and the AICPA announced that a newly established Private Company Financial Reporting Committee (PCFRC) will address the financial reporting needs of private companies and the users of their financial statements. The primary objective of the PCFRC will be to help FASB determine whether and where there should be specific differences in prospective and existing accounting standards for private companies.

The International Federation of Accountants (IFAC) strongly supports the IASB's project on PEs. The IFAC board has agreed to assist the IASB in obtaining feedback on its proposed IFRS for PEs through field testing and other means. The Australian Accounting Standards Board (AASB), the Institute of Certified Public Accountants of Ireland, and the UK Accounting Standards Board have strongly supported the IASB publication of the Exposure Draft on the IFRS for PEs. The AASB tentatively decided that Australia should adopt a two-tiered approach in relation to Australian corporate entities, as follows:

- Australian equivalents to the IFRS will be required for corporations that are publicly accountable; and
- An Australian version of the IFRS for PEs will be adopted by corporations that are not publicly accountable but that prepare general-purpose financial reports. In many European countries, a close link exists between the statutory financial statements and the results reported for income tax purposes. The successful implementation of PE standards would require breaking the mandatory link between the financial statements and the income tax return, and would also trigger a need to amend the country's applicable law.

Because it is imperative that international convergence of accounting standards be accompanied by international convergence of audit standards, differential accounting for PEs would affect regulators such as the Public Company Accounting Oversight Board (PCAOB) and the SEC. The success of the IFRS for PEs will depend on the extent to which users, preparers, and their auditors believe the standards meet their needs.

2 STATEMENT OF FINANCIAL POSITION

PERSPECTIVE AND ISSUES

As set forth by the IASB's *Framework for the Preparation and Presentation of Financial Statements ("Framework"),* the objective of financial reporting is to provide information about the financial position, performance, and changes in financial position of an entity that is useful to a wide range of users in making economic decisions. Although financial statements prepared for this purpose meet the common needs of most users, they do not provide all the information that users may need to make economic decisions since they largely portray the financial effects of past events and do not necessarily provide nonfinancial information.

The statement of financial position is a statement that presents assets, liabilities, and shareholders' equity (net assets) at a given point in time. The statement of financial position is sometimes described as a "stock" statement because it reflects the balances of the company's accounts at a moment in time, as opposed to the other basic financial statements, which are described as "flow" statements and all reflect summarized results of transactions over a period of time.

During the early era of financial reporting standard setting, throughout the nineteenth century and first half of the twentieth century, the emphasis of legislation was almost entirely on the statement of financial position (formerly most often called the balance sheet), but by the mid-twentieth century owners were asking for more and more information about operating performance, leading to presentations of an increasingly complete income statement (or profit and loss account).

There is a continuing tension between the two financial statements, since—because of double entry bookkeeping conventions—they are linked together and cannot easily serve differing objectives. The stock markets look primarily at earnings expectations, which are largely based on historic performance, as measured by the income statement. If earnings measurement drives financial reporting, this means that, of necessity, the statement of financial position carries the residuals of the earnings measurement process. For example, assets such as motor vehicles with service potential that is used up over several accounting periods will have their costs allocated to these periods through the depreciation process, with the statement of financial position left to report a residual of that allocation process, which may or may not reflect the value of those assets at the end of the reporting period. However, if reporting were truly statement of financial position driven, the reporting entity would value the vehicles at the end of each reporting period—for example by reference to their replacement costs in current condition—and the change in statement of financial position values from one year to another would be reflected in the statement of comprehensive income.

By the 1960s many national GAAP standards were being promulgated to overtly favor the income statement over the balance sheet, but the pendulum began to swing back to a balance sheet-oriented strategy when standard setters—first, the FASB in the US; later others, including the International Accounting Standards Committee, predecessor of the current IASB—developed conceptual frameworks intended to serve as the fundamental theory of financial reporting. Undertaking that exercise had the result of causing accounting theory to revert to the original purpose—namely, to measure economic activity—and to implicitly adopt the definition of income as the change in wealth from period to period. With this in mind, measurement of that wealth, as captured in the balance sheet, became more central to new standards development efforts.

In practice, IFRS as currently written are a mixture of both approaches, depending on the transaction being recognized, measured, and reported. This mixed attribute approach is partially a legacy of earlier financial reporting rule making, but also reflects the practical difficulties of value measurement for many categories of assets and liabilities. For example, many financial instruments are remeasured at the end of each reporting period, whereas property, plant, and equipment are normally held at original cost and are depreciated systematically over estimated useful lives, subject to further adjustment for impairment, as necessary.

However, while existing requirements are not entirely consistent regarding financial statement primacy, both the IASB and the FASB, when developing new accounting standards, now are formally committed to a statement of financial position (balance sheet)–oriented approach. The *Framework* is expressed in terms of measuring assets and liabilities, and reportedly the two standard-setting bodies and their respective staffs analyze transactions affected by proposed standards from the perspective of whether they increase or diminish the assets and liabilities of the entity. Overall, the IASB sees financial reporting as being based on the measuring of assets and liabilities, and has the overall goal of requiring reporting all changes to them (other than those which are a result of transactions with owners, such as the payment of dividends) in a statement of comprehensive income.

In 2003 the IASB began a project to create a new comprehensive statement of performance, to be called the *statement of comprehensive income*. Field visits suggested that the proposed statement was too far in advance of current practice to readily gain acceptance from preparers and users of financial reports, which caused the IASB to give further attention to a mode of presentation which would be more comprehensible to users and preparers. Some simplifications were subsequently agreed to, and other issues remained under discussion. In late 2004, IASB and FASB agreed to jointly conduct further consideration of these matters, effectively signaling a fresh start for this developing effort. In an Exposure Draft (ED) Proposed Amendments to IAS 1, *"Presentation of Financial Statements": A Revised Presentation,* issued in March 2006, the IASB proposed to replace the income statement with a new statement called "statement of recognized income and expense." However, in the revised IAS 1, as it was actually promulgated in 2007, the title "statement of recognized income and expense" has been replaced by "statement of comprehensive income," thereby adopting the approach imposed under US GAAP. In fact, IAS 1 (revised 2007, effective 2009) largely, but not completely, embraces the approach first established under US GAAP (in FAS 130).

The focus on earnings in the capital markets does not mean that the statement of financial position is irrelevant; clearly the financial structure of the company is an important aspect of the company's risk profile, which in turn is important to evaluating the potential return on an investment from the perspective of a current or potential shareholder. Lenders have an even greater interest in the entity's financial structure. This is why companies sometimes go to great lengths to keep some transactions off the statement of financial position, for example by using special-purpose entities and other complex financing structures. IAS 32 considers that any instrument that gives rise to a right to claim assets from an entity is a liability.

IAS 1 states that "each material class of similar items" should be presented separately in the financial statements. In addition, "items of dissimilar nature or function" should be presented separately, unless they are immaterial. The standard expresses a preference for a presentation based on the current/noncurrent distinction, but allows a presentation by liquidity if that is more reliable and relevant. An asset or liability is current if it is part of the reporting entity's normal operating cycle (e.g., customer receivables) or if it will be realized or settled within twelve months after the reporting period. Only one of these conditions needs to be satisfied, so for example, inventory that remains on hand for two years should still be classified as current, while long-term liabilities should be reclassified as current for the final year before settlement. IAS 1 includes a sample of illustrative financial statement structure in its *Guidance on Implementing IAS 1,* but use of this format is optional.

IAS 1, *PRESENTATION OF FINANCIAL STATEMENTS*

In late 2007, the IASB issued revised IAS 1, *Presentation of Financial Statements*, as part of the joint IASB/FASB project now known as "Financial Statement Presentation." The project on financial statement presentation is being conducted jointly with the FASB in three phases.

- **Phase A** addressed what constitutes a complete set of financial statement requirements to present comparative information. The IASB and FASB have completed deliberations on this Phase, and the current IAS 1 is the result of that undertaking.
- **Phase B** addresses more fundamental issues for presenting information on the face of the financial statements, including: consistent principles for aggregating information in each financial statement; the totals and subtotals that should be reported in each financial statement; whether components of other recognized income and expense should be reclassified to profit and loss; and whether the direct or the indirect method of presenting operating cash flows provides more useful information. The IASB and FASB have decided that financial statements should present information in a manner

that reflects a cohesive financial picture of an entity and which separates an entity's financing activities from its business and other activities as well as from its transactions with owners. In late 2008 a discussion paper was issued on this phase of the project, following two years' development. Portions of this discussion paper are considered later in this chapter and in Chapter 3.

- **Phase C** will address interim financial reporting. As of late 2008, the IASB has not yet begun deliberations on this topic.

The revised IAS 1 resulted from the IASB's deliberations on Phase A of the Financial Statement Presentation project, and brings IAS 1 largely into line with the corresponding US standard—Statement of Financial Accounting Standards 130 (FAS 130), *Reporting Comprehensive Income.*

The revised Standard is effective for annual periods beginning on or after January 1, 2009, with early application permitted. It should be applied by an entity preparing and presenting general-purpose financial statements in accordance with IFRS. In the past, many considered the lack of the statement of financial position and comprehensive income statement formats under IFRS as a significant impediment to achieve comparability of the financial statements.

Objective

IAS 1 prescribes the basis for presentation of general-purpose financial statements to ensure comparability both with the entity's financial statements of previous periods and with the financial statements of other entities. It sets out overall requirements for the presentation of financial statements, guidelines for their structure, and minimum requirements for their content. In revising IAS 1, IASB's main objective was to aggregate information in the financial statements on the basis of shared characteristics. Other sources of guidance on the financial statement presentation can be found in IAS 7, 8, 10, 12, 18, 24, 27, 34, and IFRS 5.

Scope

IAS 1 applies to all entities, including profit-oriented and not-for-profit entities. Not-for-profit entities in both the private and public sectors can apply this standard, however they may need to change the descriptions used for particular line items within their financial statements and for the financial statements themselves. This standard applies to those entities that present consolidated financial statements and those that present financial statements as defined in IAS 27, *Consolidated and Separate Financial Statements.* It does not apply to the structure and content of condensed interim financial statements prepared in accordance with IAS 34, *Interim Financial Reporting.*

Purpose of Financial Statements

IAS 1 refers to financial statements as "a structured representation of the financial position and financial performance of an entity" and elaborates that the objective of financial statements is to provide information about an enterprise's financial position, its financial performance, and its cash flows, which is then utilized by a wide spectrum of end users in making economic decisions. In addition, financial statements also show the results of the management's stewardship of the resources entrusted to it. All this information is communicated through a complete set of financial statements.

Presentation of Financial Statements

IAS 1 defines a complete set of financial statements to be comprised of the following:

1. A statement of financial position as at the end of the period;

a. The previous version of IAS 1 used the title "balance sheet." The current standard uses the title "statement of financial position."

2. A statement of comprehensive income for the period;

   a. Components of profit or loss may be presented either as part of a single statement of comprehensive income or in a separate income statement.
   b. When an income statement is presented, it becomes a part of a complete set of financial statements.
   c. The income statement should be displayed immediately before the statement of comprehensive income.

3. A statement of changes in equity for the period;

4. A statement of cash flows for the period;

   a. The previous version of IAS 1 used the title "cash flow statement." The revised standard uses the title "statement of cash flows."

5. Notes, comprising a summary of significant accounting policies and other explanatory information; and

6. A statement of financial position as at the beginning of the earliest comparative period when an entity applies an accounting policy retrospectively or makes a retrospective restatement of items in its financial statements, or when it reclassifies items in its financial statements.

   a. This requirement is part of the revised IAS 1.

Financial statements, except for cash flow information, are to be prepared using accrual basis of accounting.

Fairness exception under IAS 1. There is a subtle difference between US GAAP and what was required by many European countries regarding the use of an override to assure a fair presentation of the company's financial position and results of operations. While the US requires a *fair presentation in accordance with GAAP,* the European Fourth Directive requires that statements offer a *true and fair view* of the company's financial situation. If following the literal financial reporting requirements does not provide this result, then the entity should first consider the salutary effects of providing supplementary disclosures. However, if that is not seen as being sufficient to achieve a true and fair view, the entity may conclude that it must override (that is, ignore or contravene) the applicable accounting standard.

IAS 1 has a similar approach. It states the expectation that the use of IFRS will result, *in virtually all circumstances,* in financial statements that achieve a fair presentation. However, in extremely rare circumstances where management concludes that compliance with a requirement in an IFRS would be so misleading that it would conflict with the objective of financial statements set out in the *Framework,* the entity can depart from that requirement if the relevant regulatory framework requires, or otherwise does not prohibit, such a departure, and the entity discloses all of the following:

1. Management has concluded that the financial statements present fairly the entity's financial position, financial performance, and cash flows;

2. The entity has complied with all applicable IFRS, except that it has departed from a particular requirement to achieve a fair presentation;

3. The title of the IFRS from which the entity has departed, the nature of the departure, including the treatment that the IFRS would require, the reason why that treatment would be so misleading in the circumstances that it would conflict with the objective of financial statements set out in the *Framework,* and the treatment adopted; and

4. For each period presented, the financial effect of the departure on each item in the financial statements that would have been reported in complying with the requirement.

When an entity has departed from a requirement of an IFRS in a prior period, and that departure affects the amounts recognized in the current period, it shall make the disclosures as in 3. and 4. above.

The standard notes that deliberately departing from IFRS might not be permissible in some jurisdictions, in which case the entity should comply with the standard in question and disclose in the notes that it believes this to be misleading, and show the adjustments that would be necessary to avoid this distorted result. In extremely rare circumstances where management concludes that compliance with a requirement in an IFRS would be so misleading that it would conflict with the objective of financial statements set out in the *Framework,* but the relevant regulatory framework prohibits departure from the requirement, to the maximum extent possible, the entity is required to reduce the perceived misleading aspects of compliance by disclosing all of the following:

1. The title of the IFRS in question, the nature of the requirement, and the reason why management has concluded that complying with that requirement is so misleading in the circumstances that it conflicts with the objective of financial statements set out in the *Framework,* and
2. For each period presented, the adjustments to each item in the financial statements that management has concluded would be necessary to achieve a fair presentation.

When assessing whether complying with a specific requirement in an IFRS would be so misleading that it would conflict with the objective of financial statements set out in the *Framework,* management should consider the following:

1. Why the objective of financial statements is not achieved in the particular circumstances; and
2. How the entity's circumstances differ from those of other entities that comply with the requirement.

    a. If other entities in similar circumstances comply with the requirement, there is a rebuttable presumption that the entity's compliance with the requirement would not be so misleading that it would conflict with the objective of financial statements set out in the *Framework.*

It might be noted under US auditing standards there is a provision that an unqualified opinion may be rendered even when there has been a GAAP departure, if the auditor concludes that it provides a fairer presentation than would have resulted had GAAP been strictly adhered to (the so-called "Rule 203 exception"). US GAAP was recently revised to relocate the GAAP hierarchy, which was formerly incorporated in US auditing standards, to the accounting literature. The new standard does not address the auditors' duties in rendering their audit opinions, but does hold that departures from the hierarchy, if material in effect, preclude management from asserting that the financial statements comply with GAAP. Under IFRS, logic somewhat similar to the "Rule 203 exception" is built into the accounting standards themselves, and thus is not dependent upon the level of service, if any, being rendered by an independent accountant, but rather makes it a management responsibility, including the need to disclose the logic and the financial statement impact. Accordingly, it appears that IFRS now recognizes, in the accounting standards, a "fairness exception" that is now explicitly rejected by US GAAP literature.

Going concern. When preparing financial statements, management makes an assessment regarding the entity's ability to continue as a going concern. If the result of the assessment casts significant doubt upon the entity's ability to continue as a going concern, management is required to disclose that fact, together with the basis on which it prepared the financial statements and the reason why the entity is not regarded as a going concern.

Accrual basis of accounting. Financial statements, except for cash flow information, are to be prepared using accrual basis of accounting.

Materiality and aggregation. An entity should present separately each material class of similar items as well as present separately material items of dissimilar nature or function. If a line item is not individually material, it is aggregated with other items either in those statements or in the notes. It is not necessary for an entity to provide a specific disclosure required by an IFRS if the information is not material.

Offsetting. Assets and liabilities, or income and expenses, may not be offset against each other, unless required or permitted by an IFRS. However, the reduction of accounts receivable by the allowance for doubtful accounts, or of property, plant, and equipment by the accumulated depreciation, are acts that reduce these assets by the appropriate valuation accounts and are not considered to be offsetting assets and liabilities.

Frequency of reporting. An entity should present a complete set of financial statements (including comparative information) at least annually. If the reporting period changes such that the financial statements are for a period longer or shorter than one year, the entity should disclose the reason for the longer or shorter period and the fact that the amounts presented are not entirely comparable.

Comparative information. An entity is required to include a statement of financial position as at the beginning of the earliest comparative period whenever an entity retrospectively applies an accounting policy, or makes a retrospective restatement of items in its financial statements, or when it reclassifies items in its financial statements. In those limited circumstances, an entity is required to present, as a minimum, three statements of financial position and related notes, as at

1. The end of the current period;
2. The end of the previous period (which is the same as the beginning of the current period); and
3. The beginning of the earliest comparative period.

When the entity changes the presentation or classification of items in its financial statements, the entity should reclassify the comparative amounts, unless reclassification is impractical. In reclassifying comparative amounts, the required disclosure includes: (1) the nature of the reclassification; (2) the amount of each item or class of items that is reclassified; and (3) the reason for the reclassification. In situations where it is impracticable to reclassify comparative amounts, an entity should disclose: (1) the reason for not reclassifying the amounts and (2) the nature of the adjustments that would have been made if the amounts had been reclassified.

Consistency of presentation. The presentation and classification of items in the financial statements should be consistent from one period to the next. A change in presentation and classification of items in the financial statements may be required when there is a significant change in the nature of the entity's operations, another presentation or classification is more appropriate (having considered the criteria of IAS 8, *Accounting Policies, Changes in Accounting Estimates and Errors*), or when an IFRS requires a change in presentation. When making such changes in presentation, an entity should reclassify its comparative information and present adequate disclosures (see comparable information above).

The revised IAS 1 is effective for annual periods beginning on or after January 1, 2009.

Structure and content of the financial statements as well as notes in accordance with the revised IAS 1 are discussed in the remainder of this chapter (Statement of Financial Position), Chapter 3 (Statement of Comprehensive Income and Statement of Changes in Equity) and Chapter 4 (Statement of Cash Flows).

Sources of IFRS
IAS 1, 8, 10, 24, 32, 36, 38, 39, 40, 41
IFRS 5, 6
Framework for the Preparation and Presentation of Financial Statements

DEFINITIONS OF TERMS

The IASB *Framework* describes the basic concepts by which financial statements are prepared. It does so by defining the objective of financial statements; identifying the qualitative characteristics that make information in financial statements useful; and defining the basic elements of financial statements and the concepts for recognizing and measuring them in financial statements.

The elements of financial statements are the broad classifications and groupings which convey the substantive financial effects of transactions and events on the reporting entity. To be included in the financial statements, an event or transaction must meet definitional, recognition, and measurement requirements, all of which are set forth in the *Framework*.

Elements of statements of financial position.

Assets—*Probable future economic benefits obtained or controlled by a particular entity as a result of past transactions or events.*

The following three characteristics must be present for an item to qualify as an asset:

1. The asset must provide probable future economic benefit that enables it to provide future net cash inflows.
2. The entity is able to receive the benefit and restrict other entities' access to that benefit.
3. The event that provides the entity with the right to the benefit has occurred.

In addition, the asset must be capable of being measured reliably. The *Framework* states that reliable measurement means that the number must be free from material error and bias and can be depended upon by users to represent faithfully. In the Basis for Conclusions of IFRS 2, the IASB notes that the use of estimates is permitted, and that there may be a trade-off between the characteristics of being free from material error and having representational faithfulness.

Assets have features that help identify them in that they are exchangeable, legally enforceable, and have future economic benefit (service potential). It is that potential that eventually brings in cash to the entity and that underlies the concept of an asset.

Liabilities—*Probable future sacrifices of economic benefits arising from present obligations of a particular entity to transfer assets or provide services to other entities in the future as a result of past transactions or events.*

The following three characteristics must be present for an item to qualify as a liability:

1. A liability requires that the entity settle a present obligation by the probable future transfer of an asset on demand when a specified event occurs or at a particular date.
2. The obligation cannot be avoided.
3. The event that obligates the entity has occurred.

Liabilities are similarly recognized subject to the constraint that they can be measured reliably.

Liabilities usually result from transactions that enable entities to obtain resources. Other liabilities may arise from nonreciprocal transfers, such as the declaration of dividends to the owners of the entity or the pledge of assets to charitable organizations.

An entity may involuntarily incur a liability. A liability may be imposed on the entity by government or by the court system in the form of taxes, fines, or levies. A liability may arise from price changes or interest rate changes. Liabilities may be legally enforceable or they may be equitable obligations that arise from social, ethical, or moral requirements. Liabilities continue in existence until the entity is no longer responsible for discharging them.

The diagram that follows, which is taken from one of the statements produced from the conceptual framework project by the US standard setter, the FASB, identifies the three classes of events that affect an entity, and shows the relationship between assets and liabilities, on the one hand, and comprehensive income, on the other.

Equity—The residual interest in the assets that remains after deducting its liabilities. In a business enterprise, the equity is the ownership interest.

Equity arises from the ownership relation and is the basis for distributions of earnings to the owners. Distributions of enterprise assets to owners are voluntary. Equity is increased by owners' investments and comprehensive income and is reduced by distributions to owners. In practice, the distinction between equity and liabilities may be difficult to determine. Securities such as convertible debt and certain types of preference shares may have characteristics of both equity (residual ownership interest) and liabilities (nondiscretionary future sacrifices). For both the IASB and the FASB, equity, aside from exchanges with owners, is a residual of the asset/liability recognition model.

General-purpose financial statements. The financial statements intended to meet the needs of users who are not in a position to require an entity to prepare reports tailored to their particular information needs, comprising the statement of financial position, statement of comprehensive income, separate income statement (if presented), statement of changes in equity, and statement of cash flows.

Impracticable. Applying a requirement is impracticable when the entity cannot apply it after making every reasonable effort to do so.

International Financial Reporting Standards (IFRS). Standards and Interpretations adopted by the International Accounting Standards Board (IASB) which comprise

1. International Financial Reporting Standards
2. International Accounting Standards, and
3. Interpretations developed by the International Financial Reporting Interpretations Committee (IFRIC) or the former Standing Interpretations Committee (SIC).

Material omissions or misstatements. Those omissions and misstatements that could, individually or collectively, influence the economic decisions that users make on the basis of the financial statements. Materiality depends on the size and nature of the omission or misstatement judged in the surrounding circumstances. The size or nature of the item, or a combination of both, could be the determining factor.

Notes. Information provided in addition to that presented in the financial statements, which comprise a summary of significant accounting policies and other explanatory information, including narrative descriptions or disaggregations of items presented in those statements as well as information about items that do not qualify for recognition in those statements.

All transactions and other events and circumstances that affect a business enterprise during a period

A. All changes in assets and liabilities not accompanied by changes in equity

1. Exchanges of assets for assets
2. Exchanges of liabilities for liabilities
3. Acquisitions of assets by incurring liabilities
4. Settlements of liabilities by transferring assets

B. All changes in assets or liabilities accompanied by changes in equity

1. Comprehensive income

   a. Revenues
   b. Gains
   c. Expenses
   d. Losses

2. All changes in equity from transfers between a business enterprise and its owners

   a. Investments by owners
   b. Distributions to owners

C. Changes within equity that do not affect assets or liabilities

Other comprehensive income. The total of income less expenses (including reclassification adjustments) from nonowner sources that are not recognized in profit or loss as required or permitted by other IFRS or Interpretations. The components of other comprehensive income include (1) changes in revaluation surplus (IAS 16 and IAS 38); (2) actuarial gains and losses on defined benefit plans (IAS 19); (3) translation gains and losses (IAS 21); (4) gains and losses on remeasuring available-for-sale financial assets (IAS 39) and (5) the effective portion of gains and losses on hedging instruments in a cash flow hedge (IAS 39).

Profit or loss. The total of income less expenses, excluding the components of other comprehensive income.

Reclassification adjustments. Amounts reclassified to profit or loss in the current period that were recognized in other comprehensive income in the current or previous periods.

Total comprehensive income. The change in equity (net assets) of an entity during a period from transactions and other events and circumstances from nonowner sources. It includes all changes in net assets during a period, except those resulting from investments by owners and distributions to owners. It thus comprises all components of "profit or loss" and "other comprehensive income" presented in the statement of comprehensive income.

CONCEPTS, RULES, AND EXAMPLES

General Concepts

Under IFRS, assets and liabilities are recorded at fair value at inception in financial statements, which for assets and liabilities arising from arm's-length transactions will be equal to negotiated prices. Subsequent measurement is usually under the historical cost principle, although in many cases subsequent changes in values are also recognized. All assets are now subject to impairment testing. IAS 36, *Impairment of Assets,* requires assets to be reduced in value if their carrying value exceeds the higher of fair value or value in use (expected future cash flows from the asset). IAS 39, *Financial Instruments: Recognition and Measurement,* IAS 40, *Investment Property,* and IAS 41, *Agriculture,* all include some element of subsequent measurement at fair value. Where assets are classified as held for sale, they are carried at the lower of their carrying amount or fair value less selling costs (IFRS 5).

Historical exchange prices, and the amortized cost amounts that are later presented, are sometimes cited as being useful because these amounts are objectively determined and capable of being verified independently. However, critics point out that, other than at transaction date, historical cost does not result in the presentation statement of financial position numbers that are comparable between companies, so while they are reliable, they may not be relevant for decision-making purposes. This captures the fundamental conflict regarding accounting information: absolutely reliable or objective information may not be very relevant to current decision making.

Form of Statement of Financial Position

The titles commonly given to the primary financial statement that presents an entity's financial position include the statement of financial position, the balance sheet, and the statement of financial condition. (The statement of assets and liabilities, or some variant thereof, is also encountered, but usually connotes a presentation that is not consistent with IFRS or GAAP, such as that on a cash or tax basis of presentation.) The revised IAS 1 changed the title of the "balance sheet" to the "statement of financial position," the title used throughout this book. The IASB concluded that "statement of financial position" better reflects the function of the statement and is consistent with the *Framework.* In addition, the title "balance sheet" simply reflected the convention that double-entry bookkeeping requires all debits to equal credits, and did not identify the content or purpose of the statement. According to the IASB, the term "financial position" was a well-known and accepted term, and had already been used in auditors' opinions internationally for more than 20 years to describe what "the balance sheet" presents.

The three elements that are always to be displayed in the heading of a statement of financial position are

1. The entity whose financial position is being presented
2. The title of the statement
3. The date of the statement

The entity's name should appear exactly as written in the legal document that created it (e.g., the certificate of incorporation, partnership agreement, etc.). The title should also clearly reflect the legal status of the enterprise as a corporation, partnership, sole proprietorship, or division of some other entity.

The statement of financial position presents a "snapshot" of the resources and claims to resources at a moment in time. The last day of a month is normally used as the statement date (in jurisdictions where a choice is allowed) unless the entity uses a fiscal reporting period always ending on a particular day of the week, such as a Friday or Sunday (e.g., the last Friday in December, or the Sunday falling closest to December 31). In these cases, the statement of financial position can appropriately be dated accordingly (i.e., December 26, October 1, etc.). In all cases, the implication is that the statement of financial position captures the pertinent amounts as of the close of business on the date noted.

Statements of financial position should generally be uniform in appearance from one period to the next, as indeed should all of the entity's financial statements. The form, terminology, captions, and pattern of combining insignificant items should be consistent. The goal is to enhance usefulness by maintaining a consistent manner of presentation unless there are good reasons to change these and the changes are duly reported.

Classification of Assets

Assets, liabilities, and shareholders' equity are separated in the statement of financial position. IAS 1 says that companies should make a distinction between current and noncurrent assets and liabilities, except when a presentation based on liquidity provides information that is more reliable or relevant.

Current assets. An asset should be classified as a current asset when it satisfies any one of the following:

1. It is expected to be realized in, or is held for sale or consumption in, the normal course of the enterprise's operating cycle;
2. It is held primarily for trading purposes;
3. It is expected to be realized within twelve months of the end of the reporting period;
4. It is cash or a cash equivalent asset that is not restricted in its use.

If a current asset category includes items that will have a life of more than twelve months, the amount that falls into the next financial year should be disclosed in the notes. All other assets should be classified as noncurrent assets, if a classified statement of financial position is to be presented in the financial statements.

Thus, current assets include cash, cash equivalents and other assets that are expected to be realized in cash, or sold or consumed during one normal operating cycle of the business. The operating cycle of an enterprise is the time between the acquisition of materials entering into a process and its realization in cash or an instrument that is readily convertible into cash. Inventories and trade receivables should still be classified as current assets in a classified statement of financial position even if these assets are not expected to be realized within twelve months from the end of the reporting period. However, marketable securities could only be classified as current assets if they are expected to be realized (sold, redeemed, or matured) within twelve months after the end of the reporting period, even though most would deem marketable securities to be more liquid than inventories and possibly even than receivables. Management intention takes priority over liquidity potential. The following items would be classified as current assets:

1. **Inventories** are assets held, either for sale in the ordinary course of business or in the process of production for such sale, or in the form of materials or supplies to be consumed in the production process or in the rendering of services (IAS 2). The basis of valuation and the method of pricing, which is now limited to FIFO or weighted-average cost, should be disclosed.

Inventories—at the lower of cost (FIFO) or net realizable value	$xxx

    In the case of a manufacturing concern, raw materials, work in process, and finished goods should be disclosed separately on the statement of financial position or in the footnotes.

Inventories:		
Finished goods	$xxx	
Work in process	xxx	
Raw materials	xxx	$xxx

2. **Receivables** include accounts and notes receivable, receivables from affiliate companies, and officer and employee receivables. The term *accounts receivable* represents amounts due from customers arising from transactions in the ordinary course of business. Allowances due to expected lack of collectibility and any amounts discounted or pledged should be stated clearly. The allowances may be based on a relationship to sales or based on direct analysis of the receivables. If material, the receivables should be analyzed into their component parts. The receivables section may be presented as follows:

Receivables:			
Customer accounts	$xxx		
Customer notes/commercial paper	xxx	$xxxx	
Less allowance for doubtful accounts		(xxx)	$xxxx
Due from associated companies			xxx
Due from officers and employees			xxx
Total			$xxxx

3. **Prepaid expenses** are assets created by the prepayment of cash or incurrence of a liability. They expire and become expenses with the passage of time, use, or events (e.g., prepaid rent, prepaid insurance and deferred taxes). This item is frequently aggregated with others on the face of the statement of financial position with details relegated to the notes, since it is rarely a material amount.

4. **Trading investments** are those that are acquired principally for the purpose of generating a profit from short-term fluctuations in price or dealer's margin. A financial asset should be classified as held-for-trading if it is part of a portfolio for which there is evidence of a recent actual pattern of short-term profit making. Trading assets include debt and equity securities and loans and receivables acquired by the enterprise with the intention of making a short-term profit. Derivative financial assets are always deemed held-for-trading unless they are designed as effective hedging instruments.

    As required by IAS 39, a financial asset held for trading should be measured at fair value, with changes in value reflected currently in earnings. There is a presumption that fair value can be reliably measured for financial assets that are held for trading.

5. **Cash** and cash equivalents include cash on hand, consisting of coins, currency, and undeposited checks; money orders and drafts; and deposits in banks. Anything accepted by a bank for deposit would be considered cash. Cash must be available for a demand withdrawal; thus, assets such as certificates of deposit would not be considered cash because of the time restrictions on withdrawal. Also, to be classified as a current asset, cash must be available for current use. According to IAS 1, cash that is restricted in use and whose restrictions will not expire within the operating cycle, or cash restricted for a noncurrent use, would not be included in current assets. According to IAS 7, cash equivalents include short-term, highly liquid investments that (1) are readily convertible to known amounts of cash, and (2) are so near their maturity (original maturities of three months or less) that they present negligible risk of changes in value because of changes in interest rates. Treasury bills, commercial paper, and money market funds are all examples of cash equivalents.

Noncurrent assets.   IAS 1 uses the term "noncurrent" to include tangible, intangible, operating, and financial assets of a long-term nature. It does not prohibit the use of alternative descriptions, as long as the meaning is clear. The European Union (EU) uses the term *fixed assets* (which derives from nineteenth-century balance sheets, which drew a distinction between fixed and circulating assets). Noncurrent assets include held-to-maturity investments, investment property, property and equipment, intangible assets, assets held for sale, and miscellaneous other assets, as described in the following paragraphs.

Held-to-maturity investments are financial assets with fixed or determinable payments and fixed maturity that the enterprise has a positive intent and ability to hold to maturity (the term is from IAS 39, *Financial Instruments*). Examples of held-to-maturity investments are debt securities and mandatorily redeemable preference shares. This category excludes loans and receivables originated by the enterprise, which under IAS 39 constitute a separate category of asset. Held-to-maturity investments are to be measured at amortized cost. (For a detailed discussion on financial instruments, refer to Chapters 5 and 10 of this book.)

Investment property.   This denotes property being held to earn rentals, or for capital appreciation, or both, rather than for use in production or supply of goods or services, or for administrative purposes or for sale in the ordinary course of business. Investment property should be initially measured at cost. Subsequent to initial measurement an enterprise is required to elect either the fair value model or the cost model. (IAS 40 is the relevant standard: for a detailed discussion on investment property, refer to Chapter 10.)

Property, plant, and equipment.   Tangible assets that are held by an enterprise for use in the production or supply of goods or services, or for rental to others, or for administrative purposes and which are expected to be used during more than one period. Included are such items as land, buildings, machinery and equipment, furniture and fixtures, motor vehicles and equipment. These should be disclosed, with the related accumulated depreciation, as follows:

Machinery and equipment	$xxx	
Less accumulated depreciation	(xxx)	$xxx
or		
Machinery and equipment (net of $xxx accumulated depreciation)		$xxx

Accumulated depreciation should be shown by major classes of depreciable assets. In addition to showing this amount in the statement of financial position, the notes to the financial statements should contain balances of major classes of depreciable assets, by nature or function, at the date of the statement of financial position, along with a general description of the method or methods used in computing depreciation with respect to major classes of depreciable assets (IAS 16).

Illustrative example

Superconductors SA
Notes to the Consolidated Balance Sheets
December 31, 2008

Note 3—Property, Plant, and Equipment

2007 *(in thousands of euros)*	Land and buildings	Fixtures and fittings	Equipment and other	Total
Gross value at January 1, 2007	9,796	8,110	20,691	38,597
Additions	42	282	1,409	1,733
Disposals	--	(41)	(858)	(899)
Translation adjustments	--	205	(1,223)	(1,428)
Gross value at December 31, 2007	9,838	8,146	20,019	38,003
Accumulated depreciation at December 31, 2007	(7,338)	(3,837)	(17,248)	(28,423)
Net value at December 31, 2007	2,500	4,309	2,771	9,580

2008 *(in thousands of euros)*	Land and buildings	Fixtures and fittings	Equipment and other	Total
Gross value at January 1, 2008	9,838	8,146	20,019	38,003
Additions	4	98	1,577	1,679
Disposals	--	(116)	(832)	(948)
Translation adjustments	--	(158)	(858)	(1,016)
Gross value at December 31, 2008	9,842	8,014	19,862	37,718
Accumulated depreciation at December 31, 2008	(7,419)	(4,186)	(17,428)	(29,033)
Net value at December 31, 2008	2,423	3,828	2,434	8,685

Change in depreciation

2007 *(in thousands of euros)*	Land and buildings	Fixtures and fittings	Equipment and other	Total
Accumulated depreciation at January 1, 2007	(7,263)	(3,321)	(17,031)	(27,615)
Additional depreciation	(75)	(498)	(1,488)	(2,061)
Disposal of assets	--	69	723	792
Translation adjustments	--	(87)	548	461
Accumulated depreciation at December 31, 2007	(7,338)	(3,837)	(17,248)	(28,423)

2008 *(in thousands of euros)*	Land and buildings	Fixtures and fittings	Equipment and other	Total
Accumulated depreciation at January 1, 2008	(7,338)	(3,837)	(17,248)	(28,423)
Additional depreciation	(81)	(537)	(1,646)	(2,264)
Disposal of assets	--	74	778	852
Translation adjustments	--	114	688	852
Accumulated depreciation at December 31, 2008	(7,419)	(4,186)	(17,428)	(29,003)

Intangible assets. These are noncurrent assets of a business, without physical substance, the possession of which is expected to provide future benefits to the owner. Included in this category are the unidentifiable asset goodwill and the identifiable intangibles trademarks, patents, copyrights, and organizational costs.

IAS 38 stipulates that where an intangible is being amortized, it should be carried at cost net of accumulated amortization. Generally, the amortization of an intangible asset, or any impairment, is shown separately as a deduction from the asset cost, since that is a legal requirement in jurisdictions such as the EU, but IAS 38 does not require this mode of presentation.

Illustrative example

Superconductors SA
Notes to the Consolidated Balance Sheets
December 31, 2008

Note 1—Intangible Assets

2007 *(in thousands of euros)*	*Management information software*	*Patents and trademarks*	*Other intangible assets*	*Total*
Gross value at January 1, 2007	8,555	1,703	5,232	15,490
External purchases	845	177	--	1,022
Internal development costs	381	--	--	381
Write-offs and disposals	--	--	(12)	(12)
Transfers	94	--	(94)	--
Translation adjustments	(38)	--	(12)	(50)
Gross value at December 31, 2007	9,837	1,880	5,114	16,831
Amortization at December 31, 2007	(6,913)	(1,523)	(4,422)	(12,858)
Net carrying value at December 31, 2007	2,924	357	692	3,973

2008 *(in thousands of euros)*	*Management information software*	*Patents and trademarks*	*Other intangible assets*	*Total*
Gross value at January 1, 2008	9,837	1,880	5,114	16,831
External purchases	1,061	137	42	1,240
Internal development costs	404	--	--	404
Write-offs and disposals	(17)	--	--	(17)
Transfers	(15)	--	15	--
Translation adjustments	(54)	--	(4)	(58)
Gross value at December 31, 2008	11,216	2,017	5,167	18,400
Amortization at December 31, 2008	(8,367)	(1,659)	(5,018)	(15,044)
Net carrying value at December 31, 2008	(2,849)	358	149	3,356

Changes in accumulated amortization

2007 *(in thousands of euros)*	*Management information software*	*Patents and trademarks*	*Other intangible assets*	*Total*
Amortization at January 1, 2007	(5,522)	(1,407)	(3,976)	(10,905)
Amortization charges	(1,490)	(116)	(446)	(2,052)
Disposals of assets	63	--	--	63
Translation adjustments	36	--	--	36
Amortization at December 31, 2007	(6,913)	(1,523)	(4,422)	(12,858)

2008 *(in thousands of euros)*	*Management information software*	*Patents and trademarks*	*Other intangible assets*	*Total*
Amortization at January 1, 2008	(6,913)	(1,523)	(4,422)	(12,858)
Amortization charges	(1,574)	(136)	(596)	(2,306)
Disposals of assets	97	--	--	97
Translation adjustments	23	--	--	23
Amortization at December 31, 2008	(8,367)	(1,659)	(5,018)	(15,044)

Assets held for sale. Where an entity has committed to a plan to sell an asset or group of assets, these should be reclassified as assets held for sale and should be measured at the lower of their carrying amount or their fair value less selling costs. (This requirement, set forth by IFRS 5, is discussed in Chapter 8).

Other assets. An all-inclusive heading for accounts that do not fit neatly into any of the other asset categories (e.g., long-term deferred expenses that will not be consumed within one operating cycle, and deferred tax assets).

Classification of Liabilities

The liabilities are normally displayed in the statement of financial position in the order of payment due dates.

Current liabilities. According to IAS 1, a liability should be classified as a current liability when

1. It is expected to be settled in the normal course of business within the enterprise's operating cycle;
2. It is due to be settled within twelve months of the date of the statement of financial position;
3. It is held primarily for the purpose of being traded; or
4. The entity does not have an unconditional right to defer settlement beyond twelve months

All other liabilities should be classified as noncurrent liabilities. Obligations that are due on demand or are callable at any time by the lender are classified as current regardless of the present intent of the entity or of the lender concerning early demand for repayment. Current liabilities also include

1. Obligations arising from the acquisition of goods and services entering into the entity's normal operating cycle (e.g., accounts payable, short-term notes payable, wages payable, taxes payable, and other miscellaneous payables).
2. Collections of money in advance for the future delivery of goods or performance of services, such as rent received in advance and unearned subscription revenues.
3. Other obligations maturing within the current operating cycle, such as the current maturity of bonds and long-term notes.

Certain liabilities, such as trade payables and accruals for operating costs, which form part of the working capital used in the normal operating cycle of the business, are to be classified as current liabilities even if they are due to be settled after more than twelve months from the date of the statement of financial position.

Other current liabilities which are not settled as part of the operating cycle, but which are due for settlement within twelve months of the date of the statement of financial position, such as dividends payable and the current portion of long-term debt, should also be classified as current liabilities. However, interest-bearing liabilities that provide the financing for working capital on a long-term basis and are not scheduled for settlement within twelve months should not be classified as current liabilities.

IAS 1 provides another exception to the general rule that a liability due to be repaid within twelve months from the end of the reporting period should be classified as a current liability. If the original term was for a period longer than twelve months and the enterprise intended to refinance the obligation on a long-term basis prior to the date of the statement of financial position, and that intention is supported by an agreement to refinance, or to reschedule payments, which is completed before the financial statements are approved, then the debt is to be reclassified as noncurrent as of the date of the statement of financial position.

However, an entity would continue to classify as current liabilities its long-term financial liabilities when they are due to be settled within twelve months, if an agreement to refinance on a long-term basis was made after the date of the statement of financial position. Similarly if long-term debt becomes callable as a result of a breach of a loan covenant, and no agreement with the lender to provide a grace period of more than twelve months has been concluded by the date of the statement of financial position, the debt must be classified as current. (This is different than under US GAAP, which permits a determination to be made as of the date of *issuance* of the financial statements, which may be months after the date of the statement of financial position.)

The distinction between current and noncurrent liquid assets generally rests upon both the ability and the intent of the entity to realize or not to realize cash for the assets within the traditional one-year concept. Intent is not of similar significance with regard to the classification of liabilities, however, because the creditor has the legal right to demand satisfaction of a currently due obligation, and even an expression of intent not to exercise that right does not diminish the entity's burden should there be a change in the creditor's intention. Thus, whereas an entity can control its use of current assets, it is limited by its contractual obligations with regard to current liabilities, and accordingly, accounting for current liabilities (subject to the two exceptions noted above) is based on legal terms, not expressions of intent.

Noncurrent liabilities. Obligations that are not expected to be liquidated within the current operating cycle, including

1. Obligations arising as part of the long-term capital structure of the entity, such as the issuance of bonds, long-term notes, and lease obligations;
2. Obligations arising out of the normal course of operations, such as pension obligations, decommissioning provisions, and deferred taxes; and
3. Contingent obligations involving uncertainty as to possible expenses or losses. These are resolved by the occurrence or nonoccurrence of one or more future events that confirm the amount payable, the payee, and/or the date payable. Contingent obligations include such items as product warranties (see the section on provisions below).

For all long-term liabilities, the maturity date, nature of obligation, rate of interest, and description of any security pledged to support the agreement should be clearly shown. Also, in the case of bonds and long-term notes, any premium or discount should be reported separately as an addition to or subtraction from the par (or face) value of the bond or note. Long-term obligations which contain certain covenants that must be adhered to are classified as current liabilities if any of those covenants have been violated and the lender has the right to demand payment. Unless the lender expressly waives that right or the conditions causing the default are corrected, the obligation is current.

Offsetting assets and liabilities. In general, assets and liabilities may not be offset against each other. However, the reduction of accounts receivable by the allowance for doubtful accounts, or of property, plant, and equipment by the accumulated depreciation, are acts that reduce these assets by the appropriate valuation accounts and are not considered to be the result of offsetting assets and liabilities.

Only where there is an actual right of setoff is the offsetting of assets and liabilities a proper presentation. This right of setoff exists only when *all* the following conditions are met:

1. Each of the two parties owes the other determinable amounts (although they may be in different currencies and bear different rates of interest).
2. The entity has the right to set off against the amount owed by the other party.
3. The entity intends to offset.
4. The right of setoff is legally enforceable.

In particular cases, laws of certain countries, including some bankruptcy laws, may impose restrictions or prohibitions against the right of setoff. Furthermore, when maturities differ, only the party with the nearest maturity can offset because the party with the longer maturity must settle in the manner determined by the earlier maturity party.

The question of setoff is sometimes significant for financial institutions which buy and sell financial instruments, often repackaging them as part of the process. IAS 39 provides detailed rules for determining when derecognition is appropriate and when assets and liabilities must be retained on the statement of financial position.

Classification of Shareholders' Equity

Shareholders' equity represents the interests of the owners in the net assets of a corporation. It shows the cumulative net results of past transactions and other events affecting the entity since its inception.

Share capital. This consists of the par or nominal value of preference and ordinary shares. The number of shares authorized, the number issued, and the number outstanding should be clearly shown. For preference share capital, the preference features must also be stated, as the following example illustrates:

6% cumulative preference shares, $100 par value, callable at $115, 15,000 shares authorized, 10,000 shares issued and outstanding	$ 1,000,000
Ordinary shares, $10 par value per share, 2,000,000 shares authorized, 1,500,000 shares issued and outstanding	$15,000,000

Preference share capital that is redeemable at the option of the holder may not be considered a part of equity—rather, it should be reported as a liability. IAS 32 makes it clear that substance prevails over form in the case of compound financial instruments; any instrument which includes a contractual obligation for the entity to deliver cash is considered to be a liability.

Retained earnings. This represents the accumulated earnings since the inception of the enterprise, less any earnings distributed to owners in the form of dividends. In some jurisdictions, notably in continental Europe, the law requires that a portion of retained earnings, equivalent to a small proportion of share capital, be set aside as a legal reserve. Historically, this was intended to limit dividend distributions by young or ailing businesses. This practice is expected to wane, and in any event is not congruent with financial reporting in accordance with IFRS and with the distinction made between equity and liabilities.

Also included in the equity section of the statement of financial position is treasury stock representing issued shares that have been reacquired by the issuer, in jurisdictions where the purchase of the entity's own shares is permitted by law. These shares are generally stated at their cost of acquisition, as a reduction from shareholders' equity.

Finally, some elements of comprehensive income, the components of other comprehensive income, are reported in equity. These components of other comprehensive income include net changes in the fair values of available-for-sale securities portfolios, and unrealized gains or losses on translations of the financial statements of subsidiaries denominated in a foreign currency, net changes in revaluation surplus, actuarial gains and losses on defined benefit plans, and the effective portion of gains and losses on hedging instruments in a cash flow hedge. In accordance with the revised IAS 1, net changes in all items of other comprehensive income should be reported in a new statement called "statement of comprehensive income," and accumulated balances in these items are reported in equity. (For a detailed discussion on statement of comprehensive income, refer to Chapter 3.)

Noncontrolling interests should be shown separately from owners' equity of the parent company in group accounts (i.e., consolidated financial statements), but are included in the overall equity section.

Supplemental Disclosures

In addition to the recognition and measurement principles set forth under IFRS, there are also requirements for supplemental disclosures, generally shown as notes to the accounts. There is also a degree of fluidity between showing information "on the face of the accounts" (i.e., directly in the statement of financial position or income statement) and in the notes: the main categories have to be preserved (see below), but the detail underlying the reported amounts may be shown in the notes. The two basic techniques are giving parenthetical explanations on the face of the accounts, and giving additional information in the notes.

Parenthetical explanations. Supplemental information is disclosed by means of parenthetical explanations following the appropriate statement of financial position items. For example

Equity share capital ($10 par value, 200,000 shares authorized, 150,000 issued) $1,500,000

Parenthetical explanations have an advantage over both footnotes and supporting schedules, as they place the disclosure in the body of the statement, where their importance cannot be overlooked by users of the financial statements.

Footnotes. If the additional information cannot be disclosed in a relatively short and concise parenthetical explanation, a footnote should be used, with a cross-reference shown in the statement of financial position. For example

Inventories (see Note 1) $2,550,000

The notes to the financial statements would then contain the following:

Note 1: Inventories are stated at the lower of cost or market. Cost is determined by the first-in, first-out method, and market is determined on the basis of estimated net realizable value. As of the date of the statement of financial position, the market value of the inventory is $2,720,000.

To present adequate detail regarding certain statement of financial position items, or move complex detail from the face of the accounts, a supporting schedule may be provided in the notes. Current receivables may be a single line item in the statement of financial position, as follows:

Current receivables (see Note 2) $2,500,000

A separate schedule for current receivables would then be presented as follows:

Note 2
Current Receivables

Customers' accounts and notes	$2,000,000
Associated companies	300,000
Nonconsolidated affiliates	322,000
Other	18,000
	2,640,000
Less allowance for doubtful accounts	(140,000)
	$2,500,000

Valuation accounts are another form of schedule used to keep detail off the statement of financial position. For example, accumulated depreciation reduces the book value for property, plant, and equipment, and a bond premium (discount) increases (decreases) the face value of a bond payable as shown in the following illustrations. The net amount is shown in the statement of financial position, and the detail in the notes.

Property, plant, and equipment		
Equipment	$18,000,000	
Less accumulated depreciation	(1,625,000)	$16,375,000

Noncurrent liabilities		
Bonds payable	$20,000,000	
Less discount on bonds payable	(1,300,000)	$18,700,000
Bonds payable	$20,000,000	
Add premium on bonds payable	1,300,000	$21,300,000

Notes

In accordance with IAS 1 the notes should (1) present information about the basis of preparation of the financial statements and the specific accounting policies used; (2) disclose the information required by IFRS that is not presented elsewhere in the financial statements, and (3) provide information that is not presented elsewhere in the financial statements, but is relevant to an understanding of any of them.

An entity should present notes in a systematic manner and should cross-reference each item in the statements of financial position and of comprehensive income, in the separate income statement (if presented), and in the statements of changes in equity and of cash flows to any related information in the notes.

An entity normally should present notes in the following order, to help users to understand the financial statements and to compare them with financial statements of other entities:

1. Statement of compliance with IFRS
2. Summary of significant accounting policies applied
3. Supporting information for items presented in the financial statements
4. Other disclosures, including contingent liabilities and unrecognized contractual commitments; and nonfinancial disclosures (e.g., the entity's financial risk management objectives and policies).

Statement of compliance with IFRS. IAS 1 requires an entity whose financial statements comply with IFRS to make an explicit and unreserved statement of such compliance in the notes. Financial statements should not be described as complying with IFRS unless they comply with all the requirements of IFRS.

An entity might refer to IFRS in describing the basis on which its financial statements are prepared without making this explicit and unreserved statement of compliance with IFRS. For example, the EU mandated a carve-out of the financial instruments standard and other jurisdictions have carved out or altered other IFRS standards. In some cases, these differences may significantly affect the reported financial performance and financial position of the entity. This information should be disclosed in the notes.

Accounting policies. The policy note should begin with a clear statement on the nature of the comprehensive basis of accounting used. A reporting entity may only claim to follow IFRS if it complies with every single IFRS in force as of the reporting date. The EU made certain amendments to IFRS when endorsing them (a carve-out from IAS 39), and those EU companies following these directives cannot claim to follow IFRS, and instead will have to acknowledge compliance with IFRS as endorsed by the EU.

Financial statements should include clear and concise disclosure of all significant accounting policies that have been used in the preparation of those financial statements. Management must also indicate the judgments that it has made in the process of applying the accounting policies that have the most significant effect on the amounts recognized. The entity must also disclose the key assumptions about the future and any other sources of estimation uncertainty that have a significant risk of causing a material adjustment to later be made to the carrying amounts of assets and liabilities.

IAS 1 requires an entity to disclose in the summary of significant accounting policies: (1) the measurement basis (or bases) used in preparing the financial statements, and (2) the other accounting policies applied that are relevant to an understanding of the financial statements. Measurement bases may include historical cost, current cost, net realizable value, fair value or recoverable amount. Other accounting policies should be disclosed if they could assist users in understanding how transactions, other events and conditions are reported in the financial statements.

In addition, an entity should disclose the judgments that management has made in the process of applying the entity's accounting policies and that have the most significant effect on the amounts recognized in the financial statements. Management makes judgments which can significantly affect the amounts reported in the financial statements, for example, when making decisions whether investments in securities should be classified as trading, available for sale or held to maturity, or whether lease transactions transfer substantially all the significant risks and rewards of ownership of financial assets to another party.

Determining the carrying amounts of some assets and liabilities requires estimating the effects of uncertain future events on those assets and liabilities at the end of the reporting period in measuring, for example, the recoverable values of different classes of property, plant, and equipment, or future outcome of litigation in progress. The reporting entity should disclose information about the assumptions it makes about the future, and other major sources of estimation uncertainty at the end of the reporting period, which have a significant risk of resulting in a material adjustment to the carrying amount of assets and liabilities within the next financial year. The notes to the financial statements should include the nature and the carrying amount of those assets and liabilities at the end of the period.

Financial statement users must be made aware of the accounting policies used by reporting entities, so that they can better understand the financial statements and make comparisons with the financial statements of others. The policy disclosures should identify and describe the accounting principles followed by the entity and methods of applying those principles that materially affect the determination of financial position, results of operations, or changes in cash flows. IAS 1 requires that disclosure of these policies be an integral part of the financial statements.

IAS 8 (as discussed in Chapter 1) provides criteria for making accounting policy choices. Policies should be relevant to the needs of users and should be reliable (representationally faithful, reflecting economic substance, neutral, prudent, and complete).

Fairness exception under IAS 1. Accounting standard setters have commonly recognized the fact that even full compliance with promulgated financial reporting principles may, on rare occasions, still not result in financial statements that are accurate, truthful, or fair. Therefore many, but not all, standard-setting bodies have provided some form of exception whereby the higher demand of having fair presentation of the entity's financial position and results of operations may be met, even if doing so might require a technical departure from the codified body of GAAP.

In the US, this provision historically has been found in the profession's auditing literature (the "Rule 203 exception"), but under various other national GAAP there commonly was found a "true and fair view" requirement that captured this objective. Under revised IAS 1, an approach essentially identical to the true and fair view requirement (which is codified in the EU's Fourth Directive) has been formalized, as well. The rule under IFRS should be narrowly construed, with only the more serious situations dealt with by permitting departures from IFRS in order to achieve appropriate financial reporting objectives.

This matter has been addressed in greater detail in the introduction to this chapter. In the authors' view, having such a fairness exception is vital for the goal of ensuring accurate and useful financial reporting under IFRS. However, extreme caution is urged in reaching any decision to depart from the formal requirements of IFRS, since these exceptions are intended to be very few and far between in practice.

Related-party disclosures. According to IAS 24, financial statements should include disclosure of material related-party transactions that are defined by the standard as "transfer of resources or obligations between related parties, regardless of whether a price is charged."

A *related party* is essentially any party that controls or can significantly influence the financial or operating decisions of the company to the extent that the company may be prevented from fully pursuing its own interests. Such groups would include associates, investees accounted for by the equity method, trusts for the benefit of employees, principal owners, key management personnel, and immediate family members of owners or management.

Disclosures should take place even if there is no accounting recognition made for such transactions (e.g., a service is performed without payment). Disclosures should generally not imply that such related-party transactions were on terms essentially equivalent to arm's-length dealings. Additionally, when one or more companies are under common control such that the financial statements might vary from those that would have been obtained if the companies were autonomous, the nature of the control relationship should be disclosed even if there are no transactions between the companies.

The disclosures generally should include

1. Nature of relationship
2. Description of transactions and effects of such transactions on the financial statements for each period for which an income statement is presented
3. Financial amounts of transactions for each period for which an income statement is presented and effects of any change in establishing the terms of such transactions different from that used in prior periods
4. Amounts due to and from such related parties as of the date of each statement of financial position presented together with the terms and manner of settlement

Reporting comparative amounts for the preceding period. IAS 1 requires that financial statements should present corresponding figures for the preceding period. When the presentation or classification of items is changed, the comparative data must also be changed, unless it is impracticable to do so.

When an entity applies an accounting policy retrospectively or makes a retrospective restatement of items in its financial statements, or when it reclassifies items in its financial statements, at a minimum, three statements of financial position, two of each of the other statements, and related notes are required. The three statements of financial position presented are as at

1. The end of the current period;
2. The end of the previous period (which is the same as the beginning of the current period); and
3. The beginning of the earliest comparative period.

Note, however, that in circumstances where no accounting policy change is being adopted retrospectively, and no restatement (to correct an error) is being applied retrospectively, the statement of financial position as of the *beginning* of the earliest comparative period included is not required to be presented. There is no prohibition against doing so, on the other hand.

When the entity changes the presentation or classification of items in its financial statements, the entity should reclassify the comparative amounts, unless reclassification is impractical. In reclassifying comparative amounts, the required disclosure includes (1) the nature of the reclassification; (2) the amount of each item or class of items that is reclassified; and (3) the reason for the reclassification. In situations where it is impracticable to reclassify comparative amounts, an entity should disclose (1) the reason for not reclassifying the amounts; and (2) the nature of the adjustments that would have been made if the amounts had been reclassified.

The related footnote disclosures must also be presented on a comparative basis, except for items of disclosure that would be not meaningful, or might even be confusing, if set forth in such a manner. Although there is no official guidance on this issue, certain details, such as schedules of debt maturities as of the end of the previous reporting period, would seemingly be of little interest to users of the current statements and would be largely redundant with information provided for the more recent year-end. Accordingly, such details are often omitted from comparative financial statements. Most other disclosures, however, continue to be meaningful and should be presented for all years for which basic financial statements are displayed.

To increase the usefulness of financial statements, many companies include in their annual reports five- or ten-year summaries of condensed financial information. This is not required by IFRS. These comparative statements allow investment analysts and other interested readers to perform comparative analysis of pertinent information. The presentation of comparative financial statements in annual reports enhances the usefulness of such reports and brings out more clearly the nature and trends of current changes affecting the entity.

Such presentation emphasizes the fact that the statements for a series of periods are far more significant than those for a single period and that the accounts for one period are but an installment of what is essentially a continuous history.

Subsequent events. The statement of financial position is dated as of the last day of the fiscal period, but a period of time will usually elapse before the financial statements are actually prepared and issued. During this period, significant events or transactions may have occurred that materially affect the company's financial position. These events and transactions are usually referred to as subsequent events. IAS 10 refers to these as "events after the reporting period." If not disclosed, significant events occurring between the end of the reporting period and the financial statement issuance date could make the financial statements misleading to others not otherwise informed of such events.

There are two types of subsequent events described by IAS 10. The first type consists of events that provide additional evidence with respect to conditions that existed at the end of the reporting period and which affect the estimates inherent in the process of preparing financial statements: these are called adjusting events. The second type consists of events that do not provide evidence with respect to conditions that existed at the end of the reporting period, but arose subsequent to that date (and prior to the actual issuance of the financial statements): these are called nonadjusting events.

The principle is that the statement of financial position should reflect as accurately as possible conditions that existed at the end of the reporting period, but not changes in conditions that occurred subsequently, even though they have the potential to influence investors' decisions. In the latter case disclosure is to be made.

Examples of events after the reporting period

1. A loss on an uncollectible trade account receivable as a result of a customer's deteriorating financial condition leading to bankruptcy subsequent to the end of the reporting period would usually (but not always) be indicative of conditions existing at the end of the reporting period, thereby calling for adjustment of the financial statements before their issuance. On the other hand, a loss on an uncollectible trade account receivable resulting from a customer's major casualty, such as a fire or flood subsequent to the end of the reporting period, would not be indicative of conditions existing at the end of the reporting period, and adjustment of the financial statements would not be appropriate. However, if the amount is material, disclosure would be required.

2. A loss arising from the recognition after the end of the reporting period that an asset such as plant and equipment had suffered a material decline in value arising out of reduced marketability for the product or service it can produce. Such a reduction would be considered an economic event in process at the end of the reporting period and would require adjustment and recognition of the loss.

3. Nonadjusting events, which are those not existing at the end of the reporting period, require disclosure but not adjustment. These could include

    a. Sale of a bond or share capital after the end of the reporting period, even if planned before that date.
    b. Purchase of a business, if the transaction is consummated after year-end.
    c. Settlement of litigation when the event giving rise to the claim took place subsequent to the end of the reporting period. The settlement is an economic event that would be accounted for in the period of occurrence. (However, if the event occurred before the end of the reporting period, IAS 37 would require that the estimated amount of the contingency be accrued, in most instances, as discussed further in the next section of this chapter.)
    d. Loss of plant or inventories as a result of fire or flood.
    e. Losses on receivables resulting from conditions (such as a customer's major casualty) arising subsequent to the end of the reporting period.
    f. Gains or losses on certain marketable securities.

Contingent liabilities and assets. IAS 37 defines provisions, contingent assets, and contingent liabilities. Importantly, it differentiates provisions from contingent liabilities. Provisions are recognized as liabilities (if reliably estimable), inasmuch as these are present obligations with probable outflows of resources embodying economic benefits needed to settle them. Contingent liabilities, on the other hand, are not recognized as liabilities under IFRS because they are either only *possible* obligations (i.e., not yet confirmed as being present obligations), or they are present obligations that do not meet the threshold for recognition (either because resource outflows are not *probable,* or because a sufficiently reliable estimate cannot be developed). Contingent liabilities are currently disclosed, although this treatment is likely to change.

Provisions are accrued by a charge against income if

1. The reporting entity has a present obligation as a result of past events;
2. It is probable that an outflow of the entity's resources will be required; and
3. A reliable estimate can be made of the amount.

If an estimate of the obligation cannot be made with a reasonable degree of certitude, accrual is not prescribed, but rather disclosure in the notes to the financial statements is needed.

For a provision to be made, the entity has to have incurred a constructive obligation. This may be an actual legal obligation, but it may also be only an obligation that arises as a result of an entity's stated polices. However, to preclude the use of reserves for manipulative purposes ("earnings management"), provisions for restructuring are subject to additional restrictions, and a provision may only be made once a detailed plan has been agreed and its implementation has commenced.

At the present date, the key recognition issue for contingent liabilities is the probability of a future cash outflow. The probability of this occurring is the threshold condition for recognition: a probable outflow triggers recording a provision, while an unlikely or improbable outflow creates only the need for a disclosure. In its ongoing business combinations project, the IASB (and also FASB) appears likely to conclude that a contingency is usually a combination of an *unconditional* right or obligation which is linked to a *conditional* right or obligation. The unconditional element is always to be recognized, although its value will be a function of the probability of the conditional element occurring. So if a company is being sued for €1m, and it considers that it has a 10% chance of losing, under the existing financial reporting rules, no provision would be made; if the new approach under consideration were to be adopted, this could be analyzed as an unconditional obligation to pay what the court decides, and this obligation would be measured as 10% of €1m. The probability of the loss then shifts from being a recognition criterion to being a measurement tool.

In June 2005 the IASB issued an Exposure Draft (ED), *Proposed Amendments to IAS 37, "Provisions, Contingent Liabilities and Contingent Assets,"* which would eliminate the terms "provisions," "contingent liability," and "contingent asset" from the IFRS literature, and replace these with a new term, "nonfinancial liabilities." The main effect of the proposed amendments would be to require an entity to recognize items that meet the definition of a liability, unless they cannot be measured reliably. Uncertainty about the amount or timing of the economic benefits required to settle a liability would be reflected in the measurement of this liability. This proposal is a part of the IASB's *Liabilities* project, which replaced the *Nonfinancial Liabilities* project. A major change to the current practice of accounting for restructuring provisions has been introduced by this proposal. Following the general guidelines on constructive obligations, instead of recognizing one major restructuring provision at a specific time, entities would need to recognize different liabilities relating to the different costs occurring in the restructuring, which costs can occur at different points in time (see a separate paragraph in Chapter 12). As of late 2008, this draft remains outstanding and under active discussion by IASB.

Share capital. An entity is required to disclose information that enables users of its financial statements to evaluate the entity's objectives, policies, and processes for managing capital. This information should include a description of what it manages as capital, the nature of externally imposed capital requirements, if there are any, as well as how those requirements are incorporated into the management of capital. Additionally, summary quantitative data about what it manages as capital should be provided as well as any changes in the components of capital and methods of managing capital from the previous period. The consequences of noncompliance with externally imposed capital requirements should also be included in the notes. All these disclosures are based on the information provided internally to key management personnel.

An entity should also present either in the statement of financial position or in the statement of changes in equity, or in the notes, disclosures about each class of share capital as well as about the nature and purpose of each reserve within equity. Information about share capital should include the number of shares authorized and issued (fully paid or not fully paid); par value per share or that shares have no par value; the rights, preferences and restrictions attached to each class of share capital, shares in the entity held by the entity (treasury shares) or by its subsidiaries or associates; and shares reserved for issue under options and contracts.

Other disclosures required by IAS 1. The reporting entity is required to provide details of any dividends proposed or declared before the financial statements were authorized to issue but not charged to equity. It should also indicate the amount of any cumulative preference dividends not recognized in the statement of changes in equity.

If not otherwise disclosed within the financial statements, these items should be reported in the footnotes.

1. The domicile and legal form of the entity, its country of incorporation, and the address of the registered office (or principal place of business, if different);
2. A description of the nature of the reporting entity's operations and its principal activities; and
3. The name of the parent entity and the ultimate parent of the group.

These disclosures (which have been modeled on those set forth by the Fourth and Seventh EU Directives) are particularly of interest given the multinational character of many enterprises reporting in conformity with IFRS.

Statement of Financial Position Format

IAS 1 does not prescribe the order or format in which an entity presents items; however the standard stipulates the following list of minimum categories to be displayed, to the extent relevant:

1. Property, plant, and equipment;
2. Investment property;
3. Intangible assets;
4. Financial assets;
5. Investments accounted for using the equity method;
6. Biological assets;
7. Inventories;
8. Trade and other receivables;
9. Cash and cash equivalents;
10. The total of assets classified as held for sale and assets included in disposal groups classified as held for sale in accordance with IFRS 5, *Noncurrent Assets Held for Sale and Discontinued Operations;*
11. Trade and other payables:
12. Provisions;
13. Financial liabilities;
14. Liabilities and assets for current tax, as defined in IAS 12, *Income Taxes;*
15. Deferred tax liabilities and deferred tax assets, as defined in IAS 12;
16. Liabilities included in disposal groups classified as held for sale in accordance with IFRS 5;
17. Noncontrolling interest, presented within equity; and
18. Issued capital and reserves attributable to owners of the parent.

In some countries, the legislation specifies the format of the financial statements—in particular the EU Fourth Directive mandates particular presentations—but in other jurisdictions entities have a free choice. The implementation guidance to IAS 1 gives an example of a statement of financial position format in the European account format.

In general, the two types of formats are the report form and the account form. In the *report form* the statement of financial position continues line by line from top to bottom as follows:

Assets	$xxx
Liabilities	$xxx
Shareholders' equity	xxx
Total liabilities and shareholders' equity	$xxx

In the *account form* the statement of financial position appears in a balancing concept with assets on the left and liabilities and equity amounts on the right as follows:

Assets	$ xxx	Shareholders' equity	$ xxx
		Liabilities	xxx
Total assets	$ xxx	Total liabilities and shareholders' equity	$ xxx

The statement of financial position format presented in Schedule 4 to the UK Companies Act of 1985, wherein a *net* asset total is presented (as a total of assets minus liabilities) as being equal to equity plus reserves, may be seen as a third variation, and is known as the UK

GAAP format. This is, in fact, a report format, as illustrated above, with merely a minor alteration made to explicitly reveal the equality between net assets and net worth.

The format of the statement of financial position as illustrated by the appendix to IAS 1 is the following:

XYZ Limited
Consolidated Statement of Financial Position
December 31, 2008
(in thousands of currency units)

	2008	2007
Assets		
Noncurrent assets:	x	x
Property, plant, and equipment	x	x
Goodwill	x	x
Other intangible assets	x	x
Investments in associates	x	x
Available-for-sale investments	x	x
	x	x
Current assets:		
Inventories	x	x
Trade and other receivables	x	x
Other current assets	x	x
Cash and cash equivalents	x	x
Total assets	x	x
Equity and Liabilities		
Equity attributable to owners of the parent		
Share capital (Note__)	x	x
Other reserves (Note__)	x	x
Retained earnings	x	x
	x	x
Noncontrolling interest	x	x
Total equity	x	x
Noncurrent liabilities:		
Long-term borrowings	x	x
Deferred taxes	x	x
Long-term provisions	x	x
Total noncurrent liabilities		
Current liabilities:		
Trade and other payables	x	x
Short-term borrowings	x	x
Current portion of long-term borrowings	x	x
Current tax payable	x	x
Short-term provisions	x	x
Total current liabilities	x	x
Total liabilities	x	x
Total equity and liabilities	x	x

Extract from Published Financial Statements

ARCELORMITTAL AND SUBSIDIARIES
Consolidated Balance Sheets

	December 31,	
	2006*	2007
(in millions of US dollars)		
Assets		
Current assets:		
Cash and cash equivalents	6,020	7,860
Restricted cash	120	245
Short-term investments	6	--
Assets held for sale (note 4)	1,316	1,296
Trade accounts receivables (note 5)	8,769	9,533
Inventories (note 6)	19,240	21,750
Prepaid expenses and other current assets (note 7)	3,942	4,644
Total current assets	39,413	45,328
Noncurrent assets:	--	
Goodwill and intangible assets (note 8)	11,040	15,031
Property, plant, and equipment (note 9)	54,573	61,994
Investments accounted for using the equity method (note 10)	3,456	5,887
Other investments (note 11)	1,151	2,159
Deferred tax assets (note 19)	1,789	1,629
Other assets	1,259	1,597
Total noncurrent assets	73,268	88,297
Total assets	112,681	133,625

* *As required by International Financial Reporting Standards (IFRS), the 2006 information has been adjusted retrospectively for the finalization of the allocation of purchase price of Arcelor (see Note 3).*

	December 31,	
	2006*	2007
Liabilities and equity		
Current liabilities:		
Payable to banks and current portion of long-term debt (note 13)	4,922	8,542
Trade accounts payable and other (note 12)	11,342	13,991
Short-term provisions (note 20)	569	1,144
Liabilities held for sale (note 4)	239	266
Accrued expenses and other liabilities (note 21)	6,954	7,275
Income tax liabilities	534	991
Total current liabilities	24,560	32,209
Noncurrent liabilities:		
Long-term debt, net of current portion (notes 13 and 14)	21,645	22,085
Deferred tax liabilities (note 19)	7,252	7,927
Deferred employee benefits (note 18)	5,531	6,244
Long-term provisions (note 20)	2,040	2,456
Other long-term obligations	1,425	1,169
Total noncurrent liabilities	37,893	39,881
Total liabilities	62,453	72,090
Equity (note 16)		
Common shares (no par value, 1,470,000,000 shares authorized, 1,448,836,347 shares issued and 1, 421,570,646 outstanding at December 31, 2007)	--	9,269
Class A shares, (EURO 0.01 par value per share, 5,000,000,000 shares authorized, 934,818,280 shares issued and 927,778,773 share outstanding at December 31, 2006)	11	--
Class B shares, (EURO 0.10 par value per share (2005). EURO 0.01 par value per share (2006). 721,500,000 shares authorized. 457,490,210 shares issued and outstanding)	6	--
Treasury stock (7,039,547 class A shares at December 31, 2006, and 27,255,701 common shares at December 31, 2007, at cost)	(84)	(1,552)
Additional paid-in capital	25,566	20,309
Retained earnings	14,995	23,552

| | December 31, | |
	2006*	2007
Reserves	1,654	5,107
Equity attributable to the owners of the parent	42,148	56,685
Minority interest	8,080	4,850
Total equity	50,228	61,535
Total liabilities and equity	112,681	133,625
Commitments and contingencies (notes 22 and 23)		

Annual Improvements Project Finalized in 2008

The IASB adopted a strategy of issuing omnibus annual revisions to a range of existing standards in 2006. The first of these pronouncements was finalized in early 2008, consisting of 35 amendments, most of which made modest changes to presentation, recognition, and measurements. These various amendments are addressed in the appropriate chapters of this book.

Of the several changes that had been proposed for IAS 1, the only change that was ultimately adopted was the one that clarified that financial assets and financial liabilities that are classified as held for trading in accordance with IAS 39 need not necessarily be presented as current assets or current liabilities.

3 STATEMENTS OF INCOME, COMPREHENSIVE INCOME, AND CHANGES IN EQUITY

PERSPECTIVE AND ISSUES

The IASB's *Framework* emphasizes the importance of information about the performance of an entity, which is useful to assess potential changes in the economic resources that are likely to control in the future, predict future cash flows, and form judgments about the effectiveness with which the entity might employ additional resources. Since mid-2004, the IASB and the FASB have been collaboratively pursuing projects on *Financial Statement Presentation* (originally entitled *Performance Reporting),* which has resulted in fundamental changes to the format and content of what is commonly referred to as the income statement (or the profit or loss account). This joint effort has been bifurcated. The first phase of the project addressed what constitutes a complete set of financial statements and a requirement to present comparative financial statements (absent from US GAAP), and culminated in the issuance of revised IAS 1 in 2007, effective in 2009. The second phase of the project will deal with more challenging issues, such as standards for presentation on the face of the required statement(s), the so-called "recycling" problem (how to report realized gains and losses when unrealized amounts were previously reported in comprehensive income), and the use of totals and subtotals; a discussion paper on this second phase has been issued in late 2008.

IAS 1, *Presentation of Financial Statements,* as revised in 2007, resulted from the IASB and the FASB deliberations on the first phase of the financial statement presentation project and brings IAS 1 largely into line with the US standard—Statement of Financial Accounting Standards 130 (FAS 130), *Reporting Comprehensive Income.* The standard requires all non-owner changes in equity (comprehensive income) to be presented in one statement of comprehensive income or in two statements, a separate income statement and a statement of comprehensive income. Components of comprehensive income are not permitted to be presented in the statement of changes in equity (an approach that is, alas, permitted under US GAAP).

As a combined statement of income and comprehensive income became mandatory, this represents a triumph over the *all-inclusive concept* of performance reporting. While this has been officially endorsed by world standard setters for many decades, in fact many standards promulgated over the years (e.g., IAS 39 requiring exclusion of temporary changes in the fair value of investments other than trading securities from current income) have deviated from adherence to this principle. While IAS 1 allows the presentation of comprehensive income in a single statement, with net income being an intermediate caption, it remains possible to report in a two-statement format, with separate income statement and statement of comprehensive income. The statement of comprehensive income will report all nonowner changes in equity separately from owner changes in equity (investments by or distributions to owners). This Standard thus marks a notable return to an "all inclusive" concept of reporting, which had been eroded in recent decades as items such as unrealized gains and losses on available-for-sale investments became reportable directly in the equity section of the statement of financial position, which generated understandable confusion regarding what the reporting entity's "real" results of operations actually were.

Concepts of performance and measures of income have changed over the years, and current reporting still largely focuses on *realized* income and expense. However, unrealized gains and losses also reflect real economic transactions and events and are of great interest to decision makers. Under current IFRS, some of these unrealized gains and losses are *recognized*, while others are *unrecognized*. Both the financial reporting entities themselves and the financial analysts go to great lengths to identify within reported income those elements which are likely to be continuing into the future, since expected earnings and cash flows of future periods are main drivers of share prices.

IFRS rules for the presentation of income reflect a mixture of traditional realized income reporting, accompanied by fair value measures applied to unrealized gains and losses meeting certain criteria (e.g., financial instruments are accounted for differently from plant assets). For example, unrealized gains and losses arising from the translation of the foreign currency-denominated financial statements of foreign subsidiaries do not flow through the income statement. IAS 1 requires that all owner changes in equity should be reported separately from nonowner changes (deriving from performance), in a separate *statement of changes in equity.*

The traditional income statement has been known by many titles. IFRS refer to this statement as the income statement, but in the EU Fourth Directive and in many Commonwealth countries it is referred to as the *profit and loss account.* In the United States other names, such as the statement of income, statement of earnings, or statement of operations, are sometimes used to denote the income statement. For convenience, this book uses the term income statement throughout, denoting the financial statement which reports all items entering into the determination of periodic earnings, but excluding other comprehensive income items which are reported in the other comprehensive income section of the comprehensive income statement.

For many years, the income statement had been widely perceived by investors, creditors, management, and other interested parties as the single most important of an entity's basic financial statements. In fact, beginning in the mid-twentieth century, accounting theory development was largely driven by the desire to present a meaningful income statement, even to the extent that the balance sheet sometimes became the repository for balances of various accounts, such as deferred charges and credits, which could scarcely meet any reasonable definitions of assets or liabilities. This was done largely to serve the needs of investors, who are commonly thought to use the past income of a business as the most important input to their predictions for entities' future earnings and cash flows, which in turn form the basis for their predictions of future share prices and dividends.

Creditors look to the income statement for insight into the borrower's ability to generate the future cash flows needed to pay interest and eventually to repay the principal amounts of the obligations. Even in the instance of secured debt, creditors do not look primarily to the balance sheet, inasmuch as seizure and liquidation of collateral is never the preferred outcome. Rather, generation of cash flows from operations—which is generally closely correlated to income—is seen as the primary source for debt service.

Management, then, must be concerned with the income statement by virtue of the importance placed on it by investors and creditors. In many large corporations, senior management receives substantial bonuses relating to either profit targets or share price performance. Consequently, managements sometimes devote considerable efforts in order to massage what appears in the income statement, in order to present the most encouraging view of the reporting entity's future prospects. This means that standard setters need to bear in mind the abuse possibilities of the rules they impose, and for that matter, the rules have been imposed in response to previous financial reporting abuses.

IFRS formerly allowed companies to segregate in their income statement any items not expected to recur, and to designate them as extraordinary gains or losses, but this, perhaps predictably, led to abuses. As one standard setter ironically defined these items, "credits are ordinary items and debits are extraordinary items for some companies." In response, IASB eliminated the extraordinary item category entirely. On a related matter, the recognition of provisions for restructuring costs is now somewhat restricted, in an attempt to prevent companies taking a larger-than-necessary charge against earnings in one period in order to retain greater flexibility (i.e., to absorb unrelated expenses or to create earnings) in the next (a practice which has been referred to as providing "cookie jar reserves").

The importance placed on income measurement has, as is well known, influenced behavior by some management personnel, who have sought to manipulate results to, say, meet Wall Street earnings estimates. The motivation for this improper behavior is readily understandable when one observes that recent markets have severely punished companies that missed earnings estimates by as little as a penny per share. One very popular vehicle for earnings management has centered on revenue recognition. Historically, certain revenue recognition situations, such as that involving prepaid service revenue, have lacked specific financial reporting rules or have been highly subject to interpretation, opening the door to aggressive accounting by some entities. While in many businesses the revenue earning cycle is simple and straightforward and therefore difficult to manipulate, there are many other situations where it is a matter of interpretation as to when the revenue has actually been earned. Examples have included recognition by lessor of lease income from long-term equipment rental contracts that were bundled with supplies and maintenance agreements, and accruals of earnings on long-term construction contracts or software development projects having multiple deliverables.

The information provided by the income statement, relating to individual items of income and expense, as well as to the relationships between and among these items (such as the amounts reported as gross margin or profit before interest and taxes), facilitates financial analysis, especially that relating to the reporting entity's historical and possible future profitability. Even with the ascendancy of the statement of financial position as the favored financial statement, financial statement users will always devote considerable attention to the income statement.

This chapter focuses on key income measurement issues and on matters of comprehensive income, statement presentation and disclosure. It also explains and illustrates the presentation of the *statement of comprehensive income* and the *statement of changes in equity*.

Sources of IFRS
IAS 1, 8, 14, 16, 18, 19, 21, 36, 37, 38, 39, 40
IFRS 1, 5
SIC 29
Framework for the Preparation and Presentation of Financial Statements

DEFINITIONS OF TERMS

Elements of Financial Statements

Comprehensive income. The change in equity (net assets) of an entity during a period from transactions and other events and circumstances from nonowner sources. It includes all changes in net assets during a period, except those resulting from investments by owners and distributions to owners. It comprises all components of "profit or loss" and "other comprehensive income" presented in the statement of comprehensive income.

Expenses. Decreases in economic benefits during the accounting period in the form of outflows or depletions of assets or incurring liabilities that result in decreases in equity, other than those relating to distributions to equity participants. The term *expenses* is broad enough to include *losses* as well as normal categories of expenses; thus, IFRS differs from the corresponding US GAAP standard, which deems losses to be a separate and distinct element to be accounted for, denoting decreases in equity from peripheral or incidental transactions.

Income. Increases in economic benefits during the accounting period in the form of inflows or enhancements of assets that result in increases in equity, other than those relating to contributions from equity participants. The IASB's *Framework* clarifies that this definition of income encompasses both revenue and gains. As with expenses and losses, the corresponding US accounting standard holds that revenues and gains constitute two separate elements of financial reporting, with gains denoting increases in equity from peripheral or incidental transactions.

Other comprehensive income. Items of income and expense (including reclassification adjustments) that are not recognized in profit or loss as required or permitted by other IFRS. The components of other comprehensive income include (1) changes in revaluation surplus (IAS 16 and 38); (2) actuarial gains and losses on defined benefit plans (IAS 19); (3) translation gains and losses (IAS 21); (4) gains and losses on remeasuring available-for-sale financial assets (IAS 39); and (5) the effective portion of gains and losses on hedging instruments in a cash flow hedge (IAS 39).

Profit or loss. The total of income less expenses, excluding the components of other comprehensive income.

Reclassification adjustments. Amounts reclassified to profit or loss in the current period that were recognized in other comprehensive income in the current or previous periods.

Statement of changes in equity. As prescribed by IAS 1, an entity should present, as a separate financial statement, a statement of changes in equity showing

1. Total comprehensive income for the period (reporting separately amounts attributable to owners of the parent and to noncontrolling interest);
2. For each component of equity, the effect of retrospective application or retrospective restatement recognized in accordance with IAS 8;
3. The amounts of transactions with owners in their capacity as owners, showing separately contributions by and distributions to owners; and
4. A reconciliation for each component of equity (each class of share capital and each reserve) between the carrying amounts at the beginning and the end of the period, separately disclosing each movement.

Statement of comprehensive income. A statement of comprehensive income presents all components of "profit or loss" and "other comprehensive income" in a single statement, with net income being an intermediate caption. Alternatively, IAS 1 permits the use of a two-statement format, with separate income statement and statement of comprehensive income. An entity which adopts a policy of recognizing actuarial gains and losses in accordance with IAS 19 is required to present these gains and losses in the statement of comprehensive income. This statement highlights items of income and expense that are not recognized in the income statement, and it reports all changes in equity, including net income, other than those resulting from investments by and distributions to owners.

Under IFRS, a clear distinction must be maintained between transactions with nonowners and those with owners (exclusive of transactions with owners in nonowner capacities, e.g., as customers or vendors). Thus, in contrast to the parallel standard under US GAAP (upon which revised IAS 1 was heavily based), items of other comprehensive income cannot be reported in the statement of changes in equity. The "one statement" and "two statement" alternatives to reporting comprehensive income are the only permitted choices under IFRS.

Other Terminology

Discontinued operations. IFRS 5 defines a "discontinued operation" as a component of an enterprise that has been disposed of, or is classified as held for sale, and

1. Represents a separate major line of business or geographical area of operations;
2. Is part of a single coordinated disposal plan;
3. Is a subsidiary acquired exclusively with a view to resale.

Component of an entity. In the context of discontinued operations, IFRS 5 defines a component of an entity as operations and cash flows that can be clearly distinguished, operationally and for financial reporting purposes, from the rest of the entity—a cash-generating unit, or group of cash-generating units.

Net assets. Net assets are total assets minus total liabilities (synonymous to owners' equity).

Realization. The process of converting noncash resources and rights into money or, more precisely, the sale of an asset for cash or claims to cash.

Recognition. The process of formally recording or incorporating in the financial statements of an entity items that meet the definition of an element and satisfy the criteria for recognition.

Segment of a business. A distinguishable component of an enterprise which is engaged in providing products or services that are subject to risks and returns different from other "business segments" or "geographical segments." A segment may be in the form of a subsidiary, a division, a department, a joint venture, or other nonsubsidiary investee. Its assets, results of operations, and activities can be clearly distinguished (physically and operationally, and for financial reporting purposes) from the other assets, results of operations, and activities of the entity. Business segments are distinguishable components of an enterprise engaged in providing different products or services, or a different group of related products or services, primarily to customers outside an enterprise. Geographical segments are distinguishable components of an enterprise engaged in operations in different countries or group of countries within particular geographical areas as may be determined to be appropriate in an enterprise's particular circumstances.

CONCEPTS, RULES, AND EXAMPLES

Concepts of Income

Economists have generally employed a wealth maintenance concept of income. Under this concept (as specified by Hicks), income is the maximum amount that can be consumed during a period and still leave the enterprise with the same amount of wealth at the end of the period as existed at the beginning. Wealth is determined with reference to the current market values of the net productive assets at the beginning and end of the period. Therefore, the economists' definition of income would fully incorporate market value changes (both increases and decreases in wealth) in the determination of periodic income and this would correspond to measuring assets and liabilities at fair value, with the net of all the changes in net assets equating to comprehensive income.

Accountants, on the other hand, have traditionally defined income by reference to specific transactions that give rise to recognizable elements of revenue and expense during a reporting period. The events that produce reportable items of revenue and expense comprise a subset of economic events that determine economic income. Many changes in the market values of wealth components are deliberately excluded from the measurement of accounting income but are included in the measurement of economic income, although those exclusions have grown fewer as the use of fair values in financial reporting has been more widely embraced in recent years.

The discrepancy between the accounting and economic measures of income are the result of a preference on the part of accountants and financial statement users for information that is reliable, and also considerations of measurement of income for tax purposes in many jurisdictions. Since many fluctuations in the market values of assets are matters of conjecture, accountants have preferred to retain the historical cost/realization model, which generally postpones the recognition of value changes until there has been a completed transaction. While both accountants and economists understand that the earnings process occurs throughout the various stages of production, sales, and final delivery of the product, accountants have tended to stress the difficulty of measuring the precise rate at which this earnings process is taking place. That, coupled with a desire to not pay tax any earlier than necessary, has led accountants to conclude that income should be recognized only when it is fully realized.

Nonetheless, an application of the conceptual framework approach of recognizing assets and liabilities when they can be measured reliably enough is leading standard setters to experiment with the idea of recognizing transactions that are incomplete. This can be seen in IAS 39, where the changes in market value of some financial instruments are recognized, and in IAS 41, where the change in value of biological assets is recognized although not realized.

Recognition and Measurement

Recognition is signified by the inclusion of an item in the statement of financial position or the income statement. Measurement is the determination of the amount at which the recognized item should be included. The IASB's *Framework* has identified the following recognition criteria, which remain in force:

1. **Item must meet the definition of an element.** To be recognized, an item must meet the definitions of either an asset or a liability (see Chapter 1). This may also involve recognition of income and expense; as discussed above, a gain in net assets would be income and a reduction of net assets would be an expense.

2. **Assessment of degree of uncertainty regarding future economic benefits.** The asset/liability definition says there must be a probable future inflow or outflow of

future economic benefits. Recognition therefore involves consideration of the degree of uncertainty that the future economic benefits associated with an item will flow to or from the enterprise.

3. **Item's cost or value can be measured with reliability.** An item must possess a relevant attribute, such as cost or value, which can be quantified in monetary units with sufficient reliability. Measurability must be considered in terms of both relevance and reliability, the two primary qualitative characteristics of accounting information.

4. **Relevance.** An item is relevant if the information about it has the capacity to make a difference in investors', creditors', or other users' decisions. The relevance of information is affected by its nature and materiality.

5. **Reliability.** An item is reliable if the information about it is representationally faithful, free of material errors, and is neutral or free from bias. Further, to possess the quality of reliability, two more features should be present.

    a. The transactions and other events the information purports to represent should be accounted for and presented in accordance with their *substance* and economic reality and *not merely their legal form.*

    b. The preparers of financial statements, while dealing with and recognizing uncertainties, should exercise judgment or a degree of caution: in other words, *prudence.*

To be given accounting recognition, an asset, liability, or item of income or expense would have to meet the thresholds established by the above-mentioned five criteria.

Income. According to the IASB's *Framework*

Income is increases in economic benefits during the accounting period in the form of inflows or enhancements of assets or decreases of liabilities that result in increases in equity, other than those relating to contributions from equity participants. The definition of income encompasses both revenue and gains, and revenue arises in the course of ordinary activities of an enterprise and is referred to by different names, such as sales, fees, interest, dividends, royalties, and rent.

IAS 18 is the standard that deals with the accounting for revenue. It says that revenue is the gross inflow of economic benefits during the period (excluding transactions with owners).

The measurement basis is that revenue be measured at the fair value of the consideration received or receivable. *Fair value* is defined as

the amount for which an asset could be exchanged, or a liability settled, between knowledgeable, willing parties in an arm's-length transaction.

The historical cost measurement basis involves recognizing a completed marketplace transaction, in other words measuring at fair value at initial recognition. Revenue recognition is discussed in detail in Chapter 7.

Expenses. According to the IASB's *Framework*

Expenses are decreases in economic benefits during an accounting period in the form of outflows or depletions of assets or incurrences of liabilities, other than those relating to distributions to equity participants.

Expenses are expired costs, or items that were assets but are no longer assets because they have no future value. The matching principle requires that all expenses incurred in the generating of revenue be recognized in the same accounting period as the related revenues are recognized.

Costs such as materials and direct labor consumed in the manufacturing process are relatively easy to identify with the related revenue elements. These cost elements are included in inventory and expensed as cost of sales when the product is sold and revenue from the sale is recognized. This is associating cause and effect.

Some costs are more closely associated with specific accounting periods. In the absence of a cause and effect relationship, the asset's cost should be allocated to the benefited accounting periods in a systematic and rational manner. This form of expense recognition involves assumptions about the expected length of benefit and the relationship between benefit and cost of each period. Depreciation of fixed assets, amortization of intangibles, and allocation of rent and insurance are examples of costs that would be recognized by the use of a systematic and rational method.

All other costs are normally expensed in the period in which they are incurred. This would include those costs for which no clear-cut future benefits can be identified, costs that were recorded as assets in prior periods but for which no remaining future benefits can be identified, and those other elements of administrative or general expense for which no rational allocation scheme can be devised. The general approach is first to attempt to match costs with the related revenues. Next, a method of systematic and rational allocation should be attempted. If neither of these measurement principles is beneficial, the cost should be immediately expensed.

Gains and losses. The *Framework* defines the term *expenses* broadly enough to include losses. IFRS include no definition of gains and losses that enables them to be separated from income and expense. Traditionally, gains and losses are thought by accountants to arise from purchases and sales outside the regular business trading of the company, such as on disposals of noncurrent assets that are no longer required. IAS 1 used to include an extraordinary category for display of items that were clearly distinct from ordinary activities. The IASB removed this category in its 2003 Improvements Project, concluding that these items arose from the normal business risks faced by an entity and that it is the nature or function of a transaction or other event, rather than its frequency that should determine its presentation within the statement of comprehensive income.

According to the IASB's *Framework*

Gains (losses) represent increases (decreases) in economic benefits and as such are no different in nature from revenue (expenses). Hence they are not regarded as separate elements in IASB's Framework. *Characteristics of gains and losses include the following:*

1. *Result from peripheral transactions and circumstances that may be beyond entity's control*
2. *May be classified according to sources or as operating and nonoperating*

IASB Projects Affecting the Statement of Comprehensive Income

Both the FASB and the IASB have set out to create standardized formats for the income statement, to replace the current rules. These existing rules are generally thought to be unsatisfactory in that some transactions flow directly to equity while most others appear in the income statement first. Also, there is a perception that the conceptual frameworks under both sets of standards have not been rigorously applied, such that many extant standards deviate from the frameworks (and in many cases preceded the creation of the respective framework). The IASB made some progress with an initial effort to address performance reporting, the early recommendations of which involved reporting all elements of comprehensive income in a single financial statement. The IASB believes that there is an inherent inability to create a useful definition of a company's main business (e.g., as core operations, ordinary activities, etc.), and that the income statement should separate financial income and expense from all other income and expense, but that there be attempt to analyze the nonfinancial items into any core business element and the remaining "noise." The IASB field-tested the early proposals but then withdrew them in the face of opposition from constituents, recognizing that the proposals were too far in advance of business understanding of comprehensive income for acceptance of the need to abandon the traditional earnings statement format.

Subsequently, IASB entered into a cooperative venture with FASB to pursue a project entitled *Performance Reporting,* which at the joint meeting in March 2006 was retitled *Financial Statement Presentation.* This project is divided into three phases, of which the first gave rise to a revised (2007) IAS 1, *Presentation of Financial Statements* (see also the discussion in Chapter 2).

The second phase of this project is addressing issues such as recycling between net income and other comprehensive income, principles for disaggregating information and defining total and subtotals, and whether the direct or indirect method of presenting operating cash flows provides more useful information. IASB released a discussion document on the second phase in late 2008; it is summarized later in this chapter.

The third phase of the project will address interim financial reporting. Work has yet to begin on this phase.

In late 2007, the IASB issued a revised IAS 1, *Presentation of Financial Statements,* as part of the joint IASB/FASB project *Financial Statement Presentation,* which introduced as a major change the replacement of the income statement with a statement of comprehensive income. The purpose of this change is to reflect more closely the function of the statement, as cited in the *Framework.*

In accordance with IAS 1, profit or loss and total comprehensive income should be presented in the financial statements. All changes in equity arising from transactions with owners in their capacity as owners (owner changes in equity) should be presented separately from nonowner changes in equity. An entity thus is not to be permitted to present components of income and expense (nonowner changes in equity) in the statement of changes in equity. All nonowner changes in equity (other comprehensive income) should be presented in one or two statements of comprehensive income, separately from owner changes in equity. According to the IASB, these amendments will provide better information to users by requiring aggregation of items with shared characteristics. (Note that, although revised IAS 1 largely converges to the US GAAP standard, FAS 130, it differs in that the reporting of items of other comprehensive income cannot be included in the statement of changes in equity, which is, however, permitted under FAS 130.)

Statement of Comprehensive Income

The IASB's *Framework* states that comprehensive income is the change in the entity's net assets over the course of the reporting period arising from nonowner sources. An entity has the option of presenting comprehensive income in a period either in one statement or in two statements. The IASB initially intended to introduce a single format for the statement of comprehensive income, but during discussions with constituents, many of them were opposed to the concept of a single statement, stating that it could result in undue focus on the "bottom line" of the statement. Consequently, the IASB decided that presentation in a single statement was not as important as its fundamental decision that all nonowner changes in equity should be presented separately from owner changes in equity. If an entity presents the components of profit or loss in a separate statement, this separate statement of profit or loss (income statement) forms part of a complete set of financial statements and should be displayed immediately before the statement of comprehensive income.

Although IAS 1 uses the terms "profit or loss," other comprehensive income," and "total comprehensive income," an entity may use other terms to describe the totals, as long as the meaning is clear. For example, an entity may use the term "net income" to describe profit or loss.

Comprehensive income comprises all components of "profit or loss" and of "other comprehensive income."

An entity has a choice of presenting all components of comprehensive income recognized in a period either

1.   In a single statement of comprehensive income; or
2.   In two statements

   a.   A statement displaying components of profit or loss (separate income statement);
   b.   A second statement beginning with profit or loss and displaying components of other comprehensive income.

Total comprehensive income for the period reported in a statement of comprehensive income is the total of income less expenses excluding the components of other comprehensive income.

Other comprehensive income is the total of income less expenses (including reclassification adjustments) that are not recognized in profit or loss as required or permitted by other IFRS or Interpretations.

The components of *other comprehensive income* comprise

1.   Changes in revaluation surplus (see IAS 16, *Property, Plant, and Equipment,* and IAS 38, *Intangible Assets*);
2.   Actuarial gains and losses on defined benefit plans recognized in accordance with paragraph 93A of IAS 19, *Employee Benefits;*
3.   Gains and losses arising from translating the financial statements of foreign operation (see IAS 21, *The Effects of Changes in Foreign Exchange Rates*);
4.   Gains and losses on remeasuring available-for-sale financial assets (see IAS 39, *Financial Instruments: Recognition and Measurement*);
5.   The effective portion of gains and losses on hedging instruments in a cash flow hedge (see IAS 39, *Financial Instruments: Recognition and Measurement*).

IAS 1 stipulates that, at the minimum, the statement of comprehensive income must include line items that present the following amounts for the period (if they are pertinent to the entity's operations for the period in question):

1.   Revenue
2.   Finance costs
3.   Share of the profit or loss of associates and joint ventures accounted for by the equity method
4.   Tax expense
5.   Discontinued operations which include the total of

   a.   Posttax profit or loss of discontinued operations, and
   b.   Posttax gain or loss on the measurement of fair value less costs to sell or on the disposal of the assets or disposal group(s) constituting the discontinued operation
6.   Profit or loss

7. Each component of other comprehensive income classified by nature (excluding amounts in item 8. below)
8. Share of the other comprehensive income of associates and joint ventures accounted for by the equity method
9. Total comprehensive income

In addition, an entity should disclose the following items on the face of the statement of comprehensive income as allocations of

1. Profit or loss for the period attributable to

   a. Noncontrolling interest, and
   b. Owners of the parent

2. Total comprehensive income for the period attributable to

   a. Noncontrolling interest, and
   b. Owners of the parent

Items 1-6 listed above and disclosure of profit or loss attributable to noncontrolling interest and owners of the parent (listed in 1.) can be presented on the face of a separate statement of profit or loss (income statement).

The forgoing items represent the barest minimum: the standard states that additional line items, headings, and subtotals should be presented on the face of the statement when this is relevant to an understanding of the entity's financial performance (US GAAP specifies no required income statement captions). This requirement cannot be dealt with by incorporating the items into the notes to the financial statements. When items of income or expense are material, disclosures segregating their nature and amount are required in the statement of comprehensive income or in the notes.

Income Statement Classification and Presentation

In accordance with IAS 1, if an entity presents the components of profit or loss in a separate *income statement,* this separate statement should be displayed immediately before the statement of comprehensive income.

Statement title. The legal name of the entity must be used to identify the financial statements and the title "Income Statement" (or "Profit and Loss Account") used to distinguish the statement from other information presented in the annual report.

Reporting period. The period covered by the income statement must clearly be identified, such as "year ended December 31, 2009." Or "six months ended September 30, 2009." Income statements are normally presented annually (i.e., for a period of twelve months or a year). However, in some jurisdictions they may be required at quarterly or six-month intervals, and in exceptional circumstances (such as a newly acquired subsidiary harmonizing its account dates with those of its new parent), companies may need to prepare income statements for periods in excess of one year or for shorter periods as well. IAS 1 requires that when financial statements are presented for periods other than a year, the following additional disclosures should be made:

1. The reason for presenting the income statement (and other financial statements, such as the cash flow statement, statement of changes in equity, and notes) for a period other than one year; and
2. The fact that the comparative information presented (in the income statement, statement of changes in equity, cash flow statement, and notes) is not truly comparable.

Entities whose operations form a natural cycle may have a reporting period end on a specific day of the week (e.g., the last Friday of the month). Certain entities (typically retail enterprises) may prepare income statements for a fiscal period of fifty-two or fifty-three weeks instead of a year (thus, to always end on a day such as Sunday, on which no business is transacted, so that inventory may be taken). These entities should clearly state that the income statement has been presented, for instance, "for the fifty-two-week period ended March 30, 2009." IAS 1 states that it is deemed to be unlikely that the financial statements thus presented would be materially different from those that would be presented for one full year.

In order that the presentation and classification of items in the income statement be consistent from period to period, items of income and expenses should be uniform both with respect to appearance and categories from one time period through the next. If a decision is made to change classification schemes, the comparative prior period financials should be restated to conform and thus to maintain comparability between the two periods being presented together. Disclosure must be made of this reclassification, since the earlier period financial statements being presented currently will differ in appearance from those nominally same statements presented in the earlier year.

Major components of the income statement. IAS 1 stipulates that, at the minimum, the income statement must include line items that present the following items (if they are pertinent to the entity's operations for the period in question):

1. Revenue
2. Finance costs
3. Share of profits and losses of associates and joint ventures accounted for by the equity method
4. Tax expense
5. Discontinued operations
6. Profit or loss
7. Noncontrolling interest
8. Net profit attributable to equity holders in the parent

An entity should not report any items of income or expense as extraordinary items, in the separate income statement or the statement of comprehensive income. (US GAAP allows recognizing extraordinary gains and losses when specific criteria are met.) Also, an entity should present all items of income and expense in a period in the income statement unless IFRS requires or permits otherwise. For example, IAS 8 lists two such circumstances: the correction of errors and the effect of changes in accounting policies.

While the objective of the line items are uniform across all reporting entities, the manner of presentation may differ. Specifically, IAS 1 (as also does the EU Fourth Directive), offers preparers two different ways of classifying operating and other expenses: by *nature* or by *function*. While entities are encouraged to apply one or the other of these on the face of the income statement, putting it in the notes is not prohibited.

An entity should present an analysis of expenses within profit or loss using a classification based on either the nature of expenses or their function within the entity, whichever provides information that is reliable and more important.

The classification by nature identifies costs and expenses in terms of their character, such as salaries and wages, raw materials consumed, and depreciation of plant assets. On the other hand, the classification by function presents the expenses in terms of the purpose of the expenditure, such as for manufacturing, distribution, and administration. Note that finance costs must be so identified regardless of which classification is employed.

IFRS allows for expenses to be classified according to function or by nature, whichever provides more reliable and relevant information, whereas under US GAAP, expenses are classified by function only.

An example of the income statement (profit or loss) classification by the "nature of expense" method is as follows:

ABC GROUP
Income Statement
For the Year Ended December 31, 2008
(classification of expense by nature)
(in thousands of currency units)

Revenue		800,000
Other income		100,000
Changes in inventories of finished goods and work in progress	50,000	
Work performed by the entity and capitalized	60,000	
Raw materials and consumables used	110,000	
Employee benefits expense	350,000	
Depreciation expense	200,000	
Other expense	10,000	
Finance costs	30,000	
Total expenses		810,000
Profit before tax		90,000

An example of the income statement (profit or loss) classification by the "function of expense" method is as follows:

Income Statement
For the Year Ended December 31, 2008
(classification of expense by function)
(in thousands of currency units)

Revenue	800,000
Cost of sale	500,000
Gross profit	300,000
Other income	100,000
Distribution (selling) costs	100,000
Administrative expenses	170,000
Other expenses	10,000
Finance costs	30,000
Profit before tax	90,000

Under the "function of expense" or "cost of sales" method an entity should report, at a minimum, its cost of sales separately from other expenses. This method can provide more relevant information to the users of the financial statements than the classification under the "nature of expense" method, but allocating costs to functions may require arbitrary allocations based on judgment.

IAS 1 furthermore stipulates that if a reporting entity discloses expenses by function, it must also provide information on the nature of the expenses, including depreciation and amortization and staff costs (salaries and wages). The standard does not provide detailed guidance on this requirement, but companies need only provide a note indicating the nature of the allocations made to comply with the requirement.

IFRS 5 governs the presentation and disclosures pertaining to discontinued operations. This is discussed later in this chapter.

While IAS 1 does not require the inclusion of subsidiary schedules to support major captions in the income statement, it is commonly found that detailed schedules of line items are included in full sets of financial statements. These will be illustrated in the following section to provide a more expansive discussion of the meaning of certain major sections of the income statement.

Revenue. The term "ordinary activities," formerly found in IAS 1, was eliminated by the IASB's 2003 *Improvements Project.* However, companies typically show their regular trading operations first and then present any items to which they wish to direct analysts' attention.

1. **Sales or other operating revenues** are charges to customers for the goods and/or services provided to them during the period. This section of the income statement should include information about discounts, allowances, and returns, to determine net sales or net revenues.

2. **Cost of goods sold** is the cost of the inventory items sold during the period. In the case of a merchandising firm, net purchases (purchases less discounts, returns, and allowances plus freight-in) are added to beginning inventory to obtain the cost of goods available for sale. From the cost of goods available for sale amount, the ending inventory is deducted to compute cost of goods sold.

Example of schedule of cost of goods sold

ABC GROUP
Schedule of Cost of Goods Sold
For the Year Ended December 31, 2008

Beginning inventory				$xxx
Add:	Purchases		$xxx	
	Freight-in		xxx	
Cost of purchases			xxx	
Less:	Purchase discounts	$xx		
	Purchase returns and allowances	xx	(xxx)	
Net purchases			xxx	
Cost of goods available for sale			xxx	
Less:	Ending inventory		(xxx)	
Cost of goods sold			$xxx	

A manufacturing enterprise computes the cost of goods sold in a slightly different way. Cost of goods manufactured would be added to the beginning inventory to arrive at cost of goods available for sale. The ending finished goods inventory is then deducted from the cost of goods available for sale to determine the cost of goods sold. Cost of goods manufactured is computed by adding to raw materials on hand at the beginning of the period the raw materials purchases during the period and all other costs of production, such as labor and direct overhead, thereby yielding the cost of goods placed in production during the period. When adjusted for changes in work in process during the period and for raw materials on hand at the end of the period, this results in the calculation of goods produced.

Example of schedules of cost of goods manufactured and sold

ABC GROUP
Schedule of Cost of Goods Manufactured
For the Year Ended December 31, 2008

Direct materials inventory, January 1	$xxx	
Purchases of materials (including freight-in and deducting purchase discounts)	xxx	
Total direct materials available	$xxx	
Direct materials inventory, December 31	(xxx)	
Direct materials used		$xxx
Direct labor		xxx

Factory overhead:		
Depreciation of factory equipment	$xxx	
Utilities	xxx	
Indirect factory labor	xxx	
Indirect materials	xxx	
Other overhead items	xxx	xxx
Manufacturing cost incurred in 2008		$xxx
Add: Work in process, January 1		xxx
Less: Work in process, December 31		(xxx)
Cost of goods manufactured		$xxx

ABC GROUP
Schedule of Cost of Goods Sold
For the Year Ended December 31, 2008

Finished goods inventory, January 1	$xxx
Add: Cost of goods manufactured	xxx
Cost of goods available for sale	$xxx
Less: Finished goods inventory, December, 31	(xxx)
Cost of goods sold	$xxx

3. **Operating expenses** are primary recurring costs associated with central operations, other than cost of goods sold, which are incurred to generate sales. Operating expenses are normally classified into the following two categories:

   a. Distribution costs (or selling expenses)
   b. General and administrative expenses

   Distribution costs are those expenses related directly to the company's efforts to generate sales (e.g., sales salaries, commissions, advertising, delivery expenses, depreciation of store furniture and equipment, and store supplies). General and administrative expenses are expenses related to the general administration of the company's operations (e.g., officers and office salaries, office supplies, depreciation of office furniture and fixtures, telephone, postage, accounting and legal services, and business licenses and fees).

4. **Other revenues and expenses** are incidental revenues and expenses not related to the central operations of the company (e.g., rental income from letting parts of premises not needed for company operations).

5. **Separate disclosure items** are items that are of such size, nature, or incidence that their disclosure becomes important in order to explain the performance of the enterprise for the period. Examples of items that, if material, would require such disclosure are as follows:

   a. Write-down of inventories to net realizable value, or of property, plant, and equipment to recoverable amounts, and subsequent reversals of such write-downs
   b. Costs of restructuring the activities of an enterprise and any subsequent reversals of such provisions
   c. Costs of litigation settlements
   d. Other reversals of provisions

6. **Income tax expense.** The total of taxes payable and deferred taxation adjustments for the period covered by the income statement.

7. **Discontinued operations.** IFRS 5, *Noncurrent Assets Held for Sale and Discontinued Operations,* superseded IAS 35, *Discontinuing Operations,* in 2005. This standard was issued by the IASB as part of its convergence program with US GAAP, and harmonizes IFRS with those parts of the corresponding US standard, FAS 144,

Accounting for the Impairment or Disposal of Long-Lived Assets, that deal with assets held for sale and with discontinued operations.

IFRS 5 created a new "held for sale" category of asset into which should be put assets, or "disposal groups" of assets, and liabilities that are to be sold. Such assets or groups of assets are to be valued at the lower of carrying value and fair value, less selling costs. Any resulting write-down appears, net of tax, as part of the caption "discontinued operations" in the income statement.

The other component of this line is the posttax profit or loss of discontinued operations. A discontinued operation is defined as a component of an entity that either has been disposed of, or has been classified as held for sale. It must also

- Be a separate major line of business or geographical area of operations,
- Be a part of a single coordinated plan for disposal, or
- Is a subsidiary acquired exclusively with a view to resale.

The two elements of the single line of income statement have to be analyzed in the notes, breaking out the related income tax expense between the two, as well as showing the components of revenue, expense, and pretax profit of the discontinued items.

For the asset or disposal group to be classified as held for sale, and its related earnings to be classified as discontinued, IFRS 5 says that sale must be highly probable, the asset must be saleable in its current condition, and the sale price must be reasonable in relation to its fair value. The appropriate level of management in the group must be committed to a plan to sell the asset and an active program has been embarked upon. Sale should be expected within one year of classification and the standard sets out stringent conditions for any extension of this, which are based on elements outside of the control of the entity.

Where an operation meets the criteria for classification as discontinued, but will be abandoned within one year rather than be sold, it should also be included in discontinued operations. Assets or disposal groups categorized as held for sale are not depreciated further.

Example of disclosure of discontinued operations under IFRS 5

Taj Mahal Enterprises
Income Statement
For the Years Ended December 31, 2008 and 2007
(in thousands of UAE Dirhams)

	2008		2007	
Continuing Operations (Segments X & Y):				
Revenue and	10,000		5,000	
Operating expenses	(7,000)		(3,500)	
Pretax profit from operating actives	3,000		1,500	
Interest expense	(300)		(200)	
Profit before tax	2,700		1,300	
Income tax expense	(540)		(260)	
Profit after taxes		2,160		1,040
Discontinuing operation (Segment Z):				
Discontinued operations (note)		(240)		80
Total enterprise:				
Profit (loss) attributable to owners		1,920		1,120

Note: Discontinued Operations	2008	2007
Revenue	3,000	2000
Operating expenses	(1,800)	(1400)
Provision for end-of-service benefits	(900)	--
Interest expense	(100)	(100)
Pretax profit	200	500

	2008		2007	
Income tax	(40)		(100)	
Discontinued earnings		160		400
Impairment loss	(500)		(400)	
Income tax	100		(80)	
Write-down of assets		(400)		(320)
Discontinued operations, net		(240)		(80)

Aggregating items. Aggregation of items should not serve to conceal significant information, as would the netting of revenues against expenses, or the combining of other elements that are individually of interest to readers, such as bad debts and depreciation. The categories "other" or "miscellaneous expense" should contain, at maximum, an immaterial total amount of aggregated, individually insignificant elements. Once this total approaches, for example, 10% of total expenses (or any other materiality threshold), some other aggregations, together with appropriate explanatory titles, should be selected.

Information is material if its omission or misstatement or nondisclosure could influence the economic decisions of users taken on the basis of the financial statements. Materiality depends on the size of the item judged in the particular circumstances of its omission (according to IASB's *Framework*). But it is often forgotten that materiality is also linked with understandability and the level of precision in which the financial statements are to be presented. For instance, the financial statements are often rendered more understandable by rounding information to the nearest thousand currency units (e.g., US dollars). This obviates the necessity of loading the financial statements with unnecessary detail. However, it should be borne in mind that the use of the level of precision that makes presentation possible in the nearest thousands of currency units is acceptable only as long as the threshold of materiality is not surpassed.

Offsetting items of revenue and expense. Materiality also plays a role in the matter of allowing or disallowing offsetting of the items of income and expense. IAS 1 addresses this issue and prescribes rules in this area. According to IAS 1, assets and liabilities or income and expenses may not be offset against each other, unless required or permitted by an IFRS. Usually, when more than one event occurs in a given reporting period, losses and gains on disposal of noncurrent assets or foreign exchange gains and losses are seen reported on a net basis, due to the fact that they are not material individually (compared to other items on the income statement). However, if they were material individually, they would need to be disclosed separately according to the requirements of IAS 1.

However, the reduction of accounts receivable by the allowance for doubtful accounts, or of property, plant, and equipment by the accumulated depreciation, are acts that reduce these assets by the appropriate valuation accounts and are not considered to be offsetting assets and liabilities.

Views differ as to the treatment of disposal gains and losses arising from the routine replacement of noncurrent assets. Some experts believe that these should be separately disclosed as a disposal transaction, whereas others point out that if the depreciation schedule is estimated correctly, there should be no disposal gain or loss. Consequently, any difference between carrying value and disposal proceeds is akin to an adjustment to previous depreciation, and should logically flow through the income statement in the same caption where the depreciation was originally reported. Here again, the issue comes down to one of the materiality: does it affect users' ability to make economic decisions?

IAS 1 further clarifies that when items of income or expense are offset, the enterprise should nevertheless consider, based on materiality, the need to disclose the gross amounts in the notes to the financial statements. This standard gives the following examples of transactions that are incidental to the main revenue-generating activities of an enterprise and whose results when presented by offsetting or reporting on a net basis, such as netting any gains with related expenses, reflect the substance of the transaction:

1. Gains or losses on the disposal of noncurrent assets, including investments and operating assets, are reported by deducting from the proceeds on disposal the carrying amounts of the asset and related selling expenses.
2. Expenditure related to a provision that is reimbursed under a contractual arrangement with a third party may be netted against the related reimbursement.

Other Comprehensive Income

Under IAS 1, *other comprehensive income* includes items of income and expense (including reclassification adjustments) that are not recognized in profit or loss as required or permitted by other IFRS. The components of other recognized income include (1) changes in revaluation surplus (IAS 16 and IAS 38); (2) actuarial gains and losses on defined benefit plans (IAS 19); (3) translation gains and losses (IAS 21); (4) gains and losses on remeasuring available-for-sale financial assets (IAS 39); and (5) the effective portion of gains and losses on hedging instruments in a cash flow hedge (IAS 39).

The amount of income tax relating to each component of other comprehensive income, including reclassification adjustments, should be disclosed either on the face of the statement of comprehensive income or in the notes.

Components of other comprehensive income can be presented in one of two ways

1. Net of related tax effects; or
2. Before related tax effects with one amount shown for the aggregate amount of income tax relating to those components.

An entity should disclose reclassification adjustments relating to each component of other comprehensive income. Reclassification adjustments are amounts reclassified to profit or loss in the current period that were recognized in other comprehensive income in previous periods. Other IFRS specify whether and when amounts previously recognized in other comprehensive income are reclassified to profit or loss. The purpose of this requirement is to avoid double-counting items in total comprehensive income when those items are reclassified to profit or loss in accordance with other IFRS. For example, gains realized on the disposal of a foreign operation are included in profit or loss of the current period. These amounts may have been recognized in other comprehensive income as unrealized foreign currency translation gains in the current or previous periods. Those unrealized gains must be deducted from other comprehensive income in the period in which the realized gains are included in profit or loss to avoid double-counting them. In the same manner, for instance, unrealized gains or losses on available-for-sale securities should not include realized gains or losses from the sale of available-for-sale securities during the current period, which are reported in profit or loss (income statement). Reclassification adjustments arise, for example, on the following components:

*   On disposal of a foreign operation (IAS 21)
*   On derecognition of available-for-sale financial assets (IAS 39)
*   When a hedged forecast transaction affects profit or loss (IAS 39)

Reclassification adjustments *do not* arise on the following components, which are recognized in other comprehensive income, but are not reclassified to profit or loss in subsequent periods:

*   On changes in revaluation surplus (IAS 16; IAS 38)
*   On changes in actuarial gains or losses on defined benefit plans (IAS 19)

In accordance with IAS 16 and IAS 38, changes in revaluation surplus may be transferred to retained earnings in subsequent periods when the asset is sold or when it is derecognized; actuarial gains and losses are reported in retained earnings in the period that they are recognized as other comprehensive income (IAS 19).

Reclassification Adjustments: An Example

In general, the reporting of unrealized gains and losses on available-for-sale securities in comprehensive income is straightforward unless the company sells securities during the year. In such a case, double counting results when a company reports realized gains and losses as part of profit or loss (net income), but also shows the amounts as part of other comprehensive income in the current period or in previous periods.

When a sale of securities occurs, a reclassification adjustment is necessary to ensure that gains and losses are not counted twice. To illustrate, assume that ABC Group has the following two available-for-sale securities in its portfolio at the end of 2007, its first year of operations:

Investments	*Cost*	*Fair value*	*Unrealized holding gain (loss)*
Radar Ltd	€105,000	€125,000	€20,000
Konini Ltd	260,000	300,000	40,000
Total value of portfolio	265,000	425,000	60,000
Previous (accumulated) securities fair value adjustment balance			0
Securities fair value adjustment (Dr)			€60,000

ABC Group reports net income of €650,000 in 2007 and presents a statement of comprehensive income as follows:

ABC Group
Statement of Comprehensive Income
For the Year Ended December 31, 2007

Net income	€650,000
Other comprehensive income	
Holding gains on available-for-sale securities	60,000
Comprehensive income	€710,000

During 2008, ABC Group sold 50% of shares of the Konin Ltd common stock for €150,000 and realized a gain on the sale of €20,000 (€150,000 – €130,000). At the end of 2008, ABC Group reports its available-for-sale securities as follows:

Investments	*Cost*	*Fair value*	*Unrealized holding gain (loss)*
Ardara Ltd	€105,000	€130,000	€25,000
Konin Ltd	130,000	160,000	30,000
Total value of portfolio	235,000	290,000	55,000
Previous (accumulated) securities fair value adjustment balance			(60,000)
Securities fair value adjustment (Dr)			€ (5,000)

ABC Group should report an unrealized holding loss of €(5,000) in comprehensive income in 2008 and realized gain of €20,000 on the sale of the Konin common stock. Consequently, ABC recognizes a total holding gain in 2008 of €15,000 (unrealized holding loss of €5,000 plus realized holding gain of €20,000).

ABC reports net income of €830,000 in 2008 and presents the components of holding gains (losses) as follows:

ABC Group
Statement of Comprehensive Income
For the Year Ended December 31, 2007

Net income (includes €20,000 realized gain on Konin shares)		€830,000
Other comprehensive income		
Total holding gains (€5,000 + €20,000)	€15,000	
Less: Reclassification adjustment for realized gains included in net income	(20,000)	(5,000)
Comprehensive income		€815,000

In 2007, ABC included the unrealized gain on the Konin common stock in comprehensive income. In 2008, ABC sold the stock and reported the realized gain on sale in profit, which increased comprehensive income again. To prevent double-counting of this gain of €20,000 on the Konin shares, ABC makes a reclassification adjustment to eliminate the realized gain from the computation of comprehensive income in 2008.

An entity may display reclassification adjustments on the face of the financial statement in which it reports comprehensive income or disclose them in the notes to the financial statements. The IASB's view is that separate presentation of reclassification adjustments is essential to inform users clearly of those amounts that are included as income and expenses in two different periods—as income or expenses in other comprehensive income in previous periods and as income or expenses in profit or loss (net income) in the current period.

Statement of Changes in Equity

Owners' (shareholders' or stockholders') equity represents the interest of the owners (shareholders or stockholders) in the net assets of an entity and shows the cumulative net results of past transactions and other events affecting the entity since its inception. The statement of changes in equity reflects the increases and decreases in the net assets of an entity during the period. In accordance with IAS 1, all changes in equity from transactions with owners are to be presented separately from nonowner changes in equity.

IAS 1 requires an entity to present a statement of changes in equity including the following components on the face of the statement:

1. Total comprehensive income for the period, segregating amounts attributable to owners and to noncontrolling interest;
2. The effects of retrospective application or retrospective restatement in accordance with IAS 8, separately for each component of equity;
3. Contributions from and distributions to owners; and
4. A reconciliation between the carrying amount at the beginning and the end of the period, separately disclosing each change, for each component of equity.

The amount of dividends recognized as distributions to equity holders during the period, and the related amount per share should be presented either on the face of the statement of changes in equity or in the notes.

According to IAS 1, except for changes resulting from transactions with owners (such as equity contributions, reacquisitions of the entity's own equity instruments, dividends, and costs related to these transactions with owners), the change in equity during the period represents the total amount of income and expense (including gains and losses) arising from activities other than those with owners.

The following should be disclosed, either in the statement of financial position or the statement of changes in equity, or in the notes:

1. For each class of share capital

- Number of shares authorized;
- Number of shares issued and fully paid, and issued but not fully paid;
- Par value per share, or that the shares have no par value;
- Recognition of the number of shares outstanding at the beginning and at the end of the periods;
- Any rights, preferences and restrictions attached;
- Shares in the entity held by the entity or its subsidiaries; and
- Shares reserved for issue under options and contracts for the sale of shares, including terms and amounts.

2. A description of the nature and purpose of each reserve within equity

Example of the Presentation of Statements of Income, Comprehensive Income, and Changes in Equity

IAS 1, the revised standard on presentation of financial statements, has introduced the statement of comprehensive income to capture those items of gains or losses (other comprehensive income items) that are not included in the determination of profit (net income) or loss for the period. Additional footnote disclosures may also be required.

ABC Group
Income Statement
For the year ended December 31, 20X8
(Presentation of comprehensive income in two statements and classification of expenses within profit by nature)
(in thousands of currency units)

	20X8	20X7
Revenue	250,000	200,000
Other income	20,000	10,000
Changes in inventories of finished goods	(30,000)	(25,000)
Changes in inventories of work in progress	(20,000)	(15,000)
Work performed by the entity and capitalized	20,000	18,000
Raw material and consumables used	(60,000)	(55,000)
Employee benefits expense	(50,000)	(46,000)
Depreciation and amortization expense	(21,000)	(20,000)
Impairment of property, plant, and equipment	(5,000)	--
Other expenses	(8,000)	(7,000)
Finance costs	(10,000)	(12,000)
Share of profit of associates[1]	30,000	20,000
Profit before tax	116,000	68,000
Income tax expense	(29,000)	17,000
Profit for the year from continuing operations	87,000	51,000
Loss for the year from discontinued operations	--	(9,000)
Profit for the year	87,000	42,000
Profit attributable to		
Owners of the parent (80%)	69,600	33,600
Noncontrolling interest (20%)	17,400	8,400
	87,000	42,000

[1] *Share of associates' profit attributable to owners, after tax and noncontrolling interests in the associates.*

ABC Group
Statement of Comprehensive Income
For the year ended December 31, 20X8
(Presentation of comprehensive income in two statements)
(in thousands of currency units)

	20X8	20X7
Profit for the year	87,000	42,000
Other comprehensive income:		
Exchange differences on translating foreign operations	20,000	16,000
Available-for-sale financial assets:	(5,000)	24,000
Cash flow hedges	(2,000)	(1,000)
Gains on property revaluation	4,000	14,000
Actuarial gains (losses) on defined benefit pension plans	(10,000)	(8,000)
Share of other comprehensive income of associates[2]	2,000	(1,000)
Income tax relating to components of other comprehensive income[3]	(1,750)	(11,250)
Other comprehensive income for the year, net of tax	7,250	32,750
Total comprehensive income for the year	94,250	74,750
Total comprehensive income attributable to		
Owners of the parent	75,400	59,800
Noncontrolling interest	18,850	14,950
	94,250	74,750

[2] *Share of associates' other comprehensive income attributable to owners of the associates, after tax and noncontrolling interests in the associates.*
[3] *The income tax relating to each component of other comprehensive income is disclosed in the notes.*

ABC Group
Disclosure of components of other comprehensive income[4]
Notes
Year ended December 31, 20X8
(in thousands of currency units)

		20X8		20X7
Other comprehensive income:				
Exchange differences on translating foreign operations[5]		20,000		16,000
Available-for-sale financial assets:				
Gains arising during the year	(12,000)		(30,000)	
Less: Reclassification adjustments for gains (losses) included in profit or loss	(7,000)	(5,000)	(6,000)	24,000
Cash flow hedges:				
Gains (losses) arising during the year	(4,000)		(1,000)	
Less: Reclassification adjustments for gains (losses) included in profit or loss	1,800		--	
Less: Adjustments for amounts transferred to initial carrying amount of hedged items	200	(2,000)	--	(1,000)
Gains on property revaluation		4,000		14,000
Actuarial gains (losses) on defined benefit pension plans		(10,000)		(8,000)
Share of other comprehensive income of associates		2,000		(1,000)
Other comprehensive income		9,000		44,000
Income tax relating to components of other comprehensive income[6]		(1,750)		(11,250)
Other comprehensive income for the year		7,250		32,750

[4] *When an entity chooses an aggregated presentation in the statement of comprehensive income, the amounts for reclassification adjustments and current year gain or loss are presented in the notes.*
[5] *There was no disposal of a foreign operation and therefore, there is no reclassification adjustment for the years presented.*
[6] *The income tax relating to each component of other comprehensive income is disclosed in the notes.*

ABC Group
Disclosure of tax effects relating to each component of other comprehensive income
Notes
Year ended December 31, 20X8
(in thousands of currency units)

	20X8 Before-tax amount	20X8 Tax (expense) benefit	20X8 Net-of-tax amount	20X7 Before-tax amount	20X7 Tax (expense) benefit	20X7 Net-of-tax amount
Exchange differences on translating foreign operations	20,000	(5,000)	15,000	16,000	(4,000)	12,000
Available-for-sale financial assets	(5,000)	1,250	(3,750)	24,000	(6,000)	18,000
Cash flow hedges	(2,000)	500	(1,500)	(1,000)	250	(750)
Gains on property revaluation	4,000	(1,000)	3,000	14,000	(3,500)	10,500
Actuarial gains (losses) on defined benefit pension plans	(10,000)	2,500	(7,500)	(8,000)	2,000	(6,000)
Share of other comprehensive income of associates	2,000	--	2,000	(1,000)	--	(1,000)
Other comprehensive income	9,000	(1,750)	7,250	44,000	(11,250)	32,750

ABC Group
Statement of Changes in Equity
For the year ended December 31, 20X8
(in thousands of currency units)

	Share capital	Retained earnings	Translation of foreign operations	Available-for-sale financial assets	Cash flow hedges	Revaluation surplus	Total	Minority interest	Total equity
Balance at January 1, 20X7	300,000	91,000	(2,000)	1,000	1,000	--	391,000	156,000	547,000
Changes in accounting policy	--	--	--	--	--	--	--	--	--
Restated balance	300,000	91,000	(2,000)	1,000	1,000	--	391,000	156,000	547,000
Changes in equity for 20X7									
Dividends	--	(5,000)	--	--	--	--	(5,000)	--	(5,000)
Total comprehensive income for the year[7]	--	38,400	9,600	14,400	(525)	7,400	69,275	14,950	84,225
Balance at December 31, 20X7	300,000	124,400	7,600	15,400	475	7,400	455,275	170,950	626,225
Changes in equity for 20X8									
Issue of share capital	20,000	--	--	--	--	--	20,000	--	20,000
Dividends	--	(10,000)	--	--	--	--	(10,000)	--	(10,000)
Total comprehensive income for the year[8]	--	75,600	12,000	(14,400)	1,200	4,400	78,800	18,850	97,650
Transfer to retained earnings	--	200	--	--	--	(200)	--	--	--
Balance at December 31, 20X8	320,000	190,200	19,600	1,000	1,675	11,600	544,075	189,800	733,875

[7] The amount included in retained earnings for 20X7 of 38,400 represents profit attributable to owners of the parent of 33,600 plus actuarial gains on defined benefit pension plans of 4,800 (8,000 less tax 2,000, less minority interest 1,200). The amount included in the translation, available-for-sale and cash flow hedge reserves represents other comprehensive income for each component, net of tax and minority interest, (e.g., other comprehensive income related to translation of foreign operations for 20X7 of 9,600 is 16,000, less tax 4,000, less minority interest 2,400). The amount included in the revaluation surplus of 7,400 represents the share of other comprehensive income of associates of (1,000) plus gains on property revaluation of 8,400 (14,000, less tax 3,500, less minority interest 2,100). Other comprehensive income of associates relates solely to gains or losses on property revaluation.

[8] The amount included in retained earnings for 20X8 of 75,600 represents profit attributable to owners of the parent of 69,600 plus actuarial losses on defined benefit pension plans of 7,500 (10,000, less tax 2,500, less minority interest 1,500). The amount included in the translation, available-for-sale and cash flow hedge reserves represents other comprehensive income for each component, net of tax and minority interest (e.g., other comprehensive income related to the available-for-sale financial assets for 20X8 of 12,000 is 20,000, less tax 5,000, less minority interest 3,000). The amount included in the revaluation surplus of 4,400 represents the share of other comprehensive income of associates of 2,000 plus gains on property revaluation of 2,400 (4,000, less tax 1,000, less minority interest 600). Other comprehensive income of associates relates solely to gains or losses on property revaluation.

4 STATEMENT OF CASH FLOWS

PERSPECTIVE AND ISSUES

The IASC had most recently revised IAS 7, *Cash Flow Statements*, in 1992, which became effective in 1994. IAS 7 had originally required that reporting entities prepare the statement of changes in financial position (commonly referred to as the funds flow statement), which was once a widely accepted method of presenting changes in financial position, as part of a complete set of financial statements. The IASB has now amended the title of IAS 7 from *Cash Flow Statements* to *Statement of Cash Flows* (the title used in the US) as a consequence of the latest revision of IAS 1, *Presentation of Financial Statements,* a result of the IASB and the FASB deliberations on the first phase of the Financial Statement Presentation project. Phase B of the *Financial Statement Presentation* project will address more fundamental issues for presenting information on the face of the financial statements, including whether the direct or the indirect method of presenting operating cash flows provides more useful information. Historically, of course, the direct method has been strongly endorsed, yet employed by very few reporting entities. The statement of cash flows is now universally accepted and required under most national GAAP as well as IFRS. While there are some variations in terms of presentation (most of which pertain to the section in which certain captions appear), the approach is highly similar across all current sets of standards.

The purpose of the statement of cash flows is to provide information about the operating cash receipts and cash payments of an entity during a period, as well as providing insight into its various investing and financing activities. It is a vitally important financial statement, because the ultimate concern of investors is the reporting entity's ability to generate cash flows which will support payments (typically but not necessarily in the form of dividends) to the shareholders. More specifically, the statement of cash flows should help investors and creditors assess

1. The ability to generate future positive cash flows
2. The ability to meet obligations and pay dividends
3. Reasons for differences between profit or loss and cash receipts and payments
4. Both cash and noncash aspects of entities' investing and financing transactions

Sources of IFRS
IAS 7

DEFINITIONS OF TERMS

Cash. Cash on hand and demand deposits with banks or other financial institutions.

Cash equivalents. Short-term highly liquid investments that are readily convertible to known amounts of cash and which are subject to an insignificant risk of changes in value. Treasury bills, commercial paper, and money market funds are all examples of cash equivalents.

Direct method. A method that derives the net cash provided by or used in operating activities from major components of operating cash receipts and payments.

Financing activities. The transactions and other events that cause changes in the size and composition of an entity's capital and borrowings.

Indirect (reconciliation) method. A method that derives the net cash provided by or used in operating activities by adjusting profit (loss) for the effects of transactions of a noncash nature, any deferrals or accruals of past or future operating cash receipts or payments, and items of income or expense associated with investing or financing activities.

Investing activities. The acquisition and disposal of long-term assets and other investments not included in cash equivalents.

Operating activities. The transactions and other events not classified as financing or investing activities. In general, operating activities are principal revenue-producing activities of an entity that enter into the determination of profit or loss, including the sale of goods and the rendering of services.

CONCEPTS, RULES, AND EXAMPLES

Benefits of Statement of Cash Flows

The concepts underlying the statement of financial position and the statement of comprehensive income have long been established in financial reporting. They are, respectively, the stock measure or a snapshot at a point in time of an entity's resources and obligations, and a summary of the entity's economic transactions and performance over an interval of time. The third major financial statement, the statement of cash flows, is a more recent innovation but has evolved substantially since introduced. What has ultimately developed into the statement of cash flows began life as a flow statement that reconciled changes in entity resources over a period of time, but in a fundamentally different manner than did the statement of comprehensive income.

Most of the basic progress on this financial statement occurred in the United States, where during the 1950s and early 1960s a variety of formats and concepts were experimented with. By the mid-1960s the most common reporting approach used in the United States was that of sources and applications (or uses) of funds, although such reporting did not become mandatory until 1971. Even then, *funds* could be defined by the reporting entity in at least four different ways, including as cash and as net working capital (current assets minus current liabilities).

One reason why the financial statement preparer community did not more quickly embrace a cash flow concept is that the accounting profession had long had a significant aversion to the cash basis measurement of entity operating performance. This was largely the result of its commitment to accrual basis accounting, which recognizes revenues when earned and expenses when incurred, and which views cash flow reporting as a back door approach to cash basis accounting. By focusing instead on funds, which most typically was defined as net working capital, items such as receivables and payables were included, thereby preserving the essential accrual basis characteristic of the flow measurement. On the other hand, this failed to give statement users meaningful insight into the entities' sources and uses of cash, which is germane to an evaluation of the reporting entity's liquidity and solvency.

By the 1970s there was widespread recognition of the myriad problems associated with funds flow reporting, including the required use of the "all financial resources" approach, under which all major noncash (and nonfund) transactions, such as exchanges of stock or debt for plant assets, were included in the funds flow statement. This ultimately led to a renewed call for cash flow reporting. Most significantly, the FASB's conceptual framework project of the late 1970s to mid-1980s identified usefulness in predicting future cash flows as a central purpose of the financial reporting process. This presaged the nearly universal move away from funds flows to cash flows as a third standard measurement to be incorporated in financial reports.

The presentation of a statement of cash flows thus became required in the late 1980s in the United States, with the United Kingdom following soon thereafter with an approach that largely mirrored the US standard, albeit with a somewhat refined classification scheme. The international accounting standard, which was adopted a year after that of the United Kingdom (both of these were revisions to earlier requirements that had mandated the use of funds flow statements), embraces the somewhat simpler US approach but offers greater flexibility, thus effectively incorporating the UK view without adding to the structural complexity of the statement of cash flows itself.

Today, the clear consensus of national and international accounting standard setters is that the statement of cash flows is a necessary component of complete financial reporting. The perceived benefits of presenting the statement of cash flows in conjunction with the statement of financial position and the statement of comprehensive income have been highlighted by IAS 7 to be as follows:

1. It provides an insight into the financial structure of the entity (including its liquidity and solvency) and its ability to affect the amounts and timing of cash flows in order to adapt to changing circumstances and opportunities.

The statement of cash flows discloses important information about the cash flows from operating, investing, and financing activities, information that is not available or as clearly discernible in either the statement of financial position or the statement of comprehensive income. The additional disclosures which are either recommended by IAS 7 (such as those relating to undrawn borrowing facilities or cash flows that represent increases in operating capacity) or required to be disclosed by the standard (such as that about cash held by the entity but not available for use) provide a wealth of information for the informed user of financial statements. Taken together, the statement of cash flows coupled with these required or recommended disclosures provide the user with vastly more insight into the entity's performance and position, and its probable future results, than would the statement of financial position and statement of comprehensive income alone.

2. It provides additional information to the users of financial statements for evaluating changes in assets, liabilities, and equity of an entity.

When comparative statements of financial position are presented, users are given information about the entity's assets and liabilities at the end of each of the years. Were the statement of cash flows not presented as an integral part of the financial statements, it would be necessary for users of comparative financial statements either to speculate about how and why certain amounts reported in the statement of financial position changed from one period to another, or to compute (at least for the latest year presented) approximations of these items for themselves. At best, however, such a do-it-yourself approach would derive the net changes (the increase or decrease) in the individual assets and liabilities and attribute these to normally related accounts in the statement of comprehensive income. (For example, the net change in accounts receivable from the beginning to the end of the year would be used to convert reported sales to cash-basis sales or cash collected from customers.)

While basic changes in the statement of financial position can be used to infer cash flow implications, this is not universally the case. More complex combinations of events (such as the acquisition of another entity, along with its accounts receivables, which would be an increase in that asset which was not related to sales to customers by the reporting entity during the period) would not immediately be comprehensible and might lead to incorrect interpretations of the data unless an actual statement of cash flows were presented.

3. It enhances the comparability of reporting of operating performance by different entities because it eliminates the effects of using different accounting treatments for the same transactions and events.

There was considerable debate even as early as the 1960s and 1970s over accounting standardization, which led to the emergence of cash flow accounting. The principal argument in support of cash flow accounting by its earliest proponents was that it avoids the difficult to understand and sometimes seemingly arbitrary allocations inherent in accrual accounting. For example, cash flows provided by or used in operating activities are derived, under the indirect method, by adjusting profit (or loss) for items such as depreciation and amortization, which might have been computed by different entities using different accounting methods. Thus, accounting standardization will be achieved by converting the accrual-basis profit or loss to cash-basis profit or loss, and the resultant figures will become comparable across entities.

4. It serves as an indicator of the amount, timing, and certainty of future cash flows. Furthermore, if an entity has a system in place to project its future cash flows, the statement of cash flows could be used as a touchstone to evaluate the accuracy of past projections of those future cash flows. This benefit is elucidated by the standard as follows:

   a. The statement of cash flows is useful in comparing past assessments of future cash flows against current year's cash flow information, and
   b. It is of value in appraising the relationship between profitability and net cash flows, and in assessing the impact of changing prices.

Exclusion of Noncash Transactions

The statement of cash flows, as its name implies, includes only actual inflows and outflows of cash and cash equivalents. Accordingly, it excludes all transactions that do not directly affect cash receipts and payments. However, IAS 7 does require that the effects of transactions not resulting in receipts or payments of cash be disclosed elsewhere in the financial statements. The reason for not including noncash transactions in the statement of cash flows and placing them elsewhere in the financial statements (e.g., the footnotes) is that it preserves the statement's primary focus on cash flows from operating, investing, and financing activities. It is thus important that the user of financial statements fully appreciate what this financial statement does—and does not—attempt to portray.

Components of Cash and Cash Equivalents

The statement of cash flows, under the various national and international standards, may or may not include transactions in cash equivalents as well as cash. Under US standards, for example, preparers may choose to define cash as "cash and cash equivalents," as long as the same definition is used in the statement of financial position as in the statement of cash flows (i.e., the statement of cash flows must tie to a single caption in the statement of financial position). IAS 7, on the other hand, rather clearly required that the changes in both cash and cash equivalents be explained by the statement of cash flows.

Cash and cash equivalents include unrestricted cash (meaning cash actually on hand, or bank balances whose immediate use is determined by the management), other demand deposits, and short-term investments whose maturities at the date of acquisition by the entity were three months or less. Equity investments do not qualify as cash equivalents unless they fit the definition above of short-term maturities of three months or less, which would rarely, if ever, be true. Preference shares carrying mandatory redemption features, if acquired within three months of their predetermined redemption date, would meet the criteria above since they are, in substance, cash equivalents. These are very infrequently encountered circumstances, however.

Bank borrowings are normally considered as financing activities. However, in some countries, bank overdrafts play an integral part in the entity's cash management, and as such, overdrafts are to be included as a component of cash equivalents if the following conditions are met:

1. The bank overdraft is repayable on demand, and
2. The bank balance often fluctuates from positive to negative (overdraft).

Statutory (or reserve) deposits by banks (i.e., those held with the central bank for regulatory compliance purposes) are often included in the same statement of financial position caption as cash. The financial statement treatment of these deposits is subject to some controversy in certain countries, which becomes fairly evident from scrutiny of published financial statements of banks, as these deposits are variously considered to be either a cash equivalent or an operating asset. If the latter, changes in amount would be presented in the operating activities section of the statement of cash flows, and the item could not then be combined with cash in the statement of financial position. Since the appendix to IAS 7, which illustrates the application of the standard to statement of cash flows of financial institutions, does not include statutory deposits with the central bank as a cash equivalent, the authors have concluded that there is little logic to support the alternative presentation of this item as a cash equivalent. Given the fact that deposits with central banks are more or less permanent (and in fact would be more likely to increase over time than to be diminished, given a going concern assumption about the reporting financial institution) the presumption must be that these are not cash equivalents in normal practice.

Classifications in the Statement of Cash Flows

The statement of cash flows prepared in accordance with IAS 7 (and also in accordance with US GAAP) requires classification into these three categories:

1. *Investing activities* include the acquisition and disposition of property, plant and equipment and other long-term assets and debt and equity instruments of other entities that are not considered cash equivalents or held for dealing or trading purposes. Investing activities include cash advances and collections on loans made to other parties (other than advances and loans of a financial institution).

2. *Financing activities* include obtaining resources from and returning resources to the owners. Also included is obtaining resources through borrowings (short-term or long-term) and repayments of the amounts borrowed.

3. *Operating activities,* which can be presented under the (IFRS-preferred) direct or the indirect method, include all transactions that are not investing and financing activities. In general, cash flows arising from transactions and other events that enter into the determination of profit or loss are operating cash flows. Operating activities are principal revenue-producing activities of an entity and include delivering or producing goods for sale and providing services.

While both US GAAP and IFRS define these three components of cash flows, the international standards offer somewhat more flexibility in how certain types of cash flows are categorized. Differences exist between the two standards in the presentation of overdrafts, dividends, and interest. For example, under US GAAP, interest paid must be included in operating activities, but under the provisions of IAS 7 this may be consistently included in either operating or financing activities. (These and other discrepancies among the standards will be discussed further throughout this chapter.) This is a reflection of the fact that although interest expense is operating in the sense of being an item that is reported in the statement of comprehensive income, it also clearly relates to the entity's financing activities.

The following are examples of the statement of cash flows classification under the provisions of IAS 7:

	Operating	*Investing*	*Financing*
Cash inflows	• Receipts from sale of goods or rendering of services	• Principal collections from loans and sales of other entities' debt instruments	• Proceeds from issuing share capital
	• Sale of loans, debt, or equity instruments carried in trading portfolio	• Sale of equity instruments of other entities and from returns of investment in those instruments	• Proceeds from issuing debt (short-term or long-term)
	• Returns on loans (interest)	• Sale of plant and equipment	• Not-for-profits' donor-restricted cash that is limited to long-term purposes
	• Returns on equity securities (dividends)		
Cash outflows	• Payments to suppliers for goods and other services	• Loans made and acquisition of other entities' debt instruments	• Payment of dividends
	• Payments to or on behalf of employees	• Purchase of equity instruments* of other entities	• Repurchase of company's shares
	• Payments of taxes	• Purchase of plant and equipment	• Repayment of debt principal, including capital lease obligations
	• Payments of interest		
	• Purchase of loans, debt, or equity instruments carried in trading portfolio		

* *Unless held for trading purposes or considered to be cash equivalents.*

Noncash investing and financing activities should, according to IAS 7, be disclosed in the footnotes to financial statements ("elsewhere" is how the standard actually identifies this), but apparently are not intended to be included in the statement of cash flows itself. This contrasts somewhat with the US standard, FAS 95, which encourages inclusion of this supplemental information on the face of the statement of cash flows, although this may, under that standard, be relegated to a footnote as well. Examples of significant noncash financing and investing activities might include

1. Acquiring an asset through a finance lease
2. Conversion of debt to equity
3. Exchange of noncash assets or liabilities for other noncash assets or liabilities
4. Issuance of stock to acquire assets

Basic example of a classified statement of cash flows

Liquid Corporation
Statement of Cash Flows
For the Year Ended December 31, 2009

Net cash flows from operating activities		
Cash receipts from customers		
Cash paid to suppliers and employees	€ xxx	
Interest paid	(xxx)	
Income taxes paid	(xx)	
Net cash **provided** by operation activities	(xx)	
		€xxxx
Cash flows from investing activities:		
Purchase of property, plant, and equipment	€ (xxx)	
Sale of equipment	xx	
Collection of notes receivable	xx	
Net cash **used** in investing activities		(xx)
Cash flows from financing activities:		
Proceeds from issuance of share capital	xxx	
Repayment of long-term debt	(xx)	
Reduction of notes payable	(xx)	
Net cash **provided** by financing activities		xx
Effect of exchange rate changes on cash		xx
Net increase in cash and cash equivalents		€ xxx
Cash and cash equivalents at beginning of year		xxx
Cash and cash equivalents at end of year		€xxxx

Footnote Disclosure of Noncash Investing and Financing Activities

Note 4: Supplemental Statement of Cash Flows Information

Significant noncash investing and financing transactions:

Conversion of bonds into ordinary shares	€ xxx
Property acquired under finance leases	xxx
	€ xxx

Reporting Cash Flows from Operating Activities

Direct vs. indirect methods. The operating activities section of the statement of cash flows can be presented under the direct or the indirect method. However, IFRS has expressed a preference for the direct method of presenting net cash from operating activities. In this regard the IASC was probably following in the well-worn path of the FASB in the United States, which similarly urged that the direct method of reporting be adhered to. For their part, most preparers of financial statements, like those in the US, have chosen overwhelmingly to ignore the recommendation of the IASC, preferring by a very large margin to use the indirect method in lieu of the recommended direct method.

The *direct method* shows the items that affected cash flow and the magnitude of those cash flows. Cash received from, and cash paid to, specific sources (such as customers and suppliers) are presented, as opposed to the indirect method's converting accrual-basis profit (or loss) to cash flow information by means of a series of add-backs and deductions. Entities using the direct method are required by IAS 7 to report the following major classes of gross cash receipts and gross cash payments:

1. Cash collected from customers
2. Interest and dividends received[1]
3. Cash paid to employees and other suppliers
4. Interest paid[2]
5. Income taxes paid
6. Other operating cash receipts and payments

Given the availability of alternative modes of presentation of interest and dividends received, and of interest paid, it is particularly critical that the policy adopted be followed consistently. Since the face of the statement of cash flows will in almost all cases make it clear what approach has been elected, it is not usually necessary to spell this out in the accounting policy note to the financial statements, although this certainly can be done if it would be useful to do so.

An important advantage of the direct method is that it permits the user to better comprehend the relationships between the entity's profit (or loss) and its cash flows. For example, payments of expenses are shown as cash disbursements and are deducted from cash receipts. In this way the user is able to recognize the cash receipts and cash payments for the period. Formulas for conversion of various statement of comprehensive income amounts for the direct method presentation from the accrual basis to the cash basis are summarized below.

Accrual basis	*Additions*	*Deductions*	*Cash basis*
Net sales	+ Beginning AR	– Ending AR AR written off	= Cash received from customers
Cost of goods sold	+ Ending inventory Beginning AP	– Depreciation and amortization* Beginning inventory Ending AP	= Cash paid to suppliers
Operating expenses	+ Ending prepaid expenses Beginning accrued expenses	– Depreciation and amortization Beginning prepaid expenses Ending accrued expenses payable Bad debts expense	= Cash paid for operating expenses

* *Applies to a manufacturing entity only*

From the foregoing it can be appreciated that the amounts to be included in the operating section of the statement of cash flows, when the direct approach is utilized, are derived amounts that must be computed (although the computations are not onerous); they are not, generally, amounts that exist as account balances simply to be looked up and then placed in the statement. The extra effort needed to prepare the direct method operating cash flow data may be a contributing cause of why this method has been distinctly unpopular with prepar-

---

[1] *Alternatively, interest and dividends received may be classified as investing cash flows rather than as operating cash flows because they are returns on investments. In this important regard, the IFRS differs from the corresponding US rule, which does not permit this elective treatment, making the operating cash flow presentation mandatory.*

[2] *Alternatively, IAS 7 permits interest paid to be classified as a financing cash flow, because this is the cost of obtaining financing. As with the foregoing, the availability of alternative treatments differs from the US approach, which makes the operating cash flow presentation the only choice. It is not clear at this time how the alternative approaches under US GAAP and IFRS will be converged.*

ers. (There is a further reason why the direct method proved to be unpopular with entities that report in conformity with US GAAP: FAS 95 requires that when the direct method is used, a supplementary schedule be prepared reconciling profit or loss to net cash flows from operating activities, which effectively means that *both* the direct and indirect methods must be employed. This rule does not apply under international accounting standards, however.)

The *indirect method* (sometimes referred to as the reconciliation method) is the most widely used means of presentation of cash from operating activities, primarily because it is easier to prepare. It focuses on the differences between net operating results and cash flows. The indirect format begins with the amount of profit (or loss) for the year, which can be obtained directly from the statement of comprehensive income. Revenue and expense items not affecting cash are added or deducted to arrive at net cash provided by operating activities. For example, depreciation and amortization would be added back because these expenses reduce profit or loss without affecting cash.

The statement of cash flows prepared using the indirect method emphasizes changes in the components of most current asset and current liability accounts. Changes in inventory, accounts receivable, and other current accounts are used to determine the cash flow from operating activities. Although most of these adjustments are obvious (most preparers simply relate each current asset or current liability on the statement of financial position to a single caption in the statement of comprehensive income), some changes require more careful analysis. For example, it is important to compute cash collected from sales by relating sales revenue to both the change in accounts receivable and the change in the related bad debt allowance account.

As another example of possible complexity in computing the cash from operating activities, the change in short-term borrowings resulting from the purchase of equipment would not be included, since it is not related to operating activities. Instead, these short-term borrowings would be classified as a financing activity. Other adjustments under the indirect method include changes in the account balances of deferred income taxes, noncontrolling interest, unrealized foreign currency gains or losses, and the profit (loss) from investments under the equity method.

IAS 7 offers yet another alternative way of presenting the cash flows from operating activities. This could be referred to as the *modified indirect method.* Under this variant of the indirect method, the starting point is not profit (or loss) but rather revenues and expenses as reported in the statement of comprehensive income. In essence, this approach is virtually the same as the regular indirect method, with two more details: revenues and expenses for the period. There is no equivalent rule under US GAAP.

The following summary, actually simply an expanded statement of financial position equation, may facilitate understanding of the adjustments to profit or loss necessary for converting accrual-basis profit or loss to cash-basis profit or loss when using the indirect method.

	Current assets*	_	Fixed assets	=	Current liabilities	+	Long-term liabilities	+	Profit or loss	Accrual profit adjustment to convert to cash flow
1.	Increase			=					Increase	Decrease
2.	Decrease			=					Decrease	Increase
3.				=	Increase				Decrease	Increase
4.				=	Decrease				Increase	Decrease

Other than cash and cash equivalents

For example, using row 1 in the above chart, a credit sale would increase accounts receivable and accrual-basis profit but would not affect cash. Therefore, its effect must be removed from the accrual profit to convert to cash profit. The last column indicates that the increase in a current asset balance must be deducted from profit to obtain cash flow.

Similarly, an increase in a current liability, row three, must be added to profit to obtain cash flows (e.g., accrued wages are in the statement of comprehensive income as an expense, but they do not require cash; the increase in wages payable must be added back to remove this noncash flow expense from accrual-basis profit).

Under the US GAAP, when the indirect method is employed, the amount of interest and income taxes paid must be included in the related disclosures (supplemental schedule). However, under IFRS, as illustrated by the appendix to IAS 7, instead of disclosing them in the supplemental schedules, they are shown as part of the operating activities under both the direct and indirect methods. (Examples presented later in the chapter illustrate this.)

The major drawback to the indirect method involves the user's difficulty in comprehending the information presented. This method does not show from where the cash was received or to where the cash was paid. Only adjustments to accrual-basis profit (or loss) are shown. In some cases the adjustments can be confusing. For instance, the sale of equipment resulting in an accrual-basis loss would require that the loss be added to profit to arrive at net cash from operating activities. (The loss was deducted in the computation of profit or loss, but because the sale will be shown as an investing activity, the loss must be added back to profit or loss.)

Although the indirect method is more commonly used in practice, the IASC and the FASB both encouraged entities to use the direct method. As pointed out by IAS 7, a distinct advantage of the direct method is that it provides information that may be useful in estimating or projecting future cash flows, a benefit that is clearly not achieved when the indirect method is utilized instead. Both the direct and indirect methods are presented below.

Direct method

Cash flows from operating activities:		
Cash received from sale of goods	€xxx	
Cash dividends received*	xxx	
Cash provided by operating activities		€xxx
Cash paid to suppliers	(xxx)	
Cash paid for operating expenses	(xxx)	
Cash paid for income taxes**	(xxx)	
Cash disbursed for operating activities		€(xxx)
Net cash flows from operating activities		€xxx

*   *Alternatively, could be classified as investing cash flow.*
** *Taxes paid are usually classified as operating activities. However, when it is practical to identify the tax cash flow with an individual transaction that gives rise to cash flows that are classified as investing or financing activities, then the tax cash flow is classified as an investing or financing activity as appropriate.*

Indirect method

Cash flows from operating activities:	
Profit before income taxes	€ xx
Adjustments for:	
Depreciation	xx
Unrealized loss on foreign exchange	xx
Interest expense	xx
Operating profit before working capital changes***	xx
Increase in accounts receivable	(xx)
Decrease in inventories	xx
Increase in accounts payable	xx
Cash generated from operations	xx
Interest paid	(xx)
Income taxes paid (see note**above)	(xx)
Net cash flows from operating activities	€xxx

Other Requirements

Gross vs. net basis. The emphasis in the statement of cash flows is on gross cash receipts and cash payments. For instance, reporting the net change in bonds payable would obscure the financing activities of the entity by not disclosing separately cash inflows from issuing bonds and cash outflows from retiring bonds.

IAS 7 specifies two exceptions where netting of cash flows is allowed. Items with quick turnovers, large amounts, and short maturities may be presented as net cash flows. Cash receipts and payments on behalf of customers when the cash flows reflect the activities of the customers rather than those of the entity may also be reported on a net rather than a gross basis.

Foreign currency cash flows. Foreign operations must prepare a separate statement of cash flows and translate the statement to the reporting currency using the exchange rate in effect at the time of the cash flow (a weighted-average exchange rate may be used if the result is substantially the same). This translated statement is then used in the preparation of the consolidated statement of cash flows. Noncash exchange gains and losses recognized in the statement of comprehensive income should be reported as a separate item when reconciling profit or loss and operating activities. For a more detailed discussion about the exchange rate effects on the statement of cash flows, see Chapter 22.

Cash flow per share. There is presently no requirement either under the international accounting standards or under US GAAP to disclose such information in the financial statements of an entity, unlike the requirement to report earnings per share (EPS). In fact, cash flow per share is a somewhat disreputable concept, since it was sometimes touted in an earlier era as being indicative of an entity's "real" performance, when of course it is not a meaningful alternative to earnings per share because, for example, entities that are self-liquidating by selling productive assets can generate very positive total cash flows, and hence, cash flows per share, while decimating the potential for future earnings. Since, unlike a comprehensive statement of cash flows, cash flow per share cannot reveal the components of cash flow (operating, investing, and financing), its usage could be misleading.

While cash flow per share is not well regarded, it should be noted that in recent years a growing number of entities have resorted to displaying a wide range of pro forma amounts, some of which roughly correspond to cash-based measures of operating performance. These non-GAAP/non-IFRS categories should be viewed with great caution, both because they convey the message that standard, GAAP- or IFRS-based measures of performance are somehow less meaningful, and also because there are no standard definitions of the non-GAAP/non-IFRS measures, opening the door to possible manipulation. This has, in the US, caused the securities regulatory body, the SEC, to mandate that all non-GAAP measures must be explicitly reconciled to the most similar GAAP measure. The international association of securities regulators, IOSCO, has offered a similar warning and recommendation for reconciliation.

Net Reporting by Financial Institutions

IAS 7 permits financial institutions to report cash flows arising from certain activities on a net basis. These activities, and the related conditions under which net reporting would be acceptable, are as follows:

1. Cash receipts and payments on behalf of customers when the cash flows reflect the activities of the customers rather than those of the bank, such as the acceptance and repayment of demand deposits
2. Cash flows relating to deposits with fixed maturity dates

3. Placements and withdrawals of deposits from other financial institutions
4. Cash advances and loans to banks customers and repayments thereon

Reporting Futures, Forward Contracts, Options, and Swaps

IAS 7 stipulates that cash payments for and cash receipts from futures contracts, forward contracts, option contracts, and swap contracts are normally classified as investing activities, except

1. When such contracts are held for dealing or trading purposes and thus represent operating activities
2. When the payments or receipts are considered by the entity as financing activities and are reported accordingly

Further, when a contract is accounted for as a hedge of an identifiable position, the cash flows of the contract are classified in the same manner as the cash flows of the position being hedged.

Reporting Extraordinary Items in the Statement of Cash Flows

Revised IAS 1 has eliminated the extraordinary categorization of gains or losses, so this no longer will impact the presentation of the statement of cash flows under IFRS. Under IFRS, prior to revisions to IAS 1 in 2005, cash flows associated with extraordinary items were to be disclosed separately as arising from operating, investing, or financing activities in the statement of cash flows, as appropriate. By way of contrast, US GAAP permits, but does not require, separate disclosure of cash flows related to extraordinary items. If an entity reporting under US GAAP chooses to make this disclosure, however, it is expected to do so consistently in all periods.

Reconciliation of Cash and Cash Equivalents

An entity should disclose the components of cash and cash equivalents and should present a reconciliation of the difference, if any, between the amounts reported in the statement of cash flows and equivalent items reported in the statement of financial position. By contrast, under the US GAAP the definition must tie to a specific caption in the statement of financial position. For example, if short-term investments are shown as a separate caption in the statement of financial position, the definition of cash for the purposes of the statement of cash flows must include "cash" alone (and not also include short-term investments). On the other hand, if "cash and cash equivalents" is the adopted definition in the statement of cash flows, a single caption in the statement of financial position must include both "cash" and "short-term investments."

Acquisitions and Disposals of Subsidiaries and Other Business Units

IAS 7 requires that the aggregate cash flows from acquisitions and from disposals of subsidiaries or other business units should be presented separately as part of the investing activities section of the statement of cash flows. The following disclosures have also been prescribed by IAS 7 in respect to both acquisitions and disposals:

1. The total consideration included
2. The portion thereof discharged by cash and cash equivalents
3. The amount of cash and cash equivalents in the subsidiary or business unit acquired or disposed
4. The amount of assets and liabilities (other than cash and cash equivalents) acquired or disposed, summarized by major category

Other Disclosures Required or Recommended by IAS 7

Certain additional information may be relevant to the users of financial statements in gaining an insight into the liquidity or solvency of an entity. With this objective in mind, IAS 7 sets forth other disclosures that are required or in some cases, recommended.

1. **Required disclosure**—Amount of significant cash and cash equivalent balances held by an entity that are not available for use by the group should be disclosed along with a commentary by management.

2. **Recommended disclosures**—The disclosures that are encouraged are the following:

   a. Amount of undrawn borrowing facilities, indicating restrictions on their use, if any

   b. In case of investments in joint ventures, which are accounted for using proportionate consolidation, the aggregate amount of cash flows from operating, investing and financing activities that are attributable to the investment in the joint venture

   c. Aggregate amount of cash flows that are attributable to the increase in operating capacity separately from those cash flows that are required to maintain operating capacity

   d. Amount of cash flows segregated by reported industry and geographical segments

The disclosures above recommended by the IAS 7, although difficult to present, are unique since such disclosures are not required even under the US GAAP. They are useful in enabling the users of financial statements to understand the entity's financial position better.

Basic example of the preparation of the statement of cash flows under IAS 7 using a worksheet approach

Using the following financial information for ABC (Eurasia) Ltd., preparation and presentation of the statement of cash flows according to the requirements of IAS 7 are illustrated. (Note that all figures in this example are in thousands of euros.)

ABC (Eurasia) Ltd.
Statements of Financial Position
December 31, 2009 and 2008

Assets	2009	2008
Cash and cash equivalents	€ 3,000	€ 1,000
Accounts reveivable	5,000	2,500
Inventory	2,000	1,500
Prepaid expenses	1,000	1,500
Due from associates	19,000	19,000
Property, plant, and equipment, at cost	12,000	22,500
Accumulated depreciation	(5,000)	(6,000)
Property, plant, and equipment, net	7,000	16,500
Total assets	€37,000	€42,000
Liabilities		
Accounts payable	€ 5,000	€12,500
Income taxes payable	2,000	1,000
Deferred taxes payable	3,000	2,000
Total liabilities	10,000	15,500
Shareholders' equity		
Share capital	6,500	6,500
Retained earnings	20,500	20,000
Total shareholders' equity	27,000	26,500
Total liabilities and shareholders' equity	€37,000	€42,000

ABC (Eurasia) Ltd.
Statement of Comprehensive Income
For the Year Ended December 31, 2009

Sales	€ 30,000
Cost of sales	(10,000)
Gross profit	20,000
Administrative and selling expenses	(2,000)
Interest expense	(2,000)
Depreciation of property, plant and equipment	(2,000)
Amortization of intangible assets	(500)
Investment income	3,000
Profit before taxation	16,500
Taxes on income	(4,000)
Profit	€ 12,500

The following additional information is relevant to the preparation of the statement of cash flows:

1. Equipment with a net book value of €7,500 and original cost of €10,500 was sold for €7,500.
2. All sales made by the company are credit sales.
3. The company received cash dividends (from investments) amounting to €3,000, recorded as income in the statement of comprehensive income for the year ended December 31, 2009.
4. The company declared and paid dividends of €12,000 to its shareholders.
5. Interest expense for the year 2009 was €2,000, which was fully paid during the year. All administration and selling expenses incurred were paid during the year 2009.
6. Income tax expense for the year 2009 was provided at €4,000, out of which the company paid €2,000 during 2009 as an estimate.

A worksheet can be prepared to ease the development of the statement of cash flows, as follows:

Cash Flow Worksheet

	2009	2008	Change	Operating	Investing	Financing	Cash and equivalents
Cash and equivalents	3,000	1,000	2,000				2,000
Accounts receivable	5,000	2,500	2,500	(2,500)			
Inventories	2,000	1,500	500	(500)			
Prepaid expenses	1,000	1,500	(500)	500			
Due from associates	19,000	19,000	0				
Property, plant, and equipment	7,000	16,500	(9,500)	2,000	7,500		
Accounts payable	5,000	12,500	7,500	(7,500)			
Income taxes payable	2,000	1,000	1,000	1,000			
Deferred taxes payable	3,000	2,000	1,000	1,000			
Share capital	6,500	6,500	0				
Retained earnings	20,500	20,000	500	9,500	3,000	(12,000)	--
				3,500	10,500	(12,000)	2,000

ABC (Eurasia) Ltd.
Statement of Cash Flows
For the Year Ended December 31, 2009
(Direct method)

Cash flows from operating activities

Cash receipts from customers	€ 27,500	
Cash paid to suppliers and employees	(20,000)	
Cash generated from operations	7,500	
Interest paid	(2,000)	
Income taxes paid	(2,000)	
Net cash flows from operating activities		€ 3,500

Cash flows from investing activities

Proceeds from the sale of equipment	7,500	
Dividends received	3,000	
Net cash flows from investing activities		10,500

Cash flows from financing activities

Dividends paid	(12,000)	
Net cash flows used in financing activities		(12,000)
Net increase in cash and cash equivalents		2,000
Cash and cash equivalents, beginning of year		1,000
Cash and cash equivalents, end of year		€ 3,000

Details of the computations of amounts shown in the statement of cash flows are as follows:

Cash received from customers during the year

Credit sales	30,000	
Plus: Accounts receivable, beginning of year	2,500	
Less: Accounts receivable, end of year	(5,000)	
Cash received from customers during the year		€27,500

Cash paid to suppliers and employees

Cost of sales	10,000	
Less: Inventory, beginning of year	(1,500)	
Plus: Inventory, end of year	2,000	
Plus: Accounts payable, beginning of year	12,500	
Less: Accounts payable, end of year	(5,000)	
Plus: Administrative and selling expenses paid	2,000	
Cash paid to suppliers and employees during the year		€20,000
Interest paid equals interest expense charged to profit or loss (per additional information)		€ 2,000

Income taxes paid during the year

Tax expense during the year (comprising current and deferred portions)	4,000	
Plus: Beginning income taxes payable	1,000	
Plus: Beginning deferred taxes payable	2,000	
Less: Ending income taxes payable	(2,000)	
Less: Ending deferred taxes payable	(3,000)	
Cash paid toward income taxes		€ 2,000
Proceeds from sale of equipment (per additional information)		€ 7,500
Dividends received during 2009 (per additional information)		€ 3,000
Dividends paid during 2009 (per additional information)		€12,000

ABC (Eurasia) Ltd.
Statement of Cash Flows
For the Year Ended December 31, 2009
(Indirect method)

Cash flows from operating activities

Profit before taxation	€ 16,500	
Adjustments for:		
Depreciation of property, plant and equipment	2,000	
Decrease in prepaid expenses	500	
Investment income	(3,000)	
Interest expense	2,000	
Increase in accounts receivable	(2,500)	
Increase in inventories	(500)	
Decrease in accounts payable	(7,500)	
Cash generated from operations	7,500	
Interest paid	(2,000)	
Income taxes paid	(2,000)	
Net cash from operating activities		3,500

Cash flows from investing activities

Proceeds from sale of equipment	7,500	
Dividends received	3,000	

Net cash from investing activities	10,500
Cash flows from financing activities	
Dividends paid	(12,000)
Net cash used in financing activities	(12,000)
Net increase in cash and cash equivalents	2,000
Cash and cash equivalents, beginning of year	1,000
Cash and cash equivalents, end of year	€ 3,000

A Comprehensive Example of the Preparation of the Statement of Cash Flows Using the T-Account Approach

Under a cash and cash equivalents basis, the changes in the cash account and any cash equivalent account is the bottom line figure of the statement of cash flows. Using the 2008 and 2009 statements of financial position shown below, an increase of €17,000 can be computed. This is the difference between the totals for cash and cash equivalents between 2008 and 2009 (€33,000 – €16,000).

When preparing the statement of cash flows using the direct method, gross cash inflows from revenues and gross cash outflows to suppliers and for expenses are presented in the operating activities section.

In preparing the reconciliation of net profit (or loss) before taxation to net cash flow from operating activities (indirect method), changes in all accounts other than cash and cash equivalents that are related to operations are additions to or deductions from profit to arrive at net cash provided by operating activities.

A T-account analysis may be helpful when preparing the statement of cash flows. A T-account is set up for each account, and beginning (2008) and ending (2009) balances are taken from the appropriate statement of financial position. Additionally, a T-account for cash and cash equivalents from operating activities and a master or summary T-account of cash and cash equivalents should be used.

Example of preparing a statement of cash flows

The financial statements will be used to prepare the statement of cash flows.

Johnson Company
Statements of Financial Position
December 31, 2009 and 2008

	2009	*2008*
Assets		
Current assets:		
Cash and cash equivalents	€ 33,000	€ 16,000
Accounts receivable—net	9,000	11,000
Inventory	14,000	9,000
Prepaid expenses	10,000	13,000
Total current assets	€ 66,000	€ 49,000
Noncurrent assets:		
Investment in XYZ (35%)	16,000	14,000
Patent	5,000	6,000
Leased asset	5,000	--
Property, plant, and equipment	39,000	37,000
Less accumulated depreciation	(7,000)	(3,000)
Total assets	€124,000	€103,000
Liabilities		
Current liabilities:		
Accounts payable	€ 2,000	€ 12,000
Notes payable—current	9,000	--
Interest payable	3,000	2,000
Dividends payable	5,000	2,000
Income taxes payable	2,000	1,000

	2009	2008
Lease obligation	700	--
Total current liabilities	21,700	17,000
Noncurrent liabilities:		
Deferred tax liability	9,000	6,000
Bonds payable	10,000	25,000
Lease obligation	4,300	--
Total liabilities	€ 45,000	€ 48,000
Shareholders' equity		
Ordinary share $10 par value	€ 33,000	€ 26,000
Additional paid-in capital	16,000	3,000
Retained earnings	30,000	26,000
Total shareholders' equity	€ 79,000	€ 55,000
Total liabilities and shareholders' equity	€124,000	€103,000

Johnson Company
Statement of Comprehensive Income
For the Year Ended December 31, 2009

Sales	€100,000
Other income	8,000
	€108,000
Cost of goods sold, excluding depreciation	60,000
Selling, general, and administrative expenses	12,000
Depreciation	8,000
Amortization of patents	1,000
Interest expense	2,000
	€ 83,000
Income before taxes	€ 25,000
Income taxes (36%)	9,000
Profit	€ 16,000

Additional information (relating to 2009)

1. Equipment costing €6,000 with a book value of €2,000 was sold for €5,000.
2. The company received a €3,000 dividend from its investment in XYZ, accounted for under the equity method and recorded income from the investment of €5,000, which is included in other income.
3. The company issued 200 ordinary shares for €5,000.
4. The company signed a note payable for €9,000.
5. Equipment was purchased for €8,000.
6. The company converted €15,000 bonds payable into 500 ordinary shares. The book value method was used to record the transaction.
7. A dividend of €12,000 was declared.
8. Equipment was leased on December 31, 2009. The principal portion of the first payment due December 31, 2009, is €700.

Summary of Cash and Cash Equivalent					Cash and Cash Equivalents—Oper. Act.		
	Inflows	Outflows			(a)	16,000	
(d)	5,000	8,000	(g)		(b)	8,000	
(h)	5,000	9,000	(i)		(c)	1,000	3,000 (d)
(n)	9,000				(e)	3,000	5,000 (f)
(s)	15,000				(f)	3,000	
	34,000	17,000			(j)	2,000	5,000 (k)
		17,000	Net increase in cash		(l)	3,000	10,000 (m)
	34,000	34,000			(o)	1,000	
					(p)	1,000	
						38,000	23,000
							15,000 (s)
						38,000	38,000

Accounts Receivable (Net)				Inventory				Prepaid Expenses		
11,000				9,000				13,000		
		2,000 (j)	(k)	5,000						3,000 (l)
9,000				14,000				10,000		

Investment in XYZ				Patent				Leased Equipment		
	14,000			6,000			(r)	5,000		
(f)	5,000	3,000 (f)			1,000 (c)			5,000		
	16,000			5,000						

Prop., Plant, & Equip.				Accumulated Depr.				Accounts Payable		
	37,000				3,000					12,000
		6,000 (d)			8,000 (b)		(m)	10,000		
(g)	8,000		(d)	4,000						2,000
	39,000				7,000					

Notes Payable				Interest Payable				Dividends Payable		
					2,000					2,000
		9,000 (n)	(o)	1,000	2,000 (o)		(i)	9,000	12,000 (i)
		9,000			3,000					5,000

Income Taxes Payable				Deferred Tax Liability				Bonds Payable		
		1,000			6,000					25,000
(p)	5,000	6,000 (p)			3,000 (e)		(q)	15,000	
		2,000			9,000					10,000

Lease Obligation				Ordinary Share		
		5,000 (r)			26,000	
		5,000			2,000 (h)	
					5,000 (q)	
					33,000	

Additional Paid-in Capital				Retained Earnings		
		3,000			26,000	
		3,000 (h)			16,000 (a)	
		10,000 (q)	(i)	12,000		
		16,000			30,000	

Explanation of entries

a. Cash and Cash Equivalents—Operating Activities is debited for €16,000, and credited to Retained Earnings. This represents the amount of profit.

b. Depreciation is not a cash flow; however, depreciation expense was deducted to arrive at profit. Therefore, Accumulated Depreciation is credited and Cash and Cash Equivalents—Operating Activities is debited.

c. Amortization of patents is another expense not requiring cash; therefore, Cash and Cash Equivalents—Operating Activities is debited and Patent is credited.

d. The sale of equipment (additional information, item 1.) resulted in a €3,000 gain. The gain is computed by comparing the book value of €2,000 with the sales price of €5,000. Cash proceeds of €5,000 are an inflow of cash. Since the gain was included in profit, it must be deducted from profit to determine cash provided by operating activities. This is necessary to avoid counting the €3,000 gain both in cash provided by operating activities and in investing activities. The following entry would have been made on the date of sale:

Cash	5,000	
Accumulated depreciation (6,000 – 2,000)	4,000	
Property, plant, and equipment		6,000
Gain on sale of equipment (5,000 – 2,000)		3,000

Adjust the T-accounts as follows: debit Summary of Cash and Cash Equivalents for €5,000, debit Accumulated Depreciation for €4,000, credit Property, Plant, and Equipment for €6,000, and credit Cash and Cash Equivalents—Operating Activities for €3,000.

e.   The €3,000 increase in Deferred Income Taxes must be added to profit. Although the €3,000 was deducted as part of income tax expense in determining profit, it did not require an outflow of cash. Therefore, debit Cash and Cash Equivalents—Operating Activities and credit Deferred Taxes.

f.   Item 2. under the additional information indicates that the investment in XYZ is accounted for under the equity method. The investment in XYZ had a net increase of €2,000 during the year after considering the receipt of a €3,000 dividend. Dividends received (an inflow of cash) would reduce the investment in XYZ, while the equity in profit or loss XYZ would increase the investment without affecting cash. In order for the T-account to balance, a debit of €5,000 must have been made, indicating profits of that amount. The journal entries would have been

Cash (dividend received)	3,000	
Investment in XYZ		3,000
Investment in XYZ	5,000	
Equity in profit of XYZ		5,000

The dividend received (€3,000) is an inflow of cash, while the equity in profit of XYZ are not. Debit Investment in XYZ for €5,000, credit Cash and Cash Equivalents—Operating Activities for €5,000, debit Cash and Cash Equivalents—Operating Activities for €3,000, and credit Investment in XYZ for €3,000.

g.   The Property, Plant, and Equipment account increased because of the purchase of €8,000 (additional information, item 5.). The purchase of assets is an outflow of cash. Debit Property, Plant, and Equipment for €8,000 and credit Summary of Cash and Cash Equivalents.

h.   The company sold 200 ordinary shares during the year (additional information, item 3.). The entry for the sale of stock was

Cash	5,000	
Ordinary share (200 shares × €10)		2,000
Additional paid-in capital		3,000

This transaction resulted in an inflow of cash. Debit Summary of Cash and Cash Equivalents €5,000, credit Ordinary Share €2,000, and credit Additional Paid-in Capital €3,000.

i.   Dividends of €12,000 were declared (additional information, item 7.). Only €9,000 was actually paid in cash resulting in an ending balance of €9,000 in the Dividends Payable account. Therefore, the following entries were made during the year:

Retained Earnings	12,000	
Dividends Payable		12,000
Dividends Payable	9,000	
Cash		9,000

These transactions result in an outflow of cash. Debit Retained Earnings €12,000 and credit Dividends Payable €12,000. Additionally, debit Dividends Payable €9,000 and credit Summary of Cash and Cash Equivalents €9,000 to indicate the cash dividends paid during the year.

j.   Accounts Receivable (net) decreased by €2,000. This is added as an adjustment to profit in the computation of cash provided by operating activities. The decrease of €2,000 means that an additional €2,000 cash was collected on account above and beyond the sales reported in the statement of comprehensive income. Debit Cash and Cash Equivalents—Operating Activities and credit Accounts Receivable for €2,000.

k.   Inventories increased by €5,000. This is subtracted as an adjustment to profit in the computation of cash provided by operating activities. Although €5,000 additional cash was spent to increase inventories, this expenditure is not reflected in accrual-basis cost of goods sold. Debit Inventory and credit Cash and Cash Equivalents—Operating Activities for €5,000.

l.   Prepaid Expenses decreased by €3,000. This is added back to profit in the computation of cash provided by operating activities. The decrease means that no cash was spent when incurring the related expense. The cash was spent when the prepaid assets were purchased, not when they were recorded as expenses in the statement of comprehensive income. Debit Cash and Cash Equivalents—Operating Activities and credit Prepaid Expenses for €3,000.

m.   Accounts Payable decreased by $10,000. This is subtracted as an adjustment to profit. The decrease of €10,000 means that an additional €10,000 of purchases were paid for in cash; therefore, income was not affected but cash was decreased. Debit Accounts Payable and credit Cash and Cash Equivalents—Operating Activities for €10,000.

n.   Notes Payable increased by €9,000 (additional information, item 4.). This is an inflow of cash and would be included in the financing activities. Debit Summary of Cash and Cash Equivalents and credit Notes Payable for €9,000.

o.   Interest Payable increased by €1,000, but interest expense from the statement of comprehensive income was €2,000. Therefore, although €2,000 was expensed, only €1,000 cash was paid (€2,000 expense – €1,000 increase in interest payable). Debit Cash and Cash Equivalents—Operating Activities for €1,000, debit Interest Payable for €1,000, and credit Interest Payable for €2,000.

p.   The following entry was made to record the incurrence of the tax liability:

Income tax expense	9,000	
Income taxes payable		6,000
Deferred tax liability		3,000

Therefore, €9,000 was deducted in arriving at profit. The €3,000 credit to Deferred Income Taxes was accounted for in entry (e) above. The €6,000 credit to Taxes Payable does not, however, indicate that €6,000 cash was paid for taxes. Since Taxes Payable increased €1,000, only €5,000 must have been paid and €1,000 remains unpaid. Debit Cash and Cash Equivalents—Operating Activities for €1,000, debit Income Taxes Payable for €5,000, and credit Income Taxes Payable for €6,000.

q.   Item 6. under the additional information indicates that €15,000 of bonds payable were converted to ordinary share. This is a *noncash* financing activity and should be reported in a separate schedule. The following entry was made to record the transaction:

Bonds payable	15,000	
Ordinary share (500 shares × €10 par)		5,000
Additional paid-in capital		10,000

Adjust the T-accounts with a debit to Bonds Payable, €15,000; a credit to Ordinary Share, €5,000; and a credit to Additional Paid-in Capital, €10,000.

r.   Item 8. under the additional information indicates that leased equipment was acquired on the last day of 2008. This is also a noncash financing activity and should be reported in a separate schedule. The following entry was made to record the lease transaction:

Leased asset	5,000	
Lease obligation		5,000

s.   The cash and cash equivalents from operations (€15,000) is transferred to the Summary of Cash and Cash Equivalents.

Since all of the changes in the noncash accounts have been accounted for and the balance in the Summary of Cash and Cash Equivalents account of €17,000 is the amount of the year-to-year increase in cash and cash equivalents, the formal statement may now be prepared. The following classified SCF is prepared under the direct method and includes the reconciliation of profit before taxation to net cash provided by operating activities. The T-account, Cash and Cash Equivalents—Operating Activities, is used in the preparation of this reconciliation. The calculations for gross receipts and gross payments needed for the direct method are shown below.

Johnson Company
Statement of Cash Flows
For the Year Ended December 31, 2009

Cash flows from operating activities			
Cash received from customers	€102,000	(a)	
Dividends received	3,000		
Cash provided by operating activities			€105,000
Cash paid to suppliers	€ 75,000	(b)	
Cash paid for expenses	9,000	(c)	
Interest paid	1,000	(d)	
Taxes paid	5,000	(e)	
Cash paid for operating activities			(90,000)
Net cash provided by operating activities			€ 15,000
Cash flows from investing activities			
Sale of equipment	5,000		
Purchase of property, plant, and equipment	(8,000)		
Net cash used in investing activities			(3,000)
Cash flows from financing activities			
Sale of ordinary share	€ 5,000		
Increase in notes payable	9,000		
Dividends paid	(9,000)		
Net cash provided by financing activities			5,000
Net increase in cash and cash equivalents			€ 17,000
Cash and cash equivalents at beginning of year			16,000
Cash and cash equivalents at end of year			€ 33,000

Calculation of amounts for operating activities section of Johnson Co.'s statement of cash flows

(a)   Net sales + Beginning AR – Ending AR = Cash received from customers

    €100,000 + €11,000 – €9,000 = €102,000

(b)   Cost of goods sold + Beginning AP – Ending AP + Ending inventory – Beginning inventory = Cash paid to suppliers

    €60,000 + €12,000 – €2,000 + €14,000 – €9,000 = €75,000

(c)   Operating expenses + Ending prepaid expenses – Beginning prepaid expenses – Depreciation expense (and other noncash operating expenses) = Cash paid for operating expenses

    €12,000 + €10,000 – €13,000 = €9,000

(d)   Interest expense + Beginning interest payable – Ending interest payable = Interest paid

    €2,000 + €2,000 – €3,000 = €1,000

(e)   Income taxes + Beginning income taxes payable – Ending income taxes payable + Beginning deferred income taxes – Ending deferred income taxes = Taxes paid

    €9,000 + €1,000 – €2,000 + €6,000 – €9,000 = €5,000

Reconciliation of profit to net cash provided by operating activities

Profit before taxation	€16,000	
Add (deduct) items not using (providing) cash:		
Depreciation	8,000	
Amortization	1,000	
Gain on sale of equipment	(3,000)	
Increase in deferred taxes	3,000	
Equity in XYZ	(2,000)	
Decrease in accounts receivable	2,000	
Increase in inventory	(5,000)	
Decrease in prepaid expenses	3,000	
Decrease in accounts payable	(10,000)	
Increase in interest payable	1,000	
Increase in income taxes payable	1,000	
Net cash provided by operating activities		€15,000

(The reconciliation above is required by US GAAP when the direct method is used, but there is *no equivalent requirement* under IFRS. The reconciliation above illustrates the presentation of the operating section of the statement of cash flows when the indirect method is used. The remaining sections [i.e., the investing and financing sections] of the statement of cash flows are common to both methods, hence have not been presented above.)

Schedule of noncash transactions (to be reported in the footnotes)

Conversion of bonds into ordinary share	€15,000
Acquisition of leased equipment	€ 5,000

Disclosure of accounting policy

For purposes of the statement of cash flows, the company considers all highly liquid debt instruments purchased with original maturities of three months or less to be cash equivalents.

Statement of Cash Flows for Consolidated Entities

A consolidated statement of cash flows must be presented when a complete set of consolidated financial statements is issued. The consolidated statement of cash flows would be the last statement to be prepared, as the information to prepare it will come from the other consolidated statements (consolidated statement of financial position, statement of comprehensive income, and statement of changes in equity). The preparation of these other consolidated statements is discussed in Chapter 11.

The preparation of a consolidated statement of cash flows involves the same analysis and procedures as the statement for an individual entity, with a few additional items. The direct or indirect method of presentation may be used. When the indirect method is used, the additional noncash transactions relating to the business combination, such as the differential amortization, must also be reversed. Furthermore, all transfers to affiliates must be eliminated, as they do not represent a cash inflow or outflow of the consolidated entity.

All unrealized intercompany (intragroup) profits should have been eliminated in preparation of the other statements; thus, no additional entry of this sort should be required. Any profit allocated to noncontrolling parties would need to be added back, as it would have been eliminated in computing consolidated profit but does not represent a true cash outflow. Finally, any dividend payments should be recorded as cash outflows in the financing activities section.

In preparing the operating activities section of the statement by the indirect method following a purchase business combination, the changes in assets and liabilities related to operations since acquisition should be derived by comparing the consolidated statement of financial position as of the date of acquisition with the year-end consolidated statement of financial position. These changes will be combined with those for the acquiring company up to the date of acquisition as adjustments to profit. The effects due to the acquisition of these assets and liabilities are reported under investing activities. Under the pooling-of-interests method the combination is treated as having occurred at the beginning of the year. Thus, the changes in assets and liabilities related to operations should be those derived by comparing the beginning-of-the-year statement of financial position amounts on a consolidated basis with the end-of-the-year consolidated statement of financial position amounts.

Discussion Paper: Preliminary Views on Financial Statement Presentation

The IASB and the FASB have jointly published for comment a Discussion Paper (DP), *Preliminary Views on Financial Statement Presentation*, in October, 2008. A principles-based format for presenting financial statements in a manner that clearly communicates an integrated financial picture of the entity is proposed. The project is about how best to portray assets, liabilities, income, expense, cash flows and related information in financial statements.

In the statement of cash flows, the Boards recommend a direct method of preparing cash flows from operating activities rather than reconciling profit or loss or net income to net operating cash flows (an indirect method). The direct method is more consistent than an indirect method with the proposed objectives of financial statement presentation.

The new proposed financial statement presentation model includes a new schedule that reconciles cash flows to comprehensive income which should be included in the notes to financial statements. This reconciliation schedule disaggregates income into its cash, accruals other than remeasurements, and remeasurement components (for example, fair value changes), which can help users in predicting future cash flows and assessing earnings quality.

Example of cash flow reporting under IFRS

Nokia Corporation and Subsidiaries
Consolidated Statement Cash Flows
For the Years Ended December 31, 2007, 2006, and 2005

	Notes	*2007 EURm*	*2006 EURm*	*2005 EURm*
Cash flow from operating activities:				
Net profit		7,205	4,306	3,616
Adjustments total	32	1,269	1,857	1,774
Net profit before change in net working capital		8,474	6,163	5,390
Change in net working capital	32	605	(793)	(366)
Cash generated from operations		9,079	5,370	5,024
Interest received		362	235	353
Interest paid		(59)	(18)	(26)
Other financial income and expenses, net received		(43)	54	47
Income taxes paid		(1,457)	(1,163)	(1,254)
Net cash from operating activities		7,882	4,478	4,144
Cash flow from investing activities:				
Acquisition of Group companies, net of acquired cash		253	(517)	(92)
Purchase of current available-for-sale investments, liquid assets		(4,798)	(3,219)	(7,277)
Purchase of noncurrent available-for-sale investments		(126)	(88)	(89)
Purchase of shares in associated companies		(25)	(15)	(16)
Additions to capitalized development costs		(157)	(127)	(153)
Long-term loans made to customers		(261)	(11)	(56)
Proceeds from repayment and sale of long-term loans receivable		163	56	--
Proceeds from (+)/payment of (–) other long-term receivables		5	(3)	14
Proceeds from (+)/payment of (–) short-term loans receivable		(119)	199	182
Capital expenditures		(715)	(650)	(607)
Proceeds from disposal of shares in Group companies, net of disposed cash		--	--	5
Proceeds from disposal of shares in associated companies		6	1	18
Proceeds from disposal of businesses		--	--	95
Proceeds from maturities and sale of current available-for-sale investments, liquid assets		4,930	5,058	9,402
Proceeds from sale of current available-for-sale investments		--	--	247
Proceeds from sale of noncurrent available-for-sale investments		50	17	3
Proceeds from sale of fixed assets		72	29	167
Dividends received		12	--	1
Net cash used in investing activities		(710)	1,006	1,844

	Notes	2007 EURm	2006 EURm	2005 EURm
Cash flow from financing activities:				
Proceeds from stock option exercises		987	46	2
Purchase of treasury shares		(3,819)	(3,371)	(4,258)
Proceeds from long-term borrowings		115	56	5
Repayment of long-term borrowings		(16)	(7)	--
Repayment of short-term borrowings		661	(137)	212
Dividends paid		(1,760)	(1,553)	(1,531)
Net cash (used) in financing activities		(3,832)	(4,966)	(5,570)
Foreign exchange adjustment		(15)	(51)	183
Net increase (+)/decrease (–) in cash and cash equivalents		3,325	467	601
Cash and cash equivalents at beginning of period		3,525	3,058	2,457
Cash and cash equivalents at end of period		6,850	3,525	3,058
Cash and cash equivalents comprise of:				
Bank and cash		2,125	1,479	1,565
Current available-for sale investments, cash equivalents	15, 35	4,725	2,046	1,493
		6,850	3,525	3,058

See Notes to Consolidated Financial Statements.

The figures in the consolidated statement of cash flows cannot be directly traced from the statement of financial position without additional information as a result of acquisitions and disposals of subsidiaries and net foreign exchange differences arising on consolidation.

5 CASH, RECEIVABLES, AND FINANCIAL INSTRUMENTS

PERSPECTIVE AND ISSUES

Cash and receivables meet the definition of financial instruments under IFRS. The accounting for financial instruments has received a great deal of attention from the IASC—being the subject of its two most voluminous and controversial standards—and continued attention is a certainty. The original intent, which was to address all matters of recognition, measurement, derecognition, presentation, and disclosure in a single comprehensive standard, proved to be unworkable (as was also the case under US GAAP), and thus matters have been dealt with piecemeal. The first standard, IAS 32, which became effective in 1996 and has most recently been revised effective 2005, addressed only presentation and disclosure. The disclosure requirements set forth in IAS 32 have been removed from that standard, effective 2007, and are now incorporated into IFRS 7, which also includes the financial institution disclosure requirements previously set forth by IAS 30. IFRS 7 is discussed in detail in this chapter.

The more intractable problems of recognition, measurement, and derecognition were dealt with by IAS 39, which became mandatory in 2001. IAS 39 has been amended several times in the past two years, largely as IASB struggled to gain EU acceptance for IFRS and a number of highly specific financial instruments-related concerns had to be resolved. IAS 39 was intended as only an interim standard, since it failed to comprehensively embrace fair value accounting for all financial assets and liabilities, which had been held out as the goal to which the IASC was committed at the time. Fair value accounting, particularly for liabilities, was and remains a controversial topic. Subsequent to IAS 39's promulgation, IASB has indicated that any decision to impose comprehensive fair value accounting for financial assets and liabilities is likely to be several years in the future, at best, and must be viewed as a longer-term objective.

IAS 39 established extensive new requirements for the recognition, derecognition, and measurement of financial assets and liabilities, and furthermore addressed, for the first time, special hedge accounting procedures to be applied under defined sets of circumstances. Hedging has become an increasingly common business risk management practice, but had previously created serious accounting anomalies not addressed by professional standards. Hedge accounting is designed to improve the matching of recognition of related gains and losses in the statement of comprehensive income, and is made necessary by the use of a "mixed attribute" accounting model, whereby some assets and liabilities are reported at (amortized) historical costs, and others are reported at fair values. Hedge accounting for financial assets and liabilities would be neither appropriate nor necessary, therefore, if all of these assets and liabilities were simply carried at fair value. While this has been stated as the ultimate goal of IFRS, it appears that it is at least several years away from being mandated, at the minimum.

Because of the complexity of IAS 39, a number of difficult implementation issues needed to be addressed, and in response the IASC constituted an IAS 39 Implementation Guidance Committee (IGC). Several hundred questions and answers were published by this committee, and a compendium of guidance was produced in connection with the 2003 revisions to IAS 39. More recently, however, much of the guidance formerly found in materials prepared by the IGC and also in certain of the Interpretations promulgated by SIC have been directly incorporated into revised IAS 32 and IAS 39 (revised 2004, effective 2005).

In this chapter, the overall requirements of IAS 32 and 39, and IFRS 7 will be set forth, while detailed application of IAS 39 is set forth in Chapter 10. In addition, this chapter will present detailed examples on a range of topics involving cash and receivables (e.g., the accounting for factored receivables) that are derived from the most widespread and venerable practices in these areas, even if not codified in the IAS.

Sources of IFRS		
IAS 1, 32, 39	*IFRS* 7	*IFRIC* 2, 9, 10

DEFINITIONS OF TERMS

Accounts receivable. Amounts due from customers for goods or services provided in the normal course of business operations.

Aging the accounts. Procedure for the computation of the adjustment for uncollectible accounts receivable based on the length of time the end-of-period outstanding accounts have been unpaid.

Amortized cost of financial asset or financial liability. The amount at which the asset or liability was measured at original recognition, minus principal repayments, plus or minus the cumulative amortization of any premium or discount, and minus any write-down for impairment or uncollectibility.

Assignment. Formal procedure for collateralization of borrowings through the use of accounts receivable. It normally does not involve debtor notification.

Available-for-sale financial assets. Those nonderivative financial assets that are designated as available for sale or are not classified as (1) loans and receivables, (2) held to maturity investments, or (3) financial assets at fair value through profit or loss (held for trading, and those designated as at fair value through profit or loss upon initial recognition).

Carrying amount (value). The amount at which an asset is presented in the statement of financial position. For marketable equity instruments, this is fair value.

Cash. Cash on hand and demand deposits with banks or other financial institutions.

Cash equivalents. Short-term, highly liquid investments that are readily convertible to known amounts of cash and which are subject to an insignificant risk of changes in value. Examples include Treasury bills, commercial paper, and money market funds.

Control. The ability to direct the strategic financing and operating policies of an entity so as to access benefits flowing from the entity and increase, maintain, or protect the amount of those benefits.

Credit risk. The risk that a loss may occur from the failure of another party to a financial instrument to discharge an obligation according to the terms of a contract.

Current assets. An asset should be classified as current when it satisfies any of the following criteria: (1) it is expected to be realized in, or is intended for sale or consumption in, the entity's normal operating cycle; (2) it is held primarily for the purpose of being traded; (3) it is expected to be realized within twelve months after the reporting period; or (4) it is cash or cash equivalent unless it is restricted from being exchanged or used to settle a liability for at least twelve months after the reporting period.

Derecognition. Removal of a previously recognized financial asset or liability from an entity's statement of financial position.

Derivative. A financial instrument or other contract with all three of the following characteristics: (1) whose value changes in response to changes in a specified interest rate, security price, commodity price, foreign exchange rate, index of prices or rates, a credit rating or credit index, or other variable, provided in the case of a nonfinancial variable that the variable is not specific to a party to the contract (sometimes called the "underlying" or "cash" position), (2) that requires little or no initial net investment relative to other types of contracts that have a similar response to changes in market conditions, and (3) that is settled at a future date.

Effective interest method. A method of calculating the amortized cost of a financial asset or a financial liability (or group of financial instruments) and of allocating the interest income or interest expense over the relevant period. The effective interest rate used in the allocation process is the rate that exactly discounts estimated future cash flows (receipts or payments) to the net carrying amount of the financial instrument through the expected life of this instrument (or a shorter period, when appropriate).

Equity instrument. Any contract that evidences a residual interest in the assets of an entity after deducting all its liabilities.

Factoring. Outright sale of accounts receivable to a third-party financing entity. The sale may be with or without recourse.

Fair value. Amount for which an asset could be exchanged, or a liability settled, between knowledgeable willing parties in an arm's-length transaction.

Fair value through profit or loss option. An option in IAS 39 that permits an entity to irrevocably designate any financial asset or financial liability, but only upon its initial recognition, as one to be measured at fair value, with changes in fair value recognized in current profit or loss.

Financial asset. Any asset that is

1. Cash
2. An equity instrument of another entity
3. A contractual right

    a. To receive cash or another financial asset from another entity, or
    b. To exchange financial instruments with another entity under conditions that are potentially favorable

4. A contract that will be settled in the reporting entity's own equity instruments and is

    a. A nonderivative for which the entity is or may be obligated to receive a variable number of its own equity instruments, or
    b. A derivative that will or may be settled other than by the exchange of a fixed amount of cash or another financial asset for a fixed number of the entity's own equity instruments (which excludes instruments that are themselves contracts for the future receipt or delivery of the entity's equity instruments)

Financial assets (categories). Include the following four principal categories (1) those at fair value through profit or loss (held for trading, and those designated as at fair value through profit or loss [FVTPL] upon initial recognition); (2) available for sale; (3) held-to-maturity; and (4) loans and receivables originated by the entity. The following cannot be included within one of the four principal categories of financial assets, and must be measured at cost (1) investments in equity instruments which do not have quoted prices in active markets and whose value cannot be reliably measured, and (2) derivatives linked to and settled by delivery of unquoted equity instruments.

Financial asset or liability reported at fair value through current profit or loss. One which *either* is acquired or incurred for trading (i.e., is principally for the purpose of generating a profit from short-term fluctuations in price or dealer's margin, or which is part of identified commonly managed financial instruments and for which there is a pattern of short-term profit-taking by the entity, or which is a derivative unless designated for, and effective as, a hedging instrument) or upon initial recognition is designated for carrying at fair value through current profit or loss.

Fair value through profit or loss option. An option in IAS 39 that permits an entity to irrevocably designate any financial asset or financial liability, but only upon its initial recognition, as one to be measured at fair value, with changes in fair value recognized in current profit or loss.

Financial guarantee contract. A contract that requires the issuer to make specified payments to reimburse the holder for losses incurred because a specified debtor failed to make payment when due based on the original or modified terms of a debt instrument.

Financial instrument. Any contract that gives rise to both a financial asset of one entity and a financial liability or equity instrument of another entity.

Financial liability. Any liability that is

1. A contractual obligation

    a. To deliver cash or another financial asset to another entity
    b. To exchange financial instruments with another entity under conditions that are potentially unfavorable to the entity

2. A contract that will or may be settled in the entity's own equity instruments and is

    a. A nonderivative for which the entity is or may be obligated to deliver a variable number of its own equity instruments, or
    b. A derivative that will or may be settled other than by the exchange of a fixed amount of cash or another financial asset for a fixed number of the entity's own equity instruments (which excludes instruments that are themselves contracts for the future receipt or delivery of the entity's equity instruments)

Firm commitment. A binding agreement for the exchange of a specified quantity of resources at a specified price on a specified future date or dates.

Hedge effectiveness. The degree to which changes in the fair value or cash flows of the hedged item that are attributable to a hedged risk are offset by changes in the fair value or cash flows of the hedging instrument.

Hedged item. An asset, liability, firm commitment, highly probable forecast transaction or net investment in a foreign operation that (1) exposes the entity to risk of changes in fair value or future cash flows, and (2) is designated as being hedged.

Hedging. Designating one or more hedging instruments such that the change in fair value or cash flows of the hedging instrument is an offset, in whole or part, to the change in fair value or cash flows of the hedged item. The objective is to ensure that the gain or loss on the hedging instrument is recognized in profit or loss in the same period that the hedged item affects profit or loss. Types of hedges are (1) fair value, (2) cash flow, and (3) net investment.

Hedging instrument. For hedge accounting purposes, a designated derivative or (for a hedge of the risk of changes in foreign currency exchange rates only) a designated nonderivative financial asset or nonderivative financial liability whose fair value or cash flows are expected to offset changes in the fair value or cash flows of a designated hedged item.

Held-to-maturity investments. Nonderivative financial assets with fixed or determinable payments and fixed maturities, that the entity has the positive intent and ability to hold to maturity, except for (1) those at fair value through profit or loss (held for trading, and those designated as at fair value through profit or loss upon initial recognition), (2) those designated as available for sale, and (3) loans and receivables. An entity should not classify any financial assets as held to maturity if the entity has, during the current financial year or during the two preceding financial years, sold or reclassified more than an insignificant amount (in relation to the total amount of held-to-maturity investments) of held-to-maturity investments before maturity.

Liquidity risk. The risk that an entity may encounter difficulty in meeting obligations associated with financial liabilities.

Loans and receivables. Nonderivative financial assets with fixed or determinable payments that are not quoted in an active market, other than (1) held for trading, and those upon initial recognition designated as at fair value through profit or loss, (2) those designated as available for sale, and (3) those which the holder may not recover substantially all of its initial investment (other than because of credit deterioration), which should be classified as available for sale.

Market risk. The risk that the fair value or future cash flows of a financial instrument will fluctuate because of changes in market prices; it comprised three types of risk: currency risk, interest rate risk, and other price risk.

Market value. Amount obtainable from a sale, or payable on acquisition, of a financial instrument in an active market.

Marketable equity instruments. Instruments representing actual ownership interest, or the rights to buy or sell such interests, that are actively traded or listed on a national securities exchange.

Monetary financial assets and financial liabilities. Financial assets and financial liabilities to be received or paid in fixed or determinable amounts of money.

Net realizable value. Amount of cash anticipated to be produced in the normal course of business from an asset, net of any direct costs of the conversion into cash.

Operating cycle. Average time between the acquisition of materials or services and the final cash realization from the sale of products or services.

Other than temporary decline. Downward movement in the value of a marketable equity security for which there are known causes. The decline indicates the remote likelihood of a price recovery.

Percentage-of-sales method. Procedure for computing the adjustment for uncollectible accounts receivable based on the historical relationship between bad debts and gross credit sales.

Pledging. Process of using an asset as collateral for borrowings. It generally refers to borrowings secured by accounts receivable.

Realized gain (loss). Difference between the cost or adjusted cost of a marketable security and the net selling price realized by the seller, which is to be included in the determination of profit or loss in the period of the sale.

Recourse. Right of the transferee (factor) of accounts receivable to seek recovery for an uncollectible account from the transferor. It is often limited to specific conditions.

Repurchase agreement. An agreement to transfer a financial asset to another party in exchange for cash or other considerations, with a concurrent obligation to reacquire the asset at a future date for an amount equal to the cash or other consideration plus interest.

Risk of accounting loss. Includes (1) the possibility that a loss may occur from the failure of another party to perform according to the terms of a contract (credit risk), (2) the possibility that future changes in market prices may make a financial instrument less valuable (market risk), and (3) the risk of theft or physical loss.

Securitization. The process whereby financial assets are transformed into securities.

Short-term investments. Financial instruments or other assets acquired with excess cash, having ready marketability and intended by management to be liquidated, if necessary, within the current operating cycle.

Temporary decline. Downward fluctuation in the value of a marketable equity security that has no known cause which suggests that the decline is of a permanent nature.

Transaction costs. Incremental costs directly attributable to the acquisition or disposal of a financial asset or liability.

CONCEPTS, RULES, AND EXAMPLES

Cash

The only actual guidance to the accounting for cash offered by IFRS is that found in IAS 1. Common practice is to define cash as including currency on hand, as well as current and other accounts maintained with banks. However, cash that is not available for immediate use is normally given separate disclosure to prevent misleading implications. IAS 1 (as revised effective 2005) generally requires that statements of financial position be *classified* (i.e., that current and noncurrent assets and liabilities be grouped separately), unless presentation in the order of liquidity is deemed more reliable and relevant. If a classified statement of financial position is presented, cash which is restricted and not available for use within one year of the reporting period should be included in noncurrent assets. This guidance is not altered by the latest revision to IAS 1, which becomes effective for 2009 (see discussions in Chapters 2, 3, and 4).

For a current asset classification to be warranted, it must furthermore be management's intention that the cash be available for current purposes. For example, cash in a demand deposit account, being held specifically for the retirement of long-term debts not maturing currently, should be excluded from current assets and shown as a noncurrent investment. This would apply only if management's intention was clear; otherwise it would not be necessary to segregate from the general cash account the funds that presumably will be needed for a scheduled debt retirement, as those funds could presumably be obtained from alternative sources, including new borrowings.

It has become common for the caption "cash and cash equivalents" to appear in the statement of financial position. This term includes other forms of near-cash items as well as demand deposits and liquid, short-term instruments. To justify inclusion, however, cash equivalents must be available essentially upon demand (e.g., as investments which can be liquidated at once and with little risk of loss of principal). Consideration is being given to restricting the caption "cash" to only actual cash; any such limitation is not likely to be imposed within the next year, however.

In this regard, IAS 7 defines cash equivalents as short-term, highly liquid investments, readily convertible into known amounts of cash that are subject to an insignificant risk of changes in value. The reasonable, albeit arbitrary, limit of three months is placed on the maturity dates of any instruments acquired to be part of cash equivalents. (This is, not coincidentally, the same limit applied by the US standard on cash flow statements, FAS 95, promulgation of which preceded the revision of IAS 7 by several years.)

Compensating balances are cash amounts that are not immediately accessible by the owner. Pursuant to borrowing arrangements with lenders, an entity will often be required to maintain a minimum amount of cash on deposit (as a "compensating balance"). While stated to provide greater security for the loan, the actual purpose of this balance is to increase the yield on the loan to the lender. Since most organizations will need to maintain a certain working balance in their cash accounts simply to handle routine transactions and to cushion against unforeseen fluctuations in the demand for cash, borrowers often find compensating balance arrangements not objectionable and may well have sufficient liquidity to maintain these with little hardship being incurred. They may even be viewed as comprising "rotating" normal cash balances that are flowing into and out of the bank on a regular basis.

Notwithstanding how these are viewed by the debtor, however, the fact is that compensating balances are not available for unrestricted use, and penalties will result if they are withdrawn rather than being left intact, as called for under the arrangement. Therefore, the portion of an entity's cash account that is held as a compensating balance must be segregated and shown as a noncurrent asset if the related borrowings are noncurrent liabilities. If the borrowings are current liabilities, it is acceptable to show the compensating balance as a separately captioned current asset, but under no circumstances should these be included in the caption "cash."

In some jurisdictions, certain cash deposits held by banks, such as savings accounts or corporate time deposits, are subject to terms and conditions that might prevent immediate withdrawals. While not always exercised, these rights permit a delay in honoring withdrawal requests for a stated period of time, such as seven days or one month. These rules were instituted to discourage panic withdrawals and to give the depository institution adequate time to liquidate investments in an orderly fashion. Cash in savings accounts subject to a statutory notification requirement and cash in certificates of deposit maturing during the current operating cycle or within one year may be included as current assets, but as with compensating balances, should be separately captioned in the statement of financial position to avoid the misleading implication that these funds are available immediately upon demand. Typically, such items will be included in the short-term investments caption, but these could be separately labeled as time deposits or restricted cash deposits.

Petty cash and other imprest cash accounts are usually presented in financial statements with other cash accounts. Due to materiality considerations, under current rules these need not be set forth in a separate caption unless so desired.

Receivables

Receivables include trade receivables, which are amounts due from customers for goods sold or services performed in the normal course of business, as well as such other categories of receivables as notes receivable, trade acceptances, third-party instruments, and amounts due from officers, shareholders, employees, or affiliated companies.

Notes receivable are formalized obligations evidenced by written promissory notes. The latter categories of receivables generally arise from cash advances but could develop from sales of merchandise or the provision of services. The basic nature of amounts due from trade customers is often different from that of balances receivable from related parties, such as employees or shareholders. Thus, the general practice is to insist that the various classes of receivables be identified separately either on the face of the statement of financial position or in the notes. Revised IAS 1 does not explicitly require such presentation. Nonetheless, the authors believe that distinguishing among categories of receivables is an important financial reporting objective, and that the guidelines set forth in an earlier iteration of IAS 1 should continue to be observed.

IAS 39 addresses recognition and measurement of receivables. In addition, a number of international standards allude to the accounting for receivables. For example, IAS 18, *Revenue Recognition*, addresses the timing of revenue recognition, which implicitly addresses the timing of recognition of the resulting receivables.

If the gross amount of receivables includes unearned interest or finance charges, these should be deducted in arriving at the net amount to be presented in the statement of financial position. Deductions should be taken for amounts estimated to be uncollectible and also for the estimated returns, allowances, and other discounts to be taken by customers prior to or at the time of payment. In practice, the deductions that would be made for estimated returns, allowances, and trade discounts are usually deemed to be immaterial, and such adjustments are rarely made. However, if it is known that sales are often recorded for merchandise that is shipped on approval and available data suggests that a sizable proportion of such sales are returned by the customers, these estimated future returns must be accrued. Similarly, material amounts of anticipated discounts and allowances should be recorded in the period of sale.

The foregoing comments apply where revenues are recorded at the gross amount of the sale and subsequent sales discounts are recorded as debits (contra revenues). An alternative manner of recording revenue, which does away with any need to estimate future discounts, is to record the initial sale at the net amount; that is, at the amount that will be remitted if customers take advantage of the available discount terms. If customers pay the gross amount later (they fail to take the discounts), this additional revenue is recorded as income when it is remitted. The net method of recording sales, however, is rarely encountered in practice.

Bad Debt Expense

In theory, accruals should be made for anticipated sales returns, sales allowances, and discounts that pertain to sales already consummated as of the date of the financial statements. This is usually not done, however, because of materiality considerations. On the other hand, the recording of anticipated uncollectible amounts is almost always necessary, because these will be material to the presentation of the receivables in the statement of financial position and also to the determination of periodic profit or loss. The direct write-off method, in which a receivable is charged off only when it is clear that it cannot be collected, is unsatisfactory since it results in a significant mismatching of revenues and expenses, and will also cause the presentation of receivables in the statement of financial position at amounts that exceed fair (i.e., realizable) value. Proper matching can be achieved only if bad debts expense is recorded in the same fiscal period as the revenues to which they are related. Since this expense cannot be known with certainty, an estimate must be made.

There are two popular estimation techniques. The percentage-of-sales method is principally oriented toward achieving the most accurate matching between revenues and expenses. Aging the accounts, on the other hand, is more oriented toward the presentation of the correct net realizable value of the trade receivables in the statement of financial position. Both methods are acceptable and widely employed. However, with the ever-greater emphasis placed by accounting theory in the statement of financial position, one might argue that the aging of receivables (or equivalent) would be the most appropriate method to employ.

Percentage-of-sales method of estimating bad debts. Historical data are analyzed to ascertain the relationship between credit sales and bad debts. The derived percentage is then applied to the current period's sales revenues to arrive at the appropriate debit to bad debts expense for the year. The offsetting credit is made to allowance for uncollectible accounts. When specific customer accounts are subsequently identified as uncollectible, they are written off against this allowance.

Example of percentage-of-sales method

Total credit sales for year:	€7,500,000
Bad debt ratio from prior years or other data source:	× 1.75% of sales
Computed year-end adjustment for bad debts expense:	€131,250

The entry required is

Bad debts expense	131,250	
Allowance for uncollectibles		131,250

Note that the foregoing entry assumes that no bad debts expense has yet been recognized with respect to the year's credit sales. If some such expense has already been recognized, as a consequence of interim accruals, for example, the final adjusting entry would be suitably reduced.

Aging method of estimating bad debts. An analysis is prepared of the customer receivables at the date of the statement of financial position. These accounts are categorized by the number of days or months they have remained outstanding. Based on the entity's past experience or on other available statistics, historical bad debts percentages are applied to each of these aggregate amounts, with larger percentages being applicable to the older accounts. The end result of this process is a computed total dollar amount that is the proper balance in the allowance for uncollectible receivables as of the date of the statement of financial position. As a result of the difference between the previous years' adjustments to the allowance for uncollectible accounts and the actual write-offs made to the account, there will usually be a balance in this account. Thus, the adjustment needed will be an amount other than that computed by the aging.

Example of the aging method

	Under 30 days	Age of accounts 30-90 days	Over 90 days	Total
Gross receivables	€1,100,000	€425,000	€360,000	
Bad debt percentage	0.5%	2.5%	15%	
Provision required	€5,500	€10,625	€54,000	€70,125

The credit balance required in the allowance account is €70,125. Assuming that a debit balance of €58,250 already exists in the allowance account (from charge-offs during the year), the necessary entry is

Bad debts expense	128,375	
Allowance for uncollectible accounts receivable		128,375

Assuming instead that a credit balance of €58,250 already exists in the allowance account (as usually will be observed in practice) the amount in the above journal entry would be €11,875 – €58,250) instead of €128,375 (€70,125 + €58,250) as presented.

Both of the estimation techniques should produce approximately the same result. This will be true especially over the course of a number of years. Nonetheless, it must be recognized that these adjustments are based on estimates and will never be totally accurate. When facts subsequently become available to indicate that the amount provided as an allowance for uncollectible accounts was incorrect, an adjustment classified as a change in estimate is made. According to IAS 8, adjustments of this nature are never considered to be accounting errors subject to subsequent correction or restatement. Only if an actual clerical or mechanical error occurred in the recording of allowance for uncollectible accounts would treatment as a correction of an error be warranted.

Pledging, Assigning, and Factoring Receivables

An organization can alter the timing of cash flows resulting from sales to its customers by using its accounts receivable as collateral for borrowings or by selling the receivables outright. A wide variety of arrangements can be structured by the borrower and lender, but the most common are pledging, assignment, and factoring. The IFRS do not offer specific accounting guidance on these assorted types of arrangements, although the derecognition rules of IAS 39 generally apply to these as well as other financial instruments of the reporting entity.

Pledging of receivables. Pledging is an agreement whereby accounts receivable are used as collateral for loans. Generally, the lender has limited rights to inspect the borrower's records to achieve assurance that the receivables do exist. The customers whose accounts have been pledged are not aware of this event, and their payments are still remitted to the original obligee. The pledged accounts merely serve as security to the lender, giving comfort that sufficient assets exist that will generate cash flows adequate in amount and timing to repay the debt. However, the debt is paid by the borrower whether or not the pledged receivables are collected and whether or not the pattern of such collections matches the payments due on the debt.

The only accounting issue relating to pledging is that of adequate disclosure. The accounts receivable, which remain assets of the borrowing entity, continue to be shown as current assets in its financial statements but must be identified as having been pledged. This identification can be accomplished either parenthetically or by footnote disclosures. Similarly, the related debt should be identified as having been secured by the receivables.

Example of proper disclosure for pledged receivables

Current assets:
Accounts receivable, net of allowance for doubtful accounts of €600,000
  (€3,500,000 of which has been pledged as collateral for bank loans)   8,450,000

Current liabilities:
Bank loans payable (secured by pledged accounts receivable)   2,700,000

A more common practice is to include the disclosure in the notes to the financial statements.

Assignment of receivables. The assignment of accounts receivable is a more formalized transfer of the asset to the lending institution. The lender will make an investigation of the specific receivables that are being proposed for assignment and will approve those that are deemed to be worthy as collateral. Customers are not usually aware that their accounts have been assigned and they continue to forward their payments to the original obligee. In some cases, the assignment agreement requires that collection proceeds be delivered to the lender immediately. The borrower is, however, the primary obligor and is required to make timely payment on the debt whether or not the receivables are collected as anticipated. The borrowing is with recourse, and the general credit of the borrower is pledged to the payment of the debt.

Since the lender knows that not all the receivables will be collected on a timely basis by the borrower, only a fraction of the face value of the receivables will be advanced as a loan to the borrower. Typically, this amount ranges from 70% to 90%, depending on the credit history and collection experience of the borrower.

Assigned accounts receivable remain the assets of the borrower and continue to be presented in its financial statements, with appropriate disclosure of the assignment similar to that illustrated for pledging. Prepaid finance charges would be debited to a prepaid expense account and amortized to expense over the period to which the charges apply.

Factoring of receivables. This category of financing is the most significant in terms of accounting implications. Factoring traditionally has involved the outright sale of receivables to a financing institution known as a factor. These arrangements involved (1) notification to the customer to forward future payments to the factor, and (2) the transfer of receivables without recourse. The factor assumes the risk of an inability to collect. Thus, once a factoring arrangement was completed, the entity had no further involvement with the accounts except for a return of merchandise.

The classical variety of factoring provides two financial services to the business: (1) it permits the entity to obtain cash earlier, and (2) the risk of bad debts is transferred to the factor. The factor is compensated for each of the services. Interest is charged based on the anticipated length of time between the date the factoring is consummated and the expected collection date of the receivables sold, and a fee is charged based on the factor's anticipated bad debt losses.

Some companies continue to factor receivables as a means of transferring the risk of bad debts but leave the cash on deposit with the factor until the weighted-average due date of the receivables, thereby avoiding interest payments. This arrangement is still referred to as factoring, since the customer receivables have been sold. However, the borrowing entity does not receive cash but instead has created a new receivable, usually captioned "due from factor." In contrast to the original customer receivables, this receivable is essentially riskless and will be presented in the statement of financial position without a deduction for an estimated uncollectible amount.

Merchandise returns will normally be the responsibility of the original vendor, who must then make the appropriate settlement with the factor. To protect against the possibility of merchandise returns that diminish the total of receivables to be collected, very often a factoring arrangement will not advance the full amount of the factored receivables (less any interest and factoring fee deductions). Rather, the factor will retain a certain fraction of the total proceeds relating to the portion of sales that are anticipated to be returned by customers. This sum is known as the factor's *holdback*. When merchandise is returned to the borrower, an entry is made offsetting the receivable from the factor. At the end of the return privilege period, any remaining holdback will become due and payable to the borrower.

Examples of journal entries to be made by the borrower in a factoring situation

1. Thirsty Corp. on July 1, 2008, enters into an agreement with Rich Company to sell a group of its receivables without recourse. A total face value of €200,000 accounts receivable (against which a 5% allowance had been recorded) is involved. The factor will charge 20% interest computed on the (weighted) average time to maturity of the receivables of 36 days plus a 3% fee. A 5% holdback will also be retained.
2. Thirsty's customers return for credit €4,800 of merchandise.
3. The customer return privilege period expires and the remaining holdback is paid to the transferor.

The entries required are as follows:

1.	Cash	180,055	
	Allowance for bad debts (€200,000 × .05)	10,000	
	Interest expense (or prepaid) (€200,000 × .20 × 36/365)	3,945	
	Factoring fee (€200,000 × .03)	6,000	
	Factor's holdback receivable (€200,000 × .05)	10,000	
	Bad debts expense		10,000
	Accounts receivable		200,000

(Alternatively, the interest and factor's fee can be combined into a €9,945 charge to loss on sale of receivables.)

2.	Sales returns and allowances	4,800	
	Factor's holdback receivable		4,800
3.	Cash	5,200	
	Factor's holdback receivable		5,200

Transfers of Receivables with Recourse

In recent decades, a variant on traditional receivables factoring has become popular. This variation has been called factoring with recourse, the terms of which suggest somewhat of a compromise between true factoring and the assignment of receivables. Accounting practice has varied considerably because of the hybrid nature of these transactions, and a strong argument can be made, in fact, that the factoring with recourse is nothing more than the assignment of receivables, and that the proper accounting (as discussed above) is to present this as a secured borrowing, not as a sale of the receivables. While "factoring with recourse" was previously held to qualify for derecognition by the transferor, this is now seen to be consistent with the derecognition rules of IAS 39, due to the nominal transferor's continuing involvement and retention of risk.

In the most recent amendments to IAS 32 and IAS 39, the IASB at first had signaled its intent to adopt a "continuing involvement model" for purposes of financial instrument derecognition rules, but ultimately decided to retain an approach largely consistent with the previous version of IAS 39, with some modification and clarification. Under revised IAS 39, although the transfer of the contractual right to receive cash flows is the paramount criterion for derecognition of financial assets such as receivables, if not all the rewards and risks of ownership are disposed of then derecognition will not be permitted.

FINANCIAL INSTRUMENTS OTHER THAN CASH AND RECEIVABLES

Accounting for Financial Instruments: Evolution of the Current Standards

The quantity and variety of financial instruments have expanded dramatically over the recent decades. Accounting standard setters, including IASB, have lagged seriously behind "financial engineers," who have been creative in developing financial instruments which have been able to evade the presentation of the substance of these various arrangements. Compound nonderivative instruments (those having, for example, attributes of both debt and equity) and financial derivatives (e.g., options and futures) have presented the greatest challenges to standard setters. Derivative financial instruments in particular have been difficult to deal with, since traditional historical cost-based accounting does not provide satisfactory results, given the fact that many such instruments require little or no initial cash investment. Thus, under the historical cost model many if not most of these instruments would not be reported in a historical cost statement of financial position notwithstanding the often very substantial risks being taken by the investor. For these and other reasons, the IASB signaled its desire to abandon historical costing for reporting financial instruments, in favor of a universal fair value approach. However, strong opposition to this change has made such a transition unlikely in the immediate term, although, in the authors' opinion, quite likely in the intermediate term.

Standard setters have long since imposed modern financial reporting requirements for mundane instruments such as corporate shares and bonds, although even in that realm compromises were made which preserve the "mixed (historical cost and fair value) attribute" characteristic of financial reporting standards. For example (as described in Chapter 10), marketable instruments held as assets are reported in one of several different ways, depending upon management's intent. Meanwhile, accounting for financial liabilities (e.g., corporate debt obligations) remains tied to historical cost, in part due to opposition from debtors, particularly financial institutions, to the adoption of a fair value model.

Derivatives commonly employed in today's business environment include option contracts, interest rate caps, interest rate floors, fixed-rate loan commitments, note issuance facilities, letters of credit, forward contracts, forward interest rate agreements, interest rate collars, futures, swaps, mortgage-backed securities, interest-only obligations, principal-only obligations, indexed debt, and other optional characteristics which are directly incorporated within receivables and payables such as convertible bond conversion or call terms (embedded derivatives).

Derivative financial instruments are used most typically as a tool to assist in the management of some category of risk, such as possible unfavorable movements in share prices, interest rate variations, currency fluctuations and commodity price volatility. To the extent derivatives are used for hedging activities, there has long been a consensus that, within the broad framework of an essentially historical cost-based system of accounting principles, there was a need for "special" accounting to reflect the effects of hedging. This is necessitated by the fact that many of the hedging assets and liabilities are normally reported under the historical cost model, while derivatives used to hedge changes in the value of these assets and liabilities must be reported at fair value, since historical costs are not meaningful.

While IAS 32 sets requirements for the classification by issuers of financial instruments as either liabilities or equity, and for offsetting of financial assets and liabilities, as well as for the disclosure of related information in the financial statements, IAS 39 tackled the somewhat more substantive questions of recognition, derecognition, measurement, and hedge accounting. Fair value reporting has been embraced, with a few important exceptions, for financial assets, while historical cost-based reporting has been largely preserved for financial liabilities. Special hedge accounting has been endorsed for those situations when a strict set of criteria are met, with the objectives of achieving good "matching" and of ensuring that all derivative financial instruments receive formal financial statement recognition, even if some value changes are excluded from current profit or loss.

While the application of fair value accounting to all financial instruments is still in the future, the IASB did make some changes to IAS 32 and IAS 39, some of which were implemented in 2005. These already enacted and further expected changes are discussed throughout the following sections of this chapter, and in Chapter 10, as they are pertinent. Detailed discussions of hedging and of derivative financial instruments are incorporated in Chapter 10.

Reporting and Disclosure of Financial Instruments under IAS 32 and IFRS 7

IAS 32's disclosure requirements have been removed from this standard and relocated to newly issued IFRS 7, which also incorporates requirements formerly found in IAS 30. IFRS 7 is discussed later in this chapter.

When first issued, IAS 32 was an important achievement for several reasons. It represented a commitment to a strict "substance over form" approach. The most signal accomplishment, perhaps, was the requirement that disparate elements of compound financial instruments be separately presented in the statement of financial position.

Under IAS 32, financial assets and liabilities are defined as follows:

Financial asset: Any asset that is

1. Cash
2. An equity instrument of another entity
3. A contractual right to receive cash or another financial asset from another entity
4. A contractual right to exchange financial instruments with another entity under conditions that are potentially favorable
5. A contract that will be settled in the reporting entity's own equity instruments and is a nonderivative for which the entity is or may be obligated to receive a variable number of its own equity instruments
6. A contract that will be settled in the reporting entity's own equity instruments and is a derivative that will or may be settled other than by an exchange of a fixed amount of cash or another financial asset for a fixed number of the entity's own equity instruments (which excludes instruments that are themselves contracts for the future receipt or delivery of the entity's equity instruments).

Financial liability: Any liability that is

1. A contractual obligation to deliver cash or another financial asset to another entity
2. A contractual obligation to exchange financial instruments with another entity under conditions that are potentially unfavorable
3. A contract that will or may be settled in the entity's own equity instruments and is a nonderivative for which it is or may be obligated to deliver a variable number of its own equity instruments
4. A contract that will or may be settled in the entity's own equity instruments and is a derivative that will or may be settled other than by an exchange of a fixed amount of cash or another financial asset for a fixed number of the entity's own

equity instruments (which excludes instruments that are themselves contracts for the future receipt or delivery of the entity's equity instruments).

According to the foregoing definition, financial instruments encompass a broad domain within the statement of financial position. Included are both primary instruments, such as shares and bonds, and derivative instruments, such as options, forwards, and swaps. Physical assets, such as inventories or plant assets, and such long-lived intangible assets as patents and goodwill, are excluded from the definition; although control of such assets may create opportunities to generate future cash inflows, it does not grant to the holder a present right to receive cash or other financial assets. Similarly, liabilities that are not contractual in nature, such as income taxes payable (which are statutory, but not contractual, obligations), are not financial instruments either.

Some contractual rights and obligations do not involve the transfer of financial assets. For example, a commitment to deliver commodities such as agricultural products or precious metals is not a financial instrument, although in practice these contracts are often used for hedging purposes by entities and are often settled in cash (technically, the contracts are closed out by entering into offsetting transactions before their mandatory settlement dates). The fact that the contracts call for delivery of physical product, unless canceled by a closing market transaction prior to the maturity date, prevents these from being included within the definition of financial instruments.

Presentation Issues Addressed by IAS 32

Distinguishing liabilities from equity. It sometimes happens that financial instruments of a given issuer may have attributes of both liabilities and equity. From a financial reporting perspective, the central issue is whether to account for these "compound" instruments in total as *either* liabilities or equity, *in toto*, or to disaggregate them into both liabilities and equity instruments. The notion of disaggregation has long been discussed—conceptually, of course, this should not have been difficult to resolve, since the time-honored accounting tradition of substance over form provided clear guidance on this matter—but it had not been effectively dealt with prior to IAS 32. The reluctance to resolve this derived from a variety of causes, including the concern that a strict doctrine of substance over form could trigger serious legal complications.

One example of the foregoing problem pertains to mandatorily redeemable preference share, which has historically been considered part of an entity's equity base despite having important characteristics of debt. Requiring that such quasi equity issuances be recategorized as debt might have resulted in many entities being deemed to be in violation of existing debt covenants and other contractual commitments. At a minimum, their statement of financial position would imply the existence of a greater amount of leverage than previously, with possibly negative implications for lenders. Concerns such as this had previously caused the US standard setter, the FASB, to demur from adopting a strict "substance over form" approach in its financial instruments standards, despite having stated in its 1991 discussion memorandum that all debt-like instruments should be classified as debt, not equity. (In 2003, however, the FASB adopted FAS 150, which does require debt-like instruments to be classified as liabilities. However, due to strong opposition, implementation of certain aspects of that standard have been delayed, some indefinitely.) The IASC, however, resolutely dealt with this matter.

Under the provisions of IAS 32, the issuer of a financial instrument must classify it, or its component parts, if a compound instrument (defined and discussed below), in accordance with the substance of the respective contractual arrangement. Thus it is quite clear that under IFRS, when the instrument gives rise to an obligation on the part of the issuer to deliver cash or another financial asset or to exchange financial instruments on potentially unfavorable terms, it is to be classified as a liability, not as equity. Mandatorily redeemable preference share and preference share issued with put options (options that can be exercised by the holder, potentially requiring the issuer to redeem the shares at agreed-upon prices) must, under this definition, be presented as liabilities.

The presentation of ordinary share subject to a buyout agreement with the entity's shareholders is less clear. Closely held entities frequently structure *buy-sell agreements* with each shareholder, which require that upon the occurrence of defined events, such as a shareholder's retirement or death, the entity will be required to redeem the former shareholder's ownership interest at a defined or determinable price, such as fair or book value. The practical effect of buy-sell agreements is that all but the final shareholder will eventually become creditors; the last to retire or die will be, by default, the residual owner of the business, since the entity will be unable to redeem that holder's shares unless a new investor enters the picture. IAS 32 does not address this type of situation explicitly, although circumstances of this sort are clearly alluded to by the standard, which notes that "if a financial instrument labeled as a share gives the holder an option to require redemption upon the occurrence of a future event that is highly likely to occur, classification as a financial liability on initial recognition reflects the substance of the instrument." Notwithstanding this guidance, entities can be expected to be quite reluctant to reclassify the majority of shareholders' equity as debt in cases such as that described above.

IAS 32 goes beyond the formal terms of a financial instrument in seeking to determine whether it might be a liability. Thus, for example, under IAS 32, prior to amendments made in 2008 (see immediately following paragraphs), preference share which has mandatory redemption provisions, or which is "puttable" by the holder, was to be classified and accounted for as a liability upon its original issuance.

According to IAS 32, before revision, if an issuer was subject to a requirement that it pay cash or deliver another financial asset in return for redeeming or repurchasing a financial instrument, the instrument was to be classified as a financial liability. This was consistent with the long-held definition of a liability as an obligation to make a future payment as a consequence of a past action. As interpreted, this held even if the amount payable was equal to the holder's interest in the net assets of the issuer, or if the amount would only become payable at liquidation and liquidation was deemed to be certain because, for example, a fixed liquidation date for the entity was defined.

Some believed that this mandate resulted in liability treatment even where it might be unwarranted, with the result that otherwise financially healthy entities could be forced to report negative equity. This would occur, for example, where the total amount payable would equal the *market value* of the whole entity, which could well exceed the *accounting net assets* of the entity. Alternatively, where liquidation is certain or is at the option of the holder, instruments that represent the last residual interest in the entity may be recognized as financial liabilities even when the instruments have characteristics similar to equity, since not all equity can be redeemed if the entity is to be considered a going concern.

To deal with these perceived anomalies, in February 2008, amendments to IAS 32 were adopted, to provide a "short-term, limited scope amendment" to obviate these unwelcome outcomes. IASB concluded that some puttable financial instruments and financial instruments that impose on the issuer an obligation to deliver a pro-rata share of net assets of the entity only on liquidation are equity, and thus should not be presented as liabilities. The amendments are very particularized and cannot be analogized from to any other fact patterns, and very extensive detailed criteria need to be met in order to present these instruments as equity.

Puttable financial instruments. Under revised IAS 32, puttable financial instruments are now to be presented as equity, but only if *all* of the following criteria are met:

1. The holder is entitled to a pro rata share of the entity's net assets on liquidation;
2. The instruments is in the class of instruments that is the most subordinate and all instruments in that class have identical features;
3. The instrument has no other characteristics that would meet the definition of a financial liability; and
4. The total expected cash flows attributable to the instrument over its life are based substantially on the profit or loss, the change in the recognized net assets or the change in the fair value of the recognized and unrecognized net assets of the entity (excluding any effects of the instrument itself). Profit or loss or change in recognized net assets for this purpose is as measured in accordance with relevant IFRS.

In addition to the above criteria, the reporting entity is permitted to have no other instrument with terms equivalent to 4. above that has the effect of substantially restricting or fixing the residual return to the holders of the puttable financial instruments.

Based on these new requirements, it is clear that certain classifications of financial instruments issued by the reporting entity will now have to be changed. Shares that are puttable throughout their lives at fair value, that are also the most subordinate of the instruments issued by the reporting entity, and which do not contain any other obligation, and which have only discretionary (i.e., nonfixed) dividends based on profits of the issuer, will now be deemed equity, although classed as liabilities under IAS 32 prior to this amendment.

By contrast, shares that are puttable at fair value, but which are *not* the most subordinate class of instrument issued, must still be classified as liabilities under revised IAS 32.

Shares that are puttable at fair value only on liquidation, and that are also the most subordinate class of instrument, but which specify a fixed nondiscretionary dividend obligation, will now be treated as compound financial instruments (that is, as being part equity, part liability). Rules governing the allocation of proceeds among elements of compound instruments are discussed in a subsequent section of this chapter and also later in this book.

Finally, shares that are puttable at fair value only on liquidation, and that are also part of the most subordinate class of instruments issued, but are entitled to fixed, discretionary dividends, and do not contain any other obligation, are now to be deemed part of equity, and not liabilities.

If any of these instruments have been issued by a subsidiary (rather than by the reporting parent entity), and are held by noncontrolling parties, these must be reported as liabilities in the consolidated financial statements. (In separate financial statements of the subsidiary, however, the foregoing rules would need to be applied.) Thus, certain equity of the subsidiary, in its separate financial statements, to the extent held by noncontrolling interests, would have to be reclassified to liabilities in the consolidation process.

Interests in cooperatives. IFRIC 2, *Members' Shares in Cooperative Entities and Similar Instruments*, states that the contractual right of the holder of a financial instrument (including members' shares in cooperative entities) to request redemption does not, in itself, require that financial instrument to be classified as a financial liability. Rather, the entity must consider all of the terms and conditions of the financial instrument in determining its classification as a financial liability or equity, including relevant local laws, regulations, and the entity's governing charter in effect at the date of classification.

Members' shares are equity if the entity has an unconditional right to refuse redemption of the members' shares or if redemption is unconditionally prohibited by local law, regulation, or the entity's governing charter. However, if redemption is prohibited only if defined conditions—such as liquidity constraints—are met (or are not met), members' shares are not equity.

Classification of compound instruments. Compound instruments are those which are sold or acquired jointly, but which provide the holder with more than a single economic interest in the issuing entity. For example, a bond sold with share purchase warrants provides the holder with an unconditional promise to pay (the bond, which carries a rate of interest and a fixed maturity date) plus a right to acquire the issuer's shares (the warrant, which may be for common or preferred shares, at either a fixed price per share or a price based on some formula, such as a price that increases over time). In some cases, one or more of the component parts of the compound instrument may be financial derivatives, as a share purchase warrant would be. In other instances, each element might be a traditional, nonderivative instrument, as would be the case when a debenture is issued with common shares as a unit offering.

The accounting issue that is most obviously associated with compound instruments is how to allocate price or proceeds to the constituent elements. This becomes most important when the compound instrument consists of parts that are both liabilities and equity items. Proper classification of the elements is vital to accurate financial reporting, affecting potentially such matters as debt covenant compliance (if the debt to equity ratio, for example, is a covenant to be met by the debtor entity).

Under original IAS 32, the accounting issues were the same for the issuer and the holder of compound instruments. However, this is no longer the case, since revised IAS 32, effective 2005, made a significant change to the issuer's accounting for compound financial instruments. Previously, compound instruments (consisting of both liability and equity components) were to be analyzed into their constituent elements and accounted for accordingly. IAS 32, as issued, did not address recognition or measurement matters, and thus no single method of valuation for this purpose was prescribed. However, IAS 32 suggested two possible approaches: to allocate pro rata based on relative fair value, or to allocate to the more readily measured element full fair value and assign the residual to the other components. Depending on the facts and circumstances, this could have resulted in allocating fair value to the equity component, and assigning only a residual amount to the liability portion.

Under revised IAS 32, however, this has changed. Now, whether or not fair values are available for all components of the compound instrument, it is required that fair value be ascertained and then allocated to the liability components, with only the residual amount being assigned to equity. This position has been taken in order to be fully consistent with the definition of equity as instruments that evidence only a residual interest in the assets of an entity, after satisfying all of its liabilities. It therefore is no longer acceptable to assign a residual to the liability components, nor to allocate total proceeds proportionately to both liability and equity elements.

If the compound instruments include a derivative element (e.g., a put option), the value of those features, to the extent they are embedded in the compound financial instrument other than the equity component, is to be included in the liability component.

The sum of the carrying amounts assigned to the liability and equity components on initial recognition its always equal to the fair value that would be ascribed to the instrument as a whole. In other words, there can be no "day one" gains from issuing financial instruments.

Example of accounting by issuer of compound instrument

To illustrate the allocation of proceeds in a compound instrument situation, assume these facts.

1. 5,000 convertible bonds are sold by Needy Company on January 1, 2008. The bonds are due December 31, 2011
2. Issuance price is par (€1,000 per bond); total issuance proceeds are €5,000,000.
3. Interest is due in arrears, semiannually, at a nominal rate of 5%.

4. Each (€1,000 face amount) bond is convertible into 150 ordinary shares of Needy Company.
5. At issuance date, similar, nonconvertible debt must yield 8%.

Required residual value method. Under the provisions of revised IAS 32, the issuer of compound financial instruments must assign full fair value to the portion that is to be classified as a liability, with only the residual value being allocated to the equity component. The computation for the above fact situation would be as follows:

1. Use the reference discount rate, 8%, to compute the market value of straight debt carrying a 5% yield:

PV of €5,000,000 due in 4 years, discounted at 8%	€3,653,451
PV of semiannual payments of €125,000 for 8 periods, discounted at 8%	841,593
Total	€4,495,044

2. Compute the amount allocable to the conversion feature

Total proceeds from issuance of compound instrument	€5,000,000
Value allocable to debt	4,495,044
Residual value allocable to equity component	€ 504,956

Thus, Needy Company received €4,495,044 in consideration of the actual debt being issued, plus a further €504,956 for the conversion feature, which is a call option on the underlying ordinary share of the issuer. The entry to record this would be

Cash	5,000,000	
Discount on bonds payable	504,956	
Bonds payable		5,000,000
Paid-in capital—bond conversion option		504,956

The bond discount would be amortized as additional interest over the term of the debt. See Chapter 13 for a complete discussion from the debtor's perspective.

Example of accounting by acquirer of compound instrument

From the perspective of the acquirer, compound financial instruments will often be seen as containing an embedded derivative—for example, a put option or a conversion feature of a debt instrument being held for an investment. This may be required to be valued and accounted for separately (which does not necessarily imply separate presentation in the financial statements, however). Per IAS 32, separate accounting is necessary if, and only if, the economic characteristics and risks of the embedded derivative are not closely related to the host; a separate instrument with the same terms would meet the definition of a derivative; and the combined instrument is not to be measured at fair value with changes included in current profit or loss (i.e., it is neither held for trading nor subject to the "fair value option" election).

In general, the embedded derivative is measured at fair value, with the host being assigned the residual of the purchase cost. When this cannot be measured, the embedded derivative should be assigned the differential between the hybrid instrument's cost and the fair value of the host portion, assuming this can be determined. If none of these can be determined, the embedded derivative is not separated, and the hybrid is to be carried at fair value in the trading portfolio.

To illustrate the allocation of purchase cost in a compound financial asset situation, assume these facts.

1. 500 convertible Needy Company bonds are acquired by Investor Corp. January 1, 2008. The bonds are due December 31, 2011.
2. The purchase price is par (€1,000 per bond); total cost is thus €500,000.
3. Interest is due in arrears, semiannually, at a nominal rate of 5%.
4. Each bond is convertible into 150 ordinary shares of the issuer.
5. At purchase date, similar, nonconvertible debt issued by borrowers having the same credit rating as Needy Company yield 8%.
6. At purchase date, Needy Company common shares are trading at €5, and dividends over the next 4 years are expected to be €0.20 per share per year.
7. The relevant risk-free rate on 4-year obligations is 4%.

8. The historic variability of Needy Company's share price can be indicated by a standard deviation of annual returns of 25%.

Per IAS 32, the fair value of the conversion feature should be determined, if possible, and assigned to that embedded derivative. In this example, the popular Black-Scholes-Merton model will be used (but other approaches are also acceptable).

1. Compute the standard deviation of proportionate changes in the fair value of the asset underlying the option multiplied by the square root of the time to expiration of the option.

$$.25 \times \sqrt{4} = .25 \times 2 = .50$$

2. Compute the ratio of the fair value of the asset underlying the option to the present value of the option exercise price.

   a. Since the expected dividend per share is €0.20 per year, the present value of this stream over 4 years would (at the risk-free rate) be €0.726.
   b. The shares are trading at €5.00.
   c. Therefore, the value of the underlying optioned asset, stripped of the stream of dividends that a holder of an unexercised option would obviously not receive, is

   $$€5.00 - .726 = €4.274 \text{ per share.}$$

   d. The implicit exercise price is €1,000 ÷ 150 shares = €6.667 per share. This must be discounted at the risk-free rate, 4%, over 4 years, assuming that conversion takes place at the expiration of the conversion period, as follows:

   $$€6.667 \div 1.04^4 = 6.667 \div 1.170 = €5.699$$

   e. Therefore, the ratio of the underlying asset, €4.274, to the present value of the exercise price, €5.699, is .750.

3. Reference must now be made to a call option valuation table to assign a fair value to these two computed amounts (the standard deviation of proportionate changes in the fair value of the asset underlying the option multiplied by the square root of the time to expiration of the option, .50, and the ratio of the fair value of the asset underlying the option to the present value of the option exercise price, .750). For this example, assume that the table value is 13.44% (meaning that the fair value of the option is 13.44%) of the fair value of the underlying asset.

4. The valuation of the conversion option, then, is given as

   $$.1344 \times €4.274 \text{ per share} \times 150 \text{ shares/bond} \times 500 \text{ bonds} = €43,082$$

5. Since the fair value of the options (€43,082) has been determined, this is assigned to the conversion option. The difference between the cost of the hybrid investment, €500,000, and the amount allocated to the conversion feature, €43,082, or €456,918, should be attributed to the debt instrument.

6. The discount on the debt should be amortized, using the effective yield method, over the projected four-year holding period. The effective yield, taking into account the semi-annual interest payments to be received, will be about 7.54%.

If, for some reason, the value of the derivative (the conversion feature, in this case) could not be ascertained, the fair value of the debt portion would be computed, and the residual allocated to the derivative. This is illustrated as follows:

1. Use the reference discount rate, 8%, to compute the market value of straight debt carrying a 5% yield.

PV of €500,000 due in 4 years, discounted at 8%	€365,345
PV of semiannual payments of €12,500 for 8 periods, discounted at 8%	84,159
Total	€449,504

2. Compute the residual amount allocable to the conversion feature.

Total proceeds from issuance of compound instrument	€500,000
Value allocable to debt	449,504
Residual value allocable to embedded derivative	€ 50,496

Reporting interest, dividends, losses, and gains. IAS 32 establishes that income earned while holding financial instruments, and gains or losses from disposing of financial instruments should be reported in the statement of comprehensive income (or in the income statement, if it is presented separately). Dividends paid on equity instruments issued should be charged directly to equity. (These will be reported in the statement of changes in equity.) The statement of financial position classification of the instrument drives the statement of comprehensive income classification of the related interest or dividends. For example, if mandatorily redeemable preferred shares have been categorized as debt in the issuer's statement of financial position, dividend payments on those shares must be reported in the statement of comprehensive income (or income statement) in the same manner as interest expense. Gains or losses on redemptions or refinancings of financial instruments classed as liabilities would be reported similarly in the statement of comprehensive income, while gains or losses on equity are credited or charged to equity directly.

Offsetting financial assets and liabilities. Under the provisions of IAS 32, offsetting financial assets and liabilities is permitted only when the entity *both* (1) has the legally enforceable right to set off the recognized amounts, and (2) intends to settle the asset and liability on a net basis, or to realize the asset and settle the liability simultaneously. Of great significance is the fact that offsetting does not give rise to gain or loss recognition, which distinguishes it from the derecognition of an instrument (which was not dealt with by IAS 32, but was subsequently addressed by IAS 39).

Simultaneous settlement of a financial asset and a financial liability can be presumed only under defined circumstances. The most typical of such cases is when both instruments will be settled through a clearinghouse functioning for an organized exchange. Other situations may superficially appear to warrant the same accounting treatment but in fact do not give rise to legitimate offsetting. For example, if the entity will exchange checks with a single counterparty for the settlement of both instruments, it becomes exposed to credit risk for a time, however brief, when it has paid the other party for the amount of the obligation owed to it but has yet to receive the counterparty's funds to settle the amount it is owed by the counterparty. Offsetting would not be warranted in such a context.

The standard sets forth a number of other circumstances in which offsetting would *not* be justified. These include

1. When several different instruments are used to synthesize the features of another type of instrument (which typically would involve a number of different counterparties, thus violating a basic principle of offsetting).
2. When financial assets and financial liabilities arise from instruments having the same primary risk exposure (such as when both are forward contracts) but with different counterparties.
3. When financial assets are pledged as collateral for nonrecourse financial liabilities (as the intention is not typically to effect offsetting, but rather, to settle the obligation and gain release of the collateral).
4. When financial assets are set aside in a trust for the purpose of discharging a financial obligation but the assets have not been formally accepted by the creditor (as when a sinking fund is established, or when in-substance defeasance of debt is arranged).
5. When obligations incurred as a consequence of events giving rise to losses are expected to be recovered from a third party by virtue of an insurance claim (again, different counterparties means that the entity is exposed to credit risk, however slight).

Even the existence of a master netting agreement does not automatically justify the offsetting of financial assets and financial liabilities. Only if both the stipulated conditions (both the right to offset and the intention to do so) are met can this accounting treatment be employed.

Disclosure requirements under IAS 32. The disclosure requirements established by IAS 32 were later largely subsumed under those established by IAS 39. Per another revision in 2003, however, the disclosure requirements were again situated in IAS 32. Most recently (mid-2005), all disclosure requirements have been removed from IAS 32 (which continues as the authoritative source of presentation requirements) and placed in new IFRS 7. Both IAS 32 and IFRS 7 disclosure requirements are discussed later in this chapter.

IAS 39: Financial Instruments—Recognition and Measurement

Evolution of the standard. IASC (predecessor to IASB) originally attempted to develop a comprehensive standard on accounting and reporting for financial instruments, but this failed to bear fruit and the program had to be bifurcated into projects on reporting and disclosure (which resulted the issuance of IAS 32 in 1995), and recognition and measurement (which later resulted in the development of IAS 39). Regarding the latter, the two major challenges were (1) to decide whether to impose uniform measurement and reporting standards on financial assets and financial liabilities and (2) to determine whether special hedge accounting would be necessary and acceptable. The IASC's experience was similar to that of national standard-setting bodies regarding both of these; strong opposition, coupled with some perceived practical difficulties, precluded the imposition of uniform asset and liability requirements, and special hedge accounting was therefore made a necessity.

The IASC's failure to develop, at that time, a comprehensive and uniform set of standards for all financial assets and liabilities must not be judged too harshly, since it mirrors the difficulties of the major national standard-setting bodies, none of which have been able to traverse this complex issue. In addition, the then-IASC's focus was necessarily on meeting the minimum threshold for completion of the "core set of standards" so that IOSCO consideration of endorsing the IAS for cross-border securities registrations could go forward. The IASB's attention will now turn to other matters, including the application of fair value accounting to all financial assets and liabilities, although this challenging task may take several more years to achieve.

The major changes wrought by IAS 39 were to greatly expand the use of fair values for measuring and reporting financial instruments and to address the important issue of financial derivatives, requiring that these be formally recognized and measured at fair value in most cases. IAS 39 is very similar to the corresponding US standard, FAS 133, although without the vast and detailed guidance offered by that standard, as is typical of US financial reporting rules. (While there is much debate over the relative virtues and limitations of "principles-based" and "rules-based" standards, most observers agree that financial instruments topics, which tend to be quite complex, benefit from the latter approach, where detailed guidance is provided addressing a range of fact patterns.)

Financial instrument recognition and measurement. The issuance of IAS 39 was the final and, some would argue, most important component of the IASC's "core set of standards" project, making possible the qualified endorsement of the international standards for use in cross-border securities registrations. Although ambitious and quite comprehensive, especially compared to other IFRS, IAS 39 was not a perfect document. Most of the complexities, however, are the result of continued endorsement of a "mixed attribute" (historical cost and fair value) model of financial reporting. If and when a pure fair value model of reporting financial instruments is adopted, the required accounting procedures will be substantially streamlined.

Both the FASB and IASB are clearly gravitating toward a pure fair value model for all financial instruments, perhaps with changes in value included in current period profit or loss in all cases. For various reasons, this solution has not been universally greeted with enthusiasm, and as a consequence, the US standard, FAS 133 (as amended), and the international standard, IAS 39, as most recently revised, have both endorsed continuation of mixed attribute models. This has necessitated the creation of special accounting for hedging situations, which among other things requires that hedging be defined and that measures be established to evaluate the effectiveness of those hedges, in order to determine whether the special accounting is warranted in any given circumstance. A pure fair value reporting model for financial assets and liabilities would have obviated the need for these specially designed treatments.

Applicability. IAS 39 is applicable to all financial instruments *except* interests in subsidiaries, associates and joint ventures that are accounted for in accordance with IAS 27, 28, and 31, respectively; rights and obligations under operating leases, to which IAS 17 applies; most rights and obligations under insurance contracts; employers' assets and liabilities under employee benefit plans and employee equity compensation plans, to which IAS 19 applies; and equity instruments issued by the reporting entity.

IAS 39 as originally promulgated was not applicable to financial guarantee contracts, such as letters of credit, when such contracts call for payments that would have to be made only if the primary debtor fails to perform; accounting for these types of arrangements was specified by IAS 37. However, amendments to IAS 39 and IFRS 4 made in 2005 have prescribed the accounting for guarantee contracts by the guarantor. It states that financial guarantees are initially to be measured at fair value, with subsequent measurement at the greater of the initial measurement and the best estimate as defined in IAS 37. The effect of this amendment was to bring the *recognition* decision under IAS 39, while leaving *measurement* guidance under IAS 37.

IAS 39 criteria apply where the guarantor will have to make payments when a defined change in credit rating, commodity prices, interest rates, security price, foreign exchange rate, an index of rates or prices, or other underlying indicator occurs. Also, if a guarantee arises from an event leading to the derecognition of a financial instrument, the guarantee must be recognized as set forth in this standard.

IAS 39 does not apply to contingent consideration arrangements pursuant to a business combination. Also, the standard does not apply to contracts that require payments dependent upon climatic, geological, or other physical factors or events, although if other types of derivatives are embedded therein, IAS 39 would set the requirements for recognition, measurement, disclosure, and derecognition.

IAS 39 must be applied to commodity-based contracts that give either party the right to settle by cash or some other financial instrument, with the exception of commodity contracts that were entered into and continue to meet the entity's expected purchase, sale, or usage requirements and were designated for that purpose at their inception. With regard to embedded derivatives, if their economic characteristics and risks are not closely related to the economic characteristics and risks of the host contract, and if a separate instrument with the same terms as the embedded derivative would meet the definition of a derivative, they are to be separated from the host contract and accounted for as a derivative in accordance with the standard. IFRIC 9, *Reassessment of Embedded Derivatives*, provides additional interpretation concerning this matter. An entity should assess whether an embedded derivative is required to be separated from the host contract and accounted for as a derivative when the entity first becomes a party to the contract. Subsequent reassessment is *prohibited* unless there is a change in the terms of the contract that significantly modifies the cash flows that otherwise would be required under the contract; in this case reassessment is required.

A first-time IFRS adopter should assess whether an embedded derivative is required to be separated from the host contract and accounted for as a derivative on the basis of conditions existing at the later of the date it first becomes a party to the contract and the date a reassessment is required because a change in the terms of the arrangement significantly alters the cash flows otherwise mandated under the contract.

Derecognition of financial assets. Revisions made to IAS 39 in 2004 altered the derecognition accounting for financial assets. Derecognition of all or part of a financial instrument held as an asset may be warranted, depending on the facts and circumstances.

Derecognition of part of an instrument is justified only if one of the following conditions holds:

1. The part comprises specifically identified cash flows from a financial asset (or group of assets)—for example, an interest rate strip.
2. The part comprises a fully proportionate share of the cash flows from a financial asset (or group of assets)—for example, an arrangement whereby the counterparty obtains the rights to a 70% share of all cash flows of a debt instrument.
3. The part comprises a fully proportionate share of specifically identified cash flows from a financial asset (or group of assets)—for example, when an entity enters into an arrangement whereby the counterparty obtains the rights to a 70% share of interest cash flows from a financial asset.

Unless one of the foregoing conditions is met, the derecognition criteria are applied to the entire instrument.

Financial assets are to be derecognized only when (1) the contractual rights to the cash flows from the financial asset expire; or (2) the financial assets are transferred in a manner that qualifies for derecognition. A transfer of a financial asset occurs only if (1) the contractual rights to receive the cash flows of the financial asset are transferred or (2) the contractual rights to receive the cash flows of the financial asset are retained, but the entity assumes a contractual obligation to pay the cash flows to one or more recipients in an arrangement that meets the conditions set forth below.

When an entity (*transferor*) retains the contractual rights to receive the cash flows of a financial asset (referred to as the *original asset*), but assumes a contractual obligation to pay those cash flows to one or more entities (called the *eventual recipients*), the entity treats the transaction as a transfer of a financial asset only if all of the following three conditions are met:

1. The transferor has no obligation to pay amounts to the eventual recipients unless it collects equivalent amounts from the original asset.
2. The transferor is prohibited from selling or pledging the original asset except as security to the eventual recipients for the obligation to pay them cash flows.
3. The transferor has an obligation to remit any cash flows it collects on behalf of the eventual recipients without material delay; is not entitled to reinvest such cash flows, except for investments in cash or cash equivalents during the period from the collection date to the date of required remittance to the eventual recipients; and any interest earned thereon is paid to the eventual recipients.

When the reporting entity transfers a financial asset, as described in the foregoing paragraph, it is to evaluate the extent to which it retains the risks and rewards of ownership of the financial asset, which may involve consideration of control over the asset. In such a situation

1. If the reporting entity transfers substantially all the risks and rewards of ownership of the financial asset, it will derecognize the financial asset and recognize separately, as assets or liabilities, any rights and obligations created or retained in the transfer.

2.   If it retains substantially all the risks and rewards of ownership of the financial asset, continued recognition of the financial asset is required.

3.   If it neither transfers nor retains substantially all the risks and rewards of ownership of the financial asset, it must make a determination of whether it has retained control of the financial asset. In such case, (a) if it has not retained control, it is to derecognize the financial asset and recognize separately as assets or liabilities any rights and obligations created or retained in the transfer, but (b) if it has retained control, it will continue to recognize the financial asset to the extent of its continuing involvement in the financial asset.

The risks and rewards analysis, above, is effected by comparing the reporting entity's exposure, before and after the transfer, with the variability in the amounts and timing of the net cash flows of the transferred asset. Retention of substantially all the risks and rewards of ownership of a financial asset is indicated if the entity's exposure to the variability in the present value of the future net cash flows from the financial asset does not change significantly as a result of the transfer (e.g., because an asset has been sold subject to an agreement to buy it back at a fixed price or at the sale price plus a defined return to the counterparty).

On the other hand, transfer of substantially all the risks and rewards of an asset is indicated if the reporting entity's exposure to such variability is no longer significant in relation to the total variability in the present value of the future net cash flows associated with the financial asset (e.g., because the asset has been sold subject to an option to repurchase it at fair value, or a fully proportionate share of the cash flows from a larger financial asset has been sold in an arrangement, for example, a loan subparticipation, that meets the conditions set forth above).

It will often be clear that an asset transfer either did or did not involve the retention of substantially all risks and rewards of ownership. Thus, computations will commonly not be required to make this determination. However, in some instances it will be necessary to compute and compare the entity's exposure to the variability in the present value of the future net cash flows before and after the transfer. IAS 39 stipulates that the computation and comparison is to be made using an appropriate current market interest rate as the discount rate. All reasonably possible variability in net cash flows is to be considered, with greater weight being given to those outcomes that are more likely to occur.

Regarding control, IAS 39 has imposed a simple criterion. Retention of control by the reporting entity depends wholly on the transferee's ability to sell the asset. If the transferee has the practical ability to sell the asset in its entirety to an unrelated third party, and is able to exercise that ability unilaterally and without needing to impose additional restrictions on the transfer, the entity has not retained control. In all other cases, the entity has retained control.

Transfers that qualify for derecognition. IAS 39 addresses a number of circumstances that may arise in connection with a transfer of a financial instrument that is deemed to be accountable as asset derecognitions. These are discussed in the following paragraphs.

If the reporting entity retains the right to service the derecognized financial asset for a fee, it is to recognize either a servicing asset or a servicing liability for that servicing contract. If the servicing fee to be received will not compensate it adequately for performing the servicing, a servicing liability for the servicing obligation is to be recognized, measured at fair value. If the fee to be received is expected to be more than adequate compensation for the servicing, on the other hand, a servicing asset is to be recognized for the servicing right. The amount to be recognized as an asset is to be determined on the basis of an allocation of the carrying amount of the larger financial asset, discussed below.

If, because of the transfer, a financial asset is derecognized in its entirety but the transfer results in the entity obtaining a new financial asset or assuming a new financial liability, or incurring a servicing liability, the entity is to recognize the new financial asset, financial liability or servicing liability at fair value.

When a financial asset is derecognized in its entirety, the difference between the carrying amount and the sum of (1) the consideration received (including any new asset obtained less any new liability assumed) and (2) any cumulative gain or loss that had been recognized directly in equity is to be recognized in current profit or loss.

If the transferred asset is part of a larger financial asset (e.g., interest cash flows but not principal payments) and the portion that is transferred qualifies for derecognition in its entirety, the previous carrying amount of the larger financial asset must be allocated between the part that continues to be recognized and the part that is derecognized, based on the relative fair values of those parts on the date of the transfer. Any retained servicing asset is to be treated as a part that continues to be recognized for purposes of this fair value allocation process. The difference between the carrying amount allocated to the part derecognized and the sum of (1) the consideration received for the part derecognized (including any new asset obtained less any new liability assumed) and (2) any cumulative gain or loss allocated to it that had been recognized directly in equity is to be recognized currently in profit or loss. A cumulative gain or loss that was recognized directly in equity is to be allocated between the part that continues to be recognized and the part that is derecognized, based on their relative fair values.

When allocating the previous carrying amount of a larger financial asset between the part to remain recognized and that to be derecognized, the fair value of the former needs to be ascertained. If the reporting entity has a history of selling parts similar to the part that continues to be recognized, or if other market transactions exist for such parts, then recent prices of actual transactions would likely provide the best estimate of fair value. However, when there are no price quotes or recent market transactions to use as a reference, the best estimate of the fair value is the difference between the fair value of the larger financial asset as a whole and the consideration received from the transferee for the part that is derecognized.

Transfers that do not qualify for derecognition. If the reporting entity has retained substantially all the risks and rewards of ownership of the transferred asset, derecognition is not permitted. In effect, the transaction will be accounted for as a secured borrowing. Thus, the entity will continue to recognize the transferred asset in its entirety, and will also recognize a financial liability for the consideration received. In subsequent periods, the entity will recognize any income on the transferred asset and any expense incurred on the financial liability in the normal fashion.

If a transferred asset continues to be recognized, it and the corresponding liability may not be offset. Similarly, any income arising from the transferred asset and any expense incurred on the corresponding liability may not be offset.

If a transferor provides noncash collateral (e.g., debt or equity instruments) to the transferee, the accounting for the collateral by the transferor and the transferee depends on whether the transferee has the right to sell or repledge the collateral and on whether the transferor has defaulted. If the transferee has the right by contract or custom to sell or repledge the collateral, then the transferor is to reclassify that asset in its statement of financial position (e.g., as a loaned asset, pledged equity instrument or repurchase receivable), so that it is reported separately from other assets. If the transferee sells collateral pledged to it, the transferee must recognize the proceeds from the sale and a liability measured at fair value for its obligation to return the collateral.

If the transferor defaults under the terms of the contract and is no longer entitled to redeem the collateral, it will then derecognize the collateral, and the transferee is to recognize the collateral as its asset, initially measured at fair value or, if it has already sold the collateral, derecognize its obligation to return the collateral. Except for a default as just described, the transferor must continue to carry the collateral as its asset, and the transferee may not recognize the collateral as an asset.

Continuing involvement in transferred assets. If an entity neither transfers nor retains substantially all the risks and rewards of ownership of a transferred asset, but retains control of the transferred asset, it must continue to recognize the transferred asset to the extent of its continuing involvement. The extent of its continuing involvement in the transferred asset is gauged by the extent to which the entity is exposed to changes in the value of the transferred asset.

IAS 39 provides several examples that illustrate the concept of continuing involvement, indicating the amount to be reported as the asset by the transferor.

1. When the entity's continuing involvement takes the form of guaranteeing the transferred asset, the extent of the entity's continuing involvement is the lesser of (a) the amount of the asset and (b) the maximum amount of the consideration received that the entity could be required to repay (the *guarantee amount*).

2. When its continuing involvement takes the form of a written or purchased option (or both) on the transferred asset, the extent of the entity's continuing involvement is the amount of the transferred asset that the entity may repurchase. For a written put option on an asset measured at fair value, the extent of its continuing involvement is limited to the lower of the fair value of the transferred asset and the option exercise price.

3. When the entity's continuing involvement takes the form of a cash-settled option or similar provision on the transferred asset, the extent of continuing involvement is measured in the same way as that which results from non-cash-settled options, above.

When an entity continues to recognize an asset to the extent of its continuing involvement, it also must recognize a corresponding liability. The transferred asset and the corresponding liability are measured on a basis that reflects the rights and obligations that the entity has retained. The liability is to be measured in such a way that the net carrying amount of the transferred asset and the corresponding liability is either (1) the amortized cost of the rights and obligations retained by the entity, if the transferred asset is measured at amortized cost; or (2) equal to the fair value of the rights and obligations retained by the entity when measured on a stand-alone basis, if the transferred asset is measured at fair value.

The reporting entity will continue to recognize any income arising on the transferred asset to the extent of its continuing involvement, and likewise will recognize any expense incurred on the corresponding liability. As regards the subsequent measurement of the transferred asset and the corresponding liability, recognized changes in fair values are to be accounted for consistently with each other and may not be offset.

When continuing involvement is limited to only a part of a financial asset (e.g., when an entity retains an option to repurchase only a part of the transferred asset), it should allocate the previous carrying amount of the asset between the part it continues to recognize and that which is no longer recognized on the basis of the relative fair values at the date of the transfer. The difference between (1) the carrying amount allocated to the part that is no longer recognized and (2) the sum of (a) the consideration received for the part no longer recognized and (b) any cumulative gain or loss allocated to it that had been recognized directly in equity is to be recognized in current period profit or loss. A cumulative gain or loss that had been recognized in equity is allocated between the parts recognized and no longer recognized on the basis of their relative fair values.

If the transferred asset is measured at amortized cost, the "fair value option" is not applicable to the corresponding liability.

Other asset transfer guidance applicable to special situations. In some cases, a reporting entity will transfer financial assets in a securitization transaction to a special-purpose entity (SPE) that it will be required to consolidate, and the SPE subsequently transfers a portion of those financial assets to third-party investors. The evaluation of whether a transfer of a portion of financial assets meets the derecognition criteria under IAS 39 generally will not differ if the transfer is directly to investors or through an SPE that first obtains the financial assets and then transfers a portion of those financial assets to third-party investors. If a transfer by a special-purpose entity to a third-party investor meets the conditions specified for derecognition in IAS 39, the transfer would be accounted for as a sale by the special-purpose entity and those derecognized assets or portions thereof would not be brought back into the statement of financial position in the consolidated financial statements of the entity. (Note, however, that the entire subject of accounting for special-purpose entities is expected to be given renewed attention in the near future. Similar scrutiny by the US FASB has already resulted in the issuance of an important standard, Interpretation 46[R].)

In other instances there may be dispositions with full recourse for transferee. If an entity sells receivables and provides a guarantee to the buyer to pay for any credit losses that may be incurred on the receivables as a result of the failure of the debtor to pay when due, while all other substantive benefits and risks (e.g., interest rate risk) of the receivables have been transferred to the buyer, the transaction qualifies as a transfer under IAS 39. In this scenario, the transferor has lost control over the receivables because the transferee has the ability to obtain the benefits of the transferred assets, and the risk retained by the transferor is limited to credit risk in the case of default. Under IAS 39, the guarantee is treated as a separate financial instrument to be recognized as a financial liability by the transferor.

Yet another situation involves a "right of first refusal." Derecognition is warranted if the transferor retains a right of first refusal that permits the transferor to purchase the transferred assets at their fair value at the date of reacquisition should the transferee decide to sell them. This is deemed appropriate since the reacquisition price is the fair value at the time of the reacquisition.

As noted earlier in this chapter, "factoring with recourse" is a popular form of receivables financing. Under the right of recourse, the transferor is obligated to compensate the transferee for the failure of the underlying debtors to pay when due. In addition, the recourse provision often entitles the transferee to sell the receivables back to the transferor at a fixed price in the event of unfavorable changes in interest rates or credit ratings of the underlying debtors. In many cases, such financing is promoted as being a sale of the customers' accounts, but applying a substance over form approach derecognition will not generally be warranted. Instead, this type of transaction should be accounted for as a collateralized borrowing by the transferor, since it does not qualify for derecognition. While the transferor has lost control, since the transferee has the ability to obtain the benefits of the transferred asset and is free to sell or pledge approximately the full fair value of the transferred asset, the transferor has effectively granted the transferee a *put option* on the transferred asset, since the transferee may sell the receivables back to the transferor in the event of both actual credit losses and changes in underlying credit ratings or interest rates. This is similar to other situations described in IAS 39, in which a transferor has not lost control and therefore a financial asset is not derecognized if the transferor retains substantially all the risks of ownership through an unconditional put option on the transferred assets held by the transferee.

As also noted, if an entity transfers a portion of a financial asset to others while retaining a part of the asset or assumes a related liability, the carrying amount of the financial asset should be allocated between the portion retained and the part sold or amount of liability retained, based on their relative fair values on the date of sale. The best evidence of the fair value of the retained interest in the bonds is obtained by reference to market quotations.

Valuation models are generally used when market quotations do not exist. Gain or loss should be recognized based only on the proceeds for the portion sold.

If the fair value of the part of the asset retained cannot be measured reliably, then a "cost recovery" approach should be used to measure profit (that is, allocate all the cost to the portion sold). If a related liability is retained and cannot be valued, no gain should be recognized on the transfer, and the liability should be measured at the difference between the proceeds and the carrying amount of the part of the financial asset that was sold, with a loss recognized equal to the difference between the proceeds and the sum of the amount recognized for the liability and the previous carrying amount of the financial asset transferred.

Consider an example in which a portfolio of bonds is partially transferred to an unrelated party, with the balance retained by the reporting entity, with the yield to the transferee being different than that on the underlying bonds (e.g., because market rates had diverged from the coupon rates). There are two alternative methods for estimating the fair value of the retained interests in the bonds for purposes of allocating the basis in the bonds between the portion sold and the portion retained. The first method, deemed most suitable when there is no market evidence of the fair value of the bonds as a whole, requires making an estimate of the future cash flows of the underlying bonds based on their contractual payments, reduced by estimates of prepayments and credit losses. The cash flows are then discounted by an estimate of the appropriate risk-adjusted interest rate. This method produces a fair value of the retained interests in the bonds; the transferor would recognize a gain on sale computed by subtracting from the proceeds the amount allocated to the basis sold.

The other reasonable method is to obtain a market quotation on bonds that are similar to the bonds it acquired previously and are the subject of the current sale. This is prorated to the portion being sold, with a gain on sale being recognized as the difference between the prorated amount and the proceeds of the sale.

When the asset being partially transferred is one that has been originated by the transferor, some modifications in methodology might be necessary, due to a lack of an active market. However, reference to actual lending transactions of the transferor as a means of estimating the fair value of the retained beneficial interests in the loans might provide a more objective and reliable estimate of fair value than the discounted cash flow model described above, because it is based on actual market transactions. While the market interest rates may have changed between the origination dates of the loans and the subsequent sales date of a portion of the loans, the corresponding change in the value of the loans might be determined by reference to current market interest rates being charged by the transferor, or perhaps its competitors for similar loans (e.g., with similar remaining maturity, cash flow pattern, currency, credit risk, collateral, and interest basis). Alternatively, if there is no change in the credit risk of the borrowers subsequent to the origination of the loans, an estimate of the current market interest rate might be derived by using a benchmark interest rate of a higher quality than the loans, holding the credit spread constant, and adjusting for the change in the benchmark interest rate from the origination dates to the subsequent sales date.

A detailed example of accounting for partial transfers of financial assets is presented below.

Examples of allocation between asset sold and asset or liability retained

Assume that an investment in mortgage loans, carried at €14.5 million, is being sold, but the entity is retaining the "servicing rights" to these mortgages. Servicing rights entail making monthly collections of principal and interest and forwarding these to the holders of the mortgages; it also involves other activities such as taking legal action to compel payment by delinquent debtors, and so forth. For such efforts, the servicing party is compensated; in this example, the present value of future servicing income can be estimated at €1.2 million, while the mortgage portfolio, without servicing, is sold for €13.6 million. Since values of both components (the portion sold and the portion retained) can be reliably valued, gain or loss is determined by first allocating the carrying value pro rata to the two portions, as follows:

	Selling price or fair value	Percentage of total	Allocated amount
Mortgages without servicing rights	€13.6 M	91.89%	€13.32 M
Servicing rights	1.2	8.11	1.18
Total	€14.8 M	100.00%	€14.50 M

The sale of the portfolio, *sans* servicing rights, will result in a gain of €13.6 M – 13.32 M = €280,000. The servicing rights will be recorded as an asset in the amount €1.18 million.

Under other circumstances, transactions such as the foregoing will necessitate loss recognition. Assume the same facts as above, *except* that the selling price of the mortgage portfolio with servicing is only €13.1 million. In this case, the allocation of fair values and loss recognition will be as follows:

	Selling price or fair value	Percentage of total	Allocated amount
Mortgages without servicing rights	€13.1 M	91.61%	€13.28 M
Servicing rights	1.2	8.39	1.22
Total	€14.3 M	100.00%	€14.50 M

A loss on the sale of the mortgages amounting to €13.28 M – 13.1 M = €180,000 will be recognized. The servicing rights will be recorded as an asset in the amount €1.22 million.

Finally, consider a sale as above, but the obligation to continue servicing the portfolio, rather than representing an asset to the seller, is a liability, since the estimate of future costs to be incurred in carrying out these duties exceeds the future revenues to be derived therefrom. Assume this net liability has a present fair value of €1.1 million and that the selling price of the mortgages is €14.6 million. The allocation process and resulting gain or loss recognition is as follows:

	Selling price or fair value	Percentage of total	Allocated amount
Mortgages without servicing rights	€14.6 M	108.15%	€15.68 M
Servicing rights	(1.1)	(8.15)	(1.18)
Total	€14.8 M	100.00%	€14.50 M

A loss on the sale of the mortgages amounting to €15.68 M – 14.6 M = €1,080,000 will be recognized. The servicing rights will be recorded as a liability in the amount €1.1 million.

It should be added that, for the foregoing examples in which a net asset is retained, the servicing asset is deemed to be an intangible and accordingly will be accounted for under the provisions of IAS 38. Normally, this asset would be reported at amortized cost, unless impairment occurs which would necessitate a downward adjustment in carrying value. The net servicing liability would be considered similar to other liabilities and accounted for at its amortized amount.

Transfers of financial liabilities, with part of the obligation retained or with a new obligation created pursuant to the transfer, should be accounted for in a manner analogous to the foregoing examples. Using fair values and transaction prices, the carrying amount of the obligation should be allocated so that gain or loss can be computed and the liability retained or created can be appropriately recorded.

IAS 39 holds that a financial liability (or a part of a financial liability) should be removed from the statement of financial position only when it is extinguished, that is, when the obligation specified in the contract is discharged, canceled, or expires, or when the primary responsibility for the liability (or a part thereof) is transferred to another party. Among other implications, this means that in-substance defeasance (which involves segregation of assets to be used for the future retirement of specific obligations of the entity) may no longer be given accounting recognition, since this does not entail actual discharge of the liability.

As described more fully in Chapter 10, revised IAS 39 has modified the criteria for derecognition of financial instruments. While previously there were several concepts which governed this determination, the revised standard (although retaining the primary concepts of *risks and rewards* and *control*) clarifies that the evaluation of the transfer of risks and rewards of ownership precedes the evaluation of the transfer of control for all derecognition determinations. New limitations are also placed on derecognition of parts of financial assets.

Under revised IAS 39, a determination must be made as to whether a financial asset has been *transferred;* derecognition can be effected only when there has been a transfer which meets the qualifications for derecognition accounting. Even if a transfer has occurred, if the reporting entity has retained substantially all such risks and rewards of ownership, it must continue to recognize the transferred asset.

Finally, when it is determined that when the entity has neither transferred nor retained substantially all the risks and rewards of ownership of the transferred asset, it must assess whether it has retained control over the transferred asset. When control has been retained, the transferred asset remains recognized by the transferor, to the extent of its continuing involvement in the transferred asset. On the other hand, if the transferor entity has not retained control, it derecognizes the transferred asset.

Initial recognition of financial assets at fair value. Initial recognition of financial assets is to be at fair value, increased by transaction costs only for those assets that are not to be carried at fair value with changes reflected currently through profit or loss. Similarly, issuance of financial liabilities is reflected at fair value less, for those not carried at fair value, transaction costs.

For financial instruments that are carried at amortized cost (held-to-maturity investments, originated loans, and most financial liabilities) the transaction costs are included in the calculation of amortized cost using the effective interest method. In effect, transaction costs are amortized through the profit or loss over the life of the instrument. This applies to loans and receivables and held-to-maturity investments, and also to investments in equity instruments for which fair values cannot be determined by reference to quoted prices in active markets. It also applies to those derivatives that are linked to, and must be settled by delivery of, those unquoted equity instruments.

On the other hand, for financial instruments that are carried at fair value, such as available-for-sale investments and instruments held for trading, transaction costs are not included in the fair value measurement. In many instances, this will cause expense or loss recognition for the transaction costs at the date of acquisition.

For available-for-sale financial assets, if the financial asset has fixed or determinable payments and a fixed maturity (i.e., it is a debt investment), the transaction costs are amortized to net profit or loss using the effective interest method. If the financial asset does not have fixed or determinable payments and a fixed maturity (i.e., it is an equity investment), the transaction costs are recognized in income at the time of eventual sale.

Fair value option. An important change was made to IAS 39 as part of the *Improvements Project*. This amendment created the "fair value option" under which entities are granted permission to measure any financial asset or financial liability at fair value, with changes in fair value to be recognized in profit or loss. This is accomplished by designating the asset or liability, at initial recognition, as being accounted for at fair value with changes in fair value reflected currently in profit or loss. In presenting and disclosing information, the reporting entity may use an alternative caption for such instruments (e.g., "financial instruments at fair value [through net income]") instead of employing the term "trading." To prevent abuse, however, reclassification of financial instruments into (or out of) the new category during the holding period is prohibited. The purpose of the change was to simplify the application of IAS 39 (for example, for hybrid instruments and for entities with matched asset/liability positions) and to enable consistent measurement of financial assets and financial liabilities. This change obviated the need to provide the option to account for value changes in available-for-sale financial instruments through current profit or loss, so that feature of original IAS 39 has been eliminated.

Note that, because some European lenders objected to the fair value option, in order to implement IFRS-based reporting requirements in the EU in 2005 (when all publicly held companies had to begin reporting consolidated financial statements in accordance with IFRS), a modification of the fair value option was imposed, which precludes invoking this option for the reporting entity's own debt instruments. While this action by the EU authorities has not amended IFRS, per se, it will have some potential impact on comparability across entities, particularly those conforming with IFRS in their entirety, and those employing European-tailored IFRS.

When applying the fair value measure, the transaction costs which would have to be incurred if there were to be a sale of the asset are not recognized (i.e., fair value is *not* net of selling costs) and thus fair value for reporting purposes is without the impact of transaction costs on either acquisition or assumed disposition.

Example

Consider the following example of the acquisition of a financial asset. Assume an investment security is acquired as follows: 2,000 ordinary shares of Ravinia Corp., par value €5 per share, are purchased on the open market on October 15 for €76 per share, plus total commissions and fees of €1,775. The shares are held for trading and thus are recorded at [€76 × 2,000 =] €152,200, and the commissions and fees are expensed immediately. At December 31, the shares are quoted at €76 1/2, and a sale at that date would entail the payment of commissions and fees of €1,550. When the time comes to prepare the year-end statement of financial position, this investment will be presented at [€76 1/2 × 2,000 shares =] €153,000. The potential cost of a sale, which would make the net realizable amount [€153,000 – 1,550 = € 151,450] lower than fair value, as defined by IAS 39, is to be ignored in all such remeasurements.

In rare instances, when the value of consideration given or received cannot be observed directly or indirectly by means of other market values, then IAS 39 directs that value be ascribed by means of computing the present value of all future cash payments or receipts, using the prevailing market rate of similar types of instruments as the discount rate.

Trade date vs. settlement date accounting. Normal instruments trades clear or settle several days after the trade date. In practice, historically, some have recorded such transaction son the trade date, while others have waited until the settlement date to give formal recognition to the purchase or sale transaction. Under the provisions of IAS 39, as amended, an entity may elect to use either trade date accounting or settlement date accounting for purchases and sales of financial assets. However, it is required that the reporting entity apply the selected accounting policy in a consistent manner for both purchases and sales of financial assets that belong to the same statement of financial position category (i.e., financial assets held for trading, those available for sale, those to be held to maturity, and loans and receivables originated by the entity and, optionally, loans which have been purchased and which are not quoted in an active market).

When trade date accounting is used, the asset is recognized at the trade date and all subsequent changes in value will be reflected as required under IAS 39. On the other hand, if settlement date accounting is used to record purchases, there would be a failure to recognize changes in value from trade to settlement date, before formally recording the asset. For that reason, IAS 39 requires that changes in the fair value of the underlying security during the interval from trade date to settlement date must be given accounting recognition, to the extent that changes in fair value would otherwise have been accounted for, consistent with the nature of the investment. Thus, for held-to-maturity investments, fair value changes between trade and settlement dates are not reported, since these investments are accounted for at amortized historical cost, not at fair values (unless a permanent impairment occurs, which is unlikely in the brief span from trade to settlement dates). In the case of trading instruments, changes in fair value between the trade and settlement dates would be taken into profit or loss. For available-for-sale investments, the changes in fair value during the time interval from trade date to settlement date are reported in other comprehensive income.

Subsequent remeasurement issues. Before the issuance of IAS 39, the carrying values of financial instruments qualifying as investments were determined by a range of methods, varying by type of instrument, with many options available for the reporting entity to select from for any given category of investment asset. This situation was changed significantly by IAS 39, which requires that subsequent remeasurement of financial assets be at fair value excluding transaction costs, except for (1) loans and receivables, (2) held-to-maturity investments, and (3) any financial asset whose fair value cannot be reliably measured. Held-to-maturity investments and loans and receivables are to be reported at amortized cost; other financial assets which have indeterminate fair values but fixed maturities will be measured at amortized cost using the effective interest rate method, while those that do not have fixed maturities are to be measured at cost. In all cases, periodic review for possible impairment is needed, and if impairment exists, a loss is to be recognized in current period profit or loss. Derivative financial instruments that are assets must be valued at fair value.

According to IFRIC 10, *Interim Financial Reporting and Impairment*, which addresses conflicts between the requirements of IAS 34, *Interim Financial Reporting*, and those in other standards on the recognition and reversal in the financial statements of impairment losses on goodwill or an investment in either an equity instrument of a financial asset carried at cost under IAS 39, any impairment losses recognized in an interim financial statement must not be reversed in subsequent interim or annual financial statements.

One issue frequently raised pertains to how fair value should be gauged when the reporting entity owns a large enough fraction of the total class outstanding (or of the portion actively trading on a given day) such that a disposition would be expected to "move the market." The market could be affected in one of two ways: either the large block would fetch a premium price (in the nature of a "control premium" although the transferor's shares could not truly represent a controlling interest—if it did, the investment would have been accounted for under IAS 28 or 27, not under IAS 39), or it would cause a decline due to the imbalance of supply and demand. A published price quotation in an active market is the best estimate of fair value. This should be used, without adjustment for possible premiums or discounts that might result from the (hypothetical) sale of the entity's holdings.

Revised IAS 39 has provided additional guidance regarding the determination of fair values using valuation techniques. Specifically, it states that the goal is to establish what the transaction price would have been, on the measurement date, in an arm's-length exchange motivated by normal business considerations. Accordingly, any valuation technique employed must (1) incorporate all factors that market participants would consider in setting a price, and (2) be consistent with accepted economic methodologies for pricing financial instruments. The estimates and assumptions used must be consistent with available information about the estimates and assumptions that market participants would use in setting an actual price for the financial instrument.

The standard reiterates that the best estimates of fair value at initial recognition, for financial instruments that are not quoted in an active market, are the actual transaction prices. However, if fair values are evidenced by other observable market transactions, or are more usefully based on valuation techniques whose variables include only data from observable markets, those should be used instead.

Accounting for collateral held. Creditors sometimes require that debtors provide them with collateral as additional security for repayment obligations. It has often been suggested that, to enhance accountability, this collateral held be reported in the creditor's statement of financial position (which would necessitate recognition of a liability for the return of the collateral, also) for as long as it is held. This approach has, in the past, been mandated under various financial reporting standards, but has been controversial for two reasons. First, it results in a "grossing up" of the creditor's statement of financial position, since both the underlying receivable and the collateral would be shown as assets. Second, the collateral would appear in both creditor's and debtor's statements of financial position simultaneously, since it would not qualify for derecognition by the debtor, which strikes many as inappropriate although not literally banned under GAAP or IFRS.

Revised IAS 32 provides new guidance on the accounting for collateral, as follows:

1. A reporting entity is required to disclose the carrying amount of financial assets pledged as collateral for liabilities, the carrying amount of financial assets pledged as collateral for contingent liabilities, and any material terms and conditions relating to assets pledged as collateral.

2. When an entity has accepted collateral that it is permitted to sell or repledge in the absence of default by the owner of the collateral, it is now required to disclose

   a. The fair value of the collateral accepted (both financial and nonfinancial assets);
   b. The fair value of any such collateral sold or repledged and whether the entity has an obligation to return it; and
   c. Any material terms and conditions associated with its use of this collateral.

Other issues. Financial assets that are hedged against exposure in changes in fair value must be accounted for at an adjusted carrying amount that reflects changes in fair value attributable to the risk designated as being hedged, with a derivative the hedging instrument likewise accounted for at fair value, as discussed later in this chapter. Financial instruments which have values less than zero are to be accounted for as financial liabilities; that is, at fair value if held for trading or if a derivative instrument, otherwise at amortized cost in most cases.

Changes in the value of held-to-maturity investments are generally not recognized. However, the use of the held-to-maturity classification is strictly limited to situations in which both intent and ability to hold are present, and past behavior is to be used to evaluate whether the expression of intent is indeed sincere. Intent to hold for an indefinite period would not be a basis for classification as held-to-maturity, nor would a willingness to dispose of the investment if certain changes in interest rates or market risks were to occur, or if improved yields on alternative investments or other factors were to develop.

If the issuer of the instrument that the entity holds as a financial asset has the right to settle it at an amount materially below amortized cost, the use of the held-to-maturity classification is not permitted. For instance, a normal call feature will not preclude held-to-maturity classification if the holder would recover substantially the entire carrying amount if the call feature is exercised by the issuer. If the entity holding the investment has a put option (giving it the right to demand early redemption, but not the obligation to do so), classification as held-to-maturity is not possible.

As a practical matter, the held-to-maturity category will be reserved to debt instruments held as investments, since equity instruments have indefinite life (thus rendering untestable the holder's representation of its intent to hold to maturity) or else have indeterminable returns to the holder (as with warrants and options). Notwithstanding the nature of the investment, use of the held-to-maturity classification is prohibited if the reporting entity has, during the current reporting year or two prior years, sold, transferred, or exercised the put option on a significant amount of held-to-maturity investments before maturity. However, IAS 39 provides certain exceptions to the foregoing rule: sales close to maturity or an exercised call date such that market rate changes would not affect the asset's fair value; a sale after substantially all of the original principal had been recovered; and sales due to isolated events beyond the entity's control, which are nonrecurring and which could not have been reasonably anticipated by it (e.g., a significant decline in the issuer's creditworthiness, changes in tax laws, or other changes in the legal or regulatory environment). To the extent that any of these conditions exist, sales from the held-to-maturity portfolio will not taint the remaining assets.

Remeasurement of trading and available-for-sale financial assets. Changes in the value of trading investments in debt or equity instruments are reported currently in profit or loss. IAS 39 defines derivative financial instruments as being, ipso facto, financial instruments held for trading, unless held for designated hedging purposes. Available-for-sale investments are also remeasured at fair value at each date of the statement of financial position, but the changes in fair value must be reported in other comprehensive income. A formerly permitted optional treatment to show these changes in current income, is no longer permitted under revised IAS 39. However, under the fair value option, at acquisition any financial asset or liability may be designated for reporting of changes in fair value in current profit or loss, so effectively the elimination of the previous alternative accounting for available-for-sale instruments is not an impediment.

Accounting for Investments in Debt Instruments

Under IAS 39 fair value is required for debt instruments held for trading or available for sale, while amortized cost is prescribed for those in the held-to-maturity portfolio, as that is narrowly defined by the standard, as well as for those classified as loans and receivables, because these are not quoted in active markets. The held-to-maturity category is the most restrictive of the three; debt instruments can be so classified only if the reporting entity has the positive intent and the ability to hold the instruments for that length of time. A mere intent to hold an investment for an indefinite period is not adequate to permit such a classification. On the other hand, a variety of isolated causes may necessitate transferring an investment in a debt instrument from the held-for-investment category without calling into question the investor's general intention to hold other similarly classified investments to maturity. Among these are declines in the creditworthiness of a particular investment's issuer or a change in tax law or regulatory rules. On the other hand, sales of investments which were classified as held-to-maturity for other reasons will call into question the entity's assertions, both in the past and in the future, about its intentions regarding these and other similarly categorized instruments. For this reason, transfers from or sales of held-to-maturity instruments will be very rare, indeed.

If it cannot be established that a particular debt security held as an investment will be held for trading or held to maturity, or that it qualifies as a loan or a receivable, it must be classed as available-for-sale. Whatever the original classification of the investment, however, transfers among the three portfolios will be made as intentions change.

Accounting for debt instruments that are held for trading and those that are available for sale is based on fair value. Changes in the values of debt instruments in the trading portfolio are recognized in profit or loss, while changes in the values of debt instruments in the available-for-sale category are reported in other comprehensive income and the cumulative amount in equity (See paragraph "Accounting for Investments in Debt and Equity Instruments" in Chapter 10).

Reclassifications and impairments in debt and equity instruments are discussed and illustrated in Chapter 10; remeasurement of financial liabilities is discussed and illustrated in Chapter 12.

Hedge Accounting

IAS 39 provides for special hedge accounting under defined circumstances. The standard defines three types of hedging relationships: fair value hedges, cash flow hedges, and hedges of net investment in a foreign entity. These are described in IAS 39 as follows:

- **Fair value hedge.** A hedge, using a derivative or other financial instrument, of the exposure to changes in the fair value of a recognized asset, liability, or unrecognized firm commitment (or an identified portion of such an asset, liability or firm commitment), that is attributable to a particular risk and could affect profit or loss.
- **Cash flow hedge.** A hedge, using a derivative or other financial instrument, of the exposure to variability in cash flows that is attributable to a particular risk associated with a recognized asset or liability (such as all or a portion of future interest payments on variable-rate debt) or forecasted transaction (such as an anticipated purchase or sale) that could affect profit or loss. Under revised IAS 39 (effective 2005), a hedge of an unrecognized firm commitment to buy an asset at a fixed price is now to be accounted for as a fair value hedge (previously this was to be treated as a cash flow hedge). However, a hedge of the foreign currency risk of a firm commitment can be treated as either a cash flow hedge or a fair value hedge.
- **Hedge of a net investment in a foreign entity** A hedge, using a derivative or other financial instrument, of foreign currency exposed in the net assets of a foreign operation.

The most contentious issue regarding hedging has been the decision to apply special hedge accounting to such transactions. If all financial instruments were marked to market (fair) values, there would be no need for special accounting except, perhaps, for hedges of unrecognized firm commitments and forecasted transactions. However, given that fair value accounting has yet to be fully accepted for financial instruments held as assets, and is even less widely accepted for financial instruments classed as liabilities, the topic of hedge accounting must be addressed. Under the provisions of IAS 39, a hedging relationship will qualify for special hedge accounting presentation if all of the following conditions are met:

1. At the inception of the hedge there is formal documentation of the hedging relationship and the entity's risk management objective and strategy for undertaking the hedge. That documentation should include identification of the hedging instrument, the related hedged item or transaction, the nature of the risk being hedged, and how the entity will assess the hedging instrument's effectiveness if offsetting the exposure to changes in the hedged item's fair value or the hedged transaction's cash flows that is attributable to the hedged risk.
2. The hedge is expected to be highly effective in achieving offsetting changes in fair value or cash flows attributable to the hedged risk, consistent with the originally documented risk management strategy for that particular hedging relationship.
3. For cash flow hedges, a forecasted transaction that is the subject of the hedge must be probable and present an exposure to price risk that could produce variation in cash flows that will affect reported income.
4. The effectiveness of the hedge can be reliably measured, that is, the fair value or cash flows of the hedged item and the fair value of the hedging instrument can be reliably measured.
5. The hedge was assessed and determined actually to have been effective throughout the financial reporting period.

Under IAS 39, a hedging relationship could be designated for a hedging instrument taken as a whole, or, in certain specified instances, for a component of a hedging instrument. Thus, an entity could designate the change in the intrinsic value of an option as the hedge, while the remaining component of the option (its time value) is excluded.

As noted, to qualify for hedge accounting, the effectiveness of a hedge would have to be subject to effectiveness testing. The method an entity adopts for this would depend on its risk management strategy, and this could vary for different types of hedges. If the principal terms of the hedging instrument and of the entire hedged asset or liability or hedged forecasted transaction are the same, the changes in fair value and cash flows attributable to the risk being hedged offset fully, both when the hedge is entered into and thereafter until completion. An interest rate swap is likely to be an effective hedge if the notional and principal amounts, term, repricing dates, dates of interest or principal receipts and payments, and basis for measuring interest rates are the same for the hedging instrument and the hedged item.

Also, to qualify for special hedge accounting under IAS 39's provisions, the hedge would have to relate to a specific identified and designated risk, and not merely to overall entity business risks, and must ultimately affect the entity's net profit or loss, not just its equity.

The standard provides that a hedge can be judged to be highly effective if, both at inception and throughout its life, the reporting entity can expect that changes in the fair value or cash flows (depending on the type of hedge) of the hedged item will be virtually fully offset by changes in the fair value or cash flows of the underlying or hedged item, and that actual results are within a range of 80% to 125% of full offset. While there is flexibility in terms of how an entity measures and monitors effectiveness (and this may even vary within an entity regarding different types of hedges), the fact that IAS 39 provides quantified upper and lower effectiveness thresholds underlines the importance of making such a determination. The documentation of the entity's hedging strategy must stipulate how this will be achieved, and hedging effectiveness must be assessed at least as often as financial reports are prepared.

Fair value hedges. With specific regard to fair value hedges, IAS 39 prescribes the following special hedge accounting:

1. The gain or loss from remeasuring the hedging instrument at fair value is to be recognized currently in profit or loss; and
2. The gain or loss on the hedged item attributable to the hedged risk should adjust the carrying amount of the hedged item and be recognized currently in profit or loss.

These requirements apply even if a hedged item is otherwise measured at fair value with changes in fair value recognized in other comprehensive income. Hedge accounting must be discontinued, however, when the hedging instrument expires or is sold, terminated, or exercised, or when the hedge no longer meets the criteria for qualification for hedge accounting.

When there has been an adjustment made to the carrying amount of a hedged, interest-bearing instrument, it should be reclassified from equity to profit or loss as a reclassification adjustment, beginning no later than when it ceases to be adjusted for changes in fair value attributable to the risk being hedged.

Macrohedging. One of the long-standing debates regarding fair value hedging pertained to so-called "macrohedging." Historically, it was required that specific assets or liabilities be identified as the hedged items, but many financial managers have argued that actual fair value hedging is often conducted by acquiring a hedging position to protect against the effect of the value changes of the *net* asset or liability position maintained. This is known as "macrohedging" or hedging a portfolio of interest rate risks. Such an action, while sound from a management perspective, did not qualify for hedge accounting treatment under the original IAS 39.

In response to this perceived failure to address the accounting implications of common risk management strategies, IASB amended IAS 39 to permit hedge accounting for such macrohedge situations. As amended, IAS 39 permits the following rules to apply for purposes of accounting for a fair value hedge of a portfolio of interest rate risk:

1. The reporting entity identifies a portfolio of items whose interest rate risk it wishes to hedge. The portfolio may include both assets and liabilities, or could include only assets or only liabilities.

2. The reporting entity analyzes the portfolio into repricing time periods based on *expected*, rather than contractual, repricing dates.

3. The reporting entity then designates the hedged item as a percentage of the amount of assets (or liabilities) in each time period. All of the assets from which the hedged amount are drawn have to be items (a) whose fair value changes in response to the risk being hedged and (b) that could have qualified for fair value hedge accounting under the original IAS 39 had they been hedged individually. The time periods have to be sufficiently narrow to ensure that all assets (or liabilities) in a time period are homogeneous with respect to the hedged risk—that is, the fair value of each item moves proportionately to, and in the same direction as, changes in the hedged interest rate risk.

4. The reporting entity designates what interest rate risk it is hedging. This risk may be a portion of the interest rate risk in each of the items in the portfolio, such as a benchmark interest rate like LIBOR or US Prime.

5. The reporting entity designates a hedging instrument for each time period. The hedging instrument may be a portfolio of derivatives (for instance, interest rate swaps) containing offsetting risk positions.

6. The reporting entity measures the change in the fair value of the hedged item that is attributable to the hedged risk. The result is then recognized in profit or loss and in one of two separate line items in the statement of financial position. The statement of financial position line item depends upon whether the hedged item is an asset (in which case the change in fair value would be reported in a separate line item within assets) or is a liability (in which case the value change would be reported in a separate line item within liabilities). In either case this separate statement of financial position line item is to be presented on the face of the statement of financial position adjacent to the related hedged item—but it is not permissible to allocate it to individual assets or liabilities, or to separate classes of assets or liabilities (i.e., it is not acceptable to employ "basis adjustment").

7. The reporting entity measures the change in the fair value of the hedging instrument and recognized this as a gain or loss in profit or loss. It recognizes the fair value of the hedging instrument as an asset or liability in the statement of financial position.

8. Ineffectiveness will be given as the difference in profit or loss between the amounts determined in steps 6 and 7.

A change in the amounts that are expected to be repaid or mature in a time period will result in ineffectiveness, measured as the difference between (a) the initial hedge ratio applied to the initially estimated amount in a time period and (b) that same ratio applied to the revised estimate of the amount.

Cash flow hedges. Gain or loss relating to the portion of a cash flow hedge that is determined to be effective is to be recognized in other comprehensive income. The ineffective portion, if any, must be recognized currently in profit or loss.

Per IAS 39, the amount that has been recognized in other comprehensive income associated with the hedged item is to be adjusted to the lesser of two amounts: (1) the cumulative gain or loss on the hedging instrument needed to offset the cumulative change in expected future cash flows on the hedged item from inception of the hedge, less the portion associated with the ineffective component, or (2) the fair value of the cumulative change in expected future cash flows on the hedged item from inception of the hedge. Any remaining gain or loss (the ineffective portion) is recognized in profit or loss, or other comprehensive income as described above.

Revised IAS 39 requires that when a hedged forecast transaction occurs and results in the recognition of a *financial asset* or a *financial liability*, the cumulative gain or loss deferred in equity does not adjust the initial carrying amount of the asset or liability (thus, the formerly acceptable method of basis adjustment has been prohibited). This remains as a separate component of equity until subsequent derecognition or impairment, when that cumulative gain or loss should be reclassified from equity to profit or loss as a reclassification adjustment, consistent with the recognition of gains and losses on the asset or liability. On the other hand, for hedges of forecast transactions that result in the recognition of a *nonfinancial asset* or a *nonfinancial liability*, the entity may elect whether to apply basis adjustment or retain the hedging gain or loss in equity and reclassify that gain or loss from equity to profit or loss when the asset or liability affects profit or loss.

In the case of other cash flow hedges (i.e., those not resulting in recognition of assets or liabilities), amounts reflected in other comprehensive income should be reclassified from equity to profit or loss in the period or periods when the hedged firm commitment or forecasted transaction also affects profit or loss.

Hedge accounting is to be discontinued when the hedging instrument is sold, expires, is terminated or exercised. If the gain or loss was accumulated in equity, it should remain there until such time as the forecasted transaction occurs, when it is added to the asset or liability recorded or is reclassified from equity to profit or loss when the transaction impacts profit or loss. Hedge accounting is also discontinued prospectively when the hedge ceases meeting the criteria for qualification of hedge accounting. The accumulated gain or loss remains in equity until the committed or forecasted transaction occurs, whereupon it will be handled as discussed above.

Finally, if the forecasted or committed transaction is no longer expected to occur, hedge accounting is prospectively discontinued. In this case, the accumulated gain or loss included in equity must be immediately reclassified from equity to profit or loss.

Hedges of a net investment in a foreign entity. Hedges of a net investment in a foreign entity (hedges of foreign currency exposure in the net assets of a foreign operation) are accounted for similarly to cash flow hedges. To the extent it is determined to be effective, accumulated gains or losses are reflected in other comprehensive income and accumulated in equity. The ineffective portion is reported in profit or loss.

In terms of financial reporting, the gain or loss on the effective portion of these hedges should be classified in the same manner as the foreign currency translation gain or loss. According to IAS 21, translation gains and losses are not reported in profit or loss but instead are reported in other comprehensive income and the cumulative amounts in equity, with allocation being made to minority interest when the foreign entity is not wholly owned by the reporting entity. Likewise, any hedging gain or loss would be reported in other comprehensive income. When the foreign entity is disposed of, the cumulative translation gain or loss would be reclassified from equity to profit or loss, as would any related deferred hedging gain or loss.

When a hedge does not qualify for special hedge accounting (due to failure to properly document, ineffectiveness, etc.), any gains or losses are to be accounted for based on the nature of the hedging instrument. If a derivative financial instrument, the gains or losses must be reported in profit or loss.

Hedges of interest rate risk on a portfolio basis (also called macrohedging). As discussed above, revised IAS 39 permits fair value hedge accounting to be used more readily for a portfolio hedge of interest rate risk than previously was the case. In particular, for such a hedge, it allows

1. The hedged item to be designated as an amount of a currency (e.g., an amount of dollars, euros, pounds, or rands) rather than as individual assets (or liabilities)
2. The gain or loss attributable to the hedged item to be presented either

    a. In a single separate line item within assets, for those repricing time periods for which the hedged item is an asset; or
    b. In a single separate line item within liabilities, for those repricing time periods for which the hedged item is a liability.

3. Prepayment risk to be incorporated by scheduling prepayable items into repricing time periods based on expected, rather than contractual, repricing dates. However, when the portion hedged is based on expected repricing dates, the effect that changes in the hedged interest rate have on those expected repricing dates are included when determining the change in the fair value of the hedged item. Consequently, if a portfolio that contains prepayable items is hedged with a non-prepayable derivative, ineffectiveness arises if the dates on which items in the hedged portfolio are expected to prepay are revised, or actual prepayment dates differ from those expected.

Summary of Hedge Accounting

Type of transaction	Type of hedge	Accounting method	Accounting result
Hedge of a firm commitment	Fair value hedge	Recognize in profit or loss currently.	Concurrent recognition in profit or loss currently.
Hedge of a forecasted transaction	Cash flow hedge	Recognize in other comprehensive income. Reclassify from equity to profit or loss on the date the forecasted transaction actually impacts profit or loss.	Concurrent recognition in profit or loss on a delayed basis.
Hedge of an investment in subsidiary	Net investment hedge	Recognize in other comprehensive income. Reclassify from equity to profit or loss upon disposal of the investment.	Concurrent recognition in profit or loss on a delayed basis.

Assessing hedge effectiveness. Under the provisions of IAS 39, assuming other conditions are also met, hedge accounting may be applied as long as, and to the extent that, the hedge is effective. By effective, the standard is alluding to the degree to which offsetting changes in fair values or cash flows attributable to the hedged risk are achieved by the hedging instrument. A hedge is generally deemed effective if, at inception and throughout the period of the hedge, the ratio of changes in value of the underlying to changes in value of the hedging instrument are in a range of 80 to 125%.

Hedge effectiveness will be heavily impacted by the nature of the instruments used for hedging. For example, interest rate swaps will be almost completely effective if the notional and principal amounts match, and the terms, repricing dates, interest and principal payment dates, and basis for measurement are the same. On the other hand, if the hedged and hedging instruments are denominated in different currencies, effectiveness will not be 100% in most instances. Also, if the rate change is partially due to changes in perceived credit risk, there will be a lack of perfect correlation as well.

Hedges must be defined in terms of specific identified and designated risks. Overall (entity) risk cannot be the basis for hedging. Also, it must be possible to precisely measure the risk being hedged; thus, threat of expropriation (which may be an insurable risk) is not a risk that can be hedged, as that term is used in IAS 39. Similarly, investments accounted for by the equity method cannot be hedged, since that would be inconsistent with the equity method of accounting. In contrast, a net investment in a foreign subsidiary can be hedged, since this is a function of currency exchange rates alone.

If a hedge does not qualify for special hedge accounting because it is not effective, any gains or losses arising from changes in the fair value of a hedged item measured at fair value, subsequent to initial recognition, are reported as otherwise prescribed by IAS 39. That is, if an item is held for trading, changes in value are reported in profit or loss; if available for sale, the changes are reported in other comprehensive income.

Disclosures Required under IFRS 7

IAS 32 was effective in 1996 and established an expansive set of disclosure requirements. IAS 39, which became effective in 2001, carried forward these requirements with only minor changes and added further informational disclosure requirements. Both IAS 32 and IAS 39 were revised as part of the IASB's *Improvements Project* in 2003, and at that time all disclosure requirements were relocated to IAS 32. In mid-2005, IFRS 7 was promulgated, which set forth all financial instruments disclosure requirements, superseding (but not changing) the disclosure requirements previously found in both IAS 30 and IAS 32.

This to section sets forth and discusses those requirements first set forth by IAS 32 and subsequently incorporated into IFRS 7. (Bank and other financial institution disclosure requirements, as originally set forth by IAS 30, are explained and copiously illustrated in Chapter 24.)

Primacy of risk considerations. The major objective of the disclosure requirements first established by IAS 32 is to give financial statement users the ability to assess on-and off-balance-sheet risks, which prominently includes risks relating to future cash flows associated with the financial instruments. The standard presents the following typology of risk:

1. **Market risk,** which implies not merely the risk of loss but also the potential for gain, and which is in turn comprised of

   a. **Currency risk**—The risk that the value of an instrument will vary due to changes in currency exchange rates.

   b. **Interest rate risk**—The risk that the value of the instrument will fluctuate due to changes in market interest rates.

   c. **Other price risk**—A broader concept that subsumes interest rate risk, this is, the risk that the fair value or future cash flows of a financial instrument will fluctuate due to factors specific to the financial instrument or due to factors that are generally affecting all similar instruments traded in the same markets.

2. **Credit risk** is related to a loss that may occur from the failure of another party to a financial instrument to discharge an obligation according to the terms of a contract.

3. **Liquidity risk** is the risk that an entity may encounter difficulty in meeting obligations associated with financial liabilities.

The standard does address the means by which interest rate and credit risk factors are to be addressed in the financial statements, while cash flow and liquidity risk are discussed in general terms only. These matters are elaborated upon in the following paragraphs.

Interest rate risk. Interest rate risk is the risk associated with holding fixed-rate instruments in a changing interest-rate environment. As market rates rise, the price of fixed-interest-rate instruments will decline, and vice versa. This relationship holds in all cases, irrespective of other specific factors, such as changes in perceived creditworthiness of the borrower. However, with certain complex instruments such as mortgage-backed bonds (a popular form of derivative instrument), where the behavior of the underlying debtors can be expected to be altered by changes in the interest rate environment (i.e., as market interest rates decline, prepayments by mortgagors increase in frequency, raising reinvestment rate risk to the bondholders and accordingly tempering the otherwise expected upward movement of the bond prices), the inverse relationship will become distorted.

IAS 32 first required that for each class of financial asset and financial liability, both those that are recognized (i.e., on-balance-sheet) and those that are not recognized (off-balance-sheet), the reporting entity should disclose information which will illuminate its exposure to interest rate risk. This includes disclosure of contractual repricing dates or maturity dates, whichever are earlier, as well as effective interest rates, if applicable.

These data provide the user of the financial statements with an ability to predict cash flows, since fixed-rate instruments will generate cash inflows (if assets) or outflows (if liabilities) at a given rate until the maturity date or the earlier repricing date, although other features, such as optional call dates or serial retirements, can complicate this further. The combination of information on contractual (or coupon) rates, maturity dates, and changing market conditions (not provided by the financial statements, but presumably available to anyone with access to the financial press) also provides insight into the price risk of the underlying debt instruments, while for debt having floating rates of interest, knowledge of market conditions provides insight into cash flow risk.

The standard also suggests, but does not require, that when *expected repricings* are to occur at dates that differ significantly from contractual dates, such information be provided as well. An example is when the entity is an investor in fixed-rate mortgage loans and when prepayments can be reliably estimated; as the funds thereby generated will need to be reinvested at then-current market rates, altering the patterns and amounts of future cash flows from what a simple reading of the statement of financial position might otherwise suggest. Information based on management expectations should be clearly distinguished from that which is based on contractual provisions.

IAS 32 initially suggested that a meaningful way to present this information is to group financial assets and financial liabilities into categories as follows:

1. Those debt instruments that have fixed rates and thus expose the reporting entity to interest-rate (price) risk
2. Those debt instruments that have floating rates and thus expose the entity to cash flow risk
3. Those instruments, typically equity, which are not interest-rate sensitive

This guidance is carried forward by IFRS 7. Effective interest rates, in this context, means the internal rate of return, which is the discount rate that equates the present value of all future cash flows associated with the instrument with its current market price. Put another way, this is the measure of the time value of money as it relates to the financial instrument in question. It must be noted that effective interest rates cannot be determined for derivative financial instruments such as swaps, forwards and options, although these are often affected by changes in interest rates, and accordingly the effective rate disclosures do not apply in such cases. In any event, the risk characteristics of such instruments must be discussed in the footnote disclosures.

The nature of the reporting entity's business and the extent to which it holds financial assets or is obligated by financial liabilities will affect the manner in which such disclosures are presented, and no single method of making such disclosures will be suitable for every entity. The standard suggests that in many cases a tabular disclosure of amounts of financial instruments exposed to interest rate risk will be useful, with the instruments grouped according to repricing or maturity dates (e.g., within one year, from one to five years, and over five years from the date of the statement of financial position). In other cases (for financial institutions, for example), finer distinctions of maturities might be warranted. Similar tabular presentations of data on floating-rate instruments (which create cash-flow risk rather than interest-rate [price] risk) should also be presented, when pertinent. When other risk factors are also present, such as credit risk (discussed in the following section), a series of tabular presentations, segregating instruments into risk classes and then categorizing each in terms of maturities and so on, may be necessary to convey the risk dimensions adequately to readers.

Sensitivity analysis has been alluded to by a number of different accounting standards over the years. Since it has always been presented as an optional feature, it has rarely been employed in actual disclosures, despite having great potential for being useful to readers. In the context of financial instruments, sensitivity analysis would imply a discussion of the effect on portfolio value of a hypothetical change (e.g., a 1% change, plus or minus) in interest rates. There are at least two reasons why such information, unless accompanied by an adequate discussion of the particular characteristics of the financial instruments in question, might be misleading to financial statement readers.

First, because of the phenomenon known as convexity, the value change of each successive 1% change in interest rates is not a constant, but rather, a function of current market rates. For example, if the market rate at the date of the statement of financial position is 8%, a move in rates to 9% might cause a €20,000 decline in value in a given bond portfolio, but a further 1% change in the market rate, from 9% to 10%, would not have a further €20,000 effect. Instead, the effect would be an amount greater or lesser depending on the coupon (contractual) rate of interest of the underlying financial instruments. A reader, however, would rarely appreciate this fact and would probably extrapolate the sensitivity data in a linear manner, which could be materially misleading in the absence of further narrative information.

Second, sensitivity data most often are presented in a manner that suggests that they apply symmetrically. Thus, in the foregoing example, the presumption is that a 1% market rate decline would boost the portfolio value by €20,000 and that a 1% rate increase would depress it by a similar amount. However, some instruments, most notably those with embedded options (mortgage-backed bonds, having prepayment options, are the most common example cited, although exotic derivatives can be far more difficult to analyze) will not exhibit symmetrical price behavior, and the asymmetries will become exaggerated as hypothetical market rates stray further from the current rates. As a practical matter, the only way to convey these subtleties in a meaningful fashion would be to incorporate extensive tables of information into the footnotes, which many users would find to be impossibly confusing.

For these and possibly other reasons, although first recommended by IAS 32, disclosure of sensitivity data has been slow to gain popularity. Such disclosures continue to be encouraged under IFRS 7. If provided, however, any assumptions and the methodologies employed should be explained adequately, along with any needed caveats concerning the validity of extrapolation over greater ranges of market rate changes and over time.

Credit risk. For each class of financial asset, both recognized (i.e., on-balance-sheet) and unrecognized (off-balance-sheet), information is to be provided about exposure to credit risk. Specifically, the maximum amount of credit risk exposure as of the date of the statement of financial position, without considering possible recoveries from any collateral that may have been provided, should be stated and any significant concentrations of credit risk should be discussed.

Disclosure is required of the amount that best represents the maximum credit risk exposure at the date of the statement of financial position. In many cases, this is simply the carrying value of such instruments; for example, accounts receivable net of any allowance for uncollectible receivables already provided would be the measure of credit risk associated with trade receivables. In other cases, the maximum loss would be an amount less than that which is revealed in the statement of financial position, as when a legal right of offset exists but the financial asset was not presented on a net basis in the statement of financial position because one of the required conditions set forth in IAS 32 (intention to settle on a net basis) was not met. In yet other circumstances, the maximum accounting loss that could be incurred would be greater, as when the asset is unrecognized in the statement of financial position although otherwise disclosed in the footnotes as, for example, when the entity has guaranteed collection of receivables that have been sold to another party (often called factoring with recourse, discussed earlier).

There are a large number of potential combinations of factors that could affect maximum credit risk exposure, and in other than the most basic circumstances it is likely that extended narratives will be needed to convey the risks fully in the most meaningful way to users of the financial statements. For example, when an entity has financial assets owed from and financial liabilities owed to the same counter-party, with the right of offset but without having an intent to settle on a net basis, the maximum amount subject to credit risk may be lower than the carrying value of the asset. However, if past behavior suggests that the entity would probably respond to the debtor's difficulties by extending the maturity of the financial asset beyond the maturity of the related liability, it will voluntarily expose itself to greater risk since it will presumably settle its obligation and thus forfeit the opportunity to offset these related instruments.

When the maximum credit risk exposure associated with a particular financial asset or group of assets is the same as the amount presented on the face of the statement of financial position, it is not necessary to reiterate this fact in the footnotes. The presumption is that there will be disclosures made for all material items for which this fact does not hold, however.

In addition to disclosure of maximum credit risk, IFRS 7 requires disclosure of concentrations of credit risk when these are not otherwise apparent from the financial statements. Common examples of this involve trade accounts receivable that are due from debtors within one geographic region or operating within one industry segment, as when a large fraction of receivables are due from, say, housing construction contractors in the Netherlands, many of whom might find themselves in financial difficulty if economic conditions deteriorated in that narrowly defined market. In addition to geographic locale and industry, other factors to consider would include the creditworthiness of the debtors (e.g., if the reporting entity targets a market such as college students not having steady employment, or third-world governments) and the nature of the activities undertaken by the counterparties. The disclosures should provide a clear indication of the characteristics shared by the debtors.

Examples of disclosures of credit risk

Note 5: Interest Rate Swap Agreements

The differential to be paid or received is accrued as interest rates change and is recognized over the life of the agreements.

Note 8: Foreign Exchange Contracts

The corporation enters into foreign exchange contracts as a hedge against accounts payable denominated in foreign currencies. Market value gains and losses are recognized, and the resulting credit or debit offsets foreign exchange losses or gains on those payables.

Note 13: Financial Instruments with Off-Balance-Sheet Risk

In the normal course of business, the corporation enters into or is a party to various financial instruments and contractual obligations that, under certain conditions, could give rise to or involve elements of, market or credit risk in excess of that shown in the statement of financial condition. These financial instruments and contractual obligations include interest rate swaps, forward foreign exchange contracts, financial guarantees, and commitments to extend credit. The corporation monitors and limits its exposure to market risk through management policies designed to identify and reduce excess risk. The corporation limits its credit risk through monitoring of client credit exposure, reviews, and conservative estimates of allowances for bad debt and through the prudent use of collateral for large amounts of credit. The corporation monitors collateral values on a daily basis and requires additional collateral when deemed necessary.

Note 6: Interest Rate Swaps and Forward Exchange Contracts

The corporation enters into a variety of interest rate swaps and forward foreign exchange contracts. The primary use of these financial instruments is to reduce interest rate fluctuations and to stabilize costs or to hedge foreign currency liabilities or assets. Interest rate swap transactions involve the exchange of floating-rate and fixed-rate interest payment of obligations without the exchange of underlying notional amounts. The company is exposed to credit risk in the unlikely event of nonperformance by the counterparty. The differential to be received or paid is accrued as interest rates change and is recognized over the life of the agreement. Forward foreign exchange contracts represent commitments to exchange currencies at a specified future date. Gains (losses) on these contracts serve primarily to stabilize costs. Foreign currency exposure for the corporation will result in the unlikely event that the other party fails to perform under the contract.

Note 3: Financial Guarantees

Financial guarantees are conditional commitments to guarantee performance to third parties. These guarantees are primarily issued to guarantee borrowing arrangements. The corporation's credit risk exposure on these guarantees is not material.

Note 8: Commitment to Extend Credit

Loan commitments are agreements to extend credit under agreed-upon terms. The corporation's commitment to extend credit assists customers to meet their liquidity needs. These commitments generally have fixed expiration or other termination clauses. The corporation anticipates that not all of these commitments will be utilized. The amount of unused commitment does not necessarily represent future funding requirements.

Note 9: Summary of Off-Balance-Sheet Financial Instruments

The off-balance sheet financial instruments are summarized as follows (in thousands):

Financial instruments whose notional or contract amounts exceed the amount of credit risk:

	Contract or notional amount
Interest rate swap agreements	€8,765,400
Forward foreign exchange contracts	7,654,300

Financial instruments whose contract amount represents credit risk:

	Contract or notional amount
Financial guarantees	€6,543,200
Commitments to extend credit	5,432,100

Concentration of credit risk for certain entities. For certain corporations, industry or regional concentrations of credit risk may be disclosed adequately by a description of the business. Some examples of such disclosure language are

1. Credit risk for these off-balance sheet financial instruments is concentrated in Asia and in the trucking industry.
2. All financial instruments entered into by the corporation relate to Japanese government, international, and domestic commercial airline customers.

Example of disclosure of concentration of credit risk

Note 5: Significant Group Concentrations of Credit Risk

The corporation grants credit to customers throughout Europe and the Middle East. As of December 31, 2008, the five areas where the corporation had the greatest amount of credit risk were as follows:

United Kingdom	€8,765,400
Germany	7,654,300
United Arab Emirates	6,543,200
Turkey	5,432,100
France	4,321,000

Disclosure of fair values. IFRS 7 requires that for each class of financial asset and financial liability, the reporting entity should disclose information about fair value. This requirement is not operative, however, in the case of financial assets or liabilities that are already to be carried at fair value, per IAS 39. An exception is provided when the fair value cannot be reliably determined for an investment in an equity instrument, or in a derivative related to such instrument. However, when an entity avails itself of this option, it must disclose that fact, coupled with a summary of pertinent characteristics of the instrument, such that readers can make their own assessments of fair value should they so choose. IASB is currently developing guidance relative to measurement of fair values, which likely will closely hew to that already promulgated for US GAAP as FAS 157 (see complete discussion in Chapter 1).

Shareholders and others have every reason to expect that management understands the values of the assets it acquires for the business or of the obligations it incurs. Therefore, an admission in the financial statements to the effect that fair values could not be determined, if made more than infrequently, would appear either disingenuous or an admission of managerial malfeasance. For this reason, a good-faith attempt to determine the fair value data first requested by IFRS, coupled with disclosures that set forth whatever caveats are deemed necessary to make the information not misleading, is probably the best course to follow.

Beyond the basic concern of computing fair values, there is the further issue of what this information is intended to imply. This question arises most commonly in the context of financial obligations, which represent contractual commitments to repay fixed sums at fixed points in time, that are not subject to adjustment for market-driven changes in value.

For example, assume that an entity owes a bank loan carrying fixed 9.5% interest, with the principal due as a €300,000 balloon payment three years hence. If current rates are 7%, the fair value of this obligation is something greater than its face value (in fact, the computed present value of future cash flows, discounted at 7%, is €342,060, which will be the surrogate for fair value), yet the contractual obligation is unchanged at the original €300,000. What, then, is the purpose of communicating to financial statement users that the fair value is the higher, €342,060, amount?

The explanation of this disclosure is that the economic burden being borne by the entity is heavier than would have been the case had a floating market rate of interest been attached to the debt. The spread between the disclosed fair value, €342,060, and the face amount of the debt, €300,000, is the present value of the additional interest to be paid in the future under the fixed-rate agreement over the amount that would be payable at the current market rate. Thus, fair value disclosure does not measure future cash flows, per se, but rather is an indication of economic burden or benefit in the assumed absence of any restructuring or other alteration of the debt.

Fair value is the exchange price in a current transaction (other than in a forced or liquidation sale) between willing parties. If a quoted market price is available, it should be used, after adjustment for transaction costs that would normally be incurred in a real transaction of this type. If there is more than one market price, the one used should be the one from the most active market. The possible effects on market price from the sale of large holdings and/or from thinly traded issues should generally be disregarded for purposes of this determination, since it would tend to introduce too much subjectivity into this measurement process.

If quoted market prices are unavailable, management's best estimate of fair value can be used. A number of standardized techniques, which attempt to tie the prices of various financial instruments to those having readily determinable fair values, are widely employed for this purpose. Some bases from which an estimate may be made include

1. Matrix pricing models
2. Option pricing models
3. Financial instruments with similar characteristics adjusted for risks involved
4. Financial instruments with similar valuation techniques (i.e. present value) adjusted for risks involved

Fair value disclosures, by class of assets and liabilities, are to be presented in such a way that users can compare these amounts to corresponding carrying amounts.

Example

Note X: Financial Instruments Disclosures of Fair Value

The estimates of fair value of financial instruments are summarized as follows (in thousands):

Instruments for which carrying amounts approximate fair values:

	Carrying amount
Cash	€987.6
Cash equivalents	876.5
Trade receivables	765.4
Trade payables	(654.3)

Fair values approximate carrying values because of the short time until realization or liquidation.

Instruments for which fair values exceed carrying amounts:

	Carrying amount	*Fair value*
Trading investments	€876.5	€987.6
Available-for-sale investments	765.4	876.5

Estimated fair values are based on available quoted market prices, present value calculations, and option pricing models.

Instruments for which carrying amounts exceed fair values:

	Carrying amount	*Fair value*
Investment in debt instruments	(€543.2)	(€432.1)

Estimated fair values are based on quoted market prices, present value calculations, and the prices of the same or similar instruments after considering risk, current interest rates, and remaining maturities.

Unrecognized financial instruments:

	Carrying amount	Fair value
Financial guarantees	(€6,543.2)	(€7,654.3)

Estimated fair values after considering risk, current interest rates and remaining maturities were based on the following:

1. **Credit commitments**—Value of the same or similar instruments after considering credit ratings of counterparties.
2. **Financial guarantees**—Cost to settle or terminate obligations with counterparties at reporting date.

Fair value not estimated:

	Carrying amount	Fair value
Available-for-sale investment	€1,234.5	€--

Fair value could not be estimated without incurring excessive costs. Investment is carried at original cost and represents an 8% investment in the ordinary share of a privately held non-traded company that supplies the corporation. Management considers the risk of loss to be negligible.

Financial assets carried at amounts in excess of fair value. Prior to the implementation of IAS 39, there were certain circumstances in which an entity might have carried one or several financial assets at amounts that exceeded fair value, notwithstanding the general rule under accounting theory that such declines should be formally recognized in most instances. Normally, failure to recognize such declines would have been justified only when there is no objective evidence of impairment.

IAS 32 requires that when one or more financial assets are reported at amounts that exceed fair value, disclosure should be made of both carrying amount and fair value, either individually or grouped in an appropriate manner, and the reasons for not reducing the carrying value to fair value should be set forth, including the nature of the evidence that provides the basis for management's belief that the carrying value will be recovered. The purpose is to alert the financial statement readers to the risk that carrying amounts might later be reduced if a change in circumstances causes management to reassess the likelihood of recovery.

With the implementation of IAS 39, the issue of reporting investments or other financial assets at amounts in excess of fair value became virtually moot. Essentially, only held-to-maturity investments in debt instruments, loans and receivables originated by the entity, and purchased loans not quoted in an active market, might be presented at amounts in excess of fair value, for instance, when they carry a fixed interest rate that is lower than the prevailing market interest rates for similar instruments and there is no objective evidence of impairment.

Other disclosure requirements. IAS 32 initially encouraged financial statement preparers to make other disclosures as warranted to enhance the readers' understanding of the financial statements and hence, of the operations of the entity being reported on. It suggested that these further disclosures could include such matters as

1. The total amount of change in the fair value of financial assets and financial liabilities that has been recognized in income for the period, and
2. The average aggregate carrying amount during the year being reported on of recognized financial assets and financial liabilities; the average aggregate principal, stated, notional, or similar amounts of unrecognized financial assets and financial liabilities; and the average aggregate fair value of all financial assets and financial liabilities, all of which information is particularly useful when the amounts on hand at the dates of the statement of financial position are not representative of the levels of activity during the period.

Revisions to IAS 32, which became effective in 2005, added the following disclosure requirements:

- The methods and significant assumptions applied in determining fair values of financial assets and financial liabilities separately for significant classes of financial assets and financial liabilities;
- The extent to which fair values of financial assets and financial liabilities are determined directly by reference to published price quotations in an active market or recent market transactions on arm's-length terms or are estimated using a valuation technique;
- The extent to which fair values are determined in full or in part using a valuation technique based on assumptions that are not supported by observable market prices;
- If a fair value estimated using a valuation technique is sensitive to valuation assumptions that are not supported by observable market prices, a statement of this fact and the effect on the fair value of using a range of reasonably possible alternative assumptions; and
- The total amount of the change in fair value estimated using a valuation technique that was recognized in profit or loss in the reporting period.

The foregoing items were all incorporated into IFRS 7, which unifies and standardizes disclosure requirements for all financial instruments.

Categorization of financial assets and liabilities. IAS 39 establishes four categories of financial assets and liabilities, as follows:

1. Those carried at fair value through profit or loss (held for trading, and those designated as at fair value through profit or loss upon initial recognition);
2. Available-for-sale;
3. Held-to-maturity; and
4. Loans and receivables originated by the entity and not held for trading (optionally inclusive of purchased loans not quoted in an active market).

When relevant, the financial statements are required to disclose for each of these four categories of instruments, whether regular way purchases of financial instruments are accounted for at trade date or settlement date.

Also to be disclosed are a description of the reporting entity's financial risk management objectives and policies, including its policy for each major type of forecasted transaction (for example, in the case of hedges of risks relating to future sales, that description should indicate the nature of the risks being hedged, approximately how many months or years of future sales have been hedged, and the approximate percentage of sales in those future months or years); whether gain or loss on financial assets and liabilities measured at fair value subsequent to initial recognition, other than those relating to hedges, has been recognized in other comprehensive income, and if so, the cumulative amount recognized as of the date of the statement of financial position; and, when fair value cannot be reliably measured for a group of financial assets or financial liabilities that would otherwise have to be carried at fair value, that fact should be disclosed together with a description of the financial instruments, their carrying amount, and an explanation of why fair value cannot be reliably measured.

For designated fair value hedges, cash flow hedges, and hedges of net investment in a foreign entity, there are to be separate descriptions of the hedges, the financial instruments designated as hedging instruments together with fair values at the date of the statement of financial position, the nature of the risks being hedged, and for forecasted transactions, the periods in which the forecasted transactions are expected to occur, when they are expected to enter into the determination of net profit or loss (e.g., a forecasted acquisition of property may affect profit or loss over the asset's depreciable lifetime), plus a description of any forecasted transaction for which hedge accounting was previously employed but which is no longer expected to occur.

When there has been a gain or loss on derivative and nonderivative financial assets or liabilities designated as hedging instruments in cash flow hedges which has been recognized in other comprehensive income, disclosure is to be made of the amount so recognized during the current reporting period, the amount reclassified from equity and included in profit or loss for the period, and the amount reclassified from equity and included in the initial measurement of acquisition cost or carrying amount of the asset or liability in a hedged forecasted transaction during the current period.

The financial statements must also disclose the following with regard to financial instruments: the amount of any gains or losses resulting from the remeasurement of available-for-sale instruments at fair value, included in other comprehensive income in the current period, and the amount reclassified from equity and reported in current profit or loss; a description of any held-for-trading or available-for-sale financial assets for which fair value cannot be determined, together with (when possible) the range of possible fair values thereof; the carrying amount and gain or loss on sale of any financial assets whose fair value was not previously determinable; significant items of income, expense, gain and loss resulting from financial assets or liabilities, whether included in profit or loss or in other comprehensive income, with separate (gross) reporting of interest income and interest expense, and with separate reporting of realized and unrealized gains and losses resulting from available-for-sale financial assets. It is not necessary to distinguish realized and unrealized gains and losses resulting from held-for-trading financial assets, however.

If there are impaired loans, the amount of interest accrued but not received in cash must be disclosed.

If the entity has participated in securitizations or repurchase agreements, these must be described, and the nature of any collateral and key assumptions made in computing retained or new interests are to be discussed. There must be disclosure of whether the financial assets have been derecognized.

Any reclassifications of financial assets from categories reported at fair value to those reported at amortized historical cost (either because now deemed held-to-maturity, or because fair values are no longer obtainable) are to be explained.

Finally, any impairments or reversals of impairments are to be disclosed, separately for each class (held-to-maturity, etc.) of investment.

Derivatives Related to the Entity's Own Shares

Regarding derivatives based on an entity's own shares, IFRS 7 provides the following guidance:

- A derivative that is indexed to the price of an entity's own shares and requires net cash or net share settlement, or that gives the counterparty a choice of net cash or net share settlement, is to be treated as a derivative asset or derivative liability (i.e., not as an equity instrument) and is to be accounted for as such under IAS 39.
- A derivative that is indexed to the price of an entity's own shares and gives the entity a right to require net cash or net share settlement instead of gross physical settlement is to be treated as a derivative asset or derivative liability (i.e., not as an equity instrument), unless the entity has an established history of settling such contracts through a gross exchange of a fixed number of the entity's own shares for a fixed amount of cash or other financial assets.
- Changes in the fair value of a derivative that is fully indexed to the price of an entity's own shares and that will result in the receipt or delivery of a fixed number of an en-

tity's own shares in exchange for a fixed amount of cash or other financial assets are not recognized in the financial statements, since to do otherwise would be to allow changes in the value of the reporting entity's equity shares to be reflected in its profit or loss.

- When a derivative involves an obligation to pay cash in exchange for receiving an entity's own shares, there is a liability for the share redemption amount. The objective of this proposed amendment is to clarify the requirements affecting the classification of derivatives based on an entity's own shares to promote the consistent application of those requirements.

Disclosure Requirements Added by IFRS 7

IFRS 7 has superseded the disclosure requirements previously found in IAS 32, as well as the financial institution-specific disclosure requirements of IAS 30, which are accordingly withdrawn. Presentation requirements set forth in IAS 32 continue in effect under that standard. IFRS 7 became effective for years beginning in 2007.

IFRS 7 was made necessary by the increasingly sophisticated (but opaque) methods that reporting entities have begun using to measure and manage their exposure to risks arising from financial instruments. At the same time, new risk management concepts and approaches have gained acceptance. IASB concluded that users of financial statements need information about the reporting entities' exposures to risks and how those risks are being managed.

Risk management information can influence the users' assessments of the financial position and performance of reporting entities, as well as of the amount, timing, and uncertainty of the respective entity's future cash flows. In short, greater transparency regarding those risks allows users to make more informed judgments about risk and return. This is entirely consistent with the fundamental objective of financial reporting and is consistent with the widely accepted efficient markets hypothesis.

With this as background, IASB determined that certain disclosure requirements previously set forth in IAS 30 and IAS 32 needed to be revised and enhanced. A unified set of requirements was accordingly imposed, eliminating the need for a separate standard dealing only with financial institutions.

IFRS 7 applies to all risks arising from all financial instruments, with limited exceptions. It furthermore applies to all entities, including those that have few financial instruments (e.g., an entity whose only financial instruments are accounts receivable and payable), as well as those that have many financial instruments (e.g., a financial institution, most assets and liabilities of which are financial instruments). Under IFRS 7, the extent of disclosure required depends on the extent of the entity's use of financial instruments and of its exposure to risk.

IFRS 7 requires disclosure of

1. The significance of financial instruments for an entity's financial position and performance (which incorporates many of the requirements previously set forth by IAS 32); and
2. Qualitative and quantitative information about exposure to risks arising from financial instruments, including specified minimum disclosures about credit risk, liquidity risk, and market risk. The *qualitative* disclosures describe managements' objectives, policies, and processes for managing those risks. The *quantitative* disclosures provide information about the extent to which the entity is exposed to risk, based on information provided internally to the entity's key management personnel. Together, these disclosures are expected to provide an overview of the reporting entity's use of financial instruments and the exposures to risks they create.

Exceptions to applicability. IFRS 7 identifies the following types of financial instruments to which the requirements do not apply:

1. Interests in subsidiaries, associates, and joint ventures accounted for in accordance with IAS 27, IAS 28, or IAS 31, respectively. However, given that in some cases those standards permit an entity to account for an interest in a subsidiary, associate, or joint venture using IAS 39, in those cases the reporting entities are to apply the disclosure requirements in those other standards as well as those in IFRS 7. Entities are also to apply IFRS 7 to all derivatives linked to interests in subsidiaries, associates, or joint ventures, unless the derivative meets the definition of an equity instrument first established by IAS 32.

2. Employers' rights and obligations arising from employee benefit plans, to which IAS 19 applies.

3. Contracts for contingent consideration in a business combination, per IFRS 3, in financial reporting by the acquirer.

4. Insurance contracts as defined in IFRS 4. However, IFRS 7 applies to derivatives that are embedded in insurance contracts if IAS 39 requires the entity to account for them separately.

5. Financial instruments, contracts, and obligations under share-based payment transactions to which IFRS 2 applies, except that IFRS 7 applies to certain contracts that are within the scope of IAS 39.

Applicability. IFRS 7 applies to both recognized and unrecognized financial instruments. *Recognized* financial instruments include financial assets and financial liabilities that are within the scope of IAS 39. *Unrecognized* financial instruments include some financial instruments that, although outside the scope of IAS 39, are within the scope of this IFRS (such as some loan commitments). The requirements also extend to contracts involving nonfinancial items if they are subject to IAS 39.

Classes of financial instruments and level of disclosure. Many of the IFRS 7 requirements pertain to grouped data. In such cases, the grouping into classes is to be effected in the manner that is appropriate to the nature of the information disclosed and that takes into account the characteristics of the financial instruments. Importantly, sufficient information must be provided so as to permit reconciliation to the line items presented in the statement of financial position. Enough detail is required so that users are able to assess the significance of financial instruments to the reporting entity's financial position and results of operations.

IFRS 7 requires that carrying amounts of each of the following categories, as defined in IAS 39, is to be disclosed either on the face of the statement of financial position or in the notes:

1. Financial assets at fair value through profit or loss, showing separately
   a. Those designated as such upon initial recognition via the "fair value option" and
   b. Those classified as held-for-trading in accordance with IAS 39;

2. Held-to-maturity investments;

3. Loans and receivables;

4. Available-for-sale financial assets;

5. Financial liabilities at fair value through profit or loss, showing separately,
   a. Those designated as such upon initial recognition via the "fair value option" and
   b. Those classified as held-for-trading in accordance with IAS 39; and

6. Financial liabilities carried at amortized cost.

Special disclosures apply to those financial assets and liabilities accounted for by the "fair value option." If the reporting entity designated a loan or receivable (or groups thereof) to be reported at fair value through profit or loss, it is required to disclose

1. The maximum exposure to *credit risk* of the loan or receivable (or group thereof) at the reporting date.
2. The amount by which any related credit derivatives or similar instruments mitigate that maximum exposure to credit risk.
3. The amount of change, both during the reporting period *and* cumulatively, in the fair value of the loan or receivable (or group thereof) that is attributable to *changes in the credit risk* of the financial asset determined either

    a. As the amount of change in its fair value that is not attributable to changes in market conditions that give rise to market risk; or
    b. Using an alternative method the entity believes more faithfully represents the amount of change in its fair value that is attributable to changes in the credit risk of the asset.

    Changes in market conditions that give rise to market risk include changes in an observed (benchmark) interest rate, commodity price, foreign exchange rate, or index of prices or rates.
4. The amount of the change in the fair value of any related derivatives or similar instruments that has occurred during the period and cumulatively since the loan or receivable was designated.

If the reporting entity has designated a financial liability to be reported at fair value through profit or loss, it is to disclose

1. The amount of change, both during the period *and* cumulatively, in the fair value of the financial liability that is attributable to *changes in the credit risk* of that liability determined either

    a. As the amount of change in its fair value that is not attributable to changes in market conditions that give rise to market risk; or
    b. Using an alternative method the entity believes more faithfully represents the amount of change in its fair value that is attributable to changes in the credit risk of the liability.

    Changes in market conditions that give rise to market risk include changes in a benchmark interest rate, the price of another entity's financial instrument, a commodity price, a foreign exchange rate, or an index of prices or rates. For contracts that include a unit-linking feature, changes in market conditions include changes in the performance of the related internal or external investment fund.
2. The difference between the financial liability's carrying amount and the amount the entity would be contractually required to pay at maturity to the holder of the obligation.

Reclassifications. If a financial asset has been reclassified to one that is measured: (1) at cost or amortized cost, rather than at fair value; or (2) at fair value, rather than at cost or amortized cost, the amount reclassified into and out of each category and the reason for that reclassification are to be disclosed.

Certain derecognition matters. If financial assets were transferred in such a way that part or all of those assets did not qualify for derecognition under IAS 39, the following disclosures are required for each class of such financial assets:

1. The nature of the assets;
2. The nature of the risks and rewards of ownership to which the entity remains exposed;
3. When the entity continues to recognize all of the assets, the carrying amounts of the assts and of the associated liabilities; and
4. When the entity continues to recognize the assets to the extent of its continuing involvement, the total carrying amount of the original assets, the amount of the assets that the entity continues to recognize, and the carrying amount of the associated liabilities.

Collateral. The reporting entity must disclose the carrying amount of financial assets it has pledged as collateral for liabilities or contingent liabilities, including amounts that have been reclassified in accordance with the provision of IAS 39 pertaining to rights to repledge; and the terms and conditions relating to its pledge.

Conversely, if the reporting entity holds collateral (of either financial or nonfinancial assets) and is permitted to sell or repledge the collateral in the absence of default by the owner of the collateral, it must now disclose the fair value of the collateral held and the fair value of any such collateral sold or repledged, and whether it has an obligation to return it; and the terms and conditions associated with its use of the collateral.

Allowances for bad debts or other credit losses. When financial assets are impaired by credit losses and the entity records the impairment in a separate account (whether associated with a specific asset or for the collective impairment of assets), rather than directly reducing the carrying amount of the asset, it is to disclose a reconciliation of changes in that account during the period, for each class of financial assets.

Certain compound instruments. If the reporting entity is the *issuer* of compound instruments, such as convertible debt, having multiple embedded derivatives having interdependent values (such as the conversion feature and a call feature, such that the issuer can effectively force conversion), these matters must be disclosed.

Defaults and breaches. If the reporting entity is the obligor under loans payable at the date of the statement of financial position, it must disclose

1. The details of any defaults during the period, involving payment of principal or interest, or into a sinking fund, or of the redemption terms of those loans payable.
2. The carrying amount of the loans payable in default at the reporting date; and
3. Whether the default was remedied, or the terms of the loans payable were renegotiated, before the financial statements were authorized for issue.

Similar disclosures are required for any other breaches of loan agreement terms, if such breaches gave the lender the right to accelerate payment, unless these were remedied or terms were renegotiated before the reporting date.

Dislosures in the statements of comprehensive income and changes in equity. The reporting entity is to disclose the following items of revenue, expense, gains, or losses, either on the face of the financial statements or in the notes thereto:

1. Net gain or net losses on

   a. Financial assets or financial liabilities carried at fair value through profit or loss, showing separately those incurred on financial assets or financial liabilities designated as such upon initial recognition, and those on financial assets or financial liabilities that are classified as held-for-trading in accordance with IAS 39;

    b.   Available-for-sale financial assets, showing separately the amount of gain or loss recognized in other comprehensive income during the period and the amount reclassified from equity and recognized in profit or loss for the period;

    c.   Held-to-maturity investments;

    d.   Loans and receivables; and

    e.   Financial liabilities carried at amortized cost;

2. Total interest income and total interest expense (calculated using the effective interest method) for financial assets or financial liabilities that are not carried at fair value through profit or loss;

3. Fee income and expense (other than amounts included in determining the effective interest rate) arising from

    a.   Financial assets or financial liabilities that are not carried at fair value through profit or loss; and

    b.   Trust and other fiduciary activities that result in the holding or investing of assets on behalf of individuals, trusts, retirement benefit plans, and other institutions

4. Interest income on impaired financial assets accrued in accordance with the provision of IAS 39 that stipulates that, once written down for impairment, interest income thereafter is to be recognized at the rate used to discount cash flows in order to compute impairment; and

5. The amount of any impairment loss for each class of financial asset.

Accounting policies disclosure. The reporting entity is to disclose the measurement basis (or bases) used in preparing the financial statements and the other accounting policies used that are relevant to an understanding of the financial statements.

Hedging disclosures. Hedge accounting is one of the more complex aspects of financial instruments accounting under IAS 39. IFRS 7 specifies that an entity engaged in hedging must disclose, separately for each type of hedge described in IAS 39 (i.e., fair value hedges, cash flow hedges, and hedges of net investments in foreign operations)

1. A description of each type of hedge;

2. A description of the financial instruments designated as hedging instruments and their fair values at the reporting date; and

3. The nature of the risks being hedged.

In the case of cash flow hedges, the reporting entity is to disclose

1. The periods when the cash flows are expected to occur and when they are expected to affect profit or loss;

2. A description of any forecasted transaction for which hedge accounting had previously been used, but which is no longer expected to occur;

3. The amount that was recognized in other comprehensive income during the period;

4. The amount that was reclassified from equity and included in profit or loss for the period, showing the amount included in each line item in the statement of comprehensive income; and

5. The amount that was reclassified from equity during the period and included in the initial cost or other carrying amount of a nonfinancial asset or nonfinancial liability whose acquisition or incurrence was a hedged highly probable forecast transaction.

The reporting entity is to disclose separately

1. For fair value hedges, gains, or losses

    a.   From the hedging instrument; and

    b.   From the hedge item attributable to the hedged risk.

2.   The ineffectiveness recognized in profit or loss that arises from cash flow hedges; and

3.   The ineffectiveness recognized in profit or loss that arises from hedges of net investments in foreign operations.

Fair value disclosures. IFRS 7 requires that for each class of financial assets and financial liabilities, the reporting entity is to disclose the fair value of that class of assets and liabilities in a way that permits it to be compared with its carrying amount. Grouping by class is required, but offsetting assets and liabilities is generally not permitted (but will conform with statement of financial position presentation). To be disclosed are

1.   The methods and, if a valuation technique is used, the assumptions applied in determining fair values of each class of financial assets or financial liabilities (e.g., as to prepayment rates, rates of estimated credit losses, and interest rates or discount rates).

2.   Whether fair values are determined, in whole or in part, directly by reference to published price quotations in an active market or are estimated using a valuation technique.

3.   Whether the fair values recognized or disclosed in the financial statements are determined in whole or in part using a valuation technique based on assumptions that are *not* supported by prices from observable current market transactions in the same instrument (that is, without modification or repackaging) and *not* based on available observable market data. If fair values are recognized in the financial statements, and if changing one or more of those assumptions to reasonably possible alternative assumptions would change fair value significantly, then this fact must be stated, and the effect of those changes must be disclosed. Significance is to be assessed in light of the entity's profit or loss, and total assets or total liabilities, or, total comprehensive income and equity, when changes in fair value are recognized in other comprehensive income.

4.   If 3. applies, the total amount of the change in fair value estimated using such a valuation technique that was recognized in profit or loss during the period.

In instances where the market for a financial instrument is not active, the reporting entity establishes the fair value using a valuation technique. The best evidence of fair value at initial recognition is the transaction price, so there could be a difference between the fair value at initial recognition and the amount that would be determined at that date using the valuation technique. In such a case, disclosure is required, by the class of financial instrument of

1.   The entity's accounting policy for recognizing that difference in profit or loss to reflect a change in factors (including time) that market participants would consider in setting a price; and

2.   The aggregate difference yet to be recognized in profit or loss at the beginning and end of the period and a reconciliation of changes in the balance of this difference.

Disclosures of fair value are not required in these circumstances.

1.   When the carrying amount is a reasonable approximation of fair value, (e.g., for short-term trade receivables and payables);

2.   For an investment in equity instruments that do not have a quoted market price in an active market, or derivatives linked to such equity instruments, that is measured at cost in accordance with IAS 39 because its fair value cannot be measured reliably; or

3. For an insurance contract containing a discretionary participation feature if the fair value of that feature cannot be measured reliably.

In instances identified in 2. and 3. immediately above, the reporting entity must disclose information to help users of the financial statements make their own judgments about the extent of possible differences between the carrying amount of those financial assets or financial liabilities and their fair value, including

1. The fact that fair value information has not been disclosed for these instruments because their fair value cannot be measured reliably;
2. A description of the financial instruments, their carrying amount, and an explanation of why fair value cannot be measured reliably;
3. Information about the market for the instruments;
4. Information about whether and how the entity intends to dispose of the financial instruments; and
5. If financial instruments whose fair value previously could not be reliably measured are derecognized, that fact, their carrying amount at the time of derecognition, and the amount of gain or loss recognized.

Disclosures about the nature and extent of risks flowing from financial instruments. Reporting entities are required to disclose various information that will enable the users to evaluate the nature and extent of risks the reporting entity is faced with as a consequence of financial instruments it is exposed to at the date of the statement of financial position. Both qualitative and quantitative disclosures are required under IFRS 7, as described in the following paragraphs.

Qualitative disclosures. For each type of risk arising from financial instruments, the reporting entity is expected to disclose

1. The exposures to risk and how they arise;
2. Its objectives, policies and processes for managing the risk and the methods used to measure the risk; and
3. Any changes in 1. or 2. from the previous period.

Quantitative disclosures. For each type of risk arising from financial instruments, the entity must present

1. Summary quantitative data about its exposure to that risk at the reporting date. This is to be based on the information provided internally to key management personnel of the entity.
2. The disclosures required as set forth below (credit risk, et al.), to the extent not provided in 1., unless the risk is not material.
3. Concentrations of risk, if not apparent from 1. and 2.

If the quantitative data disclosed as of the date of the statement of financial position are not representative of the reporting entity's exposure to risk during the period, it must provide further information that is representative.

Specific disclosures are mandated, concerning credit risk, liquidity risk, and market risk. These are set forth as follows in IFRS 7:

Credit risk disclosures. To be disclosed, by class of financial instrument, are

1. The amount that best represents the entity's maximum exposure to credit risk at the reporting date, before taking into account any collateral held or other credit enhancements;
2. In respect of the amount disclosed in a., a description of collateral held as security and other credit enhancements;

3. Information about the credit quality of financial assets that are *neither* past due *nor* impaired; and
4. The carrying amount of financial assets that would otherwise be past due or impaired whose terms have been renegotiated.

Regarding financial assets that are either past due or impaired, the entity must disclose, again by class of financial asset

1. An analysis of the age of financial assets that are past due as of the date of the statement of financial position but which are not judged to be impaired;
2. An analysis of financial assets that are individually determined to be impaired as at the reporting date, including the factors that the entity considered in determining that they are impaired; and
3. For the amounts disclosed in 1. and 2., a description of collateral held by the entity as security and other credit enhancements and, unless impracticable, an estimate of their fair value.

Regarding any collateral and other credit enhancements obtained, if these meet recognition criteria in the relevant IFRS, the reporting entity is to disclose

1. The nature and carrying amount of the assets obtained; and
2. If the assets are not readily convertible into cash, its policies for disposing of such assets or for using them in its operations.

Liquidity risk. The entity is to disclose

1. A maturity analysis for financial liabilities that shows the remaining contractual maturities; and
2. A description of how the entity manages the liquidity risk inherent in a.

Market risk. A number of informative disclosures are mandated, as described in the following paragraphs.

Sensitivity analysis is generally required, as follows:

1. A sensitivity analysis for each type of market risk to which the entity is exposed at the reporting date, showing how profit or loss and equity would have been affected by changes in the relevant risk variable that were reasonably possible at that date;
2. The methods and assumptions used in preparing the sensitivity analysis; and
3. Changes from the previous period in the methods and assumptions used, and the reasons for such changes.

If the reporting entity prepares a sensitivity analysis, such as value-at-risk, that reflects interdependencies between risk variables (e.g., between interest rates and exchange rates and uses it to manage financial risks, it may use that sensitivity analysis in place of the analysis specified in the preceding paragraph. The entity would also have to disclose

1. An explanation of the method used in preparing such a sensitivity analysis, and of the main parameters and assumptions underlying the data provided; and
2. An explanation of the objective of the method used and of limitations that may result in the information not fully reflecting the fair value of the assets and liabilities involved.

Other market risk disclosures may also be necessary to fully inform financial statement users. When the sensitivity analyses are unrepresentative of a risk inherent in a financial instrument (e.g., because the year-end exposure does not reflect the actual exposure during the year), the entity is to disclose that fact, together with the reason it believes the sensitivity analyses are unrepresentative.

Amendments to IAS 39 Adopted in 2008

Hedge accounting. In late 2007, IASB proposed amendments to IAS 39, entitled *Exposures Qualifying for Hedge Accounting,* to clarify when an entity may designate an exposure to a financial instrument as a hedged item and to specify the following:

- The risks that may be designated as hedged risks when an entity hedges its exposure to a financial instrument
- When an entity may designate a portion of the cash flows of a financial instrument as a hedged item.

The amendments were finalized in 2008 and are effective for fiscal years beginning in 2009. As amended, IAS 39 provides expanded guidance concerning the risks that qualify for designation as hedged risks, without significantly changing existing practice. Although under US GAAP the hedged risks include benchmark interest rate risk, foreign currency risk, and credit risk, IASB specified that under IFRS any market interest rate risk, without restriction to benchmark interest rate risk, may be designated as hedged risk. This is because in practice most entities designate any market interest rate as a hedged risk, and IASB's intent is not to change the existing practice significantly. In addition, proposed amendments specify that prepayment risk (the risk that a financial asset will be repaid early) may also be designated as hedged risk. Also, the risks associated with the contractually specified cash flows of a recognized financial instrument qualify for designation as a hedged risk.

The amendments also provide specific rules when one or more portions of the cash flows of a financial instrument can be designated as a hedged item. These specific rules, according to IASB, are limited to those situations that are commonly used in practice, minimizing the impact of the proposed amendments on practice. An entity is permitted to designate as a hedged item one or more of the following portions of the cash flows of a financial instrument:

- A partial term hedge
- A proportion (%) of cash flows of a financial instrument
- The cash flows of a financial instrument associated with a one-sided risk of that instrument (for example, the cash flows resulting from a decrease in the fair value of a financial asset)
- Any contractually specified cash flows of a financial instrument that are independent from the other cash flows of that instrument
- The portion of the cash flows of an interest-bearing financial instrument that is equivalent to a financial instrument with a risk-free rate
- The portion of the cash flows of an interest-bearing financial instrument that is equivalent to a financial instrument with a quoted fixed or variable interbank rate (for example, LIBOR)

Reclassifications of financial instruments. Another amendment to IAS 39 was discussed and adopted in late 2008, effective July 1, 2008. This was stimulated by certain developments in the financial markets worldwide, leading to massive write-downs for impairments by financial institutions and other investors in financial instruments. One question arising from the debate over current conditions in the financial markets, and the impact these conditions are having on financial institutions in particular, is whether reclassifications of investments, particularly to a classification in the statement of financial position for which fair value accounting would not be mandatory, would be acceptable, especially in light of volatile market conditions that cast doubt on the validity of fair value determinations.

Suspension or modification of fair value accounting rules has been proposed by financial institutions and others, and is currently (as of late 2008) under strenuous debate in many venues. The outcome of this debate is not yet known, but it is clear that any change in fair value accounting requirements, even if framed as being temporary in nature, would have very serious implications for the accounting standard-setting process, with the risk that unintended consequences could hamper further fair value developments in financial reporting for many years. Thus, the authors do not expect that more than very minor changes to existing standards will be forthcoming.

Nonetheless, IASB has adopted (with little debate) a change to IAS 39 that permits nonderivative financial assets held for trading and available-for-sale financial assets to be reclassified in particular situations.

The proximate reason for adopting this amendment was the distinction between US GAAP and IFRS relative to transfers from the trading category (for most investments) and from the held-for-sale category (for mortgage loans). Under US GAAP transfers from those categories are restricted but still possible, whereas under IAS 39 no such reclassifications were previously permitted. IASB was asked to grant users of IFRS the same (limited) flexibility as that allowed under US GAAP.

The concern, of course, is that by granting even limited rights to transfer investments out of the category in the statement of financial position that requires fair value changes to be recognized currently in income would be to offer reporting entities the ability to manage earnings by avoiding recognition of value declines in current earnings (although probably still incorporated in comprehensive income). Given the near-unprecedented conditions affecting markets for financial instruments in late 2008, IASB did agree to adopt an amendment to IAS 39 that would largely parrot relevant US GAAP (FAS 115 and FAS 65), limited to nonderivative financial instruments held as assets. This does *not* apply to instruments for which the fair value option was elected, as those asserts must continue to be valued at fair value with changes in value reported in current earnings, since the fair value option is a one-time election that can be made only upon the original acquisition of the asset.

The impact of this amendment may be limited by the fact that the market value declines may have already largely taken place. Transfers from the trading category must be made at fair value as of the date of transfer, and cannot, for example, be back-dated to a point in time before the decline in value occurred. Thus, transfers made after the major market declines of 2008 will not avoid loss recognition, unless further declines occur after the transfers. Transfers into the fair value through current earnings category are prohibited.

If the asset is reclassified as available-for-sale, further value changes (increases or decreases) will be reported in other comprehensive income, not in current earnings. If the transfer is to the held-to-maturity category (limited to bonds and other fixed-maturity instruments, obviously), the value at the date of transfer becomes the deemed cost for subsequent accounting purposes. The amendment does not alter the requirement to report in earnings any declines in value that are deemed to be other than temporary in nature.

In addition, IASB determined that a financial asset that would have met the definition of loans and receivables (if it had not been designated as available for sale) will be permitted to be transferred from the available-for-sale category to loans and receivables, if the reporting entity intends to hold the loan or receivable for the foreseeable future or until maturity. This substantially aligns the accounting for reclassifications of loans and receivables with that permitted under US GAAP.

Furthermore, the amendment to IAS 39 also added guidance for the recognition of changes in fair values of financial instruments that are valued by reference to the present values of expected cash flows. IAS 39 provides that if an entity revises its estimates of payments or receipts, it must adjust the carrying amount of the financial asset or financial liability (or group of financial instruments) to reflect actual and revised estimated cash flows. This is accomplished by recalculating the carrying amount of the instrument by computing the present value of estimated future cash flows at the financial instrument's *original effective interest rate.* The adjustment is recognized as income or expense in current earnings.

The amendment adds a new provision to the effect that, if a financial asset is reclassified in accordance with the amendment, and the estimates of future cash receipts are later increased as a result of increased expected recoverability of those cash receipts, the effect of that increase must be recognized as an adjustment to the effective interest rate from the date of the change in estimate, rather than as an adjustment to the carrying amount of the asset at the date of the change in estimate. In other words, the increment is recognized ratably over the remaining holding period of the investment, not as an immediate gain.

Finally, IFRS 7 has been amended to expand the disclosures required whenever the amended provisions of IAS 39 are invoked. Specifically, if the reporting entity has reclassified a financial asset (in accordance with the above-described amended provisions of IAS 39) as one measured either at

1. Cost or amortized cost, rather than fair value; or
2. Fair value, rather than at cost or amortized cost

then it must disclose the amount reclassified into and out of each category and the reason for that reclassification. If the entity has reclassified a financial out of the fair value through current earnings category in accordance with the amended provisions of IAS 39, it must disclose

1. The amount reclassified into and out of each category;
2. For each reporting period until derecognition, the carrying amounts and fair values of all financial assets that have been reclassified in the current and previous reporting periods;
3. If a financial asset was reclassified in accordance with the amendment restricting such transfers to rare situations, the rare situation, and the facts and circumstances indicating that the situation was rare;
4. For the reporting period when the financial asset was reclassified, the fair value gain or loss on the financial asset recognized in profit or loss or other comprehensive income in that reporting period and in the previous reporting period;
5. For each reporting period following the reclassification (including the reporting period in which the financial asset was reclassified) until derecognition of the financial asset, the fair value gain or loss that would have been recognized in profit or loss or other comprehensive income if the financial asset had not been reclassified, and the gain, loss, income and expense recognized in profit or loss; and
6. The effective interest rate and estimated amounts of cash flows the entity expects to recover, as at the date of reclassification of the financial asset.

Annual improvements adopted in 2008. As part of its first annual improvements project, on October 11, 2007, the IASB published for comment an Exposure Draft (ED), *Proposed Improvements to International Financial Reporting Standards,* recommending miscellaneous amendments to 25 IFRS. Most of the proposed amendments were adopted in May 2008, although several were further revised after the initial proposals, and a few were not adopted at all. The changes affecting the accounting for and reporting of financial instruments are summarized in the following paragraphs:

• Since IAS 1, *Presentation of Financial Statements* (as revised in 2007), requires the statement of comprehensive income to present line items such as revenue and finance costs, and precludes the offsetting of income and expense, to resolve a potential conflict with the guidance in IFRS 7 stating that total interest income and total interest expense could be included as a component of finance costs, the amendment to the guidance in IFRS 7 requires that interest expense be disclosed separately in the statement of comprehensive income.

- Disclosure requirements in IFRS 7 for investments in associates and interests in jointly controlled entities accounted for at fair value through profit or loss have been amended as a consequence of amendments made to IAS 28, *Investments in Associates,* and IAS 31, *Interests in Joint Ventures.* Prospective application is acceptable, whereas the draft would have required retrospective application only.
- Disclosure requirements in IAS 32 for investments in associates and interests in jointly controlled entities accounted for at fair value through profit or loss have been revised to follow amendments made to IAS 28, *Investments in Associates*, and IAS 31, *Interests in Joint Ventures.*
- The language of IAS 39 has been amended to clarify that derivatives that are found to no longer be effective as hedges may be reclassified from fair value through current earnings. Specifically, these defined changes in circumstances are not precluded from necessitating reclassification of financial instruments:
  - A derivative that was previously a designated and effective hedging instrument in a cash flow hedge or net investment hedge no longer qualifies as such;
  - A derivative becomes a designated and effective hedging instrument in a cash flow hedge or net investment hedge;
  - Financial assets are reclassified when an insurance company changes its accounting policies in accordance with IFRS 4.
- Reference to the designation of hedging instruments at the segment level have been removed, to eliminate an apparent conflict with provisions of IFRS 8.
- IASB has clarified that the revised effective interest rate of a debt instrument should be used (not the original rate) when remeasuring the instrument's carrying value on the cessation of fair value hedge accounting.

Examples of Financial Statement Disclosures

Barco N.V.
Annual Report 2007

Notes to the financial statements

22. Derivative financial instruments

Derivative financial instruments are recognized initially at cost, which is the fair value of the consideration given (in the case of an asset) or received (in the case of a liability) for it. Transaction costs are considered in the initial measurement of all financial assets and liabilities. Subsequent to initial recognition, derivative financial instruments are stated at fair value. The fair values of derivative interest contracts are estimated by discounting expected future cash flows using current market interest rates and yield curve over the remaining term of the instrument. The fair value of forward exchange contracts is their market price at the end of the reporting period.

Derivative financial instruments that are either hedging instruments that are not designated or do not qualify as hedges are carried at fair value with changes in value included in profit or loss in the statement of comprehensive income. Where a derivative financial instrument is designated as a hedge of the variability in cash flows of a recognized asset or liability, or a highly probable forecasted transaction, the effective part of any gain or loss on the derivative financial instrument is recognized directly in equity with the ineffective part recognized directly in profit and loss.

Foreign currency risk

Recognized assets and liabilities. Barco incurs foreign currency risk on recognized assets and liabilities when they are denominated in a currency other than the company's local currency. Such risks may be naturally covered when a receivable in a given currency is matched with a payable in the same currency.

Forward exchange contracts and option contracts are used to manage the currency risk arising from recognized receivables and payables, which are not naturally hedged. This is particularly the case for the US dollar, for which receivables are systematically higher than payables. No hedge accounting is applied to these contracts.

The balances on foreign currency receivables and payables are valued at the rates of exchange prevailing at the end of the accounting period. Derivative financial instruments that are used to reduce the exposure of these balances are rated in the statement of financial position at fair value. Both changes in foreign currency balances and in fair value of derivative financial instruments are recognized in the statement of comprehensive income.

Forecasted transactions

Barco designates forward contracts to forecasted sales. Hedge accounting is applied to these contracts. The portion of the gain or loss on the hedging instrument that will be determined as an effective hedge is recognized directly in equity. On December 31, there were outstanding forward contracts in USD, GBP and AED.

Interest rate risk

Barco uses the following hedging instruments to manage its interest rate risk:

Swap on outstanding loan

- An outstanding loan of USD 5,695K (euro 4,324K) with variable interest swapped into fixed 4.38%
- This hedging instrument is treated as a cash-flow hedge, and gains or losses are recognized directly into equity

Cap/floor on loan agreements

Barco entered in 2003 and 2004 into the following loan agreements with variable interest rates, for which the variability is limited by a cap/floor:

- An outstanding loan of 11,250K euro, with variable interest rate which is limited between 2% and 5%;
- An outstanding loan of USD 3,680K (2,794K euro) with variable interest rate which is limited between 2.74% and 7.00%;
- The cap/floor agreements do not meet the hedging requirements of IAS 39 and are therefore treated as financial instruments held for trading. They are valued at fair value and changes in fair value are recognized in profit or loss.

Credit risk.

Credit risk on accounts receivable. Credit evaluations are performed on all customers requiring credit over a certain amount. The credit risk is monitored on a continuous basis. In a number of cases collateral is being requested before a credit risk is accepted. Specific trade finance instruments such as letters of credit and bills of exchange are regularly used in order to minimize the credit risk.

Credit risk on liquid securities and short-term investments. A policy defining acceptable counterparties and the maximum risk per counterparty is in place. Short-term investments are done in marketable securities or in fixed-term deposits with reputable banks.

adidas-AG, GERMANY
Year ended December 31, 2007

Notes to the financial statements

Summary of Significant Accounting Policies

Derivative financial instruments

The Group uses derivative financial instruments, such as interest and currency options, forward contracts, as well as interest rate swaps and cross-currency interest rate swaps to hedge its exposure to foreign exchange and interest rate risks. In accordance with its treasury policy, the Group does not hold any derivative financial instruments for trading purposes.

Derivative financial instruments are initially recognized in the statement of financial position at fair value and subsequently measured also at their fair value. The method of recognizing the resulting gain or loss is dependent on the nature of the item being hedged. On the date a derivative contract is entered into, the Group designates certain derivatives as either a hedge of a forecasted transaction (cash flow hedge), a hedge of the fair value of a recognized asset or liability (fair value hedge), or a hedge of a net investment in a foreign entity.

Changes in the fair value of derivatives that are designated and qualify as cash flow hedges, and that are 100% effective, as defined in IAS 39, are recognized in other comprehensive income and accumulated in equity. Insofar as the effectiveness is not 100%, the changes in fair value are recognized in profit or loss. Accumulated gains and losses in equity are transferred to profit or loss in the same periods during which the hedged forecasted transaction affects the statement of comprehensive income.

For derivative instruments designated as a fair value hedge, the gain or loss on the derivative and the offsetting gain or loss on the hedged item are recognized immediately in net income.

Certain derivative transactions, while providing effective economic hedges under the Group's risk management policies, do not qualify for hedge accounting under the specific rules of IAS 39. Changes in the fair values of any derivative instruments that do not qualify for hedge accounting under IAS 39 are recognized immediately in profit or loss.

Hedges of net investments in foreign entities are accounted in a similar way to cash flow hedges. If the hedging instrument is a derivative (e.g., a forward contract) or, for example, a foreign currency borrowing, effective currency gains and losses in the derivative and all gains and losses arising on the translation of the borrowing, respectively, are recognized in equity.

The Group documents the relationship between hedging instruments and hedged items at the inception of the transaction, as well as the risk management objective and strategy for undertaking various hedge transactions. This process includes linking all derivatives designated as hedges to specific forecasted transactions. The Group also documents its assessment whether the derivatives that are used in hedging transactions are highly effective in offsetting changes in cash flows of hedged items.

The fair values of forward contracts and currency options are determined on the basis of the market conditions on the reporting dates. The fair value of a currency option is determined using generally accepted models to calculate option prices. The fair market value of an option is influenced not only by the remaining term of the option but also by further determining factors, such as the actual foreign exchange rate and the volatility of the underlying foreign currency base. The fair values of interest rate options on the reporting date are assessed by generally accepted models, such as the "Markov functional model."

6 INVENTORY

PERSPECTIVE AND ISSUES

The accounting for inventories is a major consideration for many entities because of its significance on both the income statement (cost of goods sold) and the statement of financial position. Inventories are defined by IAS 2 as items that are

> ...held for sale in the ordinary course of business; in the process of production for such sale; or in the form of materials or supplies to be consumed in the production process or in the rendering of services.

The complexity of accounting for inventories arises from several factors.

1. The high volume of activity (or turnover) in the account
2. The various cost flow alternatives that are acceptable
3. The classification of inventories

There are two types of entities for which the accounting for inventories must be considered. The merchandising entity (generally, a retailer or wholesaler) has a single inventory account, usually entitled *merchandise inventory*. These are goods on hand that are purchased for resale. The other type of entity is the manufacturer, which generally has three types of inventory: (1) raw materials, (2) work in process, and (3) finished goods. *Raw materials inventory* represents the goods purchased that will act as inputs in the production process leading to the finished product. *Work in process* (WIP) consists of the goods entered into production but not yet completed. *Finished goods inventory* is the completed product that is on hand awaiting sale.

In the case of either type of entity the same basic questions need to be resolved.

1. At what point in time should the items be included in inventory (ownership)?
2. What costs incurred should be included in the valuation of inventories?
3. What cost flow assumption should be used?
4. At what value should inventories be reported (net realizable value)?

The standard that addresses these questions is IAS 2, which has been revised several times since it was first promulgated. IAS 2 discusses the definition, valuation, and classification of inventory. Over the years, the principal objective of the IASB in making amendments to this standard has been to reduce alternatives for the measurement of the carrying value of inventories. Most recently, LIFO costing has been eliminated as an acceptable pricing method.

The international accounting standards tend to be "principles-based" (as opposed to being "rules-based"), and for that reason practical application guidance contained in IAS 2 is not as comprehensive as it is under various national GAAP, such as that in the US. The materials in the body of this chapter essentially reflect the level of guidance provided under IAS 2. To supplement this material, the Appendix to this chapter contains additional guidance from other sources (specifically, from US GAAP), which provides a basis for comparing the treatment accorded to this subject in other jurisdictions.

Under the provisions of IAS 2, before its most recent revision, the first-in, first-out (FIFO) and weighted-average cost methods were defined as "benchmark treatments" with the last-in, first-out (LIFO) method cast as the "allowed alternative treatments." Since IFRS went to some length to avoid naming certain methods as being preferred or recommended (hence the term "benchmark," which was deemed to be somewhat more neutral, although the connotation was clearly that these were to be preferred), it is fair to say that all three methods were acceptable under IAS 2, prior to its recent revision. The IASB, as part of its recent Improvements Project, determined that the goals of achieving convergence among accounting standards and of promoting uniformity across entities reporting under IFRS would be served by eliminating the formerly "allowed alternative" of costing inventories by means of the last-in, first-out (LIFO) method. This has left the first-in, first-out (FIFO) and the weighted-average methods as the only two acceptable costing techniques under IFRS.

While convergence with US GAAP is now the mutual goal of FASB and IASB, the US and international standard setters, respectively, banning use of the LIFO method will complicate the achievement of this objective. Notwithstanding that LIFO rarely corresponded to the physical movement of goods (although there were exceptions, such as when new receipts of goods were placed on top of, or in front of, older stock, and thus likely to be sold before older goods), LIFO has been popular in certain jurisdictions. For example, this method has long been acceptable in the US for tax purposes, and, given the decades-long experience of rising prices, LIFO resulted in lower reportable income and therefore in lower taxes. In the US, the tax laws demand that entities using LIFO for tax purposes also do so for general-purpose financial reporting. Accordingly, the US standard setter will find it difficult or impossible to converge to revised IAS 2, unless the tax laws are also changed, which is not currently being proposed.

An interpretation (SIC 1) by the erstwhile Standing Interpretations Committee (SIC) had stated that entities should use the same cost formula for all inventories having similar nature and use. It furthermore held that mere differences in geographic location would not justify the use of different cost formulas. Revised IAS 2 has incorporated these positions into the standard, and the SIC was thus withdrawn.

Sources of IFRS
IAS 2, 18, 34, 41

DEFINITIONS OF TERMS

Absorption (full) costing. Inclusion of all manufacturing costs (fixed and variable) in the cost of finished goods inventory.

By-products. Goods that result as an ancillary product from the production of a primary good; often having minor value when compared to the value of the principal product(s).

Consignments. Marketing method in which the consignor ships goods to the consignee, who acts as an agent for the consignor in selling the goods. The inventory remains the property of the consignor until sold by the consignee.

Direct (variable) costing. Inclusion of only variable manufacturing costs in the cost of ending finished goods inventory. While often used for management (internal) reporting, this method is not deemed acceptable for financial reporting purposes.

Finished goods. Completed but unsold products produced by a manufacturing firm.

First-in, first-out (FIFO). Cost flow assumption; the first goods purchased or produced are assumed to be the first goods sold.

Goods in transit. Goods being shipped from seller to buyer at year-end.

Gross profit method. Method used to estimate the amount of ending inventory based on the cost of goods available for sale, sales, and the gross profit percentage.

Inventory. Assets held for sale in the normal course of business, or which are in the process of production for such sale, or are in the form of materials or supplies to be consumed in the production process or in the rendering of services.

Joint products. Two or more products produced jointly, where neither is viewed as being more important; in some cases additional production steps are applied to one or more joint products after a split-off point.

Last-in, first-out (LIFO). Cost flow assumption; the last goods purchased are assumed to be the first goods sold.

Lower of cost and net realizable value. Inventories must be valued at lower of cost or realizable value.

Markdown. Decrease below original retail price. A markdown cancellation is an increase (not above original retail price) in retail price after a markdown.

Markup. Increase above original retail price. A markup cancellation is a decrease (not below original retail price) in retail price after a markup.

Net realizable value. Estimated selling price in the ordinary course of business less the estimated costs of completion and the estimated costs necessary to make the sale.

Periodic. Inventory system where quantities are determined only periodically by physical count.

Perpetual. Inventory system where up-to-date records of inventory quantities are kept.

Product financing arrangements. Arrangements whereby an entity buys inventory for another firm that agrees to purchase the inventory over a certain period at specified prices which include handling and financing costs; alternatively, an entity can buy inventory from another firm with the understanding that the seller will repurchase the goods at the original price plus defined storage and financing costs.

Raw materials. For a manufacturing firm, materials on hand awaiting entry into the production process.

Replacement cost. Cost to reproduce an inventory item by purchase or manufacture. In lower of cost or market computations, the term *market* means replacement cost, subject to the ceiling and floor limitations.

Retail method. Inventory costing method that uses a cost ratio to reduce ending inventory (valued at retail) to cost.

Specific identification. Inventory system where the seller identifies which specific items are sold and which remain in ending inventory.

Standard costs. Predetermined unit costs, which are acceptable for financial reporting purposes if adjusted periodically to reflect current conditions. While useful for management (internal) reporting under some conditions, this is not an acceptable costing method for financial statements presented in accordance with IFRS.

Weighted-average. Periodic inventory costing method where ending inventory and cost of goods sold are priced at the weighted-average cost of all items available for sale.

Work in process. For a manufacturing firm, the inventory of partially completed products.

CONCEPTS, RULES, AND EXAMPLES

Basic Concept of Inventory Costing

IFRS (IAS 2) established that the lower of cost and net realizable value should be the basis for the valuation of inventories. In contrast to IFRS dealing with property, plant, and equipment (IAS 36) or investment property (IAS 40), there is no option for revaluing inventories to current replacement cost or fair value, presumably due to the far shorter period of time over which such assets are held, thereby limiting the cumulative impact of inflation or other economic factors on reported amounts.

The cost of inventories of items that are ordinarily interchangeable, and goods or services produced and segregated for specific projects, are generally assigned carrying values by using the specific identification method. For most goods, however, specific identification is not a practical alternative. In cases where there are a large number of items of inventory and where the turnover is rapid, the extant standard prescribes two more useful methods of pricing inventories, namely the first-in, first-out (FIFO) method and the weighted-average method. A third alternative formerly endorsed by IFRS, the LIFO costing method, has now been designated as being unacceptable.

FIFO and weighted-average cost are now the only acceptable cost flow assumptions under IFRS. Either method can be used to assign cost of inventories, but once selected an entity must apply that cost flow assumption consistently (unless the change to the other method can be justified under the criteria set forth by IAS 8). Furthermore, an entity is constrained from applying different cost formulas to inventories having similar nature and use to the entity. On the other hand, for inventories having different natures or uses, different cost formulas may be justified. Mere difference in location, however, cannot be used to justify applying different costing methods to otherwise similar inventories.

Ownership of Goods

Inventory can only be an asset of the reporting entity if it is an economic resource of the entity at the date of the statement of financial position. In general, an enterprise should record purchases and sales of inventory when legal title passes. Although strict adherence to this rule may not appear to be important in daily transactions, a proper inventory cutoff at the end of an accounting period is crucial for the correct determination of periodic results of operations. Thus, for accounting purposes, to obtain an accurate measurement of inventory quantity and corresponding monetary representation of inventory and cost of goods sold in the financial statements, it is necessary to determine when title has passed.

The most common error made in this regard is to assume that title is synonymous with possession of goods on hand. This may be incorrect in two ways: (1) the goods on hand may not be owned, and (2) goods that are not on hand may be owned. There are four matters that may cause confusion about proper ownership: (1) goods in transit, (2) consignment sales, (3) product financing arrangements, and (4) sales made with the buyer having generous or unusual right of return.

Goods in transit. At year-end, any *goods in transit* from seller to buyer may properly be includable in one, and only one, of those parties' inventories, based on the terms and conditions of the sale. Under traditional legal and accounting interpretation, goods are included in the inventory of the firm financially responsible for transportation costs. This responsibility may be indicated by shipping terms such as FOB, which is used in overland shipping contracts, and by FAS, CIF, C&F, and ex-ship, which are used in maritime contracts.

The term *FOB* stands for "free on board." If goods are shipped FOB destination, transportation costs are paid by the seller and title does not pass until the carrier delivers the goods to the buyer; thus these goods are part of the seller's inventory while in transit. If goods are shipped FOB shipping point, transportation costs are paid by the buyer and title passes when the carrier takes possession; thus these goods are part of the buyer's inventory while in transit. The terms *FOB destination* and *FOB shipping point* often indicate a specific location at which title to the goods is transferred, such as FOB Milan. This means that the seller retains title and risk of loss until the goods are delivered to a common carrier in Milan who will act as an agent for the buyer.

A seller who ships *FAS* (free alongside) must bear all expense and risk involved in delivering the goods to the dock next to (alongside) the vessel on which they are to be shipped. The buyer bears the cost of loading and of shipment; thus title passes when the carrier takes possession of the goods.

In a *CIF* (cost, insurance, and freight) contract the buyer agrees to pay in a lump sum the cost of the goods, insurance costs, and freight charges. In a C&F contract, the buyer promises to pay a lump sum that includes the cost of the goods and all freight charges. In either case, the seller must deliver the goods to the carrier and pay the costs of loading; thus both title and risk of loss pass to the buyer upon delivery of the goods to the carrier.

A seller who delivers goods *ex-ship* bears all expense and risk until the goods are unloaded, at which time both title and risk of loss pass to the buyer.

The foregoing is meant only to define normal terms and usage; actual contractual arrangements between a given buyer and a given seller can vary widely. The accounting treatment should in all cases strive to mirror the substance of the legal terms established between the parties.

Examples of accounting for goods in transit

The Vartan Gyroscope Company is located in Veracruz, Mexico, and obtains precision jeweled bearings from a supplier in Switzerland. The standard delivery terms are free alongside (FAS) a container ship in the harbor in Nice, France, so that Vartan takes legal title to the delivery once possession of the goods is taken by the carrier's dockside employees for the purpose of loading the goods on board the ship. When the supplier delivers goods with an invoiced value of 1,200,000 Mexican pesos to the wharf, it e-mails an advance shipping notice (ASN) and invoice to Vartan via an electronic data interchange (EDI) transaction, itemizing the contents of the delivery. Vartan's computer system receives the EDI transmission, notes the FAS terms in the supplier file, and therefore automatically logs it into the company computer system with the following entry:

Inventory	1,200,000	
Accounts payable		1,200,000

The goods are assigned an "In Transit" location code in Vartan's perpetual inventory system. When the precision jeweled bearings delivery eventually arrives at Vartan's receiving dock, the receiving staff records a change in inventory location code from "In Transit" to a code designating a physical location within the warehouse.

Vartan's secondary precision jeweled bearings supplier is located in Vancouver, British Columbia, and ships overland using free on board (FOB) Veracruz terms, so the supplier retains title until the shipment arrives at Vartan's location. This supplier also issues an advance shipping notice by EDI to inform Vartan of the estimated arrival date, but in this case Vartan's computer system notes the FOB Veracruz terms, and makes no entry to record the transaction until the goods arrive at Vartan's receiving dock.

Consignment sales. There are specifically defined situations where the party holding the goods is doing so as an agent for the true owner. In *consignments,* the consignor (seller) ships goods to the consignee (buyer), which acts as the agent of the consignor in trying to sell the goods. In some consignments, the consignee receives a commission; in other arrangements, the consignee "purchases" the goods simultaneously with the sale of the goods to the final customer. Goods out on consignment are properly included in the inventory of the consignor and excluded from the inventory of the consignee. Disclosure may be required of the consignee, however, since common financial analytical inferences, such as days' sales in inventory or inventory turnover, may appear distorted unless the financial statement users are informed. However, IFRS does not explicitly address this.

Example of a consignment arrangement

The Random Gadget Company ships a consignment of its wireless media control devices to a retail outlet of the Consumer Products Corporation. Random Gadget's cost of the consigned goods is €3,700, Random Gadget shifts the inventory cost into a separate inventory account to track the physical location of the goods. The entry follows:

Consignment out inventory	3,700	
Finished goods inventory		3,700

A third-party shipping company ships the cordless phone inventory from Random Gadget to Consumer Products. Upon receipt of an invoice for this €550 shipping expense, Random Gadget charges the cost to consignment inventory with the following entry:

Consignment out inventory	550	
Accounts payable		550

To record the cost of shipping goods from the factory to Consumer Products Corporation

Consumer Products sells half the consigned inventory during the month for €2,750 in credit card payments, and earns a 22% commission on these sales, totaling €605. According to the consignment arrangement, Random Gadget must also reimburse Consumer Products for the 2% credit card processing fee, which is €55 (€2,750 × 2%). The results of this sale are summarized as follows:

Sales price to Consumer Product's customer earned on behalf of Random Gadget	€2,750
Less: Amounts due to Consumer Product in accordance with arrangement	
22% sales commission	605
Reimbursement for credit card processing fee	55
	660
Due to Random Gadget	€2,090

Upon receipt of the monthly sales report from Consumer Products, Random Gadget records the following entries:

Accounts receivable	2,090	
Cost of goods sold	55	
Commission expense	605	
Sales		2,750

To record the sale made by Consumer Product acting as agent of Random Gadget, the commission earned by Consumer Product and the credit card fee reimbursement earned by Consumer Product in connection with the sale

Cost of goods sold	2,125	
Consignment out inventory		2,125

To transfer the related inventory cost to cost of goods sold, including half the original inventory cost and half the cost of the shipment to Consumer Product [(€3,700 + €550= €4,250) × ½ =€2,125]

Product financing arrangements. A *product financing arrangement* is a transaction in which an entity sells and agrees to repurchase inventory with the repurchase price equal to the original sales price plus the carrying and financing costs. The purpose of this transaction is to allow the seller (sponsor) to arrange financing of its original purchase of the inventory. As such, this is an alternative to other common methods of financing, such as secured working capital loans, where the ownership does not change but the lender places a lien on the inventory, which may be seized for nonpayment of the debt. The substance of a product financing transaction is illustrated by the diagram below.

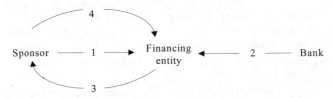

1. In the initial transaction the sponsor "sells" inventoriable items to the financing entity in return for the remittance of the sales price and at the same time agrees to repurchase the inventory at a specified price (usually the sales price plus carrying and financing costs) over a specified period of time.
2. The financing entity procures the funds remitted to the sponsor by borrowing from a bank (or other financial institution) using the newly purchased inventory as collateral.
3. The financing entity actually remits the funds to the sponsor and the sponsor presumably uses these funds to pay off the debt incurred as a result of the original purchase of the inventoriable debt.
4. The sponsor then repurchases the inventory for the specified price plus costs from the financing entity at a later time when the funds are available.

In a variant of this transaction, an entity can acquire goods from a manufacturer or dealer, with the contractual understanding that they will be resold to another entity at the same price plus handling, storage, and financing costs.

The purpose of either variation of product financing arrangement is to enable the sponsor to acquire or control inventory without incurring additional reportable debt. Transactions of this type are addressed fleetingly under IAS 18, which does note that a separate agreement to repurchase may negate the effect of a sale transaction. In effect, the substance of this type of transaction is that of a borrowing.

Under the pertinent US standard (FAS 49, *Accounting for Product Financing Arrangements*), such transactions are, in substance, no different from those where a sponsor obtains third-party financing to purchase its inventory. As a result, the FASB ruled that when an entity sells inventory with a related arrangement to repurchase it, proper accounting is to record a liability when the funds are received for the initial transfer of the inventory in the amount of the selling price. The sponsor is then to accrue carrying and financing costs in accordance with its normal accounting policies. These accruals are eliminated and the liability satisfied when the sponsor repurchases the inventory. The inventory is not to be taken off the statement of financial position of the sponsor and a sale is not to be recorded. Thus, although legal title has passed to the financing entity, for purposes of measuring and valuing inventory, the inventory is considered to be owned by the sponsor. Although the other variation on this financing arrangement with a nominee entity acquiring the goods for the ultimate purchaser is not addressed in FAS 49, logic suggests that an analogous accounting treatment be prescribed.

Example of a product financing arrangement

The Mechanical Innovations Company has borrowed the maximum amount it has available under its short-term line of credit. Mechanical Innovations obtains additional financing by selling €280,000 of its product inventory to a third-party financing entity. The third party obtains a bank loan at 6% interest to pay for its purchase of the product inventory, while charging Mechanical Innovations 8% interest and €1,500 per month to store the product inventory at a public storage facility. As Mechanical Innovations obtains product orders, it purchases inventory back from the third party, which in turn authorizes the public warehouse to drop ship the orders directly to Mechanical Innovations' customers at a cost of €35 per order. Since this is a product financing arrangement, Mechanical Innovations cannot remove the product inventory from its accounting records or record revenue for sale of its inventory to the third party. Instead, the following entry records the initial financing arrangement:

Cash	280,000	
Short-term debt		280,000

After one month, Mechanical Innovations records accrued interest of €1,867 (€280,000 × 8% interest × 1/12 year) on the loan, as well as the monthly storage fee of €1,500, as shown in the following entry:

Interest expense	1,867	
Storage expense	1,500	
Accrued interest		1,867
Accounts payable		1,500

On the first day of the succeeding month, Mechanical Innovations receives a prepaid customer order for €3,800. The margin on the order is 40%, and therefore the related inventory cost is €2,280, Mechanical Innovations pays the third party €2,280 to buy back the required inventory as well as €35 to the public storage facility to ship the order to the customer, and records the following entries:

Short-term debt	2,280	
Cash		2,280
To repurchase inventory from the third-party financing entity		
Cash	3,800	
Sales		3,800
To record the sale to the customer		
Cost of goods sold	2,280	
Inventory		2,280
To record the cost of the sale to the customer		
Freight out	35	
Accounts payable		35
To record the cost of fulfilling the order		

Right to return purchases. A related inventory accounting issue that requires special consideration is the situation that exists when the buyer holds the right to return the merchandise acquired. This is not meant to address the normal sales terms found throughout commercial transactions (e.g., where the buyer can return goods, whether found to be defective or not, within a short time after delivery, such as five days). Rather, this connotes situations where the return privileges are well in excess of standard practice, so as to place doubt on the veracity of the purported sale transaction itself.

IAS 18 notes that when the buyer has the right to rescind the transaction under defined conditions and the seller cannot, with reasonable confidence, estimate the likelihood of this occurrence, the retention of significant risks of ownership makes this transaction not a sale. Again, US GAAP usefully elaborates on this situation (FAS 48, *Revenue Recognition When Right of Return Exists*), and may provide additional insight. Under both standards the sale is to be recorded if the future amount of the returns can reasonably be estimated. If the ability to make a reasonable estimate is precluded, the sale is not to be recorded until further returns are unlikely. Although legal title has passed to the buyer, the seller must continue to include the goods in its measurement and valuation of inventory.

In some situations, a "side agreement" may grant the nominal customer greatly expanded or even unlimited return privileges, when the formal sales documents (bill of sale, bill of lading, etc.) make no such reference. These situations would be highly suggestive of financial reporting irregularities, in an apparent attempt to overstate revenues in the current period (and risk reporting high levels of sales returns in the following period, if customers do indeed avail themselves of the generous terms). In such circumstances, these sales should in all likelihood not be recognized, and the goods nominally sold should be returned to the reporting entity's inventories.

Accounting for Inventories

Introduction. The major objectives of accounting for inventories are the matching of appropriate costs against revenues in order to arrive at the proper determination of periodic income, and the accurate representation of inventories on hand as assets of the reporting entity as of the date of the statement of financial position. As it happens, these two goals are in conflict and, under any system of accounting in which the financial statements are fully articulated (i.e., where the statement of financial position and income statement are linked together mechanically), it will be virtually impossible to achieve both fully.

The accounting for inventories is done under either a periodic or a perpetual system. In a *periodic inventory system,* the inventory quantity is determined periodically by a physical count. The quantity so determined is then priced in accordance with the cost method used. Cost of goods sold is computed by adding beginning inventory and net purchases (or cost of goods manufactured) and subtracting ending inventory.

Alternatively, a *perpetual inventory system* keeps a running total of the quantity (and possibly the cost) of inventory on hand by recording all sales and purchases as they occur. When inventory is purchased, the inventory account (rather than purchases) is debited. When inventory is sold, the cost of goods sold and reduction of inventory are recorded. Periodic physical counts are necessary only to verify the perpetual records and to satisfy the tax regulations (tax regulations require that a physical inventory be taken, at least annually).

Valuation of Inventories

According to IAS 2, the primary basis of accounting for inventories is cost. *Cost* is defined as the sum of all costs of purchase, costs of conversion, and other costs incurred in bringing the inventories to their present location and condition. This definition allows for significant interpretation of the costs to be included in inventory.

For raw materials and merchandise inventory that are purchased outright and not intended for further conversion, the identification of cost is relatively straightforward. The cost of these purchased inventories will include all expenditures incurred in bringing the goods to the point of sale and putting them in a salable condition. These costs include the purchase price, transportation costs, insurance, and handling costs. Trade discounts, rebates, and other such items are to be deducted in determining inventory costs; failure to do so would result in carrying inventory at amounts in excess of true historical costs.

The impact of interest costs as they relate to the valuation of inventoriable items (IAS 23) is discussed in Chapter 8. In general, even when the allowed alternative treatment prescribed by IAS 23 is employed, borrowing costs will not be capitalized in connection with inventory acquisitions, since the period required to ready the goods for sale will not be significant. However, where a lengthy production process is required to prepare the goods for sale, the provisions of IAS 23 would be applicable and a portion of borrowing costs would become part of the cost of inventory.

Conversion costs for manufactured goods should include all costs that are directly associated with the units produced, such as labor and overhead. The allocation of overhead costs, however, must be systematic and rational, and in the case of fixed overhead costs (i.e., those which do not vary directly with level of production) the allocation process should be based on normal production levels. In periods of unusually low levels of production, a portion of fixed overhead costs must accordingly be charged directly to operations, and not taken into inventory.

Costs other than material and conversion costs are inventoriable only to the extent they are necessary to bring the goods to their present condition and location. Examples might include certain design costs and other types of preproduction expenditures if intended to benefit specific classes of customers. On the other hand, all research costs and most development costs (per IAS 38, as discussed in Chapter 8) would typically *not* become part of inventory costs. Also generally excluded from inventory would be such costs as administrative and selling expenses, which must be treated as period costs; the cost of wasted materials, labor, or other production expenditures; and most storage costs. Included in overhead, and thus allocable to inventory, would be such categories as repairs, maintenance, utilities, rent, indirect labor, production supervisory wages, indirect materials and supplies, quality control and inspection, and the cost of small tools not capitalized.

Example of recording raw material or component parts cost

Accurate Laser-Guided Farm Implements, Inc. purchases lasers, a component that it uses in manufacturing its signature product. The company typically receives delivery of all its component parts and uses them in manufacturing its finished products during the fall and early winter, and then sells its stock of finished goods in the late winter and spring. The supplier invoice for a January delivery of lasers includes the following line items:

Lasers	€5,043
Shipping and handling	125
Shipping insurance	48
Sales tax	193
Total	€5,409

Since Accurate is using the lasers as components in a product that it resells, it will not pay the sales tax. However, both the shipping and handling charge and the shipping insurance are required for ongoing product acquisition, and so are included in the following entry to record receipt of the goods:

Inventory—components	5,216	
Accounts payable		5,216

To record purchase of lasers and related costs (€5,043 +€125 + €48)

On February 1, Accurate purchases a €5,000, two-month shipping insurance (known as "inland marine") policy that applies to all incoming supplier deliveries for the remainder of the winter production season, allowing it to refuse shipping insurance charges on individual deliveries. Since the policy insures all inbound components deliveries (not just lasers) it is too time-consuming to charge the cost of this policy to individual components deliveries using specific identification, the controller can estimate a flat charge per delivery based on the number of expected deliveries during the two-month term of the insurance policy as follows:

€5,000 insurance premium ÷ 200 expected deliveries during the policy term = €25 per delivery and then charge each delivery with €25 as follows:

Inventory—components	25	
Prepaid insurance		25

To allocate cost of inland marine coverage to inbound insured components shipments

In this case, however, the controller determined that shipments are expected to occur evenly during the two-month policy period and therefore will simply make a monthly standard journal entry as follows:

Inventory—components	2,500	
Prepaid insurance		2,500

To amortize premium on inland marine policy using the straight-line method

Note that the controller must be careful, under either scenario, to ensure that perpetual inventory records appropriately track unit costs of components to include the cost of shipping insurance. Failure to do so would result in an understatement of the cost of raw materials inventory on hand at the end of any accounting period.

Joint products and by-products. In some production processes, more than one product is produced simultaneously. Typically, if each product has significant value, they are referred to as *joint products*; if only one has substantial value, the others are known as *by-products*. Under IAS 2, when the costs of each jointly produced good cannot be clearly determined, a rational allocation among them is required. Generally, such allocation is made by reference to the relative values of the jointly produced goods, as measured by ultimate selling prices. Often, after a period of joint production the goods are split off, separately incurring additional costs before being completed and ready for sale. The allocation of joint costs should take into account the additional individual product costs yet to be incurred after the point at which joint production ceases.

By-products by definition are products that have limited value when measured with reference to the primary good being produced. IAS 2 suggests that by-products be valued at net realizable value, with the costs allocated to by-products thereby being deducted from the cost pool, being otherwise allocated to the sole or several principal products.

For example, products A and B have the same processes performed on them up to the split-off point. The total cost incurred to this point is €80,000. This cost can be assigned to products A and B using their relative sales value at the split-off point. If A could be sold for €60,000 and B for €40,000, the total sales value is €100,000. The cost would be assigned on the basis of each product's relative sales value. Thus, A would be assigned a cost of €48,000 (60,000/100,000 × 80,000) and B a cost of €32,000 (400,000/100,000 × 80,000).

If inventory is exchanged with another entity for similar goods, the earnings process is generally not culminated. Accordingly, the acquired items are recorded at the recorded, or book, value of the items given up.

In some jurisdictions, the categories of costs that are includable in inventory for tax purposes may differ from those that are permitted for financial reporting purposes under international accounting standards. To the extent that differential tax and financial reporting is possible (i.e., that there is no statutory requirement that the taxation rules constrain financial reporting) this situation will result in interperiod tax allocation. This is discussed more fully in Chapter 15.

Direct costing. The generally accepted method of allocating fixed overhead to both ending inventory and cost of goods sold is commonly known as *(full) absorption costing*. IAS 2 requires that absorption costing be employed. However, often for managerial decision-making purposes an alternative to absorption costing, known as *variable or direct costing,* is utilized. Direct costing requires classifying only direct materials, direct labor, and variable overhead related to production as inventory costs. All fixed costs are accounted for as period costs. The virtue of direct costing is that under this accounting strategy there will be a predictable, linear effect on marginal contribution from each unit of sales revenue, which can be useful in planning and controlling the business operation. However, such a costing method does not result in inventory that includes all costs of production, and therefore this is deemed not to be in accordance with IFRS on inventories (IAS 2). If an entity uses direct costing for internal budgeting or other purposes, adjustments must be made to develop alternative information for financial reporting purposes.

Differences in inventory costing between IFRS and tax requirements. In certain tax jurisdictions, there may be requirements to include or exclude certain overhead cost elements which are handled differently under IFRS for financial reporting purposes. For example, in the US the tax code requires elements of overhead to be allocated to inventory, while US GAAP (consistent with IFRS) demand that these be expensed currently as period costs. Since tax laws do not dictate GAAP or IFRS, the appropriate response to such a circumstance is to treat these as temporary differences, which will create the need for interperiod income tax allocation under IAS 12. Deferred tax accounting is fully discussed in Chapter 15.

METHODS OF INVENTORY COSTING UNDER IAS 2

Specific Identification

The theoretical basis for valuing inventories and cost of goods sold requires assigning the production and/or acquisition costs to the specific goods to which they relate. For example, the cost of ending inventory for an entity in its first year, during which it produced ten items (e.g., exclusive single family homes), might be the actual production cost of the first, sixth, and eighth unit produced if those are the actual units still on hand at the date of the statement of financial position. The costs of the other homes would be included in that year's income statement (the presentation of comprehensive income in two statements) as cost of goods sold. This method of inventory valuation is usually referred to as *specific identification.*

Specific identification is generally not a practical technique, as the product will generally lose its separate identity as it passes through the production and sales process. Exceptions to this would generally be limited to those situations where there are small inventory quantities, typically having high unit value and a low turnover rate. Under IAS 2, specific identification must be employed to cost inventories that are not ordinarily interchangeable, and goods and services produced and segregated for specific projects. For inventories meeting either of these criteria, the specific identification method is mandatory and alternative methods cannot be used.

Because of the limited applicability of specific identification, it is more likely to be the case that certain assumptions regarding the cost flows associated with inventory will need to be made. One of accounting's peculiarities is that these cost flows may or may not reflect the physical flow of inventory. Over the years, much attention has been given to both the flow of physical goods and the assumed flow of costs associated with those goods. In most jurisdictions, it has long been recognized that the flow of costs need not mirror the actual flow of the goods with which those costs are associated. For example, a key provision in an early US accounting standard stated that

> ...cost for inventory purposes shall be determined under any one of several assumptions as to the flow of cost factors; the major objective in selecting a method should be to choose the one which, under the circumstances, most clearly reflects periodic income.

Under the current IFRS on inventories, revised IAS 2, there are two acceptable cost flow assumptions. These are: (1) first-in, first-out (FIFO) method and (2) the weighted-average method. There are variations of each of these cost flow assumptions that are sometimes used in practice, but if an entity presents its financial statements under IFRS it has to be careful not to apply a variant of these cost flow assumptions that would represent a deviation from the requirements of IAS 2. Furthermore, in certain jurisdictions, other costing methods, such as the last-in, first-out (LIFO) method and the base stock method, continue to be permitted. The LIFO method was an allowed alternative method of costing inventories under IAS 2 until the revision that became effective in 2005, at which time it was banned. Certain important jurisdictions such as the US still allow the use of the LIFO method, and since use of LIFO for tax purposes necessitates use for financial reporting, the elimination of LIFO in the US is a controversial topic and may hinder full convergence with IFRS. (Note, however, that the US Congress is debating a bill that would ban the use of the LIFO inventory costing method, so this impediment to convergence may be eliminated as an issue.)

First-In, First-Out (FIFO)

The FIFO method of inventory valuation assumes that the first goods purchased will be the first goods to be used or sold, regardless of the actual physical flow. This method is thought to parallel most closely the physical flow of the units for most industries having moderate to rapid turnover of goods. The strength of this cost flow assumption lies in the inventory amount reported in the statement of financial position. Because the earliest goods purchased are the first ones removed from the inventory account, the remaining balance is composed of items acquired closer to period end, at more recent costs. This yields results similar to those obtained under current cost accounting in the statement of financial position, and helps in achieving the goal of reporting assets at amounts approximating current values.

However, the FIFO method does not necessarily reflect the most accurate or decision-relevant income figure when viewed from the perspective of underlying economic performance, as older historical costs are being matched against current revenues. Depending on the rate of inventory turnover and the speed with which general and specific prices are changing, this mismatching could potentially have a material distorting effect on reported income. At the extreme, if reported earnings are fully distributed to owners as dividends, the enterprise could be left without sufficient resources to replenish its inventory stocks due to the impact of changing prices. (This problem is not limited to inventory costing; depreciation based on old costs of plant assets also may understate the true economic cost of capital asset consumption, and serve to support dividend distributions that leave the entity unable to replace plant assets at current prices.)

The following example illustrates the basic principles involved in the application of FIFO:

	Units available	Units sold	Actual unit cost	Actual total cost
Beginning inventory	100	--	€2.10	€210
Sale	--	75	--	--
Purchase	150	--	2.80	420
Sale	--	100	--	--
Purchase	50	--	3.00	150
Total	300	175		€780

Given these data, the cost of goods sold and the ending inventory balance are determined as follows:

	Units	Unit cost	Total cost
Cost of goods sold	100	€2.10	€210
	75	2.80	210
	175		€420
Ending inventory	50	3.00	€150
	75	2.80	210
	125		€360

Notice that the total of the units in cost of goods sold and ending inventory, as well as the sum of their total costs, is equal to the goods available for sale and their respective total costs.

The unique characteristic of the FIFO method is that it provides the same results under either the periodic or perpetual system. This will not be the case for any other costing method.

Weighted-Average Cost

The other acceptable method of inventory valuation under revised IAS 2 involves averaging and is commonly referred to as the weighted-average cost method. The cost of goods available for sale (beginning inventory and net purchases) is divided by the units available for sale to obtain a weighted-average unit cost. Ending inventory and cost of goods sold are then priced at this average cost. For example, assume the following data:

	Units available	Units sold	Actual unit cost	Actual total cost
Beginning inventory	100	--	€2.10	€210
Sale	--	75	--	--
Purchase	150	--	2.80	420
Sale	--	100	--	--
Purchase	50	--	3.00	150
Total	300	175		€780

The weighted-average cost is €780/300, or €2.60. Ending inventory is 125 units at €2.60, or €325; cost of goods sold is 175 units at €2.60, or €455.

When the weighted-average assumption is applied to a perpetual inventory system, the average cost is recomputed after each purchase. This process is referred to as a moving average. Sales are costed at the most recent average. This combination is called the moving average method and is applied below to the same data used in the weighted-average example above.

	Units on hand	Purchases in euros	Sales in euros	Total cost	Inventory unit cost
Beginning inventory	100	€ --	€ --	€210.00	€2.10
Sale (75 units @ 2.10)	25	--	157.50	52.50	2.10
Purchase (150 units, 420)	175	420.00	--	472.50	2.70
Sale (100 units @ 2.70)	75	--	270.00	202.50	2.70
Purchase (50 units, 150)	125	150.00	--	352.50	2.82

Cost of goods sold is 75 units at €2.10 and 100 units at €2.70, or a total of €427.50.

Net Realizable Value

As stated in IAS 2

Net realizable value is the estimated selling price in the ordinary course of business less the estimated costs of completion and the estimated costs necessary to make the sale.

The utility of an item of inventory is limited to the amount to be realized from its ultimate sale; where the item's recorded cost exceeds this amount, IFRS requires that a loss be recognized for the difference. The logic for this requirement is twofold: first, assets (in particular, current assets such as inventory) should not be reported at amounts that exceed net realizable value; and second, any decline in value in a period should be reported in that period's results of operations in order to achieve proper matching with current period's revenues. Were the inventory to be carried forward at an amount in excess of net realizable value, the loss would be recognized on the ultimate sale in a subsequent period. This would mean that a loss incurred in one period, when the value decline occurred, would have been deferred to a different period, which would clearly be inconsistent with several key accounting concepts, including conservatism.

Revised IAS 2 states that estimates of net realizable value should be applied on an item-by-item basis in most instances, although it makes an exception for those situations where there are groups of related products or similar items that can be properly valued in the aggregate. As a general principle, item-by-item comparisons of cost to net realizable value are required, lest unrealized "gains" on some items (i.e., where the net realizable values exceed historical costs) offset the unrealized losses on other items, thereby reducing the net loss to be recognized. Since recognition of unrealized gains in profit or loss is generally proscribed under IFRS, evaluation of inventory declines on a grouped basis would be an indirect or "backdoor" mechanism to recognize gains that should not be given such recognition. Accordingly, the basic requirement is to apply the tests on an individual item basis.

Recoveries of previously recognized losses. IAS 2 stipulates that a new assessment of net realizable value should be made in each subsequent period; when the reason for a previous write-down no longer exists (i.e., when net realizable value has improved), it should be reversed. Since the write-down was taken into income, the reversal should also be reflected in profit or loss. As under prior rules, the amount to be restored to the carrying value will be limited to the amount of the previous impairment recognized. (Note that, under parallel requirements imposed by some national GAAP, such as that in the US, once inventory is written down to a lower amount of net realizable value, it cannot be restored to original cost even if conditions change in later reporting periods.)

Other Valuation Methods

There are instances in which an accountant must estimate the value of inventories. Whether for interim financial statements or as a check against perpetual records, the need for an inventory valuation without an actual physical count is required. Some of the methods used, which are discussed below, are the retail method and the gross profit method.

Retail method. IAS 2 notes that the retail method may be used by certain industry groups but does not provide details on how to employ this method, nor does it address the many variations of the technique. The conventional retail method is used by retailers as a method to estimate the cost of their ending inventory. The retailer can either take a physical inventory at retail prices or estimate ending retail inventory and then use the cost-to-retail ratio derived under this method to convert the ending inventory at retail to its estimated cost. This eliminates the process of going back to original invoices or other documents to determine the original cost for each inventoriable item. The retail method can be used under either of the two cost flow assumptions discussed earlier: FIFO or average cost. As with ordinary FIFO or average cost, the LCM rule can also be applied to the retail method when either one of these two cost assumptions is used.

The key to applying the retail method is determining the cost-to-retail ratio. The calculation of this number varies depending on the cost flow assumption selected. Essentially, the cost-to-retail ratio provides a relationship between the cost of goods available for sale and the retail price of these goods. This ratio is used to convert the ending retail inventory back to cost. Computation of the cost-to-retail ratio for each of the available methods is described below.

1. **FIFO cost**—The concept of FIFO indicates that the ending inventory is made up of the latest purchases; therefore, beginning inventory is excluded from computation of the cost-to-retail ratio, and the computation becomes net purchases divided by their retail value adjusted for both net markups and net markdowns.
2. **FIFO (using a lower of cost or net realizable approach)**—The computation is basically the same as FIFO cost except that markdowns are excluded from the computation of the cost-to-retail ratio.
3. **Average cost**—Average cost assumes that ending inventory consists of all goods available for sale. Therefore, the cost-to-retail ratio is computed by dividing the cost of goods available for sale (Beginning inventory + Net purchases) by the retail value of these goods adjusted for both net markups and net markdowns.
4. **Average cost (using a lower of cost or net realizable approach)**—This is computed in the same manner as average cost except that markdowns are excluded for the calculation of the cost-to-retail ratio.

A simple example illustrates the computation of the cost-to-retail ratio under both the FIFO cost and average cost methods in a situation where no markups or markdowns exist.

	FIFO cost		*Average cost*	
	Cost	*Retail*	*Cost*	*Retail*
Beginning inventory	€100,000	€ 200,000	€100,000	€ 200,000
Net purchases	500,000	800,000	500,000	800,000
Total goods available for sale	€600,000	1,000,000	€600,000	1,000,000
Sales at retail		(800,000)		(800,000)
Ending inventory at retail		€ 200,000		€ 200,000

Cost-to-retail ratio

$$\frac{500,000}{800,000} = 62.5\% \qquad \frac{600,000}{1,000,000} = 60\%$$

Ending inventory at cost
200,000 × 0.625   € 125,000
200,000 × 0.60   € 120,000

Note that the only difference in the two examples is the numbers used to calculate the cost-to-retail ratio.

As shown above, the lower of cost or market aspect of the retail method is a result of the treatment of net markups and net markdowns. *Net markups* (defined as markups less markup cancellations) are net increases above the original retail price, which are generally caused by changes in supply and demand. *Net markdowns* (markdowns less markdown cancellations) are net decreases below the original retail price. An approximation of lower of cost or market is achieved by including net markups but excluding net markdowns from the cost-to-retail ratio.

To understand this approximation, assume that a toy is purchased for €6 and the retail price is set at €10. It is later marked down to €8. A cost-to-retail ratio including markdowns would be €6 divided by €8 or 75%, and ending inventory would be valued at €8 times 75%, or €6 (original cost). A cost-to-retail ratio excluding markdowns would be €6 divided by €10 or 60%, and ending inventory would be valued at €8 times 60%, or €4.80 (on a lower of cost or market basis). The write-down to €4.80 reflects the loss in utility that is evidenced by the reduced retail price.

The application of the lower of cost or market rule is illustrated for both the FIFO and average cost methods in the example below. Remember, if the markups and markdowns below had been included in the preceding example, *both* would have been included in the cost-to-retail ratio.

	FIFO cost (LCM)		Average cost (LCM)	
	Cost	Retail	Cost	Retail
Beginning inventory	€100,000	€ 200,000	€100,000	€ 200,000
Net purchases	500,000	800,000	500,000	800,000
Net markups	--	250,000	--	250,000
Total goods available for sale	€600,000	1,250,000	€600,000	1,250,000
Net markdowns		(50,000)		(50,000)
Sales at retail		(800,000)		(800,000)
Ending inventory at retail		€ 400,000		€ 400,000

Cost-to-retail ratio	$\dfrac{500,000}{1,050,000}$ = 47.6%	$\dfrac{600,000}{1,250,000}$ = 48%

Ending inventory at cost
400,000 × 0.476   € 190,400
400,000 × 0.48   € 192,000

Notice that under the FIFO (LCM) method all of the markups are considered attributable to the current period purchases. Although this is not necessarily accurate, it provides the most conservative estimate of the ending inventory.

There are a number of additional inventory topics and issues that affect the computation of the cost-to-retail ratio and, therefore, deserve some discussion. Purchase discounts and freight affect only the cost column in this computation. The sales figure that is subtracted from the adjusted cost of goods available for sale in the retail column must be gross sales after adjustment for sales returns. If sales are recorded at gross, deduct the gross sales figure. If sales are recorded at net, both the recorded sales and sales discount must be deducted to give the same effect as deducting gross sales (i.e., sales discounts are not included in the computation). Normal spoilage is generally allowed for in the firm's pricing policies, and for this reason it is deducted from the retail column after calculation of the cost-to-retail ratio. Abnormal spoilage, on the other hand, should be deducted from *both* the cost and retail columns *before* the cost-to-retail calculation, as it could distort the ratio. It is then generally reported as a loss separate from the cost of goods sold section. Abnormal spoilage is generally considered to arise from a major theft or casualty, while normal spoilage is usually due to shrinkage or breakage. These determinations and their treatments will vary depending on the firm's policies.

When applying the retail method, separate computations should be made for any departments that experience significantly higher or lower profit margins. Distortions arise in the retail method when a department sells goods with varying margins in a proportion different from that purchased, in which case the cost-to-retail percentage would not be representative of the mix of goods in ending inventory. Also, manipulations of income are possible by planning the timing of markups and markdowns.

The retail method is an acceptable method of valuing inventories for tax purposes in some, but not all, jurisdictions. The foregoing examples are not meant to imply that the method would be usable in any given jurisdiction; readers should ascertain whether or not it can be used.

Gross profit method. The gross profit method can be used to estimate ending inventory when a physical count is not possible or feasible. It can also be used to evaluate the reasonableness of a given inventory amount. The cost of goods available for sale is compared with the estimated cost of goods sold. For example, assume the following data:

Beginning inventory	€125,000
Net purchases	450,000
Sales	600,000
Estimated gross profit	32%

Ending inventory is then estimated as follows:

Beginning inventory	€125,000
Net purchases	450,000
Cost of goods available for sale	575,000
Cost of goods sold [€600,000 – (32% × €600,000)] or (68% × €600,000)	408,000
Estimated ending inventory	€167,000

The gross profit method, if used, should be limited to making interim reporting estimates, for analyses conducted by auditors, and for making estimates of inventory lost in fires or other catastrophes. The method is generally not acceptable for either tax or annual financial reporting purposes (and is not in conformity with IAS 2). Thus, its major purposes are for internal and interim reporting. For such purposes, however, it may prove to be extremely valuable.

Fair value as an inventory costing method. In general, inventories are to be carried at cost, although, as has been explained in the preceding sections of this chapter, cost may be ascertained by a variety of methods under IAS 2, and when recoverable amounts do not equal cost there is the further need to write down inventory to reflect such impairment. However, under defined circumstances, inventories may be carried at fair value, in excess of the actual cost of production or acquisition. Currently, IAS 41 provides that agricultural products that are carried in inventory are to be reported at fair value, subject to certain limitations.

Under the provisions of IAS 41, all biological assets are to be measured at fair value less expected point-of-sale costs at each date of the statement of financial position, unless fair value cannot be measured reliably. Agricultural produce is to be measured at fair value at the point of harvest less expected point-of-sale costs. Because harvested produce is a marketable commodity, there is no "measurable reliability" exception for produce.

Furthermore, the change in fair value of biological assets occurring during a reporting period is reported in net profit or loss, notwithstanding that these are "unrealized" as of the date of the statement of financial position. IAS 41, however, does provide an exception to this fair value model for biological assets for situations where there is no active market at time of recognition in the financial statements, and no other reliable measurement method exists. In such instances, it provides that the cost model is to be applied to the specific biological asset for which such conditions hold, only. These biological assets should be measured at depreciated cost less any accumulated impairment losses.

More generally, the quoted market prices in active markets will represent the best measure of fair value of biological assets or agricultural produce. If an active market does not exist, IAS 41 provides guidance for choosing another measurement basis. Fair value measurement stops at the moment of harvest. IAS 2 applies after that date.

The details of IAS 41 are described in Chapter 24, Specialized Industries.

Other Cost Topics

Standard costs. Standard costs are predetermined unit costs used by many manufacturing firms for planning and control purposes. Standard costs are often incorporated into the accounts, and materials, work in process, and finished goods inventories are all carried on this basis of accounting. The use of standard costs in financial reporting is acceptable if adjustments are made periodically to reflect current conditions and if its use approximates one of the recognized cost flow assumptions.

Inventories valued at net realizable value. In exceptional cases, inventories may be reported at net realizable value in accordance with well-established practices in certain industries. Such treatment is justified when cost is difficult to determine, quoted market prices are available, marketability is assured, and units are interchangeable. IAS 2 stipulates that producers' inventories of agricultural and forest products, agricultural produce after harvest, and minerals and mineral products, to the extent that they are measured at net realizable value in accordance with well-established practices, are to be valued in this manner. IAS 41 subsequently addressed this matter for biological assets only. When inventory is valued above cost, revenue is recognized before the point of sale; full disclosure in the financial statements would, of course, be required.

Inventories valued at fair value less costs to sell. In case of commodity broker-traders' inventories, IAS 2 stipulates that these inventories be valued at fair value less costs to sell. While allowing this exceptional treatment for inventories of commodity broker-traders, IAS 2 makes it mandatory that in such cases the fair value changes should be reported in profit and loss account for the period of change.

Disclosure Requirements

IAS 2 sets forth certain disclosure requirements relative to inventory accounting methods employed by the reporting entity. According to this standard, the following must be disclosed:

1. The accounting policies adopted in measuring inventories, including the costing methods (e.g., FIFO or weighted-average) employed
2. The total carrying amount of inventories and the carrying amount in classifications appropriate to the enterprise
3. The carrying amount of inventories carried at fair value less costs to sell
4. The amount of inventories recognized as expense during the period
5. The amount of any write-down of inventories recognized as an expense in the period
6. The amount of any reversal of any previous write-down that is recognized in profit or loss for the period
7. The circumstances or events that led to the reversal of a write-down of inventories to net realizable value
8. The carrying amount of inventories pledged as security for liabilities

The type of information to be provided concerning inventories held in different classifications is somewhat flexible, but traditional classifications, such as raw materials, work in progress, finished goods, and supplies, should normally be employed. In the case of service providers, inventories (which are really akin to unbilled receivables) can be described as work in progress.

In addition to the foregoing, the financial statements should disclose either the cost of inventories recognized as an expense during the period (i.e., reported as cost of sales or included in other expense categories), or the operating costs, applicable to revenues, recognized as an expense during the period, categorized by their respective natures.

Costs of inventories recognized as expense includes, in addition to the costs inventoried previously and attaching to goods sold currently, the excess overhead costs charged to expense for the period because, under the standard, they could not be deferred to future periods.

Examples of Financial Statement Disclosures

Nokia Corporation and Subsidiaries
Annual Report 2007

Notes to the Consolidated Financial Statements

1. Accounting Principles

Inventories. Inventories are stated at the lower of cost or net realizable value. Cost is determined using standard cost, which approximates actual cost, on a FIFO basis. Net realizable value is the amount that can be realized from the sale of the inventory in the normal course of business after allowing for the costs of realization. In addition to the cost of materials and direct labor, an appropriate proportion of production overhead is included in the inventory values. An allowance is recorded for excess inventory and obsolescence is based on the lower of cost or net realizable value.

18. Inventories

	2007 EURm	2006 EURm
Raw material, supplies and other	591	369
Work in progress	1,060	600
Finished goods	1,225	594
Total	2,876	1,554

Lectra S.A.
Annual Report 2007

Accounting Policies

Inventories. Inventories of raw materials are valued at the lower of purchase cost (based on weighted average cost, including related costs) and their net realizable value. Finished goods and work-in-progress are valued at the lower of standard industrial cost (adjusted at year-end on an actual cost basis) and their net realizable value.

Net realizable value is the probable sale price in the normal course of business, less estimated cost of completion or upgrading of product and unavoidable selling costs.

Industrial cost does not include interest expense.

A write-down is recorded if net realizable value is less than the book value.

Write-downs on inventories of spare parts and consumables are calculated by comparing book value and probable net realizable value after a specific analysis of the rotation and obsolescence of inventory items, taking into account the utilization of items for maintenance and after-sales services activities, and changes in the range of products marketed.

Notes to the Consolidated Financial Statements

6. Inventories

€ in thousands

	2007	2006
Raw materials	26,112	21,025
Finished goods and work-in-progress [1]	13,907	14,465
Inventories, gross value	40,019	35,490
Raw materials	(4,717)	(3,966)
Finished goods and work-in-progress [1]	(5,146)	(5,584)
Write-downs	(9,863)	(9,550)
Raw materials	21,395	17,060
Finished goods and work-in-progress [1]	8,761	8,880
Inventories, net value	30,156	25,940

[1] *Including demonstration and second-hand equipment.*

€753,000 of inventory fully written down was scrapped in the course of 2007, thereby diminishing the gross value of inventory and write-downs by the same amount.

The increase in inventories stems primarily from the launch of the new generation of Vector cutting systems and the gradual ramp-up of manufacturing capacity.

Inventory write-downs charged for the year amounted to €3,002,000. Reversals of previous write-downs relating to sales transactions amounted to €1,612,000, booked against the charges for the period.

APPENDIX

NET REALIZABLE VALUE UNDER US GAAP

In many jurisdictions, the term *lower of cost or market* is used, as contrasted to IAS 2's *lower of cost or net realizable value*. As a practical matter, this difference in terminology will have little or no impact, since *market* is usually defined operationally as being replacement cost or net realizable value. However, one important distinction is that *market* is usually defined as a conditional term that contemplates a range of values, based not only on the costs to complete and sell an item, but also, in some circumstances, on the expected or normal profit to be earned on the sale. Since IAS 2 provides only general guidance concerning the determination of net realizable value, it will be useful to look to other existing standards for insight into how these measures are to be developed in a practical situation.

Measuring the decline to net realizable value. The IAS 2 definition of net realizable value makes explicit reference only to "costs of completion and costs incurred in order to make the sale." However, as illustrated below, if expected or normal profit margins on sales of inventory items are not taken into account, excessive profits or losses might be recognized in future periods, due to an incomplete application of the net realizable value concept.

The application of these principles is illustrated in the following example. In this example, replacement cost will be used as the primary operational definition of inventory value when that amount is lower than carrying value determined by historical cost. Replacement cost is a valid measure of the future utility of the inventory item since increases or decreases in the purchase price generally foreshadow related increases or decreases in the selling price. Assume the following information for products A, B, C, D, and E:

Item	Cost	Replacement cost	Est. selling price	Cost to complete	Normal profit percentage
A	€2.00	€1.80	€ 2.50	€0.50	24%
B	4.00	1.60	4.00	0.80	24%
C	6.00	6.60	10.00	1.00	18%
D	5.00	4.75	6.00	2.00	20%
E	1.00	1.05	1.20	0.25	12.5%

Consider item A: The net realizable value defined in accordance with IAS 2 is €2.50 – 0.50 = €2.00 (estimated selling price less costs to complete and sell). As it happens, this is exactly equal to historical cost, suggesting that there would be no adjustment required. However, if no adjustment is recorded, the profit realized upon the sale next period will be €2.50 – 2.00 – 0.50 = €0, which would be an unnaturally low net margin given the historical experience of a 24% margin. To preserve the normal margin, which would amount to €0.60 (€2.50 × 24%), the inventory would have to be written down to €1.40 (€2.50 – 0.50 – 0.60). However, the actual cost to replace the item in inventory is known to be €1.80, which suggests that the normal margin of 24% cannot be replicated under current conditions.

The foregoing explains why some standards setters and accounting theoreticians (but it should be stressed, not the IASB) have concluded that inventory should be reported at the lower of cost or market, where *market* is defined as replacement cost subject to ceiling and floor values; where *ceiling* is defined as net realizable value (NRV), and *floor* as the NRV minus the normal profit margin. Using this approach (which is the standard in the United States), the amount of profit to be recognized in the period of later sale, absent other changes in the marketplace after the reporting date, will not be abnormally high or low.

To continue with this example, the data in the foregoing table are used to compute market values consistent with the definition set forth earlier. Note that the primary measure in all cases is replacement cost; if this falls between the ceiling and the floor, it becomes the measure of market, which is then compared to historical cost; the lower of cost or market is then used to actually value the inventory item. If the replacement cost exceeds the ceiling value (as for items D and E), the ceiling value becomes the market next to be compared to historical cost. On the other hand, if replacement cost is lower than the floor (as for items B and C), the floor is used as the market value to be compared next to the historical cost.

Determination of Net Realizable Value

Item	Cost	Replacement cost	NRV (ceiling)	NRV less profit (floor)	Market	LCM
A	€2.00	€1.80	€2.00	€1.40	€1.80	€1.80
B	4.00	1.60	3.20	2.24	2.24	2.24
C	6.00	6.60	9.00	7.20	7.20	6.00
D	5.00	4.75	4.00	2.80	4.00	4.00
E	1.00	1.05	0.95	0.80	0.95	0.95

Note that under a strict reading of IAS 2, NRV would be compared directly to historical cost; the other values in the above table would not be given any consideration. If a strict application of the net realizable value rule were insisted upon, in contrast, item A would be valued at €2.00 instead of €1.80, resulting in a zero profit upon sale; and item B would be valued at €3.20 instead of €2.24, also resulting in a zero profit upon ultimate disposition. In general, the impact of using net realizable value, rather than market, would be to preclude preservation of some (if not a normal amount of) profit upon later sale of the item.

7 REVENUE RECOGNITION, INCLUDING CONSTRUCTION CONTRACTS

REVENUE RECOGNITION

PERSPECTIVE AND ISSUES

The standard addressing revenue recognition principles in general terms is IAS 18. It prescribes the accounting treatment for revenue arising from certain types of transactions and events and, while useful, is not a comprehensive treatise on the peculiarities on all the diverse forms of revenue and of possible recognition strategies that could be encountered. The basic premise is that revenue should be measured at the fair value of the consideration that has been received when the product or service promised has been provided to the customer. Specific guidance applies to various categories of revenues.

Thus, in the normal sale of goods, revenue is presumed to have realized when the significant risks and rewards have been transferred to the buyer, accompanied by the forfeiture of effective control by the seller, and the amount to be received can be reliably measured. For most routine transactions (e.g., by retail merchants), this occurs when the goods have been delivered to the customer.

Revenue recognition for service transactions, as set forth in revised IAS 18, requires that the percentage-of-completion method be used unless certain defined conditions are not met. Originally, reporting entities had a choice of methods—percentage-of-completion or completed contract. Current revenue recognition standards for services transactions closely parallel those for construction contracts under IAS 11, which is also covered in this chapter.

For interest, royalties and dividends, recognition is warranted when it is probable that economic benefits will flow to the entity. Specifically, interest is recognized on a time proportion basis, taking into account the effective yield on the asset. Royalties are recognized on an accrual basis, in accordance with the terms of the underlying agreement. Dividend income is recognized when the shareholder's right to receive payment has been established.

In recent years, particularly with the advent of Web-based "e-commerce" entities, there has been a large increase in the occurrence of barter transactions. The more controversial of the barter transactions involve the swapping of advertising services (e.g., whereby two or more e-commerce (or other) operations "swap" display advertising on the others' Web sites), particularly when these were valued by reference to arbitrary prices or were seldom equaled in cash transactions conducted at arm's-length (i.e., sales of advertising for cash). The interpretation SIC 31 established the requirement that, in order for revenue to be recognized in such advertising swap situations, an objective measure of the value of the services provided by the entity seeking to recognize revenue has to be available. In the absence of such reliable data, no revenue can be recognized.

IAS 18 also established certain disclosure requirements, including the revenue recognition accounting policies of the reporting entity.

While the existing general guidance on revenue recognition under IAS actually exceeds that which has thus far been provided under various national standards, it nonetheless is modest given the broad importance of the topic.

The frequently cited contrast between principles-based IFRS and principles-based, but also rules-driven, US GAAP is perhaps most visible in the area of revenue recognition. US GAAP contains an estimated 200-plus individual revenue recognition provisions which are in many cases industry-specific and/or arrangement-specific. Those provisions are often inconsistent with fundamental principles of US GAAP and with each other. IAS 18, on the other hand, consists of a small number of authoritative general principles and contains almost no specific rules.

IASB (and the US standard setter, FASB) has been pursuing a project intended to address revenue recognition, as well as the associated topics of distinguishing liabilities from equity. This project, still not near completion, is likely to have a major impact on financial reporting, since it promises to fundamentally change revenue recognition practices. This chapter contains a summary of this project as of late 2008.

Sources of IFRS		
IASB's *Framework for Preparation and Presentation of Financial Statements*		
IAS 11, 18	*SIC* 31	*IFRIC* 12, 13, 15

DEFINITIONS OF TERMS

Fair value. An amount for which an asset could be exchanged or a liability settled, between knowledgeable, willing parties in an arm's-length transaction.

Ordinary activities. Those activities of an entity which it undertakes as part of its business and such related activities in which the entity engages in furtherance of, incidental to, or arising from those activities.

Revenue. Gross inflow of economic benefits resulting from an entity's ordinary activities is considered "revenue," provided those inflows result in increases in equity, other than increases relating to contributions from owners or equity participants. Revenue refers to the gross amount (of revenue) and excludes amounts collected on behalf of third parties.

CONCEPTS, RULES, AND EXAMPLES

Revenue. The IASB's *Framework* defines "income" to include both revenue and gains. IAS 18 deals only with revenue. Revenue is defined as income arising from the ordinary activities of an entity and may be referred to by a variety of names including sales, fees, interest, dividends and royalties. Revenue encompasses only the gross inflow of economic benefits received or receivable by the entity, on its own account. This implies that amounts collected on behalf of others—such as in the case of sales tax or value added tax, which also flow to the entity along with the revenue from sales—do not qualify as revenue. Thus, these other collections should not be included in an entity's reported revenue. Put another way, gross revenue from sales should be shown net of amounts collected on behalf of third parties.

Similarly, in an agency relationship the amounts collected on behalf of the principal is not regarded as revenue for the agent. Instead, the commission earned on such collections qualifies as revenue of the agent. For example, in the case of a travel agency, the collections from ticket sales do not qualify as revenue or income from its ordinary activities. Instead, it will be the commission on the tickets sold by the travel agency that will constitute that entity's gross revenue.

Scope of the standard. IAS 18 applies to the accounting for revenue arising from

- The sale of goods;
- The rendering of services; and
- The use of the entity's assets by others, yielding (for the entity) interest, dividends and royalties.

A sale of goods encompasses *both* goods produced by the entity for sale to others and goods purchased for resale by the entity. The rendering of services involves the performance by the entity of an agreed-upon task, based on a contract, over a contractually agreed period of time.

The use of the entity's assets by others gives rise to revenue for the entity in the form of

- **Interest,** which is a charge for the use of cash and cash equivalent or amounts due to the entity;
- **Royalties,** which are charges for the use of long-term assets of the entity such as patents or trademarks owned by the entity; and
- **Dividends,** which are distributions of profit to the holders of equity investments in the share capital of other entities.

The standard *does not* apply to revenue arising from

- Lease agreements that are subject to the requirements of IAS 17;
- Dividends arising from investments in associates which are accounted for using the equity method, which are dealt with in IAS 28;
- Insurance contracts within the scope of IFRS 4;
- Changes in fair values of financial instruments—or their disposal, which is addressed by IAS 39;

- Natural increases in herds, agriculture and forest products, which is dealt with under IAS 41;
- The extraction of mineral ores; and
- Changes in the value of other current assets.

Measurement of revenue. The quantum of revenue to be recognized is usually dependent upon the terms of the contract between the entity and the buyer of goods, the recipient of the services, or the users of the assets of the entity. Revenue should be measured at the fair value of the consideration received or receivable, net of any trade discounts and volume rebates allowed by the entity.

When the inflow of the consideration, which is usually in the form of cash or cash equivalents, is deferred, the fair value of the consideration will be an amount lower than the nominal amount of consideration. The difference between the fair value and the nominal value of the consideration, which represents the time value of money, is recognized as interest revenue.

When the entity offers interest-free extended credit to the buyer or accepts a promissory note from the buyer (as consideration) that bears either no interest or a below-market interest rate, such an arrangement would be construed as a financing transaction. In such a case the fair value of the consideration is ascertained by discounting the future inflows using an imputed rate of interest. The imputed rate of interest is either "the prevailing rate of interest for a similar instrument of an issuer with a similar credit rating, or a rate of interest that discounts the nominal amount of the instrument to the current cash sales price of the goods or services."

To illustrate this point, let us consider the following example:

> Hero International is a car dealership that is known to offer excellent packages for all new models of Japanese cars. Currently, it is advertising on the television that there is a special offer for all Year 2007 models of a certain make. The offer is valid for all purchases made on or before September 30, 2006. The special offer deal is either a cash payment in full of €20,000 or a zero down payment with extended credit terms of two years—24 monthly installments of €1,000 each. Thus, anyone opting for the extended credit terms would pay €24,000 in total.
>
> Since there is a difference of €4,000 between the cash price of €20,000 and the total amount payable if the car is paid for in 24 installments of €1,000 each, this arrangement is effectively a financing transaction (and of course a sale transaction as well). The cash price of €20,000 would be regarded as the amount of consideration attributable to the sale of the car. The difference between the cash price and the aggregate amount payable in monthly installments is interest revenue and is to be recognized over the period of two years on a time proportion basis (using the effective interest method).

Exchanges of similar and dissimilar goods and services. When goods or services are exchanged or swapped for *similar* goods or services, the earning process is not considered being complete. Thus the exchange is not regarded as a transaction that generates revenue. Such exchanges are common in certain commodity industries, such as oil or milk industries, where suppliers usually swap inventories in various locations in order to meet geographically diverse demand on a timely basis.

In contrast, when goods or services of a *dissimilar* nature are swapped, the earning process is considered to be complete, and thus the exchange is regarded as a transaction that generates revenue. The revenue thus generated is measured at the fair value of the goods or services received or receivable. If in this process cash or cash equivalents are also transferred, then the fair value should be adjusted by the amount of cash or cash equivalents transferred. In certain cases, the fair value of the goods or services received cannot be measured reliably. Under such circumstances, fair value of goods or services given up, adjusted by the amount of cash transferred, is the measure of revenue to be recognized. Barter arrangements are examples of such exchanges involving goods that are dissimilar in nature.

Identification of the transaction. While setting out clearly the criteria for the recognition of revenue under three categories—sale of goods, rendering of services and use of the entity's assets by others—the standard clarifies that these should be applied separately to each transaction. In other words, the recognition criteria should be applied to the separately identifiable components of a single transaction consistent with the principle of "substance over form."

For example, a washing machine is sold with an after-sale service warranty. The selling price includes a separately identifiable portion attributable to the after-sale service warranty. In such a case, the standard requires that the selling price of the washing machine should be apportioned between the two separately identifiable components and each one recognized according to an appropriate recognition criterion. Thus, the portion of the selling price attributable to the after-sales warranty should be deferred and recognized over the period during which the service is performed. The remaining selling price should be recognized immediately if the recognition criteria for revenue from sale of goods (explained below) are satisfied.

Similarly, the recognition criteria are to be applied to two or more separate transactions together when they are connected or linked in such a way that the commercial effect (or substance over form) cannot be understood without considering the series of transactions as a whole. For example, Company X sells a ship to Company Y and later enters into a separate contract with Company Y to repurchase the same ship from it. In this case the two transactions need to be considered together in order to ascertain whether or not revenue is to be recognized.

Revenue recognition criteria. According to the IASB's *Framework*, revenue is to be recognized when it is probable that future economic benefits will flow to the entity and reliable measurement of the quantum of revenue is possible. Based on these fundamental tenets of revenue recognition stated in the IASB's *Framework*, IAS 18 establishes criteria for recognition of revenue from three categories of transactions—the sale of goods, the rendering of services, and the use by others of the reporting entity's assets. In the case of the first two categories of transactions producing revenue, the standard prescribes certain additional criteria for recognition of revenue. In the case of revenue from the use by others of the entity's assets, the standard does not overtly prescribe additional criteria, but it does provide guidance on the bases to be adopted in revenue recognition from this source. This may, in a way, be construed as an additional criterion for revenue recognition from this source of revenue.

Revenue recognition from the sale of goods. Revenue from the sale of goods should be recognized if *all* of the five conditions mentioned below are met.

- The reporting entity has transferred significant risks and rewards of ownership of the goods to the buyer;
- The entity does not retain *either* continuing managerial involvement (akin to that usually associated with ownership) *or* effective control over the goods sold;
- The amount of revenue to be recognized can be measured reliably;
- The probability that economic benefits related to the transaction will flow to the entity exists; and
- The costs incurred or to be incurred in respect of the transaction can be measured reliably.

The determination of the point in time when a reporting entity is considered to have transferred the significant risks and rewards of ownership in goods to the buyer is critical to the recognition of revenue from the sale of goods. If upon examination of the circumstances of the transfer of risks and rewards of ownership by the entity it is determined that the entity could still be considered as having retained significant risks and rewards of ownership, the transaction could not be regarded as a sale.

Some examples of situations illustrated by the standard in which an entity may be considered to have retained significant risks and rewards of ownership, and thus revenue is not recognized, are set out below.

- A contract for the sale of an oil refinery stipulates that installation of the refinery is an integral and a significant part of the contract. Therefore, until the refinery is completely installed by the reporting entity that sold it, the sale would not be regarded as complete. In other words, until the completion of the installation, the entity that sold the refinery would still be regarded as the effective owner of the refinery even if the refinery has already been delivered to the buyer. Accordingly, revenue will not be recognized by the entity until it completes the installation of the refinery.
- Goods are sold on approval, whereby the buyer has negotiated a limited right of return. Since there is a possibility that the buyer may return the goods, revenue is not recognized until the shipment has been formally accepted by the buyer, or the goods have been delivered as per the terms of the contract, and the time stipulated in the contract for rejection has expired.
- In the case of "layaway sales," under terms of which the goods are delivered only when the buyer makes the final payment in a series of installments, revenue is not recognized until the last and final payment is received by the entity. Upon receipt of the final installment, the goods are delivered to the buyer and revenue is recognized. However, based upon experience, if it can reasonably be presumed that most such sales are consummated, revenue may be recognized when a significant deposit is received from the buyer and goods are on hand, identified and ready for delivery to the buyer.

If the reporting entity retains only an insignificant risk of ownership, the transaction is considered a sale and revenue is recognized. For example, a department store has a policy to offer refunds if a customer is not satisfied. Since the entity is only retaining an insignificant risk of ownership, revenue from sale of goods is recognized. However, since the entity's refund policy is publicly announced and thus would have created a valid expectation on the part of the customers that the store will honor its policy of refunds, a provision is also recognized for the best estimate of the costs of refunds, as explained in IAS 37.

Another important condition for recognition of revenue from the sale of goods is the existence of the probability that the economic benefits will flow to the entity. For example, for several years an entity has been exporting goods to a foreign country. In the current year, due to sudden restrictions by the foreign government on remittances of currency outside the country, collections from these sales were not made by the entity. As long as it is uncertain if these restrictions will be removed, revenue should not be recognized from these exports, since it may not be probable that economic benefits in the form of collections will flow to the entity. Once the restrictions are withdrawn and uncertainty is removed, revenue may be recognized.

Yet another important condition for recognition of revenue from the sale of goods relates to the reliability of measuring costs associated with the sale of goods. Thus, if expenses such as those relating to warranties or other postshipment costs cannot be measured reliably, then revenue from the sale of such goods should also not be recognized. This rule is based on the principle of matching of revenues and expenses.

IASB provides additional guidance on determining the point in time at which the entity transfers the significant risks and rewards of ownership, and thus when revenue from sale of goods is to be recognized. Since the law in different countries may determine the point in time at which the entity transfers ownership, this guidance accompanies IAS 18 but is not part of IAS 18. It includes the following:

Consignment sales. Revenue is recognized by the shipper (seller or consignor), not by the recipient (buyer or consignee), when the goods are sold to a third party. Goods out on consignment remain the property of the consignor and are included in its inventory. The consignee is selling the goods on behalf of the shipper for a commission.

Cash on delivery sales. In this case, revenue is recognized after delivery of goods is made and cash received.

Sales to intermediate parties, such as distributors, dealers or others for resale. In general, revenue is recognized when the risks and rewards of ownership have been transferred. In situations when the buyer is acting, in substance, as an agent, the sale is treated as a consignment sale.

Subscriptions to publications and similar items. Revenue is recognized on a straight-line basis over the period in which the items are dispatched (when items are of similar value); or on the basis of the sales value of items dispatched to total estimated sales value (when the items vary in value).

Installment sale, under which the consideration is receivable in installments. Revenue is recognized at the present value of the consideration, determined by discounting the installments receivable at the imputed rate of interest.

Real estate sales. In accordance with IFRIC 15, revenue from the construction of real estate is recognized depending on whether an agreement is for the sale of goods, the rendering of services, or a construction contract (within the scope of IAS 11 or IAS 18).

Revenue recognition from the rendering of services. When the outcome of the transaction involving the rendering of services can be estimated reliably, revenue relating to that transaction should be recognized. The recognition of revenue should be with reference to the stage of completion of the transaction at the end of the reporting period. The outcome of a transaction can be estimated reliably when each of the four conditions set out below are met.

- The amount of revenue can be measured reliably;
- The probability that the economic benefits related to this transaction will flow to the entity exists;
- The stage of completion of the transaction at the end of the reporting period can be measured reliably; and
- The costs incurred for the transaction and the costs to complete the transaction can be measured reliably.

This manner of recognition of revenue, based on the stage of completion, is often referred to as the "percentage-of-completion" method. IAS 11 also mandates recognition of revenue on this basis. Revenue is recognized only when it is probable that the economic benefits related to the transaction will flow to the reporting entity. However, when the amount of revenue cannot be estimated reliably, revenue should be recognized only to the extent of the expenses recognized that are recoverable ("cost recovery method" is fallback in this case). If there is uncertainty with regard to the collectability of an amount already included in revenue, the uncollectable amount should be recognized as an expense instead of adjusting it against the amount of revenue originally recognized. For multiperiod service contracts, differences between national GAAP (e.g., US GAAP) and IFRS can lead to timing differences in revenue recognition.

In order to be able to make reliable estimates, an entity should agree with the other party to the following:

- Each other's enforceable rights with respect to the services provided;

- The consideration to be exchanged; and
- The manner and terms of settlement.

It is important that the entity has in place an effective internal financial budgeting and reporting system. This ensures that the entity can promptly review and revise the estimates of revenue as the service is being performed. It should be noted, however, that merely because there is a later need for revisions does not by itself make an estimate of the outcome of the transaction unreliable.

Progress payments and advances received from customers are emphatically not a measure of stage of completion. The stage of completion of a transaction may be determined in a number of ways. Depending on the nature of the transaction, the method used may include

- Surveys of work performed;
- Services performed to date as a percentage of total services to be performed; or
- The proportion that costs incurred to date bear to the estimated total costs of the transaction. (Only costs that reflect services performed or to be performed are included in costs incurred to date or in estimated total costs.)

In certain cases services are performed by an indeterminable number of acts over a specified period of time. Revenue in such a case should be recognized on a straight-line basis unless it is possible to estimate the stage of completion by some other method more reliably. Similarly when in a series of acts to be performed in rendering a service, a specific act is much more significant than other acts, the recognition is postponed until the significant act is performed.

During the early stages of the transaction it may not be possible to estimate the outcome of the transaction reliably. In all such cases, where the outcome of the transaction involving the rendering of services cannot be estimated reliably, revenue should be recognized only to the extent of the expenses recognized that are recoverable. However, in a later period when the uncertainty that precluded the reliable estimation of the outcome no longer exists, revenue is recognized as usual.

NOTE: The "percentage-of-completion" method is discussed in detail in the second part of this chapter. For numerical examples illustrating the method, please refer to the second part of this chapter relating to construction contracts.

Revenue recognition from interest, royalties, and dividends. Revenue arising from the use by others of the reporting entity's assets yielding interest, royalties and dividends should be recognized when both of the following two conditions are met:

1. It is probable that the economic benefits relating to the transaction will flow to the entity; and
2. The amount of the revenue can be measured reliably.

The bases prescribed for the recognition of the revenue are the following:

1. In the case of interest—the time proportion basis that takes into account the effective yield on the assets;
2. In the case of royalties—the accrual basis in accordance with the substance of the relevant agreement; and
3. In the case of dividends—when the shareholder's right to receive payment is established.

According to IAS 18, "the effective yield on an asset is the rate of interest used to discount the stream of future cash receipts expected over the life of the asset to equate to the initial carrying amount of asset." Interest revenue includes the effect of amortization of any discount, premium or other difference between the initial carrying amount of a debt security and its amount at maturity.

When unpaid interest has accrued before an interest-bearing investment is purchased by the entity, the subsequent receipt of interest is to be allocated between preacquisition and postacquisition periods. Only the portion of interest that accrued subsequent to the acquisition by the entity is recognized as income. The remaining portion of interest, which is attributable to the preacquisition period, is treated as a reduction of the cost of the investment, as explained by IAS 39. Similarly, dividends on equity securities declared from preacquisition profits are treated as reduction of the cost of investment. If it is difficult to make such an allocation except on an arbitrary basis, dividends are recognized as revenue unless they clearly represent a recovery of part of the cost of the equity securities.

Disclosures. A reporting entity should disclose the following:

- The accounting policies adopted for the recognition of revenue including the methods adopted to determine the stage of completion of transactions involving the rendering of services;
- The amount of each significant category of revenue recognized during the period including revenue arising from
  - The sale of goods;
  - The rendering of services; and
  - Interest, royalties, and dividends.
- The amounts revenue arising from exchanges of goods or services included in each significant category of revenue.

Accounting for barter transactions. The much-heralded era of e-commerce (i.e., commerce conducted via Internet, based on commercial Web sites directed at end consumers ["B-to-C" business] or at intermediate consumers, such as wholesalers and manufacturers ["B-to-B" business]), although past its over-touted boom period, is now an established feature of business life. It is likely that growing percentages of business will be conducted via electronic commerce.

The "dot-com bubble" was accompanied by another related trend, that of investors and others finding value in new "performance" measures such as gross sales volume and the number of "hits" registered on Web sites. Concurrently, the importance (for high technology and start-up entities in particular) of traditional measure of success, particularly profits, was often unjustifiably discounted. The confluence of these two structural changes provided an unfortunate opportunity to some entities to seek ways to inflate reported revenues, if not profits. It is commonplace for Web-based businesses to swap advertising with each other. With each entity "buying" advertising and "selling" advertising, a liberal interpretation of financial reporting standards could enable each of them to inflate reported revenues by attributing any value to the exchange. While corresponding expenses were also necessarily exaggerated and net earnings affected not at all (unless revenues and expenses were reported in different fiscal periods, which also occurred), with investors mesmerized by gross revenue, the impact was to encourage overvaluation of the entities' shares in the market.

As certain financial reporting frauds have demonstrated, distortion of revenues via "swap" arrangements has hardly been constrained to the providing and acquiring of advertising (e.g., the "capacity swaps" of many US telecom and energy companies). However, the bartering of advertising services has been the first to receive the attention of the SIC, which issued SIC 31 to prescribe revenue recognition principles to be applied to these transactions.

This interpretation addresses how revenue from a barter transaction involving advertising services received or provided in a barter transaction should be reliably measured. The

SIC agreed that the entity providing advertising should measure revenue from the barter transaction based on the fair value of the advertising services it has provided to its customer, and not on the value of that received. In fact, the SIC states categorically that the value of the services received cannot be used to reliably measure the revenue generated by the services provided.

Furthermore, SIC 31 holds that the fair value advertising services provided in a barter transaction can be reliably measured only by reference to nonbarter transactions that involve services similar to that in the barter transaction, when those transactions occur frequently, are expected to continue occurring after the barter transaction, represent a predominant source of revenue from advertising similar to the advertising in the barter transaction, involve cash and/or another form of consideration (e.g., marketable securities, nonmonetary assets, and other services) that has a reliably determinable fair value, and do not involve the same counterparty as in the barter transaction. All of these conditions must be satisfied in order to value the revenue to be recognized from the advertising barter transaction.

Clearly, based on the criteria mandated by SIC 31, the more common barter transactions, involving mere "swaps" of advertising among the members of the bartering group, henceforth cannot serve as a basis for revenue recognition by any of the parties thereto.

Accounting for multiple-element revenue arrangements. The accounting for multiple-element revenue arrangements is not presently addressed under IFRS, but the IASB's project on revenue recognition does deal with this increasingly common phenomenon. When entities offer customers multiple-element revenue arrangements, these provide for the delivery or performance of multiple products, services, or rights, which may take place at different times. For example, deregulation, innovation, and competition in the telecommunication industry resulted in complex service offerings to customers, in particular for bundled (or multielement) arrangements that may include a handset. Revenue recognition is one of the most complex accounting issues this industry faces. The IASB has noted that the accounting for such arrangements has been one of the most contentious practice issues of revenue recognition. As part of its current project, it examined the application of an assets and liabilities approach to revenue recognition against the cases involving multiple-element revenue arrangements, and contrasted the impact of such an approach to the positions taken by the FASB's Emerging Issues Task Force's *Accounting for Revenue Arrangements with Multiple Deliverables* (EITF Issue 00-21, which was approved by the EITF in November 2002). The IASB noted that the EITF's approach was consistent with, but more extensive than, the revenue recognition criteria in IAS 18.

IASB compared an assets and liabilities approach with the EITF's approach, which instead focuses on when revenue is earned and whether delivering an element in an arrangement represents a separate earning process from delivery of other elements. It tentatively agreed that the case studies examined indicated that, in many cases, similar outcomes would in fact result from applying either approach. However, IASB noted that applying an assets and liabilities approach has certain advantages over the EITF's approach. First, it is not dependent on whether the delivered item is sold separately by any vendor or whether the customer could resell the deliverable. Second, the existence of rights of return does not have the potential to preclude the recognition of revenue for delivered items. Third, when a delivered asset in a multiple-element arrangement is inseparable from the undelivered items, an assets and liabilities approach avoids the need to recognize a "deferred debit" as an asset when the asset sacrificed is derecognized. Finally, the IASB approach measures the value of undelivered items by direct reference to a measurement attribute (e.g., fair value) rather than through an allocation process, which avoids assuming the same margin on each inseparable deliver-

able in a multiple-element arrangement. However, the IASB has issued no definitive literature on this topic to date.

Sales involving customer loyalty credits. Certain sales transactions involve the granting of so-called customer loyalty credits, such that customers are granted "points" toward
future purchases of goods or services. The popular airline mileage programs are perhaps the
most ubiquitous of such programs, under which frequent fliers accumulate points which can
be redeemed for future class upgrades or free flights. For a long time no special accounting
recognition was given to these very real obligations by the airlines, which resulted in a large
overhang of costly service promises. These promises clearly represented obligations (i.e.,
accounting liabilities) by the service providers (e.g., airlines), but were long ignored for two
reasons. First, they were assumed to not be material to the service providers' statements of
financial position; and second, there were legitimate concerns about how these were to be
measured (i.e., whether they should have been recorded at some average of the retail value of
the "free" services, or at the providers' cost to provide these services, which were to be delivered at some unspecified future date.

More recently, it had become clear that quite material amounts of such obligations had
been going unreported by the service providers, with the cumulative effect of possibly materially overstating current profitability and shareholders' equity (retained earnings) and understating liabilities. In the international standards arena, this has now been definitively dealt
with by the promulgation of IFRIC 13, *Customer Loyalty Programmes*. It applies to a wide
array of such programs, including those linked to individual and group buying activities, with
goods or services due to be provided by the reporting entity itself as well as rights to be redeemed by third parties. In each such instance, customers earn the right to discounted or free
goods or services, possibly after further qualifying conditions are met.

IFRIC 13 stipulates the accounting by the entity that grants the award credits. It requires
that such credits be separately identified as components of the sales transactions, thus reducing the profit recognized and resulting in the creation of a liability for the future goods or
services to be provided to its customers. The liability thereby created is liquidated when the
subsequent free or discounted service is provided, or, if a third party is to provide the later
goods or services, when the third party becomes obligated to provide such goods or services.
If the customer forfeits its right (e.g., by expiration of a contractual period for redemption of
the credits), revenue is to be recognized at that time.

This accounting requirement is, conceptually at least, straightforward. A key issue is the
proper measurement to be applied to this obligation. IFRIC 13 resolves this by specifying
that the *fair value* of the award credits is the proper measure. The interpretation stipulates
that this is given by reference to the fair value of the goods or services that would be offered
to customers who had not accumulated credits from the initial transactions. For example, if
"frequent flier" mileage points are awarded, and if, say, 25,000 mileage points result in a free
round trip flight to any domestic destination, the service provider (airline) would use the average retail price of such tickets as a basis for accruing such obligations.

Where a third party assumes this responsibility, there would usually be a contractually
agreed value, making recognition of the amount to be allocated to the program liability directly observable.

Since the amount to be allocated to the obligation to provide future discounted or free
goods or services is determined by reference to the fair value of the goods or services, the
amount allocated to this liability is a reduction in the revenue immediately recognized. It is
not an expense (such as a selling expense), because that treatment would be consistent with
measurement by reference to the reporting entity's cost of providing the future goods or ser-

vices. Put another way, the solution prescribed by IFRIC 13 is based on a revenue recognition approach, not a cost accrual approach, to financial reporting.

The only exception to the foregoing occurs when the expected cost of delivering the free or discounted goods or services is anticipated to exceed the revenue associated with that event. Consistent with practice under other IFRS, these anticipated losses must be accrued at the date the initial transactions occur.

As noted, experience suggests that some portion of the program points will be forfeited by customers (i.e., they will be earned but never redeemed). This can occur because some customers will fail to meet other qualifying conditions, such as by reaching some defined threshold such as number of miles needed to exercise the redemption, or because of the expiration of time. With experience, the reporting entity may develop the ability to accurately project the proportion of points awarded that will not be redeemed. IFRIC 13 provides that the accrual of the obligation is to be based on the fraction of points that will eventually be redeemed. This is an estimate and ultimately the facts will differ from the estimate, and as with other changes in accounting estimates, this is accounted for prospectively; it is not an error to be corrected by retroactive restatement.

For example, if customers earn one point for each €100 purchase, and need to accumulate 100 points to redeem them for a service having a fair value of €200, then the initial accounting need is to recognize €2 of revenue reduction (and an equivalent liability creation) for each €100 transaction. However, if experience shows that 25% of such loyalty program points are ultimately forfeited, then the proper accounting would be to allocate only €1.50 of each €100 transaction to this liability. If the estimate of the proportion to be forfeited is revised in later financial reporting periods, the liability for unredeemed points is adjusted in the later periods, thereby affecting profit recognized in those periods.

A final issue, not dealt with by IFRIC 13, is whether the allocation of the transaction amount should be apportioned between the initial transaction's revenue and the deferred revenue associated with the redemption of the loyalty points based on a pro rata assignment, or whether the deferred revenue should be the fair value of the future goods or services, with the residual being assigned to the initial transaction. Thus, both approaches would be acceptable—and, as usual, the reporting entity should consistently apply one or the other.

To illustrate this last matter, assume again that customers earn one point for each €100 purchase, and need to accumulate 100 points to redeem them for a service having a fair value of €200. Possible forfeitures are ignored in this example, for simplicity. The pro rata allocation method would assign [€100/(€100 + €2) =] €98.04 to the initial transaction, and would assign [€2/(€100 + €2) =] €1.96 to the obligation for future services, which will be recognized as revenue when the promised services are later performed. On the other hand, if the alternative method is used, the fair value of the future services, €2, is initially recorded, so the immediate transaction is reported as a €98 revenue event.

Service concession arrangements. In many countries, public-to-private service concession arrangements have evolved as a mechanism for providing public services. Under such arrangements, a private entity is used to construct, operate or maintain the infrastructure for public use such as roads, bridges, hospitals, airports, water distribution facilities and energy supply. IFRIC 12, *Service Concession Arrangements,* deals with a private sector entity (an operator) that provides a public service and operates and maintains that infrastructure (operation services) for a specified period of time. The interpretation was published on November 30, 2006 and should be applied for financial years beginning on or after January 1, 2008. As a change in accounting policy it is accounted for retrospectively except when it is impracticable.

This interpretation applies to service concession arrangements when the infrastructure for public use is constructed or acquired by the operator or given for use by the grantor and (1) the grantor controls what services operator must provide, to whom and at what price, and (2) the grantor controls any significant residual interest in the existing infrastructure at the end of the term of the service concession arrangement. Because the grantor continues to control the infrastructure assets within the scope of the interpretation, these assets are not recognized as property, plant, and equipment of the operator. The operator recognizes and measures revenue for the services it performs in accordance with IAS 11 or IAS 18. If more than one service is performed (e.g., construction or upgrade services and operation services) under a single contract or arrangement, consideration received or receivable is allocated based on relative fair values of the services provided, when the amounts are separately identifiable. The nature of the consideration the operator receives in exchange for the construction services determines its subsequent accounting treatment.

When the consideration received is a financial asset because the operator has an unconditional contractual right to receive from the grantor cash or other financial asset (e.g., a loan or receivable, available-for-sale financial asset, or, if so designated upon initial recognition, a financial asset at fair value through profit or loss), the subsequent accounting in accordance with IAS 32 and IAS 39 would apply. In this case the grantor bears the risk (demand risk) that the cash flows generated from the users will not recover the operator's investment. A financial asset is recognized during construction, giving rise to revenues from construction recovered during the period of use of the asset.

An intangible asset is recognized when the consideration the operator receives consists of rights to charge users of the public service, for example a license to charge users tolls for using roads or bridges, and it is accounted for within the scope of IAS 38. In this case, the operator bears the risk (demand risk) that the cash flows generated from the use of the public service will not recover its investment. The intangible asset received from the grantor in exchange for the construction services is used to generate cash flows from users of the public service.

IASB PROJECT: REVENUE RECOGNITION

Concerns over proper revenue recognition practices have long existed, and studies have shown that financial reporting irregularities that have come to light and required large restatements of previously issued reports have largely sprung from improper revenue recognition. Standard setters, including the IASB, have therefore concluded that more prescriptive guidance is needed, and are currently endeavoring to produce standards that will provide such.

According to IASB, the revenue recognition requirements in IAS 18 focus on the occurrence of critical events rather than changes in assets and liabilities. This approach may result in the creation of debits and credits that do not meet the definition of assets and liabilities under IFRS, and which in principle should not be recognized. In addition, a practical weakness of IAS 18 is that it gives insufficient guidance on contracts that provide more than one good or service to the customer (multiple-element revenue arrangements). It is unclear when contracts should be divided into components and how much revenue should be attributed to each component. As a result, the International Financial Reporting Interpretations Committee (IFRIC) receives frequent requests for guidance on the application of IAS 18.

The IASB started to work independently on the issues of revenue recognition and concepts of liabilities and equity. It subsequently, however, decided to work with the FASB as part of their joint convergence program. There are approximately 200 sources of standards and guidance on revenue recognition under US GAAP, and these are not based on consistent concepts. There currently are substantial differences between IFRS and US requirements.

The revenue recognition project has explored various different approaches and the IASB and FASB have abandoned the earning process approach and have instead embraced an asset-liability approach. Under the asset-liability approach, revenue is recognized by direct reference to changes in assets and liabilities that arises from an entity's contract (e.g., enforceable arrangement) with a customer, rather than by direct reference to critical events or activities as in the earning process approach. The idea is that where an entity has a legally enforceable, noncancelable contract, it should start to recognize the assets and liabilities inherent in that contract. While this approach does not change the final profit or loss on the completed contract, it opens up the issue of the timing of recognition, moving from the end of the transaction, where recognition has traditionally taken place, to the point where an executory contract exists, and then remeasuring as the transaction evolves towards completion.

A simple example would be where a customer sees a sofa in a furniture shop, and decides to buy it. However, he wants a different color from that available in the shop. He pays the retailer €1,000 for delivery of a similar sofa but of a different color, within one week. Assuming the contract is noncancelable, the retailer would have an asset of €1,000, plus an obligation to supply a sofa. If he could order the sofa from the manufacturer for €600 and have someone deliver it for €75, the liability is for €675, and the retailer has a surplus of €325. Arguably there is a risk that the manufacturer or delivery service will fail to perform, and the retailer might have to refund the money, but this is quantifiable in the same way as a product liability, which could be deducted from the surplus, and then released when the transaction is complete. Under this approach, the retailer can identify a "selling" profit that is distinct from the actual supplying of the item.

This approach is conceptually consistent with the *Framework,* and has the merit that it recognizes the principle that earning is a gradual process. For some businesses, the value of executory contracts is a significant indication of profits, but which is currently excluded from measurement, except in the area of financial instruments. Clearly, however, this approach depends upon being able to ascertain fair values for the different components of the earnings process. It relies upon the ability to identify the selling profit as a residual, and this often cannot be independently measured or observed, and thus there is the risk that it will be miscalculated.

The accounting model that the IASB and FASB are jointly developing in the Revenue Recognition project is an asset and liability model. A reporting entity would recognize revenue on the basis of changes in assets and liabilities arising from contracts with customers— without consideration of additional criteria, such as earning and realization, which were income statement–oriented threshold conditions. To apply this new model, the entity needs to be able to identify the separate liabilities ("performance obligations") that arise from a contract when the customer is committed to pay for the deliverables.

Under the asset and liability model, a contract is an asset to the entity if the remaining rights exceed the remaining performance obligations and it is a liability if the remaining obligations exceed the remaining rights. The criteria that should be used to identify separable obligations and the basis on which obligations should be measured have been discussed, and the IASB has recently narrowed the possible implementation to the *customer consideration* model. At contract inception, revenue is the net contractual rights and obligations measured at the amount of promised customer consideration (i.e., transaction price). Next, the transaction price is allocated to performance obligations pro rata based on the selling price (observed or estimated) of the goods or services underlying those performance obligations;

goods and services are accounted for as separate performance obligations only if they transfer to the customer at different times. An entity recognizes revenue for the resulting increase in the contract asset or decrease in the contract liabilities (or combination of both) when the promised goods or services are provided to the customer; revenue should not be recognized until those performance obligations are satisfied.

The IASB and FASB plan to develop a comprehensive standard that would apply to all business entities, although certain transactions or industries may require additional studies and may therefore be excluded from the scope of that standard, to instead be addressed separately in the future.

The IASB plans to issue a Discussion Paper—which should explain and illustrate a contract-based revenue recognition model with an allocated customer consideration measurement approach—in the fourth quarter of 2008.

Examples of Financial Statement Disclosures

Barco
Annual Report 2007

Notes to the consolidated financial statements

Accounting principles

11. Revenue recognition

Revenue is recognized when it is probable that the economic benefits will flow to the group and the revenue can be reliably measured.

For product sales, revenue is recognized when the significant risks and rewards of ownership of the goods have passed to the buyer. Sales are recognized when persuasive evidence of an arrangement exists, delivery has occurred, the fee is fixed and determinable, and collectability is probable.

For contract revenue, the percentage of completion method is used, provided that the outcome of the contract can be assessed with reasonable certainty.

For sales of services, revenue is recognized by reference to the stage of completion.

Novartis A.G.
Annual Report 2007

1. Accounting policies

Revenue recognition

Revenue is recognized when there is persuasive evidence that a sales arrangement exists, title and risks and rewards for the products are transferred to the customer, the price is fixed and determinable and collectability is reasonably assured. Provision for rebates and discounts granted to government agencies, wholesalers, retail pharmacies, managed care and other customers are recorded as a reduction of revenue at the time the related revenues are recorded or when the incentives are offered. They are calculated on the basis of historical experience and the specific terms in the individual agreements. Cash discounts are offered to customers to encourage prompt payment and are recorded as revenue deductions. Wholesaler shelf-inventory adjustments are granted to customers based on the existing inventory of a product at the time of decreases in the invoice or contract price of a product or at the point of sale if a price decline is reasonably estimable. Where there is a historical experience of Novartis agreeing to customer returns, Novartis records a provision for estimated sales returns by applying historical experience of customer returns to the amounts invoiced and the amount of returned products to be destroyed versus products that can be placed back in inventory for resale. Where shipments are made on a sale or return basis, without sufficient historical experience for estimating sales returns, revenue is only recorded when there is evidence of consumption. Provisions for revenue deductions are adjusted to actual amounts as rebates; discounts and returns are processed.

CONSTRUCTION CONTRACT ACCOUNTING

PERSPECTIVE AND ISSUES

The principal concern of accounting for long-term construction contracts involves the timing of revenue (and thus profit) recognition. It has been well accepted that, given the long-term nature of such projects, deferring revenue recognition until completion would often result in the presentation of periodic financial reports that fail to meaningfully convey the true level of activity of the reporting entity during the reporting period. In extreme cases, in fact, there could be periods of no apparent activity, and others of exaggerated amounts, when in fact the entity was operating at a rather constant rate of production during all of the periods. To avoid these distortions, the percentage of completion method was developed, which reports the revenues proportionally to the degree to which the projects are being completed, even absent full completion and, in many cases, even absent the right to collect for the work done to date.

The major challenges in using percentages of completion accounting are to accurately gauge the extent to which the projects are being finished, and to assess the ability of the entity to actually bill and collect for the work done. Since many projects are priced at fixed amounts, or in some other fashion prevent the passing through to the customers the full amount of cost overruns, the computation of periodic profits must be sensitive not merely to the extent to which the project is nearing completion, but also to the terms of the underlying contractual arrangements.

IAS 11 is the salient IFRS addressing the accounting for construction contracts and other situations in which the percentage of completion method of revenue recognition would be appropriate. This standard uses the recognition criteria established by the IASB's *Framework* as the basis for the guidance it offers on accounting for construction contracts. The various complexities in applying IAS 11, including the estimation of revenues, costs, and progress toward completion, are set forth in the following discussion.

Sources of IFRS
IAS 10, 11, 23, 37

DEFINITIONS OF TERMS

Additional asset stipulation. A special provision in a construction contract which either gives the option to the customer to require construction of an additional asset or permits amendment to the construction contract so as to include an additional asset not envisioned by the original contract should be construed as a separate construction contract when

1. The additional asset differs significantly (in design, function, or technology) from the asset(s) covered by the original contract; or
2. The extra contract price fixed for the construction of the additional asset is negotiated without regard to the original contract price.

Back charges. Billings for work performed or costs incurred by one party that, in accordance with the agreement, should have been performed or incurred by the party billed.

Billings on long-term contracts. Accumulated billings sent to the purchaser at intervals as various milestones in the project are reached.

Change orders. Modifications of an original contract that effectively change the provisions of the contract without adding new provisions; synonymous with *variations*.

Claims. Amounts in excess of the agreed-on contract price that a contractor seeks to collect from a customer (or another party) for customer-caused delays, errors in specifications and designs, disputed variations in contract work, or other occurrences that are alleged to be the causes of unanticipated costs.

Combining (grouping) contracts. Grouping two or more contracts, whether with a single customer or with several customers, into a single profit center for accounting purposes, provided that

1. The group of contracts is negotiated as a single package;
2. The contracts combined are so closely interrelated that, in essence, they could be considered as a single contract negotiated with an overall profit margin; and
3. The contracts combined are either executed concurrently or in a sequence.

Construction contract. Contract specifically entered into for the construction of an asset or a combination of assets that are closely interrelated or interdependent in terms of their design, technology, and function or their end use or purpose.

Construction-in-progress (CIP). Inventory account used to accumulate the construction costs of the contract project. For the percentage-of-completion method, the CIP account also includes the gross profit earned to date.

Contract costs. Comprised of costs directly related to a specific contract, costs that are attributable to the contract activity in general and can be allocated to the contract, and other costs that are specifically chargeable to the customer under the terms of the contract.

Contract revenue. Comprised of initial amount of revenue stipulated by the contract plus any variations in contract work, claims, and incentive payments, provided that these extra amounts of revenue meet the recognition criteria set by the IASB's *Framework* (i.e., regarding the probability of future economic benefits flowing to the contractor and reliability of measurement).

Cost-plus contract. Construction contract in which the contractor is reimbursed for allowable costs plus either a percentage of these costs or a fixed fee.

Cost-to-cost method. Percentage-of-completion method used to determine the extent of progress toward completion on a contract. The ratio of costs incurred through the end of the current year divided by the total estimated costs of the project is used to recognize income.

Estimated cost to complete. Anticipated additional cost of materials, labor, subcontracting costs, and indirect costs (overhead) required to complete a project at a scheduled time.

Fixed-price contract. Construction contract wherein the contract revenue is fixed either in absolute terms or is fixed in terms of unit rate of output; in certain cases both fixed prices being subject to any cost escalation clauses, if allowed by the contract.

Incentive payments. Any additional amounts payable to the contractor if specified performance standards are either met or surpassed.

Percentage-of-completion method. Method of accounting that recognizes income on a contract as work progresses by matching contract revenue with contract costs incurred, based on the proportion of work completed. However, any expected loss, which is the excess of total incurred and expected contract costs over the total contract revenue, is recognized immediately, irrespective of the stage of completion of the contract.

Precontract costs. Costs that are related directly to a contract and are incurred in securing a contract (e.g., architectural designs, purchase of special equipment, engineering fees, and start-up costs). They are included as part of contract costs if they can be identified separately and measured reliably and it is probable that the contract will be obtained.

Profit center. Unit for the accumulation of revenues and cost for the measurement of income.

Segmenting contracts. Dividing a single contract, which covers the construction of a number of assets, into two or more profit centers for accounting purposes, provided that

1. Separate proposals were submitted for each of the assets that are the subject matter of the single contract
2. The construction of each asset was the subject of separate negotiation wherein both the contractor and the customer were in a position to either accept or reject part of the contract pertaining to a single asset (out of numerous assets contemplated by the contract)
3. The costs and revenues pertaining to each individual asset can be separately identified

Stage of completion. Proportion of the contract work completed, which may be determined using one of several methods that reliably measures it, including

1. Percentage-of-completion method
2. Surveys of work performed
3. Physical proportion of contract work completed

Subcontractor. Second-level contractor who enters into a contract with a prime contractor to perform a specific part or phase of a construction project.

Substantial completion. Point at which the major work on a contract is completed and only insignificant costs and potential risks remain.

Variation. Instruction by the customer for a change in the scope of the work envisioned by the construction contract.

CONCEPTS, RULES, AND EXAMPLES

Construction contract revenue may be recognized during construction rather than at the completion of the contract. This "as earned" approach to revenue recognition is justified because under most long-term construction contracts, both the buyer and the seller (contractor) obtain enforceable rights. The buyer has the legal right to require specific performance from the contractor and, in effect, has an ownership claim to the contractor's work in progress. The contractor, under most long-term contracts, has the right to require the buyer to make progress payments during the construction period. The substance of this business activity is that a continuous sale occurs as the work progresses.

IAS 11 recognizes the percentage-of-completion method as the method of accounting for construction contracts (or the cost of recovery approach, when the outcome of a construction contract cannot be estimated reliably). Under an earlier version of IAS 11, both the percentage-of-completion method and the completed-contract method were recognized as being acceptable alternative methods of accounting for long-term construction activities.

The thinking worldwide on this issue is equivocal and rather confusing. Many national GAAP recognize both methods as being appropriate, although they may not be viewed as equally acceptable under given circumstances. The United States, Canada, and Japan are usually noted as protagonists of both GAAP methods on this subject. There is another set of countries whose GAAP is in line with the current IAS on the subject. The national accounting standards of the United Kingdom, Australia, China, and New Zealand recognize only the percentage-of-completion method. Germany, on the other hand, used to have taken the extreme viewpoint as a supporter of only the completed-contract method. Although it may seem that the world is completely divided on this matter, a closer look into this contentious issue offers a better insight into the diversity in approaches.

Although Germany seems to be alone in the contest of alternative methods of accounting for long-term contracts, its position is more explicable when it is recalled that this country has traditionally been known for its conservative approach and its emphasis on creditor protection and a close linkage between accounting recognition rules and the measurement of taxable income. Thus, it seems to have been guided primarily by the prudence concept in developing this accounting principle.

For countries that support both the methods, it is well known that some also express a clear preference for the percentage-of-completion method. US GAAP, for instance, exemplifies this position. It recommends the percentage-of-completion method as preferable when estimates are reasonably dependable and the following conditions exist:

1. Contracts executed by the parties normally include provisions that clearly specify the enforceable rights regarding goods or services to be provided and received by the parties, the consideration to be exchanged, and the manner and terms of settlement.
2. The buyer can be expected to satisfy its obligations under the contract.
3. The contractor can be expected to perform its contractual obligations.

The Accounting Standards Division of the AICPA believes that these two methods should not be used as acceptable alternatives for the same set of circumstances. US GAAP states that, in general, when estimates of costs to complete and extent of progress toward completion of long-term contracts are reasonably dependable, the percentage-of-completion method is preferable. When lack of dependable estimates or inherent hazards cause forecasts to be doubtful, the completed-contract method is preferable.

Percentage-of-Completion Method in Detail

A number of controversial issues are encountered when the percentage-of-completion method is used in practice. In the following paragraphs, the authors' address a number of these, offering proposed approaches to follow for those matters that have not been authoritatively resolved, or in many instances, even discussed by the international accounting standards.

IAS 11 defines the percentage-of-completion method as follows:

Under this method contract revenue is matched with the contract costs incurred in reaching the stage of completion, resulting in the reporting of revenue, expenses and profit which can be attributed to the proportion of work completed. ...Contract revenue is recognized as revenue in the statement of comprehensive income in the accounting periods in which the work is performed. Contract costs are usually recognized as an expense in the accounting periods in which the work to which they relate is performed. However, any expected excess of total revenue for the contract is recognized as an expense immediately.

Under the percentage-of-completion method, the construction-in-progress (CIP) account is used to accumulate costs and recognized income. When the CIP exceeds billings, the difference is reported as a current asset. If billings exceed CIP, the difference is reported as a current liability. Where more than one contract exists, the excess cost or liability should be determined on a project-by-project basis, with the accumulated costs and liabilities being stated separately in the statement of financial position. Assets and liabilities should not be offset unless a right of offset exists. Thus, the net debit balances for certain contracts should not ordinarily be offset against net credit balances for other contracts. An exception may exist if the balances relate to contracts that meet the criteria for combining.

Under the percentage-of-completion method, income should not be based on advances (cash collections) or progress (interim) billings. Cash collections and interim billings are based on contract terms that do not necessarily measure contract performance.

Costs and estimated earnings in excess of billings should be classified as an asset. If billings exceed costs and estimated earnings, the difference should be classified as a liability.

Contract costs. Contract costs comprise costs that are identifiable with a specific contract, plus those that are attributable to contracting activity in general and can be allocated to the contract and those that are contractually chargeable to a customer. Generally, contract costs would include all direct costs, such as direct materials, direct labor, and direct expenses and any construction overhead that could specifically be allocated to specific contracts.

Direct costs or costs that are identifiable with a specific contract include

1. Costs of materials consumed in the specific construction contract
2. Wages and other labor costs for site labor and site supervisors
3. Depreciation charges of plant and equipment used in the contract
4. Lease rentals of hired plant and equipment specifically for the contract
5. Cost incurred in shifting of plant, equipment, and materials to and from the construction site
6. Cost of design and technical assistance directly identifiable with a specific contract
7. Estimated costs of any work undertaken under a warranty or guarantee
8. Claims from third parties

With regard to claims from third parties, these should be accrued if they rise to the level of "provisions" as defined by IAS 37. This requires that an obligation that is subject to reasonable measurement exist at the end of the reporting period. However, if either of the above mentioned conditions is not met (and the possibility of the loss is not remote), this contingency will only be disclosed. Contingent losses are specifically required to be disclosed under IAS 11.

Contract costs may be reduced by incidental income if such income is not included in contract revenue. For instance, sale proceeds (net of any selling expenses) from the disposal of any surplus materials or from the sale of plant and equipment at the end of the contract may be credited or offset against these expenses. Drawing an analogy from this principle, it could be argued that if advances received from customers are invested by the contractor temporarily (instead of being allowed to lie idle in a current account), any interest earned on such investments could be treated as incidental income and used in reducing contract costs, which may or may not include borrowing costs (depending on how the contractor is financed, whether self-financed or leveraged). On the other hand, it may also be argued that instead of being subtracted from contract costs, such interest income should be added to contract revenue.

In the authors' opinion, the latter argument may be valid if the contract is structured in such a manner that the contractor receives lump-sum advances at the beginning of the contract (or for that matter, even during the term of the contract, such that the advances at any point in time exceed the amounts due the contractor from the customer). In these cases, such interest income should, in fact, be treated as contract revenue and not offset against contract costs. The reasoning underlying treating this differently from the earlier instance (where idle funds resulting from advances are invested temporarily) is that such advances were envisioned by the terms of the contract and as such were probably fully considered in the negotiation process that preceded fixing contract revenue. Thus, since negotiated as part of the total contract price, this belongs in contract revenues. (It should be borne in mind that the different treatments for interest income would in fact have a bearing on the determination of the percentage or stage of completion of a construction contract.)

Indirect costs or overhead expenses should be included in contract costs provided that they are attributable to the contracting activity in general and could be allocated to specific contracts. Such costs include construction overhead, cost of insurance, cost of design, and technical assistance that is not related directly to specific contracts. They should be allocated using methods that are systematic and rational and are applied in a consistent manner to costs having similar features or characteristics. The allocation should be based on the normal level of construction activity, not on theoretical maximum capacity.

Example of contract costs

A construction company incurs €700,000 in annual rental expense for the office space occupied by a group of engineers and architects and their support staff. The company utilizes this group to act as the quality assurance team that overlooks all contracts undertaken by the company. The company also incurs in the aggregate another €300,000 as the annual expenditure toward electricity, water, and maintenance of this office space occupied by the group. Since the group is responsible for quality assurance for all contracts on hand, its work, by nature, cannot be considered as being directed toward any specific contract but is in support of the entire contracting activity. Thus, the company should allocate the rent expense and the cost of utilities in accordance with a systematic and rational basis of allocation, which should be applied consistently to both types of expenditure (since they have similar characteristics).

Although the bases of allocation of this construction overhead could be many (such as the amounts of contract revenue, contract costs, and labor hours utilized in each contract) the basis of allocation that seems most rational is contract revenue. Further, since both expenses are similar in nature, allocating both the costs on the basis of the amount of contract revenue generated by each construction contract would also satisfy the consistency criteria.

Other examples of construction overhead or costs that should be allocated to contract costs are

1. Costs of preparing and processing payroll of employees engaged in construction activity
2. Borrowing costs capitalized under IAS 23. IASB eliminated the choice of recognizing borrowing costs immediately as an expense, in IAS 23, *Borrowing Costs*, as revised in 2007, to the extent that they are directly attributable to the acquisition, construction, or production of a qualifying asset. (See also the discussion in Chapter 8.)

Certain costs are specifically excluded from allocation to the construction contract, as the standard considers them as not attributable to the construction activity. Such costs may include

1. General and administrative costs that are not contractually reimbursable
2. Costs incurred in marketing or selling
3. Research and development costs that are not contractually reimbursable
4. Depreciation of plant and equipment that is lying idle and not used in any particular contract

Types of contract costs. Contract costs can be broken down into two categories: costs incurred to date and estimated costs to complete. The *costs incurred to date* include precontract costs and costs incurred after contract acceptance. *Precontract costs* are costs incurred before a contract has been entered into, with the expectation that the contract will be accepted and these costs will thereby be recoverable through billings. The criteria for recognition of such costs are

1. They are capable of being identified separately.
2. They can be measured reliably.
3. It is probable that the contract will be obtained.

Precontract costs include costs of architectural designs, costs of learning a new process, cost of securing the contract, and any other costs that are expected to be recovered if the contract is accepted. Contract costs incurred after the acceptance of the contract are costs incurred toward the completion of the project and are also capitalized in the construction-in-progress (CIP) account. The contract does not have to be identified before the capitalization decision is made; it is only necessary that there be an expectation of the recovery of the costs. Once the contract has been accepted, the precontract costs become contract costs incurred to date. However, if the precontract costs are already recognized as an expense in the period in which they are incurred, they are not included in contract costs when the contract is obtained in a subsequent period.

Estimated costs to complete. These are the anticipated costs required to complete a project at a scheduled time. They would be comprised of the same elements as the original total estimated contract costs and would be based on prices expected to be in effect when the costs are incurred. The latest estimates should be used to determine the progress toward completion.

Although IAS 11 does not specifically provide instructions for estimating costs to complete, practical guidance can be gleaned from other international accounting standards, as follows: The first rule is that systematic and consistent procedures should be used. These procedures should be correlated with the cost accounting system and should be able to provide a comparison between actual and estimated costs. Additionally, the determination of estimated total contract costs should identify the significant cost elements.

A second important point is that the estimation of the costs to complete should include the same elements of costs included in accumulated costs. Additionally, the estimated costs should reflect any expected price increases. These expected price increases should not be blanket provisions for all contract costs, but rather, specific provisions for each type of cost. Expected increases in each of the cost elements such as wages, materials, and overhead items should be taken into consideration separately.

Finally, estimates of costs to complete should be reviewed periodically to reflect new information. Estimates of costs should be examined for price fluctuations and should also be reviewed for possible future problems, such as labor strikes or direct material delays.

Accounting for contract costs is similar to accounting for inventory. Costs necessary to ready the asset for sale would be recorded in the construction-in-progress account, as incurred. CIP would include both direct and indirect costs but would usually not include general and administrative expenses or selling expenses since they are not normally identifiable with a particular contract and should therefore be expensed.

Subcontractor costs. Since a contractor may not be able to do all facets of a construction project, a subcontractor may be engaged. The amount billed to the contractor for work done by the subcontractor should be included in contract costs. The amount billed is directly traceable to the project and would be included in the CIP account, similar to direct materials and direct labor.

Back charges. Contract costs may have to be adjusted for back charges. Back charges are billings for costs incurred that the contract stipulated should have been performed by another party. The parties involved often dispute these charges.

Example of a back charge situation

The contract states that the subcontractor was to raze the building and have the land ready for construction; however, the contractor/seller had to clear away debris in order to begin construction. The contractor wants to be reimbursed for the work; therefore, the contractor back charges the subcontractor for the cost of the debris removal.

The contractor should treat the back charge as a receivable from the subcontractor and should reduce contract costs by the amount recoverable. If the subcontractor disputes the back charge, the cost becomes a claim. Claims are an amount in excess of the agreed contract price or amounts not included in the original contract price that the contractor seeks to collect. Claims should be recorded as additional contract revenue only if the requirements set forth in IAS 11 are met.

The subcontractor should record the back charge as a payable and as additional contract costs if it is probable that the amount will be paid. If the amount or validity of the liability is disputed, the subcontractor would have to consider the probable outcome in order to determine the proper accounting treatment.

Fixed-Price and Cost-Plus Contracts

IAS 11 recognizes two types of construction contracts that are distinguished based on their pricing arrangements: (1) fixed-price contracts and (2) cost-plus contracts.

Fixed-price contracts are contracts for which the price is not usually subject to adjustment because of costs incurred by the contractor. The contractor agrees to a fixed contract price or a fixed rate per unit of output. These amounts are sometimes subject to escalation clauses.

There are two types of cost-plus contracts.

1. **Cost-without-fee contract**—Contractor is reimbursed for allowable or otherwise defined costs with no provision for a fee. However, a percentage is added that is based on the foregoing costs.
2. **Cost-plus-fixed-fee contract**—Contractor is reimbursed for costs plus a provision for a fee. The contract price on a cost-type contract is determined by the sum of the reimbursable expenditures and a fee. The fee is the profit margin (revenue less direct expenses) to be earned on the contract. All reimbursable expenditures should be included in the accumulated contract costs account.

There are a number of possible variations of contracts that are based on a cost-plus-fee arrangement. These could include cost-plus-fixed-fee, under which the fee is a fixed monetary amount; cost-plus-award, under which an incentive payment is provided to the contractor, typically based on the project's timely or on-budget completion; and cost-plus-a-percentage-fee, under which a variable bonus payment will be added to the contractor's ultimate payment based on stated criteria.

Some contracts may have features of both a fixed-price contract and a cost-plus contract. A cost-plus contract with an agreed maximum price is an example of such a contract.

Recognition of Contract Revenue and Expenses

Percentage-of-completion accounting cannot be employed if the quality of information will not support a reasonable level of accuracy in the financial reporting process. Generally, only when the outcome of a construction contract can be estimated reliably, should the contract revenue and contract costs be recognized by reference to the stage of completion at the end of the reporting period.

Different criteria have been prescribed by the standard for assessing whether the outcome can be estimated reliably for a contract, depending on whether it is a fixed-price contract or a cost-plus contract. The following are the criteria in each case:

1. If it is a fixed-price contract

    *NOTE: **All** conditions should be satisfied.*

    a. It meets the recognition criteria set by the IASB's *Framework*; that is

       (1) Total contract revenue can be measured reliably.
       (2) It is probable that economic benefits flow to the entity.

    b. Both the contract cost to complete and the stage of completion can be measured reliably.
    c. Contract costs attributable to the contract can be identified properly and measured reliably so that comparison of actual contract costs with estimates can be done.

2. If it is a cost-plus contract

    *NOTE: **All** conditions should be satisfied.*

    a. It is probable that the economic benefits will flow to the entity.
    b. The contract costs attributable to the contract, whether or not reimbursable, can be identified and measured reliably.

When Outcome of a Contract Cannot Be Estimated Reliably

As stated above, unless the outcome of a contract can be estimated reliably, contract revenue and costs should not be recognized by reference to the stage of completion. IAS 11 establishes the following rules for revenue recognition in cases where the outcome of a contract cannot be estimated reliably:

1. Revenue should be recognized only to the extent of the contract costs incurred that are probable of being recoverable.
2. Contract costs should be recognized as an expense in the period in which they are incurred.

Any expected losses should, however, be recognized immediately.

It is not unusual that during the early stages of a contract, outcome cannot be estimated reliably. This would be particularly likely to be true if the contract represents a type of project with which the contractor has had limited experience in the past.

Contract Costs Not Recoverable Due to Uncertainties

When recoverability of contract costs is considered doubtful, the cost recovery method is applied and revenue is recognized only to the extent of cash collections, after all costs have first been recovered through cash collections. Recoverability of contract costs may be considered doubtful in the case of contracts that have any of the following characteristics:

1. The contract is not fully enforceable.
2. Completion of the contract is dependent on the outcome of pending litigation or legislation.
3. The contract relates to properties that are likely to be expropriated or condemned.
4. The contract is with a customer who is unable to perform its obligations, perhaps because of financial difficulties.
5. The contractor is unable to complete the contract or otherwise meet its obligation under the terms of the contract, as when, for example, the contractor has been experiencing recurring losses and is unable to get financial support from creditors and bankers and may be ready to declare bankruptcy.

In all such cases, contract costs should be expensed immediately. Although the implication is unambiguous, the determination that one or more of the foregoing conditions holds will be subject to some imprecision. Thus, each such situation needs to be assessed carefully on a case-by-case basis.

If and when these uncertainties are resolved, revenue and expenses should again be recognized on the same basis as other construction-type contracts (i.e., by the percentage-of-completion method). However, it is not permitted to restore costs already expensed in prior periods, since the accounting was not in error, given the facts that existed at the time the earlier financial statements were prepared.

Revenue Measurement—Determining the Stage of Completion

The standard recognizes that the stage of completion of a contract may be determined in many ways and that an entity uses the method that measures reliably the work performed. The standard further stipulates that depending on the nature of the contract, one of the following methods may be chosen:

1. The proportion that contract costs incurred bears to estimated total contract cost (also referred to as the cost-to-cost method)
2. Survey of work performed method
3. Completion of a physical proportion of contract work (also called units-of-work-performed) method.

> *NOTE: Progress payments and advances received from customers often do not reflect the work performed.*

Each of these methods of measuring progress on a contract can be identified as being either an input or an output measure. The *input measures* attempt to identify progress in a contract in terms of the efforts devoted to it. The cost-to-cost method is an example of an input measure. Under the cost-to-cost method, the percentage of completion would be estimated by comparing total costs incurred to date to total costs expected for the entire job. *Output measures* are made in terms of results by attempting to identify progress toward completion by physical measures. The units-of-work-performed method is an example of an output measure. Under this method, an estimate of completion is made in terms of achievements to date. Output measures are usually not considered to be as reliable as input measures.

When the stage of completion is determined by reference to the contract costs incurred to date, the standard specifically refers to certain costs that are to be excluded from contract costs. Examples of such costs are

1. Contract costs that relate to future activity (e.g., construction materials supplied to the site but not yet consumed during construction)
2. Payments made in advance to subcontractors prior to performance of the work by the subcontractor

Example of the percentage-of-completion method

The percentage-of-completion method works under the principle that "recognized profit (should) be that percentage of estimated total profit...that incurred costs to date bear to estimated total costs." The cost-to-cost method has become one of the most popular measures used to determine the extent of progress toward completion.

Under the cost-to-cost method, the percentage of revenue to recognize can be determined by the following formula:

$$\frac{\text{Cost to date}}{\text{Cumulative costs incurred} + \text{Estimated costs to complete}} \times \text{Contract price} - \text{Revenue previously recognized} = \text{Current revenue recognized}$$

By slightly modifying this formula, current gross profit can also be determined.

$$\frac{\text{Cost to date}}{\text{Cumulative costs incurred} + \text{Estimated costs to complete}} \times \text{Expected total gross profit} - \text{Gross profit previously recognized} = \text{Current gross profit}$$

Example of the percentage-of-completion (cost-to-cost) and completed-contract methods with profitable contract

Assume a €500,000 contract that requires 3 years to complete and incurs a total cost of €405,000. The following data pertain to the construction period:

	Year 1	*Year 2*	*Year 3*
Cumulative costs incurred to date	€150,000	€360,000	€405,000
Estimated costs yet to be incurred at year-end	300,000	40,000	--
Progress billings made during year	100,000	370,000	30,000
Collections of billings	75,000	300,000	125,000

Completed-Contract and Percentage-of-Completion Methods

	Year 1		*Year 2*		*Year 3*	
Construction in progress	150,000		210,000		45,000	
Cash, payables, etc.		150,000		210,000		45,000
Contract receivables	100,000		370,000		30,000	
Billings on contracts		100,000		370,000		30,000
Cash	75,000		300,000		125,000	
Contract receivables		75,000		300,000		125,000

Completed-Contract Method Only

Billings on contracts			500,000	
Cost of revenues earned			405,000	
Contracts revenues earned				500,000
Construction in progress				405,000

Percentage-of-Completion Method Only

Construction in progress	16,667		73,333		5,000	
Cost of revenues earned	150,000		210,000		45,000	
Contract revenues earned		166,667		283,333		50,000
Billings on contracts					500,000	
Construction in progress						500,000

Statement of Comprehensive Income Presentation

	Year 1	*Year 2*	*Year 3*	*Total*
Percentage-of-completion				
Contract revenues earned	€166,667*	€283,333**	€ 50,000***	€500,000
Cost of revenues earned	(150,000)	(210,000)	(45,000)	(405,000)
Gross profit	€ 16,667	€ 73,333	€ 5,000	€ 95,000
Completed-contract				
Contract revenues earned	--	--	€500,000	€500,000
Cost of contracts completed	--	--	(405,000)	(405,000)
Gross profit	--	--	€ 95,000	€ 95,000

$$* \quad \frac{€\,150,000}{450,000} \times 500,000 \;=\; €166,667$$

$$** \quad \frac{€\,360,000}{400,000} \times 500,000 \;-\; 166,667 \;=\; €283,333$$

$$*** \quad \frac{€405,000}{405,000} \times 500,000 \;-\; 166,667 \;-\; 283,333 \;=\; €50,000$$

Statement of Financial Position Presentation

	Year 1	Year 2	Year 3
Percentage-of-completion			
Current assets:			
Contract receivables		€25,000	€ 95,000	*
Costs and estimated earnings in excess of billings on			
uncompleted contracts			
Construction in progress	166,667**		
Less billings on long-term contracts	(100,000)	66,667	
Current liabilities:			
Billings in excess of costs and estimated earnings on			
uncompleted contracts, year 2			
(€470,000*** – €450,000****)		20,000	
Completed-contract			
Current assets:			
Contract receivables		25,000	95,000	*
Costs in excess of billings on uncompleted contracts			
Construction in progress	150,000		
Less billings on long-term contracts	(100,000)	50,000	
Current liabilities:			
Billings in excess of costs on uncompleted contracts,			
year 2 (€470,000 – €360,000)		110,000	

*   *Since the contract was completed and title was transferred in year 3, there are no amounts reported in the statement of financial position. However, if the project is complete but transfer of title has not taken place, there would be a presentation in the statement of financial position at the end of the third year because the entry closing out the Construction-in-progress account and the Billings account would not have been made yet.*

**   *€150,000 (Costs) + 16,667 (Gross profit)*

***   *€100,000 (Year 1 Billings) + 370,000 (Year 2 Billings)*

****   *€360,000 (Costs) + 16,667 (Gross profit) + 73,333 (Gross profit)*

Recognition of Expected Contract Losses

When the current estimate of total contract cost exceeds the current estimate of total contract revenue, a provision for the entire loss on the entire contract should be made. Provisions for losses should be made in the period in which they become evident under either the percentage-of-completion method or the completed-contract method. In other words, when it is probable that total contract costs will exceed total contract revenue, the expected loss should be recognized as an expense immediately. The loss provision should be computed on the basis of the total estimated costs to complete the contract, which would include the contract costs incurred to date plus estimated costs (use the same elements as contract costs incurred) to complete. The provision should be shown separately as a current liability in the statement of financial position.

In any year when a percentage-of-completion contract has an expected loss, the amount of the loss reported in that year can be computed as follows:

Reported loss = Total expected loss + All profit previously recognized

Example of the percentage-of-completion and completed-contract methods with loss contract

Using the previous information, if the costs yet to be incurred at the end of year 2 were €148,000, the total expected loss is €8,000 [= €500,000 – (360,000 + 148,000)], and the total loss reported in year 2 would be €24,667 (= €8,000 + 16,667). Under the completed-contract method, the loss recognized is simply the total expected loss, €8,000.

Journal entry at end of year 2	*Percentage-of-Completion*	*Completed-contract*
Loss on uncompleted long-term contract	24,667	8,000
Construction in progress (or estimated loss on uncompleted contact)	24,667	8,000

**Profit or Loss Recognized on Contract
(Percentage-of-Completion Method)**

	Year 1	*Year 2*	*Year 3*
Contract price	€500,000	€500,000	€500,000
Estimated total costs:			
Costs incurred to date	150,000	360,000	506,000*
Estimated cost yet to be incurred	300,000	148,000	--
Estimated total costs for the three-year period, actual for year 3	450,000	508,000	506,000
Estimated profit (loss), actual for year 3	16,667	(8,000)	(6,000)
Less profit (loss) previously recognized	--	16,667	(8,000)
Amount of estimated profit (loss) recognized in the current period, actual for year 3	€ 16,667	€ (24,667)	€ 2,000

   * *Assumed*

**Profit or Loss Recognized on Contract
(Completed-Contract Method)**

	Year 1	*Year 2*	*Year 3*
Contract price	€500,000	€500,000	€500,000
Estimated total costs:			
Costs incurred to date	150,000	360,000	506,000*
Estimated costs yet to be incurred	300,000	148,000	--
Estimated total costs for the three-year period, actual for year 3	50,000	(8,000)	(6,000)
Loss previously recognized	--	--	(8,000)
Amount of estimated profit (loss) recognized in the current period, actual for year 3	€ --	€ (8,000)	€ 2,000

   * *Assumed*

Upon completion of the project during year 3, it can be seen that the actual loss was only €6,000 (= €500,000 – 506,000); therefore, the estimated loss provision was overstated by €2,000. However, since this is a change of an estimate, the €2,000 difference must be handled prospectively; consequently, €2,000 of profit should be recognized in year 3 (= €8,000 previously recognized – €6,000 actual loss).

Combining and Segmenting Contracts

The profit center for accounting purposes is usually a single contract, but under some circumstances the profit center may be a combination of two or more contracts, a segment of a contract, or a group of combined contracts. Conformity with explicit criteria set forth in IAS 11 is necessary to combine separate contracts, or segment a single contract; otherwise, each individual contract is presumed to be the profit center.

For accounting purposes, a group of contracts may be combined if they are so closely related that they are, in substance, parts of a single project with an overall profit margin. A group of contracts, whether with a single customer or with several customers, should be combined and treated as a single contract if the group of contracts

1. Are negotiated as a single package
2. Require such closely interrelated construction activities that they are, in effect, part of a single project with an overall profit margin
3. Are performed concurrently or in a continuous sequence

Segmenting a contract is a process of breaking up a larger unit into smaller units for accounting purposes. If the project is segmented, revenues can be assigned to the different elements or phases to achieve different rates of profitability based on the relative value of each element or phase to the estimated total contract revenue. According to IAS 11, a contract may cover a number of assets. The construction of each asset should be treated as a separate construction contract when

1. The contractor has submitted separate proposals on the separate components of the project
2. Each asset has been subject to separate negotiation and the contractor and customer had the right to accept or reject part of the proposal relating to a single asset
3. The cost and revenues of each asset can be separately identified

Contractual Stipulation for Additional Asset—Separate Contract

The contractual stipulation for an additional asset is a special provision in the international accounting standard. IAS 11 provides that a contract may stipulate the construction of an additional asset at the option of the customer, or the contract may be amended to include the construction of an additional asset. The construction of the additional asset should be treated as a separate construction contract if

1. The additional asset significantly differs (in design, technology or function) from the asset or assets covered by the original contract
2. The price for the additional asset is negotiated without regard to the original contract price

Changes in Estimate

Since the percentage-of-completion method uses current estimates of contract revenue and expenses, it is normal to encounter changes in estimates of contract revenue and costs frequently. Such changes in estimate of the contract's outcome are treated on a par with changes in accounting estimate as defined by IAS 8.

Disclosure Requirements under IAS 11

IAS 11 prescribes a number of disclosures; some of them are for all the contracts and others are only for contracts in progress at the end of the reporting period. These are summarized below.

1. Disclosures relating to all contracts

    a. Aggregate amount of contract revenue recognized in the period
    b. Methods used in determination of contract revenue recognized in the period

2. Disclosures relating to contracts in progress

    a. Methods used in determination of stage of completion (of contracts in progress)
    b. Aggregate amount of costs incurred and recognized profits (net of recognized losses) to date
    c. Amounts of advances received (at the end of the reporting period)
    d. Amount of retentions (at the end of the reporting period)

Financial Statement Presentation Requirements under IAS 11

Gross amounts due from customers should be reported as an asset. This amount is the net of

1. Costs incurred plus recognized profits, less

2.   The aggregate of recognized losses and progress billings.

This represents, in the case of contracts in progress, excess of contract costs incurred plus recognized profits, net of recognized losses, over progress billings.

Gross amounts due to customers should be reported as a liability. This amount is the net of

1.   Costs incurred plus recognized profits, less
2.   The aggregate of the recognized losses and progress billings.

This represents, in the case of contract work in progress, excess of progress billings over contract costs incurred plus recognized profits, net of recognized losses.

APPENDIX

ACCOUNTING UNDER SPECIAL SITUATIONS— GUIDANCE FROM US GAAP

A number of specialized situations that are fairly common in long-term construction contracting are not addressed by international accounting standards. To provide guidance on certain of these matters, the following interpretations are offered, analogized from existing practice under US GAAP.

Joint Ventures and Shared Contracts

Many contracts obtained by long-term construction companies are shared by more than one contractor. When the owner of the contract puts it up for bids, many contractors form syndicates or joint ventures to bid on and obtain a contract under which each contractor could not perform individually.

When this transpires, a separate set of books is maintained for the joint venture. If the percentages of interest for each venture are identical in more than one contract, the joint venture might keep its records almost like another construction company. Usually, the joint venture is for a single contract and ends on completion of that contract.

A joint venture is a form of a partnership, although a partnership for a limited purpose. An agreement of the parties and the terms of the contract successfully bid on will determine the nature of the accounting records. Statements of income, in circumstances where presentation of comprehensive income is accomplished in two statements, are usually cumulative statements showing all totals from the date of contract determination until the reporting date. Each venturer records its share of the amount from the venture's comprehensive income less its previously recorded portion of the venture's income as a single line item similar to the equity method for investments. Similarly, statements of financial position of the venture give rise to a single line asset balance of investment and advances in joint ventures. In most cases, footnote disclosure is similar to the equity method in displaying condensed financial statements of material joint ventures.

Under international standards (IAS 31), a venturer's interest in a joint venture may be accounted for by either the *proportionate consolidation* or the *equity* method of accounting. See Chapter 10 for a detailed discussion of joint venture accounting.

Accounting for Change Orders

Change orders are modifications of specifications or provisions of an original contract. Contract revenue and costs should be adjusted to reflect change orders that are approved by the contractor and customer. According to US GAAP, the accounting for the change order depends on the scope and price of the change. If the customer and contractor have agreed both the scope and price, contract revenue and cost should be adjusted to reflect the change order.

According to US GAAP, accounting for unpriced change orders depends on their characteristics and the circumstances in which they occur. Under the completed-contract method, costs attributable to unpriced change orders should be deferred as contract costs if it is probable that total contract costs, including costs attributable to the change orders, will be recovered from contract revenues. Recovery should be deemed probable if the future event or events are likely to occur.

According to US GAAP, the following guidelines should be followed when accounting for unpriced change orders under the percentage-of-completion method:

1. Costs attributable to unpriced change orders should be treated as costs of contract performance in the period in which the costs are incurred if it is not probable that the costs will be recovered through a change in the contract price.

2. If it is probable that the costs will be recovered through a change in the contract price, the costs should be deferred (excluded from the cost of contract performance) until the parties have agreed on the change in contract price, or alternatively, they should be treated as costs of contract performance in the period in which they are incurred, and contract revenue should be recognized to the extent of the costs incurred.

3. If an adjustment to the contract price will be made in an amount that will exceed the costs attributable to the change order, this may be given recognition under certain circumstances. Specifically, if the amount of the excess can be reliably estimated, and if realization is probable, then the original contract price should be so adjusted. However, since the substantiation of the amount of future revenue is difficult, revenue in excess of the costs attributable to unpriced change orders should only be recorded in circumstances in which realization is assured beyond a reasonable doubt, such as circumstances in which an entity's historical experience provides such assurance or in which an entity has received a bona fide pricing offer from a customer and records only the amount of the offer as revenue.

Accounting for Contract Options

According to US GAAP, an addition or option to an existing contract should be treated as a separate contract if any of the following circumstances exist:

1. The product or service to be provided differs significantly from the product or service provided under the original contract.

2. The price of the new product or service is negotiated without regard to the original contract and involves different economic judgments.

3. The products or services to be provided under the exercised option or amendment are similar to those under the original contract, but the contract price and anticipated contract cost relationship are significantly different.

If the addition or option does not meet the foregoing circumstances, the contracts should be combined. However, if the addition or option does not meet the criteria for combining, they should be treated as change orders.

Accounting for Claims

These represent amounts in excess of the agreed contract price that a contractor seeks to collect from customers for unanticipated additional costs. The recognition of additional contract revenue relating to claims is appropriate if it is probable that the claim will result in additional revenue and if the amount can be estimated reliably. US GAAP specifies that all of the following conditions must exist for the probable and estimable requirements to be satisfied:

1. The contract or other evidence provides a legal basis for the claim; or a legal opinion has been obtained, stating that under the circumstances there is a reasonable basis to support the claim.

2. Additional costs are caused by circumstances that were unforeseen at the contract date and are not the result of deficiencies in the contractor's performance.

3. Costs associated with the claim are identifiable or otherwise determinable and are reasonable in view of the work performed.

4.   The evidence supporting the claim is objective and verifiable, not based on management's "feel" for the situation or on unsupported representations.

When the foregoing requirements are met, revenue from a claim should be recorded only to the extent that contract costs relating to the claim have been incurred. When the foregoing requirements are not met, a contingent asset should be disclosed in accordance with US GAAP governing contingencies.

8 PROPERTY, PLANT, AND EQUIPMENT

PERSPECTIVE AND ISSUES

Long-lived tangible and intangible assets (which include plant, property, and equipment as well as development costs, various intellectual property intangibles, and goodwill) hold the promise of providing economic benefits to an enterprise for a period greater than that covered by the current year's financial statements. Accordingly, these assets must be capitalized rather than immediately expensed, and their costs must be allocated over the expected periods of benefit for the reporting entity. IFRS for long-lived assets address matters such as the determination of the amounts at which to initially record the acquisitions of such assets, the amounts at which to present these assets at subsequent reporting dates, and the appropriate method(s) by which to allocate the assets' costs to future periods. Under current IFRS, while historical cost is normally assumed to be the basis for financial reporting, it is also acceptable to periodically revalue long-lived assets if certain defined conditions are met.

Long-lived nonfinancial assets are primarily operational in character, (i.e., actively used in the business rather than being held as passive investments), and they may be classified into two basic types: tangible and intangible. *Tangible assets,* which are the subject of the present chapter, have physical substance and can be further categorized as follows:

1. Depreciable assets
2. Depletable assets
3. Other tangible assets

Intangible assets, on the other hand, have no physical substance. The value of an intangible asset is a function of the rights or privileges that its ownership conveys to the business entity. Intangible assets, which are explored at length in Chapter 9, can be further categorized as being either

1. Identifiable, or
2. Unidentifiable (i.e., goodwill).

Property (such as factory buildings) is often constructed by an enterprise over an extended period of time, and during this interval, when the property has yet to be placed in productive service, the enterprise may incur interest cost on funds borrowed to finance the construction. IAS 23 provides that such cost may be added to the carrying value of the asset under construction, in line with the US treatment, or may be expensed as incurred. European companies have historically generally expensed such costs as period costs as they are incurred, because this has been a more tax-efficient strategy. IAS 23 provides for either method, but once the reporting entity adopts the allowed alternative (capitalization) as its accounting policy, interest costs should be added to the carrying value of all qualifying assets.

Long-lived assets are sometimes acquired in nonmonetary transactions, either in exchanges of assets between the entity and another business organization, or else when assets are given as capital contributions by shareholders to the entity. IAS 16 requires such transactions to be measured at fair value, unless they lack commercial substance.

Increasingly, assets may be acquired or constructed with an attendant obligation to dismantle, remediate the environment, or otherwise clean up after the end of the assets' useful lives. Decommissioning costs now have to be estimated at initial recognition of the asset and recognized, in most instances, as additional asset cost and as a long-term liability, thus causing the costs to be spread over the useful lives of the assets via depreciation charges.

Measurement and presentation of long-lived assets subsequent to acquisition or construction involves both systematic allocation of cost to accounting periods, and possible special write-downs. Concerning cost allocation to periods of use, IFRS now require a "components approach" to depreciation. Thus, elements such as roofing and heating plant are to be separated from the cost paid for a building, and amortized over the lives appropriate for those (shorter-lived) assets.

It has long been held that an entity's statement of financial position should never present assets at amounts in excess of some threshold level of economic utility; under different national GAAP standards, this was variously defined in terms of market value or an amount which could be recovered from future revenues to be derived from utilization of the asset. However, such rules were only infrequently formalized and less often enforced. For many years, there was no specific guidance within IFRS on how to account for any diminution in the value of long-lived assets that may have occurred during the reporting period. IAS 36, *Impairment of Assets*, which was introduced in 1998, significantly altered the accounting landscape by providing thorough coverage of this subject. IAS 36 is equally applicable to tangible and intangible long-lived assets, and will be accordingly addressed in both this and the immediately succeeding chapters.

Sources of IFRS			
IFRS 5	*IAS* 16, 23, 36, 37	*SIC* 21	*IFRIC* 1, 4

DEFINITIONS OF TERMS

Accumulated depreciation. The total of all prior year deductions for depreciation taken to write off the value of a fixed asset over its estimated useful life. The accumulated depreciation account is a contra asset account, which reduces the value of total fixed assets in the statement of financial position.

Asset held for sale. A noncurrent asset or a group of assets (disposal group) to be disposed of in a single transaction, together with directly associated liabilities. Assets classified as held for sale are not subject to depreciation and are carried at the lower of carrying amount and fair value less costs to sell. Separate classification of "assets and liabilities held for sale" in the statement of financial position is required.

Boot. A term sometimes applied to monetary consideration given or received as a net settle-up in what is otherwise a nonmonetary asset exchange.

Borrowing costs. Interest and other costs directly attributable to the acquisition, construction or production of qualifying assets (defined as those taking a substantial period of time to prepare for intended use or sale). Borrowing costs may include interest expense calculated using the effective interest rate method (IAS 39), finance charges in respect of finance leases (IAS 17), or exchange differences arising from foreign currency borrowings.

Carrying amount (book value). The value reported for an asset or liability in the statement of financial position. For assets, this is either cost, revalued amount, or cost minus offsets such as depreciation or allowance for bad debts. Carrying value of fixed assets is the amount at which an asset is recognized after deducting any accumulated depreciation and accumulated impairment losses. Carrying value is often different from market value because depreciation is a cost allocation rather than a means of valuation. For liabilities, the book value is the amount of the liability minus offsets such as any sums already paid or bond discounts.

Cash-generating unit. The smallest identifiable group of assets that generates cash inflows from continuing use, largely independent of the cash inflows associated with other assets or groups of assets; used for impairment testing purposes.

Commercial substance. The ability to change an entity's future cash flows; used in determining the accounting for certain nonmonetary exchanges.

Component depreciation. The systematic allocation of the cost of each part of an item of property, plant and equipment when this cost is significant in relation to the total cost of the item. An entity should allocate the amount initially recognized as an item of property, plant and equipment to its significant parts and depreciate separately each such part. For example, it may be appropriate to depreciate separately elements such as roofing and heating plant from the cost incurred to acquire a building.

Component of an entity. Operations and cash flows that can be clearly distinguished, operationally and for financial reporting purposes, from the rest of the entity.

Corporate assets. Assets, excluding goodwill, that contribute to future cash flows of the cash-generating unit under review for impairment as well as other cash-generating units of the entity.

Cost. Amount of cash or cash equivalent paid or the fair value of the other consideration given to acquire an asset at the time of its acquisition or construction or, where applicable, the amount attributed to that asset when initially recognized in accordance with the specific requirements of other IFRS (e.g., IFRS 2, *Share-Based Payment*).

Costs of disposal. The incremental costs directly associated with the disposal of an asset; these do not include financing costs or related income tax effects (IAS 36).

Costs to sell. The incremental costs directly attributed to a disposal of an asset (or disposal group), excluding finance costs and income tax expense (IFRS 5).

Current asset. An asset should be classified as a current asset when it satisfies any one of the following:

1. It is expected to be realized in, or is held for sale or consumption in, the normal operating course of the enterprise's operating cycle;
2. It is held primarily for trading purposes;
3. It is expected to be realized within twelve months after the reporting period; or
4. It is cash or a cash equivalent (as defined in IAS 7) that is not restricted in its use.

Decommissioning costs. The costs of dismantling an asset and restoring the land on which it was sited, and any other affected assets to their previous state.

Depreciable amount. Cost of an asset or the other amount that has been substituted for cost, less the residual value of the asset.

Depreciation. The process of allocating the depreciable amount (cost less residual value) of an asset over the expected useful life of the asset. This process reduces the value of an asset as a result of wear and tear, age, or obsolescence, and recognizes depreciation expense in the statement of comprehensive income. Similar to amortization, depreciation is a method of measuring the "consumption" of the value of long-term assets. It is not intended to be a valuation process. The amount allocated to depreciation expense is based on one of several accounting depreciation methods (IAS 16, IAS 36)

Depreciation method. A method of allocating the depreciable amount of an asset over its useful life. IAS 16 states that the depreciation method should reflect the pattern in which the asset's future economic benefits are expected to be consumed by the entity, and that appropriateness of the method should be reviewed at least annually in case there has been a change in the expected pattern. Beyond that, the standard leaves the choice of method to the entity, even though it does cite the following methods; straight-line, diminishing balance, and units of production methods.

Discontinued operation. A component of an entity that either has been disposed of or is classified as held for sale and satisfies any one of the following:

1. It is a separate major line of business or geographical area of operations,
2. It is part of a single coordinated plan to dispose of a separate major line of business or geographical area of operations, or
3. It is a subsidiary acquired exclusively with a view to resale.

Disposal group. A group of assets (and liabilities associated with those assets) to be disposed of, by sale or otherwise, together as a group in a single transaction. Goodwill acquired in a business combination is included in the disposal group if this group is a cash-generating unit to which goodwill has been allocated in accordance with IAS 36 or if it is an operation within such a cash-generating unit.

Exchange. Reciprocal transfer between an enterprise and another entity that results in the acquisition of assets or services, or the satisfaction of liabilities, through a transfer of other assets, services, or other obligations.

Fair value. Amount that would be obtained for an asset in an arm's-length exchange transaction between knowledgeable, willing parties.

Firm purchase commitment. An agreement with an unrelated party, binding on both parties and usually legally enforceable, that (1) specifies all important terms, including the price and timing of the transactions, and (2) includes a disincentive for nonperformance (sufficiently large) making performance highly probable.

Fixed assets. Assets used in a productive capacity that have physical substance, are relatively long-lived, and provide future benefit that is readily measurable. Also referred to as property, plant, and equipment.

Highly probable. Significantly more likely than probable.

Impairment loss. The excess of the carrying amount of an asset or a cash-generating unit over its recoverable amount.

Impairment test. Recoverability test, comparing the carrying amount of an asset in the statement of financial position to its recoverable amount to ensure that no asset is carried at more than its fair value. In general, impairment occurs when a company can no longer generate sufficient future cash inflows to recover the value of an asset. Under IAS 36, an entity must test for impairment at each financial reporting date as well as when there is an indication that an asset might be impaired.

Intangible assets. Identifiable nonmonetary assets, without physical substance.

Monetary assets. Money held and assets to be received in fixed or determinable amounts of money. Examples are cash, accounts receivable, and notes receivable.

Net selling price. The amount that could be realized from the sale of an asset by means of an arm's-length transaction, less costs of disposal.

Noncurrent asset. An asset not meeting the definition of a current asset.

Nonmonetary assets. Assets other than monetary assets. Examples are inventories; investments in common stock; and property, plant, and equipment.

Nonmonetary transactions. Exchanges and nonreciprocal transfers that involve little or no monetary assets or liabilities.

Nonreciprocal transfer. Transfer of assets or services in one direction, either from an enterprise to its owners or another entity, or from owners or another entity to the enterprise. An enterprise's reacquisition of its outstanding stock is a nonreciprocal transfer.

Property, plant, and equipment. Tangible assets with an expected useful life of more than one year, that are held for use in the process of producing goods or services for sale, that are held for rental to others, or that are held for administrative purposes; also referred to commonly as fixed assets.

Probably. More likely than not.

Provision. A liability established to recognize a probable outflow of resources, whose timing or value is uncertain, where the reporting entity has a present obligation arising out of a past event.

Qualifying asset. An asset that necessarily requires a substantial period of time to get ready for its intended use or sale. Qualifying assets can be inventories, plant and equipment, intangibles, and investment properties, unless the assets are accounted for at fair value. Financial assets or inventories produced over a very short period of time are *not* qualifying assets.

Recoverable amount. The greater of an asset's net selling price or its value in use.

Residual (salvage) value. Estimated amount that an entity would currently obtain from disposal of the asset, net of estimated costs of disposal, if the asset were already of the age and in the condition expected at the end of its useful life.

Similar productive assets. Productive assets that are of the same general type, that perform the same function, or that are employed in the same line of business.

Useful life. Period over which an asset is expected to be available for use by an entity, or the number of production or similar units expected to be obtained from the asset by an entity.

Value in use. The present value of estimated future cash flows expected to be realized from the continuing use of an asset and from its disposal at the end of its useful life.

CONCEPTS, RULES, AND EXAMPLES

Property, Plant, and Equipment

Property, plant, and equipment (also variously referred to as plant assets, fixed tangible assets, or PP&E) is the term most often used to denote tangible property to be used in a productive capacity that will benefit the enterprise for a period of greater than one year. This term is meant to distinguish these assets from intangibles, which are long-term, generally identifiable assets that do not have physical substance, or whose value is not fully indicated by their physical existence.

There are four concerns to be addressed in accounting for long-lived assets.

1. The amount at which the assets should be recorded initially on acquisition;
2. How value changes subsequent to acquisition should be reflected in the accounts, including questions of both value increases and possible decreases due to impairments;
3. The rate at which the amount the assets are recorded should be allocated as an expense to future periods; and
4. The recording of the ultimate disposal of the assets.

Initial measurement. All costs required to bring an asset into working condition should be recorded as part of the cost of the asset. Examples of such costs include sales, value added, or other nonrefundable taxes or duties, finders' fees, freight costs, site preparation and other installation costs, and setup costs. Thus, any reasonable cost incurred prior to using the asset in actual production involved in bringing the asset to the buyer is capitalized. These costs are not to be expensed in the period in which they are incurred, as they are deemed to add value to the asset and indeed were necessary expenditures to obtain the asset, provided that this does not lead to recording the asset at an amount greater than fair value.

The costs required to bring acquired assets to the place where they are to be used includes such ancillary costs as testing and calibrating, where relevant. IAS 16 aims to draw a distinction between the costs of getting the asset to the state in which it is in a condition to be exploited (which are to be included in the asset's carrying value) and costs associated with the start-up operations, such as staff training, down time between completion of the asset and the start of its exploitation, losses incurred through running at below normal capacity etc., which are considered to be operating expenses. To be netted against such costs are any revenues received during the installation process. As an example, the standard cites the sales of samples produced during this procedure.

IAS 16, as revised in 2003, distinguishes the situation described in the preceding paragraph from other situations where incidental operations unrelated to the asset may occur before or during the construction or development activities. For example, it notes that income may be earned through using a building site as a car parking lot until construction begins. Because incidental operations such as this are not necessary to bring the asset to the location and working condition necessary for it to be capable of operating in the manner intended by management, the income and related expenses of incidental operations are to be recognized in current earnings, and included in their respective classifications of income and expense in the income statement. These are not to be presented net, as in the earlier example of machine testing costs and sample sales revenues.

Administrative costs, as well as other types of overhead costs, are not normally allocated to fixed asset acquisitions, despite the fact that some such costs, such as the salaries of the personnel who evaluate assets for proposed acquisitions, are in fact incurred as part of the acquisition process. As a general principle, administrative costs are expensed in the period incurred, based on the perception that these costs are fixed and would not be avoided in the absence of asset acquisitions. On the other hand, truly incremental costs, such as a consulting fee or commission paid to an agent hired specifically to assist in the acquisition, may be treated as part of the initial amount to be recognized as the asset cost.

While interest costs incurred during the construction of certain assets must be added to the cost of the asset under (see below), if an asset is purchased on deferred payment terms, the interest cost, whether made explicit or imputed, is *not* part of the cost of the asset. Accordingly, such costs must be expensed currently as interest charges. If the purchase price for the asset incorporates a deferred payment scheme, only the cash equivalent price should be capitalized as the initial carrying amount of the asset. If the cash equivalent price is not explicitly stated, the deferred payment amount should be reduced to present value by the application of an appropriate discount rate. This would normally be best approximated by use of the enterprise's incremental borrowing cost for debt having a maturity similar to the deferred payment term.

Decommissioning costs included in initial measurement. The elements of cost to be incorporated in the initial recognition of an asset are to include the estimated costs of its eventual dismantlement ("decommissioning costs"). That is, the cost of the asset is "grossed up" for these estimated terminal costs, with the offsetting credit being posted to a liability account. It is important to stress that recognition of a liability can only be effected when all the criteria set forth in IAS 37 for the recognition of provisions are met. These stipulate that a provision is to be recognized only when (1) the reporting entity has a *present* obligation, whether legal or constructive, as a result of a *past* event; (2) it is *probable* that an outflow of resources embodying economic benefits will be required to settle the obligation; and (3) a reliable estimate can be made of the amount of the obligation. In the currently outstanding ED, *Proposed Amendment to IAS 37, "Provisions, Contingent Liabilities and Contingent Assets,"* the IASB proposes to eliminate the terms "provisions," "contingent liability," and "contingent asset" from the IFRS literature, and replace these with a new term and "nonfinancial liabilities." The draft also proposes a major change to the current practice of accounting for restructuring provisions (see a separate paragraph in Chapter 12).

For example, assume that it were necessary to secure a government license in order to construct a particular asset, such as a power generating plant, and a condition of the license is that at the end of the expected life of the property the owner would dismantle it, remove any debris, and restore the land to its previous condition. These conditions would qualify as a present obligation resulting from a past event (the plant construction), which will probably result in a future outflow of resources. The cost of such future activities, while perhaps challenging to estimate due to the long time horizon involved and the possible intervening evolution of technology, can normally be accomplished with a requisite degree of accuracy. Per IAS 37, a best estimate is to be made of the future costs, which is then to be discounted to present value. This present value is to be recognized as an additional cost of acquiring the asset.

The cost of dismantlement and similar legal or constructive obligations do not extend to operating costs to be incurred in the future, since those would not qualify as "present obligations." The precise mechanism for making these computations is addressed in Chapter 12.

If estimated costs of dismantlement, removal, and restoration are included in the cost of the asset, the effect will be to allocate this cost over the life of the asset through the depreciation process. Each period the discounting of the provision should be "unwound," such that interest cost is accreted each period. If this is done, at the expected date on which the expenditure is to be incurred it will be appropriately stated. The increase in the carrying value of the provision should be reported as interest expense or a similar financing cost.

Examples of decommissioning or similar costs to be recognized at acquisition

Example 1—Leased premises. In accordance with the terms of a lease, the lessee is obligated to remove its specialized machinery from the leased premises prior to vacating those premises, or to compensate the lessor accordingly. The lease imposes a contractual obligation on the lessee to remove the asset at the end of the asset's useful life or upon vacating the premises, and therefore in this situation an asset (i.e., deferred cost) and liability should be recognized. If the lease is a finance lease, it is added to the asset cost; if an operating lease (less likely), a deferred charge would be reported.

Example 2—Owned premises. The same machinery described in Example 1 is installed in a factory that the entity owns. At the end of the useful life of the machinery, the entity will either incur costs to dismantle and remove the asset or will leave it idle in place. If the entity chooses to do nothing (i.e., not remove the equipment), this would adversely affect the fair value of the premises should the entity choose to sell the premises on an "as is" basis. Conceptually, to apply the matching principle in a manner consistent with Example 1, the cost of asset retirement should be recognized systematically and rationally over the productive life of the asset and not in the period of retirement. However, in this example, there is no *legal obligation* on the part of the owner of the factory and equipment to retire the asset and, thus, a cost would *not* be recognized at inception for this possible future loss of value.

Example 3—Promissory estoppel. Assume the same facts as in Example 2. In this case, however, the owner of the property sold to a third party an option to purchase the factory, exercisable at the end of five years. In offering the option to the third party, the owner verbally represented that the factory would be completely vacant at the end of the five-year option period and that all machinery, furniture, and fixtures would be removed from the premises. The property owner would reasonably expect that the purchaser of the option relied to the purchaser's detriment (as evidenced by the financial sacrifice of consideration made in exchange for the option) on the representation that the factory would be vacant. While the legal status of such a promise may vary depending on local custom and law, in general this is a constructive obligation and should be recognized as a decommissioning cost and related liability.

Example of timing of recognition of decommissioning cost

Teradactyl Corporation owns and operates a chemical company. At its premises, it maintains underground tanks used to store various types of chemicals. The tanks were installed when Teradactyl Corporation purchased its facilities seven years prior. On February 1, 2008, the legislature of the nation passed a law that requires removal of such tanks when they are no longer being used. Since the law imposes a legal obligation on Teradactyl Corporation, upon enactment, recognition of a decommissioning obligation would be required.

Example of ongoing additions to the decommissioning obligation

Jermyn Manufacturing Corporation operates a factory. As part of its normal operations it stores production by-products and used cleaning solvents on-site in a reservoir specifically designed for that purpose. The reservoir and surrounding land, all owned by Jermyn, are contaminated with these chemicals. On February 1, 2008, the legislature of the nation enacted a law that requires cleanup and disposal of hazardous waste from existing production processes upon retirement of the facility. Upon the enactment of the law, immediate recognition would be required for the decommissioning obligation associated with the contamination that had already occurred. In addition, liabilities will continue to be recognized over the remaining life of the facility as additional contamination occurs.

Changes in decommissioning costs. IFRIC 1 addresses the accounting treatment to be followed where a provision for reinstatement and dismantling costs has been created when an asset was acquired. The Interpretation requires that where estimates of future costs are revised, these should be applied prospectively only, and there is no adjustment to past years' deprecation. IFRIC 1 is addressed in Chapter 13 of this book.

Initial recognition of self-constructed assets. Essentially the same principles that have been established for recognition of the cost of purchased assets also apply to self-constructed assets. All costs that must be incurred to complete the construction of the asset can be added to the amount to be recognized initially, subject only to the constraint that if these costs exceed the recoverable amount (as discussed fully later in this chapter), the excess must be expensed currently. This rule is necessary to avoid the "gold-plated hammer syndrome," whereby a misguided or unfortunate asset construction project incurs excessive costs that then find their way into the statement of financial position, consequently overstating the entity's current net worth and distorting future periods' earnings. Of course, internal (intragroup) profits cannot be allocated to construction costs. The standard specifies that "abnormal amounts" of wasted material, labor, or other resources may not be added to the cost of the asset.

Self-constructed assets should include, in addition to the range of costs discussed earlier, the cost of borrowed funds used during the period of construction. Capitalization of borrowing costs, as set forth by IAS 23, is discussed in a later section of this chapter.

The other issue that arises most commonly in connection with self-constructed fixed assets relates to overhead allocations. While capitalization of all direct costs (labor, materials, and variable overhead) is clearly required and proper, a controversy exists regarding the treatment of fixed overhead. Two alternative views of how to treat fixed overhead are to either

1. Charge the asset with its fair, pro rata share of fixed overhead (i.e., use the same basis of allocation used for inventory); or
2. Charge the fixed asset account with only the identifiable incremental amount of fixed overhead.

While international standards do not address this concern, it may be instructive to consider the nonbinding guidance to be found in US GAAP. AICPA Accounting Research Monograph 1 has suggested that

> . . . in the absence of compelling evidence to the contrary, overhead costs considered to have "discernible future benefits" for the purposes of determining the cost of inventory should be presumed to have "discernible future benefits" for the purpose of determining the cost of a self-constructed depreciable asset.

The implication of this statement is that a logic similar to what was applied to determining which acquisition costs may be included in inventory might reasonably also be applied to the costing of fixed assets. Also, consistent with the standards applicable to inventories, if the costs of fixed assets exceed realizable values, any excess costs should be written off to expense and not deferred to future periods.

Exchanges of assets. IAS 16 discusses the accounting to be applied to those situations in which assets are exchanged for other similar or dissimilar assets, with or without the additional consideration of monetary assets. This topic is addressed later in this chapter, under the heading "Nonmonetary (Exchange) Transactions."

Costs incurred subsequent to purchase or self-construction. Costs that are incurred subsequent to the purchase or construction of the long-lived asset, such as those for repairs, maintenance, or betterments, may involve an adjustment to the carrying value, or may be expensed, depending on the precise facts and circumstances.

To qualify for capitalization, costs must be associated with incremental benefits. Costs can be added to the carrying value of the related asset only when it is *probable* that future economic benefits beyond those originally anticipated for the asset will be received by the entity. For example, modifications to the asset made to extend its useful life (measured either in years or in units of potential production) or to increase its capacity (e.g., as measured by units of output per hour) would be capitalized. Similarly, if the expenditure results in an improved quality of output, or permits a reduction in other cost inputs (e.g., would result in labor savings), it is a candidate for capitalization. As with self-constructed assets, if the costs incurred exceed the defined threshold, they must be expensed currently. Where a modification involves changing part of the asset (e.g., substituting a mightier power source), the cost of the part that is removed should be treated as a disposal.

For example, roofs of commercial buildings, linings of blast furnaces used for steel making, and engines of commercial aircraft all need to be replaced or overhauled before the related buildings, furnaces, or airframes themselves must be replaced. If componentized deprecation was properly employed, the roofs, linings, and engines were being depreciated over their respectively shorter useful lives, and when the replacements or overhauls are performed, on average, these will have been fully depreciated. To the extent that undepreciated costs of these components remain, they would have to be removed from the account (i.e., charged to expense in the period of replacement or overhaul) as the newly incurred replacement or overhaul costs are added to the asset accounts, in order to avoid having, for financial reporting purposes, "two roofs on one building."

It can usually be assumed that ordinary maintenance and repair expenditures will occur on a ratable basis over the life of the asset and should be charged to expense as incurred. Thus, if the purpose of the expenditure is either to maintain the productive capacity anticipated when the asset was acquired or constructed, or to restore it to that level, the costs are not subject to capitalization.

A partial exception is encountered if an asset is acquired in a condition that necessitates that certain expenditures be incurred in order to put it into the appropriate state for its intended use. For example, a deteriorated building may be purchased with the intention that it be restored and then utilized as a factory or office facility. In such cases, costs that otherwise would be categorized as ordinary maintenance items might be subject to capitalization, subject to the constraint that the asset not be presented at a value that exceeds its recoverable amount. Once the restoration is completed, further expenditures of similar type would be viewed as being ordinary repairs or maintenance, and thus expensed as incurred.

However, costs associated with required inspections (e.g., of aircraft) could be capitalized and depreciated. These costs would be amortized over the expected period of benefit (i.e., the estimated time to the next inspection). As with the cost of physical assets, removal of any undepreciated costs of previous inspections would be required. The capitalized inspection cost would have to be treated as a separate component of the asset.

The chart on the following page summarizes the treatment of expenditures subsequent to acquisition consistent with the foregoing discussion.

IFRIC 4 describes arrangements, comprising a transaction or a series of related transactions, that does not take the legal form of a lease but nonetheless conveys a right to use an asset (e.g., an item of property, plant, or equipment) in return for a payment or series of payments. If an arrangement contains a lease, that lease should be classified as a finance lease or an operating lease, in accordance with IAS 17. Other elements of the arrangement not within the scope of IAS 17 should be accounted for in accordance with other standards (e.g., IAS 16). This topic is explored more fully in Chapter 14.

Accounting for Costs Incurred Subsequent to Acquisition of Property, Plant, and Equipment

Type of expenditure	Characteristics	Expense when incurred	Capitalize: Charge to asset	Capitalize: Charge to accum. deprec.	Other
1. Additions	• Extensions, enlargements, or expansions made to an existing asset		x		
2. Repairs and maintenance a. Ordinary	• Recurring, relatively small expenditures 1. Maintain normal operating condition 2. Do not add materially to use value 3. Do not extend useful life	x x x			
b. Extraordinary (major)	• Not recurring, relatively large expenditures 1. Primarily increase the use value 2. Primarily extend the useful life		x	x	
3. Replacements and betterments	• Major component of asset is removed and replaced with component with comparable performance capabilities (replacement) or a different type of component having superior performance capabilities (betterment)				
a. Book value of old component is known					• Remove old asset cost and accum. deprec. • Recognize any loss (or gain) on old asset • Charge asset for replacement component
b. Book value of old component is not known				x	
4. Reinstallations and rearrangements	1. Material costs incurred; benefits extend into future accounting periods 2. No measurable future benefit	x	x		

Depreciation of property, plant, and equipment. In accordance with one of the more important of the basic accounting conventions, the matching principle, the costs of fixed assets are allocated through depreciation to the periods that will have benefited from the use of the asset. Whatever method of depreciation is chosen, it must result in the systematic and rational allocation of the depreciable amount of the asset (initial cost less residual value) over the asset's expected useful life. The determination of the useful life must take a number of factors into consideration. These factors include technological change, normal deterioration, actual physical use, and legal or other limitations on the ability to use the property. The method of depreciation is based on whether the useful life is determined as a function of time or as a function of actual physical usage.

IAS 16 states that, although land normally has an unlimited useful life and is not to be depreciated, where the cost of the land includes estimated dismantlement or restoration costs, these are to be depreciated over the period of benefits obtained by incurring those costs. In some cases, the land itself may have a limited useful life, in which case it is to be depreciated in a manner that reflects the benefits to be derived from it.

Since, under the historical cost convention, depreciation accounting is intended as a strategy for cost allocation, it does not reflect changes in the market value of the asset being depreciated (except in some cases where the impairment rules have been applied in that way—as discussed below). Thus, with the exception of land, which has infinite life, all tangible fixed assets must be depreciated, even if (as sometimes occurs, particularly in periods of general price inflation) their nominal or real values increase.

Furthermore, if the recorded amount of the asset is allocated over a period of time (as opposed to actual use); it should be the expected period of usefulness to the entity, not the physical life of the property itself that governs. Thus, such concerns as technological obsolescence, as well as normal wear and tear, must be addressed in the initial determination of the period over which to allocate the asset cost. The reporting entity's strategy for repairs and maintenance will also affect this computation, since the same physical asset might have a longer or shorter economic useful life in the hands of differing owners, depending on the care with which it is intended to be maintained.

Similarly, the same asset may have a longer or shorter economic life, depending on its intended use. A particular building, for example, may have a fifty-year expected life as a facility for storing goods or for use in light manufacturing, but as a showroom would have a shorter period of usefulness, due to the anticipated disinclination of customers to shop at enterprises housed in older premises. Again, it is not physical life, but useful economic life, that should govern.

Compound assets, such as buildings containing such disparate components as heating plant, roofs, and other structural elements, are most commonly recorded in several separate accounts, to facilitate the process of amortizing the different elements over varying periods. Thus, a heating plant may have an expected useful life of twenty years, the roof a life of fifteen years, and the basic structure itself a life of forty years. Maintaining separate ledger accounts eases the calculation of periodic depreciation in such situations, although for financial reporting purposes a greater degree of aggregation is usual.

IAS 16, as revised in 2003, requires a component approach for depreciation, where, as described above, each material component of a composite asset with different useful lives or different patterns of depreciation is accounted for separately for the purpose of depreciation and accounting for subsequent expenditure (including replacement and renewal). Thus, rather than recording a newly acquired, existing office building as a single asset, it is recorded as a building shell, a heating plant, a roof, and perhaps other discrete mechanical components, subject to a materiality threshold. Allocation of cost over useful lives, instead of being based on a weighted-average of the varying components' lives, is based on separate estimated lives for each component.

IAS 16 states that the depreciation method should reflect the pattern in which the asset's future economic benefits are expected to be consumed by the entity, and that appropriateness of the method should be reviewed at least annually in case there has been a change in the expected pattern. Beyond that, the standard leaves the choice of method to the entity, even though it does cite straight-line, diminishing balance, and units of production methods.

Depreciation methods based on time.

1. Straight-line—Depreciation expense is incurred evenly over the life of the asset. The periodic charge for depreciation is given as

$$\frac{\text{Cost or amount substituted for cost, less residual value}}{\text{Estimated useful life of asset}}$$

2. Accelerated methods—Depreciation expense is higher in the early years of the asset's useful life and lower in the later years. IAS 16 only mentions one accelerated method, the diminishing balance method, but other methods have been employed in various national GAAP under earlier or contemporary accounting standards.

   a. Diminishing balance—the depreciation rate is applied to the net book value of the asset, resulting in a diminishing annual charge. There are various ways to compute the percentage to be applied. The formula below provides a mathematically correct allocation over useful life.

$$\text{Rate}\% = \left(1 - \sqrt[n]{\text{residual value/cost}}\,\right) \times 100$$

   where n is the expected useful life in years. However, companies generally use approximations or conventions influenced by tax practice, such as a multiple of the straight-line rate times the net carrying value at the beginning of the year.

$$\text{Straight-line rate} = \frac{1}{\text{Estimated useful life}}$$

   Example

   Double-declining balance depreciation (if salvage value is to be recognized, stop when book value = estimated salvage value)

   Depreciation = 2 × Straight-line rate x Book value at beginning of year

   Another method to accomplish a diminishing charge for depreciation is the sum-of-the-years' digits method, which is commonly employed in the United States and certain other venues.

   b. Sum-of-the-years' digits (SYD) depreciation =

   (Cost less salvage value) x Applicable fraction

$$\text{Where applicable fraction} = \frac{\text{Number of years of estimated life remaining as of the beginning of the year}}{\text{SYD}}$$

$$\text{and SYD} = \frac{n(n+1)}{2} \quad \text{and n = estimated useful life}$$

   Example

   An asset having a useful economic life of 5 years and no salvage value would have 5/15 (= 1/3) of its cost allocated to year 1, 4/15 to year 2, and so on.

In practice, unless there are tax reasons to employ accelerated methods, large companies tend to use straight-line depreciation. This has the merit that it is simple to apply, and where a company has a large pool of similar assets, some of which are replaced each year, the aggregate annual depreciation charge is likely to be the same, irrespective of the method chosen (consider a trucking company that has ten trucks, each costing €200,000, one of which is replaced each year: the aggregate annual depreciation charge will be €200,000 under any mathematically accurate depreciation method).

Partial-year depreciation. Although IAS 16 is silent on the matter, when an asset is either acquired or disposed of during the year, the full year depreciation calculation should be prorated between the accounting periods involved. This is necessary to achieve proper matching. However, if individual assets in a relatively homogeneous group are regularly acquired and disposed of, one of several conventions can be adopted, as follows:

1. Record a full year's depreciation in the year of acquisition and none in the year of disposal.
2. Record one-half year's depreciation in the year of acquisition and one-half year's depreciation in the year of disposal.

Example of partial-year depreciation

Assume the following:

Taj Mahal Milling Co., a calendar-year entity, acquired a machine on June 1, 2009, that cost €40,000 with an estimated useful life of four years and a €2,500 salvage value. The depreciation expense for each *full* year of the asset's life is calculated as follows:

	Straight-line			*Double-declining balance*					*Sum-of-years' digits*	
Year 1	€37,500* ÷ 4 = €9,375	50%	×	€40,000	=	€20,000	4/10	×	€37,500*	= €15,000
Year 2	€9,375	50%	×	€20,000	=	€10,000	3/10	×	€37,500	= €11,250
Year 3	€9,375	50%	×	€10,000	=	€5,000	2/10	×	€37,500	= €7,500
Year 4	€9,375	50%	×	€5,000	=	€2,500	1/10	×	€37,500	= €3,750

* *€40,000 – €2,500.*

Because the first full year of the asset's life does not coincide with the company's fiscal year, the amounts shown above must be prorated as follows:

	Straight-line			*Double-declining balance*					*Sum-of-years' digits*	
2009	7/12 × 9,375 = €5,469	7/12	×	€20,000	=	€11,667	7/12	×	€15,000	= € 8,750
2010	€9,375	5/12	×	€20,000	=	€ 8,333	5/12	×	€15,000	= € 6,250
		7/12	×	€10,000	=	€ 5,833	7/12	×	€11,250	= € 6,563
						€14,166				€12,813
2011	€9,375	5/12	×	€10,000	=	€ 4,167	5/12	×	€11,250	= € 4,687
		7/12	×	€ 5,000	=	€ 2,917	7/12	×	€ 7,500	= € 4,375
						€ 7,084				€ 9,062
2012	€9,375	5/12	×	€5,000	=	€2,083	5/12	×	€7,500	= €3,125
		7/12	×	€2,500	=	€1,458	7/12	×	€3,750	= €2,188
						€3,541				€5,313
2013	5/12 × 9,375 = €3,906	5/12	×	€2,500	=	€1,042	5/12	×	€3,750	= €1,562

Depreciation method based on actual physical use—Units of production method. Depreciation may also be based on the number of units produced by the asset in a given year. IAS 16 identifies this as the units of production method, but it is also known as the sum of the units approach. It is best suited to those assets, such as machinery, that have an expected life that is most rationally defined in terms of productive output; in periods of reduced production (such as economic recession) the machinery is used less, thus extending the number of years it is likely to remain in service. This method has the merit that the annual depreciation expense fluctuates with the contribution made by the asset each year. Furthermore, if the depreciation finds its way into the cost of finished goods, the unit cost in periods of reduced production would be exaggerated and could even exceed net realizable value unless a units of production approach to depreciation were taken.

$$\text{Depreciation rate} = \frac{\text{Cost less residual value}}{\substack{\text{Estimated number of units to be produced} \\ \text{by the asset over its estimated useful life}}}$$

$$\substack{\text{Units of} \\ \text{production} \\ \text{depreciation}} = \text{Depreciation rate} \times \substack{\text{Number of units} \\ \text{produced during} \\ \text{the period}}$$

Other depreciation methods. Although IAS 16 does not discuss other methods of depreciation (nor even all the variations noted in the foregoing paragraphs), at different times and in various jurisdictions other methods have been used. Some of these are summarized as follows:

1. **Retirement method**—Cost of asset is expensed in period in which it is retired.
2. **Replacement method**—Original cost is carried in accounts and cost of replacement is expensed in the period of replacement. (Neither the retirement nor replacement methods would be acceptable under IAS 16 because they do not reflect the pattern of consumption.)
3. **Group (or composite) method**—Averages the service lives of a number of assets using a weighted-average of the units and depreciates the group or composite as if it were a single unit. A group consists of similar assets, while a composite is made up of dissimilar assets.

$$\text{Depreciation rate} = \frac{\substack{\text{Sum of the straight-line} \\ \text{depreciation of individual assets}}}{\text{Total asset cost}}$$

$$\text{Depreciation expense} = \text{Depreciation rate} \times \text{Total group (composite) cost}$$

A peculiarity of the composite approach is that gains and losses are not recognized on the disposal of an asset, but rather, are netted into accumulated depreciation. This is because it is a presumption of this method that although dispositions of individual assets may yield proceeds greater than or less than their respective book values, the ultimate gross proceeds from a group of assets will not differ materially from the aggregate book value thereof, and accordingly, recognition of those individual gains or losses should be deferred and effectively netted out.

4. **Revenue method**—The future cash flows expected to be derived from asset are estimated, and a percentage is calculated which reflects the cost of the asset as a proportion of its expected revenue. When revenue is received, that percentage is applied to it as a depreciation charge. This is used, for example, for films, and could be considered to be a variant on the units of production method.

Residual value. Most depreciation methods discussed above require that depreciation is applied not to the full cost of the asset, but to the "depreciable amount": that is, the historical cost or amount substituted therefore (i.e., fair value) less the estimated residual value of the asset. As IAS 16 points out, residual value is often not material and in practice is frequently ignored, but it may impact upon some assets, particularly when the entity disposes of them early in their life (e.g., rental vehicles) or where the residual value is so high as to negate any requirement for depreciation (some hotel companies, for example, claim that they have to maintain their premises to such a high standard that their residual value under historical cost is higher than the original cost of the asset).

Under historical cost, residual value is defined as the expected worth of the asset, in present dollars (i.e., without any consideration of the impact of future inflation), at the end of its useful life. Residual value should, however, be measured net of any expected costs of disposal. In some cases, assets will have a negative residual value, as for example when the entity is likely to incur costs to dispose of the asset, or to return the property to an earlier condition, as in the case of certain operations, such as strip mines, that are subject to environmental protection or other laws. In such instances, periodic depreciation should total more than the asset's original cost, such that at the expected disposal date, an estimated liability has been accrued equal to the negative residual value. The residual value is, like all aspects of the depreciation method, subject to at least annual review.

If the revaluation method of measuring tangible fixed assets is chosen, residual value must be assessed anew at the date of each revaluation of the asset. This is accomplished by using data on realizable values for similar assets, ending their respective useful lives at the time of the revaluation, after having been used for purposes similar to the asset being valued. Again, no consideration can be paid to anticipated inflation, and expected future values are not to be discounted to present values to give recognition to the time value of money. As with historical cost based accounting for plant assets, if a negative residual value is anticipated, this should be effectively recognized over the useful life of the asset by charging extra depreciation, such that the estimated liability will have been accrued by the disposal date.

Useful lives. Useful life is affected by such things as the entity's practices regarding repairs and maintenance of its assets, as well as the pace of technological change and the market demand for goods produced and sold by the entity using the assets as productive inputs. If it is determined, when reviewing the depreciation method, that the estimated life is greater or less than previously believed, the change is handled as a change in accounting estimate, not as a correction of an accounting error. Accordingly, no restatement is to be made to previously reported depreciation; rather, the change is accounted for strictly on a prospective basis, being reflected in the period of change and subsequent periods.

Example of estimating the useful life

To illustrate this concept, consider an asset costing €100,000 and originally estimated to have a productive life of 10 years. The straight-line method is used, and there was no residual value anticipated. After 2 years, management revises its estimate of useful life to a total of 6 years. Since the net carrying value of the asset is €80,000 after 2 years (= €100,000 × 8/10), and the remaining expected life is 4 years (2 of the 6 revised total years having already elapsed), depreciation in years 3 through 6 will be €20,000 (= €80,000/4) each.

Tax methods. The methods of computing depreciation discussed in the foregoing sections relate only to financial reporting under IFRS. Tax laws in different nations of the world vary widely in terms of the acceptability of depreciation methods, and it is not possible for a general treatise such as this to address those in any detail. However, to the extent that depreciation allowable for income tax reporting purposes differs from that required or permitted for financial statement purposes, deferred income taxes would have to be computed. Interperiod income tax allocation is discussed more fully in Chapter 15.

Leasehold improvements. Leasehold improvements are improvements to property not owned by the party making these investments. For example, a lessee of office space may invest its funds to install partitions or to combine several suites by removing certain interior walls. Due to the nature of these physical changes to the property (done with the lessor's permission, of course), the lessee cannot remove or undo these changes and must abandon them upon termination of the lease, if the lessee does not remain in the facility.

There is no guidance under IFRS on how to account for leasehold improvements, per se. The recommendations made in the following paragraphs is derived from those under US GAAP but, in the authors' opinion, is straightforward and not subject to serious debate.

Leasehold improvements are often classified as intangibles because the reporting entity has only the (intangible) right to use the property, and does not own the physical property itself once it is attached to the leased property in a way that it cannot be removed or undone. On the other hand, leasehold improvements are not always perceived of as intangibles because they involve tangible physical enhancements made to property by or on behalf of the property's lessee. By law in many jurisdictions, when improvements are made to real property and those improvements are permanently affixed to the property, the title to those improvements automatically transfers to the owner of the property. The rationale behind this is that the improvements, when permanently affixed, are inseparable from the rest of the real estate. For purposes of the following discussion, whether leasehold improvements are depreciated or amortized is a mere semantic point, and does not alter the substance of this guidance. (The term amortization will be used here, however.)

A frequently encountered issue with respect to leasehold improvements relates to determination of the period over which they are to be amortized. Normally, the cost of long-lived assets is charged to expense over the estimated useful lives of the assets. However, the right to use a leasehold improvement expires when the related lease expires, irrespective of whether the improvement has any remaining useful life. Thus, the appropriate useful life for a leasehold improvement is the lesser of the useful life of the improvement or the term of the underlying lease.

Some leases contain a fixed, noncancelable term and additional renewal options. When considering the term of the lease for the purposes of amortizing leasehold improvements, normally only the initial fixed noncancelable term is included. There are exceptions to this general rule, however. If a renewal option is a bargain renewal option, which means that it is probable at the inception of the lease that it will be exercised and, therefore, the option period should be included in the lease term for purposes of determining the amortizable life of the leasehold improvements. Additionally, under the definition of the lease term there are other situations where it is probable that an option to renew for an additional period would be exercised. These situations include periods for which failure to renew the lease imposes a penalty on the lessee in such amount that a renewal appears, at the inception of the lease, to be reasonably assured. Other situations of this kind arise when an otherwise excludable renewal period precedes a provision for a bargain purchase of the leased asset or when, during periods covered by ordinary renewal options, the lessee has guaranteed the lessor's debt on the leased property.

Example

Mojo Corporation occupies a warehouse under a five-year operating lease commencing January 1, 2009, and expiring December 31, 2013. The lease contains three successive options to renew the lease for additional five-year periods. The options are not bargain renewals as they call for fixed rentals at the prevailing fair market rents that will be in effect at the time of exercise. When the initial calculation was made to determine whether the lease is an operating lease or a capital lease, only the initial noncancelable term of five years was included in the calculation. Consequently, for the purpose of determining the amortizable life of any leasehold improvements made by Mojo Corporation, only the initial five-year term is used. If Mojo Corporation decides, at the beginning of year four of the lease, to make a substantial amount of leasehold improvements to the leased property, it could be argued that it would now be probable that Mojo would exercise one or more of the renewal periods, since not doing so would impose the substantial financial penalty for abandoning expensive leasehold improvements. This would trigger accounting for the lease by treating the period or periods for which it is likely that the lessee will renew as a new agreement and require testing to determine whether the lease, prospectively, qualifies as a capital or operating lease.

Revaluation of Property, Plant, and Equipment

IAS 16 provides for two acceptable alternative approaches to accounting for long-lived tangible assets. The first of these is the historical cost method, under which acquisition or construction cost is used for initial recognition, subject to depreciation over the expected economic life and to possible write-down in the event of a permanent impairment in value. In many jurisdictions this is the only method allowed by statute, but a number of jurisdictions, particularly those with significant rates of inflation, do permit either full or selective revaluation and IAS 16 acknowledges this by also mandating what it calls the "revaluation model." Under the revaluation model, after initial recognition as an asset, an item of property, plant and equipment whose fair value can be measured reliably should be carried at a revalued amount, being its fair value at the date of the revaluation less any subsequent accumulated depreciation and subsequent accumulated impairment losses.

The logic of recognizing revaluations relates to both the statement of financial position and the measure of periodic performance provided by the statement of comprehensive income. Due to the effects of inflation (which even if quite moderate when measured on an annual basis can compound dramatically during the lengthy period over which fixed assets remain in use) the statement of financial position can become a virtually meaningless agglomeration of dissimilar costs.

Furthermore, if the depreciation charge to income is determined by reference to historical costs of assets acquired in much earlier periods, profits will be overstated, and will not reflect the cost of maintaining the entity's asset base. Under these circumstances, a nominally profitable enterprise might find that it has self-liquidated and is unable to continue in existence, at least not with the same level of productive capacity, without new debt or equity infusions. IAS 29, *Financial Reporting in Hyperinflationary Economies,* addresses adjustments to depreciation under conditions of hyperinflation. Use of the revaluation method is typically encountered in economies that from time to time suffer less significant inflation than that which necessitates application of the procedures specified by IAS 29.

Under the revaluation model the frequency of revaluations depends upon the changes in fair values of the items being revalued and, consequently, when the fair value of a revalued asset differs materially from its carrying amount, a further revaluation is required. Since the revaluation model is more costly to maintain than the historical cost model, the results of the survey conducted by the Institute of Chartered Accountants in England and Wales in 2005 (ICAEW, 2007) indicated that 4% of EU companies used revaluation for building (none for P&E) and 28% of EU companies with investment property used fair value (revaluation) method for this class of assets.

Fair value. As the basis for the revaluation method, the standard stipulates that it is *fair value* (defined as the amount for which the asset could be exchanged between knowledgeable, willing parties in an arm's-length transaction) that is to be used in any such revaluations. Furthermore, the standard requires that, once an entity undertakes revaluations, they must continue to be made with sufficient regularity that the carrying amounts in any subsequent statements of financial position are not materially at variance with then-current fair values. In other words, if the reporting entity adopts the revaluation method, it cannot report obsolete fair values in the statements of financial position that contain previous years' comparative data, since that would not only obviate the purpose of the allowed treatment, but would actually make it impossible for the user to meaningfully interpret the financial statements. Accordingly, the IASB recommends that a class of assets should be revalued on a rolling basis provided revaluation of the class of assets in completed within a short period and provided the revaluations are kept up-to-date.

In accordance with IAS 16, fair value is usually determined by appraisers, using market-based evidence. Market values can also be used for machinery and equipment, but since such items often do not have readily determinable market values, particularly if intended for specialized applications, they may instead be valued at depreciated replacement cost. At the moment, the term fair value is employed by several IFRS without reference to any detailed guidance as to how it is applied. Such guidance will be forthcoming, and the IASB published in November 2006 the *Fair Value Measurements* Discussion Paper, which is based on the US GAAP standard FAS 157, which the IASB used as the starting point for its deliberations, and the issuance of a new IFRS on this topic is expected in 2010. The Discussion Paper, which is presented in this book in further detail in Appendix F, "Use of Fair Value in Accounting Measurements" in Chapter 1, identifies three levels of fair value. It cited as the highest (Level 1 inputs) quoted prices in active markets for identical assets or liabilities; the second best (Level 2 inputs) being directly or indirectly observable prices in active markets for similar assets and liabilities; and the final (Level 3 inputs) being the use of valuation models having some market inputs, or some other basis. When fair value would be used, the entity would need to disclose which level of valuation had been employed, and if Level three, what actual model was being employed.

Alternative concepts of current value. A number of different concepts have been proposed over the years to achieve accounting adjusted for inflation. Methods that address changes in specific prices, in contrast to those that attempt to adjust for general purchasing power changes, have measured reproduction cost, replacement cost, sound value, exit value, entry value, and net present value.

In brief, *reproduction cost* refers to the actual current cost of exactly reproducing the asset, essentially ignoring changes in technology in favor of a strict bricks-and-mortar concept. Since the same service potential could be obtained currently, in many cases, without a literal reproduction of the asset, this method fails to fully address the economic reality that accounting should ideally attempt to measure.

Replacement cost, in contrast, deals with the service potential of the asset, which is after all what truly represents value for its owner. An obvious example can be found in the realm of computers. While the cost to reproduce a particular mainframe machine exactly might be the same or somewhat lower today versus its original purchase price, the computing capacity of the machine might easily be replaced by one or a small group of microcomputers that could be obtained for a fraction of the cost of the larger machine. To gross up the statement of financial position by reference to reproduction cost would be distorting, at the very least. Instead, the replacement cost of the service potential of the owned asset should be used to accomplish the revaluation contemplated by IAS 16.

Furthermore, even replacement cost, if reported on a gross basis, would be an exaggeration of the value implicit in the reporting entity's asset holdings, since the asset in question has already had some fraction of its service life expire. The concept of sound value addresses this concern. Sound value is the equivalent of the cost of replacement of the service potential of the asset, adjusted to reflect the relative loss in its utility due to the passage of time or the fraction of total productive capacity that has already been utilized.

Example of depreciated replacement cost (sound value) as a valuation approach

An asset acquired January 1, 2009, at a cost of €40,000 was expected to have a useful economic life of 10 years. After three years, on January 1, 2012, it is appraised as having a gross replacement cost of €50,000. The sound value, or depreciated replacement cost, would be 7/10 × €50,000, or €35,000. This compares with a book, or carrying, value of €28,000 at that same date. Mechanically, to accomplish a revaluation at January 1, 2012, the asset should be written up by €10,000 (i.e., from €40,000 to €50,000 gross cost) and the accumulated depreciation should be proportionally written up by €3,000 (from €12,000 to €15,000). Under IAS 16, the net amount of the revaluation adjustment, €7,000, would be credited to other comprehensive income and accumulated in equity as revaluation surplus.

An alternative accounting procedure is also permitted by the standard, under which the accumulated depreciation at the date of the revaluation is written off against the gross carrying value of the asset. In the foregoing example, this would mean that the €12,000 of accumulated depreciation at January 1, 2012, immediately prior to the revaluation, would be credited to the gross asset amount, €40,000, thereby reducing it to €28,000. Then the asset account would be adjusted to reflect the valuation of €35,000 by increasing the asset account by €7,000 (= €35,000 – €28,000), with the offset to other comprehensive income (and accumulated in the revaluation surplus in shareholders' equity). In terms of total assets reported in the statement of financial position, this has exactly the same effect as the first method.

Revaluation applied to all assets in the class. IAS 16 requires that if any assets are revalued, all other assets in those groupings or categories must also be revalued. This is necessary to prevent the presentation in a statement of financial position that contains an unintelligible and possibly misleading mix of historical costs and fair values, and to preclude selective revaluation designed to maximize reported net assets. Coupled with the requirement that revaluations take place with sufficient frequency to approximate fair values at the end of each reporting period, this preserves the integrity of the financial reporting process. In fact, given that a statement of financial position prepared under the historical cost method will, in fact, contain noncomparable values for similar assets (due to assets having been acquired at varying times, at differing price levels), the revaluation approach has the possibility of providing more consistent financial reporting. Offsetting this potential improvement, at least somewhat, is the greater subjectivity inherent in the use of fair values, providing an example of the conceptual framework's trade-off between relevance and reliability.

Although IAS 16 requires revaluation of all assets in a given class, the standard recognizes that it may be more practical to accomplish this on a rolling, or cycle, basis. This could be done by revaluing one-third of the assets in a given asset category, such as machinery, in each year, so that at the end of any reporting period one-third of the group is valued at current fair value, another one-third is valued at amounts that are one year obsolete, and another one-third are valued at amounts that are two years obsolete. Unless values are changing rapidly, it is likely that the statement of financial position would not be materially distorted, and therefore, this approach would in all likelihood be a reasonable means to facilitate the revaluation process.

According to the IASB, annual revaluation is necessary for those items of property, plant and equipment which experience significant and volatile changes in fair value; items with only insignificant changes in fair value may be revalued only every three or five years.

Revaluation adjustments. In general, revaluation adjustments increasing an asset's carrying amount are recognized in other comprehensive income and accumulated in equity as "*revaluation surplus.*" However, the increase should be recognized in profit or loss to the extent that it reverses a revaluation decrease of the same asset previously recognized in profit or loss. If a revalued asset is subsequently found to be impaired, the impairment loss is recognized in other comprehensive income only to the extent that the impairment loss does not exceed the amount in the revaluation surplus for the same asset. Such an impairment loss on a revalued asset is first offset against the revaluation surplus for that asset, and only when that has been exhausted, it is recognized in profit or loss.

Revaluation adjustments decreasing an asset's carrying amount, in general, are recognized in profit or loss. However, the decrease should be recognized in other comprehensive income to the extent of any credit balance existing in the revaluation surplus in respect of that asset. The decrease recognized in other comprehensive income reduces the amount accumulated in equity in the revaluation surplus account.

Under the provisions of IAS 16, the amount credited to revaluation surplus can either be transferred directly to retained earnings (but *not* through the income statement!) as the asset is being depreciated, or it can be held in the revaluation surplus account until such time as the asset is disposed of or retired from service. Some of the revaluation surplus may be transferred directly to retained earnings as the asset is used by an entity. Any transfer to retained earnings is limited to the amount equal to the difference between depreciation based on the revalued carrying amount of the asset and depreciation based on the asset's original cost. In addition, revaluation surplus may be transferred directly to retained earnings when the asset is derecognized. This would involve transferring the whole of the surplus when the asset is retired or disposed of. Important to remember is that transfers from revaluation surplus to retained earnings are not made through profit or loss!

Initial revaluation. Under the revaluation model in IAS 16, at the date of initial revaluation of an item of property, plant and equipment, revaluation adjustments are accounted for as follows: (1) Increases in an asset's carrying value are credited to other comprehensive income (gain on revaluation); and (2) Decreases in an asset's carrying value are charged to other comprehensive income (loss on revaluation in the statement of comprehensive income).

Example—Initial revaluation

Assume Henan Corporation (HC) acquired a building with a cost of €100,000. After one year the building is appraised as having a current fair value of €110,000. The journal entry to increase the carrying amount of the building to its fair value is as follows:

Building	10,000	
Other comprehensive income—gain on revaluation		10,000

At the end of the fiscal period, the increase in the carrying amount of the building is accumulated in the "revaluation surplus" in the shareholders' equity section of the statement of financial position.

Subsequent revaluation. In accordance with IAS 16, in subsequent periods, revaluation adjustments are accounted for as follows: (1) Increases in an asset's carrying value (upward revaluation) should be recognized as income in profit or loss to the extent of the amount of previous loss on revaluation accumulated in the revaluation surplus, and any excess should be credited to equity; (2) Decreases in an asset's carrying value (downward revaluation) should be charged to other comprehensive income to the extent of any previous revaluation surplus, and any excess should credited to equity.

Example—Subsequent revaluation

In the following year, HC determines that the fair value of the building is no longer €110,000. Assuming the fair value decreased to €95,000, the following journal entry is made to record downward revaluation:

Other comprehensive income—gain on revaluation	10,000	
Loss on revaluation—building (expense)	5,000	
Building		15,000

Methods of adjusting accumulated depreciation at the date of revaluation. When an item of property, plant and equipment is revalued, any accumulated depreciation at the date of the revaluation is treated in one of the following ways: (1) Restate accumulated depreciation proportionately with the change in the gross carrying amount of the asset (so that the carrying amount of the asset after revaluation equals its revalued amount); or (2) Eliminate the accumulated depreciation against the gross carrying amount of the asset.

Example—Accumulated depreciation

Konin Corporation (KC) owns buildings with a cost of €200,000 and estimated useful life of five years. Accordingly, depreciation of €40,000 per year is anticipated. After two years, KC obtains market information suggesting that a current fair value of the buildings is €300,000 and decided to write the buildings up to a fair value of €300,000. There are two approaches to apply the revaluation model in IAS 38: the asset and accumulated depreciation can be "grossed up" to reflect the new fair value information, or the asset can be restated on a "net" basis. These two approaches are illustrated below. For both illustrations, the net carrying amount (book value or depreciated cost) immediately prior to the revaluation is €120,000 [€200,000 − (2 × €40,000)]. The net upward revaluation is given by the difference between fair value and net carrying value, or €300,000 − €120,000 = €180,000.

Option 1. Applying the **"gross up" approach,** since the fair value after two years of the five-year useful life have already elapsed is found to be €300,000, the gross fair value (gross carrying amount) must be 5/3 × €300,000 = €500,000. In order to have the net carrying value equal to the fair value after two years, the balance in accumulated depreciation needs to be €200,000. Consequently, the buildings and accumulated depreciation accounts need to be restated upward as follows: buildings up €300,000 (€500,000 − €200,000) and accumulated depreciation €120,000 (€200,000 − €80,000). Alternatively, this revaluation could be accomplished by restating the buildings account and the accumulated depreciation account so that the ratio of net carrying amount to gross carrying amount is 60% (€120,000/€200,000) and the net carrying amount is $300,000. New gross carrying amount is calculated €300,000/.60 = x; x = €500,000.

The following journal entry and table illustrate the restatement of the accounts:

Buildings	300,000	
Accumulated depreciation		120,000
Other comprehensive income—gain on revaluation		180,000

	Original cost		*Revaluation*		*Total*	*%*
Gross carrying amount	€200,000	+	€300,000	=	€500,000	100
Accumulated depreciation	80,000	+	120,000	=	200,000	40
Net carrying amount	€120,000	+	€180,000	=	€300,000	60

After the revaluation, the carrying value of the buildings is €300,000 (= €500,000 − 200,000) and the ratio of net carrying amount to gross carrying amount is 60% (= €300,000/€500,000). This method is often used when an asset is revalued by means of applying an index to determine its depreciated replacement cost.

Option 2. Applying the **"netting" approach,** KC would eliminate accumulated depreciation of €80,000 and then increase the building account by €180,000 so the net carrying amount is €300,000 (= €200,000 − €80,000 + €180,000):

Accumulated depreciation	80,000	
Buildings		80,000
Buildings	180,000	
Other comprehensive income—gain on revaluation		180,000

This method is often used for buildings. In terms of total assets reported in the statement of financial position, option 2 has exactly the same effect as option 1.

However, many users of financial statements, including credit grantors and prospective investors, pay heed to the ratio of net property and equipment as a fraction of the related gross amounts. This is done to assess the relative age of the entity's productive assets and, indirectly, to estimate the timing and amounts of cash needed for asset replacements. There is a significant diminution of information under the second method. Accordingly, the first approach described above, preserving the relationship between gross and net asset amounts after the revaluation, is recommended as the preferable alternative if the goal is meaningful financial reporting.

Deferred tax effects of revaluations. As described in detail in Chapter 15, the tax effects of temporary differences must be provided. Where plant assets are depreciated over longer lives for financial reporting purposes than for tax reporting purposes, a deferred tax liability will be created in the early years and then drawn down in later years. Generally speaking, the deferred tax provided will be measured by the expected future tax rate applied to the temporary difference at the time it reverses; unless future tax rate changes have already been enacted, the current rate structure is used as an unbiased estimator of those future effects.

In the case of revaluation of plant assets, it may be that taxing authorities will not permit the higher revalued amounts to be depreciated for purposes of computing tax liabilities. Instead, only the actual cost incurred can be used to offset tax obligations. On the other hand, since revaluations reflect a holding gain, this gain would be taxable if realized. Accordingly, a deferred tax liability is still required to be recognized, even though it does not relate to temporary differences arising from periodic depreciation charges.

SIC 21 confirms that measurement of the deferred tax effects relating to the revaluation of nondepreciable assets must be made with reference to the tax consequences that would follow from recovery of the carrying amount of that asset through an eventual sale. This is necessary because the asset will not be depreciated, and hence, no part of its carrying amount is considered to be recovered through use. As a practical matter this means that if there are differential capital gain and ordinary income tax rates, deferred taxes will be computed with reference to the former.

Impairment of Tangible Long-Lived Assets

Until the promulgation of IAS 36, there had been a wide range of practices dealing with impairment recognition and measurement. Many European jurisdictions had statutory obligations to compare the carrying value of assets with their market value, but these requirements were not necessarily applied rigorously. Some jurisdictions, typically those with a British company law tradition, had no requirement to reflect impairment unless it was permanent and long-term. The much more rigorous approach of IAS 36 reflects awareness by regulators that this has been a neglected area in financial reporting.

Principal requirements of IAS 36. In general, the standard provides the procedures that an entity is required to apply to ensure that its assets are not carried at amounts higher than their recoverable amount. If an asset's carrying value is more than its recoverable amount (the amount to be recovered through use or sale of the asset), impairment loss is recognized. IAS 36 requires an entity to assess at the end of each reporting period whether there is any indication that an asset may be impaired. Tests for impairment are necessary when there is an indication that an asset might be impaired (but annually for intangible assets having an indefinite useful life and those not yet available for use, and goodwill). When carried out, the test is applied to the smallest group of assets for which the entity has identifiable cash flows, called a "cash-generating unit." The carrying amount of the asset or assets in the cash-generating unit is compared with the recoverable amount, which is the higher of the asset's (or cash-generating unit's) fair value less costs to sell and the present value of the cash flows expected to be generated by using the asset ("value in use"). If the higher of these future values is lower than the carrying amount, an impairment loss is recognized for the difference.

IAS 36 does not apply to inventories (IAS 2); assets arising from construction contracts (IAS 11); deferred tax assets (IAS 12); assets arising from employee benefits (IAS 19); financial assets within the scope of IAS 39; investment property measured at fair value (IAS 19); financial assets within the scope of IAS 39; investment property measured at fair value (IAS 40); biological assets related to agricultural activity measured at fair value less costs to sell (IAS 41); deferred acquisition costs and intangible assets under insurance contracts (IFRS 4); and noncurrent assets (or disposal groups) classified as held for sale (IFRS 5).

Identifying impairments. According to IAS 36, at each financial reporting date the reporting entity should determine whether there are conditions that would indicate that impairments may have occurred. Note that this is *not* a requirement that possible impairments be calculated for all assets at the end of each reporting period, which would be a formidable undertaking for most entities. Rather, it is the existence of conditions that might be suggestive of a heightened risk of impairment that must be evaluated. However, if such indicators are present, then further analysis will be necessary.

The standard provides a set of indicators of potential impairment and suggests that these represent a minimum array of factors to be given consideration. Other more industry- or entity-specific gauges could be devised by the reporting enterprise.

At a minimum, the following external and internal signs of possible impairment are to be given consideration on an annual basis:

- Market value declines for specific assets or cash-generating units, beyond the declines expected as a function of asset aging and use;
- Significant changes in the technological, market, economic, or legal environments in which the enterprise operates, or the specific market to which the asset is dedicated;
- Increases in the market interest rate or other market-oriented rate of return such that increases in the discount rate to be employed in determining value in use can be anticipated, with a resultant enhanced likelihood that impairments will emerge;
- Declines in the (publicly owned) entity's market capitalization suggest that the aggregate carrying value of assets exceeds the perceived value of the enterprise taken as a whole;
- There is specific evidence of obsolescence or of physical damage to an asset or group of assets;
- There have been significant internal changes to the organization or its operations, such as product discontinuation decisions or restructurings, so that the expected remaining useful life or utility of the asset has seemingly been reduced; and
- Internal reporting data suggest that the economic performance of the asset or group of assets is, or will become, worse than previously anticipated.

The mere fact that one or more of the foregoing indicators suggests that there might be cause for concern about possible asset impairment does not necessarily mean that formal impairment testing must proceed in every instance, although in the absence of a plausible explanation why the signals of possible impairment should not be further considered, the implication would be that some follow-up investigation is needed.

Computing recoverable amounts—General concepts. IAS 36 defines impairment as the excess of carrying value over recoverable amount, and defines recoverable amount as the greater of two alternative measures: net selling price and value in use. The objective is to recognize impairment when the economic value of an asset (or cash-generating unit comprised of a group of assets) is truly below its book (carrying) value. In theory, and for the most part in practice also, an entity making rational choices would sell an asset if its net selling price (fair value less costs of disposal) were greater than the asset's value in use, and would continue to employ the asset if value in use exceeded salvage value. Thus, the economic value of an asset is most meaningfully measured with reference to the greater of these two amounts, since the entity will either retain or dispose of the asset, consistent with what appears to be its highest and best use. Once recoverable amount has been determined, this is to be compared to carrying value; if recoverable amount is lower, the asset has been impaired, and this impairment must be given accounting recognition. It should be noted that value in use is an entity-specific value, in contrast to fair value, which is based on market price. Value in use is thus a much more subjective measurement than is fair value, since it takes account of factors available only to the individual business, which may be difficult to validate. If either an asset's fair value less costs to sell or its value in use exceeds the asset's carrying value, the asset is not impaired and it is not necessary to estimate the other amount.

Determining fair value less costs to sell. The determination of the fair value less costs to sell (i.e., net selling price) and the value in use of the asset being evaluated will typically present some difficulties. For actively traded assets, fair value can be ascertained by reference to publicly available information (e.g., from price lists or dealer quotations), and costs of disposal will either be implicitly factored into those amounts (such as when a dealer quote includes pick-up, shipping, etc.) or else can be readily estimated. Most common productive tangible assets, such as machinery and equipment, will not easily be priced, however, since active markets for used items will either not exist or be relatively illiquid. It will often be necessary to reason by analogy (i.e., to draw inferences from recent transactions in similar assets), making adjustments for age, condition, productive capacity, and other variables. For example, a five-year-old machine having an output rate (for a given component) of 2,000 units per day, and an estimated useful life of eight years, might be valued at 30% (=3/8 × .8) of the cost of a new replacement machine having a capacity of 2,500 units per day. In many industries, trade publications and other data sources can provide a great deal of insight into the market value of key assets.

Computing value in use. The computation of value in use involves a two-step process: first, future cash flows must be estimated; and second, the present value of these cash flows must be calculated by application of an appropriate discount rate. These will be discussed in turn in the following paragraphs.

Projection of future cash flows must be based on reasonable assumptions. Exaggerated revenue growth rates, significant anticipated cost reductions, or unreasonable useful lives for plant assets must be avoided if meaningful results are to be obtained. In general, recent past experience is a fair guide to the near-term future, but a recent sudden growth spurt should not be extrapolated to more than the very near-term future. For example, if growth over the past five years averaged 5%, but in the latest year equaled 15%, unless the recent rate of growth can be identified with factors that demonstrate it as being sustainable, a future growth rate of 5%, or slightly higher, would be more supportable.

Typically, extrapolation cannot be made to a greater number of future periods than the number of "base periods" upon which the projection is built. Thus, a five-year projection, to be sound, should be based on at least five years of actual historical performance data. Also, since no business can grow exponentially forever—even if, for example, a five-year historical analysis suggests a 20% annual (inflation adjusted) growth rate—beyond a horizon of a few years a moderation of that growth must be hypothesized. (Reversion to the mean growth rate for the industry as a whole, or of some other demographic trend, such as population growth, is usually assumed.) This is even more important for a single asset or small cash-generating unit, since physical constraints and the ironclad law of diminishing marginal returns makes it virtually inevitable that a plateau will be reached, beyond which further growth will be strictly constrained. Basic economic laws suggest that, if exceptional returns are being reaped from the assets used to produce a given product line, competitors will enter the market, driving down prices and limiting future profitability.

IAS 36 stipulates that steady or declining growth rates must be utilized for periods beyond those covered by the most recent budgets and forecasts. It further states that, barring an ability to demonstrate why a higher rate is appropriate, the growth rate should not exceed the long-term growth rate of the industry in which the entity participates.

The guidance offered by IAS 36 suggests that only normal, recurring cash inflows and outflows from the continuing use of the asset being evaluated should be considered, to which would be added any estimated salvage value at the end of the asset's useful life. Noncash costs, such as depreciation of the asset, obviously must be excluded from this calculation, since, in the case of depreciation, this would in effect double count the very item being measured. Furthermore, projections should always exclude cash flows related to financing the asset—for example, interest and principal repayments on any debt incurred in acquiring the asset—since operating decisions (e.g., keeping or disposing of an asset) are to be evaluated separately from financing decisions (borrowing, leasing, buying with equity capital funds). Also, cash flow projections must relate to the asset in its existing state and in its current use, without regard to possible future enhancements. Income tax effects are also to be disregarded (i.e., the entire analysis should be on a pretax basis). An entity should translate the present value of future cash flows estimated in the foreign currency using the spot exchange rate at the date of the value in use calculation.

Cash-generating units. Under IAS 36, when cash flows cannot be identified with individual assets, (as will frequently be the case), assets must be grouped in order to permit an assessment of future cash flows. The requirement is that this grouping be performed at the lowest level possible, which would be the smallest aggregation of assets for which discrete cash flows can be identified, and which are independent of other groups of assets. In practice, this unit may be a department, a product line, or a factory, for which the output of product and the input of raw materials, labor, and overhead can be identified.

Thus, while the precise contribution to overall cash flow made by, say, a given drill press or lathe may be impossible to surmise, the cash inflows and outflows of a department which produces and sells a discrete product line to an identified group of customers can be more readily determined. To comply with IFRS, the extent of aggregation must be the minimum necessary to develop cash flow information for impairment assessment, and no greater.

A too-high level of aggregation is prohibited for a very basic reason: doing so could permit some impairments to be concealed, by effectively offsetting impairment losses against productivity or profitability gains derived from the expected future use of other assets. Consider an entity which is, overall, quite profitable and which generates positive cash flow, although certain departments or product lines are significantly unprofitable and cash drains. If aggregation at the entity level were permitted, there would be no impairment to be recognized, which would thwart IAS 36's objectives. If impairment testing were done at the departmental or product line level, on the other hand—consistent with IAS 36 requirements—then some loss-producing assets would be written down for impairment, while the cash-generating assets would continue to be accounted for at amortized historical cost.

Put another way, excessive aggregation results (when there are both cash-generating and cash-using groups of operating assets, departments, or product lines) in the recognition of unrealized gains on some assets that nominally are being accounted for on the historical cost basis, which violates IFRS. These gains, while concealed and not reported as such, offset the impairment losses on assets (or groups of assets) whose value have suffered diminutions in value. IAS 36 does not permit this result to be obtained.

IAS 36 requires that cash-generating units be defined consistently from period to period. In addition to being necessary for consistency in financial reporting from period to period, which is an important objective per se, it is also needed to preclude the opportunistic redefining of cash-generating groups effected in order to minimize or eliminate impairment recognition.

Discount rate. The other measurement issue in computing value in use comes from identifying the appropriate discount rate to apply to projected future cash flows. The discount rate is comprised of subcomponents. The base component of the discount rate is the current market rate, which should be identical for all impairment testing at any given date. This must be adjusted for the risks specific to the asset, which thus adds the second component of discount rate.

In practice, this asset class risk adjustment can be built into the cash flows. Appendix A to the standard discusses what it describes as the *traditional approach* to present value calculation, where forecast cash flows are discounted using a rate that is adjusted for uncertainties. It also describes the *expected value* method, where the forecast cash flows are directly adjusted to reflect uncertainty and then discounted at the market rate. These are alternative approaches and care must be exercised to apply one or the other correctly. Most importantly, risk should not be adjusted for twice in computing the present value of future cash flows.

IAS 36 suggests that identifying the appropriate risk-adjusted cost of capital to employ as a discount rate can be accomplished by reference to the implicit rates in current market transactions (e.g., leasing transactions), or from the weighted-average cost of capital of publicly traded enterprises operating in the same industry grouping. Such statistics are available for certain industry segments in selected (but not all) markets. The entity's own recent transactions, typically involving leasing or borrowing to buy other long-lived assets, will be highly salient information in estimating the appropriate discount rate to use.

When risk-adjusted rates are not available, however, it will become necessary to develop a discount rate from surrogate data. The two steps to this procedure are (1) to identify the pure time value of money for the requisite time horizon over which the asset will be utilized: and (2) to add an appropriate risk premium to the pure interest factor, which is related to the variability of future cash flows. Regarding the first component, the life of the asset being tested for impairment will be critical; short-term obligations almost always carry a lower rate than intermediate or long-term ones, although there have been periods when "yield curve inversions" have been dramatic. As to the second element, projected future cash flows having greater variability (which is the technical definition of risk) will be associated with higher risk premiums.

Of these two discount rate components, the latter is likely to prove the more difficult to determine or estimate, in practice. IAS 36 provides a fairly extended discussion of the methodology to utilize, however, and this should be carefully considered before embarking on this procedure. It addresses such factors as country risk, currency risk, cash flow risk, and pricing risk.

The interest rate is considered to include an inflation risk component (i.e., to represent nominal rates, rather than real or inflation adjusted rates), and to calculate present value consistent with this fact the forecast cash flows should reflect the monetary amounts expected to be received in the future, rather than being adjusted to current price levels.

The interest rate to apply must reflect current market conditions as of the end of the reporting period. This means that during periods when rates are changing rapidly the computed value in use of assets will also change, perhaps markedly, even if projected cash flows before discounting remain stable. This is not a computational artifact, however, but rather it reflects economic reality: as discount (interest) rates decline, holdings of productive assets become more economically valuable, holding all other considerations constant; and as rates rise, such holdings lose value because of the erosion of the value of their future cash flows. The accounting implication is that long-lived assets that were unimpaired one year earlier may fail an impairment test in the current period if rates have risen during the interim.

Corporate assets. Corporate assets, such as headquarters buildings and shared equipment, which do not themselves generate identifiable cash flows, need to be tested for impairment as are all other long-lived assets. However, these present a particular problem in practice due to the inability to identify cash flows deriving from the future use of these assets. A failure to test corporate assets for impairment would permit such assets to be carried at amounts that could, under some circumstances, be at variance with requirements under IFRS. It would also permit a reporting entity to deliberately evade the impairment testing requirements by opportunistically defining certain otherwise productive assets as being corporate assets.

To avoid such results, IAS 36 requires that corporate assets be allocated among or assigned to the cash-generating unit or units with which they are most closely associated. For a large and diversified enterprise, this probably implies that corporate assets will be allocated among most or all of its cash-generating units, perhaps in proportion to annual turnover (revenue). Since ultimately an enterprise must generate sufficient cash flows to recover its investment in all long-lived assets, whether assigned to operating divisions or to administrative groups, there are no circumstances in which corporate assets can be isolated and excluded from impairment testing.

Accounting for impairments. If the recoverable amount of the cash-generating unit is lower than its carrying value, an impairment must be recognized. The mechanism for recording an impairment loss depends upon whether the entity is accounting for long-lived assets on the historical cost subject to depreciation or revaluation basis. Impairments computed for assets carried at historical cost will be recognized as charges against current period profit or loss, either included with depreciation for financial reporting, or identified separately in the income statement, if prepared separately, or in the statement of comprehensive income.

For assets grouped into cash-generating units, it will not be possible to determine which specific assets have suffered impairment losses when the unit as a whole has been found to be impaired, and so IAS 36 prescribes a formulaic approach. If the cash-generating unit in question has been allocated any goodwill, any impairment should be allocated fully to goodwill, until its carrying value has been reduced to zero. Any further impairment would be allocated proportionately to all the other assets in that cash-generating unit.

The standard does not specify whether the impairment should be credited to the asset account or to the accumulated depreciation (contra asset) account. Of course, either approach has the same effect: net book value is reduced by the accumulated impairment recognized. European practice has generally been to add impairment provisions to the accumulated depreciation account. This is consistent with the view that reducing the asset account directly would be a contravention of the general prohibition on offsetting.

If the entity employs the revaluation method of accounting for long-lived assets, the impairment adjustment will be treated as the partial reversal of a previous upward revaluation. However, if the entire revaluation account is eliminated due to the recognition of an impairment, any excess impairment should be charged to expense (and thus be closed out to retained earnings). In other words, the revaluation account cannot contain a net debit balance.

Example of accounting for impairment

Xebob Corporation (XC) has one of its (many) departments that performs machining operations on parts that are sold to contractors. A group of machines have an aggregate book value at the end of the latest reporting period (December 31, 2009) totaling €123,000. It has been determined that this group of machinery constitutes a cash-generating unit for purposes of applying IAS 36.

Upon analysis, the following facts about future expected cash inflows and outflows become apparent, based on the diminishing productivity expected of the machinery as it ages, and the increasing costs that will be incurred to generate output from the machines:

Year	Revenues	Costs, **excluding** depreciation
2010	€ 75,000	€ 28,000
2011	80,000	42,000
2012	65,000	55,000
2013	20,000	15,000
Totals	€240,000	€140,000

The fair value of the machinery in this cash-generating unit is determined by reference to used machinery quotation sheets obtained from a prominent dealer. After deducting estimated disposition costs, the fair value less costs to sell is calculated as €84,500.

Value in use is determined with reference to the above-noted expected cash inflows and outflows, discounted at a risk rate of 5%. This yields a present value of about €91,981, as shown below.

Year	Cash flows	PV factors	Net PV of cash flows
2010	€47,000	.95238	€44,761.91
2011	38,000	.90703	34,467.12
2012	10,000	.86384	8,638.38
2013	5,000	.82270	4,113.51
Total			€91,980.91

Since value in use exceeds fair value less costs to sell, value in use is selected to represent the recoverable amount of this cash-generating unit. This is lower than the carrying value of the group of assets, however, and thus an impairment must be recognized as of the end of 2009, in the amount of €123,000 − €91,981 = €31,019. This will be included in operating expenses (either depreciation or a separate caption in the statement of comprehensive income or in the income statement, if prepared separately) for 2009.

For example, under US GAAP an impairment loss should be recognized only if the carrying amount of a long-lived asset (asset group) is not recoverable and exceeds its fair value. The following two-step approach to calculating impairment losses is required: (1) Perform a recoverability test by comparing the asset's carrying value to its expected future cash flows (undiscounted); (2) Calculate an impairment loss if it is determined that the asset is not recoverable. Impairment loss is the amount by which the carrying value of the asset exceeds its fair value. In general, it is less likely to have impairment losses under US GAAP since US GAAP may not consider property, plant, and equipment impaired when the asset would be impaired under IFRS. In addition, US GAAP prohibits reversals of impairment losses.

Example—Calculation of impairment loss under IFRS and US GAAP

Assume that Henan Corporation (HC) has two cash-generating units (CGU 1 and 2) and the following information is provided for impairment testing purposes:

	CGU 1	CGU 2
Cost	€6,000,000	€8,500,000
Accumulated depreciation	3,000,000	4,500,000
Expected future cash flows (discounted)	2,800,000	3,500,000
Expected future cash flows (undiscounted)	3,100,000	3,800,000
Fair value less costs to sell	2,400,000	3,700,000
Remaining useful life of asset	4 years	4 years

Under IFRS, impairment loss of €200,000 is recognized for CGU 1 (carrying value of €3,000,000 minus discounted future cash flows of €2,800,000; and impairment loss of €300,000 is recognized for CGU 2 (carrying value of €4,000,000 minus fair value less costs to sell of €3,700,000).

Under US GAAP, no impairment loss is recognized for CGU 1 (since the carrying amount of €3,000,000 is less than the sum of the undiscounted cash flows of €3,100,000; and impairment loss of €300,000 is recognized for CGU 2 (carrying value of €4,000,000 minus fair value less costs to sell of €3,700,000) since the carrying amount is not recoverable (carrying amount of €4,000,000 exceeds undiscounted cash flows of €3,800,000).

Reversals of previously recognized impairments under historical cost method of accounting. IFRS provides for recognition of reversals of previously recognized impairments, unlike US GAAP. In order to recognize a recovery of a previously recognized impairment, a process similar to that which led to the original loss recognition must be followed. This begins with consideration, at the end of each reporting period, of whether there are indicators of possible impairment recoveries, utilizing external and internal sources of information. Data relied upon could include that pertaining to material market value increases; changes in the technological, market, economic or legal environment or the market in which the asset is employed; and the occurrence of a favorable change in interest rates or required rates of return on assets which would imply changes in the discount rate used to compute value in use. Also to be given consideration are data about any changes in the manner in which the asset is employed, as well as evidence that the economic performance of the asset has exceeded expectations and/or is expected to do so in the future.

If one or more of these indicators is present, it will be necessary to compute the recoverable amount of the asset in question or, if appropriate, of the cash-generating unit containing that asset, in order to determine if the current recoverable amount exceeds the carrying amount of the asset, where it had been previously reduced for impairment.

If that is the case, a recovery can be recognized under IAS 36. The amount of recovery to be recognized is limited, however, to the difference between the carrying value and the amount which would have been the current carrying value had the earlier impairment not been given recognition. Note that this means that restoration of the full amount at which the asset was carried at the time of the earlier impairment cannot be made, since time has elapsed between these two events and further depreciation of the asset would have been recognized in the interim.

Example of impairment recovery

To illustrate, assume an asset had a carrying value of €40,000 at December 31, 2008, based on its original cost of €50,000, less accumulated depreciation representing the one-fifth, or two years, of its projected useful life of ten years which already has elapsed. The carrying value of €40,000 is after depreciation for 2008 has been computed, but before impairment has been addressed. At that date, a determination was made that the asset's recoverable amount was only €32,000 (assume this was properly computed and that recognition of the impairment was warranted), so that an €8,000 adjustment must be made. For simplicity, assume this was added to accumulated depreciation, so that at December 31, 2008, the asset cost remains €50,000 and accumulated depreciation is stated as €18,000.

At December 31, 2009, before any adjustments are posted, the carrying value of this asset is €32,000. Depreciation for 2009 would be €4,000 (= €32,000 book value ÷ 8 years remaining life), which would leave a net book value, after current period depreciation, of €28,000. However, a determination is made that the asset's recoverable amount at this date is €37,000. Before making an adjustment to reverse some or all of the impairment loss previously recognized, the carrying value at December 31, 2009, as it would have existed had the impairment not been recognized in 2008 must be computed.

December 31, 2008 preimpairment carrying value	€40,000
2009 depreciation based on above	5,000
Indicated December 31, 2009 carrying value	€35,000

The December 31, 2009 carrying value would have been €40,000 – €5,000 = €35,000; this is the maximum carrying value which can be reflected in the December 31, 2009 statement of financial position. Thus, the full recovery cannot be recognized; instead, the 2009 income statement will reflect (net) a *negative* depreciation charge of €35,000 – €32,000 = €3,000, which can be thought of (or recorded) as follows:

Actual December 31, 2008 carrying value	€32,000
2009 depreciation based on above	4,000 (a)
Indicated December 31, 2009 carrying value	€28,000
Indicated December 31, 2009 carrying value	€28,000
Actual December 31, 2009 carrying value	35,000
Recovery of previously recognized impairment	€ 7,000 (b)

Thus, the net effect in 2009 profit or loss is (a) – (b) = €(3,000). The asset cannot be restored to its indicated recoverable amount at December 31, 2009, amounting to €37,000, as this exceeds the carrying amount that would have existed at this date had the impairment in 2008 never been recognized.

Where a cash-generating unit including goodwill has been impaired, and the impairment has been allocated first to the goodwill and then pro rata to the other assets, *only* the amount allocated to nongoodwill assets can be reversed. The standard specifically prohibits the reversal of impairments to goodwill, on the basis that the goodwill could have been replaced by internally generated goodwill, which cannot be recognized under IFRS.

Reversals of previously recognized impairments under revaluation method of accounting. Reversals of impairments are accounted for differently if the reporting entity employed the revaluation method of accounting for long-lived assets. Under this approach, assets are periodically adjusted to reflect current fair values, with the write-up being recorded in the asset accounts and the corresponding credit reported in other comprehensive income and accumulated in the revaluation surplus in shareholders' equity, and not include in profit or loss. Impairments are viewed as being downward adjustments of fair value in this scenario, and accordingly are reported in other comprehensive income as reversals of previous revaluations (to the extent of any credit balance in the revaluation surplus for that asset) and not charged against profit unless the entire remaining, unamortized portion of the revaluation surplus is eliminated as a consequence of the impairment. Any further impairment is reported in profit or loss.

When an asset (or cash-generating group of assets) had first been revalued upward, then written down to reflect impairment, and then later adjusted to convey a recovery of the impairment, the required procedure is to report the recovery as a reversal of the impairment, as with the historical cost method of accounting for long-lived assets. Since in most instances impairments will have been accounted for as reversals of upward revaluations, a still-later reversal of the impairment will be seen as yet another upward revaluation and accounted for as a credit to other comprehensive income and cumulative amount in revaluation surplus in equity, not to be reported through profit or loss. In the event that impairment will have eliminated the entire revaluation surplus account, and an excess loss will have been charged against profit, then a later recovery will be reported in profit to the extent the earlier write-down had been so reported, with any balance recorded as a credit to other comprehensive income.

Example of impairment recovery—revaluation method

To illustrate, assume an asset was acquired January 1, 2007, and it had a net carrying value of €45,000 at December 31, 2008, based on its original cost of €50,000, less accumulated depreciation representing the one-fifth, or two years, of its projected useful life of ten years, which has already elapsed, plus a revaluation write-up of €5,000, net. The increase in carrying value was recorded a year earlier, based on an appraisal showing the asset's then fair value was €56,250.

At December 31, 2009, impairment is detected, and the recoverable amount at that date is determined to be €34,000. Had this not occurred, depreciation for 2009 would have been (€45,000 ÷ 8 years remaining life =) €5,625; book value after recording 2009 depreciation would have been

(€45,000 – €5,625 =) €39,375. Thus the impairment loss recognized in 2009 is (€39,375 – €34,000 =) €5,375. Of this loss amount, €4,375 represents a reversal of the net amount of the previously recognized valuation increase remaining (i.e., undepreciated) at the end of 2009, as shown below.

Gross amount of revaluation at December 31, 2007	€6,250
Portion of the above allocable to accumulated depreciation	625
Net revaluation increase at December 31, 2007	5,625
Depreciation taken on appreciation for 2008	625
Net revaluation increase at December 31, 2008	5,000
Depreciation taken on appreciation for 2009	625
Net revaluation increase at December 31, 2009, before recognition of impairment	4,375
Impairment recognized as reversal of earlier revaluation	4,375
Net revaluation increase at December 31, 2009	€ 0

The remaining €1,000 impairment loss is recognized at December 31, 2009, in profit or loss, since it exceeds the available amount of revaluation surplus.

In 2010 there is a recovery of value that pertains to this asset; at December 31, 2008, it is valued at €36,500. This represents a €2,500 increase in carrying amount from the earlier year's balance, net of accumulated depreciation. The first €1,000 of this recovery in value is credited to profit, since this is the amount of previously recognized impairment that was charged against profit; the remaining €1,500 of recovery is accounted for as other comprehensive income and accumulated in the revaluation surplus in a shareholders' equity.

Deferred tax effects. Recognition of an impairment for financial reporting purposes will most likely not be accompanied by a deduction for current tax purposes. As a consequence of the nondeductibility of most impairment charges, the book value and tax basis of the impaired assets will diverge, with the difference thus created to gradually be eliminated over the remaining life of the asset, as depreciation for tax purposes varies from that which is recognized for financial reporting. Following the dictates of IAS 12, deferred taxes must be recognized for this new discrepancy. The accounting for deferred taxes is discussed in Chapter 15 and will not be addressed here.

Impairments that will be mitigated by recoveries or compensation from third parties. Impairments of tangible long-lived assets may result from natural or other damages, such as from floods or windstorms, and in some such instances there will be the possibility that payments from third parties (typically commercial insurers) will mitigate the gross loss incurred. The question in such circumstances is whether the gross impairment must be recognized, or whether it may be offset by the actual or estimated amount of the recovery to be received by the reporting entity.

IAS 16 holds that when property is damaged or lost, impairments and claims for reimbursements should be accounted for separately (i.e., not netted for financial reporting purposes). Impairments are to be accounted for per IAS 36 as discussed above; disposals (of damaged or otherwise impaired assets) should be accounted for consistent with guidance in IAS 16. Compensation from third parties, which are gain contingencies, should be recognized as profit only when the funds become receivable. The cost of replacement items or of restored items is determined in accordance with IAS 16.

Disclosure requirements. For each class of long-lived asset, the amount of impairment losses recognized in profit or loss for each period being reported upon must be stated, with an indication of where in the statement of comprehensive income it has been presented (i.e., as part of depreciation or with other charges). For each class of asset, the amount of any reversals of previously recognized impairment must also be stipulated, again with an identification of where in the statement of comprehensive income that this has been presented. If any impairment losses were recognized in other comprehensive income and in revaluation surplus in shareholders' equity (i.e., as a reversal of a previously recognized upward revaluation), this must be disclosed. Finally, any reversals of impairment losses that were recognized in other comprehensive income and in equity must be stated.

If the reporting entity is reporting financial information by segment (IAS 14), the amounts of impairments and of reversals of impairments, recognized in profit or loss and in other comprehensive income during the year must also be stated. Note that the segment disclosures pertaining to impairments need not be categorized by asset class, and the income statement location of the charge or credit need not be stated (but will be understood from the disclosures relating to the primary financial statements themselves).

IAS 36 further provides that if an impairment loss for an individual asset or group of assets categorized as a cash-generating unit is either recognized or reversed during the period, in an amount that is material to the financial statements taken as a whole, disclosures should be made of the following:

- The events or circumstances that caused the loss or recovery of loss;
- The amount of the impairment loss recognized or reversed;
- If for an individual asset, the nature of the asset and the reportable segment to which it belongs, using the primary format as defined under IAS 14;
- If for a cash-generating unit, a description of that unit (e.g., defined as a product line, a plant, geographical area, etc.), the amount of impairment recognized or reversed by class of asset and by reportable segment based on the primary format, and, if the unit's composition has changed since the previous estimate of the unit's recoverable amount, a description of the reasons for such changes;
- Whether fair value less costs to sell or value in use was employed to compute the recoverable amount;
- If recoverable amount is fair value less costs to sell, the basis used to determine it (e.g., whether by reference to active market prices or otherwise); and
- If the recoverable amount is value in use, the discount rate(s) used in the current and prior period's estimate.

Furthermore, when impairments recognized or reversed in the current period are material in the aggregate, the reporting entity should provide a description of the main classes of assets affected by impairment losses or reversals of losses, as well as the main events and circumstances that caused recognition of losses or reversals. This information is not required to the extent that the disclosures above are given for individual assets or cash-generating units.

Retirements and Other Disposals

In general, when an asset is no longer utilized by an entity it is removed from the statement of financial position. In the case of long-lived tangible assets, both the asset and the related contra asset, accumulated depreciation, should be eliminated. The difference between the net carrying amount and any proceeds received will be given immediate recognition as a gain or loss arising from the disposition.

If the revaluation method of accounting has been employed, and the asset and the related accumulated depreciation account have been adjusted upward, if the asset is subsequently disposed of before it has been fully depreciated, the gain or loss computed will be identical to what would have been determined had the historical cost method of accounting been used. The reason is that, at any point in time, the net amount of the revaluation (i.e., the step-up in the asset less the unamortized balance in the step-up in accumulated depreciation) will be offset exactly by the remaining balance in the revaluation surplus account. Elimination of the asset, contra asset, and revaluation surplus accounts will balance precisely, and there will be no gain or loss on this aspect of the disposition transaction. The gain or loss will be determined exclusively by the discrepancy between the net book value, based on historical cost, and the proceeds from the disposition. Thus, the accounting outcome is identical under cost and revaluation methods.

Examples of accounting for asset disposal

On January 1, 2009, Zara Corp. acquired a machine at a cost of €12,000; it had an estimated life of six years, no residual value, and was expected to provide a level pattern of utility to the enterprise. Thus, straight-line depreciation in the amount of €2,000 was charged to operations. At the end of four years, the asset was sold for €5,000. Accounting was done on a historical cost basis. The entries to record depreciation and to report the ultimate disposal on January 1, 2013, are as follows:

1/1/09	Machinery	12,000	
	Cash, etc.		12,000
12/31/09	Depreciation expense	2,000	
	Accumulated depreciation		2,000
12/31/10	Depreciation expense	2,000	
	Accumulated depreciation		2,000
12/31/11	Depreciation expense	2,000	
	Accumulated depreciation		2,000
12/31/12	Depreciation expense	2,000	
	Accumulated depreciation		2,000
1/1/13	Cash	5,000	
	Accumulated depreciation	8,000	
	Machinery		12,000
	Gain on asset disposal		1,000

Now assume the same facts as above, but that the revaluation method is used. At the beginning of year four (2012) the asset is revalued at a gross replacement cost of €15,000. A year later it is sold for €5,000. The entries are as follows (note in particular that the gain on the sale is identical to that reported under the historical cost approach):

1/1/09	Machinery	12,000	
	Cash, etc.		12,000
12/31/09	Depreciation expense	2,000	
	Accumulated depreciation		2,000
12/31/10	Depreciation expense	2,000	
	Accumulated depreciation		2,000
12/31/11	Depreciation expense	2,000	
	Accumulated depreciation		2,000
1/1/12	Machinery	3,000	
	Accumulated depreciation		1,500
	Other comprehensive income		1,500
12/31/12	Depreciation expense	2,500	
	Accumulated depreciation		2,500
	Other comprehensive income	500	
	Retained earnings—revaluation surplus		500
1/1/13	Cash	5,000	
	Accumulated depreciation	10,000	
	Revaluation surplus	1,000	
	Machinery		15,000
	Gain on asset disposal		1,000

Noncurrent Assets Held for Sale

As part of its ongoing efforts to converge IFRS with US GAAP, IASB issued IFRS 5, *Noncurrent Assets Held for Sale and Discontinued Operations*. This has introduced new and substantially revised guidance for accounting for long-lived tangible (and other) assets that have been identified for disposal, as well as new requirements for the presentation and disclosure of discontinued operations.

IFRS 5 states that where management has decided to sell an asset, or disposal group, these should be classified in the statement of financial position as "held-for-sale" and should be measured at the lower of carrying value or fair value less cost to sell. After reclassification, these assets will no longer be subject to systematic depreciation. The measurement basis for noncurrent assets classified as held-for-sale is to be applied to the group as a whole, and any resulting impairment loss will reduce the carrying amount of the noncurrent assets in the disposal group.

Assets and liabilities which are to be disposed of together in a single transaction are to be treated as a *disposal group*. In accordance with the standard, a disposal group is a group of assets (and liabilities associated with those assets) to be disposed of, by sale or otherwise, together as a group in a single transaction. Goodwill acquired in a business combination is included in the disposal group if this group is a cash-generating unit to which goodwill has been allocated in accordance with IAS 36 or if it is an operation within such a cash-generating unit.

Held-for-sale classification. The reporting entity would classify a noncurrent asset (or disposal group) as held-for-sale if its carrying amount will be recovered principally through a sale transaction rather than through continuing use. The criteria are as follows:

1. For an asset or disposal group to be classified as held-for-sale, the asset (or asset group) must be available for immediate sale in its present condition and its sale must be *highly probable*.
2. In addition, the asset (or asset group) must be currently being marketed actively at a price that is reasonable in relation to its current fair value.
3. The sale should be completed, or expected to be so, within a year from the date of the classification.
4. The actions required to complete the planned sale will have been made, and it is unlikely that the plan will be significantly changed or withdrawn.
5. For the sale to be highly probable, management must be committed to selling the asset and must be actively looking for a buyer.
6. It can be possible that the sale may not be completed within one year (i.e., absolute assurance of the sale is not necessary to comply with IFRS 5).
7. In the case that the sale may not be completed within one year, the asset could still be classified as held-for-sale if the delay is caused by events beyond the entity's control and the entity remains committed to selling the asset.

Extension of period beyond one year is allowable in the following situations:

- The reporting entity has committed itself to sell an asset, and it expects that others may impose conditions on the transfer of the asset that could not be completed until after a firm purchase commitment has been made, and a firm purchase commitment is highly probable within a year.
- A firm purchase commitment is made but a buyer unexpectedly imposes conditions on the transfer of the asset held for sale; timely actions are being taken to respond to the conditions, and a favorable resolution is anticipated.

- During the one-year period, unforeseen circumstances arise that were considered unlikely, and the asset is not sold. Necessary action to respond to the change in circumstances should be taken. The asset should be actively marketed at a reasonable price and the criteria set out for the asset to be classified as held-for-sale should have been met.

Occasionally companies acquire non-current assets exclusively with a view to disposal. In these cases, the noncurrent asset will be classified as held-for-sale at the date of the acquisition only if it is anticipated that it will be sold within the one-year period and it is highly probably that the held-for-sale criteria will be met within a short period of the acquisition date. This period normally will be no more than three months. Exchanges of noncurrent assets between companies can be treated as held-for-sale when such an exchange has commercial substance in accordance with IAS 16.

If the criteria for classifying a noncurrent asset as held-for-sale occur *after* the statement of financial position date, the noncurrent asset should *not* be shown as held-for-sale. However, certain information should be disclosed about the noncurrent assets.

Operations that are expected to be wound down or abandoned do not meet the definition of held for sale. However, a disposal group that is to be abandoned may meet the definition of a discontinued activity. *Abandonment* means that the noncurrent asset (disposal group) will be used to the end of its economic life, or the noncurrent asset (disposal group) will be closed rather than sold. The reasoning behind this is that the carrying amount of the noncurrent asset will be recovered principally through continued usage. A noncurrent asset that has been temporarily taken out of use or service cannot be classified as being abandoned.

Measurement of noncurrent assets held for sale. Assets that are classified as being held for disposal are measured differently and presented separately from other noncurrent assets. In accordance with IFRS 5, the following general principles would apply in measuring noncurrent assets that are held for sale:

- Just before an asset is initially classified as held-for-sale, it should be measured in accordance with the applicable IFRS.
- When noncurrent assets or disposal groups are classified as held-for-sale, they are measured at the *lower of the carrying amount and fair value less costs to sell.*
- When the sale is expected to occur in greater than a year's time, the entity should measure the cost to sell at its present value. Any increase in the present value of the cost to sell that arises should be shown in profit and loss as finance income.
- Any impairment loss is recognized in profit or loss on any initial or subsequent write-down of the asset or disposal group to fair value less cost to sell.
- Any subsequent increases in fair value less cost to sell of an asset can be recognized in profit or loss to the extent that it is *not in excess of the cumulative impairment loss* that has been recognized in accordance with IFRS 5 (or previously in accordance with IAS 36).
- Any impairment loss recognized for a disposal group should be applied in the order set out in IAS 36.
- Noncurrent assets or disposal groups classified as held-for-sale should not be depreciated.

Any interest or expenses of a disposal group should continue to be provided for.

The standard stipulates that, for assets not previously revalued (under IAS 16), any recorded decrease in carrying value (to fair value less cost to sell or value in use) would be an impairment loss taken as charge against income; subsequent changes in fair value would also be recognized, but not increases in excess of impairment losses previously recognized.

For an asset that is carried at a revalued amount (as permitted under IAS 16), revaluation under that standard will have to be effected immediately before it is reclassified as held-for-sale under this proposed standard, with any impairment loss recognized in profit or loss. Subsequent increases or decreases in estimated costs to sell the asset will be recognized in profit or loss. On the other hand, decreases in estimated fair value would be offset against revaluation surplus created under IAS 16, (recognized in other comprehensive income and accumulated in equity under the heading of revaluation surplus), and subsequent increases in fair value would be recognized in full as a revaluation increase under IAS 16, identical to the accounting required before the asset was reclassified as held-for-sale.

A disposal group, as defined under IFRS 5, may include some assets which had been accounted for by the revaluation method. For such disposal groups subsequent increases in fair value are to be recognized, but only to the extent that the carrying values of the noncurrent assets in the group, after the increase has been allocated, do not exceed their respective fair value less costs to sell. The increase recognized would continue to be treated as a revaluation increase under IAS 16.

Finally, IFRS 5 states that noncurrent assets classified as held-for-sale are not to be depreciated. This is logical: the concept objective of depreciation accounting is to allocate asset cost to its useful economic life, and once an asset is denoted as being held for sale, this purpose is no longer meaningful. The constraints on classifying an asset as held-for-sale are, in part, intended to prevent entities from employing such reclassification as a means of avoiding depreciation. Even after classification as held-for-sale, however, interest and other costs associated with the asset are still recognized as expenses as required under IFRS.

Change of plans. If the asset held for sale is not later disposed of, it is to be reclassified to the operating asset category it is properly assignable to. The amount to be initially recognized upon such reclassification would be the lower of (1) the asset's carrying amount before the asset (or disposal group) was classified as held-for-sale, adjusted for any depreciation or amortization that would have been recognized during the interim had the asset (disposal group) not been classified as held-for-sale, and (2) the *recoverable amount* at the date of the subsequent decision not to sell. If the asset is part of a cash-generating unit (as defined under IAS 36), its recoverable amount will be defined as the carrying amount that would have been recognized after the allocation of any impairment loss incurred from that same cash-generating unit.

Under the foregoing circumstance, the reporting entity would include, as part of income from continuing operations in the period in which the criteria for classification as held-for-sale are no longer met, any required adjustment to the carrying amount of a noncurrent asset that ceases to be classified as held-for-sale. That adjustment would be presented in income from continuing operations. It is not an adjustment to prior period results of operations under any circumstances

If an individual asset or liability is removed from a disposal group classified as held-for-sale, the remaining assets and liabilities of the disposal group still to be sold will continue to be measured as a group only if the group meets the criteria for categorization as held-for-sale. In other circumstances, the remaining noncurrent assets of the group that individually meet the criteria to be classified as held-for-sale will need to be measured individually at the lower of their carrying amounts or fair values less costs to sell at that date.

Presentation and disclosure. IFRS 5 specifies that noncurrent assets classified as held-for-sale and the assets of disposal group classified as held-for-sale must be presented separately from other assets in the statement of financial position. The liabilities of a disposal group classified as held-for-sale are also presented separately from other liabilities in the statement of financial position.

Several disclosures are required, including a description of the noncurrent assets of a disposal group, a description of the facts and circumstances of the sale, and the expected manner and timing of that disposal. Any gain or loss recognized for impairment or any subsequent increase in the fair value less costs to sell should also be shown in the applicable segment in which the noncurrent assets or disposal group is presented in accordance with IAS 14.

Discontinued Operations

Presentation and disclosure. IFRS requires an entity to present and disclose information that enables users of the financial statements to evaluate the financial effects of discontinued operations. A *discontinued operation* is a part of an entity that has either been disposed of or is classified as held-for-sale and meets the following requirements:

1. Represents a separate major line of business or geographical area of operations;
2. Is part of a single coordinated plan to dispose of separate major line of business or geographical area of operations; *or*
3. Is a subsidiary acquired exclusively with a view to resale.

An entity should present in the statement of comprehensive income a single amount comprising the total of

- The after-tax profit or loss of discontinued operations, and
- The after-tax gain or loss recognized on the measurement to fair value less costs to sell (or on the disposal) of the assets or disposal groups classified as discontinued operations.

IFRS 5 requires detailed disclosure of revenue, expenses, pretax profit or loss, and the related income tax expense, either in the notes or on the face of the income statement. If this information is presented on the face of the income statement, the information should be separately disclosed from information relating to continuing operations. Regarding the presentation in the cash flow statement, the net cash flows attributable to the operating, investing, and financing activities of the discontinued operation should be shown separately on the face of the statement or disclosed in the notes.

Any disclosures should cover both the current and all prior periods that have been shown in the financial statements. Retrospective classification as a discontinued operation, where the criteria are met after the statement of financial position date, is prohibited by IFRS. In addition, adjustments made in the current accounting period to amounts that have previously been disclosed as discontinued operations from prior periods must be separately disclosed. If an entity ceases to classify a component as held-for-sale, the results of that element must be reclassified and included in income from continuing operations.

Example—Presentation of discontinued operations in the statement of comprehensive income

IFRS 5 requires an entity to disclose a single amount in the statement of comprehensive income for discontinued operations, presented after profit for the period from continuing operations, with an analysis in the notes or in a section of the statement of comprehensive income separate from continuing operations:

Discontinued operations	20X1	20X2
Profit for the period from discontinued operations*	€600,000	€700,000
Profit for the period		
Attributable to		
Owners of the parent (80%)		
Profit for the period from discontinued operations	480,000	560,000

Discontinued operations	_20X1_	_20X2_
Noncontrolling interests (20%)		
Profit for the period from discontinued operations	120,000	140,000

*The required analysis would be provided in the notes

Forthcoming changes in accounting for discontinued operations. In September 2008, the IASB issued an Exposure Draft (ED), *Discontinued Operations,* proposing amendments to IFRS 5, *Noncurrent Assets Held for Sale and Discontinued Operations.* The ED is part of the joint project by the IASB and the US FASB to develop a common definition of discontinued operations as well as common presentation and disclosures.

The IASB proposed a change in the definition of *discontinued operation.* The new definition would hold that a discontinued operation is a *component of an entity* that

- Is an operating segment and either has been disposed of or is classified as held-for-sale, or
- Is a business that meets the criteria to be classified as held-for-sale on acquisition. The proposed change would bring IFRS 5 into conformity with IFRS 8 (which requires segment reporting by publicly accountable entities), but
- The new rules would apply to all entities; thus, reporting entities that have not previously been required to disclose segment information (i.e., privately held companies) would be required to determine whether the component to be disposed of meets the definition of an operating segment;
- The information to be reported with respect to discontinued operations would be based on the amounts presented in the statement of comprehensive income (or separate income statement, where presented), even if the segment information disclosed by an entity to comply with IFRS 8 is prepared on a different basis (i.e., the amounts reported to the chief operating decision maker, as is permitted under IFRS 8); and
- Some additional disclosures would be required for all *components* of an entity (as defined above) disposed of or classified as held-for-sale—regardless of whether or not they are presented as discontinued operations.

Special industry situations. Accounting for property, plant, and equipment in specialized industries such as mineral extraction or agriculture is dealt with in Chapter 24.

Disclosure Requirements: Property, Plant, and Equipment

The disclosures required under IAS 16 for property, plant, and equipment, and under IAS 38 for intangibles, are similar. Furthermore, IAS 36 requires extensive disclosures when assets are impaired or when formerly recognized impairments are being reversed. The requirements that pertain to property, plant, and equipment are as follows:

For each class of tangible asset, disclosure is required of

1. The measurement basis used (amortized historical cost or revaluation approaches)
2. The depreciation method(s) used
3. Useful lives or depreciation rates used
4. The gross carrying amounts and accumulated depreciation at the beginning and at the end of the period
5. A reconciliation of the carrying amount from the beginning to the end of the period, showing additions, dispositions, acquisitions by means of business combinations, increases or decreases resulting from revaluations, reductions to recognize impairments, amounts written back to recognize recoveries of prior impairments, depreciation, the net effect of translation of foreign entities' financial statements, and any other material items. (An example of such a reconciliation is presented below.)

This reconciliation need be provided for only the current period even if comparative financial statements are being presented.

In addition, the statements should also disclose the following facts:

1. Any restrictions on titles and any assets pledged as security for debt
2. The accounting policy regarding restoration costs for items of property, plant, and equipment
3. The expenditures made for property, plant, and equipment, including any construction in progress
4. The amount of outstanding commitments for property, plant, and equipment acquisitions

In addition, the statements should also disclose the following facts:

1. Whether, in determining recoverable amounts, future projected cash flows have been discounted to present values
2. Any restrictions on titles and any assets pledged as security for debt
3. The amount of outstanding commitments for property, plant, and equipment acquisitions

Example of reconciliation of asset carrying amounts

Date	Gross cost	Accumulated depreciation	Net book value
1/1/09	€4,500,000	€2,000,000	€2,500,000
Acquisitions	3,000,000		3,000,000
Disposals	(400,000)	(340,000)	(60,000)
Impairment		600,000	(600,000)
Depreciation		200,000	(200,000)
12/31/09	€7,100,000	€2,460,000	€4,640,000

Nonmonetary (Exchange) Transactions

Businesses sometimes engage in nonmonetary exchange transactions, where tangible or intangible assets are exchanged for other assets, without a cash transaction or with only a small amount of cash "settle-up." These exchanges can involve productive assets such as machinery and equipment, which are not held for sale under normal circumstances, or inventory items, which are intended for sale to customers.

IAS 16 provides authoritative guidance to the accounting for nonmonetary exchanges of tangible assets. It requires that the cost of an item of property, plant, and equipment acquired in exchange for a similar asset is to be measured at *fair value*, provided that the transaction has commercial substance. The concept of a purely "book value" exchange, formerly employed, is now prohibited under most circumstances.

Commercial substance is a new notion under IFRS, and is defined as the event or transaction causing the cash flows of the entity to change. That is, if the expected cash flows after the exchange differ from what would have been expected without this occurring, the exchange has commercial substance and is to be accounted for at fair value. In assessing whether this has occurred, the entity has to consider if the amount, timing and uncertainty of the cash flows from the new asset are different from the one given up, or if the entity-specific portion of the company's operations will be different. If either of these is significant, then the transaction has commercial substance.

If the transaction does not have commercial substance, or the fair value of neither the asset received nor the asset given up can be measured reliably, then the asset acquired is valued at the carrying amount of the asset given up. Such situations are expected to be rare.

If there is a settle-up paid or received in cash or a cash equivalent, this is often referred to as *boot;* that term will be used in the following example.

Example of an exchange involving dissimilar assets and no boot

Assume the following:

1. Jamok, Inc. exchanges an automobile with a carrying value of €2,500 with Springsteen & Co. for a tooling machine with a fair market value of €3,200.
2. No boot is exchanged in the transaction.
3. The fair value of the automobile is not readily determinable.

In this case, Jamok, Inc. has recognized a gain of €700 (= €3,200 – €2,500) on the exchange, and the gain should be included in the determination of net income. The entry to record the transaction would be as follows:

Machine	3,200	
Automobile		2,500
Gain on exchange of automobile		700

Nonreciprocal transfers. In a nonreciprocal transfer, one party gives or receives property without the other party doing the opposite. Often these involve an entity and the owners of the entity. Examples of nonreciprocal transfers with owners include dividends paid-in-kind, nonmonetary assets exchanged for common stock, split-ups, and spin-offs. An example of a nonreciprocal transaction with other than the owners is a donation of property either by or to the enterprise.

The accounting for most nonreciprocal transfers should be based on the fair market value of the asset given (or received, if the fair value of the nonmonetary asset is both objectively measurable and would be clearly recognizable under IFRS). However, nonmonetary assets distributed to owners of an enterprise in a spin-off or other form of reorganization or liquidation should be based on the recorded amount. Where no asset is given, the valuation of the transaction should be based on the fair value of the asset received.

Example of accounting for a nonreciprocal transfer

Assume the following:

1. Salaam donated property with a book value of €10,000 to a charity during the current year.
2. The property had a fair market value of €17,000 at the date of the transfer.

The transaction is to be valued at the fair market value of the property transferred, and any gain or loss on the transaction is to be recognized. Thus, Salaam should recognize a gain of €7,000 (= €17,000 – €10,000) in the determination of the current period's net income. The entry to record the transaction would be as follows:

Charitable donations	17,000	
Property		10,000
Gain on transfer of property		7,000

Capitalization of Borrowing Costs

Accounting literature says that the cost of an asset should include all the costs necessary to get the asset set up and functioning properly for its intended use in the place it is to be used. There has long been, however, a debate about whether borrowing costs should be included in the definition of all costs necessary, or whether instead such costs should be treated as purely a period expense. The concern is that two otherwise identical entities might report different asset costs simply due to decisions made regarding the financing of the enterprises, with the leveraged (debt issuing) entity having a higher reported asset cost. A corollary issue is whether an imputed cost of capital for equity financing should be treated as a cost to be capitalized, which would reduce or eliminate such a discrepancy in apparent asset costs.

The principal purposes to be accomplished by the capitalization of interest costs are as follows:

1. To obtain a more accurate original asset investment cost
2. To achieve a better matching of costs deferred to future periods with revenues of those future periods

In the US, the FASB took the position (in FAS 34) that borrowing costs, under defined conditions, are to be added to the cost of long-lived tangible assets (and inventory also, under very limited circumstances). However, the implicit cost of equity capital may not be similarly treated as an asset cost. This treatment, where defined criteria are met, is mandatory under US GAAP. Historically, the IASB has taken a different approach, offering the US GAAP rule as one alternative treatment, optional at the reporting entity's election, until the revised IAS 23 was issued in 2007.

IAS 23, as revised in 2007. In March 2007, IASB issued the revised IAS 23, *Borrowing Costs*, which eliminated the option of recognizing borrowing costs immediately as an expense, to the extent that they are directly attributable to the acquisition, construction, or production of a qualifying asset. This revision was a result of the Short-Term Convergence project with the FASB. The revised standard provides that a reporting entity should capitalize those borrowing costs that are directly attributable to the acquisition, construction, or production of a qualifying asset as part of the initial carrying value of that asset, and that all other borrowing costs should be recognized as an expense in the period in which the entity incurs them.

Key changes introduced by this revised standard include

- All borrowing costs must be capitalized if they are directly attributable to the acquisition, construction or production of a qualifying asset. The previous benchmark treatment, recognizing immediately all such financing costs as period expenses, is eliminated. Under the new approach, which was an allowable alternative treatment in the past, all these costs must be added to the carrying value of the assets, when it is probable that they will result in future economic benefits to the entity and the costs can be measured reliably, consistent with the US GAAP approach.
- Borrowing costs that do not require capitalization relate to

  - Assets measured at fair value (for example, a biological asset), although an entity can present items in profit or loss as if borrowing costs had been subject to capitalization, before measuring them at their fair values.
  - Inventories that are manufactured, or otherwise produced, in large quantities on a repetitive basis, even if they take a substantial period of time to get ready for their intended use or sale.

Borrowing costs are defined as interest and other costs directly attributable to the acquisition, construction or production of qualifying assets (defined below). Such costs may include interest expense calculated using the effective interest rate method as described in IAS 39, finance charges related to finance leases (in accordance with IAS 17, *Leases*) and exchange differences arising from foreign currency borrowings to the extent they are treated as an adjustment to interest costs.

A qualifying asset is an asset that necessarily takes a substantial period of time to get ready for its intended use and may include inventories, manufacturing plants, power generation facilities, intangible assets, properties that will become self-constructed investment properties once their construction or development is complete, and investment properties measured at cost that are being redeveloped. Other investments, and inventories that are routinely manufactured or otherwise produced in large quantities on a repetitive basis over a short period of time, as well as assets that are ready for their intended use or sale when acquired, are not qualifying assets.

Borrowing costs eligible for capitalization, directly attributable to the acquisition, construction, or production of a qualifying asset, are those borrowing costs that would have been avoided if the expenditure on this asset had not been made. They include actual borrowing costs incurred less any investment income on the temporary investment of those borrowings.

The amount of borrowing costs eligible for capitalization is determined by applying a capitalization rate to the expenditures on that asset. The capitalization rate is the weighted-average of the borrowing costs applicable to the borrowings of the entity that are outstanding during the period, other than borrowings made specifically for the purpose of obtaining a qualifying asset. The amount of borrowing costs capitalized during a period cannot exceed the amount of borrowing costs incurred.

IAS 23 does not deal with the actual or imputed cost of equity, including preferred capital not classified as a liability.

Qualifying assets are those that normally take an extended period of time to prepare for their intended uses. While IAS 23 does not give further insight into the limitations of this definition, many years' experience with FAS 34 provided certain insights that may prove germane to this matter. In general, interest capitalization has been applied to those asset acquisition and construction situations in which

1. Assets are being constructed for an entity's own use or for which deposit or progress payments are made
2. Assets are produced as discrete projects that are intended for lease or sale
3. Investments are being made that are accounted for by the equity method, where the investee is using funds to acquire qualifying assets for its principal operations which have not yet begun

Generally, inventories and land that are not undergoing preparation for intended use are not qualifying assets. When land is in the process of being developed, it is a qualifying asset. If land is being developed for lots, the capitalized interest cost is added to the cost of the land. The related borrowing costs are then matched against revenues when the lots are sold. If, on the other hand, the land is being developed for a building, the capitalized interest cost should instead be added to the cost of the building. The interest cost is then matched against future revenues as the building is depreciated.

The capitalization of interest costs would probably *not* apply to the following situations:

1. The routine production of inventories in large quantities on a repetitive basis
2. For any asset acquisition or self-construction, when the effects of capitalization would not be material, compared to the effect of expensing interest
3. When qualifying assets are already in use or ready for use
4. When qualifying assets are not being used and are not awaiting activities to get them ready for use
5. When qualifying assets are not included in a consolidated statement of financial position
6. When principal operations of an investee accounted for under the equity method have already begun
7. When regulated investees capitalize both the cost of debt and equity capital
8. When assets are acquired with grants and gifts restricted by the donor to the extent that funds are available from those grants and gifts

If funds are borrowed specifically for the purpose of obtaining a qualified asset, the interest costs incurred thereon should be deemed eligible for capitalization, net of any interest earned from the temporary investment of idle funds. It is likely that there will not be a perfect match between funds borrowed and funds actually applied to the asset production process, at any given time, although in some construction projects funds are drawn from the lender's credit facility only as vendors' invoices, and other costs, are actually paid. Only the interest incurred on the project should be included as a cost of the project, however.

In other situations, a variety of credit facilities may be used to generate a pool of funds, a portion of which is applied to the asset construction or acquisition program. In those instances, the amount of interest to be capitalized will be determined by applying an average borrowing cost to the amount of funds committed to the project. Interest cost could include the following:

1. Interest on debt having explicit interest rates
2. Interest related to finance leases
3. Amortization of any related discount or premium on borrowings, or of other ancillary borrowing costs such as commitment fees

The amount of interest to be capitalized is that portion that could have been avoided if the qualifying asset had not been acquired. Thus, the capitalized amount is the incremental amount of interest cost incurred by the entity to finance the acquired asset. A weighted-average of the rates of the borrowings of the entity should be used. The selection of borrowings to be used in the calculation of the weighted-average of rates requires judgment. In resolving this problem, particularly in the case of consolidated financial statements, the best criterion to use is the identification and determination of that portion of interest that could have been avoided if the qualifying assets had not been acquired.

The base (which should be used to multiply the weighted-average rate by) is the average amount of accumulated net capital expenditures incurred for qualifying assets during the relevant reporting period. Capitalized costs and expenditures are not synonymous terms. Theoretically, a capitalized cost financed by a trade payable for which no interest is recognized is not a capital expenditure to which the capitalization rate should be applied. Reasonable approximations of net capital expenditures are acceptable, however, and capitalized costs are generally used in place of capital expenditures unless there is a material difference.

If the average capitalized expenditures exceed the specific new borrowings for the time frame involved, the *excess* expenditures amount should be multiplied by the weighted-average of rates and not by the rate associated with the specific debt. This requirement more accurately reflects the interest cost that is actually incurred by the entity in bringing the long-lived asset to a properly functioning condition and location.

The interest being paid on the underlying debt may be either simple or subject to compounding. Simple interest is computed on the principal alone, whereas compound interest is computed on principal and on any accumulated interest that has not been paid. Compounding may be yearly, monthly, or daily. Most long-lived assets will be acquired with debt having interest compounded, and that feature should be considered when computing the amount of interest to be capitalized.

The total amount of interest actually incurred by the entity during the relevant time frame is the ceiling for the amount of interest cost capitalized. Thus, the amount capitalized cannot exceed the amount actually incurred during the period. On a consolidated financial reporting basis, this ceiling is defined as the sum of the parent's interest cost plus that incurred by its consolidated subsidiaries. If financial statements are issued separately, the interest cost capitalized should be limited to the amount that the separate entity has incurred, and that amount should include interest on intercompany borrowings, which of course would be eliminated in consolidated financial statements. The interest incurred is a gross amount and is not netted against interest earned except in rare cases.

SIC 2 states that if interest cost is capitalized, this fact must not result in the asset being reported at an amount in excess of recoverable amount. Any excess interest cost is thus an impairment, to be recognized immediately in expense.

Example of accounting for capitalized interest costs

Assume the following:

1. On January 1, 2009, Gemini Corp. contracted with Leo Company to construct a building for €20,000,000 on land that Gemini had purchased years earlier.
2. Gemini Corp. was to make five payments in 2009, with the last payment scheduled for the date of completion.
3. The building was completed December 31, 2009.
4. Gemini Corp. made the following payments during 2009:

January 1, 2009	€ 2,000,000
March 31, 2009	4,000,000
June 30, 2009	6,100,000
September 30, 2009	4,400,000
December 31, 2009	3,500,000
	€20,000,000

5. Gemini Corp. had the following debt outstanding at December 31, 2009:

   a. A 12%, 4-year note dated 1/1/08 with interest compounded quarterly. Both principal and interest due 12/31/11 (relates specifically to building project)   €8,500,000

   b. A 10%, 10-year note dated 12/31/04 with simple interest and interest payable annually on December 31   €6,000,000

   c. A 12%, 5-year note dated 12/31/06 with simple interest and interest payable annually on December 31   €7,000,000

The amount of interest to be capitalized during 2009 is computed as follows:

Average Accumulated Expenditures

Date	Expenditure	Capitalization period*	Average accumulated expenditures
1/1/09	€ 2,000,000	12/12	€2,000,000
3/31/09	4,000,000	9/12	3,000,000
6/30/09	6,100,000	6/12	3,050,000
9/30/09	4,400,000	3/12	1,100,000
12/31/09	3,500,000	0/12	--
	€20,000,000		€9,150,000

  * *The number of months between the date when expenditures were made and the date on which interest capitalization stops (December 31, 2009).*

Potential Interest Cost to Be Capitalized

(€8,500,000	×	1.12551)*	− €8,500,000	=	€1,066,840
650,000	×	0.1109**		=	72,020
€9,150,000					€1,138,860

  * *The principal, €8,500,000, is multiplied by the factor for the future amount of €1 for 4 periods at 3% to determine the amount of principal and interest due in 2009.*
  ** *Weighted-average interest rate*

	Principal	Interest
10%, 10-year note	€ 6,000,000	€ 600,000
12%, 5-year note	7,000,000	840,000
	€13,000,000	€1,440,000

$$\frac{\text{Total interest}}{\text{Total principal}} = \frac{€1,440,000}{€13,000,000} = 11.08\%$$

The actual interest is

12%, 4-year note [(€8,500,000 × 1.12551) – €8,500,000]	=	€1,066,840
10%, 10-year note (€6,000,000 × 10%)	=	600,000
12%, 5-year note (€7,000,000 × 12%)	=	840,000
Total interest		€2,506,840

The interest cost to be capitalized is the lesser of €1,138,860 (avoidable interest) or €2,506,840 (actual interest). The remaining €1,367,980 (= €2,506,840 – €1,138,860) must be expensed.

Determining the time period for capitalization of borrowing costs. An entity should begin capitalizing borrowing costs on the commencement date. Three conditions must be met before the capitalization period should begin.

1. Expenditures for the asset are being incurred
2. Borrowing costs are being incurred
3. Activities that are necessary to prepare the asset for its intended use are in progress

As long as these conditions continue, borrowing costs can be capitalized. Expenditures incurred for the asset include only those that have resulted in payments of cash, transfers of other assets or the assumption of interest-bearing liabilities, and are reduced by any progress payments and grants received for that asset.

Necessary activities are interpreted in a very broad manner. They start with the planning process and continue until the qualifying asset is substantially complete and ready to function as intended. These activities may include technical and administrative work prior to actual commencement of physical work, such as obtaining permits and approvals, and may continue after physical work has ceased. Brief, normal interruptions do not stop the capitalization of interest costs. However, if the entity intentionally suspends or delays the activities for some reason, interest costs should not be capitalized from the point of suspension or delay until substantial activities in regard to the asset resume.

If the asset is completed in a piecemeal fashion, the capitalization of interest costs stops for each part as it becomes ready to function as intended. An asset that must be entirely complete before the parts can be used as intended can continue to capitalize interest costs until the total asset becomes ready to function.

Suspension and cessation of capitalization. If there is an extended period during which there is no activity to prepare the asset for its intended use, capitalization of borrowing costs should be suspended. As a practical matter, unless the break in activity is significant, it is usually ignored. Also, if delays are normal and to be expected given the nature of the construction project (such as a suspension of building construction during the winter months), this would have been anticipated as a cost and would not warrant even a temporary cessation of borrowing cost capitalization.

Capitalization would cease when the project has been substantially completed. This would occur when the asset is ready for its intended use or for sale to a customer. The fact that routine minor administrative matters still need to be attended to would not mean that the project had not been completed, however. The measure should be *substantially* complete, in other words, not absolutely finished.

Costs in excess of recoverable amounts. When the carrying amount or the expected ultimate cost of the qualifying asset, including capitalized interest cost, exceeds its recoverable amount (if property, plant, or equipment) or net realizable value (if an item held for resale), it will be necessary to record an adjustment necessary to write the asset carrying value down. Any excess interest cost is thus an impairment, to be recognized immediately in expense.

In the case of plant, property, and equipment, a later write-up may occur due to use of the allowed alternative (i.e., revaluation) treatment, recognizing fair value increases, in which case, as described earlier, recovery of a previously recognized loss will be reported in earnings.

Disclosure requirements. With respect to an entity's accounting for borrowing costs, the financial statements must disclose (1) the amount of borrowing costs capitalized during the period and (2) the capitalization rate used to determine the amount of borrowing costs eligible for capitalization. As noted, this rate will be the weighted-average of rates on all borrowings included in an allocation pool or the actual rate on specific debt identified with a given asset acquisition or construction project.

Effective date. Revised IAS 23 should be applied for annual periods beginning on or after January 1, 2009, with earlier application permitted. If an entity applies this Standard from an earlier date, it should apply to all qualifying assets for which the commencement date for capitalization of borrowing costs is on or after that date.

Key differences between IAS 23 and FAS 34. Revised IAS 23 only achieves convergence in principle to the US GAAP equivalent, FAS 34, *Capitalization of Interest Cost*, and there is not full convergence of accounting treatments for borrowing costs. Key differences between IAS 23 and SFAS 34, as highlighted by IASB, include

- *Definition of borrowing costs.* IAS 23 uses the term "borrowing costs," which is broader than "interest costs" used in FAS 34. US GAAP also provide guidance on the capitalization of derivative gains and losses that are part of the capitalized interest cost. IASB does not address derivative gains and losses.
- *Definition of a qualifying asset.* Some assets that meet the definition of a qualifying asset under IFRS do not meet that definition under US GAAP and vice versa. For example, in some circumstances, FAS 34 includes as qualifying assets investment in investee accounted for under the equity method while under IAS 23 such investments are not qualifying assets. Also, FAS 34 does not permit the capitalization of interest costs on assets acquired with gifts or grants that are restricted by the donor or grantor but IAS 23 does not address such assets.
- *Measurement.* Under IAS 23, an entity must capitalize the actual borrowing costs incurred on that borrowing, while FAS 34 states that the rate of that borrowing may be used. Additionally, several differences exist which relate to the capitalization rate and the treatment of income earned on the temporary investment of actual borrowings.

Impact of changes. Companies that currently apply the benchmark treatment of recognizing borrowing costs as an expense will need changes in systems and processes in order to collect relevant information and calculate the amount of borrowing costs to be capitalized. Other transactions, such as foreign currency borrowings and hedging activities, may also impact the amount of borrowing costs subject to capitalization. In addition, US foreign private issuers may need to maintain two sets of capitalization information—one set under IFRS and one under US GAAP.

Improvements to IFRS

Improvements to IFRS discussed in this chapter, that the IASB published in May 2008, and which are effective for annual periods beginning on or after January 1, 2009, include

- IFRS 5, *Noncurrent Assets Held for Sale and Discontinued Operations*. When a subsidiary is held-for-sale, all of its assets and liabilities should be classified as held-for-sale even if the parent has a sale plan that will result in a loss of control of the subsidiary, while retaining a noncontrolling interest.

- IAS 16, *Property, Plant, and Equipment.* The term "net selling price" is replaced with "fair value less costs to sell" to improve consistency between IAS 16, IFRS 5, and IAS 36. Additionally, items of property, plant, and equipment that have been used for rental purposes and that are to be sold in the ordinary course of business after rental, are to be transferred to inventory when rental ceases, and held for sale. When the asset is sold, proceeds from the sale are recognized as revenues.
- IAS 23, *Borrowing Costs.* Revised definition of borrowing costs consolidated the types of items that are considered components of "borrowing costs" into one—the interest expense calculated using the effective interest rate as described in IAS 39, to emphasize the relationship between IAS 23 and IAS 39.
- IAS 36, *Impairment of Assets.* When discounted cash flows are used to estimate "fair value less costs to sell," the same disclosures are required as if discounted cash flows are calculated to estimate "value in use."

Examples of Financial Statement Disclosures

Novartis AG
Annual Report 2007

1. **Accounting policies**

    Property, plant, and equipment. Land is valued at acquisition cost less accumulated impairment, if any. Prepayments for long-term leasehold land agreements are amortized over the life of the lease.

    Other items of property, plant, and equipment have been valued at cost of acquisition or production cost and are depreciated on a straight-line basis to the income statement over the following estimated useful lives:

Buildings	20 to 40 years
Machinery and equipment	7 to 20 years
Furniture and vehicles	5 to 10 years
Computer hardware	3 to 7 years

    Additional costs which enhance the future economic benefit of property, plant, and equipment are capitalized. Borrowing costs associated with the construction of property, plant, and equipment are not capitalized. Property, plant, and equipment is reviewed for impairment whenever events or changes in circumstances indicate that the balance sheet carrying amount may not be recoverable.

    Property, plant, and equipment which are financed by leases giving Novartis substantially all the risks and rewards of ownership are capitalized at the lower of the fair value of the leased asset or the present value of minimum lease payments at the inception of the lease, and depreciated in the same manner as other assets over the shorter of the lease term or their useful life. Leases in which a significant portion of the risks and rewards of ownership are retained by the lessor are classified as operating leases. These are charged to the income statement over the life of the lease, generally on a straight-line basis.

Notes to the Novartis Group Consolidated Financial Statements

8. **Property, plant, and equipment movements**

USD millions	Land	Buildings	Plant and other equipment under construction	Other property, plant, and equipment	Totals
2007					
Cost					
January 1	570	7,154	1,545	10,434	19,703
Cost of assets related to discontinued operations	(9)	(98)	(15)	(408)	(530)
Impact of business combinations		(37)	(7)	(12)	(56)

USD millions	Land	Buildings	Plant and other equipment under construction	Other property, plant, and equipment	Totals
Reclassifications[1]	16	461	(1,053)	665	89
Additions	18	180	1,904	555	2,657
Disposals	(3)	(133)	(27)	(330)	(493)
Currency translation effects	38	460	170	762	1,430
December 31	630	7,987	2,517	11,666	22,800
Accumulated depreciation					
January 1	(7)	(2,917)		(5,834)	(8,758)
Accumulated depreciation of assets related to discontinued operations		37		211	248
Impact of business combinations		31	1	6	38
Reclassifications	2	(31)		(71)	(100)
Depreciation charge	(2)	(278)		(850)	(1,130)
Depreciation of disposals		91		265	356
Impairment charge	(4)	(87)	(23)	(41)	(155)
Currency translation effects	(1)	(211)		(454)	(666)
December 31	(12)	(3,365)	(22)	(6,768)	(10,167)
Net book value—December 31	618	4,622	2,495	4,898	12,633
Insured value—December 31					24,194
Net book value of property, plant, and equipment under finance lease contracts					9
Commitments for purchases of property, plant, and equipment					690

[1] *Reclassifications between various asset categories due to completion of plant and other requirement under construction and due to the final completion of the Chiron acquisition accounting.*

USD millions	Land	Buildings	Plant and other equipment under construction	Other property, plant, and equipment	Totals
2006					
Cost					
January 1	419	6,067	912	9,116	16,514
Cost of assets related to discontinuing operations	(4)	(79)	(18)	(179)	(280)
Impact of business combinations	117	398	259	257	1,031
Reclassifications[1]	(2)	369	(982)	615	--
Additions	17	124	1,306	393	1,840
Disposals	(5)	(109)	(18)	(464)	(596)
Currency translation effects	28	384	86	696	1,194
December 31	570	7,154	1,545	10,434	19,703
Accumulated depreciation					
January 1	(3)	(2,621)		(5,211)	(7,835)
Accumulated depreciation of assets related to discontinued operations	--	46		129	175
Depreciation charge	(3)	(244)		(769)	(1,016)
Depreciation of disposals		79		416	495
Impairment charge	(1)	1		(11)	(11)
Currency translation effects		(178)		(388)	(566)
December 31	(7)	(2,917)		(5,834)	(8,758)
Net book value—December 31	563	4,237	1,545	4,600	10,945
Insured value—December 31					19,196
Net book value of property, plant, and equipment under finance lease contracts					18
Commitments for purchases of property, plant, & equipment					563

[1] *Reclassifications between various asset categories due to completion of plant and other equipment under construction*

Lectra SA
Financial Report 2007

Summary of significant accounting policies and scope of consolidation
Property, plant, and equipment

Property, plant, and equipment are carried at cost less accumulated depreciation and impairment, if any.

When a tangible asset comprises significant components with different useful lives, the latter are analyzed separately.

Consequently, costs incurred in replacing or renewing a component of a tangible asset are booked as a distinct asset. The carrying value of the component replaced is written off. The useful life of assets is reviewed at each closing date and adjusted as required.

Subsequent expenditures relating to a tangible asset are capitalized if they increase the future economic benefits of the specific asset to which they are attached. All other costs are expensed directly at the time they are incurred.

Financial expense is not included in the cost of acquisition of tangible assets. Investment grants received are deducted from the value of tangible assets.

Depreciation is computed on the straight-line method over their estimated useful lives as follows:

Buildings and building main structures	20–35 years
Secondary structures and building installations	15 years
Fixtures and installations	5–10 years
Land arrangements	5–10 years
Technical installations, equipment, and tools	4–5 years
Office equipment and computers	3–5 years
Office furniture	5–10 years

Fixed asset impairment–impairment tests

When events or changes in the market environment, or internal factors, indicate an impairment of value of goodwill, other intangible assets or property, plant, and equipment, these are subjected to detailed scrutiny. In the case of goodwill, impairment tests are carried out systematically at least once a year.

Goodwill is tested for impairment by comparing its carrying value with its recoverable amount or value in use, which is defined as the present value of future cash flows attached to them, excluding interest and tax. The results utilized are derived from the Group's three-year plan. Beyond the time frame of the three-year plan, cash flows are projected to infinity, the assumed growth rate being dependent on the growth potential of the markets and/or products concerned by the impairment test. The discount rate is the 10-year OAT (French government bond) rate plus a risk premium specific to the activity tested. If the impairment test reveals an impairment of value relative to the carrying value, an irreversible impairment loss is recognized to reduce the carrying value of the goodwill to its recoverable amount. This charge, if any, is recognized under "Goodwill impairment" in the income statement.

Other intangible assets and property, plant, and equipment are tested by comparing the carrying value of each relevant group of assets (which may be an isolated asset or a cash-generating unit) with its recoverable amount. If the latter is less than the carrying value, an impairment charge equal to the difference between these two amounts is recognized. In the case of Lectra's new information system, impairment testing consists in periodically verifying that the initial assumptions regarding the useful life and functions of the system remain valid. The base and the schedule of amortization/depreciation of the assets concerned are reduced if a loss is recognized, the resulting charge being recorded as an amortization/depreciation charge under "Cost of goods sold," "Research and development expenses," or "Selling, general and administrative expenses" in the income statement depending on the nature and use of the assets concerned.

Notes to the consolidated financial statements

Note 3. Property, plant and equipment

(in thousands of euros) 2006	*Land and buildings*	*Fixtures and fittings*	*Equipment and other*	*Total*
Gross value at January 1, 2006	8,162	10,226	19,987	38,375
Additions	898	3,247	2,598	6,743
Write-offs and disposals	--	(325)	(1,648)	(1,973)
Transfers	--	--	109	109
Exchange rate differences	--	(58)	(338)	(396)
Gross value at December 31, 2006	9,060	13,090	20,708	42,858
Accumulated depreciation at December 31, 2006	(6,418)	(6,239)	(15,954)	(28,611)
Net value at December 31, 2006	2,642	6,851	4,754	14,247

(in thousands of euros) 2007				
Gross value at January 1, 2007	9,060	13,090	20,708	42,858
Additions	416	1,135	2,460	4,011
Write-offs and disposals	--	(80)	(857)	(937)
Exchange rate differences	--	(156)	(230)	(386)
Gross value at December 31, 2007	9,476	13,989	22,081	45,546
Accumulated depreciation at December 31, 2007	(6,482)	(7,128)	(16,700)	(30,310)
Net value at December 31, 2007	2,994	6,861	5,381	15,236

Changes in depreciation

(in thousands of euros) 2007				
Accumulated depreciation at January 1, 2007	(6,418)	(6,239)	(15,954)	(28,611)
Additional depreciation	(64)	(1,016)	(1,704)	(2,784)
Write-offs and disposals	--	69	794	863
Exchange rate differences	--	58	164	222
Accumulated depreciation at December 31, 2006	(6,482)	(7,128)	(16,700)	(30,310)

"Land and buildings" pertain solely to the Group's industrial facilities in Bordeaux-Cestas (France), amounting to €9,476,000, net of investment grants received.

The facility covers an area of 11.4 hectares (28.5 acres) and the buildings represent 27,300 m^2 (295,000 sq. ft.). Land and buildings were partly purchased outright by the company, and partly under financial leases. These have been paid for in full.

The assets purchased outright by the company (excluding fixtures and fittings) represent €5,021,000, of which €2,281,000, has been depreciated.

The assets (including fixtures and fittings) purchased under finance leases are valued at €4,745,000 including €473,000 for the land and €4,272,000 for the buildings, depreciated in full. In October 2002, the company became owner of the entire Bordeaux-Cestas land and buildings facilities.

Investments carried out at the Bordeaux-Cestas (France) industrial site in 2007 totaled €402,000. This figure mainly concerned exterior works.

Construction, fixtures and fittings and furnishings for the new facility built in 2006 on the site of the building destroyed in June 2005 represented a total figure of €3,592,000.

"Fixtures and fittings" also comprise €1,334,000 for furnishings, installation fixtures and fittings of the new premises in New York (USA).

No acquisitions of new equipment were made using finance leases in 2006 or 2007.

Other fixed assets purchased in 2006 and 2007 mainly concerned manufacturing molds and tools for the Bordeaux-Cestas (France) industrial facility.

Nestlé S.A.
Annual Report 2007

Accounting policies

Property, plant, and equipment. Property, plant, and equipment are shown in the balance sheet at their historical cost. Depreciation is provided on components that have homogenous useful lives by using the straight-line method so as to depreciate the initial cost down to the residual value over the estimated useful lives. The residual values are 30% on head offices, 20% on distribution centers for products stored at ambient temperature and nil for all other asset types.

The useful lives are as follows:

Buildings	25–35 years
Machinery and equipment	10–20 years
Tools, furniture, information technology, and sundry equipment	3–8 years
Vehicles	5 years

Land is not depreciated.

Useful lives, components and residual amounts are reviewed annually. Such a review takes into consideration the nature of the assets, their intended use and the evolution of technology.

Depreciation of property, plant, and equipment is allocated to the appropriate headings of expenses in the income statement.

Financing costs incurred during the course of construction are expensed. Premiums capitalized for leasehold land or buildings are amortized over the length of the lease.

Notes to the consolidated financial statements

11. Property, plant, and equipment

(in millions of CHF)	Land and buildings	Machinery and equipment	Tools, furniture, and other equipment	Vehicles	Totals 2006
Gross value					
At January 1	12,756	24,525	7,087	874	45,242
Currency retranslations	(210)	(344)	(87)	(11)	(652)
Capital expenditure	774	2,242	1,024	160	4,200
Disposals	(129)	(997)	(369)	(103)	(1,598)
Reclassified as held-for-sale	(69)	(99)	(11)	--	(179)
Modification of the scope of consolidation	123	128	(198)	11	64
At December 31	13,245	25,455	7,446	931	47,077
Accumulated depreciation and impairments					
At January 1	(5,111)	(15,501)	(5,159)	(481)	(26,252)
Currency retranslations	63	155	55	5	278
Depreciation	(408)	(1,295)	(769)	(109)	(2,581)
Impairments	19	(106)	(9)	--	(96)
Disposals	117	910	341	82	1,450
Reclassified as held-for-sale	48	49	8	--	105
Modification of the scope of consolidation	21	56	170	2	249
At December 31	(5,251)	(15,732)	(5,363)	(501)	26,847
Net at December 31	7,994	9,723	2,083	430	20,230

(in millions of CHF)	Land and buildings	Machinery and equipment	Tools, furniture, and other equipment	Vehicles	Totals 2007
Gross value					
At January 1	13,245	25,455	7,446	931	47,077
Currency retranslations	(156)	(478)	(171)	(86)	(891)
Capital expenditure	860	2,695	1,209	207	4,971
Disposals	(258)	(884)	(492)	(78)	(1,712)
Reclassified as held-for-sale	(30)	(38)	(3)	--	(71)
Modification of the scope of consolidation	90	51	3	(44)	100
At December 31	13,751	26,801	7,992	930	49,474

(in millions of CHF)	Land and buildings	Machinery and equipment	Tools, furniture, and other equipment	Vehicles	Totals 2007
Accumulated depreciation and impairments					
At January 1	(5,251)	(15,732)	(5,363)	(501)	(26,847)
Currency retranslations	60	284	60	14	418
Depreciation	(398)	(1,307)	(800)	(115)	(2,620)
Impairments	(26)	(148)	(50)	(1)	(225)
Disposals	165	758	468	67	1,458
Reclassified as held-for-sale	22	30	3	--	55
Modification of the scope of consolidation	80	228	12	32	352
At December 31	(5,348)	(15,887)	(5,670)	(504)	27,409
Net at December 31	8,403	10,914	2,322	426	22,065

At December 31, 2007, property, plant, and equipment include CHF 1178 million of assets under construction. Net property, plant, and equipment held under finance leases amount to CHF 354 million. Net property, plant, and equipment of CHF 117 million are pledged as security for financial liabilities. Fire risks, reasonably estimated, are insured in accordance with domestic requirements.

Nokia Corporation and Subsidiaries
For the Year Ended December 31, 2007

Accounting principles

Property, plant, and equipment. Property, plant, and equipment are stated at cost less accumulated depreciation. Depreciation is recorded on a straight-line basis over the expected useful lives of the assets as follows:

Buildings and constructions	20–33 years
Production machinery, measuring and test equipment	1–3 years
Other machinery and equipment	3–10 years

Land and water areas are not depreciated.

Maintenance, repairs, and renewals are generally charged to expense during the financial period in which they are incurred. However, major renovations are capitalized and included in the carrying amount of the asset when it is probable that future economic benefits in excess of the originally assessed standard of performance of the existing asset will flow to the Group. Major renovations are depreciated over the remaining useful life of the related asset. Leasehold improvements are depreciated over the lease term or useful life, whatever is shorter.

Gains and losses on the disposal of property, plant, and equipment items are including in operating profit/loss.

9. Depreciation and amortization

EURm	2007	2006	2005
Depreciation and amortization by function			
Cost of sales	**303**	279	242
Research and development[1]	**523**	312	349
Selling and marketing	**232**	9	9
Administrative and general	**148**	111	99
Other operating expenses	--	1	13
Total	**1,206**	712	712

[1] *In 2007, depreciation and amortization allocated to research and development and selling and marketing included amortization of acquired intangible assets of EUR 136 million and EUR 214 million, respectively.*

13. Property, plant, and equipment

EURm	*2007*	*2006*
Land and water areas		
Acquisition cost January 1	78	82
Translation differences	(2)	(1)
Additions during the period	4	--
Acquisitions	5	--
Disposals during the period	(12)	(3)
Accumulated acquisition cost December 31	73	78
Net book value January 1	78	82
Net book value December 31	73	78
Buildings and constructions		
Acquisition cost January 1	925	865
Translation differences	(15)	(11)
Additions during the period	97	123
Acquisitions	58	--
Disposals during the period	(57)	(52)
Accumulated acquisition cost December 31	1,008	925
Accumulated depreciation January 1	(230)	(244)
Translation differences	3	4
Disposals during the period	25	40
Depreciation for the period	(37)	(30)
Accumulated depreciation December 31	(239)	(230)
Net book value January 1	695	621
Net book value December 31	769	695
Machinery and equipment		
Acquisition cost January 1	3,707	3,735
Translation differences	(42)	(62)
Additions during the period	448	466
Acquisitions	264	--
Disposals during the period	(365)	(432)
Accumulated acquisition cost December 31	4,012	3,707
Accumulated depreciation January 1	(2,966)	(2,984)
Translation differences	34	48
Disposals during the period	364	429
Depreciation for the period	(539)	(459)
Accumulated depreciation December 31	(3,107)	(2,966)
Net book value January 1	741	751
Net book value December 31	905	741
Other tangible assets		
Acquisition cost January 1	22	17
Translation differences	(1)	(1)
Additions during the period	2	6
Disposals during the period	(3)	--
Accumulated acquisition cost December 31	20	22
Accumulated depreciation January 1	(7)	(6)
Translation difference	--	--
Disposals during the period	1	--
Depreciation for the period	(3)	(1)
Accumulated depreciation December 31	(9)	(7)
Net book value January 1	15	11
Net book value December 31	11	15

9 INTANGIBLE ASSETS

PERSPECTIVE AND ISSUES

Long-lived assets are those that will provide economic benefits to an enterprise for a number of future periods. Accounting standards regarding long-lived assets involve determination of the appropriate cost at which to record the assets initially, the amount at which to measure the assets at subsequent reporting dates, and the appropriate method(s) to be used to allocate the cost over the periods being benefited, if that is appropriate.

Long-lived nonfinancial assets may be classified into two basic types: tangible and intangible. Tangible assets have physical substance, while intangible assets either have no physical substance, or have a value that is not conveyed by what physical substance they do have. For example, the value of computer software is not reasonably measured by the cost of the diskettes or CDs on which these are contained.

The value of an intangible asset is a function of the rights or privileges that its ownership conveys to the business enterprise.

The accounting treatment of intangible assets is not yet in a fully settled and agreed mode. The nineteenth century model from which we draw many of our financial reporting practices was developed when productive capacity was defined by manufacturing plant and equipment. In the postindustrial, knowledge-based economy in which the more developed nations operate today there is a different perspective on what constitutes value for a business. Intellectual property, such as patents and trade names, may be more vital than manufacturing capacity to modern growth companies, typified by Dell Computers, which is a selling organization with a brand name, and whose manufacturing is done by subcontractors in low-cost nations.

The recognition and measurement of intangibles such as brand names is problematical because many brands are internally generated, over a number of years, and there is little or no historical cost to be recognized under IFRS or most national GAAP standards. Thus, the

Dell brand does not appear on Dell's statement of financial position, nor does the Nestlé brand appear on Nestlé's statement of financial position. Concepts, designs, sales networks, brands, and processes are all important elements of what enables one company to succeed while another fails, but the theoretical support for representing them on the statement of financial position is at an early stage of development. For that matter, few companies even attempt to monitor such values for internal management purposes, so it is hardly surprising that the external reporting is still evolving.

We can draw a distinction between internally generated intangibles which are difficult to measure and thus to recognize in the statement of financial position, such as research and development assets and brands, and those that are purchased externally by an entity and therefore have a historical cost. While an intangible can certainly be bought individually, most intangibles arise from acquisitions of other companies, where a bundle of assets and liabilities are acquired.

In this area of activity, we can further distinguish between identifiable intangibles and unidentifiable ones.

Identifiable intangibles include patents, copyrights, brand names, customer lists, trade names, and other specific rights that typically can be conveyed by an owner without necessarily also transferring related physical assets. Goodwill, on the other hand, is a residual which incorporates all the intangibles that cannot be reliably measured separately, and is often analyzed as containing both these and benefits that the acquiring entity expected to gain from the synergies or other efficiencies arising from a business combination and cannot normally be transferred to a new owner without also selling the other assets and/or the operations of the business.

Accounting for goodwill is addressed in IFRS 3, and is discussed in Chapter 11 in this book, in the context of business combinations. In this chapter we will address the recognition and measurement criteria for identifiable intangibles. This includes the criteria for separability and treatment of internally generated intangibles, such as research and development costs.

The subsequent measurement of intangibles depends upon whether they are considered to have indefinite economic value or a definable useful life. The standard on impairment of assets (IAS 36) pertains to both tangible and intangible long-lived assets. This chapter will consider the implications of this standard for the accounting for intangible, separately identifiable assets.

Sources of IFRS			
IFRS 3	*IAS* 23, 36, 38	*SIC* 32	*IFRIC* 4

DEFINITIONS OF TERMS

Active market. A market in which all the following conditions exist: (1) the items traded in the market are homogeneous; (2) willing buyers and sellers can normally be found at any time; and (3) prices are available to the public.

Amortization. Systematic allocation of the depreciable amount of an intangible asset over its useful life.

Asset. Resource (1) controlled by an entity as a result of past events, and (2) from which future economic benefits are expected to flow to the entity.

Carrying amount. The amount at which an asset is recognized in the balance sheet, Net of any accumulated amortization and accumulated impairment losses thereon.

Cash generating unit. The smallest identifiable group of assets that generates cash inflows from continuing use, largely independent of the cash inflows associated with other assets or groups of assets.

Corporate assets. Assets, excluding goodwill, that contribute to future cash flows of both the cash generating unit under review for impairment and other cash generating units.

Cost. Amount of cash or cash equivalent paid or the fair value of other consideration given to acquire an asset at the time of its acquisition or construction or, where applicable, the amount attributed to that asset when initially recognized in accordance with the specific requirements of other IFRS (e.g. IFRS 2, *Share-Based Payment*).

Depreciable amount. Cost of an asset or the other amount that has been substituted for cost, less the residual value of the asset.

Depreciation. Systematic and rational allocation of the depreciable amount of an asset over its useful life.

Development. The application of research findings or other knowledge to a plan or design for the production of new or substantially improved materials, devices, products, processes, systems, or services prior to commencement of commercial production or use. This should be distinguished from *research*, which must be expensed whereas development costs are capitalized.

Entity-specific value. Present value of the cash flows an entity expects to arise from the continuing use of an asset and from its disposal at the end of its useful life or expects to incur when settling a liability.

Fair value. Amount that would be obtained for an asset in an arm's-length exchange transaction between knowledgeable willing parties.

Goodwill. An asset representing the future economic benefits arising from other assets acquired in a business combination that are not individually identified and separately recognized. It is calculated as the excess of the cost of a business acquisition over the fair value of the identifiable net assets acquired.

Impairment loss. The excess of the carrying amount of an asset over its recoverable amount.

Intangible assets. Identifiable nonmonetary assets without physical substance.

Monetary assets. Money held and assets to be received in fixed or determinable amounts of money. Examples are cash, accounts receivable, and notes receivable.

Net selling price. The amount that could be realized from the sale of an asset by means of an arm's-length transaction, less costs of disposal.

Nonmonetary transactions. Exchanges and nonreciprocal transfers that involve little or no monetary assets or liabilities.

Nonreciprocal transfer. Transfer of assets or services in one direction, either from an enterprise to its owners or another entity, or from owners or another entity to the enterprise. An enterprise's reacquisition of its outstanding stock is a nonreciprocal transfer.

Recoverable amount. The greater of an asset's or a cash-generating unit's fair value less costs to sell and its value in use.

Research. The original and planned investigation undertaken with the prospect of gaining new scientific or technical knowledge and understanding. This should be distinguished from *development*, since the latter is capitalized whereas research must be expensed.

Residual value. Estimated amount that an entity would currently obtain from disposal of the asset, net of estimated costs of disposal, if the asset were already of the age and in the condition expected at the end of its useful life.

Useful (economic) life. Period over which an asset is expected to be available for use by an entity; or the number of production or similar units expected to be obtained from the asset by an entity.

CONCEPTS, RULES, AND EXAMPLES

Background

Over the years, the role of intangible assets has grown ever more important for the operations and prosperity of many types of businesses, as the "knowledge-based" economy becomes more dominant. However, until recently, accounting standards have tended to give scant attention to, or ignore entirely, the appropriate means of reporting upon such assets.

IFRS first addressed accounting for intangibles in a thorough way with IAS 38, which was promulgated in 1998 after a rather long and contentious gestation period that included the issuance of two Exposure Drafts. Research and development costs had earlier been addressed by IAS 9 (issued in 1978) and goodwill arising from a business combination was dealt with by IAS 22 (issued in 1983).

IAS 38 is the first comprehensive standard on intangibles and it superseded IAS 9. It established recognition criteria, measurement bases, and disclosure requirements for intangible assets. The standard also stipulates that impairment testing for intangible assets (as specified by IAS 36) is to be undertaken on a regular basis. This is to ensure that only assets having *recoverable values* will be capitalized and carried forward to future periods as assets of the business.

IAS 38 was modified in 2004 to acknowledge that intangible assets could have indefinite useful lives. It had been the intent, when developing IAS 38, to stipulate that intangibles should have a maximum life of twenty years, but when this standard was finally approved, it included a rebuttable presumption that an intangible would have a life of no more than twenty years. The most recent amendment to IAS 38 removed the rebuttable presumption as to maximum economic life, and brings IAS 38 into closer convergence with the corresponding US GAAP standard, FAS 142. As with the US GAAP standard, IAS 38 now includes a list of intangibles that should normally be given separate recognition, and not merely grouped with goodwill, which is to denote only the unidentified intangible asset acquired in a business combination.

The IASB and FASB have placed on their long-term joint agendas a project on accounting for intangibles.

Scope of the standard. IAS 38 applies to all reporting entities. It prescribes the accounting treatment for intangible assets, including development costs, but does not address intangible assets covered by other IFRS. For instance, deferred tax assets are covered under IAS 12; leases fall within the purview of IAS 17; goodwill arising in a business combination is dealt with by IFRS 3; assets arising from employee benefits are covered by IAS 19; and financial assets are defined by IAS 39 and covered by IAS 27, 28, 31, and 39. IAS 38 also does not apply to intangible assets arising in insurance companies from contracts with policyholders within the scope of IFRS 4, nor to exploration and evaluation assets in the extractive industries subject to IFRS 6, nor to intangible assets classified as held-for-sale under IFRS 5.

Identifiable intangible assets include patents, copyrights, licenses, customer lists, brand names, import quotas, computer software, marketing rights, and specialized know-how. These items have in common the fact that there is little or no tangible substance to them, they have an economic life of greater than one year. In many but not all cases, the asset is separable; that is, it could be sold or otherwise disposed of without simultaneously disposing of or diminishing the value of other assets held.

Intangible assets are, by definition, assets that have no physical substance. However, there may be instances where intangibles also have some physical form. For example

- There may be tangible evidence of an asset's existence, such as a certificate indicating that a patent had been granted, but this does constitute the asset itself;

- Some intangible assets may be contained in or on a physical substance such as a compact disc (in the case of computer software); and
- Identifiable assets that result from research and development activities are intangible assets because the tangible prototype or model is secondary to the knowledge that is the primary outcome of those activities.

In the case of assets that have both tangible and intangible elements, there may be uncertainty about whether classification should be as tangible or intangible assets. For example, the IASB has deliberately not specified whether mineral exploration and evaluation assets should be considered as tangible or intangible, but rather, in IFRS 6 (see Chapter 24) has established a requirement that a reporting entity consistently account for exploration and evaluation assets as either tangible or intangible.

As a rule of thumb, an asset that has both tangible and intangible elements should be classified as an intangible asset or a tangible asset based on the relative dominance or comparative significance of the tangible or the intangible components of the asset. For instance, computer software that is not an integral part of the related hardware equipment is treated as software (i.e., as an intangible asset). Conversely, certain computer software, such as the operating system, that is essential and an integral part of a computer, is treated as part of the hardware equipment (i.e., as property, plant, and equipment as opposed to an intangible asset).

Recognition Criteria

Identifiable intangible assets have much in common with tangible long-lived assets (property, plant, and equipment), and the accounting for them is accordingly very similar. Recognition depends on whether the *Framework* definition of an asset is satisfied. The key criteria for determining whether intangible assets are to be recognized are

1. Whether the intangible asset can be identified separately from other aspects of the business entity;
2. Whether the use of the intangible asset is controlled by the entity as a result of its past actions and events;
3. Whether future economic benefits can be expected to flow to the entity; and
4. Whether the cost of the asset can be measured reliably.

Identifiability. IAS 38 states that an intangible meets the identifiability requirement if

1. It is separable (i.e., is capable of being separated or divided from the entity and sold, transferred, licensed, rented or exchanged, either individually or together with a related contract, asset or liability); *or*
2. It arises from contractual or other legal rights, regardless of whether those rights are transferable or separable from the entity or form other rights and obligations.

IAS 38 provides a fairly comprehensive listing of possible separate classes of intangibles. These are

1. Brand names;
2. Mastheads and publishing titles;
3. Computer software;
4. Licenses and franchises;
5. Copyrights, patents and other industrial property rights, service and operating rights;
6. Recipes, formulae, models, designs and prototypes; and
7. Intangible assets under development

The nature of intangibles is such that, as discussed above, many are not recognized at the time that they come into being. The costs of creating many intangibles are typically expensed year by year (e.g., as research costs or other period expenses) before it is clear that an asset has been created. The cost of internal intangible asset development cannot be capitalized retrospectively, and this means that such assets remain off-balance-sheet until and unless the entity is acquired by another entity. The acquiring entity has to allocate the acquisition price over the bundle of assets and liabilities acquired, irrespective of whether those assets and liabilities had been recognized in the acquired company's statement of financial position. For that reason, the notion of identifiability is significant in enabling an allocation of the cost of a business combination to be made.

IASB prefers that as many individual assets be recognized as possible in a business acquisition, because the residual amount of unallocated acquisition cost is treated as goodwill, which provides less transparency to investors and other financial statement users. Furthermore, since goodwill is no longer subject to amortization, and its continued recognition—notwithstanding the impairment testing provision—can be indirectly justified by the creation of internally generated goodwill, improperly combining identifiable intangibles with goodwill can have long-term effects on the representational faithfulness of the entity's financial statements.

The revised IFRS 3, *Business Combinations,* issued in January 2008, introduced new approaches to measuring and recognizing the assets acquired and the liabilities assumed in business combinations. The standard reinforces the presumption that the acquirer should recognize, separately from goodwill, the acquisition-date fair value of an intangible asset acquired in a business combination if it meets the criteria provided in revised IAS 38. (This matter is discussed in detail in Chapter 11).

Control. The provisions of IAS 38 require that an enterprise should be in a position to control the use of any intangible asset that is to be presented in the entity's statement of financial position. Control implies the power to both obtain future economic benefits from the asset as well as restrict others' access to those benefits. Normally, enterprises register patents, copyrights, etc. to ensure control over these intangible assets, although entities often have to engage in litigation to preserve that control.

A patent provides the registered owner (or licensee) the exclusive right to use the underlying product or process without any interference or infringement from others. In contrast with these, intangible assets arising from technical knowledge of staff, customer loyalty, long-term training benefits, etc., will have difficulty meeting this recognition criteria in spite of expected future economic benefits to be derived from them. This is due to the fact that the enterprise would find it impossible to fully control these resources or to prevent others from controlling them.

For instance, even if an enterprise expends considerable resources on training that will supposedly increase staff skills, the economic benefits from skilled staff cannot be controlled, since trained employees could leave their current employment and move on in their career to other employers. Hence, staff training expenditures, no matter how material in amount, do not so far qualify as an intangible asset.

Future economic benefits. Generally an asset is recognized only if it is *probable* that future economic benefits specifically associated therewith will flow to the reporting entity, and the cost of the asset can be *measured reliably.* Traditionally, the probability issue acts as an on-off switch. If the future cash flow is *more likely than not* to occur, the item is recognized, but if the cash flow is less likely to occur, nothing is recognized. However, under IFRS 3, where an intangible asset is acquired as part of a business combination, it is valued at fair value, and the fair value computation is affected by the probability that the future cash flow will occur. Under the fair value approach the recorded amount is determined as the present value of the cash flow, adjusted for the likelihood of receiving it, as well as for the time value of money. Even with a low probability of cash flow ultimately occurring, fair value will have some positive measure, and an asset will be recognized.

The IASB acknowledged in the IFRS 3 Basis for Conclusions that there is a discrepancy between this standard and the concept expressed in the *Framework*, but it took the view that this will most likely be resolved in due course by amending the *Framework*. In other words, there will be a more general movement to incorporating the concept of probability in the measurement of assets, instead of using likelihood as a recognition threshold criterion.

The future economic benefits envisaged by the standard may take the form of revenue from the sale of products or services, cost savings, or other benefits resulting from the use of the intangible asset by the entity. A good example of other benefits resulting from the use of the intangible asset is the use by an entity of a secret formula (which the entity has protected legally) that leads to reduced levels of competition in the marketplace, thus enhancing the prospects for substantial and profitable future sales and reduced expenditures on such matters as product development and advertising.

Measurement of the Cost of Intangibles

The conditions under which the intangible asset has been acquired will determine the measurement of its cost.

The cost of an intangible asset acquired separately is determined in a manner largely analogous to that for tangible long-lived assets as described in Chapter 8. Thus, the cost comprises the purchase price, including any taxes and import duties, less any trade discounts and rebates, plus any directly attributable cost incurred in preparing the asset for its intended use. Directly attributable costs would include fully loaded labor costs, thus including employee benefits arising directly from bringing the asset to its working condition. It would also include outside professional fees incurred in bringing the asset to its working condition, costs of testing whether the asset is functioning properly, and other incremental costs.

As with tangible assets, capitalization of costs ceases at the point when the intangible asset is ready to be placed in service in the manner intended by management. Any costs incurred in using or redeploying intangible assets are accordingly to be excluded from the cost of those assets. Thus, any costs incurred while the asset is capable of being used in the manner intended by management, but while it has yet to be placed into service, would be expensed, not capitalized. Similarly, initial operating losses, such as those incurred while demand for the asset's productive outputs is being developed, cannot be capitalized. Examples of expenditures that are not part of the cost of an intangible asset include costs of introducing a new product or service, costs of conducting business in a new location or with a new class of customers, and administration and other general overhead costs. On the other hand, further costs incurred for the purpose of improving the asset's level of performance would qualify for capitalization. In all these particulars, guidance under IAS 38 mirrors that under IAS 16.

According to IAS 38, the cost of an intangible asset acquired as part of a business combination is its fair value as at the date of acquisition. If the intangible asset can be freely traded in an active market, then the quoted market price is the best measurement of cost. If the intangible asset has no active market, then cost is determined based on the amount that the entity would have paid for the asset in an arm's-length transaction at the date of acquisition. If the cost of an intangible asset acquired as part of a business combination cannot be measured reliably, then that asset is not separately recognized, but rather, is included in goodwill. This fall-back position is to be used only when direct identification of the intangible asset's value cannot be accomplished.

If payment for an intangible asset is deferred beyond normal credit terms, its cost is the cash price equivalent. The difference between this amount and the total payments is recognized as financing cost over the period of credit unless it is capitalized in accordance with IAS 23. Recently amended IAS 23 has eliminated the former option of recognizing financing costs immediately as an expense, to the extent that they are directly attributable to the acquisition, construction, or production of a qualifying asset. (See Chapter 8.)

IFRIC 4 describes arrangements comprising a transaction, or a series of related transactions, that does not take the legal form of a lease, but which nonetheless conveys a right to use an asset in return for a payment or series of payments. If an arrangement in substance contains a lease, that lease should be classified as a finance lease or an operating lease in accordance with IAS 17. Other elements of the arrangement, not within the scope of IAS 17, should be accounted for in accordance with other standards (e.g., IAS 38). This interpretation is discussed in Chapter 14.

Intangibles acquired through an exchange of assets. In other situations, intangible assets may be acquired in exchange or partly *in exchange for other dissimilar intangible* or other assets. The same *commercial substance* rules under IAS 16 apply under IAS 38. If the exchange will affect the future cash flows of the entity, then it has commercial substance, and the acquired asset is recognized at its fair value, and the asset given up is also measured at fair value. Any difference between carrying value of the asset(s) given up and those acquired will be given recognition as a gain or loss. However, if there is no commercial substance to the exchange, or the fair values cannot be measured reliably, then the value used is that of the asset given up.

Internally generated goodwill is not recognized as an intangible asset because it fails to meet recognition criteria including

- Reliable measurement of cost,
- An identity separate from other resources, and
- Control by the reporting entity.

In practice, accountants are often confronted with the reporting entity's desire to recognize internally generated goodwill based on the premise that at a certain point in time the market value of an enterprise exceeds the carrying value of its identifiable net assets. However, IAS 38 categorically states that such differences cannot be considered to represent the cost of intangible assets *controlled by the entity,* and hence could not meet the criteria for recognition (i.e., capitalization) of such an asset on the books of the entity. Nonetheless, standard setters are concerned that when an entity tests a cash-generating unit for impairment, internally generated goodwill cannot be separated from acquired goodwill, and that it forms a cushion against impairment of acquired goodwill. In other words, when an entity has properly recognized goodwill (i.e., that acquired in a business combination), implicitly there is the likelihood that internally generated goodwill may well achieve recognition in later periods, to the extent that this offsets the impairment of goodwill.

Intangibles acquired at little or no cost by means of government grants. If the intangible is acquired without cost or by payment of nominal consideration, as by means of a government grant (e.g., when the government grants the right to operate a radio station) or similar means, and assuming the historical cost treatment is being utilized to account for these assets, obviously there will be little or no amount reflected as an asset. If the asset is important to the reporting entity's operations, however, it must be adequately disclosed in the notes to the financial statements.

If the revaluation method of accounting for the asset is used, as permitted under IFRS, the fair value should be determined by reference to an active market. However, given the probable lack of an active market, since government grants are virtually never transferable, it is unlikely that this situation will be encountered. If an active market does not exist for this type of an intangible asset, the enterprise must recognize the asset at cost. Cost would include those that are directly attributable to preparing the asset for its intended use. Government grants, the accounting for which is under review, are addressed in Chapter 26.

Internally Generated Intangibles other than Goodwill

In many instances, intangibles are generated internally by an entity, rather than being acquired via a business combination or some other acquisitions. Because of the nature of intangibles, the measurement of the cost (i.e., the initial amounts at which these could be recognized as assets) is constrained by the fact that many of the costs have already been expensed by the time the entity is able to determine that an asset has indeed been created. For example, when launching a new magazine, an entity may have to operate the magazine at a loss in its early years, expensing large promotional and other costs which all flow through profit or loss, before such time as the magazine can be determined to have become established, and have branding that might be taken to represent an intangible asset. At the point the brand is determined to be an asset, all the costs of creating it have already been expensed, and no retrospective adjustment is allowed to create a recognized asset.

IAS 38 provides that internally generated intangible assets are to be capitalized and amortized over the projected period of economic utility, provided that certain criteria are met.

Expenditures pertaining to the creation of intangible assets are to be classified alternatively as being indicative of, or analogous to, either research activity or development activity. The former costs are entirely expensed as incurred; the latter are capitalized, if future economic benefits are reasonably likely to be received by the reporting entity. Per IAS 38,

1. Costs incurred in the *research* phase are expensed immediately; and
2. If costs incurred in the *development* phase meet the recognition criteria for an intangible asset, such costs should be capitalized. However, once costs have been expensed during the development phase, they cannot later be capitalized.

In practice, distinguishing research-like expenditures from development-like expenditures might not be easily accomplished. This would be especially true in the case of intangibles for which the measurement of economic benefits cannot be accomplished in anything approximating a direct manner. Assets such as brand names, mastheads, and customer lists can prove quite resistant to such direct observation of value (although in many industries there are rules of thumb, such as the notion that a customer list in the securities brokerage business is worth $1,500 per name, implying the amount of promotional costs a purchaser of a customer list could avoid incurring itself).

Thus, entities may incur certain expenditures in order to enhance brand names, such as engaging in image-advertising campaigns, but these costs will also have ancillary benefits, such as promoting specific products that are being sold currently, and possibly even enhancing employee morale and performance. While it may be argued that the expenditures create or add to an intangible asset, as a practical matter it would be difficult to determine what portion of the expenditures relate to which achievement, and to ascertain how much, if any, of the cost may be capitalized as part of brand names. Thus, it is considered to be unlikely that threshold criteria for recognition can be met in such a case. For this reason IAS 38 has specifically disallowed the capitalization of internally generated assets like brands, mastheads, publishing titles, customer lists, and items similar in substance to these.

Apart from the prohibited items, however, IAS 38 permits recognition of internally created intangible assets to the extent the expenditures can be analogized to the development phase of a research and development program. Thus, internally developed patents, copyrights, trademarks, franchises, and other assets will be recognized at the cost of creation, exclusive of costs which would be analogous to research, as further explained in the following paragraphs. The Basis for Conclusion to IAS 38 notes that "some view these requirements and guidance as being too restrictive and arbitrary" and that they reflect the standard setter's interpretation of the recognition criteria, but it agrees that they reflect the fact that it is difficult in practice to determine whether there is an internally generated asset separate from internally generated goodwill.

When an internally generated intangible asset meets the recognition criteria, the cost is determined using the same principles as for an acquired tangible asset. Thus, cost comprises all costs directly attributable to creating, producing, and preparing the asset for its intended use. IAS 38 closely mirrors IAS 16 with regard to elements of cost that may be considered as part of the asset, and the need to recognize the cash equivalent price when the acquisition transaction provides for deferred payment terms. As with self-constructed tangible assets, elements of profit must be eliminated from amounts capitalized, but incremental administrative and other overhead costs can be allocated to the intangible and included in the asset's cost. Initial operating losses, on the other hand, cannot be deferred by being added to the cost of the intangible, but rather must be expensed as incurred.

The standard takes this view based on the premise that an enterprise cannot demonstrate that the expenditure incurred in the research phase will generate probable future economic benefits, and consequently, that an intangible asset has been created (therefore, such expenditure should be expensed). Examples of research activities include: activities aimed at obtaining new knowledge; the search for, evaluation, and final selection of applications of research findings; and the search for and formulation of alternatives for new and improved systems, etc.

The standard recognizes that the development stage is further advanced towards ultimate commercial exploitation of the product or service being created than is the research stage. It acknowledges that an enterprise can possibly, in certain cases, identify an intangible asset and demonstrate that this asset will probably generate future economic benefits for the organization. Accordingly, IAS 38 allows recognition of an intangible asset during the development phase, provided the enterprise can demonstrate *all* of the following:

- Technical feasibility of completing the intangible asset so that it will be available for use or sale;
- Its intention to complete the intangible asset and either use it or sell it;
- Its ability to use or sell the intangible asset;
- The mechanism by which the intangible will generate probable future economic benefits;
- The availability of adequate technical, financial and other resources to complete the development and to use or sell the intangible asset; and
- The entity's ability to reliably measure the expenditure attributable to the intangible asset during its development.

Examples of development activities include: the design and testing of preproduction models; design of tools, jigs, molds, and dies; design of a pilot plant which is not otherwise commercially feasible; design and testing of a preferred alternative for new and improved systems, etc.

Recognition of internally generated computer software costs. The recognition of computer software costs poses several questions.

1. In the case of a company developing software programs for sale, should the costs incurred in developing the software be expensed, or should the costs be capitalized and amortized?

2. Is the treatment for developing software programs different if the program is to be used for in-house applications only?

3. In the case of purchased software, should the cost of the software be capitalized as a tangible asset or as an intangible asset, or should it be expensed fully and immediately?

In view of IAS 38's provisions the position can be clarified as follows:

1. In the case of a software-developing company, the costs incurred in the development of software programs are research and development costs. Accordingly, all expenses incurred in the research phase would be expensed. That is, all expenses incurred before *technological feasibility* for the product has been established should be expensed. The reporting entity would have to demonstrate both technological feasibility and a probability of its commercial success. Technological feasibility would be established if the entity has completed a detailed program design or working model. The entity should have completed the planning, designing, coding, and testing activities and established that the product can be successfully produced. Apart from being capable of production, the entity should demonstrate that it has the intention and ability to use or sell the program. Action taken to obtain control over the program in the form of copyrights or patents would support capitalization of these costs. At this stage the software program would be able to meet the criteria of identifiability, control, and future economic benefits, and can thus be capitalized and amortized as an intangible asset.

2. In the case of software internally developed for in-house use—for example, a computerized payroll program developed by the reporting entity itself—the accounting approach would be different. While the program developed may have some utility to the entity itself, it would be difficult to demonstrate how the program would generate future economic benefits to the enterprise. Also, in the absence of any legal rights to control the program or to prevent others from using it, the recognition criteria would not be met. Further, the cost proposed to be capitalized should be recoverable. In view of the impairment test prescribed by the standard, the carrying amount of the asset may not be recoverable and would accordingly have to be adjusted. Considering the above facts, such costs may need to be expensed.

3. In the case of purchased software, the treatment could differ and would need to be evaluated on a case-by-case basis. Software purchased for sale would be treated as inventory. However, software held for licensing or rental to others should be recognized as an intangible asset. On the other hand, cost of software purchased by an entity for its own use and which is integral to the hardware (because without that software the equipment cannot operate), would be treated as part of cost of the hardware and capitalized as property, plant, or equipment. Thus, the cost of an operating system purchased for an in-house computer, or cost of software purchased for computer-controlled machine tool, are treated as part of the related hardware.

    The costs of other software programs should be treated as intangible assets (as opposed to being capitalized along with the related hardware), as they are not an integral part of the hardware. For example, the cost of payroll or inventory software (purchased) may be treated as an intangible asset provided it meets the capitalization criteria under IAS 38. In practice, the conservative approach would be to expense such costs as they are incurred, since their ability to generate future economic benefits will always be questionable. If the costs are capitalized, useful lives should be conservatively estimated (i.e., kept brief) because of the well-known risk of technological obsolescence.

Example of software developed for internal use

The Hy-Tech Services Corporation employs researchers based in countries around the world. Employee time is the basis upon which charges to many customers are made. The geographically dispersed nature of its operations makes it extremely difficult for the payroll staff to collect time records, so the management team authorizes the design of an in-house, Web-based timekeeping system. The project team incurs the following costs:

Cost type	Charged to expense	Capitalized
Concept design	€ 2,500	
Evaluation of design alternatives	3,700	
Determination of required technology	8,100	
Final selection of alternatives	1,400	
Software design		€ 28,000
Software coding		42,000
Quality assurance testing		30,000
Data conversion costs	3,900	
Training	14,000	
Overhead allocation	6,900	
General and administrative costs	11,200	
Ongoing maintenance costs	6,000	
Totals	€57,700	€100,000

Thus, the total capitalized cost of this development project is €100,000. The estimated useful life of the timekeeping system is five years. As soon as all testing is completed, Hy-Tech's controller begins amortizing using a monthly charge of €1,666.67. The calculation follows:

€100,000 capitalized cost ÷ 60 months = €1,666.67 amortization charge

Once operational, management elects to construct another module for the system that issues an e-mail reminder for employees to complete their timesheets. This represents significant added functionality, so the design cost can be capitalized. The following costs are incurred:

Labor type	Labor cost	Payroll taxes	Benefits	Total cost
Software developers	€11,000	€ 842	€1,870	€13,712
Quality assurance testers	7,000	536	1,190	8,726
Totals	€18,000	€1,378	€3,060	€22,438

The full €22,438 amount of these costs can be capitalized. By the time this additional work is completed, the original system has been in operation for one year, thereby reducing the amortization period for the new module to four years. The calculation of the monthly straight-line amortization follows:

€22,438 capitalized cost ÷ 48 months = €467.46 amortization charge

The Hy-Tech management then authorizes the development of an additional module that allows employees to enter time data into the system from their cell phones using text messaging. Despite successfully passing through the concept design stage, the development team cannot resolve interface problems on a timely basis. Management elects to shut down the development project, requiring the charge of all €13,000 of programming and testing costs to expense in the current period.

After the system has been operating for two years, a Hy-Tech customer sees the timekeeping system in action and begs management to sell it as a stand-alone product. The customer becomes a distributor, and lands three sales in the first year. From these sales Hy-Tech receives revenues of €57,000, and incurs the following related expenses:

Expense type	Amount
Distributor commission (25%)	€14,250
Service costs	1,900
Installation costs	4,300
Total	€20,450

Thus, the net proceeds from the software sale is €36,550 (= €57,000 revenue less €20,450 related costs). Rather than recording these transactions as revenue and expense, the €36,550 net proceeds are offset against the remaining unamortized balance of the software asset with the following entry:

Revenue	57,000	
Fixed assets—software		36,550
Commission expense		14,250
Service expense		1,900
Installation expense		4,300

At this point, the remaining unamortized balance of the timekeeping system is €40,278, which is calculated as follows:

Original capitalized amount	€100,000
+ Additional software module	22,438
– 24 month's amortization on original capitalized amount	(40,000)
– 12 month's amortization on additional software module	(5,610)
– Net proceeds from software sales	(36,550)
Total unamortized balance	€ 40,278

Immediately thereafter, Hy-Tech's management receives a sales call from an application service provider who manages an Internet-based timekeeping system. The terms offered are so attractive that Hy-Tech abandons its in-house system at once and switches to the server system. As a result of this change, the company writes off the remaining unamortized balance of its timekeeping system with the following entry:

Accumulated amortization	45,610	
Loss on asset disposal	40,278	
Fixed assets—software		85,888

Costs Not Satisfying the IAS 38 Recognition Criteria

The standard has specifically provided that expenditures incurred for nonfinancial intangible assets should be recognized as an expense unless

1. It relates to an intangible asset dealt with in another IAS;
2. The cost forms part of the cost of an intangible asset that meets the recognition criteria prescribed by IAS 38; or
3. It is acquired in a business combination and cannot be recognized as an identifiable intangible asset. In this case, this expenditure should form part of the amount attributable to goodwill as at the date of acquisition.

As a consequence of applying the above criteria, the following costs are expensed as they are incurred:

- Research costs;
- Preopening costs for a new facility or business, and plant start-up costs incurred during a period prior to full-scale production or operation, unless these costs are capitalized as part of the cost of an item of property, plant, and equipment;
- Organization costs such as legal and secretarial costs, which are typically incurred in establishing a legal entity;
- Training costs involved in operating a business or a product line;
- Advertising and related costs;
- Relocation, restructuring, and other costs involved in organizing a business or product line;
- Customer lists, brands, mastheads, and publishing titles that are internally generated.

In some countries enterprises have previously been allowed to defer and amortize setup costs and preoperating costs on the premise that benefits from them flow to the enterprise over future periods as well. IAS 38 does not condone this view.

The criteria for recognition of intangible assets as provided in IAS 38 are rather stringent, and many enterprises will find that expenditures either to acquire or to develop intangible assets will fail the test for capitalization. In such instances, all these costs must be expensed currently as incurred. Furthermore, once expensed, these costs cannot be resurrected and capitalized in a later period, even if the conditions for such treatment are later met. This is not meant, however, to preclude correction of an error made in an earlier period if the conditions for capitalization were met but interpreted incorrectly by the reporting entity at that time.

Improvements to IFRS published by the IASB in May 2008 included two amendments to IAS 38. One improvement clarifies that certain expenditures are recognized as an expense when the entity either has access to the goods or has received the services. Examples of expenditures that are recognized as an expense when incurred include research costs, expenditure on start-up activities, training activities, advertising and promotional activities and on relocating or reorganizing part or all of an entity. Advertising and promotional activities now specifically include mail-order catalogues. Logically, these expenditures have difficult-to-measure future economic benefits (e.g., advertising), or are not controlled by the reporting entity (e.g., training), and therefore do not meet the threshold conditions for recognition as assets. For some entities this amendment may result in expenditures being recognized as an expense earlier than in the past.

In addition, a second improvement to IAS 38 removed the reference to the use of anything other than the straight-line method of amortization being rare, and makes it clear that entities may use the unit of production method of amortization even if it results in a lower amount of accumulated amortization than does the straight-line method. This would specifically apply to some service concession arrangements, where an intangible asset for the right to charge users for public service is created. Consequently, entities will have more flexibility as to the method of amortization of intangible assets and will need to evaluate a pattern of future benefits arising from those assets when selecting the method.

Subsequently Incurred Costs

Under the provisions of IAS 38, the capitalization of any subsequent costs incurred on recognized intangible assets is difficult to justify. This is because the nature of an intangible asset is such that, in many cases, it is not possible to determine whether subsequent costs are likely to enhance the specific economic benefits that will flow to the enterprise from those assets. Thus, subsequent costs incurred on an intangible asset should be recognized as an expense when they are incurred unless

1. It is probable that those costs will enable the asset to generate specifically attributable future economic benefits in excess of its assessed standard of performance immediately prior to the incremental expenditure; and
2. Those costs can be measured reliably and attributed to the asset reliably.

Thus, if the above two criteria are both met, any subsequent expenditure on an intangible after its purchase or its completion should be capitalized along with its cost. The following example should help to illustrate this point better.

Example

An enterprise is developing a new product. Costs incurred by the R&D department in 2008 on the "research phase" amounted to €200,000. In 2009, technical and commercial feasibility of the product was established. Costs incurred in 2009 were €20,000 personnel costs and €15,000 legal fees to register the patent. In 2010, the enterprise incurred €30,000 to successfully defend a legal suit to protect the patent. The enterprise would account for these costs as follows:

- Research and development costs incurred in 2008, amounting to €200,000, should be expensed, as they do not meet the recognition criteria for intangible assets. The costs do not result in an identifiable asset capable of generating future economic benefits.
- Personnel and legal costs incurred in 2009, amounting to €35,000, would be capitalized as patents. The company has established technical and commercial feasibility of the product, as well as obtained control over the use of the asset. The standard specifically prohibits the reinstatement of costs previously recognized as an expense. Thus €200,000, recognized as an expense in the previous financial statements, cannot be reinstated and capitalized.
- Legal costs of €30,000 incurred in 2010 to defend the enterprise in a patent lawsuit should be expensed. Under US GAAP, legal fees and other costs incurred in successfully defending a patent lawsuit can be capitalized in the patents account, to the extent that value is evident, because such costs are incurred to establish the legal rights of the owner of the patent. However, in view of the stringent conditions imposed by IAS 38 concerning the recognition of subsequent costs, only such subsequent costs should be capitalized which would enable the asset to generate future economic benefits *in excess of the originally assessed standards of performance*. This represents, in most instances, a very high, possibly insurmountable hurdle. Thus, legal costs incurred in connection with defending the patent, which could be considered as expenses incurred to maintain the asset at its originally assessed standard of performance, would not meet the recognition criteria under IAS 38.
- Alternatively, if the enterprise were to lose the patent lawsuit, then the useful life and the recoverable amount of the intangible asset would be in question. The enterprise would be required to provide for any impairment loss, and in all probability, even to fully write off the intangible asset. What is required must be determined by the facts of the specific situation.

Measurement subsequent to Initial Recognition

IAS 38 acknowledges the validity of two alternative measurement bases: the cost model and the revaluation model. This is entirely comparable to what is prescribed under IAS 16 relative to tangible long-lived assets.

Cost model. After initial recognition, an intangible asset should be carried at its cost less any accumulated amortization and any accumulated impairment losses.

Revaluation model. As with tangible assets, the standard for intangibles permits revaluation subsequent to original acquisition, with the asset being written up to fair value. Inasmuch as most of the particulars of IAS 38 follow IAS 16 to the letter, and were described in detail in Chapter 8, these will not be repeated here. The unique features of IAS 38 are as follows:

1. If the intangibles were not initially recognized (i.e., they were expensed rather than capitalized) it would not be possible to later recognize them at fair value.
2. Deriving fair value by applying a present value concept to projected cash flows (a technique that can be used in the case of tangible assets under IAS 16) is deemed to be too unreliable in the realm of intangibles, primarily because it would tend to commingle the impact of identifiable assets and goodwill. Accordingly, fair value of an intangible asset should *only* be determined by reference to an active market in that type of intangible asset. Active markets providing meaningful data are not expected to exist for such unique assets as patents and trademarks, and thus it is presumed that revaluation will not be applied to these types of assets in the normal course of business. As a consequence, the standard effectively restricts revaluation of intangible assets to freely tradable intangible assets.

As with the rules pertaining to plant, property, and equipment under IAS 16, if some intangible assets in a given class are subjected to revaluation, all the assets in that class should be consistently accounted for unless fair value information is not or ceases to be available. Also in common with the requirements for tangible fixed assets, IAS 38 requires that revaluations be recognized in other comprehensive income and accumulated in equity in the revaluation surplus account for that asset, except to the extent that previous impairments had been recognized by a charge against profit, in which case the recovery would also be recognized in profit. If recovery is recognized in profit, any revaluation above what the carrying value would have been absent the impairment is to be recognized in other comprehensive income.

Example of revaluation of intangible assets

A patent right is acquired July 1, 2009, for €250,000; while it has a legal life of 15 years, due to rapidly changing technology, management estimates a useful life of only five years. Straight-line amortization will be used. At January 1, 2010, management is uncertain that the process can actually be made economically feasible, and decides to write down the patent to an estimated market value of €75,000. Amortization will be taken over three years from that point. On January 1, 2012, having perfected the related production process, the asset is now appraised at a sound value of €300,000. Furthermore, the estimated useful life is now believed to be six more years. The entries to reflect these events are as follows:

7/1/09	Patent	250,000	
	Cash, etc.		250,000
12/31/09	Amortization expense	25,000	
	Patent		25,000
1/1/10	Loss from asset impairment	150,000	
	Patent		150,000
12/31/10	Amortization expense	25,000	
	Patent		25,000
12/31/11	Amortization expense	25,000	
	Patent		25,000
1/1/12	Patent	275,000	
	Gain on asset value recovery		100,000
	Other comprehensive income		175,000

Certain of the entries in the foregoing example will be explained further. The entry at year-end 2009 is to record amortization based on original cost, since there had been no revaluations through that time; only a half-year amortization is provided [(€250,000/5) × 1/2]. On January 1, 2010, the impairment is recorded by writing down the asset to the estimated value of €75,000, which necessitates a €150,000 charge against profit (carrying value, €225,000, less fair value, €75,000).

In 2010 and 2011, amortization must be provided on the new lower value recorded at the beginning of 2010; furthermore, since the new estimated life was three years from January 2010, annual amortization will be €25,000.

As of January 1, 2012, the carrying value of the patent is €25,000; had the January 2010 revaluation not been made, the carrying value would have been €125,000 (€250,000 original cost, less two-and-one-half years amortization versus an original estimated life of five years). The new appraised value is €300,000, which will fully recover the earlier write-down and add even more asset value than the originally recognized cost. Under the guidance of IAS 38, the recovery of €100,000 that had been charged to expense should be recognized as profit; the excess will be recognized in other comprehensive income and increases the revaluation surplus for the asset in shareholders' equity.

Development costs pose a special problem in terms of the application of the revaluation method under IAS 38. In general, it will not be possible to obtain fair value data from active markets, as is required by IAS 38. Accordingly, the expectation is that the cost method will be almost universally applied for development costs.

Example of development cost capitalization

Assume that Creative, Incorporated incurs substantial research and development costs for the invention of new products, many of which are brought to market successfully. In particular, Creative has incurred costs during 2009 amounting to €750,000, relative to a new manufacturing process. Of these costs, €600,000 were incurred prior to December 1, 2009. As of December 31 the viability of the new process was still not known, although testing had been conducted on December 1. In fact, results were not conclusively known until February 15, 2010, after another €75,000 in costs were incurred post–January 1. Creative, Incorporated's financial statements for 2009 were issued February 10, 2010, and the full €750,000 in research and development costs were expensed, since it was not yet known whether a portion of these qualified as development costs under IAS 38. When it is learned that feasibility had, in fact, been shown as of December 1, Creative management asks to restore the €150,000 of post–December 1 costs as a development asset. Under IAS 38 this is prohibited. However, the 2010 costs (€75,000 thus far) would qualify for capitalization, in all likelihood, based on the facts known.

If, however, it is determined that fair value information derived from active markets is indeed available, and the enterprise desires to apply the revaluation method of accounting to development costs, then it will be necessary to perform revaluations on a regular basis, such that at any reporting date the carrying amounts are not materially different from the current fair values. From a mechanical perspective, the adjustment to fair value can be accomplished either by "grossing up" the cost and the accumulated amortization accounts proportionally, or by netting the accumulated amortization, prior to revaluation, against the asset account and then restating the asset to the net fair value as of the revaluation date. In either case, the net effect of the upward revaluation will be recognized in other comprehensive income and accumulated in equity; the only exception would be when an upward revaluation is in effect a reversal of a previously recognized impairment which was reported as a charge against profit or a revaluation decrease (reversal or a yet earlier upward adjustment) which was reflected in profit or loss.

The accounting for revaluations is illustrated as follows:

Example of accounting for revaluation of development cost

Assume Breakthrough, Inc. has accumulated development costs that meet the criteria for capitalization at December 31, 2009, amounting to €39,000. It is estimated that the useful life of this intangible asset will be six years; accordingly, amortization of €6,500 per year is anticipated. Breakthrough uses the allowed alternative method of accounting for its long-lived tangible and intangible assets. At December 31, 2011, it obtains market information regarding the then-current fair value of this intangible asset, which suggests a current fair value of these development costs is €40,000; the estimated useful life, however, has not changed. There are two ways to apply IAS 38: the asset and accumulated amortization can be "grossed up" to reflect the new fair value information, or the asset can be restated on a "net" basis. These are both illustrated below. For both illustrations, the book value (amortized cost) immediately prior to the revaluation is €39,000 – (2 × €6,500) = €26,000. The net upward revaluation is given by the difference between fair value and book value, or €40,000 – €26,000 = €14,000.

If the "gross up" method is used: Since the fair value after two years of the six-year useful life have already elapsed is found to be €40,000, the gross fair value must be 6/4 × €40,000 = €60,000. The entries to record this would be as follows:

Development cost (asset)	21,000	
Accumulated amortization—development cost		7,000
Other comprehensive income		14,000

If the "netting" method is used: Under this variant, the accumulated amortization as of the date of the revaluation is eliminated against the asset account, which is then adjusted to reflect the net fair value.

Accumulated amortization—development cost	13,000	
Development cost (asset)		13,000
Development cost (asset)	14,000	
Other comprehensive income		14,000

The existing balance in other comprehensive income is closed at the end of the year and its balance accumulated in equity in the revaluation surplus account.

Amortization Period

IAS 38, as revised in 2004, requires the entity to determine whether an intangible has a finite or indefinite useful life. An indefinite future life means that there is no foreseeable limit on the period during which the asset is expected to generate future cash flows. The standard lists a number of factors to be taken into account:

1. The expected usage by the entity;
2. Typical product life cycles for the asset;
3. Technical, technological, commercial or other types of obsolescence;
4. The stability of the industry in which the asset operates;
5. Expected actions by competitors;
6. The level of maintenance expenditures required to generate the future economic benefits, and the company's ability and intention to reach such a level;
7. The period of control over the asset and legal or similar limits on the use of the asset;
8. Whether the useful life of the asset is dependent on the useful life of other assets.

Assets having a finite useful life must be amortized over that useful life, and this may be done in any of the usual ways (pro rata over time, over units of production, etc.). If control over the future economic benefits from an intangible asset is achieved through legal rights for a finite period, then the useful life of the intangible asset should not exceed the period of legal rights, unless the legal rights are renewable and the renewal is a virtual certainty. Thus, as a practical matter, the shorter legal life will set the upper limit for an amortization period in most cases.

The amortization method used should reflect the pattern in which the economic benefits of the asset are consumed by the enterprise. Amortization should commence when the asset is available for use and the amortization charge for each period should be recognized as an expense unless it is included in the carrying amount of another asset (e.g., inventory). Intangible assets may be amortized by the same systematic and rational methods that are used to depreciate tangible fixed assets. Thus, IAS 38 would seemingly permit straight-line, diminishing balance, and units of production methods. If a method other than straight-line is used, it must accurately mirror the expiration of the asset's economic service potential.

IAS 38 offers several examples of how useful life of intangibles is to be assessed. These include the following types of assets:

Customer lists. Care is urged to ensure that amortization is only over the expected useful life of the acquired list, ignoring the extended life that may be created as the acquirer adds to the list by virtue of its own efforts and costs, after acquisition. In many instances the initial, purchased list will erode in value rather quickly, since contacts become obsolete as customers migrate to other vendors, leave business, and so forth. These assets must be constantly refreshed, and that will involve expenditures by the acquirer of the original list (and whether those costs justify capitalization and amortization is a separate issue). For example, the acquired list might have a useful economic life of only two years (i.e., without additional expenditures, the value will be fully consumed over that time horizon). Two years would be the amortization period, therefore.

Patents. While a patent has a legal life (depending on jurisdiction of issuance) of as long as several decades, realistically, due to evolving technology and end-product obsolescence or changing customer tastes and preferences, the useful economic life may be much less. IAS 38 offers an example of a patent having a 15-year remaining life and a firm offer to acquire by a third party in five years, at a fixed fraction of the original acquirer's cost. In such a situation (which is probably unusual, however), amortization of the fraction not to be recovered in the subsequent sale, over a 5-year period, would be appropriate.

In other situations, it would be necessary to estimate the economic life of the patent and amortize the entire cost, in the absence of any firmly established residual value, over that period. It should be noted that there is increasing activity involving the monetizing of intellectual property values, including via the packaging of groups of patents and transferring them to special-purpose entities which then license them to third-party licensees. This shows promise of becoming an important way for patent holders to reap greater benefits from existing pools of patents held by them, but is in its infancy at this time and future success cannot be reliably predicted. Amortization of existing acquired patents or other intellectual property (intangible assets) should not be based on highly speculative values that might be obtained from such arrangements.

Additionally, whatever lives are assigned to patents for amortization purposes, these should regularly be reconsidered. As necessary, changes in useful lives should be implemented, which would be changes in estimate affecting current and future periods' amortization only, unless an accounting error had previously been made.

Copyrights. In many jurisdictions copyrights now have very lengthy terms, but for most materials so protected the actual useful lives will be very much shorter, sometimes only a year or two.

Renewable license rights. In many situations the entity may acquire license rights, such as broadcasting of radio or television signals, which technically expire after a fixed term but which are essentially renewable with little or no cost incurred as long as minimum performance criteria are met. If there is adequate evidence to demonstrate that this description is accurate and that the reporting entity has indeed been able, previously, to successfully accomplish this, then the intangible will be deemed to have an indefinite life and not be subjected to periodic amortization. However, this makes it more vital that impairment be regularly reviewed, since even if control of the rights remains with the reporting entity, changes in technology or consumer demand may serve to diminish the value of that asset. If impaired, a charge against earnings must be recognized, with the remaining unimpaired cost (if any) continuing to be recognized as an indefinite life intangible.

Similar actions would be warranted in the case of airline route authority. If readily renewable, without limitation, provided that minimal regulations are complied with (such as maintaining airport terminal space in a prescribed manner), the standard suggests that this be treated as an indefinite life intangible. Annual impairment testing would be required, as with all indefinite life intangibles (more often if there is any indication of impairment).

IAS 38 notes that a change in the governmental licensing regime may require a change in how these are accounted for. It cites an example of a change that ends perfunctory renewal and substitutes public auctions for the rights at each former renewal date. In such an instance, the reporting entity can no longer presume to have any right to continue after expiration of the current license, and must amortize its cost over the remaining term.

Residual Value

Tangible assets often have a positive residual value before considering the disposal costs because tangible assets can generally be sold, at least, for scrap, or possibly can be transferred to another user that has less need for or ability to afford new assets of that type. Intangibles, on the other hand, often have little or no residual worth. Accordingly, IAS 38 requires that a zero residual value be presumed unless an accurate measure of residual value is possible. Thus, the residual value is presumed to be zero *unless*

- There is a commitment by a third party to acquire the asset at the end of its useful life; *or*
- There is an active market for that type of intangible asset, and residual value can be measured reliably by reference to that market and it is probable that such a market will exist at the end of the useful life.

IAS 38 specifies that the residual value of an intangible asset is the estimated net amount that the reporting entity currently expects to obtain from disposal of the asset at the end of its useful life, after deducting the estimated costs of disposal, if the asset were of the age and in the condition expected at the end of its estimated useful life. Changes in estimated selling prices or other variables that occur over the expected period of use of the asset are not to be included in the estimated residual value, since this would result in the recognition of projected future holding gains over the life of the asset (via reduced amortization that would be the consequence of a higher estimated residual value).

Residual value is to be assessed at the end of each reporting period. Any change to the estimated residual, other than that resulting from impairment (accounted for under IAS 36) is to be accounted for prospectively, by varying future periodic amortization. Similarly, any change in amortization method (e.g., from accelerated to straight-line), based on an updated understanding of the pattern of future usage and economic benefits to be reaped there from, is dealt with as a change in estimate, again to be reflected only through changes in future periodic charges for amortization.

Periodic review of useful life assumptions and amortization methods employed. As for fixed assets accounted for in conformity with IAS 16, the standard on intangibles requires that the amortization period be reconsidered at the end of each reporting period, and that the method of amortization also be reviewed at similar intervals. There is the expectation that due to their nature intangibles are more likely to require revisions to one or both of these judgments. In either case, a change would be accounted for as a change in estimate, affecting current and future periods' reported earnings but not requiring restatement of previously reported periods.

Intangibles being accounted for as having an indefinite life must furthermore be reassessed periodically, as management plans and expectations almost inevitably vary over time. For example, a trademarked product, despite having wide consumer recognition and acceptance, can become irrelevant as tastes and preferences alter, and a limited horizon, perhaps a very short one, may emerge with little warning. Business history is littered with formerly valuable franchises that, for whatever reason—including management missteps—become valueless.

Impairment Losses

Where an asset is determined to have an indefinite useful life, the entity must conduct impairment tests annually, as well as whenever there is an indication that the intangible may be impaired. Furthermore, the presumption that the asset has an indefinite life must also be reviewed.

The impairment of intangible assets other than goodwill (such as patents, copyrights, trade names, customer lists, and franchise rights) should be considered in precisely the same way that long-lived tangible assets are dealt with. The impairment loss under IAS 36 is the amount by which carrying value exceeds recoverable amount. Carrying value must be compared to recoverable amount (the greater of fair value less costs to sell or value in use) when there are indications that an impairment may have been suffered. Net selling price is the price of an asset in an active market less disposal costs, and value in use is the present value of estimated future cash flows expected to arise from the continuing use of an asset and from its disposal.

Under US GAAP there are two steps in impairment testing in accordance with FAS 144 First, the carrying value and undiscounted future cash flows are compared to determine whether an asset is impaired; and, second, the impairment loss (if any is indicated) is then measured as the amount by which carrying value exceeds fair value. Impairment losses are not reversed in future periods under US GAAP.

Reversals of impairment losses under defined conditions are recognized under IFRS, by contrast. The effects of impairment recognitions and reversals will be reflected in profit or loss, if the intangible assets in question are being accounted for in accordance with the cost method.

On the other hand, if the revaluation method of accounting for intangible assets is followed (use of which is possible only if strict criteria can be met), impairments will normally be recognized in other comprehensive income to the extent that revaluation surplus exists, and only to the extent that the loss exceeds previously recognized valuation surplus will the impairment loss be reported as a charge against profit. Recoveries are handled consistent with the method by which impairments were reported, in a manner entirely analogous to the explanation in Chapter 8 dealing with impairments of plant, property, and equipment.

Unlike other intangible assets that are individually identifiable, goodwill is amorphous and cannot exist, from a financial reporting perspective, apart from the tangible and identifiable intangible assets with which it was acquired and remains associated. Thus, a direct evaluation of the recoverable amount of goodwill is not actually feasible. Accordingly, IFRS requires that goodwill be combined with other assets which together define a cash-generating unit, and that an evaluation of any potential impairment be conducted on an aggregate basis annually. A cash-generating unit (CGU) is the smallest identifiable group of assets that generates cash inflows that are largely independent of the cash inflows from other assets or groups of assets. This may not be the same as a reporting unit used for impairment testing under US GAAP.

A more detailed consideration of goodwill is presented in Chapter 11.

Example of calculating impairment losses under IFRS and US GAAP

Assume that Henan Corporation (HC) has two cash-generating units (CGU 1 and 2) and the following information is provided for impairment testing purposes:

	CGU 1	*CGU 2*
Cost	€6,000,000	€8,500,000
Accumulated amortization	3,000,000	4,500,000
Expected future cash flows (discounted)	2,800,000	3,500,000
Expected future cash flows (undiscounted)	3,100,000	3,800,000
Fair value less costs to sell	2,400,000	3,700,000
Remaining useful life of asset	4 years	4 years
Recoverable amount under IFRS	2,800,000	3,700,000
Impairment loss under IFRS	200,000	300,000
Impairment loss under US GAAP	--	300,000

What is the impairment loss for HC under IFRS and US GAAP?

Under IFRS, impairment loss of €200,000 is recognized for CGU 1 (carrying value of €3,000,000 minus recoverable amount of €2,800,000 equal to discounted future cash flows. Impairment loss of €300,000 is recognized for CGU 2 (carrying value of €4,000,000 minus recoverable amount of €3,700,000 equal to fair value less costs to sell).

Under US GAAP no impairment loss is recognized for CGU 1 since the carrying amount of €3,000,000 is less than the sum of the undiscounted cash flows of €3,100,000. Impairment loss of

€300,000 is recognized for CGU 2 (carrying value of €4,000,000 minus fair value less costs to sell of €3,700,000) since the carrying amount is not recoverable (carrying amount of €4,000,000 exceeds undiscounted cash flows of €3,800,000).

Derecognition of Intangible Assets

An intangible asset should be derecognized (1) on disposal or (2) when no future economic benefits are expected from its use or disposal. With regard to questions of accounting for the disposals of assets, the guidance of IAS 38 is consistent with that of IAS 16. Gain or loss arising from the derecognition of an intangible asset, determined as the difference between carrying amount (net, if applicable, of any remaining revaluation surplus) and the net disposal proceeds, is recognized in profit or loss (unless IAS 17 requires otherwise on a sale and leaseback) when the asset is derecognized. The 2004 amendment to IAS 38 observes that a disposal of an intangible asset may be effected either by a sale of the asset or by entering into a finance lease. The determination of the date of disposal of the intangible asset is made by applying the criteria in IAS 18 for recognizing revenue from the sale of goods, or IAS 17 in the case of disposal by a sale and leaseback. As for other similar transactions, the consideration receivable on disposal of an intangible asset is to be recognized initially at fair value. If payment for such an intangible asset is deferred, the consideration received is recognized initially at the cash price equivalent, with any difference between the nominal amount of the consideration and the cash price equivalent to be recognized as interest revenue under IAS 18, using the effective yield method.

Web Site Development and Operating Costs

With the advent of the Internet and of "e-commerce," most businesses now have their own Web sites. Web sites have become integral to doing business and may be designed either for external or internal access. Those designed for external access are developed and maintained for the purposes of promotion and advertising of an entity's products and services to their potential consumers. On the other hand, those developed for internal access may be used for displaying company policies and storing customer details.

With substantial costs being incurred by many entities for Web site development and maintenance, the need for accounting guidance became evident. The 2001 interpretation, SIC 32, concluded that such costs represent an internally generated intangible asset that is subject to the requirements of IAS 38, and that such costs should be recognized if, and only if, an enterprise can satisfy the requirements set forth in IAS 38. Therefore, Web site costs have been likened to "development phase" (as opposed to "research phase") costs.

Thus the stringent qualifying conditions applicable to the development phase, such as "ability to generate future economic benefits," have to be met if such costs are to be recognized as an intangible asset. If an enterprise is not able to demonstrate how a Web site developed solely or primarily for promoting and advertising its own products and services will generate probable future economic benefits, all expenditure on developing such a Web site should be recognized as an expense when incurred.

Any internal expenditure on development and operation of the Web site should be accounted for in accordance with IAS 38. Comprehensive additional guidance is provided in the Appendix to SIC 32 and is summarized below.

1. Planning stage expenditures, such as undertaking feasibility studies, defining hardware and software specifications, evaluating alternative products and suppliers, and selecting preferences, should be expensed;
2. Application and infrastructure development costs pertaining to acquisition of tangible assets, such as purchasing and developing hardware, should be dealt with in accordance with IAS 16;

3. Other application and infrastructure development costs, such as obtaining a domain name, developing operating software, developing code for the application, installing developed applications on the Web server and stress testing, should be expensed when incurred unless the conditions prescribed by IAS 38 are met;

4. Graphical design development costs, such as designing the appearance of Web pages, should be expensed when incurred unless recognition criteria prescribed by IAS 38 are met;

5. Content development costs, such as expenses incurred for creating, purchasing, preparing, and uploading information onto the Web site, to the extent that these costs are incurred to advertise and promote an enterprise's own products or services, should be expensed immediately, consistent with how other advertising and related costs are to be accounted for under IFRS. Thus, these costs are not deferred, even until first displayed on the Web site, but are expensed when incurred;

6. Operating costs, such as updating graphics and revising content, adding new functions, registering Web site with search engines, backing up data, reviewing security access and analyzing usage of the Web site should be expensed when incurred, unless in rare circumstances these costs meet the criteria prescribed in IAS 38, in which case such expenditure is capitalized as a cost of the Web site; and

7. Other costs, such as selling and administrative overhead (excluding expenditure which can be directly attributed to preparation of Web site for use), initial operating losses and inefficiencies incurred before the Web site achieves its planned operating status, and training costs of employees to operate the Web site, should all be expensed as incurred as required under IFRS.

Disclosure Requirements

The disclosure requirements set out in IAS 38 for intangible assets and those imposed by IAS 16 for property, plant, and equipment are very similar, and both demand extensive details to be disclosed in the financial statement footnotes. Another marked similarity is the exemption from disclosing "comparative information" with respect to the reconciliation of carrying amounts at the beginning and end of the period. While this may be misconstrued as a departure from the well-known principle of presenting all numerical information in comparative form, it is worth noting that it is in line with the provisions of IAS 1. IAS 1 categorically states that "unless a Standard permits or requires otherwise, comparative information should be disclosed in respect of the previous period for all numerical information in the financial statements...." (Another standard that contains a similar exemption from disclosure of comparative reconciliation information is IAS 37—which is dealt with in Chapter 12.)

For each class of intangible assets (distinguishing between internally generated and other intangible assets), disclosure is required of

1. Whether the useful lives are indefinite or finite and if finite, the useful lives or amortization rates used;

2. The amortization method(s) used;

3. The gross carrying amount and accumulated amortization (including accumulated impairment losses) at both the beginning and end of the period;

4. A reconciliation of the carrying amount at the beginning and end of the period showing additions (analyzed between those acquired separately and those acquired in a business combination), assets classified as held for sale, retirements, disposals, acquisitions by means of business combinations, increases or decreases resulting from revaluations, reductions to recognize impairments, amounts written back to recognize recoveries of prior impairments, amortization during the period, the net

effect of translation of foreign entities' financial statements, and any other material items; and

5. The line item in the statement of comprehensive income (or income statement, if presented separately) in which the amortization charge of intangible assets is included.

The standard explains the concept of "class of intangible assets" as a "grouping of assets of similar nature and use in an enterprise's operations." Examples of intangible assets that could be reported as separate classes (of intangible assets) are

1. Brand names;
2. Licenses and franchises;
3. Mastheads and publishing titles;
4. Computer software;
5. Copyrights, patents and other industrial property rights, service and operating right;
6. Recipes, formulae, models, designs and prototypes; and
7. Intangible assets under development.

The above list is only illustrative in nature. Intangible assets may be combined (or disaggregated) to report larger classes (or smaller classes) of intangible assets if this results in more relevant information for financial statement users.

In addition, the financial statements should also disclose the following:

1. For any asset assessed as having an indefinite useful life, the carrying amount of the asset and the reasons for considering that it has an indefinite life and the significant factors used to determine this;
2. The nature, carrying amount, and remaining amortization period of any individual intangible asset that is material to the financial statements of the enterprise as a whole;
3. For intangible assets acquired by way of a government grant and initially recognized at fair value, the fair value initially recognized, their carrying amount, and whether they are carried under the cost or revaluation method for subsequent measurement;
4. Any restrictions on title and any assets pledged as security for debt; and
5. The amount of outstanding commitments for the acquisition of intangible assets.

Where intangibles are carried using the revaluation model, the entity must disclose the effective date of the revaluation, the carrying amount of the assets, and what their carrying value would have been under the cost model, the amount of revaluation surplus applicable to the assets and the significant assumptions used in measuring fair value.

The financial statements should also disclose the aggregate amount of research and development expenditure recognized as an expense during the period. The entity is encouraged but not required to disclose any fully amortized assets still in use and any significant assets in use but not recognized because they did not meet the IAS 38 recognition criteria.

Examples of Financial Statement Disclosures

Novartis AG
For the fiscal year ending December 31, 2007

Accounting policies

Intangible assets. For business combinations, the excess of the purchase price over the fair value of net identifiable assets acquired is recorded as goodwill in the balance sheet and is denominated in the local currency of the related acquisition. Goodwill is allocated to an appropriate cash-generating unit, which is the smallest group of assets that generates cash inflows that are largely independent of the cash inflows from other assets or group of assets. All goodwill is considered to have an indefinite life and is tested for impairment at least annually. Any goodwill impairment charge is recorded in the income statement in Other Income and Expense. Goodwill that is embedded in the equity accounting for associated companies is also assessed annually for impairment with any resulting charge recorded in the results from associated companies.

All identifiable intangible assets acquired in a business combination are recognized at their fair value separate from goodwill. Furthermore, all acquired research and development assets including upfront and milestone payments on licensed or acquired compounds are capitalized as intangible assets, even if uncertainties exist as to whether the R&D projects will ultimately be successful in producing a saleable product.

All Novartis intangible assets are allocated to cash-generating units and amortized if they have a definite useful life and once they are available for use. In-Process Research & Development (IPR&D) is the only class of separately identified intangible assets which is not amortized, but tested for impairment on an annual basis or when facts and circumstances warrant an impairment test. Any impairment charge is recorded in R&D expenses. Once a project included in IPR&D has been successfully developed and is available for use, it is amortized over its useful life into Cost of Goods Sold where any related impairment charge is also recorded.

The useful lives assigned to acquired intangible assets are based on the period over which they are expected to generate economic benefits, commencing in the year in which they first generate sales. Acquired intangible assets are amortized on a straight-line basis over the following periods:

Trademarks	Over their estimated economic or legal life with a maximum of 20 years
Product and marketing rights	5 to 20 years
Core development technologies	Over their estimated useful life, typically between 15 and 30 years
Software	3 years
Others	3 to 5 years

Amortization of trademarks, product and marketing rights is charged to Cost of Goods Sold over their useful lives. Core development technologies, which represent identified and separable acquired know-how used in the development process, is amortized into Cost of Goods Sold or R & D. Any impairment charges are recorded in the income statement in the same functional cost lines as the amortization charges.

Intangible assets other than goodwill and IPR&D are reviewed for impairment whenever facts and circumstances indicate that their carrying value may not be recoverable. When evaluating an intangible asset for a potential impairment, the Group estimates the recoverable amount based on the intangible asset's fair value less cost to sell using the estimated future cash flows a market participant could generate with that asset or in certain circumstances the value in use of the intangible asset to the Group, whichever is higher. If the carrying amount of the asset exceeds the recoverable amount, an impairment loss for the difference is recognized. For purposes of assessing impairment, assets are grouped at the lowest level for which there are separately identifiable cash-generating units. Considerable management judgment is necessary to estimate discounted future cash flows and appropriate discount rates. Accordingly, actual cash flows and values could vary significantly from forecasted cash flows and related values derived using discounting techniques.

9. Intangible asset movements

2007	Goodwill USD millions	Acquired research and development USD millions	Core development technologies USD millions	Trademarks, product and marketing rights USD millions	Other intangible assets USD millions	Total USD millions
Cost						
January 1	11,404	2,471	660	9,999	1,046	25,580
Cost of assets related to discontinuing operations	(79)	--	--	(25)	(496)	(600)

2007	Goodwill USD millions	Acquired research and development USD millions	Core development technologies USD millions	Trademarks, product and marketing rights USD millions	Other intangible assets USD millions	Total USD millions
Impact of business combinations	3	--	--	38	--	41
Reclassifications	(81)	54	--	127	27	127
Additions	9	209	52	81	270	621
Disposals	--	--	--	(708)	(37)	(745)
Currency translation effects	598	102	85	553	45	1,383
December 31	11,854	2,836	797	10,065	855	25,407
Accumulated amortization						
January 1	(745)	(105)	(86)	(2,901)	(513)	(4,350)
Accumulated amortization of assets related to discontinuing operations	50	--	--	25	210	285
Reclassifications	--	--	--	34	(1)	33
Amortization charge	--	--	(54)	(919)	(118)	(1,091)
Amortization of disposals	--	--	--	704	34	738
Impairment charge	(3)	(94)	--	(360)	(25)	(482)
Currency translation effects	(46)	(13)	(14)	(196)	(22)	(291)
December 31	(744)	(212)	(154)	(3,613)	(435)	(5,158)
Net book value – December 31	11,110	2,624	643	6,452	420	21,249

2006	Goodwill USD millions	Acquired research and development USD millions	Core development technologies USD millions	Trademarks, product and marketing rights USD millions	Other intangible assets USD millions	Total USD millions
Cost						
January 1	8,080	875	508	6,455	727	16,645
Cost of assets related to discontinuing operations	(225)	--	--	(216)	(29)	(470)
Impact of business combinations	3,138	1,216	140	3,254	167	7,915
Reclassifications	--	(115)	--	114	1	--
Additions	1	407	--	12	159	579
Disposals	(59)	(1)	--	(11)	(13)	(84)
Translation effects	499	89	12	391	34	1,025
December 31	11,434	2,471	660	9,999	1,046	25,610
Accumulated amortization		660				
January 1	(801)	(37)	(10)	(2,090)	(413)	(3,351)
Accumulated amortization of assets related to discontinuing operations	49	--	--	52	10	111
Reclassifications	(1)	--	(25)	6	20	--
Amortization charge	--	--	(49)	(66)	(119)	(234)
Amortization of disposals	60	--	--	8	12	80
Impairment charge	(2)	(67)	--	(47)	(10)	(126)
Translation effects	(50)	(1)	(2)	(164)	(13)	(230)
December 31	(745)	(105)	(86)	(2,301)	(513)	(3,750)
Net book value - December 31	10,659	2,366	574	7,698	533	21,860

Goodwill, other intangible assets with indefinite useful lives and acquired R&D are tested for possible impairment annually and whenever events or changes in circumstances indicate the value may not be fully recoverable. If the initial accounting for an intangible asset acquired in the reporting period is only provisional, it is not tested for impairment and is therefore not included in the calculation of the net book values at risk from changes in the amount of discounted cash flows.

For all other intangible assets, an impairment is recognized when the balance sheet carrying amount is higher than the greater of fair value less cost to sell and value in use.

Novartis has adopted a uniform method for assessing goodwill for impairment and any other intangible asset indicated as possibly impaired. Under this method the fair value less cost to sell is calculated and only if it is lower than the balance sheet carrying amount is the value in use determined. Novartis uses the discounted cash flow method to determine the fair value less cost to sell, which starts with a forecast of all expected future cash flows. If no cash flow projections for the whole useful life of an intangible asset are available, cash flow projections for the next five years are utilized based on management's range of forecasts with a terminal value using sales projections in line or lower than inflation thereafter. Typically three probability-weighted scenarios are used. These cash flows which reflect the risks and uncertainties associated with the asset are discounted at an appropriate rate to net present value. The net present values involve highly sensitive estimates and assumptions specific to the nature of the Group's activities with regard to

- The amount and timing of projected future cash flows
- The discount rate selected
- The outcome of R&D activities (compound efficacy, results of clinical trials, etc.)
- The amount of timing of projected costs to develop the IPR&D into commercially viable products
- The probability of obtaining regulatory approval
- The long-term sales forecasts for periods of up to 20 years
- Sales price erosion rates after the end of patent protection and timing of the entry of generic competition; and
- The behavior of competitors (launch of competing products, marketing initiatives, etc.)

Factors that could result in shortened useful lives or impairment include lower than anticipated sales for acquired products or associated with patents and trademarks; or lower than anticipated future sales resulting from acquired R&D; or the closing of facilities; or changes in the planned use of property, plant or equipment. Changes in the discount rates used for these calculations also could lead to impairments. Additionally, impairments of IPR&D and product and marketing rights may also result from events such as the outcome of R&D activity, obtaining regulatory approval and the launch of competing products.

The discount rates used are based on the Group's weighted-average cost of capital adjusted for specific country and currency risks associated with the cash flow projections. Since the cash flows also take into account tax expenses a posttax discount rate is utilized. Use of the posttax discount rate approximates the results of using a pretax rate applied to pretax cash flows.

Due to the above factors, actual cash flows and values could vary significantly from the forecasted future cash flows and related values derived using discounting techniques.

The recoverable amount of a cash-generating unit and related goodwill is based on the higher of fair value less cost to sell or on the value in use which is derived from applying discounted future cash flows using the key assumptions indicated below.

	Pharmaceuticals %	Vaccines and Diagnostics%	Sandoz %	Consumer Health %
Sales growth rate assumptions after forecast period	3.0	2.5	0 to 7	-2 to 3
Discount rate	7.5	7.5	7 to 13	7 to 9

In 2007, impairment charges of USD 482 million were recorded. This is principally relating to an impairment of USD 320 million for *Famvir* product rights due to an earlier than anticipated challenge to its patent and subsequent loss of sales in the Pharmaceuticals Division. Additionally, Novartis recorded various impairment charges of USD 126 million, mainly for upfront and milestone payments in the Pharmaceuticals Division and USD 36 million for currently marketed products and other intangibles in the Sandoz and Consumer Health Divisions.

In 2006, Novartis recorded impairment charges amounting to a total of USD 126 million, principally relating to capitalized milestone payments in the Pharmaceuticals Division and marketed products and IPR&D in the Sandoz Division.

Roche Group
Consolidated Financial Statements 2007

Intangible assets

Purchased patents, licenses, trademarks and other intangible assets are initially recorded at cost. Where these assets have been acquired through a business combination, this will be the fair value allocated in the acquisition accounting. Intangible assets are amortized over their useful lives on a straight-line basis beginning from the point when they are available for use. Estimated useful life is the lower of the legal duration and the economic useful life. The estimated useful life of intangible assets is regularly reviewed.

Impairment of property, plant, and equipment and intangible assets

An impairment assessment is carried out when there is evidence that an asset may be impaired. In addition intangible assets that are not yet available for use are tested for impairment annually. When the recoverable amount of an asset, being the higher of its fair value less costs to sell and its value in use, is less than its carrying amount, then the carrying amount is reduced to its recoverable amount. This reduction is reported in the income statement as an impairment loss. Value in use is calculated using estimated cash flows, generally over a five-year period, with extrapolating projections for subsequent years. These are discounted using an appropriate long-term pretax interest rate. When an impairment loss arises, the useful life of the asset in question is reviewed and, if necessary, the future depreciation/amortization charge is accelerated. The impairment of financial assets is discussed below in the "Financial assets" policy.

Impairment of goodwill

Goodwill is assessed for possible impairment at each balance sheet date and is additionally tested annually for impairment. Goodwill is allocated to cash-generating units as described in Note 13. When the recoverable amount of the cash-generating unit, being the higher of its fair value less costs to sell or its value in use, is less than its carrying amount, then an impairment in the carrying amount is recorded. The methodology used in the impairment testing is further described in Note 13.

14. Intangible assets

Intangible assets: movements in carrying value of assets *in millions of CHF*

	Product intangibles in use	*Product intangibles not available for use*	*Technology intangibles*	*Total*
At January 1, 2006				
Cost	14,877	294	761	15,932
Accumulated amortization and impairment	(9,145)	--	(531)	(9,676)
Net book value	5,732	294	230	6,256
Year ended December 31, 2006				
At January 1, 2006	5,732	294	230	6,256
Additions	53	540	--	593
Disposals	(1)	--	--	(1)
Amortization charge	(941)	--	(36)	(977)
Impairment charge	(118)	(13)	(66)	(197)
Currency translation effects	(149)	(43)	(13)	(205)
At December 31, 2006	4,576	778	115	5,469
Cost	13,646	778	709	15,133
Accumulated amortization and impairment	(9,070)	--	(594)	(9,664)
Net book value	4,576	778	115	5,469
Year ended December 1, 2007				
At January 1, 2007	4,576	778	115	5,469
BioVeris acquisition	117	--	--	117
Tanox acquisition	613	93	--	706

	Product intangibles in use	Product intangibles not available for use	Technology intangibles	Total
Other business combinations	223	10	34	267
Additions	255	743	51	1,049
Disposals	(1)	--	--	(1)
Amortization charge	(942)	--	(34)	(976)
Impairment charge	--	(58)	--	(58)
Currency translation effects	(173)	(52)	(2)	(227)
At December 31, 2007	4,668	1,514	164	6,346
Cost	14,251	1,514	772	16,537
Accumulated amortization and impairment	(9,583)	--	(608)	(10,191)
Net book value	4,668	1,514	164	6,346
Allocation by operating segment				
-Roche Pharmaceuticals	326	1,085	52	1,463
-Genentech	955	408	35	1,398
-Chugai	440	8	--	448
-Diagnostics	2,947	13	77	3,037
Total Group	4,668	1,514	164	6,346

Significant intangible assets as at December 31, 2007 *in millions of CHF*

	Operating segment	Net book value	Remaining amortization period
Product intangibles in use			
Tanox acquisition	Genetech	553	12 years
Chugai acquistion	Chugai	436	5–13 years
Corange/Boehringer Mannheim acquisition	Diagnostics	1,590	10 years
Igen acquisition	Diagnostics	469	9 years
Product intangibles not available for use			
Alnylam alliance	Roche Pharmaceuticals	324	n/a

Classification of amortization and impairment expenses *in millions of CHF*

	2007		2006	
	Amortization	Impairment	Amortization	Impairment
Cost of sales				
- Pharmaceuticals	614	--	619	--
- Diagnostics	328	--	322	118
Research and development				
- Pharmaceuticals	31	58	27	13
- Diagnostics	3	--	9	66
Total	976	58	977	197

Internally generated intangible assets

The Group currently has no internally generated intangible assets from development as the criteria for the recognition as an asset are not met.

Impairment of intangible assets

Impairment charges arise from changes in the estimates of the future cash flows expected to result from the use of the asset and its eventual disposal. Factors such as the presence or absence of competition, technical obsolescence or lower than anticipated sales for products with capitalized rights could result in shortened useful lives or impairment.

2007. In the Genentech operating segment an impairment charge of 42 million Swiss francs was recorded in the second half of 2007, which relates to a decision to terminate development of compounds with two alliance partners. In the Roche Pharmaceuticals operating segment an impairment charge of 16 million Swiss francs was recorded in the first half of 2007, which relates to a decision to terminate development of one compound with an alliance partner. The assets concerned, which were not yet being amortized, were fully written down by these changes.

2006. In the second half of 2006 the Group recorded impairment charges of 184 million Swiss francs relating to intangible assets in the Diagnostics Division. These followed the regular updating of the division's business plans and technology assessments in the second half of 2006, which indicated anticipated recoverable amounts that were below the current carrying values for certain assets. These mainly concern certain of the intangible assets recorded following the Disetronic acquisition in 2003. These assets were written down to their recoverable amount, based on a value in use calculation using a discount rate of 10.0%. Additionally the remaining useful life of these assets was reassessed and has been reduced from 6.3 years to 3 years, effective December 31, 2006. Consequent to these matters, the 2007 amortization charge for intangible assets in the Diagnostics Division was approximately 20 million Swiss francs lower than it would otherwise have been. In the Roche Pharmaceuticals operating segment an impairment charge of 13 million Swiss francs was recorded in the second half of 2006, which relates to a decision to terminate development of one compound with an alliance partner. The asset concerned, which was not yet being amortized, was fully written down by this charge.

Intangible assets that are not yet available for use mostly represent in-process research and development assets in the Pharmaceuticals Division acquired either through in-licensing arrangements, business combinations or separate purchases. As at December 31, 2007, the carrying value of such assets in the Pharmaceuticals Division is 1,501 million Swiss francs. Of this amount approximately 40% represents projects that have potential decision points within the next twelve months which in certain circumstances could lead to impairment. Due to the inherent uncertainties in the research and development process, such assets are particularly at risk of impairment if the project in question does not result in a commercialized product.

Potential commitments from alliance collaborations

The Group is party to in-licensing and similar arrangements with its alliance partners. These arrangements may require the Group to make certain milestone or other similar payments dependent upon the achievement of agreed objectives or performance targets as defined in the collaboration agreements.

The Group's current estimate of future third-party commitments for such payments is set out in the table below. These figures are not risk adjusted, meaning that they include all such potential payments that can arise assuming all projects currently in development are successful. The timing is based on the Group's current best estimate. These figures do not include any potential commitments within the Group, such as may arise between the Roche Pharmaceuticals, Genetech and Chugai businesses.

Potential future third-party collaboration payments *in millions of CHF*

	Pharmaceuticals	*Diagnostics*	*Group*
Within one year	234	14	248
Between one and two years	112	16	128
Between two and three years	214	14	228
Total	560	44	604

Lectra
Financial Report 2006

Accounting policies

Other intangible assets

Intangible assets are carried at their purchase cost less cumulative amortization and impairment, if any. Amortization is charged on a straight-line basis depending on the estimated useful life of the intangible asset.

Management information software. The new management information system deployed on January 1, 2007, is being amortized on a straight-line basis over eight years. Other purchased management information software packages are amortized on a straight-line basis over three years, together with internal or external development costs incurred in their deployment. Costs incurred by the company in the development of software for its own use refer to direct development and configuration costs.

Patents and trademarks. Patents, trademarks and associated costs are amortized on a straight-line basis over three to ten years from the date of registration. The Group is not dependent on any patents or licenses that it does not own.

In terms of intellectual property, no patents or other industrial property rights belonging to the Group are currently under license to third parties. The rights held by the Group, notably with regard to software specific to its business as a software developer and publisher, are used under license by its customers within the framework of sales activity.

Other. Other intangible assets are amortized on a straight-line basis over two to five years.

Note 2. Other intangible assets

(In thousands of euros) **2006**	Management information *software*	Patents and *trademarks*	*Other*	*Total*
Gross value at January 1, 2006	14,653	2,278	5,336	22,267
External purchases	1,729	129	--	1,858
Internal developments	1,609	--	--	1,609
Write-offs and disposals	(39)	--	--	(39)
Transfers	(3)	7	2	6
Exchange rate differences	(53)	--	(4)	(57)
Gross value at December 31, 2006	17,896	2,414	5,334	25,644
Amortization at December 31, 2006	(12,438)	(2,093)	(5,148)	(19,679)
Net value at December 31, 2006	5,458	321	186	5,965

(In thousands of euros) **2007**	Management information *software*	Patents and *trademarks*	*Other*	*Total*
Gross value at January 1, 2007	17,896	2,414	5,334	25,644
External purchases	634	210	72	916
Internal developments	241	--	--	241
Write-offs and disposals	(47)	--	--	(47)
Exchange rate differences	(40)	--	(4)	(44)
Gross value at December 31, 2007	18,684	2,624	5,402	26,710
Amortization at December 31, 2007	(13,606)	(2,231)	(5,146)	(20,983)
Net value at December 31, 2007	5,078	393	256	5,727

Changes in amortization
2007

Amortization at January 1, 2007	(12,438)	(2,093)	(5,148)	(19,679)
Amortization charges	(1,255)	(138)	(2)	(1,395)
Amortization write-backs	47	--	--	47
Exchange rate differences	40	--	4	44
Amortization at December 31, 2007	(13,606)	(2,231)	(5,146)	(20,983)

Management information software. As part of an ongoing process of upgrading and reinforcing its information systems, in 2006 and 2007 the Group purchased licenses of new management information software together with additional licenses for software already in use in order to increase the number of users.

The company capitalized an expense of €296,000 in 2007 in respect of its IT systems upgrade project, the phase one of which became operational on January 1, 2007 and is amortized under the straight-line method over eight years. Internal development expenses amounted to €139,000. In 2006 the company capitalized an expense of €3,058,000 on this project.

The total asset value of €4,987,000 is amortized from January 1, 2007.

Nokia
Annual Report 2007

Note 1. Accounting principles

Other intangible assets. Acquired patents, trademarks, licenses, software licenses for internal use, customer relationships and developed technology are capitalized and amortized using the straight-line method over their useful lives, generally 3 to 6 years, but not exceeding 20 years.

Where an indication of impairment exists, the carrying amount of any intangible asset is assessed and written down to its recoverable amount.

Note 9. Depreciation and amortization

Depreciation and amortization by function	2007 EURm	2006 EURm	2005 EURm
Cost of sales	303	279	242
Research and development[1]	523	312	349
Selling and marketing[1]	232	9	9
Administrative and general	148	111	99
Other operating expenses	--	1	13
Total	1,206	712	712

[1] *In 2007, depreciation and amortization allocated to research and development and selling and marketing included amortization of acquired intangible assets of EUR 136 million and EUR 214 million, respectively.*

Note 12. Intangible assets

EURm	2007	2006
Capitalized development costs		
Acquisition cost January 1	1,533	1,445
Additions during the period	157	127
Acquisitions	154	--
Impairment losses	(27)	--
Disposals during the period	--	(39)
Accumulated acquisition cost December 31	1,817	1,533
Accumulated depreciation January 1	(1,282)	(1,185)
Disposals during the period	--	39
Amortization for the period	(157)	(136)
Accumulated amortization December 31	(1,439)	(1,282)
Net book value January 1	251	260
Net book value December 31	378	251
Goodwill		
Acquisition cost January 1	532	90
Translation differences	(30)	(26)
Acquisitions	882	488
Other changes	--	(20)
Accumulated acquisition cost for December 31	1,384	532
Net book value January 1	532	90
Net book value December 31	1,384	532
Other intangible assets		
Acquisition cost January 1	772	676
Translations differences	(20)	(21)
Additions during the period	102	99
Acquisitions	2,437	122
Impairment losses	--	(33)
Disposals during the period	(73)	(71)
Accumulated acquisition cost December 31	3,218	772
Accumulated amortization January 1	(474)	(465)
Translation differences	11	10
Disposals during the period	73	66
Amortization for the period	(470)	(85)
Accumulated amortization December 31	(860)	(474)
Net book value January 1	298	211
Net book value December 31	2,358	298

10 INTERESTS IN FINANCIAL INSTRUMENTS, ASSOCIATES, JOINT VENTURES, AND INVESTMENT PROPERTY

PERSPECTIVE AND ISSUES

Varying aspects of accounting for investments are addressed by several different IFRS. Previous improvements to these standards have eliminated most, but not all, options regarding how investments may be valued and presented in the financial statements. Fair value is now the predominant mode of investment valuation.

Under current standards, accounting for passive investments in financial instruments is generally at fair value, although an exception is made for held-to-maturity investments in debt instruments. Despite this general principle, the manner in which the changes in fair value are recognized in the financial statements still depends on management's intentions. Accounting for investments over which the investor has significant influence is generally by the equity method, although for the special case of joint ventures the proportional consolidation method is also permitted. Investments in real estate, other than as productive assets or goods held for sale in the ordinary course of business, are optionally accounted for at either fair value or cost.

Relevant standards include IAS 39, which provides guidance for passive investments in debt and equity instruments; IAS 28, governing the accounting for active investments in equity instruments; IAS 31, dealing with joint ventures; and IAS 40, covering investments in real property other than as productive capacity or goods to be sold to customers. A number of IFRIC (interpretations) are also relevant to the discussion below.

Sources of IAS			
IAS 28, 31, 32, 39, 40	*IFRS* 7	*SIC* 13	*IFRIC* 5, 9, 10

DEFINITIONS OF TERMS

Amortized cost of a financial asset or financial liability. The amount at which the financial asset or financial liability is initially recognized minus principal repayments, plus or minus the cumulative amortization using the effective interest method of any difference between that initial amount and the maturity amount, and minus any impairment or uncollectibility.

Associate. An entity, including an unincorporated entity such as a partnership, over which an investor has significant influence but which is neither a subsidiary nor a joint venture of the investor company.

Available-for-sale financial assets. Nonderivative financial assets that are designated as available for sale or are not classified as (1) financial assets at fair value through profit or loss (those held for trading, and those designated as at fair value through profit or loss (FVTPL) upon initial recognition); (2) held-to-maturity investments; and (3) loans and receivables originated by the entity.

Carrying amount. The amount at which an asset is currently presented in the statement of financial position.

Consolidated financial statements. Financial statements of a group presented as those of a single economic entity.

Control. The power to govern the financial and operating policies of an entity so as to obtain benefits from its activities and increase, maintain, or protect the amount of those benefits.

Cost. The amount of cash or cash equivalents paid or the fair value of other consideration given to acquire an asset at the time of its acquisition or construction or, where applicable, the amount attributed to that asset when initially recognized in accordance with the specific requirements of other IFRS, (e.g., IFRS 2, *Share-Based Payment*).

Cost method. A method of accounting for investment whereby the investment is recorded at cost; the statement of comprehensive income reflects income from the investment only to the extent that the investor receives distributions (dividends) from the investee's accumulated net profits arising after the date of acquisition. Distributions received in excess of accumulated profits are regarded as a recovery of investment and are recognized as a reduction of the cost of the investment.

Derecognition. The removal of a previously recognized financial asset or liability, or a portion thereof, from an entity's statement of financial position.

Derivative. A financial instrument (1) whose value changes in response to changes in a specified interest rate, security price, commodity price, foreign exchange rate, index of prices or rates, a credit rating or credit index, or similar variable (which is known as the "underlying"), (2) that requires no initial net investment or little initial net investment relative to other types of contracts that have a similar response to changes in market conditions, and (3) that is settled at a future date.

Differential. The difference between investment cost and the book value of underlying net assets of the investee.

Effective interest method. A method of calculating the amortized cost of a financial asset or a financial liability (or a group of financial instruments) and of allocating the interest income or interest expense over the relevant period. The effective interest rate used in the allocation process is the rate that exactly discounts estimated future cash flows (receipts or payments) to the net carrying amount of the financial instrument through the expected life of this instrument (or a shorter period, when appropriate).

Embedded derivative. A component of a hybrid (combined) financial instrument that also includes a nonderivative host contract and results in some of the cash flows of the combined instrument varying in a way similar to a stand-alone derivative. An embedded derivative should be separated from the host contract and accounted for as a derivative under IAS 39 if certain conditions are met. If an entity is required to separate an embedded derivative from its host contract, but is unable to measure the embedded derivative separately either at acquisition or at the end of a subsequent financial reporting period, it should designate the entire hybrid (combined) contract as at fair value through profit or loss (FVTPL).

Equity method. A method of accounting whereby the investment is initially recorded at cost and subsequently adjusted for the postacquisition change in the investor's share of net assets of the investee. The investor's income from investment includes the investor's share of the investee's profit or loss as well as the investor's share of the investee's other comprehensive income.

Fair value. The amount for which an asset could be exchanged between a knowledgeable, willing buyer and seller in an arm's-length transaction.

Fair value through profit or loss (FVTPL) option. An option in IAS 39 that permits an entity to irrevocably designate any financial asset or financial liability, but only upon its initial recognition, as one to be measured at fair value, with changes in fair value recognized in current profit or loss.

Financial assets. Include the following four principal categories: (1) those at fair value through profit or loss (held for trading, and those designated as at fair value through profit or loss (FVTPL) upon initial recognition); (2) available for sale; (3) held-to-maturity: and (4) loans and receivables originated by the entity. The definition does not include the following (carried at cost): (1) investments in equity instruments which do not have quoted prices in active markets and whose value cannot be reliably measured, (2) derivatives linked to and settled by delivery of unquoted equity instruments.

Financial asset or financial liability at fair value through profit or loss. A financial asset or financial liability that meets either of the following conditions: (1) is classified as held for trading, and (2) is designated as at fair value through profit or loss (FVTPL) upon initial recognition.

Financial guarantee contract. A contract that requires the issuer to make specified payments to reimburse the holder for losses incurred because a specified debtor failed to make payment when due based on the original or modified terms of a debt instrument.

Firm commitment. A binding agreement for the exchange of a specific quantity of resources at a specified price on a specified future date or dates.

Forecast transaction. An uncommitted but anticipated future transaction.

Forwards. Contracts between a buyer and a seller that require the delivery of some commodity, for example, equity instrument, or currency at a specified future date and a specified price (the exercise price). One party's gains on forward contracts result only from another party's equivalent losses (a zero-sum game). Forward contracts are commonly used for hedging purposes because the forward contracts can be customized as to duration and amounts.

Futures. Contracts that require delivery of a commodity (e.g., equity instrument, or currency) at a specified price agreed to today (the exercise price), on specified future date. Futures are similar to forward contracts except futures have standardized contract terms and are traded on organized exchanges.

Goodwill. An intangible asset acquired in a business combination representing the future economic benefits expected to be derived from the business combination that are not allocated to other individually identifiable and separately recognizable assets acquired.

Hedge effectiveness. The degree to which changes in the fair value or cash flows of the hedged item are offset by changes in the fair value or cash flows of the hedging instrument.

Hedged item. An asset, liability, firm commitment, highly probable forecast transaction or net investment in a foreign operation that (1) exposes the entity to risk of changes in fair value or future cash flows, and that (2) for hedge accounting purposes is designated as being hedged. For example, foreign currency accounts receivable arising from export transactions.

Hedging. Designating one or more hedging instruments such that the change in fair value or cash flows of the hedging instrument is an offset, in whole or part, to the change in fair value or cash flows of the hedged item. Hedge accounting recognizes the offsetting effects on profit or loss of changes in the fair values of the hedging instrument and the hedged item.

Hedging instrument. For hedge accounting purposes, a designated derivative or (in limited instances) another financial asset or liability whose fair value or cash flows are expected to offset changes in the fair value or cash flows of a designated hedged item. Nonderivative financial assets or liabilities may be designated as hedging instruments for hedge accounting purposes only if they hedge the risk of changes in foreign currency exchange rates.

Held-for-trading. A financial asset that (1) is acquired or incurred principally for the purpose of selling or repurchasing it in the near term; (2) is part of a portfolio of identified financial instruments (upon initial recognition) that are managed together and evidence exists that there is a recent actual pattern of short-term profit taking; (3) is a derivative (except for financial guarantee contracts and those designated and effective as hedging instruments).

Held-to-maturity instruments. Nonderivative financial assets with fixed or determinable payments and fixed maturities, that entity has positive intent and ability to hold to maturity, except for (1) those at fair value through profit or loss (held for trading, and those designated as at fair value through profit or loss upon initial recognition); (2) those designated as available for sale, and (3) loans and receivables originated by the entity. An entity should not classify any financial assets as held to maturity if the entity has, during the current financial year or during the two preceding financial years, sold or reclassified more than an insignificant amount (in relation to the total amount of held-to-maturity investments) of held-to-maturity investments before maturity.

Investee. An entity that issued voting share that is held by an investor.

Investee capital transaction. The purchase or sale by the investee of its own ordinary share, which alters the investor's ownership interest and is accounted for by the investor as if the investee were a consolidated subsidiary.

Investment. An asset held by an entity for purposes of accretion of wealth through distributions of interest, royalties, dividends, and rentals, or for capital appreciation or other benefits to be obtained.

Investment property. Property (land or a building, or part of a building, or both), held (by the owner or by the lessee under a finance lease), to earn rentals or for capital appreciation purposes or both, as opposed to being held as

- An owner-occupied property (i.e. for use in the production or supply of goods or services or for administrative purposes); or
- Property held for sale in the ordinary course of business.

Investor. A business entity that holds an investment in the voting shares of another entity.

Joint arrangement. A contractual arrangement whereby two or more parties undertake an economic activity together and share decision making relating to the activity. Joint arrangements can be classified into three types—joint operations, joint assets and joint ventures.

Joint control. The contractually agreed-on joint sharing of control over the operations and/or assets of an economic activity; exists only when the strategic financial and operating decisions relating to the activity require the unanimous consent of the parties sharing control (the venturers).

Joint venture. A contractual arrangement whereby two or more parties undertake an economic activity subject to their joint control.

Loans and receivables. Nonderivative financial assets with fixed or determinable payments that are not quoted in an active market other than (1) those held for trading, and those upon initial recognition designated as at fair value through profit or loss, (2) those designated as available for sale, and (3) those for which the holder may not recover substantially all of its initial investment (other than because of credit deterioration), which should be classified as available for sale.

Marketable. Assets for which there are active markets and from which fair values, or other indicators that permit determination thereof, are available.

Option. A contract that gives the buyer (option holder) the right, but not the obligation, to acquire (call option) from or sell (put option) to the option seller (option writer) a certain quantity of an underlying security or commodity, at a specified price (the strike price) and up to a specified date (the expiration date). For example, a company can exercise its call option to repurchase all of the outstanding warrants for the company's ordinary share currently held by another corporation.

Owner-occupied property. Property held by the owner (i.e., the entity itself) or by a lessee under a finance lease, for use in the production or supply of goods or services or for administrative purposes.

Proportional consolidation. A method of accounting whereby an investor's share of each of the assets, liabilities, income and expenses of the investee is combined line by line with similar items in the investor's financial statements or reported as separate line items in the investor's financial statements.

Regular way purchase or sale. A purchase or sale of a financial asset under a contract whose terms require delivery of the asset within the time frame established generally by regulation or convention in that marketplace. Marketplace is environment in which financial asset is customarily exchanged (not limited to formal stock exchange or organized OTC market).

Separate financial statements. Financial statements presented by a parent, an investor in an associate, or a venturer in a jointly controlled entity, in which the investments are accounted for on the basis of the direct equity interest rather than on the basis of the reported results and net assets of the investees.

Significant influence. The power of the investor to participate in the financial and operating policy decisions of the investee, which may be gained by share ownership, statute or agreement; however, this is less than the ability to control those policies.

Subsidiary. An entity, including an unincorporated entity such as a partnership, that is controlled by another entity (its parent).

Swap. A derivative financial instrument in which two counterparties agree to exchange streams of cash payments over time according to specified terms. Swaps can be used to hedge certain risks such as interest rate risk, exchange rate risk, or to speculate on changes in the underlying prices. The most common type is interest rate swap in which one party agrees to pay a fixed interest rate in return for receiving an adjustable rate from another party.

Transaction costs. Incremental costs that are directly attributable to the acquisition, issue or disposal of a financial asset or financial liability (costs that would not have been incurred if the entity had not acquired, issued, or disposed of the financial instrument).

Undistributed investee earnings. The investor's share of investee earnings in excess of dividends paid.

Venturer. A party to a joint venture that has control over that joint venture.

CONCEPTS, RULES, AND EXAMPLES

Accounting for Investments in Debt and Equity Instruments

IAS 39 provides rules for the accounting for investments in debt and equity instruments which differ markedly from preexisting requirements. It also addresses accounting for financial liabilities (see Chapter 12) and hedging using financial derivatives and other instruments, a subject which was introduced in Chapter 5 and which will be further explored later in the present chapter.

Under the provisions of IAS 39, the once important distinction between current and noncurrent investments is eliminated completely, even as IFRS now, for the first time (in revised IAS 1) requires presentation of classified statements of financial position in most instances. Instead, the question of "management intent" is now of paramount concern, as manifested in the tripartite distinction of investments into (1) those at fair value through profit or loss, (those held for trading, and those designated as at fair value through profit or loss upon initial recognition), (2) those available for sale albeit not held for trading purposes, and (3) those intended to be held to maturity.

The accounting for debt and equity instruments held as investments is dependent upon which of these three categories they are placed in, as was described in detail in Chapter 5. In the following sections of this chapter, illustrations of the accounting for such investments will be presented.

For convenience, some of the key provisions of IAS 39 are repeated in the following discussion, but these are less extensive than the presentation in Chapter 5, which should be referred to by the reader.

Initial recognition and measurement. An entity should recognize a financial asset or a financial liability in its statement of financial position only when the entity becomes a party to the contractual provisions of that instrument. Debt and equity instruments held as financial assets (investments) are initially measured at fair value (cost), including transactions costs directly attributable to the acquisition (e.g., fees, commissions, transfer taxes, etc.), as of the date when the investor entity becomes a party to the contractual provisions of the instrument. In general this date is readily determinable and unambiguous. Transaction costs are *not* included in initial measurement of instruments classified as at fair value through profit or loss (FVTPL).

For instruments purchased "regular way" (when settlement date follows the trade date by several days), however, recognition may be on either the trade or the settlement date. In "regular-way purchase or sale" delivery must be within the time frame generally established by regulation or convention in the market concerned (e.g., settlement on T + 3 days). An entity has a choice between the trade date or settlement date accounting rather than derivatives accounting, but a policy should be applied consistently for each category of financial assets. Any change in fair value between these dates must be recognized (strictly speaking, regular-way trades involve a forward contract, which is a derivative financial instrument, but IAS 39 does not require that these be actually accounted for as derivatives). If a transaction is considered "regular-way," a derivative is not recognized for the time period between the trade and the settlement date.

If an entity recognizes financial assets using the settlement date, any change in fair value of assets received between the trade date and the settlement date is recognized in profit or loss (if assets classified as at FVTPL) or equity (if assets classified as available for sale); changes in fair value during this period are not recognized for assets carried at cost or amortized cost.

Derecognition. IAS 39 prescribes the accounting treatment for derecognition of a financial asset. Revisions to the standard effective in 2005 altered somewhat the criteria for derecognition of investments in financial instruments. A guiding principle has become the "continuing involvement approach," which prohibits derecognition to the extent to which the transferor has continuing involvement in an asset or a portion of an asset it has transferred.

In accordance with IAS 39 there are two main concepts—risks and rewards, and control—that govern derecognition decisions. The standard makes it clear that evaluation of the transfer of risks and rewards of ownership must in all instances precede the evaluation of the transfer of control.

Appendix A to IAS 39 provides the following flowchart illustrating the evaluation of whether and to what extent a financial asset should be derecognized:

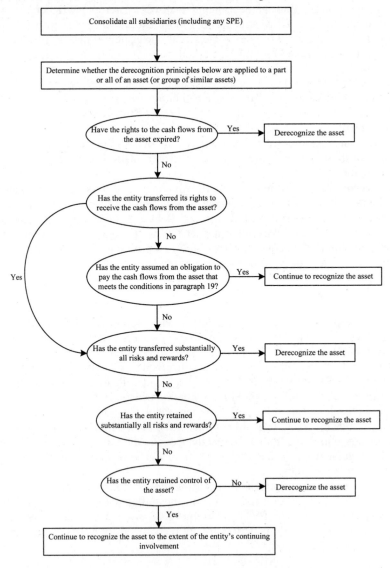

The derecognition approach should be considered at the consolidated group level after applying IAS 27 and SIC 12 prior to derecognition assessment. In accordance with IAS 27 all controlled entities should be included in the consolidated financial statements. In addition, SIC 12 requires that a special-purpose entity (SPE) be consolidated if the substance of the relationship indicates that the SPE is controlled by the reporting entity.

The term "financial asset" refers to either a part of a financial asset or a part of a group of similar assets. An entity needs to determine whether derecognition principles are applied to a part or all of a financial asset (or group of similar assets). Derecognition is applied to a part of an asset transferred only if the part comprises

- Specifically identified cash flows (e.g., an interest-only strip) when the counterparty obtains the right to interest cash flows but not the principal cash flows from a debt instrument;
- A fully proportionate (pro rata) share of cash flows (e.g., 90 % of all cash flows); and
- A fully proportionate share of specifically identified cash flows (e.g., 90 percent of interest cash flows from a financial asset).

Unless one of the foregoing criteria is satisfied, derecognition of a portion of a financial asset is not permitted. In that case, the financial asset must be considered for derecognition in its entirety.

An entity should remove (derecognize) a previously recognized financial asset from its statement of financial position *only* when (1) the contractual rights to the cash flows from the financial asset expire (e.g., expired option); or (2) it transfers the financial asset and the transfer qualifies for derecognition.

An entity transfers a financial asset only if

1. It transfers the contractual rights to receive the cash flows of the financial asset; or
2. It retains the contractual rights to receive the cash flows of the financial asset, but assumes an obligation to pay the cash flows to one or more recipients in a "pass-through arrangement."

If the entity has transferred its rights to receive the cash from the financial asset, the next step would be to consider whether risks and rewards of ownership are transferred. If rights to the cash flows are retained, an entity should consider whether a "pass-through arrangement" exists. The entity treats the transaction as a transfer of a financial asset when all of the following three conditions are met for the transaction to be a "pass-through arrangement":

1. The entity has no obligation to pay amounts not collected; short-term advances by the entity with the right of full recovery of the amount lent plus accrued interest at market rates do not violate this condition.
2. The entity is prohibited from selling or pledging the original asset other than as security to the eventual recipients for the obligation to pay them cash flows.
3. The entity has an obligation to remit any cash flows collected on behalf of the eventual recipients without material delay. In addition, the entity must not be entitled to reinvest the cash flows, except for investments in cash or cash equivalents; and interest earned (if any) on such investments must be passed on to the eventual recipients.

When an entity transfers a financial asset, the next step in applying derecognition principles is to evaluate the extent to which it retains the risks and rewards of ownership of the financial asset.

If the entity has transferred substantially all the risks and rewards of ownership of the financial asset, the entity should derecognize the financial asset and recognize separately as assets or liabilities any rights and obligations created or retained in the transfer. The entity's exposure before and after the transfer should be evaluated; risks and rewards are retained if exposure to variability in cash flows does not change significantly as a result of the transfer. Examples of transactions when the entity transfers substantially all of the risks and rewards of ownership include (1) unconditional sale of a financial asset, and (2) sale of a financial asset with an option to repurchase at fair value at the time of repurchase.

If the entity retains substantially all the risks and rewards of ownership of the financial asset, the entity should not remove this asset from its statement of financial position and continue to recognize the financial asset. Examples of transactions when substantially all risks and rewards are retained include (1) sale and repurchase transaction with repurchase price being fixed; (2) sale of a financial asset with a total return swap; (3) sale of a financial asset with a deep-in-the-money option (and it is highly unlikely to go out of the money before expiry); and sale of short-term receivables with a guarantee to compensate for likely-to-occur credit losses.

If the entity *neither* transfers *nor* retains substantially all the risks and rewards of ownership of the financial asset, the next step is to determine whether it has retained *control* of the financial asset.

- If control has not been retained, the entity derecognizes the financial asset and recognizes separately as assets or liabilities any rights and obligations created or retained in the transfer.
- If the entity has retained control, it continues to recognize the financial asset to the extent of its continuing involvement in the financial asset.

In accordance with IAS 39, whether the entity has retained control of the transferred asset depends on the transferee's ability to sell the assets to an unrelated third party; to exercise that ability unilaterally; and without needing to impose additional restrictions on the transfer. In all other cases, the entity has retained control and continues recognizing the financial asset to the extent of continuing involvement and recognizing an associated liability. Examples of continuing involvements and the requisite measurement approaches include

1. Guarantee—the transferred asset continues to be recognized at the lower of (a) the amount of the asset and (b) the maximum amount of consideration that the entity could be required to repay.
2. Written put option on asset measured at fair value—the transferred asset continues to be recognized at the lower of the fair value of the asset or the option exercise price.
3. Purchased call option—the transferred asset continues to be recognized at the amount of the transferred asset that the transferor could repurchase.

If an entity has retained control of a financial instrument, measurement of the financial asset and financial liability is on the basis that reflects rights and obligations that the entity has retained. The entity continues to recognize an asset to the extent of its continuing involvement, and also recognizes the associated liability, measured so that net carrying amount of the transferred asset and associated liability is

- Amortized cost of the rights and obligations retained by the entity, if the transferred asset is measured at amortized cost; or
- Equal to the fair value of the rights and obligations retained by the entity, if the transferred asset is measured at fair value.

Subsequent measurement. The accounting for debt and equity instruments held as investments is dependent upon whether instruments are classified as (1) at fair value through profit or loss (those held for trading and those designated as at fair value through profit or loss upon initial recognition); (2) available for sale; or (3) held to maturity.

Debt and equity instruments held as investments are to be accounted for at fair value, if classified as at fair value through profit or loss (FVTPL), or available for sale. Transaction costs are to be excluded from the fair value determinations, and thus, unless there has been an increase in value since acquisition date, there will often be a loss recognized in the first holding period, due to the fact that when originally recorded, transaction costs were included.

In the case of investments carried at FVTPL (those held for trading purposes or those otherwise designated as held at FVTPL), gains and losses arising from changes in fair value from period to period are included in profit or loss. Given the explicit presumption that these financial instruments will be disposed of in the near term, as market conditions may warrant, marking these to fair value through profit and loss is entirely logical, and mandatory.

Gains and losses arising from changes in fair value of investments classified as available-for-sale are recognized in other comprehensive income and accumulated in equity, under the caption "Available-for-Sale Financial Assets," except for impairment losses and foreign exchange gains and losses, which must be reflected in current profit or loss, until the financial asset is derecognized. Under provisions of the original IAS 39, the changes in fair value could either be included in profit or loss, or recognized in other comprehensive income, although each reporting entity had been required to make a onetime election as to which of these alternatives it would conform to thereafter. However, revised IAS 39 (effective 2005) eliminated this option, so optional recognition in profit or loss is not permitted, although the "fair value (FVTPL) option" is available and accomplishes the same objective (see discussion below).

Exceptions to the general principle of measuring financial assets at their fair values include

- Held-to-maturity investments measured at amortized cost using the effective interest method
- Loans and receivables measured at amortized cost using the effective interest method
- Investments in equity instruments that do not have a quoted market price in an active market and whose fair value cannot be reliably measured (and derivatives that must be settled by delivery of such unquoted equity instruments) measured at cost.

Debt instruments to be held to maturity are maintained at amortized cost, unless objective evidence of impairment exists. Of course, this assumes that the conditions for classification as held to maturity as set forth by IAS 39 are met; namely, that management has demonstrated both the intent and the ability to hold the instruments until the maturity date.

When an investment in bonds is classified as available-for-sale, so that fair value changes are reported in other comprehensive income and accumulated in equity until the investment is sold, the amortization of premium or discount on such an investment should nonetheless be reported in profit or loss as part of interest income or expense. Amortization cannot be included as part of the change in fair value and included in other comprehensive income. Under provisions of IAS 39, as well as under provisions of IAS 18 and IAS 32, these amounts are measured using the effective interest method, which means that the amortization of premium or discount is part of interest income or interest expense and therefore included in determining net profit or loss.

A summary of subsequent measurement of financial assets is presented in Table 1 below.

Table 1. Subsequent Measurement of Financial Assets: Summary

Category	*Measurement*
Fair value through profit and loss (FVTPL)	Fair value—through profit or loss (P&L)
Held-to-maturity (HTM)	Amortized cost—effective interest method
Loans and receivables (L&R)	Amortized cost—effective interest method
Available-for-sale (AFS)	Fair value—through other comprehensive income (OCI) and equity

The transaction costs included in the originally recorded basis of held-to-maturity financial assets are included in the calculation of effective interest rate and amortized to the P&L over the expected life of the investment, as part of any premium or discount. Transaction costs included in the carrying value of financial assets classified as available-for-sale are recognized as part of changes in fair value. If available-for-sale instruments have fixed or determinable payments, transaction costs are amortized to the P&L using the effective interest method. For those instruments listed as available-for-sale without fixed or determinable payments, costs are recognized in the P&L when the assets are derecognized or impaired.

Determining fair value. In accordance with IAS 39, fair value is the amount for which an asset could be exchanged, or a liability settled, between knowledgeable, willing parties in an arm's-length transaction, which generally equals transaction price. The best evidence of fair values is provided by quoted prices in active markets. A financial instrument is regarded as quoted in an active market if quoted prices are readily and regularly available from an exchange, dealer, broker, industry group, pricing service or regulatory agency, and those prices represent actual and regularly occurring market transactions on an arm's-length basis.

If no active market exists, valuation techniques must be used which would maximize market inputs and minimize entity-specific inputs. Valuation techniques include using recent quoted prices in active markets for similar instruments, discounted cash flow analysis and option pricing models. A separate project on fair value measurements is likely to result in the issuance of a new IFRS on this topic in 2010, based on the US GAAP standard FAS 157 which the IASB decided to use the as the starting point for its own deliberations. Appendix F, Use of Fair Value in Accounting Measurements, in Chapter 1 discusses in further detail the IASB project, *Fair Value Measurement Guidance*.

The current (2008) credit and liquidity crisis has made it difficult for many entities to determine the fair value of certain financial instruments, because the markets for many financial instruments are no longer active. In April 2008, the IASB has established an expert advisory panel to identify best practices and establish guidance on measuring and disclosing the fair value of financial instruments. In October 2008, the IASB released its final report, *Measuring and Disclosing the Fair Value of Financial Instruments in Markets That Are No Longer Active,* summarizing the discussions held by the panel. An *IASB Staff Summary* was also released, providing educational guidance on using judgment to measure the fair value of financial instruments when markets are no longer active.

The objective of fair value measurement in IAS 39 is to determine the price at which an orderly transaction (excluding forced liquidation or a distress transaction) would take place between market participants at the measurement date. An entity should consider all relevant market information that is available when measuring fair value, and when using a valuation technique, should maximize the use of relevant observable inputs and minimize the use of unobservable inputs. Determining fair value in a market that has become inactive may require the use of significant judgment and include appropriate risk adjustments that market participants would make, such as for credit quality and liquidity.

In some cases, when significant adjustments are required to available observable inputs, it might be appropriate to use a valuation technique based primarily on unobservable inputs (commonly referred to as "mark-to-model"). Multiple inputs from different sources (including broker or pricing service) might provide the best evidence of fair value, and the weighting of those inputs based on the extent to which they provide relevant information about the fair value is required. In weighing a broker quote as an input to a fair value measurement, an entity should place less reliance on quotes that do not reflect the result of market transactions and consider the nature of the quote (for example, whether the quote is an indicative price or a binding offer).

IAS 39 provides guidance about how to determine fair values using valuation techniques. A valuation technique that would be acceptable for use would (1) incorporate all factors that market participants would consider in setting a price and (2) be consistent with accepted economic methodologies for pricing financial instruments. In applying valuation techniques, the reporting entity is to use estimates and assumptions that are consistent with available information about the estimates and assumptions that market participants would use in setting a price for the financial instrument.

Fair value through profit and loss (FVTPL) option. In accordance with IAS 39, an entity can designate any financial asset or financial liability as one to be measured at fair value, with changes in fair value recognized in current profit or loss. However, this election can only be made upon its initial recognition. To preclude the obvious temptation to selectively determine which assets to treat this way from one period to the next, the reporting entity is prohibited from reclassifying financial instruments into or out of this category. Thus, the election is irrevocable upon initial recognition. Since it will not be known at the date of initial recognition whether the fair value of the instrument will increase or decrease in subsequent periods, manipulation of financial results cannot easily occur.

The fair value option can be employed in connection with either available-for-sale or held-to-maturity investments. Designation is made on an instrument-by-instrument basis and the whole instrument approach, so a portion (e.g., 80%) of a financial instrument or a component (e.g., interest rate risk only) cannot be designated. Investments in equity instruments that do not have quoted prices in active markets and whose fair value cannot be reliably measured are *not* eligible for designation as FVTPL.

Constraints on use of held-to-maturity classification. Under IAS 39, held-to-maturity investments are nonderivative financial assets having fixed or determinable payments and fixed maturity, that an entity has the positive intention and ability to hold to maturity other than those that

1. The entity designates as being carried at fair value through profit or loss at the time of initial recognition;
2. The entity designates as available for sale; or
3. Meet the definition of loans and receivables.

Importantly, an entity is not permitted to classify any financial assets as held to maturity if it has, during the current financial reporting year or during the two preceding financial reporting years, sold or reclassified more than an insignificant amount of held-to-maturity investments before maturity other than sales or reclassifications that

1. Are so close to maturity or to the asset's call date (e.g., less than three months before maturity) that changes in the market rate of interest would not have a significant effect on the financial asset's fair value over that time interval;

2. Occur after the entity has collected substantially all of the financial asset's original principal through scheduled payments (e.g., from payments on serial bonds) or prepayments; or
3. Are attributable to an isolated event that is beyond the entity's control, is nonrecurring and could not have been reasonably anticipated by the entity.

In applying the foregoing rule, *more than insignificant* is evaluated in relation to the total amount of held-to-maturity investments.

It is clear that an entity cannot have a demonstrated ability to hold an investment to maturity if it is subject to a constraint that could frustrate its intention to hold the financial asset to maturity. One question that arises is whether a debt security that has been pledged as collateral or transferred to another party under a repurchase agreement ("repo") or instruments lending transaction and continues to be recognized by the reporting entity, can still be classified as a held-to-maturity investment. Accordingly to the IGC (IASB's Implementation Guidance Committee), an entity's intent and ability to hold debt instruments to maturity is not necessarily constrained if those instruments have been pledged as collateral or are subject to a repurchase agreement or instruments lending agreement. However, an entity does not have the positive intent and ability to hold the debt instruments until maturity if it does not expect to be able to maintain or recover access to the instruments. Thus, the specific facts and circumstances of the repo arrangement must be given careful consideration in concluding on the classification of the instruments.

The strictures against early sales of instruments that had been classified as held-to-maturity are quite severe. For example, if an investor sells a significant amount of financial assets classified as held-to-maturity, and does not thereafter classify any financial assets acquired subsequently as held-to-maturity, but maintains that it still intends to hold the remaining investments originally categorized as held-to-maturity to their respective maturities and accordingly does not reclassify them, the reporting entity will be deemed to be not in compliance with IAS 39. Thus, whenever a sale or transfer of more than an insignificant amount of financial assets classified as held-to-maturity results in the conditions in IAS 39 not being satisfied, no instruments should continue to be classified in that category. Any remaining held-to-maturity assets must be reclassified as available-for-sale. The reclassification is recorded in the reporting period in which the sales or transfers occurred and is accounted for as a change in classification as prescribed by the standard. Once this violation has occurred, at least two full years must pass before an entity can again classify financial assets as held-to-maturity.

Another question concerning continuing classification of investments as held-to-maturity relates to sales that are triggered by a change in the management of the investor entity. According to the IGC, such sales would definitely compromise the classification of other financial assets as held-to-maturity. A change in management is not identified under IAS 39 as an instance where sales or transfers from held-to-maturity do not compromise the classification as held-to-maturity. Sales that are made in response to such a change in management would, therefore, call into question the entity's intent to hold any of its investments to maturity.

The IGC cited an example similar to the following. A company held a portfolio of financial assets that was classified as held-to-maturity. In the current period, at the direction of the board of directors, the entire senior management team was replaced. The new management wishes to sell a portion of the held-to-maturity financial assets in order to carry out an expansion strategy designated and approved by the board, as part of its recovery strategy. Although the previous management team had been in place since the entity's inception and the company had never before undergone a major restructuring, the sale will nevertheless call into question this entity's intent to hold remaining held-to-maturity financial assets to maturity. If the sale goes forward, all held-to-maturity instruments would have to be reclassified, and the entity will be precluded from using that classification for investments for another two years.

Another example of the stringency of the requirements for classifying instruments as held-to-maturity is suggested by an IGC position on sales made to satisfy regulatory authorities. In some countries, regulators of banks or other industries may set capital requirements on an entity-specific basis based on an assessment of the risk in that particular entity. IAS 39 indicates that an entity that sells held-to-maturity investments in response to an unanticipated significant increase by the regulator of the industry's capital requirements may do so under that standard without necessarily raising a question about its intention to hold other investments to maturity. The IGC has ruled, however, that sales of held-to-maturity investments that are due to a significant increase in *entity-specific* capital requirements imposed by regulators will indeed "taint" the entity's intent to hold other financial assets as held-to-maturity. Thus, unless it can be demonstrated that the sales fulfill the condition in IAS 39 in that the sales were the result of an increase in capital requirements which was an isolated event that was beyond the entity's control and that is nonrecurring and could not have been reasonably anticipated by the entity.

Held-to-maturity investments disposed of before maturity. As noted above, an entity may not classify any financial asset as held-to-maturity unless it has both the positive intent and ability to hold it to maturity. To put teeth into this threshold criterion, IAS 39 stipulates that, if a sale of a held-to-maturity financial asset occurs, it calls into question the entity's intent to hold all other held-to-maturity financial assets to maturity. However, IAS 39 provides exceptions for held-to-maturity investments that can be disposed of before maturity under certain conditions: for sales "close enough to maturity," and after collection of "substantially all" of the original principal.

Questions have arisen in practice on how these conditions should be interpreted. The IGC has offered certain insights into the application of these exception criteria. As interpreted, these conditions relate to situations in which an entity can be expected to be indifferent whether to hold or sell a financial asset because movements in interest rates—occurring after substantially all of the original principal has been collected or when the instrument is close to maturity—will not have a significant impact on its fair value. In such situations, a sale would not affect reported net profit or loss and no price volatility would be expected during the remaining period to maturity.

More specifically, the condition "close enough to maturity" addresses the extent to which interest rate risk is substantially eliminated as a pricing factor. According to the IGC, if an entity sells a financial asset less than three months before its scheduled maturity, which would generally qualify for use of this exception. The impact on the fair value of the instrument for a difference between the stated interest rate and the market rate generally would be small for an instrument that matures in three months, in contrast to an instrument that matures in several years, for example.

The condition of having collected "substantially all" of the original principal provides guidance as to when a sale is for not more than an insignificant amount. Thus, if an entity sells a financial asset after it has collected 90% or more of the financial asset's original principal through scheduled payments or prepayments, the requirements of IAS 39 would probably not be deemed to have been violated. However, if the entity has collected only 10% of the original principal, then that condition clearly is not met. The 90% threshold is apparently not meant to be absolute, so some judgment is still needed to operationalize this exception.

In some cases a debt instrument will have a put option associated with it; this gives the holder (the investor) the right, but not the obligation, to require that the issuer redeem the debt, under defined conditions. The existence of the put option need not be an impediment to held-to-maturity classification. IAS 39 permits an entity to classify a puttable debt instrument as held-to-maturity, provided that the investor has the positive intent and ability to hold the investment until maturity and does not intend to exercise the put option. However, if an entity has sold, transferred, or exercised a put option on more than an insignificant amount of other held-to-maturity investments, the continued use of the held-to-maturity classification would be prohibited, subject to exceptions for certain sales (very close to maturity, after substantially all principal has been recovered, and due to certain isolated events). The IGC has stated that these same exceptions apply to transfers and exercises (rather than outright sales) of put options in similar circumstances. The IGC cautions, however, that classification of puttable debt as held-to-maturity requires great care, as it seems inconsistent with the likely intent when purchasing a puttable debt instrument. Given that the investor presumably would have paid extra for the put option, it would seem counter intuitive that the investor would be willing to represent that it does not intend to exercise that option.

In addition to debt instruments being held to maturity, any financial asset that does not have a quoted market price in an active market, fair value of which cannot be reliably measured, will of necessity also be maintained at cost, unless there is evidence of impairment in value. Furthermore, loans or receivables which are originated by the reporting entity, and which are *not* held for trading purposes, are also to be maintained at cost, per IAS 39. Loans or receivables that are acquired from others, however, are accounted for in the same manner as other debt instruments (i.e., they must be classified as at fair value through profit or loss, available-for-sale, or held-to-maturity, and accounted for accordingly).

Under IAS 39, held-to-maturity financial assets (i.e., debt instruments held for long-term investment) and originated loans are measured at amortized cost, using the effective interest method. This requires that any premium or discount be amortized not on the straight-line basis, but rather by the effective interest method, in order to achieve a constant yield on the amortized carrying value. One question that arises is how discount or premium arising in connection with the purchase of a variable-rate debt instrument should be amortized (i.e., whether it should be amortized to maturity or to the next repricing date.)

The IGC has ruled that this depends generally on whether, at the next repricing date, the fair value of the financial asset will be its par value. In theory, of course, a constantly repricing variable-rate instrument will sell at or very close to par value, since it offers a current yield fully reflective of market rates and the issuer's credit risk. Accordingly, the IGC notes that there are two potential reasons for the discount or premium: it either (1) could reflect the timing of interest payments—for instance, because interest payments are in arrears or have otherwise accrued since the most recent interest payment date or market rates of interest have changed since the debt instrument was most recently repriced to par—or (2) the market's required yield differs from the stated variable rate, for instance, because the credit spread required by the market for the specific instrument is higher or lower than the credit spread that is implicit in the variable rate.

Thus, a discount or premium that reflects interest that has accrued on the instrument since interest was last paid or changes in market rates of interest since the debt instrument was most recently repriced to par is to be amortized to the date that the accrued interest will be paid and the variable interest rate will be reset to the market rate. On the other hand, to the extent the discount or premium results from a change in the credit spread over the variable rate specified in the instrument, it is to be amortized over the remaining term to maturity of the instrument. In this case, the date the interest rate is next reset is not a market-based repricing date of the entire instrument, since the variable rate is not adjusted for changes in the credit spread for the specific issue.

Example

To illustrate, a twenty-year bond is issued at €10,000,000, which is the principal (i.e., par) amount. The debt requires quarterly interest payments equal to current three-month LIBOR plus 1% over the life of the instrument. The interest rate reflects the market-based required rate of return associated with the bond issue at issuance. Subsequent to issuance, the credit quality of the issuer deteriorates, resulting in a bond rating downgrade. Thereafter, the bond trades at a significant discount. Columbia Co. purchases the bond for €9,500,000 and classifies it as held-to-maturity. In this case, the discount of €500,000 is amortized to profit or loss over the period to the maturity of the bond. The discount is not amortized to the next date interest rate payments are reset. At each reporting date, Columbia assesses the likelihood that it will not be able to collect all amounts due (principal and interest) according to the contractual terms of the instrument, to determine the need for recognizing an impairment loss as a charge against profit or loss.

With the foregoing principles in mind, a basic example of the accounting for investments in equity instruments is next presented.

Example of accounting for investments in equity instruments

Assume that Raphael Corporation acquires the following equity instruments for investment purposes during 2009:

Security description	Acquisition cost	Fair value at year-end
1,000 shares Belarus Steel common stock	€ 34,500	€ 37,000
2,000 shares Wimbledon pfd. "A" share	125,000	109,500
1,000 shares Hillcrest common stock	74,250	88,750

Assume that, at the respective dates of acquisition, management of Raphael Corporation designated the Belarus Steel and Hillcrest common stock investments as being for trading purposes, while the Wimbledon preferred shares were designated as having been purchased for long-term investment purposes (and will thus be categorized as available-for-sale rather than trading). Accordingly, the entries to record the purchases were as follows:

Investment in equity instruments—held-for-trading	108,750	
Cash		108,750
Investment in equity instruments—available-for-sale	125,000	
Cash		125,000

At year-end, both portfolios are adjusted to fair value; the decline in Wimbledon preferred share, series A, is judged to be a temporary market fluctuation because there is no objective evidence of impairment. The entries to adjust the investment accounts at December 31, 2009, are as follows:

Investment in equity instruments—held-for-trading	17,000	
Gain on holding equity instruments		17,000
Unrealized loss on equity instruments (OCI)—available-for-sale		
(other comprehensive income account)	15,500	
Investment in equity instruments—available-for-sale		15,500

Thus, the change in value of the portfolio of trading financial assets is recognized in profit or loss, whereas the change in the value of the available-for-sale financial assets is reflected in other comprehensive income and accumulated in equity.

Reclassifications

Amendments to IAS 39—reclassifications from the held-for-trading category. There is a limited ability to revise the classification of investments in financial instruments under IAS 39. This limitation is to avoid providing a vehicle by which to manipulate profit or loss by, for example, deciding period-by-period which value changes will be reflected in profit or loss and which will be reported in other comprehensive income (and accumulated in equity). Entities cannot reclassify instruments that were designated as at fair value through profit or loss using the fair value option, nor derivatives.

In October 2008, the IASB published amendments to IAS 39 and IFRS 7 to allow reclassification of certain financial instruments from held-for-trading to either held-to-maturity, loans and receivables, or available-for-sale categories under certain circumstances. The amendments were made in response to requests by regulators to allow banks to measure instruments which are no longer traded in an active market at amortized cost, and consequently reducing reported profit or loss volatility. Under US GAAP, transfers from those categories are restricted but still possible, whereas under IAS 39 no such reclassifications were previously permitted.

Entities are allowed to reclassify certain financial instruments out of the held-for-trading category if the original intent has changed and they are no longer held for sale in the near future. The amended IAS 39 distinguishes between those financial assets which are eligible for classification as loans and receivables and those which are not. Financial assets are eligible for classification as loans and receivables if they are held for trading and, in addition, have fixed or determinable payments, are not quoted in an active market, and are those for which the holder should recover substantially all of its initial investment, other than as might be impacted by credit deterioration.

Financial assets that are not eligible for classification as loans and receivables can be transferred from the held-for-trading category to held-to-maturity or to available-for-sale only in "rare" circumstances. The Basis for Conclusions to IAS 39 states that "rare" circumstances arise from a single event that is "unusual and highly unlikely to recur in the near term." On its Web site, the IASB has confirmed that the deterioration of world markets that has occurred during the third quarter of 2008 is a possible example of rare circumstances.

In addition, concerning loans and receivables, if an entity has the intention and the ability to hold the asset for the "foreseeable future" or until maturity

- Financial assets that would *not* meet the criteria to be classified as loans and receivables may be transferred from held-for-trading to loans and receivables, and
- Financial assets that would now meet the criteria to be classified as loans and receivables may be reclassified out of the available-for-sale category to loans and receivables.

The reclassification should be based on the fair value on the date of reclassification, which becomes the new cost (or amortized cost). For example, an instrument that was acquired at its par value of €1,000 had declined in fair value to €700, and is now reclassified as held-to-maturity, should be measured at amortized cost of €700. Any difference between the new amortized cost and the instrument's expected recoverable amount is amortized using the new effective interest rate over the expected remaining life, similar to the amortization of a premium or discount. Gain or loss that has already been recognized in profit or loss should not be reversed. Therefore, in the above example, the loss of €300 recognized previously, would not be reversed through profit or loss, either on reclassification or in future, except through adjustments to interest income.

Any reclassified instruments are subsequently tested for impairments in accordance with the IAS 39 impairment requirements for the categories into which they are reclassified. For example, any subsequent changes in fair value of an instrument reclassified into the available-for-sale category (other than amortization of interest using the new effective interest rate) from the date of reclassification will be recorded in other comprehensive income and accumulated in equity as revaluation surplus until the instrument is derecognized or impaired.

The effective date of the amended standard is July 1, 2008. Reclassifications before this date are not permitted, so on the first application of the amended standard entities can reclassify instruments as early as July 1, 2008. The amendments to IFRS 7 require substantial disclosure which would permit a user of the financial statements to understand the results of the reclassification as well as of what would have been the accounting results had the reclassification not been made. Amendments to IFRS 7 are discussed in Chapter 5.

Reclassifications from the held-to-maturity to available-for-sale category. IAS 39 requires that a held-to-maturity investment must be reclassified as available-for-sale and remeasured at fair value as of the date of transfer if there is a change of intent or ability. Note that this may well be at an interim date, and fair value as of the next reporting date would not necessarily suffice to gauge the gain or loss to be recognized. Transfers from the held-to-maturity category to available-for-sale are measured at fair value at the date of transfer with the difference between the financial instrument's carrying amount and fair value recognized in other comprehensive income (and accumulated in equity)

Reclassifications out of the held-to-maturity category may jeopardize all other similar classifications. The IGC has addressed the issue of whether such a reclassification might call into question the classification of other held-to-maturity investments. It finds that such reclassifications could well raise the specter of having to reclassify all similarly categorized investments. IAS 39's requirements concerning early sales of some held-to-maturity investments apply not only to sales, but also to transfers of such investments. The term "transfer" comprises any reclassification out of the held-to-maturity category. Thus, the transfer of more than an insignificant portion of held-to-maturity investments into the available-for-sale category would not be consistent with an intent to hold other held-to-maturity investments to maturity.

Consequently, investments classified as held-to-maturity may be mandatorily reclassified to available-for-sale if the entity, during the current year or the two prior years, has sold, transferred, or exercised a put option on more than an insignificant amount of similarly classified instruments before maturity date. However, sales very close to the maturity dates (or exercised call dates) will not "taint" the classification of other held-to-maturity financial assets, nor will sales occurring after substantially all of the asset's principal has been collected (e.g., in the case of serial bonds or mortgage instruments), or when made in response to isolated events beyond the entity's control (e.g., the debtor's impending financial collapse) when nonrecurring in nature and not subject to having been forecast by the entity.

Reclassification from the available-for-sale to held-to-maturity category. An entity is permitted, as a result of a change in intention or ability and because the two-year "tainting period" has passed, to reclassify any financial assets from the available-for-sale category to the held-to-maturity category. Transfers from the available-for-sale to the held-to-maturity category are measured at fair value at the date of transfer with the fair value on the date of reclassification becoming the amortized cost.

Reclassifications from the available-for-sale category to cost. Any financial asset classified as available-for-sale that does not have a quoted market price in an active market or has fair value which cannot be reliably measured, will of necessity be carried at cost, unless there is evidence of impairment in value. Furthermore, on the date when a quoted price in active markets becomes available or its fair value can be reliably measured, the financial asset must be reclassified to the available-for-sale category, with changes in fair value recognized in other comprehensive income and accumulated in equity.

Reclassifications from or to the fair value through profit or loss (FVTPL) category. Historically, under the provisions of IAS 39, financial instruments classified as at fair value through profit or loss (held-for-trading, and those designated as at fair value through profit or loss upon initial recognition) could not later be reclassified out of this category; conversely, transfers to the FVTPL category are also prohibited (whereas previously there were permitted but were expected to be infrequent, occurring only when there was evidence of trading behavior by the entity which strongly suggested that the investment in question will indeed be traded in the short term).

Amendments to IAS 39 published in 2008 permit the reclassification of securities out of the held-for-trading category in rare circumstances as well as reclassification of loans and receivables out of held-for-trading (or available-for-sale) if the entity has the intention and ability to hold the asset for the foreseeable future or until maturity (see discussion in paragraph Amendments to IAS 39—Reclassification out of the "held-for-trading" category). This treatment does not apply to those instruments carried at FVTPL which have been designated under the "fair value option" at acquisition, since this election cannot later be revoked. Consequently, neither those investments which were at first denoted as carried at FVTPL using the fair value option, nor derivatives, can ever be later defined as held-to-maturity or as available-for-sale, and those investments not originally classed as at FVTPL using the fair value option cannot later be so categorized, under IAS 39. This is a direct consequence of the desire to not permit changes in designation of investments in any way that would alter which value changes are being reported in profit or loss.

Example of accounting for reclassifications of investments

Marseilles Corporation purchases the following debt instruments as investments in 2009:

Issue	Face value	Price paid*
DeLacroix Chemical 8% due 2014	€200,000	€190,000
Forsythe Pharmaceutical 9.90% due 2024	500,000	575,000
Luckystrike Mining 6% due 2011	100,000	65,000

* *Accrued interest is ignored in these amounts; the normal entries for interest accrual and receipt are assumed.*

Management has stated that Marseilles's objectives differed among the various investments. Thus, the DeLacroix bonds are considered to be suitable as a long-term investment, with the intention that they will be held until maturity. The Luckystrike bonds are a speculation; the significant discount from par value was seen as very attractive, despite the low coupon rate. Management believes the bonds were depressed because mining shares and bonds have been out of favor, but believes the economic recovery will lead to a surge in market value, at which point the bonds will be sold for a quick profit. The Forsythe Pharmaceutical bonds are deemed a good investment, but with a maturity date sixteen years in the future, management is unable to commit to holding these to maturity.

Based on the foregoing, the appropriate accounting for the three investments in bonds would be as follows:

DeLacroix Chemical 8% due 2014

These should be accounted for as held-to-maturity; maintain at cost, with the discount (€10,000) to be amortized over term to maturity using the effective interest method.

Forsythe Pharmaceutical 9.90% due 2024

Account for these as available-for-sale, since neither the held-for-trading nor held-to-maturity criteria apply. These should be reported at fair value at the end of each reporting period, with any unrealized gain or loss included in the other comprehensive income account (consistent with the entity's normal accounting practice), unless an impairment occurs.

Luckystrike Mining 6% due 2011

As an admitted speculation, these should be accounted for as part of the trading portfolio, and also reported at fair value in the statement of financial position. All adjustments to carrying value will be included in profit or loss each year, whether the fair value fluctuations are temporary or permanent in nature.

Transfers between portfolio categories are to be accounted for at fair value at the date of the transfer, as described above. However, only certain types of transfers are permitted under IAS 39. For example, transfers out of the trading category are permitted only in rare circumstances, since there is a strong presumption that trading instruments are properly defined at the date of their acquisition.

To better understand the limited opportunity for reclassification of financial assets held as trading, available-for-sale or held-to maturity investments by the entity, and the accounting for such transfers as are permitted, consider the following events:

1. Marseilles management decides in 2010, when the Forsythe bonds have a market (fair) value of €604,500, that the bonds will be disposed of in the short term, hopefully when the price hits €605,000. Under revised IAS 39, the decision to sell a financial asset does not make it a financial asset held for trading, and transfers into the trading portfolio are not allowed. Therefore, these bonds will continue to be held in the available-for-sale portfolio, and fair value changes will be recognized in other comprehensive income, unless this investment was denoted under the "fair value option" at acquisition date.

2. In 2010, Marseilles management also made a decision about its investment in DeLacroix Chemical bonds. These bonds, which were originally designated as held-to-maturity, were accounted for at amortized cost. Assume the amortization in 2009 was €2,000 (because the bonds were not held for a full year), so that the book value of the investment at year-end 2009 was €192,000. In 2010, at a time when the value of these bonds was €198,000, management concluded that it was no longer certain that they would be held to maturity. While the change in management's intention could be seen as providing support for a reclassification of this investment to the available-for-sale portfolio, to do so would raise a tainting concern which would jeopardize any classification of further investments as held-to-maturity.

According to IAS 39, investments in debt instruments may be categorized as held-to-maturity only when there is a positive intent to do so. The intent is absent when the reporting entity stands ready to sell that asset in response to changes in market conditions or the entity's liquidity needs, among other considerations. As described here, Marseilles management seemingly has reacted to either market conditions or its own liquidity needs in effectively retracting its commitment to hold the DeLacroix bonds to maturity. If reclassification were effected, there would be a virtually certain presumption that no other fixed maturity investment could thereafter be classified as held-to-maturity—there would be tainting which would preclude usage of that classification. This would apply even to other investments being held currently, where no intent to dispose before maturity had even been manifested. Thus (as interpreted by the IGC), the tainting issue must be taken extremely seriously.

It should also be understood that transfers into the held-to-maturity category would be feasible in rare circumstances.

Impairments and Uncollectibility

Accounting for impairments—general concerns. A financial asset or group of financial assets (except those carried at FVTPL) need to be assessed at the end of each reporting period, whether there is any objective evidence that the assets are impaired. This is to be assessed as a result of one or more events that occurred after the initial recognition of the asset (a "loss event") and that loss event (or events) impacts the estimated future cash flows of the financial asset(s) that can be reliably estimated. Loss events include any significant financial difficulties of the issuer, a contractual breach (default or delinquency) by the issuer, the probability of a bankruptcy or financial reorganization, or the disappearance of an active market for the issuer's instruments (although the fact that an entity has "gone private" does not create the presumption of impairment).

If there is an objective evidence of impairment, measurement of impairment losses presented in Table 2 is as follows:

Table 2. Measurement of Impairment Losses

Financial assets carried at	*Measurement of impairment loss*
Amortized cost (Loans & receivables; Held to maturity)	Difference between the carrying amount and the present value of expected future cash flows, discounted using the instrument's original discount rate
Fair value (Available for sale)	Difference between the acquisition cost (net of any principal repayment and amortization) and current fair value, less any impairment loss previously recognized in profit or loss.
Cost (Fair value cannot be reliably measured)	Difference between the carrying amount of the financial asset and the present value of estimated future cash flows discounted at the current market rate of return for similar financial asset.

For financial assets being reported at amortized cost (those held to maturity, plus loans or receivables originated by the entity), the amount of the impairment to be recognized is the difference between the carrying amount and the present value of expected future cash flows, discounted using the instrument's original discount rate. Unquoted equity instruments carried at cost (because its fair value cannot be reliably measured) are also tested for impairment and the amount of impairment loss is calculated as the difference between the carrying amount of the financial asset and the present value of estimated future cash flows discounted at the current market rate of return for similar financial asset. If a decline in the fair value of an available-for-sale financial asset has been recognized in other comprehensive income and there is objective evidence that the asset is impaired, the cumulative impairment loss should be reclassified from equity to profit or loss.

Evidence of impairment. A financial asset (or a group of assets) is impaired only if there is objective evidence of impairments as a result of one or more events that occurred after the initial recognition of the asset (which IAS 39 calls a "loss event") and that loss event (or events) has an impact on the estimated future cash flows of the financial asset (or group of assets) that can be reliably estimated. Losses that are anticipated to occur as a result of future events, no matter how likely this may appear to be, cannot be given current recognition. (This is consistent with guidance on provisions and contingencies under IAS 37.)

In practice, it may not be possible to identify a single, specific event that causes an impairment. Rather, the combined effect of several events may be the cause. Revised IAS 39 does offer a useful tabulation of such factors, however. These include the following matters:

1. Significant financial difficulty of the issuer or obligor;
2. A default or delinquency in interest or principal payments, or other breach of contract by the borrower;
3. The lender, for economic or legal reasons relating to the borrower's financial difficulty, granting an otherwise unlikely concession to the borrower;
4. A growing likelihood that the borrower will enter bankruptcy or reorganize;
5. The elimination of an active market for the asset because of financial difficulties; or
6. Observable data about a measurable decrease in the estimated future cash flows from a *group* of financial assets since their initial recognition, although the decrease cannot yet be identified with the individual financial assets in the group, including

    a. Adverse changes in the payment status of borrowers in the group (e.g., an increased number of late payments; increased frequency of credit card borrowers reaching their credit limits and that are paying monthly minimums); or

b. National or local economic indicators that correlate with defaults on the assets in the group (e.g., increased unemployment rate in the geographical area of the borrowers; decreased property prices (for mortgage assets); decreased commodity process (for loans to commodity producers); adverse changes in other industry conditions).

In addition to the above loss events, objective evidence of impairment for an investment in an equity instrument includes information about changes in technological, economic, and legal environments. A significant or prolonged decline in the fair value of an investment in equity instruments below its cost may also constitute objective evidence of impairment.

The disappearance of an active market because an entity's financial instruments are no longer publicly traded, and a decline in the fair value of a financial asset below its cost or amortized cost, is not necessarily evidence of impairment, although it may be evidence of impairment when considered with other available information. In some cases experienced professional judgment must be used to estimate the amount of impairment losses, for example when a borrower is in financial difficulties and there are few available historical data relating to similar borrowers.

Impairment of financial assets carried at amortized cost. IAS 39 requires that impairment be recognized for financial assets carried at amortized cost (loans and receivables or held-to-maturity investments) if there is objective evidence that an impairment has been incurred. That impairment may be measured and recognized individually or, for a group of similar financial assets, on a portfolio basis. As noted above, the amount of the loss is measured as the difference between the asset's carrying amount and the present value of estimated future cash flows discounted at the financial asset's original effective interest rate. Future credit losses that have not been incurred cannot be included in this computation (again, the concepts underlying IAS 37 must be observed). The original effective rate is not the nominal or contractual rate of the debt, but rather is the effective interest rate computed at the date of initial recognition of the investment. If an impairment is determined to exist, the carrying amount of the asset may either be reduced directly or via the use of an allowance (reserve) account. Any loss is to be recognized currently in profit or loss.

Where there is no ability to individually assess financial assets accounted for at amortized cost for impairment, IAS 39 directs that these assets be grouped and assessed on a portfolio basis. The following additional guidance is provided to evaluate impairment inherent in a group of loans, receivables or held-to-maturity investments that cannot be identified with any individual financial asset in the group:

• Assets individually assessed for impairment and found to be impaired should not be included in a group of assets that are collectively assessed for impairment
• Assets individually assessed for impairment and found *not* to be individually impaired should be included in a collective assessment of impairment
• When performing a collective assessment of impairment, an entity groups assets by similar credit risk characteristics
• Expected cash flows are estimated based on contractual cash flows and historical loss experience (adjusted on the basis of relevant observable data reflecting current economic conditions)
• Impairment loss should not be recognized on the initial recognition of an asset.

A reversal of a previously recognized impairment is permitted when there is clear evidence that the reversal occurred subsequent to the initial impairment recognition and is the result of a discrete event, such as the improved credit rating of the debtor. This reversal is accounted for consistent with the impairment—that is, it is recognized in current period profit or loss. However, the amount of recovery recognition is limited, so that the new carrying value of the asset is no greater than what its carrying value would have been had the impairment not occurred, adjusted for any amortization over the intervening period. For example, consider an asset that was carried at €8,000 and being accreted, at €500 per year, to a maturity value of €10,000 at the time it was found to be impaired and written down to €5,000. Two years later the credit-related problem was resolved and the fair value was assessed as €9,500. However, it can only be restored to a carrying value of €9,000, which is what would have been the carrying value had two further years' amortization (at €500 per year) been accreted.

If an asset has been individually assessed for impairment and was found not be individually impaired, according to IAS 39 it should be included in the collective assessment of impairment. According to the standard, this is to reflect that, in the light of the law of large numbers, impairment may be evident in a group of assets, but not yet meet the threshold for recognition when any individual asset in that group is assessed.

However, it is not permissible to avoid addressing impairment on an individual asset basis in order to use group assessment, in a deliberate effort to benefit from the implicit offsetting described above. If one asset in the group is impaired but the fair value of another asset in the group is above its amortized cost, nonrecognition of the impairment of the first asset is not permitted. If it is known that an individual financial asset carried at amortized cost is impaired, IAS 39 requires that the impairment of that asset be recognized. Measurement of impairment on a portfolio basis under IAS 39 is applicable *only* when there is indication of impairment in a group of similar assets, and impairment cannot be identified with an individual asset in that group.

In actually assessing impairment on a portfolio basis (a "collective assessment of impairment"), care should be taken to include only assets having similar credit risk characteristics, indicative of the debtors' ability to pay all amounts due according to the contractual terms. While contractual cash flows and historical loss experience will provide a basis for estimating *expected* cash flows, these historical data must be adjusted for relevant observable data reflecting current (i.e., as of the end of the reporting period) economic conditions.

IAS 39 further cautions that whatever methodology is used to measure impairment, it should ensure that an impairment loss is not recognized at the initial recognition of an asset. Put another way, the imputed interest rate on a newly acquired debt instrument should be the rate that equates the net carrying amount of the financial instrument and the present value of future cash flows, and this rate is used consistently thereafter in valuing the asset as future cash flow expectations change. An impairment on "day one" thus cannot exist, and would indicate an error in methodology should it occur.

Assessment and recognition of loan impairment. If an originated loan with fixed interest rate payments is hedged against the exposure to interest rate risk by a "receive-variable, pay-fixed" interest rate swap, the hedge relationship qualifies for fair value hedge accounting and is reported as a fair value hedge. Thus, the carrying amount of the loan includes an adjustment for fair value changes attributable to movements in interest rates. According to an interpretive finding by the IGC, an assessment of impairment in the loan should take into account the fair value adjustment for interest rate risk. Since the loan's original effective interest rate prior to the hedge is made irrelevant once the carrying amount of the loan is adjusted for any changes in its fair value attributable to interest rate movements, the original effective interest rate and amortized cost of the loan are adjusted to take into account recognized fair value changes. The adjusted effective interest rate is calculated using the adjusted carrying amount of the loan. An impairment loss on the hedged loan should therefore be calculated as the difference between its carrying amount after adjustment for fair value changes attributable to the risk being hedged and the expected future cash flows of the loan discounted at the adjusted effective interest rate.

Assume that, due to financial difficulties of Knapsack Co., one of its customers, the Galactic Bank, becomes concerned that Knapsack will not be able to make all principal and interest payments due on an originated loan when they become due. Galactic negotiates a restructuring of the loan, and it now expects that Knapsack will be able to meet its obligations under the restructured terms. Whether Galactic Bank will recognize an impairment loss—and in what magnitude—will depend, according to the IGC, on the specifics of the restructured terms. The IGC offers the following guidelines.

If, under the terms of the restructuring, Knapsack Co. will pay the full principal amount of the original loan five years after the original due date, but none of the interest due under the original terms, an impairment must be recognized, since the present value of the future principal and interest payments discounted at the loan's original effective interest rate (i.e., the recoverable amount) will be lower than the carrying amount of the loan.

If, on the other hand, Knapsack Co.'s restructuring agreement calls for it to pay the full principal amount of the original loan on the original due date, but none of the interest due under the original terms, the same result as the foregoing will again hold. The impairment will be measured as the difference between the former carrying amount and the present value of the future principal and interest payments discounted at the loan's original effective interest rate.

As yet another variation on the restructuring theme, if Knapsack will pay the full principal amount on the original due date with interest, only at a lower interest rate than the interest rate inherent in the original loan, again the same guidance is offered by the IGC, so that an impairment must be recognized.

This same outcome prevails if Knapsack agrees to pay the full principal amount five years after the original due date and all interest accrued during the original loan term, but no interest for the extended term. Since the present value of future cash flows is lower than the loan's carrying amount, impairment is to be recognized.

As a final option, the IGC offers the loan restructuring situation whereby Knapsack is to pay the full principal amount five years after the original due date and all interest, including interest for both the original term of the loan and the extended term. In this scenario, even though the amount and timing of payments has changed, Galactic Bank will nonetheless receive interest on interest, so that the present value of the future principal and interest payments discounted at the loan's original effective interest rate will equal the carrying amount of the loan. Therefore, there is no impairment loss.

Impairment of financial assets carried at cost. Impairment losses on unquoted equity instruments that are not carried at fair value because the fair value cannot be reliably measured, or on a derivative asset that is linked to and must be settled by delivery of such an unquoted equity instrument, are recognized if there is objective evidence that impairment losses have occurred. These are measured as the difference between the carrying amount of the financial asset and the present value of estimated future cash flows discounted at the current market rate of return for similar financial asset. Note that current rates, not the original effective rate, are the relevant reference, since these investments were being maintained at cost by default (i.e., due to the absence of reliable fair value data), not because they qualified for amortized cost due to being held to maturity. Accordingly, the application of fair value accounting, or a reasonable surrogate for it, is valid in such instances. No reversals of prior impairment losses are allowed for financial assets measured at cost.

Impairment of financial assets carried at fair value. The fair value of an equity security that is classified as available-for-sale may fall below its carrying amount and that is not necessarily evidence of impairment. When an entity reports fair value changes on available-for-sale financial assets in other comprehensive income and equity in accordance with IAS 39, it continues to do so until there is objective evidence of impairment, such as the circumstances identified in the standard. If objective evidence of impairment exists, any cumulative impairment loss that has been recognized in other comprehensive income should be reclassified from equity to profit or loss for the period.

The amount of the cumulative impairment loss that is reclassified from equity to profit or loss is the difference between the acquisition cost (net of any principal repayment and amortization) and current fair value, less any impairment loss previously recognized in profit or loss.

Reversals of impairment losses recognized in profit or loss for an investment in *equity* instruments are *not* allowed. Since no reversal of the impairment loss is allowed for equity instruments, so that, if subsequent to impairment recognition there is an increase in the fair value of the available-for-sale investment, that increase is recognized in other comprehensive income and not in profit or loss.

Reversals of impairment losses recognized in profit or loss for an investment in *debt* instruments should be reversed, with the amount of the reversal recognized in profit or loss if the increase in the fair value is objectively linked to an event occurring after the impairment loss was recognized.

No assessment of impairment is conducted for investments in debt and equity instruments classified as at FVTPL since these instruments are valued at fair value with mark-to-market adjustments recognized in profit or loss.

IFRIC 10, *Interim Financial Reporting and Impairment*, addressing conflicts between the requirements of IAS 34, *Interim Financial Reporting*, and those in other standards on the recognition and reversal in the financial statements of impairment losses in respect of goodwill or an investment in either an equity instrument or a financial asset carried at cost under IAS 39, states that any impairment losses recognized in an interim financial statement must not be reversed in subsequent interim or annual financial statements.

Example of impairment of investments

Given the foregoing, assume now, with reference again to the Raphael Corporation example first presented earlier in this chapter, that in January 2010 new information comes to Raphael Corporation management regarding the viability of Wimbledon Corp. Based on this information, it is determined that the decline in Wimbledon preferred share is probably not a temporary one, but rather is an impairment of the asset as that term is used in IAS 39. The standard prescribes that such a decline be reflected in profit or loss. The share's fair value has remained at the amount last reported, €109,500, but this value is no longer viewed as being only a market fluctuation. Accordingly, the entry to recognize the fact of the investment's permanent impairment is as follows:

Impairment loss on holding equity instruments	15,500	
Unrealized loss on equity instruments—available-for-sale (other		
comprehensive income)		15,500

Any later recovery of impairment losses on available-for-sale equity instruments cannot be reversed. Later market fluctuations will be reported in other comprehensive income.

To illustrate this point, assume that in March 2010 new information comes to management's attention, which suggests that the decline in Wimbledon preferred had indeed been only a temporary decline; in fact, the value of Wimbledon now rises to €112,000. It would not be permitted under revised IAS 39 to reverse the impairment loss that had been included in profit or loss. The carrying value after the recognition of the impairment was €109,500, and the current period increase to €112,000 will have to be accounted for as an increase to be reflected in other comprehensive income, rather than in profit or loss. The entry required to reflect this is

Investment in equity instruments—available-for-sale	2,500	
Unrealized gain on equity instruments—available-for-sale (other comprehensive income)		2,500

However, if this investment is a debt instrument classified as available-for-sale, evidence of any specific event occurring after the date of the impairment loss recognized in profit or loss that is responsible for this recovery in value can be reversed through profit or loss. Any increases in value above the original cost basis would not be taken into profit or loss, but rather recognized in other comprehensive income, since the investment is classified as available-for-sale.

Structured notes as held-to-maturity investments. Among the more complex of what are commonly referred to as "engineered" financial products, which have become commonplace over the last decade, are "structured notes." Structured notes and related products are privately negotiated and not easily marketable once acquired. These instruments often appear to be straightforward debt investments, but in fact contain provisions which have the potential to greatly increase or decrease the return to the investor, based on (typically) the movement of some index related to currency exchange rates, interest rates, or, in some cases, share price indices. The IGC has addressed the question of whether these assets can be considered as held-to-maturity investments. The IGC offers as an example a structured note tied to an equity price index, upon which the following illustration is based.

Example of structured debt instrument

Cartegena Co. purchases a five-year "equity-index-linked note" with an original issue price of €1,000,000 at its market price of €1,200,000 at the time of purchase. The note requires no interest payments prior to maturity. At maturity, the note requires payment of the original issue price of €1,000,000 plus a supplemental redemption amount that depends on whether a specified share price index (e.g. the Dow Jones Industrial Average) exceeds a predetermined level at the maturity date. If the share index does not exceed or is equal to the predetermined level, no supplemental redemption amount is paid. If the share index exceeds the predetermined level, the supplemental redemption amount will equal 115% of the difference between the level of the share index at maturity and the level of the share index at original issuance of the note divided by the level of the share index at original issuance.

Obviously, the investment is largely a gamble on an increase in the Dow Jones average over the five-year term, since Cartegena is paying a substantial premium and, as a worst-case scenario, could lose its entire premium plus the opportunity cost of lost interest over the five years. Structured notes such as this are very difficult to dispose of on the secondary (i.e., resale) market, having been created (structured) to fit the unique needs or desires of the issuer and investor. Determining a fair value at any intermediate point in the five-year holding period would be difficult or impossible, absent arm's-length bids, particularly if the underlying index has yet to advance to a level at which a gain will be reaped by the investor.

In the present example, assume that Cartegena has the positive intent and ability to hold the note to maturity. According to guidance issued by the IGC, it can indeed classify this note as a held-to-maturity investment, because it has a fixed payment of €1,000,000 and a fixed maturity, and because Cartegena Co. has the positive intent and ability to hold it to maturity. However, the equity index feature is a call option not closely related to the debt host, and accordingly, it must be separated as an embedded derivative under IAS 39. The purchase price of €1,200,000 must be allocated between the host debt instrument and the embedded derivative. For instance, if the fair value of the embedded option at acquisition is €400,000, the host debt instrument is measured at €800,000 on initial recognition. In this case, the discount of €200,000 that is implicit in the host bond is amortized to net profit or loss over the term to maturity of the note using the effective interest method.

A similar situation arises if the investment is a bond with a fixed payment at maturity and a fixed maturity date, but with variable interest payments indexed to the price of a commodity or equity (commodity-indexed or equity-indexed bonds). If the entity has the positive intent and ability to hold the bond to maturity, it can be classified as held-to-maturity. However, as confirmed in an interpretation offered by the IGC, the commodity-indexed or equity-indexed interest payments result in an embedded derivative that is separated and accounted for as a derivative at fair value. The special exception in IAS 39, under which, if the two components cannot be reasonably separated the entire financial asset is classified as held for trading purposes, is found not to be applicable. According to the IGC, it should be straightforward to separate the host debt investment (the fixed payment at maturity) from the embedded derivative (the index-linked interest payments).

Accounting for sales of investments in financial instruments. In general, sales of investments are accounted for by eliminating the carrying value and recognizing a gain or loss for the difference between carrying amount and sales proceeds. Derecognition will occur only when the entity transfers control over the contractual rights which comprise the financial asset, or a portion thereof. IAS 39 sets forth certain conditions to define an actual transfer of control. Thus, for example, in most cases if the transferor has the right to reacquire the transferred asset, derecognition will not be warranted, unless the asset is readily obtainable in the market or reacquisition is to be at then-fair value. Arrangements which are essentially repurchase (repo) arrangements are similarly not sales and do not result in derecognition. In general, the transferee must obtain the benefits of the transferred asset in order to warrant derecognition by the transferor.

In accordance with IAS 39 there are two main concepts—risks and rewards, and control—that govern derecognition decisions. However, the standard clarifies that evaluation of the transfer of risks and rewards of ownership must in all instances precede the evaluation of the transfer of control (see discussion in the paragraph, "Derecognition of Financial Asset" earlier in this chapter).

In some instances, the asset will be sold as part of a compound transaction in which the transferor either retains part of the asset, obtains another financial instrument, or incurs a financial liability. If the fair values of all components of the transaction (asset retained, new asset acquired, etc.) are known, computing the gain or loss will be no problem. However, if one or more elements are not subject to an objective assessment, special requirement apply. In the unlikely event that the fair value of the component retained cannot be determined, it should be recorded at zero, thereby conservatively measuring the gain (or loss) on the transaction. Similarly, if a new financial asset is obtained and it cannot be objectively valued, it must be recorded at zero value.

On the other hand, if a financial liability is assumed (e.g., a guarantee) and it cannot be measured at fair value, then the initial carrying amount should be such (i.e., large enough) that no gain is recognized on the transaction. If necessitated by IAS 39's provisions, a loss should be recognized on the transaction. For example, if an asset carried at €4,000 is sold for €4,200 in cash, with the transferor assuming a guarantee obligation which cannot be valued (admittedly, such a situation is unlikely to occur in the context of a truly "arm's-length" transaction), no gain would be recognized and the financial liability would accordingly be initially recorded at €200. On the other hand, if the selling price were instead only €3,800, a loss of €200 would be immediately recognized, and the guarantee obligation would be given no value (but would be disclosed).

Presentation and Disclosure Issues

Presentation in the statement of comprehensive income. Under IAS 32 and IAS 39, significant items of income, expense, gain and loss deriving from financial assets and financial liabilities are to be given sufficient disclosure. (Note that disclosure requirements formerly set forth by IAS 39 were moved to IAS 32 in the revisions of these standards, effective 2005, and were subsequently moved from IAS 32 to IFRS 7, effective 2007.) This applies equally to those items recognized in profit or loss, and those recognized in other comprehensive income. Interest income and interest expense are to be disclosed on a "gross" basis (i.e., interest income is not to be netted against interest expense). Additional disclosure is required of interest accrued on impaired loans.

With regard to available-for-sale financial assets which have been adjusted to fair value, a distinction is to be maintained between the total gain or loss associated with derecognition (typically, from disposition) which is included in profit or loss for the period, and gains and losses which are recognized in other comprehensive income for the period. The most common terminology is to denote the former as realized and the latter as unrealized gains and losses.

Other disclosures required. In addition to the distinctions to be made in the statement of comprehensive income or the notes thereto, IFRS 7 (which incorporates the disclosure requirements formerly found in IAS 32) now also specifies a number of other mandatory disclosures. These include

- The methods and key assumptions used in determining fair values of financial assets and liabilities, separately by major class
- A statement as to whether trade date or settlement date accounting is used for "regular-way" trades, for each of the four categories of financial assets
- Disclosures pertaining to hedging, including describing the entity's risk management objectives and policies and policy for hedging each major type of forecasted transaction
- For designated fair value hedges, cash flow hedges, and hedges of net investments in a foreign entity (separately), descriptions of the hedges and of the hedging instruments used, and the fair values thereof, the nature of the risks being hedged, and for forecasted transactions that are expected to occur, when the forecasted transactions are expected to enter into the determination of profit or loss as well as descriptions of hedges of forecasted transactions that are no longer anticipated
- For gains and losses on financial assets and liabilities that are designated as hedges that have been recognized in other comprehensive income: the amount so recognized in the current reporting period, the amount of other comprehensive income reclassified from equity to profit or loss, and the amount reclassified from equity and added to the carrying value of an acquired asset or incurred liability during the reporting period
- The amounts of fair value adjustments pertaining to available-for-sale financial assets recognized in other comprehensive income or reclassified from equity during the period
- The carrying amount and description of any trading or available-for-sale instruments for which fair values could not be determined, with an explanation of why such assessments could not be made, including (where possible) ranges of likely fair values, as well as the amount of any gain or loss incurred on sales of assets for which previously fair values could not be determined
- For each securitization or repo agreement occurring during the period, and for remaining retained interests in earlier such transactions, the nature and extent of those transactions, including descriptions of collateral and quantitative information about key as-

sumptions used in calculating fair values thereof, and a statement as to whether the financial assets had been derecognized

- Information about reclassifications of instruments previously carried at fair value to the amortized cost basis
- The nature and amount of any impairment loss or reversals thereof, separately for each significant class of financial asset

Revised IAS 32 (effective 2005) clarified certain disclosure requirements for investments in financial assets. (Note that the disclosure requirements formerly found in IAS 32 were relocated to IFRS 7, effective 2007.) Disclosure was required of the extent to which fair values are estimated using a valuation technique, and the extent to which valuations using valuation techniques are based on assumptions that are not supported by observable market prices. Also required is information about the sensitivity of the estimated fair values to changes in those assumptions, based on a range of *reasonably possible* alternative assumptions that could be made.

Furthermore, the changes in fair values estimated using valuation techniques and recognized in profit or loss during the reporting period must be stated. Finally, revised IAS 32 (now IFRS 7) required disclosures about the nature and extent of transfers of financial assets that *do not* qualify for derecognition, along with an explanation of the risks inherent in any component that continues to be recognized after a transfer of financial assets that does not qualify for derecognition. (See also Chapter 5 and the Disclosure Checklist.)

Accounting for Hedging Activities

The topic of hedging is almost inextricably intertwined with the subject of financial derivatives, since most (but not all) hedging is accomplished using derivatives. Revised IAS 39 addresses both of these matters extensively, and the IGC has provided yet more instructional materials on these issues. In the following sections, a basic review of, first, derivative financial instruments, and second, hedging activities, will be presented.

Derivatives. As defined by IAS 39, a derivative is a financial instrument with all the following characteristics:

1. Its value changes in response to the change in a specified interest rate, security price, commodity price, foreign exchange rate, index of prices or rates, a credit rating or credit index, or similar variable (sometimes called the underlying);
2. It requires no initial net investment or little initial net investment relative to other types of contracts that have a similar response to changes in market conditions; and
3. It is settled at a future date.

Examples of financial instruments that meet the foregoing definition include the following, along with the underlying variable which affects the derivative's value.

Type of contract	*Main pricing—settlement variable (underlying variable)*
Interest rate swap	Interest rates
Currency swap (foreign exchange swap)	Currency rates
Commodity swap	Commodity prices
Equity swap (equity of another entity)	Equity prices
Credit swap	Credit rating, credit index, or credit price
Total return swap	Total fair value of the reference asset and interest rates
Purchased or written treasury bond option (call or put)	Interest rates
Purchased or written currency option (call or put)	Currency rates
Purchased or written commodity option (call or put)	Commodity prices
Purchased or written share option (call or put)	Equity prices (equity of another entity)

Type of contract	Main pricing—settlement variable (underlying variable)
Interest rate futures linked to government debt (treasury futures)	Interest rates
Currency futures	Currency rates
Commodity futures	Commodity prices
Interest rate forward linked to government debt (treasury forward)	Interest rates
Currency forward	Currency rates
Commodity forward	Commodity prices
Equity forward	Equity prices (equity of another entity)

The issue of what is meant by "little or no net investment" has been explored by the IGC. According to the IGC, professional judgment will be required in determining what constitutes little or no initial net investment, and is to be interpreted on a relative basis—the initial net investment is less than that needed to acquire a primary financial instrument with a similar response to changes in market conditions. This reflects the inherent leverage features typical of derivative agreements compared to the underlying instruments. If, for example, a "deep in the money" call option is purchased (that is, the option's value consists mostly of intrinsic value), a significant premium is paid. If the premium is equal or close to the amount required to invest in the underlying instrument, this would fail the "little initial net investment" criterion.

A margin account is not part of the initial net investment in a derivative instrument. Margin accounts are a form of collateral for the counterparty or clearinghouse and may take the form of cash, instruments, or other specified assets, typically liquid ones. Margin accounts are separate assets that are to be accounted for separately. Accordingly, in determining whether an arrangement qualifies as a derivative, the margin deposit is not a factor in assessing whether the "little or no net investment" criterion has been met.

A financial instrument can qualify as a derivative even if the settlement amount does not vary proportionately. An example of this phenomenon was provided by the IGC.

Example of derivative transaction

Accurate Corp. enters into a contract that requires it to pay Aimless Co. €2 million if the share of Reference Corp. rises by €5 per share or more during a six-month period. Conversely, Accurate Corp. will receive from Aimless Co. a payment of €2 million if the share of Reference Corp. declines by €5 or more during that same six-month period. If price changes are within the ± €5 collar range, no payments will be made or received by the parties. This arrangement would qualify as a derivative instrument, the underlying being the price of Reference Corp. common share. IAS 39 provides that "a derivative could require a fixed payment as a result of some future event that is unrelated to a notional amount."

In some instances what might first appear to be normal financial instruments are actually derivative transactions. The IGC offers the example of offsetting loans, which serve the same purpose and should be accounted for as an interest rate swap. The example is as follows:

Example of apparent loans that qualify as derivative transaction

Aguilar S.A. makes a five-year *fixed-rate* loan to Battapaglia Spa, while Battapaglia at the same time makes a five-year *variable-rate* loan for the same amount to Aguilar. There are no transfers of principal at inception of the two loans, since Aguilar and Battapaglia have a netting agreement. While superficially these appear to be two unconditional debt obligations, in fact this meets the definition of a derivative. Note that there is an underlying variable, no or little initial net investment, and future settlement, such that the contractual effect of the loans is the equivalent of an interest rate swap arrangement with no initial net investment. Nonderivative transactions are aggregated and treated as a derivative when the transactions result, in substance, in a derivative.

Indicators of this situation would include (1) the transactions are entered into at the same time and in contemplation of one another, (2) they have the same counterparty, (3) they relate to the same risk, and (4) there is no apparent economic need or substantive business purpose for structuring the transactions separately that could not also have been accomplished in a single transaction. Note that even in the absence of a netting agreement, the foregoing arrangement would have been deemed to be a derivative.

Difficulty of identifying whether certain transactions involve derivatives. The definition of derivatives has already been addressed. While seemingly straightforward, the almost limitless and still expanding variety of "engineered" financial products often makes definitive categorization more difficult than this at first would appear to be. The IGC illustrates this with examples of two variants on interest rate swaps, both of which involve prepayments. The first of these, a prepaid interest rate swap (fixed-rate payment obligation prepaid at inception or subsequently) qualifies as a derivative; the second, a variable-rate payment obligation prepaid at inception or subsequently) would not be a derivative. The reasoning is set forth in the next paragraphs, which are adapted from the IGC guidance.

Example of interest rate swap to be accounted for as a derivative

First consider the "pay-fixed, receive-variable" interest rate swap that the party prepays at inception. Assume Agememnon Corp. enters into a €100 million notional amount five-year pay-fixed, receive-variable interest rate swap with Baltic Metals, Inc. The interest rate of the variable part of the swap resets on a quarterly basis to the three-month LIBOR. The interest rate of the fixed part of the swap is 10% per year. Agememnon Corp. prepays its fixed obligation under the swap of €50 million (= €100 million × 10% × 5 years) at inception, discounted using market interest rates, while retaining the right to receive interest payments on the €100 million reset quarterly based on three-month LIBOR over the life of the swap.

The initial net investment in the interest rate swap is significantly less than the notional amount on which the variable payments under the variable leg will be calculated. The contract requires little initial net investment relative to other types of contracts that have a similar response to changes in market conditions, such as a variable-rate bond. Therefore, the contract fulfills the "no or little initial net investment" provision of IAS 39. Even though Agememnon Corp. has no future performance obligation, the ultimate settlement of the contract is at a future date and the value of the contract changes in response to changes in the LIBOR index. Accordingly, the contract is considered to be a derivative contract. The IGC further notes that if the fixed-rate payment obligation is prepaid subsequent to initial recognition, which would be considered a termination of the old swap and an origination of a new instrument, which would have to be evaluated under IAS 39.

Now consider the opposite situation, a prepaid pay-variable, receive-fixed interest rate swap, which the IGC concludes is *not* a derivative. This result obtains because it provides a return on the prepaid (invested) amount comparable to the return on a debt instrument with fixed cash flows.

Example of interest rate swap *not* to be accounted for as a derivative

Assume that Synchronous Ltd. enters into a €100 million notional amount five-year "pay-variable, receive-fixed" interest rate swap with counterparty Cabot Corp. The variable leg of the swap resets on a quarterly basis to the three-month LIBOR. The fixed interest payments under the swap are calculated as 10% times the swap's notional amount, or €10 million per year. Synchronous Ltd. prepays its obligation under the variable leg of the swap at inception at current market rates, while retaining the right to receive fixed interest payments of 10% on €100 million per year.

The cash inflows under the contract are equivalent to those of a financial instrument with a fixed annuity stream, since Synchronous Ltd. knows it will receive €10 million per year over the life of the swap. Therefore, all else being equal, the initial investment in the contract should equal that of other financial instruments that consist of fixed annuities. Thus, the initial net investment in the pay-variable, receive-fixed interest rate swap is equal to the investment required in a nonderivative contract that has a similar response to changes in market conditions. For this reason, the instrument fails the "no or little net investment" criterion of IAS 39. Therefore, the contract is *not* to be accounted for as a derivative under IAS 39. By discharging the obligation to pay variable interest rate payments, Synchronous Ltd. effectively extends an annuity loan to Cabot Corp. In this situation, the instrument is accounted for as a loan originated by the entity unless Synchronous Ltd. has the intent to sell it immediately or in the short term.

In yet other instances arrangements that technically meet the definition of derivatives are not to be accounted for as such.

Example of derivative not to be settled for cash

Assume National Wire Products Corp. enters into a fixed-price forward contract to purchase two million kilograms of copper. The contract permits National Wire to take physical delivery of the copper at the end of twelve months or to pay or receive a net settlement in cash, based on the change in fair value of copper. While such a contract meets the definition of a derivative, it is not necessarily accounted for as a derivative. The contract is a derivative instrument because there is no initial net investment, the contract is based on the price of an underlying, copper, and it is to be settled at a future date. However, if National Wire intends to settle the contract by taking delivery and has no history of settling in cash, the contract is not accounted for as a derivative under IAS 39. Instead, it is accounted for as an executory contract for the purchase of inventory.

Just as some seemingly derivative transactions may be accounted for as not involving a derivative instrument, the opposite situation can also occur, where some seemingly nonderivative transactions would be accounted for as being derivatives.

Example of nonfinancial derivative to be settled for cash

Argyle Corp. enters into a forward contract to purchase a commodity or other nonfinancial asset that contractually is to be settled by taking delivery. Argyle has an established pattern of settling such contracts prior to delivery by contracting with a third party. Argyle settles any market value difference for the contract price directly with the third party. This pattern of settlement prohibits Argyle Corp. from qualifying for the exemption based on normal delivery; the contract is accounted for as a derivative. IAS 39 applies to a contract to purchase a nonfinancial asset if the contract meets the definition of a derivative and the contract does not qualify for the exemption for delivery in the normal course of business. In this case, Argyle does not expect to take delivery. Under the standard, a pattern of entering into offsetting contracts that effectively accomplishes settlement on a net basis does not qualify for the exemption on the grounds of delivery in the normal course of business.

Forward contracts. Forward contracts to purchase, for example, fixed-rate debt instruments (such as mortgages) at fixed prices are to be accounted for as derivatives. They meet the definition of a derivative because there is no or little initial net investment, there is an underlying variable (interest rates), and they will be settled in the future. However, such transactions are to be accounted for as a regular way transaction, if regular-way delivery is required. "Regular-way" delivery is defined by IAS 39 to include contracts for purchases or sales of financial instruments that require delivery in the time frame generally established by regulation or convention in the marketplace concerned. Regular-way contracts are explicitly defined as *not* being derivatives.

Future contracts. Future contracts are financial instruments that require delivery of a commodity, for example an equity instrument or currency, at a specified price agreed to on the contract inception date (exercise price), on a specified future date. Futures are similar to forward contracts except futures have standardized contract terms and are traded on organized exchanges.

Options. Options are contracts that give the buyer (option holder) the right, but not the obligation, to acquire from or sell to the option seller (option writer) a certain quantity of an underlying financial instrument or other commodity, at a specified price (the strike price) and up to a specified date (the expiration date). An option to buy is referred to as a "call"; an option to sell is referred is call a "put."

Swaps. Interest rate (and currency) swaps have become widely used financial arrangements. Swaps are to be accounted for as derivatives whether an interest rate swap settles gross or net. Regardless of how the arrangement is to be settled, the three key defining characteristics are present in all interest rate swaps—namely, that value changes are in response to changes in an underlying variable (interest rates or an index of rates), that there is little or no initial net investment, and that settlements will occur at future dates. Thus, swaps are always derivatives.

Derivatives that are not based on financial instruments. Not all derivatives involve financial instruments. Consider Corboy Co., which owns an office building and enters into a put option, with a term of five years, with an investor that permits it to put the building to the investor for €15 million. The current value of the building is €17.5 million. The option, if exercised, may be settled through physical delivery or net cash, at Corboy's option. Corboy's accounting depends on Corboy's intent and past practice for settlement. Although the contract meets the definition of a derivative, Corboy does not account for it as a derivative if it intends to settle the contract by delivering the building if it exercises its option, and there is no past practice of settling net.

The investor, however, cannot conclude that the option was entered into to meet the investor's expected purchase, sale, or usage requirements because the investor does not have the ability to require delivery. Therefore, the investor has to account for the contract as a derivative. Regardless of past practices, the investor's intention does not affect whether settlement is by delivery or in cash. The investor has written an option, and a written option in which the holder has the choice of physical delivery or net cash settlement can never satisfy the normal delivery requirement for the exemption from IAS 39 for the investor. However, if the contract required physical delivery and the reporting entity had no past practice of settling net in cash, the contract would not be accounted for as a derivative.

Embedded derivatives. In certain cases, IAS 39 requires that an embedded derivative be separated from a host contract. The embedded derivative must then be accounted for separately as a derivative, at fair value. That does not, however, require separating them in the statement of financial position, IAS 39 does not address the presentation in the statement of financial position of embedded derivatives. However, IAS 32 required (and IFRS 7 now requires) separate disclosure of financial assets carried at cost and financial assets carried at fair value, although this could be in the notes rather than in the statement of financial position.

IFRIC 9, *Reassessment of Embedded Derivatives*, states that an entity should assess whether an embedded derivative is required to be separated from the host contract and accounted for as a derivative when the entity first becomes a party to the contract. Subsequent reassessment is prohibited unless there is a change in the terms of the contract that significantly modifies the cash flows that otherwise would be required under the contract; in this case reassessment is required.

The concept of embedded derivatives embraces such elements as conversion features, such as are found in convertible debts. For example, an investment in a bond (a financial asset) may be convertible into shares of the issuing entity or another entity at any time prior to the bond's maturity, at the option of the holder. The existence of the conversion feature in such a situation generally precludes classification as a held-to-maturity investment because that would be inconsistent with paying for the conversion feature—the right to convert into equity shares before maturity.

An investment in a convertible bond can be classified as an available-for-sale financial asset provided it is not purchased for trading purposes. The equity conversion option is an embedded derivative. If the bond is classified as available-for-sale with fair value changes recognized in other comprehensive income until the bond is sold, the equity conversion option (the embedded derivative) is generally separated. The amount paid for the bond is split between the debt security without the conversion option and the equity conversion option itself. Changes in the fair value of the equity conversion option are recognized in profit or loss unless the option is part of a cash flow hedging relationship. If the convertible bond is carried at fair value with changes in fair value reported in profit or loss, separating the embedded derivative from the host bond is not permitted.

When an evaluation made using the criteria in IAS 39 leads to a conclusion that the embedded derivative must be separately accounted for, the initial carrying amounts of a host and the embedded derivative must be determined. Since the embedded derivative must be recorded at fair value with changes in fair value reported in profit or loss, the initial carrying amount assigned to the host contract on separation is determined as the difference between the cost (i.e., the fair value of the consideration given) for the hybrid (combined) instrument and the fair value of the embedded derivative.

IAS 32, as revised and effective 2005, requires that in separating the liability and equity components contained in a compound financial instrument, the issuer must first allocate fair value to the liability component, leaving only the residual (the difference between aggregate fair value and that allocated to liabilities) to be assigned to the equity component. However, IAS 32 is not applicable to the separation of a derivative from a hybrid instrument under IAS 39. It would be inappropriate to allocate the basis in the hybrid instrument under IAS 39 to the derivative and nonderivative components based on their relative fair values, since that might result in an immediate gain or loss being recognized in profit or loss on the subsequent measurement of the derivative at fair value.

Example of separate contracts that cannot be deemed an embedded derivative

Erehwon AG acquires a five-year floating-rate debt instrument issued by Spacemaker Co. At the same time, it enters into a five-year "pay-variable, receive-fixed" interest rate swap with the St. Helena Bank. Erehwon argues that the combination of the debt instrument and swap is a "synthetic fixed-rate instrument" and accordingly classifies the instrument as a held-to-maturity investment, since it has the positive intent and ability to hold it to maturity. Erehwon contends that separate accounting for the swap is inappropriate, since IAS 39 requires an embedded derivative to be classified together with its host instrument if the derivative is linked to an interest rate that can change the amount of interest that would otherwise be paid or received on the host debt contract.

The company's analysis is not correct. Embedded derivative instruments are terms and conditions that are included in nonderivative host contracts. It is generally inappropriate to treat two or more separate financial instruments as a single combined instrument (synthetic instrument accounting) for the purposes of applying IAS 39. Each of the financial instruments has its own terms and conditions and each may be transferred or settled separately. Therefore, the debt instrument and the swap are classified separately.

Hedging Accounting under IAS 39

When there is a hedging relationship between a hedging instrument and another item (the underlying), and certain conditions are met, then special "hedging accounting" will be applied. The objective is to ensure that the gain or loss on the hedging instrument is recognized in profit or loss in the same period that the hedged item affects profit or loss. Hedge accounting recognizes the offsetting effects on profit or loss of changes in the fair values of the hedging instrument and the hedged item. Hedging instruments are often financial derivatives, such as forwards, options, swaps or futures, but this is not a necessary condition. Hedging may be engaged in to protect against changes in fair values, changes in expected cash flows, or changes in the value of an investment in a foreign operation, such as a subsidiary, due to currency rate movements. There is no requirement that entities engage in hedging, but the principles of good management will often dictate that this be done.

For a simplistic example of the need for, and means of, hedging, consider an entity that holds US Treasury bonds as an investment. The bonds have a maturity some ten years in the future, but the entity actually intends to dispose of these in the intermediate term, for example, within four years to partially finance a plant expansion currently being planned. Obviously, an unexpected increase in general interest rates during the projected four-year holding period would be an unwelcome development, since it would cause a decline in the market value of the bonds and could accordingly result in an unanticipated loss of principal. One means of guarding against this would be to purchase a put option on these bonds, permitting the entity to sell them at an agreed-upon price, which would be most valuable should there be a price decline. If interest rates do indeed rise, the increasing value of the "put" will (if properly structured) offset the declining value of the bonds themselves, thus providing an effective fair value hedge. (Other hedging strategies are also available, including selling short Treasury bond futures, and the entity of course could have reduced or eliminated the need to hedge entirely by having invested in Treasury bonds having a maturity more closely matched to its anticipated cash need.)

Special hedge accounting is necessitated by the fact that fair value changes in not all financial instruments are reported in current profit or loss. Thus, if the entity in the foregoing example holding the Treasuries has elected to report changes in available-for-sale investments (which would include the Treasury bonds in this instance) in other comprehensive income, but the changes in the hedging instrument's fair value were to be reported in profit or loss, there would be a fundamental mismatching which would distort the real hedging relationship that had been established. To avoid this result, the entity may elect to apply special hedge accounting as prescribed by IAS 39, as was discussed in some detail in Chapter 5. It should be noted, though, that hedge accounting is optional. An entity that carries out hedging activities for risk management purposes may well decide not to apply hedge accounting for some hedging transactions if it wishes to reduce the cost and burden of complying with the hedge accounting requirements in IAS 39.

Accounting for gains and losses from fair value hedges. The accounting for qualifying gains and losses on fair value hedges is as follows:

1. On the hedging instrument, they are recognized in profit or loss.
2. On the hedged item, they are recognized in profit or loss even if the gains or losses would normally have been recognized in other comprehensive income if not hedged.

The foregoing rule applies even in the case of investments (classified as available-for-sale) for which unrealized gains and losses are being recognized in other comprehensive income, if that method was appropriately elected by the reporting entity, as permitted by IAS 39. In all instances, to the extent that there are differences between the amounts of gain or loss on hedging and hedged items, these will be due either to amounts excluded from assessment effectiveness, or to hedge ineffectiveness; in either event, these are recognized currently in profit or loss.

As an example, consider an available-for-sale (AFS) financial asset, the carrying amount of which is adjusted by the amount of gain or loss resulting from the hedged risk, a fair value hedge. It is assumed that the entire investment was hedged, but it is also possible to hedge merely a portion of the investment. The facts are as follows:

Hedged item:	Available-for-sale financial asset
Hedging instrument:	Put option
Underlying:	Price of the security
Notional amount:	100 shares of the financial asset

Example 1

On July 1, 2008, Gardiner Company purchased 100 shares of Dizzy Co. ordinary shares at €15 per share and classified it as an available-for-sale financial asset. On October 1, Gardiner Company purchased an at-the-money put on Dizzy with an exercise price of €25 and an expiration date of April 2009. This put purchase locks in a profit of €650, as long as the price is equal to €25 or lower, but allows continued profitability if the price of the Dizzy share goes above €25. (In other words, the put cost a premium of €350, which if deducted from the locked-in gain [= €2,500 market value less €1,500 cost] leaves a net gain of €650 to be realized.)

The premium paid for an at-the-money option (i.e., where the exercise price is current fair value of the underlying) is the price paid for the right to have the entire remaining option period in which to exercise the option. In the present example, Gardiner Company specifies that only the intrinsic value of the option is to be used to measure effectiveness. Thus, the time value decreases of the put will be charged against profit or loss of the period, and not offset against the change in value of the underlying, hedged item. Gardiner Company then documents the hedge's strategy, objectives, hedging relationships, and method of measuring effectiveness. The following table shows the fair value of the hedged item and the hedging instrument.

Case One

	10/1/08	12/31/08	3/31/09	4/17/09
Hedged item:				
Dizzy share price	€ 25	€ 22	€ 20	€ 20
Number of shares	100	100	100	100
Total value of shares	€2,500	€2,200	€2,000	€2,000
Hedging instrument:				
Put option (100 shares)				
Intrinsic value	€ 0	€ 300	€ 500	€ 500
Time value	350	215	53	0
Total	€ 350	€ 515	€ 553	€ 500
Intrinsic value				
Gain (loss) on put from last measurement date	€ 0	€ 300	€ 200	€ 0

Entries to record the foregoing changes in value, ignoring tax effects and transaction costs, are as follows:

7/1/08	Purchase:	Available-for-sale investment	1,500	
		Cash		1,500
9/30/08	End of quarter:	Valuation allowance—available-for-sale investment	1,000	
		Other comprehensive income		1,000
10/1/08	Put purchase:	Put option	350	
		Cash		350
12/31/08	End of year:	Put option	300	
		Hedge gain/loss (intrinsic value gain)		300
		Gain/loss	162	
		Put option (time value loss)		162
		Hedge gain/loss	300	
		Available-for-sale investment (market value loss)		300
3/31/09	End of quarter:	Put option	200	
		Hedge gain/loss (intrinsic value changes)		200
		Gain/loss	162	
		Put option (time value loss)		162
		Hedge gain/loss	200	
		Available-for-sale investment (market value loss)		200

4/17/09	Put expires:	Put option	0	
		Hedge gain/loss (intrinsic value changes)		0
		Gain/loss	53	
		Put option (time value changes)		53
		Hedge gain/loss	0	
		Available-for-sale investment (market value changes)		0

An option is said to be "in-the-money" if the exercise price is above the market value (for a put option) or below the market value (for a call option). At or before expiration, an in-the-money put should be sold or exercised (to let it simply expire would be to effectively discard a valuable asset). It should be stressed that this applies to so-called "American options," which may be exercised at any time prior to expiration; so-called "European options" can only be exercised at the expiration date. Assuming that the put option is sold immediately before its expiration date, the entry would be

4/17/09	Put sold:	Cash	500	
		Put option		500

On the other hand, if the put is exercised (i.e., the underlying instrument is delivered to the counterparty, which is obligated to pay €25 per share), the entry would be

4/17/09		Cash	2,500	
		Other comprehensive income	1,000	
		Valuation allowance—available-for-sale investment		1,000
		Available-for-sale investment		1,000
		Put option		500
		Gain on sale of investment		1,000

The cumulative effect on retained earnings of the hedge and sale is a net gain of €650 (= €1,000 – €350).

Example 2

To further illustrate fair value hedge accounting, the facts in the preceding example will now be slightly modified. Now, the share price increases after the put option is purchased, thus making the put worthless, since the shares could be sold for a more advantageous price on the open market.

Case Two

	10/1/08	*12/31/08*	*3/31/09*	*4/17/09*
Hedged item:				
Dizzy share price	€ 25	€ 28	€ 30	€ 31
Number of shares	100	100	100	100
Total value of shares	€2,500	€2,800	€3,000	€3,100
Hedging instrument:				
Put option (100 shares)				
Intrinsic value	€ 0	€ 0	€ 0	€ 0
Time value	350	100	25	0
Total	€ 350	€ 100	€ 25	€ 0
Intrinsic value				
Gain (loss) on put from last measurement date	€ 0	€ 0	€ 0	€ 0

Entries to record the foregoing changes in value, ignoring tax effects and transaction costs, are as follows:

7/1/08	Purchase:	Available-for-sale investment	1,500	
		Cash		1,500
9/30/08	End of quarter:	Valuation allowance—available-for-sale investment	1,000	
		Other comprehensive income		1,000
10/1/08	Put purchase:	Put option	350	
		Cash		350

12/31/08	End of year:	Put option	0	
		Hedge gain/loss (intrinsic value gain)		0
		Hedge gain/loss	250	
		Put option (time value loss)		250
		Available-for-sale investment	300	
		Other comprehensive income		300
3/31/09	End of quarter:	Put option	0	
		Hedge gain/loss (intrinsic value change)		0
		Hedge gain/loss	75	
		Put option (time value loss)		75
		Available-for-sale investment	200	
		Other comprehensive income		200
4/17/09	Put expires:	Put option	0	
		Hedge gain/loss (intrinsic value change)		0
		Hedge gain/loss	25	
		Put option (time value change)		25
		Available-for-sale investment	100	
		Other comprehensive income		100

The put expired unexercised and Gardiner Company must decide whether to sell the investment. If it continues to hold, normal IAS 39 accounting would apply. In this example, since it was hypothesized that Gardiner had elected to record the effects of value changes (apart from those which were hedging related) in other comprehensive income, it would continue to apply this accounting after the expiration of the put option. Assuming, however, that the investment is instead sold, the entry would be

4/17/09	Cash	3,100	
	Other comprehensive income	1,600	
	Available-for-sale investment		1,500
	Valuation allowance—available-for-sale investment		1,600
	Gain on sale of investment		1,600

Accounting for gains and losses from cash flow hedges. Cash flow hedges generally involve forecasted transactions or events. The intention is to defer the recognition of gains or losses arising from the hedging activity itself until the forecasted transaction takes place, and then to have the formerly deferred gain or loss affect profit or loss when the forecasted transaction affects profit or loss. While overwhelmingly it will be derivative financial instruments that are used to hedge cash flows relating to forecasted transactions, IAS 39 contemplates the use of nonderivatives for this purpose as well in the case of hedges of foreign currency risk. Forecasted transactions may include future cash flows arising from presently existing, recognized assets or liabilities—for example, future interest rate payments to be made on debt carrying floating interest rates are subject to cash flow hedging.

The accounting for qualifying gains and losses on cash flow hedges is as follows:

1. On the hedging instrument, the portion of the gain or loss that is determined to be an effective hedge will be recognized in other comprehensive income.
2. Also on the hedging instrument, the ineffective portion should be reported in profit or loss, if the instrument is a derivative; otherwise, it should be reported in a manner consistent with the accounting for other financial assets or liabilities as set forth in IAS 39. Thus, if an available-for-sale financial asset has been used as the hedging instrument in a particular cash flow hedging situation, and the entity has elected to report value changes in other comprehensive income, then any ineffective portion of the hedge should continue to be recorded in other comprehensive income.

According to IAS 39, the separate component of equity associated with the hedged item should be adjusted to the lesser (in absolute terms) of either the cumulative gain or loss on the hedging instrument necessary to offset the cumulative change in expected future cash flows on the hedged item from hedge inception, excluding the ineffective portion, or the fair value of the cumulative change in expected future cash flows on the hedged item from inception of the hedge. Furthermore, any remaining gain or loss on the hedging instrument (i.e., the ineffective portion) must be recognized currently in profit or loss or in other comprehensive income, as dictated by the nature of the instrument and entity's accounting policy (for available-for-sale instruments, where there is a choice of reporting in other comprehensive income or in profit or loss). If the entity's policy regarding the hedge is to exclude a portion from the measure of hedge effectiveness (e.g., time value of options in the preceding example in this section of Chapter 10), then any related gain or loss must be recognized in either profit or loss or other comprehensive income based on the nature of the item and the elected policy.

Example of "plain vanilla" interest rate swap

On July 1, 2008, Abbott Corp. borrows €5 million with a fixed maturity (no prepayment option) of June 30, 2012, carrying interest at the US prime interest rate + 1/2%. Interest payments are due semiannually; the entire principal is due at maturity. At the same date, Abbott Corp. enters into a "plain-vanilla-type" swap arrangement, calling for fixed payments at 8% and the receipt of prime + 1/2%, on a notional amount of €5 million. At that date prime is 7.5%, and there is no premium due on the swap arrangement since the fixed and variable payments are equal. (Note that swaps are privately negotiated and, accordingly, a wide range of terms will be encountered in practice; this is simply intended as an example, albeit a very typical one.)

The foregoing swap qualifies as a cash flow hedge under IAS 39. Given the nature of this swap, it is reasonable to assume no ineffectiveness, but in real world situations this must be carefully evaluated with reference to the specific circumstances of each case; IAS 39 does not provide a short-cut method (which contrasts with the corresponding US GAAP standard). IAS 39 defines effectiveness in terms of results: if at inception and throughout the life of the hedge, the entity can expect an almost complete offset of cash flow variations, and in fact (retrospectively) actual results are within a range of 80 to 125%, the hedge will be judged highly effective.

In the present example, assume that in fact the hedge proves to be highly effective. Also, assume that the prime rate over the four-year term of the loan, as of each interest payment date, is as follows, along with the fair value of the remaining term of the interest swap at those dates:

Date	Prime rate (%)	Fair value of swap*
December 31, 2008	6.5	€(150,051)
June 30, 2009	6.0	(196,580)
December 31, 2009	6.5	(111,296)
June 30, 2010	7.0	(45,374)
December 31, 2010	7.5	0
June 30, 2011	8.0	23,576
December 31, 2011	8.5	24,038
June 30, 2012	8.0	0

* *Fair values are determined as the present values of future cash flows resulting from expected interest rate differentials, based on current prime rate, discounted at 8%.*

Regarding the fair values presented in the foregoing table, it should be assumed that the fair values of the swap contract are precisely equal to the present value, at each valuation date (assumed to be the interest payment dates), of the differential future cash flows resulting from utilization of the swap. Future variable interest rates (prime + 1/2%) are assumed to be the same as the existing rates at each valuation date (i.e., the yield curve is flat and there is no basis for any expectation of rate changes, and therefore, the best estimate at any given moment is that the current rate will persist over time). The discount rate, 8%, is assumed to be constant over time.

Thus, for example, the fair value of the swap at December 31, 2008, would be the present value of an annuity of seven payments (the number of remaining semiannual interest payments due) of €25,000 each (pay 8%, receive 7%, based on then-existing prime rate of 6.5%) to be made to the swap counterparty, discounted at an annual rate of 8%. (Consistent with the convention for quoting interest rates as bond-equivalent yields, 4% is used for the semiannual discounting, rather than the rate that would compound to 8% annually.) The present value of a stream of seven €25,000 payments to the swap counterparty amounts to €150,051 at December 31, 2008, which is the swap liability to be reported by Abbott Corp. at that date. The offset is a debit to other comprehensive income, since the hedge is continually judged to be 100% effective in this case.

The semiannual accounting entries will be as follows:

December 31, 2008

Interest expense	175,000	
Accrued interest (or cash)		175,000

To accrue or pay interest on the debt at the variable rate of prime + 1/2% (7.0%)

Interest expense	25,000	
Accrued interest (or cash)		25,000

To record net settle-up on swap arrangement [8.0 – 7.0%]

Other comprehensive income	150,051	
Obligation under swap contract		150,051

To record the fair value of the swap contract as of this date (a net liability because fixed rate payable is below expected variable rate based on current prime rate)

June 30, 2009

Interest expense	162,500	
Accrued interest (or cash)		162,500

To accrue or pay interest on the debt at the variable rate of prime + 1/2% (6.5%)

Interest expense	37,500	
Accrued interest (or cash)		37,500

To record net settle-up on swap arrangement [8.0 – 6.5%]

Other comprehensive income	46,529	
Obligation under swap contract		46,529

To record the fair value of the swap contract as of this date (increase in obligation because of further decline in prime rate)

December 31, 2009

Interest expense	175,000	
Accrued interest (or cash)		175,000

To accrue or pay interest on the debt at the variable rate of prime + 1/2% (7.0%)

Interest expense	25,000	
Accrued interest (or cash)		25,000

To record net settle-up on swap arrangement [8.0 – 7.0%]

Obligation under swap contract	85,284	
Other comprehensive income		85,284

To record the fair value of the swap contract as of this date (decrease in obligation due to increase in prime rate)

June 30, 2010

Interest expense	187,500	
Accrued interest (or cash)		187,500

To accrue or pay interest on the debt at the variable rate of prime + 1/2% (7.5%)

Interest expense	12,500	
Accrued interest (or cash)		12,500

To record net settle-up on swap arrangement [8.0 – 7.5%]

Obligation under swap contract	65,922	
Other comprehensive income		65,922

To record the fair value of the swap contract as of this date (further increase in prime rate reduces fair value of derivative)

December 31, 2010

Interest expense	200,000	
Accrued interest (or cash)		200,000

To accrue or pay interest on the debt at the variable rate of prime + 1/2% (8.0%)

Interest expense	0	
Accrued interest (or cash)		0

To record net settle-up on swap arrangement [8.0 – 8.0%]

Obligation under swap contract	45,374	
Other comprehensive income		45,374

To record the fair value of the swap contract as of this date (further increase in prime rate eliminates fair value of the derivative)

June 30, 2011

Interest expense	212,500	
Accrued interest (or cash)		212,500

To accrue or pay interest on the debt at the variable rate of prime + 1/2% (8.5%)

Accrued interest (or cash)	12,500	
Interest expense		12,500

To record net settle-up on swap arrangement [8.0 – 8.5%]

Receivable under swap contract	23,576	
Other comprehensive income		23,576

To record the fair value of the swap contract as of this date (increase in prime rate creates net asset position for derivative)

December 31, 2011

Interest expense	225,000	
Accrued interest (or cash)		225,000

To accrue or pay interest on the debt at the variable rate of prime + 1/2% (9.0%)

Accrued interest (or cash)	25,000	
Interest expense		25,000

To record net settle-up on swap arrangement [8.0 – 9.0%]

Receivable under swap contract	462	
Other comprehensive income		462

To record the fair value of the swap contract as of this date (increase in asset value due to further rise in prime rate)

June 30, 2012

Interest expense	212,500	
Accrued interest (or cash)		212,500

To accrue or pay interest on the debt at the variable rate of prime + 1/2% (8.5%)

Accrued interest (or cash)	12,500	
Interest expense		12,500

To record net settle-up on swap arrangement [8.0 – 8.5%]

Other comprehensive income	24,038	
Receivable under swap contract		24,038

To record the fair value of the swap contract as of this date (value declines to zero as expiration date approaches)

Example of option on an interest rate swap

The facts of this example are a further variation on the previous one (the "plain vanilla" swap). Abbott Corp. anticipates, as of June 30, 2008, that as of June 30, 2010, it will become a borrower of €5 million with a fixed maturity four years hence (i.e., at June 30, 2014). Based on its current credit rating, it will be able to borrow at the US prime interest rate + 1/2%. As of June 30, 2008, it is able to purchase a "swaption" (an option on an interest rate swap, calling for fixed pay at 8% and variable receipt at prime + 1/2%, on a notional amount of €5 million, for a term of four years) for a single payment of €25,000. The option will expire in two years. At June 30, 2008, the prime is 7.5%.

NOTE: The interest rate behavior in this example differs somewhat from the prior example, to better illustrate the "one-sideness" of options, versus the obligation under a plain vanilla swap arrangement or of other non-option contracts, such as futures and forwards.

It will be assumed that the time value of the swaption expires ratably over the two years.

This swaption qualifies as a cash flow hedge under IAS 39. However, while the change in fair value of the contract is an effective hedge of the cash flow variability of the prospective debt issuance, the premium paid is a reflection of the time value of money and would not be an effective part of the hedge. Accordingly, it is to be expensed as incurred, rather than being deferred.

The table below gives the prime rate at semiannual intervals including the two-year period prior to the debt issuance, plus the four years during which the debt (and the swap, if the option is exercised) will be outstanding, as well as the fair value of the swaption (and later, the swap itself) at these points in time.

Date	Prime rate (%)	Fair value of swaption/swap*
December 31, 2008	7.5	€ 0
June 30, 2009	8.0	77,925
December 31, 2009	6.5	0
June 30, 2010	7.0	(84,159)
December 31, 2010	7.5	0
June 30, 2011	8.0	65,527
December 31, 2011	8.5	111,296
June 30, 2012	8.0	45,374
December 31, 2012	8.0	34,689
June 30, 2013	7.5	0
December 31, 2013	7.5	0
June 30, 2014	7.0	0

* *Fair value is determined as the present value of future expected interest rate differentials, based on current prime rate, discounted at 8%. An "out-of-the-money" swaption is valued at zero, since the option does not have to be exercised. Since the option is exercised on June 30, 2010, the value at that date is recorded, although negative.*

The value of the swaption contract is only recorded (unless and until exercised, of course, at which point it becomes a contractually binding swap) if it is positive, since if "out-of-the-money," the holder would forego exercise in most instances and thus there is no liability by the holder to be reported. This illustrates the asymmetrical nature of options, where the most that can be lost by the option holder is the premium paid, since exercise by the holder is never required, unlike the case with futures and forwards, in which both parties are obligated to perform.

The present example is an illustration of counterintuitive (but not really illogical) behavior by the holder of an out-of-the-money option. Despite having a negative value, the option holder determines that exercise is advisable, presumably because it expects that over the term of the debt unfavorable movements in interest rates will occur.

At June 30, 2010, the swaption is an asset, since the reference variable rate (prime + 1/2%) is greater than the fixed swap rate, and thus the expectation is that the option will be exercised at expiration. This would (if present rates hold steady, which is the naïve assumption) result in a series of eight semiannual payments from the swap counterparty in the amount of €12,500. Discounting this at a nominal 8%, the present value as of the debt origination date (to be June 30, 2010) would be €84,159, which, when further discounted to June 30, 2009, yields a fair value of €77,925.

Note that the following period (at December 31, 2009) prime drops to such an extent that the value of the swaption evaporates entirely. Actually, the value becomes negative, which will not be reported since the holder is under no obligation to exercise the option under unfavorable conditions; the carrying value is therefore eliminated as of that date.

At the expiration of the swaption contract, the holder does (for this example) exercise, notwithstanding a negative fair value, and from that point forward the fair value of the swap will be reported, whether positive (an asset) or negative (a liability). Once exercised, the swap represents a series of forward contracts, the fair value of which must be fully recognized under IAS 39. (Note that, in the real world, the holder would have likely had another choice: to let the unfavorable swaption expire unexercised, but to negotiate a new interest rate swap, presumably at more favorable terms given that prime is only 7% at that date; for example, a swap of 7.5% fixed versus prime + 1/2% would likely be available at little or no cost.)

As noted above, assume that, at the option expiration date, despite the fact that prime + 1/2% is below the fixed pay rate on the swap, the management is convinced that rates will climb over the four-year term of the loan, and thus it does exercise the swaption at that date. Given this, the accounting journal entries over the entire six years are as follows:

June 30, 2008

Swaption contract	25,000	
Cash		25,000

To record purchase premium on swaption contract

December 31, 2008

Gain/loss on hedging arrangement	6,250	
Swaption contract		6,250

To record change in time value of swaption contract—charge premium to income since this represents payment for time value of money, which expires ratably over two-year term

June 30, 2009

Swaption contract	77,925	
Other comprehensive income		77,925

To record the fair value of the swaption contract as of this date

Gain/loss on hedging arrangement	6,250	
Swaption contract		6,250

To record change in time value of swaption contract—charge premium to profit or loss since this represents payment for time value of money, which expires ratably over two-year term

December 31, 2009

Other comprehensive income	77,925	
Swaption contract		77,925

To record the change in fair value of the swaption contract as of this date; since contract is out-of-the-money, it is not written down below zero (i.e., a net liability is not reported)

Gain/loss on hedging arrangement	6,250	
Swaption contract		6,250

To record change in time value of swaption contract—charge premium to profit or loss since this represents payment for time value of money, which expires ratably over two-year term

June 30, 2010

Other comprehensive income	84,159	
Swaption contract		84,159

To record the fair value of the swaption contract as of this date—a net liability is reported since swap option was exercised

Gain/loss on hedging arrangement	6,250	
Swaption contract		6,250

To record change in time value of swaption contract—charge premium to profit or loss since this represents payment for time value of money, which expires ratably over two-year term

December 31, 2010

Interest expense	200,000	
Accrued interest (or cash)		200,000

To accrue or pay interest on the debt at the variable rate of prime + 1/2% (8.0%)

Interest expense	0	
Accrued interest (or cash)		0

To record net settle-up on swap arrangement [8.0 – 8.0%]

Swap contract	84,159	
Other comprehensive income		84,159

To record the change in the fair value of the swap contract as of this date

June 30, 2011

Interest expense	212,500	
Accrued interest (or cash)		212,500

To accrue or pay interest on the debt at the variable rate of prime + 1/2% (8.5%)

Accrued interest (or cash)	12,500	
Interest expense		12,500

To record net settle-up on swap arrangement [8.0 – 8.5%]

Swap contract	65,527	
Other comprehensive income		65,527

To record the fair value of the swap contract as of this date

December 31, 2011

Interest expense	225,000	
Accrued interest (or cash)		225,000

To accrue or pay interest on the debt at the variable rate of prime + 1/2% (9.0%)

Accrued interest (or cash)	25,000	
Interest expense		25,000

To record net settle-up on swap arrangement [8.0 – 9.0%]

Swap contract	45,769	
Other comprehensive income		45,769

To record the fair value of the swap contract as of this date

June 30, 2012

Interest expense	212,500	
Accrued interest (or cash)		212,500

To accrue or pay interest on the debt at the variable rate of prime + 1/2% (8.5%)

Accrued interest (cash)	12,500	
Interest expense		12,500

To record net settle-up on swap arrangement [8.0 – 8.5%]

Other comprehensive income	65,922	
Swap contract		65,922

To record the change in the fair value of the swap contract as of this date (declining prime rate causes swap to lose value)

December 31, 2012

Interest expense	212,500	
Accrued interest (or cash)		212,000

To accrue or pay interest on the debt at the variable rate of prime + 1/2% (8.5%)

Accrued interest (or cash)	12,500	
Interest expense		12,500

To record net settle-up on swap arrangement [8.0 – 8.5%]

Other comprehensive income	10,685	
Swap contract		10,685

To record the fair value of the swap contract as of this date (decline is due to passage of time, as the prime rate expectations have not changed from the earlier period)

June 30, 2013

Interest expense	200,000	
Accrued interest (or cash)		200,000

To accrue or pay interest on the debt at the variable rate of prime + 1/2% (8.0%)

Accrued interest (or cash)	0	
Interest expense		0

To record net settle-up on swap arrangement [8.0 – 8.5%]

Other comprehensive income	34,689	
Swap contract		34,689

To record the fair value of the swap contract as of this date

December 31, 2013

Interest expense	200,000	
Accrued interest (or cash)		200,000

To accrue or pay interest on the debt at the variable rate of prime + 1/2% (8.0%)

Accrued interest (or cash)	0	
Interest expense		0

To record net settle-up on swap arrangement [8.0 – 8.0%]

Swap contract	0	
Other comprehensive income		0

No change to the fair value of the swap contract as of this date

June 30, 2014

Interest expense	187,500	
Accrued interest (or cash)		187,500

To accrue or pay interest on the debt at the variable rate of prime + 1/2% (7.5%)

Interest expense	12,500	
Accrued interest (or cash)		12,500

To record net settle-up on swap arrangement [8.0 – 7.5%]

Other comprehensive income	0	
Swap contract		0

No change to the fair value of the swap contract, which expires as of this date

Example of using options to hedge a future purchase of inventory

Friendly Chemicals Corp. uses petroleum as a feedshare from which it produces a range of chemicals for sale to producers of synthetic fabrics and other consumer goods. It is concerned about the rising price of oil and decides to hedge a major purchase it plans to make in mid-2009 Oil futures and options are traded on the New York Mercantile Exchange and in other markets; Friendly decides to use options rather than futures because it is only interested in protecting itself from a price increase; if prices decline, it wishes to reap that benefit rather than suffer the loss which would result from holding a futures contract in a declining market environment.

At December 31, 2008, Friendly projects a need for 10 million barrels of crude oil of a defined grade to be purchased by mid-2009; this will suffice for production through mid-2010. The current world price for this grade of crude is €64.50 per barrel, but prices have been rising recently. Management desires to limit its crude oil costs to no higher than €65.75 per barrel, and accordingly purchases, at a cost of €2 million, an option to purchase up to 10 million barrels at a cost of €65.55 per barrel, at any time through December 2009. When the option premium is added to this €65.55 per barrel cost, it would make the total cost €65.75 per barrel if the full 10 million barrels are acquired.

Management has studied the behavior of option prices and has concluded that changes in option prices that relate to time value are not correlated to price changes and hence are ineffective in hedging price changes. On the other hand, changes in option prices that pertain to pricing changes (intrinsic value changes) are highly effective as hedging vehicles. The table below reports the value of these options, analyzed in terms of time value and intrinsic value, over the period from December 2008 through December 2009.

Date	Price of oil/barrel	Fair value of option relating to Time value*	Intrinsic value
December 31, 2008	€64.50	€2,000,000	€ 0
January 31, 2009	64.90	1,900,000	0
February 28, 2009	65.30	1,800,000	0
March 31, 2009	65.80	1,700,000	2,500,000
April 30, 2009	66.00	1,600,000	4,500,000
May 31, 2009	65.85	1,500,000	3,000,000
June 30, 2009**	66.00	700,000	2,250,000
July 31, 2009	65.60	650,000	250,000
August 31, 2009	65.50	600,000	0
September 30, 2009	65.75	550,000	1,000,000
October 31, 2009	65.80	500,000	1,250,000
November 30, 2009	65.85	450,000	1,500,000
December 31, 2009***	65.90	400,000	1,750,000

* This example does not address how the time value of options would be computed in practice.
** Options for five million barrels exercised; remainder held until end of December, then sold.
*** Values cited are immediately prior to sale of remaining options.

At the end of June 2009, Friendly Chemicals exercises options for five million barrels, paying €65.55 per barrel for oil that is then selling on world markets for €66.00 each. It holds the remaining options until December, when it sells these for an aggregate price of €2.1 million, a slight discount to the nominal fair value at that date.

The inventory acquired in mid-2009 is processed and included in goods available for sale. Sales of these goods, in terms of the five million barrels of crude oil which were consumed in their production, are as follows:

Date	Equivalent barrels sold in month	Equivalent barrels on hand at month end
June 30, 2009	300,000	4,700,000
July 31, 2009	250,000	4,450,000
August 31, 2009	400,000	4,050,000
September 30, 2009	350,000	3,700,000
October 31, 2009	550,000	3,150,000
November 30, 2009	500,000	2,650,000
December 31, 2009	650,000	2,000,000

Based on the foregoing facts, the journal entries prepared on a *monthly* basis (for illustrative purposes) for the period December 2008 through December 2009 are as follows:

December 31, 2008

Option contract	2,000,000	
Cash		2,000,000

To record purchase premium on option contract for up to 10 million barrels of oil at price of €65.55 per barrel

January 31, 2009

Gain/loss on hedging transaction	100,000	
Option contract		100,000

To record change in time value of option contract—charge premium to profit or loss since this represents payment for time value of money, which expires ratably over two-year term and does not qualify for hedge accounting treatment

Option contract	0	
Other comprehensive income		0

To reflect change in intrinsic value of option contracts (no value at this date)

February 28, 2009

Gain/loss on hedging transaction	100,000	
Option contract		100,000

To record change in time value of option contract—charge premium to profit or loss since this represents payment for time value of money, which expires ratably over two-year term and does not qualify for hedge accounting treatment

Option contract	0	
Other comprehensive profit or loss		0

To reflect change in intrinsic value of option contracts (no value at this date)

March 31, 2009

Gain/loss on hedging transaction	100,000	
Option contract		100,000

To record change in time value of option contract—charge premium to profit or loss since this represents payment for time value of money, which expires ratably over two-year term and does not qualify for hedge accounting treatment

Option contract	2,500,000	
Other comprehensive profit or loss		2,500,000

To reflect change in intrinsic value of option contracts

April 30, 2009

Gain/loss on hedging transaction	100,000	
Option contract		100,000

To record change in time value of option contract—charge premium to profit or loss since this represents payment for time value of money, which expires ratably over two-year term and does not qualify for hedge accounting treatment

Option contract	2,000,000	
Other comprehensive profit or loss		2,000,000

To reflect change in intrinsic value of option contracts (further increase in value)

May 31, 2009

Gain/loss on hedging transaction	100,000	
Option contract		100,000

To record change in time value of option contract—charge premium to profit or loss since this represents payment for time value of money, which expires ratably over two-year term and does not qualify for hedge accounting treatment

Other comprehensive profit or loss	1,500,000	
Option contract		1,500,000

To reflect change in intrinsic value of option contracts (decline in value)

June 30, 2009

Gain/loss on hedging transaction	800,000	
Option contract		800,000

To record change in time value of option contract—charge premium to profit or loss since this represents payment for time value of money, which expires ratably over two-year term and does not qualify for hedge accounting treatment; since one-half the options were exercised in June, the remaining unexpensed time value of that portion is also entirely written off at this time

Option contracts	1,500,000	
Other comprehensive income		1,500,000

To reflect change in intrinsic value of option contracts (further increase in value) before accounting for exercise of options on five million barrels

June 30 value of options before exercise	4,500,000
Allocation to oil purchased at €65.55	2,250,000
Remaining option valuation	2,250,000

The allocation to exercised options will be used to adjust the carrying value of the inventory, and ultimately will be transferred to cost of goods sold as a contra cost, as the five million barrels are sold, at the rate of 45¢ per equivalent barrel.

Inventory	327,750,000	
Cash		327,750,000

To record purchase of five million barrels of oil at option price of €65.55/barrel

Inventory	2,250,000	
Option contract		2,250,000

To increase the recorded value of the inventory to include the fair value of options given up in acquiring the oil (taken together, the cash purchase price and the fair value of options surrendered add to €66.00 per barrel, the world market price at date of purchase)

Other comprehensive income	2,250,000	
Inventory		2,250,000

To reclassify deferred gain from equity and include in initial measurement of inventory

Cost of goods sold	19,665,000	
Inventory		19,665,000

To record cost of goods sold

July 31, 2009

Gain/loss on hedging transaction	50,000	
Option contract		50,000

To record change in time value of option contract—charge premium to profit or loss since this represents payment for time value of money, which expires ratably over two-year term, and does not qualify for hedge accounting treatment

Other comprehensive income	2,000,000	
Option contract		2,000,000

To reflect change in intrinsic value of remaining option contracts (decline in value)

Cost of goods sold	16,387,500	
Inventory		16,387,500

To record cost of goods sold

August 31, 2009

Loss on hedging transaction	50,000	
Option contract		50,000

To record change in time value of option contract—charge premium to profit or loss since this represents payment for time value of money, which expires ratably over two-year term, and does not qualify for hedge accounting treatment

Other comprehensive income	250,000	
Option contract		250,000

To reflect change in intrinsic value of remaining option contracts (decline in value)

Cost of goods sold	26,220,000	
Inventory		26,220,000

To record cost of goods sold

September 30, 2009

Gain/loss on hedging transaction	50,000	
Option contract		50,000

To record change in time value of option contract—charge premium to profit or loss since this represents payment for time value of money, which expires ratably over two-year term, and does not qualify for hedge accounting treatment

Option contract	1,000,000	
Other comprehensive income		1,000,000

To reflect change in intrinsic value of remaining option contracts (increase in value)

Cost of goods sold	22,942,500	
Inventory		22,942,500

To record cost of goods sold

October 31, 2009

Gain/loss on hedging transaction	50,000	
Option contract		50,000

To record change in time value of option contract—charge premium to profit or loss since this represents payment for time value of money, which expires ratably over two-year term, and does not qualify for hedge accounting treatment

Option contract	250,000	
Other comprehensive income		250,000

To reflect change in intrinsic value of remaining option contracts (further increase in value)

Cost of goods sold	36,052,500	
Inventory		36,052,500

To record cost of goods sold

November 30, 2009

Gain/loss on hedging transaction	50,000	
Option contract		50,000

To record change in time value of option contract—charge premium to profit or loss since this represents payment for time value of money, which expires ratably over two-year term, and does not qualify for hedge accounting treatment

Option contract	250,000	
Other comprehensive income		250,000

To reflect change in intrinsic value of remaining option contracts (further increase in value)

Cost of goods sold	32,775,000	
Inventory		32,775,000

To record cost of goods sold

December 31, 2009

Gain/loss on hedging transaction	50,000	
Option contract		50,000

To record change in time value of option contract—charge premium to profit or loss since this represents payment for time value of money, which expires ratably over two-year term, and does not qualify for hedge accounting treatment

Option contract	250,000	
Other comprehensive income		250,000

To reflect change in intrinsic value of remaining option contracts (further increase in value) before sale of options

Cost of goods sold	42,607,500	
Inventory		42,607,500

To record cost of goods sold

Cash	2,100,000	
Loss on sale of options	50,000	
Option contract		2,150,000
Other comprehensive income	1,750,000	
Gain on sale of options		1,750,000

To record sale of remaining option contracts; the cash price was €50,000 lower than carrying value of asset sold (options having unexpired time value of €400,000 plus intrinsic value of €1,750,000), but reclassification from equity to profit or loss recognizes formerly deferred gain; since no further inventory purchases are planned in connection with this hedging activity, the unrealized gain is recognized in profit or loss

Example of hedging of a net investment in a foreign subsidiary

IAS 39 permits hedging of a net investment in foreign subsidiaries ("net investment hedge"). For example, Swartzwald GmbH has a net investment of $100,000 in its US subsidiary, Simpsons Inc., for which it paid €110,000 on January 1, 2009. Swartzwald could hedge its net asset investment by entering, for example, into a forward exchange contract to sell US dollars, or the company could incur a US dollar-based liability. IAS 39 states that the gain or loss on the effective portion of a hedge of a net investment is reported in other comprehensive income and accumulated in equity as part of the foreign currency translation adjustment. However, the amount of offset to other comprehensive income is limited to the translation adjustment for the net investment. For example, if the forward exchange rate is used to measure hedge effectiveness, the amount of offset is limited to the change in spot rates during the period. Any excess of the ineffective portion of the hedge must be recognized currently in profit or loss.

On January 1, 2009, Swartzwald decided to hedge its investment in Simpsons for the amount equal to the book value of the US company's net investment (net assets). Swartzwald is unsure whether the exchange rate for the dollar will increase or decrease for the year and wants to hedge its net asset investment. On January 1, 2009, Swartzwald's ownership share of Simpson's net assets is equal to $100,000 ($80,000 share capital and $20,000 retained earnings). On that day Swartzwald borrows $100,000, at a 5% rate of interest, to hedge its equity investment in the US company, and the principal and interest are due and payable on January 1, 2010.

The spot exchange rates are: January 1, 2009 $1 = €.90
                                  December 31, 2009 $1 = €.80

The average exchange rate for the year 2009 is: $1 = €.85

The journal entries on Swartzwald's Euro-denominated books to account for this hedge of a net investment are as follows:

January 1, 2009

Cash	90,000	
Loan payable ($ denominated debt)		90,000

To record a dollar-denominated loan to hedge net investment in US subsidiary €90,000 = $100,000 × €.90 spot rate

December 31, 2009

Loan payable ($ denominated debt)	10,000	
Other comprehensive income (OCI)		10,000

To revalue foreign currency-denominated payable to end-of-period spot rate €10,000 = $100,000 × (€.90 – €.80)

Interest expense	4,250	
Foreign currency exchange gain		250
Interest payable		4,000

To accrue interest expense and payable on dollar loan
€4,250 = $100,000 × 0.05 interest × €.85 average exchange rate
€4,000 = $100,000 × 0.05 interest × €.80 ending spot rate

Other comprehensive income (OCI)	10,000	
Foreign currency exchange gain	250	
Profit or loss summary (retained earnings)		250
Translation adjustment—accumulated OCI		10,000

To record closing of nominal accounts related to hedge of net investment in foreign subsidiary

January 1, 2010

Interest payable ($ denominated debt)	4,000	
Loan payable ($ denominated debt)	80,000	
Cash		84,000

To record repayment of principal and interest. €80,000 = €90,000 – €10,000

During 2009 the euro has strengthened relative to the dollar (the direct exchange rate has decreased from €.90 to €.80) and Swartzwald would recognize a loss on a net asset investment in dollars and gain on a liability payable in dollars. Without this hedge of the net investment, Swartzwald would report a €10,850 debit balance in other comprehensive income (the cumulative translation adjustment portion of accumulated other comprehensive income equals €10,000 + €850 differential adjustment). With the hedge of its net investment, Swartzwald will report only €850 (€10,850 – €10,000 effect of hedge) as the change in the cumulative translation adjustment for 2009. Note also that the amount of the offset to other income is limited to the effective portion of the hedge based on the revaluation of the net assets. Any excess, in this case the €250 gain on the revaluation of the interest payable, is reported currently in the profit or loss.

Hedging on a "net" basis and "macrohedging." The IGC has addressed the issue of whether a reporting entity can group financial assets together with financial liabilities for the purpose of determining the net cash flow exposure to be hedged for hedge accounting purposes. It ruled that while an entity's hedging strategy and risk management practices may assess cash flow risk on a net basis, IAS 39 does not permit designating a net cash flow exposure as a hedged item for hedge accounting purposes. IAS 39 provides an example of how a bank might assess its risk on a net basis (with similar assets and liabilities grouped together) and then qualify for hedge accounting by hedging on a gross basis.

In 2004 IASB amended IAS 39 to permit "macrohedging" (more formally, hedging a portfolio hedge of interest rate risk). This permits an entity to apply *fair value* hedging (but not cash flow hedging) to a grouping of assets and/or liabilities, which essentially means that the net exposure can be hedged, without a need to separately put hedge positions on for each of the individual assets and/or liabilities. (See discussion in Chapter 5.)

Partial term hedging. IAS 39 indicates that a hedging relationship may not be designated for only a portion of the time period in which a hedging instrument is outstanding. On the other hand, it is permitted to designate a derivative as hedging only a portion of the time period to maturity of a hedged item. For example, if Aquarian Corp. acquires a 10% fixed-rate government bond with a remaining term to maturity of ten years, and classifies the bond as available-for-sale, it may hedge itself against fair value exposure on the bond associated with the present value of the interest rate payments until year five by acquiring a five-year "pay-fixed, receive-floating" swap. The swap may be designated as hedging the fair value exposure of the interest rate payments on the government bond until year five and the change in value of the principal payment due at maturity to the extent affected by changes in the yield curve relating to the five years of the swap.

Interest rate risk managed on a net basis should be designated as hedge of gross exposure. If an entity manages its exposure to interest rate risk on a net basis, a number of complex financial reporting issues must be addressed, regarding the ability to use hedge accounting. The IGC has offered substantial guidance on a number of matters, the more generally applicable of which are summarized in the following paragraphs.

The IGC has concluded that a derivative that is used to manage interest rate risk on a net basis be designated as a hedging instrument in a fair value hedge or a cash flow hedge of a gross exposure under IAS 39. An entity may designate the derivative used in interest rate risk management activities either as a fair value hedge of assets or liabilities or as a cash flow hedge of forecasted transactions, such as the anticipated reinvestment of cash inflows, the anticipated refinancing or rollover of a financial liability, and the cash flow consequences of the resetting of interest rates for an asset or a liability.

The IGC also notes that firm commitments to purchase or sell assets at fixed prices create fair value exposures, but are accounted for as cash flow hedges. (Note, however, the IASB has proposed to reverse the former rule, such that hedges of firm commitments will henceforth be accounted for as fair value hedges.) In economic terms, it does not matter whether the derivative instrument is considered a fair value hedge or a cash flow hedge. Under either perspective of the exposure, the derivative has the same economic effect of reducing the net exposure. For example, a receive-fixed, pay-variable interest rate swap can be considered to be a cash flow hedge of a variable-rate asset or a fair value hedge of a fixed-rate liability. Under either perspective, the fair value or cash flows of the interest rate swap offsets the exposure to interest rate changes. However, accounting consequences differ depending on whether the derivative is designated as a fair value hedge or a cash flow hedge, as discussed below.

Consider the following illustration. Among its financial resources and obligations, a bank has the following assets and liabilities having maturities of two years:

	Variable interest	*Fixed interest*
Assets	60,000	100,000
Liabilities	(100,000)	(60,000)
Net	(40,000)	40,000

The bank enters into a two-year interest rate swap with a notional principal of €40,000 to receive a variable interest rate and pay a fixed interest rate, in order to hedge the net exposure of the two-year maturity financial assets and liabilities. According to the IGC, this may be designated either as a fair value hedge of €40,000 of the fixed-rate assets or as a cash flow hedge of €40,000 of the variable-rate liabilities. It cannot be designated as a hedge of the net exposure, however.

Determining whether a derivative that is used to manage interest rate risk on a net basis should be designated as a hedging instrument in a fair value hedge or a cash flow hedge of a gross exposure is based on a number of critical considerations. These include the assessment of hedge effectiveness in the presence of prepayment risk, and the ability of the information systems to attribute fair value or cash flow changes of hedging instruments to fair value or cash flow changes, respectively, of hedged items. For accounting purposes, the designation of the derivative as hedging a fair value exposure or a cash flow exposure is important because both the qualification requirements for hedge accounting and the recognition of hedging gains and losses differ for each of these categories. The IGC has observed that it will often be easier to demonstrate high effectiveness for a cash flow hedge than for a fair value hedge.

Another important issue involves the effects of prepayments on the fair value of an instrument and the timing of its cash flows, as well as the impacts on the effectiveness test for fair value hedges and the probability test for cash flow hedges, respectively. Effectiveness is often more difficult to achieve for fair value hedges than for cash flow hedges when the instrument being hedged is subject to prepayment risk. For a fair value hedge to qualify for hedge accounting, the changes in the fair value of the derivative hedging instrument must be expected to be highly effective in offsetting the changes in the fair value of the hedged item. This test may be difficult to meet if, for example, the derivative hedging instrument is a forward contract having a fixed term, and the financial assets being hedged are subject to prepayment by the borrower.

Also, it may be difficult to conclude that, for a portfolio of fixed-rate assets that are subject to prepayment, the changes in the fair value for each individual item in the group will be expected to be approximately proportional to the overall changes in fair value attributable to the hedged risk of the group. Even if the risk being hedged is a benchmark interest rate, to be able to conclude that fair value changes will be proportional for each item in the portfolio, it may be necessary to disaggregate the asset portfolio into categories based on term, coupon, credit, type of loan, and other characteristics.

In economic terms, a forward derivative instrument could be used to hedge assets that are subject to prepayment, but it would be effective only for small movements in interest rates. A reasonable estimate of prepayments can be made for a given interest rate environment and the derivative position can be adjusted as the interest rate environment changes. However, for accounting purposes, the expectation of effectiveness has to be based on existing fair value exposures and the potential for interest rate movements, without consideration of future adjustments to those positions. The fair value exposure attributable to prepayment risk can generally be hedged with options.

For a cash flow hedge to qualify for hedge accounting, the forecasted cash flows, including the reinvestment of cash inflows or the refinancing of cash outflows, must be highly probable, and the hedge expected to be highly effective in achieving offsetting changes in the cash flows of the hedged item and hedging instrument. Prepayments affect the timing of cash flows and, therefore, the probability of occurrence of the forecasted transaction. If the hedge is established for risk management purposes on a net basis, an entity may have sufficient levels of highly probable cash flows on a gross basis to support the designation for accounting purposes of forecasted transactions associated with a portion of the gross cash flows as the hedged item. In this case, the portion of the gross cash flows designated as being hedged may be chosen to be equal to the amount of net cash flows being hedged for risk management purposes.

The IAS 39 Implementation Guidance Committee has also emphasized that there are important systems considerations relating to the use of hedge accounting. It notes that the accounting differs for fair value hedges and cash flow hedges. It is usually easier to use existing information systems to manage and track cash flow hedges than it is for fair value hedges.

Under fair value hedge accounting, the assets or liabilities that are designated as being hedged are remeasured for those changes in fair values during the hedge period that are attributable to the risk being hedged. Such changes adjust the carrying amount of the hedged items and, for interest-sensitive assets and liabilities, may result in an adjustment of the effective yield of the hedged item. As a consequence of fair value hedging activities, the changes in fair value have to be allocated to the hedged assets or liabilities being hedged in order to be able to recompute their effective yield, determine the subsequent amortization of the fair value adjustment to net profit or loss, and determine the amount that should be recognized in net profit or loss when assets are sold or liabilities extinguished. To comply with the requirements for fair value hedge accounting, it generally will be necessary to establish a system to track the changes in the fair value attributable to the hedged risk, associate those changes with individual hedged items, recompute the effective yield of the hedged items, and amortize the changes to net profit or loss over the life of the respective hedged item.

Under cash flow hedge accounting, the cash flows relating to the forecasted transactions that are designated as being hedged reflect changes in interest rates. The adjustment for changes in the fair value of a hedging derivative instrument is initially recognized in other comprehensive income. To comply with the requirements for cash flow hedge accounting, it is necessary to determine when the adjustments from changes in the fair value of a hedging instrument should be recognized in profit or loss. For cash flow hedges, it is not necessary to create a separate system to make this determination. The system used to determine the extent of the net exposure provides the basis for scheduling out the changes in the cash flows of the derivative and the recognition of such changes in profit or loss. The timing of the recognition in profit or loss can be predetermined when the hedge is associated with the exposure to changes in cash flows.

The forecasted transactions that are being hedged can be associated with a specific principal amount in specific future periods, composed of variable-rate assets and cash inflows being reinvested or variable-rate liabilities and cash outflows being refinanced, each of which create a cash flow exposure to changes in interest rates. The specific principal amounts in specific future periods are equal to the notional amount of the derivative hedging instruments and are hedged only for the period that corresponds to the repricing or maturity of the derivative hedging instruments so that the cash flow changes resulting from changes in interest rate are matched with the derivative hedging instrument. IAS 39 specifies that the amounts recognized in other comprehensive income should be included in profit or loss in the same period or periods during which the hedged item affects profit or loss.

If a hedging relationship is designated as a cash flow hedge relating to changes in cash flows resulting from interest rate changes, the documentation required by IAS 39 would include information about the hedging relationship; the entity's risk management objective and strategy for undertaking the hedge; the type of hedge; the hedged item; the hedged risk; the hedging instrument; and the method of assessing effectiveness.

Information about the hedging relationship would include the maturity schedule of cash flows used for risk management purposes, to determine exposures to cash flow mismatches on a net basis would provide part of the documentation of the hedging relationship. The entity's risk management objective and strategy for undertaking the hedge would be addressed in terms of the entity's overall risk management objective and strategy for hedging exposures to interest rate risk would provide part of the documentation of the hedging objective and strategy. The fact that the hedge is a cash flow hedge would also be noted.

The hedged item will be documented as a group of forecasted transactions (interest cash flows) that are expected to occur with a high degree of probability in specified future periods, for instance, scheduled on a monthly basis. The hedged item may include interest cash flows resulting from the reinvestment of cash inflows, including the resetting of interest rates on assets, or from the refinancing of cash outflows, including the resetting of interest rates on liabilities and rollovers of financial liabilities. The forecasted transactions meet the probability test if there are sufficient levels of highly probable cash flows in the specified future periods to encompass the amounts designated as being hedged on a gross basis.

The risk designated as being hedged is documented as a portion of the overall exposure to changes in a specified market interest rate, often the risk-free interest rate or an interbank offered rate, common to all items in the group. To help ensure that the hedge effectiveness test is met at inception of the hedge and subsequently, the designated hedged portion of the interest rate risk could be documented as being based off the same yield curve as the derivative hedging instrument.

Each derivative hedging instrument is documented as a hedge of specified amounts in specified future time periods corresponding with the forecasted transactions occurring in the specified future periods designated as being hedged.

The method of assessing effectiveness is documented by comparing the changes in the cash flows of the derivatives allocated to the applicable periods in which they are designated as a hedge to the changes in the cash flows of the forecasted transactions being hedged. Measurement of the cash flow changes is based on the applicable yield curves of the derivatives and hedged items.

When a hedging relationship is designated as a cash flow hedge, the entity might satisfy the requirement for an expectation of high effectiveness in achieving offsetting changes by preparing an analysis demonstrating high historical and expected future correlation between the interest rate risk designated as being hedged and the interest rate risk of the hedging instrument. Existing documentation of the hedge ratio used in establishing the derivative contracts may also serve to demonstrate an expectation of effectiveness.

If the hedging relationship is designated as a cash flow hedge, an entity may demonstrate a high probability of the forecasted transactions occurring by preparing a cash flow maturity schedule showing that there exist sufficient aggregate gross levels of expected cash flows, including the effects of the resetting of interest rates for assets or liabilities, to establish that the forecasted transactions that are designated as being hedged are highly probable of occurring. Such a schedule should be supported by management's stated intent and past practice of reinvesting cash inflows and refinancing cash outflows.

For instance, an entity may forecast aggregate gross cash inflows of €10,000 and aggregate gross cash outflows of €9,000 in a particular time period in the near future. In this case, it may wish to designate the forecasted reinvestment of gross cash inflows of €1,000 as the hedged item in the future time period. If more than €1,000 of the forecasted cash inflows are contractually specified and have low credit risk, the entity has very strong evidence to support an assertion that gross cash inflows of €1,000 are highly probable of occurring and support the designation of the forecasted reinvestment of those cash flows as being hedged for a particular portion of the reinvestment period. A high probability of the forecasted transactions occurring may also be demonstrated under other circumstances.

If the hedging relationship is designated as a cash flow hedge, an entity will assess and measure effectiveness under IAS 39, at a minimum, at the time an entity prepares its annual or interim financial reports. However, an entity may wish to measure it more frequently on a specified periodic basis, at the end of each month or other applicable reporting period. It is also measured whenever derivative positions designated as hedging instruments are changed or hedges are terminated to ensure that the recognition in net profit or loss of the changes in the fair value amounts on assets and liabilities and the recognition of changes in the fair value of derivative instruments designated as cash flow hedges are appropriate.

Changes in the cash flows of the derivative are computed and allocated to the applicable periods in which the derivative is designated as a hedge and are compared with computations of changes in the cash flows of the forecasted transactions. Computations are based on yield curves applicable to the hedged items and the derivative hedging instruments and applicable interest rates for the specified periods being hedged. The schedule used to determine effectiveness could be maintained and used as the basis for determining the period in which the hedging gains and losses recognized initially in other comprehensive income are reclassified out of equity and recognized in profit or loss.

If the hedging relationship is designated as a cash flow hedge, an entity will account for the hedge as follows: (1) the portion of gains and losses on hedging derivatives determined to result from effective hedges is recognized in other comprehensive income whenever effectiveness is measured and (2) the ineffective portion of gains and losses resulting from hedging derivatives is recognized in net profit or loss.

The amounts recognized in other comprehensive income should be included in net profit or loss in the same period or periods during which the hedged item affects net profit or loss. Accordingly, when the forecasted transactions occur, the amounts previously recognized in other comprehensive income are reclassified from equity to profit or loss. For instance, if an interest rate swap is designated as a hedging instrument of a series of forecasted cash flows, the changes in the cash flows of the swap are recognized in net profit or loss in the periods when the forecasted cash flows and the cash flows of the swap offset each other.

If the hedging relationship is designated as a cash flow hedge, the treatment of any net cumulative gains and losses recognized in other comprehensive income if the hedging instrument is terminated prematurely, the hedge accounting criteria are no longer met, or the hedged forecasted transactions are no longer expected to take place, will be as described in the following. If the hedging instrument is terminated prematurely or the hedge no longer meets the criteria for qualification for hedge accounting (for instance, the forecasted transactions are no longer highly probable), the net cumulative gain or loss reported in other comprehensive income remains in equity until the forecasted transaction occurs. If the hedged forecasted transactions are no longer expected to occur, the net cumulative gain or loss is reclassified from equity to profit or loss for the period.

IAS 39 states that a hedging relationship may not be designated for only a portion of the time period in which a hedging instrument is outstanding. If the hedging relationship is designated as a cash flow hedge, and the hedge subsequently fails the test for being highly effective, IAS 39 does not preclude redesignating the hedging instrument. The standard indicates that a derivative instrument may not be designated as a hedging instrument for only a portion of its remaining period to maturity but does not refer to the derivative instrument's original period to maturity. If there is a hedge effectiveness failure, the ineffective portion of the gain or loss on the derivative instrument is recognized immediately in net profit or loss and hedge accounting based on the previous designation of the hedge relationship cannot be continued. In this case, the derivative instrument may be redesignated prospectively as a hedging instrument in a new hedging relationship, provided this hedging relationship satisfies the necessary conditions. The derivative instrument must be redesignated as a hedge for the entire time period it remains outstanding.

For cash flow hedges, IAS 39 states that "if the hedged firm commitment or forecasted transaction results in the recognition of an asset or liability, then at the time the asset or liability is recognized the associated gains or losses that were recognized in other comprehensive income should enter into the initial measurement of the carrying amount of the asset or liability" (basis adjustment). If a derivative is used to manage a net exposure to interest rate risk and the derivative is designated as a cash flow hedge of forecasted interest cash flows or portions thereof on a gross basis, there will be no basis adjustment when the forecasted cash flow occurs. There is no basis adjustment because the hedged forecasted transactions do not result in the recognition of assets or liabilities and the effect of interest rate changes that are designated as being hedged is recognized in net profit or loss in the period in which the forecasted transactions occur. Although the types of hedges described herein would not result in basis adjustment if instead the derivative is designated as a hedge of a forecasted purchase of a financial asset or issuance of a liability, the derivative gain or loss would be an adjustment to the basis of the asset or liability upon the occurrence of the transaction.

IAS 39 permits a portion of a cash flow exposure to be designated as a hedged item. While IAS 39 does not specifically address a hedge of a portion of a cash flow exposure for a forecasted transaction, it specifies that a financial asset or liability may be a hedged item with respect to the risks associated with only a portion of its cash flows or fair value, if effectiveness can be measured. The ability to hedge a portion of a cash flow exposure resulting from the resetting of interest rates for assets and liabilities suggests that a portion of a cash flow exposure resulting from the forecasted reinvestment of cash inflows or the refinancing or rollover of financial liabilities can also be hedged. The basis for qualification as a hedged item of a portion of an exposure is the ability to measure effectiveness.

Furthermore, IAS 39 specifies that a nonfinancial asset or liability can be hedged only in its entirety or for foreign currency risk but not for a portion of other risks because of the difficulty of isolating and measuring the risks attributable to a specific risk. Accordingly, assuming effectiveness can be measured, a portion of a cash flow exposure of forecasted transactions associated with, for example, the resetting of interest rates for a variable-rate asset or liability can be designated as a hedged item.

Since forecasted transactions will have different terms when they occur, including credit exposures, maturities, and option features, there may be an issue over how an entity can satisfy the tests in IAS 39 requiring that the hedged group have similar risk characteristics. According to the IGC, the standard provides for hedging a group of assets, liabilities, firm commitments, or forecasted transactions with similar risk characteristics. IAS 39 provides additional guidance and specifies that portfolio hedging is permitted if two conditions are met, namely: the individual items in the portfolio share the same risk for which they are designated and the change in the fair value attributable to the hedged risk for each individual item in the group will be expected to be approximately proportional to the overall change in fair value.

When an entity associates a derivative hedging instrument with a gross exposure, the hedged item typically is a group of forecasted transactions. For hedges of cash flow exposures relating to a group of forecasted transactions, the overall exposure of the forecasted transactions and the assets or liabilities that are repricing may have very different risks. The exposure from forecasted transactions may differ based on the terms that are expected as they relate to credit exposures, maturities, option, and other features. Although the overall risk exposures may be different for the individual items in the group, a specific risk inherent in each of the items in the group can be designated as being hedged.

The items in the portfolio do not necessarily have to have the same overall exposure to risk, providing they share the same risk for which they are designated as being hedged. A common risk typically shared by a portfolio of financial instruments is exposure to changes in the risk-free interest rate or to changes in a specified rate that has a credit exposure equal to the highest credit-rated instrument in the portfolio (that is, the instrument with the lowest credit risk). If the instruments that are grouped into a portfolio have different credit exposures, they may be hedged as a group for a portion of the exposure. The risk they have in common that is designated as being hedged is the exposure to interest rate changes from the highest credit-rated instrument in the portfolio. This ensures that the change in fair value attributable to the hedged risk for each individual item in the group is expected to be approximately proportional to the overall change in fair value attributable to the hedged risk of the group. It is likely there will be some ineffectiveness if the hedging instrument has a credit quality that is inferior to the credit quality of the highest credit-rated instrument being hedged, since a hedging relationship is designated for a hedging instrument in its entirety.

For example, if a portfolio of assets consists of assets rated A, BB, and B, and the current market interest rates for these assets are LIBOR + 20 basis points, LIBOR + 40 basis points, and LIBOR + 60 basis points, respectively, an entity may use a swap that pays fixed interest rate and for which variable interest payments are made based on LIBOR to hedge the exposure to variable interest rates. If LIBOR is designated as the risk being hedged, credit spreads above LIBOR on the hedged items are excluded from the designated hedge relationship and the assessment of hedge effectiveness.

Equity Method of Accounting for Investments

The preceding discussion addressed investments in which the investor has essentially a passive position, due to holding only a small minority ownership interest (or, in the case of debt, no actual ownership interest at all). In such situations, the investor is unable to control or materially influence decisions to be made by management of the investee. The use of fair value accounting has been deemed most appropriate in such circumstances.

In other situations an investor will have active control over the decisions taken by the management of the investee, or have joint control over those decisions, to be made in conjunction with its coinvestors. A third logical possibility is that the investor will have something less than control (or joint control), but will clearly also not be a mere passive investor. This last named circumstance is that where there is significant influence over an investee.

The notion of applying what is now known as equity-method accounting to investment situations where the investor is able to exercise significant influence developed in the early 1950s, as an application of the "substance over form" philosophy of financial reporting. It was not actually made mandatory, however, until the late 1960s, in the US. Because the actual determination of the existence of significant influence was anticipated to be difficult, a somewhat arbitrary, refutable presumption of such influence was set at a 20% voting interest in the investee. This became the de facto standard for all later accounting requirements seeking to emulate the pioneering one set forth under US GAAP.

The necessity of applying a method of accounting such as the equity method, when significant influence over the investee is held by the investor, can easily be understood when one considers how readily manipulation of the investor's financial position and results of operations could be achieved in its absence. If an investee has substantial profit or loss, but the investor, employing the cost method of accounting for the investment, uses its influence to defer the investee's declaration of dividends, the result would be that the investor would not be reporting its share of the investee's economic operating results, even though it had been in a position to cause a distribution of dividends, had it chosen to do so. This might be motivated, for example, by a desire to put aside future earnings to compensate for an expected, or feared, decline in the investor's own operations.

Conversely, the investor could effect or encourage a dividend distribution even in the absence of earnings by the investee. This could be motivated by a need for reportable earnings, perhaps to offset disappointing performance in the investor's own operations. In either case, the opportunity to manipulate reported results of operations would be of great concern.

More importantly, however, the use of the cost method would simply not reflect the economic reality of the investor's interest in an entity whose operations were indicative, in part at least, of the reporting entity's (i.e., the investor's) management decisions and operational skills. Thus, the clearly demonstrable need to reflect substance, rather than mere form, made the development of the equity method highly desirable.

The pure equity method is not the only possible means of accomplishing the goal of reporting the economic performance of the investor. Other suggested solutions include the expanded equity method and proportionate consolidation. IASB and the various national standard-setting bodies have directed differing levels of attention to these alternatives over the years; the simple equity method has received the most universal support.

The equity method permits an entity (the investor) controlling a certain share of the voting interest in another entity (the investee) to incorporate its pro rata share of the investee's operating results into its profit or loss. However, rather than include its share of each component of the investee's revenues, expenses, assets and liabilities into its financial statements, the investor will only include its share of the investee's profit or loss as a separate line item in its statement of comprehensive income. Similarly, only a single line in the investor's balance is presented, but this reflects, to a degree, the investor's share in each of the investee's assets and liabilities. For this reason, the equity method has been referred to as "one-line consolidation."

It is important to recognize that the bottom-line impact on the investor's financial statements is identical whether the equity method or full consolidation is employed; only the amount of detail presented within the statements will differ. An understanding of this principle will be useful as the need to identify the "goodwill" component of the cost of the investment is explained below.

Expanded equity method. Less commonly presented than the pure equity method of accounting are the expanded equity method and the proportionate consolidation method. These alternative approaches effectively are successive points along a continuum ranging from a pure historical cost basis to full consolidation. In contrast to the one-line consolidation approach of the simple equity method, the expanded equity method is an attempt to provide more meaningful detail about the various assets and liabilities, and revenues and expenses, in which the investor has an economic interest. Thus, if using the expanded equity method, the investor's interest in the investee's aggregate current assets would be presented, as a single number, in the current asset section of the investor's statement of financial position. Similarly, the investor's share of the investee's noncurrent assets, current liabilities, and noncurrent liabilities would be captioned separately in the corresponding section of the investor's statement of financial position.

In the statement of comprehensive income, using this expanded equity method, the investor's share of significant items of revenue, expense, gains, and losses would be set forth separately. This would not extend to every item of the statement of comprehensive income, but would highlight the major ones. Greater or lesser degrees of detail would be possible, depending on the investor's preferences, since there are no definitive standards governing this method.

A major advantage of this method of reporting an investor's interest in the investee is that the investor's financial statements will provide a more meaningful insight into the true economic scope of its operations, including indications of the gross volume of business being transacted. Furthermore, financial position will not be distorted by, for example, effectively merging the investee's current assets with the investor's noncurrent assets, which would be the result of placing equity in investee in the noncurrent asset section, as is required under common practice. As the amount of detail expands, the expanded equity method edges into proportionate consolidation, however.

The expanded equity method has not been endorsed, as such, although the equity method as defined by US GAAP (in APB Opinion 18) does incorporate elements of this approach. Specifically, APB 18 mandates one-line consolidation for the statement of financial position, but requires that certain components of the investee's statement of comprehensive income (such as items related to discontinued operations) retain their character when incorporated into the investor's statement of comprehensive income. Thus APB 18's requirements do go beyond a strict application of the equity method.

Proportionate consolidation. This is a more fully developed variant of the expanded equity method, whereby the investor's share of each element of the investee's statement of financial position and statement of comprehensive income is reported in the investor's statements. Although there is nonauthoritative GAAP in the United States supporting this method of accounting for investments in joint ventures, and under IFRS (as discussed later in the chapter) this method is prescribed optionally for joint ventures, it has not been widely advocated for investments in which the investor does not exercise, at a minimum, joint control. Nonetheless, from a conceptual perspective, it does have appeal since it would convey the full scope of economic activities over which the reporting entity could be said to have either direct control or indirect yet significant impact.

Equity method as prescribed by IAS 28. The equity method is generally not available to be used as a substitute for consolidation. Consolidation is required when a majority voting interest is held by the reporting entity (the parent) in another entity (the subsidiary). The equity method is intended for use where the reporting entity (the investor) has significant influence over the operations of the other entity (the investee), but lacks control.

In general, significant influence is inferred when the investor owns between 20% and 50% of the investee's voting common stock. However, the 20% threshold stipulated in IAS 28 is not an absolute one. Specific circumstances may suggest that significant influence exists even though the investor's level of ownership is under 20%, in which case the equity method should be applied. In other instances, significant influence may be absent despite a level of ownership above 20%. Therefore, the existence of significant influence in the 20% to 50% ownership range should be treated as a refutable presumption. This 20% lower threshold is identical to that prescribed under US GAAP.

In considering whether significant influence exists, IAS 28 identifies the following factors as evidence that such influence is present: (1) investor representation on the board of directors or its equivalent, (2) participation in policy-making processes, (3) material transactions between the investor and investee, (4) interchange of managerial personnel, and (5) provision of essential technical information. There may be other factors present that suggest a lack of significant influence, such as organized opposition by the other shareholders, majority ownership by a small group of shareholders not inclusive of the investor, and inability to achieve representation on the board or to obtain information on the operations of the investee. Whether sufficient contrary evidence exists to negate the presumption of significant influence is a matter of judgment and requires a careful evaluation of all pertinent facts and circumstances, over an extended period of time in some cases.

When equity method is required. IAS 28 stipulates that the equity method should be employed by the investor for all investments in associates, unless the investment is acquired and held exclusively with a view to its disposal within twelve months from acquisition, or if it is in reorganization or in bankruptcy, or operates under severe long-term restrictions that would preclude making distributions to investors. In the latter cases, the use of the equity method of accounting would not be deemed appropriate; rather, the investment would be carried at its historical cost.

The IASB's Improvements Project made a number of changes to IAS 28 (effective 2005), among which is an exclusion from IAS 28's requirements for investments in associates held by venture capital organizations, mutual funds, unit trusts, and similar entities that are measured at fair value in accordance with IAS 39, when such measurement is well-established practice in those industries. When those investments are measured at fair value, changes in fair value are included in profit or loss in the period of the change.

When considering whether the investor has significant influence—and thus must apply the equity method of accounting—a number of factors must be taken into consideration. For example, beyond the mere 20% threshold of ownership, relevant indicia of significant influence would often include these factors.

1. Representation on the board of directors or equivalent governing body of the investee;
2. Participation in policy-making processes;
3. Material transactions between the investor and the investee;
4. Interchange of managerial personnel; or
5. Provision of essential technical information.

Another complicating factor in ascertaining whether the reporting entity has significant influence over the investee is that the investor may own instruments such as share warrants, share call options, or other debt or equity instruments that are convertible into ordinary shares, or other similar instruments that have the potential, if exercised or converted, to give the entity additional voting power or reduce another party's relative power over the financial and operating policies of another entity (i.e., potential voting rights). The existence and effect of potential voting rights that are currently exercisable or currently convertible, including potential voting rights held by other entities, must be considered when assessing whether an entity has the power to have significant influence in the financial and operating policy decisions of the investee. This issue is discussed in greater detail later in this chapter.

The standard does distinguish between the accounting for investments in associates in consolidated financials and that in separate financials of the investor. As amended by IAS 39, IAS 28 provides that in the separate financials of the investor the investment in the associate may be carried at either cost, by the equity method, or as an available-for-sale financial asset consistent with IAS 39's provisions, if the investor also prepares consolidated financial statements. If the investor does not issue consolidated financial statements, the choices are expanded to include, if warranted by the facts, treating the investment as a trading security as well.

In practice, many parent-only financial statements apply equity method accounting to subsidiaries and significant influence investees alike. This probably does provide the most meaningful reporting, avoiding detailed inclusion of any assets, liabilities, revenues, or expenses other than the parent company's own in its financial statements, while not distorting the bottom line measure of economic performance.

Complications in applying equity method accounting. Complexities in the use of the equity method arise in two areas. First, the cost of the investment to the investor might not be equal to the fair value of the investor's share of investee net assets; this is analogous to the existence of goodwill in a purchase business combination. Or the fair value of the investor's share of the investee's net assets may not be equal to the book value thereof; this situation is analogous to the purchase cost allocation problem in consolidations. Since the ultimate statement of comprehensive income result from the use of equity method accounting must generally be the same as full consolidation, an adjustment must be made for each of these differentials.

The second major complexity relates to interperiod income tax allocation. The equity method causes the investor to reflect current earnings based on the investee's operating results; however, for income tax purposes the investor reports only dividends received and gains or losses on disposal of the investment. Thus, temporary differences result, and IAS 12 provides guidance as to the appropriate method of computing the deferred tax effects of these differences.

In the absence of these complicating factors, use of the equity method by the investor is straightforward: The original cost of the investment is increased by the investor's share of the investee's earnings and is decreased by its share of investee losses and by dividends received. The basic procedure is illustrated below.

Example of a simple case ignoring deferred taxes

Assume the following information:

On January 2, 2008, Regency Corporation (the investor) acquired 40% of Elixir Company's (the investee) voting common stock on the open market for €100,000. Unless demonstrated otherwise, it is assumed that Regency Corporation can exercise significant influence over Elixir Company's operating and financing policies. On January 2, Elixir's shareholders' equity is comprised of the following accounts:

Common stock, par €1, 100,000 shares authorized, 50,000 shares issued and outstanding	€ 50,000
Additional paid-in capital*	150,000
Retained earnings	50,000
Total shareholders' equity	€250,000

> * *Note that IAS 1 (revised 2007) does not require any distinction between share capital and any excess over a stated value, historically called additional paid-in capital. However, some legal jurisdictions may distinguish between these and thus this bifurcation will be maintained in these examples.*

Note that the cost of Elixir Company common stock was equal to 40% of the book value of Elixir's net assets. Assume also that there is no difference between the book value and the fair value of Elixir Company's assets and liabilities. Accordingly, the balance in the investment account in Regency's records represents exactly 40% of Elixir's shareholders' equity (net assets). Assume further that Elixir Company reported a 2008 net profit of €30,000 and paid cash dividends of €10,000. Its shareholders' equity at year-end would be as follows:

Common stock, par €1, 100,000 shares authorized, 50,000 shares issued and outstanding	€ 50,000
Additional paid-in capital	150,000
Retained earnings	70,000
Total shareholders' equity	€270,000

Regency Corporation would record its share of the increase in Elixir Company's net assets during 2008 as follows:

Investment in Elixir Company	12,000	
Equity in Elixir profit or loss (€30,000 × 40%)		12,000
Cash	4,000	
Investment in Elixir Company (€10,000 × 40%)		4,000

When Regency's statement of financial position is prepared at December 31, 2008, the balance reported in the investment account would be €108,000 (= €100,000 + €12,000 − €4,000). This amount represents 40% of the book value of Elixir's net assets at the end of the year (40% ×

€270,000). Note also that the equity in Elixir profit or loss is reported as one amount on Regency's income statement under the caption "Other income and expense."

IAS 12 established the requirement that deferred income taxes be provided for the tax effects of timing differences. Under this standard, discussed in detail in Chapter 15, the liability method must be employed, under which the provision of a net deferred tax asset or liability is adjusted at the end of each reporting period to reflect the current expectations regarding the amount that ultimately is to be received or paid.

In order to compute the deferred tax effects of profit or loss recognized by an investor employing the equity method of accounting for its investment, it must make an assumption regarding the means by which undistributed earnings of its investee will be realized. Earnings can generally be realized either through subsequent receipt of dividends, or by disposition of the investment at a gain, which presumably would reflect the investee's undistributed earnings as of that date. In many jurisdictions, these alternative modes of income realization will have differing tax implications. For example, in many jurisdictions the assumption of future dividends would result in taxes at the investor's marginal income tax rate (net of any dividends received deduction or exclusion permitted by the local taxing authorities). If the sale of the investment is expected to be the route by which earnings are realized, this would commonly result in a capital gain, which in some jurisdictions is taxed at a different rate, or not taxed at all.

Example of a simple case including deferred taxes

Assume the same information as in the example above. In addition, assume that Regency Corporation has a combined (federal, state, and local) marginal income tax rate of 34% and that it anticipates realization of Elixir Company earnings through future dividend receipts. In Regency's tax jurisdiction, there is an 80% deduction for dividends received from nonsubsidiary investees, meaning that only 20% of profits is subject to tax. Regency Corporation's entries at year-end 2008 will be as follows:

1.	Investment in Elixir Company	12,000	
	Equity in Elixir profit or loss		12,000
2.	Income tax expense	816	
	Deferred taxes		816

(Taxable portion of investee earnings to be received in the future as dividends times marginal tax rate: €12,000 × 20% × 34% = €816)

3.	Cash	4,000	
	Investment in Elixir Company		4,000
4.	Deferred taxes	272	
	Taxes payable—current		272

[Fraction of investee earnings currently taxed (€4,000/12,000) × 816 = €272]

Under the liability method of interperiod income tax allocation, as required by IAS 12, the tax provision should be based on the projected tax effect of the temporary difference reversal, and this may be subsequently adjusted for a variety of reasons, including alterations in tax rates and revision to management expectations (see Chapter 15 for a complete discussion).

Furthermore, when the taxable income (from dividends or the sale of the investment) is ultimately realized, the actual incidence of tax may still differ from the amount of deferred tax provided, as adjusted. This may occur because, assuming graduated rates and other complexities apply, the actual tax effect is a function of the entity's other income and expense items in the year of realization. Also, notwithstanding good-faith expectations, the realization of the investee's profits may come in a manner other than anticipated (e.g., a sudden decision to sell rather than hold the investment could precipitate capital gains when future dividend income was planned for).

To illustrate this last point, assume that in 2009, before any further profits or dividends are reported by the investee, the investor sells the entire investment for €115,000. The tax impact is

Selling price	€115,000
Less cost	100,000
Gain	€ 15,000
Capital gain rate (marginal corporate rate)	× 34%
Tax liability	€ 5,100

The entries to record the sale, the tax thereon, and the amortization of deferred taxes provided previously on the undistributed 2008 earnings are as follows:

1.	Cash	115,000	
	Investment in Elixir Company		108,000
	Gain on sale of investment		7,000
2.	Income tax expense	4,556	
	Deferred tax liability	544	
	Taxes payable—current		5,100

In the above, income tax expense of €4,556 is the sum of two factors: (1) the capital gains rate of 34% applied to the actual book gain realized (€115,000 selling price less €108,000 carrying value), for a tax of €2,380, and (2) the difference between the capital gains tax rate (34%) and the effective rate on dividend income (20% × 34% = 6.8%) on the undistributed 2007 earnings of Elixir Company previously recognized as other income by Regency Corporation [€8,000 × (34% − 6.8%) = €2,176].

Note that if the realization through a sale of the investment had been anticipated at the time the 2008 statement of financial position was being prepared, the deferred tax liability account would have been adjusted (possibly to the entire €5,100 amount of the ultimate obligation), with the offsetting entry applied to 2008 ordinary tax expense. The example above explicitly assumes that sale of the investment was not anticipated prior to 2009.

Accounting for a differential between cost and book value. The simple examples presented thus far avoided the major complexity of equity method accounting, the allocation of the differential between the cost to the investor and the investor's share in the net equity (net assets at book value) of the investee. Since the net impact of equity method accounting must equal that of full consolidation accounting, this differential must be analyzed into the following components and accounted for accordingly:

1. The difference between the book and fair values of the investee's net assets at the date the investment is made.
2. The remaining difference between the fair value of the net assets and the cost of the investment, that is generally attributable to goodwill.

According to IAS 28, any difference between the cost of the investment and the investor's share of the fair values of the net identifiable assets of the associate should be identified and accounted for in accordance with IFRS 3 (as detailed in Chapter 11). Thus, the differential should be allocated to specific asset categories, and these differences will then be amortized to the income from investee account as appropriate, for example, over the economic lives of fixed assets whose fair values exceeded book values. The difference between fair value and cost will be treated like goodwill and, in accordance with the provisions of IFRS 3 not subject to amortization, but rather will be reviewed for impairment on a regular basis, with write-downs taken for any impairment identified, to be included in earnings of the investor in the period of impairment.

Example of a complex case ignoring deferred taxes

Assume again that Regency Corporation acquired 40% of Elixir Company's shares on January 2, 2008, but that the price paid was €140,000. Elixir Company's assets and liabilities at that date had the following book and fair values:

	Book value	*Fair value*
Cash	€ 10,000	10,000
Accounts receivable (net)	40,000	40,000
Inventories (FIFO cost)	80,000	90,000
Land	50,000	40,000
Plant and equipment (net of accumulated depreciation)	140,000	220,000
Total assets	€320,000	400,000
Liabilities	(70,000)	(70,000)
Net assets (shareholders' equity)	€250,000	€330,000

The first order of business is the calculation of the differential, as follows:

Regency's cost for 40% of Elixir's ordinary share	€140,000
Book value of 40% of Elixir's net assets (€250,000 × 40%)	(100,000)
Total differential	€ 40,000

Next, the €40,000 is allocated to those individual assets and liabilities for which fair value differs from book value. In the example, the differential is allocated to inventories, land, and plant and equipment, as follows:

Item	*Book value*	*Fair value*	*Difference debit (credit)*	*40% of difference debit (credit)*
Inventories	€ 80,000	€ 90,000	€ 10,000	€ 4,000
Land	50,000	40,000	(10,000)	(4,000)
Plant and equipment	140,000	220,000	80,000	32,000
Differential allocated				€32,000

The difference between the allocated differential of €32,000 and the total differential of €40,000 is essentially identical to goodwill of €8,000. As shown by the following computation, goodwill represents the excess of the cost of the investment over the fair value of the net assets acquired.

Regency's cost for 40% of Elixir's ordinary share	€140,000
40% of Elixir's net assets (€330,000 × 40%)	(132,000)
Excess of cost over fair value (goodwill)	€ 8,000

At this point it is important to note that the allocation of the differential is not recorded formally by either Regency Corporation or Elixir Company. Furthermore, Regency does not remove the differential from the investment account and allocate it to the respective assets, since the use of the equity method (one-line consolidation) does not involve the recording of individual assets and liabilities. Regency leaves the differential of €40,000 in the investment account, as part of the balance of €140,000 at January 2, 2008. Accordingly, information pertaining to the allocation of the differential is maintained by the investor, but this information is outside the formal accounting system, which is comprised of journal entries and account balances.

After the differential has been allocated, the amortization pattern is developed. To develop the pattern in this example, assume that Elixir's plant and equipment have 10 years of useful life remaining and that Elixir depreciates its fixed assets on a straight-line basis. Under the provisions of IFRS 3, Regency may not amortize the unallocated differential, which is akin to goodwill, but must consider its possible impairment whenever preparing financial statements to conform with IFRS. Regency would prepare the following amortization schedule:

Item	*Differential debit (credit)*	*Useful life*	*2008*	*Amortization 2009*	*2010*
Inventories (FIFO)	€ 4,000	Sold in 2008	€4,000	€ --	€ --
Land	(4,000)	Indefinite	--	--	--
Plant and equipment (net)	32,000	10 years	3,200	3,200	3,200
Goodwill	8,000	N/A	--	--	--
Totals	€40,000		€7,200	€3,200	€3,200

Note that the entire differential allocated to inventories is amortized in 2008 because the cost flow assumption used by Elixir is FIFO. If Elixir had been using weighted-average costing instead of FIFO, amortization might have been computed on a different basis. Prior to the 2003 revision to IAS 2, LIFO costing was also permitted and this would have had an even more dramatically different impact on the pattern of eliminating the differential. However, now LIFO has been banned and this will simplify addressing the differential between cost of the investment and fair value of the underlying net identifiable assets. Note also that the differential allocated to Elixir's land is not amortized, because land is not a depreciable asset. Goodwill likewise is no longer subject to amortization.

The amortization of the differential, to the extent required under IFRS, is recorded formally in the accounting system of Regency Corporation. Recording the amortization adjusts the equity in Elixir's income that Regency recorded based on Elixir's statement of comprehensive income. Elixir's income must be adjusted because it is based on Elixir's book values, not on the cost that Regency incurred to acquire Elixir. Regency would make the following entries in 2008, assuming that Elixir reported profit of €30,000 and paid cash dividends of €10,000:

1.	Investment in Elixir	12,000	
	Equity in Elixir income (€30,000 × 40%)		12,000
2.	Equity in Elixir income (amortization of differential)	7,200	
	Investment in Elixir		7,200
3.	Cash	4,000	
	Investment in Elixir (€10,000 × 40%)		4,000

The balance in the investment account on Regency's records at the end of 2008 is €140,800 [= €140,000 + €12,000 – (€7,200 + €4,000)], and Elixir's shareholders' equity, as shown previously, is €270,000. The investment account balance of €140,000 is not equal to 40% of €270,000. However, this difference can easily be explained, as follows:

Balance in investment account at December 31, 2008		€140,800
40% of Elixir's net assets at December 31, 2008		108,000
Difference at December 31, 2008		€ 32,800
Differential at January 2, 2008	€40,000	
Differential amortized during 2008	(7,200)	
Unamortized differential at December 31, 2008		€ 32,800

As the years go by, the balance in the investment account will come closer and closer to representing 40% of the book value of Elixir's net assets. After twenty years, the remaining difference between these two amounts would be attributed to the original differential allocated to land (a €4,000 credit) and the amount analogous to goodwill (€8,000), unless written off due to impairment. This €4,000 difference would remain until Elixir sold the property.

To illustrate how the sale of land would affect equity method procedures, assume that Elixir sold the land in the year 2028 for €80,000. Since Elixir's cost for the land was €50,000, it would report a gain of €30,000, of which €12,000 (= €30,000 × 40%) would be recorded by Regency, when it records its 40% share of Elixir's reported profit, ignoring income taxes. However, from Regency's viewpoint, the gain on sale of land should have been €40,000 (€80,000 – €40,000) because the cost of the land from Regency's perspective was €40,000 at January 2, 2008. Therefore, besides the €12,000 share of the gain recorded above, Regency should record an additional €4,000 gain [(= €40,000 – €30,000) × 40%] by debiting the investment account and crediting the equity in Elixir income account. This €4,000 debit to the investment account will negate the €4,000 differential allocated to land on January 2, 2008, since the original differential was a credit (the fair value of the land was €10,000 less than its book value).

Example of a complex case including deferred taxes

The impact of interperiod income tax allocation in the foregoing example is similar to that demonstrated earlier in the simplified example. However, a complication arises with regard to the portion of the differential allocated to goodwill, since in some jurisdictions amounts representing goodwill are not amortizable for tax purposes and, therefore, will be a permanent (not a timing) difference that does not give rise to deferred taxes. The other components of the differential in this example are all generally defined as being timing differences.

The entries recorded by Regency Corporation in 2008 would be

1.	Investment in Elixir	12,000	
	Equity in Elixir income		12,000

2.	Income tax expense	816	
	Deferred tax liability (€12,000 × 20% × 34%)		816
3.	Cash	4,000	
	Investment in Elixir		4,000
4.	Deferred tax liability	272	
	Taxes payable—current (€4,000/€12,000 × €816)		272
5.	Equity in Elixir income	7,200	
	Investment in Elixir		7,200
6.	Deferred tax liability	490	
	Income tax expense (€7,200 × 20% × 34%)		490

Reporting disparate elements of the investee's statement of comprehensive income. As suggested earlier in this section, the expanded equity method would require that the major captions in the investee's statement of comprehensive income maintain their character when reported, pro rata, by the investor. In addition, adjustments to the investment carrying value may also be necessary for changes in the investor's proportionate interest in the investee arising from changes in the investee's equity that have not been recognized in the investee's profit or loss. Such changes include those arising from the revaluation of property, plant, and equipment and from foreign exchange translation differences (other comprehensive income items). Although the standard is silent on separate reporting in financial statements, the authors are of the opinion that, to the extent that certain items would be a material part of the investor's statement of comprehensive income and thus have the potential to mislead users of those financial statements, it would be prudent and fully consistent with the spirit of IAS 28 to report these separately. For example, if corrected prior period financial statements are reported by the investee to address accounting errors made in the originally released financial statements, the investor's share of those corrections, if material, might be identified separately (or via footnote explanation) rather than simply be included in the equity in the investee company profit or loss.

One solution, of course, is to include the investor's share of these items with similar items in the investor's financial statements. That is, the expanded equity method concept should be applied, judiciously, to the investor's statement of comprehensive income. This would not extend, however, to separate reporting of any items of operating income or expense (gross sales, salaries, depreciation, etc.).

Example of accounting for separately reportable items

Assume that a correction of an accounting error is reported in an investee's statement of comprehensive income as reissued in the current period (e.g., as a comparative financial statement), and this item is considered material from the investor's viewpoint.

Investee's statement of comprehensive income:

Net profit as originally reported	€ 80,000
Correction of accounting error —failure to record depreciation	(18,000)
Net profit as corrected	€ 62,000

If an investor owned 30% of the voting common stock of this investee, the investor would make the following journal entries:

1.	Investment in investee company	24,000	
	Equity in investee income before correction of accounting error		24,000
	(€80,000 × 30%)		
2.	Equity in investee correction of accounting error	5,400	
	Investment in investee company		5,400
	(€18,000 × 30%)		

The equity in the investee's correction of an accounting error should be reported separately in the appropriate section on the investor's statement of comprehensive income.

Intercompany transactions between investor and investee. Transactions between the investor and the investee may require that the investor make certain adjustments when it records its share of the investee earnings. According to the realization concept, profits can be recognized by an entity only when realized through a sale to outside (unrelated) parties in arm's-length transactions (sales and purchases) between the investor and investee. Similar problems can arise when sales of fixed assets between the parties occur. In all cases, there is no need for any adjustment when the transfers are made at book value (i.e., without either party recognizing a profit or loss in its separate accounting records).

In preparing consolidated financial statements, all intercompany (parent-subsidiary) transactions are eliminated. However, when the equity method is used to account for investments, only the *profit component* of intercompany (investor-investee) transactions is eliminated. This is because the equity method does not result in the combining of all statement of comprehensive income accounts (such as sales and cost of sales) and therefore will not cause the financial statements to contain redundancies. In contrast, consolidated statements would include redundancies if the gross amounts of all intercompany transactions were not eliminated.

IAS 28 as originally issued was not explicit regarding the percentage of unrealized profits on investor-investee transactions to be eliminated. Logical arguments can be made to eliminate 100% of intercompany profits not realized through a subsequent transaction with unrelated third parties, that would replicate the approach used when preparing consolidated financial statements. However, good arguments can also be presented for the elimination of only the percentage held by the investor. Now-superseded interpretation SIC 3 held that when applying the equity method, unrealized profits should be eliminated for both "upstream" and "downstream" transactions (i.e., sales from investee to investor, and from investor to investee) to the extent of the investor's interest in the investee. Revised IAS 28 has incorporated the guidance formerly found in SIC 3 into the text of the revised standard itself.

Elimination of the investor's interest in the investee, rather than the entire unrealized profit on the transaction, is based on the logic that in an investor-investee situation, the investor does not have control (as would be the case with a subsidiary), and thus the nonowned percentage of profit is effectively realized through an arm's-length transaction. This is essentially the same logic as is set forth in IAS 31, dealing with joint venture accounting. For joint ventures, IAS 31 prescribes proportionate consolidation, which implies likewise that profits on intercompany transactions be eliminated only to the extent of the investor's interest in the venture. However, notwithstanding the use of proportionate elimination of intercompany profits, to the extent that losses are indicative of impairment in the value of the investment, this rule would not apply.

For purposes of determining the percentage interest in unrealized profit or loss to be eliminated, a group's interest in an associate is the aggregate of the holdings in that associate by the parent and its subsidiaries (excluding any interests held by minority interests of subsidiaries). Any holdings of the group's other associates (i.e., equity method investees) or joint ventures are ignored for the purpose of applying the equity method. When an associate has subsidiaries, associates, or joint ventures, the profits or losses and net assets taken into account in applying the equity method are those recognized in the associate's consolidated financial statements (including the associate's share of the profits or losses and net assets of its associates and joint ventures), after any adjustments necessary to give effect to the investor's accounting policies.

Example of accounting for intercompany transactions

Continue with the same information from the previous example and also assume that Elixir Company sold inventory to Regency Corporation in 2009 for €2,000 above Elixir's cost. Thirty percent of this inventory remains unsold by Regency at the end of 2009. Elixir's net profit for 2009, including the gross profit on the inventory sold to Regency, is €20,000; Elixir's income tax rate is 34%. Regency should make the following journal entries for 2009 (ignoring deferred taxes):

1.	Investment in Elixir	8,000	
	Equity in Elixir income (€20,000 × 40%)		8,000
2.	Equity in Elixir income (amortization of differential)	3,600	
	Investment in Elixir		3,600
3.	Equity in Elixir income	158	
	Investment in Elixir (€2,000 × 30% × 66% × 40%)		158

The amount in the last entry needs further elaboration. Since 30% of the inventory remains unsold, only €600 of the intercompany profit is unrealized at year-end. This profit, net of income taxes, is €396. Regency's share of this profit (€158) is included in the first (€8,000) entry recorded. Accordingly, the third entry is needed to adjust or correct the equity in the reported net income of the investee.

Eliminating entries for intercompany profits in fixed assets are similar to those in the examples above. However, intercompany profit is realized only as the assets are depreciated by the purchasing entity. In other words, if an investor buys or sells fixed assets from or to an investee at a price above book value, the gain would only be realized piecemeal over the asset's remaining depreciable life. Accordingly, in the year of sale the pro rata share (based on the investor's percentage ownership interest in the investee, regardless of whether the sale is upstream or downstream) of the unrealized portion of the intercompany profit would have to be eliminated. In each subsequent year during the asset's life, the pro rata share of the gain realized in the period would be added to income from the investee.

Example of eliminating intercompany profit on fixed assets

Assume that Radnor Co., that owns 25% of Empanada Co., sold to Empanada a fixed asset having a five-year remaining life, at a gain of €100,000. Radnor Co. expects to remain in the 34% marginal tax bracket. The sale occurred at the end of 2008; Empanada Co. will use straight-line depreciation to amortize the asset over the years 2009 through 2013.

The entries related to the foregoing are

2008

1.	Gain on sale of fixed asset	25,000	
	Deferred gain		25,000
	To defer the unrealized portion of the gain		
2.	Deferred tax benefit	8,500	
	Income tax expense		8,500
	Tax effect of gain deferral		

Alternatively, the 2008 events could have been reported by this single entry.

Equity in Empanada income	16,500	
Investment in Empanada Co.		16,500

2009 through 2013 (each year):

1.	Deferred gain	5,000	
	Gain on sale of fixed assets		5,000
	To amortize deferred gain		
2.	Income tax expense	1,700	
	Deferred tax benefit		1,700
	Tax effect of gain realization		

The alternative treatment would be

Investment in Empanada Co.	3,300	
Equity in Empanada income		3,300

In the example above, the tax currently paid by Radnor Co. (34% × €25,000 taxable gain on the transaction) is recorded as a deferred tax benefit in 2008 since taxes will not be due on the book gain recognized in the years 2009 through 2013. Under provisions of IAS 12, deferred tax benefits should be recorded to reflect the tax effects of all deductible timing differences. Unless Radnor Co. could demonstrate that future taxable amounts arising from existing temporary differences exist, this deferred tax benefit might be offset by an equivalent valuation allowance in Radnor Co.'s statement of financial position at year-end 2008, because of the doubt that it will ever be realized. Thus, the deferred tax benefit might not be recognizable, net of the valuation allowance, for financial reporting purposes unless other temporary differences not specified in the example provided future taxable amounts to offset the net deductible effect of the deferred gain.

NOTE: *The deferred tax impact of an item of income for book purposes in excess of tax is the same as a deduction for tax purposes in excess of book.*

This is discussed more fully in Chapter 15.

Accounting for a partial sale or additional purchase of the equity investment. This section covers the accounting issues that arise when the investor either sells some or all of its equity or acquires additional equity in the investee. The consequence of these actions could involve discontinuation of the equity method of accounting, or resumption of the use of that method.

Example of accounting for a discontinuance of the equity method

Assume that Plato Corp. owns 10,000 ordinary shares (30%) of Xenia Co. for which it paid €250,000 ten years ago. On July 1, 2008, Plato sells 5,000 Xenia shares for €375,000. The balance in the Investment in Xenia Co. account at January 1, 2008, was €600,000. Assume that all the original differential between cost and book value has been amortized. To calculate the gain (loss) on the sale of 5,000 shares, it is necessary first to adjust the investment account so that it is current as of the date of sale. Assuming that the investee reported net profit of €100,000 for the six months ended June 30, 2008, the investor should record the following entries:

1.	Investment in Xenia Co.	30,000	
	Equity in Xenia income (€100,000 × 30%)		30,000
2.	Income tax expense	2,040	
	Deferred tax liability (€30,000 × 20% × 34%)		2,040

The gain on sale can now be computed, as follows:

Proceeds on sale of 5,000 shares	€375,000
Book value of the 5,000 shares (€630,000 × 50%)	315,000
Gain from sale of investment in Xenia Co	€ 60,000

Two entries will be needed to reflect the sale: one to record the proceeds, the reduction in the investment account, and the gain (or loss); the other to record the tax effects thereof. Recall that the investor must have computed the deferred tax effect of the undistributed earnings of the investee that it had recorded each year, on the basis that those earnings either would eventually be paid as dividends or would be realized as capital gains. When those dividends are ultimately received or when the investment is disposed of, the deferred tax liability recorded previously must be amortized.

To illustrate, assume that the investor in this example, Plato Corp., provided deferred taxes at an effective rate for dividends (considering the assumed 80% exclusion of intercorporate dividends) of 6.8%. The realized capital gain will be taxed at an assumed 34%. For tax purposes, this gain is computed as (€375,000 – €125,000 =) €250,000, giving a tax effect of €85,000. For accounting purposes, the deferred taxes already provided are 6.8% × (€315,000 – €125,000), or €12,920. Accordingly, an additional tax expense of €72,080 is incurred on the sale, due to the fact that an additional gain was realized for book purposes (€375,000 – €315,000 = €60,000; tax at 34% = €20,400) *and* that the tax previously provided for at dividend income rates was lower than the real capital gains rate [€190,000 × (34% – 6.8%) = €51,680 extra tax due]. The entries are as follows:

1.	Cash	375,000	
	Investment in Xenia Co.		315,000
	Gain on sale of investment in Xenia Co.		60,000

2. Deferred tax liability	12,920	
Income tax expense	72,080	
Taxes payable—current		85,000

The gains (losses) from sales of investee equity instruments are reported on the investor's income statement in the other income and expense section, assuming that an entity presents the components of profit or loss in a separate income statement.

According to IAS 28, an investor should discontinue use of the equity method when (1) it ceases to have significant influence in an associate while retaining some or all of its investment, or (2) the use of the equity method is no longer deemed to be appropriate because the associate is operating under severe and long-lasting restrictions that will limit its ability to transfer funds to the investor entity. When the equity method of accounting is discontinued due to a loss of significant influence, the carrying amount of the investment at the date that it ceases to be an associate shall be regarded as its cost on initial measurement as a financial asset under IAS 39.

In the foregoing example, the sale of shares reduced the percentage of the investee owned by the investor to 15%. In a situation such as this, discontinuation of the equity method is generally prescribed, although it is not inconceivable that significant influence can still be demonstrated at that ownership level, which would require continued application of equity method accounting.

The balance in the investment account on the date the equity method is suspended (€315,000 in the example) continues as an asset, but it then becomes subject to the IAS 39 requirement that it be accounted for at fair value. Passive equity investments are classified as either held-for-trading or available-for-sale; in this fact situation, categorization as available-for-sale is most likely. Under IAS 39, changes in fair value of available-for-sale investments are reported either in profit or loss or in other comprehensive income, depending on the election made by the reporting entity upon first adoption. For purposes of this example, assume election of reporting changes in the fair value of available-for-sale investments will be shown in equity.

The change in ownership precipitates a change in accounting principle from equity method to fair value. This change does not require computation of a cumulative effect or any retroactive disclosures in the investor's financial statements. In periods subsequent to this change, the investor records cash dividends received from the investment as dividend revenue. Any dividends received in excess of the investor's share of post–disposal date earnings of the investee (which are unlikely) should be credited to the investment account rather than to income, as they would represent a return of capital, rather than income.

An entity may hold an investment in another entity's ordinary share that is below the level that would create a presumption of significant influence, which it later increases so that the threshold for application of the equity method is exceeded. The guidance of IAS 28 would suggest that when the equity method is first applied, the difference between the carrying value of the investment and the fair value of the underlying net identifiable assets must be computed (as described earlier in the chapter). Even though IAS 39's fair value provisions were being applied, there will likely be a difference between the fair value of the passive investment (gauged by market prices for publicly-traded instruments) and the fair value of the investee's underlying net assets (which are driven by the ability to generate cash flows, etc.). Thus, when the equity method accounting threshold is first exceeded for a formerly passively held investment, determination of the "goodwill-like" component of the investment will typically be necessary.

Example of accounting for a return to the equity method of accounting

Continuing the same example, Xenia Co. reported profit for the second half of 2008 and all of 2009, respectively, of €150,000 and €350,000; Xenia paid dividends of €100,000 and €150,000 in December of those years. During the period from July 2008 through December 2009, Plato Corp. accounted for its investment in Xenia Co. as an investment in marketable instruments, at fair value, with changes in carrying value being reflected directly in equity. At December 31, 2008, the fair value of Plato's holding of Xenia's share is assessed at €335,000; at December 31, 2009, the fair value is €365,000.

In January 2010, the Plato Corp. purchased 10,000 Xenia shares in the open market for €700,000, thereby increasing its ownership share to 45% and necessitating a return to equity method accounting. The fair value of Plato's interest in the underlying identifiable net assets of Xenia at this date is €1,000,000. The relevant entries are as follows:

1. Cash   15,000
        Income from Xenia dividends   15,000
    To report dividends paid in 2008

2. Investment in Xenia Corp.   20,000
        Unrealized gain on available-for-sale investment   20,000
    To reflect increased value of investment

3. Income tax expense   1,020
    Unrealized gain on available-for-sale investment   6,800
        Taxes payable—current   1,020
        Taxes payable—deferred   6,800
    To record taxes on dividends at current effective tax rate [€15,000 × .068] and deferred taxes on value increase [€20,000 × .34] in 2008

4. Cash   22,500
        Income from Xenia dividends   22,500
    To report dividends paid in 2009

5. Investment in Xenia Corp.   30,000
        Unrealized gain on available-for-sale investment   30,000
    To reflect increased value of investment

6. Income tax expense   1,530
    Unrealized gain on available-for-sale investment   10,200
        Taxes payable—current   1,530
        Taxes payable—deferred   10,200
    To record taxes on dividends at current effective tax rate [€22,500 × .068] and deferred taxes on value increase [€30,000 × .34] in 2009

7. Investment in Xenia Co.   700,000
        Cash   700,000
    To record additional investment in Xenia

8. Unrealized gain on available-for-sale investment   33,000
        Income from investment   33,000
    See explanation for this entry below

The explanation for the last entry above is as follows. IAS 28 does not suggest that a return to the previously discontinued equity method would result in a restatement of the investment account and the additional equity and retained earnings accounts to "catch up" to what the balances would have been had that not taken place. Accordingly, the authors believe that the new cost basis of the investment at the time the equity method is reestablished should be the adjusted carrying amount immediately prior thereto. In the present example, the carrying amount was as follows:

Balance 6/30/08	€	315,000
Adjust to fair value 12/08		20,000
Adjust to fair value 12/09		30,000
Balance, 12/09	€	365,000
Additional investment, 1/10		700,000
Carrying value, 1/10		€1,065,000

The difference between the new cost basis, €1,065,000, and Plato's equity in Xenia's net identifiable assets, (€1,065,000 – €1,000,000 =) €65,000, would be treated similar to goodwill. Since goodwill is no longer subject to amortization, this must be assessed for impairment each year, as described in IFRS 3.

It would not be appropriate to carry forward the amount reflected in the additional equity account, €33,000, since the investment is no longer to be accounted for under IAS 39. Accordingly, in the authors' opinion, this should be reported as current period profit or loss, analogous to how the disposition of any other available-for-sale investment would be accounted for (where the unrealized gain or loss had been reported in other comprehensive income, not in profit or loss during the holding period). The income will have been realized by adoption or readoption of the equity method. Note that the €33,000 balance is the net of the cumulative €50,000 upward revaluation recognized in 2008 and 2009 and the €17,000 tax provision, at capital gain rates (assumed in this example to be 34%), which was expected to pertain to the ultimate realization of this value increase. If, at the time the equity method is resumed, the effective tax rate is expected to differ from that used to compute deferred taxes earlier (e.g., due to the effect of the significant influence over the investee's dividend decisions), then there would be a need for an adjustment to the deferred tax provision.

To illustrate the latter point, assume that Plato now expects to realize all its income from Xenia in the form of dividends, to be taxed at an effective rate of 6.8%. The entry to adjust the deferred tax liability would be

Taxes payable—deferred	13,600	
Tax expense		13,600
To record adjustment to deferred taxes		

Note that the offset to the deferred tax adjustment is to current period (i.e., 2010) tax expense, under the rules of IAS 12, as described more fully in Chapter 15.

The foregoing illustration adjusts the additional equity account to profit or loss, since the resumption of equity method accounting is seen as an economic event of that period, similar to an outright sale of the investment. However, IAS 28 is silent on this matter and an argument could perhaps be made that this adjustment should be made to retained earnings directly, in effect as an adjustment to prior periods' profit or loss. This is the accounting prescribed under US GAAP.

Investor accounting for investee capital transactions. Investor accounting for investee capital transactions that affect the worth of the investor's investment is not addressed by IAS 28. However, given that ultimately the effect of using equity method accounting is intended to mirror full consolidation, it is logical that investee transactions of a capital nature, which affect the investor's share of the investee's shareholders' equity, should be accounted for as if the investee were a consolidated subsidiary. These transactions principally include situations where the investee purchases treasury shares from, or sells unissued shares or shares held in the treasury to, outside shareholders (i.e., owners other than the reporting entity). (Note that, if the investor participates in these transactions on a pro rata basis, its percentage ownership will not change and no special accounting would be necessary.) Similar results will be obtained when holders of outstanding options or convertible instruments acquire additional investee ordinary shares via exercise or conversion.

When the investee engages in one of the foregoing capital transactions, the investor's ownership percentage will be altered. This gives rise to a gain or loss, depending on whether the price paid (for treasury shares acquired) or received (for shares issued) is greater or lesser than the per share carrying value of the investor's interest in the investee. However, since no gain or loss can be recognized on capital transactions, these purchases or sales will be reflected in paid-in capital and/or retained earnings directly, without being reported in the investor's profit or loss. This method is consistent with the treatment that would be accorded to a consolidated subsidiary's capital transactions.

Example of accounting for an investee capital transaction

Assume that Roger Corp. purchases, on 1/2/08, 25% (2,000 shares) of Energetic Corp.'s outstanding shares for €80,000. The cost is equal to both the book and fair values of Roger's interest in Energetic's underlying net assets (i.e., there is no differential to be accounted for as goodwill). One week later, Energetic Corp. acquires 1,000 own shares from other shareholders, in a treasury share transaction, for €50,000. Since the price paid (€50/share) exceeded Roger Corp.'s per share carrying value of its interest, (€80,000 ÷ 2,000 shares =) €40, Roger Corp. has in fact suffered economic harm by virtue of this transaction. Also, Roger's percentage ownership of Energetic Corp. has increased, because the number of shares held by third parties, and total shares outstanding, have been reduced.

Roger Corp.'s new interest in Energetic's net assets is

$$\frac{2{,}000 \text{ shares held by Roger Corp}}{7{,}000 \text{ shares outstanding in total}} \times \text{Energetic Corp net assets}$$

$$= .2857 \times (€320{,}000 - €50{,}000) = €77{,}143$$

The interest held by Roger Corp. has thus been diminished by €80,000 − €77,143 = €2,857. Therefore, Roger Corp. should make the following entry:

Paid-in capital (or retained earnings)	2,857	
Investment in Energetic Corp.		2,857

Roger Corp. should charge the loss against paid-in capital only if paid-in capital from past transactions of a similar nature exists; otherwise, the debit must be made to retained earnings. Had the transaction given rise to a gain, it would have been credited to paid-in capital only (never to retained earnings) following the accounting principle that transactions in one's own shares cannot produce reportable earnings.

Note that the amount of the charge to paid-in capital (or retained earnings) in the entry above can be verified as follows: Roger Corp.'s share of the posttransaction net equity (2/7) times the excess price paid to outside interests (€50 − €40 = €10) times the number of shares purchased = 2/7 × €10 × 1,000 = €2,857.

Other-than-temporary impairment in value of equity method investments. IAS 28 provides that if there is a decline in value of an investment accounted for by the equity method which is determined to be "other-than-temporary" in nature, the carrying value of the investment should be adjusted downward. This criterion must be applied on an individual investment basis.

Other requirements of IAS 28. The standard requires that there be disclosure of the percentage of ownership that is held by the investor in each investment and, if it differs, the percentage of voting rights that are controlled. The method of accounting that is being applied to each significant investment should also be identified.

In addition, there may have been certain assumptions or adjustments made in developing information so that the equity method was applied. For example, the investee may have used different accounting principles than the investor, for which the investor made allowances in determining its share of the investee's operating results. The reported results of an investee that formerly used LIFO inventory accounting, for instance, may have been adjusted by the investor to conform to its FIFO costing method. Also, the investee's fiscal year may have differed from the investor's, and the investor may have converted this to its fiscal year by adding and subtracting stub period data. Revised IAS 28, effective 2005, states that a fiscal year-end difference of no more than three months will be permissible if unadjusted investee financial statements are to be employed. In any such case, if the impact is material, the fact of having made these adjustments should be disclosed, although it would be unusual to report the actual amount of such adjustments to users of the investor's financial statements.

If an associate has outstanding cumulative preferred share, held by interests other than the investor, the investor should compute its equity interest in the investee's earnings after deducting dividends due to the preferred shareholders, whether or not declared. If material, this should be explained in the investor's financial statements.

When, due to the investor's recognition of recurring investee losses, the carrying value of the equity method investment has been reduced to zero, normally the investor will not recognize any share of further investee losses. If an investor ceases recognition of its share of losses of an investee, disclosure must be made in the notes to the financial statements of the unrecognized share of losses, both incurred during the current reporting period and cumulatively to date. The reason for the disclosure of cumulative unrecognized losses is that this is a measure of the amount of future investee earnings that will have to be realized before any further income will be reported in earnings by the investor.

There are certain exceptions to this rule. If the investor has incurred obligations or made payments on behalf of the associate to satisfy obligations of the associate that the investor has guaranteed or to which it is otherwise committed, whether funded or not, it should record further losses up to the amount of the guarantee or other commitment.

There are many common situations in which this occurs. For example, in the case of some closely held companies the investor negotiates banking facilities (both funded and unfunded) on the basis of the financial strength of the entire controlled group, not solely on the basis of the financial condition of the investee utilizing the borrowed funds. Where the investor has participated in the lending arrangements, even if its commitment is only moral, rather than contractual, it should be assumed that it will suffer losses beyond the nominal limit of its actual investment in the investee's shares, should that be necessary. For purposes of determining the total amount of losses which can be reflected in the investor's earnings, the interest in an associate is the carrying amount of the investment under the equity method plus items that, in substance, form part of the investor's investment in equity of the associate. Thus, for example, an item for which settlement is neither planned nor likely to occur in the foreseeable future is, in substance, an extension to or deduction from the entity's investment in equity. These additional investment items may include preferred shares and long-term receivables or loans; they would not include trade receivables or trade payables.

Impact of Potential Voting Interests on Application of Equity Method Accounting for Investments in Associates

Historically, actual voting interests in equity method investees has been the criterion used to determine (1) if equity method accounting for investees is to be employed; and (2) what percentage to apply in determining the allocation of the equity method investee's earnings to be included in the earnings of the equity method investor. However, the SIC has now addressed the situation in which the equity method investor has, in addition to its actual voting shareholder interest, a further potential voting interest in the investee.

The potential interest may exist in the form of options, warrants, convertible shares, or a contractual arrangement to acquire additional shares, including shares that it may have sold to another shareholder in the investee or to another party, with a right or contractual arrangement to reacquire the shares transferred.

As to whether the potential shares should be considered in reaching a decision as to whether significant influence is present, and thus whether reporting entity is to be regarded as the equity method investor and should therefore apply equity method accounting. Revised

IAS 28 holds that this is indeed a factor to weigh (a position first taken by the now-withdrawn SIC 33). It has concluded that the existence and effect of potential voting rights that are presently exercisable or presently convertible should be considered, in addition to the other factors set forth in IAS 28, when assessing whether an entity significantly influences another entity. All potential voting rights should be considered, including potential voting rights held by other entities (which would counter the impact of the reporting entity's potential voting interest).

For example, an entity holding a 15% voting interest in another entity, but having options, not counterbalanced by options held by another party, to acquire another 15% voting interest, would thus effectively have a 30% current and potential voting interest, making use of the equity method of accounting for the investment required, under the provisions of revised IAS 28.

Regarding whether the potential share interest should be considered when determining what fraction of the investee's income should be allocated to the investor, the general answer is no. The proportion allocated to an investor that accounts for its investment using the equity method under IAS 28 should be determined based solely on present ownership interests.

However, the entity may, in substance, have a present ownership interest when it sells and simultaneously agrees to repurchase some of the voting shares it had held in the investee, but does not lose control of access to economic benefits associated with an ownership interest. In this circumstance, the proportion allocated should be determined taking into account the eventual exercise of potential voting rights and other derivatives that, in substance, presently give access to the economic benefits associated with an ownership interest. Note that the right to reacquire shares alone is not enough to have those shares included for purposes of determining the percentage of the investee's income to be reported by the investor. Rather, the investor must have ongoing access to the economic benefits of ownership of those shares.

Revised IAS 28 provides that losses recognized under the equity method in excess of the investor's equity interest will be applied to the other components of the investor's interest in an associate in the order of their seniority (i.e., in order of priority in liquidation). The investor will apply the requirements of IAS 39 to determine whether any additional impairment loss is recognized with respect to the other component of the investor's interest.

Once the investor's interest has been reduced to zero by its absorption of investee losses, any additional losses are provided for, and a liability is recognized, only to the extent that the investor has incurred obligations or made payments on behalf of the associate. If the associate subsequently reports profits, the investor would resume recognizing its share of those profits only after its share of the profits equals the share of net losses not recognized.

Apart from the foregoing considerations of investee loss recognition, the investor must assess possible impairment of value of the investment as required under IAS 36. This requires that the "value in use" of the investment be ascertained. In making such a determination, the investor must estimate

1. Its share of the present value of the estimated future cash flows expected to be generated by the investee as a whole, including the cash flows from the operations of the investee and the proceeds on the ultimate disposal of the investment; or
2. The present value of the estimated future cash flows expected to arise from dividends to be received from the investment and from its ultimate disposal.

Under appropriate assumptions (given a perfectly functioning capital market), both methods give the same result. Any resulting impairment loss for the investment is allocated in accordance with IAS 36. Accordingly, it would first be allocated to that component of the investment carrying value that reflects any underlying, remaining goodwill, as described earlier in this chapter.

Disclosure Requirements

IAS 28, as most recently revised (effective 2005), provides for extensive disclosures. These include

1. The fair value of investments in associates for which there are published price quotations;
2. Summarized financial information of associates, including the aggregated amounts of assets, liabilities, revenues, and profit or loss;
3. The reasons why the presumption that an investor does not have significant influence is overcome if the investor holds, directly or indirectly through subsidiaries, less than 20% of the voting or potential voting power of the investee but concludes that it has significant influence;
4. The reasons why the presumption that an investor has significant influence is overcome if the investor holds, directly or indirectly through subsidiaries, 20% or more of the voting or potential voting power of the investee but concludes that is does not have significant influence;
5. The reporting date of the financial statements of an associate when such financial statements are used in applying the equity method and are as of a reporting date or for a period that is different from that of the investor, and the reasons for using a different reporting date or different period;
6. The nature and extent of any restrictions on the ability of associates to transfer funds to the investor in the form of cash dividends, repayment of loans or advances (i.e., borrowing arrangements, regulatory restraint, etc.);
7. The unrecognized share of net losses of an associate, both for the period and cumulatively, if an investor has discontinued recognition of its share of losses of an associate.

Investments in associates accounted for using the equity method must be classified as long-term assets and disclosed as a separate item in the statement of financial position. The investor's share of the after-tax profit or loss of such associates investments should be disclosed as a separate item in the statement of comprehensive income. The investor's share of any discontinuing operations of such associates also should be separately disclosed. Furthermore, the investor's share of changes in the associate's equity recognized directly in equity by the investor is to be disclosed in the statement of changes in equity required by IAS 1.

To comply with the requirements of IAS 37, the investor must disclose

1. Its share of the contingent liabilities of an associate for which it is also contingently liable; and
2. Those contingent liabilities that arise because the investor is severally liable for all liabilities of the associate.

Accounting for Investments in Joint Ventures

IFRS address accounting for interests in joint ventures as a topic separate from accounting for other investments. Joint ventures share many characteristics with investments that are accounted for by the equity method: The investor clearly has significant influence over the investee but does not have absolute control, and hence full consolidation is typically unwarranted. According to the provisions of IAS 31, two different methods of accounting are possible, although not as true alternatives for the same fact situations: the proportional consolidation method and the equity method.

Joint ventures can take many forms and structures. Joint ventures may be created as partnerships, as corporations, or as unincorporated associations. The standard identifies three distinct types, referred to as jointly controlled operations, jointly controlled assets, and jointly controlled entities. Notwithstanding the formal structure, all joint ventures are characterized by certain features: having two or more venturers that are bound by a contractual arrangement, and by the fact that the contractual agreement establishes joint control of the entity.

The contractual provision(s) establishing joint control most clearly differentiates joint ventures from other investment scenarios in which the investor has significant influence over the investee. In fact, in the absence of such a contractual provision, joint venture accounting would not be appropriate, even in a situation in which two parties each have 50% ownership interests in an investee. The actual existence of such a contractual provision can be evidenced in a number of ways, although most typically it is in writing and often addresses such matters as the nature, term of existence, and reporting obligations of the joint venture; the governing mechanisms for the venture; the capital contributions by the respective venturers; and the intended division of output, income, expenses, or net results of the venture.

The contractual arrangement also establishes joint control over the venture. The thrust of such a provision is to ensure that no venturer can control the venture unilaterally. Certain decision areas will be stipulated as requiring consent by all the venturers, while other decision areas may be defined as needing the consent of only a majority of the venturers. There is no specific set of decisions that must fall into either grouping, however.

Typically, one venturer will be designated as the manager or operator of the venture. This does not imply the absolute power to govern; however, if such power exists, the venture would be a subsidiary, subject to the requirements of IAS 27 and not accounted for properly under IAS 31. IAS 31 (as amended by the IASB's Improvements Project in late 2003) does not apply to interests in jointly controlled entities held by venture capital organizations, mutual funds, unit trusts, and similar entities that are measured at fair value in accordance with IAS 39, when such measurement is well established practice in those industries. When such investments are measured at fair value, changes in fair value are included in profit or loss in the period of the change.

Specific accounting guidance is dependent on whether the entity represents jointly controlled operations, jointly controlled assets, or a jointly controlled entity.

Jointly controlled operations. The first of three types of joint ventures, this is characterized by the assigned use of certain assets or other resources, in contrast to an establishment of a new entity, be it a corporation or partnership. Thus, from a formal or legal perspective, this variety of joint venture may not have an existence separate from its sponsors; from an economic point of view, however, the joint venture can still be said to exist, which means that it may exist as an accounting entity. Typically, this form of operation will utilize assets owned by the venture partners, often including plant and equipment as well as inventories, and the partners will sometimes incur debt on behalf of the operation. Actual operations may be conducted on an integrated basis with the partners' own, separate operations, with certain employees, for example, devoting a part of their efforts to the jointly controlled operation. The European consortium Airbus may be a prototype of this type of entity.

IAS 31 is concerned not with the accounting by the entity conducting the jointly controlled operations, but by the venturers having an interest in the entity. Each venturer should recognize in its separate financial statements all assets of the venture that it controls, all liabilities that it incurs, all expenses that it incurs, and its share of any revenues produced by the venture. Often, since the assets are already owned by the venturers, they would be included in their respective financial statements in any event; similarly, any debt incurred will be reported by the partner even absent this special rule. Perhaps the only real challenge, from a measurement and disclosure perspective, would be the revenues attributable to each venture's efforts, which will be determined by reference to the joint venture agreement and other documents.

Note that joint control may be precluded when an investee is in legal reorganization or in bankruptcy, or operates under severe long-term restrictions on its ability to transfer funds to the venturer; in such cases, application of IAS 31 would not be appropriate.

Jointly controlled assets. In certain industries, such as oil and gas exploration and transmission and mineral extraction, jointly controlled assets are frequently employed. For example, oil pipelines may be controlled jointly by a number of oil producers, each of which uses the facilities and shares in its costs of operation. Certain informal real estate partnerships may also function in this fashion.

IAS 31 stipulates that in the case of jointly controlled assets, each venturer must report in its own financial statements its share of all jointly controlled assets, appropriately classified according to their natures. It must also report any liabilities that it has incurred on behalf of these jointly controlled assets, as well as its share of any jointly incurred liabilities. Each venturer will report any profit earned from the use its share of the jointly controlled assets, along with the pro rata expenses and any other expenses it has incurred directly.

Jointly controlled entities. The major type of joint venture is the jointly controlled entity, which is really a form of partnership (although it may well be structured legally as a corporation) in which each partner has a form of control, rather than only significant influence. The classic example is an equal partnership of two partners; obviously, neither has a majority and either can block any important action, so the two partners must effectively agree on each key decision. Although this may be the model for a jointly controlled entity, it may in practice have more than two venturers and, depending on the partnership or shareholders' agreement, even minority owners may have joint control. For example, a partnership whose partners have 30%, 30%, 30%, and 10% interests, respectively, may have entered into a contractual agreement that stipulates that investment or financing actions may be taken only if there is unanimity among the partners.

Jointly controlled entities control the assets of the joint venture and may incur liabilities and expenses on its behalf. As a legal entity, it may enter into contracts and borrow funds, among other activities. In general, each venturer will share the net results in proportion to its ownership interest. As an entity with a distinct and separate legal and economic identity, the jointly controlled entity will normally produce its own financial statements and other tax and legal reports.

IAS 31 provides alternative accounting treatments that may be applied by the venture partners to reflect the operations and financial position of the venture. The objective is to report economic substance, rather than mere form, but there is not universal agreement on how this may best be achieved.

The benchmark treatment under the standard is the use of proportionate consolidation, which requires that the venture partner reflect its share of all assets, liabilities, revenues, and expenses on its financial statements as if these were incurred or held directly. In fact, this technique is very effective at conveying the true scope of an entity's operations, when those operations include interests in one or more jointly controlled entities. In this regard, IFRS are more advanced than US, UK, or other national standards, which at best permit proportionate consolidation but do not mandate this accounting treatment.

If the venturer employs the proportionate consolidation method, it will have a choice between two presentation formats that are equally acceptable. First, the venture partner may include its share of the assets, liabilities, revenues, and expenses of the jointly controlled entity with similar items under its sole control. Thus, under this method, its share of the venture's receivables would be added to its own accounts receivable and presented as a single total in its statement of financial position. Alternatively, the items that are undivided interests in the venture's assets, and so on, may be shown on separate lines of the venture's financial statements, although still placed within the correct grouping. For example, the venture's receivables might be shown immediately below the partner's individually owned accounts receivable. In either case, the same category totals (aggregate current assets, etc.) will be presented; the only distinction is whether the venture-owned items are given separate recognition. Even if presented on a combined basis, however, the appropriate detail can still be shown in the financial statement footnotes, and indeed to achieve a fair presentation, this might be needed.

The proportionate consolidation method should be discontinued when the partner no longer has the ability to control the entity jointly. This may occur when the interest is held for disposal within twelve months from acquisition date, or when external restrictions are placed on the ability to exercise control. In some cases a partner will waive its right to control the entity, possibly in exchange for other economic advantages, such as a larger interest in the operating results. In such instances, IAS 39 should be used to guide the accounting for the investment.

Under the provisions of IAS 31, a second accounting method, the equity method, is also considered to be acceptable. The equity method in this context is as described in IAS 28 and as explained in the preceding section. As with the proportionate consolidation method, use of the equity method must be discontinued when the venturer no longer has joint control or significant influence over the jointly controlled entity. In such a case, IAS 39 would be the relevant accounting requirement.

Accounting for jointly controlled entities as passive investments. Although the expectation is that investments in jointly controlled entities will be accounted for by the proportionate consolidation or equity method (the benchmark and allowed alternative treatments, respectively), in certain circumstances the venturer should account for its interest following the guidelines of IAS 39, that is, as a passive investment. This would be the prescription when the investment has been acquired and is being held with a view toward disposition within twelve months of the acquisition, or when the investee is operating under severe long-term restrictions that severely impair its ability to transfer funds to its venturer owners.

If the investment is seen as being strictly temporary, effectively it is being held for trading purposes in the same manner as a temporary investment in marketable instruments would be. In such a situation it would not be logical to apply either the proportionate consolidation or equity method, since it would not be the venture's share of the operating results of the venture that provided value to the venturer, but rather, the change in fair value.

Similarly, if the venture were operating under such severe restrictions, expected to persist beyond a short time horizon, that transfers of funds from the jointly controlled entity to its venture parents were precluded, it would be misleading and conceptually invalid to treat the venture's operating results as bearing directly on the venture parents' earnings results. In such a case, an inability to transfer funds would mean that the venture partners would be unable to obtain any benefit, in the short run at least, from their investment in the jointly controlled entity.

As amended by IAS 39, IAS 31 provides that in the separate financial statements of an investor that issues consolidated financial statements as well, the cost method may alternatively be employed to present the investment in the joint venture.

Change from joint control to full control status. If one of the venturers' interest in the jointly controlled entity is increased, whether by an acquisition of some or all of another of the venturers' interest, or by action of a contractual provision of the venture agreement (resulting from a failure to perform by another venturer, etc.), the proportionate consolidation method of accounting ceases to be appropriate and full consolidation will become necessary. Guidance on preparation of consolidated financial statements is provided by IAS 27 and is discussed fully in Chapter 11.

Accounting for Transactions between Venture Partner and Jointly Controlled Entity

Transfers at a gain to the transferor. A general, underlying principle of financial reporting is that earnings are to be realized only by engaging in transactions with outside parties. Thus, gains cannot be recognized by transferring assets (be they productive assets or goods held for sale in the normal course of the business) to a subsidiary, affiliate, or joint venture, to the extent this really would represent a transaction by an entity with itself. Were this not the rule, entities would establish a range of related entities to sell goods to, thereby permitting the reporting of profits well before any sale to real, unrelated customers ever took place. The potential for abuse of the financial reporting process in such a scenario is too obvious to need elaboration.

IAS 31 stipulates that when a venturer sells or transfers assets to a jointly controlled entity, it may recognize profit only to the extent that the venture is owned by the other venture partners, and then only to the extent that the risks and rewards of ownership have indeed been transferred to the jointly controlled entity. The logic is that a portion of the profit has in fact been realized, to the extent that the purchase was agreed on by unrelated parties that jointly control the entity making the acquisition. For example, if venturers A, B, and C jointly control venture D (each having a 1/3 interest), and A sells equipment having a book value of €40,000 to the venture for €100,000, only 2/3 of the apparent gain of €60,000, or €40,000, may be realized. In its statement of financial position immediately after this transaction, A would report its share of the asset reflected in the statement of financial position of D, $1/3 \times €100,000 = €33,333$, minus the unrealized gain of €20,000, for a net of €13,333. This is identical to A's remaining 1/3 interest in the pretransaction basis of the asset ($1/3 \times €40,000 = €13,333$). Thus, there is no step-up in the carrying value of the proportionate share of the asset reflected in the transferor's statement of financial position.

If the asset is subject to depreciation, the deferred gain on the transfer ($1/3 \times €60,000 = €20,000$) would be amortized in proportion to the depreciation reflected by the venture, such that the depreciated balance of the asset reported by A is the same as would have been reported had the transfer not taken place. For example, assume that the asset has a useful economic life of five years after the date of transfer to D. The deferred gain (€20,000) would be amortized to profit or loss at a rate of €4,000 per year. At the end of the first posttransfer year, D would report a net carrying value of $€100,000 – €20,000 = €80,000$; A's proportionate interest is $1/3 \times €80,000 = €26,667$. The unamortized balance of the deferred gain is $€20,000 – €4,000 = €16,000$. Thus the net reported amount of A's share of the jointly controlled entity's asset is $€26,667 – €16,000 = €10,667$. This amount is precisely what A would have reported the remaining share of its asset at on this date: $1/3 \times (€40,000 – €8,000) = €10,667$.

Of course, A has also reported a gain of €40,000 as of the date of the transfer of its asset to joint venture D, but this represents the gain that has been realized by the sale of 2/3 of the asset to unrelated parties B and C, the coventures in D. In short, two-thirds of the asset has been sold at a gain, while one-third has been retained and is continuing to be used and depreciated over its remaining economic life and is reported on the cost basis in A's financial statements.

The matters described above have been further emphasized by the Standing Interpretation Committee's interpretation, SIC 13, which holds that gains or losses will result from contributions of nonmonetary assets to a jointly controlled entity *only* when significant risks and rewards of ownership have been transferred, and the gain or loss can be reliably measured. However, no gain or loss would be recognized when the asset is contributed in exchange for an equity interest in the jointly controlled entity when the asset is similar to assets contributed by the other venturers. Any unrealized gain or loss should be netted against the related assets, and not presented as deferred gain or loss in the venture's consolidated financial statements.

Transfers of assets at a loss. The foregoing illustration was predicated on a transfer to the jointly controlled entity at a nominal gain to the transferor, of which a portion was realized for financial reporting purposes. The situation when a transfer is at an amount below the transferor's carrying value is not analogous; rather, such a transfer is deemed to be confirmation of a permanent decline in value, which must be recognized by the transferor immediately rather than being deferred. This reflects the conservative bias in accounting: Unrealized losses are often recognized, while unrealized gains are deferred.

Assume that venturer C (a 1/3 owner of D, as described above) transfers an asset it had been carrying at €150,000 to jointly controlled entity D at a price of €120,000. If the decline is deemed to be other than temporary in nature (that presumptively it is, since C would not normally have been willing to engage in this transaction if the decline were expected to be reversed in the near term), C must recognize the full €30,000 at the time of the transfer. Subsequently, C will pick up its 1/3 interest in the asset held by D (1/3 × €120,000 = €40,000) as its own asset in its statement of financial position, before considering any depreciation, and so on.

Accounting for Assets Purchased from a Jointly Controlled Entity

Transfers at a gain to the transferor. A similar situation arises when a venture partner acquires an asset from a jointly controlled entity: The venturer cannot reflect the gain recognized by the joint venture, to the extent that this represents its share in the results of the venture's operations. For example, again assuming that A, B, and C jointly own D, an asset having a book value of €200,000 is transferred by D to B for a price of €275,000. Since B has a 1/3 interest in D, it would (unless an adjustment were made to its accounting) report €25,000 of D's gain as its own, which would violate the realization concept under GAAP.

To avoid this result, B will record the asset at its cost, €275,000, less the deferred gain, €25,000, for a net carrying value of €250,000, which represents the transferor's basis, €200,000, plus the increase in value realized by unrelated parties (A and C) in the amount of €50,000.

As the asset is depreciated, the deferred gain will be amortized apace. For example, assume that the useful life of the asset in B's hands is ten years. At the end of the first year, the carrying value of the asset is €275,000 – €27,500 = €247,500; the unamortized balance of the deferred gain is €25,000 – €2,500 = €22,500. Thus the net carrying value, after offsetting the remaining deferred gain, will be €247,500 – €22,500 = €225,000. This corresponds to the remaining life of the asset (9/10 of its estimated life) times its original net carrying amount, €250,000. The amortization of the deferred gain should be credited to depreciation expense to offset the depreciation charged on the nominal acquisition price and thereby to reduce it to a cost basis as required by GAAP.

Transfers at a loss to the transferor. If the asset was acquired by B at a loss to D, on the other hand, and the decline was deemed to be indicative of an other-than-temporary diminution in value, B should recognize its share of this decline. This contrasts with the gain scenario discussed immediately above, and as such is entirely consistent with the accounting treatment for transfers from the venture partner to the jointly controlled venture.

For example, if D sells an asset carried at €50,000 to B for €44,000, and the reason for this discount is an other than temporary decline in the value of said asset, the venture, D, records a loss of €6,000 and each venture partner will in turn recognize a €2,000 loss. B would report the asset at its acquisition cost of €44,000 and will also report its share of the loss, €2,000. This loss will not be deferred and will not be added to the carrying value of the asset in B's hands (as would have been the case if B treated only the €4,000 loss realized by unrelated parties A and C as being recognizable).

Disclosure Requirements

A venture partner is required to disclose in the notes to the financial statements its ownership interests in all significant joint ventures, including its ownership percentage and other relevant data. If the venturer uses proportionate consolidation and merges its share of the assets, liabilities, revenues, and expenses of the jointly controlled entity with its own assets, liabilities, revenues, and expenses, or if the venturer uses the equity method, the notes should disclose the amounts of the current and long-term assets, current and long-term liabilities, revenues, and expenses related to its interests in jointly controlled ventures.

Furthermore, the joint venture partner should disclose any contingencies that the venturer has incurred in relation to its interests in any joint ventures, noting any share of contingencies jointly incurred with other joint venturers. In addition, the venturer's share of any contingencies of the joint venture (as distinct from contingencies incurred in connection with its investment in the venture) for which it may be contingently liable must be reported. Finally, those contingencies that arise because the venturer is contingently liable for the liabilities of the other partners in the jointly controlled entity must be set forth. These disclosures are a logical application of the rules set forth in IAS 37, which is discussed in Chapter 12 of this publication.

A venture partner should also disclose in the notes to her/his financial statements information about any commitments s/he has outstanding in respect to interests s/he has in joint ventures. These include any capital commitments s/he has and her/his share of any joint commitments s/he may have incurred with other venture partners, as well as her/his share of the capital commitments of the joint ventures themselves, if any.

Exposure Draft 9—Joint Arrangements

On September 13, 2007, IASB issued Exposure Draft (ED) 9, *Joint Arrangements,* which should supersede both IAS 31, *Interests in Joint Ventures,* and SIC 13, *Jointly Controlled Entities: Nonmonetary Contributions by Ventures.* This ED is a result of the Board's Short-Term Convergence project with the FASB and should bring convergence in principle with requirements set forth by US GAAP.

The main changes in proposed IFRS include

- An entity would be required to recognize only those assets that it controls and only those liabilities that are present obligations. Currently, the accounting approach under IAS 31 can lead to the recognition of assets that are not controlled and liabilities that are not obligations.
- A choice in accounting for interests in jointly controlled entities would be removed, improving comparability of financial reports. IASB proposes to eliminate proportionate consolidation, a method not officially endorsed under US GAAP (although used by certain construction contractors and others). If the parties only have a right to

share in the outcome of the activities (e.g., profit or loss), their net interest will be recognized using the equity method.

This proposed IFRS establishes a core principle that parties in a joint arrangement should recognize their contractual rights and obligations arising from the arrangement. It applies to joint arrangements, except interests in joint ventures held by venture capital organizations, mutual funds, unit trusts and similar entities, including investment-linked insurance funds, when those interest are measured at fair value through profit or loss or are classified as held for trading and accounted for in accordance with IAS 39.

ED 9 defines a "joint arrangement," subject to the requirements of proposed IFRS, as a contractual arrangement whereby two or more parties undertake an economic activity together and share *decision-making* relating to that activity, as distinct from having actual *control.* Joint arrangements are classified into three types: joint operations, joint assets and joint ventures, based on the rights and obligations that arise from the contractual arrangement. The draft also proposes that "joint operations" and "joint assets" will replace the terms "jointly controlled operations" and "jointly controlled assets," which are used in IAS 31.

A *joint operation* is a joint arrangement, or part of joint arrangement, that involves using the assets and other resources of the parties, incurring liabilities and raising its own finance, sharing revenues and expenses incurred in common while undertaking an economic activity, often manufacturing or selling joint products. A *joint asset* is an asset to which each party has rights, often with joint ownership, and each party shares the output from the asset as well as the costs to operate the asset. ED 9 retains the term "joint venture," which will replace the term "jointly controlled entity," used in IAS 31, to describe a joint arrangement, or part of joint arrangement, which is jointly controlled by the venturers. The venturers have an interest only in a share of the outcome (e.g., profit or loss) and do not have rights to individual assets or obligations for expenses of the venture.

The type of joint arrangement an entity is a party to depends on the rights and obligations that arise from the contractual arrangement. IASB has proposed that a party to a joint arrangement should recognize its contractual rights and obligations arising from the arrangement. The legal form of the arrangement, which IAS 31 follows, is only one of the factors in assessing the rights and obligations. An entity can recognize only assets that it controls and obligations that it currently has.

Under the provisions of ED 9, each party should recognize each asset and liability (and related income and expenses) in accordance with applicable IFRS—for example, IAS 16, IAS 18, IAS 37, IAS 38 and IAS 39. Any remaining assets and liabilities should be recognized using the equity method. These remaining assets and liabilities of the joint arrangement are those for which the parties have an interest only in a share of the outcome of the activities carried on by those assets and liabilities, and the parties jointly control the activities.

A venturer, having no rights to individual assets or obligations, should recognize its interest in a joint venture using the equity method. ED 9 also has proposed to eliminate the use of the proportionate consolidation method of accounting. According to IASB, although some argue that proportionate consolidation is a practical way to present a venturer's interest in a joint venture, the Board believes that it is misleading for users of financial statements if an entity recognizes as assets items that are not actually controlled, and as liabilities items that are not present obligations, and present these together with items it controls or items that are present obligations.

ED 9 also provides proposed accounting for the loss of control of an interest in a joint venture. The accounting approach is based on the upcoming revisions to IAS 27, *Consolidated and Separate Financial Statements.* An entity should discontinue the use of the equity method from the date on which it ceases to have joint control over a joint venture, except when it retains significant influence. If an investor loses joint control but retains significant influence, the investor should account for its investment using the equity method both before and after the loss of joint control.

In situations where joint control is lost and the investment does not become a subsidiary or associate, any retained investment is measured at fair value. The gain or loss (recognized in profit or loss) on the loss of control is calculated as the difference between

1. The sum of the fair value of the retained interest and any proceeds from the interest disposed of; and
2. The carrying amount of the interest at the date joint control is lost.

When joint control is lost and any remaining interest is accounted for under IAS 39, the fair value of the interest when it ceases to be a joint venture should be measured at its fair value on initial recognition as a financial asset in accordance with IAS 39. Any amounts related included in "other comprehensive income" or another component of equity should be recognized as if the joint venture disposed of the related assets and liabilities directly. Reclassification adjustments in accordance with IAS 1, as revised in 2007, should be taken to profit or loss.

ED 9 provides examples illustrating the application of the requirements of the proposed IFRS to arrangements in which parties have interests in joint operations, joint assets and joint ventures.

The proposed IFRS may affect significantly the accounting for the jointly controlled entities using the proportionate consolidation in accordance with IAS 31. Venturers will need to examine the contractual arrangements to determine whether the parties have contractual rights and obligations to individual assets and liabilities, which should be recognized separately in the financial statements, before converting to the equity method of accounting.

The following decision tree, adapted from the IASB Exposure Draft, shows how financial reporting entities will decide how to apply this standard, if and when it is finalized. As of late 2008, IASB is indicating that this will be finalized before mid-2009.

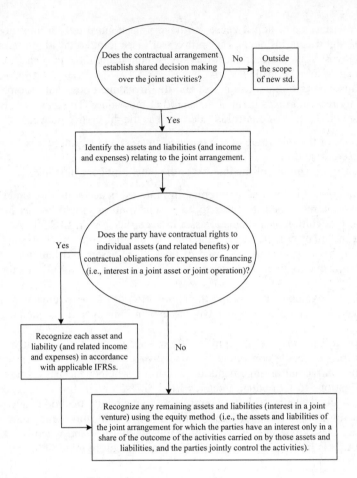

Accounting for Investment Property

Investment property. An investment in land or a building, part of a building, or both, if held by the owner (or a lessee under a finance lease) with the intention of earning rentals or for capital appreciation or both, is defined by IAS 40 as an investment property. An investment property is capable of generating cash flows independently of other assets held by the entity. Investment property is sometimes referred to as being "passive" investments, to distinguish it from actively managed property such as plant assets, the use of which is integrated with the rest of the entity's operations. This characteristic is what distinguishes investment property from owner-occupied property, which is property held by the entity or a lessee under a finance lease, for use in its business (i.e., for use in production or supply of goods or services or for administrative purposes).

Revised IAS 40, effective in 2005, for the first time permits property interests held in the form of operating leases to be classified and accounted for as investment property. This may be done if

1. The other elements of the definition of investment property (see below) are met;
2. The operating lease is accounted for as if it were a finance lease in accordance with IAS 17 (that is, it is capitalized); and
3. The lessee uses the fair value model set out in IAS 40 for the asset recognized.

This classification option—to report the lessee's property interest as investment property—is available on a property-by-property basis. On the other hand, IAS 40 requires that all investment property should be consistently accounted for, employing either the fair value or cost model. Given these requirements, it is held that once the investment alternative is selected for one leased property, all property classified as investment property must be accounted for consistently, on the fair value basis.

The best way to understand what investment property constitutes is to look at examples of investments that are considered by the standard as investment properties, and contrast these with those investments that do not qualify for this categorization.

According to the standard, examples of investment property are

- Land held for long-term capital appreciation as opposed to short-term purposes like land held for sale in the ordinary course of business;
- Land held for an undetermined future use;
- Building owned by the reporting entity (or held by the reporting entity under a finance lease) and leased out under one or more operating leases; and
- Vacant building held by an entity to be leased out under one or more operating leases.

According to IAS 40, investment property does *not* include

- Property employed in the business, (i.e., held for use in production or supply of goods or services or for administrative purposes, the accounting for which is governed by IAS 16);
- Property being constructed or developed on behalf of others, the accounting of which is outlined in IAS 11;
- Property held for sale in the ordinary course of the business, the accounting for which is specified by IAS 2; and
- Property under construction or being developed for future use as investment property. IAS 16 is applied to such property until the construction or development is completed, at which time, IAS 40 governs. However, existing investment property that is being redeveloped for continued future use would qualify as investment property.

Apportioning property between investment property and owner-occupied property. In many cases it will be clear what constitutes investment property as opposed to owner-occupied property, but in other instances making this distinction might be less obvious. Certain properties are not held entirely for rental purposes or for capital appreciation purposes. For example, portions of these properties might be used by the entity for manufacturing or for administrative purposes. If these portions, earmarked for different purposes, could be sold separately, then the entity is required to account for them separately. However, if the portions cannot be sold separately, the property would be deemed as investment property if an insignificant portion is held by the entity for business use.

When ancillary services are provided by the entity and these ancillary services are a relatively insignificant component of the arrangement, as when the owner of a residential building provides maintenance and security services to the tenants, the entity treats such an investment as investment property. On the other hand, if the service provided is a comparatively significant component of the arrangement, then the investment would be considered as an owner-occupied property.

For instance, an entity that owns and operates a motel and also provides services to the guests of the motel would be unable to argue that it is an investment property as that term is used by IAS 40. Rather, such an investment would be classified as an owner-occupied property. Judgment is therefore required in determining whether a property qualifies as investment property. It is so important a factor that if an entity develops criteria for determining when to classify a property as an investment property, it is required by this standard to disclose these criteria in the context of difficult or controversial classifications.

Property leased to a subsidiary or a parent company. Property leased to a subsidiary or its parent company is considered an investment property from the perspective of the entity. However, for the purposes of consolidated financial statements, from the perspective of the group as a whole, it will not qualify as an investment property, since it is an owner-occupied property when viewed from the parent company level.

Recognition and measurement. Investment property will be recognized when it becomes probable that the entity will enjoy the future economic benefits which are attributable to it, and when the cost or fair value can be reliably measured. In general, this will occur when the property is first acquired or constructed by the reporting entity. In only unusual circumstances would it be concluded that the owner's likelihood of receipt of the economic benefits would be less than probable, necessitating deferral of initial recognition of the asset.

Initial measurement will be at cost, which is equivalent to fair value, assuming that the acquisition was the result of an arm's-length exchange transaction. Included in the purchase cost will be such directly attributable expenditure as legal fees and property transfer taxes, if incurred in the transaction. If the asset is self-constructed, cost will include not only direct expenditures on product or services consumed, but also overhead charges which can be allocated on a reasonable and consistent basis, in the same manner as these are allocated to inventories under the guidelines of IAS 2. To the extent that the acquisition cost includes an interest charge, if the payment is deferred, the amount to be recognized as an investment asset should not include the interest charges. Furthermore, start-up costs (unless they are essential in bringing the property to its working condition), initial operating losses (incurred prior to the investment property achieving planned level of occupancy) or abnormal waste (in construction or development) do not constitute part of the capitalized cost of an investment property. If an investment property is acquired in exchange for equity instruments of the reporting entity, the cost of the investment property is the fair value of the equity instruments issued, although the fair value of the investment property received is used to measure its cost if it is more clearly evident than the fair value of the equity instruments issued.

Subsequent expenditures. In some instances there may be further expenditure incurred on the investment property after the date of initial recognition. Consistent with similar situations arising in connection with plant, property and equipment (dealt with under IAS 16), if it can be demonstrated that the subsequent expenditure will enhance the generation of future economic benefits to the entity, then those costs may be added to the carrying value of the investment property. That is, the cost can be capitalized only when it is probable that it increases the future economic benefits, in excess of its standard of performance assessed immediately before the expenditure was made. By implication, all other subsequent expenditure should be expensed in the periods they are incurred.

Sometimes, the appropriate accounting treatment for subsequent expenditure would depend upon the circumstances that were considered in the initial measurement and recognition of the investment property. For example, if a property (e.g., an office building) is acquired for investment purposes in a condition that makes it incumbent upon the entity to perform significant renovations thereafter, then such renovation costs (which would constitute subsequent expenditures) will be added to the carrying value of the investment property when incurred later.

Fair value model vs. cost. Analogous to the financial reporting of plant and equipment under IAS 16, IAS 40 provides that investment property may be reported at either fair value or at depreciated cost less accumulated impairment. The cost model is the benchmark treatment prescribed by IAS 16 for plant assets. The fair value approach under IAS 40 more closely resembles that used for financial instruments than it does the allowed alternative (revaluation) method for plant assets, however. Also, under IAS 40 if the cost method is used, fair value information must nonetheless be disclosed.

Fair value. When investment property is carried at fair value, at each subsequent financial reporting date the carrying amount must be adjusted to the then-current fair value, with the adjustment being reported in the profit or loss for the period in which it arises. The inclusion of the value adjustments in earnings—in contrast to the revaluation approach under IAS 16, whereby adjustments are generally reported in other comprehensive income—is a reflection of the different roles played by plant assets and by other investment property. The former are used, or consumed, in the operation of the business, which is often centered upon the production of goods and services for sale to customers. The latter are held for possible appreciation in value, and hence those value changes are highly germane to the assessment of periodic operating performance. With this distinction in mind, the decision was made to not only permit fair value reporting, but to require value changes to be included in profit or loss.

IAS 40 represents the first time that fair value accounting is being embraced as an accounting model for nonfinancial assets. This has been a matter of great controversy, and to address the many concerns voiced during the exposure draft stage, the IASC added more guidance on the subject to the final standard. This standard is quite comprehensive, and it includes some very insightful and practical hints on applying the standard.

Fair value is defined by the standard as the most probable price reasonably obtainable in the marketplace at the end of the reporting period. Fair value would not be appropriately measured with reference to either a past or a future date. Further, the definition envisions "knowledgeable, willing parties" as being the arbiters of fair value. This presupposes that both the buyer and seller are willing to enter into the transaction, and that they each have reasonable knowledge about the nature and characteristics of the investment property, its potential uses, and the state of the market as of the valuation date. Put another way, fair value presumes that neither the buyer nor the seller is acting under coercion; and fair value is not a price that is based on a "distress sale."

The standard goes into great detail to explain the concept of a "willing buyer" (i.e., one who is motivated but not compelled to buy) and a "willing seller" (i.e., one who is neither overeager nor a forced seller). For instance, in explaining the concept of a "willing seller," the standard clarifies that the motivation to sell at market terms for the best price obtainable in the open market is derived "after proper marketing." This expression has been explained very eloquently by the standard to mean that in order to be considered as "after proper marketing," the investment property would need to be "exposed to the market" in the most appropriate manner to effect its disposal at the best price obtainable. The length of exposure time, according to the standard, must be "sufficient" to allow the investment property to be brought to the attention of an "adequate number" of potential purchasers.

As if there were not enough unknowns in the equation, the standard further qualifies this by stating that the "exposure period" is assumed to occur "prior to the end of the reporting period." With respect to the length of the exposure period, the standard opines that "it may vary with market conditions." Some may find this an example of "overkill" which confuses, rather than clarifies the standard and impedes attempts to apply it. However, given that this is the maiden attempt by the IASC to mandate fair value accounting for nonfinancial assets, it may in hindsight be warranted.

The standard *encourages* an entity to determine the fair value based on a valuation by an independent valuer who holds a recognized and relevant professional qualification and who has had recent experience in the location and category of the investment property being valued. While terms such as "relevant" are not defined, IAS 40 does offer a significant amount of practical guidance on issues relating to the determination of fair values. These practical hints will likely greatly facilitate the correct application of the principles enshrined in the standard. They are summarized as follows:

- Factors that could distort the value, such as the incorporation of particularly favorable or unfavorable financing terms, the inclusion of sale and leaseback arrangements, or any other concession by either buyer or seller, are not to be given any consideration in the valuation process;
- On the other hand, the actual conditions in the marketplace at the valuation date, even if these represent somewhat atypical climatic factors, will govern the valuation process. For example, if the economy is in the midst of a recession and rental properties' prices are depressed, no attempt should be made to normalize fair value, since that would add a subjective element and depart from the concept of fair value as of the end of the reporting period;
- Fair values should be determined without any deduction for transaction costs that the entity may incur on the sale or other disposal of the investment property;
- Fair value should reflect the actual state of the market and circumstances as of the end of the reporting period, not as of either a past or a future date;
- In the absence of current prices on an active market, an entity should use information from a variety of sources, including: current prices on an active market of dissimilar properties with suitable adjustments for the differences, recent prices on less active markets, with necessary adjustments, and discounted cash flow projections based on reliable estimates of future cash flows using an appropriate discount rate;
- Fair value differs from "value in use" as defined in IAS 36. Whereas fair value is reflective of market knowledge and estimates of participants in the market in general, value in use reflects the entity's knowledge and estimates that are entity-specific and are thus not applicable to entities in general. In other words, value in use is an estimate at the entity level or at a "microlevel," while fair value is a "macrolevel" concept that is reflective of the perceptions of the market participants in general;
- Entities are alerted to the possibility of double counting in determining the fair value of certain types of investment property. For instance, when an office building is leased on a furnished basis, the fair value of office furniture and fixtures is generally included in the fair value of the investment property (in this case the office building). The IASC's apparent rationale is that the rental income relates to the furnished office building; when fair values of furniture and fixtures are included along with the fair value of the investment property, the entity does not recognize them as separate assets; and
- Lastly, the fair value of investment property should neither reflect the future capital expenditure (that would improve or enhance the property), nor the related future benefits from this future expenditure.

Inability to measure fair value reliably. There is a rebuttable presumption that, if an entity acquires or constructs property that will qualify as investment property under this standard, it will be able to assess fair value reliably on an ongoing basis. In rare circumstances, however, when an entity acquires for the first time an investment property (or when an existing property first qualifies to be classified as investment property following the completion of development or construction, or when there has been change of use), there may be clear evidence that the fair value of the investment property cannot reliably be determined, on a continuous basis.

Under such exceptional circumstances, the standard stipulates that the entity should measure that investment property using the benchmark treatment in IAS 16 until the disposal of the investment property. According to IAS 40, the residual value of such investment property measured under the benchmark treatment in IAS 16 should be presumed to be zero. The standard further states that under the exceptional circumstances explained above, in the case of an entity that uses the fair value model, the entity should measure the other investment properties held by it at fair values. In other words, notwithstanding the fact that one of the investment properties, due to exceptional circumstances, is being carried under the benchmark (cost) treatment in IAS 16, an entity that uses the fair value model should continue carrying the other investment properties at fair values. While this results in a mixed measure of the aggregate investment property, it underlines the perceived importance of the fair value method.

Transfers to or from investment property. Transfers to or from investment property should be made only when there is demonstrated "change in use" as contemplated by the standard. A change in use takes place when there is a transfer

- From investment property to owner-occupied property, when owner-occupation commences;
- From investment property to inventories, on commencement of development with a view to sale;
- From an owner-occupied property to investment property, when owner-occupation ends;
- Of inventories to investment property, when an operating lease to a third party commences; or
- Of property in the course of development or construction to investment property, at end of the construction or development.

In the case of an entity that employs the cost model, transfers between investment property, owner-occupied property and inventories do not change the carrying amount of the property transferred and thus do not change the cost of that property for measurement or disclosure purposes. When the investment property is carried under the fair value model, vastly different results follow as far as recognition and measurement is concerned. These are explained below.

1. **Transfers from (or to) investment property to (or from) plant and equipment (in the case of investment property carried under the fair value model).** In some instances, property that at first is appropriately classified as investment property under IAS 40 may later become plant, property, and equipment as defined under IAS 16. For example, a building is obtained and leased to unrelated parties, but at a later date the entity expands its own operations to the extent that it now chooses to utilize the building formerly held as a passive investment for its own purposes, such as for the corporate executive offices. The amount reflected in the accounting records as the fair value of the property as of the date of change in status would become the cost basis for subsequent accounting purposes. Previously recognized changes in value, if any, would not be reversed.

   Similarly, if property first classified as owner-occupied property and treated as plant and equipment under the benchmark treatment of IAS 16 is later redeployed as investment property, it is to be measured at fair value at the date of the change in its usage. If the value is lower than the carrying amount (i.e., if there is a previously unrecognized decline in its fair value) then this will be reflected in profit or loss in the period of redeployment as an investment property. On the other hand, if there has been an unrecognized increase in value, the accounting will depend on whether this is a reversal of a previously recognized value impairment. If the increase is a reversal of a decline in value, the increase should be recognized currently in profit or loss; the amount so reported, however, should not exceed the amount needed to restore the carrying amount to what it would have been, net of depreciation, had the earlier impairment loss not occurred.

If, on the other hand, there was no previously recognized impairment which the current value increase is effectively reversing (or, to the extent that the current increase exceeds the earlier decline), then the increase should be reported directly in equity, by means of the statement of changes in equity. If the investment property is later disposed of, any resultant gain or loss computation should *not* include the effect of the amount reported directly in equity.

2. **Transfers from inventory to investment property (in the case of investment property carried under the fair value model).** It may also happen that property originally classified as inventory, originally held for sale in the normal course of the business, is later redeployed as investment property. When reclassified, the initial carrying amount should be fair value as of that date. Any gain or loss resulting from this reclassification would be reported in current period's profit or loss. IAS 40 does not contemplate reclassification from investment property to inventory, however. When the entity determines that property held as investment property is to be disposed of, that property should be retained as investment property until actually sold. It should not be derecognized (eliminated from the statement of financial position) or transferred to an inventory classification.

3. **Transfer on completion of construction or development of self-constructed investment property (to be carried at fair value).** On completion of construction or development of self-constructed investment property that will be carried at fair value, any difference between the fair value of the property at that date and its previous carrying amount should be recognized in profit or loss for the period.

Disposal and retirement of investment property. An investment property should be derecognized (i.e., eliminated from the statement of financial position of the entity) on disposal or when it is permanently withdrawn from use and no future economic benefits are expected from its disposal. The word "disposal" has been used in the standard to mean not only a sale but also the entering into of a finance lease by the entity. Any gains or losses on disposal or retirement of an investment property should be determined as the difference between the net disposal proceeds and the carrying amount of the asset and should be recognized in profit or loss for the period.

Disclosure requirements. It is anticipated that in certain cases investment property will be property that is owned by the reporting entity and leased to others under operating-type lease arrangements. The disclosure requirements set forth in IAS 17 (and discussed in Chapter 14) continue unaltered by IAS 40. In addition, IAS 40 stipulates a number of new disclosure requirements set out below.

1. **Disclosures applicable to all investment properties**

    - When classification is difficult, an entity that holds an investment property will need to disclose the criteria used to distinguish investment property from owner-occupied property and from property held for sale in the ordinary course of business.
    - The methods and any significant assumptions that were used in ascertaining the fair values of the investment properties are to be disclosed as well. Such disclosure also includes a statement about whether the determination of fair value was supported by market evidence or relied heavily on other factors (which the entity

needs to disclose as well) due to the nature of the property and the absence of comparable market data.

- If investment property has been revalued by an independent appraiser, having recognized and relevant qualifications, and who has recent experience with properties having similar characteristics of location and type, the extent to which the fair value of investment property (either used in case the fair value model is used or disclosed in case the cost model is used) is based on valuation by such an independent valuer. If there is no such valuation, that fact should be disclosed as well.
- The following should be disclosed in the statement of comprehensive income:

  - The amount of rental income derived from investment property;
  - Direct operating expenses (including repairs and maintenance) arising from investment property that generated rental income;
  - Direct operating expenses (including repairs and maintenance) arising from investment property that did not generate rental income;
  - The existence and the amount of any restrictions which may potentially affect the realizability of investment property or the remittance of income and proceeds from disposal to be received; and
  - Material contractual obligations to purchase or build investment property or for repairs, maintenance or improvements thereto.

2. **Disclosures applicable to investment property measured using the fair value model**

   - In addition to the disclosures outlined above, the standard requires that an entity that uses the fair value model should also present a reconciliation of the carrying amounts of the investment property, from the beginning to the end of the reporting period. The reconciliation will separately identify additions resulting from acquisitions, those resulting from business combinations, and those deriving from capitalized expenditures subsequent to the property's initial recognition. It will also identify disposals, gains or losses from fair value adjustments, the net exchange differences, if any, arising from the translation of the financial statements of a foreign entity, transfers to and from inventories and owner-occupied properties, and any other movements. (Comparative reconciliation data for prior periods need not be presented).
   - Under exceptional circumstances, due to lack of reliable fair value, when an entity measures investment property using the benchmark treatment under IAS 16, the above reconciliation should disclose amounts separately for that investment property from amounts relating to other investment property. In addition, an entity should also disclose

     - A description of such a property,
     - An explanation of why fair value cannot be reliably measured,
     - If possible, the range of estimates within which fair value is highly likely to lie, and
     - On disposal of such an investment property, the fact that the entity has disposed of investment property not carried at fair value along with its carrying amount at the time of disposal and the amount of gain or loss recognized.

3. **Disclosures applicable to investment property measured using the cost model**

   - In addition to the disclosure requirements outlined in 1. above, the standard requires that an entity that applies the cost model should also disclose: the depreciation methods used, the useful lives or the depreciation rates used, and the gross carrying amount and the accumulated depreciation (aggregated with accumulated impairment losses) at the beginning and end of the period. It should also disclose a reconciliation of the carrying amount of investment property at the beginning and the end of the period showing the following details: additions resulting from acquisitions, those resulting from business combinations, and those deriving from capitalized expenditures subsequent to the property's initial recognition. It should also disclose disposals, depreciation, impairment losses recognized and reversed, the net exchange differences, if any, arising from the translation of the financial statements of a foreign entity, transfers to and from inventories and owner-occupied properties, and any other movements. (Comparative reconciliation data for prior periods need not be presented.)

- The fair value of investment property carried under the cost model should also be disclosed. In exceptional cases, when the fair value of the investment property cannot be reliably estimated, the entity should instead disclose

  - A description of such property,
  - An explanation of why fair value cannot be reliably measured, and
  - If possible, the range of estimates within which fair value is highly likely to lie.

Transitional Provisions

Fair value model. Under the fair value model, an entity should report the effect of adopting this standard on its effective date (or earlier) as an adjustment to the opening balance of retained earnings for the period in which the standard is first adopted. In addition

- If the entity has previously disclosed publicly (in financial statements or otherwise) the fair value of its investment property in earlier periods (determined on a basis that satisfies the definition of fair value given in the standard), the entity is encouraged, but not required, to

  - Adjust the opening balance of retained earnings for the earliest period presented for which such fair value was disclosed publicly; and
  - Restate comparative information for those periods.

- If the entity has not previously disclosed publicly the information described in 1., the entity should not restate comparative information and should disclose that fact.

Cost model. IAS 8 applies to any change in accounting policies that occurs when an entity first adopts this standard and chooses to use the cost model. The effect of the change in accounting policies includes the reclassification of any amount held in revaluation surplus for investment property.

Rights to Interests Arising from Decommissioning, Restoration, and Environmental Rehabilitation Funds

As discussed in Chapter 8, when an obligation exists for decommissioning or otherwise removing or remediating damages caused by a long-lived asset at the end of its useful economic life, this must be accounted for as a cost of the asset, depreciated or amortized over its useful life. The corresponding obligation, recorded at inception at the present value of the amount estimated to be incurred at the termination date, is accreted for time value of money (i.e., interest) and, subject to the usual uncertainties of the estimation process, will equal the amount due at that point.

The required accounting is independent of whether or not funds are set aside to pay for the expected decommissioning or other costs. However, in some cases, funds are provided by the entity over the course of the asset's use so that there will be little or no risk that the entity would be unable to meet its terminal obligation. In some cases, providing a sinking fund is simply a matter of prudent financial management, but in other instances payments into a fund, not under the control of the reporting entity, may be mandated by law or regulation. IFRIC 5, which became effective in 2006, addresses the accounting for the entities' interests in such funds.

The purpose of various decommissioning, restoration and environmental rehabilitation funds ("decommissioning funds") is to segregate assets to fund some or all of the costs of decommissioning, or in undertaking environmental rehabilitation. The funds typically have one of the following structures:

1. They are established by a single contributor to fund its own decommissioning obligations, whether for a particular site, or for a number of geographically dispersed sites.

2. They are established with multiple contributors, to fund their individual or joint decommissioning obligations, and the contributors will be entitled to reimbursement for decommissioning expenses to the extent of their contributions plus any actual earnings on those contributions less pro rata costs of administering the fund. Contributors may be contingently obligated to make additional contributions, as in the event of the bankruptcy of another contributor.

3. They are established with multiple contributors to fund their individual or joint decommissioning obligations when the required level of contributions is based on the current activity of a contributor and the benefit obtained by that contributor is based on its past activity. In such cases there is a potential mismatch in the amount of contributions made by a contributor (based on current activity) and the value realizable from the fund (based on past activity).

The guidance in IFRIC 5 was intended to apply to those situations where

1. The fund is separately administered by independent trustees.

2. The entities make contributions to the fund, which are invested in a range of assets that may include both debt and equity investments, and are available to help pay these entities' decommissioning costs. The fund trustees determine how contributions are invested, within the constraints set by the fund's governing documents and any applicable legislation or other regulations.

3. The contributing entities retain the obligation to pay their decommissioning costs. However, they are able to obtain reimbursement of decommissioning costs from the fund up to the lower of the decommissioning costs incurred and the contributor's share of assets of the fund.

4. The contributing entities may have restricted access or no access to any surplus of assets of the fund over those used to meet eligible decommissioning costs.

IFRIC 5 directs the accounting for the fund contributions in the financial statements of the contributing entities, if both of the following features are present:

1. The assets are administered separately (either by being held in a separate legal entity or as segregated assets within *another* entity); *and*

2. The contributing entity's right to access the assets is restricted.

If there is a residual interest in the fund, that goes beyond a right to reimbursement (e.g., a contractual right to distributions once all decommissioning has been completed, or on winding up the fund), this may be an equity instrument within the scope of IAS 39. Accordingly, accounting for such an interest is not within the scope of IFRIC 5.

Consistent with underlying principles of IFRS, offsetting is not permitted. Therefore, the entity making contributions to a fund must recognize its obligation to pay decommissioning costs as a liability, and separately recognize its interest in the fund, unless the entity has been relieved of its obligation and would not be liable to pay decommissioning costs even if the fund fails to pay.

The reporting entity is to determine whether it has control, joint control or significant influence over the fund by reference to IAS 27, IAS 28, IAS 31 and SIC12. If one of these conditions exists, the entity is required to account for its interest in the fund in accordance with the applicable standard (i.e., equity method accounting might be necessary, etc.).

In most cases, significant influence or control will not be in the hands of the contributing entity. IFRIC 5 status that, when the entity does not have control, joint control, or significant influence over the fund, it is to recognize the right to receive reimbursement from the fund as a reimbursement in accordance with IAS 37. This is to be measured at the lesser of

1. The amount of the decommissioning obligation recognized; and
2. The contributor's share of the fair value of the net assets of the fund attributable to contributors.

Any changes in the carrying value of the right to receive reimbursement, other than contributions to and payments from the fund, are to be recognized in profit or loss in the period in which these changes occur.

In some instances the entity making contributions to a fund has an obligation to make additional contributions in the future. For example, in a multicontributor fund, entities might be contingently liable for further contributions if other fund participants declare bankruptcy, or if the value of the investment assets held by the fund decreases to an extent that they are insufficient to fulfill the fund's reimbursement obligations. IFRIC 5 states that such an obligation is a contingent liability within the scope of IAS 37. Accordingly, the entity would need to recognize a liability only if it is deemed *probable* that additional contributions will have to be made.

Disclosures required. The reporting entity that makes contributions to such a fund is required to disclose the nature of its interest in a fund and any restrictions on access to the assets in the fund. When there is an obligation to make potential additional contributions that is not recognized as a liability (i.e., it was not deemed probable of occurrence), the reporting entity is required to make the disclosures required by IAS 37.

If the contributor accounts for its interest in the fund as set forth above, it must also make the disclosures required under IAS 37.

APPENDIX

Schematic Summarizing Treatment of Investment Property

(*Source: IAS 40, Appendix A*)

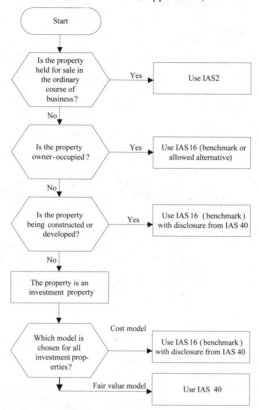

Examples of Financial Statement Disclosures

Barco
Annual Report 2007

Accounting principles

Investments in associated companies

Investments in associated companies over which the Company has significant influence (typically those that are 20-50% owned) are accounted for under the equity method of accounting and are carried in the statement of financial position at the lower of the equity method amount and the recoverable amount, and the pro rata share of income (loss) of associated companies is included in income.

Joint ventures

The Company's interest in the jointly controlled entity is accounted for by proportionate consolidation, which involves recognizing a proportionate share of the joint venture's assets, liabilities, income and expenses with similar items in the consolidated financial statements on a line-by-line basis.

Nokia
Annual Report 2007

Notes o the consolidated financial statements

15. Investments in associated companies

EURm	2007	2006
Net carrying amount January 1	224	193
Translation differences	--	(2)
Additions	19	19
Acquisitions	67	--
Deductions	(6)	(1)
Impairments	(7)	--
Share of results	44	28
Dividends	(12)	--
Other movements	(4)	(13)
Net carrying amount December 31	325	224

Shareholdings in associated companies are comprised of investments in unlisted companies in all periods presented.

Novartis Group
For the years ended December 31, 2007 and 2006

10. Associated companies

Novartis has the following significant investments in associated companies which are accounted for using the equity method:

	Balance sheet value		Net income statement effect	
	2007	2006	2007	2006
	USD millions	USD millions	USD millions	USD millions
Roche Holding AG, Switzerland	6,817	6,020	391	290
Chiron Corporation, USA				(44)
Others	128	91	21	18
Total	6,945	6,111	412	264

The results of the Group's associated companies are adjusted to be in accordance with IFRS in cases where IFRS is not already used.

A survey of analyst estimates is used to predict the Group's share of net income in Roche Holding AG ("Roche"). Any differences between these estimates and actual results will be adjusted in the 2008 financial statements.

The following table shows summarized financial information of the major associated company for the year ended December 31, 2006, since the 2007 data is not yet available:

	Assets CHF billions	Liabilities CHF billions	Revenue CHF billions	Net profit CHF billions
Roche	74.4	27.6	43.5	9.2

Roche Holding AG

The Group's holding in Roche voting shares was 33.3% at December 31, 2007 and 2006. This investment represents approximately 6.3% of the total outstanding voting and nonvoting equity instruments. In order to apply the equity method of accounting, independent appraisers were used to estimate the fair value of Roche's identifiable assets and liabilities at the time of acquisition and, therefore, the amount of residual goodwill. The purchase price allocations were made on publicly available information at the time of acquisition of the shares.

The balance sheet value allocation is as follows:

	USD millions
Novartis share of Roche's reported net assets	2,347
Novartis share of net book value of additional appraised intangible assets	2,211
Net book value of Novartis goodwill	2,509
Total residual value of purchase price	7,067
Accumulated equity accounting adjustments and translation effects	(250)
December 31, 2006 balance sheet value	6,817

The identified intangible assets principally relate to the value of currently marketed products and are being amortized straight-line over their estimated average useful life of 20 years.

The income statement effects from applying Novartis accounting for Roche in 2007 and 2006 are as follows:

	2007 USD millions	2006 USD millions
Depreciation and amortization of fair value adjustments relating to property plant & equipment and intangible assets net of taxes of USD 36 million (2006: USD 34 million)	(118)	(114)
Prior year adjustment	13	13
Novartis share of estimated Roche current year consolidated net income	496	391
Net income effect	391	290

The market value of the Novartis interest in Roche at December 31, 2007, was USD 10.0 billion (Reulers symbol: RO.S).

Chiron Corporation

The recording of the results was based on the Group's weighted-average holdings in Chiron until the acquisition of the remaining shares of Chiron in April 2006. The interest in Chiron has been accounted for using the equity method for the period from January 1, 2006 to the date of acquisition and thereafter it is fully consolidated.

The income statement effects from applying Novartis accounting policies to Chiron up to its date of full acquisition in April 2006 are as follows:

	2006 USD millions
Prior year adjustment	24
Novartis share of Chiron consolidated net income	(68)
Net income effect	(44)

11 BUSINESS COMBINATIONS AND CONSOLIDATED FINANCIAL STATEMENTS

PERSPECTIVE AND ISSUES

Background and Historical Perspective

A longstanding topic of debate in financial reporting theory has been about the accounting for business combinations and the determination of when it is more informative and meaningful to present the financial statements of multiple entities together, as a single economic entity.

In January 2008, the IASB issued revised versions of two key standards, IFRS 3, *Business Combinations,* and IAS 27, *Consolidated and Separate Financial Statements.* These significantly change the accounting for business combinations and transactions with noncontrolling interests. The revised standards are a result of the second phase of the Business Combinations project, conducted jointly with the US Financial Accounting Standards Board (FASB), to improve financial reporting while promoting the international convergence of accounting standards. Revised IFRS 3 will be denoted as IFRS 3(R) in this chapter, for clarity.

The first phase of the Business Combinations project, which FASB and IASB deliberated separately, concluded with the FASB issuing Statement 141, *Business Combinations,* in 2001, and the IASB issuing the previous version of IFRS 3, *Business Combinations,* in 2004. Their primary conclusion in the first phase of the project was that since virtually all business combinations are acquisitions, only one method of accounting for business combinations is warranted—the acquisition method. Consequently, IFRS 3, like SFAS 141, ended the use of pooling-of-interests accounting, and treats goodwill arising from an acquisition as an intangible asset with an indefinite life, not subject to periodic amortization, but instead to be tested periodically for impairment. IFRS 3 also requires that, where there is a noncontrolling interest (formerly, minority interest), the assets and liabilities in a subsidiary are to be valued at full fair value, including the noncontrolling interest's portion. (Under SFAS 141, before the changes made by SFAS 141[R], the noncontrolling interest was to be valued at book value, but this has now been conformed to IFRS practice.)

IFRS had traditionally permitted two distinct methods of accounting for business combinations. The purchase accounting method required that the actual cost of the acquisition be recognized, including any excess over the amounts allocable to the fair value of identifiable net assets, commonly known as goodwill. The pooling-of-interests method, available only when a set of stringent criteria were all met, resulted in combining the book values of the merging entities, without any adjustment to reflect the fair values of acquired assets and liabilities, and without any recognition of goodwill. Since pooling-of-interests accounting required that the mergers be achieved by means of exchanges of ordinary(common) shares, the use of this method was largely restricted to publicly held acquirers, which greatly preferred poolings since this averted step-ups in the carrying value of depreciable assets and goodwill recognition, the amortization of which would reduce future reported earnings.

Pooling accounting was widely seen as not being reflective of economic reality, since mergers which were "marriages of equals" rarely, if ever, occurred, notwithstanding that this was the theoretical basis for using this method of accounting. Ultimately, the pooling method was eliminated, but gaining support for this change required a significant compromise on the related matter of goodwill accounting: under the rules established in IFRS 3 (and in US by SFAS 141 and SFAS 142), goodwill would no longer be amortized, and the impact of business combinations on reported profit would often more closely resemble that of the now-banned pooling method than the traditional purchase accounting method. However, although periodic amortization is no longer reported, goodwill must be tested annually for impairment and, when impairment is found to have occurred, goodwill must be written down to fair value, with the adjustment reflected as a charge against the profit of that period.

While goodwill impairment must be regularly assessed, the actual application of IFRS 3 can result in recognizing goodwill created by the reporting entity subsequent to the purchase combination, to the extent that this replaces or offsets impaired goodwill. Consequently, in many cases impairments will not be recognized even when the value of the acquired operations has declined. This approach—which effectively reverses the longstanding ban on recognizing internally created (as opposed to purchased) goodwill—was necessitated by the virtual impossibility of separately identifying elements of goodwill having alternative derivations. Even with this simplified approach, measurement of goodwill impairment is a fairly difficult task, often requiring the services of independent valuation consultants.

IFRS 3 contained significant differences from SFAS 141 and 142, and both the IASB and the FASB believed their respective standards could be improved and converged. Consequently the Boards conducted jointly the second phase of the Business Combination project to converge their respective standards that addressed the guidance for applying the acquisition method. The second phase culminated with the issuance of the revised IFRS 3(R) and IAS 27(R), which are effective prospectively for business combinations for which the acquisition date is on or after the beginning of the first annual reporting period beginning on or after July 1, 2009. While the revised IFRS more closely resemble the equivalent US GAAP standards, differences still remain. Accountants who are responsible for preparing financial statements using both sets of standards or who are responsible for reconciling or converting financial statements must be cognizant of these differences.

IFRS 3(R) and IAS 27(R) introduce a number of changes in accounting for business combinations and preparation of consolidated financial statements. These changes will impact the amounts of goodwill and noncontrolling interest recognized, and operating results in the year that acquisition occurs and future years. In accordance with the revised standards, entities will have a choice for each business combination entered into to measure noncontrolling interest in the acquiree either at its full fair value or at its proportionate share of the acquiree's identifiable net assets. This choice will result in either recognizing goodwill relating to 100% of the business (applying the full fair value option and allocating implied goodwill to noncontrolling interest) or recognizing goodwill relating only to the percentage interest acquired.

In accordance with IFRS 3(R) and IAS 27(R), all business combinations are accounted for as an acquisition. The assets acquired and liabilities assumed are recorded on the acquirer's books at their respective fair values using *acquisition accounting* (formerly, *purchase accounting*). Goodwill is measured initially as the difference between (1) the acquisition-date fair value of the consideration transferred plus the fair value of any noncontrolling interest in the acquiree, plus the fair value of the acquirer's previously held equity interest in the acquiree, if any; and (2) the acquisition-date fair values (or other amounts recognized in accordance with IFRS 3(R) of the identifiable assets acquired and liabilities assumed. Goodwill can arise only in the context of a business combination, and cannot arise from purchases of an asset or group of assets.

The core principles adopted in IFRS 3(R) are that an acquirer of a business recognizes assets acquired and liabilities assumed at their acquisition-date fair values, and discloses information that enables users to evaluate the nature and financial effects of the acquisition. While fair values of many assets and liabilities can readily be determined (and in an arm's-length transaction should be known to the parties), certain recognition and measurement problems do inevitably arise. Among these are the value of contingent consideration (e.g., earn-outs) promised to former owners of the acquired entity, and the determination as to whether certain expenses that arise by virtue of the transaction, such as those pertaining to elimination of duplicate facilities, should be treated as part of the transaction or as an element of postacquisition accounting.

This chapter addresses in detail the application of the acquisition method of accounting for business combinations and, to a lesser extent, the accounting for goodwill. Chapter 9 presents the accounting for all intangible assets, including goodwill, with greater specificity. This chapter addresses the two allowed options of measuring noncontrolling interest in the acquiree under IFRS 3(R): (1) the new option to measure noncontrolling interest at its fair value and to allocate implied goodwill to the noncontrolling interest, and (2) the option to measure the noncontrolling interest at its proportionate share of the acquiree's identifiable net assets—which was the only option allowable under previous IFRS 3.

While the presentation of consolidated financial statements is required under IFRS, there is no parallel requirement to present combined financial statements for entities under common control (brother/sister entities). However, in certain cases, it is desirable that combined financial statements be prepared for such entities. This process is very similar to an accounting consolidation using the formerly permitted pooling accounting, except that the equity accounts for the combining entities are carried forward intact.

Consolidation of many "special-purpose entities" (SPE)—which under US GAAP are now named "variable interest entities" (VIE) by FIN 46(R)—has increased substantially under these requirements, which were in part spurred on by the financial reporting scandals of the early 2000s. Rules governing consolidation of SPEs and VIEs are complex and are continuing to evolve further in response to an ongoing credit market turmoil that is (as of late 2008) being experienced worldwide.

The IASB is currently pursuing a project (recently renamed *Consolidation*) to address both the basis (policy) on which a parent entity should consolidate its investments in subsidiaries and enhanced disclosures about consolidated and nonconsolidated entities. The objective of the project is to publish a single IFRS on consolidation that would replace IAS 27, *Consolidated and Separate Financial Statements,* and SIC-12, *Consolidation—Special-Purpose Entities.* It is intended that this will provide more rigorous guidance on the concept of control, which is the basis for consolidation under IAS 27, including a revision of the control definition (in order to apply the same control criteria to all legal entities), as well as improved guidance in relation to power with less than a majority of the voting rights, potential voting rights, veto rights, and economic dependence. The project will also focus on the consolidation of structured entities (for example, SPEs) which are utilized for "off the books" financings, leasing activities, and other purposes. The objective is to force adherence to the "substance over form" practice of consolidating SPEs when they are, effectively, economically integrated with the reporting entity.

NOTE: SIC 12 sets forth the current IFRS requirements in this area, which call for consolidation when the SPE is controlled by the reporting entity.

Major accounting issues affecting business combinations and the preparation of consolidated or combined financial statements pertain to the following:

1. The proper recognition and measurement of the assets and liabilities of the combining entities
2. The accounting for goodwill or gain from a bargain purchase (negative goodwill)
3. The elimination of intercompany balances and transactions in the preparation of consolidated financial statements
4. The manner of reporting the noncontrolling interest

The accounting for the assets and liabilities of entities acquired in a business combination is largely dependent on the fair values assigned to them at the transaction date. (The now-obsolete pooling method relied upon book values.) The US GAAP standard, FAS 157, *Fair Value Measurements,* introduced a framework for measuring fair value, and its provisions provide important guidance when assigning values as part of a business combination. In essence, it favors valuations determined on the open market, but allows other methodologies if open market valuation is not practicable. The IASB added this topic to its agenda in September 2005 and decided to use the US standard as the starting point for its own deliberation. In November 2006, the IASB issued a Discussion Paper on Fair Value Measurements aimed at establishing a concise definition of fair value as well as a single source of guidance for all fair value measurements required by IFRS. The fair value concepts and procedures are discussed in greater detail in Chapter 1 (and Appendix).

Sources of IFRS			
IFRS 3(R)	*IAS* 27(R), 36, 37, 38	*SIC* 12, 32	*IFRIC* 5, 9, 10

DEFINITIONS OF TERMS

Accounting consolidation. The process of combining the financial statements of a parent company and one or more legally separate and distinct subsidiaries as a single economic entity for financial reporting purposes.

Acquiree. One or more businesses in which an acquirer obtains control in a business combination.

Acquirer. An entity that obtains control over one or more businesses in a business combination. When the acquiree is a special-purpose entity (SPE), the creator or sponsor of the SPE (or the entity on whose behalf the SPE was created) is always the acquirer.

Acquisition. A business combination in which one entity (the acquirer) obtains control over the net assets and operations of another (the acquiree) in exchange for the transfer of assets, incurrence of liability, or issuance of equity.

Acquisition date. The date on which control of the acquiree is obtained by the acquirer (i.e., the date of exchange effecting the acquisition).

Acquisition method. The method of accounting for each business combination under IFRS. Applying the acquisition method requires: (1) identifying the acquirer; (2) determining the acquisition date; (3) recognizing and measuring the identifiable assets acquired, the liabilities assumed, and any noncontrolling interest in the acquiree; and (4) recognizing and measuring goodwill or a gain from a bargain purchase. It establishes a new basis of accountability for the acquiree.

Acquisition-related costs. Costs incurred by an acquirer to enter into a business combination.

Asset. A present economic resource: (1) controlled by an entity, through an enforceable right or other means, as a result of past events; and (2) from which future economic benefits are expected to flow to the entity (*Framework,* IAS 38).

The following three characteristics must be present for an item to qualify as an asset:

1. An economic resource is scarce and capable of producing cash inflows or reducing cash outflows, directly or indirectly, alone or together with other economic resources.
2. The entity has an enforceable right or other means to use the economic resource directly or indirectly, or can limit the access of others.
3. The economic resource and the enforceable right or other means both exist at the financial statement date (Conceptual Framework Project).

In addition, the asset must be capable of being measured reliably.

Bargain purchase. A business combination in which the net of the acquisition-date amounts of the identifiable assets acquired and the liabilities assumed, measured in accordance with IFRS 3(R), exceeds the aggregate of the acquisition-date fair value of the consideration transferred, plus the amount of any noncontrolling interest in the acquiree, plus the acquisition-date fair value of the acquirer's previously held equity interest in the acquiree.

Business. An integrated set of assets and activities capable of being conducted and managed in order to provide a return directly to investors or other owners, members, or participants. The return can be in the form of dividends, lower costs, or other economic benefits. A development stage enterprise is not precluded from qualifying as a business under this definition, and the guidance that accompanies it is provided in IFRS 3(R) (Appendix B).

Business combination. A transaction or other event that results in an acquirer obtaining control over one or more businesses. Transactions that are sometimes referred to as "true mergers" or "mergers of equals" are also considered to be business combinations with an acquirer and one or more acquirees.

Closing date. The day on which an acquirer legally transfers consideration, acquires the assets, and assumes the liabilities of an acquiree.

Combined financial statements. The financial statements presenting the financial position and/or results of operations of legally separate entities, related by common ownership, as if they were a single entity. A combined statement is distinguished from a consolidated financial statement of a company and subsidiaries, which must reconcile investment and capital accounts.

Consideration transferred. The acquirer measures the consideration transferred in a business combination in exchange for the acquiree (or control of the acquiree) at fair value, which is calculated as the aggregate of the acquisition-date fair values of the assets transferred, liabilities incurred to former owners of the acquiree, and the equity interests issued by the acquirer. The acquisition-date fair value of contingent consideration should also be recognized as part of the consideration transferred in exchange for the acquiree. Acquisition-related costs are expenses recognized when incurred in profit or loss.

Consolidated financial statements. The financial statements of a group (a parent and all its subsidiaries) presented as those of a single economic entity.

Contingency. An existing, unresolved condition, situation, or set of circumstances that will eventually be resolved by the occurrence or nonoccurrence of one or more future events. A potential gain or loss to the reporting entity can result from the contingency's resolution.

Contingent consideration. Generally, an acquirer's obligation to transfer additional assets or equity interests to the acquiree's former owners if specified future events occur or conditions are met. The contingent obligation is incurred as part of a business combination in order to obtain control of an acquiree. Contingent consideration might also arise when the terms of the business combination provide a requirement that the acquiree's former owners return previously transferred assets or equity interests to the acquirer under certain specified conditions.

Control. The power to govern the financing and operating policies of an entity so as to obtain benefits from its activities and increase, maintain, or protect the amount of those benefits. Control of an entity can be obtained either by (1) obtaining ownership of a majority of its outstanding voting power; or (2) obtaining contractual rights to receive the majority of the financial benefits and/or by assuming contractual obligations to bear the majority of the financial consequences that occur in the future from the entity outperforming or underperforming its expectations (the controlled entity being referred to as a special-purpose entity, or

SPE). IAS 27 indicates several circumstances which result in control even in cases where an entity owns less than one-half of the voting power of another entity.

Cost method. A method of accounting whereby the investment is recognized at cost. The investor recognizes income from the investment only to the extent that the investor receives distributions from accumulated net profits of the investee (dividends) arising after the date of acquisition. Distributions received in excess of such profits are regarded as a recovery of investment and are recognized as a reduction of the cost of the investment.

Creator (or sponsor) of SPE. The entity on whose behalf a special-purpose entity (SPE) was created and which retains a significant beneficial interest in the SPE's activities, even though it may own little or none of the SPE's equity.

Equity interests. For the purposes of IFRS 3(R), equity interests is used broadly to mean ownership interests (or instruments evidencing rights of ownership) of investor-owned entities. In a mutual entity, equity interests means instruments evidencing ownership, membership, or participation rights.

Fair value. The amount for which an asset could be exchanged, or a liability settled, between knowledgeable, willing parties in an arm's-length transaction.

Favorable contract. From the perspective of a counterparty, a contract is favorable if its terms are more lucrative than current market terms.

Gain from a bargain purchase. In a business combination resulting in a bargain purchase, the difference between: (1) the acquisition-date fair values (or other amounts measured in accordance with IFRS 3[R]) of the identifiable assets acquired and liabilities assumed; and (2) the acquisition-date fair value of the consideration transferred plus the amount of any noncontrolling interest in the acquiree plus the acquisition-date fair value of the acquirer's previously held equity interest in the acquiree. A gain from a bargain purchase is recognized when (1) exceeds (2). Goodwill arises when (2) exceeds (1). After the acquirer's reassessment of whether all the assets acquired and all the liabilities assumed have been correctly identified, the resulting gain from a bargain purchase is recognized in profit or loss on the acquisition date. Gain from a bargain purchase is also referred to in accounting literature as negative goodwill.

Goodwill. An intangible asset acquired in a business combination representing the future economic benefits expected to be derived from the business combination that are not allocated to other individually identifiable and separately recognizable assets acquired. In accordance with IFRS 3(R), the acquirer measures goodwill initially as the difference between: (1) the acquisition-date fair value of the consideration transferred plus the amount of any noncontrolling interest in the acquiree plus the acquisition-date fair value of the acquirer's previously held equity interest in the acquiree; and (2) the acquisition-date fair values (or other amounts measured in accordance with IFRS 3[R]) of the identifiable assets acquired and liabilities assumed. Goodwill is recognized when (1) exceeds (2). A bargain purchase arises when (2) exceeds (1). After initial recognition, goodwill is measured at cost less any accumulated impairment losses. Entities have a choice for each business combination to measure noncontrolling interest in the acquiree either at its fair value (and recognizing goodwill relating to 100% of the business) or at its proportionate share of the acquiree's net assets.

Group. A parent and all its subsidiaries.

Identifiable asset. An asset that is identifiable if it either: (1) is separable from the entity that holds it; or (2) represents a legal and/or contractual right. An asset is considered separable if it is capable of being separated or divided from the entity that holds it for the purpose of the asset's sale, transfer, license, rental, or exchange, by itself or together with a related contract, or other identifiable asset or liability, irrespective of whether management of the entity intends to do so. A legal and/or contractual right is considered identifiable irrespective of whether it is transferrable or separable from the entity or from other rights and obligations.

Intangible asset. A identifiable nonmonetary asset that lacks physical substance.

Liability. A present unconditional economic obligation, the settlement of which is expected to result in an outflow from the entity of resources embodying economic benefits (IAS 37, *Framework*).

The following three characteristics must be present for an item to qualify as a liability:

1. An economic obligation is expected to result in cash outflows, or reduced cash inflows, directly or indirectly, alone or together with other economic obligations.
2. Obligations are enforceable against the entity by legal or other means and cannot be avoided.
3. The economic obligation exists on the date of the financial statements (Conceptual Framework Project).

In addition, liabilities are recognized subject to the constraint that the amount at which the settlement will take place can be measured reliably.

Market participants. Buyers and sellers in the principal or most advantageous market for an asset or liability who are

1. Independent of the reporting entity (i.e., they are not related parties).
2. Knowledgeable to the extent that they have a reasonable understanding about the asset or liability and the transaction based on all available information, including information that is obtainable through the performance of usual and customary due diligence efforts.
3. Able to buy or sell the asset or liability.
4. Willing to enter into a transaction for the asset or liability (i.e., they are not under duress that would force or compel them to enter into the transaction).

Mutual entity. An entity that is not investor-owned, organized for the purpose of providing dividends, reduced costs, or other economic benefits directly to its owners, members, or participants. Examples of mutual entities include mutual insurance companies, credit unions, and cooperative entities.

Noncontrolling interest. The equity (net assets) in a subsidiary not directly or indirectly attributable to its parent. In accordance with IFRS 3(R), entities have a choice for each business combination entered into to measure noncontrolling interest in the acquiree either (1) at its fair value, or (2) as its proportionate share of the value of the identifiable assets and liabilities (net assets) of the acquiree, measured as required by that standard. The first choice will result in recognizing goodwill constituting all of the goodwill of the acquired business (applying the fair value option and allocating implied goodwill to noncontrolling interest), while the second choice will result in recognizing goodwill associated with only the percentage of interest acquired. Noncontrolling interests were formerly referred to in accounting literature as minority interests.

Owners. For the purposes of IFRS 3(R), the term *owners* is used broadly to include holders of equity interests (ownership interests) in investor-owned or mutual entities. Owners include parties referred to as shareholders, partners, proprietors, members, or participants.

Parent. An entity that has one or more subsidiaries.

Reporting entity. An entity for which there are users who rely on the entity's general-purpose financial statements as their major source of financial information about the entity that will be useful to them for making decisions about the allocation of resources. A reporting entity can be a single entity or a group comprising a parent and all of its subsidiaries.

Reverse acquisition. An acquisition when one entity, nominally the acquirer, issues so many shares to the former owners of the target entity that they become the majority owners of the successor entity.

Reverse spin-off. A spin-off transaction in which the nominal or legal spinnor is to be accounted for as the spinnee, in order to reflect the economic reality of the spin-off transaction.

Roll-up or put-together transaction. A business combination that is effected by two or more entities transferring the net assets of their businesses to a newly formed entity. These transactions can also be effected by the owners of the entities transferring their equity interests in those entities to the newly formed entity.

Separate financial statements. The financial statements presented by a parent, an investor in an associate or a venture in a jointly controlled entity, in which the investments are accounted for on the basis of the direct interest rather than on the basis of the reported results and net assets of the investees. An entity accounts for such investments either (1) at cost; or (2) in accordance with IAS 39.

Special-purpose entity (SPE). An entity created to accomplish a narrow and well-defined objective (e.g., to effect a lease, research and development activities, or a securitization of financial assets), which can be a corporation, trust, partnership or unincorporated entity. SIC 12 requires consolidation when the SPE is controlled by the reporting entity (the sponsor or creator of the SPE). Under IFRS 3(R), this party is also referred to as a "parent" and the SPE is also referred to as a "subsidiary."

Spin-off. The creation of an independent entity through the sale or distribution of new shares of an existing business/division of a parent company. For example, occasionally an entity may dispose of a wholly or partially owned subsidiary, or of an investee, by transferring it unilaterally to the entity's shareholders.

Stapling arrangement. An arrangement in which two or more legal entities contractually agree to combine their securities so that they are quoted at a single price and cannot be traded or transferred independently.

Subsidiary. An entity, including an unincorporated entity such as a partnership that is controlled by another entity (known as the parent).

Unfavorable contract. From the perspective of a counterparty, a contract is unfavorable if its terms are less lucrative than current market terms. An unfavorable contract is not necessarily a contract that will result in a loss to the counterparty.

Unrealized intercompany profit. The excess of the transaction price over the carrying value of an item (usually inventory or long-lived assets) transferred from (or to) a parent to (or from) the subsidiary, or among subsidiaries, and not sold to an outside entity as of the end of the reporting period. For purposes of consolidated financial statements, recognition must be deferred until subsequent realization through a transaction with an unrelated party.

CONCEPTS, RULES, AND EXAMPLES

IFRS 3(R) and IAS 27(R) and International Accounting Convergence

In January 2008, the IASB issued a revised version of IFRS 3, *Business Combinations*, which in this book will be referred to as IFRS 3(R), and an amended version of IAS 27, *Consolidated and Separate Financial Statements,* which will be referred to as IAS 27(R). These standards were the product of the first major joint project undertaken by IASB and FASB. In December 2007, FASB released a revised standard, FAS 141(R), *Business Combinations,* and a newly developed companion standard FAS 160, *Noncontrolling Interests in Consolidated Financial Statements.* The FASB thus made fundamental changes to its accounting for business combination and noncontrolling interests, most of which brought US accounting into line with IFRS 3 and IAS 27. Other improvements change both IFRS and US GAAP. The tandem sets of standards substantially converge IFRS and US GAAP, although differences still remain between them, as the two standards setters did not agree on all of their conclusions (See Appendix C, Comparison of IFRS and US GAAP).

Key changes introduced by IFRS 3(R) include

- Option to measure noncontrolling interest at fair value
- Acquisition-related costs recognized in profit or loss as incurred
- In step acquisitions, previously held equity interest in the acquiree is remeasured at its acquisition-date fair value, with the resulting gains and losses recognized in profit or loss
- Reassessing the classification or designation of all assets and liabilities acquired as required by other IFRS
- Contingent consideration measured at fair value at the date of business combination, with subsequent changes (gains, losses) recognized in profit or loss
- Contingent liabilities (present obligations that arise from past events) of the acquiree recognized at fair value
- Reacquired rights recognized as intangible assets, separately from goodwill
- Separate accounting for preexisting relationships
- Indemnification assets measured on the same basis as the related liability

Key changes introduced by IAS 27(R) are

- Changes in a parent's controlling ownership interest that do not result in a loss of control are accounted for as equity transactions (transactions with owners in their capacity as owners). Consequently, no gain or loss, and no changes in the carrying values of the subsidiary's assets (including goodwill) or liabilities are recognized.
- Losses incurred by the subsidiary are allocated between controlling and noncontrolling interests, even if losses attributed to the noncontrolling interests exceed the noncontrolling interests in the subsidiary's equity.
- On loss of control of a subsidiary, the parent derecognizes the individual assets, liabilities, and equity related to that subsidiary (including any noncontrolling interests and amounts previously recognized in other comprehensive income). Any retained interest in the former subsidiary should be valued at fair value at the date that control is lost; any resulting gain or loss is recognized in profit or loss.

Organization of This Chapter and Its Appendix

In general, IFRS 3(R) and IAS 27(R) should be applied prospectively, although early application is permitted. Consequently, guidance included in many of the pronouncements that were amended by the new standards will continue to apply during the transition period to those business combinations predating the new standards. To aid the reader/researcher in navigating this maze, we have divided this chapter into two discrete sections. The main portion of the chapter is devoted to the interpretation and application of IFRS 3(R) and IAS 27(R).

To augment the main portion of the chapter to provide the currently applicable guidance to those who still are required to follow it, guidance regarding the former standards has been placed in Appendix A. This may, to some extent, be duplicative, but this method of organizing the material will result in the most effective and complete research relative to a given aspect of the standards during this transition period.

Effective Date and Transition Provisions

IFRS 3(R) and IAS 27(R) come into effect for the first annual reporting period beginning on or after July 1, 2009. Early application is permitted, although the new pronouncements may not be applied to periods beginning prior to June 30, 2007. If an entity elects early adoption, both IFRS 3(R) and IAS 27(R) must be applied at the same time.

Thus reporting entities must apply IFRS 3(R) prospectively to business combinations for which the acquisition date is on or after the beginning of the annual period in which the standard is adopted. Further, reporting entities are not permitted to retrospectively adjust the carrying amounts of assets and liabilities from previously recognized business combinations for the effects of the new pronouncements. Special transition provisions apply to mutual entities and with respect to amendments made to paragraph 68 of IAS 12, governing the accounting for current and deferred income taxes. After the date this IFRS is adopted, any change in a deferred tax benefit acquired in a business combination does not adjust goodwill, but is recognized in profit or loss for the period (or, if IAS 12 requires, outside profit or loss). These are discussed later in this chapter and in Chapter 15, Income Taxes.

Objectives

IFRS 3(R) and IAS 27(R) follow a revised drafting convention, intended to be more principles-based than rules-based in approach. Thus, each major section of these pronouncements is preceded by a prominent statement of the main principles embodied by that section, presented in a boldfaced font for emphasis. All paragraphs and the appendices containing implementation guidance, whether boldfaced or not, are of equal authority, however.

The overriding objective of the new standards is to improve the relevance, representational faithfulness, transparency, and comparability of information provided in financial statements about business combinations and their effects on the reporting entity by establishing principles and requirements with respect to how an acquirer, in its consolidated financial statements

1. Recognizes and measures identifiable assets acquired, liabilities assumed, and the noncontrolling interest in the acquiree, if any,
2. Recognizes and measures acquired goodwill or a gain from a bargain purchase,
3. Determines the nature and extent of disclosures sufficient to enable the reader to evaluate the nature of the business combination and its financial effects on the consolidated reporting entity,
4. Accounts for and reports noncontrolling interests in subsidiaries, and
5. Deconsolidates a subsidiary when it ceases to hold a controlling interest in it.

Scope

Transactions or other events that meet the definition of a business combination are subject to IFRS 3(R) and IAS 27(R). Excluded from the scope of these standards, however, are

1. Formation of a joint venture
2. Acquisition of an asset or group of assets that does not represent a business, as that term is newly defined
3. Combinations between entities or businesses under common control

Mutual entities (i.e., credit unions, cooperatives, etc.), those achieved by contract alone (providing control without ownership—i.e., dual-listed entities, stapled entity structures), those achieved in stages (step acquisitions), those transferring less than 100% ownership, and bargain purchases are within the scope of the revised standards.

Business Combinations

The revised standard IFRS 3(R) replaces the cost principle of accounting for business combinations with the fair value principle. Under the cost principle, which is applied in the current practice (IFRS 3), the exchange transaction is recorded at cost. That cost is allocated to the assets acquired and liabilities assumed; and goodwill is recognized for the difference between the cost and the fair value of the net assets acquired. In contrast, based on the fair value principle, upon obtaining control of the subsidiary, the exchange transaction is measured at fair value. Also assets, liabilities, and equity (except equity acquired by the controlling interest) of the acquired entity are measured at fair value. However, several exceptions to this principle are provided in IFRS 3(R).

Determining Fair Values

Accounting for acquisitions requires a determination of the fair value for each of the acquired entity's identifiable tangible and intangible assets and for each of its liabilities at the date of combination (except for assets which are to be resold and which are to be accounted for at fair value less costs to sell under IFRS 5; and for those items to which limited exceptions to recognition and measurement principles apply). IFRS 3(R) provides illustrative examples of how to treat certain assets, particularly intangibles, but provides no general guidance on determining fair value. A separate project on fair value measurements is likely to result in the issuance of a new IFRS on this topic in 2010, very likely to be heavily based on the recent US GAAP standard, FAS 157, which the IASB decided to use as the starting point for its deliberations. As the first stage of its project, the IASB published in November 2006, the *Fair Value Measurements* Discussion Paper setting forth its preliminary views on the principal issues contained in SFAS 157. To assist readers, the following were reproduced in the Discussion Paper: (1) excerpts of fair value measurement guidance in IFRSs and (2) the text of SFAS 157, together with the related application guidance, present value guidance, and basis for conclusions. Based on the comments received on the Discussion Paper, the IASB plans to publish an Exposure Draft of an IFRS on fair value measurement guidance in the first half of 2009. Appendix F, Use of Fair Value in Accounting Measurements, in Chapter 2 discusses in further detail the IASB project, *Fair Value Measurement Guidance*.

Transactions and Events Accounted for as Business Combinations

A business combination results from the occurrence of a transaction or other event that results in an acquirer obtaining control of one or more businesses. This can occur in many different ways that include the following examples individually or in some cases, in combination:

1. Transfer of cash, cash equivalents, or other assets, including the transfer of assets of another business of the acquirer,
2. Incurring liabilities,
3. Issuance of equity instruments,
4. Providing more than one type of consideration, or
5. By contract alone without the transfer of consideration, such as when

    a. An acquiree business repurchases enough of its own shares to cause one of its existing investors (the acquirer) to obtain control over it
    b. There is a lapse of minority veto rights that had previously prevented the acquirer from controlling an acquiree in which it held a majority voting interest
    c. An acquirer and acquiree contractually agree to combine their businesses without a transfer of consideration between them.

Qualifying as a Business

IFRS 3(R) substantively redefines the previous definition of a business that was set forth for the first time in IFRS 3, which may increase the number of acquisition transactions that will be accounted for as a business combination. Under IFRS 3(R), in order to be considered a business, an integrated group of activities and assets must be *capable* of being conducted and managed to provide a return directly to investors, *owners, members, or participants*. The return can be in the form of dividends, reduced costs, or other economic benefits. The word *capable* was added to emphasize the fact that the definition does not preclude a development stage enterprise from qualifying as a business. *Other owners, members, or participants* were included to emphasize the applicability of IFRS 3(R) to mutual entities (e.g., credit unions and cooperatives) that previously used the pooling-of-interests method of accounting for business combinations and to noncorporate entities.

The definition and related guidance elaborate further that a business consists of inputs and processes applied to those inputs that have the ability to create outputs. Clarification is provided that, while outputs are usually present in a business, they are not required to qualify as a business as long as there is the *ability* to create them.

An input is an economic resource that creates or has the ability to create outputs when one or more processes are applied to it. Examples of inputs include fixed assets, intangible rights to use fixed assets, intellectual property or other intangible assets, and access to markets in which to hire employees or purchase materials.

A process is a system, protocol, convention, or rule with the ability to create outputs when applied to one or more inputs. Processes are usually documented; however, an organized workforce with the requisite skills and experience may apply processes necessary to create outputs by following established rules and conventions. In evaluating whether an activity is a process, IFRS 3(R) indicates that functions such as accounting, billing, payroll, and other administrative systems do not meet the definition. Thus, processes are the types of activities that an entity engages in to produce the products and/or services that it provides to the marketplace rather than the internal activities it follows in operating its business.

An output is simply the by-product resulting from applying processes to inputs. An output provides, or has the ability to provide, the desired return to the investors, members, participants, or other owners.

In analyzing a transaction or event to determine whether it is a business combination, it is not necessary that the acquirer retain, postcombination, all of the inputs or processes used by the seller in operating the business. If market participants could, for example, acquire the business in an arm's-length transaction and continue to produce outputs by integrating the business with their own inputs and processes, then that subset of remaining inputs and processes still meets the definition of a business from the standpoint of the acquirer.

The guidance in IFRS 3(R) provides additional flexibility by providing that it is not necessary that a business have liabilities, although that situation is expected to be rare. The broad scope of the term "capable of" requires judgment in determining whether an acquired set of activities and assets constitutes a business, to be accounted for applying the acquisition method.

As discussed previously, development stage enterprises are not precluded from meeting the criteria to be a business. This is true even if they do not yet produce outputs. If there are no outputs being produced, the acquirer is to determine whether the enterprise constitutes a business by considering whether it

1. Has started its planned principal activities,
2. Has hired employees,
3. Has obtained intellectual property,

4. Has obtained other inputs,
5. Has implemented processes that could be applied to its inputs,
6. Is pursuing a plan to produce outputs,
7. Will have the ability to obtain access to customers that will purchase the outputs.

It is important to note, however, that it is not required that all of these factors be present for a given set of development stage activities and assets to qualify as a business. Again, the relevant question to ask is whether a market participant would be capable of conducting or managing the set of activities and assets as a business irrespective of whether the seller did so or the acquirer intends to do so.

Finally, IFRS 3(R) provided, what it acknowledged was circular logic in asserting that, absent evidence to the contrary, if goodwill is included in a set of assets and activities, it can be presumed to be a business. The circularity arises from the fact that, in order to apply IFRS to determine whether to initially recognize goodwill, the accountant would be required to first determine whether there had, in fact, been an acquisition of a business. Otherwise, it would not be permitted to recognize goodwill. It is not necessary, however, that goodwill be present in order to consider a set of assets and activities to be a business.

Techniques for Structuring Business Combinations

A business combination can be structured in a number of different ways that satisfy the acquirer's strategic, operational, legal, tax, and risk management objectives. Some of the more frequently used structures are

1. One or more businesses become subsidiaries of the acquirer. As subsidiaries, they continue to operate as legal entities.
2. The net assets of one or more businesses are legally merged into the acquirer. In this case, the acquiree entity ceases to exist (in legal vernacular, this is referred to as a statutory merger and normally the transaction is subject to approval by a majority of the outstanding voting shares of the acquiree).
3. The owners of the acquiree transfer their equity interests to the acquirer entity or to the owners of the acquirer entity in exchange for equity interests in the acquirer.
4. All of the combining entities transfer their net assets or their owners transfer their equity interests into a new entity formed for the purpose of the transaction. This is sometimes referred to as a roll-up or put-together transaction.
5. A former owner or group of former owners of one of the combining entities obtains control of the combined entities collectively.
6. An acquirer might hold a noncontrolling equity interest in an entity and subsequently purchase additional equity interests sufficient to give it control over the investee. These transactions are referred to as step acquisitions or business combinations achieved in stages.
7. A business owner organizes a partnership, S corporation, or LLC to hold real estate. The real estate is the principal location of the commonly owned business and that business entity leases the real estate from the separate entity.

Accounting for Business Combinations under the Acquisition Method

The acquirer is to account for a business combination using the acquisition method. This term, new to IFRS, represents an expansion of the now-outdated term, "purchase method." The change in terminology was made in order to emphasize that a business combination can occur even when a purchase transaction is not involved.

The following steps are required to apply the acquisition method:

1. Identify the acquirer.
2. Determine the acquisition date.
3. Identify the assets and liabilities, if any, requiring separate accounting because they result from transactions that are not part of the business combination, and account for them in accordance with their nature and the applicable IFRS.
4. Identify assets and liabilities that require acquisition date classification or designation decisions to facilitate application of IFRS in postcombination financial statements and make those classifications or designations based on (a) contractual terms, (b) economic conditions, (c) acquirer operating or accounting policies, and (d) other pertinent conditions existing at the acquisition date.
5. Recognize and measure the identifiable tangible and intangible assets acquired and liabilities assumed.
6. Recognize and measure any noncontrolling interest in the acquiree.
7. Measure the consideration transferred.
8. Recognize and measure goodwill or, if the business combination results in a bargain purchase, recognize a gain from the bargain purchase.

Step 1—Identify the acquirer. IFRS 3(R), as did the predecessor standard, strongly emphasizes the concept that every business combination has an acquirer. In the "basis for conclusions" that accompanies IFRS 3(R), IASB asserted that

> ..."true mergers" or "mergers of equals" in which none of the combining entities obtain control of the others are so rare as to be virtually nonexistent...[1]

The provisions of IAS 27, *Consolidated and Separate Financial Statements,* should be used to identify the acquirer—the entity that obtains *control* of the acquiree. IFRS 3 carried forward the principle of IAS 22 that in a business combination accounted for using the acquisition method the acquirer is the combining entity that obtains control of the other combining entities. According to the IASB, using the control concept for identifying the acquirer is consistent with using the control concept in IAS 27 to define the boundaries of the reporting entity and to provide the basis for establishing a parent-subsidiary relationship.

While IAS 27 provides, that in general, control is presumed to exist when the parent owns, directly or indirectly, a majority of the voting power of another entity, this is not an absolute rule to be applied in all cases. In fact, IAS 27 explicitly provides that in exceptional circumstances, it can be clearly demonstrated that majority ownership does not constitute control, but rather that the minority ownership may constitute control (related IFRS guidance is provided later in this chapter in the paragraph titled *Scope of Consolidated Financial Statements*).

Exceptions to the general majority ownership rule include, but are not limited to the following situations:

1. An entity that is in legal reorganization or bankruptcy
2. An entity subject to uncertainties due to government-imposed restrictions, such as foreign exchange restrictions or controls, whose severity casts doubt on the majority owner's ability to control the entity
3. If the acquiree is a special-purpose entity (SPE), the creator or sponsor of the SPE is always considered to be the acquirer. Accounting for SPEs is discussed later in this chapter.

---

[1]   *IFRS 3(R), paragraph B35.*

If applying the guidance in IAS 27(R) does not clearly indicate the party that is the acquirer, IFRS 3(R) provides factors to consider in making that determination under different facts and circumstances.

1. *Relative size*—Generally, the acquirer is the entity whose relative size is significantly larger than that of the other entity or entities. Size can be compared by using measures such as assets, revenues, or net income.

2. *Initiator of the transaction*—When more than two entities are involved, another factor to consider (besides relative size) is which of the entities initiated the transaction.

3. *Roll-ups or put-together transactions*—When a new entity is formed to issue equity interests to effect a business combination, one of the preexisting entities is to be identified as the acquirer. If, instead, a newly formed entity transfers cash or other assets, or incurs liabilities as consideration to effect a business combination, that new entity may be considered to be the acquirer.

4. *Nonequity consideration*—In business combinations accomplished primarily by the transfer of cash or other assets, or by incurring liabilities, the entity that transfers the cash or other assets, or incurs the liabilities is usually the acquirer.

5. *Exchange of equity interests*—In business combinations accomplished primarily by the exchange of equity interests, the entity that issues its equity interests is generally considered to be the acquirer. One notable exception that occurs frequently in practice is sometimes referred to as a reverse acquisition, discussed in detail later in this chapter. In a reverse acquisition, the entity issuing equity interests is legally the acquirer, but for accounting purposes is considered the acquiree. There are, however, other factors that should be considered in identifying the acquirer when equity interests are exchanged. These include

   a. *Relative voting rights in the combined entity after the business combination*—Generally, the acquirer is the entity whose owners, as a group, retain or obtain the largest portion of the voting rights in the consolidated entity. This determination must take into consideration the existence of any unusual or special voting arrangements as well as any options, warrants, or convertible securities.

   b. *The existence of a large minority voting interest in the combined entity in the event no other owner or organized group of owners possesses a significant voting interest*—Generally, the acquirer is the entity whose owner or organized group of owners holds the largest minority voting interest in the combined entity.

   c. *The composition of the governing body of the combined entity*—Generally, the acquirer is the entity whose owners have the ability to elect, appoint, or remove a majority of members of the governing body of the combined entity.

   d. *The composition of the senior management of the combined entity*—Generally the acquirer is the entity whose former management dominates the management of the combined entity.

   e. *Terms of the equity exchange*—Generally, the acquirer is the entity that pays a premium over the precombination fair value of the equity interests of the other entity or entities.

Step 2—Determine the acquisition date. By definition, the acquisition date is that on which the acquirer obtains control of the acquiree. As discussed previously, this concept of control is not always evidenced by ownership of voting rights. Thus, control can be obtained contractually by an acquirer absent that party holding any voting ownership interests.

The general rule is that the acquisition date is the date on which the acquirer legally transfers consideration, acquires the assets, and assumes the liabilities of the acquiree. This date, in a relatively straightforward transaction, is referred to as the closing date. Not all transactions are that straightforward, however. All pertinent facts and circumstances are to be considered in determining the acquisition date. The parties to a business combination might, for example, execute a contract that entitles the acquirer to the rights and obligates the acquirer with respect to the obligations of the acquiree prior to the actual date of the closing. Thus, in evaluating economic substance over legal form, the acquirer will have contractually acquired the target on the date it executed the contract.

Example of acquisition date preceding closing date

In 2005, Henan Corporation (HC), a China-based holding company, purchased more than 20 wine brands and specified distribution assets from a French company. In its annual report, HC disclosed that the acquired assets were transferred to a subsidiary of the seller, in which HC received, in connection with the transaction, economic rights (these were structured as "tracker shares" in the holding subsidiary of the seller) with respect to the acquired assets prior to their actual legal transfer to the company. In addition, HC obtained the contractual right to manage the acquired assets prior to their legal transfer to HC, resulting in the acquirer obtaining control of the acquiree on the date before the closing date. Among the reasons HC cited for entering into these arrangements was their commercial desire to obtain the economic benefits associated with owning and operating the acquired assets as soon as possible after funding the purchase price for them.

Until the assets were legally transferred to HC, the transaction was accounted for under SIC 12, *Consolidation—Special-Purpose Entities*, and consequently, HC's interests in the tracker shares of the seller's subsidiary were consolidated since HC was considered the sponsor of that subsidiary. The seller's residual interest in the holding subsidiary was reported in the consolidated financial statements of HC as a noncontrolling interest.

Step 3—Recognize and measure the identifiable tangible and intangible assets acquired and liabilities assumed. In general, the measurement principle is that an acquirer measures the identifiable tangible and intangible assets acquired, and the liabilities assumed, at their fair values on the acquisition date. IFRS 3(R) provides the acquirer with a choice of two methods to measure noncontrolling interests arising in a business combination: (1) to measure the noncontrolling interest at fair value (recognizing the acquired business at fair value), or (2) to measure the noncontrolling interest at the noncontrolling interest's share of the acquiree's net assets.

Exceptions to the recognition and/or measurement principles. IFRS 3(R) provides certain exceptions to its general principles for recognizing assets acquired and liabilities assumed at their acquisition date fair values. These can be summarized as follows:

Nature of exception	*Recognition*	*Measurement*
Contingent liabilities	x	
Income taxes	x	x
Employee benefits	x	x
Indemnification assets	x	x
Reacquired rights		x
Share-based payment awards		x
Assets held for sale		x

Exceptions to the recognition principle.

Contingent liabilities of the acquiree. In accordance with IAS 37, *Provisions, Contingent Liabilities and Contingent Assets,* a contingent liability is defined as

1. A possible obligation that arises from past events and whose existence will be confirmed only by the occurrence or nonoccurrence of one or more uncertain future events not wholly within the control of the entity; or

2. A present obligation that arises from past events but is not recognized because

  a. It is not probable that an outflow of resources embodying economic benefits will be required to settle the obligation, or
  b. The amount of the obligation cannot be measured with sufficient reliability.

Under IFRS 3(R) the acquirer recognizes as of the acquisition date a contingent liability assumed in a business combination if it is a present obligation that arises from past events and its fair value can be measured reliably, regardless of the probability of cash flow arising (contrary to IAS 37). This differs from the current IFRS 3, in that possible obligations of the acquiree were also recognized at fair value. As a result, more careful analysis will be necessary to determine whether or not a past event has occurred and contingent liability of the acquiree is a present obligation, which is a matter of judgment, and can result in fewer contingent liabilities to be recognized. A potential gain or loss to the reporting entity can result from the contingency's resolution.

Exceptions to both the recognition and measurement principles.

Income taxes. The basic principle that applies to income tax accounting in a business combination (carried forward without change by IFRS 3[R]) is that the acquirer is to recognize in accordance with IAS 12, *Income Taxes,* as of the acquisition date, deferred income tax assets or liabilities for the future effects of temporary differences and carryforwards of the acquiree that either

1. Exist on the acquisition date, *or*
2. Are generated by the acquisition itself.

However, IAS 12 has been amended in order to accommodate the new business combinations framework and, consequently, management must carefully assess the reasons for changes in the deferred tax benefits during the measurement period. As a result of these amendments, deferred tax benefits that do not meet the recognition criteria at the date of acquisition are subsequently recognized as follows:

- Acquired deferred tax benefits recognized within the measurement period (within one year after the acquisition date) that result from new information regarding the facts and circumstances existing at the acquisition date, are accounted for as a reduction of goodwill related to this acquisition. If goodwill is reduced to zero, any remaining portion of the adjustment is recorded as a gain from a bargain purchase.
- All other acquired deferred tax benefits realized are recognized in profit or loss.

In addition, IAS 12 has been amended to require any tax benefits arising from the difference between the income tax basis and IFRS carrying amount of goodwill to be accounted for as any other temporary difference at the date of acquisition.

IASB and FASB are currently pursuing a joint project to converge IFRS and US GAAP with respect to accounting for income taxes, and that project will be subject to the Boards' due process procedures that provide constituents an opportunity to provide feedback.

Employee benefits. Liabilities (and assets, if applicable), associated with acquiree employee benefit arrangements are to be recognized and measured in accordance with IAS 19, *Employee Benefits.* Any amendments to a plan (and their related income tax effects) that are made as a result of business combination are treated as a postcombination event and recognized in the acquirer's postcombination financial statements in the periods in which the changes occur.

Indemnification assets. Indemnification provisions are usually included in the voluminous closing documents necessary to effect a business combination. Indemnifications are contractual terms designed to fully or partially protect the acquirer from the potential adverse effects of an unfavorable future resolution of a contingency or uncertainty that exists at the acquisition date (e.g., legal or environmental liabilities, or uncertain tax positions). Frequently the indemnification is structured to protect the acquirer by limiting the maximum amount of postcombination loss that the acquirer would bear in the event of an adverse outcome. A contractual indemnification provision results in the acquirer obtaining, as a part of the acquisition, an indemnification asset and simultaneously assuming a contingent liability of the acquiree.

Exceptions to the measurement principle.

Reacquired rights. An acquirer and acquiree may have engaged in preacquisition business transactions such as leases, licenses, franchises, trade name or technology that resulted in the acquiree paying consideration to the acquirer to use tangible and/or intangible assets of the acquirer in the acquiree's business. The acquisition results in the acquirer reacquiring that right. The acquirer measures the value of a reacquired right recognized as an intangible asset. If the terms of the contract giving rise to a reacquired right are favorable or unfavorable compared with current terms and prices for the same or similar items, a settlement gain or loss will be recognized in profit or loss.

The IFRS accounting requirements after acquisition, on subsequently measuring and accounting for reacquired rights, contingent liabilities, and indemnification assets are discussed later in this chapter in the paragraph entitled "Subsequent measurement and accounting."

Share-based payment awards. In connection with a business combination, the acquirer often replaces acquiree's share-based payment awards with share-based payment awards of the acquirer. Obviously, there are many valid business reasons for the exchange, not the least of which is ensuring smooth transition and integration as well as retention of valued employees. The acquirer measures a liability or an equity instrument related to the replacement of an acquiree's share-based payment awards with the acquirer's share-based awards in accordance with IFRS 2, *Share-Based Payment.*

Assets held for sale. Assets classified as held for sale individually or as part of a disposal group are to be measured at acquisition date fair value less cost to sell consistent with IFRS 5, *Noncurrent Assets Held for Sale and Discontinued Operations* (discussed in detail in Chapter 8). In determining fair value less cost to sell, it is important to differentiate costs to sell from expected future losses associated with the operation of the long-lived asset or disposal group to which it belongs.

In postacquisition periods, long-lived assets classified as held for sale are not to be depreciated or amortized. If the assets are part of a disposal group (discussed in detail in Chapter 8), interest and other expenses related to the liabilities included in the disposal group are to continue to be accrued.

In determining fair value less cost to sell, it is important to differentiate costs to sell from expected future losses associated with the operation of the long-lived asset or disposal group to which it belongs.

Costs to sell are defined as the incremental direct costs necessary to transact a sale. To qualify as costs to sell, the costs must result directly from the sale transaction, incurring them needs to be considered essential to the transaction, and the cost would not have been incurred by the entity absent the decision to sell the assets. Examples of costs to sell include brokerage commissions, legal fees, title transfer fees, and closing costs necessary to effect the transfer of legal title. Costs to sell are expressly not permitted to include any future losses that are expected to result from operating the assets (or disposal group) while it is classified as held for sale. If the expected timing of the sale exceeds one year from the end of the reporting period, which is permitted in limited situations by paragraph 27 of IFRS 5, the costs to sell are to be discounted to their present value.

Should a loss be recognized in subsequent periods due to declines in the fair value less cost to sell, such losses may be restored by future periods' gains only to the extent to which the losses have been recognized cumulatively from the date the asset (or disposal group) was classified as held for sale.

During deliberations on IFRS 3(R) and FAS 141(R), IASB's and FASB's tentative conclusion was that assets held for sale should be measured in the same manner as other acquired assets—that is, at their acquisition-date fair value. If the final standard had contained this provision, however, it would have caused a practical dilemma because, technically, on the day after the acquisition date, the new consolidated reporting entity would be required to apply paragraph 16 of IFRS 5 and write down the newly acquired assets to their fair value *less cost to sell,* resulting in recognizing a loss equal to the selling costs (referred to as a *day 2 loss* because in theory it would be recognized on the day after the acquisition date). This anomaly could have been remedied by incorporating an amendment to IFRS 5 in IFRS 3(R), but IASB believed such an amendment should be made in a separate project in order to provide its constituents an opportunity to submit comments on the proposed change.

The IASB thus deemed this treatment to be a *temporary* exception to the measurement principle under IFRS 3(R). As of mid-2008, however, IASB and FASB had each removed from their respective agendas similar projects that would have, in the case of the IASB standards, amended IFRS 5 to require assets held for sale to be measured at fair value and presumably remove the temporary exception to the measurement principle currently included in IFRS 3(R). Thus this measurement principle exception will not be resolved in the near future.

IFRS guidance on recognizing and measuring the identifiable assets acquired and liabilities assumed is discussed later in this chapter in the paragraph entitled "Additional guidance in applying the acquisition method."

Step 4—Identify assets and liabilities requiring separate accounting. IFRS 3(R) provides a basic recognition principle that, as of the acquisition date, the acquirer is to recognize, separately from goodwill, the identifiable assets acquired (whether tangible or intangible), the liabilities assumed, and, if applicable, any noncontrolling interest (previously referred to as "minority interest") in the acquiree.

In applying the recognition principle to a business combination, the acquirer may recognize assets and liabilities that had not been recognized by the acquiree in its precombination financial statements but which meet the definitions of assets and liabilities in the *Framework for the Preparation and Presentation of Financial Statements* at the acquisition date. IFRS 3(R) continues to permit recognition of acquired intangibles (e.g., patents, customer lists) that would not be granted recognition if they were internally developed.

The pronouncement elaborates on the basic principle by providing that recognition is subject to the following conditions:

1. At the acquisition date, the identifiable assets acquired and liabilities assumed must meet the definitions of assets and liabilities as set forth in *Framework for the Preparation and Presentation of Financial Statements.*[2]
2. The assets and liabilities recognized must be part of the exchange transaction between the acquirer and the acquiree (or the acquiree's former owners) and not part of a separate transaction or transactions.

---

[2] *Assets are defined as "present economic resources: (1) controlled by an entity, through an enforceable right or other means, as a result of past events; and (2) from which future economic benefits are expected to flow to the entity" (IAS 38, Framework). Liabilities are defined as "present unconditional economic obligations, the settlement of which is expected to result in an outflow from the entity of resources embodying economic benefits" (IAS 37, Framework).*

Restructuring or exit activities. Frequently, in a business combination, the acquirer's plans include the future exit of one or more of the activities of the acquiree or the termination or relocation of employees of the acquiree. Since these exit activities are discretionary on the part of the acquirer and the acquirer is not obligated to incur the associated costs, the costs do not meet the definition of a liability and are not recognized at the acquisition date. Rather, the costs will be recognized in postcombination financial statements in accordance with other IFRS, and discussed in detail in Chapter 3.

Boundaries of the exchange transaction. Preexisting relationships and arrangements often exist between the acquirer and acquiree prior to beginning negotiations to enter into a business combination. Furthermore, while conducting the negotiations, the parties may enter into separate business arrangements. In either case, the acquirer is responsible for identifying amounts that are not part of the exchange for the acquiree. Recognition under the acquisition method is only given to the consideration transferred for the acquiree and the assets acquired and liabilities assumed in exchange for that consideration. Other transactions outside the scope of the business combination are to be recognized by applying other relevant IFRS.

The acquirer is to analyze the business combination transaction and other transactions with the acquiree and its former owners to identify the components that comprise the transaction in which the acquirer obtained control over the acquiree. This distinction is important to ensure that each component is accounted for according to its economic substance, irrespective of its legal form.

The imposition of this condition was based on an observation that, upon becoming involved in negotiations for a business combination, the parties may exhibit characteristics of related parties. In so doing, they may be willing to execute agreements designed *primarily* for the benefit of the acquirer of the combined entity that might be designed to achieve a desired financial reporting outcome after the business combination has been consummated. Thus, the imposition of this condition is expected to curb such abuses.

In analyzing a transaction to determine inclusion or exclusion from a business combination, consideration should be given to which of the parties will reap its benefits. If a precombination transaction is entered into by the acquirer, or on behalf of the acquirer, or *primarily* to benefit the acquirer (or to benefit the to-be-combined entity as a whole) rather than for the benefit of the acquiree or its former owners, the transaction most likely would be considered to be a "separate transaction" outside the boundaries of the business combination and for which the acquisition method would not apply.

The acquirer is to consider the following factors, which IASB states "are neither mutually exclusive nor individually conclusive," in determining whether a transaction is a part of the exchange transaction or recognized separately:

1. *Purpose of the transaction*—Typically, there are many parties involved in the management, ownership, operation, and financing of the various entities involved in a business combination transaction. Of course, there are the acquirer and acquiree entities, but there are also owners, directors, management, and various parties acting as agents representing their respective interests. Understanding the motivations of the parties in entering into a particular transaction potentially provides insight into whether or not the transaction is a part of the business combination or a separate transaction.

2. *Initiator of the transaction*—Identifying the party that initiated the transaction may provide insight into whether or not it should be recognized separately from the business combination. IASB believes that if the transaction was initiated by the acquirer, it would be less likely to be part of the business combination and, con-

versely, if it were initiated by the acquiree or its former owners, it would be more likely to be part of the business combination.

3. *Timing of the transaction*—Examining the timing of the transaction may provide insight into whether, for example, the transaction was executed in contemplation of the future business combination in order to provide benefits to the acquirer or the postcombination entity. IASB believes that transactions that take place during the negotiation of the terms of a business combination may be entered into in contemplation of the eventual combination for the purpose of providing future economic benefits *primarily* to the acquirer of the to-be-combined entity and, therefore, should be accounted for separately.

IFRS 3(R) provides the following presumption after analyzing the economic benefits of a precombination transaction:

Primarily *for the benefit of*	*Transaction likely to be*
Acquirer or combined entity	Separate transaction
Acquiree or its former owners	Part of the business combination

IFRS 3(R) provides three examples of separate transactions that are *not* to be included in applying the acquisition method.

1. A settlement of a preexisting relationship between acquirer and acquiree,
2. Compensation to employees or former owners of the acquiree for future services, and
3. Reimbursement to the acquiree or its former owners for paying the acquirer's acquisition-related costs.

The paragraph entitled, "Determining what is part of the business combination transaction," later in this chapter, will discuss related application guidance for these transactions that are separate from the business combination (i.e., not part of the exchange for the acquiree).

In a departure from the previous IFRS 3, acquisition-related costs, under IFRS 3(R), are generally expensed through profit or loss at the time the services are received, which will generally be prior to, or at the date of the acquisition.

Step 5—Classify or designate identifiable assets acquired and liabilities assumed. In order to facilitate the combined entity's future application of IFRS in its postcombination financial statements, management is required to make decisions on the acquisition date relative to the classification or designation of certain items. These decisions are to be based on the contractual terms, economic and other conditions, and the acquirer's operating and accounting policies as they exist *on the acquisition date*. Examples include, but are not limited to, the following:

1. Classification of investments in certain debt and equity securities as trading, available for sale, or held to maturity under IAS 39, *Financial Instruments: Recognition and Measurement,*
2. Designation of a derivative instrument as a hedging instrument under the provisions of IAS 39,
3. Assessment of whether an embedded derivative is to be separated from the host contract under IAS 39.

In applying Step 5, specific exceptions are provided for lease contracts and insurance contracts: classification of a lease contract as either an operating lease or a finance lease in accordance with IAS 17, *Leases,* and classification of a contract as an insurance contract in accordance with IFRS 4, *Insurance Contracts.* Generally, these contracts are to be classified by reference to the contractual terms and other factors that were applicable *at their inception* rather than at the acquisition date. If, however, the contracts were modified subsequent to their inception and those modifications would change their classification at that date, then the accounting for the contracts will be determined by the modification date facts and circumstances. Under these circumstances, the modification date could be the same as the acquisition date.

Step 6—Recognize and measure any noncontrolling interest in the acquiree. The term "noncontrolling interest" replaces the term "minority interest" in referring to the portion of the acquiree, if any, that is not controlled by the parent subsequent to the acquisition. The term "minority interest" became an inadequate descriptor because under IAS 27(R) and SIC 12, *Consolidation—Special-Purpose Entities*, an entity can possess a controlling financial interest in another entity without possessing a majority of the voting interests of that entity. Thus it would be inaccurate, in many cases, to refer to the party that does not possess a controlling financial interest as a "minority" since that party could, in fact, hold a majority of the voting equity of the acquiree.

IFRS 3(R) provides the acquirer with a choice of two methods to measure noncontrolling interests arising in a business combination.

1. To measure the noncontrolling interest at *fair value* (also recognizing the acquired business at fair value), or
2. To measure the noncontrolling interest at the *noncontrolling interest's share of the value of net assets acquired.*

The choice of the method to measure the noncontrolling interest should be made separately for each business combination rather than as an accounting policy. In making this election, management must carefully consider all factors since the two methods may result in significantly different amounts of goodwill as well as different accounting for changes in ownership interest in a subsidiary. One important factor would be the entity's future intent to acquire noncontrolling interest, because of the potential effects on equity when the outstanding noncontrolling interest is acquired. Contrary to the previous practice under the original IFRS 3, the subsequent acquisition of the outstanding noncontrolling interest under IFRS 3(R) would not result in additional goodwill being recognized since the transaction is considered as taking place between shareholders.

Measuring noncontrolling interest at fair value. IFRS 3(R) allows the noncontrolling interest in the acquiree to be measured at fair value at the acquisition date, determined based on market prices for equity shares not held by the acquirer, or, if not available, by using a valuation technique. If the acquirer is not acquiring all of the shares in the acquiree and there is an active market for the remaining outstanding shares in the acquiree, the acquirer may be able to use the market price to measure the fair value of the noncontrolling interest. Otherwise, the acquirer would measure fair value using other valuation techniques. Under this approach, recognized goodwill represents all of the goodwill of the acquired business, not just the acquirer's share, as currently recognized under IFRS 3.

In applying the appropriate valuation technique to determine the fair value of the noncontrolling interest, it is likely that there will be a difference in the fair value per share of the noncontrolling interest and the fair value per share of the controlling interest (the acquirer's interest in the acquiree). This difference is likely to be the inclusion of a control premium in the per-share fair value of the controlling interest or, similarly, what has been referred to as a "noncontrolling interest discount" applicable to the noncontrolling shares. Obviously, an investor would be unwilling to pay the same amount per share for equity shares in an entity that did not convey control of that entity than it would pay for shares that did convey control. For this reason the amount of consideration transferred by an acquirer is not usually indicative of the fair value of the noncontrolling interest, since the consideration transferred by the acquirer often includes a control premium.

Example of measuring noncontrolling interest at fair value

Konin Corporation (KC) acquires a 75% interest in Bartovia Corporation (BC), in exchange for cash of €360,000. BC has 25% of its shares traded on an exchange; KC acquired the 60,000 non–publicly traded shares outstanding, at €6 per share. The fair value of BC's identifiable net assets is €300,000; the shares of BC at the acquisition date are traded at €5 per share.

Under the full fair value approach, the noncontrolling interest is measured based on the trading price of the shares of entity BC at the date control is obtained by KC (€5 per share) and a value of €100,000 is assigned to the 25% noncontrolling interest, indicating that KC has paid a control premium of €60,000 (€360,000 – [€5 × 60,000])

Equity – Noncontrolling interest in net assets (€5 × 20,000) = €100,000

It is important to note from this analysis that, from the perspective of the acquirer, the computation of the acquisition-date fair value of the noncontrolling interest in the acquiree is not computed by simply multiplying the same fair value per share that the acquirer paid for its controlling interest. Such a calculation would have yielded a different result.

Equity – Noncontrolling interest in net assets (€6 × 20,000) = €120,000

If this method had been used, the noncontrolling interest would be overvalued by €20,000 (the difference between €120,000 and €100,000).

Under the fair value approach to measure noncontrolling interest, the acquired business will be recognized at fair value, with the controlling share of total goodwill assigned to the controlling interest and the noncontrolling share allocated to the noncontrolling interest.

Measuring noncontrolling interest at its share of the identifiable net assets of the acquiree, calculated in accordance with IFRS 3(R). Under this approach, noncontrolling interest is measured as the noncontrolling interest's proportionate interest in the value of the identifiable assets and liabilities of the acquiree, determined under current requirements of IFRS 3(R).

Example of measuring noncontrolling interest at share of net assets of the acquiree

Konin Corporation (KC) acquires a 75% interest in Bartovia Corporation (BC), in exchange for cash of €360,000. BC has 25% of its shares traded on an exchange; KC acquired the 60,000 non–publicly traded shares outstanding, at €6 per share. The fair value of BC's identifiable net assets is €300,000; the shares of entity BC at the acquisition date are traded at €5 per share. The consideration transferred indicates that KC has paid a control premium of €60,000 (€360,000 – [€5 × 60,000])

Since KC elects to measure noncontrolling interest in BC at its share of the acquiree's net assets, a value of €75,000 is assigned to the 25% noncontrolling interest.

Equity – Noncontrolling interest in net assets (€300,000 × 25%) = €75,000

Under this approach to measure noncontrolling interest, goodwill recognized will represent only the acquirer's share, as was the practice prior to the effective date of IFRS 3(R)

IAS 27(R) settles the long-controversial issue of how the noncontrolling interest is to be classified in the consolidated statement of financial position by requiring that it be reported within the equity section, separately from the equity of the parent company, and clearly identified with a caption such as "noncontrolling interest in subsidiaries." Should there be noncontrolling interests attributable to more than one consolidated subsidiary, the amounts may be aggregated in the consolidated statement of financial position.

Only equity-classified instruments issued by the subsidiary may be classified as equity in this manner. If, for example, the subsidiary had issued a financial instrument that, under applicable IFRS, was classified as a liability in the subsidiary's financial statements, that instrument would not be classified as a noncontrolling interest since it does not represent an ownership interest.

Step 7—Measure the consideration transferred. In general, consideration transferred by the acquiree is measured at its acquisition-date fair value. Examples of consideration that could be transferred include cash, other assets, a business, a subsidiary of the acquirer, contingent consideration, ordinary or preference equity instruments, options, warrants, and member interests of mutual entities. The aggregate consideration transferred is the sum of the following elements measured at the acquisition date:

1. The fair value of the assets transferred by the acquirer,
2. The fair value of the liabilities incurred by the acquirer to the former owners of the acquiree, and
3. The fair value of the equity interests issued by the acquirer subject to the measurement exception discussed earlier in this chapter for the portion, if applicable, of acquirer share-based payment awards exchanged for awards held by employees of the acquiree that is included in consideration transferred.

To the extent the acquirer transfers consideration in the form of assets or liabilities with carrying amounts that differ from their fair values at the acquisition date, the acquirer is to remeasure them at fair value and recognize a gain or loss on the acquisition date. If, however, the transferred assets or liabilities remain within the consolidated entity postcombination, with the acquirer retaining control of them, no gain or loss is recognized, and the assets or liabilities are measured at their carrying amounts to the acquirer immediately prior to the acquisition date. This situation can occur, for example, when the acquirer transfers assets or liabilities to the entity being acquired rather than to its former owners.

The structure of the transaction may involve the exchange of equity interests between the acquirer and either the acquiree or the acquiree's former owners. If the acquisition-date fair value of the acquiree's equity interests is more reliably measurable than the equity interests of the acquirer, the fair value of the acquiree's equity interests is to be used to measure the consideration transferred.

When a business combination is effected without transferring consideration, for example by contract alone, the acquisition method of accounting also applies to those combinations. Examples of such combinations include

- The acquiree repurchases a sufficient number of its own shares for an existing investor (the acquirer) to obtain control
- Minority veto rights lapse that kept the acquirer, holding the majority voting rights, from controlling an acquiree
- The acquirer and acquiree agree to combine their businesses by contract alone (e.g., a stapling arrangement or dual-listed corporation)

In a business combination achieved by contract alone, the entities involved are not under common control and the combination does not involve one of the combining entities obtaining an ownership interest in another combining entity. Consequently, there is a 100% noncontrolling interest in the acquiree's net assets since the acquirer must contribute the fair value of the acquiree's assets and liabilities to the owners of the acquiree. Depending on the option elected to measure noncontrolling interest (at fair value or share of the acquiree's net assets), this may result in recognizing goodwill allocated only to the noncontrolling interest or recognizing no goodwill at all.

Contingent consideration. In many business combinations, the acquisition price is not completely fixed at the time of the exchange, but is instead dependent on the outcome of future events. There are two major types of future events that might commonly be used to modify the acquisition price: the performance of the acquired entity (acquiree), and the market value of the consideration initially given for the acquisition.

The most frequently encountered contingency involves the postacquisition performance of the acquired entity or operations. The contractual agreement dealing with this is often referred to as an "earn out" provision. It typically calls for additional payments to be made to the former owners of the acquiree if defined revenue or earnings thresholds are met or exceeded. These may extend for several years after the acquisition date, and may define varying thresholds for different years. For example, if the acquiree, during its final pretransaction year generated revenues of €4 million, there might be additional sums due if the acquired operations produced €4.5 million or greater revenues in year one after the acquisition, €5 million or greater in year two, and €6 million in year three.

Contingent consideration arrangements in connection with business combinations can be structured in many different ways and can result in the recognition of either assets or liabilities under IFRS 3(R). An acquirer may agree to transfer (or receive) cash, additional equity instruments, or other assets to (or from) former owners of an acquiree after the acquisition date, if certain specified events occur in the future. In either case, the acquirer is to include contingent assets and liabilities as part of the consideration transferred, measured at acquisition-date fair value, which represents a significant change from current practice under IFRS 3 (the previous standard). In accordance with IFRS 3, contingent consideration can only be recognized when the contingency is probable and can be reliably measured.

If the contingent consideration includes a future payment obligation, that obligation is to be classified as either a liability or equity under the provisions of

- Paragraph 11 of IAS 32, *Financial Instrument: Presentation,* or
- Other applicable IFRS.

The acquirer is to carefully consider information obtained subsequent to the acquisition-date measurement of contingent consideration. Additional information obtained during the measurement period that relates to the facts and circumstances that existed at the acquisition date result in measurement period adjustments to the recognized amount of contingent consideration and a corresponding adjustment to goodwill or gain from bargain purchase. The IFRS accounting requirements on subsequently measuring and accounting for contingent consideration in the postcombination periods is discussed later in this chapter in the paragraph entitled, "Subsequent measurement and accounting."

Step 8—Recognize and measure goodwill or gain from a bargain purchase. The last step in applying the acquisition method is the measurement of goodwill or a gain from a bargain purchase. Goodwill represents an intangible that is not specifically identifiable. It results from situations when the amount the acquirer is willing to pay to obtain its controlling interest exceeds the aggregate recognized values of the net assets acquired measured following the principles of IFRS 3(R). It arises largely from the synergies and economies of scale expected from combining the operations of the acquirer and acquiree. Goodwill's elusive nature as an unidentifiable, residual asset means that it cannot be measured directly but rather can only be measured by reference to the other amounts measured as a part of the business combination. In accordance with IFRS 3(R) management must select, for each acquisition, the option to measure the noncontrolling interest, and consequently the amount recognized as goodwill (or gain on a bargain purchase) will depend on whether noncontrolling interest is measured at fair value (option 1), or at the noncontrolling interest's share of the acquiree's net assets (option 2).

GW	=	Goodwill
GBP	=	Gain from a bargain purchase
NI	=	Noncontrolling interest in the acquiree, if any, measured at fair value (option 1); or as the noncontrolling interest's share of the acquiree's net assets (option 2)
CT	=	Consideration transferred, generally measured at acquisition-date fair value
PE	=	Fair value of the acquirer's previously held interest in the acquiree if the acquisition was achieved in stages
NA	=	Net assets acquired—consisting of the acquisition-date fair values (or other amounts recognized under the requirements of IFRS 3[R] as described in the chapter) of the identifiable assets acquired and liabilities assumed.
GW (or GBP)	=	(CT + NI + PE) – NA

Thus, when application of the formula yields an excess of the acquisition-date fair value of the consideration transferred plus the amount of any noncontrolling interest and plus fair value of the acquirer's previously held equity interest over the net assets acquired, this means that the acquirer has paid a premium for the acquisition and that premium is characterized as goodwill.

When the opposite is true, that is, when the formula yields a negative result, a gain from a bargain purchase (sometimes referred to as negative goodwill) is recognized, since the acquirer has, in fact, obtained a bargain purchase as the value the acquirer obtained in the exchange exceeded the fair value of what it surrendered.

In a business combination in which no consideration is transferred, the acquirer is to use one or more valuation techniques to measure the acquisition-date fair value of its equity interest in the acquiree and substitute that measurement in the formula for "CT," the consideration transferred. The techniques selected require the availability of sufficient data to properly apply them and are to be appropriate for the circumstances. If more than one technique is used, management of the acquirer is to evaluate the results of applying the techniques including the extent of data available and how relevant and reliable the inputs (assumptions) used are. Guidance on the use of valuation techniques is provided in Discussion Paper, *Fair Value Measurements*, presented in Chapter 1, Appendix F.

Example of recognizing goodwill—noncontrolling interest measured at fair value

Konin Corporation (KC) acquires a 75% interest in Danube Corporation (DC), in exchange for cash of €350,000. DC has 25% of its shares traded on an exchange; KC acquired the 60,000 non–publicly traded shares outstanding. The fair value of DC's identifiable net assets is €300,000; the shares of DC at the acquisition date are traded at €5 per share. The consideration transferred indicates that KC has paid a control premium of €50,000 (€350,000 – [€5 × 60,000])

Management elects the option to measure noncontrolling interest at fair value and a value of €100,000 is assigned to the 25% noncontrolling interest. The amount of goodwill accruing to the controlling interest is €125,000, which is equal to the consideration transferred, €350,000, for the controlling interest minus the controlling interest's share in the fair value of the identifiable net assets acquired, €225,000 (€300,000 × 75%). The amount of goodwill accruing to the noncontrolling interest is €25,000 (€150,000 total goodwill less €125,000 allocated to the controlling interest). The acquirer (KC) would record its acquisition of DC in its consolidated financial statement as follows:

Identifiable net assets acquired, at fair value	300,000	
Goodwill (€450,000 – €300,000)	150,000	
Equity—Noncontrolling interest		100,000
Cash		350,000

Under the approach to measure noncontrolling interest at fair value, the acquired business is recognized at €450,000 (€350,000 + 100,000) fair value and full goodwill (€150,000 = €450,000 – €300,000) is recognized. The amount of goodwill associated with the controlling interest is €125,000 (€150,000 × 75%), and the amount of goodwill associated with noncontrolling interest is €25,000 (€150,000 × 25%).

Example of recognizing goodwill—noncontrolling interest measured at the noncontrolling interest's proportionate share of the acquiree's net assets

Konin Corporation (KC) acquires a 75% interest in Donna Corporation (DC), in exchange for cash of €350,000. DC has 25% of its shares traded on an exchange; KC acquired the 60,000 non–publicly traded shares outstanding. The fair value of DC's identifiable net assets is €300,000; the shares of DC at the acquisition date are traded at €5 per share. The consideration transferred indicates that KC has paid a control premium of €50,000 (€350,000 – [€5 × 60,000])

Management elects the option to measure noncontrolling interest at its share of the acquiree's net assets and a value assigned to the noncontrolling interest is €75,000 (€300,000 × 25%).

The amount of goodwill recognized is only €125,000, the accruing to the controlling interest is €125,000, which is equal to the consideration transferred €350,000 for the controlling interest minus the controlling interest's share in the fair value of the identifiable net assets acquired €225,000 (€300,000 × 75%). No goodwill is assigned to the noncontrolling interest. The acquirer (KC) would record its acquisition of DC in its consolidated financial statement as follows.

Identifiable net assets acquired, at fair value	300,000	
Goodwill (€450,000 – 300,000)	125,000	
Equity—Noncontrolling interest		75,000
Cash		350,000

Under the approach to measure noncontrolling interest at the proportionate share of the acquiree's net assets, goodwill recognized (€125,000) represents only the acquirer's share of the goodwill, as it is recognized in the current practice.

Bargain purchases. A bargain purchase occurs when the value of net assets acquired is in excess of the acquisition-date fair value of the consideration transferred plus the amount of any noncontrolling interest and plus fair value of the acquirer's previously held equity interest. This can happen, for example, in a business combination that is a forced sale, when the seller is acting under compulsion.

Under IFRS 3(R), when a bargain purchase occurs, a gain on acquisition is recognized in the profit or loss at the acquisition date, as part of income from continuing operations.

Before recognizing a gain on a bargain purchase, IASB prescribed a verification protocol for management to follow given the complexity of the computation involved. If the computation initially yields a bargain purchase, management of the acquirer is to perform the following procedures before recognizing a gain on the bargain purchase:

1. Perform a completeness review of the identifiable tangible and intangible assets acquired and liabilities assumed to reassess whether all such items have been correctly identified. If any omissions are found, recognize the assets and liabilities that had been omitted.
2. Perform a review of the procedures used to measure all of the following items. The objective of the review is to ensure that the acquisition-date measurements appropriately considered all available information available at the acquisition date.

   a. Identifiable assets acquired
   b. Liabilities assumed
   c. Consideration transferred
   d. Noncontrolling interest in the acquiree, if applicable

e. Acquirer's previously held equity interest in the acquiree for a business combination achieved in stages

Example of a bargain purchase

On January 1, 2009, Konin Corporation (KC) acquires 75% of the equity interests of Laska Corporation (LC), a private entity, in exchange for cash of €250,000. The former owners of LC were forced to sell their investments within a short period of time and unable to market LC to multiple potential buyers in the marketplace. The management of KC initially measures at the acquisition date in accordance with IFRS 3(R) the separately recognizable identifiable assets acquired at €500,000 and liabilities at €100,000. KC engages an independent valuation specialist who determines that the fair value of the 25% noncontrolling interest in LC is €110,000.

Since the amount of KC identifiable net assets (€400,000 calculated as €500,000 – €100,000) exceeds the fair value of the consideration transferred (€250,000) plus the fair value of the noncontrolling interest (€110,000), the acquisition initially results in a bargain purchase. In accordance with the requirements of IFRS 3(R), KC must perform a review to ensure whether all assets, liabilities, consideration transferred, and noncontrolling interest have been correctly measured. KC concludes that the procedures and resulting measures are correct.

The acquirer (KC) recognizes the gain on its acquisition of the 75% interest as follows:

Identifiable net assets acquired, at fair value		400,000
Less: Fair value of the consideration transferred for 75% interest in LC Plus:	250,000	
Fair value of noncontrolling interest in LC	110,000	360,000
Gain on bargain purchase		40,000

The acquirer (KC) would record its acquisition of LC in its consolidated financial statements as follows:

Identifiable net assets acquired	400,000	
Cash		250,000
Gain on the bargain purchase		40,000
Equity—Noncontrolling interest in LC		110,000

If the acquirer (KC) elects to measure the noncontrolling interest in LC on the basis of its proportionate interest in the identifiable net assets of the acquiree, the recognized amount of the noncontrolling interest would be €100,000 (€400,000 × 25%); the gain on the bargain purchase would be €50,000 (€400,000 – [€250,000 + €100,000]).

Measurement period. More frequently than not, management of the acquirer does not obtain all of the relevant information needed to complete the acquisition-date measurements in time for the issuance of the first set of interim or annual financial statements subsequent to the business combination. If the initial accounting for the business combination has not been completed by that time, the acquirer is to report provisional amounts in the consolidated financial statements for any items for which the accounting is incomplete. IFRS 3(R) provides for a "measurement period" during which any adjustments to the provisional amounts recognized at the acquisition date are to be retrospectively adjusted to reflect new information that management obtains regarding facts and circumstances existing as of the acquisition date. Information that has a bearing on this determination must not relate to postacquisition events or circumstances. The information is to be analyzed to determine whether, if it had been known at the acquisition date, it would have affected the measurement of the amounts recognized as of that date.

In evaluating whether new information obtained is suitable for the purpose of adjusting provisional amounts, management of the acquirer is to consider all relevant factors. Critical in this evaluation is the determination of whether the information relates to facts and circumstances as they existed at the acquisition date or instead, the information results from events occurring after the acquisition date. Relevant factors include

1. The timing of the receipt of the additional information, *and*
2. Whether management of the acquirer can identify a reason that a change is warranted to the provisional amounts.

Obviously, information received shortly after the acquisition date has a higher likelihood of relevance to acquisition-date circumstances than information received months later. However, the measurement period should not exceed one year from the acquisition date.

Example of consideration of new information obtained during the measurement period

Konin Corporation (KC) acquired Automotive Industries, Inc.. (AI) on September 30, 2008. KC hired independent valuation specialists to determine valuation for an asset group acquired in the combination, but the valuation was not complete by the time KC authorized for issue its 2008 consolidated financial statements. As a result, KC assigned a provisional fair value of €40 million to an asset group acquired, consisting of a factory and related machinery that manufactures engines used in large trucks and sport utility vehicles (SUVs).

As of the acquisition date, the average cost of gasoline in the markets served by the customers of AI was €4.30 per gallon. For the first six months subsequent to the acquisition, the per-gallon price of gasoline was relatively stable and only fluctuated slightly up or down on any given day. Upon further analysis, management was able to determine that, during that six-month period, the production levels of the asset group and related order backlog did not vary substantially from the acquisition date.

In April 2009, however, due to an accident on April 3, 2009, at a large refinery, the average cost per gallon skyrocketed to more than €6.00. As a result of this huge spike in the price of fuel, AI's largest customers either canceled orders or sharply curtailed the number of engines they had previously ordered.

Scenario 1: On March 31, 2009, management of KC received the independent valuation, which estimated the assets' acquisition-date fair value as €30 million. Given the fact that management was unable to identify any changes that occurred during the measurement period that would have accounted for a change in the acquisition-date fair value of the asset group, management determines that it will retrospectively reduce the provisional fair value assigned to the asset group to €30 million.

In its financial statements for the year ended December 31, 2009, KC retrospectively adjust the 2008 prior year information as follows:

1. The carrying amount of assets is decreased by €10,600. That adjustment is measured as the fair value adjustment at the acquisition date of €10,000 plus the reduced depreciation that would have been recognized if the asset's fair value at the acquisition date had been recognized from that date (€600 for three months' depreciation)
2. The carrying amount of goodwill as of December 31, 2008 is increased by €10,000.
3. Depreciation expense for 2008 is decreased by €600.

Scenario 2: KC has not received the independent valuation of assets until May 2009. On April 15, 2009, management of KC signed a sales agreement with Jonan International (JI) to sell the asset group for €30 million. Given the intervening events that affected the price of fuel and the demand for AI's products, management determines that the €10 million decline in the fair value of the asset group from the provisional fair value it was originally assigned resulted from those intervening changes and, consequently does not adjust the provisional fair value assigned to the asset group at the acquisition date.

In addition to adjustments to provisional amounts recognized, the acquirer may determine during the measurement period that it omitted recognition of additional assets or liabilities that existed at the acquisition date. During the measurement period, any such assets or liabilities identified are also to be recognized and measured on a retrospective basis.

In determining adjustments to the provisional amounts assigned to assets and liabilities, management should be alert for interrelationships between recognized assets and liabilities.

For example, new information that management obtains that results in an adjustment to the provisional amount assigned to a liability for which the acquiree carries insurance could also result in an adjustment, in whole or in part, to a provisional amount recognized as an asset representing the claim receivable from the insurance carrier. In addition, as discussed in this chapter and Chapter 15, changes in provisional amounts assigned to assets and liabilities frequently will also affect temporary differences between the items' income tax basis and IFRS carrying amount, which in turn will affect the computation of deferred income assets and liabilities.

Adjustments to the provisional amounts that are made during the measurement period are recognized retrospectively as if the accounting for the business combination had actually been completed as of the acquisition date. This will result in the revision of comparative information included in the financial statements for prior periods including any necessary adjustments to depreciation, amortization, or other effects on profit or loss or other comprehensive income related to the adjustments.

The measurement period ends on the earlier of

1. The date management of the acquirer receives the information it seeks regarding facts and circumstances as they existed at the acquisition date or learns that it will be unable to obtain any additional information, *or*
2. One year after the acquisition date.

After the end of the measurement period, the only revisions that are permitted to be made to the initial acquisition-date accounting for the business combination are restatements for corrections of prior period errors in accordance with IAS 8, *Accounting Policies, Changes in Accounting Estimates and Errors,* discussed in detail in Chapter 3.

Acquisition-related costs. In a departure from the standard IFRS 3, acquisition-related costs are, under IFRS 3(R), generally to be charged to expense of the period in which the costs are incurred and the related services received. Examples of these costs include

Accounting fees	Internal acquisitions department
Advisory fees	Legal fees
Consulting fees	Other professional fees
Finder's fees	Valuation fees

Under the previous IFRS 3, such costs are included in the cost of the business combination and included in the calculation of goodwill. In accordance with the revised standard, since such costs are not part of the fair value exchange between the buyer and the seller for the acquired business, they are accounted for separately, as operating costs in the period in which services are received. This departure from current practice (under IFRS 3) may significantly affect the operating results reported for the period of any acquisition.

IFRS 3(R) makes an exception to the general rule of charging acquisition-related costs against profit with respect to costs to register and issue equity or debt securities. These costs are to be recognized in accordance with IAS 32 and IAS 39. Share issuance costs are normally charged against the gross proceeds of the issuance (see Chapter 17). Debt issuance costs are treated as a reduction of the amount borrowed or as an expense of the period in which they are incurred; however, some reporting entities have treated these costs as deferred charges and amortized them against profit during the term of the debt (see Chapter 13).

Postcombination measurement and accounting. In general, in accordance with IFRS 3(R) in postcombination periods an acquirer should measure and account for assets acquired, liabilities assumed or incurred and equity instruments issued in a business combination on the basis consistent with other applicable IFRS for those items, which include

- IAS 38 prescribes the accounting for identifiable intangible assets acquired in a business combination
- IAS 36 provides guidance on recognizing impairment losses
- IFRS 4 prescribes accounting for an insurance contract acquired in a business combination
- IAS 12 prescribes the postcombination accounting for deferred tax assets and liabilities acquired in a business combination.
- IFRS 2 provides guidance on subsequent measurement and accounting for share-based payment awards
- IAS 27 prescribes accounting for changes in a parent's ownership interest in a subsidiary after control is obtained.

IFRS 3(R) provides special guidance on accounting for the following items arising in a business combination:

1. Reacquired rights
2. Contingent liabilities recognized as of the acquisition date
3. Indemnification assets, and
4. Contingent consideration

After acquisition, a *reacquired right* recognized as an intangible asset is amortized over the remaining contractual term, without taking into consideration potential renewal periods. If an acquirer subsequently sells a reacquired right to a third party, the carrying amount of the right should be included in calculating the gain or loss on the sale.

In postcombination periods, until the liability is settled, cancelled or expires, the acquirer measures a *contingent liability* recognized as of the acquisition date at the higher of

1. The amount that would be recognized in accordance with IAS 37, and
2. The amount initially recognized, less, if appropriate, cumulative amortization recognized in accordance with IAS 18, *Revenue.*

This requirement would not apply to contracts accounted for under the provisions of IAS 39. In accordance with this standard, the financial liability is to be measured at fair value at each reporting date, with changes in value recognized either in profit or loss or in other comprehensive income in accordance with IAS 39.

At each reporting date subsequent to the acquisition date, the acquirer should measure an **indemnification asset** recognized as part of the business combination using the same basis as the indemnified item, subject to any limitations imposed contractually on the amount of the indemnification. If an indemnification asset is not subsequently measured at fair value (because to do so would be inconsistent with the basis used to measure the indemnified item), management is to assess the collectibility of the asset. Any changes in the measurement of the asset (and the related liability) are recognized in profit or loss.

The acquirer needs to carefully consider information obtained subsequent to the acquisition-date measurement of *contingent consideration.* Some changes in the fair value of contingent consideration result from additional information obtained during the measurement period that relates to the facts and circumstances that existed at the acquisition date. Such changes are measurement period adjustments to the recognized amount of contingent consideration and a corresponding adjustment to goodwill or gain from bargain purchase. However, changes that result from events occurring after the acquisition date, such as meeting a specified earnings target, reaching a specified share price, or reaching an agreed-upon milestone on a research and development project, do not constitute measurement period adjustments, and no longer result in changes to goodwill. This approach represents another significant change from current practice under IFRS 3 (previous version of IFRS 3[R]).

Changes in the fair value of contingent consideration that do not result from measurement period adjustments are to be accounted for as follows:

1. If the contingent consideration is classified as equity, it is not to be remeasured, and subsequent settlement of the contingency is to be reflected within equity.
2. If the contingent consideration is classified as an asset or liability that is a financial instrument within the scope of IAS 39, it is to be remeasured at fair value at each reporting date, with changes in value recognized either in profit or loss or in other comprehensive income in accordance with IAS 39.
3. If the contingent consideration is classified as an asset or liability that is not a financial instrument within the scope of IAS 39, it is to be measured in accordance with IAS 37 or other applicable standards, with changes in value recognized in profit or loss.

Since subsequent measurement and accounting for contingent consideration represents significant change from current practice under IFRS 3, it is important that the management provides reliable estimates of the acquisition-date fair values. The potential impact of post-acquisition remeasurements on subsequent profit or loss as well as on debt covenants or management remuneration should be analyzed at the date of acquisition.

IFRS guidance on recognizing and measuring reacquired rights, contingent liabilities and indemnification assets on the acquisition date was discussed earlier in this chapter in the paragraph entitled, "Accounting for Business Combinations under the Acquisition Method, Step 5–Classify or designate the identifiable assets acquired and liabilities assumed"; and guidance on contingent consideration in "Step 7– Measure the consideration transferred."

Disclosure Requirements

The acquirer should disclose information that enables users of its financial statements to evaluate

-   The nature as well as financial effect of a business combination that occurs either (1) during the current period; or (2) after the end of the reporting period but before the financial statements are authorized to issue.
-   The financial effects of adjustments recognized in the current reporting period that relate to business combinations that occurred during (1) the current period; or (2) previous reporting periods.

The disclosure requirements of the new standards are quite extensive and, for the reader's convenience, are presented in detail in the disclosure checklist in Appendix A to this publication.

Additional guidance in applying the acquisition method. Due to the complexity of many business combinations and the varying structures used to effect them, IASB provided supplemental guidance to aid practitioners in applying the standard.

Recognizing and measuring the identifiable assets acquired and liabilities assumed.

The following guidance is to be followed in applying the recognition and measurement principles (subject to certain specified exceptions).

Assets with uncertain cash flows (valuation allowances). Since fair value measurements take into account the effects of uncertainty regarding the amounts and timing of future cash flows, the acquirer is not to recognize a separate valuation allowance for assets subject to such uncertainties (e.g., acquired receivables, including loans). This may be a departure from current practice, especially for entities operating in the financial services industry.

Assets subject to operating leases in which the acquiree is the lessee. Irrespective of whether the acquiree is the lessee or lessor, the acquirer is to evaluate, as of the acquisition date, each of the acquiree's operating leases to determine whether its terms are favorable or unfavorable compared to the market terms of leases of identical or similar items. If the acquiree is the lessee and the lease terms are favorable, the acquirer is to recognize an intangible asset; if the lease terms are unfavorable, the acquirer is to recognize a liability.

Even when the lease is considered to be at market terms, there nevertheless may be an identifiable intangible associated with it. This would be the case if market participants would be willing to pay to obtain it (i.e., to obtain the rights and privileges associated with it). Examples of this situation are leases for favorable positioned airport gates, or prime retail space in an economically favorable location. If, from the perspective of marketplace participants, acquiring the lease would entitle them to future economic benefits that qualify as identifiable intangible assets (discussed later in this chapter), the acquirer would recognize, separately from goodwill, the associated identifiable intangible asset.

Assets subject to operating leases in which the acquiree is the lessor. The fair value of assets owned by the acquiree that are subject to operating leases with the acquiree being the lessor are to be measured separately from the underlying lease to which they are subject. Consequently, the acquirer does not recognize a separate asset or liability if the terms of an operating lease are either favorable or unfavorable when compared with market terms, as required for leases in which the acquiree is the lessee.

Assets the acquirer plans to idle or to use in a way that is different from the way other market participants would use them. If the acquirer intends, for competitive or other business reasons, to idle an acquired asset (e.g., a research and development intangible asset) or use it in a manner that is different from the manner in which other market participants would use it, the acquirer is still required to initially measure the asset at fair value determined in accordance with its use by other market participants.

Identifiable intangibles to be recognized separately from goodwill. Intangible assets acquired in a business combination are to be recognized separately from goodwill if they meet either of two criteria to be considered *identifiable.* These criteria are

1. *Separability criterion*—The intangible asset is capable of being separated or divided from the entity that holds it, and sold, transferred, licensed, rented, or exchanged, regardless of the acquirer's intent to do so. An intangible asset meets this criterion even if its transfer would not be alone, but instead would be accompanied or bundled with a related contract, other identifiable asset, or a liability.
2. *Legal/contractual criterion*—The intangible asset results from contractual or other legal rights. An intangible asset meets this criterion even if the rights are not transferable or separable from the acquiree or from other rights and obligations of the acquiree.

Illustrative Examples to IFRS 3(R) carry forward from the original IFRS 3 a lengthy, though not exhaustive, listing of intangible assets that FASB believes have characteristics that meet one of these two criteria (legal/contractual or separability). A logical approach in practice would be for the acquirer to first consider whether the intangibles specifically included on the IASB list are applicable to the particular acquiree and then to consider whether there may be other unlisted intangibles included in the acquisition that meet one or both of the criteria for separate recognition.

IFRS 3(R) organizes groups of identifiable intangibles into categories related to or based on

1. Marketing
2. Customers or clients
3. Artistic works
4. Contractual
5. Technological

These categorizations are somewhat arbitrary. Consequently, some of the items listed could fall into more than one of the categories. Examples of identifiable intangibles included in each of the categories are as follows:

Marketing-related intangible assets.

1. *Trademarks, service marks, trade names, collective marks, certification marks.* A trademark represents the right to use a name, word, logo, or symbol that differentiates a product from products of other entities. A service mark is the equivalent of a trademark for a service offering instead of a product. A collective mark is used to identify products or services offered by members affiliated with each other. A certification mark is used to designate a particular attribute of a product or service such as its geographic source (e.g., Columbian coffee or Italian olive oil) or the standards under which it was produced (e.g., ISO 9000 Certified).

2. *Trade dress.* The overall appearance and image (unique color, shape, or package design) of a product.

3. *Newspaper mastheads.* The unique appearance of the title page of a newspaper or other periodical.

4. *Internet domain names.* The unique name that identifies an address on the Internet. Domain names must be registered with an Internet registry and are renewable.

5. *Noncompetition agreements.* Rights to assurances that companies or individuals will refrain from conducting similar businesses or selling to specific customers for an agreed-upon period of time.

Customer-related intangible assets.

1. *Customer lists.* Names, contact information, order histories, and other information about a company's customers, that a third party, such as a competitor or a telemarketing firm would want to use in its own business.

2. *Order or production backlogs.* Unfilled sales orders for goods and services in amounts that exceed the quantity of finished goods and work-in-process on hand for filling the orders.

3. *Customer contracts and related customer relationships.* When a company's relationships with its customers arise primarily through contracts and are of value to buyers who can "step into the shoes" of the sellers and assume their remaining rights and duties under the contracts, and which hold the promise that the customers will place future orders with the entity or relationships between entities and their customers for which

   a. The entities have information about the customers and have regular contacts with the customers, and

   b. The customers have the ability to make direct contact with the entity.

4. *Noncontractual customer relationships.* Customer relationships that arise through means such as regular contacts by sales or service representatives, the value of which are derived from the prospect of the customers placing future orders with the entity.

Artistic-related intangible assets.

1. *Plays, operas, ballets.*
2. *Books, magazines, newspapers, and other literary works.*
3. *Musical works such as compositions, song lyrics, and advertising jingles.*
4. *Pictures and photographs.*
5. *Video and audiovisual material including motion pictures or films, music videos and television programs.*

Contract-based intangible assets.

1. *License, royalty, standstill agreements.* License agreements represent the right, on the part of the licensee, to access or use property that is owned by the licensor for a specified period of time at an agreed-upon price. A royalty agreement entitles its holder to a contractually agreed-upon portion of the income earned from the sale or license of a work covered by patent or copyright. A standstill agreement conveys assurances that a company or individual will refrain from engaging in certain activities for specified periods of time.

2. *Advertising, construction, management, service or supply contracts.* For example a contract with a newspaper, broadcaster, or Internet site to provide specified advertising services to the acquiree.

3. *Lease agreements* (irrespective of whether the acquiree is the lessee or lessor). A contract granting use or occupation of property during a specified period in exchange for a specified rent.

4. *Construction permits.* Rights to build a specified structure at a specified location.

5. *Construction contracts.* Rights to become the contractor responsible for completing a construction project and benefit from the profits it produces, subject to the remaining obligations associated with performance (including any past-due payments to suppliers and/or subcontractors).

6. *Construction management, service, or supply contracts.* Rights to manage a construction project for a fee, procure specified services at a specified fee, or purchase specified products at contractually agreed-upon prices.

7. *Broadcast rights.* Legal permission to transmit electronic signals using specified bandwidth in the radio frequency spectrum, granted by the operation of communication laws.

8. *Franchise rights.* Legal rights to engage in a trade-named business, to sell a trade-marked good, or to sell a service-marked service in a particular geographic area.

9. *Operating rights.* Permits to operate in a certain manner, such as those granted to a carrier to transport specified commodities.

10. *Use rights, such as drilling, water, air, timber cutting and route authorities.* Permits to use specified land, property, or air space in a particular manner, such as the right to cut timber, expel emissions, or to land airplanes at specified gates at an airport.

11. *Servicing contracts.* The contractual right to service a loan. Servicing entails activities such as collecting principal and interest payments from the borrower, maintaining escrow accounts, paying taxes and insurance premiums when due, and pursuing collection of delinquent payments.

12. *Employment contract.* The right to succeed the acquiree as the employer under a formal contract to obtain an employee's services in exchange for fulfilling the employer's remaining duties, such as payment of salaries and benefits, as specified by the contract.

Technology-based intangible assets.

1. *Patented or copyrighted software.* Computer software source code, program specifications, procedures, and associated documentation that is legally protected by patent or copyright.

2. *Computer software and mask works.* Software permanently stored on a read-only memory chip as a series of stencils or integrated circuitry. Mask works may be provided statutory protection in some countries.

3. *Unpatented technology.* Access to knowledge about the proprietary processes and workflows followed by the acquiree to accomplish desired business results.

4. *Databases, including title plants.* Databases are collections of information generally stored digitally in an organized manner. A database can be protected by copyright (e.g., the database contained on the CD-ROM version of this publication). Many databases, however, represent information accumulated as a natural by-product of a company conducting its normal operating activities. Examples of these databases are plentiful and include title plants, scientific data, and credit histories. Title plants (discussed in detail in Chapter 25) represent historical records with respect to real estate parcels in a specified geographic location.

5. *Trade secrets.* Trade secrets are proprietary, confidential information, such as a formula, process, or recipe.

One commonly cited intangible asset deliberately omitted by the IASB from its list of identifiable intangibles is an "assembled workforce." IASB decided that the replacement cost technique that is often used to measure the fair value of an assembled workforce does not faithfully represent the fair value of the intellectual capital acquired. It was thus decided that an exception to the recognition criteria would be made, and that the fair value of an acquired assembled workforce would remain part of goodwill.

Research and development assets. IFRS 3(R) requires the acquirer to recognize and measure all tangible and intangible assets used in research and development (R&D) activities acquired individually or in a group of assets as part of the business combination. This prescribed treatment is to be followed even if the assets are judged to have no alternative future use. These assets are to be measured at their acquisition-date fair values. Fair value measurements are to be made based on the assumptions that would be made by market participants in pricing the asset. Assets that the acquirer does not intend to use or intends to use in a manner that is different from the manner other market participants would use them are, nevertheless, required to be measured at fair value.

Intangible R&D assets. Upon initial recognition, the *intangible* R&D assets are to be classified as indefinite-lived assets until the related R&D efforts are either completed or abandoned. In the reporting periods during which the R&D intangible assets are classified as indefinite-lived, they are not to be amortized. Instead, they are to be tested for impairment in the same manner as other indefinite-lived intangibles. Upon completion or abandonment of the related R&D efforts, management is to determine the remaining useful life of the intangibles and amortize them accordingly. In applying these requirements, assets that are temporarily idled are not to be considered abandoned.

Tangible R&D assets. Tangible R&D assets acquired in a business combination are to be accounted for according to their nature (e.g., supplies, inventory, depreciable assets, etc.).

Determining what is part of the business combination transaction. Transactions entered into by or on behalf of the acquirer or primarily for the benefit of the acquirer or the combined entity, rather than primarily for the benefit of the acquiree (or its former owners), before the combination, are likely to be separate transactions, not accounted for under the acquisition method. In applying the acquisition method to account for a business combination, the acquirer must recognize only the consideration transferred for the acquiree and the assets acquired and liabilities assumed in the exchange for the acquiree. IFRS 3(R) provides the following examples of separate transactions that are not to be included in applying the acquisition method:

1. A transaction that in effect settles preexisting relationships between the acquirer and acquiree,

2. A transaction that remunerates employees or former owners of the acquiree for future services, and

3.   A transaction that reimburses the acquiree or its former owners for paying the acquirer's acquisition-related costs.

The amount of the gain or loss measured as a result of settling a preexisting relationship will, of course, depend on whether the acquirer had previously recognized related assets or liabilities with respect to that relationship.

Example of settlement of preexisting contractual supplier relationship; contract unfavorable to acquirer

Konin Corporation (KC) and Banham Corporation (BC) are parties to a 3-year supply contract that contains the following provisions:

1.   KC is required to annually purchase 3,000 flat-panel displays from BC at a fixed price of €400 per unit for an aggregate purchase price of €1,200,000 for each of the three years.
2.   KC is required to pay BC the annual €1,200,000 irrespective of whether it takes delivery of all 3,000 units and the required payment is nonrefundable.
3.   The contract contains a penalty provision that would permit KC to cancel it at the end of the second year for a lump-sum payment of €500,000.
4.   In each of the first two years of the contract, KC took delivery of the full 3,000 units.

At December 31, 2008, the supply contract was unfavorable to KC because KC would be able to purchase flat-panel displays with similar specifications and of similar quality from another supplier for €350 per unit. Therefore, in accordance with ARB 43, KC accrued a loss of €150,000 (3,000 units remaining under the firm purchase commitment × €50 loss per unit).

On January 1, 2009, KC acquires BC for €30 million, which reflects the fair value of BC based on what other marketplace participants would be willing to pay. On the acquisition date, the €30 million fair value of BC includes €750,000 related to the contract with KC that consists of

Identifiable intangibles[3]	€600,000	Representing the remaining year of the contract, at prevailing market prices
Favorable pricing	150,000	Representing the portion of the contract price that is favorable to BC and unfavorable to KC
	€750,000	

BC has no other identifiable assets or liabilities related to the supply contract with KC. KC would compute its gain or loss on settlement of this preexisting relationship as follows:

1. Amount of unfavorableness to acquirer (KC) at acquisition date	€150,000
2. Lump-sum settlement amount available to KC	500,000
3. Lessor of 1. or 2.	150,000
4. Amount by which 1. exceeds 2.	N/A

Since KC had already recognized an unrealized loss on the firm purchase commitment as of December 31, 2008, upon its acquisition of BC, its loss of €150,000 from recognizing the lesser of 1. and 2. above would be offset by the elimination of the liability for the unrealized loss on the firm purchase commitment in the same amount of €150,000. Thus, under these circumstances, KC would have neither a gain nor a loss on the settlement of its preexisting relationship with BC. The entries to record these events are not considered part of the business combination accounting. It is important to note that, from the perspective of KC, when it applies the acquisition method to record the business combination, it will characterize the €600,000 "at-market" component of the contract as part of goodwill and not as identifiable intangibles. This is the case because of the obvious fallacy of KC recognizing customer-relationship intangible assets that represent a relationship with itself.

---

[3]   *In computing the valuation of BC, these amounts would represent such identifiable customer-related intangible assets as customer contract, related customer relationship, production backlog, etc.*

Example of settlement of preexisting contractual supplier relationship; contract favorable to acquirer

Using the same facts as the KC/BC example above, assume that, instead of the contract being favorable to the acquirer KC, it was unfavorable to BC in the amount of €150,000 and that there was a cancellation provision in the contract that would permit BC to pay a penalty after year two of €100,000 to cancel the remainder of the contract.

On the acquisition date, the €30 million fair value of BC, under this scenario would include €750,000 related to the contract with KC that consists of

Identifiable intangibles	€600,000	Representing the remaining year of the contract, at prevailing market prices
Unfavorable pricing	(150,000)	Representing the portion of the contract price that is unfavorable to BC and favorable to KC
	€450,000	

Under these changed assumptions, KC would not have incurred or recorded an unrealized loss on the firm purchase commitment with BC since the contract terms were favorable to KC. The determination of KC's gain or loss would be as follows:

1.	Amount of favorability to acquirer (KC) at acquisition date	€150,000
2.	Lump-sum settlement amount available to BC	100,000
3.	Lessor of 1. or 2.	100,000
4.	Amount by which 1. exceeds 2.	50,000

Under this scenario, unless BC believed that the market would change in the near term, it would be economically advantageous, absent a business combination, for BC to settle the remaining contract at the acquisition date by paying the €100,000 penalty because BC would be able to sell the remaining 3,000 units covered by the contract for an aggregate price of €150,000 more than it was committed to sell those units to KC.

At the acquisition date, KC would record a gain of €100,000 to settle its preexisting relationship with BC. The entry to record the gain is not considered part of the business combination accounting.

In addition, however, since 2. is less than 1., the €50,000 difference is included in the accounting for the business combination, since economically, in postcombination periods, the combined entity will not benefit from that portion of the acquisition date favorability of the contract.

As was the case in the first example, the portion of the purchase price allocated to the contract in the business combination accounting would be accounted for as goodwill for the same reason.

Contingent payments to employees or former owners of the acquiree. The acquirer is to assess whether arrangements to make contingent payments to employees or selling owners of the acquiree represent contingent consideration that is part of the business combination transaction or represent separate transactions to be excluded from the application of the acquisition method to the business combination. In general, the acquirer is to consider the reasons why the terms of the acquisition include the payment provision, the party that initiated the arrangement, and when (at what stage of the negotiations) the arrangement was entered into by the parties. When those considerations do not provide clarity regarding whether the transaction is separate from the business combination, the acquirer considers the following indicators:

1. *Postcombination employment*—Consideration is to be given to the terms under which the selling owners will be providing services as key employees of the combined entity. The terms may be evidenced by a formal employment contract, by provisions included in the acquisition documents, or by other documents. If the arrangement provides that the contingent payments are automatically forfeited upon termination of employment, the consideration is to be characterized as compensa-

tion for postcombination services. If, instead, the contingent payments are not affected by termination of employment, this would be an indicator that the contingent payments represent additional consideration that is part of the business combination transaction and not compensation for services.

2. *Duration of postcombination employment*—If the employee is contractually bound to remain employed for a period that equals or exceeds the period during which the contingent payments are due, this may be an indicator that the contingent payments represent compensation for services.

3. *Amount of compensation*—If the amount of the employee's compensation that is not contingent is considered to be reasonable in relation to other key employees of the combined entity, this may indicate that the contingent amounts represent additional consideration and not compensation for services.

4. *Differential between amounts paid to employees and selling owners who do not become employees of the combined entity*—If, on a per-share basis, the contingent payments due to former owners of the acquiree that did not become employees are lower than the contingent payments due to the former owners that did become employees of the combined entity, this may indicate that the incremental amounts paid to the employees are compensation.

5. *Extent of ownership*—The relative ownership percentages (e.g., number of shares, units, percentage of membership interest) owned by the selling owners who remain employees of the combined entity serve as an indicator of how to characterize the substance of the contingent consideration. If, for example, the former owners of substantially all of the ownership interests in the acquiree are continuing to serve as key employees of the combined entity, this may be an indicator that the contingent payment arrangement is substantively a profit-sharing vehicle designed with the intent of providing compensation for services to be performed postcombination. Conversely, if the former owners that remained employed by the combined entity collectively owned only a nominal ownership interest in the acquiree and all of the former owners received the same amount of contingent basis on a per-share basis, this may be an indicator that the contingent payments represent additional consideration. In considering the applicability of this indicator, care must be exercised to closely examine the effects, if any, of transactions, ownership interests, and employment relationships, precombination and postcombination, with respect to parties related to the selling owners of the acquiree.

6. *Relationship of contingent arrangements to the valuation approach used*—The payment terms negotiated in many business combinations provide that the amount of the acquisition date transfer of consideration from acquirer to acquiree (or the acquiree's former owners) is computed near the lower end of a range of valuation estimates the acquirer used in valuing the acquiree. Furthermore, the formula for determining future contingent payments is derived from or related to that valuation approach. When this is the case, it may be an indicator that the contingent payments represent additional consideration. Conversely, if the formula for determining future contingent payments more closely resembles prior profit-sharing arrangements, this may be an indicator that the substance of the contingent payment arrangement is to provide compensation for services.

7. *Formula prescribed for determining contingent consideration*—Analyzing the formula to be used to determine the contingent consideration may provide insight into the substance of the arrangement. Contingent payments that are determined on the basis of a multiple of earnings may be indicative of being, in substance, contingent consideration that is part of the business combination transaction. Alternatively,

contingent consideration that is determined as a prespecified percentage of earnings would be more suggestive of a routine profit-sharing arrangement for the purposes of providing additional compensation to employees for postcombination services rendered.

8. *Other considerations*—Given the complexity of a business combination transaction and the sheer number and girth of the legal documents necessary to effect it, the financial statement preparer is charged with the daunting, but unavoidable task of performing a comprehensive review of the terms of all the associated agreements. These can take the form of noncompete agreements, consulting agreements, leases, guarantees, indemnifications, and, of course, the formal agreement to combine the businesses. Particular attention should be paid to the applicable income tax treatment afforded to the contingent payments. The income tax treatment of these payments may be an indicator that tax avoidance was a primary motivator in characterizing them in the manner that they are structured. An acquirer might, for example, simultaneous to a business combination, execute a property lease with one of the key owners of the acquiree. If the lease payments were below market, some or all of the contingent payments to that key owner/lessor under the provisions of the other legal agreements might, in substance, be making up the shortfall in the lease and thus should be recharacterized as lease payments and accounted for separately from the business combination in the combined entity's postcombination financial statements. If this were not the case, and the lease payments were reflective of the market, this would be an indicator pointing to a greater likelihood that the contingent payment arrangements actually did represent contingent consideration associated with the business combination transaction.

Example of contingent payments to employees

Henan Corporation (HC) hired a new Accounting Director in charge of the conversion to IFRS under a five-year contract. The terms of the contract stated that HC will pay the Director €1 million annually if HC is acquired before the expiration of this contract, up to the maximum amount of €5 million. After four years, Konin Corporation (KC) acquires HC. Since the Director was still working for HC at the acquisition date, he will receive €1 million payment under the contract.

In this example, the contract for the employment of the Accounting Director was entered into much before the negotiations of the business combination were initiated, and the purpose of the contract was to receive the services of the Director. Therefore, there is no evidence that this contract was primarily entered into to provide benefits to KC or the combined entity. As a result, the liability for the payment of €1 million is included in the application of the acquisition method.

Alternatively, HC might enter into the contract at the recommendation of KC, as part of the negotiations for the business combination, with the intent to provide severance pay to the Director. Therefore, the contract may primarily benefit KC and the combined entity rather than HC or its former owners. Consequently, the acquirer KC must account for the liability of €1 million to the Director since the payment is considered a separate transaction, excluded from the application of the acquisition method to this business combination.

Replacement awards—Acquirer share-based payment awards exchanged for acquiree awards held by its employees. In connection with a business combination, the acquirer often awards share options or other share-based payments (i.e., replacement awards) to the employees of the acquiree in exchange for the employees' acquiree awards. Obviously, there are many valid business reasons for the exchange, not the least of which is ensuing smooth transition and integration, retention and motivation of valued employees, and maintaining controlling interests in the acquiree.

IFRS 3(R) provides guidance on determining whether equity instruments (e.g., share-based payments awards) issued in a business combination are part of the consideration transferred in exchange for control of the acquiree (and accounted for in accordance with IFRS 3[R]) or are in return for continued service in the postcombination periods (and accounted for under IFRS 2, *Share-Based Payment,* as a modification of a plan).

Acquirer not obligated to exchange. Accounting for the replacement awards under IFRS 3(R) is dependent on whether the acquirer is obligated to replace the acquiree awards. The acquirer is obligated to replace the acquiree awards if the acquiree or its employees can enforce replacement through rights obtained from the terms of the acquisition agreement, the acquiree awards, or applicable laws or regulations.

If the acquirer is not obligated to replace the acquiree awards, all of the market-based measure (MBM) of the replacement awards is recognized as remuneration cost in the post-combination financial statements.

Example of acquirer replacing acquiree awards without the obligation to do so

Konin Corporation (KC) acquired Henan Corporation (HC) on January 1, 2009. Because of the business combination, the share-based payment awards of the subsidiary that had been previously granted by HC to its employees expired on the acquisition date.

Although KC was not obligated, legally or contractually, to replace the expired awards, its Board of Directors approved a grant of KC awards designed so that the employees of HC would not be financially disadvantaged by the acquisition transaction.

Since the replacement awards were voluntary on the part of KC, the market-based measure of the replacement award is attributed wholly to postcombination service and therefore recognized as remuneration cost in KC's postcombination consolidated financial statements.

Acquirer obligated to replace acquiree awards. If the acquirer is obligated to replace the awards of the acquiree, either all or a portion of the market-based measure of the replacement awards are included in measuring the consideration transferred by the acquirer in the business combination. To the extent a portion of the replacement awards are not allocated to consideration transferred, they are attributable to postcombination services and therefore recognized as remuneration cost in the acquirer's consolidated financial statements, thus having no impact on goodwill and equity.

For the purposes of illustrating the allocation computations, the following conventions and abbreviations are used:

MBM_{RA}	Acquisition date market-based measure of acquirer replacement award
MBM_{AA}	Acquisition date market-based measure of acquiree award that is being replaced by the acquirer
VP_{AA}	Original vesting period[4] of acquiree awards at acquisition date
VP_{RA}	Vesting period of the acquirer replacement awards at their acqusition date
CVP_{AA}	Portion of vesting period completed at the acquisition date by employees under the acquiree awards

---

[4] *The term "vesting period" is defined as the period during which all the specified vesting conditions of a share-based payment arrangement are to be satisfied. Vesting conditions are the conditions that determine whether the entity receives the services that entitle the counterparty to receive cash, other assets, or equity instruments of the entity, under a share-based payment arrangement. Vesting conditions are either service conditions or performance conditions. These terms are defined in IFRS2, discussed in detail in Chapter 17.*

TVP   Total vesting period—The vesting period already satisfied by the employees at the acquisition date under the acquiree awards plus the vesting period, if any, required by the acquirer replacement awards

PRE   Portion of MBM_{RA} attributable to precombination services performed by the employees of the acquiree

PRC   Postcombination remuneration cost

$$TVP = CVP_{AA} + VP_{RA}$$

The following steps are followed to determine the portion of the market-based measure of the replacement award that is to be included as part of the consideration transferred by the acquirer:

1. Compute both MBM_{RA} and MBM_{AA} by following the provision of IFRS 2, as discussed in detail in Chapter 17.

2. Compute the portion of the replacement award that is attributable to precombination services rendered by the acquiree's employees as follows:

   a.   If $VP_{AA} > TVP$, then

$$PRE = MBM_{AA} \left(\frac{CVP_{AA}}{VP_{AA}} \right)$$

   b.   If $VP_{AA} < TVP$, then

$$PRE = MBM_{AA} \left(\frac{CVP_{AA}}{TVP} \right)$$

3. Compute the portion of the nonvested replacement award attributable to postcombination service as follows:

$$PRC = MBM_{RA} - PRE$$

This amount is to be recognized as remuneration cost in the acquirer's postcombination consolidated financial statements since, at the acquisition date, the vesting conditions had not been met.

The following examples are adapted from IFRS 3(R), Illustrative Examples:

Example 1

Example of acquirer replacement awards requiring no postcombination services exchanges for fully vested acquiree awards where the employees have rendered all required services by the acquisition date

Acquiree awards   Vesting period *completed* before the business combination

Replacement awards   Additional employee services *are not* required after the acquisition date

Konin Corporation (KC) acquired Henan Corporation (HC) on January 1, 2009. In accordance with the acquisition agreement, KC agreed to replace share-based awards that had previously been issued by HC. Details are as follows:

	a. Acquiree awards	*b. Acquirer awards*
1. Acquisition date market-based measure of awards	$MBM_{AA} = €100$	$MBM_{RA} = €110$
2. Original vesting period of acquiree awards at their grant date	$VP_{AA} = 4$ years	--
3. Portion of 2a. completed by the acquisition date by employees of the acquiree	$CVP_{AA} = 4$ years	--

	a. Acquiree awards	*b. Acquirer awards*
4. Vesting period of acquirer replacement awards at the acquisition date	--	$VP_{RA} = 0$
5. Total vesting period (3a. + 4b.)	--	$TVP = 4$ years
6. The greater of the total vesting period (5b.) or the original vesting period of the acquiree awards (2a.)	--	4 years

Since the acquiree's employees had completed all of the services required under the prior awards, applying the formula yields a result that attributes 100% of the market-based value of the acquiree award that is being replaced to precombination services rendered.

$$PRE = 1a. \left(\frac{3a.}{6b.} \right)$$

$$PRE = €100 \left(\frac{4 \text{ years}}{4 \text{ years}} \right)$$

$$PRE = €100$$

The €100 result, attributed to precombination services, is included by the acquirer in its computation of the consideration transferred in exchange for control of the acquiree.

The final step in the computation is to account for the difference between the acquisition date market-based measure of the replacement awards and the acquiree awards as follows:

Market-based measure of replacement awards—MBM_{RA}	€110
– Allocated to consideration transferred per above	100
= Additional remuneration cost recognized in postcombination consolidated financial statements	€ 10

This result illustrates the basic principle in IFRS 3(R) that any excess of MBM_{RA} over the MBM_{AA} is to be attributed to postcombination services and recognized as remuneration cost in the acquirer's postcombination consolidated financial statements.

Example 2

Example of acquirer replacement awards requiring performance of postcombination services exchanged for full vested acquiree awards where the employees have rendered all required services by the acquisition date

Acquiree awards	Vesting period *completed* before the business combination
Replacement awards	Additional employee services *are* required after the acquisition date

The acquisition agreement referred to in the previous example governing the KC acquisition of HC that occurred on January 1, 2009, contained the following provisions regarding exchange of outstanding HC awards at acquisition date for KC replacement awards:

	a. Acquiree awards	*b. Acquirer awards*
1. Acquisition date market-based measure of awards	$MBM_{AA} = €100$	$MBM_{RA} = €100$
2. Original vesting period of acquiree awards at their grant date	$VP_{AA} = 4$ years	--
3. Portion of 2a. completed by the acquisition date by employees of the acquiree (the acquiree employees in this example had actually completed a total of 7 years of services by the acquisition date)	$CVP_{AA} = 4$ years	--
4. Vesting period of acquirer replacement awards at the acquisition date	--	$VP_{RA} = 1$ year

		a. Acquiree awards	*b. Acquirer awards*
5.	Total vesting period (3a. + 4b.)	--	TVP = 5 years
6.	The greater of the total vesting period (5b.) or the original vesting period of the acquiree awards (2a.)	--	5 years

Even though the acquiree's employees had completed all the vesting period required by the acquiree's awards three years prior to the acquisition, the imposition of an additional year of required service by the acquirer's replacement awards results in an allocation between the amount attributable to precombination services and, separately, to postcombination services as follows:

$$ PRE = 1a. \left(\frac{3a.}{6b.} \right) $$

$$ PRE = €100 \left(\frac{4 \text{ years}}{5 \text{ years}} \right) $$

$$ PRE = €80 $$

The €80 result, attributed to precombination services, is included by the acquirer in its computation of the consideration transferred in exchange for control of the acquiree.

The €20 difference between the €100 market value of the replacement awards and the €80 allocated to precombination services (and included in consideration transferred) is accounted for as remuneration cost in the postcombination consolidated financial statements of KC.

Example 3

Example of acquirer replacement awards requiring performance of postcombination services exchanged for acquiree awards with remaining unsatisfied vesting period as of the acquisition date

Acquiree awards	Vesting period *not completed* before the business combination
Replacement awards	Additional employee services *are* required after the acquisition date

The acquisition agreement referred to in the previous examples governing the KC acquisition of HC that occurred on January 1, 2009, contained the following provisions regarding exchange of outstanding HC awards at acquisition date for KC replacement awards:

		a. Acquiree awards	*b. Acquirer awards*
1.	Acquisition date market-based measure of awards	$MBM_{AA} = €100$	$MBM_{RA} = €100$
2.	Original vesting period of acquiree awards at their grant date	$VP_{AA} = 4$ years	--
3.	Portion of 2a. completed by the acquisition date by employees of the acquiree	$CVP_{AA} = 2$ years	--
4.	Vesting period of acquirer replacement awards at the acquisition date	--	$VP_{RA} = 1$ year
5.	Total vesting period (3a. + 4b.)	--	TVP = 3 years
6.	The greater of the total vesting period (5b.) or the original vesting period of the acquiree awards (2a.)	--	4 years

The portion of the market-based measure of the replacement awards attributable to precombination services already rendered by the acquiree employees is computed as follows:

$$PRE = 1a. \left(\frac{3a.}{6b.} \right)$$

$$PRE = €100 \left(\frac{2 \text{ years}}{4 \text{ years}} \right)$$

$$PRE = €50$$

Based on the computation above, at the acquisition date, KC, the acquirer includes €50 as consideration transferred to obtain control of HC, the acquiree. The remaining €50 is attributed to postcombination services and, accordingly, recognized as remuneration cost in the postcombination consolidated financial statements of KC.

Example 4

Example of acquirer replacement awards that do not require postcombination services exchanged for acquiree awards with remaining unsatisfied vesting period as of the acquisition date

Acquiree awards	Vesting period *completed* before the business combination
Replacement awards	Additional employee services *are not* required after the acquisition date

The acquisition agreement referred to in the previous examples governing the KC acquisition of HC that occurred on January 1, 2009, contained the following provisions regarding exchange of outstanding HC awards at acquisition date for KC replacement awards:

		a. Acquiree awards	*b. Acquirer awards*
1.	Acquisition date market-based measure of awards	$MBM_{AA} = €100$	$MBM_{RA} = €100$
2.	Original vesting period of acquiree awards at their grant date	$VP_{AA} = 4$ years	--
3.	Portion of 2a. completed by the acquisition date by employees of the acquiree	$CVP_{AA} = 2$ years	--
4.	Vesting period of acquirer replacement awards at the acquisition date		$VP_{RA} = 0$
5.	Total vesting period (3a. + 4b.)	--	$TVP = 2$ years
6.	The greater of the total vesting period (5b.) or the original vesting period of the acquiree awards (2a.)	--	4 years

Under this scenario, the terms of the replaced HC awards did not contain a change-in-control provision which would eliminate any remaining vesting period upon a change in control and would fully vested them upon the acquisition by KC. If the HC awards had included a provision eliminating any remaining vesting period upon a change in control, the guidance in Example 1 would apply and the outcome would be the same as the Example 1 (where neither the acquiree awards nor the replacement rewards required the completion of any service on the part of the acquiree's employees).

Since, at the acquisition date, the acquiree employees had completed only two out of the four years of required services and the replacement awards do not extend the duration of postcombination services required, the total vesting period (TVP) in 5b. is the 2 years already completed by the acquiree's employees under their original awards in 3a. (CVP_{AA}).

The portion of the market-based measure of the replacement awards attributable to precombination services already rendered by the acquiree employees is computed as follows:

$$PRE = 1a. \quad \left(\begin{array}{c} \underline{3a.} \\ 6b. \end{array} \right)$$

$$PRE = €100 \quad \left(\begin{array}{c} \underline{2 \text{ years}} \\ 4 \text{ years} \end{array} \right)$$

$$PRE = €50$$

Consequently, €50 of the market-based measure of the replacement awards is attributable to precombination services already performed by the acquiree employees and is, therefore, included in computing the consideration transferred in exchanges for obtaining control of the acquiree.

The remaining €50 of the market-based measure of the replacement awards is attributable to postcombination services. However, since the acquiree's employees are not required to provide any postcombination services under the terms of the replacement awards, the entire €50 is immediately recognized by KC, the acquirer, in its postcombination consolidated financial statements.

Although not illustrated in the preceding examples, IFRS 3(R) requires the acquirer to estimate the number of its replacement awards for which the vesting is expected to occur. To the extent that service is not expected to occur due to employees terminating prior to meeting the replacement award's vesting requirements, the portion of the market-based measure of the replacement awards included in consideration transferred in the business combination is to be reduced accordingly. For example, if the market-based measure of the portion of replacement awards attributed to precombination services is €100 and the acquirer expects that only 90% of the awards will vest, the amount included as consideration transferred in the business combination is €90. Changes in the estimated number of replacement awards expected to vest are recognized in the acquirer's postcombination financial statements in the periods in which the changes occur, not as adjustments to the amount of consideration transferred in the business combination.

Finally, it is important to note that the same requirements for apportioning the replacement award between precombination and postcombination service apply to replacement awards that are classified as equity or as liabilities in accordance with the provisions of IFRS 2. All postacquisition-date changes in the market-based measure of liability awards (and their related income tax effects recognized in accordance with the provision of IAS 12) are recognized in the acquirer's postcombination financial statements in the periods in which the changes occur.

Goodwill and Gain from a Bargain Purchase

Goodwill. Goodwill represents the difference between the acquisition-date fair value of the consideration transferred plus the amount of any noncontrolling interest in the acquiree plus the acquisition-date fair value of the acquirer's previously held equity interest in the acquiree; and the acquisition-date fair values of the identifiable assets acquired and liabilities assumed. Presumable, when an acquiring entity pays this premium price for the acquiree, it sees value that transcends the worth of the tangible assets and the identifiable intangibles, or else the deal would not have been consummated on such terms. This goodwill arising from acquisitions often consists largely of the synergies and economies of scale expected from combining the operations of the acquirer and acquiree. Goodwill must be recognized as an asset.

The balance in the goodwill account should be reviewed at the end of each reporting period to determine whether the asset has suffered any impairment. If goodwill is no longer deemed probable of being fully recovered through the profitable operations of the acquired business, it should be partially written down or fully written off. Any write-off of goodwill must be charged to expense. Once written down, goodwill cannot later be restored as an asset, again reflecting the concern that the independent measurement of goodwill is not possible and the acquired goodwill may, in the postacquisition periods, be replaced by internally generated goodwill, which is not to be recognized.

It should be noted that in acquisitions of less than 100% of the equity interests, IFRS 3(R) provides the acquirer with a choice of two options to measure noncontrolling interests arising in a business combination: (1) to measure the noncontrolling interest at *fair value* (also recognizing the acquired business at fair value), or (2) to measure the noncontrolling interest at *the noncontrolling interest's share of the value of net assets acquired.* Under the fair value approach to measure noncontrolling interest, the acquired business will be recognized at fair value, with the controlling share of total goodwill assigned to the controlling interest and the noncontrolling share allocated to the noncontrolling interest. Under the second approach to measure noncontrolling interest, while the net identifiable assets attributable to the noncontrolling interest are written up to the fair values implied by the acquisition transaction, goodwill will not be imputed for the noncontrolling share.

Example of acquisition transaction—goodwill

Oman Heating Corp. acquired 100% the equity interests of Euro Boiler Manufacturing Co. on January 2, 2008, in exchange for cash of €15 million and the balance represented by a long-term note to former Euro shareholders. As of January 2, 2008, immediately prior to the transaction, Euro's statement of financial position is as follows, with both book and fair values indicated (in thousands of €):

	Book value	Fair value		Book value	Fair value
Cash	€ 1,000	€ 1,000	Current liabilities	€26,200	€26,200
Accounts receivable, net	12,200	12,000	Long-term debt	46,000	41,500
Inventory	8,500	9,750	Guarantee of debt	--	75
Other current assets	500	500			
Property, plant, and equipment, net	38,500	52,400			
Customers list	--	1,400			
Patents	2,400	3,900			
In-process research and development	--	8,600	Shareholders' equity (deficit)	(9,100)	21,775
Totals	€63,100	€89,550		€63,100	€89,550

The fair value of inventory exceeded the corresponding book value because Euro Boiler had been using LIFO for many years to cost its inventory, prior to revised IAS 2's banning this method, and actual replacement cost was therefore somewhat higher than carrying value at the date of the acquisition. The long-term debt's fair value was slightly lower than carrying value (cost) because the debt carries a fixed interest rate and the market rates have risen since the debt was incurred. Consequently, Euro Boiler benefits economically by having future debt service requirements which are less onerous than they would be if it were to borrow at current rates. Conversely, of course, the fair value of the lender's note receivable has declined since it now represents a loan payable at less than market rates. Finally, the fair values of Euro Boiler's receivables have also declined from their carrying amount, due to both the higher market rates of interest and to the greater risk of noncollectibility because of the change in ownership. The higher interest rates impact the valuation in two ways: (1) when computing the discounted present value of the amounts to be received, the higher interest rate reduces the computed present value, and (2) the higher interest rates may serve as an incentive for customers to delay payments to Euro rather than borrow the money to repay the receivables, with that delay resulting in cash flows being received later than anticipated thus causing the present value to decline.

Euro Boiler's customer list has been appraised at €1.4 million and is a major reason for the company's acquisition by Oman Heating. Having been internally developed over many years, the customer list is not recorded as an asset by Euro, however. The patents have been amortized down to €2.4 million in Euro Boiler's accounting records, consistent with IFRS, but an appraisal finds that on a fair value basis the value is somewhat higher.

Similarly, property, plant, and equipment has been depreciated down to a book value of €38.5 million, but has been appraised at a sound value (that is, replacement cost new adjusted for the fraction of the useful life already elapsed) of €52.4 million.

A key asset being acquired by Oman Heating, albeit one not formally recognized by Euro Boiler, is the in-process research and development (IPR&D), which pertains to activities undertaken over a period of several years aimed at making significant process and product improvements which would enhance Euro Boiler's market position and will be captured by the new combined operations. It has been determined that duplicating the benefits of this ongoing R&D work would cost Oman Heating €8.6 million. The strong motivation to make this acquisition, and to pay a substantial premium over book value, is based on Euro Boiler's customer list and its IPR&D. Euro Boiler has previously expensed all R&D costs incurred, as required under IFRS, since it conservatively believed that these costs were in the nature of research, rather than development.

Euro Boiler had guaranteed a €1.5 million bank debt of a former affiliated entity, but this was an "off the books" event since guarantees issued between corporations under common control were commonly deemed exempt from recognition. The actual contingent obligation has been appraised as having a fair value (considering both the amount and likelihood of having to honor the commitment) of €75,000.

Thus, although Euro Boiler's statement of financial position reflects a shareholders' deficit (including share capital issued and outstanding, and accumulated deficit) of €9.1 million, the value of the acquisition, including the IPR&D, is much higher. The preliminary computation of goodwill is as follows:

Consideration transferred		€32,000,000
Net working capital	€(2,950,000)	
Property, plant, and equipment	52,400,000	
Customer list	1,400,000	
Patents	3,900,000	
In-process research and development	8,600,000	
Guarantee of indebtedness of others	(75,000)	
Long-term debt	(41,500,000)	21,775,000
Goodwill		€10,225,000

Under IFRS 3(R), the fair value allocated to the in-process research and development must be expensed unless it is separately identifiable, is a resource that is controlled, is a probable source of future economic benefits, and has a reliably measurable fair value. Oman Heating determines that €1,800,000 of the cost of IPR&D meets all these criteria and supports capitalization. All other assets and liabilities are recorded by Oman Heating at the allocated fair values, with the excess consideration transferred being assigned to goodwill. The entry to record the acquisition (for preparation of consolidated financial statements, for example) is as follows:

Cash	1,000,000	
Accounts receivable, net	12,000,000	
Inventory	9,750,000	
Other current assets	500,000	
Property, plant, and equipment	52,400,000	
Customer list	1,400,000	
Patents	3,900,000	
Development costs capitalized	1,800,000	
Research and development expense	6,800,000	
Goodwill	10,225,000	
Current liabilities		26,200,000
Guarantee of indebtedness of others		75,000
Long-term debt		41,500,000
Notes payable to former shareholders		17,000,000
Cash		15,000,000

Note that, while the foregoing example is for a share acquisition, an asset and liability acquisition would be accounted for in the exact same manner. Also, since the debt is recorded at fair value, which will often differ from face (maturity) value, the differential (premium or discount) must be amortized using the effective yield method from acquisition date to the maturity date of the debt, and thus there will be differences between actual payments of interest and the amounts recognized in profit or loss as interest expense. Finally, note that property, plant, and equipment is recorded "net"—that is, the allocated fair value becomes the "cost" of these assets; accumulated depreciation previously recorded in the accounting records of the acquired entity does not carry forward to the postacquisition financial statements of the consolidated entity.

Impairment of goodwill. Assume that an entity acquires another entity and that goodwill arises from this acquisition. Also assume that, for purposes of impairment, it is determined that the acquired business comprises seven discrete cash-generating units. Cash-generating unit is the smallest level of identifiable group of assets that generates cash inflows that are largely independent of the cash inflows from other assets or groups of assets (not larger than an operating segment). The goodwill recorded on the acquisition must be allocated to some or all of those seven cash-generating units. If it is the case that the goodwill is associated with only some of the seven cash-generating units, the goodwill recognized in the statement of financial position should be allocated to only those assets or groups of assets.

Three steps are required for goodwill impairment testing. First, the recoverable amount of a *cash-generating unit* which is the higher of the cash-generating unit's fair value less costs to sell (net selling price) and its value in use, which is the present value of the estimated future cash flows expected to be derived from the cash-generating unit must be determined. Second, the recoverable amount of the cash-generating unit is compared to its carrying value. If the recoverable value exceeds the carrying value, then there is no goodwill impairment, and the third testing step is not required.

IAS 36 requires that if the recoverable amount is less than the carrying value, an impairment write-down must be made. In this third step in goodwill impairment testing, the recoverable value of the cash-generating unit as of the testing date is allocated to its assets (including intangible assets) and liabilities, with the remainder (if any) being assigned to goodwill. If the amount of goodwill resulting from this calculation is less than the carrying amount of goodwill, then the difference is impaired goodwill and must be charged to expense in the current period.

An impairment loss is first absorbed by goodwill, and only when goodwill has been eliminated entirely is any further impairment loss credited to other assets in the group (on a pro rata basis, unless it is possible to measure the recoverable amounts of the individual assets). This is perhaps somewhat arbitrary, but it is also logical, since the excess earnings power represented by goodwill must be deemed to have been lost if the recoverable amount of the cash-generating unit is less than its carrying amount. It is also a conservative approach, and will diminish or eliminate the display of that often misunderstood and always suspiciously viewed asset, goodwill, before the carrying values of identifiable intangible and tangible assets are adjusted.

Reversal of previously recognized impairment of goodwill. In general under IFRS, reversal of an impairment identified with a cash-generating unit is permitted. However, due to the special character of this asset, IAS 36 has imposed a requirement that reversals may not be recognized for previous write-downs in goodwill. Thus, a later recovery in value of the cash-generating unit will be allocated to assets other than goodwill. (The adjustments to those assets cannot be for amounts greater than would be needed to restore them to the carrying amounts at which they would be currently stated had the earlier impairment not been recognized—i.e., at the former carrying values less the depreciation that would have been recorded during the intervening period.)

IFRIC 10, *Interim Financial Reporting and Impairment*, addresses conflicts between the requirements of IAS 34, *Interim Financial Reporting*, and those in other standards on the recognition and reversal in the financial statements of impairment losses on goodwill and certain financial assets. In conformity with IFRIC 10, any impairment losses recognized in an interim financial statement must not be reversed in subsequent interim or annual financial statements.

Gain from a bargain purchase. In certain business combinations, the consideration transferred is less than the fair value of the net assets acquired. These are often identified as being "bargain purchase" transactions. This difference has traditionally (if illogically) been referred to as "negative goodwill." IFRS 3(R) suggests that, since arm's-length business acquisition transactions will usually favor neither party, the likelihood of the acquirer obtaining a bargain is considered remote. According to this standard, apparent instances of bargain purchases giving rise to a gain from a bargain purchase are more often the result of measurement error (i.e., where the fair values assigned to assets and liabilities were incorrect to some extent) or of a failure to recognize a contingent or actual liability (such as for employee severance payments). However, a gain from a bargain purchase can also derive from the risk of future losses, recognized by both parties and incorporated into the transaction price. (One such example was the case of the sale by BMW of its Rover car division to a consortium for £1. It did indeed suffer subsequent losses and eventually failed.)

IFRS 3(R) requires that, before a gain from a bargain purchase is recognized, the allocation of fair values is to be revisited, and that all liabilities—including contingencies—be reviewed. After this is completed, if indeed the fair values of identifiable assets acquired net of all liabilities assumed exceeds the total consideration transferred, then a gain from a bargain purchase will be acknowledged. The accounting treatment of negative goodwill has passed through a number of evolutionary stages beginning with the original IAS 22, which was later twice revised with major changes to the prescribed accounting treatment of negative goodwill.

Under IFRS 3(R), a gain from a bargain purchase is taken immediately into profit. Essentially, this is regarded, for financial reporting purposes, as a gain realized upon the acquisition transaction, and accounted for accordingly.

Example of acquisition transaction—gain from a bargain purchase

Hoegedorn Corp. acquires, on March 4, 2008, all of the outstanding ordinary shares of Gemutlicheit Co. in exchange for cash of €800,000. A formerly successful entity, Gemutlicheit had recently suffered from declining sales and demands for repayment of its outstanding bank debt, which were threatening its continued existence. Hoegedorn management perceived an opportunity to make a favorable purchase of a company operating in a related line of business, and accordingly made this modest offer, which was accepted by the shareholders of Gemutlicheit, the acquiree. Gemutlicheit's statement of financial position at the date of acquisition is as follows, with both book and fair values indicated (in thousands of €):

	Book value	Fair value		Book value	Fair value
Cash	€ 800	€ 800	Current liabilities	€ 2,875	€ 2,875
Accounts receivable, net	3,600	3,400	Long-term debt	11,155	11,155
Inventory	1,850	1,800			
Property, plant, and equipment	6,800	7,200	Shareholders'		
Net operating loss carryforwards	--	2,400	equity (deficit)	(980)	1,570
Totals	€13,050	€15,600		€13,050	€15,600

Gemutlicheit had provided a valuation allowance for the deferred income tax asset attributable to the net operating loss carryforward tax benefit, since recurring and increasing losses made it probable that these benefits would not be realized, consistent with IFRS (IAS 12). Hoegedorn Corp., which is highly profitable, is in the same line of business, and intends to continue Gemutlicheit's operation, expects to be able to realize these benefits, and therefore will have no valuation allowance against this asset.

Thus, although Gemutlicheit's statement of financial position reflects a shareholders' deficit (including share capital and accumulated deficit in retained earnings) of €980,000, the value of the acquisition is much higher, and furthermore the acquirer is able to negotiate a bargain purchase. The preliminary computation of negative goodwill is as follows:

Net working capital	€ 3,125,000	
Property, plant, and equipment	7,200,000	
Net operating loss carryforward	2,400,000	
Long-term debt	(11,155,000)	1,570,000
Consideration transferred		800,000
Gain from bargain purchase		€ 770,000

IFRS 3(R) requires that a gain from a bargain purchase be taken into profit or loss immediately, after first verifying that all acquired or assumed liabilities, including contingencies, have been fully accounted for, and that assets acquired were not overstated. In the present example, these matters were reviewed and the amounts shown above were fully supported.

The entry to record the acquisition is therefore as follows:

Cash	800,000	
Accounts receivable, net	3,400,000	
Inventory	1,800,000	
Property, plant, and equipment	7,200,000	
Deferred income tax asset	2,400,000	
Current liabilities		2,875,000
Long-term debt		11,155,000
Cash		800,000
Gain from bargain purchase		770,000

Business combinations achieved in stages (step acquisitions). *A step acquisition is a business combination in which the acquirer held an equity interest in the acquiree prior to the acquisition date on which it obtained control.* In some instances, control over another entity is not achieved in a single transaction, but rather, after a series of transactions. For example, one entity may acquire a 25% interest in another entity, followed by another 20% some time later, and then followed by another 10% at yet a later date. The last step gives the acquirer a 55% interest and, thus, control. The accounting issue is to determine at what point in time the business combination took place and how to measure the acquisition.

IFRS 3(R) requires the acquirer to remeasure its previous holdings of the acquiree's equity at acquisition-date fair value. Any gain or loss on remeasurement is recognized in profit or loss on that date.

Example of a step acquisition

On December 31, 2008, Konin Corporation (KC) owns 5% of the 30,000 outstanding voting common shares of Henan Corporation (HC). On KC's December 31, 2008 statement of financial position, it classified its investment in HC as available for sale. On March 31, 2009, KC acquired additional equity shares in HC sufficient to provide KC with a controlling interest in HC and, thus, become HC's parent company.

The following table summarizes KC's initial holdings in HC, the subsequent increase in those holdings, and the computation of the gain on remeasurement at the acquisition date of March 31, 2009:

Date	# of Shares	Percent interest	Per share Cost	Per share Fair value	Aggregate investment Cost	Aggregate investment Fair value	Unrealized appreciation included in accumulated other compre-hensive income
12/31/2008	1,500	5%	$10	$16	$ 15,000	$ 24,000	$9,000
3/31/2009	21,000	70%	20	20	420,000	420,000	
	22,500	75%					

Computation of gain (loss) on remeasurement at acquisition date:

Fair value per share on 4/1/2009	$ 20
Number of preacquisition shares	× 1,500
Aggregate fair value of preacquisition shares on 4/1/2009	30,000
Carrying amount of preacquisition shares on 4/1/2009	24,000
Appreciation attributable to the 1st quarter of 2009	6,000
Pre-2009 appreciation reclassified from accumulated OCI	9,000
Gain on remeasurement of HC stock on 3/31/2009	$ 15,000

If the acquirer had previously recognized changes in the carrying value of its equity interest in the acquiree in other comprehensive income (e.g., because the investment was classified as available for sale), that amount is to be reclassified and included in the computation of the acquisition date gain or loss from remeasurement.

Footnote Disclosure: Acquisitions

IFRS 3(R) provides an illustrative example of footnote disclosures about acquisitions which an acquirer should present in the financial statements.

Footnote XX: Acquisitions

On March 30, 20X7, Konin Corporation (KC) acquired 10% of the outstanding ordinary shares of Henan Corporation (HC). On September 30, 20X8 KC acquired 65% of the outstanding ordinary shares of HC and obtained control of HC. HC is the provider of electrical distribution products and as a result of the acquisition, KC is expected to be the leading provider of energy sufficiency solutions in Central and Eastern Europe.

The goodwill of €2,500 arising from the acquisition consists largely of the synergies and economies of scale expected from combining the operations of KC and HC. None of the goodwill recognized is expected to be deductible for income tax purposes.

The following information summarizes the consideration paid for HC and the fair values of the assets acquired and liabilities assumed recognized at the acquisition date, as well as the acquisition date fair value of the noncontrolling interest in HC.

Consideration (at September 30, 20X8)

Cash	€5,000
Equity instruments (65,000 ordinary shares of KC)	6,500
Contingent consideration	1,000
Total consideration transferred	12,500
Fair value of KC's equity interest in HC held before the business combination	2,000
	14,500

Acquisition-related costs (included in selling, general and administrative expenses in KC's statement of comprehensive income for the year ended December 31, 20X8)	1,100

Recognized amounts of identifiable assets acquired and liabilities assumed

Financial assets	4,000
Inventory	3,000
Property, plant, and equipment	9,000
Identifiable intangible assets	2,500
Total assets	18,500
Financial liabilities	(3,500)

Contingent liability	(1,000)
Total identifiable net assets	14,000
Noncontrolling interest in HC	(3,500)
Goodwill	4,000
	14,500

The fair value of the 65,000 ordinary shares issued as part of the consideration paid for HC (€6,500) was determined on the basis of the acquisition-date closing market price of KC's ordinary shares.

The contingent consideration arrangement requires KC to pay the former owners of HC 4% of the revenues of HC in excess of €25,000 for 20X9, up to a maximum amount of €2,000 (undiscounted). The potential undiscounted amount of all future payments that KC could be required to make under the contingent consideration arrangement is between €0 and €2,000. The fair value of the contingent consideration arrangement (€1,000) was estimated by applying the income approach. The fair value estimates are based on an assumed discount rate range of 15–20% and assumed probability-adjusted revenues in HC of €20,000–€30,000. As of December 31, 20X8, the amount recognized for the contingent consideration and the range of outcomes and assumptions used to develop the estimates have not changed.

The fair value of the financial assets acquired includes receivables from industrial control services provided to a new customer. The gross amount due under the contracts is €2,100 of which €250 is expected to be uncollectible.

The fair value of the acquired identifiable intangibles assets (licenses) of €2,500 is based on a receipt of the final valuations for those assets.

A contingent liability of €1,000 has been recognized for expected future services to satisfy warranty claims on industrial control products sold by HC during the last four years. It is expected that the majority of this expenditure will be incurred in 20X9 and that all will be incurred by the end of 2011. The estimate of potential undiscounted amount of all future payments that HC could be required to make under the warranty claims is between €750 and €1,250. As of December 31, 20X8, there has been no change since September 30, 20X8 in the amount estimated for the liability or any change in the range of outcomes or assumptions used to develop the estimates.

The fair value of the noncontrolling interest in HC, an unlisted company, was estimated by applying a market approach and an income approach. The fair value estimates are based on

1.   An assumed discount rate range of 15–20%
2.   An assumed terminal value based on a range of terminal EBITDA multiples between 3 and 5 times (or, if appropriate, based on long-term sustainable growth rates ranging from 3 to 6%);
3.   Assumed financial multiples of companies deemed to be similar to HC; and
4.   Assumed adjustments because of the lack of control or lack of marketability that market participants would consider when estimating the fair value of the noncontrolling interest in HC.

KC recognized a gain of €500 as a result of measuring at fair value its 15% equity interest in HC held before the business combination. The gain is included in other income in KC's statement of comprehensive income for the year ending December 31, 20X8.

The revenue included in the consolidated statement of comprehensive income since September 30, 20X8, contributed by HC was €5,550 and profit of €1,100 was generated over the same period. HC reported revenue of €20,200 and profit of €3,910 for 20X8.

Consolidated Financial Statements

The revised standard IAS 27(R) introduced a major change to accounting for noncontrolling interest and consolidated financial statements: mandatory adoption of the economic entity model. Currently, under IFRS, a mixed model is adopted with the parent entity approach used predominantly and some elements of an economic entity approach (e.g., classifying noncontrolling interest in equity). The economic entity model considers all providers of equity capital as owners of the consolidated entity, even if they are not shareholders of the parent company and have no decision-making ability. As a result, the revised standard introduced major changes to accounting for noncontrolling interest, accounting for increases and decreases in the level of controlling ownership, and accounting for the loss of control of a subsidiary.

Presentation and scope. IAS 27(R) follows the fundamental approach to consolidation of subsidiaries used in current practice in accordance with IAS 27. A parent must consolidate its investments in subsidiaries. This requirement also applies to venture capital organizations, mutual funds, unit trusts, and similar organizations. There is only a limited exception available to some nonpublic entities.

IASB provides only the following four situations in which a parent need not present consolidated financial statements:

1. The parent is itself a wholly owned subsidiary, or is a partially owned subsidiary of another entity and its other owners, including those not otherwise entitled to vote, have been informed about, and do not object to, the parent not presenting consolidated financial statements;
2. The parent's debt or equity instruments are not traded in a public market (a domestic or foreign stock exchange or an over-the-counter market, including local and regional markets);
3. The parent did not file, nor is it in the process of filing, its financial statements with a securities commission or other regulatory organization for the purpose of issuing any class of instruments in a public market; and
4. The ultimate or any intermediate parent of the parent produces consolidated financial statements available for public use that comply with IFRS.

Consolidated financial statements should include all subsidiaries of the parent. While IAS 27(R) provides that, in general, control is presumed to exist when the parent owns, directly or indirectly, a majority of the voting power of another entity, this is not an absolute rule to be applied in all cases. In fact, IAS 27(R) explicitly provides that in exceptional circumstances, it can be clearly demonstrated that majority ownership does not constitute control as well as minority ownership may constitute control.

Control also exists when the parent owns one-half or less of the voting power of an entity but obtains power

1. Over more than one-half of the voting rights of the other entity by virtue of agreement with the other investors (e.g., voting trust arrangements or other contractual provisions)
2. To govern the financial and operating policies of the other entity, under a statute or agreement
3. To appoint and remove the majority of the board of directors or equivalent governing body of the other entity
4. To cast the majority of votes at meetings of the board of directors or equivalent body

Historically, actual voting interest in subsidiaries has been the criterion used to determine

1. If consolidated financial statements are to be presented; and
2. What percentage to apply in determining the allocation of a subsidiary's income, included in consolidated earnings, between the parent and the noncontrolling interests.

However, the revised standard, IAS 27(R), also addresses the situation where the parent entity has, in addition to its actual voting shareholder interest, a further potential voting interest in the subsidiary. (This was first addressed by SIC 33, which was withdrawn when IAS 27 was revised.)

A potential interest may exist due to the existence of options, warrants, convertible shares, or a contractual agreement to acquire additional shares, including shares that the investor or parent entity may have sold to another shareholder in the subsidiary or to another party, with a right or contractual arrangement to reacquire the shares transferred at a later date.

As to whether the potential shares should be considered in reaching a decision as to whether control is present, and thus whether the reporting entity is to be regarded as the parent company and should therefore prepare consolidated financial statements, IAS 27(R) holds that this is indeed a factor to weigh. It concluded that the existence and effect of potential voting rights that are *currently* exercisable or *currently* convertible should be considered, in addition to the other factors set forth in IAS 27(R), when assessing whether an entity controls another entity. All potential voting rights should be considered, including any potential voting rights held by other entities, which would mitigate or even eliminate the impact of the reporting entity's potential voting interest.

For example, an entity holding 40% voting rights in another entity, but having options to acquire another 15% voting interest, the effect of which is not offset by options held by another party, would effectively have a 55% current and potential voting interest, making consolidation required under IAS 27(R).

On the other hand, concerning whether the potential share interest should be taken into account when determining what fraction of the subsidiary's income should be allocated to the parent, the general answer is no. IAS 27(R) states that the proportion allocated to the parent and to noncontrolling interests, respectively, when preparing consolidated financial statements should be determined solely on present ownership interests. That is, potential ownership may necessitate consolidated financial reporting, but profit or loss allocation is still to be based on actual, not potential, ownership percentages.

However, the entity may, in substance, have a present ownership interest when it sells and simultaneously agrees to repurchase some of the voting shares it had held in the subsidiary. In such a situation, it does not lose control of access to economic benefits associated with an ownership interest. In this circumstance, the proportion allocated should be determined by taking into account the eventual exercise of potential voting rights and other derivatives that, in substance, give present access to the economic benefits associated with an ownership interest. Note that the right to reacquire shares alone is not enough to have those shares included for purposes of determining the percentage of the subsidiary's profit to be reported by the parent. Rather, the parent must have ongoing access to the economic benefits of ownership of those shares.

A subsidiary is not excluded from consolidation simply because the investor is a venture capital organization, mutual fund unit trust, or similar entity. Also, a subsidiary is not excluded from consolidation because its business activities are dissimilar from those of the other entities included in the group. In such cases, disclosure in accordance with IFRS 8, *Operating Segments,* helps in providing additional relevant information to investors.

Allocation of losses to noncontrolling interests. As a result of adopting the economic entity concept, the consolidated financial statements present noncontrolling interests in the profit or loss of consolidated subsidiaries for the reporting period, separately from the controlling interests (the parent's ownership interests). Also, noncontrolling interests in the net assets of consolidated subsidiaries are identified separately from the controlling interests in them.

Losses allocated to the parent and to the noncontrolling interest may exceed their respective interests in the equity of the subsidiary. When this occurs, and if it continues to occur in subsequent periods, the excess as well as any further losses are to continue to be allocated to the parent and noncontrolling interest even if this allocation results in a deficit balance in noncontrolling interest (losses in excess of the noncontrolling interests in the net assets of the subsidiary).

This is a major departure from the current practice, since the original IAS 27 allows these losses to be allocated to the minority interests only if minority interests have a binding obligation to cover the funding. Under the new approach in IAS 27(R), the controlling interests will be higher in such situations.

Noncontrolling interests in the net assets consist of (1) the amount recognized at the date of the original business combination (calculated in accordance with IFRS 3[R]), and (2) the noncontrolling interests' share of changes in equity (net assets) of the subsidiary since the date of combination.

Changes in ownership interest without loss of control. Subsequent to a business combination, the parent may increase or decrease its ownership percentage in the subsidiary. The parent entity may purchase or sell shares of the subsidiary after the acquisition date without a loss of control of the subsidiary. In addition, the subsidiary may issue new shares or repurchase some of its own shares as treasury shares or for retirement.

In accordance with IAS 27(R), changes in the parent's ownership interest that do not result in a loss of control of the subsidiary are accounted for as equity transactions (transactions with owners acting in their capacity as owners) with no gain or loss recognized in profit or loss (consolidated net income) or in other comprehensive income. Also, no change in the carrying amounts of the subsidiary's assets (including goodwill) or liabilities are to be recognized as a result of such transactions. The carrying amount of the noncontrolling interest in the subsidiary is to be adjusted to reflect the change in ownership interest. Any difference between the fair value of the consideration received or paid in the transaction and the amount by which the noncontrolling interest is adjusted is to be recognized in equity attributable to the parent.

In current practice, as a result of the lack of guidance in IFRS, most common practice has been to account for changes in ownership interest similar to an acquisition or disposal of goodwill. The new approach in IAS 27(R) differs significantly from current practice because IASB acknowledged that obtaining control in a business combination is a significant event and this is the event causing the initial recognition and measurement of all the assets acquired (including goodwill) and liabilities assumed. Subsequent transactions with owners within one economic entity should not affect the measurement of those assets and liabilities. Consequently, changes in a parent's ownership interest (without loss of control) are accounted for within equity.

Example of recognizing changes in the level of the parent's controlling ownership interest

Konin Corporation (KC) owns a 75% interest in Donna Corporation (DC). KC decided to acquire an additional 10% interest in DC from the noncontrolling shareholders in exchange for cash of €100,000. DC has net assets of €800,000. KC accounts for this transaction in the consolidated financial statements as follows:

Equity—Noncontrolling interest	80,000	
Equity—Controlling interest	20,000	
Cash		100,000

In the case of a subsidiary that has accumulated other comprehensive income (AOCI), if there is a change in the parent's ownership interest, the carrying amount of AOCI is to be adjusted through a corresponding charge or credit to equity attributable to the parent.

Changes in ownership interest resulting in loss of control. Control of a subsidiary can be lost as a result of a parent's decision to sell its shares in the subsidiary to a third party or as a result of a subsidiary selling its shares in the marketplace. If a parent company ceases to have a controlling financial interest in a subsidiary, the parent is required to deconsolidate the subsidiary as of the date on which its control ceased. Examples of situations that can result in a parent being required to deconsolidate a subsidiary include

1. Sale by the parent of all or a portion of its ownership interest in the subsidiary resulting in the parent no longer holding a controlling financial interest,
2. Expiration of a contract that granted control of the subsidiary to the parent,
3. Issuance by the subsidiary of shares that reduces the ownership interest of the parent to a level not representing a controlling financial interest,
4. Loss of control of the subsidiary by the parent because the subsidiary becomes subject to control by a governmental body, court, administrator, or regulator.

When control of a subsidiary is lost and a noncontrolling interest is retained, consistent with the approach applied in step acquisitions, the parent should measure that retained interest at fair value and recognize, in profit or loss, a gain or loss on disposal of the controlling interest. The gain or loss is measured as follows:

FVCR = Fair value of consideration received, if any
FVNIR = Fair value of any noncontrolling investment retained by the former parent at the derecognition date (the date control is lost)
CVNI = Carrying value of the noncontrolling interest in the former subsidiary on the derecognition date, including any accumulated other comprehensive income attributable to the noncontrolling interest
CVAL = Carrying value of the former subsidiary's assets and liabilities at the derecognition date

$$(FVCR + FVNIR + CVNI) - CVAL = Gain\ (Loss)$$

Example of accounting for the parent's loss of control of a subsidiary

Konin Corporation (KC) owns an 85% interest in Donna Corporation (DC). On December 31, 2008, in the KC's consolidated financial statements the carrying value of DC's net assets is €1,000,000 and the carrying value of the noncontrolling interest in DC (including the noncontrolling interest's share of accumulated other comprehensive income) is €100,000. On January 1, 2009, KC decided to sell a 50% interest in DC to a third party in exchange for cash of €600,000. As a result of this transaction, KC loses control of DC but retains a 35% interest in the former subsidiary, valued at €400,000 on that date. The gain or loss on the disposal of 50% interest in DC is calculated as follows:

Cash received	€ 600,000
Fair value of retained noncontrolling interest	350,000
Carrying value of DC's noncontrolling interest	100,000
	1,050,000
Less: Carrying value of DC's net assets	1,000,000
Gain on disposal	€ 50,000

Should the parent's loss of controlling financial interest occur through two or more transactions, management of the former parent is to consider whether the transactions should be accounted for as a single transaction. In evaluating whether to combine the transactions, management of the former parent is to consider all of the terms and conditions of the transactions as well as their economic impact. The presence of one or more of the following indicators may lead to management concluding that it should account for multiple transactions as a single transaction:

1. The transactions are entered into simultaneously or in contemplation of one another,
2. The transactions, when considered in tandem, are in-substance, a single transaction designed to achieve an overall commercial objective,
3. The occurrence of one transaction depends on the occurrence of at least one other transaction,
4. One transaction, when considered on its own merits, does not make economic sense, but when considered together with the other transaction or transactions would be considered economically justifiable.

Obviously, this determination requires the exercise of sound judgment and attention to economic substance over legal form.

Separate financial statements. The revised standard IAS 27(R), in addition to consolidated financial statements, address also issues related to accounting for investments in subsidiaries, jointly controlled entities, and associates in separate financial statements. An entity, preparing its separate financial statements, should account for investments in subsidiaries, jointly controlled entities and associates either

1. At cost; or
2. In accordance with IAS 39.

The same accounting should be applied for each category of investments presented in separate financial statements. Investments accounted for at cost, classified as held for sale (or included in a disposal group that is classified as held for sale) are accounted for in accordance with IFRS 5, *Noncurrent Assets Held for Sale and Discontinued Operations* (measured at fair value less costs to sell). However, investments accounted for in accordance with IAS 39 are excluded from IFRS 5's measurement requirements. Consequently, an entity should continue to account for such investments in accordance with IAS 39 even if they meet the held-for-sale criteria in IFRS 5.

IASB identified an inconsistency with IFRS 5 related to the accounting by a parent in its separate financial statements for investments accounted for under IAS 39 classified as held for sale in accordance with IFRS 5. Paragraph BC13 of the Basis for Conclusions on IFRS 5 states that noncurrent assets should be excluded from the measurement scope of IFRS 5 only "if (i) they are already carried at fair value with changes in fair value recognized in profit or loss; or (ii) there would be difficulties in determining their fair value less costs to sell." IASB acknowledged that not all financial assets within the scope of IAS 39 are recognized at fair value through profit or loss, but did not want to make more changes to the accounting for financial assets at that time. This created the need to amend paragraph 38 in IAS 27(R) by *Improvements to IFRS* issued in May 2008, which allowed the practice of accounting for such investments in accordance with IAS 39 to continue, even if they are classified as held-for-sale under IFRS 5.

The IASB noted that although the equity method provides users with some profit or loss information similar to that presented in consolidated financial statements, such information does not need to be provided to the users in separate financial statements. Since the focus in separate statements is on the performance of the investments, separate financial statements prepared using either the fair value method in accordance with IAS 39 or the cost method would be relevant.

An entity should recognize a dividend from a subsidiary, jointly controlled entity or associate in profit or loss in its separate financial statements when it has the right to receive the dividend. Under the cost model, distributions are recognized as income only if they came from postacquistion retained earnings. To apply this method retrospectively upon first-time adoption of IFRS would require information available about the subsidiary's preacquisition retained earnings in accordance with IFRS. Entities adopting IFRS for the first time ("first-time adopters") have received an exemption from restating the retained earnings of the subsidiary at the date of acquisition for the purpose of applying the cost method (*Cost of an Investment in a Subsidiary, Jointly Controlled Entity or Associate* issued in May 2004), since restating preacquisition retained earnings would be a difficult or impossible task. Consequently, the IASB decided to remove the definition of the cost method from IAS 27(R).

Disclosure requirements. IAS 27(R) has its own its own disclosure requirements in addition to those set out in IFRS 3(R) (discussed earlier in the chapter).

If an entity over which the parent does not own, directly or indirectly through subsidiaries, more than half of the voting power is included in the consolidated financial statements, the nature of the relations between the parent and a subsidiary must be explained. If any subsidiary is not included in the consolidated financial statements, the reason why the ownership, directly or indirectly through subsidiaries, more than half of the voting power or potential voting power of an investee does not constitute control, must be set forth.

The financial statements must disclose if the reporting date for a subsidiary is different from that of the parent, and if so, why this is the case. If there are any significant restrictions on the subsidiary's ability to transfer funds to the parent, this must be explained.

If a subsidiary was acquired or disposed of during the period, the effect of the event on the consolidated financial statements should be discussed. If parent-only financial statements are being presented (which is permitted, but not as a substitute for consolidated financial reporting), the method of accounting for interests in subsidiaries should be stated.

Additional disclosures introduced in the revised IAS 27(R) include the amount of any gain or loss arising on the loss of control of a subsidiary. This should include the portion of the gain or loss attributable to recognizing any investment retained in the former subsidiary at its fair value at the date when control is lost, and the line item presenting gains and losses in the statement of comprehensive income.

Also, the IASB decided to converge with the FASB to require that if a parent has equity transactions with noncontrolling interests, it should disclose in a separate schedule the effects of those transactions on the equity of the owners of the parent.

The disclosure requirements of the new standards are quite extensive and, for the reader's convenience, are presented in detail in the disclosure checklist in Appendix A to this publication.

Impact of key changes on the financial statements. The revised standards IFRS 3(R) and IAS 27(R) will have a significant impact on profit or loss reported in the year of the acquisition and in future periods, as well as on the amount of goodwill recognized in the acquirer's consolidated statement of financial position. The impact of certain changes (e.g., the option to measure noncontrolling interest at fair value, or accounting for changes in a parent's controlling ownership interest accounted for as equity transactions) will depend on (1) the accounting method applied in the past to recognize the noncontrolling interest, and (2) the option chosen to measure the noncontrolling interest in accordance with the revised standards.

The revisions to accounting for contingent consideration, which is measured at the acquisition-date fair value, with subsequent changes recognized in profit or loss, may reduce future earnings and increase volatility in earnings. Additionally, expensing acquisition costs when incurred decreases current earnings. Management, taking into consideration its future intentions to acquire the noncontrolling interest, will need to elect for each business combination the appropriate option of measuring the noncontrolling interest, as a result of the potentially negative impact on equity which future acquisitions of noncontrolling interest might have.

The application of IFRS 3(R) and IAS 27(R) will require more efforts (and costs) to identify and measure separately different elements in the acquisition transaction. For example, there is additional guidance on measurement and determination of whether replacement share awards are part of the consideration for the business combination or compensation for postcombination services. The revised standards have increased disclosure requirements, including information about contingent liabilities, contingent consideration, and the assumptions used in determining fair values.

Consolidation Procedures

Presentation of noncontrolling interests. In preparing consolidated financial statements an entity combines the items presented in the financial statements line by line, adding together like items of assets, liabilities, equity, income and expenses. When less than 100% of the shares of the acquired entity are owned by the acquirer, a complication arises in the preparation of consolidated statements, and a noncontrolling interest must be determined and presented. The acquired assets and liabilities are still fully included in the parent's consolidated financial statements and are valued at fair value, which has implications for the presentation of noncontrolling interest.

In order to present financial information about the group as that of a single economic entity, the following basic eliminating entries are needed:

1. The carrying amount of the parent's investment in each subsidiary is eliminated against the parent's portion of equity of each subsidiary;
2. Noncontrolling interests in the profit or loss of consolidated subsidiaries is recognized;
3. Noncontrolling interests in the net assets (equity) of consolidated subsidiaries are recognized separately from the controlling (parent's) ownership interests, measured at the acquisition-date fair value, or at the noncontrolling interest's proportionate share of the subsidiaries, net identifiable assets, plus its share of changes in equity since acquisition.

Noncontrolling interests must be presented in the consolidated statement of financial position within equity, separately from the equity of controlling interests (the owners of the parent).

Intercompany transactions and balances. In preparing consolidated financial statements, any transactions among members of the group (intragroup or intercompany transactions) must be eliminated. For example, a parent may sell merchandise to its subsidiary, at cost or with a profit margin added, before the subsidiary ultimately sells the merchandise to unrelated parties in arm's-length transactions. Furthermore, any balances due to or from members of the consolidated group at the end of the reporting period must also be eliminated. The reason for this requirement is to avoid grossing up the financial statements for transactions or balances that do not represent economic events with outside parties. Were this rule not in effect, a consolidated group could create the appearance of being a much larger entity than it is in reality, merely by engaging in multiple transactions with itself.

If assets have been transferred among the entities in the controlled group at amounts in excess of the transferor's cost, and they have not yet been further transferred to outside parties (e.g., inventories) or not yet consumed (e.g., plant assets subject to depreciation) by the end of the reporting period, the amount of profit not yet realized through an arm's-length transaction must be eliminated.

Different fiscal periods of parent and subsidiary. A practical consideration in preparing consolidated financial statements is to have information on all constituent entities current as of the parent's year-end. If the subsidiaries have different fiscal years, they may prepare updated information as of the parent's year-end, to be used for preparing consolidated statements. Failing this, IAS 27(R) permits combining information as of different dates, as long as this discrepancy does not exceed three months. Of course, if this option is elected, the process of eliminating intercompany transactions and balances may become a bit more complicated, since reciprocal accounts (e.g., sales and cost of sales) will be out of balance for any events occurring after the earlier fiscal year-end but before the later one.

Uniformity of accounting policies. There is a presumption that all the members of the consolidated group should use the same accounting principles to account for similar events and transactions. However, in many cases this will not occur, as, for example, when a subsidiary is acquired that uses FIFO costing for its inventories while the parent has long employed the LIFO method. (Note that LIFO is no longer permitted under provisions of revised IAS 2. The average cost method is still permitted as an alternative to FIFO.) IAS 27 does not demand that one or the other entity change its method of accounting; rather, it merely requires that there be adequate disclosure of the accounting principles employed.

If a subsidiary was acquired during the period, the results of the operations of the subsidiary should be included in consolidated financial statements only for the period it was owned. Since this may cause comparability with earlier periods presented to be impaired, there must be adequate disclosure in the accompanying footnotes to make it possible to interpret the information properly. The posttax profits or losses of operations that have been sold or classified as held for sale during the period should be disclosed separately on the face of the statement of comprehensive income as discontinued operations.

Consolidated Financial Statements with Noncontrolling Interests

When an entity acquires some, but not all, of the voting share of another entity, the shares held by third parties represent a *noncontrolling interest* in the acquired entity. Under IFRS, if a parent entity controls another entity in some other way (as discussed above), the two should be consolidated for financial statement purposes (there is only a limited exception available to some nonpublic entities). The noncontrolling interest in equity and profit of the consolidated entity must also be accounted for.

IAS 27(R) states that when consolidated statements are prepared, the full amount of assets and liabilities (in the statement of financial position) and income and expenses (in the statement of comprehensive income) of the subsidiary are presented. Accordingly, equity attributable to noncontrolling interest should be separately presented in the statement of financial position, representing the noncontrolling interest in consolidated equity (net assets) of the subsidiary entity. A debit (negative) balance in noncontrolling interest could result when the subsidiary has a deficit in its shareholders' equity even if the noncontrolling interests do not have a binding obligation to cover the funding. This is a major departure from the previous practice under the original IAS 27 when this negative equity attributable to noncontrolling interests would be recorded only if there is reason to believe that the noncontrolling owners will make additional capital contributions to erase that deficit. (This situation could occur when the entities were closely held and the noncontrolling owners were related parties having other business relationships with the parent company and/or its shareholders; in other circumstances, a debit in noncontrolling interest would be charged against parent company retained earnings under the concept that the loss will be borne by that company.

In acquisitions of less than 100% of the equity interests in the acquired entity IFRS 3(R) provides the acquirer with a choice of two options to measure noncontrolling interests arising in a business combination: (1) to measure the noncontrolling interest at *fair value* (also recognizing the acquired business at fair value), or (2) to measure the noncontrolling interest at *the noncontrolling interest's share of the value of the net assets acquired.* Under the fair value approach to measure noncontrolling interest, the acquired business will be recognized at fair value, with the controlling share of total goodwill assigned to the controlling interest and the noncontrolling share allocated to the noncontrolling interest. Under the second approach to measure noncontrolling interest, while the net identifiable assets attributable to the noncontrolling interest are written up to the fair values implied by the acquisition transaction, goodwill will not be imputed for the noncontrolling share.

IAS 27 as revised stipulates that noncontrolling interest be presented in the consolidated statement of financial position as a separate component of, but within, shareholders' equity. In the past, IAS 27 permitted noncontrolling interest to be shown in a separate caption positioned between liabilities and equity. However, IASB determined that it did not meet the definition of a liability and should be included within equity.

In accordance with IAS 27(R), income attributable to noncontrolling interest should be separately presented in the statement of comprehensive income. Generally, this is accomplished by presenting profit and total comprehensive income, attributable separately to owners of the parent (controlling interest) and noncontrolling interest.

Example of consolidation process—noncontrolling interest measured at fair value

Assume that on January 1, 2008, Alto Ltd acquired 90% of the equity interest in Bass Ltd in exchange for 5,400 shares having a fair value of €120,600 on that day. Management elects the option to measure noncontrolling interest at fair value and a value of €13,400 is assigned to the 10% noncontrolling interest. The following shows the financial positions of the companies before business combination at January 1, 2008.

Alto Ltd and Bass Ltd
Statements of Financial Position at January 1, 2008
(before combination)

	Alto Ltd	*Bass Ltd*
Assets		
Cash	€ 30,900	€ 37,400
Accounts receivable (net)	34,200	9,100
Inventories	22,900	16,100
Equipment	200,000	50,000
Less accumulated depreciation	(21,000)	(10,000)
Patents	--	10,000
Total assets	€267,000	€112,600
Liabilities and shareholders' equity		
Accounts payable	€ 4,000	€ 6,600
Bonds payable, 10%	100,000	--
Share capital	115,000	65,000
Retained earnings	48,000	41,000
Total liabilities and shareholders' equity	€267,000	€112,600

Note that in the foregoing, the net assets (equity) of Bass Ltd may be computed by one of two methods.

Method 1: Subtract the book value of the liability from the book value of the assets.

€112,600 – €6,600 = €106,000

Method 2: Add the book value of the components of Bass Ltd's shareholders' equity.

€50,000 + €15,000 + €41,000 = €106,000

At the date of the combination, the fair values of the assets and liabilities of Bass were determined by appraisal, as follows:

Bass Ltd Item	Book value (BV)	Fair market value (FMV)	Difference between BV and FMV
Cash	€ 37,400	€ 37,400	€ --
Accounts receivable (net)	9,100	9,100	--
Inventories	16,100	17,100	1,000
Equipment (net)	40,000	48,000	8,000
Patents	10,000	13,000	3,000
Accounts payable	(6,600)	(6,600)	--
Totals	€106,000	€118,000	€12,000

The equipment has a book value of €40,000 (€50,000 less 20% depreciation of €10,000). An appraisal concluded that the equipment's replacement cost was €60,000 less 20% accumulated depreciation of €12,000, resulting in a net fair value of €48,000.

When a noncontrolling interest is measured at fair value, the concept employed is to record the acquired business at fair value. All the assets and liabilities of Bass Ltd are recorded at their fair values as of the date of the acquisition, including the revaluation portion accruing to the non-controlling interest's ownership share. In addition, full goodwill will be recognized: the parent's share of total goodwill is assigned to the controlling interest and the imputed noncontrolling share of total goodwill is allocated to the noncontrolling interest.

In our example, goodwill (€16,000) is calculated as follows: consideration transferred, at fair value (€120,600) plus noncontrolling interest (€13,400) minus the net assets of Bass Ltd, at fair value (€118,000). The amount allocated to the parent's interest is €14,400 (90% × €16,000) and the amount allocated to the noncontrolling interest is €1,600 (10% × €16,000).

Bass's identifiable (i.e., before goodwill) net assets will be reported in the Alto consolidated statement of financial position at €118,000. These amounts are computed as follows:

Bass Ltd net assets, at FMV	€118,000	
90% thereof (majority interest)		€106,200
Bass Ltd net assets, at FMV	118,000	
10% thereof (noncontrolling interest)		11,800
Total identifiable net assets		€118,000

Goodwill is calculated as follows:

Consideration transferred (at fair value)	€120,600
Noncontrolling interest (at fair value)	13,400
Total	134,000
Fair value of Bass Ltd net assets	(118,000)
Goodwill (total)	16,000
Goodwill allocated to controlling interests (90%)	14,400
Goodwill allocated to noncontrolling interests (10%)	1,600

Working papers for the consolidated statement of financial position as of the date of the transaction will be as shown below.

Alto Ltd and Bass Ltd Consolidated Working Papers
As of the Date of Combination—1/1/08

Acquisition accounting
90% interest

	Alto Ltd	Bass Ltd	Adjustments and eliminations Debit	Credit	Noncontrolling interest	Consolidated balances
Statement of financial position, 1/1/08						
Cash	€ 30,900	€ 37,400				€ 68,300
Accounts receivable	34,200	9,100				43,300
Inventories	22,900	16,100	€ 1,000[b]			40,000
Equipment	200,000	50,000	10,000[b]			260,000
Accumulated depreciation	(21,000)	(10,000)		€ 2,000[b]		(33,000)
Investment in Bass Ltd	120,600			120,600[a]		
Difference between fair and book value			12,000[a]	12,000[b]		
Goodwill			16,000[a]			16,000
Patents		10,000	3,000[b]			13,000
Total assets	€387,600	€112,600				€407,600
Accounts payable	€ 4,000	€ 6,600				€ 10,600
Bonds payable	100,000					100,000
Share capital	235,600	65,000	58,500[a]		€ 6,500	235,600
Retained earnings	48,000	41,000	36,900[a]		4,100	48,000
Share of revaluation				1,200[a]	1,200	
Share of goodwill				1,600[a]		
Noncontrolling interest						13,400 NI
Total liabilities and equity	€387,600	€112,600	€137,400	€137,400		€407,600

Based on the foregoing, the consolidated statement of financial position of the date of acquisition will be as follows:

Alto Ltd and Bass Ltd
Consolidated Statement of Financial Position at January 1, 2008
(immediately after combination)

Assets

Cash	€ 68,300
Accounts receivable, net	43,300
Inventories	40,000
Equipment	260,000
Less accumulated depreciation	(33,000)
Goodwill	16,000
Patents	13,000
Total assets	€407,600

Liabilities and shareholders' equity

Accounts payable	€ 10,600
Bonds payable, 10%	100,000
Total liabilities	110,600
Share capital	235,600
Retained earnings	48,000
Owners of parent	283,600
Noncontrolling interest	13,400
Total equity	297,000
Total liabilities and equity	€407,600

1. Investment on Alto Ltd's books

The entry to record the 90% acquisition in Bass Ltd on Alto Ltd's books was

Investment in share of Bass Ltd	120,600	
Share capital		120,600

To record the issuance of 5,400 shares of capital to acquire a 90% interest in Bass Ltd

Although share capital is issued for the consideration in our example, Alto could have transferred cash, debentures, or any other form of consideration acceptable to Bass Ltd's shareholders to make the purchase combination.

2. Allocation of step-up of Bass's net assets to fair value is calculated as follows:

Adjustment of asset values to fair values			
Book value of Bass Ltd at acquisition date			
Share capital	€ 65,000		
Retained earnings	41,000		
	€106,000		
Parent's share (% stock ownership)	× 90%		
Acquired share of book value	(a) 95,400		
Allocation of step up to fair value of net assets			
Fair value of net assets	€118,000		
Book value of net assets	106,000		
Excess fair value over book value (step-up)	12,000		
Parent's share (% share ownership)	× 90%		
Parent's share of step up	(b) 10,800		
Parent's share of net assets at fair value (a) + (b)	€106,200	€106,200	
Noncontrolling interest's share of net assets at fair value		€ 1,800	

Adjustment of asset values (the workpaper entry [b])		
Inventory	1,000	
Equipment	10,000	
Patents	3,000	
Accumulated depreciation		2,000
Differential*		12,000

   * *Differential represents excess fair value over book value (the difference between the fair value and book value of Bass Ltd's net assets)*

3. Elimination entries on preceding workpaper (the workpaper entry [a])

The basic reciprocal accounts are the investment in subsidiary account on the parent's books and the subsidiary's shareholders' equity accounts. Only the parent's share of the subsidiary's accounts may be eliminated as reciprocal accounts. The remaining 10% portion is allocated to the noncontrolling interest. The entries below include documentation showing the company source for the information. The workpaper entry to eliminate the basic reciprocal accounts is as follows:

Share capital—Bass Ltd.	58,500	
Retained earnings—Bass Ltd.	36,900*	
Differential	12,000	
Goodwill	16,000	
Investment in share of Bass Ltd		120,600
Noncontrolling interest in revaluation		1,200
Noncontrolling interest in goodwill		1,600

   * *90% × €41,000 = €36,900*

The noncontrolling interest column includes the 10% interest of Bass Ltd's net assets owned by outside third parties €10,600 (noncontrolling interest's proportionate share of Bass's equity) plus the noncontrolling interest's share in revaluation of net assets to fair values €1,200 (10% × €12,000) and plus imputed goodwill allocated to the noncontrolling interest (10% × €16,000).

This example does not include any other intercompany accounts as of the date of combination. If any existed, they would be eliminated to present the consolidated entity fairly. Several examples of other reciprocal accounts will be shown later for the preparation of consolidated financial statements subsequent to the date of acquisition.

Example of consolidation process—noncontrolling interest measured at the noncontrolling interest's proportionate share of the acquiree's net assets

Assume that on January 1, 2008, Alto Ltd acquired 90% of the equity interests in Bass Ltd in exchange for 5,400 shares having a fair value of €120,600 on that day. Management elects the option to measure noncontrolling interest at the noncontrolling interest's proportionate share of the Bass Ltd net assets. The following shows the financial positions of the companies before business combination at January 1, 2008:

Alto Ltd and Bass Ltd
Statements of Financial Position at January 1, 2008
(before combination)

	Alto Ltd	*Bass Ltd*
Assets		
Cash	€ 30,900	€ 37,400
Accounts receivable (net)	34,200	9,100
Inventories	22,900	16,100
Equipment	200,000	50,000
Less accumulated depreciation	(21,000)	(10,000)
Patents	--	10,000
Total assets	€267,000	€112,600
Liabilities and shareholders' equity		
Accounts payable	€ 4,000	€ 6,600
Bonds payable, 10%	100,000	--
Share capital	115,000	65,000
Retained earnings	48,000	41,000
Total liabilities and shareholders' equity	€267,000	€112,600

At the date of the combination, the fair values of the assets and liabilities of Bass Ltd were determined by appraisal, as follows:

Bass Ltd Item	*Book value (BV)*	*Fair market value (FMV)*	*Difference between BV and FMV*
Cash	€ 37,400	€ 37,400	€ --
Accounts receivable (net)	9,100	9,100	--
Inventories	16,100	17,100	1,000
Equipment (net)	40,000	48,000	8,000
Patents	10,000	13,000	3,000
Accounts payable	(6,600)	(6,600)	--
Totals	€106,000	€118,000	€12,000

The equipment has a book value of €40,000 (€50,000 less 20% depreciation of €10,000). An appraisal concluded that the equipment's replacement cost was €60,000 less 20% accumulated depreciation of €12,000, resulting in a net fair value of €48,000.

When a noncontrolling interest is measured at the noncontrolling interest's proportionate share of the acquiree's net assets, the concept employed is to record all the assets and liabilities of Bass Ltd at their fair values as of the date of the acquisition, including the portion represented by the noncontrolling interest's ownership share. There will be no mixture of costs for the net identifiable assets acquired in the business combination in the consolidated statement of financial position; all items will be presented at fair values as of the acquisition date. Goodwill, however, will be recognized only to the extent that the acquirer paid more than the fair values of the net identifiable assets acquired; there will not be any imputed goodwill attributable to the noncontrolling interest.

In the present example, Bass's identifiable (i.e., before goodwill) net assets will be reported in the Alto consolidated statement of financial position at €118,000. These amounts are computed as follows:

Bass Ltd net assets, at FMV	€118,000	
90% thereof (Parent's interest)		€106,200
Bass Ltd net assets, at FMV	118,000	
10% thereof (noncontrolling interest)		11,800
Total identifiable net assets		€118,000

Working papers for the consolidated statement of financial position as of the date of the transaction will be as shown below.

Alto Ltd and Bass Ltd Consolidated Working Papers
As of the Date of Combination—1/1/08

Acquisition accounting
90% interest

Statement of financial position, 1/1/08	Alto Ltd	Bass Ltd	Adjustments and eliminations Debit	Credit	Noncontrolling interest	Consolidated balances
Cash	€ 30,900	€ 37,400				€ 68,300
Accounts receivable	34,200	9,100				43,300
Inventories	22,900	16,100	€ 1,000[b]			40,000
Equipment	200,000	50,000	10,000[b]			260,000
Accumulated depreciation	(21,000)	(10,000)		€ 2,000[b]		(33,000)
Investment in Bass Ltd	120,600			120,600[a]		
Difference between fair and book value			12,000[a]	12,000[b]		
Goodwill			14,400[a]			14,400
Patents		10,000	3,000[b]			13,000
Total assets	€387,600	€112,600				€406,000
Accounts payable	€ 4,000	€ 6,600				€ 10,600
Bonds payable	100,000					100,000
Share capital	235,600	65,000	58,500[a]		€ 6,500	235,600
Retained earnings	48,000	41,000	36,900[a]		4,100	48,000
Share of revaluation				1,200[a]	1,200	
Noncontrolling interest					€11,800	11,800 NI
Total liabilities and equity	€387,600	€112,600	€135,800	€135,800		€406,000

Based on the foregoing, the consolidated statement of financial position of the date of acquisition will be as follows:

Alto Ltd and Bass Ltd
Consolidated Statement of Financial Position at January 1, 2008
(immediately after combination)

Assets

Cash	€ 68,300
Accounts receivable, net	43,300
Inventories	40,000
Equipment	260,000
Less accumulated depreciation	(33,000)
Goodwill	14,400
Patents	13,000
Total assets	€406,000

Liabilities and shareholders' equity

Accounts payable	€ 10,600
Bonds payable, 10%	100,000
Total liabilities	110,600
Share capital	235,600
Retained earnings	48,000
Owners of parent	283,600
Noncontrolling interest	11,800
Total equity	295,400
Total liabilities and equity	€406,000

1. Investment on Alto company's books
    The entry to record the 90% acquisition in Bass Ltd on Alto company's books was

Investment in share of Bass Ltd	120,600	
Share capital		120,600

    To record the issuance of 5,400 shares of capital to acquire a 90% equity interest in Bass Ltd

Although share capital is issued for the consideration in our example, Alto could have transferred cash, debentures, or any other form of consideration acceptable to Bass Ltd's shareholders to make the purchase combination.

2. Difference between consideration transferred (at fair value) and fair value of net assets acquired.

The difference between the acquisition-date fair value of the consideration transferred and the acquisition-date fair values of the assets acquired and liabilities assumed is computed as follows:

Consideration transferred (fair value of shares)			€120,600
Computation of goodwill			
Book value of Bass Company at acquisition date			
Share capital		€ 65,000	
Retained earnings		41,000	
		€106,000	
Parent's share (% share ownership)		× 90%	
Acquired share of book value	(a)	95,400	
Allocation of step-up to fair value of net assets			
Fair value of net assets		€118,000	
Book value of net assets		106,000	
Excess fair value over book value (step-up)		12,000	
Parent's share (% share ownership)		× 90%	
Parent's share of step-up	(b)	10,800	
Parent's share of net assets at fair value (a) + (b)		€106,200	€106,200
Goodwill to be recognized			€ 14,400
Adjustment of asset values (the workpaper entry [b])			
Inventory		1,000	
Equipment		10,000	
Patents		3,000	
Accumulated depreciation			2,000
Differential*			12,000

Differential represents excess fair value over book value (the difference between the fair value and book value of Bass Ltd's net assets)

3. Elimination entries on preceding workpaper (the workpaper entry [a])

The basic reciprocal accounts are the investment in subsidiary account on the parent's books and the subsidiary's shareholders' equity accounts. Only the parent's share of the subsidiary's accounts may be eliminated as reciprocal accounts. The remaining 10% portion is allocated to the minority interest. The entries below include documentation showing the company source for the information. The workpaper entry to eliminate the basic reciprocal accounts is as follows:

Share capital—Bass Ltd.	58,500	
Retained earnings—Bass Ltd.	36,900*	
Differential	12,000	
Goodwill	16,000	
Investment in share of Bass Co.—Alto Co.		120,600
Noncontrolling interest in revaluation		1,200

*   *€41,000 × 90%= €36,900*

Note that only 90% of Bass Ltd shareholders' equity accounts are eliminated.

The noncontrolling interest column includes the 10% interest of Bass Ltd's net assets owned by outside third parties (noncontrolling interest's proportionate share of Bass's equity) plus the noncontrolling interest's share in revaluation of net assets to fair values. Consequently, 100% of the fair values of Bass Ltd's assets and liabilities are included in the consolidated statements, but no goodwill is allocated to the noncontrolling interest.

This example does not include any other intercompany accounts as of the date of combination. If any existed, they would be eliminated to present the consolidated entity fairly. Several examples of other reciprocal accounts will be shown in the next paragraph presenting the preparation of consolidated financial statements subsequent to the date of acquisition.

Consolidation process in periods subsequent to acquisition. The approach followed to prepare a complete set of consolidated financial statements subsequent to a business combination is quite similar to that used to prepare a consolidated statement of financial position as of the date of acquisition. Because consolidation subsequent to a subsidiary's acquisition involves changes that take place over time, the resulting financial statements rest heavily on the concepts of consolidated comprehensive income and consolidated retained earnings.

This paragraph follows the example of the consolidation process as of the date of acquisition with noncontrolling interest measured at the noncontrolling interest's proportionate share of the acquiree's net assets, discussed in the previous section. The following additional information is available in the first year after the acquisition (2008):

1. Alto Ltd uses the partial equity method to record changes in the value of the investment account. The partial equity method means that the parent reports its share of earnings, and so on, of the subsidiary on its books using the equity method, but any differential between acquisition cost and underlying fair value of net assets, and so on, is not addressed on an ongoing basis; rather, these matters await the typical year-end accounting adjustment process.

2. During 2008, Alto Ltd sold merchandise to Bass Ltd that originally cost Alto Ltd €15,000, and the sale was made for €20,000. On December 31, 2008, Bass Ltd's inventory included merchandise purchased from Alto Ltd at a cost to Bass Ltd of €12,000.

3. Also during 2008, Alto Ltd acquired €18,000 of merchandise from Bass Ltd. Bass Ltd uses a normal markup of 25% above its cost. Alto Ltd's ending inventory includes €10,000 of the merchandise acquired from Bass Ltd.

4. Bass Ltd reduced its intercompany account payable to Alto Ltd to a balance of €4,000 as of December 31, 2008, by making a payment of €1,000 on December 30. This €1,000 payment was still in transit on December 31, 2008.

5. On January 2, 2008, Bass Ltd acquired equipment from Alto Ltd for €7,000. The equipment was originally purchased by Alto Ltd for €5,000 and had a book value of €4,000 at the date of sale to Bass Ltd. The equipment had an estimated remaining life of four years as of January 2, 2008.

6. On December 31, 2008, Bass Ltd purchased for €44,000, 50% of the outstanding bonds issued by Alto Ltd. The bonds mature on December 31, 2010, and were originally issued at par. The bonds pay interest annually on December 31 of each year, and the interest was paid to the prior investor immediately before Bass Ltd's purchase of the bonds.

The worksheet for the preparation of consolidated financial statements as of December 31, 2008, is presented on the following pages.

The investment account balance at the statement date should be reconciled to ensure that the parent company made the proper entries under the method of accounting used to account for the investment. Any adjustments (e.g., depreciation) made with respect to the step-up to fair values will be recognized only in the worksheets.

An analysis of the investment account at December 31, 2008, is as presented below.

	Investment in Share of Bass Ltd		
Original cost	120,600		
% of Bass Ltd's income			% of Bass Ltd's dividends
(€9,400 × 90%)	8,460	3,600	declared (€4,000 × 90%)
Balance, 12/31/08	125,460		

Any errors will require correcting entries before the consolidation process is continued. Correcting entries will be posted to the books of the appropriate company; eliminating entries are not posted to either company's books.

The difference between the consideration transferred in business combination and the book value of the assets acquired and liabilities assumed was determined and allocated in the preparation of the acquisition-date consolidated statements presented earlier. The same computations are used in preparing financial statements for as long as the investment is owned and the acquiree controlled.

The following adjusting and eliminating entries will be required to prepare consolidated financial statements as of December 31, 2008. Note that a consolidated statement of comprehensive income is required, and therefore, the nominal (i.e., income and expense) accounts are still open. The number or letter in parentheses to the left of the entry corresponds to the key used on the worksheets presented after the following discussion.

Step 1—Complete the transaction for any intercompany items in transit at the end of the year.

(a)	Cash	1,000	
	Accounts receivable		1,000

This adjusting entry will now properly present the financial positions of both companies, and the consolidation process may be continued.

Step 2—Prepare the eliminating entries.

(a)	Sales	38,000	
	Cost of goods sold		38,000

Total intercompany sales of €38,000 include €20,000 in a downstream transaction from Alto Ltd to Bass Ltd and €18,000 in an upstream transaction from Bass Ltd to Alto Ltd.

(b)	Cost of goods sold	5,000	
	Inventory		5,000

The ending inventories are overstated because of the unrealized profit from the intercompany sales. The debit to cost of goods sold is required because a decrease in ending inventory will increase cost of goods sold to be deducted on the income statement. Supporting computations for the entry are as follows:

	In ending inventory of	
	Alto Ltd	Bass Ltd
Intercompany sales not resold, at selling price	€10,000	€12,000
Cost basis of remaining intercompany merchandise		
From Bass to Alto (÷ 125%)	(8,000)	
From Alto to Bass (÷ 133 1/3%)	_____	(9,000)
Unrealized profit	€_2,000	€_3,000

NOTE: When preparing consolidated working papers for 2009 (the next fiscal period), an additional eliminating entry will be required if the goods in 2008's ending inventory are sold to outsiders during 2009. The additional entry will recognize the profit for 2009 that was eliminated as unrealized in 2008. This entry is necessary since the entry at the end of 2008 was made only on the worksheet. The 2009 entry will be as follows:

Retained earnings—Bass Ltd, 1/1/09	*2,000*	
Retained earnings—Alto Ltd, 1/1/09	*3,000*	
Cost of goods sold, 2009		*5,000*

(c)	Accounts payable	4,000	
	Accounts receivable		4,000

This entry eliminates the remaining intercompany receivable/payable owed by Bass Ltd to Alto Ltd. This eliminating entry is necessary to avoid overstating the consolidated entity's statement of financial position. The receivable/payable is not extinguished, and Bass Ltd must still transfer €4,000 to Alto Ltd in the future.

(d)	Gain on sale of equipment	3,000	
	Equipment		2,000
	Accumulated depreciation		250
	Depreciation expense		750

This entry eliminates the gain on the intercompany sale of the equipment, eliminates the overstatement of equipment, and removes the excess depreciation taken on the gain. Supporting computations for the entry are as follows:

	Cost	At date of intercompany sale accum. depr.	2008 depr. exp.	End of period accum. depr.
Original basis				
(to seller, Alto Co.)	€5,000	€(1,000)	€ 1,000	€(2,000)
New basis				
(to buyer, Bass Co.)	7,000	--	1,750	(1,750)
Difference	€(2,000)		€(750)	€ 250

If the intercompany sale had not occurred, Alto Ltd would have depreciated the remaining book value of €4,000 over the estimated remaining life of four years. However, since Bass Ltd's acquisition price (€7,000) was more than Alto Ltd's basis in the asset (€4,000), the depreciation recorded on the books of Bass Ltd will include part of the intercompany unrealized profit. The equipment must be reflected on the consolidated statements at the original cost to the consolidated entity. Therefore, the write-up of €2,000 in the equipment, the excess depreciation of €750, and the gain of €3,000 must be eliminated. The ending balance of accumulated depreciation must be shown at what it would have been if the intercompany equipment transaction had not occurred. In future periods, a retained earnings account will be used instead of the gain account; however, the other concepts will be extended to include the additional periods.

(e)
Bonds payable	50,000	
Investment in bonds of Alto Ltd		44,000
Gain on extinguishment of debt		6,000

This entry eliminates the book value of Alto Ltd's debt against the bond investment account of Bass Ltd. On a consolidated entity basis, this transaction must be shown as a retirement of debt, even though Alto Ltd has the outstanding intercompany debt to Bass Ltd. Any gains or losses on debt extinguishment will be reported in the statement of comprehensive income. In future periods Bass Ltd will amortize the discount, thereby bringing the investment account up to par value. In future periods the retained earnings account will be used in the eliminating entry instead of the gain account, as the gain is closed out with other nominal accounts.

(f)
Equity in subsidiary's profit—Alto Ltd.	8,460	
Dividends declared—Bass Ltd.		3,600
Investment in share of Alto Ltd.		4,860

This elimination entry adjusts the investment account back to its balance at the beginning of the period and also eliminates the subsidiary profit or loss account.

(g)
Share capital—Bass Ltd.	58,500	
Retained earnings—Bass Ltd.	36,900	
Noncontrolling interest in revaluation		1,200
Differential	12,000	
Goodwill	14,400	
Investment in share of Bass Ltd—Alto Ltd.		120,600

This entry eliminates 90% of Bass Ltd's shareholders' equity at the beginning of the year, 1/1/08. Note that the changes during the year were eliminated in entry (f).

(h)
Adjustment of asset book values to fair values		
Inventory	1,000	
Equipment	10,000	
Patents	3,000	
Accumulated depreciation		2,000
Differential		12,000

This entry allocates the differential (excess of fair value over the book values of the assets acquired) to step up the carrying values of Bass's net assets to their fair values. Note that this entry is similar to the allocation entry made to prepare consolidated financial statements for January 1, 2008, the date of acquisition.

(i)	Cost of goods sold	1,000	
	Depreciation expense	2,000	
	Other operating expenses—patent amortization	300	
	Inventory		1,000
	Accumulated depreciation		2,000
	Patents		300

The elimination entry amortizes the revaluations to fair market value made in entry (h). The inventory has been sold and therefore becomes part of cost of goods sold. The remaining revaluations will be amortized as follows:

	Revaluation	*Amortization period*	*Annual amortization*
Equipment (net)	€8,000	4 years	€2,000
Patents	3,000	10 years	300

The amortizations will continue to be made on future worksheets. For example, at the end of the next year (2009), the amortization entry (i) would be as follows:

Differential	3,300	
Depreciation expense	2,000	
Other operating expenses—patent amortization	300	
Inventory		1,000
Accumulated depreciation		4,000
Patents		600

The initial debit of €3,300 to differential is an aggregation of the prior period's charges to profit or loss (€1,000 + €2,000 + €300). During subsequent years, some accountants prefer reducing the allocated amounts in entry (h) for prior period's charges. In this case the amortization entry in future periods would reflect just that period's amortizations.

In adjusting for the noncontrolling interest in the consolidated entity's equity and earnings, the following guidelines should be observed:

1. Only the parent's share of the subsidiary's shareholders' equity is eliminated in the basic eliminating entry. The noncontrolling interest's share is presented separately.
2. The entire amount of intercompany reciprocal items is eliminated. For example, all receivables/payables and sales/cost of sales with a 90% subsidiary are eliminated.
3. For intercompany transactions in inventory and fixed assets, the possible effect on noncontrolling interest depends on whether the original transaction affected the subsidiary's profit or loss. Noncontrolling interest is adjusted only if the subsidiary is the selling entity. In this case, the noncontrolling interest is adjusted for its percentage ownership of the share capital of the subsidiary. The noncontrolling interest is not adjusted for unrealized profits on downstream sales. The effects of downstream transactions are confined solely to the parent's (i.e., controlling) ownership interests.

The noncontrolling interest's share of the subsidiary's profit is shown as a deduction on the consolidated statement of comprehensive income since 100% of the subsidiary revenues and expenses are combined, even though the parent company owns less than a 100% interest. For our example, the noncontrolling interest deduction on the income statement is computed as follows:

Bass Ltd's reported profit	€9,400
Less unrealized profit on an upstream inventory sale	(2,000)
Bass Ltd's profit for consolidated financial purposes	€7,400
Noncontrolling interest share	× 10%
Noncontrolling interest in profit	€ 740

The noncontrolling interest's share of the net assets of Bass Ltd is shown in the consolidated statement of financial position within Bass's shareholders' equity. The computation for the noncontrolling interest shown in the statement of financial position for our example is as follows:

Bass Ltd's share capital, 12/31/08	€65,000	
Noncontrolling interest share	× 10%	€ 6,500
Bass Ltd's retained earnings, 1/1/08	€41,000	
Noncontrolling interest share	× 10%	4,100
Bass Ltd's 2008 profit for consolidated purposes	€ 7,400	
Noncontrolling interest share of profit	× 10%	740
Bass Ltd's dividends during 2008	€ 4,000	
Noncontrolling interest share	× 10%	(400)
Total noncontrolling interest, 12/31/08		€10,940

Alto Ltd and Bass Ltd Consolidated Working Papers
Year Ended December 31, 2008

Acquisition accounting
90% owned subsidiary
Subsequent year

	Alto Ltd	Bass Ltd	Adjustments and eliminations Debit	Credit	Noncontrolling interest	Consolidated balances
Statements of comprehensive income for year ended 12/31/08						
Sales	€750,000	€420,000	€ 38,000[a]			€1,132,000
Cost of sales	581,000	266,000	5,000[b] 1,000[i]	€ 38,000[a]		815,000
Gross margin	169,000	154,000				317,000
Depreciation and interest expense	28,400	16,200	2,000[i]	750[d]		45,850
Other operating expenses	117,000	128,400	300[i]			245,700
Profit from continuing operations	23,600	9,400				25,450
Gain on sale of equipment	3,000		3,000[d]			
Gain on bonds				6,000[e]		6,000
Equity in subsidiary's profit	8,460		8,460[f]			
Noncontrolling interest in profit (€7,400 × .10)					€ 740	(740)
Profit for the year	€ 35,060	€ 9,400	€ 57,760	€ 44,750	€ 740	€ 30,710
Statement of retained earnings for year ended 12/31/08 1/1/08 retained earnings						
Alto Ltd	€ 48,000					€ 48,000
Bass Ltd		€ 41,000	€ 36,900[g]		€ 4,100	
Add profit (from above)	35,060	9,400	57,760	€ 44,750	740	30,710
Total	83,060	50,400			4,840	78,710
Deduct dividends	15,000	4,000		3,600[f]	400	15,000
Balance, 12/31/08	€ 68,060	€ 46,400	€ 94,660	€ 48,350	€ 4,440	€ 63,710

	Alto Ltd	Bass Ltd	Adjustments and eliminations Debit	Credit	Noncontrolling interest	Consolidated balances
Statement of financial position						
Cash	€ 45,300	€ 6,400	€ 1,000[l]			€ 52,700
Accounts receivable (net)	43,700	12,100		€ 1,000[l]		50,800
				4,000[c]		
Inventories	38,300	20,750	1,000[h]	5,000[b]		54,050
				1,000[i]		
Equipment	195,000	57,000	10,000[h]	2,000[d]		260,000
Accumulated depreciation	(35,200)	(18,900)		250[d]		(58,350)
				2,000[h]		
				2,000[i]		
Investment in share of Bass Ltd				4,860[f]		
	125,460			120,600[g]		
Differential			2,000[g]	2,000[h]		
Goodwill			14,400[g]			14,400
Investment in bonds of Alto Ltd		44,000		44,000[e]		
Patents		9,000	3,000[h]	300[i]		11,700
	€412,560	€130,350				€ 385,300
Accounts payable	€ 8,900	€ 18,950	4,000[c]			€ 23,850
Bonds payable	100,000		50,000[e]			50,000
Share capital	235,600	65,000	58,500[g]		€ 6,500	235,600
Retained earnings (from above)	68,060	46,400	94,660	48,350	4,440	63,710
Noncontrolling share of revaluation				1,200	1,200	
Noncontrolling interest in equity					€10,940	12,140
	€412,560	€130,350	€238,560	€238,560		€385,300

The remainder of the consolidation process consists of the following worksheet techniques:

1. Take all income items across horizontally, and foot the adjustments, noncontrolling interest, and consolidated columns down to the net income line.
2. Take the amounts on the profit or loss line (on the statement of comprehensive income) in the adjustments, noncontrolling interest, and consolidated balances columns down to retained earnings items across the consolidated balances column. Foot and crossfoot the retained earnings statement.
3. Take the amounts of ending retained earnings in each of the four columns down to the ending retained earnings line in the statement of financial position. Foot the noncontrolling interest column and place its total in the consolidated balances column. Take all the statement of financial position items across to consolidated balances column.

Other Accounting Issues Arising in Business Combinations

Depending on the tax jurisdiction, an acquirer may or may not succeed to the available tax loss carryforward benefits of an acquired entity. IFRS requires that a liability approach be used in accounting for the tax effects of temporary differences, which includes the tax effects of tax loss carryforwards. If an acquirer is permitted to use the predecessor's tax benefits, the amount to be reflected in its statement of financial position will be measured in accordance with IAS 12, which is the amount of the benefits expected to be realized. As expectations change over time, this amount will be amended, with any such adjustments being taken into tax expense of the period in which expectations change. If the acquirer can only utilize the benefits to offset taxes on earnings of the operations acquired (i.e., it cannot shelter other sources of earnings), it will be necessary to project profitable operations to support recording this benefit as an asset.

Subsequent identification of, or changes in value of, assets and liabilities acquired. IFRS 3(R) stipulates that individual assets and liabilities should be recognized in an acquisition to the extent that there are probable future economic benefits that will flow to the acquirer and a reliable measure is available of the fair value. In some cases, due to one or both of these criteria not being met at the date of the transaction, some assets or liabilities may not be recognized (which would normally have the ramification that goodwill would be larger). The standard stipulates that where the acquirer knows that there are possible assets and liabilities which cannot be recognized certainly at acquisition date, it may assign provisional values for a maximum of twelve months from the date of acquisition. In these circumstances adjustments may be made to the acquisition transaction, and these should be done as at the acquisition date. Deferred tax assets that did not meet the criteria for recognition at the time of acquisition but are subsequently realized should trigger a change in goodwill. The only other adjustment possible is the correction of an error. Changes in estimates flow through the statement of comprehensive income in the period where they are recognized.

The reason for this requirement is to avoid having changes made to goodwill or gain on a bargain purchase over an unlimited time horizon.

Combined Financial Statements

When a group of entities is under common ownership, control, or management, it is often useful to present combined (or combining, showing the separate as well as the combined entities) financial statements. In this situation, the economic substance of the nominally independent entities' operations may be more important to statement users than is the legal form of those entities. When consolidated statements are not presented, combined statements may be used to show the financial position, or operating results, of a group of companies that are each subsidiaries of a common parent.

As described in the main part of this chapter, the revised IFRS 3(R) and IAS 27(R) include within their scope combinations involving only mutual entities and combinations achieved by contract alone. In accordance with IFRS 3(R), mutual entities are to be accounted for in the same way as a commercial acquisition, and on the basis that one of the entities was an acquirer. Where there is no consideration, as in a combination by contract, the fair value of the assets and liabilities of the acquiree would be attributed to the noncontrolling interest (which in this scenario are actually the acquiree's unrelated shareholders). Where two mutual entities combine, the aggregate of the fair value of the acquiree's net assets and of any assets given, liabilities assumed or equity issued by the acquirer would be added to the acquirer's equity issued (contributed capital).

Combinations of Entities under Common Control

IFRS 3(R) explicitly does *not* apply to entities under common control (e.g., brother-sister corporations). A question arises, however, when a parent (Company P) transfers ownership in one of its subsidiaries (Company B) to another of its subsidiaries (Company A) in exchange for additional shares of Company A. In such an instance, A's carrying value for the investment in B should be P's basis, not B's book value. Furthermore, if A subsequently retires the interests of noncontrolling owners of B, the transaction should be accounted for as an acquisition, whether it is effected through a share issuance by A or by a cash payment to the selling shareholders.

Furthermore, when an acquisition transaction is closely followed by a sale of the parent's subsidiary to the newly acquired (target) entity, these two transactions should be viewed as a single transaction. Accordingly, the parent should recognize gain or loss on the sale of its subsidiary to the target company, to the extent of noncontrolling interest in the target entity. As a result, there will be a new basis (step-up) not only for the target company's assets and liabilities, but also for the subsidiary company's net assets. Basis is stepped up to the extent of noncontrolling participation in the target entity to which the subsidiary company was transferred.

Accounting for Special-Purpose Entities

An issue related to the accounting for entities under common control arises when one entity has been created solely or largely for the purpose of accommodating the other's need for financing or for engaging in certain strictly limited transactions with or on behalf of the sponsoring entity. Common objectives are to affect a lease, conduct research and development activities, or to securitize financial assets. These special-purpose entities (SPE) or special-purpose vehicles (SPV) have received a good deal of attention in recent years, largely as a consequence of several notable financial frauds, which utilized SPE to conceal large amounts of the reporting entity's debt and/or to create the appearance of revenues and/or earnings which did not actually exist.

SPEs have often been used to escape the requirements of lease capitalization or other financial reporting requirements that the sponsoring entity wishes to evade. While there are often legitimate (i.e., those not driven by financial reporting) reasons for the use of special-purpose entities (SPE), at least a side effect, if not the main one, is that the sponsoring entity's apparent financial strength (e.g., leverage) will be distorted.

In many instances an adroitly structured SPE will not be owned, or majority owned, by the true sponsor. Were ownership the only criterion for determining whether entities need to be consolidated for financial reporting purposes, this factor could result in a "form over substance" decision to not consolidate the SPE with its sponsor. However, under the provisions of SIC 12, ownership is not the critical element in determining the need for consolidation; rather, a "beneficial interest" test is used to determine whether the SPE should be consolidated. Beneficial interest can take various forms, including ownership of debt instruments, or even a lessee relationship.

SIC 12 states that consolidation of an SPE should be effected if the substance of its relationship with another entity indicates that it is effectively controlled by the other entity. Control can derive from the nature of the predetermined activities of the SPE (what the interpretation refers to as being on "autopilot"), and emphatically can exist even when the sponsor has less than a majority interest in the SPE. SIC 12 specifically notes that the following conditions would suggest that the sponsor controls the SPE:

1. The activities of the SPE are conducted so as to provide the sponsor with the benefits thereof;
2. The sponsor in substance has decision-making powers to obtain most of the benefits of the SPE, or else an autopilot mechanism has been established such that the decision-making powers have been delegated;
3. The sponsor has the right to obtain the majority of the benefits of the SPE and consequently is exposed to risks inherent in the SPE activities; or
4. The sponsor retains the majority of the residual or ownership risks of the SPE or its assets, in order to obtain the benefits of the SPE activities.

SIC 12 is particularly concerned that autopilot arrangements may have been put into place specifically to obfuscate the determination of control. It cautions that although difficult to assess in some situations, control is to be attributed to the entity having the principal beneficial interest. The entity which arranged the autopilot mechanism would generally have had, and continue to have, control, and thus the need for consolidation with the sponsor for financial reporting purposes would accordingly be indicated. SIC 12 offers a number of examples of conditions which would be strongly indicative of control and thus of a need to consolidate the SPE financial statements with those of its sponsor.

Common SPE situations involve entities set up to facilitate a lease, to engage in a securitization of financial assets, or to conduct research and development activities. The concept of control used in IAS 27 requires having the ability to direct or dominate decision making accompanied by the objective of obtaining benefits from the SPE's activities. Thus, determining whether a given SPE should be consolidated by the sponsor or beneficiary reporting entity remains a matter of judgment under IFRS. Note that under US GAAP (FIN 46[R]), which replaced the concept of SPEs with a similar but more complex concept of variable interest entities (VIE), consolidation questions are resolved by mechanical, but complex, analyses.

Some entities will separately evaluate the matter of asset derecognition, as when assets are transferred to an SPE. In certain circumstances, a transfer of assets may result in those assets being derecognized and the transfer will be accounted for as a sale, with gain or loss recognition being warranted. Even if the transfer qualifies as a sale, however, the provisions of IAS 27(R) and SIC 12 may necessitate that the entity consolidate the SPE, thus reversing or obviating sale recognition and elimination of any gain or loss. SIC 12 does not address the circumstances where sale treatment would apply for the reporting entity or when the consequences of such a sale would have to be eliminated upon consolidation.

SIC 12 was modified by IFRIC in late 2004 to clarify the scope exclusion for postemployment benefit plans and extend this to other long-term employee benefit plans. The IASB is currently pursuing a project (recently renamed *Consolidation*) to address both the basis (policy) on which a parent entity should consolidate its investments in subsidiaries and enhanced disclosures about consolidated and nonconsolidated entities. The project will also focus on the consolidation of structured entities (for example, SPEs). The objective of the project is to publish a single IFRS on consolidation that would replace IAS 27(R), *Consolidated and Separate Financial Statements* and SIC-12, *Consolidation—Special-Purpose Entities*.

Accounting for Leveraged Buyouts

Possibly one of the most complex accounting issues has been the appropriate accounting for leveraged buyouts (LBO). At the center of this issue is the question of whether a new basis of accountability is created by the LBO transaction. If so, a step-up in the reported value of assets and/or liabilities is warranted. If not, the carryforward bases of the predecessor entity should continue to be reported in the company's financial statements.

IFRS do not address this issue directly. However, guidance can be gleaned from the decisions made by the standard setters in the United States, which have dealt with this question. Although this guidance is neither definitive nor binding on preparers of IFRS-based financial reports, it is instructive.

Under relevant US GAAP, partial or complete new basis accounting is appropriate only when the LBO transaction is characterized by a change in control of voting interest. A series of mechanical tests were developed by which this change in interest is to be measured. Three groups of interests were identified: the shareholders in the newly created company, management, and the shareholders in the old company (who may or may not also have an interest in the new company). Depending on the relative interests of these groups in the old entity (referred to as OLDCO) and in the new entity (NEWCO), there will be either (1) a finding that the transaction was a purchase (new basis accounting applies) or (2) that it was a recapitalization or a restructuring (carryforward basis accounting applies).

Among the test decreed to determine proper accounting for any given LBO transaction is the *monetary test*. This test requires that at least 80% of the net consideration paid to acquire

OLDCO interest must be monetary. In this context, monetary means cash, debt, and the fair value of any equity securities given by NEWCO to selling shareholders of OLDCO. Loan proceeds provided by OLDCO to assist in the acquisition of NEWCO shares by NEWCO shareholders are excluded from this definition. If the portion of the purchase that is effective through monetary consideration is less than 80%, but other criteria are satisfied, there will be a step-up. This step-up will be limited to the percentage of the transaction represented by monetary consideration.

US GAAP guidance also present an extensive series of examples illustrating the circumstances that would and would not meet the purchase accounting criteria to be employed in LBO. These examples should be consulted as needed when addressing an actual LBO transaction accounting issue. It is not known whether IFRS will eventually address this type of acquisition transaction.

Reverse Acquisitions

A reverse acquisition occurs when one entity, the legal parent, issues such a large proportion of its outstanding shares to the owners of the legal subsidiary that control passes to the legal subsidiary due to the number of additional shares issued by the legal parent and the owners of the subsidiary effectively become the majority owners of the combined economic entity. Thus, in a reverse acquisition, one entity—the one whose equity interests are acquired—obtains economic (although not legal) control over the other entity and is therefore the acquirer. The consequence of such a transaction is that the legal and accounting treatments will diverge, with the legal subsidiary being the accounting acquirer for financial reporting purposes. While often the legal parent (accounting acquirer) will adopt the subsidiary's name, thus alerting users of the statements to the nature of the organizational change, this does not necessarily occur, and, in any event, it will be critical that the financial statements contain sufficient disclosure so that users are not misled. This will be important particularly in the periods immediately following the transaction, and especially when comparative financial statements are presented which include some periods prior to the acquisition, since comparability will be affected.

A typical reverse acquisition would occur when a "shell" entity, which often is a publicly held but dormant company, merges with an operating company, which often will be nonpublic. The objective is for the operating entity to "go public" without the usual time-consuming and expensive registration process. However, reverse acquisitions are not limited to such situations, and there have been many such transactions involving two public or two nonpublic companies. The legal subsidiary (accounting acquirer) may have substantial operations of its own, although of lesser scope or with lower growth prospects than those of the accounting acquiree.

A number of difficult questions arise in reverse acquisitions, and there is no definitive guidance in IFRS on these important issues. Among the matters to be considered, and which will be discussed in the following paragraphs, are these:

1. What circumstances signal a reverse acquisition?
2. How should the consolidated financial statements be presented in the subsequent periods?
3. How should the acquisition cost be computed and allocated in a reverse acquisition?
4. What would the shareholders' equity section of the statement of financial position be immediately following the reverse acquisition?
5. What would be the impact on computation of earnings per share?
6. How will noncontrolling interest be presented in the financial statements?

Reverse acquisitions occur when the former shareholders of the legal subsidiary become the majority owners of the postcombination consolidated entity, and most commonly this will result when a share-for-share swap occurs. If the former owners of the legal subsidiary in a business combination become the majority owners of the consolidated entity following the transactions, it will be deemed to have been a reverse acquisition.

Following a reverse acquisition, consolidated financial statements will be presented. Although the financial statements will be identified as being those of the accounting acquirer (which will be the legal owner of the accounting acquiree), in substance these will be the financial statements of the acquiree company, with the assets and liabilities, and revenues and expenses, of the legal parent being included effective with the date of the transaction. Put another way, the legal parent will be deemed to be a continuation of the business of the legal subsidiary, notwithstanding the formal structure of the transaction or the name of the successor entity. For this reason, if the legal parent does not change its name to that of the acquiree, it would be appropriate for the financial statement titles to be captioned in a way that most clearly communicates the substance of the transaction to the readers. For example, the statements may be headed "ABC Company, Inc.—successor to XYZ Corporation."

Given the foregoing, it is clear that the shareholders' equity section of the posttransaction consolidated statement of financial position is to be that of the subsidiary, not the parent, with appropriate modification for the new shares issued in the transaction and ancillary adjustments, if any. Comparative financial statements for earlier periods, if presented, are to be consistent, meaning that these would be the financial statements of the legal subsidiary. Since in some instances the subsidiary's name is different than that shown in the heading, care must be taken to fully communicate with the readers. The fact that the prior period's financial information identified as being that of the legal parent is really that of the legal subsidiary obviously is extremely pertinent to a reader's understanding of these statements.

Consistent with the accounting imposed on other business combinations, the cost of reverse acquisitions is measured at the fair value of the net assets acquired, or the value of the consideration paid, if more determinable. A special rule is that, if fair value cannot be determined for the issuer's equity instruments, and the transaction is valued at the fair value of the issuer's net assets, no goodwill is recognized in the transaction. In addition, in the special case of a publicly held shell company and a privately held acquiree, the SEC has ruled that no goodwill can be recognized in any event. Clearly, in such instances there is substantial doubt about the true existence of goodwill and unusual difficulty in valuing the transaction, and this prohibition is prudent under the circumstances.

If the fair value of the shares of the legal subsidiary (accounting acquirer) is used to determine the cost of the transaction, it is suggested that a calculation be made to determine the number of shares that the acquiree would have issued in order to provide the same level of ownership in the combined entity to the shareholders of the legal parent (accounting acquiree) as they have as a consequence of the reverse acquisition. The fair value of the number of shares thus determined is used to value the transaction, as illustrated later in this section.

In some instances, the market price of acquiree shares may not be fairly indicative of the value of the transaction. In such cases, the most feasible alternative would be to use the fair value of all the outstanding shares of the ostensible acquirer, prior to the transaction, to value the purchase transaction. In some instances, adjustments would have to be made for trading volume, price fluctuations, etc., to most accurately reflect the substance of the acquisition.

In other cases, particularly where the acquirer is a dormant shell entity, market price of its shares may not be meaningful. If it is possible to determine, utilizing the fair value of the net assets of the acquirer may be a more meaningful technique.

Whatever technique is employed under the circumstances, the total purchase cost is to be allocated to the net assets of the acquirer (not the acquiree) following the principles set forth in IFRS 3. If the acquisition cost exceeds the fair value of net identifiable assets, the excess is allocated to goodwill, which will be tested for impairment, and written down or eliminated when and if impairment is detected. The financial statements of the consolidated entity following the reverse acquisition would reflect the assets and liabilities of the legal parent (nominal acquirer) at fair value, and those of the legal subsidiary (nominal acquiree) at historical cost.

Since for financial reporting purposes the accounting acquirer is the parent company, the retained earnings or deficit of the acquirer will be carried forward in the equity section of the successor entity's consolidated statement of financial position The retained earnings or deficit of the accounting acquiree will not be presented. The amount shown for issued equity interests would be measured by adding the issued equity of the legal subsidiary immediately before the business combination, plus the fair value of the consideration transferred, as described above and illustrated below. However, in the consolidated financial statements, the equity structure (e.g., the number and type of equity interests issued) must reflect the equity structure of the legal parent (which was the accounting acquiree). An example of accounting for a reverse acquisition follows.

Assume that Belmont Corporation, which is the legal subsidiary, acquires Dakar Corporation, the entity issuing equity instruments and therefore the legal parent, in a reverse acquisition.

The statements of financial position of the two entities at the end of 2008 and as of September 30, 2009, the date of the transaction, are given as follows:

Dakar Corporation
(legal parent, accounting agquiree)

	December 31, 2008	September 30, 2009
Current assets	€ 800,000	€1,000,000
Plant, property, and equipment, net	2,400,000	2,600,000
	€3,200,000	€3,600,000
Current liabilities	€ 400,000	€ 600,000
Long-term debt	600,000	400,000
Deferred tax liabilities	200,000	200,000
	1,200,000	1,200,000
Stockholders' equity		
8% redeemable preferred stock, 2,000 shs.	200,000	200,000
Common stock, 100,000 shs.	600,000	600,000
Retained earnings	1,200,000	1,600,000
	€3,200,000	€3,600,000

Belmont Corporation
(legal subsidiary, accounting acquirer)

	December 31, 2008	September 30, 2009
Current assets	€2,500,000	€1,750,000
Property, plant, and equipment, net	5,000,000	7,500,000
	€7,500,000	€9,250,000
Current liabilities	€1,250,000	€1,500,000
Long-term debt	1,750,000	2,000,000
Deferred tax liabilities	500,000	750,000
	3,500,000	4,250,000
Stockholders' equity		
Common stock, 60,000 shs.	1,500,000	1,500,000
Retained earnings	2,500,000	3,500,000
	€7,500,000	€9,250,000

Dakar had profit of €400,000 for the nine months ended September 30, 2009, while Belmont Co. enjoyed earnings of €1,000,000 for that period. Neither company paid any dividends during this period.

The fair value of each share of Belmont common stock was €100 at the date of the acquisition. Dakar shares were quoted at €24 on the date.

Dakar's identifiable net assets had fair values equal to their respective book values, with the exception of the property, plant, and equipment, which were appraised at €3,000,000 at September 30, 2009.

In effecting the acquisition, Dakar issues 150,000 new shares of its common stock to the owners of Belmont in exchange for all outstanding Belmont shares. Thus, former Belmont owners become the owners of a majority of the ordinary shares of Dakar after this transaction.

To compute the cost of the reverse acquisition, the number of shares of Belmont, which would have had to have been issued to acquire Dakar, must be computed. This is done as follows:

Actual Dakar shares issued to former Belmont owners	150,000
Dakar shares outstanding prior to transaction	100,000
Total Dakar shares outstanding after transaction	250,000
Fraction held by former Belmont owners (150,000/250,000)	60%
Number of Belmont shares outstanding before transaction	60,000
Number of Belmont shares that could have been issued in transaction if 60% of total would have remained with original Belmont shareholders	40,000

Belmont would have had to issue 40 shares for the ratio of ownership interest in the combined entity to be the same ([60,000/.60] − 40,000).

If Belmont had issued 40,000 of its shares to effect the acquisition of Dakar, the cost would have been (given the fair value of Belmont shares at September 30, 2008) €100 × 40,000 = €4,000,000. This acquisition cost would have been allocated to Dakar's assets and liabilities as follows:

Current assets		€1,000,000
Property, plant, and equipment		3,000,000
		€4,000,000
Current liabilities	€600,000	
Long-term debt	400,000	
Deferred tax liabilities	200,000	1,200,000
		2,800,000
8% redeemable preferred stock, 2,000 shares		200,000
		2,600,000
Cost of purchase (from above)		4,000,000
Goodwill to be recognized		€1,400,000

Goodwill is measured as the excess of the fair value of the consideration effectively transferred (€4,000,000) over the net amount of Dakar's identifiable assets and liabilities (€2,600,000).

From the foregoing, the information needed to construct a consolidated statement of financial position as of the date of the transaction, September 30, 2008, can be determined.

Dakar Corporation
Consolidated Statement of Financial Position
September 30, 2009

Current assets	€ 2,750,000
Property, plant, and equipment, net	10,500,000
Goodwill	1,400,000
	€14,650,000
Current liabilities	€ 2,100,000
Long-term liabilities	2,400,000
Deferred tax liabilities	950,000
	5,450,000
Shareholders' equity	
8% redeemable preferred stock, 2,000 shares	200,000
Ordinary share, 250,000 shares (€1,500,00 + 4,000,000)	5,500,000
Retained earnings	3,500,000
	9,200,000
	€14,650,000

The amount recognized as issued equity interests in the consolidated financial statements (€5,500,000) is determined by adding the issued equity of the legal subsidiary immediately before the business combination (€1,500,000) and the fair value of the consideration transferred (€4,000,000). However, the equity structure presented in the consolidated financial statements (e.g., the number and type of shares issued) must reflect the equity structure of the legal parent, including shares issued by the legal parent to the effect this combination (€100,000 + €150,000).

Computing earnings per share after a reverse acquisition poses special problems, particularly so in the year in which the transaction occurs and in any subsequent years when comparative financial statements are presented that include those of pretransaction periods.

For this purpose, the number of shares outstanding for the period from the beginning of the current reporting year until the date of the reverse acquisition is the number of shares issued by the accounting acquiree (the legal parent company) to the shareholders of the accounting acquirer (the legal subsidiary). For the period after the transaction, the number of shares considered to be outstanding is the actual number of shares of the legal parent company outstanding during that period. The average number of shares outstanding for the full year being reported upon would be computed by averaging these two amounts. Other appropriate adjustments would be made to deal with changes in numbers of shares issued during the period, as is done under other circumstances (as described in Chapter 18), if necessary. Under the current standard for computing earnings per share (IAS 33), the calculation of basic earnings per share (replacing the former measure, primary earnings per share) is simplified for all entities.

Earnings per share for any earlier periods presented for comparative purposes is likewise complicated by the occurrence of a reverse acquisition. Restated earnings for earlier periods would be calculated as the earnings of the legal subsidiary divided by the number of ordinary shares issued in the reverse acquisition.

Continuing with the Dakar-Belmont acquisition example above, earnings per share can be computed. Assume that consolidated net income for the year ended December 31, 2009, after deducting preference shares, equals €1,600,000. This includes Belmont's earnings for the full year 2009, plus Dakar's earnings from the date of acquisition, September 30, 2009, until year-end. Remember that, notwithstanding that the new entity is called Dakar, from an accounting perspective this is Belmont Corporation.

Earnings per share would thus be computed as follows:

Number of shares outstanding from the acquisition date (Sept. 30) to December 2009	250,000
Number of shares deemed outstanding before 30 September—the number of Dakar's shares issued to Belmont	150,000

Average number of shares

$$[(150,000 \times 9) + (250,000 \times 3)] \div 12 = 175,000$$

Earnings per share for 2008

$$€1,600,000 \div 175,000 = €9.14 \text{ per share}$$

For 2009, assuming Belmont alone had earnings of €1,400,000 for the year, earnings per share would be

$$€1,400,000 \div 150,000 = €9.33 \text{ per share}$$

Finally, there is the question of noncontrolling interest. In a reverse acquisition situation, the noncontrolling interest is comprised of the former shareholders of the legal subsidiary who do not exchange their shares for those of the new parent company, but continue on as stockholders in the legal subsidiary entity. Note that this holds even though from the accounting perspective they are shareholders in an entity that acquired another company. In other words, the identity of the noncontrolling interest is determined by the legal structure of the transaction, not the accounting substance. Since the net assets of the legal subsidiary are included in the consolidated financial statements at the old book values, noncontrolling interest is likewise computed based on the book value of the legal subsidiary's net assets.

For example, in the present case all shareholders of Belmont might not agree to tender their shares in exchange for Dakar's share, and if so they will continue on as noncontrolling owners of the legal subsidiary, Belmont. To illustrate, consider these assumed facts.

Dakar offered 2.5 shares for each share of Belmont ordinary share. In the example above, 150,000 shares of Dakar were exchanged for 60,000 Belmont shares. Now, however, assume that owners of 4,000 Belmont shares decline to participate in this transaction, so Dakar issues only 140,000 shares in exchange for 56,000 Belmont shares. After the exchange, former Belmont owners hold 140,000 of a total of 240,000 Dakar's shares, or 58.33% of the total outstanding; still a majority and thus enough to define this as a reverse acquisition.

The cost of the purchase is computed similar to what was illustrated above. Since the owners of 56,000 Belmont shares participated and the transaction resulted in these owners obtaining a 58.33% interest in the successor entity, the calculation of the number of Belmont shares hypothetically required to be issued in a "straight" acquisition of Dakar is as follows:

56,000 shares outstanding ÷ .5833 = 96,000 total shares after transaction

96,000 total shares − 56,000 shares outstanding = 40,000 new shares to be issued

Thus, it can be seen that the cost of the purchase, determined in the manner that is necessary when a reverse acquisition takes place, remains $40,000 \times €100 = €4,000,000$ even given the existence of the noncontrolling interest.

The noncontrolling interest is 4,000 shares ÷ 60,000 shares = 6.6667%. It consists, as of the acquisition date, of 6.6667% of the book value of Belmont ordinary share and retained earnings, as follows:

6.6667% × €1,500,000	=	$100,000
6.6667% × €3,500,000	=	233,310
Total noncontrolling interest		$333,310

The consolidated statement of financial position at the acquisition date would differ from that shown above only as follows: a noncontrolling interest of €333,310 would be presented (under current GAAP, as a liability, as equity, or in a semiequity account); common stock would be only €5,400,000, comprised of 93.33% (1 − 6.66667%) of Belmont's €1,500,000, plus the €4 million purchase cost); and retained earnings would be only 93.33% or Belmont's pretransaction balance of €3.5 million, or €3,266,655. All other asset and liability account balances would be identical to the presentation above.

Spin-Offs

Occasionally, an entity disposes of a wholly or partially owned subsidiary or of an investee by transferring it unilaterally to the entity's shareholders. The proper accounting for such a transaction, generally known as a spin-off, depends on the percentage of the company that is owned.

If the ownership percentage is relatively minor, 25% for example, the transfer to shareholders would be viewed as a *dividend in kind* and would be accounted for at the fair value of the property (i.e., shares in the investee) transferred.

However, when the entity whose shares are distributed is majority or wholly owned, the effect is not merely to transfer a passive investment, but to remove the operations from the former parent and to vest them with the parent's shareholders. This transaction is a true spin-off transaction, not merely a property dividend. Although international accounting standards have not addressed this matter, as a point of reference, US GAAP requires that spin-offs and similar nonreciprocal transfers to owners be accounted for at the recorded book values of the assets and liabilities transferred.

If the operations (or subsidiary) being spun off are distributed during a fiscal period, it may be necessary to estimate the results of operations for the elapsed period prior to spin-off to ascertain the net book value as of the date of the transfer. Stated another way, the operating results of the subsidiary to be disposed of should be included in the reported results of the parent through the actual date of the spin-off.

In most instances, the subsidiary being spun off will have a positive net book value. This net worth represents the cost of the nonreciprocal transfer to the owners, and like a dividend, will be reflected as a charge against the parent's retained earnings at the date of spin-off. In other situations, the operations (or subsidiary) will have a net deficit (negative net book value). Since it is unacceptable to recognize a credit to the parent's retained earnings for other than a culmination of an earnings process, the spin-off should be recorded as a credit to the parent's paid-in capital. In effect, the shareholders (the recipients of the spun-off subsidiary) have made a capital contribution to the parent company by accepting the operations having a negative book value. As with other capital transactions, this would *not* be presented in the statement of comprehensive income, only in the statement of changes in owners' equity (and in the statement of cash flows).

Push-Down Accounting

The term push-down accounting (also known as "new basis accounting") refers to the practice of revaluing to fair value the assets and liabilities of a purchased subsidiary directly on that subsidiary's books at the date of acquisition. Therefore, these revaluations are not made in the consolidation working papers each time consolidated financial statements are prepared. As a result, push-down accounting can simplify the consolidation procedure.

Under new basis accounting, the amounts allocated to various assets and liabilities can be adjusted to reflect the arm's-length valuation reflected in a significant transaction, such as the sale of a majority interest in the entity. For example, the sale of 90% of the shares of a company by one shareholder to a new investor—which under the entity concept would not alter the accounting by the company itself—would, under new basis accounting, be "pushed down" to the entity. The logic is that, as under purchase method accounting for business combinations, the most objective gauge of "cost" is that arising from a recent arm's-length transaction.

Traditionally, push-down accounting has not been permitted, in part because of the practical difficulty of demonstrating that the reference transaction was indeed arm's-length in nature. (Obviously, the risk is that a series of sham transactions could be used to grossly distort the "cost" and hence carrying values of the entity's assets, resulting in fraudulent financial reporting.) Also heavily debated has been where the threshold should be set (a 50% change in ownership, an 80% change, etc.) to denote when a significant event had occurred that would provide valid information on the valuation of the entity's assets and liabilities for financial reporting purposes.

Many of the more general issues of push-down accounting (those applicable to traditional business acquisitions) have yet to be dealt with. For example, proponents of push-down accounting point out that in a purchase business combination a new basis of accounting is established, and that this new basis should be pushed down to the acquired entity and should be used when presenting that entity's own, separate financial statements. However, practical problems remain: for example, while push-down accounting makes some sense in the case where a major block of the investee's shares is acquired in a single free-market transaction, if new basis accounting were to be used in the context of a series of step transactions, continual adjustment of the investee's carrying values for assets and liabilities would be necessary. Furthermore, the price paid for a fractional share of ownership of an investee may not always be meaningfully extrapolated to a value for the investee company as a whole.

For example, in the US, the SEC's position has been that push-down accounting would be required if 95% or more of the shares of the company have been acquired (unless the company has outstanding public debt or preference share that may impact the acquirer's ability to control the form of ownership of the company); that it would be permitted, but not mandated, if 80% to 95% has been acquired; and it would be prohibited if less than 80% of the company is acquired.

While there is no requirement under US GAAP to apply the push-down concept, the SEC position is substantial authoritative support and can be referenced even for nonpublic company financial reporting. It would be defensible in any instance where there is a change in control and/or a change in ownership of a majority of the ordinary shares, when separate financial statements of the subsidiary are to be presented. Full disclosure is to be made of the circumstances whenever push-down accounting is applied.

Example of push-down accounting

Assume that Dakar acquires, in an open market arm's-length transaction, 90% of the common stock of Bari Co. for $464.61 million. At that time, Bari Co.'s net book value was $274.78 million (for the entire company). Book and fair values of selected assets and liabilities of Bari Co. as of the transaction date are summarized as follows ($000,000 omitted):

	Book value		Fair value of	Excess of
	100% of entity	*90% interest*	*90% interest*	*FV over book*
Assets				
Receivables	$ 24.6	$ 22.14	$ 29.75	$ 7.61
Inventory	21.9	19.71	24.80	5.09
Property, plant &				
equipment, net	434.2	390.78	488.20	97.42
All others	223.4	201.06	201.06	0.00
Additional goodwill			120.00	120.00
Total assets	$704.1	$633.69	$863.81	$230.12
Liabilities				
Bonds payable	104.9	94.41	88.65	5.76
All other liabilities	325.0	292.50	310.55	18.05
Total liabilities	429.9	386.91	399.20	12.29
Equity				
Preferred stock	40.0	36.00	36.00	0.00
Ordinary share	87.4	78.66	78.66	0.00
Equity-Revaluation*			217.83	217.83
Retained earnings	146.8	132.12	132.12	0.00
Total equity	274.2	246.88	464.61	217.83
Liabilities + Equity	$704.1	$633.69	$863.81	$230.12

* *Net premium paid over book value by arm's-length of "almost all" ordinary share*

Assuming that "new basis" accounting is deemed to be acceptable and meaningful, since Bari Co. must continue to issue separate financial statements to its creditors and holders of its preference shares, and also assuming that a revaluation of the share of ownership that did not change hands (i.e., the 10% noncontrolling interest in this example) should not be revalued based on the majority transaction, the entries by the subsidiary (Bari Co.) for purposes only of preparing separate stand-alone financial statements would be as follows:

Accounts receivable	7,610,000	
Inventory	5,090,000	
Plant, property and equipment (net)	97,420,000	
Goodwill	120,000,000	
Discount on bonds payable	5,760,000	
Other liabilities		18,050,000
Equity—revaluation		217,830,000

The foregoing entry would only be made for purposes of preparing separate financial statements of Bari Co. If consolidated financial statements of Dakar Corp. are also presented, essentially the same result will be obtained. The additional equity issued account would be eliminated against the parent's investment account, however, since in the context of the consolidated financial statements this would be a cash transaction rather than a mere accounting revaluation.

There is also a body of opinion holding that the separate financial statements of Bari Co. in this example should be "grossed up" for the imputed premium that would have been achieved on the transfer of the remaining 10% ownership interest. This is less appealing, however, given the absence of a "real" transaction involving that last 10% ownership stake, making the price at which it would have traded somewhat speculative.

The foregoing example obviously also ignored the tax effects of the transaction. Since the step-ups in carrying value would not, in all likelihood, alter the corresponding tax bases of the assets and liabilities, deferred tax effects would also require recognition. This would be done following the procedures set forth in IAS 12, as described fully in Chapter 15. The revisions to IAS 27 that require presenting consolidated financial statements in accordance with a single economic entity concept should facilitate the use of push-down accounting, simplify the consolidation procedure and lead to more transparency in financial reporting.

Non-Sub Subsidiaries

An issue that has sometimes been of concern to accountants is the use of what have been called *non-sub subsidiaries*. This situation arises when an entity plays a major role in the creation and financing of what is often a start-up or experimental operation but does not take an equity position at the outset. For example, the parent might finance the entity by means of convertible debt or debt with warrants for the later purchase of ordinary shares. The original equity partner in such arrangements most often will be the creative or managerial talent that generally exchanges its talents for an equity interest. If the operation prospers, the parent will exercise its rights to a majority voting share position; if it fails, the parent presumably avoids reflecting the losses in its statements.

Although this strategy may seem to avoid the requirements of equity accounting or consolidation, the economic substance clearly suggests that the operating results of the subsidiary should be reflected in the financial statements of the real parent, even absent ownership. In theory the control criteria of IAS 27 should apply, and where the "parent" entity's interest includes convertible debt, there may well be latent control.

Examples of Financial Statement Disclosures

adidas AG
Annual Report 2007

2. Summary of significant accounting policies

The consolidated financial statements are prepared in accordance with the consolidation, accounting, and valuation principles described below.

Principles of consolidation. The consolidated financial statements include the accounts of adidas AG and its direct and indirect subsidiaries, which are prepared in accordance with uniform accounting principles.

A company is considered a subsidiary if adidas AG directly or indirectly governs the financial and operating policies of the respective enterprise.

The number of consolidated subsidiaries evolved as follows for the years ending December 31, 2007 and 2006 respectively.

Number of consolidated companies

	2007	2006
January 1	168	94
Newly founded/consolidated companies	6	2
Divestments/exclusion from consolidation	(1)	(4)
Merged companies	(2)	(1)
Purchased companies	--	77
December 31	171	168

A schedule of the shareholdings of adidas AG is shown in Attachment II to these notes. Further, a schedule of these shareholdings will be published on the electronic platform of the German Federal Gazette.

The first-time consolidation of purchased companies had a material impact in 2006. (See note 4.)

Within the scope of the first-time consolidation, all acquired assets and liabilities are recognized in the balance sheet at fair value. A debit difference between the investment book value and the proportionate fair value of the assets and liabilities is shown as goodwill. A credit difference is recorded in the income statement. No fair value adjustments are recognized at the first-time consolidation of acquired minority interests in companies accounted for using the purchase method. A debit difference between the cost for such an additional investment and the carrying amount of the net assets at the acquisition date is shown as goodwill. A credit difference is recorded in the income statement.

All intercompany transactions and balances, as well as any unrealized gains and losses arising from intercompany transactions are eliminated in preparing the consolidated financial statements.

20. Minority interests

This line item within equity comprises the equity of third parties in a number of our consolidated companies. Minority interests are attributable to three subsidiaries as at December 31, of both 2007 and 2006. (see Shareholdings, Attachment II to these Notes)

These subsidiaries were mainly purchased as part of the acquisition of the Reebok business.

In accordance with IAS 32, the following minority interests are not reported within minority interests: GEV Grundstüksgesellschaft Herzogenaurach mbH & Co. KG (Germany), as the company is a limited partnership, and adidas Hellas A.E. (Greece), as this minority is held with a put option. The fair value of these minorities is shown within other liabilities. The difference between the fair value and the minority interests is shown as goodwill less accumulated amortization. The result for these minorities is reported within the financial expenses.

Novartis Group
Annual Report 2007

1. Accounting policies

Principles of consolidation. The annual closing date of the individual financial statements is December 31. The purchase method of accounting is used to account for business combinations by the Group in transactions where the Group takes control of another entity. The cost of an acquisition is measured as the fair value of the assets transferred to the seller and liabilities incurred or assumed at the date of exchange, plus costs directly attributable to the acquisition. Identifiable assets acquired and liabilities and contingent liabilities assumed in a business combination are measured initially at their full fair values at the acquisition date, irrespective of the extent of any minority interest. The excess of the cost of acquisition over the fair value of the Group's share of identifiable net assets acquired is recorded as goodwill. Companies acquired or disposed of during the year are included in the consolidated financial statements from the date of acquisition or up to the date of disposal.

Intercompany income and expenses, including unrealized profits from internal Novartis transactions and intercompany receivables and payables are eliminated.

2. **Divestments, business combinations and other significant transactions**

The following divestments, business combinations and other significant transactions occurred during 2007 and 2006. See notes 3 and 23 for further details of the impact of these transactions on the consolidated financial statements.

Divestments/discontinued operations—2007

Consumer health—Gerber Business Unit. On September 1, Novartis completed the divestment of the Gerber infant products Business Unit for approximately USD 5.5 billion to Nestlé S.A. resulting in a pretax divestment gain of approximately USD 4.0 billion and an after-tax gain of USD 3.6 billion.

Consumer health—Medical Nutrition Business Unit. On July 1, Novartis completed the divestment of the remainder of the Medical Nutrition Business Unit for approximately USD 2.5 billion for Nestlé S.A. resulting in a pretax divestment gain of USD 1.8 billion and an after-tax gain of USD 1.6 billion

Both the Gerber and Medical Nutrition Business Units (which included the Nutrition & Santé business divested in February 2006) are reported as discontinued operations in all periods in the Group's consolidated financial statements. These businesses had combined 2007 net sales of USD 1.7 billion (2006: USD 2.6 billion) and operating income of USD 311 million (2006: USD 403 million) before their divestment.

Other significant transactions—2007

Pharmaceuticals—Betaseron® agreement related to Chiron acquisition. On September 14, 2007, Novartis and Bayer Schering Pharma AG received regulatory approval to complete an agreement related to various rights for the multiple scelrosis treatment Betaseron® under an earlier agreement between Schering and Chiron Corporation, transferred to Novartis in April 2006. Under the new agreement, Novartis received a onetime payment and approximately USD 200 million, principally for manufacturing facilities transferred to Bayer Schering, as well as receiving the rights to market its own branded version of Betaseron® starting in 2009 (pending regulatory approvals). As a result of clarification of the intangible product rights, a reassessment was made of the related assets from the Chiron acquisition as of April 20, 2006. This resulted in an increase of USD 235 million in identified net assets. After taking this into account, Pharmaceuticals Division goodwill for the Chiron acquisition at December 31, 2007, amounted to USD 1.9 billion.

Vaccines and diagnostics—Intercell agreement. On September 28, 2007, Novartis entered into a strategic alliance with Intercell AG, an Austrian biotechnology company focused on vaccines development. As a consequence of the agreement, Novartis paid USD 383 million (EUR 270 million) and recorded USD 207 million (EUR 146 million) of intangible assets and acquired an additional 4.8 million shares for USD 176 million (EUR 124 million), which increased the Novartis holding in Intercell to 15.9%.

The equity investment is accounted for as an available-for-sale marketable security within the financial assets of the Division.

23. **Acquisitions and divestments of businesses**

23.1. **Assets and liabilities arising from acquisitions**

The following is a summary of the cash flow impact of the major divestments and acquisitions of businesses.

2007	Fair value USD millions	Revaluation due to purchase accounting[1] USD millions	Acquirer's carrying amount USD millions
Currently marketed products including trademarks	38	38	
Inventories	16	5	11
Trade receivables and other current assets	12		12
Marketable securities and cash	5		5
Trade payables and other liabilities including deferred tax liabilities	(17)		(17)
Net identifiable assets acquired	54	43	11
Less acquired liquidity	(5)		
Goodwill	3		
Net assets recognized as a result of business combinations	52		

2006	Fair value[1] USD millions	Revaluation due to purchase accounting[1] USD millions	Acquirer's carrying amount USD millions
Property, plant & equipment	1,031	123	908
Currently marketed products including trademarks	3,256	2,699	557
In-process research and development	1,216	1,216	--
Other intangible assets	307	307	--
Financial assets including deferred tax assets	438	33	405
Inventories	540	224	316
Trade accounts receivable and other current assets	535	11	524
Marketable securities and cash	1,771	--	1,771
Long-term and short-term financial debts	(1,462)	(18)	(1,444)
Trade payables and other liabilities including deferred tax liabilities	(2,346)	(1,656)	(690)
Net identifiable assets acquired	5,286	2,939	2,347
Goodwill	3,155		
Net assets recognized as a result of business combinations	8,441		

[1] *The acquisition of Chiron Corporation was the principal acquisition during 2006. The fair value adjustments also include USD 637 million of IPR&D arising on the NeuTec Pharma plc acquisition which also contributed USD 129 million of goodwill and reclassification reducing Hexal AG's IPR&D by USD 221 million with a corresponding increase to goodwill of USD 134 million and reclassification of USD 87 million to other categories of assets and liabilities including a reduction on the purchase price of USD 6 million.*

The 2006 goodwill arising out of the acquisitions reflects mainly the value of expected buyer specific synergies, future products and the acquired assembled workforce. No goodwill is expected to be deductible for tax purposes.

Professional fees and related costs capitalized for the acquisitions amounts to USD 43 million in 2006. Amounts in 2007 were insignificant.

23.2. Assets and liabilities related to discontinued operations.

Assets related to discontinued operations

	2006 USD millions
Property, plant, and equipment	69
Intangible assets	370
Deferred tax assets	10
Other financial assets	8
Total noncurrent assets reclassified as assets related to discontinued operations	457
Inventories	120
Trade receivables	139
Other current assets	16
Cash and cash equivalents	4
Total current assets reclassified as assets related to discontinued operations	279
Total assets related to discontinued operations	736

Liabilities related to discontinued operations

	2006 USD millions
Financial debts	2
Deferred tax liabilities	18
Provisions and other noncurrent liabilities	31
Total noncurrent liabilities reclassified as liabilities related to discontinued operations	51
Trade payables	69
Financial debts	5
Current income tax liabilities	17
Provisions and other current liabilities	65
Total current liabilities reclassified as liabilities related to discontinued operations	156
Total liabilities related to discontinued operations	207

12 CURRENT LIABILITIES, PROVISIONS, CONTINGENCIES, AND EVENTS AFTER THE REPORTING PERIOD

PERSPECTIVE AND ISSUES

Accounting for all of a reporting entity's liabilities is clearly necessary in order to accurately convey its financial position to investors, creditors and other stakeholders. Different kinds of liabilities have differing implications: *short-term trade payables* indicate a near-term outflow, while *long-term debt* covers a wide range of periods, and *provisions* have yet other significance to those performing financial analysis. At the same time, a company with a long operating cycle will have operating liabilities that stretch for more than a year ahead, and some long-term debt may call for repayment within one year, so the distinction is not so clear, and presentation in the statement of financial position is an issue. Transparency of disclosure will also be a consideration, beyond mere questions of current or noncurrent classification.

Historically, it has long been recognized that prudence would normally necessitate the recognition of even uncertain liabilities, while uncertain assets were not to be recognized. IAS 37, the key standard on provisions, addresses the boundaries of recognition. In general, IASB is also evolving to a new position on contingent liabilities, where the assessed probability of occurrence will be built into the measurement of liabilities, thereby changing the boundaries of accounting recognition for liabilities.

The recognition and measurement of provisions can have a major impact on the way in which the financial position of an entity is viewed. IAS 37 addresses so-called "onerous contract" provisions, which require a company to take into current earnings the entire cost of fulfilling contracts that continue into the future under defined conditions. This can be a very sensitive issue for a company experiencing trading difficulties. In June 2005 the IASB issued an Exposure Draft (ED), *Proposed Amendments to IAS 37: Provisions, Contingent Liabilities and Contingent Assets,* which proposed to eliminate the terms "provisions," "contingent liability," and "contingent asset" from the IFRS literature and replace these with a new term, "nonfinancial liabilities." As of late 2008, this remains under consideration. A major change to the current practice of accounting for restructuring provisions has been introduced (see discussion at the end of this chapter).

Another sensitive issue is the accounting for decommissioning or similar asset retirement costs, which increasingly are becoming a burden for companies engaged in mineral extraction and manufacturing, but also potentially for those engaged in agriculture and other industry segments. Where historically it was assumed that these costs were future events to be recognized in later periods, it is now clear that these are costs of asset ownership and operation that need to be reflected over the productive lives of the assets, and that the estimated costs are to be recognized as a formal obligation of the reporting entity.

The reporting entity's financial position may also be affected by events, both favorable and unfavorable, which occur between the end of the reporting period and the date when the financial statements are authorized for issue. Under IAS 10, such post–reporting period date events require either formal recognition or only disclosure, depending on the character and timing of the event in question, which are referred to as "adjusting" and "nonadjusting," respectively.

In practice, there may be some ambiguity as to when the financial statements are actually "authorized for issuance." For this reason, the revised standard recognizes that the process involved in authorizing the financial statements for issue will vary and may be dependent upon the reporting entity's management structure, statutory requirements, and the procedures prescribed for the preparing and finalizing of the financial statements. Thus, IAS 10 illustrates in detail the principles governing the determination of the financial statements' authorization date, which date is required to be disclosed.

Sources of IFRS	
IAS 1, 10, 37, 39	*IFRIC* 1, 6

DEFINITIONS OF TERMS

Adjusting events after the reporting period. Those post–reporting period events that provide evidence of conditions that existed at the end of the reporting period and require that the financial statements be adjusted.

Authorization date. The date when the financial statements would be considered legally authorized for issue.

Constructive obligation. An obligation resulting from an entity's actions such that the entity

- By an established pattern of past practice, published policies or a sufficiently specific current statement, has indicated to third parties that it will accept certain responsibilities; and
- As a result, has created a valid expectation in the minds of third parties that it will discharge those responsibilities.

Contingent asset. A possible asset that arises from past events and whose existence will be confirmed only by the occurrence or nonoccurrence of one or more uncertain future events not wholly within the control of the reporting entity.

Contingent liability. An obligation that is either

- A possible obligation arising from past events, the outcome of which will be confirmed only on the occurrence or nonoccurrence of one or more uncertain future events which are not wholly within the control of the reporting entity; or
- A present obligation arising from past events which is not recognized either because it is not probable that an outflow of resources will be required to settle an obligation, or where the amount of the obligation cannot be measured with sufficient reliability.

Current liabilities. Entity obligations whose liquidation is reasonably expected to require the use of existing resources properly classified as current assets or the creation of other current liabilities. Obligations that are due on demand or will be due on demand within one year or the operating cycle, if longer, are current liabilities.

Estimated liability. An obligation that is known to exist, although the obligee may not be known, and the amount and timing of payment is subject to uncertainty. Now referred to as provisions.

Events after the reporting period. Events that occur after an entity's accounting year-end (also referred to as the end of the reporting period or as the date of the statement of financial position) and the date the financial statements are authorized for issue that would necessitate either adjusting the financial statements or disclosure. The concept is comprehensive enough to cover both favorable and unfavorable post–reporting period events.

Guarantee. A commitment to honor an obligation of another party in the event certain defined conditions are not met.

Indirect guarantee of indebtedness of others. A guarantee under an agreement that obligates one entity to transfer funds to a second entity upon the occurrence of specified events under conditions whereby (1) the funds are legally available to the creditors of the second entity, and (2) those creditors may enforce the second entity's claims against the first entity.

Legal obligation. An obligation that derives from the explicit or implicit terms of a contract, or from legislation or other operation of law.

Liability. A present obligation of the reporting entity arising from past events, the settlement of which is expected to result in an outflow from the entity of resources embodying economic benefits.

Nonadjusting events after the reporting period. Those post–reporting period events that are indicative of conditions that arose *after* the end of the reporting period and which thus would not necessitate adjusting financial statements. Instead, if significant, these would require disclosure.

Obligating event. An event that creates a legal or constructive obligation that results in an entity having no realistic alternative but to settle that obligation.

Onerous contract. A contract in which the unavoidable costs of meeting the obligations under the contract exceed the economic benefits expected to be received therefrom.

Operating cycle. The average length of time necessary for an entity to convert inventory to receivables to cash.

Possible loss. A contingent loss based on the occurrence of a future event or events whose likelihood of occurring is more than remote but less than likely.

Probable loss. A contingent loss based on the occurrence of a future event or events that are likely to occur.

Provision. Liabilities having uncertain timing or amount.

Remote loss. A contingent loss based on the occurrence of a future event or events whose likelihood of occurring is slight.

Restructuring. A program that is planned and controlled by management and which materially changes either the scope of business undertaken by the entity or the manner in which it is conducted.

CONCEPTS, RULES, AND EXAMPLES

Current Liabilities

Classification of statements of financial position. IAS 1 requires that the reporting entity must present current and noncurrent assets, and current and noncurrent liabilities, as separate classifications on the face of its statement of financial position, except when a liquidity presentation provides more relevant and reliable information. In those exceptional instances, all assets and liabilities are to be presented broadly in order of liquidity. Whether classified or employing the order of liquidity approach, for any asset or liability reported as a discrete line item that combines amounts expected to be recovered or settled within no more than twelve months after the end of the reporting period and more than twelve months after the end of the reporting period, the reporting entity must disclose the amount expected to be recovered or settled after more than twelve months.

IAS 1 also makes explicit reference to the requirements imposed by IAS 32 concerning financial assets and liabilities. Since such common statement of financial position items as trade and other receivables and payables are within the definition of financial instruments, information about maturity dates is already required under IFRS. While most trade payables and accrued liabilities will be due within thirty to ninety days, and thus are understood by all financial statement readers to be current, this requirement would necessitate additional disclosure, either in the statement of financial position or in the footnotes thereto, when this assumption is not warranted.

The other purpose of presenting a classified statement of financial position is to highlight those assets and obligations that are "continuously circulating" in the phraseology of IAS 1. That is, the goal is to identify specifically resources and commitments that are consumed or settled in the normal course of the operating cycle. In some types of businesses, such as certain construction entities, the normal operating cycle may exceed one year. Thus, some assets or liabilities might fail to be incorporated into a definition based on the first goal of reporting, providing insight into liquidity, but be included in one that meets the second goal.

As a compromise, if a classified statement of financial position is indeed being presented, the convention for financial reporting purposes is to consider assets and liabilities current if they will be realized and liquidated within one year or one operating cycle, whichever is longer. Since this may vary in practice from one reporting entity to another, however, it is important for users to read the accounting policies set forth in notes to the financial statements. The classification criterion should be set forth there, particularly if it is other than the rule most commonly employed: one-year threshold.

Nature of current liabilities. Current liabilities are generally perceived to be those that are due within a brief time span. The convention has long been to use one year from the end of the reporting period as the threshold for categorization as current, subject to the operating cycle issue for liabilities linked to operations. Examples of liabilities which are not expected to be settled in the normal course of the operating cycle but which, if due within twelve months would be deemed current, are current portions of long-term debt and bank overdrafts, dividends declared and payable, and various nontrade payables.

Current liabilities would almost always include not only obligations that are due on demand (typically including bank lines of credit, other demand notes payable, and certain overdue obligations for which forbearance has been granted on a day-to-day basis), but also the currently scheduled payments on longer-term obligations, such as installment notes. Also included in this group would be trade credit and accrued expenses, and deferred revenues and advances from customers for which services are to be provided or product delivered within one year. If certain conditions are met (described below), short-term obligations that are intended to be refinanced may be excluded from current liabilities.

Like all liabilities, current liabilities may be known with certainty as to amount, due date, and payee, as is most commonly the case. However, one or more of these elements may be unknown or subject to estimation. Consistent with basic principles of accrual accounting, however, the lack of specific information on, say, the amount owed, will not serve to justify a failure to record and report on such obligations. The former commonly used term "estimated liabilities" has been superseded per IAS 37 by the term "provisions." Provisions and contingent liabilities are discussed in detail later in this chapter.

Offsetting current assets against related current liabilities. IAS 1 states that current liabilities are not to be reduced by the deduction of a current asset (or vice versa) unless required or permitted by another IAS. In practice, there are few circumstances that would meet this requirement; certain financial institution transactions are the most commonly encountered exceptions. As an almost universal rule, therefore, assets and liabilities must be shown "broad," even where the same counterparties are present (e.g., amounts due from and amounts owed to another entity).

Types of liabilities. Current obligations can be divided into those where

1. Both the amount and the payee are known;
2. The payee is known but the amount may have to be estimated;
3. The payee is unknown and the amount may have to be estimated; and
4. The liability has been incurred due to a loss contingency.

These types of liabilities are discussed in the following sections.

Amount and Payee Known

Accounts payable arise primarily from the acquisition of materials and supplies to be used in the production of goods or in conjunction with providing services. Payables that arise from transactions with suppliers in the normal course of business, which customarily are due in no more than one year, may be stated at their face amount rather than at the present value of the required future cash flows.

Notes payable are more formalized obligations that may arise from the acquisition of materials and supplies used in operations or from the use of short-term credit to purchase capital assets. Although international accounting standards do not explicitly address the matter, it is widely agreed that monetary obligations, other than those due currently, should be presented at the present value of the amount owed, thus giving explicit recognition to the time value of money. However, most would agree that this exercise would not be needed to present current obligations fairly. (Of course, if the obligations are interest-bearing at a reasonable rate determined at inception, this is not an issue.)

Dividends payable become a liability of the entity when a dividend has been declared. However, jurisdictions vary as to how this is interpreted. Under most continental European company law, only the shareholders in general meeting can declare a dividend, and so the function of the directors is to propose a dividend, which itself does not give rise to a liability. In other jurisdictions, the decision of the board of directors would trigger recognition of a liability. Since declared dividends are usually paid within a short period of time after the declaration date, they are classified as current liabilities, should a statement of financial position be prepared at a date between the two events.

Unearned revenues or advances result from customer prepayments for either performance of services or delivery of product. They may be required by the selling entity as a condition of the sale or may be made by the buyer as a means of guaranteeing that the seller will perform the desired service or deliver the product. Unearned revenues and advances should be classified as current liabilities at the end of the reporting period if the services are to be performed or the products are to be delivered within one year or the operating cycle, whichever is longer.

Returnable deposits may be received to cover possible future damage to property. Many utility companies require security deposits. A deposit may be required for the use of a reusable container. Refundable deposits are classified as current liabilities if the firm expects to refund them during the current operating cycle or within one year, whichever is longer.

Accrued liabilities have their origin in the end-of-period adjustment process required by accrual accounting. They represent economic obligations, even when the legal or contractual commitment to pay has not yet been triggered, and as such must be given recognition if the matching concept is to be adhered to. Commonly accrued liabilities include wages and salaries payable, interest payable, rent payable, and taxes payable.

Agency liabilities result from the legal obligation of the entity to act as the collection agent for employee or customer taxes owed to various federal, state, or local government units. Examples of agency liabilities include value-added tax, sales taxes, income taxes withheld from employee paychecks, and employee social security contributions, where mandated by law. In addition to agency liabilities, an employer may have a current obligation for unemployment taxes. Payroll taxes typically are not legal liabilities until the associated payroll is actually paid, but in keeping with the concept of accrual accounting, if the payroll has been accrued, the associated payroll taxes should be as well.

Obligations that are, by their terms, due on demand or will become due on demand within one year (or operating cycle, if longer) from the end of the reporting period, even if liquidation is not expected to occur within that period, must be classified as current liabilities. Current IAS are not explicit as to how long-term obligations having features such as subjective acceleration provisions, or acceleration based on covenant violations which are deemed likely to occur over the following year, should be accounted for.

However, when the reporting entity breaches an undertaking or covenant under a long-term loan agreement, thereby causing the liability to become due and payable on demand, it must be classified as current at the end of the reporting period, even if the lender has agreed, after the end of the reporting period and before the authorization of the financial statements for issue, not to demand payment as a consequence of the breach (i.e., to give forbearance to the borrower).

On the other hand, if the lender has granted forbearance before the end of the reporting period (extending for at least one year from the end of the reporting period), then noncurrent classification would be warranted. Similarly, if the lender has agreed by the end of the reporting period to provide a grace period within which the entity can rectify a breach of an undertaking or covenant under a long-term loan agreement and during that time the lender cannot demand immediate repayment, the liability is to be classified as noncurrent if it is due for settlement, without that breach of an undertaking or covenant, at least twelve months after the reporting period *and either*

1. The entity rectifies the breach within the period of grace; *or*
2. When the financial statements are authorized for issue, the grace period is incomplete and it is probable that the breach will indeed be rectified.

Failure to rectify the breach confirms that current classification of the liability was warranted, and the financial statements would be adjusted to conform to that fact.

Short-term obligations expected to be refinanced. Long-term financial liabilities within twelve months of maturity are current liabilities in a classified balance sheet. In some cases, the reporting entity has plans or intentions to refinance the debt (to "roll it over") and thus does not expect its maturity to cause it to deploy its working capital. Under provisions of IAS 1, this debt must be shown as current when due to be settled within twelve months of the end of the reporting period, notwithstanding that its original term was for a period of more than twelve months; and that an agreement to refinance, or to reschedule payments, on a long-term basis is completed after the reporting period and before the financial statements are authorized for issuance. Note that this rule contrasts with the corresponding provision under US GAAP, which does (if certain additional conditions are met) permit noncurrent presentation. The two Boards are unlikely to try to converge in the short term.

However, if the reporting entity has the ability, unilaterally, to refinance or "roll over" the debt for at least twelve months after the end of the reporting period, under the terms of an existing loan facility, it is classified an noncurrent, even if it is otherwise due to be repaid within twelve months of the end of the reporting period, if a "rollover" is the entity's intent. This differs from the situation in which refinancing or "rolling over" the obligation is not at the discretion of the entity (as when there is no agreement to refinance), in which case the potential to refinance (which is no more than the borrower's hope in such instance) is not considered and the obligation is classified as current.

Example of short-term obligations to be refinanced

The Marrakech Warehousing Company has obtained a €3,500,000 bridge loan to assist it in completing a new warehouse. All construction is completed by the end of the reporting period, after which Marrakech has the following three choices for refinancing the bridge loan:

- Enter into a 30-year fixed-rate mortgage for €3,400,000 at 7% interest, leaving Marrakech with a €100,000 obligation to fulfill from short-term funds. Under this scenario, Marrakech reports as current debt the €100,000, as well as the €50,000 portion of the mortgage due within one year, with the remainder of the mortgage itemized as long-term debt. The presentation follows:

Current liabilities	
Short-term notes	100,000
Current portion of long-term debt	50,000
Noncurrent liabilities	
7% mortgage note due in 2037	3,350,000

- Pay off the bridge loan with Marrakech's existing variable rate line of credit (LOC), which expires in two years. The maximum amount of the LOC is 80% of Marrakech's accounts receivable. Over the two-year remaining term of the LOC, the lowest level of qualifying accounts receivable is expected to be €2,700,000. Thus only €2,700,000 of the debt can be classified as long-term, while €800,000 is classified as a short-term obligation. The presentation follows:

Current liabilities
    Short-term note—variable rate line of credit   800,000

Noncurrent liabilities
    Variable rate line of credit due in 2009   2,700,000

- Obtain a loan bearing interest at 10% from Marrakech's owner, with a balloon payment due in five years. Under the terms of this arrangement, the owner can withdraw up to €1,500,000 of funding at any time, even though €3,500,000 is currently available to Marrakech. Under this approach, €1,500,000 is callable, and therefore must be classified as a short-term obligation. The remainder is classified as long-term debt. The presentation follows:

Current liabilities
    Short-term note—majority stockholder   1,500,000

Noncurrent liabilities
    10% balloon note payable to majority stock-
        holder, due in 2012   2,000,000

Long-term debt subject to demand for repayment. What may be thought of as the polar opposite of short-term debt to be refinanced long-term is the situation where the entity is obligated under a long-term (noncurrent) debt arrangement where the lender has either the right to demand immediate or significantly accelerated repayment, or such acceleration rights vest with the lender upon the occurrence of certain events. For example, long-term (and even many short-term) debt agreements typically contain covenants, which effectively are negative or affirmative restrictions on the borrower as to undertaking further borrowings, paying dividends, maintaining specified levels of working capital, and so forth. If a covenant is breached by the borrower, the lender will typically have the right to call the debt immediately, or to otherwise accelerate repayment.

In other cases, the lender will have certain rights under a "subjective acceleration clause" inserted into the loan agreement, giving it the right to demand repayment if it perceives that its risk position has deteriorated as a result of changes in the borrower's business operations, liquidity, or other sometimes vaguely defined factors. Obviously, this gives the lender great power and subjects the borrower to the real possibility that the nominally long-term debt will, in fact, be short-term.

IAS 1 addresses the matter of breach of loan covenants, but does not address the less common phenomenon of subjective acceleration clauses in loan agreements. As to the former, it provides that continued classification of the debt as noncurrent, when one or more of the stipulated default circumstances has occurred, is contingent upon meeting two conditions: First, the lender has agreed, prior to approval of the financial statements, not to demand payment as a consequence of the breach (giving what is known as a debt compliance waiver); and second, that it is considered not probable that further breaches will occur within twelve months of the end of the reporting period. If one or both of these cannot be met, the debt must be reclassified to current status if a classified statement of financial position is, as is generally required under IAS 1, to be presented.

Logic suggests that the existence of subjective acceleration clauses convert nominally long-term debt into currently payable debt. US GAAP, in fact, formally recognizes this reality, requiring current presentation whenever such clauses are present. The authors therefore suggest that in the presence of these or similar provisions, it would be misleading to categorize debt as noncurrent, regardless of the actual maturity date, since continued forbearance by the lender would be required, and this cannot be controlled by the obligor. Such debt should be shown as current, with sufficient disclosure to inform the reader that the debt could effectively be "rolled over" until the nominal maturity date, at the sole discretion of the lender.

Payee Known but Amount May Need to Be Estimated

Provisions. Under IAS 37, *Provisions, Contingent Liabilities, and Contingent Assets*, those liabilities for which amount or timing of expenditure is uncertain are deemed to be provisions.

IAS 37 provides a comprehensive definition of the term "provision." It mandates, in a clear-cut manner, that a provision should be recognized *only* if

- The entity has a present obligation (legal or constructive) as a result of a past event;
- It is probable that an outflow of resources embodying economic benefits will be required to settle the obligation; and
- A reliable estimate can be made of the amount of the obligation.

Thus, a whole range of vaguely defined reserves found in financial statements in days past are clearly not permitted under IFRS. This includes the oft-manipulated restructuring reserves commonly found created during the business combination process when purchase accounting was used (the only acceptable method of accounting for such transactions now; IASB has recently proposed to call this the "acquisition method"). Now, unless there is a *present obligation* as of the purchase combination date, such reserves cannot be established—in most instances, any future restructuring costs will be recognized after the merger event and charged against the successor entity's earnings.

Many other previously employed reserves are likewise barred by the strict conditions set forth by IAS 37. However, the mere need to estimate the amount to be reflected in the provision is not evidence of a failure to qualify for recognition. If an actual obligation exists, despite one or more factors making the amount less than precisely known, recognition is required.

IAS 37 offers in-depth guidance on the topic of provisions. Each of the key words in the definition of the term "provision" is explained in detail by the standard. Explanations and clarifications offered by the standard are summarized below.

- **Present obligation.** The standard opines that in almost all cases it will be clear when a present obligation exists. The notion of an obligation in the standard includes not only a legal obligation (e.g., deriving from a contract or legislation) but also a constructive obligation. It explains that a constructive obligation exists when the entity from an established pattern of past practice or stated policy has created a valid expectation that it will accept certain responsibilities.
- **Past event.** There must be some past event which has triggered the present obligation—for example, an accidental oil spillage. An accounting provision cannot be created in anticipation of a future event. The entity must also have no realistic alternative to settling the obligation caused by the event.
- **Probable outflow of resources embodying economic benefits.** For a provision to qualify for recognition it is essential that it is not only a present obligation of the reporting entity, but also it should be probable that an outflow of resources embodying benefits used to settle the obligation will in fact result. For the purposes of this standard, probable is defined as "more likely than not." A footnote to the standard states that this interpretation of the term "probable" does not necessarily apply to other IAS. The use of terms such as probable, significant, or impracticable creates problems of interpretation, both within a given set of standards (e.g., IFRS) and across different

sets. The IASB and FASB are intending to converge on their interpretation and use of such terms in order to reduce the level of confusion.

- **Reliable estimate of the obligation.** The standard recognizes that using estimates is common in the preparation of financial statements and suggest that by using a range of possible outcomes, an entity will usually be able to make an estimate of the obligation that is sufficiently reliable to use in recognizing a provision. Where no reliable estimate can be made, though, no liability is recognized.

Other salient features of provisions explained by the standard include the following:

1. For all estimated liabilities that are included within the definition of provisions, the amount to be recorded and presented in the statement of financial position should be the *best estimate*, at the end of the reporting period, of the amount of expenditure that will be required to settle the obligation. This is often referred to as the "expected value" of the obligation, which may be operationally defined as the amount the entity would pay, currently, to either settle the actual obligation or provide consideration to a third party to assume it (e.g., as a single occurrence insurance premium). For estimated liabilities comprised of large numbers of relatively small, similar items, weighting by probability of occurrence can be used to compute the aggregate expected value; this is often used to compute accrued warranty reserves, for example. For those estimated liabilities consisting of only a few (or a single) discrete obligations, the most likely outcome may be used to measure the liability when there is a range of outcomes having roughly similar probabilities; but if possible outcomes include amounts much greater (and lesser) than the most likely, it may be necessary to accrue a larger amount if there is a significant chance that the larger obligation will have to be settled, even if that is not the most likely outcome as such.

    The concept of "expected value" can be best explained through a numeric illustration.

    > Good Samaritan Inc. manufactures and sells pinball machines under warranty. Customers are entitled to refunds if they return defective machines with valid proof of purchase. Good Samaritan Inc. estimates that if all machines sold and still in warranty had major defects, total replacement costs would equal €1,000,000; if all those machines suffered from minor defects, the total repair costs would be €500,000. Good Samaritan's past experience, however, suggests that only 10% of the machines sold will have major defects, and that another 30% will have minor defects. Based on this information, the expected value of the product warranty costs to be accrued at year-end would be computed as follows:
    >
    > Expected value of the cost of refunds:
    >
    > | | | | |
    > |---|---|---|---|
    > | Resulting from major defects: | €1,000,000 × 0.10 | = | €100,000 |
    > | Resulting from minor defects: | € 500,000 × 0.30 | = | 150,000 |
    > | No defects: | €   0 × 0.60 | = | -- |
    > | | Total | = | €250,000 |

2. The "risks and uncertainties" surrounding events and circumstances should be taken into account in arriving at the best estimate of a provision. However, as pointedly noted by the standard, uncertainty should not be used to justify the creation of excessive provisions or a deliberate overstatement of liabilities.

3. The standard also addresses the use of present values or discounting (i.e., recording the estimated liability at present value, after taking into account the time value of money). While the entire subject of present value measurement in accounting has

been widely debated, in practice there is a notable lack of consistency (with some standards requiring it, others prohibiting it, and many others remaining silent on the issue). IAS 37 has stood firm on the subject of present value measurement, despite some opposition voiced in response to the Exposure Draft and an ongoing plea for more guidance on how this is to be determined. The standard requires the use of discounting when the effect would be material, but it can be ignored if immaterial in effect. Thus, provisions estimated to be due farther into the future will have more need to be discounted than those due currently. As a practical matter, all but trivial provisions should be discounted unless the timing is unknown (which makes discounting a computational impossibility).

IAS 37 clarifies that the discount rate applied should be consistent with the estimation of cash flows (i.e., if cash flows are projected in nominal terms). That is, if the estimated amount expected to be paid out reflects whatever price inflation is anticipated to occur between the end of the reporting period and the date of ultimate settlement of the estimated obligation, then a nominal discount rate should be used. If future cash outflows are projected in real terms, net of any price inflation, then a real interest rate should be applied. In either case, past experience must be used to ascertain likely timing of future cash flows, since discounting cannot otherwise be performed.

4. Future events that may affect the amount required to settle an obligation should be reflected in the provision amount where there is sufficient objective evidence that such future events will in fact occur. For example, if an entity believes that the cost of cleaning up a plant site at the end of its useful life will be reduced by future changes in technology, the amount recognized as a provision for cleanup costs should reflect a reasonable estimate of cost reduction resulting from any anticipated technological changes. In many instances making such estimates will not be possible, however.

5. IFRIC 1 mandates that changes in decommissioning provisions should be recognized prospectively (i.e., by amending future depreciation charges).

6. Gains from expected disposals of assets should not be taken into account in arriving at the amount of the provision (even if the expected disposal is closely linked to the event giving rise to the provision).

7. Reimbursements by other parties should be taken into account when computing the provision, only if it is virtually certain that the reimbursement will be received. The reimbursement should be treated as a separate asset on the balance sheet, not netted against the estimated liability. However, in the statement of comprehensive income or in the income statement, if prepared separately, the provision may be presented net of the amount recognized as a reimbursement. In the authors' observation, recognition of such contingent assets would be very rare in practice due to the long time horizons and concerns about the viability of the parties promising to make reimbursement payments over the long term. A government-backed fund, on the other hand, could probably be deemed reliable.

8. Changes in provisions should be considered at the end of each reporting period, and provisions should be adjusted to reflect the current best estimate. If upon review it appears that it is no longer probable that an outflow of resources embodying economics will be required to settle the obligation, then the provision should be reversed through current period results of operations.

9. Use of provision is to be restricted to the purpose for which it was recognized originally. A reserve for plant dismantlement, for example, cannot be used to absorb environmental pollution claims or warranty payments. If an expenditure is set against

a provision that was originally recognized for another purpose, that would camouflage the impact of the two different events, distorting income performance and possibly constituting financial reporting fraud.

10. Provisions for future operating losses should not be recognized. This is explicitly proscribed by the standard, since future operating losses do not meet the definition of a liability at the end of the reporting period (as defined in the standard) and the general recognition criteria set forth in the standard.

11. Present obligations under *onerous contracts* should be recognized and measured as a provision. The standard introduces the concept of onerous contracts, which it defines as contracts under which the unavoidable costs of satisfying the obligations exceed the economic benefits expected. Executory contracts that are not onerous do not fall within the purview of this standard. In other words, the expected negative implications of such contracts (executory contracts which are not onerous) cannot be recognized as a provision.

    The standard mandates that unavoidable costs under a contract represent the "least net costs of exiting from the contract." Such unavoidable costs should be measured at the *lower* of

    - The cost of fulfilling the contract; *or*
    - Any compensation or penalties arising from failure to fulfill the contract.

12. Provisions for restructuring costs are recognized only when the general recognition criteria for provisions are met. A constructive obligation to restructure arises only when an entity has a *detailed formal plan* for the restructuring which identifies at least: the business or the part of the business concerned, principal locations affected, approximate number of employees that would need to be compensated for termination resulting from the restructuring (along with their function and location), expenditure that would be required to carry out the restructuring, and information as to when the plan is to be implemented.

    Furthermore, the recognition criteria also require that the entity should have raised a valid expectation among those affected by the restructuring that it will, in fact, carry out the restructuring by starting to implement that plan or announcing its main features to those affected by it. Thus, until both the conditions mentioned above are satisfied, a restructuring provision cannot be made based upon the concept of constructive obligation. In practice, given the strict criteria of IAS 37, restructuring costs are more likely to become recognizable when actually incurred in a subsequent period.

    Only *direct* expenditures arising from restructuring should be provided for. Such direct expenditures should be both necessarily incurred for the restructuring *and* not associated with the ongoing activities of the entity. Thus, a provision for restructuring would not include costs like: cost of retraining or relocating the entity's current staff members or costs of marketing or investments in new systems and distribution networks (such expenditures are in fact categorically disallowed by the standard, as they are considered to be expenses relating to the future conduct of the business of the entity, and thus are not liabilities relating to the restructuring program). Also, identifiable future operating losses up to the date of an actual restructuring are not to be included in the provision for a restructuring (unless they relate to an onerous contract). Furthermore, in keeping with the general measurement principles relating to provisions outlined in the standard, the specific guidance in IAS 37 relating to restructuring prohibits taking into account any gains on expected disposal of assets in measuring a restructuring provision, even if the sale of the assets is envisaged as part of the restructuring.

A management decision or a board resolution to restructure taken before the end of the reporting period does not automatically give rise to a constructive obligation at the end of the reporting period unless the entity has, before end of the reporting period: either started to implement the restructuring plan, or announced the main features of the restructuring plan to those affected by it in a sufficiently specific manner such that a valid expectation is raised in them (i.e., that the entity will in fact carry out the restructuring and that benefits will be paid to them).

Examples of events that may fall within the definition of restructuring are

- A fundamental reorganization of an entity that has a material effect on the nature and focus of the entity's operations;
- Drastic changes in the management structure—for example, making all functional units autonomous;
- Removing the business to a more strategic location or place by relocating the headquarters from one country or region to another; and
- The sale or termination of a line of business (if certain other conditions are satisfied, such that a restructuring could be considered a discontinued operation under IFRS 5).

13. Disclosures mandated by the standard for provisions are the following:

- For each class of provision, the carrying amount at the beginning and the end of the period, additional provisions made during the period, amounts used during the period, unused amounts reversed during the period, and the increase during the period in the discounted amount arising from the passage of time and the effect of change in discount rate (comparative information is not required).
- For each class of provision, a brief description of the nature of the obligation and the expected timing of any resulting outflows of economic benefits, an indication of the uncertainties regarding the amount or timing of those outflows (including, where necessary in order to provide adequate information, disclosure of major assumptions made concerning future events), and the amount of any expected reimbursement, stating the amount of the asset that has been recognized for that expected reimbursement.
- In extremely rare circumstances, if the above disclosures as envisaged by the standard are expected to seriously prejudice the position of the reporting entity in a dispute with third parties on the subject matter of the provision, then the standard takes a lenient view and allows the reporting entity to disclose the general nature of the dispute together with the fact that, and reason why, the information has not been disclosed. This is to satisfy the concerns of those who believe that mere disclosure of certain provisions will encourage potential claimants to assert themselves, thus becoming a "self-fulfilling prophecy."

For the purposes of making the above disclosures, it may be essential to group or aggregate provisions. The standard also offers guidance on how to determine which provisions may be aggregated to form a class. As per the standard, in determining which provisions may be aggregated to report as a class, the nature of the items should be sufficiently similar for them to be aggregated together and reported as a class. For example, while it may be appropriate to aggregate into a single class all provisions relating to warranties of different products, it may not be appropriate to group and present, as a single class, amounts relating to normal warranties and amounts that are subject to legal proceedings.

Example footnote illustrating disclosures required under IAS 37 with respect to provisions

Provisions

At December 31, 2009, provisions consist of the following (all amounts in euros):

	Opening balance	Additions	Provision utilized	Unutilized provision reversed	Closing balance
Provision for environmental costs	1,000,000	900,000	(800,000)	(100,000)	1,000,000
Provision for staff bonus	2,000,000	1,000,000	(900,000)	--	2,100,000
Provision for restructuring costs	1,000,000	500,000	(100,000)	(200,000)	1,200,000
Provision for decommissioning costs	5,000,000	500,000	(2,000,000)	--	3,500,000
	9,000,000	2,900,000	(3,800,000)	(300,000)	7,800,000

Provision for environmental costs. Statutory decontamination costs relating to old chemical manufacturing sites are determined based on periodic assessments undertaken by environmental specialists employed by the company and verified by independent experts.

Provision for staff bonus. Provisions for staff bonus represents contractual amounts due to the company's middle management, based on one month's basic salary, as per current employment contracts.

Provision for restructuring costs. Restructuring provisions arise from a fundamental reorganization of the company's operations and management structure.

Provision for decommissioning costs. Provision is made for estimated decommissioning costs relating to oilfields operated by the company based on engineering estimates and independent experts' reports.

The following paragraphs provide examples of provisions that would need to be recognized, based on the rules laid down by the standard. It also discusses common provisions and the accounting treatment that is often applied to these particular items.

Dry-docking costs. In some countries it is required by law, for the purposes of obtaining a certificate of seaworthiness, that ships must periodically (e.g., every three to five years) undergo extensive repairs and incur maintenance costs that are customarily referred to as "dry-docking costs." Depending on the type of vessel and its remaining useful life, such costs could be significant in amount. Before IAS 37 came into effect, some argued that dry-docking costs should be periodically accrued (in anticipation) and amortized over a period of time such that the amount is spread over the period commencing from the date of accrual to the date of payment. Using this approach, if every three years a vessel has to be dry-docked at a cost of €5 million, then such costs could be recognized as a provision at the beginning of each triennial period and amortized over the following three years.

Under the requirements set forth by IAS 37, provisions for future dry-docking expenditures cannot be accrued, since these future costs are not contractual in nature and can be avoided (e.g., by disposing of the vessel prior to its next overhaul). In general, such costs are to be expensed when incurred. However, consistent with IAS 16, if a separate component of the asset cost was recognized at inception (e.g., at acquisition of the vessel) and depreciated over its (shorter) useful life, then the cost associated with the subsequent dry-docking can likewise be capitalized as a separate asset component and depreciated over the interval until the next expected dry-docking. While the presumption is that this asset component would be included in the property and equipment accounts, in practice, some entities record major inspection or overhaul costs as a deferred charge (a noncurrent prepaid expense account) and amortize them over the expected period of benefit, which has the same impact on total assets and periodic results of operations.

Unlawful environmental damage. Cleanup costs and penalties resulting from unlawful environmental damage (e.g., an oil spill by a tanker ship which contaminates the water near the sea port) would need to be provided for in those countries which have laws requiring cleanup, since it would lead to an outflow of resources embodying economic benefits in settlement regardless of the future actions of the entity.

In case the entity which has caused the environmental damage operates in a country that has not yet enacted legislation requiring cleanup, in some cases a provision may still be required based on the principle of constructive obligation (as opposed to a legal obligation). This may be possible if the entity has a widely publicized environmental policy in which it undertakes to clean up all contamination that it causes and the entity has a clean track record of honoring its published environmental policy. The reason a provision would be needed under the second situation is that the recognition criteria have been met—that is, there is a present obligation resulting from a past obligating event (the oil spill) and the conduct of the entity has created a valid expectation on the part of those affected by it that the entity will clean up the contamination (a constructive obligation) and the outflow of resources embodying economic benefits is probable.

The issue of determining what constitutes an "obligating event" under IAS 37 has recently been addressed, in a highly particularized setting, by IFRIC 6, *Liabilities Arising from Participating in a Specific Market—Waste Electrical and Electronic Equipment.* This was in response to a European Union Directive on Waste Electrical and Electronic Equipment (WE&EE), which regulates the collection, treatment, recovery and environmentally sound disposal of waste equipment. Such items contain toxic metals and other materials and have become a concern in recent years, due to the large quantities (e.g., obsolete computers) of goods being dumped by household and business consumers.

The EU Directive deals only with private household WE&EE sold before August 13, 2005 ("historical household equipment"). Assuming enactment of legislation by member states, it is to be mandated that the cost of waste management for this historical household equipment will be borne by the producers of that type of equipment, with levies being assessed on them in proportion to their market shares. This will be done with reference to those manufacturers that are in the market during a period to be specified in the applicable legislation of each EU member state (the "measurement period").

The accounting issue is simply this: what is the obligating event that creates the liabilities for these producers of the defined historical household equipment, which of course all has already been sold by the producers in months and years gone by. IFRIC 6 concludes that it is participation in the market during the measurement period that will be the obligating event, rather than the earlier event (manufacture of the equipment) or a later event (incurrence of costs in the performance of waste management activities). Accordingly, initial recognition of the liability will occur when the measurement period occurs.

While IFRIC 6 was promulgated in response to a specific, and unusual, situation, it does well illustrate how significant making such determinations (the obligating event, in this instance) can be with regard to presentation in the financial statements.

Provision for restructuring costs. An entity which publicly announces, before the end of the reporting period, its plans to shut down a division in accordance with a board decision and a detailed formal plan, would need to recognize a provision for the best estimate of the costs of closing down the division. In such a case the recognition criteria are met as follows: a present obligation has resulted from a past obligating event (public announcement of the decision to the public at large) which gives rise to a constructive obligation from that date, since it creates a valid expectation that the division will be shut down and an outflow of resources embodying economic benefits in settlement is probable.

On the other hand, if the entity had not publicly announced its plans to shut down the division before the end of the reporting period, or did not start implementing its plan before the end of the reporting period, no provision would need to be made since the board decision alone would not give rise to a constructive obligation at the end of the reporting period (since no valid expectation has in fact been raised in those affected by the restructuring that the entity will start to implement that plan). When a reporting entity commences implementation of a restructuring plan, or announces its main features to those affected, only after the end of the reporting period, disclosure is required by the provisions of IAS 10. Applying the materiality logic common in financial reporting, such disclosure would only be mandatory if the restructuring is material and if nondisclosure could reasonably be expected to influence the economic decisions made by users on the basis of the financial statements.

Onerous contracts. An entity relocates its offices to a more prestigious office complex because the old office building that it was occupying (and has been there for the last twenty years), does not suit the new corporate image it wants to project. However, the lease of the old office premises cannot be canceled at the present time since it continues for the next five years. This is a case of an onerous contract wherein the unavoidable costs of meeting the obligations under the contract exceed the economic benefits under it. A provision is thus required to be made for the best estimate of unavoidable lease payments.

Decommissioning costs. An oil company installed an oil refinery on leased land. The installation was completed before the end of the reporting period. Upon expiration of the lease contract, seven years hence, the refinery will have to be relocated to another strategic location that would ensure uninterrupted supply of crude oil. These estimated relocation or decommissioning costs would need to be recognized at the end of the reporting period. Accordingly, a provision should be recognized for the present value of the estimated decommissioning costs to take place after seven years.

In 2004, the IASB's committee dealing with implementation issues (IFRIC) issued a final interpretation, IFRIC 1, *Changes in Decommissioning, Restoration and Similar Liabilities,* which provides further guidance on this topic. Specifically, this interpretation specifies how the following matters would be accounted for:

1. Changes in the estimated outflows of resources embodying economic benefits (e.g., cash flows) required to settle the obligation;
2. Changes in current market assessments of the discount rate as defined in IAS 37 (i.e., including changes in both the time value of money and the risks specific to the liability); and
3. Increases that reflect the passage of time (also referred to as the unwinding of the discount, or as accretion of the estimated liability amount).

The interpretation holds that, regarding changes in either the estimated future cash flows or in the assessed discount rate, these would be added to (or deducted from) the related asset to the extent the change relates to the portion of the asset that will be depreciated in future periods. These charges or credits will thereafter be reflected in periodic results of operations over future periods. Thus, no prior period adjustments will be permitted in respect to such changes in estimates, consistent with IAS 8.

Regarding accretion of the discount over the asset's useful life, so that the liability for decommissioning costs reaches full value at the date of decommissioning, the interpretation holds that this must be included in current income, presumably as a finance charge. Importantly, the interpretation states that this cannot be capitalized as part of the asset cost.

Example of adjustment for changes in discount rate

To illustrate the accounting for this change, assume an oil refinery was recorded inclusive of an estimated removal cost, at present value, of €2,333,000. Now assume that, after two years have elapsed, the relevant discount rate is assessed at 6%. There have been no changes in the estimated ultimate removal costs, which are still expected to total €4,000,000. The accreted recorded liability value at this date is €2,722,000, but given the new discount rate, it needs to be adjusted to €2,989,000, for an increase of €267,000 as of the beginning of the third year. The provision account must be credited by this amount, as shown in the journal entry below.

The asset account and accumulated depreciation must also be adjusted for this change in discount rate. Under the proposed requirement, this would be done by recomputing the amount that would have been capitalized, using the initial discount rate for the first two years, followed by the new discount rate over the remaining five years (note that the new rate is not imposed on the period already elapsed, because the rate originally used was correct during those earlier periods). If the €4,000,000 future value were discounted for five years at 6% and two years at 8%, the adjusted initial present value would have been €2,563,000, instead of the €2,333,000 actually recorded. To adjust for this, the asset must be increased by (€2,563,000 – €2,333,000 =) €230,000.

Had the revised present value of the removal costs been capitalized, €732,286 (= €2,563,000 × 2/7) would have been depreciated to date, instead of the €666,571 (= €2,333,000 × 2/7) that was in fact recorded, for a net difference in accumulated depreciation of €65,715. This amount must be credited to the contra asset account.

Asset	230,000	
Expense	102,715	
Accumulated depreciation		65,715
Decommissioning liability		267,000

The remaining part of the entry above, a debit to expense totaling €102,715, is the net effect of the increase in the net book value of the asset (€230,000 – €65,715 =) €164,285, offset by the increased provision, €267,000, which is an expense of the period.

Taxes payable include federal or national, state or provincial, and local income taxes. Due to frequent changes in the tax laws, the amount of income taxes payable may have to be estimated. That portion deemed currently payable must be classified as a current liability. The remaining amount is classified as a long-term liability. Although estimated future taxes are broadly includable under the category "provisions," specific rules in IAS 12 prohibit discounting these amounts to present values.

Property taxes payable represents the unpaid portion of an entity's obligation to a state or other taxing authority that arises from ownership of real property. Often these taxes are levied in arrears, based on periodic reassessments of value and on governmental budgetary needs. Accordingly, the most acceptable method of accounting for property taxes is a monthly accrual of property tax expense during the fiscal period of the taxing authority for which the taxes are levied. The fiscal period of the taxing authority is the fiscal period that includes the assessment or lien date.

A liability for property taxes payable arises when the fiscal year of the taxing authority and the fiscal year of the entity do not coincide or when the assessment or lien date and the actual payment date do not fall within the same fiscal year. For example, XYZ Corporation is a calendar-year corporation that owns real estate in a state that operates on a June 30 fiscal year. In this state, property taxes are assessed and become a lien against property on July 1, although they are not payable until April 1 and August 1 of the next calendar year. XYZ Corporation would accrue an expense and a liability on a monthly basis beginning on July 1. At year-end (December 31), the firm would have an expense for six months' property tax in profit or loss and a current liability for the same amount.

Bonus payments may require estimation since the amount of the bonus payment may be affected by the amount of income taxes currently payable.

Compensated absences refer to paid vacation, paid holidays, and paid sick leave. IAS 19 addresses this issue and requires that an employer should accrue a liability for employees' compensation of future absences if the employees' right to receive compensation for future absences is attributable to employee services already rendered, the right vests or accumulates, ultimate payment of the compensation is probable, and the amount of the payment can be reasonably estimated.

If an employer is required to compensate an employee for unused vacation, holidays, or sick days, even if employment is terminated, the employee's right to this compensation is said to vest. Accrual of a liability for nonvesting rights depends on whether the unused rights expire at the end of the year in which earned or accumulated and are carried forward to succeeding years. If the rights expire, a liability for future absences should not be accrued at year-end because the benefits to be paid in subsequent years would not be attributable to employee services rendered in prior years. If unused rights accumulate and increase the benefits otherwise available in subsequent years, a liability should be accrued at year-end to the extent that it is probable that employees will be paid in subsequent years for the increased benefits attributable to the accumulated rights, and the amount can reasonably be estimated.

Pay for employee leaves of absence that represent time off for past services should be considered compensation subject to accrual. Pay for employee leaves of absence that will provide future benefits and that are not attributable to past services rendered would not be subject to accrual. Although in theory such accruals should be based on expected future rates of pay, as a practical matter these are often computed on current pay rates that may not materially differ and have the advantage of being known. Also, if the payments are to be made some time in the future, discounting of the accrual amounts would seemingly be appropriate, but again this may not often be done for practical considerations.

Similar arguments can be made to support the accrual of an obligation for post-employment benefits other than pensions if employees' rights accumulate or vest, payment is probable, and the amount can be reasonably estimated. If these benefits do not vest or accumulate, these would be deemed to be contingent liabilities. Contingent liabilities are discussed in IAS 37 and are considered later in this chapter.

Short sale obligations. When an individual or entity sells securities that are not owned, this is referred to as a "short sale," and is usually accomplished by means of securities borrowed from a brokerage firm. In such cases, the borrowed securities are not recorded as an asset by the borrower. The IASC's IAS 39 Implementation Guidance Committee has noted that a short seller accounts for the obligation to deliver securities that it has sold as a "liability held for trading." Therefore, if an entity sells an unrecorded financial asset that is subject to a securities borrowing agreement, the entity recognizes the proceeds from the sale as an asset, and the obligation to return the asset as a liability held for trading. Liabilities held for trading, just like held for trading securities that are assets of the entity, must be measured at fair value. Changes in fair value will be reflected currently in earnings.

Payee Unknown and the Amount May Have to Be Estimated

The following are further examples of estimated liabilities, which also will fall within the definition of provisions under IAS 37. Accordingly, discounting should be applied to projected future cash flows to determine the amounts to be reported in the statement of financial position if the effect of discounting is material, and if timing can be estimated with sufficient accuracy to accomplish this process.

Premiums are usually offered by an entity to increase product sales. They may require the purchaser to return a specified number of box tops, wrappers, or other proofs of purchase. They may or may not require the payment of a cash amount. If the premium offer terminates at the end of the current period but has not been accounted for completely if it extends into the next accounting period, a current liability for the estimated number of redemptions expected in the future period will have to be recorded. If the premium offer extends for more than one accounting period, the estimated liability must be divided into a current portion and a long-term portion.

Product warranties providing for repair or replacement of defective products may be sold separately or may be included in the sale price of the product. If the warranty extends into the next accounting period, a current liability for the estimated amount of warranty expense anticipated for the next period must be recorded. If the warranty spans more than the next period, the estimated liability must be partitioned into a current and long-term portion.

Example of product warranty expense accrual

The River Rocks Corporation manufactures clothes washers. It sells €900,000 of washing machines during its most recent month of operations. Based on its historical warranty claims experience, it reserves an estimated warranty expense of 2% of revenues with the following entry:

Warranty expense	18,000	
Reserve for warranty claims		18,000

During the following month, River Rocks incurs €10,000 of actual labor and €4,500 of actual materials expenses to repair warranty claims, which it charges to the warranty claims reserve with the following entry:

Reserve for warranty claims	14,500	
Labor expense		10,000
Materials expense		4,500

River Rocks also sells three-year extended warranties on its washing machines that begin once the initial one-year manufacturer's warranty is completed. During one month, it sells €54,000 of extended warranties, which it records with the following entry:

Cash	54,000	
Unearned warranty revenue		54,000

This liability remains unaltered for one year from the purchase date, during the period of normal warranty coverage, after which the extended warranty servicing period begins. River Rocks recognizes the warranty revenue on a straight-line basis over the 36 months of the warranty period, using the following entry each month:

Unearned warranty revenue	1,500	
Warranty revenue		1,500

Other customer incentives are usually offered by an entity to increase product sales. They may require the customers to accumulate "points" earned in proportion to products or services purchased or consumed. A common example is airline frequent flyer mileage programs, which reward loyal passengers with free trips following a threshold amount of paid travel, usually gauged by mileage traveled. Over time, airlines accumulate experience which lets them accurately predict what fraction of earned miles will eventually be redeemed for "free" travel. A provision must be made for the cost of such travel, if and when redemption occurs.

Example of an accrued sales incentive cost

Central European Airlines, a specialty airline offering flights to Central Europe's wine producing regions, offers frequent flier miles to its passengers. Anyone remitting 15,000 mileage points earns a free flight on Central European, which costs the airline €120 per flight granted, or approximately €0.008 per mileage point remitted. In April, the airline granted 23,000,000 mileage points, having a total value of €184,000 (=23,000,000 miles flown × €0.008). Central European's history of mileage claims remitted over the past three years suggests that 40% of all mileage points are eventually remitted. Thus, Central European records the following liability in April, based on recognition of 40% of the total value of points granted:

Passenger transportation expense	73,600	
Unremitted mileage points liability		73,600

Also in April, 8,475,000 mileage points are remitted by Central European passengers for free flights. The implicit cost of these remittances is as follows:

Mileage points remitted		8,475,000
Cost per mileage point	×	€ 0.008
Total liability reduction	=	€ 67,800

Central European records the liability with the following entry:

Unremitted mileage points liability	67,800	
Passenger transportation expense		67,800

The actual cost of transportation of passengers paid or accrued by Central European at the time the flights occur is thus reduced by the amount accrued at the time the points currently being redeemed were awarded.

A year later, Central European finds that the mileage points remittance rate has risen from 40% to 42%. At this time, there are 163,000,000 mileage points outstanding. Central European records a liability for the incremental increase of 2% in the remittance level with the following entry:

Passenger transportation expense	26,080	
Unremitted mileage points liability		26,080

The entry is based on the following calculation:

Mileage points outstanding		163,000,00
Net increase in remittance percentage	×	2%
Cost per mileage point	×	€ 0.008
Total liability	=	€26,080

Central European receives an offer to sell 20,000,000 mileage points to the Wine Tourist branded credit card, which in turn sells the points to its cardholders in exchange for purchases made with its credit card. The sale price is €0.005 per mile sold, resulting in the following entry:

Cash	100,000	
Revenue		100,000

Central European must also record the related cost of this transaction. Based on its estimated 42% mileage points remittance rate and €0.008 cost per mileage point, Central European arrives at the following estimated cost of this transaction:

Mileage points sold		20,000,000
Mileage remittance percentage	×	42%
Cost per mileage point	×	€ 0.008
Total estimated cost	=	€67,200

Central European records the following entry to record the expense associated with the mileage points sale:

Passenger transportation expense	67,200	
Unremitted mileage points liability		67,200

Contingent Liabilities

The term contingent liability is used differently under IFRS than under US GAAP. IAS 37 defines a contingent liability as an obligation that is either

- A *possible* obligation arising from past events, the outcome of which will be confirmed only on the occurrence or nonoccurrence of one or more uncertain future events which are not wholly within the control of the reporting entity; *or*
- A *present* obligation arising from past events, which is not recognized either because it is not probable that an outflow of resources will be required to settle an obligation or the amount of the obligation cannot be measured with sufficient reliability.

Under IAS 37, the reporting entity is not to give formal recognition to a contingent liability. Instead, it should disclose in the notes to the financial statements the following information:

1. An estimate of its financial effect;
2. An indication of the uncertainties relating to the amount or timing of any outflow; and
3. The possibility of any reimbursement.

Disclosure of this information may be foregone if the possibility of any outflow in settlement is remote, or if the information cannot be obtained without undue cost or effort.

Contingent liabilities may develop in a way not initially anticipated. Thus, it is imperative that they be reassessed continually to determine whether an outflow of resources embodying economic benefits has become probable. If the outflow of future economic benefits becomes probable, then a provision is required to be recognized in the financial statements of the period in which the change in such a probability occurs (except in extremely rare cases, when no reliable estimate can be made of the amount needed to be recognized as a provision).

Contingent liabilities must be distinguished from estimated liabilities, although both involve uncertainties that will be resolved by future events. However, an estimate exists because of uncertainty about the amount of an event requiring an acknowledged accounting recognition. The event is known and the effect is known, but the amount itself is uncertain. For example, depreciation is an estimate, but not a contingency, because the actual fact of physical depreciation is acknowledged, although the amount is obtained by an assumed accounting method.

In a contingency, whether there will be an impairment of an asset or the occurrence of a liability is the uncertainty that will be resolved in the future. The amount is also usually uncertain, although that is not an essential characteristic defining the contingency. Collectibility of receivables is a contingency because both the amount of loss and the identification of which customer will not pay as promised in the future is unknown. Similar logic would hold for obligations related to product warranties. Both the amount and the customer are currently unknown.

Assessing the likelihood of contingent events. It is tempting to express quantitatively the likelihood of the occurrence of contingent events (e.g., an 80% probability), but this exaggerates the degree of precision possible in the estimation process. For this reason, accounting standards have not been written to require quantification of the likelihood of contingent outcomes. Rather, qualitative descriptions, ranging along the continuum from remote to probable, have historically been prescribed.

IAS 37 sets the threshold for accrual at "more likely than not," which most experts have defined as being a probability of very slightly over a 50% likelihood. Thus, if there is even a hint that the obligation is more likely to exist than to not exist, it will need to be formally recognized if an amount can be reasonably estimated for it. The impact will be both to make it much less ambiguous when a contingency should be recorded, and to force recognition of far more of these obligations at earlier dates than they are being given recognition at present. (Note that under longstanding US GAAP, only "probable" contingent losses are accrued, although less likely outcomes, called "reasonably possible" contingencies, must be given disclosure in the financial statement footnotes.)

When a loss is probable and no estimate is possible, these facts should be disclosed in the current period. The accrual of the loss should be made in the period in which the amount of the loss can be estimated. This accrual of a loss in future periods is a change in estimate. It is **not** to be presented as a prior period adjustment.

Disappearance of contingent liabilities and assets. In the context of Phase II of its Business Combinations project, the IASB has extensively redebated the accounting for contingent items. It has concluded that a contingent liability consists of both a certain obligation and an uncertain obligation. For example, a premium or reward to be claimed by buyers of a sufficient quantity of the entity's goods involves a certain liability, the obligation to pay the premium when claimed correctly, and an uncertain obligation, which is a function of how many people are likely to claim it. The certain obligation meets the *Framework* definition of a liability, while the uncertain obligation provides an input into the measurement of this liability. This approach has been incorporated into the amendment to IFRS 3 that was adopted in early 2008 (see full discussion in Chapter 11), and thus the probability of the obligation coming to fruition is no longer the trigger for recognition; it has become instead the basis of measurement. In the case of the premiums owed to customers, the entity should work out the expected value of the future cash flows by combining the probabilities, and this would determine the value of the liability. In the future, therefore, contingent assets and contingent liabilities will no longer exist: the same events will trigger an actual asset or liability, and the level of uncertainty will be factored into the carrying value.

Remote contingent losses. With the exception of certain remote contingencies for which disclosures have traditionally been given, contingent losses that are deemed remote in terms of likelihood of occurrence are not accrued or disclosed in the financial statements. For example, every business risks loss by fire, explosion, government expropriation, or guarantees made in the ordinary course of business. These are all contingencies because of the uncertainty surrounding whether the future event confirming the loss will or will not take place. The risk of asset expropriation exists, but this has become less common an occurrence in recent decades and, in any event, would be limited to less developed or politically unstable nations. Unless there is specific information about the expectation of such occurrences, which would thus raise the item to the possible category in any event, thereby making it subject to disclosure, these are not normally discussed in the financial statements.

Litigation. The most difficult area of contingencies accounting involves litigation. In some nations there is a great deal of commercial and other litigation, some of which exposes reporting entities to risks of incurring very material losses. Accountants must generally rely on attorneys' assessments concerning the likelihood of such events. Unless the attorney indicates that the risk of loss is remote or slight, or that the impact of any loss that does occur would be immaterial to the company, the accountant will require that the entity add explanatory material to the financial statements regarding the contingency. In cases where judgments have been entered against the entity, or where the attorney gives a range of expected losses or other amounts, certain accruals of loss contingencies for at least the minimum point of the range must be made. Similarly, if the reporting entity has made an offer in settlement of unresolved litigation, that offer would normally be deemed the lower end of the range of possible loss and, thus, subject for accrual. In most cases, however, an estimate of the contingency is unknown and the contingency is reflected only in footnotes.

Example of illustrative footnotes—contingent liabilities

1. A former plant manager of the establishment has filed a claim related to injuries sustained by him during an accident in the factory. The former employee is claiming approximately €3.5 million as damages for permanent disability, alleging that the establishment had violated a safety regulation. At the end of the reporting period, no provision has been made for this claim, as management intends to vigorously defend these allegations and believes the payment of any penalty is not probable.

2. Based on allegations made by a competitor, the company is currently the subject of a government investigation relating to antitrust matters. If the company is ultimately accused of violations of the country's antitrust laws, fines could be assessed. Penalties

would include sharing of previously earned profits with a competitor on all contracts entered into from inception. The competitor has indicated to the governmental agency investigating the company that the company has made excessive profits ranging from €50 million to €75 million by resorting to restrictive trade practices that are prohibited by the law of the country. No provision for any penalties or other damages has been made at the end of the reporting period since the company's legal counsel is confident that these allegations will not be sustained in a court of law.

Financial Guarantee Contracts

Guarantees are commonly encountered in the commercial world; these can range from guarantees of bank loans made as accommodations to business associates to negotiated arrangements made to facilitate sales of the entity's goods or services. Guarantees had not been comprehensively addressed by IFRS prior to the mid-2005 amendment to IAS 39 and IFRS 4, which was made to explicitly deal with certain financial guarantee contracts. In contrast, under US GAAP (FAS 5, in particular) there had long been a tradition of, at minimum, disclosure of guarantees, and in many circumstances the accrual of the anticipated loss to be suffered by the guarantor. Most recently, US GAAP saw the promulgation of a detailed standard, FIN 45, which established a new regime for measuring, recording, and reporting all guarantees.

IFRS has been revised to provide guidance on the accounting for all financial guarantees—those which are in effect insurance, the accounting for which is therefore to be guided by the provisions of IFRS 4, and those which are not akin to insurance, and which are to be accounted for consistent with IAS 39, which has been amended appropriately. For purposes of applying the new guidance, a financial guarantee contract is defined as a contract that requires the issuer to make specified payments to reimburse the holder for a loss it incurs because a specified debtor fails to make payment when due. These are generally to be accounted for under provisions of amended IAS 39, as follows:

- Financial guarantee contracts are initially recognized at fair value. For those financial guarantee contracts issued in stand-alone arm's-length transactions to unrelated parties, fair value at inception will be equal to the consideration received, unless there is evidence to the contrary.
- In subsequent periods, the guarantee is to be reported at the higher of (1) the amount determined in accordance with IAS 37, or (2) the amount initially recognized less, if appropriate, the cumulative amortization (to income) that was recognized in accordance with IAS 18.

If certain criteria are met, the issuer (guarantor) may elect to use the fair value option set forth in IAS 39. That is, the guarantee may be designated as simply being carried at fair value, with all changes being reported currently in profit or loss. (See Chapter 5 for discussion of the *fair value option*, as most recently revised.)

The original (2004) proposal, would have dealt with a class of arrangement that required the guarantor to make payments in response to adverse changes in the debtor's credit rating, even if no event of default occurred. However, in the amendments to IAS 39 and IFRS 4 that were actually adopted, these were excluded from the definition of financial guarantees. Rather, these credit derivatives (as they are often known) are to be accounted for at fair value under IAS 39. These are derivative financial instruments, not insurance. The accounting for such derivatives is not affected by the amendments.

The amended language of IAS 39 observes that financial guarantee contracts can have various legal forms (e.g., a guarantee, some types of letter of credit, a credit default contract, or an insurance contract), but that the proper accounting treatment does not depend on legal form.

The basic requirement of these amendments is that financial guarantee contracts, as defined, are to be accounted for under IAS 39, not under IFRS 4. However, there is an important exception: if the guarantor/issuer had previously asserted explicitly that it regarded those as insurance contracts, and had accounted for them consistent with such a declaration, then it is permitted to make a onetime election (on a contract-by-contract basis) as to whether the contracts will be accounted for as insurance or as financial instruments. This is an irrevocable election.

Apart from this special optional treatment, all financial guarantees are to be accounted for as set forth above. Free-standing guarantees (e.g., when a party other than the merchandise vendor guarantees the customer's borrowings made to effect the transaction), if arm's length, will typically be priced at fair value. For instance, if a €10,000 loan is drawn down so that the borrower can acquire machinery from a dealer, and a third party agrees to guarantee this debt to the bank for a onetime premium of €250, for a loan term of four years, that amount probably represents the fair value of the loan guarantee, which should be recorded accordingly. If it qualifies under IAS 18 for recognition as revenue on a straight-line basis, it would be amortized to income at the rate of €62.50 per year.

Assume that, subsequently, the machinery purchaser's creditworthiness is impaired by a severe downturn in its industry segment performance, so that, by the end of the second year, the fair value of this guarantee (which has two more years to run) is €200. That could be measured, among other ways, by the onetime premium that would be charged to transfer this risk to another arm's-length guarantor. Since the carrying value of the liability is €125 after two years' amortization has occurred, the *higher* of the amount determined under IAS 37 or the carrying value, €200 must be reported in the statement of financial position as the guarantee obligation. An expense of (€200 – €125 =) €75 must be recognized in the current (second) year as the cost of the additional risk borne by the reporting entity (but note that €62.50 in fee income is also being recognized in that year). The new book value, €200, will be amortized over the remaining two years ratably, assuming that no default occurs.

Note that IAS 37 stipulates that the "best estimate" of the amount to be reported as a provision is the amount that would rationally be offered to eliminate the obligation. In general, this should comport well with the notion of "fair value." Both imply a probability-weighted assessment, which may be made explicitly or implicitly depending upon the circumstances. Both also imply a present value equivalent of future resource outflows, assuming that the timing of such outflows could be estimated.

When the guarantor is not "arm's-length," determining the fair value of the guarantee at inception may be more difficult, since there is no "onetime premium" being paid to secure this arrangement. Typically, the guarantee is a sales inducement (e.g., when the machinery dealer finds it must guarantee the buyer's bank loan in order to consummate the sale), and thus is effectively a discount on the price otherwise obtainable for the merchandise (or services). The full expense would be recognized at the date of the transaction since this expense was incurred in order to generate the sale; thus it is best "matched" against revenue recognized in the current reporting period. The guarantee liability is accounted for as set forth above (adjusted to the higher of fair value or amortized original value, if amortization is proper under IAS 18).

Example of estimating the fair value of a guarantee

Paso Robles Company guarantees a €1,000,000 debt of Sauganash Company for the next three years in conjunction with selling equipment to Sauganash. Paso Robles evaluates its risk of payment as follows:

1. There is no possibility that Paso Robles will pay to honor the guarantee during year 1 (or, equivalently, there is zero risk of default by Sauganash in year 1).
2. There is a 15% chance that Paso Robles will pay during year 2 (i.e., that there will be a partial or complete default by Sauganash that year). If it has to pay, there is a 30% chance that it will have to pay €500,000 and a 70% chance that it will have to pay only €250,000.
3. There is a 20% chance that Paso Robles will pay during year 3. If it has to pay, there is a 25% chance that it will have to pay €600,000 and a 75% chance that it will have to pay €300,000.

The expected cash outflows from the guarantor are computed as follows:

Year 1   100% chance of paying €0 = €0

Year 2   85% chance of paying €0 and a 15% chance of paying (.30 × €500,000 + .70 × €250,000) = (€325,000 × 15%) = €48,750

Year 3   80% chance of paying €0 and a 20% chance of paying (.25 × €600,000 + .75 × €300,000) = (€375,000 × 20%) = €75,000

The present value of the expected cash flows is computed as the sum of the years' probability-weighted cash flows, here assuming an appropriate discount rate of 8%.

Year 1	€ 0	×	$1/1.08$	=	€ 0
Year 2	€48.750	×	$1/(1.08)^2$	=	41,795
Year 3	€75,000	×	$1/(1.08)^3$	=	59,537
	Fair value of the guarantee				€101,332

Based on the foregoing, a liability of €101,332 should be recognized at inception. This would effectively reduce the net selling price of the equipment sold to Sauganash by a like amount, thereby reducing the profit to be reported on the sale transaction. Assume that the equipment cost was €650,000; the entry recording the sale (assume specific identification is used for inventory costing) and the guarantee is as follows:

Cash	1,000,000	
Cost of goods sold	650,000	
Sales expense—guarantee of customer debt	101,332	
Revenue		1,000,000
Guarantee liability		101,332
Inventory		650,000

The profit reported in the current period would be €1,000,000 – €650,000 – €101,332 = €248,668. The guarantee liability would be amortized to income over the term of the three-year loan; if no default occurs, the dealer recovers the full sales expense it incurred by offering the discount.

Contingent Assets

Per IAS 37, a contingent asset is a possible asset that arises from past events and whose existence will be confirmed only by the occurrence or nonoccurrence of one or more uncertain future events that are not wholly within the control of the reporting entity.

Contingent assets usually arise from unplanned or unexpected events that give rise to the possibility of an inflow of economic benefits to the entity. An example of a contingent asset is a claim against an insurance company that the entity is pursuing legally.

Contingent assets should not be recognized; instead, they should be disclosed if the inflow of the economic benefits is probable. As with contingent liabilities, contingent assets need to be continually assessed to ensure that developments are properly reflected in the financial statements. For instance, if it becomes virtually certain that the inflow of economic benefits will arise, the asset and the related income should be recognized in the financial statements of the period in which the change occurs. If, however, the inflow of economic benefits has become probable (instead of virtually certain), then it should be disclosed as a contingent asset.

Example of illustrative footnotes—gain contingency/contingent asset

1.   During the current year, a trial court found that a major multinational company had infringed on certain patents and trademarks owned by the company. The court awarded €100 million in damages for these alleged violations by the defendant. In accordance with the court order, the defendant will also be required to pay interest on the award amount and legal costs as well. Should the defendant appeal to an appellate court, the verdict of the trial court could be reduced or the amount of the damages could be reduced. Therefore, at the end of the reporting period, the company has not recognized the award amount in the accompanying financial statements since it is not virtually certain of the verdict of the appellate court.

2.   In June 2008, the company settled its longtime copyright infringement and trade secrets lawsuit with a competitor. Under the terms of the settlement, the competitor paid the company €2.5 million, which was received in full and final settlement in October 2008, and the parties have dismissed all remaining litigation. For the year ended December 31, 2008, the company recognized the amount received in settlement as "other income," which is included in the accompanying financial statements.

The IASB's project dealing with business combinations (described in Chapter 11) has recently revised the definition of contingent asset to converge with the US GAAP definition. This defines a contingent asset as "a present right that arises from past events that may result in future cash inflow (or other economic benefits) based on the occurrence or nonoccurrence of one or more uncertain future events not wholly within the control of the entity." As discussed under contingent liabilities, in the future it is likely that the category contingent assets would disappear, to be replaced by a measurement which factors in uncertainty.

Disclosures Prescribed by IAS 37 for Contingent Liabilities and Contingent Assets

For the moment, an entity should disclose, for each class of contingent liability at the end of the reporting period, a brief description of the nature of the contingent liability and, where practicable, an estimate of its financial effect measured in the same manner as provisions, an indication of the uncertainties relating to the amount or timing of any outflow, and the possibility of any reimbursement.

In aggregating contingent liabilities to form a class, it is essential to consider whether the nature of the items is sufficiently similar to each other such that they could be presented as a single class.

In the case of contingent assets where an inflow of economic benefits is probable, an entity should disclose a brief description of the nature of the contingent assets at the end of the reporting period and, where practicable, an estimate of their financial effect, measured using the same principles as provisions.

Where any of the above information is not disclosed because it is not practical to do so, that fact should be disclosed. In extremely rare circumstances, if the above disclosures as envisaged by the standard are expected to seriously prejudice the position of the entity in a dispute with third parties on the subject matter of the contingencies, then the standard takes a lenient view and allows the entity to disclose the general nature of the dispute, together with the fact that, and reason why, the information has not been disclosed.

Reporting Events Occurring After the Reporting Period

The issue addressed by IAS 10 is to what extent anything that happens during the post-year-end period when the financial statements are being prepared should be reflected in those financial statements. The standard distinguishes between events that provide information about the state of the entity at the end of the reporting period, and those that concern the next financial period. A secondary issue is the cutoff point beyond which the financial statements are considered to be finalized.

Authorization date. The determination of the authorization date (i.e., the date when the financial statements could be considered legally authorized for issuance, generally by action of the board of directors of the reporting entity) is critical to the concept of events after the reporting period. It serves as the cutoff point after the reporting period, up to which the post–reporting period events are to be examined in order to ascertain whether such events qualify for the treatment prescribed by IAS 10. This standard explains the concept through the use of illustrations.

The general principles that need to be considered in determining the authorization date of the financial statements are set out below.

- When an entity is required to submit its financial statements to its shareholders for approval after they have already been issued, the authorization date in this case would mean the date of original issuance and not the date when these are approved by the shareholders; and
- When an entity is required to issue its financial statements to a supervisory board made up wholly of nonexecutives, authorization date would mean the date on which management authorizes them for issue to the supervisory board.

Consider the following examples:

1. The preparation of the financial statements of Xanadu Corp. for the accounting period ended December 31, 2009, was completed by the management on February 15, 2010. The draft financial statements were considered at the meeting of the board of directors held on February 18, 2010, on which date the Board approved them and authorized them for issuance. The annual general meeting (AGM) was held on March 28, 2010, after allowing for printing and the requisite notice period mandated by the corporate statute. At the AGM the shareholders approved the financial statements. The approved financial statements were filed by the corporation with the Company Law Board (the statutory body of the country that regulates corporations) on April 6, 2010.

   Given these facts, the date of authorization of the financial statements of Xanadu Corp. for the year ended December 31, 2009, is February 18, 2010, the date when the board approved them and authorized them for issue (and not the date they were approved in the AGM by the shareholders). Thus, all post–reporting period events between December 31, 2009, and February 18, 2010, need to be considered by Xanadu Corp. for the purposes of evaluating whether or not they are to be accounted or reported under IAS 10.

2. Suppose in the above cited case the management of Xanadu Corp. was required to issue the financial statements to a supervisory board (consisting solely of nonexecutives including representatives of a trade union). The management of Xanadu Corp. had issued the draft financial statements to the supervisory board on February 16, 2010. The supervisory board approved them on February 17, 2010 and the shareholders approved them in the AGM held on March 28, 2010. The approved financial statements were filed with the Company Law Board on April 6, 2010.

   In this case the date of authorization of financial statements would be February 16, 2010, the date the draft financial statements were issued to the supervisory board. Thus, all post–reporting period events between December 31, 2009, and February 16, 2010, need to be considered by Xanadu Corp. for the purposes of evaluating whether or not they are to be accounted or reported under IAS 10.

Adjusting and nonadjusting events (after the reporting period). Two kinds of events after the reporting period are distinguished by the standard. These are, respectively, "adjusting events after the reporting period" and "nonadjusting events after the reporting period." Adjusting events are those post–reporting period events that provide evidence of conditions that actually existed at the end of the reporting period, albeit they were not known at the time. Financial statements should be adjusted to reflect adjusting events after the reporting period.

Examples of *adjusting events*, given by the standard, are the following:

1. Resolution after the reporting period of a court case that confirms a present obligation requiring either an adjustment to an existing provision or recognition of a provision instead of mere disclosure of a contingent liability;
2. Receipt of information after the reporting period indicating that an asset was impaired or that a previous impairment loss needs to be adjusted. For instance, the bankruptcy of a customer subsequent to the end of the reporting period usually confirms the existence of loss at the end of the reporting period, and the disposal of inventories after the reporting period provides evidence (not always conclusive, however) about their net realizable value at the date of the statement of financial position;
3. The determination after the reporting period of the cost of assets purchased, or the proceeds from assets disposed of, before the date of the statement of financial position;
4. The determination subsequent to the end of the reporting period of the amount of profit sharing or bonus payments, where there was a present legal or constructive obligation at the date of the statement of financial position to make the payments as a result of events before that date; and
5. The discovery of frauds or errors, after the reporting period, that show that the financial statements were incorrect at year-end before the adjustment.

Commonly encountered situations of adjusting events are illustrated below.

*   During the year 2009 Taj Corp. was sued by a competitor for €10 million for infringement of a trademark. Based on the advice of the company's legal counsel, Taj accrued the sum of €5 million as a provision in its financial statements for the year ended December 31, 2009. Subsequent to the date of the statement of financial position, on February 15, 2010, the Supreme Court decided in favor of the party alleging infringement of the trademark and ordered the defendant to pay the aggrieved party a sum of €7 million. The financial statements were prepared by the company's management on January 31, 2010, and approved by the Board on February 20, 2010. Taj Corp. should adjust the provision by €2 million to reflect the award decreed by the Supreme Court (assumed to be the final appellate authority on the matter in this example) to be paid by Taj Corp. to its competitor. Had the judgment of the Supreme Court been delivered on February 25, 2010, or later, this post–reporting period event would have occurred after the cutoff point (i.e., the date the financial statements were authorized for original issuance). If so, adjustment of financial statements would not have been required.
*   Penn Corp. carries its inventory at the lower of cost and net realizable value. At December 31, 2009, the cost of inventory, determined under the first-in, first-out (FIFO) method, as reported in its financial statements for the year then ended, was €5 million. Due to severe recession and other negative economic trends in the market, the inventory could not be sold during the entire month of January 2010. On February 10, 2010, Penn Corp. entered into an agreement to sell the entire inventory to a competitor for €4 million. Presuming the financial statements were authorized for issuance on February 15, 2010, the company should recognize a write-down of €1 million in the financial statements for the year ended December 31, 2009.

In contrast with the foregoing, nonadjusting events are those post–reporting period events that are indicative of conditions that arose after the date of the statement of financial position. Financial statements should not be adjusted to reflect nonadjusting events after the end of the reporting period. An example of a nonadjusting event is a decline in the market value of investments between the date of the statement of financial position and the date when the financial statements are authorized for issue. Since the fall in the market value of investments after the reporting period is not indicative of their market value at the date of the statement of financial position (instead it reflects circumstances that arose subsequent to the end of the reporting period) the fall in market value need not, and should not, be recognized in the financial statements at the date of the statement of financial position.

Not all nonadjusting events are significant enough to require disclosure, however. The revised standard gives examples of nonadjusting events that would impair the ability of the users of financial statements to make proper evaluations or decisions if not disclosed. Where nonadjusting events after the reporting period are of such significance, disclosure should be made for each such significant category of nonadjusting event, of the nature of the event and an estimate of its financial effect or a statement that such an estimate cannot be made. Examples given by the standard of such significant nonadjusting post–reporting period events are the following:

1. A major business combination or disposing of a major subsidiary;
2. Announcing a plan to discontinue an operation;
3. Major purchases and disposals of assets or expropriation of major assets by government;
4. The destruction of a major production plant by fire;
5. Announcing or commencing the implementation of a major restructuring;
6. Abnormally large changes in asset prices or foreign exchange rates;
7. Significant changes in tax rates and enacted tax laws;
8. Entering into significant commitments or contingent liabilities; and
9. Major litigation arising from events occurring after the reporting period.

Dividends proposed or declared after the reporting period. Dividends on equity shares proposed or declared after the reporting period should not be recognized as a liability at the end of the reporting period. Such declaration is a nonadjusting subsequent event, in other words. While at one time IFRS did permit accrual of post–balance sheet dividend declarations, this has not been permissible for quite some time. Furthermore, the revisions made to IAS 10 as part of the IASB's Improvements Project in late 2003 (which became effective 2005) also eliminated the display of post–reporting period dividends as a separate component of equity, as was formerly permitted. Footnote disclosure is, on the other hand, required unless immaterial.

A further clarification has been added by the 2008 *Improvements*, a collection of major and minor changes made in 2008 (largely endorsing proposals made in late 2007). It states that, if dividends are declared (i.e., the dividends are appropriately authorized and no longer at the discretion of the entity) after the reporting period but before the financial statements are authorized for issue, the dividends are not recognized as a liability at the end of the reporting period, for the very simple reason that *no obligation exists at that time*. This rudimentary expansion of the language of IAS 10 was deemed necessary because it had been asserted that a *constructive obligation* could exist under certain circumstances, making formal accrual of a dividend liability warranted. The *Improvements* language makes it clear that this is never the case.

Going concern considerations. Deterioration in an entity's financial position after the end of the reporting period could cast substantial doubts about an entity's ability to continue as a going concern. IAS 10 requires that an entity should not prepare its financial statements on a going concern basis if management determines after the end of the reporting period either that it intends to liquidate the entity or cease trading, or that it has no realistic alternative but to do so. IAS 10 notes that disclosures prescribed by IAS 1 under such circumstances should also be complied with.

Disclosure requirements. The following disclosures are mandated by IAS 10:

1. The date when the financial statements were authorized for issue and who gave that authorization. If the entity's owners have the power to amend the financial statements after issuance, this fact should be disclosed;
2. If information is received after the reporting period about conditions that existed at the date of the statement of financial position, disclosures that relate to those conditions should be updated in the light of the new information; and
3. Where nonadjusting events after the reporting period are of such significance that nondisclosure would affect the ability of the users of financial statements to make proper evaluations and decisions, disclosure should be made for each such significant category of nonadjusting event, of the nature of the event and an estimate of its financial effect or a statement that such an estimate cannot be made.

In *Improvements to International Financial Reporting Standards* issued in October 2007, which was adopted in May, 2008, IASB proposed to amend IAS 10, *Events after the Reporting Period,* to clarify why dividends declared after the reporting period does not result in the recognition of a liability. Dividends declared to holders of equity instruments after the reporting period but before the financial statements are authorized for issue are not recognized as a liability at the end of the reporting period because no obligation exists at that time.

Accounting for Financial Liabilities and IAS 39

IAS 39 established new requirements for accounting for financial liabilities that are held for trading and those that are derivatives. These have to be accounted for at fair value and are addressed in detail in Chapters 5, 10, and 13. However, other financial liabilities continue to be reported at amortized historical cost. The Joint Working Group of standard setters, which in the 1990s discussed a possible successor to IAS 39, suggested the notion of employing fair value to account for all financial assets and liabilities. Some standard setters, both internationally and in the US, are enthusiastic for the extension of the use of fair value, because they believe it provides more comparable and representationally faithful information. However, a move towards the use of full fair value is undoubtedly many years away.

Initial measurement of financial liabilities. IAS 39 stipulates that all financial liabilities are to be initially measured at cost, which (assuming they are each incurred in an arm's-length transaction) is also fair value. Any related transaction costs are included in this initial measurement. In rare instances when the fair value of the consideration received is not reliably determinable, resort is to be made to a computation of the present value of all future cash flows related to the liability. In such a case, the discount rate to apply would be the prevailing rate on similar instruments issued by a party having a similar credit rating.

Remeasurement of financial liabilities. IAS 39 provides that, subsequent to initial recognition, an entity should measure all financial liabilities, other than liabilities held for trading purposes and derivative contracts that are liabilities, at amortized cost. Where the initial recorded amount is not the contractual maturity value of the liability (e.g., as when transaction costs are added to the issuance price, or when there was a premium or discount upon issuance) periodic amortization should be recorded, using the constant effective yield method.

In its 2003 revisions, the IASB introduced what is known as the "fair value option," which allowed entities to designate any liability as being held at fair value, with changes in fair value flowing through profit or loss. However, this widening of the standard, intended to provide flexibility, has been strenuously opposed by banking regulators and by some EU authorities, and in response (to gain support for the EU mandate that all publicly held entities begin reporting consolidated financial statements prepared in accordance with IFRS in 2005) the IASB issued an amendment which constrains its use in respect of liabilities.

Exposure Draft of Proposed Amendments to IAS 37, *Provisions, Contingent Liabilities, and Contingent Assets*

In June 2005, IASB issued an Exposure Draft (ED), *Proposed Amendments to IAS 37, "Provisions, Contingent Liabilities, and Contingent Assets,"* as a result of two current projects: the second phase of the Business Combinations project and the Short-term Convergence project. The proposed amendments are principally concerned with definitions and recognition criteria in IAS 37, but have also required some amendments to the measurement requirements. IASB proposed to eliminate the terms "provisions," "contingent liability," and "contingent asset" from the IFRS literature and replace these with a new term, "nonfinancial liabilities." The proposals provide a consistent approach to dealing with contingencies within and outside a business combination, and also provide a comprehensive approach to the accounting for nonfinancial liabilities which represents a significant change in principle for accounting for obligations. IASB believes that "...the most significant effect of the proposed amendments is to require entities to recognize, as nonfinancial liabilities, items that were not previously recognized (and, in some cases, not considered to be liabilities)."

Provisions. Following IASB's focus on assets and liabilities as the primary elements of the financial statements, the ED proposed that the term "provision" be eliminated and replaced with the term "nonfinancial liability," which includes items previously described as provisions as well as other liabilities. IASB is unwilling to maintain the concept of "provision" as a separate statement of financial position item, since it believes that the current IAS 37 does not provide a clear conceptual rationale for distinguishing a provision from a liability. The IASB also clarifies that, except in specified cases, IAS 37 should be applied to all nonfinancial liabilities that are not within the scope of other Standards. Consequently, a clear distinction was made between liabilities within the scope of IAS 39 and those within the scope of IAS 37. It is also interesting to note that the ED includes a statement that IFRS do not specify how items should be described in financial statements and thus reporting entities may continue to describe some liabilities as provisions in their financial statements.

Contingent liabilities. The Exposure Draft proposes to eliminate the term "contingent liability" and to replace it with the term "nonfinancial liability." The IASB argues that liabilities arise only from unconditional (or noncontingent) obligations, and consequently a liability (i.e., an unconditional obligation) cannot be contingent or conditional.

In general, most agree that a liability should be recognized where there is a present obligation on the part of the entity as a result of past events. When there is no contingency, the point at which this occurs is determinable. In cases where there is a contingency, the ED proposed to divide the obligation into two obligations: an unconditional obligation, which is the "stand ready" obligation, and a conditional obligation. The "stand ready" obligation requires the recognition of a liability and the conditional obligation affects the amount that will be required to settle the liability.

The term "stand ready" obligation is derived from US GAAP and is defined as "liabilities for which the amount that will be required in settlement is contingent on the occurrence or nonoccurrence of a future event." This is because the entity has an unconditional obligation to stand ready to fulfill the conditional obligation if the uncertain future event occurs (or fails to occur).

An example of a stand ready obligation provided by IASB is a product warranty. An entity issuing a product warranty has an unconditional obligation to provide warranty coverage over the term of the warranty and a conditional obligation to repair or replace the product if it develops a fault. The IASB concluded that the only uncertainty relates to whether the product will develop a fault and require repair or replacement. Therefore, the contingency does not determine whether the entity has a liability to provide warranty coverage (as this is an unconditional obligation), but it affects the amount that will be required to settle the obligation. Uncertainties about the future event should be reflected in the measurement but not in the recognition.

Similarly, according to IASB, an entity that is involved in defending a lawsuit should recognize the liability arising from its unconditional obligation to stand ready to perform as the court directs. Uncertainties about the possible penalties the court may impose (i.e., the conditional obligation) are reflected in the measurement of the liability.

The application of this ED may lead to the recognition of liabilities that have a remote possibility of leading to a future outflow of economic benefits. There are certain stand-ready obligations (such as an "obligation to stand-ready to perform as the court directs" of an entity that knows itself to be not guilty of the charge brought against it) that would have to be recognized under the amended guidance.

Contingent assets. As a result of analyzing items previously described as contingent assets into conditional and unconditional rights, the IASB proposed to eliminate the term "contingent assets," since it believes that the term is troublesome and confusing, and that assets arise only from unconditional (i.e., noncontingent) rights. Thus, an asset that embodies an unconditional right could not be identified as contingent or conditional. Consequently, in accordance with the *Framework*, contingent or conditional rights should not be recognized as assets, even if it is "virtually certain" that they will become unconditional or noncontingent. As a result, instead of using the term "contingent" to refer to uncertainty about whether an asset exists, the IASB decided that the term should refer to one or more uncertain future events, the occurrence (or nonoccurrence) of which affects the amount of the future economic benefits from an asset.

The ED proposes to remove the recognition requirement "virtual certainty" for reimbursement rights in IAS 37, and requires such rights to be recognized unless they cannot be measured reliably. The IASB also decided that items previously described as contingent assets under IAS 37 that satisfy the definition of an asset should be in the future within the scope of IAS 38, *Intangible Assets*. This is because such assets would be nonmonetary assets without physical form, and those which are identifiable (i.e., if separable or arise from contractual or other legal rights) meet the definition of an intangible asset.

This analysis of conditional rights and obligations can be illustrated with an example of an entity that is pursuing a lawsuit, where the outcome of this lawsuit is uncertain. In accordance with IAS 37, an entity would recognize an asset if the outcome is virtually certain. Under the proposed ED, the lawsuit would be split into two rights: (1) the entity's conditional right to receive compensation (i.e., conditional on the outcome of the legal process) and (2) the entity's unconditional right to have its claim for recovery of the damages caused by the defendant considered by the court. Consequently, although the compensation that the entity might receive as a result of a successful pursued claim is a conditional right, the pursuit of the lawsuit satisfies the definition of an asset. Therefore, the costs incurred in pursuing the lawsuit are considered an intangible asset and the IAS 38 should be applied in this case.

Constructive obligations. It appears that IASB wants to heighten the threshold for, and consequently delay recognition of, constructive obligations in order to converge more with US GAAP. Under IAS 37, there must be a valid expectation in those affected that the plan will be carried out before a provision for a constructive obligation is recognized. The newly proposed definition states that there must be "a valid expectation in those parties that they can reasonably rely on it to discharge those responsibilities."

IASB has noted that the threshold for determining whether an entity's past actions have created a constructive obligation is higher under US GAAP than under IAS 37. Under FAS

143, which applies the doctrine of "promissory estoppel," a constructive obligation is recognized only if that obligation is a legal obligation and could be enforced by a court. However, IASB decided that it would be premature to make such an amendment in advance of reconsidering liabilities more generally. Consequently, it proposed to introduce into a definition of a constructive obligation the notion that the counterparty should be reasonably able to rely on the entity to discharge its responsibilities.

In the Basis for Conclusion, the IASB pointed out that the "proposed amendment should not alter existing practice for well-understood examples of constructive obligations (for example, some environmental cleanup obligations and warranty obligations) because in such cases there is usually a counterparty that is relying on the entity to discharge its responsibilities. However, items that were previously determined to be constructive obligations, but leave the entity discretion to avoid settling the item, will no longer be recognized as liabilities." The ED does not provide any examples of such items or examples which could assist in developing a consistent understanding as to what type of communication is required before another party can be considered to "reasonably rely" on the entity's actions.

Probability recognition criterion. Under the current IAS 37, a provision is recognized "if it is probable that an outflow of resources embodying economic benefits will be required to settle the obligation." IASB proposed to omit the probability recognition criterion from the Standard after having refined its analysis of items previously described as contingent liabilities. IASB concluded that applying this criterion to "conditional obligation" conflicted with the *Framework*, which requires an entity to determine whether a liability exists before considering whether that liability should be recognized.

The ED explains that if an entity has a nonfinancial liability arising from an unconditional obligation that is accompanied by a conditional obligation, the probability recognition criterion should be applied to the unconditional obligation rather than the conditional obligation. For example, in the case of a product warranty, the criterion should be applied to the unconditional obligation to stand ready to provide warranty coverage and in such case the probability recognition criterion is always satisfied.

Measurement. In accordance with the current IAS 37, a provision should be measured at the best estimate of the expenditure required to settle the present obligation at the date of the statement of financial position. The proposed amendments to IAS 37 replaced this principle with the requirement that "a nonfinancial liability should be measured at the amount that an entity would rationally pay to settle the present obligation or to transfer it to a third party at the end of the reporting period." The ED also proposes that an expected cash flow approach can be used as the basis for measuring a nonfinancial liability for both a class of similar obligations and a single obligation. As a result, the ED moved the method of measurement of provisions (nonfinancial liabilities) from "best estimate" towards a more "fair value" approach.

Some express concerns that this measurement guidance may result in nonfinancial liabilities being recognized at their legal layoff amount (or "relief value"), the amount that has just been rejected as an appropriate measurement basis for obligations incurred within a revenue-generating context in the joint project on revenue recognition. Adopting the legal layoff approach for all nonfinancial liabilities but rejecting if for purposes of revenue recognition may create a measurement inconsistency.

Reimbursement. Under the current IAS 37, when an expenditure required to settle a provision is expected to be reimbursed by another party, the reimbursement should only be recognized when it is virtually certain that the reimbursement will be received. The ED proposes to remove the recognition requirement "virtual certainty" for reimbursement rights in IAS 37 and requires such rights to be recognized unless they cannot be measured reliably.

IASB noted that most reimbursements arise from insurance contracts, indemnity clauses or suppliers' warranties. In such cases an entity has a conditional right (the reimbursement itself) and an unconditional right (e.g., the insurance contract) that satisfies the definition of an asset. As a result, any uncertainty relates to the measurement of economic benefits that will flow from the assets (and not to unconditional right).

Onerous contracts. In conformity with the current IAS 37, an onerous contract is one in which the unavoidable costs of meeting its obligations exceed the economic benefits expected. The entity should recognize as a provision the present obligation under contract but no guidance is provided when the provision should be recognized.

The ED proposes that if a contract would become onerous as a result of an entity's own action, the liability should be recognized only when that action is taken. In the case of an onerous operating lease, the unavoidable costs of the contract should be based on the unavoidable lease commitment less any sublease rentals that the entity could reasonably obtain for the property, regardless whether the entity intends to sublease the property. Hence, IASB has proposed adopting the "cease-use" principle of FAS 146, *Accounting for Costs Associated with Exit or Disposal Activities*, as the recognition principle for onerous operating leases in its efforts to achieve convergence with US GAAP.

Restructuring provisions. Under the current IAS 37, an entity recognizes a restructuring provision when: (1) it has a detailed formal plan for restructuring and (2) it has raised a valid expectation in those affected that it will carry out the restructuring. The ED proposed that a nonfinancial liability for a cost associated with a restructuring should be recognized only when the definition of a liability has been satisfied for that cost. Hence, the ED removed the application guidance in IAS 37, deemphasizing the restructuring plan as the critical recognition issue; this could lead to a major change to the current practice of accounting for restructuring provisions. Following the general guidelines on constructive obligations, instead of recognizing one major restructuring provision at a specific time, in the future entities may need to recognize individual liabilities relating to the different costs occurring in restructuring, which can occur in different accounting periods.

The Exposure Draft discussed in the preceding paragraphs has been debated at numerous IASB meetings since being proposed, but has not yet been finalized as an amended standard. Current IASB plans do not call for this to be completed before 2010.

Examples of Financial Statement Disclosures

Novartis Group
Annual Report 2007

Notes to the consolidated financial statements

19. Provisions and other noncurrent liabilities

	2007 (USD millions)	2006 (USD millions)
Accrued liability for employee benefits:		
– defined benefit pension plans	1,108	1,343
– other long-term employee benefits and deferred compensation	788	993
– other postemployment benefits	386	343
Liabilities for life insurance subsidiary activities	--	638
Environmental provisions	848	239
Provision for product liability and other legal matters	677	634
Other noncurrent liabilities	465	344
Total	4,272	4,534

21. Provisions and other current liabilities

	2007	2006
	(USD millions)	*(USD millions)*
Taxes other than income taxes	508	335
Restructuring provisions	458	86
Accrued expenses for goods and services received but not invoiced	761	737
Provisions for royalties	274	269
Provisions for revenue deductions	1,512	1,428
Potential claims from life insurance activities	--	172
Provisions for compensation and benefits including social security and pension funds	1,011	878
Environmental liabilities	26	14
Deferred income relating to government grants	91	77
Deferred purchase consideration	--	9
Provision for legal matters	349	269
Accrued share-based payments	129	--
Other payables	1,668	1,462
Total provisions and other current liabilities	6,787	5,736

Provisions are based upon management's best estimate and adjusted for actual experience. Such adjustments to the historic estimates have not been material.

29. Commitments and contingencies

Leasing commitments. Commitments arising from fixed-term operational leases in effect at December 31 are as follows:

	2007
	($ millions)
2008	301
2009	232
2010	164
2011	108
2012	93
Thereafter	301
Total	1,199
Expense of current year	350

Research and development commitments. The Group has entered into long-term research agreements with various institutions, including potential milestone payments and other payments by Novartis which may be capitalized. As of December 31, 2007, the Group's commitments to may payments under those agreements were as follows:

	Unconditional commitments 2007	Potential milestone payments 2007	Total 2007
	($ millions)	*($ millions)*	*($ millions)*
2008	19	303	322
2009	13	519	532
2010	13	379	392
2011	9	569	578
2012	5	704	709
Thereafter	3	704	707
Total	62	3,178	3,240

Other commitments. The Novartis Group entered into various purchase commitments for services and materials as well as for equipment in the ordinary course of business. These commitments are not in excess of current market prices in all material respects and reflect on normal business operations.

Contingencies. Group companies have to observe the laws, government orders, and regulations of the country in which they operate.

The Group's potential environmental liability is assessed based on a risk assessment and investigation of the various sites identified by the Group as at risk for environmental exposure. The Group's future remediation expenses are affected by a number of uncertainties. These uncertainties include, but are not limited to, the method and extent of remediation, the percentage of material attributable to the Group at the remediation sites relative to that attributable to other parties, and the financial capabilities of the other potentially responsible parties.

A number of Group companies are currently involved in administrative proceedings, litigations and investigations arising out of the normal conduct of their business. These litigations include certain legal and product liability claims. Whilst provisions have been made for probable losses that Management deems to be reasonable or appropriate, there are uncertainties connected with these estimates. Note 19 contains a more extensive discussion of these matters.

In the opinion of management, however the outcome of these actions will not materially affect the Group's financial position, but could be material to the results of operations or cash flow in a given period.

Clariant International Ltd.
Consolidated Financial Statements
Annual Report 2007

19. Movements in provisions for current liabilities

CHF mn	Environmental provisions	Restructuring provisions	Current personnel provisions	Other current provisions	Total provisions current liabilities 2007	Total provisions for current liabilities 2006
At January 1	19	54	152	126	351	431
Additions and reclassifications	27	114	152	103	396	305
Effects of disposals	--	--	--	--	--	(5)
Reclassified from/to held for sale	--	--	--	5	5	(19)
Amounts used	(16)	(30)	(166)	(74)	286	(319)
Unused amounts reversed	(3)	(4)	(11)	(21)	(39)	(43)
Exchange rate differences	--	(3)	2	2	1	1
At December 31	27	131	129	141	428	351

Environmental provisions. Environmental provisions for environmental liabilities are made when there is a legal or constructive obligation for the Group, which will result in an outflow of economic resources. It is difficult to estimate the action required by Clariant in the future to correct the effects on the environment of prior disposal or release of chemical substances by Clariant or other parties, and the associated costs, pursuant to environmental laws and regulations. The material components of the environmental provisions consist of the cost to fully clean and refurbish contaminated sites and to treat and contain contamination at sites where the environmental exposure is less severe. The Group's future remediation expenses are affected by a number of uncertainties which include, but are not limited to, the method and extent of remediation and the percentage of material attributable to Clariant at the remediation sites relative to that attributable to other parties.

The environmental provisions reported in the balance sheet concern a number of different obligations, mainly in Switzerland, the United States, Germany, the United Kingdom, Brazil and Italy.

Provisions are made for remedial work where there is an obligation to remedy environmental damage, as well as for containment work where required by environmental regulations. All provisions relate to environmental liabilities arising in connection with activities that occurred prior to the date when Clariant took control of the relevant site.

Restructuring provisions. Restructuring provisions are established where there is a legal or constructive obligation for the Group that will result in the outflow of economic resources and which is expected to occur with the next twelve months. The term restructuring refers to activities that have as a consequence, staff redundancies and the shutdown of production lines or entire sites. However, expenses for termination benefits which are borne by the pension and termination plans are included in pension plan liabilities.

Personnel provisions. Personnel provisions include holiday entitlements, compensated long-term absences such as annual leave, profit sharing and bonuses payable within twelve months. Such provisions are provided for in proportion to the services rendered by the employee concerned.

Other provisions. Other current provisions are recorded for liabilities (comprising tax, legal and other items in various countries) falling due within twelve months, for which no invoice has been received at the reporting date and/or for which the amount can only be reliably estimated.

33. Commitments and contingencies

Leasing commitments. The Group leases land, buildings, machinery and equipment, furniture, and vehicles under fixed-term agreements. The leases have varying terms, escalation clauses, and renewal rights.

Commitments arising from fixed-term operating leases mainly concern buildings in Switzerland and Germany. The most important partners for operating leases of buildings in Germany are the Infraserv companies.

CHF mn	2007	2005
2007	--	70
2008	66	54
2009	48	39
2010	24	21
2011	16	13
2012	13	--
Thereafter	37	20
Total	204	217
Guarantees in favor of third parties	63	53

Expenses for operating leases were CHF 86 million in 2007 and CHF 85 million in 2006.

Purchase commitments. In the regular course of business, Clariant enters into relationships with suppliers whereby the Group commits itself to purchase certain minimum quantities of materials in order to benefit from better pricing conditions. These commitments are not in excess of current market prices and reflect normal business operations. At present, the purchase commitments on such contracts amount to about CHF 106 million (2006: CHF 176 million).

Contingencies. Clariant operates in countries where political, economic, social, legal and regulatory developments can have an impact on the operational activities. The effects of such risks on the Company's results, which arise during the normal course of business, are not foreseeable and are therefore not included in the accompanying financial statements.

In 2006 Clariant sold its Pharmaceutical Fine Chemicals business to Archimica, a company pertaining to Towerbrook Capital Partners. On October 25, 2007, Archimica Group Holdings B.V. filed a request for arbitration against Clariant before the Zurich Chamber of Commerce, raising various claims under the purchase agreement in an amount of EUR 42 million. Clariant fully contests such claims. Based on the situation no liability has been booked for these claims.

In the ordinary course of business, Clariant is involved in lawsuits, claims, investigations and proceedings, including product liability, intellectual property, commercial, environmental and health and safety matters. Although the outcome of any legal proceedings cannot be predicted with certainty, management is of the opinion that there are no such matters pending which would be likely to have any material adverse effect in relation to its business, financial position, or results of operations.

Environmental risk. Clariant is exposed to environmental liabilities and risks relating to its past operations, principally in respect of remediation costs. Provisions for nonrecurring remediation costs are made when there is a legal or constructive obligation and the cost can be reliably estimated. It is difficult to estimate the action required by Clariant in the future to correct the effects on the environment of prior disposal or release of chemical substances by Clariant or other parties, and the associated costs, pursuant to environmental laws and regulations. The material components of the environmental provisions consist of costs to fully clean and refurbish contaminated sites and to treat and contain contamination at sites where the environmental exposure is less severe.

The Group's future remediation expenses are affected by a number of uncertainties which include, but are not limited to, the method and extent of remediation and the percentage of material attributable to Clariant at the remediation sites relative to that attributable to other parties. The Group permanently monitors the various sites identified at risk for environmental exposure. Clariant believes that its provisions are adequate based upon currently available information; however, given the inherent difficulties in estimating liabilities in this area, there is no guarantee that additional costs will not be incurred.

Nestlé Group
Annual Report 2007

17. Provisions

CHF mn	Restructuring	Environmental	Litigation	Other	2006 Total
At January 1	950	41	2,070	286	3,347
Currency retranslations	6	(2)	(59)	(6)	(61)
Provisions made in the period	437	2	327	73	839
Amounts used	(326)	(3)	(591)	(87)	(1,007)
Unused amounts reversed	(34)	--	(100)	(80)	(214)
Modification of the scope of consolidation	1	--	103	31	135
At December 31	1,034	38	1,750	217	3,039

CHF mn	Restructuring	Environmental	Litigation	Other	2007 Total
At January 1	1,034	38	1,750	217	3,039
Currency retranslations	2	(2)	(44)	--	(44)
Provisions made in the period	392	7	510	121	1,030
Amounts used	(393)	(4)	(77)	(64)	(538)
Unused amounts reversed	(28)	--	(271)	(47)	(346)
Modification in the scope of consolidation	--	--	31	44	175
At December 31	1,007	39	1,999	271	3,316

Restructuring. Restructuring provisions arise from a number of projects across the Group. These include plans to optimize production, sales, and administration structures, mainly in Europe. Restructuring provisions are expected to result in future cash outflows when implementing the plans (usually over the following two to three years) and are consequently not discounted.

Litigation. Litigation provisions have been set up to cover legal and administrative proceedings that arise in the ordinary course of business. These provisions concern numerous cases that are not of public knowledge and whose detailed disclosure could seriously prejudice the interests of the Group. Reversal of such provisions refers to cases resolved in favor of the Group. The timing of cash outflows of litigation provisions is uncertain as it depends upon the outcome of the proceedings. These provisions are therefore not discounted because their present value would not represent meaningful information. Group Management does not believe it is possible to make assumptions on the evolution of the cases beyond the balance sheet date.

Other. Other provisions are mainly constituted by onerous contracts, liabilities for partial refund of selling prices of divested businesses, and various damage claims having occurred during the period but not covered by insurance companies. Onerous contracts result from unfavorable leases or supply agreements above market prices in which the unavoidable costs of meeting the obligations under the contract exceed the economic benefits expected to be received or for which no benefits are received. These agreements have been entered into as a result of selling and closing inefficient facilities and have an average duration of 2.5 years.

31. Contingent assets and liabilities

The group is exposed to contingent liabilities amount to CHF 1,016 million (2006: CHF 957 million) representing various potential litigations (CHF 956 million) and other items (CHF 60 million).

Contingent assets for litigation claims in favor of the Group amount to CHF 252 million (2006: CHF 267 million).

Lectra Group
Annual Report 2007

Notes to the consolidated financial statements

Provisions for other liabilities and charges. All known risks at balance sheet date are reviewed in detail and a provision is recognized if an obligation exists, if the costs entailed to settle this obligation are probable or certain, and if they can be measured reliably.

In view of the short-term nature of the risks covered by these provisions, the discounting impact is immaterial and therefore not recognized.

At the time of the effective payment, the provision is deducted from the corresponding expenses.

Provisions for warranties. A provision for warranties covers, on the basis of historical data, probable costs arising from warranties granted by the Group to its customers at the time of the sale of CAD/CAM equipment, for replacement of parts, travel of technicians, and labor. This provision is recorded at the time the sale is booked by the company.

13 FINANCIAL INSTRUMENTS— NONCURRENT LIABILITIES

PERSPECTIVE AND ISSUES

Noncurrent liabilities represent future sacrifices of economic benefits to be repaid over a period of more than twelve months after the reporting period or, if longer, over more than one operating cycle. Noncurrent liabilities include such familiar obligations as bonds and notes payable, lease obligations, pension and deferred compensation plan obligations, and deferred income tax liabilities. The accounting for debt instruments, such as bonds and long-term notes is covered in this chapter. Since at present, IFRS explicitly address only a few of these topics, the accounting recommendations herein are those of the authors, based on long-endorsed practices under GAAP of many nations. Most of these are commonsense suggestions, not likely to prove controversial.

The proper valuation basis for noncurrent liabilities is the present value of future payments using the market rate of interest, either that stated or implied in the transaction, at the date the debt was incurred. An exception to the use of the market rate of interest stated or implied in the transaction in valuing long-term notes occurs when it is necessary to use an imputed interest rate, if the debt is either noninterest-bearing or bears a clearly nonmarket rate of interest.

Changes were made in 2003 to IAS 32 and IAS 39 which pertain to a number of matters addressed in this chapter, including the classification of instruments with contingent settlement provisions, and the method to be employed in allocating proceeds from the issuance of compound financial instruments. The "fair value option" grants entities the right to designate any financial asset or financial liability, at acquisition or issuance, respectively, to be accounted for at fair value, with changes in fair value being included in profit or loss. The objective in adopting this provision was to provide the entities making this election the opportunity to eliminate the otherwise tedious computations associated with hedge accounting (such as determining hedge effectiveness each period). However, this option proved to be controversial and became an issue in the process of gaining EU endorsement of IFRS, necessary to facilitate the 2005 mandate for all publicly held companies to report consolidated financial statements on the basis of IFRS.

Sources of IFRS	
IAS 32, 39	*IFRIC* 1

DEFINITIONS OF TERMS

Amortization. The process of allocating an amount (e.g., bond issue costs) to expense over the periods benefited.

Bond. A written agreement whereby a borrower agrees to pay a sum of money at a designated future date plus periodic interest payments at the stated rate.

Bond issue costs. Costs related to issuing a bond (i.e., legal, accounting, underwriting fees, and printing and registration costs).

Bonds outstanding method. The method of accounting for serial bonds that assumes the discount or premium applicable to each bond of the issue is the same dollar amount per bond per year.

Book value approach. The method of recording the share issued from a bond conversion at the carrying value of the bonds converted.

Callable bond. A bond in that the issuer reserves the right to call and retire the bond prior to its maturity.

Carrying value. The face amount of a debt issue increased or decreased by the applicable unamortized premium or discount plus unamortized issue costs.

Collateral. Asset(s) pledged to settle the obligation to repay a loan, if not repaid.

Contingent settlement provisions. A requirement in a financial instrument that could result in the payment of cash, depending upon the occurrence or nonoccurrence of an event, or on the outcome of uncertain circumstances that are beyond the control of the obligor.

Convertible debt. Debt that may be converted into ordinary share at the holder's option after specific criteria are met.

Covenant. A clause in a debt instrument (or preferred share) contract written for the protection of the lender (or investor in preferred share) that outlines the rights and actions of the parties involved when certain conditions occur (e.g., when the debtor's current ratio declines below a specified level).

Current liabilities. A liability that (a) is expected to be settled in the normal operating cycle (b) is held primarily for the purpose of trading (c) is due to be settled within twelve months after the reporting period or (d) the entity does not have an unconditional right to defer its settlement for at least twelve months after the reporting period. All other liabilities an entity should classify as noncurrent.

Debenture. Long-term debt instrument not secured by collateral.

Defeasance. Extinguishment of debt by creating a trust to service it.

Discount. Created when a debt instrument sells for less than face value and occurs because the stated rate on the instrument is less than the market rate at the date of issue.

Effective interest method. A method of calculating the amortized cost of a financial asset or a financial liability (or group of financial instruments) and of allocating the interest income or interest expense over the relevant period. The effective interest rate used in the allocation process is the rate that exactly discounts estimated future cash flows (receipts or payments) to the net carrying amount of the financial instrument through the expected life of this instrument (or, a shorter period, when appropriate).

Effective rate. See market rate.

Face value. The stated or principal amount due on the maturity date.

Imputation. The process of interest rate approximation that is accomplished by examining the circumstances under which the note was issued.

Market rate. The current rate of interest available for obligations issued under the same terms and conditions.

Market value approach. The method of recording the shares issued from a bond conversion at the current market price of the bonds converted or the shares issued.

Maturity date. The date on which the face value (principal) of the bond or note becomes due.

Maturity value. See face value.

Noncurrent liabilities. Probable future sacrifices of economic benefits arising from present obligations that are not currently payable within twelve months after the reporting period or one operating cycle of the business, whichever is longer. All liabilities other than current liabilities are noncurrent.

Premium. Created when a debt instrument sells for more than its face value and occurs because the stated rate on the instrument is greater than the market rate at the time of issue.

Principal. See face value.

Secured debt. Debt instrument that has collateral to satisfy the obligation (i.e., a mortgage on specific property), if not otherwise repaid.

Serial bond. Debt instrument whose face value matures in installments.

Stated rate. The interest rate written on the face of the debt instrument.

Straight-line method. The method of amortizing the premium or discount to interest expense such that there is an even allocation of interest expense over the life of the debt, instrument causing the effective rate to vary from one period to the next.

Take-or-pay contract. A contract in which a purchaser of goods agrees to pay specified fixed or minimum amounts periodically in return for products, even if delivery is not taken. It results from a project financing arrangement where the project produces the products.

Throughput agreement. An agreement similar to a take-or-pay contract except that a service is provided by the project under the financing arrangement.

Troubled debt restructuring. Occurs when the creditor, for economic or legal reasons related to the debtor's financial difficulties, grants a concession to the debtor (deferment or reduction of interest or principal) that it would not otherwise consider.

Unconditional purchase obligation. An obligation to transfer a fixed or minimum amount of funds in the future or to transfer goods or services at fixed or minimum prices.

Yield. See market rate.

CONCEPTS, RULES, AND EXAMPLES

Recognition and Measurement of Financial Liabilities

In accordance with IAS 39, financial liabilities are initially measured at fair value, including transactions costs directly attributable to the issue of the financial liability (e.g., fees, commissions, taxes, etc.), as of the date when the entity becomes a party to the contractual provisions of the debt. Transaction costs are *not* included in initial measurement of financial liabilities classified as at fair value through profit or loss (FVTPL).

After initial recognition, financial liabilities are subsequently measured at amortized cost, using the effective interest method. Exceptions to the general rule of measuring financial liabilities at amortized cost include

- Financial liabilities classified as at fair value through profit or loss, including derivatives that are liabilities, are accounted for at fair value, with changes in fair value recognized in profit or loss in the current period (except for a derivative liability, measured at cost, that is linked and must be settled by delivery of unquoted equity instrument whose fair value cannot be reliably determined).

- Financial liabilities recognized when a transfer of a financial asset does not qualify for derecognition or when the continuing involvement approach applies (See Derecognition covered in Chapters 5 and 10).
- Financial guarantee contracts measured at the higher of (1) the amount determined in accordance with IAS 37 and (2) the amount initially recognized less cumulative amortization (IAS 18).
- Commitments to provide a loan at a below-market interest rate measured at the higher of (1) the amount determined in accordance with IAS 37 and (2) the amount initially recognized less cumulative amortization (IAS 18)

In addition, financial liabilities designated as hedge items are accounted for in accordance with the hedge accounting requirements.

Notes and Bonds

Noncurrent liabilities generally take one of two forms: notes or bonds. *Notes* generally represent debt issued to a single investor without intending for the debt to be broken up among many investors. Their maturity, usually lasting one to seven years, tends to be shorter than that of a bond. *Bonds* also result from a single agreement. However, a bond is intended to be broken up into various subunits, for example, €1,000 (or equivalent) each, which can be issued to a variety of investors.

Notes and bonds share common characteristics: a written agreement stating the amount of the principal, the interest rate, when the interest and principal are to be paid, and the restrictive covenants, if any, that must be met. The interest rate is affected by many factors including the cost of money, the business risk factors, and the inflationary expectations associated with the business.

Nominal vs. effective rates. The stated rate on a note or bond often differs from the market rate at the time of issuance. When this occurs, the present value of the interest and principal payments will differ from the maturity, or face value. If the market rate exceeds the stated rate, the cash proceeds will be less than the face value of the debt because the present value of the total interest and principal payments discounted back to the present yields an amount that is less than the face value. Because an investor is rarely willing to pay more than the present value, the bonds must be issued at a discount. The discount is the difference between the issuance price (present value) and the face, or stated, value of the bonds. This discount is then amortized over the life of the bonds to increase the recognized interest expense so that the total amount of the expense represents the actual bond yield.

When the stated rate exceeds the market rate, the bond will sell for more than its face value (at a premium) to bring the effective rate to the market rate and will decrease the total interest expense. When the market and stated rates are equivalent at the time of issuance, no discount or premium exists and the instrument will sell at its face value. Changes in the market rate subsequent to issuance are irrelevant in determining the discount or premium or the amount of periodic amortization.

Notes are a common form of exchange in business transactions for cash, property, goods, and services. Most notes carry a stated rate of interest, but it is not uncommon for noninterest-bearing notes or notes bearing an unrealistic rate of interest to be exchanged. Notes such as these, which are long-term in nature, do not reflect the economic substance of the transaction since the face value of the note does not represent the present value of the consideration involved. Not recording the note at its present value will misstate the cost of the asset or services to the buyer, as well as the selling price and profit to the seller. In subsequent periods, both the interest expense and revenue will be misstated.

In general, the transaction price (cash, or the fair value of any noncash consideration) will define the fair value of a financial instrument, including liabilities, at initial recognition. For most liabilities, this will be equivalent to the present value of all associated contractual cash flows, discounted at the relevant interest rate. However, when part of the consideration is other than the instrument, fair value may be estimated using a valuation technique (e.g., option pricing models). When a long-term loan is received which bears no interest or a nonmarket rate of interest, the present value must be computed with reference to contractual cash flows and current market rates. Any extra amount given is reflected in current earnings unless some other asset has been obtained.

Accordingly, it is suggested that all commitments to pay (and receive) money at a determinable future date be subjected to present value calculations and, if necessary, interest imputation, with the exceptions of the following:

1. Normal accounts payable due within one year
2. Amounts to be applied to purchase price of goods or services or that provide security to an agreement (e.g., advances, progress payments, security deposits, and retainages)
3. Obligations payable at some indeterminable future date (warranties)
4. Lending and depositor savings activities of financial institutions whose primary business is lending money
5. Transactions where interest rates are affected by prescriptions of a governmental agency (e.g., revenue bonds, tax exempt obligations, etc.)

Notes issued solely for cash. When a note is issued solely for cash, its present value is assumed to be equal to the cash proceeds. The interest rate is that rate which equates the cash proceeds to the amounts to be paid in the future (i.e., *no* interest rate is to be imputed). For example, a €1,000 note due in three years that sells for €889 has an implicit rate of 4% (€1,000 × .889, where .889 is the present value factor of a lump sum at 4% for three years). This rate is to be used when amortizing the discount.

Notes issued for cash and a right or privilege. Often when a note bearing an unrealistic rate of interest is issued in exchange for cash, an additional right or privilege is granted, such as the issuer agreeing to sell merchandise to the purchaser at a reduced rate. The difference between the present value of the receivable and the cash loaned should logically be regarded as an addition to the cost of the products purchased for the purchaser/lender and as unearned revenue to the issuer. This treatment stems from the desire to match revenue and expense in the proper periods and to differentiate between those factors that affect profit or loss from continuing operations and profit or loss from nonoperating sources. In the situation above, the discount (difference between the cash loaned and the present value of the note) will be amortized to interest revenue or expense, while the unearned revenue or contractual right is amortized to sales and inventory, respectively. The discount affects profit or loss from nonoperational sources, while the unearned revenue or contractual right affects the gross profit computation. This differentiation is necessary because the amortization rates used differ for the two amounts.

Example of accounting for a note issued for both cash and a contractual right

1. Miller borrows €10,000 via a noninterest-bearing 3-year note from Krueger.
2. Miller agrees to sell €50,000 of merchandise to Krueger at less than the ordinary retail price for the duration of the note.
3. The fair rate of interest on a note such as this is 10%.

As set forth in the discussion above, the difference between the present value of the note and the face value of the loan is to be regarded as part of the cost of the products purchased under the agreement. The present value factor for an amount due in 3 years at 10% is .75132. Therefore, the present value of the note is €7,513 (= €10,000 × .75132). The €2,487 (= €10,000 − €7,513) difference between the face value and the present value is to be recorded as a discount on the note payable and as unearned revenue on the future purchases. The following entries would be made to record the transaction:

Miller				*Krueger*		
Cash	10,000			Note receivable	10,000	
Discount on note payable	2,487			Contract right with supplier	2,487	
Note payable		10,000		Cash		10,000
Unearned revenue		2,487		Discount on note receivable		2,487

The discount on note payable (and note receivable) should be amortized using the effective interest (constant yield) method, while the unearned revenue account and contract right with supplier account are amortized on a pro rata basis as the right to purchase merchandise is used up. Thus, if Krueger purchased €20,000 of merchandise from Miller in the first year, the following entries would be necessary:

Miller				*Krueger*		
Unearned revenue	995[*]			Inventory (or cost of sales)	995	
Sales		995		Contract right with supplier		995
Interest expense	751			Discount on note receivable	751	
Discount on note payable		751[**]		Interest revenue		751

[*] €2,487 × (20,000/50,000)
[**] €7,513 × 10%

The amortization of unearned revenue and contract right with supplier accounts will fluctuate with the amount of purchases made. If there is a balance remaining in the account at the end of the loan term, it is amortized to the appropriate account in that final year.

Noncash transactions. When a note is issued for consideration such as property, goods, or services, and the transaction is entered into at arm's length, the stated interest rate is presumed to be fair unless (1) no interest rate is stated, (2) the stated rate is unreasonable, or (3) the face value of the debt is materially different from the consideration involved or the current market value of the note at the date of the transaction. As discussed above, it is recommended that when the rate on the note is not considered fair, the note is to be recorded at the fair market value of the property, goods, or services received or at an amount that reasonably approximates the market value of the note, whichever is the more clearly determinable. When this amount differs from the face value of the note, the difference is to be recorded as a discount or premium and amortized to interest expense.

Example of accounting for a note exchanged for property

1.   Alpha sells Beta a machine that has a fair market value of €7,510.
2.   Alpha receives a 3-year noninterest-bearing note having a face value of €10,000.

In this situation, the fair market value of the consideration is readily determinable and thus represents the amount at which the note is to be recorded. The following entry is necessary:

Machine	7,510	
Discount on notes payable	2,490	
Notes payable		10,000

The discount will be amortized to interest expense over the 3-year period using the interest rate implied in the transaction.

If the fair market value of the consideration or note is not determinable, the present value of the note must be determined using an *imputed* interest rate. This rate will then be used to establish the present value of the note by discounting all future payments on the note at this rate. General guidelines for imputing the interest rate include the prevailing rates of similar instruments from creditors with similar credit ratings and the rate the debtor could obtain for similar financing from other sources. Other determining factors include any collateral or restrictive covenants involved, the current and expected prime rate, and other terms pertaining to the instrument. The objective is to approximate the rate of interest that would have resulted if an independent borrower and lender had negotiated a similar transaction under comparable terms and conditions. This determination is as of the issuance date, and any subsequent changes in interest rates would be irrelevant.

Bonds represent a promise to pay a sum of money at a designated maturity date plus periodic interest payments at a stated rate. Bonds are used primarily to borrow funds from the general public or institutional investors when a contract for a single amount (a note) is too large for one lender to supply. Dividing up the amount needed into €1,000 or €10,000 units makes it easier to sell the bonds.

In most situations, a bond is issued at a price other than its face value. The amount of the cash exchanged is equal to the total of the present value of the interest and principal payments. The difference between the cash proceeds and the face value is recorded as a premium if the cash proceeds are greater or a discount if they are less. The journal entry to record a bond issued at a premium follows:

Cash	(proceeds)	
Premium on bonds payable		(difference)
Bonds payable		(face value)

The premium will be recognized over the life of the bond issue. If issued at a discount, "Discount on bonds payable" would be debited for the difference. As the premium is amortized, it will reduce interest expense on the books of the issuer (a discount will increase interest expense). The premium (discount) would be added to (deducted from) the related liability when a statement of financial position is prepared.

The *effective interest method* is the prescribed method of accounting for a discount or premium arising from a note or bond, although some other method may be used (e.g., straight-line) if the results are not materially different. Under the effective interest method, the discount or premium is to be amortized over the life of the debt so as to produce a constant rate of interest when applied to the amount outstanding at the beginning of any given period. Therefore, interest expense is equal to the market rate of interest at the time of issuance multiplied by this beginning figure. The difference between the interest expense and the cash paid represents the amortization of the discount or premium. The effective rate is a required disclosure under IAS 32.

As with other aspects of financial reporting requirements, if alternative methods do not result in material disparities versus the prescribed approaches to measurement, they may also be used. Thus, where use of the straight-line amortization method does not result in a material distortion as compared to the effective interest method, it would also be acceptable, although not endorsed under IFRS. Interest expense under the *straight-line method* is equal to the cash interest paid plus the amortized portion of the discount or minus the amortized portion of the premium. The amortized portion is equal to the total amount of the discount or premium divided by the life of the debt from issuance in months multiplied by the number of months the debt has been outstanding that year.

Example of applying the effective interest method

1. A three-year, 12%, €10,000 bond is issued at 1/1/09 with interest payments due semiannually.
2. The market rate is 10%.

The amortization table would appear as follows:

Date	Credit cash	Debit int. exp.	Debit premium	Unamoritized prem. bal.	Carrying Value
1/1/09				€507.61	€10,507.61(a)
7/1/09	€ 600.00(b)	€ 525.38(c)	€ 74.62(d)	432.99(e)	10,432.99(f)
1/1/10	600.00	521.65	78.35	354.64	10,354.64
7/1/10	600.00	517.73	82.27	272.37	10,272.37
1/1/11	600.00	513.62	86.38	185.99	10,185.99
7/1/11	600.00	509.30	90.70	95.29	10,095.29
1/1/12	600.00	504.71(g)	95.29	--	€10,000.00
	€3,600.00	€3,092.39	€507.61		

(a)*PV of principal and interest payments*

$€10,000(.74622)$ = €7,462.20

$€   600(5.07569)$ = $\underline{3,045.41}$

$\underline{€10,507.61}$

(b) $€10,000.00 \times .06$

(c) $€10,507.61 \times .05$

(d $€600.00 - €525.38$

(e) $€507.61 - €74.62$

(f) $€10,507.61 - €74.62$

(or $€10,000 + €432.99$)

(g) *Rounding error = €.05*

When the interest date does not coincide with the year-end, an adjusting entry must be made. The proportional share of interest payable should be recognized along with the amortization of the discount or premium. Within the amortization period, the discount or premium can be amortized using the straight-line method, as a practical matter, or can be computed more precisely as described above.

If the bonds are issued between interest dates, discount or premium amortization must be computed for the period between the sale date and the next interest date. This is accomplished by "straight-lining" the period's amount calculated using the usual method of amortization. In addition, the purchaser prepays the seller the amount of interest that has accrued since the last interest date. This interest is recorded as a payable by the seller. At the next interest date, the buyer then receives the full amount of interest regardless of how long the bond has been held. This procedure results in interest being paid equivalent to the time the bond has been outstanding.

Various costs may be incurred in connection with issuing bonds. Examples include legal, accounting, and underwriting fees; commissions; and engraving, printing, and registration costs. These costs should be deducted from the initial carrying amount of the bonds and amortized using the effective interest method; generally the amount involved is insignificant enough that use of the simpler straight-line method would not result in a material difference. These costs do not provide any future economic benefit and therefore should not be considered an asset. Since these costs reduce the amount of cash proceeds, they in effect increase the effective interest rate and probably should be accounted for the same as an unamortized discount. Current liabilities that are expected to be refinanced on a long-term basis, and that accordingly are classified as noncurrent liabilities according to IAS 1, are discussed in Chapter 12.

The diagram below illustrates the recommended accounting treatments for monetary assets (and liabilities).

ACCOUNTING FOR MONETARY ASSETS AND LIABILITIES

Monetary assets and liabilities recorded at PV of future cash flows

- Notes received or issued solely for cash
- Notes received or issued for cash plus some right or privilege
- Notes received or issued in a noncash exchange for property, goods, or services

Cash exchanged = Present value of note

- Face amount = Cash exchanged
  - No discount or premium recorded; Face rate = Yield rate
- Face amount > Cash exchanged
  - Discount recorded; Face rate < Yield rate
- Face amount < Cash exchanged
  - Premium recorded; Face rate> Yield rate

Difference between PV of the note and the cash exchanged is the amount assigned to the right or privilege

Discount or premium corresponds to the amount assigned to the right or privilege

Interest rate not assumed fair

- No interest is stated
- Stated interest rate is unreasonable
- Stated face amount of the note is materially different from the current cash sales price for the same or similar items or from the FMV of the note at the date of the transaction

Interest rate assumed fair

- Record note at face amount, which is assumed to be the FMV of the property, goods, or services

Recognize interest at other than stated rate

- FMV of property, goods, or services exchanged is known or the FMV of the note is known
  - Use FMV of goods, property, or services. If there is no reliable FMV of the goods, property, or services, use FMV of note
  - Rate of interest equates future payments of the note with the FMV of the goods, property, or services or the FMV of the note
- FMV of property, goods, or services exchanged is not known and the FMV of note not known
  - Use imputed interest rate to calculate PV of the note and determine interest expense/income

Derecognition of Financial Liabilities

According to IAS 39, removing a financial liability (or part of a financial liability) from the reporting entity's statement of financial position is warranted only when the obligation is *extinguished*. This will be deemed to have occurred when the obligation specified in the contract is discharged or canceled or expires.

In some instances, the debt issuer exchanges newly issued debt carrying different terms (as to maturities, interest rates, etc.) for outstanding debt. Under IAS 39, under such circumstances the original debt will be deemed extinguished, and a new liability will be deemed to have been incurred. Likewise, substantial modifications to the terms of existing financial liabilities, or to a part of that debt, whether this is attributable to financial exigencies or not, are now to be accounted for as extinguishments.

If there is a difference between the carrying amount (i.e., book value) of a financial liability extinguished or transferred (or relevant portion thereof) and the consideration paid to accomplish this, including the fair value of noncash assets transferred or liabilities assumed, this gain or loss will be recognized in profit or loss.

When only a part of an existing liability is repurchased, the carrying value is allocated pro rata between the part extinguished and the part that remains outstanding. This allocation is to be based upon relative fair values. Gain on loss is recognized as the difference between the carrying value allocated to the portion extinguished and the consideration paid to accomplish this extinguishment, using the same approach as described above.

Substantial modification of the terms of existing debt instruments. When an existing borrower and lender of debt exchange instruments with substantially different terms, this represents an extinguishment of the old debt and results in derecognition of that debt and recognition of a new debt instrument. IAS 39 defines "substantial modification of the terms" of an existing debt instrument and the standard requires that those modifications should be accounted for as extinguishments, provided that the discounted present value of cash flows under the terms of the new debt differs by at least 10% from the discounted present value of the remaining cash flows of the original debt instrument.

In computing the discounted present values for determining whether the 10% limit has been exceeded, the effective interest rate of the (old) debt being modified or exchanged is to be used. If the difference in present values is at least 10% the transaction is to be accounted for as an extinguishment of the old debt. In such case, the new, modified debt is initially recognized at fair value. On the other hand, a difference of less than 10%, is to be amortized over the remaining term of the debt instrument. In this instance, the debt is not to be remeasured at fair value and any costs or fees incurred adjust the carrying value of the debt and will be amortized by the effective interest method.

If an exchange of debt instruments, or if a modification of terms is accounted for under IAS 39 as an extinguishment, costs or fees incurred are to be recognized as part of the gain or loss incurred in the extinguishment. In nonextinguishment instances, any costs or fees incurred in the transaction are to be accounted for as adjustments to the carrying amount of the liability, to be amortized over the remaining term of the modified loan.

Under IAS 39, the reasons for the debt modification or exchange are irrelevant to the determination of the accounting to be applied. In this regard, IFRS contrasts with US GAAP, which historically had applied different accounting to those debt modifications which were identified as "troubled debt restructurings."

Example of accounting for debt exchange or restructuring with gain recognition

Assume that Debtor Corp. owes Friendly Bank €90,000 on a 5% interest-bearing non-amortizing note payable in five years, plus accrued and unpaid interest, due immediately, of €4,500. Friendly Bank agrees to a restructuring to assist Debtor Corp., which is suffering losses and is threatening to declare bankruptcy. The interest rate is reduced to 4%, the principal is reduced to €72,500, and the accrued interest is forgiven outright. Future payments will be on normal terms.

Whether there is recognition of a gain on the restructuring depends on the 10% threshold. The relevant discount rate to be used to compare the present values of the old and the new debt obligations is 5%. The present value of the old debt is simply the principal amount, €90,000, plus the interest due at present, €4,500, for a total of €94,500.

The present value of the replacement debt is the discounted present value of the reduced principal and the reduced future interest payments; the forgiven interest does not affect this. The new principal, €72,500, discounted at 5%, equals €56,806. The stream of future interest payments (€72,500 × .04 = €2,900 annually in arrears), discounted at 5%, equals €12,555. The total present value, therefore, is €69,361, which is about 27% below the present value of the old debt obligation. Thus, the 10% threshold is exceeded, and a gain will be recognized at the date of the restructuring.

However, given Debtor's current condition, the market rate of interest for its debt would actually be 12%, and since the new obligation must be recorded at fair value, this must be computed. The present value of the reduced principal, €72,500, discounted at 12%, has a present value of €41,138. The stream of future interest payments (€72,500 × .04 = €2,900 annually, in arrears), discounted at 12%, has a present value of €10,454. The total obligation thus has a fair value of €51,592.

The entry to record this event would be

Debt obligation (old) payable	90,000	
Interest payable	4,500	
Discount on debt obligation (new)	20,908	
Debt obligation (new) payable		72,500
Gain on debt restructuring		42,908

Note that the new debt obligation is recorded at a net of €51,592, not at the face value of €72,500. The difference, €20,908, is a discount to be amortized to interest expense over the next five years, in order to reflect the actual market rate of 12%, rather than the nominal 4% being charged. Amortization should be accomplished on the effective yield method.

Example of accounting for debt exchange or restructuring with gain deferral

Assume now that Hopeless Corp. owes Callous Bank €90,000 on a 5% interest-bearing non-amortizing note payable in five years, plus accrued and unpaid interest, due immediately, of €4,500. Callous Bank agrees to a restructuring to assist Hopeless Corp., which is also suffering losses and is threatening to declare bankruptcy. However, Callous is only willing to reduce the principal amount from €90,000 to €85,000, and reduce interest to 4.5% from 5%. It is not willing to forego the currently owed €4,500 interest payment, and furthermore requires that the loan maturity be shortened to three years, from five, in order to limit its risk. Hopeless agrees to the new terms.

In order to comply with IAS 39, the present value of the new debt must be compared to the present value of the old, existing obligation. As in the preceding example, the present value of the old debt is simply the principal amount, €90,000, plus the interest due at present, €4,500, for a total of €94,500.

The present value of the replacement debt is the discounted present value of the reduced principal and the reduced future interest payments, plus the interest using a 5% discount factor (= .86384 for the new three-year term), has a present value of €73,426. The stream of future interest payments (€85,000 × .045 = €3,825 annually in arrears), discounted at 5% (= 2.7231 annuity factor), has a present value of €10,416. The total present value, therefore, is (€73,426 + €10,416 + €4,500 =) €88,342, which is about 7% below the present value of the old debt obligation. Accordingly, since the 10% threshold is not exceeded, the difference of (€94,500 − €88,342 =) €6,158 is not recognized as a gain at the date of the restructuring, but rather is deferred and amortized over the new three-year term of the restructured loan.

The entry to record this event would be

Debt obligation (old) payable	90,000	
Discount on debt obligation (new)	1,158	
Debt obligation (new) payable		85,000
Deferred gain on debt restructuring		6,158

Note that the new debt obligation is recorded at a net of €83,842, not at the face value of €85,000. The difference of €1,158 represents a discount to be amortized to interest expense over the subsequent three years; this will result in an interest expense at the actual market rate of 5%, rather than at the nominal 4.5% rate. Amortization should be computed on the effective yield method, although if the discrepancy is not material the straight-line method may be employed.

The deferred gain, €6,158, will be amortized over the three-year revised term. While the discount amortization will be added to interest expense. IAS 39 is silent as to how the amortization of the deferred gain should be handled. However, by reference to how a gain in excess of the 10% threshold (and thus been subject to immediate recognition) would have been reported, it is thought likely that this amortization should be included in "other income," and should not be offset against interest expense.

Presentation of the gain or loss from debt restructurings is not explicitly dealt with under IFRS. However, since IAS 8 has been revised, as part of the IASB's Improvements Project to eliminate the presentation of extraordinary items in profit or loss, there is no difficulty in making the appropriate decision. Gain or loss on debt extinguishments should, in the authors' opinion, be displayed as items of "other" income or expense in profit or loss.

Defeasance of debt instruments. Defeasance refers to the practice of effectively eliminating an obligation by pledging assets to the satisfaction thereof. For a period, it was in vogue to eliminate the display in the statement of financial position of the liabilities "satisfied" and the assets pledged for that purpose, notwithstanding that the issuer remained legally obligated for the debt's satisfaction (For example, if the assets pledged prove to be insufficient to the task, the obligor must fulfill the obligation). This technique, *in-substance defeasance,* enjoyed some popularity, largely due to the accounting treatment that had been permitted under earlier standards, particularly under US GAAP. By permitting the obligor to remove both the segregated assets and the debt from its statement of financial position, a more positive financial leverage situation was implied, even though reported net worth would be unaffected.

This financial reporting practice was subsequently prohibited under US GAAP. More recently, in-substance defeasance was considered by IAS 39 and was rejected as an appropriate financial reporting option. According to this standard, payments to a third party (including a trust) do not relieve the debt or of its primary obligation to the creditor of record, in the absence of legal release. Accordingly, in-substance defeasance cannot be accounted for as elimination of debt and of the segregated assets.

Gain or loss on derecognition of financial liabilities. The difference between the net carrying value and the consideration paid, including any noncash assets transferred or liabilities assumed, is recorded as a gain or loss. If the acquisition price is greater than the carrying value, a loss is incurred and must be accounted for. A gain is generated if the acquisition price is less than the carrying value. These gains or losses are to be recognized in the period in which the extinguishment takes place. These should be reported as "other" income or expense, because this is the same profit or loss category where interest expense is normally reported. It would not be appropriate, however, to include any gain or loss in the interest pool from which capitalized interest is computed under IAS 23 (discussed in Chapter 8).

The unamortized premium or discount and issue costs should be amortized to the acquisition date and recorded prior to determination of the gain or loss. If the extinguishment of debt does not occur on the interest date, the interest payable accruing between the last interest date and the acquisition date must also be recorded.

Example of accounting for the extinguishment of debt

1. A 10%, ten-year, €200,000 bond is dated and issued on 1/1/09 at €98, with the interest payable semiannually.
2. Associated bond issue costs of €14,000 are incurred.
3. Four years later, on 1/1/13 the entire bond issue is repurchased at €102 per €100 face value and is retired.
4. The straight-line method of amortization is used since the result is not materially different from that when the effective interest method is used.

The gain or loss on the repurchase is computed as follows:

Reacquisition price [(102/100) × €200,000]		€204,000
Net carrying amount:		
Face value	€200,000	
Unamortized discount [2% × €200,000 × (6/10)]	(2,400)	
Unamortized issue costs [€14,000 × (6/10)]	(8,400)	189,200
Loss on bond repurchase		€ 14,800

Convertible Debt Instruments

Bonds are frequently issued with the right to convert them into ordinary shares of the company at the holder's option when certain terms and conditions are met (i.e., a target market price is reached). Convertible debt is used for two reasons. First, when a specific amount of funds is needed, convertible debt often allows fewer shares to be issued (assuming that conversion ultimately occurs) than if the funds were raised by directly issuing the shares. Thus, less dilution is suffered by the other shareholders. Second, the conversion feature allows debt to be issued at a lower interest rate and with fewer restrictive covenants than if the debt were issued without it. That is because the bondholders are receiving the benefit of the conversion feature in lieu of higher current interest returns.

This dual nature of debt and equity, however, creates a question as to whether the equity element should receive separate recognition. Support for separate treatment is based on the assumption that this equity element has economic value. Since the convertible feature tends to lower the rate of interest, it can easily be argued that a portion of the proceeds should be allocated to this equity feature. On the other hand, a case can be made that the debt and equity elements are inseparable, and thus that the instrument is either all debt or all equity. IFRS had not previously addressed this matter directly, although the focus of the IASB *Framework* on "true and fair presentation" could be said to support the notion that the proceeds of a convertible debt offering be allocated between debt and equity accounts. The promulgation of IAS 32 resulted in the defining of convertible bonds (among other instruments) as being compound financial instruments, the component parts of which must be classified according to their separate characteristics.

Features of convertible debt instruments. Revised IAS 32 addresses the accounting for compound financial instruments from the perspective of issuers. Convertible debt probably accounts for most of the compound instruments that will be of concern to those responsible for financial reporting. IAS 32 requires the issuer of such a financial instrument to present the liability component and the equity component separately in the statement of financial position. Allocation of proceeds between liability and equity proceeds as follows:

1. Upon initial recognition, the fair value of the liability component of compound (convertible) debt instruments is computed as the present value of the contractual stream of future cash flows, discounted at the rate of interest applied at inception by the market to instruments of comparable credit status and providing substantially the same cash flows, on the same terms, but absent the conversion option. For example, if a 5% interest-bearing convertible bond would have commanded an 8% yield if issued without the conversion feature, the contractual cash flows are to be discounted at 8% in order to calculate the fair value of the unconditional debt component of the compound instrument.

2. The equity portion of the compound instrument is actually an embedded option to convert the liability into equity of the issuer. The fair value of the option is determined by time value and by the intrinsic value, if there is any. This option has value on initial recognition even when it is out of the money.

The issuance proceeds from convertible debt should be assigned to the components as described below.

Features of convertible debt typically include (1) a conversion price 15% to 20% greater than the market value of the share when the debt is issued; (2) conversion features (price and number of shares) that protect against dilution from share dividends, splits, and so on; and (3) a callable feature at the issuer's option that is usually exercised once the conversion price is reached (thus forcing conversion or redemption).

Convertible debt also has its disadvantages. If the share price increases significantly after the debt is issued, the issuer would have been better off simply by issuing the share. Additionally, if the price of the share does not reach the conversion price, the debt will never be converted (a condition known as overhanging debt).

Accounting for Compound Instruments

For purposes of accounting decisions, the most important compound instruments are those which incorporate some elements of liability and other elements of equity instruments. Convertible bonds, and bonds with detachable share purchase warrants, are the most common such instruments. In some cases, one or more of the component parts of the compound instrument may be financial derivatives, as a share purchase warrant would be. In other instances, each element might be a traditional, nonderivative instrument, as would be the case when a debenture is issued with common shares as a unit offering.

The accounting issue that is most obviously associated with compound instruments is how to allocate the proceeds among the constituent elements. When the compound instrument consists of parts which are both liabilities and equity items, proper classification of the elements is vital to accurate financial reporting, affecting potentially such matters as debt covenant compliance (if the debt to equity ratio, for example, is a covenant to be met by the debtor entity.)

Revised IAS 32, as revised effective 2005, made a significant change to the *issuer's* accounting for compound financial instruments. Previously, under original IAS 32, compound instruments were to be analyzed into their constituent elements and accounted for by either allocating the proceeds pro rata based on relative fair values, or allocating to the more readily measured element full fair value and assigning only the residual to the other components. Depending on the facts and circumstances, this could have resulted in allocating fair value to the equity component, and assigning only a residual amount to the liability portion.

Under revised IAS 32, however, it is required that whether or not fair values are available for all components of the compound instrument, full fair value be allocated to the liability components, with only the residual being assigned to equity. This position has been taken in order to be fully consistent with the definition of equity instruments. Equity evidences the residual interest in the assets of an entity after deducting all of its liabilities. To be consistent, liabilities must be stated at their full amounts, which in this instance is developed from the allocated proceeds upon issuance, at fair value, as subsequently adjusted for amortization of any associated discount or premium. To have assigned a lower amount to the debt would thus understate the interest of creditors in the entity's assets, and overstate the interest of the shareholders, in violation of IFRS.

It will no longer be acceptable to assign a residual to the liability components after first assigning a "fair value" measure to the equity. It will also be unacceptable to allocate total proceeds proportionately to both liability and equity elements.

If the compound instruments include a derivative element (e.g., a put option), the value of those features, to the extent they are embedded in the compound financial instrument other than the equity component, is to be included in the liability component.

The sum of the carrying amounts assigned to the liability and equity components on initial recognition is always equal to the fair value that would be ascribed to the instrument as a whole. In other words, there can be no "day one" gains from issuing financial instruments.

Residual allocation method. As noted, the only acceptable method of allocating proceeds from the issuance of convertible debt is to assign to the equity component (e.g., the conversion feature) the residual amount, after first assigning the full fair value of the debt, minus the conversion feature, to the liability component. To illustrate this approach, consider the following fact situation.

Example of the residual allocation method

Istanbul Corp. sells convertible bonds having aggregate par (face) value of €25 million to the public at a price of €98 on January 2, 2009. The bonds are due December 31, 2016, but can be called at €102 anytime after January 2, 2012. The bonds carry a coupon of 6% and are convertible into Istanbul Corp. common shares at an exchange ratio of twenty-five shares per bond (each bond having a face value of €1,000). Taking the discount on the offering price into account, the bonds were priced to yield about 6.3% to maturity.

The company's investment bankers have advised it that without the conversion feature, Istanbul's bonds would have had to carry an interest yield of 8% to have been sold in the current market environment. Thus, the market price of a pure bond with a 6% coupon at January 2, 2009, would have been about €883.48 (the present value of a stream of semiannual interest payments of €30 per bond, plus a terminal value of €1,000, discounted at a 4% semiannual rate).

This suggests that of the €980 being paid for each bond, €883.48 is being paid for the pure debt obligation, and another €96.52 is being offered for the conversion feature. Given this analysis, the entry to record the original issuance of the €25 million in debt securities on January 2, 2009, would be as follows:

Cash	24,500,000	
Discount on bonds payable	2,913,000	
Bonds payable		25,000,000
Paid-in capital—conversion feature		2,413,000

The discount should be amortized to interest expense, ideally by the effective yield method (constant return on increasing base) over the eight years to the maturity date. For purposes of this example, however, straight-line amortization (€2,913,000 ÷ 16 periods = €182,000 per semiannual period) will be used. Thus, the entry to record the June 30, 2009 interest payment would be as follows:

Interest expense	932,000	
Discount on bonds payable		182,000
Cash		750,000

The paid-in capital account arising from the foregoing transaction would form a permanent part of the capital of Istanbul Corp. If the bonds are later converted, this would be transferred to the common share accounts, effectively forming part of the price paid for the shares ultimately issued. If the bondholders *decline* to convert and the bonds are eventually paid off at maturity, the paid-in capital from the conversion feature will form a type of "donated capital" to the entity, since the bondholders effectively will have forfeited this capital that they had contributed to the company.

If the bonds are not converted, the discount on the bonds payable will continue to be amortized until maturity. However, if they are converted, the remaining unamortized balance in this account, along with the face value of the bonds, will constitute the "price" being paid for the shares to be issued.

To illustrate this, assume the following:

On July 1, 2012, all the bonds are tendered for conversion to common shares of Istanbul Corp. The remaining book value of the bonds will be converted into common shares, which does not carry any par or stated value. The first step is to compute the book value of the debt.

Bonds payable		€25,000,000
Discount on bonds payable		
Original discount	€2,913,000	
Less amortization to date (4.4 yrs.)	(1,638,000)	1,275,000
Net book value of obligation		€23,725,000

The entry to record the conversion, given the foregoing information, is as follows:

Bonds payable	25,000,000	
Contributed capital—Conversion feature	2,413,000	
Discount on bonds payable		1,275,000
Share capital		26,138,000

Note that in the foregoing entry, the effective price recorded for the shares being issued is the book value of the remaining debt, adjusted by the price previously recorded to reflect the sale of the conversion feature. In the present instance, given the book value at the conversion date (a function of when the conversion privilege was exercised), and given the conversion ratio of twenty-five shares per bond, an effective price of €41.82 per share is being paid for the shares to be issued. This is determined without any reference to the market value at the date of the conversion. Presumably, the market price is higher, as it is unlikely that the bondholders would surrender an asset earning 6%, with a fixed maturity date, for another asset having a lower value and having an uncertain future worth (although if the dividend yield were somewhat higher than the equivalent bond interest, an unlikely event, this might happen).

Induced Conversion of Debt Instruments

A special situation may occur in that the conversion privileges of convertible debt are modified after issuance of the debt. These modifications may take the form of reduced conversion prices or additional consideration paid to the convertible debt holder. The debtor offers these modifications or "sweeteners" to induce prompt conversion of the outstanding debt. This is in addition to the normal strategy of calling the convertible debt to induce the holders to convert, assuming the underlying economic values make this attractive (debtors often do this when only a small fraction of the originally issued convertible debt remains outstanding). The issuance of these "sweeteners" should be accounted for as a reduction in the proceeds of the share offering, thereby reducing contributed capital from the transaction.

A previously acceptable alternative accounting treatment, recording the sweetener payments as an expense in the period of conversion, is no longer deemed appropriate given the proceeds allocation scheme mandated by revised IAS 32. That latter approach derived from a recognition that if it had been part of the original arrangement, a change in the exchange ratio or other adjustment would have affected the allocation of the original proceeds between debt and equity, and the discount or premium originally recognized would have been different in amount, and hence periodic amortization would have differed as well.

Debt Instruments Issued with Share Warrants

Warrants are certificates enabling the holder to purchase a stated number of shares of capital at a certain price within a certain period. They are often issued with bonds to enhance the marketability of the bonds and to lower the bond's interest rate.

Detachable warrants are similar to other features, such as the conversion feature discussed earlier, which under IAS 32 make the debt a compound financial instrument and which necessitates that there is an allocation of the original proceeds among the constituent elements. Since warrants, which will often be traded in the market, are easier to value than are conversion features, prior to the most recent revision to IAS 32 it was logical to employ pro rata allocation based on relative market values. However, since revised IAS 32 requires allocation of only residual value to the equity element of compound instruments consisting of both liability and equity components, that approach is no longer acceptable.

Accounting for Collateral Given by Debtor to Creditor

In some instances, the borrower (debtor) will provide the lender (creditor) with valuable assets, most typically highly liquid assets such as marketable securities, to further secure the lending relationship and to provide the creditor with added protection. Under the provisions of IAS 39, the borrower is required to disclose the carrying amount of financial assets pledged as collateral for liabilities, as well as any significant terms and conditions relating to pledged assets. If the debtor delivers collateral to the creditor and the creditor is permitted to sell or repledge the collateral without constraints, then the debtor should disclose the collateral separately from other assets not used as collateral.

In other instances, the collateral is in the form of a security interest or mortgage deed. In those instances disclosure is still required, but the creditor is not able to take actions such as repledging or selling the collateral, as would be possible if actual assets such as negotiable instruments had been delivered.

Instruments Having Contingent Settlement Provisions

Some financial instruments are issued which have contingent settlement provisions— that is, which may or may not require the issuer/obligor to utilize its resources in subsequent settlement. For example, a note can be issued that will be payable either in cash or in the issuer's shares, depending on whether certain contingent events, such as the share price exceeding a defined target over a defined number of days immediately preceding the maturity date of the note, are met or not. This situation differs from convertible debt, which is exchangeable into the shares of the borrower, at the holder's option.

Revised IAS 32 incorporates the conclusion previously set forth separately in SIC 5, *Classification of Financial Instruments—Contingent Settlement Provisions*, that a financial instrument is a financial liability when the manner of settlement depends on the occurrence or nonoccurrence of uncertain future events or on the outcome of uncertain circumstances that are beyond the control of *both* the issuer and the holder. Contingent settlement provisions are ignored when they apply only in the event of liquidation of the issuer or are not genuine.

Examples of such contingent conditions would be changes in a stock market index, the consumer price index, a reference interest rate or taxation requirements, or the issuer's future revenues, profit or loss or debt to equity ratio. The issuer cannot impact these factors and thus cannot unilaterally avoid settlement as a liability, delivering cash or other assets to resolve the obligation.

Under revised IAS 32, certain exceptions to the foregoing rule have been established. These exist when

1. The part of the contingent settlement provision that could require settlement in cash or another financial asset (or otherwise in such a way that it would be a financial liability) is not genuine; or
2. The issuer can be required to settle the obligation in cash or another financial asset (or otherwise to settle it in such a way that it would be a financial liability) only in the event of liquidation of the issuer.

By "not genuine," IAS 32 means that there is no reasonable expectation that settlement in cash or other asset will be triggered. Thus, a contract that requires settlement in cash or a variable number of the entity's own shares only on the occurrence of an event that is extremely rare, highly abnormal and very unlikely to occur is an equity instrument. Similarly, settlement in a fixed number of the entity's own shares may be contractually precluded in circumstances that are outside the control of the entity, but if these circumstances have no genuine possibility of occurring, classification as an equity instrument is appropriate.

If the settlement option is only triggered upon liquidation, this possibility is ignored in classifying the instrument, since the going concern assumption, underlying IFRS-basis financial reporting, presumes ongoing existence rather than liquidation.

In other instances the instrument includes a "put" option (i.e., an option that gives the holder the right, but not the obligation, to cause the issuer to redeem it at a fixed or determinable price). Notwithstanding certain prominent features suggesting an equity ownership, under the provisions of the revised IAS 32, any such instruments would have to be classified as liabilities. Again, this is because the issuer does not retain an unconditional right to avoid settlement using cash or other resources of the entity.

It also happens that entities will enter into contractual obligations of a fixed amount or of an amount that fluctuates in part or in full in response to changes in a variable other than the market price of the entity's own equity instruments, but which the entity must or can settle by delivery of its own equity instruments, the number of which depends on the amount of the obligation. Under revised IAS 32, such an obligation must be reported as a financial liability of the entity, unless the terms are such that this is deemed "not genuine." The reasoning is that if the number of an entity's own shares or other own equity instruments required to settle an obligation varies with changes in their fair value so that the total fair value of the entity's own equity instruments to be delivered always equals the amount of the contractual obligation, then the counterparty does not hold a true residual interest in the entity. Furthermore, settlement in shares could require the issuing entity to deliver more or fewer of its own equity instruments than would be the case at the date of entering into the contractual arrangement. This leads the IASB to conclude that such an obligation is a financial liability of the entity even though the entity must or can settle it by delivering its own equity instruments.

Changes in Noncurrent Estimated Liabilities

Increasingly, due to environmental and other concerns, entities are obligated to dismantle, remove and restore items of property, plant, and equipment during or at the end of the useful lives of the assets. The cost of such dismantlement or remediation is, per IAS 16, deemed to be a part of the cost of the assets and will be expensed via depreciation over the periods of use of these assets. IAS 37 contains requirements on how to measure decommissioning, restoration and similar liabilities, which will generally be presented in the statement of financial position as noncurrent liabilities. IFRIC 1 provides guidance on how to account for the effect of changes in the measurement of existing decommissioning, restoration and similar liabilities.

Changes in these estimated liabilities may occur for two principal reasons. First, there likely may be one or more revisions to the estimated outflows of resources embodying economic benefits. Given the long-term nature of these obligations, and the constantly changing factors, such as technology, which will impact these costs, it would indeed be peculiar if such estimates did not change over time. For example, the estimated costs of decommissioning a nuclear-powered electric generating plant may vary significantly both in timing and amount as the plan is being used and as remediation technology advances. Timing is important because the *present value* of projected future cash outflows is used to measure this obligation; as the horizon lengthens or shortens, this will have a material effect on the amount of the liability to be reported.

Second, there may be revisions to the current market-based discount rate. As the discount rate rises, the present value of future cash outflows declines; as rates decline, present value of future costs increases.

IFRIC 1 applies to changes in the measurement of any existing decommissioning, restoration or similar liability that is *both* (1) recognized as part of the cost of an item of property, plant, and equipment in accordance with IAS 16; and (2) recognized as a liability in accordance with IAS 37. If the changes result from changes in the estimated timing or amount of the outflow of resources embodying economic benefits required to settle the obligation, or a change in the discount rate, this change is to be accounted for as explained in the following paragraphs.

Under provisions of IAS 16, plant assets can be carried either at depreciated cost or at revalued amounts. If the related asset is measured using the cost model, then changes in the liability are to be added to (if estimated cost increases), or deducted from (if estimated cost decreases), the cost of the related asset in the current period, subject to the reasonable condition, however, that the amount deducted from the cost of the asset cannot exceed the asset's carrying amount. In other words, the carrying value of the long-lived assets cannot "go negative." If the indicated decrease in the estimated liability in the current period, due to a reduction in the remediation or dismantlement obligation, were to exceed the carrying amount of the asset, the excess is to be recognized immediately in results of operations.

If the adjustment to the estimated liability results in an addition to the cost of an asset, it must be determined whether the new, higher carrying amount of the asset is deemed to be fully recoverable. If there is indication of a possible inability to recover this carrying value, then the reporting entity is required to test the asset for impairment by estimating its recoverable amount, and to account for the impairment loss, if any, in accordance with IAS 36. (See Chapter 8 for a full discussion.)

On the other hand, if the related asset is measured using the permitted revaluation model, then any changes in the liability will modify the revaluation surplus or deficit previously recognized in connection with that asset. Accordingly, a decrease in the liability will be recognized in other comprehensive income, in the statement of comprehensive income, and accumulated in the equity section of the statement of financial position under the heading revaluation surplus, with the exception that it is to be recognized in current period profit or loss to the extent that it reverses a revaluation deficit on the asset that was previously recognized in profit or loss. Similarly, an increase in the liability is to be recognized in profit or loss, subject to the requirement that it is recognized in other comprehensive income to the extent of any credit balance existing in the revaluation surplus arising from the asset.

In the event that a decrease in the liability (due to a reduction in estimated remediation or dismantlement costs, measured at present value) exceeds the carrying amount that would have been recognized had the asset been carried under the cost model, this excess must be recognized immediately in profit or loss.

The objectives of the revaluation model, where used, have to be borne in mind when estimated dismantlement or other costs are revised. A change in this liability is an indication that the asset may have to be revalued in order to ensure that the carrying amount does not differ materially from that which would be determined using fair value at the end of the reporting period. Any such revaluation must be taken into account in determining the amounts to be recognized in profit or loss or in other comprehensive income. If revaluation is indeed necessary, IFRIC 1 stipulates that all the assets of that class are to be revalued.

IAS 1, as revised in 2007, requires disclosure in the statement of comprehensive income of each item of other comprehensive income. In complying with this requirement, the change in the revaluation surplus arising from a change in the liability is to be separately identified and disclosed as to its source.

Under IFRS, the adjusted depreciable amount of the asset is depreciated over its respective useful life. Thus, once the related asset has reached the end of its useful economic life, all subsequent changes in the liability are to be recognized in profit or loss as they occur.

This rule applies to both assets accounted for under the cost model and those reported in accordance with the revaluation model.

As time advances, of course, the present value of the obligation for dismantlement and similar costs, holding other factors constant, will increase. This periodic "unwinding of the discount" is to be recognized in current profit or loss according to its character, which is a finance cost. The required capitalization of interest cost under IAS 23 is not relevant to this situation (it is intended to address construction period finance costs which are deemed part of the original cost of plant assets, only).

Examples of Financial Statement Disclosures

adidas Group AG
Annual Report 2007

15. Borrowings and credit lines

With settlement on October 8, 2003, adidas issued a €400 million convertible bond through its wholly owned Dutch subsidiary, adidas International Finance B.V. The bond was guaranteed by adidas AG and issued in tranches of €50,000 each with a maturity up to 15 years. The bond is, at the option of the respective holder, subject to certain conditions, convertible from and including November 18, 2003, up to and including September 20, 2018, into ordinary no-par-value bearer shares of adidas AG at the conversion price of €25.50 which was fixed upon issue. The coupon of the bond is 2.5% and is payable annually in arrears on October 8 of each year, commencing on October 8, 2004. The bond is convertible into approximately 16 million no-par-value shares.

The convertible bond is not callable by the issuer until October 2009. It is callable thereafter, subject to a 130% trigger between October 2009 and October 2012 and subject to a 115% trigger between October 2012 and 2015. The convertible bond is unconditionally callable thereafter. Investors have the right to convert the bond in October 2009, October 2012, and October 2015.

The fair values of the liability component and the equity conversion component were determined on the issuance of the bond. The fair value of the liability component, included in long-term borrowings, was calculated using a market interest rate of approximately 4.6% for an equivalent straight bond without conversion rights. Due to the retrospective application of the amendment to IAS 39 and IAS 32, the liability and equity split of the convertible bond changed. As a result, the liability component as at the date of issuance increased by €71.1 million with an equivalent decrease in equity. The amount of the equity component, which is included in equity in the capital reserve, amounts to €44.1 million (less transactions costs of €0.9 million). The liability component is valued using the "effective interest method."

The adidas AG share first traded above 110% (€28.05) of the conversion price of €25.50 on more than 20 trading days within the last 30 trading days in the fourth quarter of 2004. Consequently, bondholders have had the right to convert their convertible bonds into equity since January 1, 2005. An early redemption or conversion of the convertible bond is currently not expected.

Gross borrowing decreased by €432 million in 2007 compared to an increase of €1.543 billion in 2006.

Borrowings are denominated in a variety of currencies in which the Group conducts its business. The largest portions of effective gross borrowings (before liquidity swaps for cash management purposes) as at December 31, 2007, are denominated in euros (2007:51%; 2006: 51%) and US dollars (2007:45%; 2006: 44%).

Month-end weighted-average interest rates on borrowings in all currencies ranged from 5.2% to 5.6% in 2007 and from 4.2% to 5.3% in 2006.

As at December 31, 2007, the Group had cash credit lines and other long-term financing arrangements totaling €6.3 billion (2006: €6.9 billion); thereof unused credit lines accounted for €4.1 billion (2006: €4.4 billion). In addition, the Group had separate lines for the issuance of letters of credit in an amount of approximately €0.2 billion (2006: €0.3 billion).

The Group's outstanding financings are unsecured.

The private placement and convertible bond documentation each contain a negative-pledge clause. Additionally, the private placement documentation contains minimum equity covenants and net loss covenants. As at December 31, 2007, actual shareholders' equity was well above the amount of the minimum equity covenant.

The amounts disclosed as borrowings represent outstanding borrowings under the following arrangements with aggregated expiration dates as follows:

Gross Borrowings as at December 31, 2007

€ in millions	Up to 1 year	Between 1 and 3 years	Between 3 and 5 years	After 5 years	Total
Bank borrowings incl. commercial paper	--	--	198	--	198
Private placements	186	583	376	419	1,564
Convertible bond	--	384	--	--	384
Total	186	967	574	419	2,146

Gross Borrowings as at December 31, 2006

€ in millions	Up to 1 year	Between 1 and 3 years	Between 3 and 5 years	After 5 years	Total
Bank borrowings includ- ing commercial paper	144	--	275	--	419
Private placements	109	610	474	591	1,784
Convertible bond	--	--	375	--	375
Total	253	610	1,124	591	2,578

As all short-term borrowings are based upon long-term arrangements, the Group reports them as long-term borrowings.

The borrowings related to our outstanding convertible bond changed in value, reflecting the accruing interest on the debt component in accordance with IFRS requirements.

Novartis
Annual Report 2007

18. Noncurrent financial debts

	2007 USD million	2006 USD million
Straight bonds	--	1,318
Liabilities to banks and other financial institutions [1]	693	666
Finance lease obligations	8	12
Total (including current portion of noncurrent financial debt)	701	1,996
Less current portion of noncurrent financial debt	(24)	(1,340)
Total noncurrent financial debts	677	656

Straight bonds		
EUR 3.75% EUR 1 billion bond 2002/2007 of Novartis Securities Investment Ltd., Hamilton, Bermuda		1,318
Total straight bonds		1,318

[1] *Average interest rate 2.1% (2006: 2.3%)*

Breakdown by maturity:		
2007	--	1,340
2008	24	32
2009	557	528
2010	20	17
2011	20	16
2012	18	--
Thereafter	62	63
Total	701	1,996

Breakdown by currency:		
USD	2	6
EUR	157	1,473
JPY	530	504
Others	12	13
Total	701	1,996

Fair value comparison	2007 Balance sheet USD million	2007 Fair values USD million	2006 Balance sheet USD million	2006 Fair values USD million
Straight bonds	--	--	1,318	1,318
Others	701	701	678	678
Total	701	701	1,996	1,996

Collateralized noncurrent financial debts and pledged assets	2007 USD million	2006 USD million
Total amount of collateralized noncurrent financial debts	63	29
Total net book value of property, plant, and equipment pledged as collateral for noncurrent financial debts	112	118

The Group's collateralized noncurrent financial debt consists of overdraft facilities at usual market conditions.

The percentage of fixed-rate financial debt to total financial debt was 11% and 27% at December 31, 2007 and 2006, respectively.

The financial debts, including current financial debts, contain only general default covenants. The Group is in compliance with these covenants.

The average interest rate on total financial debt is 3.4% (2006: 3.0%)

Clariant International Limited
Annual Report 2007

16. Movements in provisions for noncurrent liabilities

CHFm	Environmental provisions	Personnel provisions	Restructuring provisions	Other provisions	Total provisions for noncurrent liabilities 2007	Total provisions for noncurrent liabilities 2006
At January 1	134	41	1	68	244	289
Additions	16	10	3	21	50	57
Effect of acquisitions	--	--	--	--	--	1
Effect of disposals	--	--	--	--	--	(23)
Reclassifications	(25)	(10)	(1)	--	(36)	(25)
Reclassified to held for sale	--	--	--	--	--	(4)
Amounts used	(1)	(6)	--	(7)	(14)	(16)
Unused amounts reversed	(6)	(1)	--	(14)	(21)	(35)
Changes due to the passage of time and changes in discount rates	1	--	--	2	3	1
Exchange rate differences	--	2	--	3	5	(1)
At December 31	119	36	3	73	231	244

Environmental provisions. Environmental provisions for environmental liabilities are made when there is a legal or constructive obligation for the Group which will result in an outflow of economic resources. It is difficult to estimate the action required by Clariant in the future to correct the effects on the environment of prior disposal or release of chemical substances by Clariant or other parties and the associated costs, pursuant to environmental laws and regulations. The material components of the environmental provisions consist of the costs to fully clean and refurbish contaminated sites and to treat and contain contamination at sites where the environmental exposure is less severe. The Group's future remediation expenses are affected by a number of uncertainties which include, but are not limited to, the method and extent of remediation and the percentage of material attributable to Clariant at the remediation sites relative to that attributable to other parties.

The environmental provisions reported in the balance sheet concern a number of different obligations, mainly in Switzerland, the United States, Germany, the United Kingdom, Brazil and Italy.

Provisions are made for remedial work where there is an obligation to remedy environmental damage, as well as for containment work where required by environmental regulations. All provisions relate to environmental liabilities arising in connection with activities that occurred prior to the date when Clariant took control of the relevant site. At each balance sheet date Clariant critically reviews all provisions and makes adjustments where required.

Personnel provisions. Personnel provisions include compensated long-term absences such as sabbatical leave, jubilee or other long-service benefits, noncurrent disability benefits, profit sharing and bonuses payable twelve months or more after the end of the period in which they were earned.

Restructuring provisions. Restructuring provisions are established where there is a legal or constructive obligation for the Group that will result in the outflow of economic resources and which is expected to occur twelve months or more after the end of the reporting period. The term restructuring refers to the activities that have as a consequence, staff redundancies and the shutdown of production lines or entire sites. However, expenses for termination benefits which are borne by the pension and termination plans are included in pension plan liabilities (see note 15).

Other provisions. Other provisions include provisions for obligations relating to tax and legal cases in various countries where settlement is expected after twelve months or more.

All noncurrent provisions are discounted to reflect the time value of money where material. Discount rates reflect current market assessments of the time value of money and the risk specific to the provisions in the respective countries.

14 LEASES

PERSPECTIVE AND ISSUES

Leasing has long been a popular financing option for the acquisition of business property. During the past few decades, however, the business of leasing has experienced staggering growth, and much of this volume is reported in the statements of financial position. The tremendous popularity of leasing is quite understandable, as it offers great flexibility, often coupled with a range of economic advantages over ownership. Thus, with leasing, a lessee (borrower) is typically able to obtain 100% financing, whereas under a traditional credit purchase arrangement the buyer would generally have to make an initial equity investment. In many jurisdictions, a leasing arrangement offers tax benefits compared to the purchase option. The lessee is protected to an extent from the risk of obsolescence, although the lease terms will vary based on the extent to which the lessor bears this risk. For the lessor, there will be a regular stream of lease payments, which include interest that often will be at rates above commercial lending rates, and, at the end of the lease term, usually some residual value.

The accounting for lease transactions involves a number of complexities, which derive partly from the range of alternative structures that are available to the parties. For example, in many cases leases can be configured to allow manipulation of the tax benefits, with other features such as lease term and implied interest rate adjusted to achieve the intended overall economics of the arrangement. Leases can be used to transfer ownership of the leased asset, and they can be used to transfer some or all of the risks normally associated with ownership. The financial reporting challenge is to have the economic substance of the transaction dictate the accounting treatment.

The accounting for lease transactions is one of the best examples of the application of the principle of substance over form, as set forth in the IASB's *Framework*. If the transaction effectively transfers ownership to the lessee, the substance of the transaction is that of a sale of the underlying property, which should be recognized as such even though the transaction takes the contractual form of a lease, which is only a right to use the property at issue.

Modest changes were made to IAS 17 as part of the Improvements Project undertaken by IASB beginning in 2002, with the most recent amendments becoming effective in 2005. These serve to clarify the classification of leases jointly granting rights to use land and buildings, and also to reduce available alternatives for accounting for initial direct costs in the financial statements of lessors. An earlier revision restricted the recognition of finance income by lessors, which may now only be based on net book investment (i.e., carrying value). Several interpretations pertain to application of IAS 17, and IFRIC 4 identifies criteria which, if satisfied, establish whether specific arrangements are or contain a lease agreement.

The guidance on lease accounting under IFRS is not as fully elaborated as is that provided under certain national GAAP, consistent with a somewhat more "principles-based" approach. Even with such a perspective, however, IFRS does not result in capitalization (treatment as assets and related debt) of all lease arrangements, and there are variations in lease terms that can be made to achieve operating (noncapitalization) treatment, which is often desired by lessees, in particular. Because of the significance of this area of practice in all developed economies, and the remaining divergence of requirements under alternative sets of standards, IASB undertook a joint project with the U.K.'s Accounting Standards Board to thoroughly review the entire subject area. The likely outcome of this (and a further joint effort with the US's FASB) will be to reduce the amount of mechanical rules or tests currently found in all lease accounting standards, perhaps with the ultimate result that a mandate that all (perhaps excluding very short-term) leases will be subject to capitalization.

While almost any type of arrangement that satisfies the definition of a lease is covered by this standard, the following specialized types of lease agreements are specifically excluded:

1. Lease agreements to explore for or use natural resources, such as oil, gas, timber, metals, and other mineral rights
2. Licensing agreements for such items as motion picture films, video recordings, plays, manuscripts, patents, and copyrights

The accounting for rights to explore and develop natural resources has yet to be formally addressed by IAS; IFRS 6, which deals with exploration and evaluation assets arising in the mineral exploration process, offers no accounting guidance for leases. Licensing agreements are addressed by IAS 38, which is discussed in Chapter 9.

IASB has been conducting a joint project with FASB on lease accounting, and this ultimately could result in a fundamental change in accounting for leases by both lessors and lessees. It is possible that, to eliminate subjective assessments or the use of criteria subject to manipulation, IASB and FASB may simply conclude that all leases, apart from a defined short-term category of leases (e.g., having terms under one year), represent the transfer of property rights and related debt obligations, and thus should be subject to capitalization by the lessee.

Sources of IFRS		
IAS 17, 24, 36	*SIC* 15, 27	*IFRIC* 4

DEFINITIONS OF TERMS

Bargain purchase option (BPO). A provision in the lease agreement allowing the lessee the option of purchasing the leased property for an amount that is sufficiently lower than the fair value of the property at the date the option becomes exercisable. Exercise of the option must appear reasonably assured at the inception of the lease.

Contingent rentals. Those lease rentals that are not fixed in amount but are based on a factor other than simply the passage of time; for example, if based on percentage of sales, price indices, market rates of interest, or degree of use of the leased asset.

Economic life of leased property. Either the period over which the asset is expected to be economically usable by one or more users, or the number of production or similar units expected to be obtained from the leased asset by one or more users.

Executory costs. Costs such as insurance, maintenance, and taxes incurred for leased property, pertaining to the current period, whether paid by the lessor or lessee. If the obligation of the lessee, these are excluded from the minimum lease payments.

Fair value of leased property (FMV). The amount for which an asset could be exchanged between a knowledgeable, willing buyer and a knowledgeable, willing seller in an arm's-length transaction. When the lessor is a manufacturer or dealer, the fair value of the property at the inception of the lease will ordinarily be its normal selling price, net of any volume or trade discounts. When the lessor is not a manufacturer or dealer, the fair value of the property at the inception of the lease will ordinarily be its cost to the lessor, unless a significant amount of time has elapsed between the acquisition of the property by the lessor and the inception of the lease, in which case fair value should be determined in light of market conditions prevailing at the inception of the lease. Thus, fair value may be greater or less than the lessor's cost or the carrying amount of the property.

Finance lease. A lease that transfers substantially all the risks and rewards associated with the ownership of an asset. The risks related to ownership of an asset include the possibilities of losses from idle capacity or technological obsolescence, and that flowing from variations in return due to changing economic conditions; rewards incidental to ownership of an asset include an expectation of profitable operations over the asset's economic life and expectation of gain from appreciation in value or the ultimate realization of the residual value. Title may or may not eventually be transferred to the lessee under finance lease arrangements.

Gross investment in the lease. The sum total of (1) the minimum lease payments under a finance lease (from the standpoint of the lessor), plus (2) any unguaranteed residual value accruing to the lessor.

Inception of the lease. The date of the written lease agreement or, if earlier, the date of a commitment by the parties to the principal provisions of the lease.

Initial direct costs. Initial direct costs, such as commissions and legal fees, incurred by lessors in negotiating and arranging a lease. These generally include (1) costs to originate a lease incurred in transactions with independent third parties that (a) result directly from and are essential to acquire that lease and (b) would not have been incurred had that leasing transaction not occurred; and (2) certain costs directly related to specified activities performed by the lessor for that lease, such as evaluating the prospective lessee's financial condition; evaluating and recording guarantees, collateral, and other security arrangements; negotiating lease terms; preparing and processing lease documents; and closing the transaction.

Lease. An agreement whereby a lessor conveys to the lessee, in return for payment or series of payments, the right to use an asset (property, plant, equipment, or land) for an agreed-upon period of time. Other arrangements essentially similar to leases, such as hire-purchase contracts, bare-boat charters, and so on, are also considered leases for purposes of the standard.

Lease term. The initial noncancelable period for which the lessee has contracted to lease the asset together with any further periods for which the lessee has the option to extend the lease of the asset, with or without further payment, which option it is reasonably certain (at the inception of the lease) that the lessee will exercise.

Lessee's incremental borrowing rate. The interest rate that the lessee would have to pay on a similar lease, or, if that is not determinable, the rate that at the inception of the lease the lessee would have incurred to borrow over a similar term (i.e., a loan term equal to the lease term), and with a similar security, the funds necessary to purchase the leased asset.

Minimum lease payments (MLP).

1. *From the standpoint of the lessee.* The payments over the lease term that the lessee is or can be required to make in connection with the leased property. The lessee's obligation to pay executory costs (e.g., insurance, maintenance, or taxes) and contingent rents are excluded from minimum lease payments. If the lease contains a bargain purchase option, the minimum rental payments over the lease term plus the payment called for in the bargain purchase option are included in minimum lease payments.

    If no such provision regarding a bargain purchase option is included in the lease contract, the minimum lease payments include the following:

    a. The minimum rental payments called for by the lease over the lease contract over the term of the lease (excluding any executory costs), plus
    b. Any guarantee of residual value, at the expiration of the lease term, to be paid by the lessee or a party related to the lessee.

2. *From the standpoint of the lessor.* The payments described above plus any guarantee of the residual value of the leased asset by a third party unrelated to either the lessee or lessor (provided that the third party is financially capable of discharging the guaranteed obligation).

Net investment in the lease. The difference between the lessor's gross investment in the lease and the unearned finance income.

Noncancelable lease. A lease that is cancelable only

1. On occurrence of some remote contingency
2. With the concurrence (permission) of the lessor
3. If the lessee enters into a new lease for the same or an equivalent asset with the same lessor
4. On payment by the lessee of an additional amount such that at inception, continuation of the lease appears reasonably assured

Nonrecourse (debt) financing. Lending or borrowing activities in which the creditor does not have general recourse to the debtor but rather has recourse only to the property used for collateral in the transaction or other specific property.

Operating lease. A lease that does not meet the criteria prescribed for a finance lease.

Penalty. Any requirement that is imposed or can be imposed on the lessee by the lease agreement or by factors outside the lease agreement to pay cash, incur or assume a liability, perform services, surrender or transfer an asset or rights to an asset, or otherwise forego an economic benefit or suffer an economic detriment.

Rate implicit in the lease. The discount rate that at the inception of the lease, when applied to the minimum lease payments, and the unguaranteed residual value accruing to the benefit of the lessor, causes the aggregate present value to be equal to the fair value of the leased property to the lessor, net of any grants and tax credits receivable by the lessor.

Related parties in leasing transactions. Entities that are in a relationship where one party has the ability to control the other party or exercise significant influence over the operating and financial policies of the related party. Examples include the following:

1. A parent company and its subsidiaries
2. An owner company and its joint ventures and partnerships
3. An investor and its investees

Significant influence may be exercised in several ways, usually by representation on the board of directors but also by participation in the policy-making process, material intercompany transactions, interchange of managerial personnel, or dependence on technical information. The ability to exercise significant influence must be present before the parties can be considered related.

Renewal or extension of a lease. The continuation of a lease agreement beyond the original lease term, including a new lease where the lessee continues to use the same property.

Residual value of leased property. The fair value, estimated at the inception of the lease, that the enterprise expects to obtain from the leased property at the end of the lease term.

Sale and leaseback accounting. A method of accounting for a sale-leaseback transaction in which the seller-lessee records the sale, removes all property and related liabilities from its statement of financial position, recognizes gain or loss from the sale, and classifies the leaseback in accordance with this section.

Unearned finance income. The excess of the lessor's gross investment in the lease over its present value.

Unguaranteed residual value. Part of the residual value of the leased asset (estimated at the inception of the lease) the realization of which by the lessor is not assured or is guaranteed by a party related to the lessor.

Useful life. The estimated remaining period over which the economic benefits embodied by the asset are expected to be consumed, without being limited to the lease term. (The former definition of this term, as employed in the original standard IAS 17, has now been assigned to the term **economic life**.)

CONCEPTS, RULES, AND EXAMPLES

Classification of Leases—Lessee

For accounting and reporting purposes the lessee has two alternatives in classifying a lease.

1. Operating
2. Finance

Finance leases (which are known as *capital* leases under the corresponding US GAAP, because such leased property is treated as owned, and accordingly, capitalized in the statement of financial position) are those that essentially are alternative means of financing the acquisition of property or of substantially all the service potential represented by the property. Due to the relative paucity of guidance on lease accounting under IFRS there will be many issues on which informal direction will be taken from US GAAP. Accordingly, the terms *finance* and *capital* when used to characterize leases will be treated as synonymous in this chapter.

The proper classification of a lease is determined by the circumstances surrounding the leasing transaction. According to IAS 17, whether a lease is a finance lease or not will have to be judged based on the *substance* of the transaction, rather than on its mere *form*. If substantially all of the benefits and risks of ownership have been transferred to the lessee, the lease should be classified as a finance lease; such a lease is normally noncancelable and the lessor is assured (subject to normal credit risk) of recovery of the capital invested plus a reasonable return on its investment. IAS 17 stipulates that substantially all of the risks or benefits of ownership are deemed to have been transferred if *any one* of the following four criteria has been met:

1. The lease transfers ownership to the lessee by the end of the lease term.
2. The lease contains a bargain purchase option (an option to purchase the leased asset at a price that is expected to be substantially lower than the fair value at the date the option becomes exercisable) and it is reasonably certain that the option will be exercisable.
3. The lease term is for the *major part* of the economic life of the leased asset; title may or may not eventually pass to the lessee.
4. The present value (PV), at the inception of the lease, of the minimum lease payments is at least equal to *substantially all* of the fair value of the leased asset, net of grants and tax credits to the lessor at that time; title may or may not eventually pass to the lessee.
5. The leased assets are of a specialized nature such that only the lessee can use them without major modifications being made.

Further indicators which suggest that a lease *might* be properly considered to be a finance lease are

6. If the lessee can cancel the lease, the lessor's losses associated with the cancellation are to be borne by the lessee.
7. Gains or losses resulting from the fluctuations in the fair value of the residual will accrue to the lessee.
8. The lessee has the ability to continue the lease for a supplemental term at a rent that is substantially lower than market rent (i.e., there is a bargain renewal option).

Thus, under IAS 17, an evaluation of all eight of the foregoing criteria would be required to properly assess whether there is sufficient evidence to conclude that a given arrangement should be accounted for as a finance lease. Of the eight criteria set forth in the standard, the first five are essentially determinative in nature; that is, meeting *any one* of these would normally result in concluding that a given arrangement is in fact a finance lease. The final three criteria, however, are more suggestive in nature, and the standard states that these could lead to classification as a finance lease.

The interest rate used to compute the present value should be the lessee's *incremental borrowing rate*, unless it is practicable to determine the rate *implicit* in the lease, in which case that implicit rate should be used. It is interesting to note that under US GAAP, in order to use the rate implicit in the lease to discount the minimum lease payments, this rate must be lower than the lessee's incremental borrowing rate. Logically, of course, if the lessee's incremental borrowing rate were lower than a rate offered implicitly in a lease, and the prospective lessee was aware of this fact, it would be more attractive to borrow and purchase, so the limitation under the US rule may be somewhat superfluous. IAS 17 does not set this as a condition, however.

In general, if a lease agreement meets one of the eight criteria set forth above, it is likely to be classified as a finance lease in the financial statements of the lessee. Prior to the most recent revisions to IAS 17, leases involving both land and buildings could only be considered finance leases if title were expected to transfer at the end of the lease term. However, the *Improvements Project* resulted in an amendment that revised IAS 17 regarding this issue. Separate analyses of the land and building components of the lease are now required, and capital treatment of the building lease component is not dependent on, nor does it require, the land portion of the lease being capitalized. If title to the land is not expected to transfer to the lessee (i.e., there is no automatic title transfer at lease termination, nor any bargain purchase option), the land component will be treated as an operating lease, which does not limit the accounting for the building component to also being an operating lease. (This conforms to the corresponding rule under US GAAP.)

The language used in the third and fourth lease accounting criteria, as set forth above, makes them rather subjective and somewhat difficult to apply in practice. Thus, given the same set of facts, it is possible for two reporting entities to reach different conclusions regarding the classification of a given lease. The IAS 17 approach differs from that adopted by the corresponding US standard, FAS 13, in that more subjective criteria are established under IFRS. Note, however, that both IASB and FASB are addressing lease accounting and may well promulgate a "converged" and more unambiguous set of requirements within the next several years.

The purpose of the third criterion is to define leases covering essentially all of the asset's useful life as being financing arrangements. Under the US standard, a clearly defined threshold of 75% of the useful life has been specified for classifying a lease as a finance lease, which thus creates a "bright line" test that can be applied mechanically. The corresponding language under IAS 17 stipulates that capitalization results when the lease covers a "major part of the economic life" of the asset. Reasonable persons obviously can debate whether "major part" implies a proportion lower than 75% (say, as little as 51%), or implies a higher proportion (such as 90%).

The fourth criterion defines what are essentially arrangements to fully compensate the lessor for the entire value of the leased property as financing arrangements. In contrast to US GAAP, this quantitative threshold is not provided under IFRS. A threshold, "the present value of minimum lease payments equaling at least 90% of leased asset fair value," is set under the US standard, while the corresponding language, "substantially all of the fair value of the leased asset," is employed under IFRS. Again, there is room for debate over whether "substantially all" implies a threshold lower than 90% or, less likely, an even higher one.

IAS 17 addresses the issue of change in lease classification resulting from alterations in lease terms, stating that if the parties agree to revise the terms of the lease, other than by means of renewing the lease, in a manner that would have resulted in a different classification of the lease had the changed terms been in effect at inception of the lease, then the revised lease is to be considered a new lease agreement.

Leases Involving Land and Buildings

IAS 17, addresses leases involving both land and buildings. In general, the accounting treatment of such leases is the same as for simple leases of other types of assets. As revised, the standard requires that leases for land and buildings be analyzed into their component parts, with each element separately accounted for, unless title to both elements is expected to pass to the lessee by the end of the lease term. It continues the operating lease treatment requirement for the land portion of the lease, unless title is expected to pass to the lessee by the end of the lease term, in which case finance lease treatment is warranted. The buildings element is to be classified as a finance or operating lease in accordance with IAS 17's provisions.

Under revised IAS 17, the minimum lease payments at the inception of a lease of land and buildings (including any up-front payments) are to be allocated between the land and the buildings elements in proportion to their relative fair values at the inception of the lease. In those circumstances where the lease payments cannot be allocated reliably between these two elements, the entire lease is to be classified as a finance lease, unless it is clear that both elements are operating leases.

Furthermore, the amendment to IAS 17 has specified that for a lease of land and buildings in which the value of the land element at the inception of the lease is immaterial, the land and buildings may be treated as a single unit for the purpose of lease classification, in which case the criteria set forth in IAS 17 will govern the classification as a finance or operating lease. If this is done, the economic life of the buildings is regarded as the economic life of the entire leased asset.

Additional guidance, drawn from US GAAP, and an example of accounting for a combined land and building lease, are presented in Appendix A.

Classification of Leases—Lessor

The lessor has the following alternatives in classifying a lease:

1. Operating lease
2. Finance lease

   a. Plain or regular finance lease, hereinafter referred to as *direct financing* lease, which is the term used by US GAAP
   b. Finance lease by manufacturers or dealers, hereinafter referred to as *sales-type* lease, the term used by US GAAP
   c. *Leveraged* lease, wherein financing is through a third-party creditor instead of the lessor

Consistent accounting by lessee and lessor. Since the events or transactions that take place between the lessor and the lessee are based on an agreement (the lease) that is common to both the parties, it is normally appropriate that the lease be classified in a consistent manner by both parties. Thus, if any one of the eight criteria specified above for classification of a finance lease by the lessee is met, the lease should also be classified as a finance lease by the lessor. If the lease qualifies as a finance lease from the standpoint of the lessor, it would be classified either as a sales-type lease, a direct financing lease, or a leveraged lease, depending on the conditions present at the inception of the lease. Of course, neither party to the lease can control whether the other applies proper accounting to the transaction.

Notwithstanding this general observation, IAS 17 alludes to an exception to this rule when it speaks about the "differing circumstances" sometimes resulting in the same lease being classified differently by the lessor and lessee. This could occur, for example, when the lessor benefits by having a third-party residual value guarantee in place. The standard does not elaborate on such circumstances, unfortunately, but once again it is possible to be informed by reference to US GAAP, which clearly sets forth the conditions or factors which, if not satisfied from the standpoint of the lessor, would lead to different classifications by the lessor and the lessee.

It may be instructive to note that US GAAP (FAS 13) stipulates that the following two conditions *both* need to be satisfied in addition to meeting any one of the criteria established for capitalization determination by the lessee, before a lease could be classified as a finance (capital) lease from the standpoint of a lessor:

1. Collectibility of the minimum lease payments is reasonably predictable.
2. No important uncertainties surround the amount of nonreimbursable costs yet to be incurred by the lessor under the lease.

Under US GAAP, therefore, if a lease transaction does not meet the criteria for classification as a sales-type lease, a direct financing lease, or a leveraged lease as specified above (by satisfying both of the above noted extra criteria), it is to be classified in the financial statements of the lessor as an operating lease. Accordingly, if the lessee has accounted for the lease as a capital lease, the asset being leased may appear in the statements of financial position of both lessee and lessor. This is an anomaly which may trouble some, but it is not actually a serious problem, since rarely will those using or relying on the financial statements of one party (lessor or lessee) also be relying on the financial statements of the other party.

Although guidance under IAS 17 does not establish additional conditions that must be fulfilled for the lessor to treat a lease as a financing transaction, as the US standard does, use of the "differing circumstances" language opens up the possibility that in any given situation, additional subjective considerations could be defined. This remains a matter for each reporting entity to address on an individual basis, however, inasmuch as interpretive guidance on this issue has not been forthcoming.

Distinction among Sales-Type, Direct Financing, and Leveraged Leases

A lease is classified as a sales-type lease when the criteria set forth above have been met and the lease transaction is structured such that the lessor (generally a manufacturer or dealer) recognizes a profit or loss on the transaction in addition to interest revenue. For this to occur, the fair value of the property, or if lower, the sum of the present values of the minimum lease payments and the estimated unguaranteed residual value, must differ from the cost (or carrying value, if different). The essential substance of this transaction is that of a sale, thus its name. Common examples of sales-type leases: (1) when an automobile dealership opts to lease a car to its customers in lieu of making an actual sale, and (2) the re-lease of equipment coming off an expiring lease.

A direct financing lease differs from a sales-type lease in that the lessor does not realize a profit or loss on the transaction other than the interest revenue to be earned over the lease term. In a direct financing lease, the fair value of the property at the inception of the lease is equal to the cost (or carrying value, if the property is not new). This type of lease transaction most often involves entities regularly engaged in financing operations. The lessor (usually a bank or other financial institution) purchases the asset and then leases the asset to the lessee. This mode of transaction is merely a replacement for the conventional lending transaction, where the borrower uses the borrowed funds to purchase the asset.

There are many economic reasons why a lease transaction may be considered. These include

1. The lessee (borrower) is often able to obtain 100% financing.
2. There may be tax benefits for the lessee, such as the ability to expense the asset over its lease term, instead of over a longer depreciable life.

3. The lessor receives the equivalent of interest as well as an asset with some remaining value at the end of the lease term (unless title transfers as a condition of the lease).
4. The lessee is protected from risk of obsolescence (although presumably this risk protection is priced into the lease terms).

In summary, it may help to visualize the following chart when considering the classification of a lease:

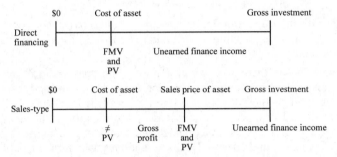

One specialized form of a direct financing lease is a *leveraged lease*. This type is mentioned separately both here and in the following section on how to account for leases because it is to receive a different accounting treatment by a lessor. A leveraged lease meets all the definitional criteria of a direct financing lease, but differs because it involves at least three parties: a lessee, a long-term creditor, and a lessor (commonly referred to as the equity participant). Other characteristics of a leveraged lease are as follows:

1. The financing provided by the long-term creditor must be without recourse as to the general credit of the lessor, although the creditor may hold recourse with respect to the leased property. The amount of the financing must provide the lessor with substantial leverage in the transaction.
2. The lessor's net investment declines during the early years and rises during the later years of the lease term before its elimination.

Accounting for Leases—Lessee

As discussed in the preceding section, there are two classifications under IAS 17 that apply to a lease transaction in the financial statements of the lessee. They are as follows:

1. Operating
2. Finance

Operating leases. The accounting treatment accorded an operating lease is relatively simple; rental expense should be charged to profit or loss as the payments are made or become payable. IAS 17 stipulates that rental expense be "recognized on a systematic basis that is representative of the time pattern of the user's benefits, even if the payments are not on that basis." In many cases, the lease payments are being made on a straight-line basis (i.e., equal payments per period over the lease term), and recognition of rental expense would normally also be on a straight-line basis.

However, even if the lease agreement calls for an alternative payment schedule or a scheduled rent increase over the lease term, the lease expense should still be recognized on a straight-line basis unless another systematic and rational basis is a better representation of actual physical use of the leased property. In such instances it will be necessary to create either a prepaid asset or a liability, depending on the structure of the payment schedule. In

SIC 15, it has been held that all incentives relating to a new or renewed operating lease are to be considered in determining the total cost of the lease, to be recognized on a straight-line basis over the term of the lease. Thus, for example, a rent holiday for six months, offered as part of a five-year lease commitment, would not result in the reporting of only six months' rent expense during the first full year. Rather, four and one-half years' rent would be allocated over the full five-year term, such that monthly expense would equal 90% (=54 months' payments/60-month term) of the stated monthly rental payments that begin after the holiday ends. This accounting method would apply to both lessor and lessee.

The accounting would differ if rental increases were directly tied to expanded space utilization, however, but not if related merely to the extent that the property were being used. For example, if the lease agreement provides for a scheduled increase(s) in contemplation of the lessee's increased (i.e., more intensive) physical use of the leased property (e.g., more sustained usage of machinery after an initial set-up period), the total amount of rental payments, including the scheduled increase(s), should be charged to expense over the lease term on a straight-line basis; the increased rent should not impact the accounting. On the other hand, if the scheduled increase(s) is due to additional leased property (e.g., expanding to adjacent space after two years), recognition should be proportional to the amount of leased property, with the increased rents recognized over the years that the lessee has control over the use of the additional leased property. (These suggestions, and many other recommendations made in this chapter, are based on guidance from US GAAP, since IFRS does not address these detailed implementation matters at the present time.) Scheduled increases could envision more than one of these events occurring, making the accounting more complex.

Notice that in the case of an operating lease there is no recognition in the statement of financial position of the leased asset because the substance of the lease is merely that of a rental. There is no reason to expect that the lessee will derive any future economic benefit from the leased asset beyond the lease term. There may, however, be a deferred charge or credit in the statement of financial position if the payment schedule under terms of the lease does not correspond with the expense recognition, as suggested in the preceding paragraph.

Finance leases. Assuming that the lease agreement satisfies one of the eight criteria set forth above (while recognizing that the last three of the eight are not absolutely determinative, but are instead merely suggestive or persuasive), it must be accounted for as a finance lease.

According to IAS 17, the lessee is to record a finance lease as an asset and an obligation (liability) at an amount equal to the lesser of (1) the fair value of the leased property at the inception of the lease, net of grants and tax credits receivable by the lessors, or (2) the present value of the minimum lease payments.

For purposes of this computation, the minimum lease payments are considered to be the payments that the lessee is obligated to make or can be required to make, excluding contingent rent and executory costs such as insurance, maintenance, and taxes. The minimum lease payments generally include the minimum rental payments, and any guarantee of the residual value made by the lessee or a party related to the lessee. If the lease includes a bargain purchase option (BPO), the amount required to be paid under the BPO is included in the minimum lease payments. The present value shall be computed using the incremental borrowing rate of the lessee unless it is practicable for the lessee to determine the implicit rate computed by the lessor, in which case it is to be employed, whether higher or lower than the incremental borrowing rate.

(Note that under US GAAP, an important exception is made when the FMV of the leased asset is lower than the PV of the minimum lease payments, but this is an exception that has not yet been considered under IAS 17. In such a case an implicit rate is computed through a series of trial-and-error calculations. This rule is entirely logical, since it is well established in GAAP that assets are not to be recorded at amounts greater than fair value or net realizable value at acquisition. This exception has been illustrated in a detailed case study that follows in Appendix A.)

The lease term to be used in the present value computation is the fixed, noncancelable term of the lease, plus any further terms for which the lessee has the option to continue to lease the asset, with or without further payment, provided that it is reasonably certain, as of the beginning of the lease, that lessee will exercise such a renewal option.

Depreciation of leased assets. The depreciation of the leased asset will depend on which criterion resulted in the lease being qualified as a finance lease. If the lease transaction met the criteria as either transferring ownership or containing a bargain purchase option, the asset arising from the transaction is to be depreciated over the estimated useful life of the leased property, which will, after all, be used by the lessee (most likely) after the lease term expires. If the transaction qualifies as a finance lease because it met either the criterion of encompassing the major part of the asset's economic life, or because the present value of the minimum lease payments represented substantially all of the fair value of the underlying asset, then it must be depreciated over the shorter of the lease term or the useful life of the leased property. The conceptual rationale for this differentiated treatment arises because of the substance of the transaction. Under the first two criteria, the asset actually becomes the property of the lessee at the end of the lease term (or on exercise of the BPO). In the latter situations, title to the property remains with the lessor.

Thus, the leased asset is to be depreciated (amortized) over the shorter of the lease term or its useful life if title does not transfer to the lessee, but when it is reasonably certain that the lessee will obtain ownership by the end of the lease term, the leased asset is to be depreciated over the asset's useful life. The manner in which depreciation is computed should be consistent with the lessee's normal depreciation policy for other depreciable assets owned by the lessee, recognizing depreciation on the basis set out in IAS 16. Therefore, the accounting treatment and method used to depreciate (amortize) the leased asset is very similar to that used for an owned asset. The leased asset should not be depreciated (amortized) below the estimated residual value.

In some instances when the property is to revert back to the lessor, there may be a guaranteed residual value. This is the value at lease termination that the lessee guarantees to the lessor. If the fair value of the asset at the end of the lease term is greater than or equal to the guaranteed residual amount, the lessee incurs no additional obligation. On the other hand, if the fair value of the leased asset is less than the guaranteed residual value, the lessee must make up the difference, usually with a cash payment. The guaranteed residual value is often used as a device to reduce the periodic payments by substituting the lump-sum amount at the end of the term that results from the guarantee. In any event the depreciation (amortization) must still be based on the estimated residual value. This results in a rational and systematic allocation of the expense through the periods and avoids having to recognize a disproportionately large expense (or loss) in the last period as a result of the guarantee.

The annual (periodic) rent payments made during the lease term are to be apportioned between the reduction in the obligation and the finance charge (interest expense) in a manner such that the finance charge (interest expense) represents a constant periodic rate of interest on the remaining balance of the lease obligation. This is commonly referred to as the *effective rate* interest method. However, it is to be noted that IAS 17 also recognizes that an approximation of this pattern can be made, as an alternative. The effective rate method, which is used in many other applications, such as mortgage amortization, is almost universally understood, and therefore should be applied in virtually all cases.

At the inception of the lease the asset and the liability relating to the future rental obligation are reported in the statement of financial position of the lessee at the same amounts. However, since the depreciation charge for use of the leased asset and the finance expense during the lease term differ due to different policies being used to recognize them, as explained above, it is likely that the asset and related liability balances would not be equal in amount after inception of the lease.

The following examples illustrate the treatment described in the foregoing paragraphs:

Example of accounting for a finance lease—asset returned to lessor at termination

Assume the following:

1. The lease is initiated on January 1, 2009, for equipment with an expected useful life of three years. The equipment reverts back to the lessor on expiration of the lease agreement.
2. The FMV of the equipment is €135,000.
3. Three payments are due to the lessor in the amount of €50,000 per year beginning December 31, 2009. An additional sum of €1,000 is to be paid annually by the lessee for insurance.
4. Lessee guarantees a €10,000 residual value on December 31, 2011, to the lessor.
5. Irrespective of the €10,000 residual value guarantee, the leased asset is expected to have only a €1,000 salvage value on December 31, 2011.
6. The lessee's incremental borrowing rate is 10% (lessor's implicit rate is unknown).
7. The present value of the lease obligation is as follows:

PV of guaranteed residual value	=	€10,000 × 0.7513*	=	€ 7,513
PV of annual payments	=	€50,000 × 2.4869**	=	124,345
				€131,858

* *The present value of an amount of €1 due in three periods at 10% is 0.7513.*
** *The present value of an ordinary annuity of €1 for three periods at 10% is 2.4869.*

The first step in accounting for any lease transaction is to classify the lease. In this case, the lease term is for three years, which is equal to 100% of the expected useful life of the asset. Notice that the test of fair value versus present value is also fulfilled, as the PV of the minimum lease payments (€131,858) could easily be considered as being equal to substantially all the FMV (€135,000), being equal to 97.7% of the FMV. Thus, this lease should be accounted for as a finance lease.

In assumption 7 above the present value of the lease obligation is computed. Note that the executory costs (insurance) are not included in the minimum lease payments and that the incremental borrowing rate of the lessee was used to determine the present value. This rate was used because the implicit rate was not determinable.

NOTE: To have used the implicit rate it would have to have been known to the lessee.

The entry necessary to record the lease on January 1, 2009, is

Leased equipment	131,858	
Lease obligation		131,858

Note that the lease is recorded at the present value of the minimum lease payments, which in this case is less than the fair value. If the present value of the minimum lease payments had exceeded the fair value, the lease would be recorded at fair value, as defined under IAS 36, dealing with impairment of long-lived assets.

The next step is to determine the proper allocation between interest and a reduction in the lease obligation for each lease payment. This is done using the effective interest method as illustrated below.

Year	Cash payment	Interest expense	Reduction in lease obligation	Balance of lease obligation
Inception of lease				€131,858
1	€50,000	€13,186	€36,814	95,044
2	50,000	9,504	40,496	54,548
3	50,000	5,452	44,548	10,000

The interest is calculated at 10% (the incremental borrowing rate) of the balance of the lease obligation for each period, and the remainder of the €50,000 payment is allocated to a reduction in the lease obligation. The lessee is also required to pay €1,000 for insurance on an annual basis. The entries necessary to record all payments relative to the lease for each of the three years are shown below.

	December 31, 2009		December 31, 2010		December 31, 2011	
Insurance expense	1,000		1,000		1,000	
Interest expense	13,186		9,504		5,452	
Lease obligation	36,184		40,496		44,548	
Cash		51,000		51,000		51,000

The leased equipment recorded as an asset must also be amortized (depreciated). The balance of this account is €131,858; however, as with any other asset, it cannot be depreciated below the estimated residual value of €1,000 (note that it is depreciated down to the actual estimated residual value, *not* the guaranteed residual value). In this case, the straight-line depreciation method is applied over a period of three years. This three-year period represents the lease term, *not* the life of the asset, because the asset reverts back to the lessor at the end of the lease term. Therefore, the following entry will be made at the end of each year:

Depreciation expense	43,619	
Accumulated depreciation		43,619 [(€131,858 – €1,000) ÷ 3]

Finally, on December 31, 2011, we must recognize the fact that ownership of the property has reverted back to the owner (lessor). The lessee made a guarantee that the residual value would be €10,000 on December 31, 2011; as a result, the lessee must make up the difference between the guaranteed residual value and the actual residual value with a cash payment to the lessor. The following entry illustrates the removal of the leased asset and obligation from the books of the lessee:

Lease obligation	10,000	
Accumulated depreciation	130,858	
Cash		9,000
Leased equipment		131,858

The foregoing example illustrated a situation where the asset was to be returned to the lessor. Another situation exists (where there is a bargain purchase option or automatic transfer of title) where the asset is expected to remain with the lessee. Recall that, under IAS 17, leased assets are amortized over their useful life when title transfers or a bargain purchase option exists. In such a circumstance, the lease liability will not be amortized completely as of the termination date, in many cases. At the end of the lease, the balance of the lease obligation should equal the guaranteed residual value, the bargain purchase option price, or a termination penalty.

Example of accounting for a finance lease—asset ownership transferred to lessee *and* fair market value of leased asset lower than present value of minimum lease payments

Assume the following:

1. A three-year lease is initiated on January 1, 2009, for equipment with an expected useful life of five years.
2. Three annual lease payments of €52,000 are required beginning on January 1, 2009, (note that the payment at the beginning of the year changes the PV computation). The lessor pays €2,000 per year for insurance on the equipment.

3. The lessee can exercise a bargain purchase option on December 31, 2011, for €10,000. The expected residual value at December 31, 2013, is €1,000.
4. The lessee's incremental borrowing rate is 10% (lessor's implicit rate is unknown).
5. The fair market value of the property leased is €140,000.

Once again, the classification of the lease must take place prior to the accounting for it. This lease is classified as a finance lease because it contains a bargain purchase option (BPO). Note that in this case, the PV versus FMV test is also clearly fulfilled.

The PV of the lease obligation is computed as follows:

PV of bargain purchase option	=	€10,000	×	0.7513*	=	€ 7,513
PV of annual payments	=	(€52,000 – €2,000)	×	2.7355**	=	136,755
						€144,288

* *The present value of an amount of €1 due in three periods at 10% is 0.7513.*
** *The present value of an annuity due of €1 for three periods at 10% is 2.7355.*

Notice that in the example above, the present value of the lease obligation is greater than the fair value of the asset. Also notice that since the lessor pays €2,000 a year for insurance, this payment is treated as executory costs and hence excluded from calculation of the present value of annual payments. In conclusion, since the PV is greater than the fair value, the lease obligation (as well as the leased asset) must be recorded at the fair value of the asset leased (being the lower of the two). The entry on January 1, 2009, is as follows:

Leased equipment	140,000	
Obligation under finance lease		140,000

According to IAS 17, the apportionment between interest and principal is to be such that interest recognized reflects the use of a constant periodic rate of interest applied to the remaining balance of the obligation. As noted above, a special rule applies under US GAAP (which are illustrated here) when the present value of the minimum lease payments exceeds the fair value of the leased asset (i.e., when the asset is impaired) at lease inception. When the PV exceeds the fair value of the leased asset, a new, effective rate must be computed through a series of trial-and-error calculations. (Note, however, that an impairment after the inception date would be recognized as expense in the period of the impairment, following the procedures set forth in IAS 36, and this would not affect the recorded amount of the lease obligation (i.e., the liability) and thus would not alter the initially determined interest rate. In this example, the interest rate was determined to be 13.265%. The amortization of the lease takes place as follows:

Year	Cash payment	Interest expense	Reduction in lease obligation	Balance of lease obligation
Inception of lease				€140,000
January 1, 2009	€50,000	€ --	€50,000	90,000
January 1, 2010	50,000	11,939	38,061	51,939
January 1, 2011	50,000	6,890	43,110	8,829
December 31, 2011	10,000	1,171	8,829	--

The following entries are required in years 2009 through 2011 to recognize the payment and depreciation (amortization).

		2009		2010		2011	
January 1	Operating expense	2,000		2,000		2,000	
	Obligation under finance lease	50,000		38,061		43,110	
	Accrued interest payable			11,939		6,890	
	Cash		52,000		52,000		52,000
December 31	Interest expense	11,939		6,890		1,171	
	Accrued interest payable		11,939		6,890		
	Obligation under finance lease						1,171
December 31	Depreciation expense	27,800		27,800		27,800	
	Accumulated depreciation		27,800		27,800		27,800
	(€139,000, five years)						

		2009	2010	2011
December 31	Obligation under finance lease			10,000
	Cash			10,000

Impairment of leased asset. IAS 17 did not originally address the issue of how impairments of leased assets are to be assessed or, if determined to have occurred, how they would need to be accounted for. Subsequently, IAS 17 was revised to note that the provisions of IAS 36 should be applied to leased assets in the same manner as they would be applied to owned assets. Impairments to the leased asset (occurring after the inception of the lease) are recognized by charges to expense in the current reporting period. IAS 36 is discussed more fully in Chapter 8.

Accounting for Leases—Lessor

As illustrated above, there are four classifications of leases with which a lessor must be concerned.

1. Operating
2. Sales-type
3. Direct financing
4. Leveraged

Operating leases. As is the case for the lessee, the operating lease requires a less complex accounting treatment than does a finance lease. The payments received by the lessor are to be recorded as rent income in the period in which the payment is received or becomes receivable. As with the lessee, if the rentals vary from a straight-line basis, or if the lease agreement contains a scheduled rent increase over the lease term, the revenue is nonetheless to be recognized on a straight-line basis unless an alternative basis of systematic and rational allocation is more representative of the time pattern of earning process contained in the lease.

Additionally, if the lease agreement provides for a scheduled increase(s) in contemplation of the lessee's increased (i.e., more intensive) physical use of the leased property, the total amount of rental payments, including the scheduled increase(s), is allocated to revenue over the lease term on a straight-line basis. However, if the scheduled increase(s) is due to additional leased property (e.g., larger space, more machines), recognition should be proportional to the leased property, with the increased rents recognized over the years that the lessee has control over use of the additional leased property.

The lessor must report the leased property in the statement of financial position under the caption "Investment in leased property." This account should be displayed with or near the property, plant, and equipment owned by the lessor, and depreciation should be determined in the same manner as for the rest of the lessor's owned property, plant, and equipment. IAS 17 stipulates that "when a significant portion of the lessor's business comprises operating leases, the lessor should disclose the amount of assets by each major class of asset together with the related accumulated depreciation at the end of each reporting period." Further, "assets held for operating are usually included as property, plant, and equipment in the statement of financial position."

Previously, lessors under operating leases were given the choice of either amortizing initial direct costs over the term of the lease or expensing such costs immediately. Under amended IAS 17, however, this choice was eliminated, and now all initial direct costs incurred must be added to the carrying amount of the leased asset and recognized as an expense over the lease term on the same basis as the lease income. Initial direct costs are incurred by lessors in negotiating and arranging an operating lease, and may include commissions, legal fees, and those internal costs that are actually incremental (i.e., would not exist if the lease were not being negotiated) and directly attributable to negotiating and arranging the lease.

Although there is no guidance on this matter under IFRS, logically any incentives granted by the lessor to the lessee are to be treated as reductions of rent and recognized on a straight-line basis over the term of the lease. This is also the position taken under US GAAP.

Depreciation of leased assets should be on a basis consistent with the lessor's normal depreciation policy for similar assets, and the depreciation expense should be computed on the basis set out in IAS 16.

Finance leases. The accounting by the lessor for finance leases depends on which variant of finance lease is at issue. In sales-type leases, an initial profit, analogous to that earned by a manufacturer or dealer, is recognized, whereas a direct financing lease does not give rise to an initial recognition of profit.

Sales-type leases. In the accounting for a sales-type lease, it is necessary for the lessor to determine the following amounts:

1. Gross investment
2. Fair value of the leased asset
3. Cost

From these amounts, the remainder of the computations necessary to record and account for the lease transaction can be made. The first objective is to determine the numbers necessary to complete the following entry:

Lease receivable	xx	
Cost of goods sold	xx	
Sales		xx
Inventory		xx
Unearned finance income		xx

The gross investment (lease receivable) of the lessor is equal to the sum of the minimum lease payments (excluding contingent rent and executory costs) from the standpoint of the lessor, plus the nonguaranteed residual value accruing to the lessor. The difference between the gross investment and the present value of the two components of gross investment (i.e., minimum lease payments and nonguaranteed residual value) is recorded as "unearned finance income" (also referred to as "unearned interest revenue"). The present value is to be computed using the lease term and implicit interest rate (both of which were discussed earlier).

IAS 17 stipulates that the resulting unearned finance income is to be amortized and recognized into income using the effective rate (or yield) interest method, which will result in a constant periodic rate of return on the "lessor's net investment" (which is computed as the "lessor's gross investment" less the "unearned finance income"). A choice of amortization approaches was offered under the original standard, but the selection of options has since been eliminated, so that the constant effective rate on book (carrying) value is now the only acceptable method of income recognition.

Consideration of "prudence" is called for by IAS 17 in recognizing finance income, which is in any event an underlying, qualitative characteristic or attribute of financial statements prepared under the IAS. The IASB's *Framework* makes it incumbent on financial statement preparers to exercise prudence. In other words, it requires caution in the exercise of judgment. IAS 17 clarifies this in the context of spreading income on a systematic basis, by giving the example of recognition of uncertainties relative to collectibility of lease rentals or to fluctuation of interest rates in the future. For instance, the uncertainties surrounding collectibility of lease rentals usually increase with the lease term (i.e., the longer the lease term, the greater are the risks involved), and thus in keeping with the principle of prudence, modification of the pattern of income recognition may be required to compensate.

For example, a lessor may decide to delay the recognition of finance income into the later years in the case of leases with terms spread over twenty years and above, as opposed to short-term leases with terms of three to five years, since predicting with certainty long-term collectibility, which depends on a number of factors such as the future financial position of the lessee, is a very difficult task. Effectively, more of the earlier collections might be seen as returns on investment, rather than income, until longer-term viability has been demonstrated.

Recall that the fair value of the leased property is by definition equal to the normal selling price of the asset adjusted by any residual amount retained (including any unguaranteed residual value, investment credit, etc.). According to IAS 17, the selling price to be used for a sales-type lease is equal to the fair value of the leased asset, or if lower, the sum of the present values of the MLP and the estimated unguaranteed residual value accruing to the lessor, discounted at a commercial rate of interest. In other words, the normal selling price less the present value of the unguaranteed residual value is equal to the present value of the MLP. (Note that this relationship is sometimes used while computing the MLP when the normal selling price and the residual value are known; this is illustrated in a case study that follows.)

Under IAS 17, initial direct costs incurred in connection with a sales-type lease (i.e., where the lessor is a manufacturer or dealer) must be expensed as incurred. This is a reasonable requirement, since these costs offset some of the profit recognized at inception, as do other selling expenses. Thus, the costs recognized at the inception of such lease arrangements would include the carrying value of the equipment or other items being leased, as well as incidental costs of negotiating and executing the lease. The profit recognized at inception would be the gross profit on the sale of the leased asset, less all operating costs, including the initial direct costs of creating the lease arrangement.

The estimated unguaranteed residual values used in computing the lessor's gross investment in a lease should be reviewed regularly. In case of a permanent reduction (impairment) in the estimated unguaranteed residual value, the income allocation over the lease term is revised and any reduction with respect to amounts already accrued is recognized immediately.

To attract customers, manufacturer or dealer lessors sometimes quote artificially low rates of interest. This has a direct impact on the recognition of initial profit, which is an integral part of the transaction and is inversely proportional to the finance income to be generated by it. Thus, if finance income is artificially low, this results in recognition of excessive profit from the transaction at the time of the sale. Under such circumstances, the standard requires that the profit recognized at inception, analogous to a cash sale of the leased asset, be restricted to that which would have resulted had a commercial rate of interest been used in the deal. Thus, the substance, not the form, of the transaction should be reflected in the financial statements. (The present value of the scheduled lease payments, discounted at the appropriate commercial rate, must be computed to derive the effective selling price of the leased asset under these circumstances. See Appendix D to Chapter 1 for a discussion of present value calculations.)

The difference between the selling price and the amount computed as the cost of goods sold is the gross profit recognized by the lessor on the inception of the lease (sale). Manufacturer or dealer lessors often give an option to their customers of either leasing the asset (with financing provided by them) or buying the asset outright. Thus, a finance lease by a manufacturer or dealer lessor, also referred to as a sales-type lease, generates two types of revenue for the lessor.

1. The gross profit (or loss) on the sale, which is equivalent to the profit (or loss) that would have resulted from an outright sale at normal selling prices, adjusted if necessary for a noncommercial rate of interest.

2. The finance income or interest earned on the lease receivable to be spread over the lease term based on a pattern reflecting a constant periodic rate of return on either the lessor's net investment outstanding or the net cash investment outstanding in respect of the finance lease.

The application of these points is illustrated in the example below.

Example of accounting for a sales-type lease

XYZ Inc. is a manufacturer of specialized equipment. Many of its customers do not have the necessary funds or financing available for outright purchase. Because of this, XYZ offers a leasing alternative. The data relative to a typical lease are as follows:

1. The noncancelable fixed portion of the lease term is five years. The lessor has the option to renew the lease for an additional three years at the same rental. The estimated useful life of the asset is ten years. Lessee guarantees a residual value of €40,000 at the end of five years, but the guarantee lapses if the full three renewal periods are exercised.

2. The lessor is to receive equal annual payments over the term of the lease. The leased property reverts back to the lessor on termination of the lease.

3. The lease is initiated on January 1, 2009. Payments are due on December 31 for the duration of the lease term.

4. The cost of the equipment to XYZ Inc. is €100,000. The lessor incurs cost associated with the inception of the lease in the amount of €2,500.

5. The selling price of the equipment for an outright purchase is €150,000.

6. The equipment is expected to have a residual value of €15,000 at the end of five years and €10,000 at the end of eight years.

7. The lessor desires a return of 12% (the implicit rate).

The first step is to calculate the annual payment due to the lessor. Recall that the present value (PV) of the minimum lease payments is equal to the selling price adjusted for the present value of the residual amount. The present value is to be computed using the implicit interest rate and the lease term. In this case, the implicit rate is given as 12% and the lease term is 8 years (which includes the fixed noncancelable portion plus the renewal period, since the lessee guarantee terms make renewal virtually inevitable). Thus, the structure of the computation would be as follows:

Normal selling price – PV of residual value = PV of minimum lease payment

Or, in this case,

€150,000	–	(0.40388* × €10,000)	=	4.96764** × Minimum lease payment
€145,961.20	÷	4.96764	=	Minimum lease payment
		€29,382.40	=	Minimum lease payment

* *0.40388 is the present value of an amount of €1 due in eight periods at a 12% interest rate.*
** *4.96764 is the present value of an annuity of €1 for eight periods at a 12% interest rate.*

Prior to examining the accounting implications of a lease, we must determine the lease classification. In this example, the lease term is eight years (discussed above) while the estimated useful life of the asset is 10 years; thus this lease qualifies as something other than an operating lease. (Note that it also meets the FMV versus PV criterion because the PV of the minimum lease payments of €145,961.20, which is 97% of the FMV [€150,000], could be considered to be equal to substantially all of the fair value of the leased asset.) Now it must be determined if this is a sales-type, direct financing, or leveraged lease. To do this, examine the FMV or selling price of the asset and compare it to the cost. Because the two are not equal, we can determine this to be a sales-type lease.

Next, obtain the figures necessary to record the entry on the books of the lessor. The gross investment is the total minimum lease payments plus the unguaranteed residual value, or

$$(€29,382.40 × 8) + €10,000 = €245,059.20$$

The cost of goods sold is the historical cost of the inventory (€100,000) plus any initial direct costs (€2,500) less the PV of the unguaranteed residual value (€10,000 × 0.40388). Thus, the cost of goods sold amount is €98,461.20 (€100,000 + €2,500 − €4,038.80). Note that the initial direct costs will require a credit entry to some account, usually accounts payable or cash. The inventory account is credited for the carrying value of the asset, in this case €100,000.

The adjusted selling price is equal to the PV of the minimum payments, or €145,961.20. Finally, the unearned finance income is equal to the gross investment (i.e., lease receivable) less the present value of the components making up the gross investment (the minimum lease payment of €29,382.40 and the unguaranteed residual of €10,000). The present value of these items is €150,000 [(€29,382.40 × 4.96764) + (€10,000 × 0.40388)]. Therefore, the entry necessary to record the lease is

Lease receivable	245,059.20	
Cost of goods sold	98,461.20	
Inventory		100,000.00
Sales		145,961.20
Unearned finance income		95,059.20
Accounts payable (initial direct costs)		2,500.00

The next step in accounting for a sales-type lease is to determine proper handling of the payment. Both principal and interest are included in each payment. According to IAS 17, interest is recognized on a basis such that a constant periodic rate of return is earned over the term of the lease. This will require setting up an amortization schedule as illustrated below.

Date or year ended	Cash payment	Interest	Reduction in principal	Balance of net investment
January 1, 2009				€150,000.00
December 31, 2009	€ 29,382.40	€18,000.00	€ 11,382.40	138,617.00
December 31, 2010	29,382.40	16,634.11	12,748.29	125,869.31
December 31, 2011	29,382.40	15,104.32	14,278.08	111,591.23
December 31, 2012	29,382.40	13,390.95	15,991.45	95,599.78
December 31, 2013	29,382.40	11,471.97	17,910.43	77,689.35
December 31, 2014	29,382.40	9,322.72	20,059.68	57,629.67
December 31, 2015	29,382.40	6,915.56	22,466.84	35,162.83
December 31, 2016	29,382.40	4,219.57	25,162.83	10,000.00
	€235,059.20	€95,059.20	€140,000.00	

A few of the columns need to be elaborated on. First, the net investment is the gross investment (lease receivable) less the unearned finance income. Notice that at the end of the lease term, the net investment is equal to the estimated residual value. Also note that the total interest earned over the lease term is equal to the unearned interest (unearned finance income) at the beginning of the lease term.

The entries below illustrate the proper treatment to record the receipt of the lease payment and the amortization of the unearned finance income in the year ended December 31, 2009.

Cash	29,382.40	
Lease receivable		29,382.40
Unearned finance income	18,000.00	
Interest revenue		18,000.00

Notice that there is no explicit entry to recognize the principal reduction. This is done automatically when the net investment is reduced by decreasing the lease receivable (gross investment) by €29,382.40 and the unearned finance income account by only €18,000. The €18,000 is 12% (implicit rate) of the net investment. These entries are to be made over the life of the lease.

At the end of the lease term, December 31, 2016, the asset is returned to the lessor and the following entry is required:

Asset	10,000	
Leased receivable		10,000

If the estimated residual value has changed during the lease term, the accounting computations would have also changed to reflect this.

Direct financing leases. The accounting for a direct financing lease exhibits many similarities to that for a sales-type lease. Of particular importance is that the terminology used is much the same; however, the treatment accorded these items varies greatly. Again, it is best to preface the discussion by determining the objectives in the accounting for a direct financing lease. Once the lease has been classified, it must be recorded. To do this, the following amounts must be determined:

1. Gross investment
2. Cost
3. Residual value

As noted, a direct financing lease generally involves a leasing company or other financial institution and results in only interest revenue being earned by the lessor. This is because the FMV (selling price) and the cost are equal, and therefore no dealer profit is recognized on the actual lease transaction. Note how this is different from a sales-type lease, which involves both a profit on the transaction and interest revenue over the lease term. The reason for this difference is derived from the conceptual nature underlying the purpose of the lease transaction. In a sales-type lease, the manufacturer (distributor, dealer, etc.) is seeking an alternative means to finance the sale of his product, whereas a direct financing lease is a result of the consumer's need to finance an equipment purchase. Because the consumer is unable to obtain conventional financing, he or she turns to a leasing company that will purchase the desired asset and then lease it to the consumer. Here the profit on the transaction remains with the manufacturer while the interest revenue is earned by the leasing company.

Like a sales-type lease, the first objective is to determine the amounts necessary to complete the following entry:

Lease receivable	xxx	
Asset		xxx
Unearned finance income		xxx

The gross investment is still defined as the minimum amount of lease payments (from the standpoint of a lessor) exclusive of any executory costs, plus the unguaranteed residual value. The difference between the gross investment as determined above and the cost (carrying value) of the asset is to be recorded as the unearned finance income because there is no manufacturer's/dealer's profit earned on the transaction. The following entry would be made to record initial direct costs:

Initial direct costs	xx	
Cash		xx

Under IAS 17, the net investment in the lease is defined as the gross investment less the unearned income plus the unamortized initial direct costs related to the lease. Initial direct costs are incremental costs that are directly attributable to negotiating and arranging a lease, except for such costs incurred by manufacturer or dealer lessors. Originally, initial direct costs could optionally either be amortized over the lease term, or charged to expense immediately. Revisions made to IAS 17, effective 2005, eliminated the choice of how a lessor accounts for initial direct costs incurred in negotiating a lease, and it is now a requirement that costs that are incremental and directly attributable to the lease are to be capitalized and allocated over the lease term.

Employing initial direct cost capitalization, the unearned lease (i.e., interest) income and the initial direct costs will be amortized to income over the lease term so that a constant periodic rate is earned either on the lessor's net investment outstanding or on the net cash investment outstanding in the finance lease (i.e., the balance of the cash outflows and inflows in respect of the lease, excluding any executory costs that are chargeable to the lessee). Thus, the effect of the initial direct costs is to reduce the implicit interest rate or, yield, to the lessor over the life of the lease.

An example follows that illustrates the preceding principles.

Example of accounting for a direct financing lease

Emirates Refining needs new equipment to expand its manufacturing operation; however, it does not have sufficient capital to purchase the asset at this time. Because of this, Emirates Refining has employed Consolidated Leasing to purchase the asset. In turn, Emirates will lease the asset from Consolidated. The following information applies to the terms of the lease:

1. A three-year lease is initiated on January 1, 2009, for equipment costing €131,858, with an expected useful life of five years. FMV at January 1, 2009, of equipment is €131,858.
2. Three annual payments are due to the lessor beginning December 31, 2009. The property reverts back to the lessor on termination of the lease.
3. The unguaranteed residual value at the end of year three is estimated to be €10,000.
4. The annual payments are calculated to give the lessor a 10% return (the implicit rate).
5. The lease payments and unguaranteed residual value have a PV equal to €131,858 (FMV of asset) at the stipulated discount rate.
6. The annual payment to the lessor is computed as follows:

PV of residual value	=	€10,000 × .7513* = €7,513
PV of lease payments	=	Selling price – PV of residual value
	=	€131,858 – €7,513 = €124,345
Annual payment	=	€124,345 ÷ 2.4869** = €50,000

   * *.7513 is the PV of an amount due in three periods at 10%.*
   ** *2.4869 is the PV of an ordinary annuity of €1 per period for three periods, at 10% interest.*

7. Initial direct costs of €7,500 are incurred by ABC in the lease transaction.

As with any lease transaction, the first step must be to classify the lease appropriately. In this case, the PV of the lease payments (€124,345) is equal to 94% of the FMV (€131,858), thus could be considered as equal to substantially all of the FMV of the leased asset. Next, the unearned interest and the net investment in lease are to be determined.

Gross investment in lease [(3 × €50,000) + €10,000]	€160,000
Cost of leased property	131,858
Unearned finance income	€ 28,142

The unamortized initial direct costs are to be added to the gross investment in the lease, and the unearned finance income is to be deducted to arrive at the net investment in the lease. The net investment in the lease for this example is determined as follows:

Gross investment in lease	€160,000
Add:	
Unamortized initial direct costs	7,500
Less:	
Unearned finance income	28,142
Net investment in lease	€139,358

The net investment in the lease (Gross investment – Unearned finance income) has been increased by the amount of initial direct costs. Therefore, the implicit rate is no longer 10%, and the implicit rate must be recomputed, which is the result of performing an internal rate of return calculation. The lease payments are to be €50,000 per annum and a residual value of €10,000 is available at the end of the lease term. In return for these payments (inflows), the lessor is giving up equipment (an outflow) and incurring initial direct costs (also an outflow), with a net investment of €139,358 (€131,858 + €7,500). The way to obtain the new implicit rate is through a trial-

and-error calculation as set up below (or employ a calculator or computer routine that does this iterative computation automatically).

$$\frac{50,000}{(1+i)} \; 1 + \; \frac{50,000}{(1+i)} \; 2 + \; \frac{50,000}{(1+i)} \; 3 + \; \frac{10,000}{(1+i)} \; 3 = €139,358$$

Where: i = implicit rate of interest

In this case, the implicit rate is equal to 7.008%. Thus, the amortization table would be set up as follows:

	(a) Lease payments	(b) Reduction in unearned Interest	(c) PV x Implicit rate (7.008%)	(d) Reduction in initial direct costs (b-c)	(e) Reduction in PVI net in- vestment (a-b + d)	(f) PVI net investment in lease $(f)_{(n+1)} = (f)_n - (e)$
At inception						€139,358
2008	€ 50,000	€13,186 (1)	€ 9,766	€3,420	€ 40,234	99,124
2009	50,000	9,504 (2)	6,947	2,557	43,053	56,071
2010	50,000	5,455 (3)	3,929	1,526	46,071	10,000
	€150,000	€28,145*	€20,642	€7,503	€129,358	

Rounded

(b.1) €131,858 × 10% = €13,186
(b.2) [€131,858 − (€50,000 − 13,186)] × 10% = €9,504
(b.3) [€95,044 − (€50,000 − 9,504)] × 10% = €5,455

Here the interest is computed as 7.008% of the net investment. Note again that the net investment at the end of the lease term is equal to the estimated residual value.

The entry made initially to record the lease is as follows:

Lease receivable** [(€50,000 × 3) + €10,000]	160,000	
Asset acquired for leasing		131,858
Unearned lease revenue		28,142

When the payment (or obligation to pay) of the initial direct costs occurs, the following entry must be made:

Initial direct costs	7,500	
Cash		7,500

Using the schedule above, the following entries would be made during each of the indicated years:

	2009		2010		2011	
Cash	50,000		50,000		50,000	
Lease receivable**		50,000		50,000		50,000
Unearned finance income	13,186		9,504		5,455	
Initial direct costs		3,420		2,557		1,526
Interest income		9,766		6,947		3,929

Finally, when the asset is returned to the lessor at the end of the lease term, it must be recorded on the books. The necessary entry is as follows:

Used asset	10,000	
Lease receivable**		10,000

**Also commonly referred to as the "gross investment in lease."*

Leveraged leases. Leveraged leases are discussed in detail in Appendix B of this chapter because of the complexity involved in the accounting treatment based on guidance available under US GAAP, where this topic has been given extensive coverage. Under IFRS, this concept has been defined, but with only a very brief outline of the treatment to be accorded to this kind of lease. A leveraged lease is defined in IAS 17 as a finance lease which is structured such that there are at least three parties involved: the lessee, the lessor, and one or more long-term creditors who provide part of the acquisition finance for the leased asset, usually without any general recourse to the lessor. Succinctly, this type of a lease is given the following unique accounting treatment:

1. The lessor records his or her investment in the lease net of the nonrecourse debt and the related finance costs to the third-party creditor(s).
2. The recognition of the finance income is based on the lessor's net cash investment outstanding in respect of the lease.

Sale-Leaseback Transactions

Sale-leaseback describes a transaction where the owner of property (the seller-lessee) sells the property and then immediately leases all or part of it back from the new owner (the buyer-lessor). These transactions may occur when the seller-lessee is experiencing cash flow or financing problems or because there are tax advantages in such an arrangement in the lessee's tax jurisdiction. The important consideration in this type of transaction is recognition of two separate and distinct economic transactions. However, it is important to note that there is not a physical transfer of property. First, there is a sale of property, and second, there is a lease agreement for the same property in which the original seller is the lessee and the original buyer is the lessor. This is illustrated as follows:

A sale-leaseback transaction is usually structured such that the sales price of the asset is greater than or equal to the current market value. The higher sales price has the concomitant effect of a higher periodic rental payment over the lease term than would otherwise have been negotiated. The transaction is usually attractive because of the tax benefits associated with it, and because it provides financing to the lessee. The seller-lessee benefits from the higher price because of the increased gain on the sale of the property and the deductibility of the lease payments, which are usually larger than the depreciation that was previously being taken. The buyer-lessor benefits from both the higher rental payments and the larger depreciable basis.

Under IAS 17, the accounting treatment depends on whether the leaseback results in a finance lease or an operating lease. If it results in a finance lease, any excess of sale proceeds over previous carrying value may not be recognized immediately as income in the financial statements of the seller-lessee. Rather, it is to be deferred and amortized over the lease term.

Accounting for a sale-leaseback that involves the creation of an operating lease depends on whether the sale portion of the compound transaction was on arm's-length terms. If the leaseback results in an operating lease, and it is evident that the transaction is established at fair value, then any profit or loss should be recognized immediately. On the other hand, if the sale price is *not* established at fair value, then

a. If sale price is *below* fair value, any profit or loss should be recognized immediately, except that when a loss is to be compensated by below fair market future rentals, the loss should be deferred and amortized in proportion to the rental payments over the period the asset is expected to be used.
b. If the sale price is *above* fair value, the excess over fair value should be deferred and amortized over the period for which the asset is expected to be used.

IAS 17 stipulates that, in case of operating leasebacks, if at the date of the sale and leaseback transaction the fair value is less than the carrying amount of the leased asset, the difference between the fair value and the carrying amount should immediately be recognized. In other words, impairment is recognized first, before the actual sale-leaseback transaction is given recognition.   This logically follows from the fact that impairments are essentially catch-up depreciation charges, belated recognition that the consumption of the utility of the assets had not been correctly recognized in earlier periods.

However, in case the sale and leaseback result in a finance lease, no such adjustment is considered necessary unless there has been an impairment in value, in which case the carrying value should be reduced to the recoverable amount in accordance with the provisions of IAS 36.

The guidance under IFRS pertaining to sale-leaseback transactions is limited, and many variations in terms and conditions are found in actual practice. To provide further insight, albeit not with the suggestion that this constitutes IFRS, selected guidance found under US GAAP is offered in Appendix A to this chapter.

Other leasing guidance. SIC 27 addresses arrangements between an enterprise and an investor that involve the legal form of a lease. SIC 27 establishes that the accounting for such arrangements is in all instances to reflect the substance of the relationship. All aspects of the arrangement are to be evaluated to determine its substance, with particular emphasis on those that have an economic effect. To assist in doing this, SIC 27 identifies certain indicators that may demonstrate that an arrangement might not involve a lease under IAS 17. For example, a series of linked transactions that in substance do not transfer control over the asset, and which keep the right to receive the benefits of ownership with the transferor, would not be a lease. Also, transactions arranged for specific objectives, such as the transfer of tax attributes, would generally not be accounted for as leases.

SIC 27 deals most specifically with those arrangements that have characteristics of leases coupled with corollary subleases, whereby the lessor is the sublessee and the lessee is the sublessor, which may also involve a purchase option. The financing party (the lessee-sublessor) is often guaranteed a certain economic return on such transactions, further revealing that the substance might in fact be that of a secured borrowing rather than a series of lease arrangements. Since nominal lease and sublease payments will net to zero, the exchange of funds is often limited to the fee given by the property owner to the party providing financing; tax advantages are often the principal objective of these transactions. Accounting questions arising from the transactions include recognition of fees received by the financing party; the presentation of separate investment and sublease payment obligation accounts as an asset and a liability, respectively; and the accounting for resulting obligations.

SIC 27 imposes a substance over form solution to this problem. Accordingly, when an arrangement is found to not meet the definition of a lease, a separate investment account and a lease payment obligation would not meet the definitions of an asset and a liability, and should not be recognized by the entity. It presents certain indicators which imply that a given arrangement is not a lease (e.g., when the right to use the property for a given term is not in fact transferred to the nominal lessee) and that lease accounting cannot be applied.

The interpretation provides that the fee paid to the financing provider should be recognized in accordance with IAS 18. Fees received in advance would generally be deferred and recognized over the lease term when future performance is required in order to retain the fee, when limitations are placed on the use of the underlying asset, or when the nonremote likelihood of early termination would necessitate some fee repayment.

Finally, SIC 27 identifies certain factors that would suggest that other obligations of an arrangement, including any guarantees provided and obligations incurred upon early termination, should be accounted for under either IAS 37 (contingent liabilities) or IAS 39 (financial obligations), depending on the terms.

IFRIC 4 describes arrangements, comprising transactions or series of related transactions, that do not take the legal form of a lease, but which convey rights to use assets in return for series of payments. Examples of such arrangements include

- Outsourcing arrangements (e.g., the outsourcing of the data processing functions of an entity).
- Various arrangements in the telecommunications industry, in which suppliers of network capacity enter into contracts to provide other entities with rights to capacity.
- "Take-or-pay" and similar contracts, in which purchasers must make specified payments regardless of whether they take delivery of the contracted products or services (these often are styled as capacity contracts, giving one party exclusive rights to the counterparty's output).

IFRIC 4 provides guidance for determining whether such arrangements are, or contain, leases that should be accounted for in accordance with IAS 17. (It does not address how such arrangements, if determined to be leases, should be classified). In some of these arrangements, the underlying asset that is the subject of the lease is a portion of a larger asset. IFRIC 4 does not address how to ascertain if the portion of a larger asset is itself the underlying asset for the purposes of applying IAS 17. However, arrangements in which the underlying asset would represent a unit of account under either IAS 16 or IAS 38 are within the scope of this interpretation. Leases which would be excluded from IAS 17 (as noted earlier in this chapter) are not subject to the provisions of IFRIC 4.

Determining whether an arrangement is, or contains, a lease is required to be based on the substance of the arrangement. It requires an assessment of whether

1. Fulfillment of the arrangement is dependent on the use of a specific asset or assets; *and*
2. The arrangement conveys a right to use the asset.

An arrangement is not the subject of a lease if its fulfillment is not dependent on the use of the specified asset. Thus, if terms call for delivery of a specified quantity of goods or services, and the entity has the right and ability to provide those goods or services using other assets not specified in the arrangement, it is not subject to this interpretation. On the other hand, a warranty obligation that permits or requires the substitution of the same or similar assets when the specified asset is not operating properly, or a contractual provision (whether or not contingent) permitting or requiring the supplier to substitute other assets for any reason on or after a specified date, do not preclude lease treatment before the date of substitution.

IFRIC 4 states that an asset has been *implicitly specified* if, for example, the supplier owns or leases only one asset with which to fulfill the obligation, and it is not economically feasible to perform its obligation through the use of alternative assets.

An arrangement conveys the right to use the asset if the arrangement conveys to the purchaser (putatively, the lessee) the right to control the use of the underlying asset. This occurs if

1. The purchaser has the ability or right to operate the asset (or direct others to operate the asset) in a manner it determines while obtaining or controlling more than an insignificant amount of the output or other value of the asset;
2. The purchaser has the ability or right to control physical access to the underlying asset while obtaining or controlling more than an insignificant amount of the output or other utility of the asset; or

3. Fact and circumstances suggest that it is remote that one or more parties other than the purchaser will take more than an insignificant amount of the output of the asset, or other value that will be produced or generated by the asset during the term of the arrangement, and the price that the purchaser will pay for the output is neither contractually fixed per unit of output nor equal to the current market price per unit of output as of the time of delivery of the output.

According to IFRIC 4, the assessment of whether an arrangement contains a lease is to be made at the inception of the arrangement. This is defined as the earlier of the date of the arrangement or the date the parties commit to the principal terms of the arrangement, on the basis of all of the facts and circumstances. Once determined, a reassessment is permitted only if

1. There is a change in the contractual terms, unless the change only renews or extends the arrangement;
2. A renewal option is exercised or an extension is agreed to by the parties, unless the term of the renewal or extension had initially been included in the lease term in accordance with IAS 17 (a renewal or extension of the arrangement that does not include modification of any of the terms in the original arrangement before the end of the term of the original arrangement is to be evaluated only with respect to the renewal or extension period);
3. There is a change in the determination of whether fulfillment is dependent on a specified asset; or
4. There is a substantial change to the asset, (e.g., a substantial physical change to property, plant, or equipment).

Any reassessment of an arrangement is to be based on the facts and circumstances as of the date of reassessment, including the remaining term of the arrangement. Changes in estimate (e.g., as to the expected output to be delivered) may not be used to trigger a reassessment. If the reassessment concludes that the arrangement contains (or does not contain) a lease, lease accounting is to be applied (or cease to be applied) from when the change in circumstances giving rise to the reassessment occurs (if other than exercise of a renewal or extension), or the inception of the renewal or extension period.

If an arrangement is determined to contain a lease, both parties are to apply the requirements of IAS 17 to the lease element of the arrangement. Accordingly, the lease must be classified as a finance lease or an operating lease. Other elements of the arrangement, not within the scope of that standard, are to be accounted for as required by relevant IFRS. For the purpose of applying IAS 17, payments and other consideration required must be separated, at inception or upon a reassessment of the arrangement, into that being made for the lease and that applicable to the other elements, on the basis of relative fair values. Minimum lease payments (per IAS 17) include only payments for the lease itself.

In some instances it will be necessary to make assumptions and estimates in order to separate the payments for the lease from payments for the other elements. IFRIC 4 suggests that a purchaser might estimate the lease payment portion by reference to a lease for a comparable asset that contains no other elements, or might estimate the payments for the other elements by reference to comparable agreements, deriving the payments for the other component by deduction. However, if a purchaser concludes that it is impracticable to separate the payments reliably, the procedure to be followed depends on whether the lease is operating or finance in nature.

If a finance lease, the purchaser/lessee is to recognize an asset and a liability at an amount equal to the fair value of the underlying asset that was identified as being the subject of the lease. As payments are later made, the liability will be reduced and an imputed finance charge on the liability will be recognized using the purchaser's incremental borrowing rate of interest (as described earlier in this chapter).

If an operating lease, the purchaser/lessee is to treat all payments as lease payments for the purposes of complying with the disclosure requirements of IAS 17, but (1) disclose those payments separately from minimum lease payments of other arrangements that do not include payments for nonlease elements, and (2) state that the disclosed payments also include payments for nonlease elements in the arrangement.

IASB Lease Accounting Project

The concept of accounting for leases as the simultaneous acquisitions of assets and obligations under a long-term debt agreement is long-established. Various financial reporting standards, going back more than 40 years, have attempted to incrementally move accounting principles toward a uniform treatment of all leases, but this has been met with opposition from financial statement preparers, which often prefer to not acknowledge the amount of debt owed (and the impact on debt to equity ratios, often viewed as key statistics revealing financial riskiness of the reporting entities), as well as by the lease financing industry, which has become a major source of business for banks and other financial institutions.

The major modern-era financial reporting standards to deal with leasing, US GAAP's FAS 13 (and its many subsequent interpretations and amendments) and IASB's IAS 17, attempt to impose capitalization requirements, but both sets of standards provide largely formulaic criteria which result in many such arrangements still being reported as operating leases, with only current rent being reported, and the rights to use long-lived assets, and the related debt obligations, not being represented in the statement of financial position.

As part of the IASB's convergence efforts undertaken in conjunction with FASB, the matter of lease accounting is again being considered. The objective is to amend or replace IAS 17 to better conform to the IASB's *Framework* definitions of asset and liability. Simply put, this would, if uniformly applied, result in capitalization of virtually all leases, with the possible (perhaps expedient) exception of very short-term ones (say, of under one year's duration). Such a standard would facilitate elimination of much guidance found in US GAAP, most of which is absent from the somewhat more "principles-based" IFRS.

The IASB/FASB joint project on lease accounting should result in a fundamental change in accounting for leases by both lessors and lessees by providing a model for the recognition and measurement of assets and liabilities arising under lease contracts. In 2006, the Boards established the Joint Working Group on Lease Accounting to provide expert advice on future proposals and implementation issues. The first step in the development of new accounting standards on leases will be the publication of a discussion paper which is now anticipated in early 2009.

DISCLOSURE REQUIREMENTS UNDER IAS 17

Lessee Disclosures

1. **Finance Leases**

    IAS 17 mandates the following disclosures for lessees under finance leases, in addition to disclosures required under IAS 32 for all financial instruments:

    a. For each class of asset, the net carrying amount at the end of the reporting period (the date of the statement of financial position)
    b. A reconciliation between the total of minimum lease payments at the end of the reporting period, and their present value. In addition, an enterprise should dis-

close the total of the minimum lease payments at the end of the reporting period, their present value, for each of the following periods:

(1) Due in one year or less
(2) Due in more than one but no more than five years
(3) Due in more than five years

c. Contingent rents included in profit or loss for the period
d. The total of minimum sublease payments to be received in the future under noncancelable subleases at the end of the reporting period
e. A general description of the lessee's significant leasing arrangements including, but not necessarily limited to the following:

(1) The basis for determining contingent rentals
(2) The existence and terms of renewal or purchase options and escalation clauses
(3) Restrictions imposed by lease arrangements such as on dividends or assumptions of further debt or further leasing

2. **Operating Leases**

IAS 17 sets forth in greater detail the disclosure requirements that will be applicable to lessees under operating leases. While some of these were suggested under original IAS 17 or are implicitly needed to provide adequate disclosure, the revised standard offers preparers more explicit guidance.

Lessees should, in addition to the requirements of IAS 32, make the following disclosures for operating leases:

a. Total of the future minimum lease payments under noncancelable operating leases for each of the following periods:

(1) Due in one year or less
(2) Due in more than one year but no more than five years
(3) Due in more than five years

b. The total of future minimum sublease payments expected to be received under noncancellable subleases at the end of the reporting period
c. Lease and sublease payments included in profit or loss for the period, with separate amounts of minimum lease payments, contingent rents, and sublease payments
d. A general description of the lessee's significant leasing arrangements including, but not necessarily limited to the following:

(1) The basis for determining contingent rentals
(2) The existence and terms of renewal or purchase options escalation clauses
(3) Restrictions imposed by lease arrangements such as on dividends or assumption of further debt or on further leasing

Lessor Disclosures

1. **Finance Leases**

IAS 17 requires enhanced disclosures compared to the original standard. Lessors under finance leases are required to disclose, in addition to disclosures under IAS 32, the following:

a. A reconciliation between the total gross investment in the lease at the end of the reporting period, and the present value of minimum lease payments receivable at the end of the reporting period, categorized into

(1) Those due in one year or less
(2) Those due in more than one year but not more than five years
(3) Those due beyond five years

b. Unearned finance income
c. The accumulated allowance for uncollectible minimum lease payments receivable
d. Total contingent rentals included in income
e. A general description of the lessor's significant leasing arrangements

2. **Operating Leases**

For lessors under operating leases, IAS 17 has prescribed the following expanded disclosures:

a. For each class of asset, the gross carrying amount, the accumulated depreciation and accumulated impairment losses at the end of the reporting period

(1) Depreciation recognized in profit or loss for the period
(2) Impairment losses recognized in profit or loss for the period
(3) Impairment losses reversed in profit or loss for the period

b. Depreciation recognized on assets held for operating lease use during the period
c. The future minimum lease payments under noncancellable operating leases, in the aggregate and classified into

(1) Those due in no more than one year
(2) Those due in more than one but not more than five years
(3) Those due in more than five years

d. Total contingent rentals included in profit or loss for the period
e. A general description of leasing arrangements to which it is a party

Examples of Financial Statement Disclosures

Nestlé SA
Year Ended December 31, 2007

Accounting Policies
Leased Assets

Assets acquired under finance leases are capitalized and depreciated in accordance with the Group's policy on property, plant, and equipment unless the lease term is shorter. Land and building leases are recognized separately provided an allocation of the lease payments between these categories is reliable.

The associated obligations are included in financial liabilities.

Rentals payable under operating leases are expensed.

The costs of the agreements that do not take the legal form of a lease but convey the right to use an asset are separated into lease payments and other payments if the entity has the control of the use or of the access to the asset or takes essentially all the output of the asset. Then the entity determines whether the lease component of the agreement is a finance or an operating lease.

28. Lease commitments

Operating leases

In millions of CHF	Minimum lease payments future value	
	2007	*2006*
Within one year	559	480
In the second year	425	389
In the third to the fifth year inclusive	859	702
After the fifth year	571	555
	2,414	2,126

Finance leases

	2007		2006	
	Minimum lease payments			
In millions of CHF	*Present value*	*Future value*	*Present value*	*Future value*
Within one year	78	88	78	87
In the second year	100	120	81	97
In the third to the fifth year inclusive	146	208	166	229
After the fifth year	122	264	159	331
	446	680	484	744

The difference between the future value of the minimum lease payments and their present value represents the discount on the lease obligations.

Novartis Group
For the year ended December 31, 2007

Property, plant, and equipment. Land is valued at acquisition cost less accumulated impairment, if any. Prepayments for long-term leasehold land agreements are amortized over the life of the lease. Other items of property, plant, and equipment are valued at cost of acquisition or production cost and are depreciated on a straight-line basis to the income statement over the following estimated useful lives:

Buildings	20 to 40 years
Other property, plant & equipment	
- Machinery and equipment	7 to 20 years
- Furniture and vehicles	5 to 10 years
- Computer hardware	3 to 7 years

Additional costs which enhance the future economic benefit of property, plant, and equipment are capitalized. Borrowing costs associated with the construction of property, plant & equipment are not capitalized. Property, plant, and equipment is reviewed for impairment whenever events or changes in circumstances indicate that the balance sheet carrying amount may not be recoverable. Property, plant, and equipment which are financed by leases giving Novartis substantially all the risks and rewards of ownership are capitalized at the lower of the fair value of the leased asset or the present value of minimum lease payments at the inception of the lease, and depreciated in the same manner as other assets over the shorter of the lease term or their useful life. Leases in which a significant portion of the risks and rewards of ownership are retained by the lessor are classified as operating leases. These are charged to the income statement over the life of the lease, generally, on a straight-line basis.

18. Noncurrent financial debts

	2007 USD millions	2006 USD millions
Straight bonds		1,318
Liabilities to banks and other financial institutions[1]	693	666
Finance lease obligations	8	12
Total (including current portion of noncurrent debt)	**701**	**1,996**
Less current portion of noncurrent debt	(24)	(1,340)
Total noncurrent debts	**677**	**656**

Straight bonds

EUR	3.75% EUR 1 billion bond 2002/2007 of Novartis Securities Investments Ltd., Hamilton, Bermuda		1,318
Total straight bonds			**1,318**

[1] *Average interest rate 2.1% (2006; 2.3%)*

		2007 *USD millions*	2006 *USD millions*
Breakdown by maturity	2007		1,340
	2008	24	32
	2009	557	528
	2010	20	17
	2011	20	16
	2012	18	--
	Thereafter	62	63
Total		**701**	**1,996**

		2007 *USD millions*	2006 *USD millions*
Breakdown by currency	USD	2	6
	EUR	157	1,473
	JPY	530	504
	Others	12	13
Total		**701**	**1,996**

Fair value comparison	*2007 Balance sheet USD millions*	*2007 Fair values USD millions*	*2006 Balance sheet USD millions*	*2006 Fair values USD millions*
Straight bonds			1,318	1,318
Others	701	701	678	678
Total	**701**	**701**	**1,996**	**1,996**

	2007 *USD millions*	2006 *USD millions*
Collateralized non-current financial debt and pledged assets		
Total amount of collateralized noncurrent financial debts	63	29
Total net book value of property, plant & equipment pledged as collateral for non-current financial debts	112	118

The Group's collateralized noncurrent financial debt consists of overdraft facilities at usual market conditions.

The percentage of fixed rate financial debt to total financial debt was 11% and 27% at December 31, 2007 and 2006, respectively.

The financial debts, including current financial debts, contain only general default covenants. The Group is in compliance with these covenants.

The average interest rate on total financial debt is 3.4% (2006: 3.0%).

29. Commitments and Contingencies

Leasing commitments

Commitments arising from fixed-term operational leases in effect at December 31 are as follows:

	2007 *USD millions*
2008	301
2009	232
2010	164
2011	108
2012	93
Thereafter	301
Total	**1199**
Expense of current year	**350**

APPENDIX A

SPECIAL SITUATIONS NOT ADDRESSED BY IAS 17 BUT WHICH HAVE BEEN INTERPRETED UNDER US GAAP

In the following section, a number of interesting and common problem areas that have not been addressed by IFRS are briefly considered. The guidance found in US GAAP is referenced, as this is likely to represent the most comprehensive source of insight into these matters. However, it should be understood that this constitutes only possible approaches to selected fact situations, and is not authoritative guidance.

Sale-Leaseback Transactions

The accounting treatment from the seller-lessee's perspective will depend on the degree of rights to use retained by the seller-lessee. The degree of rights to use retained may be categorized as follows:

1. Substantially all
2. Minor
3. More than minor but less than substantially all

The guideline for the determination substantially all is based on the classification criteria presented for the lease transaction. For example, a test based on the 90% recovery criterion seems appropriate. That is, if the present value of fair rental payments is equal to 90% or more of the fair value of the sold asset, the seller-lessee is presumed to have retained substantially all the rights to use the sold property. The test for retaining minor rights would be to substitute 10% or less for 90% or more in the preceding sentence.

If substantially all the rights to use the property are retained by the seller-lessee and the agreement meets at least one of the criteria for capital lease treatment, the seller-lessee should account for the leaseback as a capital lease, and any profit on the sale should be deferred and either amortized over the life of the property or treated as a reduction of depreciation expense. If the leaseback is classified as an operating lease, it should be accounted for as one, and any profit or loss on the sale should be deferred and amortized over the lease term. Any loss on the sale would also be deferred unless the loss were perceived to be a real economic loss, in which case the loss would be recognized immediately and not deferred.

If only a minor portion of the rights to use are retained by the seller-lessee, the sale and the leaseback should be accounted for separately. However, if the rental payments appear unreasonable based on the existing market conditions at the inception of the lease, the profit or loss should be adjusted so that the rentals are at a reasonable amount. The amount created by the adjustment should be deferred and amortized over the life of the property if a capital lease is involved or over the lease term if an operating lease is involved.

If the seller-lessee retains more than a minor portion but less than substantially all the rights to use the property, any excess profit on the sale should be recognized on the date of the sale. For purposes of this paragraph, excess profit is derived as follows:

1. If the leaseback is classified as an operating lease, the excess profit is the profit that exceeds the present value of the minimum lease payments over the lease term. The seller-lessee should use its incremental borrowing rate to compute the present value of the minimum lease payments. If the implicit rate of interest in the lease is known, it should be used to compute the present value of the minimum lease payments.
2. If the leaseback is classified as a capital (i.e., finance) lease, the excess profit is the amount greater than the recorded amount of the leased asset.

When the fair value of the property at the time of the leaseback is less than its undepreciated cost, the seller-lessee should immediately recognize a loss for the difference. In the example below, the sales price is less than the book value of the property. However, there is no economic loss because the FMV is greater than the book value.

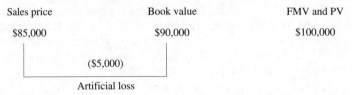

Sales price	Book value	FMV and PV
$85,000	$90,000	$100,000

($5,000)

Artificial loss

The artificial loss must be deferred and amortized as an addition to depreciation.

The following diagram summarizes the accounting for sale-leaseback transactions.

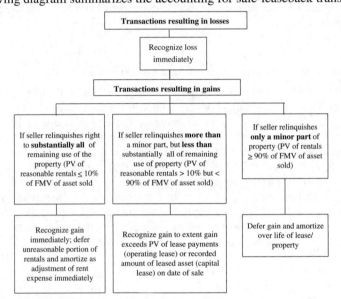

In the foregoing circumstances, when the leased asset is land only, any amortization should be on a straight-line basis over the lease term, regardless of whether the lease is classified as a capital or an operating lease.

Executory costs are not to be included in the calculation of profit to be deferred in a sale-leaseback transaction. The buyer-lessor should account for the transaction as a purchase and a direct financing lease if the agreement meets the criteria of *either* a direct financing lease **or** a sales-type lease. Otherwise, the agreement should be accounted for as a purchase and an operating lease.

Sale-leaseback involving real estate. Under US GAAP, three requirements are necessary for a sale-leaseback involving real estate (including real estate with equipment) to qualify for sale-leaseback accounting treatment. Those sale-leaseback transactions not meeting the three requirements should be accounted for as a deposit or as a financing. The three requirements are

1. The lease must be a normal leaseback.
2. Payment terms and provisions must adequately demonstrate the buyer-lessor's initial and continuing investment in the property.

3. Payment terms and provisions must transfer all the risks and rewards of ownership as demonstrated by a lack of continuing involvement by the seller-lessee.

A normal leaseback involves active use of the leased property in the seller-lessee's trade or business during the lease term.

The buyer-lessor's initial investment is adequate if it demonstrates the buyer-lessor's commitment to pay for the property and indicates a reasonable likelihood that the seller-lessee will collect any receivable related to the leased property. The buyer-lessor's continuing investment is adequate if the buyer is contractually obligated to pay an annual amount at least equal to the level of annual payment needed to pay that debt and interest over no more than (1) twenty years for land and (2) the customary term of a first mortgage loan for other real estate.

Any continuing involvement by the seller-lessee other than normal leaseback disqualifies the lease from sale-leaseback accounting treatment. Some examples of continuing involvement other than normal leaseback include

1. The seller-lessee has an obligation or option (excluding the right of first refusal) to repurchase the property.
2. The seller-lessee (or party related to the seller-lessee) guarantees the buyer-lessor's investment or debt related to that investment or a return on that investment.
3. The seller-lessee is required to reimburse the buyer-lessor for a decline in the fair value of the property below estimated residual value at the end of the lease term based on other than excess wear and tear.
4. The seller-lessee remains liable for an existing debt related to the property.
5. The seller-lessee's rental payments are contingent on some predetermined level of future operations of the buyer-lessor.
6. The seller-lessee provides collateral on behalf of the buyer-lessor other than the property directly involved in the sale-leaseback.
7. The seller-lessee provides nonrecourse financing to the buyer-lessor for any portion of the sales proceeds or provides recourse financing in which the only recourse is the leased asset.
8. The seller-lessee enters into a sale-leaseback involving property improvements or integral equipment without leasing the underlying land to the buyer-lessor.
9. The buyer-lessor is obligated to share any portion of the appreciation of the property with the seller-lessee.
10. Any other provision or circumstance that allows the seller-lessee to participate in any future profits of the buyer-lessor or appreciation of the leased property.

Example of accounting for a sale-leaseback transaction

To illustrate the accounting treatment in a sale-leaseback transaction, suppose that Lessee Corporation sells equipment that has a book value of €80,000 and a fair value of €100,000 to Lessor Corporation, and then immediately leases it back under the following conditions:

1. The sale date is January 1, 2009, and the equipment has a fair value of €100,000 on that date and an estimated useful life of 15 years.
2. The lease term is 15 years, noncancelable, and requires equal rental payments of €13,109 at the beginning of each year.
3. Lessee Corp. has the option annually to renew the lease at the same rental payments on expiration of the original lease.
4. Lessee Corp. has the obligation to pay all executory costs.
5. The annual rental payments provide the lessor with a 12% return on investment.
6. The incremental borrowing rate of Lessee Corp. is 12%.
7. Lessee Corp. depreciates similar equipment on a straight-line basis.

Lessee Corp. should classify the agreement as a capital lease since the lease term exceeds 75% (which is deemed to be a major part) of the estimated economic life of the equipment, and because the present value of the lease payments is greater than 90% (deemed to be substantially all) of the fair value of the equipment. Assuming that collectibility of the lease payments is reasonably predictable and that no important uncertainties exist concerning the amount of nonreimbursable costs yet to be incurred by the lessor, Lessor Corp. should classify the transaction as a direct financing lease because the present value of the minimum lease payments is equal to the fair market value of €100,000 (€13,109 × 7.62817).

Lessee Corp. and Lessor Corp. would normally make the following journal entries during the first year:

Upon Sale of Equipment on January 1, 2009

Lessee Corp.			*Lessor Corp.*		
Cash	100,000		Equipment	100,000	
Equipment*		80,000	Cash		100,000
Unearned profit on					
sale-leaseback		20,000			
Leased equipment	100,000		Lease receivable		
Lease obligations		100,000	(€13,109 × 15)	196,635	
			Equipment		100,000
			Unearned interest		96,635

Assumes new equipment

To Record First Payment on January 1, 2009

Lessee Corp.			*Lessor Corp.*		
Lease obligations	13,109		Cash	13,109	
Cash		13,109	Lease receivable		13,109

To Record Incurrence and Payment of Executory Costs

Lessee Corp.			*Lessor Corp.*	
Insurance, taxes, etc.	xxx		(No entry)	
Cash (accounts payable)		xxx		

To Record Depreciation Expense on the Equipment, December 31, 2009

Lessee Corp.			*Lessor Corp.*	
Depreciation expense	6,667		(No entry)	
Accum. depr.— capital				
leases (€100,000 ÷ 15)		6,667		

To Amortize Profit on Sale-Leaseback by Lessee Corp., December 31, 2009

Lessee Corp.			*Lessor Corp.*	
Unearned profit on sale-			(No entry)	
leaseback	1,333			
Depr. expense				
(€20,000 ÷ 15)		1,333		

To Record Interest for December 31, 2009

Lessee Corp.			*Lessor Corp.*		
Interest expense	10,427		Unearned interest		
Accrued interest			income	10,427	
payable		10,427	Interest income		10,427

Partial Lease Amortization Schedule

Date	Cash payment	Interest expense	Reduction of obligation	Lease obligation
Inception of lease				€100,000
January 1, 2009	€13,109	€ --	€13,109	86,891
January 1, 2010	13,109	10,427	2,682	84,209

Leases Involving Real Estate—Guidance under US GAAP

While required practice regarding lease accounting is rather clearly set forth under IAS 17, as is typical under IFRS this is presented in rather general terms. US GAAP, by contrast, offers a great deal of very specific guidance on this topic. It is instructive to at least consider the US GAAP rules for lease accounting, which may provide some further insight and, in some circumstances, offer operational guidance to those attempting to apply IAS 17 to particular fact situations. Under US GAAP (which consists of many discrete standards and a large volume of interpretive literature), leases involving real estate are categorized into four groups:

1. Leases involving land only
2. Leases involving land and building(s)
3. Leases involving real estate and equipment
4. Leases involving only part of a building

Leases Involving Land Only

Lessee accounting. If the lease agreement transfers ownership or contains a bargain purchase option, the lessee should account for the lease as a capital lease and record an asset and related liability in an amount equal to the present value of the minimum lease payments. If the lease agreement does not transfer ownership or contain a bargain purchase option, the lessee should account for the lease as an operating lease.

Lessor accounting. If the lease gives rise to dealer's profit (or loss) and transfers ownership (i.e., title), the standards require that the lease shall be classified as a sales-type lease and accounted for under the provisions of the US standard dealing with sales of real estate, in the same manner as would a seller of the same property. If the lease transfers ownership, both the collectibility and the no material uncertainties criteria are met, but if it does not give rise to dealer's profit (or loss), the lease should be accounted for as a direct financing or leveraged lease, as appropriate. If the lease contains a bargain purchase option and both the collectibility and no material uncertainties criteria are met, the lease should be accounted for as a direct financing, leveraged, or operating lease as appropriate. If the lease does not meet the collectibility and/or no material uncertainties criteria, the lease should be accounted for as an operating lease.

Leases Involving Land and Building

Lessee accounting. Under US GAAP, if the agreement transfers title or contains a bargain purchase option, the lessee should account for the agreement by separating the land and building components and capitalize each separately. The land and building elements should be allocated on the basis of their relative fair market values measured at the inception of the lease. The land and building components are accounted for separately because the lessee is expected to own the real estate by the end of the lease term. The building should be depreciated over its estimated useful life without regard to the lease term.

When the lease agreement neither transfers title nor contains a bargain purchase option, the fair value of the land must be determined in relation to the fair value of the aggregate properties included in the lease agreement. If the fair value of the land is less than 25% of the fair value of the leased properties in aggregate, the land is considered immaterial. Conversely, if the fair value of the land is 25% or greater of the fair value of the leased properties in aggregate, the land is considered material.

When the land component of the lease agreement is considered immaterial (FMV land < 25% total FMV), the lease should be accounted for as a single lease unit. The lessee should capitalize the lease if one of the following occurs:

1. The term of the lease is 75% or more of the economic useful life of the real estate
2. The present value of the minimum lease payments equals 90% or more of the fair market value of the leased real estate less any lessor tax credits

If neither of the two criteria above is met, the lessee should account for the lease agreement as a single operating lease.

When the land component of the lease agreement is considered material (FMV land ≥ 25% total FMV), the land and building components should be separated. By applying the lessee's incremental borrowing rate to the fair market value of the land, the annual minimum lease payment attributed to land is computed. The remaining payments are attributed to the building. The division of minimum lease payments between land and building is essential for both the lessee and lessor. The lease involving the land should *always* be accounted for as an operating lease. Under US GAAP, the lease involving the building(s) must meet either the 75% (of useful life) or 90% (of fair value) test to be treated as a capital lease. If neither of the two criteria is met, the building(s) will also be accounted for as an operating lease.

Lessor accounting. The lessor's accounting depends on whether the lease transfers ownership, contains a bargain purchase option, or does neither of the two. If the lease transfers ownership and gives rise to dealer's profit (or loss), US GAAP requires that the lessor classify the lease as a sales-type lease and account for the lease as a single unit under the provisions of FAS 66 in the same manner as a seller of the same property. If the lease transfers ownership, meets both the collectibility and no important uncertainties criteria, but does not give rise to dealer's profit (or loss), the lease should be accounted for as a direct financing or leveraged lease as appropriate.

If the lease contains a bargain purchase option and gives rise to dealer's profit (or loss), the lease should be classified as an operating lease. If the lease contains a bargain purchase option, meets both the collectibility and no material uncertainties criteria, but does not give rise to dealer's profit (or loss), the lease should be accounted for as a direct financing lease or a leveraged lease, as appropriate.

If the lease agreement neither transfers ownership nor contains a bargain purchase option, the lessor should follow the same rules as the lessee in accounting for real estate leases involving land and building(s).

However, the collectibility and the no material uncertainties criteria must be met before the lessor can account for the agreement as a direct financing lease, and in no such case may the lease be classified as a sales-type lease (i.e., ownership must be transferred).

The treatment of a lease involving both land and building can be illustrated in the following examples.

Example of accounting for land and building lease containing transfer of title

Assume the following:

1. The lessee enters into a ten-year noncancelable lease for a parcel of land and a building for use in its operations. The building has an estimated useful life of 12 years.
2. The FMV of the land is €75,000, while the FMV of the building is €310,000.
3. A payment of €50,000 is due to the lessor at the beginning of each of the 10 years of the lease.
4. The lessee's incremental borrowing rate is 10%. (Lessor's implicit rate is unknown.)
5. Ownership will transfer to the lessee at the end of the lease.

The present value of the minimum lease payments is €337,951 (€50,000 × 6.75902*). The portion of the present value of the minimum lease payments that should be capitalized for each of the two components of the lease is computed as follows:

FMV of land		€ 75,000
FMV of building		310,000
Total FMV of leased property		€385,000

Portion of PV allocated to land €337,951 × $\frac{75,000}{385,000}$ = € 65,835

Portion of PV allocated to building €337,951 × $\frac{310,000}{385,000}$ = 272,116

Total PV to be capitalized €337,951

The entry made to record the lease initially is as follows:

Leased land	65,835	
Leased building	272,116	
Lease obligation		337,951

*6.75902 is the PV of an annuity due for ten periods at 10%.

Subsequently, the obligation will be decreased in accordance with the effective interest method. The leased building will be amortized over its expected useful life.

Example of accounting for land and building lease without transfer of title or bargain purchase option

Assume the same facts as in the previous example except that title does not transfer at the end of the lease.

The lease is still a capital lease because the lease term is more than 75% of the useful life. Since the FMV of the land is less than 25% of the leased properties in aggregate, (€75,000/€385,000 = 19%), the land component is considered immaterial and the lease will be accounted for as a single lease. The entry to record the lease is as follows:

Leased property	337,951	
Lease obligation		337,951

Assume the same facts as in the previous example except that the FMV of the land is €110,000 and the FMV of the building is €275,000. Once again, title does not transfer.

Because the FMV of the land exceeds 25% of the leased properties in aggregate (€110,000/€385,000 = 28%), the land component is considered material and the lease would be separated into two components. The annual minimum lease payment attributed to the land is computed as follows:

FMV of land $\frac{€100,000}{6.75902^*}$ = €16,275
PV factor

The remaining portion of the annual payment is attributed to the building.

Annual payment	€ 50,000
Less amount attributed to land	(16,275)
Annual payment attributed to building	€33,725

The present value of the minimum annual lease payments attributed to the building is then computed as follows:

Minimum annual lease payment attributed to building	€ 33,725
PV factor	× 6.75902*
PV of minimum annual lease payments attributed to building	€227,948

The entry to record the capital portion of the lease is as follows:

Leased building	227,948	
Lease obligation		227,948

*6.75902 is the PV of an annuity due for ten periods at 10%.

There would be no computation of the present value of the minimum annual lease payment attributed to the land since the land component of the lease will be treated as an operating lease. For this reason, each year, €16,275 of the €50,000 lease payment will be recorded as land rental expense. The remainder of the annual payment (€33,725) will be applied against the lease obligation using the effective interest method.

Leases involving real estate and equipment. When real estate leases also involve equipment or machinery, the equipment component should be separated and accounted for as a separate lease agreement by both lessees and lessors. According to US GAAP, "the portion of the minimum lease payments applicable to the equipment element of the lease shall be estimated by whatever means are appropriate in the circumstances." The lessee and lessor should apply the capitalization requirements to the equipment lease independently of accounting for the real estate lease(s). The real estate leases should be handled as discussed in the preceding two sections. In a sale-leaseback transaction involving real estate with equipment, the equipment and land are not separated.

Leases involving only part of a building. It is common to find lease agreements that involve only part of a building, as, for example, when a floor of an office building is leased or when a store in a shopping mall is leased. A difficulty that arises in this situation is that the cost and/or fair market value of the leased portion of the whole may not be determinable objectively.

For the lessee, if the fair value of the leased property is objectively determinable, the lessee should follow the rules and account for the lease as described in "leases involving land and building." If the fair value of the leased property cannot be determined objectively but the agreement satisfies the 75% test, the estimated economic life of the building in which the leased premises are located should be used. If this test is not met, the lessee should account for the agreement as an operating lease.

From the lessor's position, both the cost and fair value of the leased property must be objectively determinable before the procedures described under "leases involving land and building" will apply. If either the cost or the fair value cannot be determined objectively, the lessor should account for the agreement as an operating lease.

Termination of a Lease

The lessor shall remove the remaining net investment from his or her books and record the leased equipment as an asset at the lower of its original cost, present fair value, or current carrying value. The net adjustment is reflected in income of the current period.

The lessee is also affected by the terminated agreement because he or she has been relieved of the obligation. If the lease is a capital lease, the lessee should remove both the obligation and the asset from his or her accounts and charge any adjustment to the current period income. If accounted for as an operating lease, no accounting adjustment is required.

Renewal or Extension of an Existing Lease

The renewal or extension of an existing lease agreement affects the accounting of both the lessee and the lessor. US GAAP specifies two basic situations in this regard: (1) the renewal occurs and makes a residual guarantee or penalty provision inoperative or (2) the renewal agreement does not do the foregoing and the renewal is to be treated as a new agreement. The accounting treatment prescribed under the latter situation for a lessee is as follows:

1. If the renewal or extension is classified as a capital lease, the (present) current balances of the asset and related obligation should be adjusted by an amount equal to the difference between the present value of the future minimum lease payments un-

der the revised agreement and the (present) current balance of the obligation. The present value of the minimum lease payments under the revised agreement should be computed using the interest rate that was in effect at the inception of the original lease.

2. If the renewal or extension is classified as an operating lease, the current balances in the asset and liability accounts are removed from the books and a gain (loss) recognized for the difference. The new lease agreement resulting from a renewal or extension is accounted for in the same manner as other operating leases.

Under the same circumstances, US GAAP prescribes the following treatment to be followed by the lessor:

1. If the renewal or extension is classified as a direct financing lease, then the existing balances of the lease receivable and the estimated residual value accounts should be adjusted for the changes resulting from the revised agreement.

   NOTE: Remember that an upward adjustment of the estimated residual value is not allowed.

   The net adjustment should be charged or credited to an unearned income account.

2. If the renewal or extension is classified as an operating lease, the remaining net investment under the existing sales-type lease or direct financing lease is removed from the books and the leased asset recorded as an asset at the lower of its original cost, present fair value, or current carrying amount. The difference between the net investment and the amount recorded for the leased asset is charged to profit or loss of the period. The renewal or extension is then accounted for as for any other operating lease.

3. If the renewal or extension is classified as a sales-type lease *and* it occurs at or near the end of the existing lease term, the renewal or extension should be accounted for as a sales-type lease.

   NOTE: A renewal or extension that occurs in the last few months of an existing lease is considered to have occurred at or near the end of the existing lease term.

If the renewal or extension causes the guarantee or penalty provision to be inoperative, the lessee adjusts the current balance of the leased asset and the lease obligation to the present value of the future minimum lease payments (according to the relevant standard, "by an amount equal to the difference between the PV of future minimum lease payments under the revised agreement and the present balance of the obligation"). The PV of the future minimum lease payments is computed using the implicit rate used in the original lease agreement.

Given the same circumstances, the lessor adjusts the existing balance of the lease receivable and estimated residual value accounts to reflect the changes of the revised agreement (remember, no upward adjustments to the residual value). The net adjustment is charged (or credited) to unearned income.

Leases between Related Parties

Leases between related parties are classified and accounted for as though the parties are unrelated, except in cases where it is clear that the terms and conditions of the agreement have been influenced significantly by the fact of the relationship. When this is the case, the classification and/or accounting is modified to reflect the true economic substance of the transaction rather than the legal form.

If a subsidiary's principal business activity is leasing property to its parent or other affiliated companies, consolidated financial statements are presented. The US GAAP standard on related parties requires that the nature and extent of leasing activities between related parties be disclosed.

TREATMENT OF SELECTED ITEMS IN ACCOUNTING FOR LEASES UNDER US GAAP

	Lessor		*Lessee*	
	Operating	*Direct financing and sales-type*	*Operating*	*capital*
Initial direct costs	Capitalize and amortize over lease term in proportion to rent revenue recognized (normally SL basis)	Direct financing: Record in separate account; Add to net investment in lease; Compute new effective rate that equates gross amt. of min. lease payments and unguar. residual value with net invest. Amortize so as to produce constant rate of return over lease term. Sales-type: Expense in period incurred	N/A	N/A
Investment tax credit retained by lessor	N/A	Reduces FMV of leased asset for 90% test	N/A	Reduces FMV of leased asset for 90% test
Bargain purchase option	N/A	Include in: Minimum lease payments 90% test	N/A	Include in: Minimum lease payments 90% test
Guaranteed residual value	N/A	Include in: Minimum lease payments 90% test; Sales-type: Include PV in sales revenues	N/A	Include in: Minimum lease payments 90% test
Unguaranteed residual value	N/A	Include In: "Gross Investment in Lease"; Not included in: Minimum lease payments 90% test; Sales-type: Exclude from sales revenue; Deduct PV from cost of sales	N/A	Include in: Minimum lease payments 90% test
Contingent rentals	Revenue in period earned	Not part of minimum lease payments; revenue in period earned	Expense in period incurred	Not part of minimum lease payments; expense in period incurred
Amortization period	Amortize down to estimated residual value over estimated economic life of asset	N/A	N/A	Amortize down to estimated residual value over lease term or estimated economic life[c]
Revenue (expense)[a]	Rent revenue (normally SL basis); Amortization (depreciation expense)	Direct financing: Interest revenue on net investment in lease (gross investment less unearned interest income); Sales-type: Dealer profit in period of sale (sales revenue less cost of leased asset); Interest revenue on net investment in lease	Rent expense (normally SL basis)[b]	Interest expense and depreciation expense

[a] Elements of revenue (expense) listed for the items above are not repeated here (e.g., treatment of initial direct costs).

[b] If payments are not on a SL basis, recognize rent expense on a SL basis unless another systematic and rational method is more representative of use benefit obtained from the property; in which case, the other method should be used.

[c] If lease has automatic passage of title or bargain purchase option, use estimated economic life; otherwise, use the lease term.

Accounting for Leases in a Business Combination

A business combination, in and of itself, has no effect on the classification of a lease. However, if, in connection with a business combination, the lease agreement is modified to change the original classification of the lease, it should be considered a new agreement and reclassified according to the revised provisions.

In most cases, a business combination that is accounted for by the pooling-of-interest method or by the purchase method will not affect the previous classification of a lease unless the provisions have been modified as indicated in the preceding paragraph.

The acquiring company should apply the following procedures to account for a leveraged lease in a business combination accounted for by the purchase method:

1. The classification of leveraged lease should be kept.
2. The net investment in the leveraged lease should be given a fair market value (present value, net of tax) based on the remaining future cash flows. Also, the estimated tax effects of the cash flows should be given recognition.
3. The net investment should be broken down into three components: net rentals receivable, estimated residual value, and unearned income.
4. Thereafter, the leveraged lease should be accounted for as described above in the section on leveraged leases.

Sale or Assignment to Third Parties—Nonrecourse Financing

The sale or assignment of a lease or of property subject to a lease that was originally accounted for as a sales-type lease or a direct financing lease will not affect the original accounting treatment of the lease. Any profit or loss on the sale or assignment should be recognized at the time of transaction except under the following two circumstances:

1. When the sale or assignment is between related parties, apply the provisions presented above under "Leases between Related Parties."
2. When the sale or assignment is with recourse, it should be accounted for using the provisions of the US GAAP standard on sale of receivables with recourse.

The sale of property subject to an operating lease should not be treated as a sale if the seller (or any related party to the seller) retains substantial risks of ownership in the leased property. A seller may retain substantial risks of ownership by various arrangements. For example, if the lessee defaults on the lease agreement or if the lease terminates, the seller may arrange to do one of the following:

1. Acquire the property or the lease
2. Substitute an existing lease
3. Secure a replacement lessee or a buyer for the property under a remarketing agreement

A seller will not retain substantial risks of ownership by arrangements where one of the following occurs:

1. A remarketing agreement includes a reasonable fee to be paid to the seller
2. The seller is not required to give priority to the releasing or disposition of the property owned by the third party over similar property owned by the seller

When the sale of property subject to an operating lease is not accounted for as a sale because the substantial risk factor is present, it should be accounted for as a borrowing. The proceeds from the sale should be recorded as an obligation on the seller's books. Rental payments made by the lessee under the operating lease should be recorded as revenue by the seller even if the payments are paid to the third-party purchaser. The seller shall account for each rental payment by allocating a portion to interest expense (to be imputed in accordance with the provisions of APB 21), and the remainder will reduce the existing obligation. Other normal accounting procedures for operating leases should be applied except that the depreciation term for the leased asset is limited to the amortization period of the obligation.

The sale or assignment of lease payments under an operating lease by the lessor should be accounted for as a borrowing as described above.

Nonrecourse financing is a common occurrence in the leasing industry whereby the stream of lease payments on a lease is discounted on a nonrecourse basis at a financial institution with the lease payments collateralizing the debt. The proceeds are then used to finance future leasing transactions. Even though the discounting is on a nonrecourse basis, US GAAP prohibits the offsetting of the debt against the related lease receivable unless a legal right of offset exists or the lease qualified as a leveraged lease at its inception.

Money-Over-Money Lease Transactions

In cases where a lessor obtains nonrecourse financing in excess of the leased asset's cost, a technical bulletin states that the borrowing and leasing are separate transactions and should not be offset against each other unless a right of offset exists. Only dealer profit in sales-type leases may be recognized at the beginning of the lease term.

Acquisition of Interest in Residual Value

Recently, there has been an increase in the acquisition of interests in residual values of leased assets by companies whose primary business is other than leasing or financing. This generally occurs through the outright purchase of the right to own the leased asset or the right to receive the proceeds from the sale of a leased asset at the end of its lease term.

In instances such as these, the rights should be recorded by the purchaser at the fair value of the assets surrendered. Recognition of increases in the value of the interest in the residual (i.e., residual value accretion) to the end of the lease term are prohibited. However, a nontemporary write-down of the residual value interest should be recognized as a loss. This guidance also applies to lessors who sell the related minimum lease payments but retain the interest in the residual value. Guaranteed residual values also have no effect on this guidance.

Accounting for a Sublease

A sublease is used to describe the situation where the original lessee re-leases the leased property to a third party (the sublessee), and the original lessee acts as a sublessor. Normally, the nature of a sublease agreement does not affect the original lease agreement, and the original lessee/sublessor retains primary liability.

The original lease remains in effect, and the original lessor continues to account for the lease as before. The original lessee/sublessor accounts for the lease as follows:

1. If the original lease agreement transfers ownership or contains a bargain purchase option and if the new lease meets any one of the four criteria specified in US GAAP (i.e., transfers ownership, BPO, the 75% test, or the 90% test) and both the collectibility and uncertainties criteria, the sublessor should classify the new lease as a sales-type or direct financing lease; otherwise, as an operating lease. In either situation, the original lessee/sublessor should continue accounting for the original lease obligation as before.

2. If the original lease agreement does not transfer ownership or contain a bargain purchase option, but it still qualified as a capital lease, the original lessee/sublessor

should (with one exception) apply the usual criteria set by US GAAP in classifying the new agreement as a capital or operating lease. If the new lease qualifies for capital treatment, the original lessee/sublessor should account for it as a direct financing lease, with the unamortized balance of the asset under the original lease being treated as the cost of the leased property. The one exception arises when the circumstances surrounding the sublease suggest that the sublease agreement was an important part of a predetermined plan in which the original lessee played only an intermediate role between the original lessor and the sublessee. In this situation, the sublease should be classified by the 75% and 90% criteria as well as collectibility and uncertainties criteria. In applying the 90% criterion, the fair value for the leased property will be the fair value to the original lessor at the inception of the original lease. Under all circumstances, the original lessee should continue accounting for the original lease obligation as before. If the new lease agreement (sublease) does not meet the capitalization requirements imposed for subleases, the new lease should be accounted for as an operating lease.

3. If the original lease is an operating lease, the original lessee/sublessor should account for the new lease as an operating lease and account for the original operating lease as before.

APPENDIX B

LEVERAGED LEASES UNDER US GAAP

One of the most complex accounting subjects regarding leases is the accounting for a leveraged lease. Once again, as with both sales-type and direct financing, the classification of the lease by the lessor has no effect on the accounting treatment accorded the lease by the lessee. The lessee simply treats it as any other lease and thus is interested only in whether the lease qualifies as an operating or a capital lease. The lessor's accounting problem is substantially more complex than that of the lessee.

Leveraged leases are not directly addressed under IFRS. However, such three-party leasing transactions may be encountered occasionally. This guidance under US GAAP is therefore offered to fill a void in IFRS literature.

To qualify as a leveraged lease, a lease agreement must meet the following requirements, and the lessor must account for the investment tax credit (when in effect) in the manner described below.

NOTE: Failure to do so will result in the lease being classified as a direct financing lease.

1. The lease must meet the definition of a direct financing lease. (The 90% of FMV criterion does not apply.)[1]
2. The lease must involve at least three parties.

    a. An owner-lessor (equity participant)
    b. A lessee
    c. A long-term creditor (debt participant)

3. The financing provided by the creditor is nonrecourse as to the general credit of the lessor and is sufficient to provide the lessor with substantial leverage.
4. The lessor's net investment (defined below) decreases in the early years and increases in the later years until it is eliminated.

The last characteristic (item 4) poses the accounting problem.

The leveraged lease arose as a result of an effort to maximize the tax benefits associated with a lease transaction. To accomplish this, it was necessary to involve a third party to the lease transaction (in addition to the lessor and lessee), a long-term creditor. The following diagram illustrates the existing relationships in a leveraged lease agreement:

The leveraged lease arrangement*

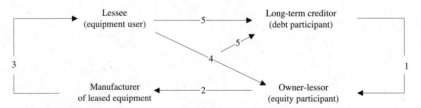

*   *Adapted from "A Straightforward Approach to Leveraged Leasing" by Pierce R. Smith,* **The Journal of Commercial Bank Lending**, *July 1973, pp. 40-47.*

---

[1] *A direct financing lease must have its cost or carrying value equal to the fair value of the asset at the inception of the lease. Thus, even if the amounts are not significantly different, leveraged lease accounting should not be used.*

1. The owner-lessor secures long-term financing from the creditor, generally in excess of 50% of the purchase price. US GAAP indicates that the lessor must be provided with sufficient leverage in the transaction; thus the 50%.
2. The owner then uses this financing along with his or her own funds to purchase the asset from the manufacturer.
3. The manufacturer delivers the asset to the lessee.
4. The lessee remits the periodic rent to the lessor.
5. The debt is guaranteed by either using the equipment as collateral, the assignment of the lease payments, or both, depending on the demands established by the creditor.

The FASB concluded that the entire lease agreement be accounted for as a single transaction and not a direct financing lease plus a debt transaction. The feeling was that the latter did not readily convey the net investment in the lease to the user of the financial statements. Thus, the lessor is to record the investment as a net amount. The gross investment is calculated as a combination of the following amounts:

1. The rentals receivable from the lessee, net of the principal and interest payments due to the long-term creditor
2. A receivable for the amount of the investment tax credit (ITC) to be realized on the transaction (repealed in the United States but may yet exist in other jurisdictions)
3. The estimated residual value of the leased asset
4. The unearned and deferred income, consisting of

   a. The estimated pretax lease income (or loss), after deducting initial direct costs, remaining to be allocated to income
   b. The ITC remaining to be allocated to profit or loss over the remaining term of the lease

The first three amounts described above are readily obtainable; however, the last amount, the unearned and deferred income, requires additional computations. To derive this amount, it is necessary to create a cash flow (income) analysis by year for the entire lease term. As described in item 4 above, the unearned and deferred income consists of the pretax lease income (Gross lease rentals – Depreciation – Loan interest) and the unamortized investment tax credit. The total of these two amounts for all the periods in the lease term represents the unearned and deferred income at the inception of the lease.

The amount computed as the gross investment in the lease (foregoing paragraphs) less the deferred taxes relative to the difference between pretax lease income and taxable lease income is the net investment for purposes of computing profit or loss for the period. To compute the periodic profit or loss, another schedule must be completed that uses the cash flows derived in the first schedule and allocates them between income and a reduction in the net investment.

The amount of profit or loss is first determined by applying a rate to the net investment. The rate to be used is the rate that will allocate the entire amount of cash flow (income) when applied in the years in which the net investment is positive. In other words, the rate is derived in much the same way as the implicit rate (trial and error), except that only the years in which there is a positive net investment are considered. Thus, income is recognized only in the years in which there is a positive net investment.

The profit or loss recognized is divided among the following three elements:

1. Pretax accounting income
2. Amortization of investment tax credit
3. The tax effect of the pretax accounting income

The first two are allocated in proportionate amounts from the unearned and deferred income included in calculation of the net investment. In other words, the unearned and deferred income consists of pretax lease accounting income and any investment tax credit. Each of these is recognized during the period in the proportion that the current period's allocated income is to the total income (cash flow). The last item, the tax effect, is recognized in the tax expense for the year. The tax effect of any difference between pretax lease accounting income and taxable lease income is charged (or credited) to deferred taxes.

When tax rates change, all components of a leveraged lease must be recalculated from the inception of the lease, using the revised after-tax cash flows arising from the revised tax rates.

If, in any case, the projected cash receipts (income) are less than the initial investment, the deficiency is to be recognized as a loss at the inception of the lease. Similarly, if at any time during the lease period the aforementioned method of recognizing income would result in a future period loss, the loss shall be recognized immediately.

This situation may arise as a result of the circumstances surrounding the lease changing. Therefore, any estimated residual value and other important assumptions must be reviewed on a periodic basis (at least annually). Any change is to be incorporated into the income computations; however, there is to be no upward revision of the estimated residual value.

The following example illustrates the application of these principles to a leveraged lease.

Example of simplified leveraged lease

Assume the following:

1. A lessor acquires an asset for €100,000 with an estimated useful life of 3 years in exchange for a €25,000 down payment and a €75,000 3-year note with equal payments due on December 31 each year. The interest rate is 18%.
2. The asset has no residual value.
3. The PV of an ordinary annuity of €1 for three years at 18% is 2.17427.
4. The asset is leased for 3 years with annual payments due to the lessor on December 31 in the amount of €45,000.
5. The lessor uses the ACRS method of depreciation for tax purposes and elects to reduce the ITC rate to 4%, as opposed to reducing the depreciable basis.
6. Assume a constant tax rate throughout the life of the lease of 40%.

Chart 1 analyzes the cash flows generated by the leveraged leasing activities. Chart 2 allocates the cash flows between the investment in leveraged leased assets and income from leveraged leasing activities. The allocation requires finding that rate of return which, when applied to the investment balance at the beginning of each year that the investment amount is positive, will allocate the net cash flow fully to net income over the term of the lease. This rate can be found only by a computer program or by an iterative trial-and-error process. The example that follows has a positive investment value in each of the three years, and thus the allocation takes place in each time period. Leveraged leases usually have periods where the investment account turns negative and is below zero.

Allocating principal and interest on the loan payments is as follows:

€75,000 ÷ 2.17427 = €34,494

Year	Payment	Interest 18%	Principal	Balance
Inception of lease	€ --	€ --	€ --	€75,000
1	34,494	13,500	20,994	54,006
2	34,494	9,721	24,773	29,233
3	34,494	5,261	29,233	--

Chart 1

	A	B	C	D	E	F	G	H	I
					Income tax payable (rcvbl.)	*Loan principal*		*Cash flow (A+G-C*	*Cumulative cash*
			Interest	*Taxable income*					
	Rent	*Depr.*	*on loan*	*(A-B-C)*	*Dx40%*	*payments*	*ITC*	*-E-F)*	*flow*
Initial	€ --	€ --	€ --	€ --	€ --	€ --	€ --	€(25,000)	€(25,000)
Year 1	45,000	25,000	13,500	6,500	2,600	20,994	4,000	11,906	(13,094)
Year 2	45,000	38,000	9,721	(2,721)	(1,088)	24,773	--	11,594	(1,500)
Year 3	45,000	37,000	5,261	2,739	1,096	29,233	--	9,410	7,910
Total	€135,000	€100,000	€28,482	€ 6,518	€ 2,608	€75,000	€4,000	€ 7,910	

The chart below allocates the cash flows determined above between the net investment in the lease and income. Recall that the income is then allocated between pretax accounting income and the amortization of the investment for credit. The income tax expense for the period is a result of applying the tax rate to the current periodic pretax accounting income.

The amount to be allocated in total in each period is the net cash flow determined in column H above. The investment at the beginning of year 1 is the initial down payment of €25,000. This investment is then reduced on an annual basis by the amount of the cash flow not allocated to income.

Chart 2

	1	2	3	4	5	6	7
		Cash Flow Assumption				*Income Analysis*	
	Investment beginning of year	*Cash flow*	*Allocated to investment*	*Allocated to income*	*Pretax income*	*Income tax expense*	*Investment tax credit*
Year 1	€25,000	€11,906	€ 7,964	€ 3,942	€3,248	€1,300	€1,994
Year 2	17,036	11,594	8,908	2,686	2,213	885	1,358
Year 3	8,128	9,410	8,128	1,282	1,057	423	648
		€32,910	€25,000	€7,910	€6,518	€2,608	€4,000

Rate of return = 15.77%

1. Column 2 is the net cash flow after the initial investment, and columns 3 and 4 are the allocation based on the 15.77% rate of return. The total of column 4 is the same as the total of column H in Chart 1.

2. Column 5 allocates column D in Chart 1 based on the allocations in column 4. Column 6 allocates column E in Chart 1, and column 7 allocates column G in Chart 1 in the same basis.

The journal entries below illustrate the proper recording and accounting for the leveraged lease transaction. The initial entry represents the cash down payment, investment tax credit receivable, the unearned and deferred revenue, and the net cash to be received over the term of the lease.

The remaining journal entries recognize the annual transactions that include the net receipt of cash and the amortization of income.

	Year 1	*Year 2*	*Year 3*
Rents receivable [Chart 1 (A-C-F)]	31,518		
Investment tax credit receivable	4,000		
Cash		25,000	
Unearned and deferred income		10,518	
[Initial investment, Chart 2 (5+7) totals]			
Cash	10,506	10,506	10,506
Rent receivable		10,506	10,506	10,506

	Year 1	Year 2	Year 3
[Net for all cash transactions, Chart 1 (A-C-F) line by line for each year]			
Income tax receivable (cash)	4,000		
Investment tax credit receivable		4,000	
Unearned and deferred income	5,242	3,571	1,705
Income from leveraged leases		5,242	3,571	1,705
[Amortization of unearned income, Chart 2 (5+7) line by line for each year]			

The following schedules illustrate the computation of deferred income tax amount. The annual amount is a result of the temporary difference created due to the difference in the timing of the recognition of income for book and tax purposes. The income for tax purposes can be found in column D in Chart 1, while the income for book purposes is found in column 5 of Chart 2. The actual amount of deferred tax is the difference between the tax computed with the temporary difference and the tax computed without the temporary difference. These amounts are represented by the income tax payable or receivable as shown in column E of Chart 1 and the income tax expense as shown in column 6 of Chart 2. A check of this figure is provided by multiplying the difference between book and tax income by the annual rate.

Year 1

Income tax payable	€ 2,600	
Income tax expense	(1,300)	
Deferred income tax (Dr)		€1,300
Taxable income	€ 6,500	
Pretax accounting income	(3,248)	
Difference	€ 3,252	
€3,252 × 40% = €1,300		

Year 2

Income tax receivable	€ 1,088	
Income tax expense	885	
Deferred income tax (Cr)		€1,973
Taxable loss	€ 2,721	
Pretax accounting income	2,213	
Difference	€ 4,934	
€4,934 × 40% = €1,973		

Year 3

Income tax payable	€ 1,096	
Income tax expense	(423)	
Deferred income tax (Dr)		€ 673
Taxable income	€ 2,739	
Pretax accounting income	(1,057)	
Difference	€ 1,682	
€1,682 × 40% = €673		

15 INCOME TAXES

PERSPECTIVE AND ISSUES

Income taxes are an expense incurred in operating most businesses, and as such are to be reflected in the entity's operating results. However, accounting for income taxes is complicated by the fact that, in most jurisdictions, the amounts of revenues and expenses recognized in a given period for taxation purposes will not fully correspond to what is reported in the financial statements (whether prepared in accordance with various national GAAP or IFRS). The venerable matching principle (still having some relevance, although it is no longer a central concept underlying financial reporting rules) implies that for financial reporting purposes the amount presented as current period tax expense should bear an appropriate relationship to the amount of pretax accounting income being reported. That expense will normally not equal—and may differ markedly from—the amount of the current period's tax payment obligation. The upshot is that deferred income tax assets and/or liabilities must be recognized. These are measured, approximately, as the difference between the amounts currently owed and the amounts recognizable for financial reporting purposes.

Various theories of interperiod income tax allocation have been proposed and mandated over the years, both by various national GAAP and by IFRS. Under the current provisions of IAS 12, which was substantially revised effective in 1998 (with further limited revisions made in 2000), the *liability method* of computing interperiod income tax allocation is required. This method is oriented toward the statement of financial position, rather than the statement of operations, and has as its highest objective the accurate, appropriate measurement of assets and liabilities, so that the statement of financial position representation of deferred tax benefits and obligations will comply with the definitions of assets and liabilities set forth by the IASB's *Framework*. In order to achieve this, at each statement of financial position date the amounts in the deferred tax asset and/or liability accounts must be assessed, with whatever adjustment(s) are needed to achieve the correct balance(s) being reported in the tax provisions for the period. In other words, tax expense is a residual, with the primary objective being achieving the correct balances in the deferred tax asset and liability accounts.

Under revised IAS 12, deferred tax assets and liabilities are to be presented at the amounts that are expected to flow to or from the reporting entity when the tax benefits are ultimately realized or the tax obligations are settled. IAS 12 does not distinguish operating losses from other types of deductible temporary differences, and requires that both be given recognition, when realization is deemed to be *probable*. Discounting of these amounts to present values is not permitted, as debate continues about the role of discounting in the presentation of assets and liabilities on the statement of financial position. (Uncertainty about the timing of deferred tax realization or settlement makes discounting a practical challenge, also).

Both deferred tax assets and liabilities are measured by reference to expected tax rates, which in general are the enacted, effective rates as of the date of the statement of financial position. IAS 12 has particular criteria to be used for the recognition of the tax effects of temporary differences arising from ownership interests in investees and subsidiaries, and for the accounting related to goodwill and negative goodwill arising from business acquisitions. Presentation of deferred tax assets or liabilities as current assets or liabilities is prohibited by the standard, which also establishes extensive financial statement disclosures.

Sources of IFRS
IAS 12   *SIC* 21, 25

DEFINITIONS OF TERMS

Accounting profit. Net profit or loss for the reporting period before deducting income tax expense.

Current tax expense (benefit). The amount of income taxes payable (recoverable) in respect of the taxable profit (tax loss) for a period.

Deductible temporary differences. Temporary differences that result in amounts that are deductible in determining future taxable profit when the carrying amount of the asset or liability is recovered or settled.

Deferred tax asset. The amounts of income taxes recoverable in future periods in respect of deductible temporary differences, carryforwards of unused tax losses, and carryforwards of unused tax credits.

Deferred tax expense (benefit). The change during a reporting period in the deferred tax liabilities and deferred tax assets of an entity.

Deferred tax liability. The amounts of income taxes payable in future periods in respect of taxable temporary differences.

Gains and losses included in nonowner movements in equity but excluded from net income. Certain items which, under IFRS, are events occurring currently but which are reported directly in equity, such as changes in market values of available-for-sale portfolios of marketable equity securities.

Interperiod tax allocation. The process of apportioning income tax expense among reporting periods without regard to the timing of the actual cash payments for taxes. The objective is to reflect fully the tax consequences of all economic events reported in current or prior financial statements and, in particular, to report the expected tax effects of the reversals of temporary differences existing at the reporting date.

Operating loss carryback or carryforward. The excess of tax deductions over taxable income. To the extent that this results in a carryforward (to be offset against future periods' taxable income under local laws), the tax effect thereof is included in the entity's deferred tax asset, unless this is not expected to be realized.

Permanent differences. Differences between accounting profit and taxable profit as a result of the treatment accorded certain transactions by the income tax regulations which differs from the accounting treatment. Permanent differences will not reverse in subsequent periods, and accordingly, do not create a need for deferred tax recognition.

Tax basis. The amount attributable (explicitly or implicitly) to an asset or liability by the taxation authorities in determining taxable profit.

Tax credits. Reductions in the tax liability as a result of certain expenditures accorded special treatment under the tax regulations.

Tax expense. The aggregate of current tax expense and deferred tax expense for a reporting period.

Taxable profit (loss). The profit (loss) for a taxable period, determined in accordance with the rules established by the pertinent taxing authorities, which determine income taxes payable (recoverable).

Taxable temporary differences. Temporary differences that result in taxable amounts in determining taxable profit of future periods when the carrying amount of the asset or liability is recovered or settled.

Temporary differences. The differences between tax and financial reporting bases of assets and liabilities that will result in taxable or deductible amounts in future periods. Temporary differences include "timing differences" as previously defined under IFRS as well as certain other differences, such as those arising from business combinations. There are some temporary differences that cannot be associated with particular assets or liabilities, but nonetheless do result from events that received financial statement recognition, and will have tax effects in future periods.

Unrecognized tax benefits. Deferred tax benefits that have not been recognized because they are not deemed probable of being realized.

CONCEPTS, RULES, AND EXAMPLES

Basic Concepts of Interperiod Income Tax Allocation

Over the years, various theories have been advanced regarding the appropriate reporting of income tax expense when there are differences in the timing of recognition of revenue and expense for tax and financial reporting purposes. The most popular of these were the *deferral* method and the *liability* method. (A third approach, the *net of tax* method, for a time received a moderate amount of academic support but was far less widely employed [or understood] by practitioners; its only actual widespread use was as a valuation technique to record assets and liabilities acquired in purchase business combinations under now-superseded accounting standards.)

The deferral method, which was widely employed from the 1960s until about 1990, was soundly based on the then-important matching principle and was never misrepresented as being designed to produce the most meaningful statement of financial position. However, in practice, the deferral method suffered from great complexity and sometimes also resulted in material distortions of the statement of financial position. This was considered an acceptable, if regrettable, side effect, particularly during the late 1960s and 1970s, a period when more attention was directed at direct income measurement than at meaningfulness of statements of financial position. (Income measurement obviously remains of great importance, but under current financial reporting concepts it is increasingly being measured indirectly, as the by-product of changes in assets and liabilities. This emphasis will only increase under proposed new standards, including the expected changes to revenue recognition now being developed.)

Following the adoption of the IASC's *Framework*, which is conceptual underpinning for financial reporting standards promulgated by IASB, it was inevitable that substantial changes in accounting for income taxes would be made. That follows because the deferred charges and credits resulting from the application of the deferral method (as permitted by the original IAS 12) were generally not true assets or liabilities, as defined by the *Framework*. Accordingly, it became indefensible to continue to place these items on the statement of financial position. The liability method (explained below), which completely avoids this problem, became the method of choice.

A separate, but also important, debate had been waged regarding which items of timing differences for which deferred tax effects were to be computed and reported. At one extreme were proponents of no allocation, who favored reporting in the financial statements only the amount of taxes currently payable as income tax expense. Occupying the middle ground were advocates of partial allocation, who accepted the need to provide deferred taxes, but only for those timing differences whose ultimate reversal could be reasonably predicted. At the other extreme were those favoring comprehensive allocation, which holds that deferred tax effects are to be reported for all timing differences, even if ultimate reversal is far in the future or cannot be predicted at all. Reported earnings would often vary markedly depending on which of these approaches were employed. Over time, comprehensive allocation became the approach endorsed by most major standard-setting bodies.

As was true with many early IASC-issued standards, the original IAS 12 permitted use of a wide variety of techniques, which produced highly disparate results. IASC's goal, however, was to ultimately narrow the range of alternatives that would be deemed acceptable in accounting for given economic events, and it has accomplished that with regard to income tax accounting. The current version of IAS 12 demands that the liability method be employed, using comprehensive allocation, and no alternative methodologies are permitted.

Measurement of Tax Expense

Current tax expense. Income tax expense will be comprised of two components: current tax expense and deferred tax expense. Either of these can be a benefit (i.e., a credit amount in the statement of comprehensive income), rather than an expense (a debit), depending on whether there is taxable profit or loss for the period. For convenience, the term "tax expense" will be used to denote either an expense or a benefit. Current tax expense is easily understood as the tax effect of the entity's reported taxable income or loss for the period, as determined by relevant rules of the various taxing authorities to which it is subject. Deferred tax expense, in general terms, arises as the tax effect of timing differences occurring during the reporting period.

Using the liability method, the reporting entity's current period total income tax expense cannot be computed directly (except when there are no temporary differences). Rather, it must be calculated as the sum of the two components: current tax expense and deferred tax expense. This total will not, in general, equal the amount that would be derived by applying the current tax rate to pretax accounting profit. The reason is that deferred tax expense is defined as the change in the deferred tax asset and liability accounts occurring in the current period, and this change may encompass more than the mere effect of the current tax rate times the net temporary differences arising or being reversed in the present reporting period.

Under provisions of IAS 12, current period deferred tax expense incorporates the effects of changing tax rates on the as-yet-unreversed temporary differences which originated in prior periods. In other words, current period tax expense may include not merely the tax effects of currently reported revenue and expense items, but also certain tax effects relating to items reported previously.

Although the primary objective of income tax accounting is no longer the proper matching of current period revenue and expenses, the once-critical matching principle retains some importance in financial reporting theory. Therefore, the tax effects of items excluded from the statement of income are also excluded from the statement of income. For example, the tax effects of items reported in other comprehensive income are likewise reported in other comprehensive income. (Under revised IAS 1, discussed in Chapter 3, preparers have a choice of reporting comprehensive income in two separate financial statements or in one.) This is referred to as *intraperiod* tax allocation, and is to be distinguished from the *interperiod* allocation that is the major subject of IAS 12 and of this chapter.

An Overview of the Liability Method

The liability method is statement of financial position oriented. Therefore, the primary goal of the liability method is to present the estimated actual taxes to be payable in current and future periods as the income tax liability on the statement of financial position. (This equally applies in the case of current and future tax refunds.) To accomplish this goal, it is necessary to consider the effect of certain enacted future changes in the tax rates when computing the current period's tax provision. The computation of the amount of deferred taxes is based on the rate expected to be in effect when the temporary differences reverse. The annual computation is considered a tentative estimate of the liability (or asset) that is subject to change as the statutory tax rate changes or as the taxpayer moves into other tax rate brackets.

The IASB's *Framework* defines liabilities as obligations resulting from past transactions and involving "giving up resources embodying economic benefits in order to satisfy the claim of [another] party." Assets are defined as "the potential to contribute, directly or indirectly, to the flow of cash . . . to the enterprise." The fact that the deferred debits and credits generated through the use of the formerly-permitted deferral method did not meet the strict definitions of assets and liabilities prescribed by the *Framework* was one of the primary reasons for the IASC's mid-1990s reconsideration of IAS 12, which culminated in the issuance of the 1996 revision to IAS 12, which became mandatory in 1998.

Application of the liability method is, in concept at least, relatively simple when compared to the deferral method. Unlike the deferral method, there is no need to maintain a historical record of the timing of origination of the various unreversed differences, since the effective rates at which the various components were established is not relevant. As the liability method is strictly a statement of financial position approach, the primary concern is to state the obligation for taxes payable (or tax benefits receivable) as accurately as possible, based on expected tax impact of future reversals. This is accomplished by multiplying the aggregate unreversed temporary differences, including those originating in the current period, by the tax rate(s) expected to be in effect in the future to determine the expected future liability (or benefit). This expected liability (or benefit) is the amount presented on the statement of financial position at the end of the period. The difference between this amount and the amount on the books at the beginning of the period, to greatly simplify the actual process, is the deferred tax expense or benefit to be reported in operating results for the current reporting period.

An example of application of the liability method of deferred income tax accounting follows.

Simplified example of interperiod allocation using the liability method

Ghiza International has no permanent differences in either years 2008 or 2009. The company has only two temporary differences, arising in connection with depreciation and prepaid rent. No consideration is given to the nature of the deferred tax account (i.e., current or long-term) as it is not considered necessary for purposes of this example. Ghiza has a credit balance in its deferred tax account at the beginning of 2008 in the amount of €180,000. This balance consists of €228,000 (€475,000 depreciation temporary difference × 48% tax rate) of deferred taxable amounts and €48,000 (€100,000 prepaid rent temporary difference × 48% tax rate) of deferred deductible amounts.

For purposes of this example, it is assumed that there was a constant effective 48% tax rate in all periods prior to 2008. The pretax accounting income and the temporary differences originating and reversing in 2008 and 2009 are as follows:

Ghiza International

		2008		*2009*	
Pretax accounting income		€800,000		€1,200,000	
Timing differences:					
Depreciation:	originating	€(180,000)		€(160,000)	
	reversing	60,000	(120,000)	100,000	(60,000)
Prepaid rental income:	originating	75,000		80,000	
	reversing	(25,000)	50,000	(40,000)	40,000
Taxable income			€730,000		€1,180,000

The tax rates for years 2008 and 2009 are 46% and 38%, respectively. These rates are assumed to be independent of one another, and the 2009 change in the rate was not known until it actually took place in 2009.

Computation of tax provision—2008

Balance of deferred tax account, 1/1/08

Depreciation (€475,000 × 48%)	€228,000
Prepaid rental income (€100,000 × 48%)	(48,000)
	180,000

Aggregate temporary differences, 12/31/08

Depreciation (€475,000 + €120,000)	€595,000	
Prepaid rental income (€100,000 + €50,000)	(150,000)	
	445,000	
Expected future rate (2008 rate)	× 46%	
Balance required in the deferred tax account, 12/31/08		204,700
Required addition to the deferred tax account		24,700
Income taxes currently payable (€730,000 × 46%)		335,800
Total tax provision		€360,500

Computation of tax provision—2009

Balance of deferred tax account, 1/1/09

Depreciation (€595,000 × 46%)		€273,700
Prepaid rental income (€150,000 × 46%)		(69,000)
		€204,700
Aggregate timing differences, 12/31/09		
Depreciation (€595,000 + €60,000)	€655,000	
Prepaid rental income (€150,000 + €40,000)	(190,000)	
	465,000	
Expected future rate (2009 rate)	× 38%	
Balance required in the deferred tax account, 12/31/09		176,700
Required reduction in the deferred tax account		(28,000)
Income taxes currently payable (€1,180,000 × 38%)		448,400
Total tax provision		€420,400

Liability Method Explained in Detail

While conceptually the liability method is straightforward, in practice there are a number of complexities that need to be addressed. In the following discussion, these measurement and reporting issues will be discussed in greater detail.

1. Nature of temporary differences
2. Treatment of operating loss carryforwards
3. Measurement of deferred tax assets and liabilities
4. Valuation allowance for deferred tax assets that are not assured of realization
5. Effect of tax law changes on previously recorded deferred tax assets and liabilities
6. Effect of tax status changes on previously incurred deferred tax assets and liabilities
7. Tax effects of business combinations
8. Intercorporate income tax allocation
9. Exceptions to the general rules of IAS 12

Detailed examples of deferred income tax accounting under IAS 12 are presented throughout the following discussion of these issues.

Nature of Temporary Differences

The preponderance of the typical reporting entity's revenue and expense transactions are treated identically for tax and financial reporting purposes. Some transactions and events, however, will have different tax and accounting implications. In many of these cases, the difference relates to the period in which the income or expense will be recognized. Under earlier iterations of IAS 12, the latter differences were referred to as *timing differences* and were said to originate in one period and to reverse in a later period. Common timing differences included those relating to depreciation methods, deferred compensation plans, percentage-of-completion accounting for long-term construction contracts, and cash versus accrual accounting methods.

The latest revisions to IAS 12 introduced the concept of *temporary differences*, which is a somewhat more comprehensive concept than that of timing differences. Temporary differences include all the categories of items defined under the earlier concept, and add a number of additional items, as well. Temporary differences are thus defined to include *all* differences between the tax and financial reporting bases of assets and liabilities, if those differences will result in taxable or deductible amounts in future years.

Examples of temporary differences that were also deemed to be timing differences under the original IAS 12 are the following:

1. **Revenue recognized for financial reporting purposes before being recognized for tax purposes.** Examples include revenue accounted for by the installment method for tax purposes, but reflected in income currently; certain construction-related revenue recognized on a completed-contract method for tax purposes, but on a percentage-of-completion basis for financial reporting; earnings from investees recognized by the equity method for accounting purposes but taxed only when later distributed as dividends to the investor. These are taxable temporary differences, which give rise to deferred tax liabilities.

2. **Revenue recognized for tax purposes prior to recognition in the financial statements.** These include certain types of revenue received in advance, such as prepaid rental income and service contract revenue. Referred to as deductible temporary differences, these items give rise to deferred tax assets.

3. **Expenses that are deductible for tax purposes prior to recognition in the financial statements.** This results when accelerated depreciation methods or shorter useful lives are used for tax purposes, while straight-line depreciation or longer useful economic lives are used for financial reporting; and when there are certain preoperating costs and certain capitalized interest costs that are deductible currently for tax purposes. These items are taxable temporary differences and give rise to deferred tax liabilities.

4. **Expenses that are reported in the financial statements prior to becoming deductible for tax purposes.** Certain estimated expenses, such as warranty costs, as well as such contingent losses as accruals of litigation expenses, are not tax deductible until the obligation becomes fixed. These are deductible temporary differences, and accordingly give rise to deferred tax assets.

In addition to these familiar and well-understood timing differences, temporary differences include a number of other categories that also involve differences between the tax and financial reporting bases of assets or liabilities. These are

1. **Reductions in tax deductible asset bases arising in connection with tax credits.** Under tax provisions in certain jurisdictions, credits are available for certain qualifying investments in plant assets. In some cases, taxpayers are permitted a choice of either full accelerated depreciation coupled with a reduced investment tax credit, or a full investment tax credit coupled with reduced depreciation allowances. If the taxpayer chose the latter option, the asset basis is reduced for tax depreciation, but would still be fully depreciable for financial reporting purposes. Accordingly, this election would be accounted for as a taxable timing difference, and give rise to a deferred tax liability.

2. **Increases in the tax bases of assets resulting from the indexing of asset costs for the effects of inflation.** Occasionally, proposed and sometimes enacted by taxing jurisdictions, such a tax law provision allows taxpaying entities to finance the replacement of depreciable assets through depreciation based on current costs, as

computed by the application of indices to the historical costs of the assets being re-measured. This reevaluation of asset costs gives rise to deductible temporary differences that would be associated with deferred tax benefits.

3. **Certain business combinations accounted for by the acquisition method.** Under certain circumstances, the costs assignable to assets or liabilities acquired in purchase business combinations will differ from their tax bases. The usual scenario under which this arises is when the acquirer must continue to report the predecessor's tax bases for tax purposes, although the price paid was more or less than book value. Such differences may be either taxable or deductible and, accordingly, may give rise to deferred tax liabilities or assets. These differences were treated as timing differences under the original IAS 12, and will now be recognized as temporary differences by revised IAS 12.

4. **Assets which are revalued for financial reporting purposes although the tax bases are not affected.** This is analogous to the matter discussed in the preceding paragraph. Under certain IFRS (such as IAS 16 and IAS 40), assets may be upwardly adjusted to current fair values (revaluation amounts), although for tax purposes these adjustments are ignored until and unless the assets are disposed of. The discrepancies between the adjusted book carrying values and the tax bases are temporary differences under IAS 12, and deferred taxes are to be provided on these variations. This is required even if there is no intention to dispose of the assets in question, or if, under the salient tax laws, exchanges for other similar assets (or reinvestment of proceeds of sales in similar assets) would effect a postponement of the tax obligation.

There are other items that would not have been deemed timing differences under the original IAS 12, but which are temporary differences under revised IAS 12. These include the following:

1. **Assets and liabilities acquired in transactions that are not business combinations which are not deductible or taxable in determining taxable profit.** In some tax jurisdictions, the cost of certain assets are never deductible in computing taxable profit. Depending on jurisdiction, buildings, intangibles, or other assets may not be subject to depreciation or amortization. Thus, the asset in question has a differing accounting basis than tax basis, and this defines a temporary difference under revised IAS 12. Similarly, certain liabilities may not be recognized for tax purposes. While IAS 12 agrees that these represent temporary differences and that, under the principles of interperiod tax allocation using the liability method, this should result in the recognition of deferred tax liabilities or assets, the decision was made to not permit this. The reason given is that the new result would be to "gross up" the recorded amount of the asset or liability to offset the recorded deferred tax liability or benefit, and this would make the financial statements "less transparent." It could also be argued that when an asset has, as one of its attributes, nondeductibility for tax purposes, the price paid for this asset would have been affected accordingly, so that any such "gross-up" would cause the asset to be reported at an amount in excess of fair value.

2. **Assets and liabilities acquired in business combinations.** When assets and liabilities are valued at fair value, as required under IFRS 3, but the tax basis is not adjusted (i.e., there is a carryforward basis for tax purposes), there will be differences between the tax and financial reporting bases of these assets and liabilities, which will constitute temporary differences. Deferred tax benefits and obligations need to be recognized for these differences.

3. **Goodwill that cannot be amortized (deducted) for tax purposes.** Prior to IFRS 3, goodwill was subject to amortization for financial reporting purposes but in some tax jurisdictions this could not be deducted, so there was a question regarding the deferred tax effects to be recognized. Goodwill or negative goodwill were residual amounts, and any attempt to compute the deferred tax effects thereof would have resulted in "grossing up" the financial statement balance of that very account (goodwill or negative goodwill, as the case may be). Although such a presentation could have been rationalized, it would have been of dubious usefulness to the users of the financial statements. For this reason, IAS 12 held that no deferred taxes were to be provided on the difference between the tax and book bases of nondeductible goodwill or nontaxable negative goodwill. Under the provisions of IFRS 3, goodwill is no longer subject to amortization, and negative goodwill is included in income upon consummating a business acquisition that is deemed to be a bargain purchase. There is less likely to be any issue of tax/book differences under the current requirements.

Measurement of Deferred Tax Assets and Liabilities

The procedure to compute the gross deferred tax provision (i.e., before addressing whether the deferred tax asset is probable of being realized and therefore should be recognized) is as follows:

1. Identify (i.e., take an inventory of) all temporary differences existing as of the reporting date.
2. Segregate the temporary differences into those that are taxable and those that are deductible. This step is necessary because under IAS 12 only those deferred tax benefits which are probable of being realized are recognized, whereas all deferred obligations are given full recognition.
3. Accumulate information about the *deductible* temporary differences, particularly the net operating loss and credit carryforwards that have expiration dates or other types of limitations.
4. Measure the tax effect of aggregate *taxable* temporary differences by applying the appropriate expected tax rates (federal plus any state, local, and foreign rates that are applicable under the circumstances).
5. Similarly, measure the tax effects of *deductible* temporary differences, including net operating loss carryforwards.

It should be emphasized that separate computations should be made for each tax jurisdiction, since in assessing the propriety of recording the tax effects of deductible temporary differences it is necessary to consider the entity's ability to absorb deferred tax benefits against tax liabilities. Inasmuch as benefits receivable from one tax jurisdiction will not reduce taxes payable to another jurisdiction, separate calculations will be needed. Also, for purposes of statement of financial position presentation (discussed below in detail), the offsetting of deferred tax assets and liabilities is permissible only within jurisdictions, since there would never be a legal right to offset obligations due to and from different taxing authorities. Similarly, separate computations should be made for each taxpaying component of the business. Thus, if a parent company and its subsidiaries are consolidated for financial reporting purposes but file separate tax returns, the reporting entity comprises a number of components, and the tax benefits of any one will be unavailable to reduce the tax obligations of the others.

The principles set forth above are illustrated by the following examples.

Basic example of the computation of deferred tax liability and asset

Assume that Noori Company has pretax financial income of €250,000 in 2009, a total of €28,000 of taxable temporary differences, and a total of €8,000 of deductible temporary differences. Noori has no operating loss or tax credit carryforwards. The tax rate is a flat (i.e., not graduated) 40%. Also assume that there were no deferred tax liabilities or assets in prior years.

Taxable income is computed as follows:

Pretax financial income	€250,000
Taxable temporary differences	(28,000)
Deductible temporary differences	8,000
Taxable income	€230,000

The journal entry to record required amounts is

Current income tax expense	92,000	
Deferred tax asset	3,200	
Income tax expense—deferred	8,000	
Deferred tax liability		11,200
Income taxes currently payable		92,000

Current income tax expense and income taxes currently payable are each computed as taxable income times the current rate (€230,000 × 40%). The deferred tax asset of €3,200 represents 40% of deductible temporary differences of €8,000. The deferred tax liability of €11,200 is calculated as 40% of taxable temporary differences of €28,000. The deferred tax expense of €8,000 is the *net* of the deferred tax liability of €11,200 and the deferred tax asset of €3,200.

In 2010, Noori Company has pretax financial income of €450,000, aggregate taxable and deductible temporary differences are €75,000 and €36,000, respectively, and the tax rate remains a flat 40%. Taxable income is €411,000, computed as pretax financial income of €450,000 minus taxable differences of €75,000 plus deductible differences of €36,000. Current income tax expense and income taxes currently payable each are €164,400 (€411,000 × 40%).

Deferred amounts are calculated as follows:

	Deferred tax liability	*Deferred tax asset*	*Income tax expense—deferred*
Required balance at 12/31/10			
€75,000 × 40%	€30,000		--
€36,000 × 40%		€14,400	--
Balances at 12/31/09	11,200	3,200	--
Adjustment required	€18,800	€11,200	€7,600

The journal entry to record the deferred amounts is

Deferred tax asset	11,200	
Income tax expense—deferred	7,600	
Deferred tax liability		18,800

Because the *increase* in the liability in 2009 is larger (by €7,600) than the increase in the asset for that year, the result is a deferred tax *expense* for 2009.

Considerations for Recognition of Deferred Tax Assets

Although the case for presentation in the financial statements of any amount computed for deferred tax liabilities is clear, it can be argued that deferred tax assets should be included in the statement of financial position only if they are, in fact, very likely to be realized in future periods. Since realization will almost certainly be dependent on the future profitability of the reporting entity, it may become necessary to ascertain the likelihood that the enterprise will be profitable. Absent convincing evidence of that, the concepts of conservatism and realization would suggest that the asset be treated as a contingent gain, and not accorded recognition until and unless ultimately realized.

Under IAS 12, deferred tax assets resulting from temporary differences and from tax loss carryforwards are to be given recognition only if realization is deemed to be *probable*. To operationalize this concept, the standard sets forth several criteria, which variously apply to deferred tax assets arising from temporary differences and from tax loss carryforwards. The standard establishes that

1. It is *probable* that future taxable profit will be available against which a deferred tax asset arising from a deductible temporary difference can be utilized when there are sufficient taxable temporary differences relating to the same taxation authority which will reverse either

    a. In the same period as the reversal of the deductible temporary difference, or
    b. In periods into which the deferred tax asset can be carried back or forward; or

2. If there are insufficient taxable temporary differences relating to the same taxation authority, it is probable that the enterprise will have taxable profits in the same period as the reversal of the deductible temporary difference or in periods to which the deferred tax can be carried back or forward, or there are tax planning opportunities available to the enterprise that will create taxable profit in appropriate periods.

Thus, there necessarily will be an element of judgment in making an assessment about how probable the realization of the deferred tax asset is, for those circumstances in which there is not an existing balance of deferred tax liability equal to or greater than the amount of the deferred tax asset. If it cannot be concluded that realization is probable, the deferred tax asset is not given recognition.

As a practical matter, there are a number of positive and negative factors which may be evaluated in reaching a conclusion as to amount of the deferred tax asset to be recognized. Positive factors (those suggesting that the full amount of the deferred tax asset associated with the gross temporary difference should be recorded) might include

1. Evidence of sufficient future taxable income, exclusive of reversing temporary differences and carryforwards, to realize the benefit of the deferred tax asset
2. Evidence of sufficient future taxable income arising from the reversals of existing taxable temporary differences (deferred tax liabilities) to realize the benefit of the tax asset
3. Evidence of sufficient taxable income in prior year(s) available for realization of an operating loss carryback under existing statutory limitations
4. Evidence of the existence of prudent, feasible tax planning strategies under management control which, if implemented, would permit the realization of the tax asset. These are discussed in greater detail below.
5. An excess of appreciated asset values over their tax bases, in an amount sufficient to realize the deferred tax asset. This can be thought of as a subset of the tax strategies idea, since a sale or sale/leaseback of appreciated property is once rather obvious tax planning strategy to salvage a deferred tax benefit which might otherwise expire unused.
6. A strong earnings history exclusive of the loss that created the deferred tax asset. This would, under many circumstances, suggest that future profitability is likely and therefore that realization of deferred tax assets is probable.

Although the foregoing may suggest that the reporting entity will be able to realize the benefits of the deductible temporary differences outstanding as of the date of the statement of financial position, certain negative factors should also be considered in determining whether realization of the full amount of the deferred tax benefit is probable under the circumstances. These factors could include

1. A cumulative recent history of accounting losses. Depending on extent and length of time over which losses were experienced, this could reduce the assessment of likelihood of realization below the important "probable" threshold.
2. A history of operating losses or of tax operating loss or credit carryforwards that have expired unused
3. Losses that are anticipated in the near future years, despite a history of profitable operations

Thus, the process of determining how much of the computed gross deferred tax benefit should be recognized involves the weighing of both positive and negative factors to determine whether, based on the preponderance of available evidence, it is probable that the deferred tax asset will be realized. IAS 12 notes that a history of unused tax losses should be considered "strong evidence" that future taxable profits might prove elusive. In such cases, it would be expected that primary reliance would be placed on the existence of taxable temporary differences which, upon reversal, would provide taxable income to absorb the deferred tax benefits that are candidates for recognition in the financial statements. Absent those taxable temporary differences, recognition would be much more difficult.

Example

To illustrate this computation in a more specific fact situation, assume the following facts:

1. Malpasa Corporation reports on a calendar year and adopted revised IAS 12 in 2005.
2. As of the December 31, 2008 statement of financial position, Malpasa has taxable temporary differences of €85,000 relating to depreciation, deductible temporary differences of €12,000 relating to deferred compensation arrangements, a net operating loss carryforward (which arose in 2004) of €40,000, and a capital loss carryover of €10,000. Note that capital losses can only be offset against capital gains (not ordinary income), but may be carried forward until used.
3. Malpasa's expected tax rate for future years is 40% for ordinary income, and 25% for net long-term capital gains.

The first steps are to compute the required balances of the deferred tax asset and liability accounts, without consideration of whether the tax asset would be probable of realization. The computations would proceed as follows:

Deferred tax liability	
Taxable temporary difference (depreciation)	€85,000
Effective tax rate	× 40%
Required balance	€34,000
Deferred tax asset	
Deductible temporary differences	€12,000
Deferred compensation	40,000
Net operating loss	€52,000
Effective tax rate	× 40%
Required balance (a)	€20,800
Capital loss	€10,000
Effective tax rate	× 25%
Required balance (b)	€ 2,500
Total deferred tax asset	
Ordinary (a)	€20,800
Capital (b)	2,500
Total required balance	€23,300

The next step would be to consider whether realization of the deferred tax asset is probable. Malpasa management must evaluate both positive and negative evidence to determine this matter. Assume now that management identifies the following factors which may be relevant:

1. Before the net operating loss deduction, Malpasa reported taxable income of €5,000 in 2008. Management believes that taxable income in future years, apart from NOL deductions, should continue at about the same level experienced in 2008.
2. The taxable temporary differences are not expected to reverse in the foreseeable future.
3. The capital loss arose in connection with a transaction of a type that is unlikely to recur. The company does not generally engage in activities that have the potential to result in capital gains or losses.
4. Management estimates that certain productive assets have a fair value exceeding their respective tax bases by about €30,000. The entire gain, if realized for tax purposes, would be a recapture of depreciation previously taken. Since the current plans call for a substantial upgrading of the company's plant assets, management feels that it could easily accelerate those actions to realize taxable gains, should it be desirable to do so for tax planning purposes.

Based on the foregoing information, Malpasa Corporation management concludes that a €2,500 adjustment to deferred tax assets is required. The reasoning is as follows:

1. There will be some taxable operating income generated in future years (€5,000 annually, based on the earnings experienced in 2008), which will absorb a modest portion of the reversal of the deductible temporary difference (€12,000) and net operating loss carryforward (€40,000) existing at year-end 2008.
2. More important, the feasible tax planning strategy of accelerating the taxable gain relating to appreciated assets (€30,000) would certainly be sufficient, in conjunction with operating income over several years, to permit Malpasa to realize the tax benefits of the deductible temporary difference and NOL carryover.
3. However, since capital loss carryovers are only usable to offset future capital gains and Malpasa management is unable to project future realization of capital gains, the associated tax benefit accrued (€2,500) will probably not be realized, and thus cannot be recognized.

Based on this analysis, deferred tax benefits in the amount of €20,800 should be recognized.

The criterion prescribed by IAS 12 is significantly different than that which is employed under the corresponding US GAAP standard, FAS 109. In conformity with that standard, all deferred tax assets are first recorded, after which a valuation allowance or reserve is established to offset that portion which is not deemed "more likely than not" to be realizable. The net effect will be generally similar under either approach, but the consensus opinion is that the US GAAP realization threshold, "more likely than not," represents a somewhat lower boundary than does IAS 12's "probable." While the former is acknowledged to imply a probability of just slightly over 50%, the latter is thought to connote a likelihood in the range of at least 75-80%, or possibly higher. Worded yet another way, it would seemingly be more difficult to support the existence of a valid deferred tax asset under IFRS than under US GAAP rules as they now exist.

Future temporary differences as a source for taxable profit to offset deductible differences. In some instances, an entity may have deferred tax assets that will be realizable when future tax deductions are taken, but it cannot be concluded that there will be sufficient taxable profits to absorb these future deductions. However, the enterprise can reasonably predict that if it continues as a going concern, it will generate other temporary differences such that taxable (if not book) profits will be created. It has indeed been argued that the going concern assumption underlying much of accounting theory is sufficient rationale for the recognition of deferred tax assets in such circumstances.

However, IAS 12 makes it clear that this is not valid reasoning. The new taxable temporary differences anticipated for future periods will themselves reverse in even later periods; these cannot do "double duty" by also being projected to be available to absorb currently existing deductible temporary differences. Thus, in evaluating whether realization of currently outstanding deferred tax benefits is probable, it is appropriate to consider the currently outstanding taxable temporary differences, but not taxable temporary differences which are projected to be created in later periods.

Tax planning opportunities that will help realize deferred tax assets. When an entity has deductible temporary differences and taxable temporary differences pertaining to the same tax jurisdiction, there is a presumption that realization of the relevant deferred tax assets is probable, since the relevant deferred tax liabilities should be available to offset these. However, before concluding that this is valid, it will be necessary to consider further the *timing* of the two sets of reversals. If the deductible temporary differences will reverse, say, in the very near term, and the taxable differences will not reverse for many years, it is a matter for concern that the tax benefits created by the former occurrence may expire unused prior to the latter event occurring. Thus, when the existence of deferred tax obligations serves as the logical basis for the recognition of deferred tax assets, it is also necessary to consider whether, under pertinent tax regulations, the benefit carryforward period is sufficient to assure that the benefit will not be lost to the reporting enterprise.

For example, if the deductible temporary difference is projected to reverse in two years but the taxable temporary difference is not anticipated to occur for another ten years, and the tax jurisdiction in question offers only a five-year tax loss carryforward, then (absent other facts suggesting that the tax benefit is probable of realization) the deferred tax benefit could not be given recognition under IAS 12.

However, the entity might have certain tax planning opportunities available to it, such that the pattern of taxable profits could be altered to make the deferred tax benefit, which might otherwise be lost, probable of realization. For example, again depending on the rules of the salient tax jurisdiction, an election might be made to tax interest income on an accrual rather than a cash received basis, which might accelerate income recognition such that it would be available to offset or absorb the deductible temporary differences. Also, claimed tax deductions might be deferred to later periods, similarly boosting taxable profits in the short term.

More subtly, a reporting entity may have certain assets, such as buildings, which have appreciated in value. It is entirely feasible, in many situations, for an enterprise to take certain steps, such as selling the building to realize the taxable gain thereon and then either leasing back the premises or acquiring another suitable building, to salvage the tax deduction that would otherwise be lost to it due to the expiration of a loss carryforward period. If such a strategy is deemed to be reasonably available, even if the entity does not expect to have to implement it (for example, because it expects other taxable temporary differences to be originated in the interim), it may be used to justify recognition of the deferred tax benefits.

Consider the following example of how an available tax planning strategy might be used to support recognition of a deferred tax asset that otherwise might have to go unrecognized.

Example of the impact of a qualifying tax strategy

Assume that Kirloski Company has a €180,000 operating loss carryforward as of 12/31/09, scheduled to expire at the end of the following year. Taxable temporary differences of €240,000 exist that are expected to reverse in approximately equal amounts of €80,000 in 2010, 2011, and 2012. Kirloski Company estimates that taxable income for 2010 (exclusive of the reversal of existing temporary differences and the operating loss carryforward) will be €20,000. Kirloski Company expects to implement a qualifying tax planning strategy that will accelerate the total of

€240,000 of taxable temporary differences to 2010. Expenses to implement the strategy are estimated to approximate €30,000. The applicable expected tax rate is 40%.

In the absence of the tax planning strategy, €100,000 of the operating loss carryforward could be realized in 2010 based on estimated taxable income of €20,000 plus €80,000 of the reversal of taxable temporary differences. Thus, €80,000 would expire unused at the end of 2010 and the net amount of the deferred tax asset at 12/31/10 would be recognized at €40,000, computed as €72,000 (= €180,000 × 40%) minus the valuation allowance of €32,000 (€80,000 × 40%).

However, by implementing the tax planning strategy, the deferred tax asset is calculated as follows:

Taxable income for 2010	
Expected amount without reversal of taxable temporary differences	€ 20,000
Reversal of taxable temporary differences due to tax planning strategy, net of costs	210,000
	230,000
Operating loss to be carried forward	(180,000)
Operating loss expiring unused at 12/31/10	€ 0

The deferred tax asset to be recorded at 12/31/09 is €54,000. This is computed as follows:

Full benefit of tax loss carryforward		
	€180,000 × 40% =	€72,000
Less:	Net-of-tax effect of anticipated expenses related to implementation of the strategy	
	€30,000 – (€30,000 × 40%) =	18,000
Net		€54,000

Kirloski Company will also recognize a deferred tax liability of €96,000 at the end of 2008 (40% of the taxable temporary differences of €240,000).

Subsequently revised expectations that a deferred tax benefit is realizable. It may happen that, in a given reporting period, a deferred tax asset is deemed not probable of being realized and accordingly is not recognized, but in a later reporting period the judgment is made that the amount is in fact realizable. If this change in expectation occurs, the deferred tax asset previously not recognized will now be recorded. This does not constitute a prior period adjustment because no accounting error occurred. Rather, this is a change in estimate and is to be included in current earnings. Thus, the tax provision in the period when the estimate is revised will be affected.

Similarly, if a deferred tax benefit provision is made in a given reporting period, but later events suggest that the amount is, in whole or in part, not probable of being realized, the provision should be partially or completely reversed. Again, this adjustment will be included in the tax provision in the period in which the estimate is altered, since it is a change in an accounting estimate. Under either scenario the footnotes to the financial statements will need to provide sufficient information for the users to make meaningful interpretations, since the amount reported as tax expense will seemingly bear an unusual relationship to the reported pretax accounting profit for the period.

If the deferred tax provision in a given period is misstated due to a clerical error, such as miscalculation of the effective expected tax rate, this would constitute an accounting error, and this must be accounted for according to IAS 8's provisions; as revised, this standard requires restatement of prior period financial statements and does not permit adjusting opening retained earnings for the effect of the error. Errors are thus distinguished from changes in accounting estimate, as the latter are accounted for prospectively, without restatement of prior period financial statements. Correction of accounting errors is discussed in Chapter 21.

Example of determining the extent to which the deferred tax asset is realizable

Assume that Zacharias Corporation has a deductible temporary difference of €60,000 at December 31, 2009. The applicable tax rate is a flat 40%. Based on available evidence, management of Zacharias Corporation concludes that it is probable that all sources will not result in future taxable income sufficient to realize more than €15,000 (i.e., 25%) of the deductible temporary difference. Also, assume that there were no deferred tax assets in previous years and that prior years' taxable income was inconsequential.

At 12/31/09 Zacharias Corporation records a deferred tax asset in the amount of €6,000 (= €60,000 × 25% × 40%). The journal entry at 12/31/09 is

Deferred tax asset	6,000	
Income tax benefit—deferred		6,000

The deferred income tax benefit of €6,000 represents the tax effect of that portion of the deferred tax asset (25%) that is probable of being realized. For 2010 assume that Zacharias Corporation's results are

Pretax financial loss	€(32,000)
Reversing deductible differences from 2008	(10,000)
Loss carryforward for tax purposes	€(42,000)

The total of the loss carryforward (€42,000, as computed above) plus the amount of deductible temporary differences from 2009 not reversing in 2010 (€50,000) equals €92,000. Before considering how much of the benefit is probable of being realized, a deferred tax asset of €36,800 (= €92,000 × 40%) is computed at the end of 2010. However, the management of Zacharias Corporation has to consider what portion of this deferred tax asset is probable of being realized. It concludes that it is probable that €25,000 of the tax loss carryforward will *not* be realized. Thus, the net tax loss carryforward that is *probable* of being realized is €92,000 − €25,000 = €67,000, which yields a tax benefit of €26,800 (= €67,000 × 40%).

Since the balance in the deferred tax asset account had been €6,000, the adjustment needed is now as follows. The journal entry at 12/31/10 is

Deferred tax asset	20,800	
Income tax benefit—deferred		20,800

Effect of Tax Law Changes on Previously Recorded Deferred Tax Assets and Liabilities

The statement of financial position oriented measurement approach of IAS 12 necessitates the reevaluation of the deferred tax asset and liability balances at each year-end. Although IAS 12 does not directly address the question of changes to tax rates or other provisions of the tax law (e.g., deductibility of items) which may be enacted that will affect the realization of future deferred tax assets or liabilities, the effect of these changes should be reflected in the year-end deferred tax accounts in the period the changes are enacted. The offsetting adjustments should be made through the current period tax provision.

When revised tax rates are enacted, they may affect not only the unreversed effects of items which were originally reported in the continuing operations section of the statement of income (under revised IAS 1, the income statement section of a combined statement of comprehensive income), but also the unreversed effects of items first presented as other comprehensive income. Although it might be conceptually superior to report the effects of tax law changes on such unreversed temporary differences in these same statement of comprehensive income captions, as a practical matter the complexities of identifying the diverse treatments of these originating transactions or events would make such an approach unworkable. Accordingly, remeasurements of the effects of tax law changes should generally be reported in the tax provision associated with continuing operations.

Example of the computation of a deferred tax asset with a change in rates

Assume that the Fanuzzi Company has €80,000 of deductible temporary differences at the end of 2008, which are expected to result in tax deductions of approximately €40,000 each on tax returns for 2009-2011. Enacted tax rates are 50% for the years 2004-2008, and 40% for 2009 and thereafter.

The deferred tax asset is computed at 12/31/08 under each of the following independent assumptions:

1. If Fanuzzi Company expects to offset the deductible temporary differences against taxable income in the years 2009-2011, the deferred tax asset is €32,000 (€80,000 × 40%).
2. If Fanuzzi Company expects to realize a tax benefit for the deductible temporary differences by loss carryback refund, the deferred tax asset is €40,000 (= €80,000 × 50%).

Assume that Fanuzzi Company expects to realize a tax asset of €32,000 at the end of 2008. Also assume that taxes payable in each of the years 2004-2007 were €8,000 (or 50% of taxable income). Realization of €24,000 of the €32,000 deferred tax asset is assured through carryback refunds even if no taxable income is earned in the years 2009-2010. Whether some or all of the remaining €8,000 will be recognized depends on Fanuzzi Company's assessment of the levels of future taxable earnings (i.e., whether the probable threshold is exceeded).

The foregoing estimate of the certain tax benefit, based on a loss carryback to periods of higher tax rates than are statutorily in effect for future periods, should be utilized only when future losses (for tax purposes) are expected. This restriction applies since the benefit thus recognized exceeds benefits that would be available in future periods, when tax rates will be lower.

Changes in tax law may affect rates, and may also affect the taxability or deductibility of income or expense items. While the latter type of change occurs infrequently, the impact is similar to the more common tax rate changes.

Example of effect of change in tax law

Leipzig Corporation has, at December 31, 2008, gross receivables of €12,000,000 and an allowance for bad debts in the amount of €600,000. Also assume that expected future taxes will be at a 40% rate. Effective January 1, 2009, the tax law is revised to eliminate deductions for accrued bad debts, with existing allowances required to be taken into income ratably over three years (a three-year spread). A statement of financial position of Leipzig Corporation prepared on January 1, 2009, would report a deferred tax benefit in the amount of €240,000 (i.e., €600,000 × 40%, which is the tax effect of future deductions to be taken when specific receivables are written off and bad debts are incurred for tax purposes); a current tax liability of €80,000 (one-third of the tax obligation); and a noncurrent tax liability of €160,000 (two-thirds of the tax obligation). Under the requirements of IAS 12, the deferred tax benefit must be entirely reported as noncurrent in classified statements of financial position, inasmuch as no deferred tax benefits or obligations can be shown as current.

Reporting the Effect of Tax Status Changes

Changes in the tax status of the reporting entity should be reported in a manner that is entirely analogous to the reporting of enacted tax law changes. When the tax status change becomes effective, the consequent adjustments to deferred tax assets and liabilities are reported in current tax expense as part of the tax provision relating to continuing operations.

The most commonly encountered changes in status are those attendant to an election, where permitted, to be taxed as a partnership or other flow-through enterprise. (This means that the corporation will not be treated as a taxable entity but rather as an enterprise that "flows through" its taxable income to the owners on a current basis. This favorable tax treatment is available to encourage small businesses, and often will be limited to entities having sales revenue under a particular threshold level, or to entities having no more than a maximum number of shareholders.) Enterprises subject to such optional tax treatment may also request that a previous election be terminated. When a previously taxable corporation becomes a nontaxed corporation, the stockholders become personally liable for taxes on the company's earnings, whether the earnings are distributed to them or not (similar to the relationship among a partnership and its partners).

As issued, IAS 12 did not explicitly address the matter of reporting the effects of a change in tax status, although (as discussed in earlier editions of this book) the appropriate treatment was quite obvious given the underlying concepts of that standard. This ambiguity was subsequently resolved by the issuance of SIC 25, which stipulates that in most cases the current and deferred tax consequences of the change in tax status should be included in net profit or loss for the period in which the change in status occurs. The tax effects of a change in status are included in results of operations because a change in a reporting entity's tax status (or that of its shareholders) does not give rise to increases or decreases in the pretax amounts recognized directly in equity.

The exception to the foregoing general rule arises in connection with those tax consequences which relate to transactions and events that result, in the same or a different period, in a direct credit or charge to the recognized amount of equity. For example, an event that is recognized directly in equity is a change in the carrying amount of property, plant, or equipment revalued under IAS 16. Those tax consequences that relate to change in the recognized amount of equity, in the same or a different period (not included in net profit or loss) should be charged or credited directly to equity.

The most common situation giving rise to a change in tax status would be the election by a corporation, in those jurisdictions where it is permitted to do so, to be taxed as a partnership, trust, or other flow-through entity. If a corporation having a net deferred tax liability elects nontaxed status, the deferred taxes will be eliminated through a credit to current period earnings. That is because what had been an obligation of the corporation has been eliminated (by being accepted directly by the shareholders, typically); a debt thus removed constitutes earnings for the formerly obligated party.

Similarly, if a previously nontaxed corporation becomes a taxable entity, the effect is to assume a net tax benefit or obligation for unreversed temporary differences existing at the date the change becomes effective. Accordingly, the financial statements for the period of such a change will report the effects of the event in the current tax provision. If the entity had at that date many taxable temporary differences as yet unreversed, it would report a large tax expense in that period. Conversely, if it had a large quantity of unreversed deductible temporary differences, a substantial deferred tax benefit (if probable of realization) would need to be recorded, with a concomitant credit to the current period's tax provision in the statement of comprehensive income. Whether eliminating an existing deferred tax balance or recording an initial deferred tax asset or liability, the income tax footnote to the financial statements will need to fully explain the nature of the events that transpired.

In some jurisdictions, nontaxed corporation elections are automatically effective when filed. In such a case, if a reporting entity makes an election before the end of the current fiscal year, it is logical that the effects be reported in current year income to become effective at the start of the following period. For example, an election filed in December 2008 would be reported in the 2008 financial statements to become effective at the beginning of the company's next fiscal year, January 1, 2009. No deferred tax assets or liabilities would appear on the December 31, 2008 statement of financial position, and the tax provision for the year then ended would include the effects of any reversals that had previously been recorded. Practice varies, however, and in some instances the effect of the elimination of the deferred tax assets and liabilities would be reported in the year the election actually becomes effective.

Reporting the Effect of Accounting Changes Made for Tax Purposes

Occasionally, an entity will initiate or be required to adopt changes in accounting that affect income tax reporting, but that will not impact on financial reporting. For example, in certain jurisdictions at varying times, the following changes have been mandated: use of the direct write-off method of bad debt recognition instead of providing an allowance for bad debts, while continuing to use the reserve method as required by GAAP for financial reporting; the "full costing" method of computing inventory valuations for tax purposes (adding some items that are administrative costs to overhead), while continuing to expense currently those costs not inventoriable under GAAP; and use of accelerated capital recovery (depreciation) methods for tax reporting while continuing to use normal methods for financial reporting. Often, these changes really involve two distinct temporary differences. The first of these is the onetime, catch-up adjustment which either immediately or over a prescribed time period affects the tax basis of the asset or liability in question (net receivables or inventory, in the examples above), and which then reverses as these assets or liabilities are later realized or settled and are eliminated from the statement of financial position. The second change is the ongoing differential in the amount of newly acquired assets or incurred liabilities being recognized for tax and accounting purposes; these differences also eventually reverse. This second type of change is the normal temporary difference which has already been discussed. It is the first change that differs from those previously discussed earlier in the chapter.

Implications of Changes in Tax Rates and Status Made in Interim Periods

Tax rate changes may occur during an interim reporting period, either because a tax law change mandated a midyear effective date, or because tax law changes were effective at year-end but the reporting entity has adopted a fiscal year-end other than the natural year (December 31). The IFRS on interim reporting, IAS 34 (addressed in detail in Chapter 19), has essentially embraced a mixed view on interim reporting—with many aspects conforming to a "discrete" approach (each interim period standing on its own) but others, including accounting for income taxes, conforming to the "integral" manner of reporting. Whatever the philosophical strengths and weaknesses of the discrete and integral approaches in general, the integral approach was clearly warranted in the matter of accounting for income taxes.

The fact that income taxes are assessed annually is the primary reason for concluding that taxes are to be accrued based on an entity's estimated average annual effective tax rate for the full fiscal year. If rate changes have been enacted to take effect later in the fiscal year, the expected effective rate should take into account the rate changes as well as the anticipated pattern of earnings to be experienced over the course of the year. Thus, the rate to be applied to interim period earnings (or losses, as discussed further below) will take into account the expected level of earnings for the entire forthcoming year, as well as the effect of enacted (or substantially enacted) changes in the tax rates to become operative later in the fiscal year. In other words, and as expressed by IAS 34, the estimated average annual rate would "reflect a blend of the progressive tax rate structure expected to be applicable to the full year's earnings enacted or substantially enacted changes in the income tax rates scheduled to take effect later in the financial year."

While the principle espoused by IAS 34 is both clear and logical, a number of practical issues can arise. The standard does address in detail the various computational aspects of an effective interim period tax rate, some of which are summarized in the following paragraphs.

Many modern business entities operate in numerous nations or states and therefore are subject to a multiplicity of taxing jurisdictions. In some instances the amount of income subject to tax will vary from one jurisdiction to the next, since the tax laws in different jurisdictions will include and exclude disparate items of income or expense from the tax base.

For example, interest earned on government-issued bonds may be exempted from tax by the jurisdiction which issued them, but be defined as fully taxable by other tax jurisdictions the entity is subject to. To the extent feasible, the appropriate estimated average annual effective tax rate should be separately ascertained for each taxing jurisdiction and applied individually to the interim period pretax income of each jurisdiction, so that the most accurate estimate of income taxes can be developed at each interim reporting date. In general, an overall estimated effective tax rate will not be as satisfactory for this purpose as would a more carefully constructed set of estimated rates, since the pattern of taxable and deductible items will fluctuate from one period to the next.

Similarly, if the tax law prescribes different income tax rates for different categories of income, then to the extent practicable, a separate effective tax rate should be applied to each category of interim period pretax income. IAS 34, while mandating such detailed rules of computing and applying tax rates across jurisdiction or across categories of income, nonetheless recognized that such a degree of precision may not be achievable in all cases. Thus, IAS 34 allows usage of a weighted-average of rates across jurisdictions or across categories of income provided it is a reasonable approximation of the effect of using more specific rates.

In computing an expected effective tax rate given for a tax jurisdiction, all relevant features of the tax regulations should be taken into account. Jurisdictions may provide for tax credits based on new investment in plant and machinery, relocation of facilities to backward or underdeveloped areas, research and development expenditures, levels of export sales, and so forth, and the expected credits against the tax for the full year should be given consideration in the determination of an expected effective tax rate. Thus, the tax effect of new investment in plant and machinery, when the local taxing body offers an investment credit for qualifying investment in tangible productive assets, will be reflected in those interim periods of the fiscal year in which the new investment occurs (assuming it can be forecast to occur later in a given fiscal year), and not merely in the period in which the new investment occurs. This is consistent with the underlying concept that taxes are strictly an annual phenomenon, but it is at variance with the purely discrete view of interim financial reporting.

IAS 34 notes that, although tax credits and similar modifying elements are to be taken into account in developing the expected effective tax rate to apply to interim earnings, tax benefits which will relate to onetime events are to be reflected from the interim period when those events take place. This is perhaps most likely to be encountered in the context of capital gains taxes incurred in connection with occasional dispositions of investments and other capital assets; since it is not feasible to project the timing of such transactions over the course of a year, the tax effects should be recognized only as the underlying events actually do transpire.

While in most cases tax credits are to be handled as suggested in the foregoing paragraphs, in some jurisdictions tax credits, particularly those which relate to export revenue or capital expenditures, are in effect government grants. Accounting for government grants is set forth in IAS 20; in brief, grants are recognized in income over the period necessary to properly match them to the costs which the grants are intended to offset or defray. Thus, compliance with both IAS 20 and IAS 34 would require that tax credits be carefully analyzed to identify those which are in substance grants, and that credits be accounted for consistent with their true natures.

When an interim period loss gives rise to a tax loss carryback, it should be fully reflected in that interim period. Similarly, if a loss in an interim period produces a tax loss carryforward, it should be recognized immediately, but only if the criteria set forth in IAS 12 are met. Specifically, it must be deemed probable that the benefits will be realizable before the loss benefits can be given formal recognition in the financial statements. In the case of interim period losses, it may be necessary to assess not only whether the enterprise will be profitable enough in future fiscal years to utilize the tax benefits associated with the loss, but furthermore, whether interim periods later in the same year will provide earnings of sufficient magnitude to absorb the losses of the current period.

IAS 12 provides that changes in expectations regarding the realizability of benefits related to net operating loss carryforwards should be reflected currently in tax expense. Similarly, if a net operating loss carryforward benefit is not deemed probable of being realized until the interim (or annual) period when it in fact becomes realized, the tax effect will be included in tax expense of that period. Appropriate explanatory material must be included in the notes to the financial statements, even on an interim basis, to provide users with an understanding of the unusual relationship reported between pretax accounting income and the provision for income taxes.

Income Tax Consequences of Dividends Paid

Historically, some taxing jurisdictions have levied income tax rates on corporate earnings at differential rates, depending on whether the earnings are retained by the entity or are distributed to shareholders. Typically, the rationale for this disparate treatment is that it motivates business entities to make distributions to shareholders, which is deemed a socially worthwhile goal by some (although it doesn't really alter wealth accumulation unless distortions are introduced by fiscal policy). A secondary reason for such rules is that this partially ameliorates the impact of the double taxation of corporate profits (which are typically first taxed at the corporate level, then taxed again as distributed to shareholders as taxable dividends). IAS 12 specifically abstained from addressing the issue of how to account for this phenomenon, but this was subsequently dealt with by a 2001 amendment.

Under the provisions of IAS 12, tax effects are to be provided for current taxable earnings without making any assumptions about future dividend declarations. In other words, the tax provision is to be computed using the tax rate applicable to undistributed earnings, even if the enterprise has a long history of making earnings distributions subsequent to year-end, which when made will generate tax savings. If dividends are later declared, the tax effect of this event will be accounted for in the period in which the proposed dividend is paid or becomes accruable as a liability by the enterprise, if earlier. Since there is typically no legal requirement to declare distributions to shareholders, this approach is clearly appropriate because to recognize tax benefits associated with dividend payments before declaration would be to anticipate income (in the form of tax benefits) before it is earned.

The standard holds that the tax effect of the dividend declaration (or payment) is to be included in the current period's tax provision, not as an adjustment to the earlier period's earnings, taken through the retained earnings account. This is true even when it is clear that the dividend is a distribution being made out of the earlier period's profits. The logic of this requirement is that the tax benefits are more closely linked to events reported in the statement of comprehensive income (i.e., the past or current transactions producing net income) than they are to the dividend distribution. In other words, it is the transactions and events resulting in earnings and not the act of distributing some of these earnings to shareholders that is of the greatest pertinence to financial statement users.

If dividends are declared before the end of the year, but are payable after year-end, the dividends become a legal liability of the reporting entity and taxes should be computed at the appropriate rate on the amount thus declared. If the dividend is declared after year-end but before the financial statements are issued, under IAS 10 a liability cannot be recognized on the statement of financial position at year-end, and thus the tax effect related thereto also cannot be given recognition. Disclosure would be made, however, of this post-year-end event.

To illustrate the foregoing, consider the following example:

> Amir Corporation operates in a jurisdiction where income taxes are payable at a higher rate on undistributed profits than on distributed earnings. For the year 2009, the company's taxable income is €150,000. Amir also has net taxable temporary differences amounting to €50,000 for the year, thus creating the need for a deferred tax provision. The tax rate on distributed profits is 25%, and the rate on undistributed profits is 40%; the difference is refundable if profits are later distributed. As of the date of the statement of financial position no liability for dividends proposed or declared has been reflected on the statement of financial position. March 31, 2009, however, the company distributes dividends of €50,000.
>
> The tax consequences of dividends on undistributed profits, current and deferred taxes for the year 2009, and the recovery of 2009 income taxes when dividends are subsequently declared would be as follows:
>
> 1. Amir Corporation recognizes a current tax liability and a current tax expense for 2009 of €150,000 × 40% = €160,000;
> 2. No asset is recognized for the amount that will be (potentially) recoverable when dividends are distributed;
> 3. Deferred tax liability and deferred tax expense for 2009 would be €50,000 × 40% = €20,000, and
> 4. In the following year (2010) when the company recognizes dividends of €50,000, the company will also recognize the recovery of income taxes of €50,000 × (40% − 25%) = €7,500 as a current tax asset and a reduction of the current income tax expense.

The only exception to the foregoing accounting for tax effects of dividends that are subject to differential tax rates arises in the situation of a dividend-paying corporation which is required to withhold taxes on the distribution and remit these to the taxing authorities. In general, withholding tax is offset against the amounts distributed to shareholders, and is later forwarded to the taxing bodies rather than to the shareholders, so that the total amount of the dividend declaration is not altered. However, if the corporation pays the tax in addition to the full amount of the dividend payments to shareholders, some might view this as a tax falling on the corporation and, accordingly, add this to the tax provision reported on the statement of comprehensive income. IAS 12, however, makes it clear that such an amount, if paid or payable to the taxing authorities, is to be charged to equity as part of the dividend declaration if it does not affect income taxes payable or recoverable by the enterprise in the same or a different period.

Finally, IAS 12 provides that disclosure will be required of the potential income tax consequences of dividends. The reporting enterprise should disclose the amounts of the potential income tax consequences which are practically determinable, and whether there are any potential income tax consequences not practically determinable.

Accounting for Income Taxes in Business Combinations

One of the more complex aspects of interperiod income tax accounting occurs when business combinations are consummated and are treated as acquisitions as now defined by IFRS 3, which superseded former IAS 22 in 2004. The principal complexity relates to the recognition, at the date of the purchase, of the deferred tax effects of the differences between the tax and financial reporting bases of assets and liabilities acquired. Further difficulties arise in connection with the recognition of goodwill and negative goodwill. If the reporting entity expects that the ultimate tax allocation will differ from the initial one (such as when disallowance by the tax authorities of an allocation made to identifiable intangibles is anticipated by the taxpayer), yet another complex accounting matter must be dealt with.

Under the provisions of IAS 12, the tax effects of any differences in tax and financial reporting bases are to be reflected, from the date of the purchase, as deferred tax assets and liabilities. The same rules that apply to the recognition of deferred tax assets and liabilities arising under other circumstances (i.e., the origination of temporary differences by the reporting entity) are equally applicable to such instances, *except* for the initial recognition of an asset or liability in a transaction other than a business combination when, at the time of the transaction, neither accounting profit nor taxable profit is affected. Accordingly, if deferred tax assets are not deemed to be probable of ultimate realization, they are not recognized in any of these circumstances.

·Depending on the tax jurisdictions in which they occur, and how the transactions are structured, acquisitions may be either taxable or nontaxable in nature. In a taxable acquisition, the total purchase price paid will be allocated to assets and liabilities for both tax and financial reporting purposes, although under some circumstances the specifics of these allocations may differ, and to the extent the allocation is made to nondeductible goodwill there will be differences in future periods' taxable and accounting profit. In a nontaxable acquisition, the predecessor entity's tax bases for the various assets and liabilities will be carried forward, while for financial reporting purposes the purchase price will be allocated to the assets and liabilities acquired. Thus, in most cases, there may be significant differences between the tax and financial reporting bases. For this reason, both taxable and nontaxable acquisitions can involve the application of deferred income tax accounting.

Accounting for Purchase Business Combinations at Acquisition Date

IAS 12 requires that the tax effects of the tax-book basis differences of all assets and liabilities generally be presented as deferred tax assets and liabilities as of the acquisition date. In general, this grossing-up of the statement of financial position is a straightforward matter.

Example of temporary differences in business acquisition

An example, in the context of the business acquisition of Windlass Corp., follows:

1. The income tax rate is a flat 40%.
2. The acquisition of a business is effected at a cost of €500,000.
3. The fair values of assets acquired total €750,000.
4. The carryforward tax bases of assets acquired total €600,000.
5. The fair and carryforward tax bases of the liabilities assumed in the purchase are €250,000.
6. The difference between the tax and fair values of the assets acquired, €150,000, consists of taxable temporary differences of €200,000 and deductible temporary differences of €50,000.
7. There is no doubt as to the realizability of the deductible temporary differences in this case.

Based on the foregoing facts, allocation of the purchase price is as follows:

Gross purchase price	€ 500,000
Allocation to identifiable assets and (liabilities):	
Assets other than goodwill and deferred tax benefits	750,000
Deferred tax benefits	20,000
Liabilities, other than deferred tax obligations	(250,000)
Deferred tax obligations	(80,000)
Net of the above allocations	440,000
Allocation to goodwill	€ 60,000

Goodwill and negative goodwill. Goodwill arises when part of the price paid in a business combination accounted for as a purchase cannot be allocated to identifiable assets; what was formerly known as negative goodwill results from bargain purchases. Accounting for goodwill and for negative goodwill has been substantially altered by IFRS 3. Goodwill is no longer subject to periodic amortization, but must be regularly tested for impairment and, if impaired, written down to fair value, with the adjustment being reflected in current period earnings. Negative goodwill (more properly, the excess of fair value over cost), which is much less commonly encountered, is now reported in current period earnings, rather than being deferred and amortized as under prior IFRS.

Goodwill may be tax deductible, depending on tax jurisdiction, or may be nondeductible. If it is deductible, the mandated amortization period will cause the carrying value for tax purposes over time to differ from that reflected in the financial statements prepared in conformity with IFRS. Since under IFRS goodwill is no longer to be amortized over its expected economic life, a temporary difference will develop, with the book carrying value being greater than the tax carrying amount, absent any impairment recognition for financial reporting purposes. If impairment charges are taken, however, book carrying value may be lower than the corresponding tax basis.

The situation with negative goodwill is as follows: if the fair value of net assets acquired exceeds the cost of the acquisition, it is first incumbent upon the acquirer to reassess values assigned. However, in the (likely) case that this does not lead to the elimination of what appeared to be negative goodwill, that amount is to be reported currently in income. This will likely result in a difference between tax and book carrying value for the negative goodwill (depending on local tax rules, of course), and this also is a timing difference to be considered in computing deferred taxes for the entity.

If goodwill or negative goodwill is not deductible or taxable, respectively, in a given tax jurisdiction (that is, it is a permanent difference), in theory its tax basis is zero, and thus there is a difference between tax and financial reporting bases, to which one would logically expect deferred taxes would be attributed. However, given the residual nature of goodwill or negative goodwill, recognition of deferred taxes would in turn create yet more goodwill, and thus more deferred tax, etc. There would be little purpose achieved by loading up the statement of financial position with goodwill and related deferred tax in such circumstances, and the computation itself would be quite challenging. Accordingly, IAS 12 prohibits grossing up goodwill in such a fashion. Similarly, no deferred tax benefit will be computed and presented in connection with the financial reporting recognition of negative goodwill.

The accounting for a taxable purchase business combination is essentially similar to that for a nontaxable one. However, unlike the previous example, in which there were numerous assets with different tax and financial reporting bases, there are likely to be only a few differences in the case of taxable purchases. In jurisdictions in which goodwill is not deductible, attempts are often made for tax purposes to allocate excess purchase cost to tangible assets as well as to other intangibles, such as covenants not to compete. (Such attempts may or not survive review by the tax authorities, of course.) In jurisdictions where goodwill is deductible, presumably this is not a motivation, although because goodwill is often viewed as a suspect asset, entities will still be more comfortable if purchase cost can be attributed to "real" assets, even when goodwill can be amortized for tax purposes.

IAS 12 does not permit recognition of deferred tax effects associated with goodwill. It is true that some book-tax temporary differences in goodwill would, if any other asset or liability were at issue, give rise to deferred tax assets or liabilities. For example, in some tax jurisdictions goodwill is not only not subject to period expensing (via amortization), but also the goodwill cannot be considered part of the tax basis in the subsidiary, so that when the parent ultimately sells the acquired entity, including its goodwill, the gain or loss on the transaction has to be adjusted so that goodwill is not deducted at that time. In other words, the tax basis of the goodwill is zero at acquisition and throughout the holding period of the business acquired. This differs from the book basis (under IFRS 3, goodwill is not subject to amortization, so absent any impairment the original amount allocated to goodwill remains intact until disposed of), which is the normal definition of a temporary difference. Nonetheless, no deferred tax can be associated with this.

This requirement applies equally to any subsequent change in the carrying value of goodwill, which is deemed to relate to the original acquisition of the goodwill. For example, if the book goodwill is later written down in value due to an assessed impairment, this does not generate deferred tax recognition.

A similar situation arises if assets other than goodwill are acquired and are not subject to depreciation for tax purposes (unusual, but not an impossible situation, given the wide disparity of local income tax laws). For example, if an asset is acquired and depreciated for book (financial reporting) purposes, and has an expected residual value of zero, but neither depreciation nor capital gains or losses are recognized for tax purposes, the tax basis of the asset is zero. The book-tax difference is in effect a permanent difference, and no deferred tax effects can be recognized under provisions of IAS 12.

Accounting for Purchase Business Combinations After the Acquisition

Under the provisions of the revised IAS 12, net deferred tax benefits are not to be carried forward as assets unless the deferred tax assets are deemed *probable* of being realized. The assessment of this probability was discussed earlier in the chapter.

In an example (Windlass) given above, it was specified that all deductible temporary differences were fully realizable, and therefore the deferred tax benefits associated with those temporary differences were recorded as of the acquisition date. In other situations there may be substantial doubt concerning realizability; that is, it may not be probable that the benefits will be realized. Accordingly, under IAS 12, the deferred tax asset would not be recognized at the date of the business acquisition. If so, the allocation of the purchase price would have to reflect that fact, and more of the purchase cost would be allocated to goodwill than would otherwise be the case.

If, at a later date, it is determined that some or all of the deferred tax asset that was not recognized at the date of the acquisition is, in fact, probable of being ultimately realized, the effect of that reevaluation will be reflected in tax expense (benefit) in the period during which the reevaluation is made. Furthermore, the portion of the extra goodwill recognized at the time of the business acquisition must be written off to expense.

Example of revising estimate of tax benefit realizability in business combination

To illustrate this last concept, assume that a business acquisition occurs on January 1, 2008, and that deferred tax assets of €100,000 are *not* recognized at that time, due to an assessment that realization is not probable. The unrecognized tax benefit is implicitly allocated to goodwill during the purchase price assignment process. On January 1, 2010, the likelihood of ultimately realizing the tax benefit is reassessed as being probable, with realization projected for later years. The entries at that date are as follows:

Deferred tax benefit	100,000	
Goodwill		100,000

In some situations, the amount of deferred tax benefits will, upon reassessment, exceed the balance in the goodwill account, or there may have been no goodwill recognized in connection with the business acquisition at all. IAS 12 stipulates that this reassessment cannot result in the recognition of negative goodwill. The implication is that, while negative goodwill could have been first recognized at the time of a business acquisition which involved recognition of deferred assets (and, under IFRS 3, reported immediately in earnings), it will not be possible to later recognize deferred tax benefits under such circumstances.

A related issue arises when the acquirer had unrecognized deferred tax benefits unrelated to the impending business combination. The asset was unrecognized because it was not probable that this benefit could be realized by that entity. As a result of the acquisition, however, this previously unrecognized asset becomes probable of realization, for example, because under relevant tax laws the earnings of the acquired entity will provide the acquirer with an opportunity to utilize its deductible temporary differences. According to IAS 12, the acquirer's deferred tax asset will now be given recognition, with the consequence that goodwill otherwise to be recorded in the transaction will be reduced, or negative goodwill will be increased or first given recognition (if negative goodwill is created, of course, this will be recognized immediately in income under IFRS 3).

Tax Allocation for Business Investments

As noted in Chapter 10, there are two basic methods of accounting for passive or minority investments in the common stock of other corporations: (1) the cost method and (2) the equity method. The *cost method* requires that the investing corporation (investor) record the investment at its purchase price, and no additional entry is made to the account over the life of the asset (this does not include any valuation contra accounts). The cost method is used in instances where the investor is not considered to have significant influence over the investee. The ownership threshold generally used is 20% of ownership. This figure is not considered an absolute, but it will be used to identify the break between application of the cost and equity methods. Under the cost method, ordinary income is recognized as dividends are declared by the investee, and capital gains (losses) are recognized on disposal of the investment. For tax purposes, no provision is made during the holding period for the allocable undistributed earnings of the investee. Deferred tax computation is not necessary when using the cost method because there is no temporary difference.

The *equity method* is generally used whenever an investor owns more than 20% of an investee or has significant influence over its operations. The equity method calls for recording the investment at cost and then increasing this carrying amount by the allocable portion of the investee's earnings. The allocable portion of the investee's earnings is then included in the pretax accounting income of the investor. Dividend payments are no longer included in pretax accounting income but are considered to be a reduction in the carrying amount of the investment. However, for tax purposes, dividends are the only revenue realized. As a result, the investor needs to recognize deferred income tax expense on the undistributed earnings of the associate that will be taxed in the future.

IAS 28 distinguishes between an associate and a subsidiary and prescribes different accounting treatments for each. An associate is considered to be a corporation whose stock is owned by an investor which holds more than 20% but no greater than 50% of the outstanding stock. An association situation occurs when the investor has significant influence but not control over the corporation in which it has invested. A subsidiary, on the other hand, exists when one enterprise exerts control over another, which is presumed when it holds more than 50% of the stock of the other entity.

In an important exception to the general rule that deferred taxes must be recognized for all book-tax basis differences, IAS 12 provides that when the parent, investor, or joint venturer can prevent the taxable event from occurring, deferred taxes are not recognized. Specifically, under IAS 12, two conditions must *both* be satisfied to justify *not* reflecting deferred taxes in connection with the earnings of a subsidiary (a control situation), branches and associates (significant influence), and joint ventures. These are (1) that the parent, investor or venturer is able to control the timing of the reversal of the temporary difference and (2) it is probable that the difference will not reverse in the foreseeable future. Unless *both* conditions are met, the tax effects of these temporary differences must be given recognition.

When a parent company that has the ability to control the dividend and other policies of its subsidiary determines that dividends will not be declared, and thus that the undistributed profit of the subsidiary will not be taxed at the parent company level, no deferred tax liability is to be recognized. If this intention is later altered, the tax effect of this change in estimate would be reflected in the current period's tax provision.

On the other hand, an investor, even one having significant influence, cannot absolutely determine the associate's dividend policy. Accordingly, it has to be presumed that earnings will eventually be distributed and that these will create taxable income at the investor company level. Therefore, deferred tax liability must be provided for the reporting entity's share of all undistributed earnings of its associates for which it is accounting by the equity method, unless there is a binding agreement for the earnings of the investee to not be distributed within the foreseeable future.

In the case of joint ventures there are a wide range of possible relationships between the venturers, and in some cases the reporting entity has the ability to control the payment of dividends. As in the foregoing, if the reporting entity has the ability to exercise this level of control and it is probable that distributions will not be made within the foreseeable future, no deferred tax liability will be reported.

In all these various circumstances, it will be necessary to assess whether distributions within the foreseeable future are probable. The standard does not define "foreseeable future" and thus this will remain a matter of subjective judgment. The criteria of IAS 12, while subjective, are less ambiguous than under the original standard, which permitted nonrecognition of deferred tax liability when it was "reasonable to assume that (the associate's) profits will not be distributed."

Example of tax allocation for investee and subsidiary income

To illustrate the application of these concepts, assume that Parent Company owns 30% of the outstanding common stock of Investee Company and 70% of the outstanding common stock of Subsidiary Company. Additional data for the year 2008 are as follows:

	Investee Company	Subsidiary Company
Net income	€50,000	€100,000
Dividends paid	20,000	60,000

How the foregoing data are used to recognize the tax effects of the stated events is discussed below.

Income tax effects from investee company. The 2009 accounting profit of Parent Company will include equity in its associate's income equal to €15,000 (= €50,000 × 30%). Parent's taxable income, however, will include dividend income of €6,000 (= €20,000 × 30%), and, under applicable tax law, a credit of 80% of the €6,000, or €4,800, will also be allowed for the dividends received. This 80% dividends received deduction is a permanent difference between accounting and taxable profits.

The amount of the deferred tax credit in 2008 depends on the expectations of Parent Company as to the manner in which the €9,000 of undistributed income will be received. In many tax jurisdictions, the effective tax rate will differ based on method of realization; dividend income may be taxed at a different rate than capital gains (achieved on the sale of an investment in an associate, for example). If the expectation of receipt is via dividends, the temporary difference is 20% of €9,000, or €1,800, and the deferred tax credit for this originating temporary difference in 2008 is the current tax rate times €1,800. However, if the expectation is that receipt will be through future sale of the investment, the gain on which would be fully taxed, the temporary difference is €9,000 and the deferred tax credit is the current capital gains rate times the €9,000.

The entries below illustrate these alternatives. A tax rate of 34% is used for both ordinary income and for capital gains. Note that the amounts in the entries below relate only to Investee Company's incremental impact on Parent Company's tax accounts.

	Expectations for undistributed income	
	Dividends	*Capital gains*
Income tax expense	1,020	2,208
Deferred tax liability	612[b]	1,800[c]
Income taxes payable	408[a]	408[a]

[a]*Computation of income taxes payable:*

Dividend income—30% × (€20,000)	€6,000
Less 80% dividends received deduction	(4,800)
Amount included in Parent's taxable income	€1,200
Tax liability—34% × (€1,200)	€ 408

[b]*Computation of deferred tax liability (dividend assumption):*

Originating temporary difference:	
Parent's share of undistributed income—30% × (€30,000)	€9,000
Less 80% dividends received deduction	(7,200)
Originating temporary difference	€1,800
Deferred tax liability—34% × (€1,800)	€ 612

	Expectations for undistributed income	
	Dividends	*Capital gains*

[c]*Computation of deferred tax liability (capital gain assumption):*

Originating temporary difference: Parent's share of undistributed income—30% × (€30,000)	€9,000
Deferred tax liability—20% × (€9,000)	€1,800

Income tax effects from subsidiary company. The accounting profit of Parent Company will also include equity in Subsidiary income of €70,000 (= 70% × €100,000). This €70,000 will be included in pretax consolidated income if Parent and Subsidiary issue consolidated financial statements. Depending on the rules of the particular tax jurisdiction, it may be the case that for tax purposes, Parent and Subsidiary will not file a consolidated tax return (e.g., because the prescribed minimum level of control, that is, 80%, is not present). In the present example, assume that it will not be possible to file consolidated tax returns. Consequently, the taxable income of Parent will include dividend income of €42,000 (= 70% × €60,000). Assume further that there will be an 80% dividends received deduction, which will amount to €33,600. The originating temporary difference results from Parent's equity (€28,000) in Subsidiary's undistributed earnings of €40,000.

The amount of the deferred tax credit in 2009 depends on the expectations of Parent Company as to the manner in which this €28,000 of undistributed income will be received. The same expectations can exist as discussed previously, for Parent's equity in Investee's undistributed earnings (i.e., through future dividend distributions or capital gains).

The entries below illustrate these alternatives. A marginal tax rate of 34% is assumed. The amounts in the entries below relate only to Subsidiary Company's incremental impact on Parent Company's tax accounts.

	Expectations for undistributed income	
	Dividends	*Capital gains*
Income tax expense	4,760	12,376
Deferred tax liability	1,904[b]	9,520[c]
Income taxes payable	2,856[a]	2,856[a]

[a]*Computation of income taxes payable:*

Dividend income—70% × (€60,000)	€42,000
Less 80% dividends received deduction	(33,600)
Amount included in Parent's taxable income	€ 8,400
Tax liability—34% × (€5,600)	€ 2,856

[b]*Computation of deferred tax liability (dividend assumption):*

Originating temporary difference:	
Parent's share of undistributed income—70% × (€40,000)	€28,000
Less 80% dividends received deduction	(22,400)
Originating temporary difference	€ 5,600
Deferred tax liability—34% × (€5,600)	€ 1,904

[c]*Computation of deferred tax liability (capital gain assumption):*

Originating temporary difference: Parent's share of undistrib-	
uted income—70% × (€40,000)	€28,000
Deferred tax liability—34% × (€28,000)	€ 9,520

If a parent company owns a large enough percentage of the voting stock of a subsidiary and the parent, so that it may consolidate the subsidiary for both financial and tax reports, no temporary differences exist between pretax consolidated income and taxable income. Under the rules in some jurisdictions, it may be possible to submit separate tax returns even if consolidated returns could alternatively be filed; in such circumstances, there may be a tax rule that grants a 100% dividends received deduction, to avoid imposing double taxation. If, in the circumstances noted above, consolidated financial statements are prepared but a consolidated tax return is not, it would be the case that a dividends received deduction of 100% would be allowed. Accordingly, the temporary difference between pretax consolidated income and taxable income is zero if the parent assumes that the undistributed income will be realized in dividends.

Note that, as of late 2007, IASB has determined that the exception to the required recognition of deferred taxes, when the parent or investor or venturer entity is both able to control the timing of the reversal of the temporary difference and it is probable that the temporary difference will not reverse in the foreseeable future, will be removed from IAS 12. Accounting for income taxes is one of the remaining convergence projects being jointly pursued by IASB and FASB, and an exposure-stage document is still promised by year end 2008 (which appears unlikely to occur on schedule) with a final revised IAS 12 to be issued in 2009.

Tax Effects of Compound Financial Instruments

IAS 32 established the important notion that when financial instruments are compound, the separately identifiable components are to be accounted for according to their distinct natures. For example, when an entity issues convertible debt instruments, those instruments have characteristics of both debt and equity securities, and accordingly, the issuance proceeds should be allocated among those components. (Originally the allocation was to be proportional to fair values of the components, but as amended, IAS 32 requires that the full fair value of the liability component be recognized, with only the residual allocated to equity, consistent with the concept that equity is only the residual interest in an entity.) A problem arises when the taxing authorities do not agree that a portion of the proceeds should be allocated to a secondary instrument. For example, when convertible bonds are sold, for tax reporting purposes the entire proceeds are considered to be the basis of the debt instrument in most jurisdictions, with no basis being allocated to the conversion feature. Accordingly this will create a temporary difference between the interest expense to be recognized for financial reporting purposes and interest to be recognized for income tax purposes, because of the amortization of discount or premium, and in turn this will create deferred tax implications.

Example of tax effects of compound financial instrument at issuance

Consider the following scenario. Tamara Corp. issues 6% convertible bonds with a face value of €3,000,000, due in ten years, with the bonds being convertible into Tamara common stock at the holders' option. Proceeds of the offering amount to €3,200,000, for an effective yield of approximately 5.13% at a time when "straight" debt with similar risks and time to maturity is yielding just under 6.95% in the market. Since the fair value of the debt component is thus €2.8 million out of the actual proceeds of €3.2 million, the convertibility feature is seemingly worth €400,000 in the financial marketplace. Under revised IAS 32, the full fair value of the liability component must be allocated to it, with only the residual value being attributed to equity.

The entry to record the issuance of the bonds follows:

Cash	3,200,000	
Unamortized debt discount	200,000	
Debt payable		3,000,000
Equity—paid-in capital account		400,000

Unamortized debt discount will be amortized as additional interest cost over the life of the bonds (ten years, in this example) for financial reporting purposes, but for tax purposes the deductible interest cost will be limited, typically, to the actual interest paid. In this example, the "originating" phase of the temporary difference will be when the compound security is first sold; the "reversing" of this temporary difference will occur as the debt discount is amortized, until the net carrying value of the debt equals the face value.

Example of tax effects of compound financial instrument in subsequent periods

To illustrate, continue the preceding example and assume that the tax rate is 30%, and for simplicity, also assume that the debt discount will be amortized on a straight-line basis over the ten-year term (€200,000 ÷ 10 = €20,000 per year), although in theory amortization using the "effective yield" method is preferred. The tax effect of the total debt discount is €200,000 × 30% = €60,000. Annual interest expense is €20,000 + (€3,000,000 × 6%) = €200,000. The entries to establish deferred tax liability accounting at inception, and to reflect interest accrual and reversal of the deferred tax account are as follows:

At inception (in addition to the entry shown above)

Equity—paid-in capital account	60,000	
Deferred tax payable		60,000

Each year thereafter

Interest expense	200,000	
Interest payable		180,000
Unamortized debt discount		20,000
Deferred tax payable	6,000	
Tax expense—deferred		6,000

Note that the offset to deferred tax liability at inception is a charge to equity, in effect reducing the credit to paid-in capital for the equity portion of the compound financial instrument to a net of tax basis, since allocating a portion of the proceeds to the equity component caused the creation of a nondeductible deferred charge, debt discount. When the deferred charge is later amortized, however, the reversing of the temporary difference leads to a reduction in tax expense to better "match" the higher interest expense reported in the financial statements than on the tax return.

Intraperiod Tax Allocation

While IAS 12 is concerned predominantly with the requirements of *interperiod* income tax allocation (deferred tax accounting), it also addresses the questions of *intraperiod* tax allocation. Intraperiod tax allocation relates to the matching in the income (or other financial) statement of various categories of comprehensive income or expense (continuing operations, corrections of errors, etc.) with the tax effects of those items. The general principle is that tax effects should follow the items to which they relate. The computation of the tax effects of these items is, however, complicated by the fact that many, if not most, jurisdictions feature progressive tax rates. For that reason, a question arises as to whether overall "blended" rates should be apportioned across all the disparate elements (ordinary income, corrections of errors, etc.), or whether the marginal tax effects of items other than ordinary income should be reported instead.

IAS 12 does not answer this question, or even address it. It might, however, be instructive to consider the two approaches, since this will affect the presentation of the statement of comprehensive income and, in the case of errors, the statement of shareholders' equity as well.

The blended rate approach would calculate the average, or effective, rate applicable to all an entity's taxable earnings for a given year (including the deferred tax effects of items that will be deductible or taxable in later periods, but that are being reported in the current year's financial statements). This effective rate is then used to compute income taxes on each of the individually reportable components. For example, if an entity has an effective blended rate of 46% in a given year, after considering the various tax brackets and any available credits against the gross amount of the tax computed, this rate is used to calculate the taxes on ordinary income, extraordinary income, the results of discontinued operations, the correction of fundamental errors, and the effects of changes in accounting principles, if any.

The alternative to the blended rate approach is what can be called the marginal tax effect approach. Using this computational technique, a series of "with-and-without" calculations will be made to identify the marginal, or incremental, effects of items other than those arising from ordinary, continuing operations. This is essentially the approach dictated under US GAAP (FAS 109 and its predecessor standards) and is the primary approach employed under UK GAAP as well. Since the prescription of this with-and-without method is detailed most extensively in current US GAAP, that explanation is referred to extensively in the following discussion.

Prior to the promulgation of current US GAAP, the with-and-without technique was applied under prior US standards in a step-by-step fashion proceeding down the face of the statement of comprehensive income. For example, an entity having continuing operations, discontinued operations, and extraordinary items would calculate tax expense as follows:

1. Tax would be computed for the aggregate results and for continuing operations. The difference between the two amounts would be allocated to the total of discontinued operations and extraordinary items.
2. Tax expense would be computed on discontinued operations. The residual amount (i.e., the difference between tax on the discontinued operations and the tax on the total of discontinued operations and extraordinary items) would then be allocated to extraordinary items.

Thus, the amount of tax expense allocated to any given classification in the statement of income (and the other financial statements, if relevant) was partially a function of the location in which the item was traditionally presented in the income and retained earnings statements.

Under current US GAAP, total income tax expense or benefit for the period is allocated among continuing operations, discontinued operations, extraordinary items, and stockholders' equity. The standard creates a few anomalies since, as defined in current US GAAP, the tax provisions on income from continuing operations include not only taxes on the income earned from continuing operations, as expected, but also a number of other tax effects including the following:

1. The impact of changes in tax laws and rates, which includes the effects of such changes on items that were previously reflected directly in stockholders' equity
2. The impact of changes in tax status
3. Changes in estimates about whether the tax benefits of deductible temporary differences or net operating loss or credit carryforwards are probable of realization

> *NOTE: Under current US GAAP the actual criterion is "more likely than not," which differs from IAS's "probable" criterion.*

Under current US GAAP, stockholders' equity is charged or credited with the initial tax effects of items that are reported directly in stockholders' equity, including that related to corrections of the effects of accounting errors of previous periods, which under the international standards are known as fundamental errors. The effects of tax rate or other tax law changes on items for which the tax effects were originally reported directly in stockholders' equity are reported in continuing operations if they occur in any period after the original event. This approach was adopted by current US GAAP because of the presumed difficulty of identifying the original reporting location of items that are affected possibly years later by changing rates; the expedient solution was to require all such effects to be reported in the tax provision allocated to continuing operations.

Example of intraperiod allocation using a "with-and-without" approach

Assume that there were €50,000 in deductible temporary differences at 12/31/08; these remain unchanged during the current year, 2009.

Income from continuing operations	€400,000
Loss from discontinued operations	(120,000)
Gain on involuntary conversion	60,000
Correction of accounting error:	
understatement of depreciation in 2008	(20,000)
Tax credits	5,000

- Tax rates are: 15% on first €100,000 of taxable income; 20% on next €100,000; 25% on next €100,000; 30% thereafter.
- Effective (average) future tax rates were expected to be 20% at December 31, 2008, but are expected to be 28% at December 31, 2009.
- Retained earnings at December 31, 2008, totaled €650,000.

Intraperiod tax allocation proceeds as follows:

Step 1 — Tax on total taxable income of €320,000 (= €400,000 − €120,000 + €60,000 − €20,000) is €61,000 (that is, €66,000 based on rate structure, less tax credit of €5,000).

Step 2 — Tax on income from continuing operations, which includes the gain on the involuntary conversion (which can no longer be deemed extraordinary, since that classification has been eliminated by revised IAS 8) of €460,000 is €103,000, net of the tax credit.

Step 3 — The difference, €42,000, is allocated pro rata to discontinued operations, and the correction of the error in prior year depreciation, which for this example is deemed not practical to account for by restating the earlier year (in practice, this would not be readily accepted). Note the effect of these intraperiod allocations are both at 30%, the marginal rate.

Step 4 — Adjustment of the deferred tax asset, amounting to a €4,000 increase due to an effective tax rate estimate change [= €50,000 × (.28 − .20)] is allocated to continuing operations, regardless of the actual source of the temporary difference.

A summary combined income and retained earnings statement is presented below.

Income from continuing operations,		
before income taxes		€460,000
Income taxes on income from continuing operations:		
Current	€108,000	
Deferred	(4,000)	
Tax credits	(5,000)	99,000
Income from continuing operations, net		361,000
Loss from discontinued operations,		
net of tax benefit of €36,000		(84,000)
Net income		277,000
Retained earnings, January 1, 2009		650,000
Correction of accounting error, net of tax effects (€6,000)		(14,000)
Retained earnings, December 31, 2009		€913,000

Applicability to international accounting standards. Since IAS 12 is silent on the method to be used to compute the tax effects of individual captions in the statement of income and the statement of retained earnings (or changes in stockholders' equity), in the authors' opinion financial statement preparers have the option of using essentially a with-and-without or blended rate approach. Both can be rationalized from either practical or theoretical perspectives. The blended rate method would clearly be easier to apply, since only one set of computations using progressive tax rates would be needed. The blended rate method also avoids the implication that items other than income from continuing operations represented the "last units of currency" earned, since the rates applicable to those items would not be the highest marginal rates. On the other hand, the with-and-without method averts the situation where the blended rate applied to income from continuing operations is subject to wide variation due simply to the occasional existence of extraordinary and other unusual items.

On balance, and given the lack of a prescribed methodology in IAS 12, the authors slightly favor the blended rate approach. Whichever methodology is employed, however, it is vital that the notes to the financial statements clearly describe how the computation was made and disclose the tax effects of the various components presented. IAS 12 does, however, permit the tax effects of all extraordinary items to be presented in one amount, if computation of each extraordinary item is not readily accomplished.

Statement of Financial Position Classification of Deferred Taxes

Somewhat surprisingly, IAS 12 stated that should the reporting entity classify its statement of financial position (into current and noncurrent assets and liabilities), deferred tax assets and liabilities should never be included in the current category. (Subsequent to the most recent revision to IAS 12, revised IAS 1 was promulgated, which essentially requires presentation of a classified statement of financial position unless a liquidation ordering is deemed more meaningful; the prohibition against current classification of deferred taxes remains.) While not articulated in the standard, presumably the anticipated difficulties of assessing the amount and pattern of temporary difference reversals led to this decision. Arguably, the extent of any required scheduling would have been rather limited, since the only concern would have been to assess whether the expected reversals would occur before or after the one-year demarcation line between current and noncurrent. However, having established this clear prohibition, IAS 12 is undeniably easier to apply.

However, IASB had determined, as part of its convergence efforts to eliminate differences between IFRS and US GAAP, that IAS 12 will be amended so that both current and noncurrent deferred tax assets and liabilities may be presented in the statement of financial position. As of late 2008, IASB was still planning on finalizing this change in 2009.

Deferred tax assets pertaining to certain tax jurisdictions may be fully or partially recognizable under IFRS rules, while those pertaining to others may not be recognized at all, based on the circumstances. Applying IAS 12's "probable" criterion to the expected timing and availability of taxable temporary differences and other items entering into the computation of taxable profit in each jurisdiction is necessary to make these determinations.

The offsetting of tax assets and liabilities is never allowed in the statement of financial position, except to the extent that they pertain to taxes levied by, and refund due from, the same taxing authority. Amounts due to or from independent taxing bodies would not be subject to offsetting, inasmuch as amounts due to one agency cannot be withheld because refunds are due from others. In practice, offsetting is almost never applied even when the same authority is the counterparty, since due dates of amounts owed may not coincide with expected refund dates.

Finally, when entities included in consolidated financial statements are taxed separately, a tax asset recognized by one member of the group should not be offset against a liability recognized by another member of the same group, unless a legal right of offset exists, which would be rare. For example, in some jurisdictions the tax loss carryforward of an acquired affiliate entity cannot be used to reduce taxable profit of another member of the group, even if consolidated tax returns are being prepared. In such a case, the deferred tax asset recognized in connection with the tax loss carryforward cannot be offset against a deferred tax liability of another member of the consolidated group. Further, in evaluating whether realization of the tax asset is probable, the existence of the tax liability could not be considered.

Financial Statement Disclosures

Revised IAS 12 mandated a number of disclosures, including some which had not been required under earlier practice. The purpose of these disclosures is to provide the user with an understanding of the relationship between pretax accounting profit and the related tax effects, as well as to aid in predicting future cash inflows or outflows related to tax effects of assets and liabilities already reflected in the statement of financial position. The more recently imposed disclosures were intended to provide greater insight into the relationship between deferred tax assets and liabilities recognized, the related tax expense or benefit recognized in earnings, and the underlying natures of the related temporary differences resulting in those items. There is also enhanced disclosure for discontinued operations under IAS 12. Finally, when deferred tax assets are given recognition under defined conditions, there will be disclosure of the nature of the evidence supporting recognition. The specific disclosures are presented in greater detail in the following paragraphs.

Statement of financial position disclosures. A reporting entity is required to disclose the amount of a deferred tax asset and the nature of evidence supporting its recognition, when

1. Utilization of the deferred tax asset is dependent on future taxable profits in excess of the profits arising from the reversal of the existing taxable temporary differences; *and*
2. The enterprise has suffered a loss in the same tax jurisdiction to which the deferred tax assets relate in either the current or preceding period.

Statement of comprehensive income disclosures. IAS 12 places primary emphasis on disclosure of the components of income tax expense or benefit. The following information must be disclosed about the components of tax expense for each year for which a statement of comprehensive income is presented.

The components of tax expense or benefit, which may include some or all of the following:

1. Current tax expense or benefit
2. Any adjustments recognized in the current period for taxes of prior periods
3. The amount of deferred tax expense or benefit relating to the origination and reversal of temporary differences
4. The amount of deferred tax expense or benefit relating to changes in tax rates or the imposition of new taxes
5. The amount of the tax benefit arising from a previously unrecognized tax loss, tax credit, or temporary difference of a prior period that is used to reduce current period tax expense
6. The amount of the tax benefit from a previously unrecognized tax loss, tax credit, or temporary difference of a prior period that is used to reduce deferred tax expense
7. Deferred tax expense arising from the write-down of a deferred tax asset because it is no longer deemed probable of realization

In addition to the foregoing, IAS 12 also requires that disclosures be made of the following items which are to be separately stated:

1. The aggregate current and deferred tax relating to items that are charged or credited to equity
2. The relationship between tax expense or benefit and accounting profit or loss either (or both) as

    a. A numerical reconciliation between tax expense or benefit and the product of accounting profit or loss times the applicable tax rate(s), with disclosure of how the rate(s) was determined; or
    b. A numerical reconciliation between the average effective tax rate and applicable rate, also with disclosure of how the applicable rate was determined

3. An explanation of changes in the applicable rate vs. the prior reporting period
4. The amount and date of expiration of unrecognized tax assets relating to deductible temporary differences, tax losses and tax credits
5. The aggregate amount of any temporary differences relating to investments in subsidiaries, branches, and associates and interests in joint ventures for which deferred liabilities have not been recognized
6. For each type of temporary difference, including unused tax losses and credits, disclosure of

    a. The amount of the deferred tax assets and liabilities included in each statement of financial position presented; and
    b. The amount of deferred income or expense recognized in the statement of comprehensive income, if not otherwise apparent from changes in the statements of financial position

7. Disclosure of the tax expense or benefit related to discontinued operations

Finally, disclosure must be made of the amount of deferred tax asset and the evidence supporting its presentation in the statement of financial position, when both these conditions exist: utilization is dependent upon future profitability beyond that assured by the future reversal of taxable temporary differences, *and* the entity has suffered a loss in either the current period or the preceding period in the jurisdiction to which the deferred tax asset relates.

Examples of informative disclosures about income tax expense

The disclosure requirements imposed by IAS 12 are extensive and in some instances complicated. The following examples have been adapted from the standard itself, with some modifications.

Note: Income tax expense

Major components of the provisions for income taxes are as follows:

	2008	*2009*
Current tax expense	€75,500	€82,450
Deferred tax expense (benefit), relating to the origination and reversal of temporary differences	12,300	(16,275)
Effect on previously provided deferred tax assets and liabilities resulting from increase in statutory tax rates	--	7,600
Total tax provision for the period	€87,800	€73,775

The aggregate current and deferred income tax expense (benefit) which was charged (credited) to stockholders' equity for the periods

	2008	*2009*
Current tax, related to correction of error	€(5,200)	€ --
Deferred tax, related to revaluation of investments	--	45,000
Total	€(5,200)	€45,000

The relationship between tax expense and accounting profit is explained by the following reconciliations:

NOTE: Only one required.

	2008	*2009*
Accounting profit	€167,907	€132,398
Tax at statutory rate (43% in 2006; 49% in 2008)	€ 72,200	€ 64,875
Tax effect of expenses which are not deductible:		
Charitable contributions	600	1,300
Civil fines imposed on the entity	15,000	
Effect on previously provided deferred tax assets and liabilities resulting from increase in statutory rates	--	7,600
Total tax provision for the period	€ 87,800	€ 73,775
Statutory tax rate	43.0%	49.0%
Tax effect of expenses which are not deductible:		
Charitable contributions	0.4	1.0
Civil fines imposed on the entity	8.9	--
Effect on previously provided deferred tax assets and liabilities resulting from increase in statutory rates	--	5.7
Total tax provision for the period	52.3%	55.7%

In 2009, the federal government imposed a 14% surcharge on the income tax, which has affected 2009 current tax expense as well as the recorded amounts of deferred tax assets and liabilities, since when these benefits are ultimately received or settled, the new higher tax rates will be applicable.

Deferred tax assets and liabilities included in the accompanying statements of financial position as of December 31, 2008 and 2009 are as follows, as classified by categories of temporary differences:

	2008	*2009*
Accelerated depreciation for tax purposes	€26,890	€22,300
Liabilities for postretirement health care that are deductible only when paid	(15,675)	(19,420)
Product development costs deducted from taxable profits in prior years	2,500	--
Revaluation of fixed assets, net of accumulated depreciation	--	2,160
Deferred tax liability, net	€13,715	€ 5,040

IASB–FASB Convergence Efforts Affecting Accounting for Income Taxes

Beginning in 2002, and reaffirmed in 2006, IASB and FASB, the US standard-setting body, formally agreed upon a program designed to eliminate, over a relatively few years, many or most of the remaining disparities between US GAAP and IFRS. One of the major areas being addressed is that of income tax accounting—where there are a significant number of inconsistencies that need to be resolved. Both US GAAP and IFRS pertaining to income tax accounting are firmly grounded in the statement of financial position–oriented *liability method* of computing deferred tax assets and liabilities. Discrepant guidance exists, however, with regard to certain scope exceptions; measurement criteria for both deferred tax assets and liabilities; recognition criteria for deferred tax assets; required allocations of tax effects to stockholders' equity; the statement of financial position classifications of deferred tax assets and liabilities; certain disclosures; and tax effects of equity instruments. The current statuses of IASB deliberations on these topics are set forth in the following paragraphs.

Scope exceptions. IAS 12 provides a general exception that relates to the initial recognition of certain assets and liabilities, such as for those that are not given any tax recognition. While technically this creates a basis difference (i.e., zero basis for tax purposes, but recognition for financial reporting purposes), which in general necessitates interperiod income tax allocation, when such situations are encountered (other than in connection with business combinations) no deferred tax asset or liability is to be recognized, according to IAS 12. IASB has tentatively decided to eliminate this exception from IAS 12 in connection with its convergence efforts.

Another scope exception pertains to goodwill. As a residual arising from the allocation of a business combination's total cost to assets acquired and liabilities assumed, were this to also be tax-effected, it would only result in inflating the statement of financial position, without providing any useful additional information. For that reason, no deferred tax effects are to be recognized associated with goodwill (or negative goodwill, to the limited extent that is recognized). US GAAP has essentially the same exception, and both FASB and IASB have tentatively decided to retain this exception to the general principle of interperiod tax allocation.

Under current IFRS, when an investor controls the timing of distributions from equity investees such that temporary differences between financial and tax reporting of the investor's share of investee earnings can be postponed indefinitely, no interperiod tax allocation is required (i.e., no deferred tax liability is to be provided by the investor). A parallel situation can arise with a parent entity, if (say) earnings of a foreign subsidiary will not be taxed until distributed, and the parent entity intends to not effect such distributions. The exception would apply in joint venture situations only if the venturers have an agreement that distributions will not occur. (The same exception exists under US GAAP.) IASB will probably eliminate this exception, so that deferred taxes will henceforth have to be provided for such temporary differences, even if ultimate reversals are under the reporting entity's control. However, given the goal of convergence, this action may be viewed as counterproductive and thus the final outcome cannot yet be predicted.

Measurement criteria. Deferred tax assets and liabilities are adjusted at each date of the statement of financial position to reflect anticipated tax effects given the tax rates that have been enacted. In some circumstances, rate changes have been "substantially enacted" but are not fully in effect and may be subject to some slight uncertainty. US GAAP applies a somewhat different criterion in this regard, and the IASB is seeking to have FASB adopt IASB's approach.

Also, IAS 12 directs that, when there are differential tax rates on distributed and undistributed profits, deferred taxes are to be computed based on the rate applicable to undistributed profits in all cases. The corresponding requirement under US GAAP permits the use of the distributed profit tax rate where, and to the extent that, there is an obligation to make distributions. IASB's preference is to retain its current approach, and for FASB to "converge" its standard to IFRS.

Recognition criteria. A basic principle of interperiod tax allocation is that deferred tax assets or liabilities are to be provided for *all* temporary differences (although limited exceptions have already been noted, above). However, while recognizing all tax liabilities is beyond question, the recognition of tax-related assets is subject to concern over realizability (or, equivalently, impairment). Here, US GAAP and IFRS differ in approach, with US GAAP requiring recognition of the gross amount of deferred tax assets, with a possible allowance (contra asset) established to recognize the benefits that are not "more likely than not" going to be realized. There is no parallel requirement under IAS 12 for a contra asset to reduce the gross deferred tax asset to a net realizable amount. Instead, IFRS prescribes that the deferred tax asset be recognized to the extent that realization is "probable." IASB has concluded that its term, probable, is equivalent to "more likely than not," and thus that the net amounts of deferred tax assets reported in the statement of financial condition would not differ under the two sets of standards (in effect, the contra asset provided under US GAAP is already netted in the deferred tax asset under IFRS). A change is likely to be made to the wording of IAS 12 to clarify the equivalence of the different terms used.

Allocation to shareholders' equity. While most deferred tax effects are reflected in the statement of operations, those arising from items reported directly in equity are also reported in equity, not earnings. One example often cited is revaluation of long-lived assets, as permitted by IAS 16. Since the revaluation adjustments are taken directly to equity, the tax effects are also shown in equity. As a practical matter, "tracing" the tax effects in the current period to items recorded directly in equity in prior periods can be challenging. IASB has thus far continued in its position that allocation to equity should continue to the extent possible. The ultimate resolution of this issue cannot yet be predicted with any assurance.

Uncertain tax positions. US GAAP enacted a requirement (FASB Interpretation 48) that tax benefits of uncertain tax positions (generally, aggressive use of deductions or deferrals which might not survive examination by the taxing authorities) can only be given financial statement recognition if a defined threshold of probability (more likely than not) is met. IASB is considering this development and may adopt similar requirements as it converges with US GAAP. It can be argued that other existing requirements (recognition of contingent obligations) already in substance require that the tax obligation associated with uncertain tax positions should be accrued, in any event, although this is not common in practice.

Statement of financial position classification. US GAAP requires that deferred tax assets and liabilities be classified as current and noncurrent consistent with the classifications of the assets and liabilities with which they are associated. IAS 12 prohibits current classification of deferred taxes, however. IASB intends to converge to the US GAAP position on this matter.

Disclosures. A number of specific aspects of US GAAP and IFRS disclosure requirements are being debated, and come changes in the interperiod, tax allocation disclosures under IAS 12 may be enacted as the project proceeds.

Examples of Financial Statement Disclosures

Clariant Group
Period ending December 2007

Accounting policies

1.18 Current income tax

The taxable profit (loss) of Group companies, on which the reporting period's income tax payable (recoverable) is calculated using applicable tax rates, is determined in accordance with the rules established by the taxation authorities of the countries in which they operate. Current income taxes for current and prior periods, to the extent they are unpaid, are recognized as liabilities. In case income taxes already paid in respect of current and prior periods exceed the income tax liability amount of those periods, the exceeding amounts are recognized as assets. Current income tax receivables and current income tax liabilities are offset if there is a legally enforceable right to set off the recognized amounts and if there is the intention to settle on a net basis or to realized the asset and settle the liability simultaneously.

1.19 Deferred income tax

Deferred income tax is calculated using the comprehensive liability method. This method calculates a deferred tax asset or liability on the temporary differences that arise between the recognition of items in the balance sheets of Group companies used for tax purposes and one prepared for consolidation purposes. An exception is that no deferred income tax is calculated for the temporary differences in investments in Group companies and associates, provide that the investor (parent company) is able to control the timing of the reversal of the temporary difference and it is probable that the temporary difference will not reverse in the foreseeable future. Furthermore, withholding taxes or other taxes on the eventual distribution of retained earnings of Group companies are only taken into account when a dividend has been planned, since generally the retained earnings are reinvested.

Deferred taxes, calculated using applicable local tax rates, are included in noncurrent assets and noncurrent liabilities, with any changes during the year recorded in the income statement. Changes in deferred taxes on items that are recognized in equity are recorded in equity.

Deferred income tax is determined using tax rates (and laws) that have been enacted by the balance sheet date and are expected to apply when the related deferred income tax asset is realized or the deferred income tax liability is settled.

Deferred income tax assets are recognized to the extent that it is probable that future taxable profit will be available against which the temporary differences or the tax losses carried forward can be utilized.

Taxes

CHF mn	*2006*	*2005**
Current income taxes	(164)	(77)
Deferred income taxes	20	(12)
	(144)	(89)

*Restated for discontinued operations

The main elements contributing to the difference between the Group's overall expected tax expense/rate and effective tax expense/rate for continuing operations are

	2006		2005*	
	CHF mn	%	CHF mn	%
Income before tax	275		351	
Expected tax expense/rate	(74)	6.9	(110)	31.3
Effect of taxes on items not tax-deductible	(57)	20.7	(37)	10.5
Effect of utilization and changes in recognition of tax losses and tax credits	(11)	4.0	41	(11.7)
Effect of tax losses and tax credits of current year not recognized	(8)	2.9	(3)	0.9
Effect of adjustments to current taxes due to prior periods	6	(2.2)	5	(1.4)
Effect of tax-exempt income	6	(2)	5	(1.4)
Effect of other items	(6)	2.2	10	(2.8)
Effective tax expense/rate	(144)	52.4	(89)	25.4

Compared to 2005 the expected tax rate was significantly lower in 2006 due to a larger part of the profit in countries with lower tax rates and also as a result of European reorganization.

The movement of the net deferred tax balance is as follows:

CHF mn	2006	2005*
Beginning of the year	(140)	(129)
Effect of acquisitions	(1)	
Effect of disposals	(4)	
Effect of discontinued operations	24	2
Tax on disposal result of discontinued operations	20	
Reclassification to held for sale	(6)	
Tax on vested equity share based payments reversed to equity	(4)	
Income statement charge	20	(12)
Exchange rate differences	(3)	(1)
End of the year	(94)	(140)

*Restated

Deferred tax assets and liabilities are offset when there is a legally enforceable right to offset current tax assets against current tax liabilities and when the deferred income taxes related to the same fiscal authority.

CHF mn	2006	2005*
Deferred tax liabilities on		
PPE and intangible assets	286	380
Prepaid pensions, other accruals and provisions	11	10
Total deferred tax liabilities	297	390
Thereof offset with deferred tax assets within the same jurisdiction	114	144
Net deferred tax liabilities	183	246
Deferred tax assets on		
PPE and intangible assets	50	68
Retirement benefit obligations	80	84
Tax losses carried forward and tax credits	40	41
Other accruals and provisions	33	57
Total deferred tax assets	250	259
Thereof offset with deferred tax liabilities within the same jurisdiction	114	144
Net deferred tax assets	89	106
Net deferred tax balance	(94)	(140)

Of the deferred tax assets capitalized, CHF 10 million refer to tax losses of the French subsidiaries (2005: CHF 18 million) and CHF 20 million to the tax losses of the Italian subsidiaries (2005: 0). Clariant is confident it can recover these tax losses as a result of the efforts made both in the restructuring program and in the implementation of the new principal structure.

The total of temporary differences on investments in subsidiaries, for which no deferred taxes were calculated, was CHF 764 million at December 31, 2006 (CHF 1,024 million at December 31, 2005).

Tax losses on which no deferred tax was calculated are as follows:

CHF mn	2006	2005
Expiry by		
2006	--	32
2007	128	31
2008	129	699
2009	642	640
2010	46	--
After 2010		
(2005: after 2009)	883	753
Total	1,828	2,155
Unrecognized tax credits	8	6

The tax credits expire between 2007 and 2012.

Nestlé SA
Year Ended December 31, 2006

Accounting policies

Taxes

The Group is subject to taxes in different countries all over the world. Taxes and fiscal risks recognized in the Consolidated Financial Statements reflect Group Management's best estimate of the outcome based on the facts known at the balance sheet date in each individual country. Any differences between tax estimates and final tax assessments are charged to the income statement in the period in which they are incurred, unless anticipated. Taxes include current taxes on profit and other taxes such as taxes on capital. Also included are actual or potential withholding taxes on current and expected transfers of income from Group companies and tax adjustments relating to prior years. Income tax is recognized in the income statement, except to the extent that it relates to items directly taken to equity, in which case it is recognized against equity. Deferred taxation is the tax attributable to the temporary differences that arise when taxation authorities recognize and measure assets and liabilities with rules that differ from those of the Consolidated Financial Statements.

Deferred taxes are calculated under the liability method at the rates of tax expected to prevail when the temporary differences reverse subject to such rates being substantially enacted at the balance sheet date. Any changes of the tax rates are recognized in the income statement unless related to items directly recognized against equity. Deferred tax liabilities are recognized on all taxable temporary differences excluding nondeductible goodwill. Deferred tax assets are recognized on all deductible temporary differences provided that it is probable that future taxable income will be available.

For share-based payments, a deferred tax asset is recognized against the income statement over the vesting period, provided that a future reduction of the tax expense is both probable and can be reliably estimated. The deferred tax asset for the future tax deductible amount exceeding the total share-based payment cost is recognized against equity.

5. **Taxes**

In millions of CHF	2006	2005[a]
Components of tax expense		
Current tax	2,457	2,272
Deferred tax	647	166
Transfers (from)/to unrecognized tax assets	(38)	(179)
Changes in deferred tax rates	40	8
Prior years' tax	(105)	(119)
Taxes reclassified to equity	(230)	(57)
Taxes reclassified to discontinued operations	31	5
Other taxes[b]	491	351
	3,293	2,647
Deferred tax by types		
Property, plant, and equipment	82	(86)
Goodwill and intangible assets	(43)	304
Employee benefits	261	114
Inventories, receivables, payables, and provisions	(6)	(23)
Unused tax losses and tax credits	194	(50)
Other	159	(93)
	647	166
Reconciliation of tax expense		
Tax at the theoretical domestic rates applicable to profits of taxable entities in the countries concerned[c]	3,051	2,939
Tax effect of nondeductible amortization and impairment of goodwill	21	41
Tax effect of nondeductible or nontaxable items	(173)	(391)
Transfers (from)/to unrecognized tax assets	(38)	(179)
Difference in tax rates	46	5
Other taxes[b]	386	232
	3,293	2,647

[a] 2005 comparatives have been restated following the first application of the option of IAS 19, **Employee Benefit§ 93A ss. and IFRIC 4, Determining Whether an Arrangement Contains a Lease,** as well as the decision to transfer the fresh cheese activities in Italy to Nestlé Nutrition (refer to Note 29).

[b] Includes withholding tax levied on transfers of income and taxes on capital.

[c] The applicable Group tax rate varies from one year to the other depending on the weight of each individual company in the taxable Group profit.

22. **Deferred taxes**

In millions of CHF	2006	2005[a]
Tax assets by types of temporary difference		
Property, plant, and equipment	317	311
Goodwill and intangible assets	297	148
Employee benefits	1,905	2,171
Inventories, receivables, payables, and provisions	997	1,018
Unused tax losses and tax credits	288	536
Other	565	564
	4,369	4,748
Tax liabilities by types of temporary difference		
Property, plant, and equipment	1,239	1,150
Goodwill and intangible assets	952	905
Employee benefits	52	33
Inventories, receivables, payables, and provisions	99	110
Other	300	324
	2,642	**2,522**
Net assets	**1,727**	**2,226**

In millions of CHF	*2006*	*2005*[a]
Reflected in the balance sheet as follows:		
Deferred tax assets	2,433	2,466
Deferred tax liabilities	(706)	(240)
Net assets	**1,727**	**2,226**
Temporary differences for which no deferred tax is recognized		
On investments in affiliated companies (taxable temporary difference)	19,436	15,441
On unused tax losses, tax credits, and other items [b]	2,175	2,026

[a] *2005 comparatives restated following first application of the option of IAS 19,* **Employee Benefits,** *and IFRIC 4,* **Determining Whether an Arrangement Contains a Lease.**

[b] *Of which more than half expire in more than five years.*

APPENDIX

ACCOUNTING FOR INCOME TAXES IN INTERIM PERIODS

Interim Reporting

IAS 34, *Interim Financial Reporting*, established new requirements for interim reporting, while not making the reporting of interim results mandatory. While the DSOP preceding this standard's promulgation essentially endorsed a discrete approach (applying measurement principles to each interim period on a stand-alone basis), the final standard represents a judicious mix of integral and discrete viewpoints. As noted in the main body of this chapter, IAS 34 adopts an integral viewpoint with regard to income tax expense, as indeed was necessitated by the fact that taxing authorities almost universally apply their requirements to a full year, taken as a whole, with no attempt at interim measurement of results of operations.

In this appendix, supplementary guidance is offered, largely based on US GAAP, to assist in applying the principles of income tax accounting set forth in IAS 12 to interim periods when the enterprise elects (or is required by local law) to report on such as basis. This guidance should be understood as being illustrative rather than authoritative. Care should be taken in particular regarding areas of financial reporting which are guided by recently issued or revised international accounting standards (such as that for discontinuing operations).

The general consensus is that the appropriate perspective for interim period reporting is to view the interim period as an integral part of the year rather than as a discrete period. For purposes of computing income tax provisions, this objective is usually achieved by projecting income for the full annual period, computing the tax thereon, and applying the effective rate to the interim period income or loss, with quarterly (or monthly) revisions to the expected annual results and the tax effects thereof, as necessary.

Notwithstanding this general principle, however, there are certain complexities that arise only in the context of interim financial reporting. Included in this group of issues are (1) recognizing the tax benefits of losses based on expected earnings of later interim or annual periods, (2) reporting the benefits of net operating loss carryforwards in interim periods, and (3) reporting the effects of tax law changes in interim periods. Other matters requiring interpretation include the classification of deferred taxes on interim statements of financial position and the allocation of interim period tax provisions between current and deferred expense.

Basic example of interim period accounting for income taxes

Andorra Woolens, Inc. estimates that accounting profit for the full fiscal year ending June 30, 2009, will be €400,000. The company expects the annual premium on an officer's life insurance policy to be €12,000, and dividend income (from a less than 20% ownership interest) is expected to be €100,000. Under pertinent tax rules, premiums paid on officer's life insurance is not an expense. Furthermore, there is a dividends received deduction of 70% for intercorporate investments of under 20%. Deferred organization costs are being amortized for financial reporting purposes (having been assessed as having limited life), but cannot be deducted for tax purposes in the company's jurisdiction. Organization cost amortization is €30,000 per year.

The company recognized income of €75,000 in the first quarter of the year. The deferred tax liability arises solely in connection with depreciation temporary differences; these differences totaled €150,000 at the beginning of the year and are projected to equal €280,000 at year-end. The effective rate expected to apply to the reversal at both year beginning and year-end is 34%. The change in the taxable temporary difference during the current interim period is €30,000.

Andorra Woolens must first calculate its estimated effective income tax rate for the year. This rate is computed using all the tax planning alternatives available to the company (e.g., tax credits, foreign rates, capital gains rates, etc.).

Estimated pretax accounting income		€ 400,000
Permanent differences:		
Add: Nondeductible officer's life insurance premium	€12,000	
Nondeductible amortization of organization costs	30,000	42,000
		442,000
Less: Dividends received deduction (€100,000 × 70%)		(70,000)
Estimated book taxable income		372,000
Less: Change in taxable temporary difference		(130,000)
Estimated taxable income for the year		242,000
Tax on estimated taxable income (see below)		€ 70,530
Effective tax rate for **current** tax provision		
[€70,530/(€400,000 – €130,000)]		26.1%

Tax rate schedule			Taxable	
At least	*Not more than*	*Rate*	*income*	*Tax*
€ --	€50,000	15%	€ 50,000	€ 7,500
50,000	75,000	25%	25,000	6,250
75,000	--	34%	167,000	56,780
				€70,530

The deferred tax provision for the interim period should be based on the actual change in the temporary difference (depreciation, in this example) during the interim period. In this case the depreciation temporary difference grew by €30,000 during the period, and the expected tax rate that will apply to the reversal, in future years, is the marginal rate of 34%. Accordingly, the tax provision for the period is as follows:

Ordinary income for the interim period	€75,000
Less: Change in temporary difference	30,000
Net ordinary income	45,000
Applicable tax rate	26.1%
Current tax provision	11,755
Tax effect of temporary difference (€30,000 × 34%)	10,200
Total provision	€21,955

Therefore, the entry necessary to record the income tax expense at the end of the first quarter is as follows:

Income tax expense	21,955	
Income taxes payable—current		11,755
Deferred tax liability		10,200

The financial statement presentation would remain the same as has been illustrated in prior examples.

In the second quarter, Andorra Woolens, Inc. revises its estimate of income for the full fiscal year. It now anticipates only €210,000 of book income, including only €75,000 of dividend income, because of dramatic changes in the national economy. Other permanent differences are still expected to total €42,000.

Estimated pretax accounting income		€ 210,000
Permanent differences:		
Add: Nondeductible officer's life insurance premium	€12,000	
Nondeductible amortization of organization costs	30,000	42,000
		252,000
Less: Dividends received deduction (€75,000 × 70%)		(52,500)
Estimated book taxable income		199,500
Less: Change in taxable temporary difference		(130,000)
Estimated taxable income for the year		69,500
Tax on estimated taxable income (see below)		€ 12,375
Effective tax rate for *current* tax provision		
[€12,375/(€210,000 – €130,000)]		15.5%

| Tax rate schedule | | | Taxable | |
At least	Not more than	Rate	income	Tax
€ --	€50,000	15%	€50,000	€ 7,500
50,000	75,000	25%	19,500	4,875
				€12,375

The actual earnings for the second quarter were €22,000, and the change in the temporary difference was only €10,000. The tax provision for the second quarter is computed as follows:

Ordinary income for the half year	€97,000
Less: Change in temporary difference	40,000
Net ordinary income	57,000
Applicable tax rate	15.5%
Current tax provision	8,835
Tax effect of temporary difference (€40,000 × 34%)	13,600
Total provision	€22,435

Under the general principle that changes in estimate are reported prospectively, the results of prior quarters are not restated for changes in the estimated effective annual tax rate. Given the provision for current and deferred income taxes that was made in the first interim period, shown above, the following entry is required to record the income taxes as of the end of the second quarter:

Income tax expense	480	
Income taxes payable—current	2,920	
Deferred tax liability		3,400

The foregoing illustrates the basic problems encountered in applying the promulgated US GAAP to interim reporting. In the following paragraphs, we discuss some items requiring modifications to the approach described above.

Net Operating Losses in Interim Periods

The tax effects of operating losses are treated no differently than any other temporary differences; if probable of being realized, the tax effects are reflected as deferred tax benefits in the period the loss is incurred. If not deemed probable, no tax effects are recognized; if the estimation of realizability changes in a later period, the deferred tax benefit is then recorded, with the offset being included in current period tax expense. However, given the desire to treat interim periods as integral parts of the annual period of which they are a component, the accounting treatment of net operating losses raises a number of issues. These include (1) calculation of the expected annual tax rate for purposes of interim period income tax provisions and (2) recognition of an asset for the tax effects of a loss carryforward.

Carryforward from prior years. Loss carryforward benefits from prior years first given recognition (i.e., by recordation of a deferred tax benefit when none had been recognized in the period the loss was incurred) in interim periods are included in the ordinary tax provision. Common practice is to compute the expected annual effective tax rate on ordinary income at each interim reporting date, and use this rate to provide income taxes on ordinary income on a cumulative basis at each interim date. The tax effects of extraordinary items, discontinued operations, and other nonoperating categories were excluded from this computation; those tax effects are typically separately determined on a with-and-without basis, as explained later in this appendix.

Recognition of a previously unrecognized tax benefit should be included as a credit in the tax provision of the interim period when there is a reevaluation of the likelihood of future tax benefits being realized. Similarly, a reduction of the deferred tax benefit resulting from a revised judgment that the benefits are not probable of being realized would cause a catch-up adjustment to be included in the current interim period's ordinary tax provision. In either situation, the effect is *not* prorated to future interim periods by means of the effective tax rate estimate. To illustrate, consider the following example.

Example of carryforward from prior years

Dacca Corporation has a previously unrecognized €50,000 net operating loss carryforward; a flat 40% tax rate for current and future periods is assumed. Income for the full year (before NOL) is projected to be €80,000; in the first quarter a pretax loss of €10,000 will be reported.

Projected annual income	€80,000
× Tax rate	40%
Projected tax liability	€32,000

Accordingly, in the statement of comprehensive income for the first fiscal quarter, the pretax operating loss of €10,000 will give rise to a tax *benefit* of €10,000 × 40% = €4,000.

In addition, a tax benefit of €20,000 (€50,000 loss carryforward × 40%) is given recognition and is included in the current interim period tax provision relating to continuing operations. Thus, total tax benefit for the first fiscal quarter will be €24,000 (= €4,000 + €20,000).

If Dacca's second quarter results in a pretax operating income of €30,000, and the expectation for the full year remains unchanged (i.e., operating income of €80,000), the second quarter tax provision is €12,000 (€30,000 × 40%).

The tax provision for the fiscal first half-year will be a benefit of €12,000, as follows:

Cumulative pretax income through second quarter	
(€30,000 – €10,000)	€ 20,000
× Effective rate	40%
Tax provision before recognition of NOL carryforward benefit	8,000
Benefit of NOL carryforward first recognized in first quarter	(20,000)
Total tax provision (benefit)	€(12,000)

The foregoing example assumes that during the first quarter, Dacca's judgment changed as to the full realizability of the previously unrecognized benefit of the €50,000 loss carryforward. Were this *not* the case, however, the benefit would have been recognized only as actual tax liabilities were incurred (through current period earnings) in amounts to offset the NOL benefit.

To illustrate the latter situation, assume the same facts about earnings for the first two quarters, and assume now that Dacca's judgment about realizability of prior period NOL does not change. Tax provisions for the first quarter and first half are as follows:

	First quarter	*First half-year*
Pretax income (loss)	€(10,000)	€20,000
× Effective rate	40%	40%
Tax provision before recognition of NOL carryforward benefit	(4,000)	8,000
Benefit of NOL carryforward recognized	0	(8,000)
Tax provision (benefit)	€(4,000)	€ 0

Notice that recognition of a tax benefit of €4,000 in the first quarter is based on the expectation of at least a breakeven full year's results. That is, the benefit of the first quarter's loss was deemed probable of realization. Otherwise, no tax benefit would have been reported in the first quarter.

Estimated loss for the year. When the full year is expected to be profitable, it will be irrelevant that one or more interim periods results in a loss, and the expected effective rate for the full year should be used to record interim period tax benefits, as illustrated above. However, when the full year is expected to produce a loss, computation of the expected annual tax benefit rate must logically take into account the extent to which a deferred tax asset will be recordable at year-end. For the first set of examples, below, assume that the realization of tax benefits related to operating loss carryforwards are not entirely probable. That is, only a portion of the benefits will be recognized.

For each of the following examples we assume that the L'avventura Corporation is anticipating a loss for the fiscal year of €150,000. A deferred tax liability of €30,000 is currently recorded on the company's books; all of the credits will reverse in the fifteen-year carryforward period permitted by applicable tax law. Assume that future taxes will be at a 40% rate.

Example 1

Assume that the company can carry back the entire €150,000 to the preceding three years. The tax potentially refundable by the carryback would (remember, this is only an estimate until year-end) amount to €48,000 (an assumed amount). The effective rate is then 32% (€48,000/€150,000).

	Ordinary income (loss)			*Tax (benefit) expense*	
				Less	
Reporting	*Reporting*	*Year-*	*Year-*	*previously*	*Reporting*
period	*period*	*to-date*	*to-date*	*provided*	*period*
1st qtr.	€ (50,000)	€ (50,000)	€(16,000)	€ --	€(16,000)
2nd qtr.	20,000	(30,000)	(9,600)	(16,000)	6,400
3rd qtr.	(70,000)	(100,000)	(32,000)	(9,600)	(22,400)
4th qtr.	(50,000)	(150,000)	(48,000)	(32,000)	(16,000)
Fiscal year	€(150,000)				€(48,000)

Note that both the income tax expense (2nd quarter) and benefit are computed using the estimated annual effective rate. This rate is applied to the year-to-date numbers just as in the previous examples, with any adjustment being made and realized in the current reporting period. This treatment is appropriate because the accrual of tax benefits in the first, third, and fourth quarters is consistent with the effective rate estimated at the beginning of the year; in contrast to those circumstances in which a change in estimate is made in a quarter relating to the realizability of tax benefits not provided previously (or provided for only partially).

Example 2

In this case assume that L'avventura Corporation can carry back only €50,000 of the loss and that the remainder must be carried forward. Realization of income to offset the loss is not deemed to be probable. The estimated carryback of €50,000 would generate a tax refund of €12,000 (again assumed). The company is assumed to be in the 40% tax bracket (a flat rate is used to simplify the example). The benefit of the operating loss carryforward is recognized only to the extent that it is deemed to be probable of realization. In this example, management has concluded that only one-fourth of the gross benefit will be realized in future years. Accordingly, only €10,000 of estimated tax benefit related to the carryforward of the projected loss is recordable. Considered in conjunction with the carryback of €12,000, the company will obtain a €22,000 tax benefit relating to the projected current year loss, for an effective tax benefit rate of 14.7%. The calculation of the estimated annual effective rate is as follows:

Expected net loss			€150,000
Tax benefit from carryback		€12,000	
Benefit of carryforward			
(€100,000 × 40%)	€40,000		
Portion not deemed to be			
probable of realization	(30,000)	10,000	
Total recognized benefit			€ 22,000
Estimated annual effective rate			
(€22,000 ÷ €150,000)			14.7%

	Ordinary income (loss)			*Tax (benefit) expense*		
				Year-to-date	*Less*	
Reporting	*Reporting*	*Year-*			*previously*	*Reporting*
period	*period*	*to-date*	*Computed*	*Limited to*	*provided*	*period*
1st qtr.	€ 10,000	€ 10,000	€ 1,470	€ --	€ --	€ 1,470
2nd qtr.	(80,000)	(70,000)	(11,733)	--	1,470	(10,263)
3rd qtr.	(100,000)	(170,000)	(14,667)	(22,000)	(10,263)	(4,404)
4th qtr.	20,000	(150,000)	(22,000)	--	(22,000)	--
Fiscal year	€(150,000)					€(22,000)

In the foregoing, the tax expense (benefit) is computed by multiplying the year-to-date income or loss by the estimated annual effective rate, and then subtracting the amount of tax liability or benefit provided in prior interim periods. It makes no difference if the current period indicates an income or a loss, assuming of course that the full-year estimated results are not being revised. However, if the cumulative loss for the interim periods to date exceeds the projected loss for the full year on which the effective tax benefit rate had been based, no further tax benefits can be recorded, as illustrated above in the provision for the third quarter.

Operating loss occurring during an interim period. An instance may occur in which the company expects net income for the year and incurs a net loss during one of the reporting periods. In this situation, the estimated annual effective rate, which was calculated based on the expected net income figure, is applied to the year-to-date income or loss to arrive at a total year-to-date tax provision. The amount previously provided is subtracted from the year-to-date figure to arrive at the provision for the current reporting period. If the current period operations resulted in a loss, the tax provision for the period will reflect a tax benefit.

Tax Provision Applicable to Discontinuing Operations Occurring in Interim Periods

Discontinuing operations are to be shown net of the related tax effects. The interim treatment accorded discontinuing operations does not differ from the fiscal year-end reporting required by GAAP. However, common practice is not to include these items in computation of the estimated annual tax rate. These items are generally recognized in the interim period in which they occur; that is, they are not annualized. Recognition of the tax effects of a loss due to any of the aforementioned situations would be made if the benefits are expected to be realized during the year or if they will be recognizable as a deferred tax asset at year-end under the provisions of IAS 12.

If a situation arises where realization is not probable in the period of occurrence but becomes assured in a subsequent period in the same fiscal year, the previously unrecognized tax benefit should be reported in income until it reduces the tax provision to zero, with any excess reported in other categories of income (e.g., discontinuing operations) that provided a means of realization for the tax benefit.

If the decision to dispose of operations occurs in any interim period other than the first period, the income (loss) applicable to the discontinuing segment has already been used in computing the estimated annual effective tax rate. Therefore, a recomputation of the total tax is not required. However, the total tax is to be divided into two components.

1. That tax applicable to income (loss) before discontinuing operations
2. That tax applicable to the income (loss) from the discontinuing segment

This division is accomplished as follows: A revised estimated annual effective rate is calculated for the income (loss) before discontinuing operations. This recomputation is then applied to the income (loss) from the preceding periods. The total tax applicable to the discontinuing segment is then composed of the difference between the total tax originally computed and the tax recomputed on remaining income before discontinuing operations.

Example

Realtime Corporation anticipates net income of €150,000 during the fiscal year. The net permanent differences for the year will be €10,000. The company also anticipates tax credits of €10,000 during the fiscal year. For purposes of this example, we assume a flat statutory rate of 50%. The estimated annual effective rate is then calculated as follows:

Estimated pretax income	€150,000
Net permanent differences	(10,000)
Taxable income	140,000
Statutory rate	50%

Tax	70,000
Anticipated credits	(10,000)
Total estimated tax	€ 60,000
Estimated effective rate (€60,000 ÷ €150,000)	40%

The first two quarters of operations were as follows:

Reporting period	Income (loss) Reporting period	Year-to-date	Tax provision Year-to-date	Less previously provided	Reporting period
1st qtr.	€30,000	€30,000	€12,000	€ --	€12,000
2nd qtr.	25,000	55,000	22,000	12,000	10,000

In the third quarter, Realtime made the decision to dispose of Division X. During the third quarter, the company earned a total of €60,000. The company expects the disposal to result in a onetime charge to income of €50,000 and estimates that losses subsequent to the disposal will be €25,000. The company estimates revised income in the fourth quarter to be €35,000. The two components of pretax accounting income (discontinuing operations and revised income before discontinuing operations) are shown below.

Reporting period	Revised income before discontinuing operations	Division X Loss from operations	Provision for loss on disposal
1st qtr.	€ 40,000	€(10,000)	€ --
2nd qtr.	40,000	(15,000)	--
3rd qtr.	80,000	(20,000)	(75,000)
4th qtr.	35,000	--	--
Fiscal year	€195,000	€(45,000)	€(75,000)

Realtime must now recompute the estimated annual tax rate. Assume that all the permanent differences are related to the revised continuing operations. However, €3,300 of the tax credits were applicable to machinery used in Division X. Because of the discontinuance of operations, the credit on this machinery would not be allowed. Any recapture of prior period credits must be used as a reduction in the tax benefit from either operations or the loss on disposal. Assume that the company must recapture €2,000 of investment tax credit which is related to Division X.

The recomputed estimated annual rate for continuing operations is as follows:

Estimated (revised) ordinary income	€195,000
Less net permanent differences	(10,000)
	185,000
Tax at statutory rate of 50%	€ 92,500
Less anticipated credits from continuing operations	(6,700)
Tax provision	€ 85,800
Estimated annual effective tax rate (€85,800 ÷ €195,000)	44%

The next step is then to apply the revised rate to the quarterly income from continuing operations as illustrated below.

Reporting period	Income before discontinuing operations Reporting period	Year-to-date	Estimated annual effective rate	Tax provision Year-to-date	Less previously provided	Reporting period
1st qtr.	€ 40,000	€ 40,000	44%	€17,600	€ --	€17,600
2nd qtr.	40,000	80,000	44%	35,200	17,600	17,600
3rd qtr.	80,000	160,000	44%	70,400	35,200	35,200
4th qtr.	35,000	195,000	44%	85,800	70,400	15,400
Fiscal year	€195,000					€85,800

The tax benefit applicable to the operating loss from discontinuing operations and the loss from the disposal must now be calculated. The first two quarters are calculated on a differential basis as shown below.

Reporting period	Tax applicable to ordinary income		Tax (benefit) expense applicable to Division X
	Previously reported	*Recomputed (above)*	
1st qtr.	€12,000	€17,600	€ (5,600)
2nd qtr.	10,000	17,600	(7,600)
			€(13,200)

The only calculation remaining applies to the third quarter tax benefit pertaining to the operating loss and the loss on disposal of the discontinuing segment. The calculation of this amount is made based on the revised estimate of annual ordinary income, both including and excluding the effects of the Division X losses. This is shown below.

	Loss from operations of Division X	Provision for loss on Disposal
Estimated annual income from continuing operations	€195,000	€195,000
Net permanent differences	(10,000)	(10,000)
Loss from Division X operations	(45,000)	--
Provision for loss on disposal of Division X	--	(75,000)
Total	140,000	110,000
Tax at the statutory rate of 50%	70,000	55,000
Anticipated credits (from continuing operations)	(6,700)	(6,700)
Recapture of previously recognized tax credits as a result of disposal	--	2,000
Taxes after effect of Division X losses	63,300	50,300
Taxes computed on estimated income before the effect of Division × losses	85,800	85,800
Tax benefit applicable to Division X	(22,500)	(35,500)
Amounts recognized in quarters one and two (€5,600 + €7,600)	(13,200)	--
Tax benefit to be recognized in the third quarter	€ (9,300)	€ (35,500)

The quarterly tax provisions can be summarized as follows:

Reporting period	Pretax income (loss)			Tax (benefit) applicable to		
	Continuing operations	*Operations of Division X*	*Provision for loss on disposal*	*Continuing operations*	*Operations of Division X*	*Provision for loss on disposal*
1st qtr.	€ 40,000	€(10,000)	€ --	€17,600	€ (5,600)	€ --
2nd qtr.	40,000	(15,000)	--	17,600	(7,600)	--
3rd qtr.	80,000	(20,000)	(75,000)	35,200	(9,300)	(35,500)
4th qtr.	35,000	--	--	15,400	--	--
Fiscal year	€195,000	€(45,000)	€(75,000)	€85,800	€(22,500)	€(35,500)

The following statement of comprehensive income shows the proper financial statement presentation of these unusual and infrequent items. The notes to the statement indicate which items are to be included in the calculation of the annual estimated rate.

Statement of Comprehensive Income

Net sales*		€xxxx
Other income*		xxx
		xxxx
Costs and expenses		
Cost of sales*	€xxxx	
Selling, general, and administrative expenses*	xxx	
Interest expense*	xx	
Other deductions*	xx	
Unusual items	xxx	
Infrequently occurring items	xxx	xxxx
Income (loss) from continuing operations before income taxes and other items listed below		xxxx
Provision for income taxes (benefit)**		xxx
Income (loss) from continuing operations before items listed below		xxxx

Discontinued operations:

Income (loss) from operations of discontinued Division X (less applicable income taxes of €xxxx)	xxxx	
Income (loss) on disposal of Division X, including provision of €xxxx for operating losses during phaseout period (less applicable taxes of €xxxx)	<u>xxxx</u>	<u>xxxx</u>
Net income (loss)		€<u>xxxx</u>

* *Components of ordinary income (loss).*

** *Consists of total income taxes (benefit) applicable to ordinary income (loss), unusual items, and infrequent items.*

*** *This amount is shown net of income taxes. Although the income taxes are generally disclosed (as illustrated), this is not required.*

16 EMPLOYEE BENEFITS

PERSPECTIVE AND ISSUES

The prescribed rules for the accounting for employee benefits under IFRS have evolved markedly over the past twenty-five years. The current standard, IAS 19, was last subjected to a major revision in 1998, with further limited amendments made in 2000, 2002, 2004, and 2008. IAS 19 provides broad guidance, applicable to all employee benefits, not merely to pension plans. The approach set forth by IAS 19 is largely consistent with that of major national accounting standard setters. Compared to pre-1998 iterations of IAS 19, the range of acceptable alternative accounting treatments has been narrowed substantially. Further modifications will likely continue as the process of "convergence" moves forward, and also, perhaps, as the full extent of defined benefit plan obligations and assets becomes disclosable on the face of plan sponsor statements of financial position.

The objective of employee benefit accounting is primarily the appropriate determination of periodic cost. Under current IAS 19, only one basic method, the "projected unit credit" variation on the *accrued benefit valuation* method, is permitted for the periodic determination of this cost. IAS 19 endorses a smoothing methodology, and thus creates a "corridor" approach to recognition of actuarial gains and losses. It requires annual valuations, whereas the earlier mandate had been for triennial valuations. It also addresses past service cost recognition and other matters that had not been given any attention in earlier standards. Revised IAS 19 is more precise in defining the extent to which components of pension cost are to be disclosed in the financial statements, and it reduces the latitude formerly given to financial statement preparers regarding amortizing certain cost elements, such as that associated with plan amendments.

IAS 19 identifies and provides accounting direction for four categories of employee benefits: short-term benefits such as wages, bonuses, and emoluments such as medical care; postemployment benefits such as pensions and other postretirement benefits; other long-term benefits such as sabbatical leave; and termination benefits. Meaningful IFRS guidance is provided on each of these, whereas the earlier standards focused only on pensions. Nonetheless, the most explicit and detailed of these instructions are for defined benefit pension and other postretirement benefits plans, with less detailed instructions given on the other types of employee benefits; this is understandable given the extreme complexity of both the plans and the accounting therefor. Another major category of employee benefit program, stock-based compensation arrangements, is now dealt with by a separate standard, IFRS 2, which is addressed in detail in Chapter 17.

Pension plans traditionally have existed in two basic varieties: defined contribution and defined benefit. The accounting for the latter is, by far, the more difficult. Given the central role that accounting estimates play in the accounting for defined benefit plans, some diversity in financial reporting will be unavoidable, and full disclosure of key assumptions and methods is the best means of preventing misunderstandings by financial statement users. Defined benefit plan accounting in particular remains a controversial subject because of the heavy impact that various management assumptions have on expense determination, and also because IAS 19 embraces the concept of expense smoothing to a much greater extent than do other accounting standards. Many believe any smoothing strategy to be inappropriate, and a number of financial reporting frauds (not related to pension accounting) uncovered in recent years used improper smoothing as a central component of their respective schemes. It remains possible that future revisions to IAS 19 and its corresponding standards under US and other national GAAP may reduce or eliminate the extent to which periodic defined benefit pension cost determinations rely on such techniques.

Because of the long-term nature of employee benefit plans, IAS 19 accepted the need for delayed recognition of certain cost components, such as those resulting from changes in actuarial estimates. Thus, certain changes are not recognized immediately but instead are recognized over subsequent years in a gradual and systematic way. Estimates and averages may be used as long as material differences are not created as a result. Explicit assumptions and estimates of future events should be made for each specified variable included in pension costs.

IAS 19 also establishes requirements for disclosures to be made by employers when defined contribution or defined benefit pension plans are settled, curtailed, or terminated. Some previously deferred amounts are required to be recognized immediately under such circumstances.

IAS 19 defines all postemployment benefits other than pensions as defined benefit plans and, thus, all the accounting complications of defined benefit pension plans are mirrored here. These difficulties may be exacerbated, in the case of postretirement health care plans, by the need to project the future escalation in health care costs over a rather lengthy time horizon, which is a famously difficult exercise to undertake.

IAS 19 was amended in mid-2002 to prohibit the recognition of gains or losses that arise solely from past service cost and actuarial losses or gains, respectively, when a surplus in the plan exists. This amendment to IAS 19 addressed what some viewed as a counterintuitive result produced by the interaction of two aspects of the standard; namely, the option to defer the gains and losses in the pension fund and the limit on the amount that can be recognized as an asset (the "asset ceiling"). The effect of the amendment, which is viewed as an interim solution only, is to prevent such counterintuitive loss or gain recognition. The asset ceiling requirement was left unchanged.

While accounting for employee benefits by the various national standards and IFRS has been in the process of converging for many years, a number of important differences remain. IASB concluded that the differences between IAS 19 and the national standards would best be addressed in a broad-scope convergence project. This is an ongoing effort, with resolution tied to certain other IASB projects, including one that is attempting to address how comprehensive income should be reported. The major issues being addressed are discussed later in this chapter.

In June 2002, IASB began a limited convergence project on postemployment benefits. It resulted in the promulgation of an amendment dealing with the recognition of actuarial gain and losses, and in proposals (not acted upon) on the treatment of group defined benefit plans in the individual or separate financial statements of entities within a consolidated group, and additional disclosures. IASB now projects that an exposure draft will be released in 2009 and that a final standard may follow in 2011.

In July 2007, IFRIC 14 was issued, addressing the problems that arise from the interaction between the limitation on defined benefit plan asset recognition by employers/plan sponsors under IAS 19 and the statutory minimum funding requirements that exist under some jurisdictions.

Sources of IFRS
IAS 19   *IFRIC* 14

DEFINITIONS OF TERMS

Accrued benefit obligation. Actuarial present value of benefits (whether vested or nonvested) attributed by the pension benefit formula to employee service rendered before a specified date and based on employee service and compensation (if applicable) prior to that date.

Accrued benefit valuation methods. Actuarial valuation methods that reflect retirement benefits based on service rendered by employees to the date of the valuation. Assumptions about projected salary levels to the date of retirement must be incorporated, but service to be rendered after the end of the reporting period is not considered in the calculation of pension cost or of the related obligation.

Accrued pension cost. Cumulative net pension cost accrued in excess of the employer's contributions.

Accrued postretirement benefit obligation. The actuarial present value of benefits attributed to employee service rendered as of a particular date. Prior to an employee's full eligibility date, the accrued postretirement benefit obligation as of a particular date for an employee is the portion of the expected postretirement benefit obligation attributed to that employee's service rendered to that date. On and after the full eligibility date, the accrued and expected postretirement benefit obligations for an employee are the same.

Actuarial gains and losses. Include (1) experience adjustments (the effects of differences between the previous actuarial assumptions and what has actually occurred); and (2) the effects of changes in actuarial assumptions.

Actuarial present value. Value, as of a specified date, of an amount or series of amounts payable or receivable thereafter, with each amount adjusted to reflect (1) the time value of money (through discounts for interest) and (2) the probability of payment (by means of decrements for events such as death, disability, withdrawal, or retirement) between the date specified and the expected date of payment.

Actuarial valuation. The process used by actuaries to estimate the present value of benefits to be paid under a retirement plan and the present values of plan assets and sometimes also of future contributions.

Amortization. Usually refers to the process of reducing a recognized liability systematically by recognizing revenues or reducing a recognized asset systematically by recognizing expenses or costs. In pension accounting, amortization is also used to refer to the systematic recognition in net pension cost over several periods of previously unrecognized amounts, including unrecognized prior service cost and unrecognized actuarial gain or loss.

Asset ceiling. The maximum amount of defined benefit asset that can be recognized is the lower of

1. The surplus or deficit in the benefit plan plus (minus) any unrecognized losses (gains) or
2. The total of
   a. Any cumulative unrecognized net actuarial losses and past service cost, and
   b. The present value of any economic benefits available in the form of refunds from the plan or reductions in future contributions to the plan, determined using the discount rate that reflects market yields at the end of the reporting period on high-quality corporate bonds or, if necessary, on government bonds.

Attribution. Process of assigning pension benefits or cost to periods of employee service.

Career-average-pay formula (career-average-pay plan). Benefit formula that bases benefits on the employee's compensation over the entire period of service with the employer. A career-average-pay plan is a plan with such a formula.

Contributory plan. Pension plan under which employees contribute part of the cost. In some contributory plans, employees wishing to be covered must contribute; in other contributory plans, employee contributions result in increased benefits.

Current service cost. The increase in the present value of the defined benefit obligation resulting from services rendered by employees during the period, exclusive of cost elements identified as past service cost, experience adjustments, and the effects of changes in actuarial assumptions.

Curtailment. Event that significantly reduces the expected years of future service of present employees or eliminates, for a significant number of employees, the accrual of defined benefits for some or all of their future services. Curtailments include (1) termination of employee's services earlier than expected, which may or may not involve closing a facility or discontinuing a segment of a business, and (2) termination or suspension of a plan so that employees do not earn additional defined benefits for future services. In the latter situation, future service may be counted toward vesting of benefits accumulated based on past services.

Defined benefit pension plan. Any postemployment benefit plan other than a defined contribution plan. These are generally retirement benefit plans under which amounts to be paid as retirement benefits are determinable, usually by reference to employees' earnings and/or years of service. The fund (and/or employer) is obligated either legally or constructively to pay the full amount of promised benefits whether or not sufficient assets are held in the fund.

Defined contribution pension plan. Benefit plans under which amounts to be paid as retirement benefits are determined by the contributions to a fund together with accumulated investment earnings thereon; the plan has no obligation to pay further sums if the amounts available cannot pay all benefits relating to employee services in the current and prior periods.

Employee benefits. All forms of consideration to employees in exchange for services rendered.

Equity compensation benefits. Benefits under which employees are entitled to receive employer's equity financial instruments, or which compensate employees based on the future value of such instruments.

Equity compensation plans. Formal or informal arrangements to provide equity compensation benefits.

Expected long-term rate of return on plan assets. Assumption as to the rate of return on plan assets reflecting the average rate of earnings expected on the funds invested, or to be invested, to provide for the benefits included in the projected benefit obligation.

Expected postretirement benefit obligation. The actuarial present value as of a particular date of the benefits expected to be paid to or for an employee, the employee's beneficiaries, and any covered dependents pursuant to the terms of the postretirement benefit plan.

Expected return on plan assets. Amount calculated as a basis for determining the extent of delayed recognition of the effects of changes in the fair value of assets. The expected return on plan assets is determined based on the expected long-term rate of return on plan assets and the market related value of plan assets.

Experience adjustments. Adjustments to benefit costs arising from the differences between the previous actuarial assumptions as to future events and what actually occurred.

Fair value. Amount that an asset could be exchanged for between willing, knowledgeable parties in an arm's-length transaction.

Final-pay plan. A defined benefit plan that promises benefits based on the employee's remuneration at or near the date of retirement. It may be the compensation of the final year, or of a specified number of years near the end of the employee's service period.

Flat-benefit formula (flat-benefit plan). Benefit formula that bases benefits on a fixed amount per year of service, such as €20 of monthly retirement income for each year of credited service. A flat-benefit plan is a plan with such a formula.

Fund. Used as a verb, to pay over to a funding agency (as to fund future pension benefits or to fund pension cost). Used as a noun, assets accumulated in the hands of a funding agency for the purpose of meeting pension benefits when they become due.

Funding. The irrevocable transfer of assets to an entity separate from the employer's entity, to meet future obligations for the payment of retirement benefits.

Gain or loss. Change in the value of either the projected benefit obligation or the plan assets resulting from experience different from that assumed or from a change in an actuarial assumption.

Interest cost component (of net periodic pension cost). Increase in the present value of the accrued benefit obligation due to the passage of time.

Measurement date. Date as of which plan assets and obligations are measured.

Mortality rate. Proportion of the number of deaths in a specified group to the number living at the beginning of the period in which the deaths occur. Actuaries use mortality tables, which show death rates for each age, in estimating the amount of pension benefits that will become payable.

Multiemployer plans. Defined contribution plans or defined benefit plans, other than state plans, that (1) pool the assets contributed by various entities that are not under common control; and (2) use those assets to provide benefits to employees of more than one entity, on the basis that contribution and benefit levels are determined without regard to the identity of the entity that employs the employees concerned.

Net periodic pension cost. Amount recognized in an employer's financial statements as the cost of a pension plan for a period. Components of net periodic pension cost are service cost, interest cost (which is implicitly presented as part of service cost), actual return on plan assets, gain or loss, amortization of unrecognized prior service cost, and amortization of the unrecognized net obligation or asset existing at the date of initial application of IAS 19.

Other long-term employee benefits. Benefits other than postemployment, termination and stock equity compensation benefits, that are not due to be settled within one year of the end of the period in which service was rendered.

Past service cost. The actuarially determined change in the present value of the defined benefit obligation arising on the introduction of a retirement benefit plan, on the making of improvements to such a plan, or on the completion of minimum service requirements for eligibility in such a plan, all of which give employees credit for benefits for service prior to the occurrence of one or more of these events. Past service cost may be either positive (when benefits are introduced or changed so that the present value of the defined benefit obligation increases) or negative (when existing benefits are changed so that the present value of the defined benefit obligation decreases).

Pay-as-you-go. A method of recognizing the cost of retirement benefits only at the time that cash payments are made to employees on or after retirement.

Plan amendment. Change in terms of an existing plan or the initiation of a new plan. A plan amendment may increase benefits, including those attributed to years of service already rendered.

Plan assets. The assets held by a long-term employee benefit fund, and qualifying insurance policies. Regarding assets held by a long-term employee benefit fund, these are assets (other than nontransferable financial instruments issued by the reporting entity) that both

1. Are held by a fund that is legally separate from the reporting entity and exists solely to pay or fund employee benefits, and
2. Are available to be used only to pay or fund employee benefits, are not available to the reporting entity's own creditors (even in the event of bankruptcy), and cannot be returned to the reporting entity unless either

   a. The remaining assets of the fund are sufficient to meet all related employee benefit obligations of the plan or the entity, or
   b. The assets are returned to the reporting entity to reimburse it for employee benefits already paid by it.

Regarding the qualifying insurance policy, this must be issued by a nonrelated party if the proceeds of the policy both

1. Can be used only to pay or fund employee benefits under a defined benefit plan, and
2. Are not available to the reporting entity's own creditors (even in the event of bankruptcy) and cannot be returned to the reporting entity unless either

a. The proceeds represent surplus assets that are not needed for the policy to meet all related employee benefit obligations, or

b. The proceeds are returned to the reporting entity to reimburse it for employee benefits already paid by it.

Postemployment benefits. Employee benefits, other than termination benefits, which are payable after the completion of employment.

Postemployment benefit plans. Formal or informal arrangements under which an entity provides postemployment benefits for one or more employees.

Postretirement benefits. All forms of benefits, other than retirement income, provided by an employer to retirees. Those benefits may be defined in terms of specified benefits, such as health care, tuition assistance, or legal services, that are provided to retirees as the need for those benefits arises, or they may be defined in terms of monetary amounts that become payable on the occurrence of a specified event, such as life insurance benefits.

Prepaid pension cost. Cumulative employer contributions in excess of accrued net pension cost.

Present value of a defined benefit obligation. Present value, without deducting any plan assets, of expected future payments required to settle the obligation resulting from employee service in the current and prior periods.

Prior service cost. Cost of retroactive benefits granted in a plan amendment.

Projected benefit obligation. The actuarial present value as of a date of all benefits attributed by the pension benefit formula to employee service rendered prior to that date. The projected benefit obligation is measured using assumptions as to future compensation levels if the pension benefit formula is based on those future compensation levels (pay-related, final-pay, final-average-pay, or career-average-pay plans).

Projected benefit valuation methods. Actuarial valuation methods that reflect retirement benefits based on service both rendered and to be rendered by employees, as of the date of the valuation. Contrasted with accumulated benefit valuation methods, projected benefit valuation methods will result in a more level assignment of costs to the periods of employee service, although this will not necessarily be a straight-line allocation. Assumptions about projected salary levels must be incorporated. This was the allowed alternative method under the prior version of IAS 19, but is prohibited under the current standard.

Retirement benefit plans. Formal or informal arrangements whereby employers provide benefits for employees on or after termination of service, when such benefits can be determined or estimated in advance of retirement from the provisions of a document or from the employers' practices.

Retroactive benefits. Benefits granted in a plan amendment (or initiation) that are attributed by the pension benefit formula to employee services rendered in periods prior to the amendment. The cost of the retroactive benefits is referred to as prior service cost.

Return on plan assets. Interest, dividends and other revenues derived from plan assets, together with realized and unrealized gains or losses on the assets, less administrative costs (other than those included in the actuarial assumptions used to measure the defined benefit obligation) including taxes payable by the plan.

Service. Employment taken into consideration under a pension plan. Years of employment before the inception of a plan constitute an employee's past service; years thereafter are classified in relation to the particular actuarial valuation being made or discussed. Years of employment (including past service) prior to the date of a particular valuation constitute prior service.

Settlement. Transaction that (1) is an irrevocable action, (2) relieves the employer (or the plan) of primary responsibility for a pension benefit obligation, and (3) eliminates significant risks related to the obligation and the assets used to effect the settlement. Examples include making lump-sum cash payments to plan participants in exchange for their rights to receive specified pension benefits and purchasing nonparticipating annuity contracts to cover vested benefits.

Short-term employee benefits. Benefits other than termination and equity compensation benefits that are due to be settled within one year after the end of the period in which the employees rendered the related service.

Terminal funding. A method of recognizing the projected cost of retirement benefits only at the time an employee retires.

Termination benefits. Employee benefits payable as a result of the entity's termination of employment before normal retirement or the employee's acceptance of early retirement inducements.

Unrecognized prior service cost. Portion of prior service cost that has not been recognized as a part of net periodic pension cost.

Vested benefits. Those benefits that, under the conditions of a retirement benefit plan, are not conditional on continued employment.

CONCEPTS, RULES, AND EXAMPLES

Importance of Pension and Other Benefit Plan Accounting

For a variety of cultural, economic, and political reasons, the existence of private pension plans has increased tremendously over the past forty years, and these arrangements are the most common and desired of the assorted "fringe benefits" offered by employers in many nations. Under the laws of some nations, employers may be required to have such programs in place for their permanent employees. For many entities, pension costs have become a very material component of the total compensation paid to employees. Unlike for wages and other fringe benefits, the timing of the payment of cash to either the plan's administrators or to the plan beneficiaries can vary substantially from the underlying economic event (that is, the plans are not always fully funded on a current basis). This creates the possibility of misleading financial statement representation of the true costs of conducting business, unless a valid accrual method is employed. For this reason, and also because of the complexity of these arrangements and the impact they have on the welfare of the workers, accounting for the cost of pension plans and similar schemes (postretirement benefits other than pensions, etc.) has received a great deal of attention from national and international standards setters.

Basic Objectives of Accounting for Pension and Other Benefit Plan Costs

Need for pension accounting rules. The principal objectives of pension accounting are to measure the compensation cost associated with employees' benefits and to recognize that cost over the employees' respective service periods. The relevant standard, IAS 19, is concerned only with the accounting aspects of pensions (and other benefit plans). The funding of pension benefits is considered to be financial management and legal concerns, and accordingly, is not addressed by this pronouncement.

When an entity provides benefits, the amounts of which can be estimated in advance, to its retired employees and their beneficiaries, the arrangement is deemed to be a pension plan. The typical plan is written, and the amounts of future benefits can be determined by reference to the plan documents. However, the plan and its provisions can also be implied from unwritten but established past practices. The accounting for most types of retirement plans is suggested by, if not heavily detailed in, IAS 19. Plans may be unfunded, insured, trust fund, defined contribution and defined benefit plans, and deferred compensation contracts, if equivalent. Independent (i.e., not employer-sponsored) deferred profit-sharing plans and pension payments which are made to selected employees on a case-by-case basis are not considered pension plans.

The establishment of a pension plan represents a long-term financial commitment to employees. Although some entities manage their own plans, this commitment usually takes the form of contributions that are made to an independent trustee or, in some countries, to a governmental agency. These contributions are used by the trustee to acquire plan assets of various kinds, although the available types of investments may be restricted by governmental regulations in certain jurisdictions. Plan assets are used to generate a financial return, which typically consists of earned interest and/or appreciation in asset values.

The earnings from the plan assets (and occasionally, the proceeds from their liquidation) provide the trustee with cash to pay the benefits to which the employees become entitled at the date of their retirements. These benefits in turn are defined by the terms of the pension plan, which is known as the plan's benefit formula. In the case of defined benefit plans, the benefit formula incorporates many factors, including the employee's current and future compensation, service longevity, age, and so on. The benefit formula is the best indictor of the plan's obligations at any point in time. It is used as the basis for determining the pension cost to be recognized each fiscal year.

Statement of comprehensive income vs. statement of financial position objectives. As the accounting requirements for pensions and other forms of postemployment benefits have evolved over the years, the primary objective has been to assign the periodic costs of such plans properly to the periods in which the related benefits are received by the employers incurring these costs. These benefits are obviously received when the workers are productively working at their jobs, not during the later years when they are enjoying their retirements. Matching expected future costs to currently occurring revenues is the central challenge of pension accounting.

For this reason, accounting long ago recognized that the "pay-as-you-go" method of expense recognition, under which expense recognition would be deferred until the benefit payments to retirees were actually made, would cause an unacceptable mismatching of costs and benefits and a significant distortion of profit or loss, as well as an underreporting of legal or constructive obligations and corresponding overstatement of equity. The probable result of this mismatching would be the overstating of earlier years' results of operations and understating those of later years when large retirement payments are being made. As pensions and other fringe benefits expanded over the past generation to become a material and ever-increasing fraction of workers' compensation, this problem could no longer be ignored by accounting standards setters.

The reason that pay-as-you-go accounting had not been eliminated long ago is that many pension plans and similar employee benefit plan arrangements are rather complex, and the accounting necessary to report on them properly is also difficult and was slow in evolving. Most significantly, in the case of defined benefit plans, actual costs may not be known for many years, even decades, since a variety of future events (employee turnover, performance of investments, salary increases, etc.) will affect the ultimate burden on the employer. Accordingly, the measurement of expense on a current basis demands that many complicated estimates be made, some involving actuarial computations, and accountants have often been reluctant to anchor the financial statements to estimates that are potentially very imprecise. Only when the distortions of pay-as-you-go accounting became unacceptably great, due to the growing occurrence and magnitude of these benefit plans, were professional standards revised to prohibit continued use of that mode of accounting.

As pensions became an almost universal fixture of the employment landscape (in some nations, private pensions are mandated by law; in other countries, participation in government-sponsored plans is required), the failure to require such accounting became an impediment to meaningful financial reporting. Notwithstanding the limitations of actuarial and other estimates, financial statements incorporating the accrual of pension costs are vastly more accurate and useful than those based on a pay-as-you-go approach.

Evolution of IFRS on pension costs. About thirty years ago, major accounting standard-setting bodies began urging that pension costs be accrued properly in financial statements. At first, a wide range of actuarial methods were permitted, each of which could produce more meaningful results than the pay-as-you-go method, but over time the range of options permitted has been narrowed in major jurisdictions.

As presently constituted, pension accounting rules have tended to focus overwhelmingly on the income statement. That is, the dominant objective has been to match income and expense properly on a current basis, so that the periodic measurement of operating performance is within the bounds of material accuracy.

The meaningful presentation of the statement of financial position has been somewhat less of a priority, however. Thus, even when an employer has retained full responsibility for the ultimate payment of pension benefits (as with defined benefit plans), the employer's statement of financial position has usually not set forth the assets and obligations of the pension scheme. This has been due partly to the fact that various "smoothing" approaches have been made to expense measurement, making the statement of financial position (given the rigors of double entry bookkeeping) a repository for the resulting deferred charges and credits, inevitably making an accurate depiction from the statement of financial position side less meaningful. Furthermore, accountants and other have been genuinely ambivalent about the validity of presenting information about the assets and obligations of the pension plan in the employer's statement of financial position, believing that the pension plan constitutes a separate economic and reporting entity even when the ultimate legal (or at least, moral) obligation belongs to the employer.

IAS 19 is a substantial advance over its predecessor standards and is very similar in approach to the corresponding US GAAP standards (FAS 87, 88, 106, and more recently 132[R] and 158). In fact, it offers broader coverage than the US standards, touching on compensated absences and stock compensation arrangements (which are the subjects of more extensive coverage in separate US GAAP standards, however), and on various short-term arrangements as well. IAS 19 broke with the past IFRS practice of permitting a range of methodologies resulting in potentially quite different financial statement results. Finally, IAS 19 greatly expanded the disclosures required by employers having defined benefit plans, again largely mimicking the US requirements.

By mandating one specific actuarial costing method, IAS 19 effectively required employers sponsoring defined benefit plans to engage in annual actuarial valuations, which has increased the cost of compliance for those having such plans. Overall, the effect of IAS 19 has been to significantly increase the comparability of financial statements of entities with a wide range of employee benefit plans and thus, from a standard-setting perspective, must be deemed a success.

Basic Principles of IAS 19

Applicability: pension plans. IAS 19 is applicable to both defined contribution and defined benefit pension plans. The accounting for *defined contribution* plans is normally straightforward, with the objective of matching the cost of the program with the periods in which the employees earn their benefits. Since contributions are formula-driven (e.g., as a percentage of wages paid), typically the payments to the plan will be made currently; if they do not occur by the end of the reporting period, an accrual will be recognized for any unpaid current contribution liability. Once made or accrued, the employer has no further obligation for the value of the assets held by the plan or for the sufficiency of fund assets for payment of the benefits, absent any violation of the terms of the agreement by the employer. Employees thus suffer or benefit from the performance of the assets in which the contributions made on their behalf were invested; often the employees themselves are charged with responsibility for selecting those investments.

IAS 19 requires that disclosure be made of the amount of expense recognized in connection with a defined contribution pension plan. If not explicitly identified in the statement of income, this should therefore be disclosed in the notes to the financial statements.

Compared to defined contribution plans, the accounting for *defined benefit* plans is vastly more complex, because the employer (sponsor) is responsible not merely for the current contribution to be made to the plan on behalf of participants, but additionally for the sufficiency of the assets in the plan for the ultimate payments of benefits promised to the participants. Thus the current contribution is at best a partial satisfaction of its obligation, and the amount of actual cost incurred is not measured by this alone. The measurement of pension cost under a defined benefit plan necessarily involves the expertise of actuaries— persons who are qualified to estimate the numbers of employees who will survive (both as employees, in the case of vesting requirements which some of them may not yet have met; and as living persons who will be present to receive the promised retirement benefits), the salary levels at which they will retire (if these are incorporated into the benefit formula, as is commonly the case), their expected life expectancy (since benefits are typically payable for life), and other factors which will influence the amount of resources needed to satisfy the employer's promises. Actuarial determinations cannot be made by accountants, who lack the training and credentials, but the results of actuaries' efforts will be critical to the ability to properly account for defined benefit plan costs. Accounting for defined benefit plans is described at length in the following pages.

Applicability: other employee benefit plans. IAS 19 explicitly applies to not merely pension plans (which were dealt with by earlier iterations of this standard as well, although in rather less detail), but also four other categories of employee and postemployment benefits. These are

1. *Short-term employee benefits,* which include normal wages and salaries as well as compensated absences, profit sharing and bonuses, and such nonmonetary fringe benefits as health insurance, housing subsidies, and employer-provided automobiles, to the extent these are granted to current (not retired) employees.
2. *Other long-term employee benefits,* such as long-term (sabbatical) leave, long-term disability benefits and, if payable after twelve months beyond the end of the reporting period, profit sharing and bonus arrangements and deferred compensation.
3. *Termination benefits,* which are payments to be made upon termination of employment under defined circumstances, generally when employees are induced to leave employment before normal retirement age.
4. *Equity compensation benefits,* which are stock option plans, phantom stock plans, and similar compensation schemes which reward employees based upon the performance of the companies' share prices.

Each of the foregoing categories of employee benefits will be explained later in this chapter.

IAS 19 also addresses postemployment benefits *other than pensions,* such as retiree medical plan coverage, as part of its requirements for pension plans, since these are essentially similar in nature. These are also discussed further later in this chapter.

IAS 19 considers all plans other than those explicitly structured as defined contribution plans to be defined benefit plans, with the accounting and reporting complexities that this implies. Unless the employer's obligation is strictly limited to the amount of contribution currently due, typically driven by a formula based on entity performance or by employee wages or salaries, the obligations to the employees (and the amount of recognizable expense) will have to be estimated in accordance with actuarial principles.

Cost recognition distinguished from funding practices. Although it is arguably a sound management practice to fund retirement benefit plans on a current basis, in some jurisdictions the requirement to do this is either limited or absent entirely. Furthermore, in some jurisdictions the currently available tax deduction for contributions to pension plans may be limited, reducing the incentive to make such contributions until such time as the funds are actually needed for making payouts to retirees. Since the objective of periodic financial reporting is to match costs and revenues properly on a current basis, the pattern of funding is obviously not always going to be a useful guide to proper accounting for pension costs.

"Pay-as-you-go," accrued benefit, and projected benefit methods of accounting for postretirement benefits. Before the establishment of strict accounting and financial reporting rules, it was not uncommon to account for pensions and other similar costs on the "pay-as-you-go" basis. Briefly, this methodology recognized current period expense equal to only the amounts of benefits actually paid out to retirees and other beneficiaries in the reporting period. In support of this approach, the argument was usually made (1) it was very difficult, or expensive, to accurately measure (i.e., on an actuarial basis) the real cost of such plans and (2) the effect on periodic earnings would not be much different in any event. However, pay-as-you-go obviously violates the concept of accrual basis accounting, and the presumption that periodic expense is not materially distorted is often not supported in fact. This method of accounting for pensions and other postretirement programs has accordingly been barred since the first version of IAS 19 was promulgated in 1983.

While adherence to the accrual concept precluded pay-as-you-go accounting for the cost of employee benefit plans, for plans other than those which qualify as defined contribution arrangements there remained a range of acceptable, accrual-basis-consistent methods. Earlier versions of IAS 19 granted wide discretion in selection of costing methods, for which it was rightly criticized. The various techniques all fall within two general groupings which are known as the *accrued benefit* and *projected benefit* methods. While IAS 19 has now ended the acceptability of the projected benefit methods, an understanding of the two approaches will be helpful to gaining a fuller comprehension of the intricacies of the financial reporting of pension plan related costs in the financial statements of the sponsoring entity.

The *accrued (or accumulated) benefit methods* are based on services provided by employees through the date of valuation (i.e., the date of the statement of financial position), without considering future services to be rendered by them. Periodic pension cost is a function of services that are provided in the current period. Since the obligation for future pension payments is computed as the discounted present value of the amounts to be paid in later years, accrued benefit methods will calculate increasing charges (even if wage levels are constant) as employees approach retirement, since the present values of future payments will increase as the time to retirement shortens. Periodic charges also increase, in most actual instances, because attrition rates (employees who leave, thereby forfeiting their rights to retirement payments) decline over time, inasmuch as older employees show less inclination to change employment. While wages will typically increase over time as employees age, both as a result of compensation increases due to seniority and performance improvements, and also as a result (if the past is any guide) of ongoing wage inflation, this should not be the cause of increasing pension costs as time to retirement grows shorter, since even accrued benefit valuation methods must be based on assumptions about future salary progression.

Notwithstanding that over time these assumptions and expectations cannot be precisely accurate, the presumption should be that "estimation errors" will be randomly distributed, and that over the long run, good-faith estimates of salary progression and the resultant effects on periodic pension costs will be reasonably accurate. Consequently, periodic pension costs should not drift upward as employees age because of wage increases.

The *projected benefit valuation method*, on the other hand, uses actuarial estimation techniques that consider the services already rendered as well as those to be rendered by the employees. The goal is to allocate the entire retirement cost smoothly over each employee's respective working life. The pension obligation at any point in time is computed as the present value of the aggregate future payments earned by the end of the reporting period. As with accrued benefit valuation methods, future salary progression must be taken into account in determining periodic pension costs over the working lives of employees. The difference, however, is that future costs are spread more evenly over the full period of employment (although this does not imply that straight-line allocation would be an absolute requirement) as compared to the accrued benefit valuation methods, and in particular, pension-related costs will not show the constantly increasing pattern exhibited by the alternative approach simply due to the shortening time horizon as retirement dates draw near.

Proponents of both accrued and projected benefit valuation approaches cite the matching concept for theoretical support. In fact, for major employers having a workforce comprised of individuals of all ages, which typically replace older retiring workers with younger ones, pension costs will be similar under either methodology on an aggregate basis. While pension costs relative to older workers will be higher and costs relating to younger workers will be lower, if the accrued benefit valuation method is used versus what would be reflected if the projected benefit valuation method were used, with a stable mix of ages of workers, total periodic pension cost will not significantly vary. For smaller employers, or those with a workforce skewed toward younger or older workers, the periodic pattern of pension costs will diverge under these two methods, holding all other considerations constant.

Example of accrued and projected benefit methods

To understand the essential difference between accrued benefit and projected benefit methods, consider a simple case of a single employee hired today with no expectation of future salary increases, and promised a total retirement benefit of €10,000 if he retires after at least 10 years' service, or €14,000 if after 20 years' service. Ignoring present valuing (which does have to be taken into account in the actual accounting for employee benefit costs, however), the accrued benefit method would allocate 1/10 of the €10,000 = €1,000 in promised benefits to each of the first 10 years of service, and then 1/10 of the €4,000 increment = €400 to each of the next 10 years, since accrued benefit methods would not assume the employee would continue employment beyond the tenth year until after that threshold is surpassed. Projected benefit methods, on the other hand, would assign 1/20 of the €14,000 = €700 to each of the first 20 years' employment, being based on service rendered and to be rendered until expected retirement. This all presumes the employee is expected to work at least 20 years (based on experience, the employee's age, etc.). In actual practice, with multiple employees, statistical estimates are used such that full accrual of benefits is normally not made for all employees, given that a certain fraction will opt out before becoming vested, etc.

The foregoing discussion was introduced merely to provide a background about the alternative methods which, conceptually, could be proposed to address the measurement of periodic pension (and similar) costs, and also to report on the alternatives which had been authorized for use previously under IFRS. Under revised IAS 19, promulgated in 1998 and modified in several respects in more recent years, only the accrued benefit valuation method may be utilized. This will reflect retirement benefits based on service already rendered by employees to the date of the valuation. Assumptions about projected salary levels to the date of retirement must be incorporated, but service to be rendered after the end of the reporting period is not. The following discussion will detail this method.

Net Periodic Pension Cost

General discussion. Absent specific information to the contrary, it is assumed that a company will continue to provide retirement benefits well into the future. The accounting for the plan's costs should be reflected in the financial statements and these amounts should not be discretionary. All pension costs—with the exception noted below—should be charged against income. No amounts should be charged directly to retained earnings. The principal focus of IAS 19 is on the allocation of cost to the periods being benefited, which are the periods in which the covered employees provide service to the reporting entity.

In a limited amendment to IAS 19 enacted in 2004, entities now have the option to fully recognize actuarial gains and losses in the period in which they occur, in other comprehensive income in the statement of comprehensive income, outside of operating results. This eliminates these gains and losses from profit or loss determination but includes them in a "middle step" statement, and not directly as charges or credits to retained earnings.

Periodic measurement of cost for defined contribution plans. Under the terms of a defined contribution plan (in some cases referred to as a "money purchase" plan), the employer will be obligated for fixed or determinable contributions in each period, often computed as a percentage of the wage and salary base paid to the covered employees during the period. For one example, contributions might be set at 4% of each employee's wages and salaries, up to €50,000 wages per annum. Generally, the contributions must actually be made by a specific date, such as ninety days after the end of the reporting entity's fiscal year, consistent with local law. The expense must be accrued for accounting purposes in the year the cost is incurred, whether the contribution is made currently or not.

IAS 19 requires that contributions payable to a defined contribution plan be accrued currently, even if not paid by year-end. If the amount is due over a period extending more than one year from the end of the reporting period, the long-term portion should be discounted at the rate applicable to long-term corporate bonds, if that information is known, or applicable to government bonds in the alternative.

Employers may choose to make further discretionary contributions to benefit plans in certain periods. For example, if the entity enjoys a particularly profitable year, the board of directors may vote to grant another 2% of wages as a bonus contribution to the employees' benefit plan. The extent to which this is done will depend, among other factors, on the tax laws of the relevant jurisdiction. Normally, an entity making such a discretionary contribution does not do so simply to reward past performance by its workers. Rather, it does so in the belief that the gesture will cause its employees to be motivated to be more productive and loyal in the forthcoming years. IAS 19 addresses profit sharing and bonus plans as a subset of its requirements concerning short-term compensation arrangements; it stipulates that such a payment should be recognized only when paid or when the entity has a legal or constructive obligation to make it, and when the payment can be reliably estimated. There appears to be no basis for deferring recognition of the expense after that point, however, even though longer-term benefits to the entity might be hoped for.

Past service costs arise when a plan is amended retroactively, so that additional attribution for benefits is given to services rendered in past years. When plans are amended in this fashion, it is generally management's belief that doing so will provide an incentive for greater efforts in the future. For that reason, expense related to past service cost is recognized over the remaining period until these benefits become vested. Despite characterization as relating to past service, no adjustment or restatement is made to prior periods' reported costs, nor is a "catch-up" adjustment made in the period that the plan is amended—unless the benefit increase is fully vested when granted. The manner by which these past service costs are funded, of course, is an issue separate from the accounting for the additional expense. The measure of past service cost is the change in the pension liability resulting from the plan amendment. (In rare cases, past service cost may be a negative amount, if attribution for benefits is reduced.)

IAS 19 does not explicitly address retroactive amendments to defined contribution plans, but by analogizing from the requirements concerning similar amendments to defined benefit plans, it is clear that, if fully vested immediately (as would almost inevitably be the case), these would have to be expensed currently.

Terminations of defined contribution plans generally provide no difficulties from an accounting perspective, since costs have been recognized currently in most instances. However, if certain costs, such as those associated with past services and with discretionary bonus contributions made in past years, have not yet been fully amortized, the remaining unrecognized portions of those costs must be expensed in the period when it becomes probable that the plan is to be terminated. This should be the period when the decision to terminate is made, which on occasion may precede the actual termination of the plan.

Periodic measurement of cost for defined benefit plans. Defined benefit plans present a far greater challenge to accountants than do defined contribution plans, since the amount of expense to be recognized currently will need to be determined on an actuarial basis. Under current IFRS, only the accrued benefit valuation method may be used to measure defined benefit plan pension cost. Furthermore, only a single variant of the accrued benefit method—the "projected unit credit" method—is permitted. A number of alternative approaches, which also fell under the general umbrella of the accrued benefit method are no longer accepted under IFRS. Accordingly, only the projected unit credit method will be discussed in the following presentation.

Net periodic pension cost will consist of the sum of the following six components:

1. Current (pure) service cost
2. Interest cost for the current period on the accrued benefit obligation
3. The expected return on plan assets
4. Actuarial gains and losses, to the extent recognized
5. Past service costs, to the extent recognized
6. The effects of any curtailments or settlements

Disclosures required by IAS 19 effectively require that these cost components be displayed in the notes to the financial statements.

It is important to stress that current service cost, the core cost element of all defined benefit plans, must be determined by a qualified actuary. While the other items to be computed and presented are also developed by actuaries in most cases, they can be verified or even calculated directly by others, including the entity's internal or external accountants. The current service cost, however, is not an immediately apparent computation, as it relies upon a detailed census of employees (age, expected remaining working life, etc.) and the employer's experience (turnover, etc.), and is an intricate and elaborate computational exercise in many cases. Current service cost can only be developed by this careful, employee-by-employee analysis, and this is best left to those with the expertise to complete it.

Current service cost. Current service cost must be determined by an actuarial valuation and will be affected by assumptions such as expected turnover of staff, average retirement age, the plan's vesting schedule, and life expectancy after retirement. The probable progression of wages over the employees' remaining working lives will also have to be taken into consideration if retirement benefits will be affected by levels of compensation in later years, as will be true in the case of career average and final pay plans, among others.

It is worth stressing this last point: when pension arrangements call for benefits to be based on the employees' ultimate salary levels, experience will show that those benefits will increase, and any computation based on current salary levels will surely understate the actual economic commitment to the future retirees. Accordingly, IFRS requires that, for such plans, future salary progression must be considered in determining current period pension costs. This is why the services of a consulting actuary are vital; it is not something to be assigned to accountants. While future salary progression (where appropriate to the plan's benefit formula) must be incorporated (via estimated wage increase rates), current pension cost is a function of the services provided by the employee in the reporting period, emphatically not including services to be provided in later periods.

Under IAS 19, service cost is based on the present value of the defined benefit obligation, and is attributed to periods of service without regard to conditional requirements under the plan calling for further service. Thus, vesting is not taken into account in the sense that there is no justification for nonaccrual prior to vesting. However, in the actuarial determination of pension cost, the statistical probability of employees leaving employment prior to vesting must be taken into account, lest an overaccrual of these costs result.

Example of service cost attribution

To explain the concept of service cost, assume a single employee is promised a pension of €1,000 per year for each year worked before retirement, for life, upon retirement at age sixty or thereafter. Further assume that this is the worker's first year on the job, and he is 30 years of age. The consulting actuary determines that if the worker, in fact, retires at age 60, he will have a life expectancy of 15 years, and at the present value of the required benefits (€1,000/yr × 15 years = €15,000) discounted at the long-term corporate bond rate, 8%, equals €8,560. In other words, based on the work performed thus far (one year's worth), this employee has earned the right to a lump-sum settlement of €8,560 at age 60. Since this is 30 years into the future, this amount must be reduced to present value, which at 8% is a mere €851, which is the pension cost to be recognized currently.

In year two, this worker earns the right to yet another annuity stream of €1,000 per year upon retirement, which again has a present value of €8,560 at the projected retirement age of 60. However, since age 60 is now only 29 years hence, the present value of that promised benefit at the end of the current (second) year is €919, which represents the service cost in year two. This pattern will continue: As the employee ages, the current cost of pension benefits grows apace with, for example, the cost in the final working year being €8,560, before considering interest on the previously accumulated obligation—which would, however, add another €18,388 of expense, for a total cost for this one employee in his final working year of €26,948. It should be noted, however, that in "real-life" situations for employee groups in the aggregate, this may not hold, since new younger employees will be added as older employees die or retire, which will tend to smooth out the annual cost of the plan.

Interest on the accrued benefit obligation. As noted, since the actuarial determination of current period cost is the present value of the future pension benefits to be paid to retirees by virtue of their service in the current period, the longer the time until the expected retirement date, the lower will be the service cost recognized. However, over time this accrued cost must be further increased, until at the employees' respective retirement dates the full amounts of the promised payments have been accreted. In this regard, the accrued pension liability is much like a sinking fund that grows from contributions plus the earnings thereon.

Consider the example of service cost presented in the preceding section. The €851 obligation recorded in the first year of that example will have grown to €919 by the end of the second year. This €68 increase in the obligation for future benefits due to the passage of time is reported as a component of pension cost, denoted as interest cost.

While service cost and interest are often the major components of expense recognized in connection with defined benefit plans, there are other important elements of benefit cost to be accounted for. IAS 19 identifies the expected return on plan assets, actuarial gains and losses, past service costs, and the effects of any curtailments or settlements as categories to be explicitly addressed in the disclosure of the details of annual pension cost for defined benefit plans. These will be discussed in the following sections, in turn.

The expected return on plan assets. IAS 19 has adopted the approach of the corresponding US standard in accepting the notion that since pension plan assets are intended as long-term investments, the random and perhaps sizable fluctuations from period to period should not be allowed to excessively distort the operating results reported by the sponsoring entity. This standard identifies the expected return rather than the actual return on plan assets as the salient component of pension cost, with the difference between actual and expected return being an *actuarial gain or loss* to be dealt with as described below (deferred to future periods or, if significant, partially recognized in the current period). Expected return for a given period is determined at the start of that period, and is based on long-term rates of return for assets to be held over the term of the related pension obligation. Expected return is to incorporate anticipated dividends, interest, and changes in fair value, and is furthermore to be reduced in respect of expected plan administration costs.

For example, assume that at the start of 2009 the plan administrator expects, over the long term, and based on historical performance of plan assets, that the plan's assets will receive annual interest and dividends of 6%, net of any taxes due by the fund itself, and will enjoy a market value gain of another 2.5%. It is also noted that plan administration costs will average .75% of plan assets, measured by fair value. With this data, an expected rate of return for 2009 would be computed as $6.00\% + 2.50\% - .75\% = 7.75\%$. This rate would be used to calculate the return on assets, which would be used to offset service cost and other benefit plan cost components for the year 2009.

The difference between this assumed rate of return, 7.75% in this example, and the actual return enjoyed by the plan's assets would be added to or subtracted from the cumulative actuarial gains and losses. In theory, over the long run, if the expected returns are accurately estimated, these gains and losses will largely offset, inasmuch as they are the result of random, short-term fluctuations in market returns and of demographic and other changes in the group covered by the plan (such as unusual turnover, mortality, or changes in salaries). Since these are expected to largely offset, and given the very long time horizon over which pension benefit plan performance is to be judged, the notion of deferring and thus smoothing recognition of these net gains or losses was appealing, although certainly subject to criticism since actual economic results will not be reported as they occur.

Prior to a 2000 amendment to IAS 19, assets were properly considered to be plan assets only if *all* of the following three conditions were met:

1. The pension or other benefit plan is an entity which is legally separate from the sponsoring employer or entity;
2. The assets of the plan are only to be used to settle employee benefit obligations, are not available to the sponsoring entity's creditors, and either cannot be returned to the sponsor at all or can be returned only to the extent that assets remaining in the fund are sufficient to meet the plan's obligations; and
3. The sponsor will have no legal or constructive obligation to directly pay the employee benefit obligations, assuming that the fund contains sufficient assets to satisfy those obligations.

The 2000 amendment modified IAS 19's definition of plan assets to explicitly include certain insurance policies, and to eliminate the condition relating to sufficiency of assets in the funds. It also slightly amended and reworded the balance of the former definition. The new definition includes assets held by a long-term employee benefit fund, and qualifying insurance policies. Regarding assets held by a fund, these are assets (other than nontransferable financial instruments issued by the reporting entity) that both

1. Are held by a fund that is legally separate from the reporting entity and exist solely to pay or fund employee benefits, and
2. Are available to be used only to pay or fund employee benefits, are not available to the reporting entity's own creditors (even in the event of bankruptcy), and cannot be returned to the reporting entity unless either

   a. The remaining assets of the fund are sufficient to meet all related employee benefit obligations of the plan or the entity, or
   b. The assets are returned to the reporting entity to reimburse it for employee benefits already paid by it.

Regarding the qualifying insurance policy, this must be issued by a nonrelated party if the proceeds of the policy both

1. Can be used only to pay or fund employee benefits under a defined benefit plan, and
2. Are not available to the reporting entity's own creditors (even in the event of bankruptcy), and cannot be returned to the reporting entity unless either

   a. The proceeds represent surplus assets that are not needed for the policy to meet all related employee benefit obligations, or
   b. The proceeds are returned to the reporting entity to reimburse it for employee benefits already paid by it.

It should be stressed that the definition of plan assets is significant for several reasons: plan assets are excluded from the sponsoring employer's statement of financial position and will also serve as the basis for determining the actual and expected rates of return, which impact on the periodic determination of pension cost. By adopting a somewhat more expansive definition of plan assets, the amended IAS 19 affected the future computation of pension costs.

The IAS 19 amendment adopted in 2000 also added certain new requirements which relate to recognition and measurement of the right of reimbursement of all or part of the expenditure to settle a defined benefit obligation. It established that only when it is virtually certain that another party will reimburse some or all of the expenditure required to settle a defined benefit obligation, the sponsoring entity would recognize its right to reimbursement as a separate asset, which would be measured at fair value. In all other respects, however, the asset (amount due from the pension plan) is to be treated in the same way as plan assets. In the statement of comprehensive income or separate income statement presented, defined benefit plan expense may be presented net of the reimbursement receivable recognized.

In some situations, a plan sponsor would be able to look to another entity to pay some or all of the cost to settle a defined benefit obligation, but the assets held by that other party were not deemed to be plan assets as defined in IAS 19 (prior to the revision in 2000). For example, when an insurance policy would match postemployment benefits, the assets of the insurer were not included in plan assets because the insurer was not established solely to pay or fund employee benefits. In such cases, the sponsor recognized its right to reimbursement as a separate asset, rather than as a deduction in determining the defined benefit liability (i.e., no right of offset was deemed to exist in such instances); in all other respects (e.g., the use of the corridor), the sponsoring entity would treat that asset in the same way as plan assets. In particular, the defined benefit liability recognized under IAS 19 had been increased (reduced) to the extent that net cumulative actuarial gains (losses) on the defined benefit obligation and on the related reimbursement remain unrecognized under this standard, as explained earlier in this chapter. A brief description of the link between the reimbursement and the related obligation would be required.

If the right to reimbursement arises under an insurance policy that exactly matches the amount and timing of some or all of the benefits payable under a defined benefit plan, the fair value of the reimbursement was formerly deemed to be present value of the related obligation (subject to any reduction required if the reimbursement was not recoverable in full).

As amended, however, qualifying insurance policies are now to be included in plan assets, arguably because those plans have similar economic effects to funds whose assets qualify as plan assets under the revised definition.

Actuarial gains and losses, to the extent recognized. Changes in the amount of the actuarially determined pension obligation and differences in the actual versus the expected yield on plan assets, as well as demographic changes (e.g., composition of the workforce, changes in life expectancy, etc.) contribute to actuarial (or "experience") gains and losses. While immediate recognition of these gains or losses could clearly be justified conceptually (because these are real and have already occurred), there are both theoretical arguments opposed to such immediate recognition (the distorting effects on the measure of current operating performance resulting from very long-term investments, much of which will reverse of their own accord over time), as well as great opposition by financial statement preparers and users. For this reason, IAS 19 does not require such immediate recognition, unless the fluctuations are so great that deferral is not deemed to be wise. It essentially acceded to the US approach and defined a 10% "corridor" as representing the range of variation deemed to be "normal." While the use of a 10% threshold is arbitrary, it does carry an aura of acceptability, since it had been employed for over a decade previously under US GAAP.

Thus, if the unrecognized actuarial gain or loss is no more than 10% of the larger of the present value of the defined benefit obligation or the fair value of plan assets, measured at the beginning of the reporting period, no recognition in the current period will be necessary (i.e., there will be continued deferral of the accumulated net actuarial gain or loss). On the other hand, if the accumulated net actuarial gain or loss exceeds this 10% corridor, the magnitude creates greater doubt that future losses or gains will offset these, and for that reason some recognition will be necessary.

It is suggested by IAS 19 that this excess be amortized over the expected remaining working lives of the then-active employee participants, but the standard actually permits any reasonable method of amortization as long as (1) recognition is at no slower a pace than would result from amortization over the working lives of participants, and (2) that the same method is used for both net gains and net losses. It is also acceptable to fully recognize all actuarial gains or losses immediately, without regard to the 10% corridor.

The corridor and the amount of any excess beyond this corridor must be computed anew each year, based on the present value of defined benefits and the fair value of plan assets, each determined as of the beginning of the year. Thus, there may have been an unrecognized actuarial gain of €450,000 at the end of year one, which exceeds the 10% corridor boundary by €210,000, and is therefore to be amortized over the average twenty-one-year remaining working life of the plan participants, indicating a €10,000 reduction in pension cost in year two. If, at the end of year two, market losses or other actuarial losses reduce the accumulated actuarial gain below the threshold implied by the 10% corridor, accordingly, in year three there will be no further amortization of the net actuarial gain. This determination, therefore, must be made at the beginning of each period. Depending on the amount of unrecognized actuarial gain or loss at the end of year three, there may or may not be amortization in year four, and so on.

Past service costs, to the extent recognized. Past service costs refer to increases in the amount of a defined benefit liability that results from the initial adoption of a plan, or from a change or amendment to an existing plan which increases the benefits promised to the participants with respect to previous service rendered. Less commonly, a plan amendment could reduce the benefits for past services, if local laws permit this. Employers will amend plans for a variety of reasons, including competitive factors in the employment marketplace, but often it is done with the hope and expectation that it will engender goodwill among the workers and thus increase future productivity. For this reason, it is sometimes the case that these added benefits will not vest immediately, but rather must be earned over some defined time period.

IAS 19 requires immediate recognition of past service cost as an expense when the added benefits vest immediately. However, when these are not immediately vested, recognition is to be on a straight-line basis over the period until vesting occurs. For example, if at January 1, 2009, the sponsoring entity grants an added €4,000 per employee in future benefits, and given the number of employees expected to receive these benefits this computes to a present value of €455,000, but vesting will not be until January 1, 2014, then a past service cost of €455,000 ÷ 5 years = €91,000 per year will be recognized. (To this amount interest must be added, as with service cost as described above.)

The effects of any curtailments or settlements. Periodic defined benefit plan expense is also affected by any curtailments or settlements which have been incurred. The standard defines a curtailment as arising in connection with isolated events such as plant closings, discontinuations of operations, or termination or suspension of a benefit plan. Curtailments may also result from changes in plan features that tie future salary progressions to benefits that will be payable for past service. Often, corporate restructurings will be accompanied by curtailments in benefit plans. Recognition can be given to the effect of a curtailment when the sponsor is demonstrably committed to make a material reduction in the number of covered employees, or it amends the terms of the plan such that a material element of future service by existing employees will no longer be covered or will receive reduced benefits. The curtailment must actually occur for it to be given recognition.

Settlements occur when the entity enters into a transaction which effectively transfers the obligation to another entity, such as an insurance company, so that the sponsor has no legal or constructive obligation to fund any benefit shortfall. Merely acquiring insurance which is intended to cover the benefit payments does not constitute a settlement, since a funding mechanism does not relieve the underlying obligation.

Under the current standard's predecessor, curtailment and settlement gains were recognized when the event occurred, but losses were to be recognized when probable of occurrence. Revised IAS 19 concluded that being *probable* was not sufficient under IFRS to warrant expense or loss recognition in the context of pension plan curtailments or settlements. Thus, both gains and losses are to be recognized when the event occurs.

The effect of a curtailment or settlement is measured with reference to the change in present value of the defined benefits, any change in fair value of related assets (normally there is none), and any related actuarial gains or losses and past service cost which had not yet been recognized. The net amount of these elements will be charged or credited to pension expense in the period the curtailment or settlement actually occurs.

Example of a settlement

Assume that a company's pension plan, at the current date, reports obligations amounting to €1,150 in vested future benefits and another €400 in nonvested benefits. It settles the €1,150 vested benefit portion of its projected benefit obligation by using plan assets to purchase a non-participating annuity contract at a cost of €1,150. After this settlement, nonvested benefits and the effects of projected future compensation levels remain in the plan. In accordance with IAS 19, a pro rata amount of the unrecognized net actuarial loss on assets and unrecognized past service cost are recognized due to settlement. Because the projected benefit obligation is reduced from €1,550 to €400, for a decrease of 74%, the pro rata amount used for recognition purposes is 74%. These changes are noted in the following table:

	Before settlement	Effect of settlement	After settlement
Assets and obligations			
Vested benefit obligation	€(1,150)	€1,150	€ 0
Nonvested benefits	(400)		(400)
Pension benefit obligation before salary increases projection	(1,550)	1,150	(400)
Effects of projected future salary increases	(456)		(456)
Pension benefit obligation	(2,006)	1,150	(856)
Plan assets at fair value	1,159	(1,150)	369
Items not yet recognized in profit or loss			
Funded status	(487)		(487)
Unrecognized net actuarial loss on assets	174	(129)	45
Unrecognized prior service cost	293	(217)	76
Unamortized net asset at IAS 19 adoption	(3)	0	(3)
Prepaid (accrued) benefit cost	€ (23)	€ (346)	€(369)

The entry used by the company to record this transaction does not include the purchase of the annuity contract, since the pension plan acquires the contract with existing funds. The recognition of the pro rata amount of the unrecognized net actuarial loss on assets and unrecognized prior service cost is recorded with the following entry:

Loss from settlement of pension obligation	346	
Accrued/prepaid pension cost		346

Example of a curtailment

Use information from the previous example, assume that the company shuts down one of its factories, which terminates the employment of a number of its staff. The terminated employees have nonvested benefits of €120 and a projected benefit obligation of €261. As a result of this curtailment of the plan, 19% of the pension benefit obligation has been eliminated (€381 obligation reduction resulting from the curtailment, divided by the beginning €2,006 pension benefit obligation). Accordingly, 19% of the unrecognized past service cost will also be recognized. The analysis follows:

	Before curtailment	Effect of curtailment	After curtailment
Assets and obligations			
Vested benefit obligation	€(1,150)	€ 0	€(1,150)
Nonvested benefits	(400)	120	(280)
Pension benefit obligation before salary increases projection	(1,550)	120	(1,430)
Effects of projected future salary increases	(456)	261	(195)
Pension benefit obligation	(2,006)	381	(1,625)
Plan assets at fair value	1,159		1,159

Items not yet recognized in profit or loss			
Funded status	(487)	381	(106)
Unrecognized net actuarial loss on assets	174	(33)	141
Unrecognized prior service cost	293	(56)	237
Unamortized net asset at IAS 19 adoption	(3)	0	(3)
Prepaid (accrued) benefit cost	€ (23)	€ 292	€ 269

The company records the recognition of the pro rata amount of the unrecognized prior service cost and unamortized net actuarial loss, which is offset against the net gain of €381 resulting from the reduction in the pension benefit obligation.

Accrued/prepaid pension cost	292	
Gain from curtailment of pension obligation		292

Transition adjustment. The final element of periodic pension cost under IAS 19 related to the effect of first adopting the accounting standard, which was mandatory for years beginning 1999. The transition amount was to be the present value of the benefit obligation at the date the standard was adopted, less the fair value of plan assets at that date, less any past service cost that was to be deferred to later periods, if the criterion regarding vesting period was met. If the transitional liability was greater than the liability which would have been recognized under the entity's previous policy for accounting for pension costs, it was required to make an *irrevocable* choice to either

1. Recognize the increase in the pension obligation immediately, with the expense included in employee benefit cost for the period; *or*
2. Amortize the transition amount over no longer than a five-year period, on the straight-line basis. Note that the five-year maximum transition would have concluded by 2004, if the entity adopted IAS 19 in 1999. The unrecognized transition amount was not to be formally included in the statement of financial position, but was required to be disclosed.

If the second method were elected, and the entity had a *negative* transitional liability (that is, an asset, resulting from a surplus of pension assets over the related obligation), it was limited in the amount of such asset to present in its statement of financial position to the total of any unrecognized actuarial losses plus past service cost, and the present value of economic benefits available as refunds from the plan or reductions in future contributions, with the present value determined by reference to the rate on high-quality corporate bonds. Furthermore, the amount of unrecognized transitional gain or loss at the end of each reporting period was required to have been presented, as was the amount recognized in the current period profit or loss.

Finally, if the second method was employed, recognition of actuarial gains (which did not include negative past service cost) was limited in two ways. If an actuarial gain was being recognized because it exceeded the 10% limit, or because the entity had elected a more rapid method of systematic recognition, then the actuarial gain was required to be recognized only to the extent the net cumulative gain exceeded the unrecognized transitional liability. And, in determining the gain or loss on any later settlement or curtailment, the related part of the unrecognized transitional liability was required to be incorporated.

IAS 19 also stipulated that if the transitional liability was lower than the amount which would have been recognized under previous accounting rules, the adjustment was to have been taken into profit or loss immediately (i.e., amortization was not permitted).

Upon adoption of the current revised IAS 19, the reporting entity was not permitted to retrospectively compute the effect of the 10% limit on actuarial gain or loss recognition. It was clear that retrospective application would have been impracticable to accomplish and would not have generated useful information, and that was accordingly prohibited by the revised standard.

Employer's Liabilities and Assets

IAS 19 has as its primary concern the measurement of periodic expense incurred in connection with pension plans of employers. One source of dissatisfaction with the standard is its general failure to address the assets or liabilities that may be recognized in the employers' statements of financial position as a consequence of expense recognition, which may include deferral of certain items (e.g., past service costs). In fact, the amounts that may find their way into the statement of financial position will often not meet the strict definition of assets or liabilities, but rather, will be "deferred charges or credits." This will consist of the cumulative difference between the amount funded and the amount expensed over the life of the plan.

Thus, IAS 19 has been criticized for not requiring, under appropriate circumstances, recognition of an additional or minimum liability when plans are materially underfunded. The point of comparison is US GAAP standard FAS 87, which does demand that a minimum liability be reported in the employer's statement of financial position, when both the accumulated (accrued) benefit obligation exceeds the fair value of plan assets, and a liability at least in the amount of this difference is not already recorded as unfunded accrued pension cost. Under that standard, the additional minimum liability is recognized by an offset to an intangible asset up to the amount of unrecognized prior service cost. Any additional debit needed is considered a loss and is recognized in other comprehensive income in the statement of comprehensive income. The IASB concluded that additional measures of liability were potentially confusing and did not promise to provide relevant information. Accordingly, with the exception of any liability to be accrued under IAS 37 (regarding contingencies), the decision was made to dispense with such an item.

IAS 19 does, nonetheless, require that a defined benefit liability or asset be included in the sponsor's statement of financial position when certain conditions are met. Specifically, under the provisions of IAS 19, the amount recognized as a defined benefit liability in the employer's statement of financial position is the net total of

1. The present value of the defined benefit obligation at the end of the reporting period,
2. Any actuarial gains (less any actuarial losses) not recognized because of the "corridor" approach described elsewhere in this chapter,
3. Any past service cost not yet recognized; and
4. The fair value of plan assets at the end of the reporting period.

If this amount nets to a negative sum, it represents the defined benefit asset to be reported in the employer's statement of financial position. However, the amount of asset that can be displayed, per IAS 19, is subject to a *ceiling requirement*.

The asset ceiling defined in IAS 19 is the lower of

1. The amount computed in the preceding paragraph, or
2. The total of

    a. Any cumulative unrecognized net actuarial losses and past service cost, and
    b. The present value of any economic benefits available in the form of refunds from the plan or reductions in future contributions to the plan, determined using the discount rate that reflects market yields at the end of the reporting period on high-quality corporate bonds or, if necessary, on government bonds.

In 2002 the IASB amended IAS 19 in response to concerns raised about the perceived interaction of the deferred recognition and the asset ceiling provisions of IAS 19, and the risk that this was creating counterintuitive results. The issue affects only those entities that have, at the beginning or end of the financial reporting period, a surplus in a defined benefit plan that, based on the current terms of the plan, the entity cannot fully recover through refunds or reductions in future contributions. Such situations created financial reporting anomalies, as follows:

1. *Gains* were being reported in the financial statements based on the occurrence of actuarial *losses* in the pension plans, or
2. *Losses* were being reported on occurrence of actuarial *gains* in the pension plans.

More specifically, the issue was the wording of the asset ceiling provision in IAS 19. This wording, without regard to the limitation imposed by the amendment in 2002, sometimes caused, as a consequence of deferring the recognition of an actuarial loss (gain), the recognition of a gain (loss) in profit or loss.

The problem occurred when an entity defers recognition of actuarial losses or past service cost in determining the amount specified in IAS 19's provision for the measurement of defined benefit liability or asset, but is required to measure the defined benefit asset at the net total of

1. Any cumulative unrecognized net actuarial losses and past service cost, and
2. The present value of any economic benefits available in the form of refunds from the plan or reductions in future contributions to the plan.

In particular, the cumulative unrecognized net actuarial losses and past service cost could result in the entity recognizing an increased asset because of actuarial losses or past service cost in the period. This increase in the asset would be reported as a gain in income.

To resolve this, IAS 19 was amended to prevent gains (losses) from being recognized solely as a result of the deferred recognition of past service cost or actuarial losses (gains). This was done because it was concluded that recognizing gains (losses) arising from past service cost and actuarial losses (gains) would not be representationally faithful. The solution devised in the amendment was to require the reporting entity, to ascertain the defined benefit asset, to recognize immediately the following—but only to the extent that these items arise while the defined benefit asset is determined in accordance with the asset ceiling provision limiting it to the sum of the cumulative unrecognized net actuarial losses and past service cost and the present value of any economic benefits available in the form of refunds from the plan or reductions in future contributions to the plan:

1. The net actuarial losses of the current period and past service cost of the current period, to the extent that they exceed any reduction in the present value of the economic benefits. If there is no change or an increase in the present value of economic benefits, the entire net actuarial losses of the current period and past service cost of the current period should be recognized immediately.
2. The net actuarial gains of the current period after the deduction of past service cost of the current period to the extent that they exceed any increase in the present value of the economic benefits. If there is no change or a decrease in the present value of the economic benefits, the entire net actuarial gains of the current period after the deduction of past service cost of the current period should be recognized.

The foregoing applies to a reporting entity only if it has, at the beginning or end of the accounting period, a surplus in a defined benefit plan and cannot, based on the current terms of the plan, recover that surplus fully through refunds or reductions in future contributions.

A surplus is an excess of the fair value of the plan assets over the present value of the defined benefit obligation. In such cases, past service cost and actuarial losses that arise in the period, the recognition of which is deferred, will increase the amount of the unrecognized net actuarial loss and past service cost determined in accordance with IAS 19. If that increase is not offset by an equal decrease in the present value of economic benefits identified also in IAS 19, there will be an increase in the net total specified by that provision and, hence, a recognized gain. The language added by the amendment prohibits the recognition of a gain in these circumstances.

The opposite effect arises with actuarial gains that arise in the period, the recognition of which is deferred under the standard, to the extent that the actuarial gains reduce cumulative unrecognized actuarial losses. The current language of IAS 19 prohibits the recognition of a loss in these circumstances.

The limitation on asset recognition—to the total of (1) any cumulative unrecognized net actuarial losses and past service cost, and (2) the present value of any economic benefits available in the form of refunds from the plan or reductions in future contributions to the plan—does not override the delayed recognition of certain actuarial losses and certain past service cost, except to the extent that the limitation on asset recognition is driven by the provision pertaining to basic computation of the defined benefit liability or asset in IAS 19. However, that limit does override the transitional option set forth by the standard (i.e., where straight-line amortization over a period not longer than five years is employed). The reporting entity must disclose any amount not recognized as an asset because of the limit stated at the beginning of this paragraph.

To illustrate this immediately previous matter, consider a defined benefit plan with the following characteristics:

Present value of the obligation	€ 550
Fair value of plan assets	(595)
	(45)
Unrecognized actuarial losses	(55)
Unrecognized past service cost	(35)
Unrecognized increase in the liability on initial adoption of IAS 19	(25)
Negative amount determined under defined benefit liability or asset definition	(160)
Present value of available future refunds and reductions in future contributions.	45
The limit is computed as follows:	
Unrecognized actuarial losses	55
Unrecognized past service cost	35
Present value of available future refunds and reductions in future contributions	45
Limit	€ 135

The limit, €135 in this example, is less than the amount determined under the basic definition of defined benefit asset, €160. Therefore, the reporting entity would recognize an asset of €135 and discloses that application of the limit had reduced the carrying amount of the asset by €25.

This amendment to IAS 19 added an appendix that provides several examples that illustrate how to apply this somewhat complex modification to the asset recognition ceiling under the standard.

IFRIC 14: IAS 19—*The Limit on a Defined Benefit Asset, Minimum Funding Requirements and Their Interaction*. In July 2007, IFRIC issued Interpretation 14 to provide guidance on the limitation on asset recognition and the statutory minimum funding requirements. Although funding requirements would not normally affect the accounting for a defined benefit plan, however the asset ceiling test in IAS 19 limits the recognition of the net pension asset to the sum of (1) any cumulative unrecognized net actuarial losses and past service costs and (2) the present value of available to the employer economic benefits in the form of refunds from the plan or reduction in future contributions to the plan. According to IASB, the interaction of this limit and minimum funding requirement has two possible effects:

1. The minimum funding requirement may restrict the economic benefits available as a reduction in future contributions, and
2. The limit may make the minimum funding requirement onerous because contributions payable under the requirement for services already received may not be available once they have been paid, either as a refund or as a reduction in future contributions.

In some jurisdictions, there are jurisdictions, there are statutory, (or contractual) minimum funding requirements (an increasingly common phenomenon, given the public's growing awareness that many defined benefit plans are underfunded, raising concern that retirees will find insufficient assets to pay their benefits after, for example, the plan sponsor has ceased operations or been sold) that require sponsors to make future contributions. The question is thus whether those requirements should limit the amount of plan assets the employer may report in its statement of financial position in those situations where application of IAS 19 would otherwise permit asset recognition, as discussed in the preceding paragraphs. In other words, the problem is that IAS 19-based asset might not be available to the entity (and thus not be an asset of the reporting entity) if future minimum funding requirements exist.

IFRIC 14 addresses the extent to which the economic benefit, via refund or reduction in future contributions, is constrained by contractual or statutory minimum funding obligations. It also addresses the calculation of the available benefits under such circumstances, as well as the effect of the minimum funding requirement on the measurement of defined benefit plan asset or liability.

IFRIC 14 addresses the following issues:

1. When refunds or reductions in future contributions should be regarded as "available to the employer"
2. The economic benefit available as a reduction in future contributions
3. The effect of a minimum funding requirement on the economic benefit available as a reduction in future contributions
4. When a minimum funding requirement may give rise to a liability

Economic benefit available as a refund. IFRIC 14 specifies that the availability of a refund of surplus or a reduction in future contributions would be determined in accordance with the terms and conditions of the plan and any statutory requirements in its jurisdiction. An economic benefit, in the form of a refund of surplus or a reduction in future contributions, would be deemed available (and hence an asset of the sponsor) if it will be realizable at some point during the life of the plan or when the plan liabilities are finally settled. Most importantly, an economic benefit, in the form of a refund from the plan or reduction in future contributions, may still be deemed available even if it is not realizable immediately at the end of the reporting period, as long as the refunds from the plan will be realizable during the life of a plan or at final settlement.

In cases where the question to be resolved is the amount of asset that is deemed to be an economic benefit to be received via a refund, this is to be measured as the amount that will be refunded to the entity *either*

1. During the life of the plan, without assuming that the plan liabilities have to be settled in order to get the refund (e.g., in some jurisdictions, the entity may have a

contractual right to a refund during the life of the plan, irrespective of whether the plan liability is settled); or

2. Assuming the gradual settlement of the plan liabilities over time until all members have left the plan; or

3. Assuming the full settlement of the plan liabilities in a single event (i.e., as a plan termination and settlement).

The amount of the economic benefit is to be determined on the basis of the approach that is the *most advantageous* to the entity. It is thus to be measured as the amount of the surplus (i.e., the fair value of the plan assets less the present value of the defined benefit obligation) that, at the end of the reporting period, the reporting entity has a right to receive as a refund after all the associated costs (such as taxes other than those on income) are paid.

If the refund is calculated using the approach in subparagraph (3) above, then the costs associated with the settlement of the plan liabilities and making the refund are to be taken into account. These could include professional fees to be paid by the plan, as well as the costs of any insurance premiums that might be required to secure the liability upon plan settlement.

Since under IAS 19 the surplus at the end of the reporting period is measured at present value, even if the refund is realizable only at a future date no further adjustment will need to be made for the time value of money.

Economic benefit available as a reduction in future contributions. When there is no minimum funding requirement, an entity should determine the economic benefit available as a reduction in future contributions as the lower of (1) the surplus in the plan and, (2) the present value of the future service cost to the entity.

Interpretation 14 requires that, in accordance with IAS 1, the entity disclose information about the key sources of estimation uncertainty at the end of the reporting period, if there is a significant risk of material adjustment to the carrying amount of the net asset or liability in the statement of financial position. This might include disclosure of any restrictions on the current realizability of the plan assets, or disclosure of the basis used to determine the amount of the economic benefit available as a refund.

The effect of a minimum funding requirement on the economic benefit available as a reduction in future contributions. In cases where there is a minimum funding requirement, the question to be resolved is the amount of asset that is deemed to be an economic benefit to be received via a future contribution reduction, and this would be measured as the present value, using IAS 19 assumptions applicable at the end of the reporting period, of

1. The estimated future service cost to the entity in each year (excluding any part of the total cost that is borne by employees), *less*

2. Any future minimum funding contribution requirements in respect of the future accrual of benefits in that year, over the expected life of the plan.

Any expected changes in the future minimum funding contributions as a result of the entity paying the minimum contributions due would be reflected in the measurement of the available contribution reduction. However, no allowance could be made for expected changes in the terms and conditions of the minimum funding requirement that are not substantively enacted at the end of the reporting period. Any allowances for expected future changes in the demographic profile of the workforce would have to be consistent with the assumptions underlying the calculation of the present value of the defined benefit obligation itself at the end of the reporting period.

If the future minimum funding contribution requirement in respect of the future accrual of benefits exceeds the future IAS 19 service cost in any given year, the present value of that excess would be used to reduce the amount of the asset available as a contribution reduction at the end of the reporting period. The amount of the total asset available as a reduction in future contributions can never be less than zero.

When a minimum funding requirement may give rise to a liability. If an entity has a statutory or contractual obligation under a minimum funding requirement to pay additional contributions to cover an existing shortfall on the minimum funding requirements in respect of services already received by the end of the reporting period, the entity would have to ascertain whether the contributions payable will be available as a refund or reduction in future contributions after they are paid into the plan. To the extent that the contributions payable will not be available once paid into the plan, the reporting entity would be required to recognize a liability. The liability would reduce the defined benefit asset or increase the defined benefit liability when the obligation arises, so that no gain or loss results when the contributions are later paid.

The adjustment to the defined benefit asset or liability in respect of the minimum funding requirement, and any subsequent remeasurement of that adjustment, would be recognized immediately in accordance with the entity's adopted policy for recognizing the effect of the limit set forth by IAS 19 (see discussion above). In particular

1. A reporting entity that recognizes the effect of the limit in profit or loss would also recognize the adjustment immediately in profit or loss, whereas
2. An entity that recognizes the effect of the limit in other comprehensive income would likewise recognize the adjustment immediately in other comprehensive income in the statement of comprehensive income.

IFRIC 14 provides a number or examples illustrating how to calculate the economic benefit available or not available when an entity has a certain funding level on the minimum funding requirement.

IFRIC 14 should be applied for annual periods beginning on or after January 1, 2008, with earlier application permitted. IFRIC 14 should be applied from the beginning of the first year presented in the first financial statements to which it applies. Any initial adjustment arising from the application of IFRIC 14 should be recognized as an adjustment to retained earnings at the beginning of that period.

IFRIC 14 requires entities to reexamine how they determine their asset ceiling. As a result, entities may have to make changes concerning the amount of pension assets recognized or even may need to recognize pension liabilities, possibly having a significant impact in the sponsors' statements of financial position.

Other Pension Considerations

Multiple and multiemployer plans. If an entity has more than one plan, IAS 19 provisions should be applied separately to each plan. Offsets or eliminations are not allowed unless there clearly is the right to use the assets in one plan to pay the benefits of another plan.

Participation in a multiemployer plan (to which two or more unrelated employers contribute) requires that the contribution for the period be recognized as net pension cost and that any contributions due and unpaid be recognized as a liability. Assets in this type of plan are usually commingled and are not segregated or restricted. A board of trustees usually administers these plans, and multiemployer plans are generally subject to a collective bargaining agreement. If there is a withdrawal from this type of plan and if an arising obligation is either probable or reasonably possible, the provisions of IFRS that address contingencies (IAS 37) apply.

Some plans are, in substance, a pooling or aggregation of single employer plans and are ordinarily without collective bargaining agreements. Contributions are usually based on a selected benefit formula. These plans are not considered multiemployer plans, and the accounting is based on the respective interest in the plan.

Business combinations. When an entity that sponsors a single-employer defined benefit plan is acquired and must therefore be accounted for under the provisions of IFRS 3 (revised 2008), the purchaser should assign part of the purchase price to an asset if plan assets exceed the projected benefit obligation, or to a liability if the projected benefit obligation exceeds plan assets. The projected benefit obligation should include the effect of any expected plan curtailment or termination. This assignment eliminates any existing unrecognized components, and any future differences between contributions and net pension cost will affect the asset or liability recognized when the purchase took place.

Disclosure of Pension and Other Postemployment Benefit Costs

For defined contribution plans, IAS 19 requires only that the amount of expense included in current period earnings be disclosed. Good practice would suggest that disclosure be made of the general description of each plan, identifying the employee groups covered, and of any other significant matters related to retirement benefits that affect comparability with the previous period reported on.

For defined benefit plans, as would be expected, much more expansive disclosures are mandated. These include

1. A general description of each plan identifying the employee groups covered
2. The accounting policy regarding recognition of actuarial gains or losses
3. A reconciliation of the plan-related assets and liabilities recognized in the statement of financial position, showing at the minimum

   a. The present value of wholly unfunded defined benefit obligations
   b. The present value (gross, before deducting plan assets) of wholly or partly unfunded obligations
   c. The fair value of plan assets
   d. The net actuarial gain or loss not yet recognized in the statement of financial position
   e. The past service cost not yet recognized in the statement of financial position
   f. Any amount not recognized as an asset because of the limitation to the present value of economic benefits from refunds and future contribution reductions
   g. The amounts which are recognized in the statement of financial position

4. The amount of plan assets represented by each category of the reporting entity's own financial instruments or by property which is occupied by, or other assets used by, the entity itself
5. A reconciliation of movements (i.e., changes) during the reporting period in the net asset or liability reported in the statement of financial position
6. The amount of, and location in profit or loss of, the reported amounts of current service cost, interest cost, expected return on plan assets, actuarial gain or loss, past service cost, and effect of any curtailment or settlement
7. The total amount recognized in other comprehensive income
8. The cumulative amount of actuarial gains and losses recognized in other comprehensive income
9. The actual return earned on plan assets for the reporting period

10. The principal actuarial assumptions used, including (if relevant) the discount rates, expected rates of return on plan assets, expected rates of salary increases or other index or variable specified in the pension arrangement, medical cost trend rates, and any other material actuarial assumptions utilized in computing benefit costs for the period. The actuarial assumptions are to be explicitly stated in absolute terms, not merely as references to other indices.

Amounts presented in the sponsor's statement of financial position cannot be offset (presented on a net basis) unless legal rights of offset exist. Furthermore, even with a legal right to offset (which itself would be a rarity), unless the intent is to settle on a net basis, such presentation would not be acceptable. Thus, a sponsor having two plans, one being in a net asset position, and another in a net liability position, cannot net these in most instances.

Comprehensive example

In the following example, the various components of pension cost are reviewed in detail. Note that only a qualified actuary can compute the service cost component, which depends on numerous assumptions regarding mortality, tenure, and other factors. The remaining elements can be (but usually are not) addressed by nonactuaries, such as accountants. Amounts are keyed to summary of pension cost at end of the following discussion.

Service cost. Future compensation is considered in the calculation of the service cost component to the extent specified by the benefit formula. If part of the benefit formula, future compensation includes changes due to advancement, expected turnover of employees, inflation, etc. Indirect effects, such as predictable bonuses based on compensation levels, and automatic increases specified by the plan also need to be considered. The effect of *retroactive* amendments is included in the calculation at the point when the employer has contractually agreed to them. Service costs attributed (i.e., charged to expense) during the period increase the pension benefit obligation, since they result in additional benefits that are payable in the future.

	January 1, 2009	*2009 Service cost*
Benefit obligation based on current salary	€(1,500)	€ (90)
Effect of expected progression of salary	(400)	(24)
Actuarially determined benefit obligation	€(1,900)	€(114) (a)*

* *Component of net periodic pension cost, summarized later in this example.*

The current period service cost component is found in the actuarial report.

Interest cost. The actuarially computed benefit obligation is a discounted amount. It represents the present value, at the date of the valuation, of all benefits attributed under the plan's formula to employee service rendered prior to that date. Each year the end-of-year pension obligation becomes one year closer to the year in which the benefits attributed in prior years will begin to be paid to plan participants. Consequently, the present value of those previously attributed benefits will have increased to take into account the time value of money. This annual increment is computed by multiplying the assumed settlement discount rate times the pension obligation at the beginning of the year; this increases net periodic pension cost and the pension obligation. Since this imputed interest cost is accounted for as part of pension cost, it is not reported as interest in the financial statements, and accordingly cannot be included as interest for the purposes of computing capitalized interest under IAS 23.

	January 1, 2009	*2009 Service cost*	*2009 Interest cost*
Benefit obligation based on current salary	€(1,500)	€ (90)	€(210)
Effect of expected progression of salary	(400)	(24)	(32)
Actuarially determined benefit obligation	€(1,900)	€(114) (a)*	€(152) (b)*

* *Component of net periodic pension cost, summarized later in this example.*

In this example, the applicable discount rate has been assumed at 8%. The interest cost component is calculated by multiplying the start-of-the-year obligation balances by the 8% settlement rate. This amount is found in the actuarial report, although obviously readily computed.

Benefits paid. Benefits paid to retirees are deducted from the above to arrive at the end of the reporting period amounts of the accumulated benefit obligation and the projected benefit obligation.

	January 1, 2009	2009 Service cost	2009 Interest cost	2009 Benefits paid	December 31, 2009
Benefit obligation based on current salary	€(1,500)	€ (90)	€(120)	€160	€(1,550)
Effect of expected progression of salary	(400)	(24)	(32)	--	(456)
Actuarially determined benefit obligation	€(1,900)	€(114) (a)	€(152) (b)	€160	€(2,006)

Benefits of €160 were paid to retirees during the current year. This amount is found in the report of the pension plan trustee.

Actual return on plan assets. This component is the difference between the *fair value* of the plan assets at the end of the period and the fair value of the plan assets at the beginning of the period adjusted for contributions and payments during the period. Another way to express the result is that it is the net (realized and unrealized) appreciation and depreciation of plan assets plus earnings from the plan assets for the period.

	January 1, 2009	2009 Actual return on plan assets	2009 Employer funding	2009 Benefits paid	December 31, 2009
Plan assets	€1,376	€158 (c)*	€145	€(160)	€1,519

* *Component of net periodic pension cost, summarized later in this example.*

The actual return on plan assets of €158, cash deposited with the trustee of €145, and benefits paid (€160) are amounts found in the report of the pension plan trustee. These items increase the plan assets to €1,519 at the end of the year. For purposes of reporting periodic pension cost, however, the actual return on plan assets is adjusted to the expected long-term rate (9%, which is assumed in this example and should be based on empirical data for the classes of assets held in the plan) of return on plan assets (€1,376 × 9% = €124). The difference (€158 – €124 = €34) is an actuarial gain (loss) and is deferred as a gain (loss) to be recognized, or not recognized, in future periods (as explained below).

Gain or loss. Gains (losses) result from (1) changes in plan assumptions, (2) changes in the amount of plan assets, and (3) changes in the amount of the actuarially determined benefit obligation. As discussed previously, even though these gains or losses are economic events that impact the sponsoring entity's obligations under the plan, their immediate recognition in the sponsor's financial statements is not required by IAS 19. Instead, to provide "smoothing" of the effects of short-term fluctuations, unrecognized net gain (loss) may be amortized if the deferred amount meets the criteria specified below. Unlike under the comparable US GAAP standard, however, immediate recognition is permitted under IFRS, if the reporting entity elects to do so.

Since actuarial cost methods are based on numerous assumptions (employee compensation, mortality, turnover, earnings of the pension plan, etc.), it is not unusual for one or more of these assumptions to be invalidated by changes over time. Adjustments will invariably be necessary to bring prior estimates back in line with actual events. These adjustments are known as actuarial gains (losses). The accounting issue regarding the recognition of actuarial adjustments is their timing. All pension costs must eventually be recognized as expense. Actuarial gains (losses) are not considered prior period adjustments since they result from a refinement of estimates arising from obtaining subsequent information. Thus, under IAS 8, they are considered changes in an estimate to be recognized in current and future periods.

Plan asset gains (losses) result from both realized and unrealized amounts. They represent periodic differences between the actual return on assets and the expected return. The expected return is generated by multiplying the *expected long-term rate of return* by the *fair value* of plan assets as of the beginning of the reporting period. The expected rate of return is generally best determined by those having access to relevant data and an understanding of financial matters; this is often provided by the consulting actuary or investment advisor responsible for the pension fund asset management. Whatever method is used, it should be done consistently, which means from year to year for each asset class (i.e., bonds, equities), since different classes of assets may have their market-related value calculated in a different manner (i.e., fair value in one case, moving average in another case). There appears to be flexibility permitted under IFRS.

IFRS permits deferral of unrecognized gains or losses, but only to the extent that this does not exceed certain limits (defined under the parallel US GAAP requirement as a "corridor"). This limit is the *greater* of 10% of the present value of the defined benefit obligation at the end of the preceding reporting period (before deducting plan assets), or 10% of the fair value of plan assets as of the same date.

To the extent that the unrecognized net gain (loss) exceeds this limit, the *excess* over 10% is divided by the average remaining service period of active employees and included as a component of net pension costs. Average remaining life expectancies of inactive employees may be used if that is a better measure due to the demographics of the plan participants.

Net pension costs include only the expected return on plan assets, unless immediate recognition of actuarial gains and losses is elected by the reporting entity. The difference between actual and expected returns is deferred through the gain (loss) component of net pension cost. If actual return is greater than expected return, net pension cost is increased to adjust the actual return to the lower expected return. If expected return is greater than actual return, the adjustment results in a decrease to net pension cost to adjust the actual return to the higher expected return.

As noted, if the unrecognized net gain (loss) is large enough, it is amortized. Conceptually, the expected return represents the best estimate of long-term performance of the plan's investments. In any given year, however, an unusual short-term result may occur given the volatility of financial markets.

The expected long-term rate of return used to calculate the expected return on plan assets is the average rate of return expected to be earned on invested funds to provide for pension benefits included in the defined benefit pension obligation. Present rates of return and expected future reinvestment rates of return are considered in arriving at the rate to be used.

To summarize, net periodic pension cost includes a gain (loss) component consisting of *both* of the following, if applicable:

1. As a minimum, the portion of the unrecognized net gain (loss) from previous periods that exceeds the *greater* of 10% of the beginning balances of the pension obligation *or* the fair value of plan assets, amortized over the average remaining service period of active employees expected to receive benefits (or more rapidly, if so elected).
2. The difference between the expected return and the actual return on plan assets.

	January 1, 2009	2009 Return on asset adjustment	2009 Amortization	December 31, 2009
Unrecognized actuarial gain (loss)	€(210)	€34 (d)*	€2 (d)*	€(174)

* *Component of net periodic pension cost, summarized later in this example.*

The return on asset adjustment of €34 is the difference between the actual return of €158 and the expected return of €124 on plan assets. The actuarial loss at the start of the year (€210 assumed for this example) is amortized if it exceeds a limit of the larger of 10% of the pension benefit obligation at the beginning of the period (€1,900 × 10% = €190) or 10% of the fair value of plan assets (€1,376 × 10% = €138). In this example, €20 (€210 – €190) is amortized by dividing the years of average remaining service (twelve years assumed), with a result rounded to €2.

Past service cost. Past service costs are incurred when the sponsor adopts plan amendments (or a new plan, in its entirety) that increase plan benefits attributable to services rendered by plan participants in the past. Under IAS 19, these costs are to be recognized over the period until the benefits have become vested. Even though these pertain to past service, they are not handled as immediate charges (unless immediately vested) or as corrections of prior periods' reported results. Unlike for actuarial gains or losses, IAS 19 offers no option for more rapid recognition of these costs.

Under the rare situation where benefits are reduced, resulting in negative past service cost, this, too, is amortized (as a reduction in periodic pension cost) over the average term until vesting.

Note that, under the corresponding US GAAP standard, prior service cost (equivalent to past service cost) may be amortized using various methods, generally over the remaining service lives (working periods) of employees at the date of the amendment to the plan. IFRS requires only that the straight-line method of amortization be used, and that this be over the vesting period. For example, if an improved benefit is granted to only employees having five years' service, the portion applicable to those workers already meeting this threshold test will be immediately expensed, while the portion applicable to those having less seniority will be amortized over the *average* term to vesting for that subgroup.

	January 1, 2009	2009 Amortization	December 31, 2009
Unrecognized prior service cost	€320	€27 (e)*	€293

* *Component of net periodic pension cost, summarized later in this example.*

Unrecognized prior service cost (€320) is amortized over the time to full vesting. In this example, that term is almost 12 years, but in practice this might be much shorter. The straight-line method must be used. These amounts are found in the actuarial report.

Transitional issues. When IAS 19 was enacted, it provided that the initial obligation was to be measured as the present value of the pension obligation, less the fair value of plan assets, less any past service cost to be amortized in later periods, as described above. When this amount exceeded what was reportable under prior GAAP used by the entity (whether an actual standard or the policy adopted by the entity in absence of definitive accounting rules), the entity had to make an irrevocable election to either immediately recognize that increased liability via a charge against profit or loss, or recognize the adjustment over a period of up to five years from date of adoption. A negative transition adjustment was to be recognized immediately in profit or loss.

Since IAS 19 was implemented effective 1999, all transition amounts should have been fully amortized by 2004, making this issue now moot. However, *solely for the purpose of completing the current comprehensive example*, the following amortization of transitional liability is included.

	January 1, 2009	2009 Amortization	December 31, 2009
Unamortized net obligation (asset) existing at IAS 19 application	€(6)	€3 (f)*	€(3)

* *Component of net periodic pension cost, summarized later in this example.*

At initial adoption of IAS 19, the "transition amount" was computed, and was being amortized using the straight-line method at a rate of €3 per year. The assumed unamortized balance at January 1, 2009, was €6 and the amortization for 2009 was €3. These amounts are found in the actuarial report.

NOTE: All such transitions should now be complete, in practice.

Summary of net periodic pension cost. The components that were identified in the above examples are summed as follows to determine the amount defined as net periodic pension cost:

		2009
Service cost	(a)	€114
Interest cost	(b)	152
Actual return on plan assets	(c)	(158)
Unrecognized gain (loss)	(d)	36
Amortization of unrecognized past service cost	(e)	27
Amortization of unrecognized net obligation (asset) existing at IAS 19 adoption	(f)	(3)
Total net periodic pension cost		€168

One possible source of confusion is the actual return on plan assets (€158) and the unrecognized gain of €36, which net to €122. The actual return on plan assets reduces pension cost. This is because, to the extent that plan assets generate earnings, those earnings help the plan sponsor subsidize the cost of providing the benefits. Thus, the plan sponsor will not have to fund benefits as they become due, to the extent that plan earnings provide the plan with cash to pay those benefits. This reduction, however, is adjusted by increasing pension cost by the difference between actual and expected return of €34 and the amortization of the excess actuarial loss of €2, for a total of €36. The net result is to include the expected return of €124 (= €158 – €34) less the amortization of the excess of €2 for a total of €122 (= €158 – €36).

In terms of reporting the results of operations, IAS 19 requires disclosure of total pension cost, with details as to the amounts of

- Current service cost
- Interest cost
- Expected return on plan assets
- Expected return on any reimbursement right recognized as an asset
- Actuarial gains and losses
- Past service cost
- The effect of any curtailment or settlement

Regarding the statement of financial position, IAS 19 requires a reconciliation of pension-related assets and liabilities presented, showing

- The present value of the defined benefit pension obligation that is wholly unfunded
- The present value of the defined benefit pension obligation that is partially or fully funded, before offsetting pension assets
- The fair value of pension assets
- Net actuarial gain or loss not recognized by the end of the reporting period
- Past service cost not recognized by the end of the reporting period
- Fair value of a reimbursement right recognized as an asset
- Any other amounts recognized in the statement of financial position

Reconciliation of Beginning and Ending Pension Obligation and Plan Assets

The following table summarizes the 2009 activity affecting the defined benefit pension obligation and the plan assets, and reconciles the beginning and ending balances per the actuarial report:

	Benefit obligation before salary progression	Effect of progression of salaries and wages	Actuarial defined benefit obligation	Fair value of plan assets
Balance, January 1, 2009	€(1,500)	€(400)	€(1,900)	€1,376
Service cost	(90)	(24)	(114) (a)	
Interest cost	(120)	(32)	(152) (b)	
Benefits paid to retired participants	160		160	(160)
Actual return on plan assets				158 (c)
Sponsor's contributions				145
Balance, December 31, 2008	€(1,550)	€(456)	€(2,006)	€1,519

Postemployment Benefits: Limited Convergence Project

In 2002, IASB undertook a limited convergence project on postemployment benefits. The stated objectives of the project did not extend to a comprehensive reexamination of the accounting for postemployment benefits—which, however, IASB believes is warranted in the near to immediate term. Rather, the goal was to build on the principles that are common to most existing national standards on benefit accounting, and to seek improvements to IAS 19 in certain specific areas. In 2004 an Exposure Draft was issued and an amendment was adopted by year-end 2004, which addressed only a few of the several topics first broached by IASB, the most important of which dealt with the reporting of actuarial gains and losses. A proposed amendment to IAS 37, containing minor, consequential proposed amendments to IAS 19, was announced in mid-2005 but, as of late 2008, has yet to be enacted.

Under IAS 19, before this amendment, actuarial gains and losses could either be taken into income immediately, or, as was more popular with preparers of financial statements, could be deferred and later taken into income over an extended period of time. IASB had expressed its dislike for the latter approach, which is an artificial smoothing technique (albeit modeled after the very similar one under US GAAP) that is probably not conceptually logical. The amendment's solution, however, may also be subject to serious criticism.

As amended, IAS 19 now offers yet a third alternative technique for recognition of actuarial gains and losses: recognition of the entire amount of any actuarial gain or loss may be effected immediately, in the *other comprehensive income* section of a statement of comprehensive income, without "recycling" to income.

In other words, for those electing this new option, actuarial gains or losses will be reported as other comprehensive income items (as are, for example, unrealized gains and losses on investments which are available for sale) but will *not* be included in profit or loss for any period (as are, for example, realized gains and losses on available for sale investments). According to this amendment, gains or losses so recognized will not later be "recycled" through profit or loss. Thus, actuarial gain or loss would *never* impact profit or loss, although these would affect retained earnings after passing through the newly designated statement of comprehensive income. While the mechanism for a "recycling" strategy is not obvious, the fact that this would exclude from profit or loss determination these potentially sizeable gains and losses does trouble some observers.

Additionally, the fact that this was adopted as yet a new alternative method was unsettling. Rather than narrowing the range of available alternative ways to treat a given economic phenomenon, this widened it, contrary to one of the fundamental goals of IASB. As adopted, entities now have the unfettered right to choose from among three very different methods: to recognize, *in current period income*, the entire amount of any actuarial gain or loss, to recognize, *outside of income*, the entire amount of any actuarial gain or loss, or to defer and amortize actuarial gain or loss as part of pension cost (in profit or loss), over an extended period of years. Those reporting entities electing to apply this new, third approach to actuarial gains and losses will permanently avoid reporting these elements of pension cost in earnings.

The amendment to IAS 19 was perhaps motivated by the desire to converge with UK GAAP, which offers essentially this option to preparers. IASB stated, in the Exposure Draft preceding this amendment, that actuarial gains and losses are economic events of the reporting period, and therefore recognizing these when they occur provides a more faithful representation of the events. On the other hand, when recognition is deferred, as is optionally the case under both US GAAP and IFRS, the information provided to users of financial statements is partial and potentially misleading. IASB noted also that the net cumulative deferred actuarial losses may result in displaying a debit item in the statement of financial position that does not conform to the definition of an asset, and a net cumulative gain results in displaying a credit which is not an actual liability. Thus, it concluded that its new approach was preferable to the deferral method widely employed (but that remains an acceptable method under amended IAS 19).

The amendment also added significant new disclosure requirements to IAS 19. These are as follows:

1. Reconciliations showing the changes in plan assets and in the defined benefit obligation for the period. It was thought that this mode of reconciliation will provide a clearer picture of the plan than the previously required reconciliation, which reported the changes in the recognized net liability or asset. The new reconciliation, which superseded the previously mandated reconciliation, will include amounts for which recognition has been deferred.
2. Information about plan assets will include

    a. Percentages that the major classes of assets held by the plan constitute of the total fair value of plan assets;

    b. Expected rates of return for each class of asset; and

    c. A description of the basis for determination of the overall expected rate of return on assets.

3. Information about the sensitivity of defined health care benefit plans to changes in medical cost trend rates. This was deemed useful by IASB because of the widely understood difficulties of assessing the effects of changes in a plan's medical cost trend rate, in part due to such complexities as the ways in which health care cost assumptions interact with caps, cost-sharing provisions, and other factors in plans. IASB concluded that the mere disclosure of a one percentage point change could be appropriate for plans operating in low-inflation environments, but would not provide useful information for plans operating in high-inflation environments.

4. Information about trends in the plan, intended to provide financial statement users with a view of the plan over time, not simply its position at the reporting date. In the absence of such information, misinterpretation of future cash flow implications of the plan can occur. The IASB requirement thus is for disclosure of five-year histories of the plan liabilities, plan assets, the plan's surplus or deficit, and experience adjustments.

5. Information about contributions to the plan, to provide insight into the entity's immediate future cash flows, beyond what can be determined from other required disclosures about the plan. The required disclosures include the employer's best estimate, as soon as this can reasonably be determined, of contributions expected to be paid to the plan during the fiscal year beginning after the end of the reporting period.

6. Improved information about the nature of the plan, including all the terms of the plan that are used in the determination of the defined benefit obligation.

In July 2006, the IASB announced that it has added three new projects to its agenda: the first two include comprehensive reviews of the standards on leases and employee benefits; the purpose of the third will be to amend related-party disclosures.

The project aimed to improving the quality of financial reporting for pension plans and other employee benefits will be conducted in two phases. The first phase will consider revisions that could achieve significant improvements in IAS 19 in the short term, with a plan for an interim standard in 2010, while the other aspects of the project will be considered in the second phase. The FASB is also undertaking a two-phase postretirement benefits project, and the two Boards are committed to arrive at a common approach at the end of the second phase. These projects are expected to take several years to complete. IASB plans to publish a Discussion Paper on Phase I of this project in 2008.

Other Benefit Plans

Short-term employee benefits. According to IAS 19, short-term benefits are those falling due within twelve months from the end of the period in which the employees render their services. These include wages and salaries, as well as short-term compensated absences (vacations, annual holiday, paid sick days, etc.), profit sharing and bonuses if due within twelve months after the end of the period in which these were earned, and such nonmonetary benefits as health insurance and housing or automobiles. The standard requires that these be reported as incurred. Since they are accrued currently, no actuarial assumptions or computations are needed and, since due currently, discounting is not to be applied.

Compensated absences may provide some accounting complexities, if these accumulate and vest with the employees. Under the terms of the new employee benefits standard, accumulating benefits can be carried forward to later periods when not fully consumed currently; for example, when employees are granted two weeks' leave per year, but can carry forward to later years an amount equal to no more than six weeks, the compensated absence benefit can be said to be subject to limited accumulation. Depending on the program, accumulation rights may be limited or unlimited; and, furthermore, the usage of benefits may be defined to occur on a last-in, first-out (LIFO) basis, which in conjunction with limited accumulation rights further limits the amount of benefits which employees are likely to use, if not fully used in the period earned.

The cost of compensated absences should be accrued in the periods earned. In some cases (as when the plans subject employees to limitations on accumulation rights with or without the further restriction imposed by a LIFO pattern of usage), it will be understood that the amounts of compensated absences to which employees are contractually entitled will exceed the amount that they are likely to actually utilize. In such circumstances, the accrual should be based on the *expected* usage, based on past experience and, if relevant, changes in the plan's provisions since the last reporting period.

Example of compensated absences

Consider an entity with 500 workers, each of whom earns two weeks' annual leave, with a carryforward option limited to a maximum of six weeks, to be carried forward no longer than four years. Also, this employer imposes a LIFO basis on any usages of annual leave (e.g., a worker with two weeks' carryforward and two weeks earned currently, taking a three-week leave, will be deemed to have consumed the two currently earned weeks plus one of the carryforward weeks, thereby increasing the risk of ultimately losing the older carried-forward compensated absence time). Based on past experience, 80% of the workers will take no more than two weeks' leave in any year, while the other 20% take an average of four extra days. At the end of the year, each worker has an average of five days' carryforward of compensated absences. The amount accrued should be the cost equivalent of $[(.80 \times 0 \text{ days}) + (.20 \times 4 \text{ days})] \times 500 \text{ workers} = 400 \text{ days' leave}$.

Other postretirement benefits. Other postretirement benefits include medical care and other benefits offered to retirees partially or entirely at the expense of the former employer. These are essentially defined benefit plans very much like defined benefit pension plans. Like the pension plans, these require the services of a qualified actuary in order to estimate the true cost of the promises made currently for benefits to be delivered in the future. As with pensions, a variety of determinants, including the age composition, life expectancies, and other demographic factors pertaining to the present and future retiree groups, and the course of future inflation of medical care (or other covered) costs (coupled with predicted utilization factors), need to be projected in order to compute current period costs. Developing these projections requires the skills and training of actuaries; the projected pattern of future medical costs has been particularly difficult to achieve with anything approaching accuracy. Unlike most defined benefit pension plans, other postretirement benefit plans are more commonly funded on a pay-as-you-go basis, which does not alter the accounting but does eliminate earnings on plan assets as a cost offset.

Other long-term employee benefits. These are defined by IAS 19 as including any benefits other than postemployment benefits (pensions, retiree medical care, etc.), termination benefits and equity compensation plans. Examples would include sabbatical leave, "jubilee" or other long-service benefits, long-term profit-sharing payments, and deferred compensation arrangements. Executive deferred compensation plans have become common in nations where these are tax-advantaged (i.e., not taxed to the employee until paid), and these give rise to deferred tax accounting issues as well as measurement and reporting questions, as benefit plans. In general, measurement will be less complex than for defined benefit pension or other postretirement benefits, although some actuarial measures may be needed.

Reportedly for reasons of simplicity, IAS 19 decided to not provide the corridor approach to nonrecognition of actuarial gains and losses for other long-term benefits, under which (as described above) only the gain or loss in excess of a threshold level has to be recognized in profit or loss. It also requires that past service cost (resulting from the granting of enhanced benefits to participants on a retroactive basis) and the transition gain or loss (from adoption of IAS 19) all must be reported in earnings in the period in which these are granted or occur. In other words, deferred recognition via amortization is not acceptable for these various long-term benefit programs.

For liability measurement purposes, IAS 19 stipulates that the present value of the obligation be presented in the statement of financial position, less the fair value of any assets that have been set aside for settlement thereof. The long-term corporate bond rate is used here, as with defined benefit pension obligations, to discount the expected future payments to present value. As to expense recognition, the same cost elements as are set forth for pension plan expense should be included, with the exceptions that, as noted, actuarial gains and losses and past service cost must be recognized immediately, not amortized over a defined time horizon.

Termination benefits. Termination benefits are to be recognized only when the employer has demonstrated its commitment either to terminate the employee or group of employees before normal retirement date, or provide benefits as part of an inducement to encourage early retirements. Generally, a detailed, formal plan will be necessary to support a representation that such a commitment exists. According to IAS 19, the plan should, as a minimum, set forth locations, functions, and numbers of employees to be terminated; the benefits for each job class or other pertinent category; and the time when the plan is to be implemented; with inception to be as soon as possible and completion soon enough to largely eliminate the chance that any material changes to the plan will be necessary.

Since termination benefits do not confer any future economic benefits on the employing entity, these must be expensed immediately. If the payments are to fall due more than twelve months after the end of the reporting period, however, discounting to present value is required (again, using the long-term corporate bond rate). Estimates, such as the number of employees likely to accept voluntary early retirement, may need to be made in many cases involving termination benefits. To the extent that accrual is based on such estimates (the possibility that greater numbers may accept, thereby triggering additional costs) further disclosure of loss contingencies may be necessary to comply with IAS 37.

Equity compensation benefits. IAS 19 included equity compensation programs in the benefits to which the standard's reporting requirements applied, when revised IAS 19 was promulgated in 1998. However, since then the IASB developed a comprehensive standard on share-based payments, IFRS 2, which supersedes the guidance of IAS 19. IFRS 2 is addressed in Chapter 17.

Proposed Amendments to IAS 19, *Employee Benefits*

In June 2005, the IASB issued an Exposure Draft, *Proposed Amendments to IAS 19, "Employee Benefits,"* as a result of a short-term convergence project with the FASB and to complement the proposed amendments to the requirements addressing restructurings in IAS 37, *Provisions, Contingent Liabilities, and Contingent Assets.* IASB considered the US GAAP requirements under FASB Statement 146, *Accounting for Costs Associated with Exit or Disposal Activities* (FAS 146) and proposed amendments to IAS 37 relating to the recognition of liabilities for costs associated with a restructuring that would serve to converge IFRS with FAS 146 and improve IAS 37. Since FAS 146 also addresses the accounting for a class of termination benefits known as "onetime termination benefits," IASB decided to also amend the accounting for termination benefits in IAS 19 consistent with its amendments to IAS 37. Its intention was to not reconsider the fundamental approach to the accounting for employee benefits covered in IAS 19, which is the subject of a more substantial project expected to take several years to complete. As of late 2008, this matter remains unresolved and under active deliberations.

Definition of Termination Benefits

The current IAS 19 defines *termination benefits* as employee benefits that are payable as a result of an employee's decision to accept voluntary redundancy in exchange for those benefits. The Exposure Draft proposed to amend this definition to clarify that benefits that are offered in exchange for an employee's decision to accept voluntary termination of employment are termination benefits only if they are offered for a short period of time. Other employee benefits that are offered over more extended periods to encourage employees to leave service before normal retirement date are postemployment benefits.

The Exposure Draft defines termination benefits as employee benefits provided in connection with the termination of an employee's employment which may be either

- Involuntary termination benefits, which are benefits provided as a result of an entity's decision to terminate an employee's employment before the normal retirement date; or
- Voluntary termination benefits, which are benefits offered for a short period in exchange for an employee's decision to accept voluntary termination of employment.

The *minimum retention period* is the period of notice that an entity is required to provide to employees in advance of terminating their employment. The notice period may be specified by law, contract, or union agreement, or may be implied as a result of customary business practice.

Recognition of Termination Benefits

In accordance with the current IAS 19, a liability for termination benefits is recognized when the entity is demonstrably committed to the termination. But in the basis for conclusions of the 2005 Exposure Draft, the IASB agreed with the FASB (in FAS 146) that in some cases termination benefits, although they constitute compensation for the early termination of services, are provided in exchange for employees' future services. For example, the Board observed that following a business acquisition an entity will sometimes terminate the employment of the workers at the acquired entity. However, since the acquiring entity needs the skills and knowledge of those employees for a certain period of time, it may offer enhanced termination benefits as an inducement for those employees to provide services for that period. Consequently, the IASB decided that, like FAS 146, IAS 19 should specify different recognition requirements for termination benefits that are provided in exchange for future services.

The Exposure Draft proposes that

- An entity should recognize a liability and expense for voluntary termination benefits when the employee accepts the entity's offer of those benefits
- An entity should recognize a liability and expense for involuntary termination benefits when the entity has a plan of termination and has communicated to the affected employees and the plan meets specified criteria, unless the involuntary termination benefits are provided in exchange for employees' future services (i.e., in substance they are a "retention bonus"). In such cases, an entity should recognize the termination

benefits as a liability and an expense over the future service period (from the date the plan was communicated to the date that employment is terminated).

The plan of termination would be required to

- Identify the number of employees whose employment is to be terminated, their job classifications or functions and their locations, and the expected completion date; and
- Establish the benefits that employees will receive upon termination of employment (including but not limited to cash payments) in sufficient detail to enable employees to determine the type and amount of benefits they will receive when their employment is terminated.

In the Exposure Draft, involuntary termination benefits are considered to be provided in exchange for employees' future services if those benefits

- Are incremental to what the employees would otherwise be entitled to receive (i.e., the benefits are not provided in accordance with the terms of an ongoing benefit plan);
- Do not vest until the employment is terminated; and
- Are provided to employees who will be retained beyond the minimum retention period.

Measurement

The IASB decided to retain the existing measurement requirement in IAS 19, which is to discount termination benefits due more than 12 months after the end of the reporting period and subsequently to follow the recognition and measurement requirements for postemployment benefits. The rationale behind this decision was that this measurement requirement can be applied to all termination benefits, regardless of whether those benefits are provided through or outside an ongoing benefit plan.

In the basis for conclusions of the Exposure Draft, the IASB acknowledged that this approach creates measurement differences with US GAAP. FAS 146 states that onetime termination benefits should be measured at fair value, except when the liability is recognized over time. In such cases, the fair value measurement date is modified to the termination date (i.e., the fair value of the liability at termination date is recognized over the future service period). However, IASB observed that, as a practical matter, most onetime termination benefits that are not recognized over a service period would be likely to vest relatively quickly, and the effect of discounting might be immaterial.

Example

Following a recent acquisition, Conduit SRL plans to close an acquired factory and terminate the employment of all the employees in 10 months. Since it needs the knowledge and expertise of the employees to complete certain ongoing contracts, it announces the termination benefit plan. Under this plan each employee who stays on the job and renders services for the full 10-month period will receive as a termination benefit on the termination date a cash payment of €50,000 in addition to the amount specified by employment legislation in its jurisdiction.

Under employment legislation, the usual practice is to pay only €11,000 minimum termination benefits per employee, and to give 50 days' notice of the intent to terminate employment. There are 150 employees at the factory; 110 decide to provide services for the 10-month period and 40 decide to leave voluntarily before closure. The Exposure Draft requires Conduit SRL to account for the termination benefits under ongoing benefit plan (i.e., employment legislation) and incremental benefits separately.

With regard to the ongoing benefit plan, a liability and expense of €1,650,000 (= 150 × €11,000) for the termination benefits is to be accrued, in accordance with employment legislation, and will be fully recognized when the plan is announced.

Concerning the incremental benefits, the expected cash flows, which relate to future services, are €5,500,000 (= 110 × $50,000). In this example, discounting is not required (12 months or less) and a liability and expense of €550,000 (= €5,500,000/10) is recognized in each month during the future service period of 10 months. If the number of employees expected to leave voluntarily changes, the company changes its estimate of the expected cash flows for termination benefits and the liability and expense recognized.

Revisions to IAS 19 Made by 2008 Improvements Project

In October 2007, as part of its first annual improvements project, the IASB published for comment an Exposure Draft (ED), *Proposed Improvements to International Financial Reporting Standards*, recommending miscellaneous amendments to 25 IFRS. In May 2008, this was finalized, making the following changes to IAS 19:

- Revised the definition of "past service costs" to include reductions in benefits for *past* services (negative past service costs) and to exclude reductions in benefit for future services (curtailments)
- Amended the definition of return on plan assets to exclude any plan administration costs that are included in the actuarial assumptions used to measure the defined benefit obligation
- Replaced the term "fall due" in the definition of short-term employee benefits and other long-term employee benefits. The definition proposed is that "Short-term employee benefits are employee benefits (other than termination benefits) to which the employee becomes entitled within twelve months after the end of the period in which the employee renders the related service."
- Removed guidance in IAS 19 which incorrectly refers to the recognition of contingent liabilities, to ensure consistency with IAS 37, which does not permit the recognition of contingent liabilities.

Examples of Financial Statement Disclosures

adidas Group AG, Germany
Year ended December 31, 2007

Summary of Significant Accounting Policies

Pensions and similar obligations. Provisions for pensions and similar obligations comprise the Group provision obligation under defined benefit and contribution plans. Obligations under defined benefit plans are calculated separately for each plan by estimating the benefit amount that employees have earned in return for their service in the current and prior periods. That benefit is discounted to determine its present value, and all unrecognized past service costs and the fair value of any plan assets are deducted. The discount rate is the yield at the balance sheet date on high-quality corporate bonds. Calculations are performed by qualified actuaries using the projected unit credit method in accordance with IAS 19. Obligations for contributions to defined contribution plans are recognized as an expense in the income statement when they are due.

18. Pensions and Similar Obligations

The Group has obligations both from defined contribution and defined benefit pension plans. The benefits are provided pursuant to the legal, fiscal, and economic conditions in each respective country.

Pensions and Similar Obligations (€ in millions)

	Year ending December 31	
	2007	*2006*
Defined benefit plans	115	126
Thereof: adidas AG	99	109
Similar obligations	9	8
Pensions and similar obligations	124	134

Defined Contribution Plans

The total expense for defined contribution plans amounted to €39 million in 2007 (2006: €12 million). All other pension plans are defined benefit plans, which are partly funded by plan assets.

Defined Benefit Plans

Given the diverse Group structure, different defined benefit plans exist, comprising both pension payments and widow's and orphan's pensions as well as other postemployment benefits for employees and members of the Executive Board. These plans are partly funded.

Actuarial assumptions in %

	Year ending December 31	
	2007	*2006*
Discount rate	5.6	4.5
Salary increases	3.5	3.5
Pension increases	1.8	1.5
Expected return on plan asset	5.7	3.0

The actuarial valuations of the defined benefit plans are made at the end of each reporting period. The assumptions for employee turnover and mortality are based on empirical data, the latter for Germany on the 2005 G version of the mortality tables of Dr. Heubeck. The actuarial assumptions in Germany and in other countries are not materially different.

As of January 1, 2005, due to application of the amendment to IAS 19, *Employee Benefits,* issued in December 2004, the Group recognizes actuarial gains or losses of defined benefit plans arising during the financial year immediately outside the income statement in the statement of recognized income and expense. The actuarial gain recognized in the statement of recognized income and expense for 2007 was €18 million (2006: €2 million). The cumulative recognized actuarial losses amount to €12 million (2006: €30 million) (see also Note 21).

Pension Expenses for Defined Benefit Plans (€ in millions)

	Year ending December 31	
	2007	*2006*
Current service cost	12	7
Interest cost	7	5
Expected return on plan assets	(4)	(1)
Pensions expenses	15	11

Of the total pension expenses, an amount of €12 million (2006: €7 million) relates to employees in Germany. Contributions to postemployment benefit plans for employees living in Germany for the year ending December 31, 2008, are expected to amount to €7 million. The pension expense is recorded within the operating expenses whereas the production-related part thereof is recognized within the cost of sales.

Defined Benefit Obligation (€ in millions)

	2007	*2006*
Defined benefit obligation as at January 1	170	131
Increase in companies consolidated	--	34
Currency translation differences	2	1
Current service cost	12	7
Interest cost	7	5
Pensions paid	(6)	(6)
Actuarial gain	(14)	(2)
Defined benefit obligation as at December 31	171	170

Status of Funded and Unfunded Obligations (€ in millions)

	Dec. 31 2007	Dec. 31 2006
Present value of unfunded obligation	114	110
Present value of funded obligation	57	60
Present value of total obligations	171	170
Fair value of plan assets	(56)[1]	(44)
Recognized liability for defined benefit obligations	115	126

[1] *Part of the 46 million total of plan assets cannot be deducted, as it is not possible to use the exceeding amount for another plan.*

The calculations of the recognized assets and liabilities from defined benefit plans are based upon statistical and actuarial calculations. In particular, the present value of the defined benefit obligation is impacted by assumptions on discount rates used to arrive at the present value of future pension liabilities and assumptions on future increases in salaries and benefits. Furthermore, the Group's independent actuaries use statistically based assumptions covering areas such as future participant plan withdrawals and estimates on life expectancy. The actuarial assumptions used may differ materially from actual results due to changes in market and economic conditions, higher or lower withdrawal rates or longer or shorter life spans of participants and other changes in the factors being assessed. These differences could impact the assets or liabilities recognized in the balance sheet in future periods.

Movement in Plan Assets (€ in millions)

	2007	2006
Fair value of plan assets at January 1	46	--
Increase in companies consolidated	--	25
Currency translation differences	(3)	
Pension paid	(1)	
Contributions paid into the plan	10	20
Actuarial gains	4	
Expected return on plan assets	4	1
Fair value of plan assets at December 31	60	46

Contributions into the plan are only paid by the employer. The plan assets are invested in several pension funds. The return on plan assets is in conformity with the current strategy of the pension funds. In 2007, the actual return on plan assets was €7 million (2006: €2 million).

Constitution of Plan Assets

€ in millions	December 31, 2007
Equity instruments	28
Bonds	6
Pension plan reinsurance	16
Other assets	11
Fair value of plan assets	60

Historical Development

€ in millions	Dec. 31 2007	Dec. 31 2006	Dec. 31 2005	Dec. 31 2004	Dec. 31 2003
Defined benefit obligation	171	170	131	118	100
Plan assets	60	46	--	--	--
Nondeductible plan assets	(4)	(2)	--	--	--
Deficit in plan	115	126	131	118	100
Experience adjustments	(1)	4	1	--	--

Novartis AG
For the year ended December 31, 2007

26. Employee Benefits

Defined benefit plans

The Group has, apart from the legally required social security schemes, numerous independent pension and other postemployment benefit plans. In most cases these plans are externally funded vehicles which are legally separate from the Group. For certain Group companies, however, no independent assets exist for the pension and other long-term benefit obligations of associates. In these cases the related liability is included in the balance sheet.

Defined benefit pension plans cover a significant number of the Group's associates. The defined benefit obligations and related assets of all major plans are reappraised annually by independent actuaries. Plan assets are recorded at fair values and their actual return in 2007 was USD 808 million (2006: USD 771 million). The defined benefit obligation of unfunded pension plans was USD 327 million at December 31, 2007 (2006: USD 324 million). The measurement dates for the pension plans and the other postemployment benefits were between September 30, 2007, and December 31, 2007, depending on the plan. Any changes between the measurement date and year-end are monitored and adjusted, if necessary.

The following is a summary of the status of the main funded and unfunded pension and other postemployment benefit plans of associates at December 31, 2007 and 2006:

	Pension plans		Other postemployment benefit plans	
	2007	2006	2007	2006
	(USD millions)			
Benefit obligation at beginning of the year	16,767	15,632	987	1,024
Benefit obligations related to discontinuing operations	(197)	(49)	(163)	(10)
Service cost	424	417	51	51
Interest cost	615	559	42	50
Actuarial losses	(586)	(144)	(96)	(81)
Plan amendments	(94)	(7)	--	4
Translation effects	1,056	1,076	7	--
Benefit payments	(996)	(865)	(44)	(51)
Contributions of associates	116	63	--	--
Effect of acquisitions or divestments	--	85	--	--
Benefit obligation at end of the year	17,105	16,767	784	987
Fair value of plan assets at beginning of the year	17,515	16,059	20	24
Plan assets related to discontinuing operations	(199)	(21)	--	--
Expected return on plan assets	804	758	2	1
Actuarial gains	4	13	--	--
Translation effects	1,088	1,094	--	--
Novartis Group contributions	59	388	39	46
Contributions of associates	116	63	--	--
Plan amendments	(36)	--	--	--
Benefit payments	(996)	(865)	(44)	(51)
Effect of acquisitions or divestments	--	26	--	--
Fair value of plan assets at end of the year	18,355	17,515	17	20
Funded status	1,250	748	(767)	(967)
Unrecognized past service cost	3	11	(21)	(26)
Limitation on recognition of fund surplus	(52)		--	
Net asset/(liability) in the balance sheet	<u>1,201</u>	<u>759</u>	<u>(788)</u>	<u>(993)</u>

The movement in the net asset and the amounts recognized in the balance sheet were as follows:

	Pension plans		Other postemployment benefit plans	
	2007	2006	2007	2006
		(USD millions)		
Movement in net asset or (liability)				
Net asset or (liability) in the balance sheet at				
beginning of the year	759	439	(993)	(1,033)
Net asset or (liability) related to discontinued operations	(2)	28	163	10
Net periodic benefit cost	(186)	(199)	(88)	(96)
Novartis Group contributions	59	388	39	46
Plan amendments, net	1	(13)	2	3
Effect of acquisitions or divestments	--	(59)	--	(4)
Change in actuarial gains	590	157	96	81
Currency translation effects	32	18	(7)	--
Limitation on recognition of fund surplus	(52)	--	--	--
Net asset or (liability) in the balance sheet at the end				
of the year	1,201	759	(788)	(993)
Amounts recognized in the balance sheet				
Prepaid benefit cost	2,309	2,102	--	--
Accrued benefit liability	(1,108)	(1,343)	(788)	(993)
Net asset or (liability) in the balance sheet at the end				
of the year	1,201	759	(788)	(993)

The net periodic benefit cost recorded in the income statement consists of the following components:

	Pension plans		Other postemployment benefit plans	
	2007	2006	2007	2006
		(USD millions)		
Components of net periodic benefit cost				
Service cost	424	417	51	51
Interest cost	615	559	42	50
Expected returns on plan assets	(804)	(758)	(2)	(1)
Recognized past service cost	(20)	(11)	(3)	(4)
Curtailment/settlement gains	(29)	(8)	--	--
Net periodic benefit cost[1]	186	199	88	96

[1] *The 2007 net periodic benefit cost excludes all amounts for the discontinued operations. In 2006, the net periodic benefit costs include items for Gerber. Included are net periodic pension benefits of USD 14 million (comprised of USD 3 million service cost, USD 14 million interest costs and an expected return on plan assets of USD 31 million) and other postemployment benefit plan costs of USD 12 million (comprised of USD 5 million service cost, USD 8 million interest costs and an expected return on plan assets of USD 1 million).*

The principal actuarial weighted-average assumptions used for calculating defined benefit plans and other postemployment benefits of associates are as follows:

	Pension plans		Other postemployment benefit plans	
	2007 %	2006 %	2007 %	2005 %
Weighted-average assumptions used to determine benefit obligations at the end of the year				
Discount rate	4.1	3.6	5.8	5.8
Expected rate of salary increase	3.7	3.7		
Current average life expectancy for a 65 year old male/female	19/22 years	19/22 years	18/21 years	18/21 years

	Pension plans		Other postemployment benefit plans	
	2007 %	2006 %	2007 %	2005 %
Weighted-average assumptions used to determine net periodic pension cost for the year ended				
Discount rate	3.6	3.4	5.8	5.5
Expected return on plan assets	4.6	4.5		
Expected rate of salary increase	3.7	2.7		
Current average life expectancy for a 65 year old male/female	19/22 years	19/22 years	18/21 years	18/21 years

The following shows a five-year summary reflecting the funding of defined benefit pensions and the impact of historical deviations between expected and actual return on plan assets and actuarial adjustments on plan liabilities.

	2007 USD millions	2006 USD millions	2005 USD millions	2004 USD millions	2003 USD millions
Plan assets	18,355	17,515	16,059	17,663	16,128
Defined benefit obligation	(17,105)	(16,767)	(15,362)	(16,488)	(13,865)
Surplus	1,250	748	427	1,175	2,263
Differences between expected and actual return on plan assets	4	13	367	23	120
Actuarial adjustments on plan liabilities	586	144	(869)	(1,401)	(695)

The weighted-average asset allocation of funded defined benefit plans at December 31, 2007 and 2006 were as follows:

	Long-term target %	2007 %	2006 %
Equity securities	15-40	42	30
Debt securities	45-70	39	54
Real estate	0-15	9	8
Cash and other investments	0-15	10	8
Total		100	100

Strategic pension plan asset allocations are determined with the objective of achieving an investment return which, together with the contributions paid, is sufficient to maintain reasonable control over the various funding risks of the plans. Based upon current market and economic environments, actual asset allocation may periodically be permitted to deviate from policy targets. Expected return assumptions are reviewed periodically and are based on each plan's strategic asset mix. Factors considered in the estimate of the expected return are the risk-free interest rate together with risk premiums on the assets of each pension plan.

The expected future cash flows to be paid by the Group in respect of pension and other postemployment benefit plans at December 31, 2007, were as follows:

	Pension plans	Other postemployment benefit plans
Novartis Group contributions	*(USD millions)*	
2008 (estimated)	113	44
Expected future benefit payments		
2008	1,039	44
2009	1,062	45
2010	1,057	46
2011	1,075	47
2012	1,091	48
2013-2017	5,485	259

The health-care cost trend rate assumptions for other postemployment benefits are as follows:

	2007	2006
Health-care cost trend rate assumptions used		
Health-care cost trend rate assumed for next year	8.0%	9.0%
Rate to which the cost trend rate is assumed to decline	4.8%	4.8%
Year that the rate reaches the ultimate trend rate	2012	2012

A one-percentage-point change in the assumed health-care cost trend rates compared to those used for 2006 would have the following effects:

	1% point increase	*1% point decrease*
	(USD millions)	
Effects on total of service and interest cost components	14	(12)
Effect on postemployment benefit obligations	93	(78)

The number of Novartis AG shares held by pension and similar benefit funds at December 31, 2006, was 21.6 million shares with a market value of USD 1.2 billion (2005: 21.6 million shares with a market value of USD 1.2 billion). These funds sold no Novartis AG shares during the years ended December 31, 2007 and 2006. The amount of dividends received on Novartis AG shares held as plan assets by these funds was USD 26 million for the year ended December 31, 2007 (2006: USD 20 million).

Defined contribution plans

In some Group companies, associates are covered by defined contribution plans and other long-term benefits of associates. The liability of the Group for these benefits is reported in other long-term benefits of associates and deferred compensation and at December 31, 2007, amounts to USD 386 million (2006: USD 343 million). In 2007 contributions charged to the consolidated income statement for the defined contribution plans were USD 141 million (2006: USD 123 million).

17 SHAREHOLDERS' EQUITY

PERSPECTIVE AND ISSUES

The IASB's *Framework* defines equity as the residual interest in the assets of an entity after deducting all its liabilities. Shareholders' equity is comprised of all capital contributed to the entity (including share premium, also referred to as capital paid-in in excess of par value) plus retained earnings (which represents the entity's cumulative earnings less all distributions that have been made therefrom).

IAS 1, which was substantially revised in late 2007, suggests that shareholders' interests be subcategorized into three broad subdivisions: issued share capital, retained earnings (accumulated profits or losses) and other components of equity (reserves). Depending on jurisdiction, issued share capital may need to be further categorized as par or stated capital and as additional contributed capital. This standard also sets forth requirements for disclosures about the details of share capital for corporations and the various capital accounts of other types of entities, such as partnerships.

Equity represents an interest in the net assets (i.e., assets less liabilities) of the entity. It is not a claim on those assets in the sense that liabilities are, however. Upon the liquidation of the business, an obligation arises for the entity to distribute any remaining assets to the shareholders, but only after the creditors are first fully paid.

Earnings are not generated by transactions in an entity's own equity (e.g., by the issuance, reacquisition, or reissuance of its common or preferred shares). Depending on the laws of the jurisdiction of incorporation, distributions to shareholders may be subject to various limitations, such as to the amount of retained (accounting basis) earnings. In other cases, limitations may be based on values not presented in the financial statements, such as the net solvency of the entity as determined on a market value basis; in such instances, IFRS-basis financial statements will not provide information needed for making such determination.

In recent years the matter of share-based payments (e.g., share option plans and other arrangements whereby employees or others, such as vendors, are compensated via issuance of shares) has received great amounts of attention. IASB imposed a comprehensive standard, IFRS 2, which requires a fair value-based measurement of all such schemes.

A major objective of the accounting for shareholders' equity is the adequate disclosure of the sources from which the capital was derived. For this reason, a number of different contributed capital accounts may be presented in the statement of financial position. The rights of each class of shareholder must also be disclosed. Where shares are reserved for future issuance, such as under the terms of share option plans, this fact must also be made known.

Sources of IFRS		
IFRS 2	*IAS* 1, 8, 16, 32, 38	*IFRIC* 2, 8, 11

DEFINITIONS OF TERMS

Cash-settled share-based payment transaction. A share-based payment transaction in which the entity acquires goods or services by incurring a liability to transfer cash or other assets to the supplier of those goods or services for amounts that are based on the price (or value) of the entity's shares or other equity instruments of the entity.

Employees and others providing similar services. Individuals who render personal services to the entity and either (1) the individuals are regarded as employees for legal or tax purposes, (2) the individuals work for the entity under its direction in the same way as individuals who are regarded as employees for legal or tax purposes, or (3) the services rendered are similar to those rendered by employees. For example, the term encompasses all management personnel (i.e., those persons having authority and responsibility for planning, directing and controlling the activities of the entity, including nonexecutive directors).

Equity instrument. A contract that evidences a residual interest in the assets of an entity after deducting all of its liabilities, where liabilities are defined as the present obligations of the entity arising from past events, the settlement of which are expected to result in an outflow from the entity of resources embodying economic benefits (i.e., an outflow of cash or other assets of the entity).

Equity instrument granted. The right (conditional or unconditional) to an equity instrument of the entity conferred by the entity on another party, under a share-based payment arrangement.

Equity-settled share-based payment transaction. A share-based payment transaction in which the entity receives goods or services as consideration for equity instruments of the entity (including shares or share options).

Fair value. The amount for which an asset could be exchanged, a liability settled, or an equity instrument granted could be exchanged, between knowledgeable, willing parties in an arm's-length transaction.

Grant date. The date at which the entity and another party (including an employee) agree to a share-based payment arrangement, being when the entity and the counterparty have a shared understanding of the terms and conditions of the arrangement. At grant date the entity confers on the counterparty the right to cash, other assets, or equity instruments of the entity, provided the specified vesting conditions, if any, are met. If that agreement is subject to an approval process (for example, by shareholders), grant date is the date when that approval is obtained.

Intrinsic value. The difference between the fair value of the shares to which the counterparty has the (conditional or unconditional) right to subscribe or which it has the right to receive, and the price (if any) the counterparty is (or will be) required to pay for those shares.

Market condition. A condition upon which the exercise price, vesting or exercisability of an equity instrument depends that is related to the market price of the entity's equity instruments, such as attaining a specified share price or a specified amount of intrinsic value of a share option, or achieving a specified target that is based on the market price of the entity's equity instruments relative to an index of market prices of equity instruments of other entities.

Measurement date. The date at which the fair value of the equity instruments granted is measured for the purposes of this IFRS. For transactions with employees and others providing similar services, the measurement date is grant date. For transactions with parties other than employees (and those providing similar services), the measurement date is the date the entity obtains the goods or the counterparty renders service.

Puttable financial instruments. Shares which the holders can "put" back to the issuing entity; that is, the holders can require that the entity repurchases the shares, at defined amounts that can include fair value.

Reload feature. A feature that provides for an automatic grant of additional share options whenever the option holder exercises previously granted options using the entity's shares, rather than cash, to satisfy the exercise price.

Reload option. A new share option granted when a share is used to satisfy the exercise price of a previous share option.

Share-based payment arrangement. An agreement between the entity and another party (including an employee) to enter into a share-based payment transaction, which thereby entitles the other party to receive cash or other assets of the entity for amounts that are based on the price of the entity's shares or other equity instruments of the entity, or to receive equity instruments of the entity, provided the specified vesting conditions, if any, are met.

Share-based payment transaction. A transaction in which the entity receives goods or services as consideration for equity instruments of the entity (including shares or share options), or acquires goods or services for amounts that are based on the price of the entity's shares or other equity instruments of the entity.

Share option. A contract that gives the holder the right, but not the obligation, to subscribe to the entity's shares at a fixed or determinable price for a specified period of time.

Vest. To become an entitlement. Under a share-based payment arrangement, a counterparty's right to receive cash, other assets, or equity instruments of the entity vests upon satisfaction of any specified vesting conditions.

Vesting conditions. The conditions that must be satisfied for the counterparty to become entitled to receive cash, other assets or equity instruments of the entity, under a share-based payment arrangement. Vesting conditions include service conditions, which require the other party to complete a specified period of service, and performance conditions, which require specified performance targets to be met (such as a specified increase in the entity's profit over a specified period of time).

Vesting period. The period during which all the specified vesting conditions of a share-based payment arrangement are to be satisfied.

CONCEPTS, RULES, AND EXAMPLES

IFRS have dealt primarily with presentation and disclosure requirements relating to shareholders' equity and have yet to resolve or even address matters pertaining to the actual accounting for the various components of shareholders' equity (i.e., recognition and measurement issues). The promulgation of IFRS 2, which thoroughly addresses the accounting for share-based payments, was a major step forward. It should be noted that in many jurisdictions company law sets out specific requirements as regards accounting for equity, which may limit the application of IFRS.

Because of the absence of any promulgated IFRS on many details of this area, this chapter makes use of certain guidance that exists under US GAAP. The IAS 8 hierarchy requires that in the absence of a standard, the preparer should refer to the *Framework* and thereafter to national GAAP based on the same conceptual framework. In the light of the IASB's *Norwalk Agreement,* US GAAP would normally be seen as being most authoritative in such a case. Also, given the intent to converge US GAAP and IFRS, it is certainly possible that IFRS may formally adopt at least some of the US GAAP guidance, rather than attempt to create unique IFRS to deal with these matters. In the following discussion, therefore, certain guidance under US GAAP will be invoked where IFRS is silent regarding the accounting for specific types of transactions involving the entity's shareholders' equity. Since this is a rapidly evolving area, care should be taken to verify the current status of relevant developments.

Presentation and Disclosure Requirements under IFRS

Equity includes reserves such as statutory or legal reserves, general reserves and contingency reserves, and revaluation surplus. IAS 1 categorizes shareholders' interests in three broad subdivisions: issued share capital, retained earnings (accumulated profits or losses) and other components of equity (reserves). This standard also sets forth requirements for disclosures about the details of share capital for corporations and of the various capital accounts of other types of entities.

Disclosures relating to share capital.

1. *The number or amount of shares authorized, issued, and outstanding.* It is required that a company disclose information relating to the number of shares authorized, issued, and outstanding. Authorized share capital is defined as the maximum number of shares that a company is permitted to issue, according to its articles of association, its charter, or its bylaws. The number of shares issued and outstanding could vary, based on the fact that a company could have acquired its own shares and is holding them as treasury shares (discussed below under reacquired shares).
2. *Capital not yet paid in (or unpaid capital).* In an initial public offering (IPO), subscribers may be asked initially to pay in only a portion of the par value, with the balance due in installments, which are known as *calls.* Thus, it is possible that at the end of the reporting period a certain portion of the share capital has not yet been paid in. The amount not yet collected must be shown as a contra (i.e., a deduction) in the equity section, since that portion of the subscribed capital has yet to be issued. For example, while the gross amount of the share subscription increases capital, if the due date of the final call falls on February 7, 2007, following the accounting year-end of December 31, 2006, the amount of capital not yet paid in should be shown as a deduction from shareholders' equity. In this manner, only the net

amount of capital received as of the end of the reporting period will be properly included in shareholders' equity, averting an overstatement of the entity's actual equity.

IAS 1 requires that a distinction be made between shares that have been issued and fully paid, on the one hand, and those that have been issued but not fully paid, on the other hand. The number of shares outstanding at the beginning and at the end of each period presented must also be reconciled.

3. *Par value per share.* This is also generally referred to as legal value or face value per share. The par value of shares is specified in the corporate charter or bylaws and referred to in other documents, such as the share application and prospectus. Par value is the smallest unit of share capital that can be acquired unless the prospectus permits fractional shares (which is very unusual for commercial entities). In certain jurisdictions, including the United States, it is also permitted for corporations to issue no-par share (i.e., shares that are not given any par value). In such cases, again depending on local corporation laws, sometimes a stated value is determined by the board of directors, which is then accorded effectively the same treatment as par value. IAS 1 requires disclosure of par values or of the fact that the shares were issued without par values.

Historically, companies often issued shares at par value in cases where shares are issued immediately on incorporation or soon thereafter. This was partially due to laws, now rare, holding share owners contingently liable in the event of business failure, up to the amount of any discount from par value at the original issuance of shares. The prohibition against issuing shares at discount was thought to protect creditors and others, who could rely on aggregate par value as having been contributed in cash to the entity. It did not restrict any subsequent sale of the shares, however. As a practical matter, par values have had a much diminished importance as corporation laws have been modernized in many jurisdictions. Additionally, often the par values will be made trivial, such as when set at €1 or even €0.01 per share, such that the concern over an original-issuance discount is made moot, since issuance prices even at inception of a new corporation will be substantially above par value.

4. *Movements in share capital accounts during the year.* This information is usually disclosed in the financial statements or the footnotes to the financial statements, generally in a tabular or statement format, although in some circumstances merely set forth in a narrative. If a statement is presented, it is generally referred to as the Statement of Changes in Shareholders' (or Stockholders') Equity. It highlights the changes during the year in the various components of shareholders' equity. It also serves the purpose of reconciling the beginning and the ending balances of shareholders' equity, as shown in the statements of financial position. Under the provisions of revised IAS 1, reporting entities must present a statement showing the changes in all the equity accounts (including issued capital, retained earnings and reserves (See Chapter 3). Transactions with owners are reported in this statement, while all changes other than those resulting from transactions with owners are to be reported in the statement of comprehensive income. The former practice of including items of other comprehensive income in the statement of changes in equity is no longer permitted under revised IAS 1 (which becomes mandatorily effective in 2009).

5. *Rights, preferences, and restrictions with respect to the distribution of dividends and to the repayment of capital.* When there is more than one class of share capital having varying rights, adequate disclosure of the rights, preferences, and restrictions

attached to each such class of share capital will enhance understandability of the information provided by the financial statements.

6. *Cumulative preference dividends in arrears.* If an entity has preferred share outstanding, and does not pay *cumulative* dividends on the preference shares annually when due, it will be required by statute to pay these arrearages in later years, before any distributions can be made on common (ordinary) shares. When there are several series of preferred shares, the individual share indentures will spell out the relative preference order, so that, for example, senior preferred series may be paid dividends even though junior preferred shares has several years' arrearages. Although practice varies, most preference shares are cumulative in nature. Preference shares that do not have this feature are called *noncumulative preference shares.*

7. *Reacquired shares.* Shares that are issued but then reacquired by a company are referred to as *treasury shares.* The entity's ability to reacquire shares may be limited by its corporate charter or by covenants in its loan and/or preferred share agreements (for example, it may be restricted from doing so as long as bonded debt remains outstanding). In those jurisdictions where the company law permits the repurchase of shares, such shares, on acquisition by the company or its consolidated subsidiary, become legally available for reissue or resale without further authorization. *Shares outstanding* refers to shares other than those held as treasury shares. That is, treasury shares does not reduce the number of shares issued, but affects the number of shares outstanding. It is to be noted that certain countries prohibit companies from purchasing their own shares, since to do so is considered as a reduction of share capital that can be achieved only with the express consent of the shareholders in an extraordinary general meeting, and then only under certain defined conditions.

IAS 1 requires that shares in the entity held in its treasury or by its subsidiaries be identified for each category of share capital and be deducted from contributed capital. IAS 32 states that the treasury share acquisition transaction is to be reported in the statement of changes in equity. When later resold, any difference between acquisition cost and ultimate proceeds represents a change in equity, and is therefore not to be considered a gain or loss to be reported in the statement of comprehensive income. Accounting for treasury shares is discussed in further detail later in this chapter.

IAS 32 also specifies that the costs associated with equity transactions are to be accounted for as reductions of equity if the corresponding transaction was a share issuance, or as increases in the contra equity account when incurred in connection with treasury share reacquisitions. Relevant costs are limited to incremental costs directly associated with the transactions. If the issuance involves a compound instrument, the issuance costs should be associated with the liability and equity components, respectively, using a rational and consistent basis of allocation.

8. *Shares reserved for future issuance under options and sales contracts, including the terms and amounts.* Companies may issue share options that grant the holder of these options rights to a specified number of shares at a certain price. Share options have become a popular means of employee remuneration, and often the top echelon of management is offered this noncash perquisite as a major part of their remuneration packages. The options grant the holder the right to acquire shares over a defined time horizon for a fixed price, which may equal fair value at the grant date or, less commonly, at a price lower than fair value. Granting options usually is not legal unless the entity has enough authorized but unissued shares to satisfy the holders' demands, if made, although in some instances this can be done, with manage-

ment thus becoming bound to the reacquisition of enough shares in the market (or by other means) to enable it to honor these new commitments. If a company has shares reserved for future issuance under option plans or sales contracts, it is necessary to disclose the number of shares, including terms and amounts, so reserved. These reserved shares are not available for sale or distribution to others during the terms of the unexercised options.

IAS 32 deals with situations in which entity obligations are to be settled in cash or in equity securities, depending on the outcome of contingencies not under the issuer's control. In general, these should be classed as liabilities, unless the part that could require settlement in cash is not genuine, or settlement by cash or distribution of other assets is available only in the event of the liquidation of the issuer. If the optionee can demand cash, the obligation is a liability, not equity.

The accounting for share options, which was introduced by IFRS 2, is dealt with later in this chapter. As will be seen, it presents many intriguing and complex issues.

Disclosures relating to other equity.

1. *Capital contributed in excess of par value.* This is the amount received on the issuance of shares that is the excess over the par value. It is called "additional contributed capital" in the United States, while in many other jurisdictions, including the European Union, it is referred to as "share premium." Essentially the same accounting would be required if a stated value is used in lieu of par value, where permitted.

2. *Revaluation reserve.* When a company carries property, plant, and equipment under the revaluation model, as is permitted by IAS 16 (revaluation to fair value), the difference between the cost (net of accumulated depreciation) and the fair value is recognized in other comprehensive income and accumulated in equity as the Revaluation Surplus.

   IAS 1, as revised in 2007, requires that movements of this reserve during the reporting period (year or interim period) be disclosed in the other comprehensive income section of the statement of comprehensive income. Increases in an asset's carrying value are recognized in other comprehensive income and accumulated in equity. Decreases are recognized in other comprehensive income only to the extent of any credit balance existing in the revaluation surplus in respect of that asset, and additional decreases are taken to profit or loss. Also, restrictions as to any distributions of this reserve to shareholders should be disclosed. Note that in some jurisdictions the directors may be empowered to make distributions in excess of recorded book capital, and this often will require a determination of fair values.

3. *Reserves.* Reserves include capital reserves as well as revenue reserves. Also, statutory reserves and voluntary reserves are included under this category. Finally, special reserves, including contingency reserves, are included herein. The use of general reserves and statutory reserves, once common or even required under company laws in many jurisdictions, is now in decline.

   Statutory reserves (or legal reserves, as they are called in some jurisdictions) are created based on the requirements of the law or the statute under which the company is incorporated. For instance, many corporate statutes in Middle Eastern countries require that companies set aside 10% of their net income for the year as a "statutory reserve," with such appropriations to continue until the balance in this reserve account equals 50% of the company's equity capital. The intent is to provide an extra "cushion" of protection to creditors, such that even significant losses incurred in later periods will not reduce the entity's actual net worth below zero, which would, were it to occur, threaten creditors' ability for repayment of liabilities.

Sometimes a company's articles, charter, or bylaws may require that each year the company set aside a certain percentage of its net profit (income) by way of a contingency or general reserve. Unlike statutory or legal reserves, contingency reserves are based on the provisions of corporate bylaws. The use of general reserves is not consistent with IFRS and some national GAAP, such as that in the US.

The standard requires that movements in these reserves during the reporting period be disclosed, along with the nature and purpose of each reserve presented within owners' equity.

4. *Retained earnings.* By definition, retained earnings represents a corporation's accumulated profits (or losses) less any distributions that have been made therefrom. However, based on provisions contained in IFRS, other adjustments are also made to the amount of retained earnings. IAS 8 requires the following to be shown as adjustments to retained earnings:

    a. Correction of accounting errors that relate to prior periods should be reported by adjusting the opening balance of retained earnings. Comparative information should be restated, unless it is impracticable to do so.

    b. The adjustment resulting from a change in accounting policy that is to be applied retrospectively should be reported as an adjustment to the opening balance of retained earnings. Comparative information should be restated unless it is impracticable to do so.

When dividends have been proposed but not formally approved, and hence when such intended dividends have not yet become reportable as a liability of the entity, disclosure is required by IAS 1. Dividends declared after the end of the reporting period, but prior to the issuance of the financial statements, must be disclosed but cannot be formally recognized via a charge against retained earnings (as was sometimes done in the past, and as remains normal practice in certain jurisdictions such as the UK under national rules). Also, the amount of any cumulative preference dividends not recognized as charges against accumulated profits must be disclosed (i.e., arrearages), either parenthetically or in the footnotes.

Major changes were wrought by the issuance, in late 2007, of revised IAS 1. This standard now mandates that an entity should present in a statement of changes in equity the amount of total comprehensive income for the period, showing separately the total amounts attributable to owners of the parent (controlling interest) and to the noncontrolling interest. Comprehensive income (a new term under IFRS, adopted from the corresponding standard under US GAAP) includes all components of what was formerly denoted as "profit or loss" and of "other recognized income and expense." The latter category will henceforth be known as "other comprehensive income."

The components of other comprehensive income comprise

1. Changes in revaluation surplus (see IAS 16, *Property, Plant, and Equipment*, and IAS 38, *Intangible Assets*);
2. Gains and losses arising from translating the financial statements of a foreign operation (see IAS 21, *The Effects of Changes in Foreign Exchange Rates*)
3. Gains and losses on remeasuring available-for-sale financial assets (see IAS 39, *Financial Instruments: Recognition and Measurement*);
4. The effective portion of gains and losses on hedging instruments in a cash flow hedge (see IAS 39); and

5. Actuarial gains and losses on defined benefit plans recognized in accordance with paragraph 93A of IAS 19, *Employee Benefits*.

This topic is covered in more detail in a separate discussion at the end of Chapter 3.

Classification between Liabilities and Equity, Including Puttable Shares

A longstanding challenge under IFRS and various national GAAP standards has been to discern between instruments that are liabilities and those that truly represent permanent equity in an entity. This has been made more difficult as various hybrid instruments have been invented over recent decades. IAS 32 requires that the issuer of a financial instrument should classify the instrument, or its components, as a liability or as equity, according to the substance of the contractual arrangement on initial recognition.

The standard defines a financial liability as a contractual obligation

1. To deliver cash or another financial asset to another entity, or
2. To exchange financial instruments with another entity under conditions that are potentially unfavorable.

An equity instrument, on the other hand, has been defined by the standard as any contract that evidences a residual interest in the assets of an entity after deducting all its liabilities.

A special situation arises in connection with cooperatives, which are member-owned organizations having capital which exhibits certain characteristics of debt, since it is not permanent in nature. IFRIC 2 addresses the accounting for members' shares in cooperatives. It holds that where a member of a cooperative has a contractual right to request redemption of shares, this does not necessarily require the shares to be classified as a liability. Members' shares are to be classified as equity if the entity has an unconditional right to refuse redemption, or if national law prohibits redemption. On the other hand, if the law prohibits redemption only conditionally (e.g., if minimum capital requirements are not maintained), this does not alter the general rule that cooperative shares are to be deemed a liability, not equity, of the entity.

IASB also considered the special case of shares which are puttable to the entity for a proportion of the fair value of the entity. Under then-existing IFRS, when this right was held by the shareholder, redemption could be demanded, and accordingly the shares were to be classified as a liability and to be measured at fair value. This created what was viewed by many as an anomalous situation whereby a successful entity using historical cost would have a liability that increases every year and leaves the reporting entity with, potentially, no equity at all in its statement of financial position. The logic was that, since the equity in the business would not be truly permanent in nature, and would represent a claim on the assets of the entity, it would not be properly displayed as a liability—although clearly this must be adequately explained to users of the financial statements. (An anomalous situation arose under US GAAP with the issuance of FAS 150, and the strong negative reaction to that standard ultimately led the FASB to indefinitely postpone its application, in certain circumstances.)

In responding to the foregoing concern, in June 2006, the IASB issued Exposure Draft (ED), *Proposed Amendments to IAS 32 and IAS 1: Financial Instruments Puttable at Fair Value and Obligations Arising on Liquidation*, proposing that financial instruments puttable at fair value, as well as obligations to deliver to another entity a pro rata share of the net assets of the entity upon its liquidation, should be classified as equity. Under prior practice these instruments were classified as financial liabilities. After extended debate, IASB issued amendments to IAS 1 and IAS 32 in early 2008.

Puttable shares. As amended, *certain* puttable shares, which under IAS 32 before its amendment in early 2008 (effective 2009) were classified as liabilities in the statement of financial position, are not to be presented as equity if strict conditions are met. The purpose is to avoid anomalous results when residual equity interests, which would be entitled to a pro rata share of the entity's net assets upon liquidation, are puttable throughout the life of the entity at fair value.

The conditions that must be met should limit the application of this exception to the general, and fundamental, rule that instruments that obligate the entity to the payment of cash must be reported as liabilities. The conditions are that

- The instrument's holders are entitled to their pro rata share of the entity's net assets upon the liquidation of the entity.
- The instrument is in the class of instruments that is most subordinate (i.e., is among the residual equity interests in the entity) and all instruments in that class have identical features.
- The instrument has no other features that would require classification as a liability.
- The total expected cash flows attributable to the instrument, over its life, are based substantially on profit or loss, or change in recognized net assets, or change in the fair value of recognized or unrecognized net assets; there must be no other instruments outstanding that have equivalent terms that would effectively restrict or fix the residual returns to these instrument holders.

The amendments result in equity classification of puttable shares having the foregoing characteristics, whether the shares are puttable throughout the instrument's life at fair value or only upon liquidation. Puttable instruments not meeting the criteria must be presented as liabilities.

IAS 1 has been amended to also require expanded disclosures in circumstances when puttable instruments are included in equity. These disclosures include summary quantitative data about the amount classified as equity; the entity's objectives, policies, and processes for managing the obligation to repurchase or redeem such instruments, including changes therein; the expected cash outflow on redemption or repurchase; and information on the means of determining such cash outflows.

Compound financial instruments. Increasingly, corporations issue financial instruments that exhibit attributes of both equity and liabilities. IAS 32 stipulates that an entity that issues such financial instruments, which are technically known as compound instruments, should classify the component parts of the financial instrument separately as equity or liability as appropriate. (For a detailed discussion on financial instruments, refer to Chapters 5 and 10.) The full fair value of the liability component(s) must be reported as liabilities, and only the residual value, at issuance, can be included as equity, according to a recent amendment to IAS 32.

Additional Guidance Relative to Share Issuances and Related Matters

As noted, IFRS provides only minimal guidance regarding the actual accounting for share capital transactions, including the issuance of shares of various classes of equity instruments. In the following paragraphs, the authors offer suggestions concerning the accounting for such transactions, which are within the spirit of IFRS, although largely drawn from other authoritative sources. This is done to provide guidance which conforms to the requirements under IAS 8 (hierarchy of professional standards), and to illustrate a wide array of actual transactions that often need to be accounted for.

Preferred shares. Ownership interest in a corporation is made up of ordinary (common) shares and, optionally, preferred (preference) shares. The ordinary shares represent the residual risk-taking ownership of the corporation after the satisfaction of all claims of creditors and senior classes of equity. It is important that the actual common ownership be accurately identified, since the computation of earnings per share (described in Chapter 18) requires that the ultimate residual ownership class be properly associated with that calculation, regardless of what the various equity classes are nominally called.

Preferred shareholders are owners who have certain rights superior to those of common shareholders. These rights will pertain either to the earnings or the assets of the corporation. Preferences as to earnings exist when the preferred shareholders have a stipulated dividend rate (expressed either as a dollar amount or as a percentage of the preferred share's par or stated value). Preferences as to assets exist when the preferred shares have a stipulated liquidation value. If a corporation were to liquidate, the preferred holders would be paid a specific amount before the ordinary shareholders would have a right to participate in any of the proceeds.

In practice, preferred shares are more likely to have preferences as to earnings than as to assets. Some classes of preferred shares may have both preferential rights, although this is rarely encountered. Preferred shares may also have the following features: participation in earnings beyond the stipulated dividend rate; a cumulative feature, affording the preferred shareholders the protection that their dividends in arrears, if any, will be fully satisfied before the ordinary shareholders participate in any earnings distribution; and convertibility or callability by the corporation. Whatever preferences exist must be disclosed adequately in the financial statements, either in the statement of financial position or in the notes.

In exchange for the preferences, the preferred shareholders' rights or privileges are limited. For instance, the right to vote may be limited to ordinary shareholders. The most important right denied to the preferred shareholders, however, is the right to participate without limitation in the earnings of the corporation. Thus, if the corporation has exceedingly large earnings for a particular period, these earnings would accrue to the benefit of the ordinary shareholders. This is true even if the preferred shares are participating (itself a fairly uncommon feature) because even participating preferred shares usually have some upper limitation placed on its degree of participation. For example, preferred may have a 5% cumulative dividend with a further 3% participation right, so in any one year the limit would be an 8% return to the preferred shareholders (plus, if applicable, the 5% per year prior year dividends not paid).

Occasionally, as discussed in the chapter, several classes of share capital will be categorized as ordinary (e.g., Class A ordinary, Class B ordinary, etc.). Since there can be only one class of shares that constitutes the true residual risk-taking equity interest in a corporation, it is clear that the other classes, even though described as ordinary shares, must in fact have some preferential status. Not uncommonly, these preferences relate to voting rights, as when a control group holds ordinary shares with "super voting" rights (e.g., ten votes per share). The rights and responsibilities of each class of shareholder, even if described as ordinary, must be fully disclosed in the financial statements.

Accounting for the issuance of shares. The accounting for the sale of shares by a corporation depends on whether the share capital has a par or stated value. If there is a par or stated value, the amount of the proceeds representing the aggregate par or stated value is credited to the ordinary or preferred share capital account. The aggregate par or stated value is generally defined as legal capital not subject to distribution to shareholders. Proceeds in excess of par or stated value are credited to an additional contributed capital account. The additional contributed capital represents the amount in excess of the legal capital that may, under certain defined conditions, be distributed to shareholders. A corporation selling shares below par value credits the share capital account for the par value and debits an offsetting discount account for the difference between par value and the amount actually received.

If there is a discount on original issue of share capital, it serves to notify the actual and potential creditors of the contingent liability of those investors. As a practical matter, corporations avoided this problem by reducing par values to an arbitrarily low amount. This reduction in par eliminated the chance that shares would be sold for amounts below par. Where corporation laws make no distinction between par value and amounts in excess of par, the entire proceeds from the sale of shares may be credited to the ordinary share capital account without distinction between the share capital and the additional contributed capital accounts. The following entries illustrate these concepts:

Facts: A corporation sells 100,000 shares of €5 par ordinary share for €8 per share cash.

Cash	800,000	
Ordinary share		500,000
Additional contributed capital		300,000

Facts: A corporation sells 100,000 shares of no-par ordinary share for €8 per share cash.

Cash	800,000	
Ordinary share		800,000

Preferred shares will often be assigned a par value because in many cases the preferential dividend rate is defined as a percentage of par value (e.g., 5%, €25 par value preferred share will have a required annual dividend of €1.25). The dividend can also be defined as a euro amount per year, thereby obviating the need for par values.

Share capital issued for services. If the shares in a corporation are issued in exchange for services or property rather than for cash, the transaction should be reflected at the fair value of the property or services received. If this information is not readily available, the transaction should be recorded at the fair value of the shares that were issued. Where necessary, appraisals should be obtained to properly reflect the transaction. As a final resort, a valuation by the board of directors of the shares issued can be utilized. Shares issued to employees as compensation for services rendered should be accounted for at the fair value of the services performed, if determinable, or the value of the shares issued. (See discussion of IFRS 2 later in this chapter.)

Occasionally, particularly for start-up operations having limited working capital, the controlling owners may directly compensate certain vendors or employees. If shares are given by a major shareholder directly to an employee for services performed for the entity, this exchange should be accounted for as a capital contribution to the company by the major shareholder and as compensation expense incurred by the company. Only when accounted for in this manner will there be conformity with the general principle that all costs incurred by an entity, including compensation, should be reflected in its financial statements.

Issuance of share units. In certain instances, ordinary and preferred shares may be issued to investors as a unit (e.g., a unit of one share of preferred and two ordinary shares can be sold as a package). Where both of the classes of shares are publicly traded, the proceeds from a unit offering should be allocated in proportion to the relative market values of the securities. If only one of the securities is publicly traded, the proceeds should be allocated to the one that is publicly traded based on its known market value. Any excess is allocated to the other. Where the market value of neither security is known, appraisal information might be used. The imputed fair value of one class of security, particularly the preferred shares, can be based on the stipulated dividend rate. In this case, the amount of proceeds remaining after the imputing of a value of the preferred shares would be allocated to the ordinary shares.

The foregoing procedures would also apply if a unit offering were made of an equity and a nonequity security such as convertible debentures, or of shares and rights to purchase additional shares for a fixed time period.

Share subscriptions. Occasionally, particularly in the case of a newly organized corporation, a contract is entered into between the corporation and prospective investors, whereby the latter agree to purchase specified numbers of shares to be paid for over some installment period. These share subscriptions are not the same as actual share issuances, and the accounting differs accordingly. In some cases, laws of the jurisdiction of incorporation will govern how subscriptions have to be accounted for (e.g., when pro rata voting rights and dividend rights accompany partially paid subscriptions).

The amount of share subscriptions receivable by a corporation is sometimes treated as an asset in the statement of financial position and is categorized as current or noncurrent in accordance with the terms of payment. However, most subscriptions receivable are shown as a reduction of shareholders' equity in the same manner as treasury shares. Since subscribed shares do not have the rights and responsibilities of actual outstanding shares, the credit is made to a shares subscribed account instead of to the share capital accounts.

If the ordinary shares have par or stated value, the ordinary shares subscribed account are credited for the aggregate par or stated value of the shares subscribed. The excess over this amount is credited to additional contributed capital. No distinction is made between additional contributed capital relating to shares already issued and shares subscribed for. This treatment follows from the distinction between legal capital and additional contributed capital. Where there is no par or stated value, the entire amount of the ordinary share subscribed is credited to the shares subscribed account.

As the amount due from the prospective shareholders is collected, the share subscriptions receivable account is credited and the proceeds are debited to the cash account. Actual issuance of the shares, however, must await the complete payment of the share subscription. Accordingly, the debit to ordinary share subscribed is not made until the subscribed shares are fully paid for and the shares are issued.

The following journal entries illustrate these concepts:

1. 10,000 shares of €50 par preferred are subscribed at a price of €65 each; a 10% down payment is received.

Cash	65,000	
Share subscriptions receivable	585,000	
Preferred share subscribed		500,000
Additional contributed capital		150,000

2. 2,000 shares of no par ordinary shares are subscribed at a price of €85 each, with one-half received in cash.

Cash	85,000	
Share subscriptions receivable	85,000	
Ordinary share subscribed		170,000

3. All preferred subscriptions are paid, and one-half of the remaining ordinary subscriptions are collected in full and subscribed shares are issued.

Cash [€585,000 + (€85,000 × 0.50)]	627,500	
Shares subscriptions receivable		627,500
Preferred shares subscribed	500,000	
Preferred share		500,000
Ordinary shares subscribed	127,500	
Ordinary shares (€170,000 × 0.75)		127,500

When the company experiences a default by the subscriber, the accounting will follow the provisions of the jurisdiction in which the corporation is chartered. In some of these, the subscriber is entitled to a proportionate number of shares based on the amount already paid on the subscriptions, sometimes reduced by the cost incurred by the corporation in selling the remaining defaulted shares to other shareholders. In other jurisdictions, the subscriber forfeits the entire investment on default. In this case the amount already received is credited to an additional contributed capital account that describes its source.

Distinguishing additional contributed capital from the par or stated value of the shares. For largely historical reasons, entities sometimes issue share capital having par or stated value, which may be only a nominal value, such as €1 or even €0.01. The actual share issuance will be at a much higher (market driven) amount, and the excess of the issuance price over the par or stated value might be assigned to a separate equity account referred to as *premium on capital (ordinary) shares* or *additional contributed (paid-in) capital*. Generally, but not universally, the distinction between ordinary shares and additional contributed capital has little legal import, but may be maintained for financial reporting purposes nonetheless.

Additional contributed capital represents all capital contributed to a corporation other than that defined as par or stated value. Additional contributed capital can arise from proceeds received from the sale of ordinary and preferred shares in excess of their par or stated values. It can also arise from transactions relating to the following:

1. Sale of shares previously issued and subsequently reacquired by the corporation (treasury shares)
2. Retirement of previously outstanding shares
3. Payment of share dividends in a manner that justifies the dividend being recorded at the market value of the shares distributed
4. Lapse of share purchase warrants or the forfeiture of share subscriptions, if these result in the retaining by the corporation of any partial proceeds received prior to forfeiture
5. Warrants that are detachable from bonds
6. Conversion of convertible bonds
7. Other gains on the company's own shares, such as that which results from certain share option plans

When the amounts are material, the sources of additional contributed capital should be described in the financial statements.

Examples of various transactions giving rise to (or reducing) additional contributed capital accounts are set forth below.

Examples of additional contributed capital transactions

Alta Vena Company issues 2,000 shares of ordinary shares having a par value of €1, for a total price of €8,000. The following entry records the transaction:

Cash	8,000	
Ordinary shares		2,000
Additional contributed capital		6,000

Alta Vena Company buys back 2,000 shares of its own ordinary share for €10,000 and then sells these shares to investors for €15,000. The following entries record the buyback and sale transactions, respectively, assuming the use of the cost method of accounting for treasury share:

Treasury shares	10,000	
Cash		10,000
Cash	15,000	
Treasury shares		10,000
Additional contributed capital		5,000

Alta Vena Company buys back 2,000 shares of its own €1 par value ordinary shares (which it had originally sold for €8,000) for €9,000 and retires the shares, which it records with the following entry:

Ordinary shares	6,000	
Additional contributed capital	2,000	
Retained earnings	1,000	
Cash		10,000

Alta Vena Company issues a small share dividend of 5,000 ordinary shares at the market price of €8 per share. Each share has a par value of €1. The following entry records the transaction:

Retained earnings	40,000	
Ordinary shares		5,000
Additional contributed capital		35,000

Alta Vena Company previously has recorded €1,000 of share options outstanding as part of a compensation agreement. The options expire a year later, resulting in the following entry:

Share options outstanding	1,000	
Additional contributed capital		1,000

Alta Vena Company sells 2,000 of par €1,000 bonds, as well as 2,000 attached warrants having a market value of €15 each. Pro rata apportionment of the €2,000,000 cash received between the bonds and warrants results in the following entry:

Cash	2,000,000	
Discount on bonds payable	29,557	
Bonds payable		2,000,000
Additional contributed capital—warrants		29,557

Alta Vena's bondholders convert a €1,000 bond with an unamortized premium of €40 and a market value of €1,016 into 127 shares of €1 par ordinary share whose market value is €8 per share. This results in the following entry:

Bonds payable	1,000	
Premium on bonds payable	40	
Ordinary shares		913
Additional contributed capital—warrants		127

Donated capital. Donated capital can result from an outright gift to the corporation (e.g., a major shareholder donates land or other assets to the company in a nonreciprocal transfer) or may result when services are provided to the corporation. Under current US GAAP, such nonreciprocal transactions will be recognized as revenue in the period the contribution is received. IFRS does not, at present, address contributions or donations.

In these situations, historical cost is not adequate to reflect properly the substance of the transaction, since the historical cost to the corporation would be zero. Accordingly, these events should be reflected at fair value. If long-lived assets are donated to the corporation, they should be recorded at their fair value at the date of donation, and the amount so recorded should be depreciated over the normal useful economic life of such assets. If donations are conditional in nature, they should not be reflected formally in the accounts until the appropriate conditions have been satisfied. However, disclosure might still be required in the financial statements of both the assets donated and the conditions required to be met.

Example of donated capital

A board member of the for-profit organization Village Social Services donates land to the organization that has a fair market value of €1 million. Village Social Services records the donation with the following entry:

Land	1,000,000	
Revenue—donations		1,000,000

The same board member donates one year of accounting labor to Village Social Services. The fair value of services rendered is €75,000. Village Social Services records the donation with the following entry:

Salaries—accounting department	75,000	
Revenue—donations		75,000

The board member also donates one year of free rent of a local building to Village Social Services. The annual rent in similar facilities is €45,000. Village Social Services records the donation with the following entry:

Rent expense	45,000	
Revenue—donations		45,000

Finally, the board member pays off a €100,000 debt owed by Village Social Services. Village Social Services records the donation with the following entry:

Notes payable	100,000	
Revenue—donations		100,000

Following the closing of the fiscal period, the effect of all the foregoing donations will be reflected in Village Social Services' retained earnings account.

Note that IFRS explicitly addresses the proper accounting for government grants (see discussion in Chapter 26), which may differ from the foregoing illustrative example, which involved private donations only. Readers should be alert to further developments in this area.

Compound and Convertible Equity Instruments

Entities sometimes issue preferred shares which is convertible into ordinary shares. Given that both the preferred and ordinary shares represent equity in the issuer, there is no real concern regarding the proper accounting, as the entire proceeds of the offering are credited to equity accounts. The treatment of convertible preferred shares at its issuance is no different from that of nonconvertible preferred. When it is converted, the book value approach is used to account for the conversion. Use of the market value approach would entail a gain or loss for which there is no theoretical justification, since the total amount of contributed capital does not change when the share capital is converted. When the preferred shares are converted, the "Preferred shares" and related "Additional contributed capital—preferred share" accounts are debited for their original values when purchased, and "Ordinary share" and "Additional contributed capital—ordinary shares" (if an excess over par or stated value exists) are credited. If the book value of the preferred shares is less than the total par value of the ordinary shares being issued, retained earnings is charged for the difference. This charge is supported by the rationale that the preferred shareholders are offered an additional return to facilitate their conversion to ordinary share. Some jurisdictions require that this excess instead reduce additional contributed capital from other sources.

On the other hand, the issuance of debt that is convertible into equity (almost always into ordinary shares) does trigger accounting complexities. Under IAS 32, it is necessary for the issuer of nonderivative financial instruments to ascertain whether it contains both liability and equity components. If the instrument does contain both elements (e.g., debentures convertible into ordinary shares), these components must be separated and accounted for according to their respective natures.

In the case of convertible debt, the instrument is viewed as being constituted of both an unconditional promise to pay (a liability) and an option granting the holder the right, but not the obligation, to obtain the issuer's shares under a fixed conversion ratio arrangement. (Under provisions of IAS 32, unless the number of shares that can be obtained on conversion is fixed, the conversion option is not an equity instrument.) This option, at issuance date, is an equity instrument and must be accounted for as such by the issuer, whether subsequently exercised or not.

The amount allocated to equity is the residual derived by deducting the fair value of the liability component (typically, by discounting to present value the future principal and interest payments on the debt by the relevant interest rate) from the total proceeds of issuance. It would not be acceptable to derive the amount to be allocated to debt as a residual, on the other hand—a conservative rule that effectively maximizes the allocation to debt and minimizes the allocation to equity.

Retained Earnings

Accounting traditionally has clearly distinguished between equity contributed by owners (including donations from owners) and that resulting from the operating results of the reporting entity, consisting mainly of accumulated earnings since the entity's inception less amounts distributed to shareholders (i.e., dividends). Equity in each of these two categories is generically distinct from the other, and financial statement users need to be informed of the composition of shareholders' equity so that, for example, the cumulative profitability of the entity can be accurately gauged.

Legal capital (the defined aggregate par or stated value of the issued shares), additional contributed capital, and donated capital, collectively represent the contributed capital of the corporation. The other major source of capital is retained earnings, which represents the accumulated amount of earnings of the corporation from the date of inception (or from the date of reorganization) less the cumulative amount of distributions made to shareholders and other charges to retained earnings (e.g., from treasury share transactions). The distributions to shareholders generally take the form of dividend payments, but may take other forms as well, such as the reacquisition of shares for amounts in excess of the original issuance proceeds. They key events impacting retained earnings are as follows:

- Dividends
- Certain sales of shares held in the treasury at amounts below acquisition cost
- Certain share retirements at amounts in excess of book value
- Prior period adjustments
- Recapitalizations and reorganizations

Examples of retained earnings transactions

Baking Bread Co. declares a dividend of €84,000, which it records with the following entry:

Retained earnings	84,000	
Dividends payable		84,000

Baking Bread acquires 3,000 shares of its own €1 par value ordinary shares for €15,000, and then resells it for €12,000. The following entries record the buyback and sale transactions, respectively, assuming the use of the cost method of accounting for treasury shares:

Treasury shares	15,000	
Cash		15,000
Cash	12,000	
Retained earnings	3,000	
Treasury shares		15,000

Baking Bread buys back 12,000 shares of its own €1 par value ordinary shares (which it had originally sold for €60,000) for €70,000 and retires the shares, which it records with the following entry:

Ordinary shares	12,000	
Additional contributed capital	48,000	
Retained earnings	10,000	
Cash		70,000

Baking Bread's accountant makes a mathematical mistake in calculating depreciation, requiring a prior period reduction of €30,000 to the accumulated depreciation account, and corresponding increases in its income tax payable and retained earnings accounts. Baking Bread's income tax rate is 35%. It records this transaction with the following entry:

Accumulated depreciation	30,000	
Income taxes payable		10,500
Retained earnings		19,500

Retained earnings are also affected by action taken by the corporation's board of directors. Appropriation serves disclosure purposes and serves to restrict dividend payments but does nothing to provide any resources for satisfaction of the contingent loss or other underlying purpose for which the appropriation has been made. Any appropriation made from retained earnings must eventually be returned to the retained earnings account. It is not permissible to charge losses against the appropriation account nor to credit any realized gain to that account. The use of appropriated retained earnings has diminished significantly over the years.

An important rule relating to retained earnings is that transactions in a corporation's own shares can result in a reduction of retained earnings (i.e., a deficiency on such transactions can be charged to retained earnings) but cannot result in an increase in retained earnings (any excesses on such transactions are credited to contributed capital, never to retained earnings).

If a series of operating losses have been incurred or distributions to shareholders in excess of accumulated earnings have been made and if there is a debit balance in retained earnings, the account is generally referred to as accumulated deficit.

Dividends and Distributions

Cash dividends. Dividends represent the pro rata distribution of earnings to the owners of the corporation. The amount and the allocation between the preferred and ordinary shareholders is a function of the stipulated preferential dividend rate, the presence or absence of (1) a participation feature, (2) a cumulative feature, and (3) arrearages on the preferred shares, and the wishes of the board of directors. Dividends, even preferred share dividends where a cumulative feature exists, do not accrue. Dividends become a liability of the corporation only when they are declared by the board of directors.

Traditionally, corporations were not allowed to declare dividends in excess of the amount of retained earnings. Alternatively, a corporation could pay dividends out of retained earnings and additional contributed capital but could not exceed the total of these categories (i.e., they could not impair legal capital by the payment of dividends). Local company law obviously dictates, directly or by implication, the accounting to be applied in many of these situations. In the US, states that have adopted the Model Business Corporation Act grant more latitude to the directors. Corporations can now, in certain US jurisdictions, declare and pay dividends in excess of the book amount of retained earnings if the directors conclude that, after the payment of such dividends, the fair value of the corporation's net assets will still be a positive amount. Thus, directors can declare dividends out of unrealized appreciation, which, in certain industries, can be a significant source of dividends beyond the realized and recognized accumulated earnings of the corporation. This action, however, represents a major departure from traditional practice and demands both careful consideration and adequate disclosure.

Three important dividend dates are

1. The declaration date
2. The record date
3. The payment date

The declaration date governs the incurrence of a legal liability by the corporation. The record date refers to that point in time when a determination is made as to which specific registered shareholders will receive dividends and in what amounts. Finally, the payment date relates to the date when the distribution of the dividend takes place. These concepts are illustrated in the following example:

Example of payment of dividends

On May 1, 2009, the directors of River Corp. declare a €75 per share quarterly dividend on River Corp.'s 650,000 outstanding ordinary shares. The dividend is payable May 25 to holders of record May 15.

May 1	Retained earnings (or Dividends)	487,500	
	Dividends payable		487,500
May 15	No entry		
May 25	Dividends payable	487,500	
	Cash		487,500

If a dividends account is used, it is closed directly to retained earnings at year-end.

Dividends may be made in the form of cash, property, or scrip, which is a form of short-term note payable. Cash dividends are either a given dollar amount per share or a percentage of par or stated value. Property dividends consist of the distribution of any assets other than cash (e.g., inventory or equipment). Finally, scrip dividends are promissory notes due at some time in the future, sometimes bearing interest until final payment is made.

Occasionally, what appear to be disproportionate dividend distributions are paid to some but not all of the owners of closely held corporations. Such transactions need to be analyzed carefully. In some cases these may actually represent compensation paid to the recipients. In other instances, these may be a true dividend paid to all shareholders on a pro rata basis, to which certain shareholders have waived their rights. If the former, the distribution should not be accounted for as a dividend but as compensation or some other expense category and included in the statement of comprehensive income. If the latter, the dividend should be grossed up to reflect payment on a proportional basis to all the shareholders, with an offsetting capital contribution to the company recognized as having been effectively made by those to whom payments were not made.

Upon occasion, dividends may be paid in property other than cash. For example, a merchandising firm may distribute merchandise to shareholders in lieu of cash, although this makes it more difficult to assure absolute proportionality. When, say, inventory is used to distribute earnings to shareholders, the accounting is similar to that shown above, except inventory is credited rather than cash. IFRS does not address this situation, but a reasonable interpretation of other IFRS and of national GAAP standards would suggest that these distributions should be measured at fair value, and thus there will be some revenue to be recognized by the dividend-paying entity. For example, if inventory carried at cost of $100,000, and having a fair value of $125,000, is distributed to shareholders as a dividend, the entity would record profit of $25,000 and a dividend payment of $125,000.

Share dividends. In many jurisdictions, corporations may issue "dividends" in the form of additional shares in the entity itself. Since these are pro rata for all shareholders (most jurisdictions prohibit nonproportional dividend payments, whether in cash or additional shares), effectively these do not actually give the shareholders anything of value. Indeed, a shareholder holding, say, 2% of the entity's outstanding ordinary shares before the share dividend will still hold 2% of the new, larger number of outstanding shares after the dividend.

Share dividends represent neither an actual distribution of the assets of the corporation nor a promise to distribute those assets. For this reason, a share dividend is not considered a legal liability when declared (in contrast to cash dividends, which are generally viewed as legal obligations once declared) or a taxable transaction. However, these are legal, not accounting determinations and may vary from one jurisdiction to another.

Notwithstanding the foregoing, share dividends are often viewed by shareholders as being indicative of company success, particularly when these are of minor amount, say 5% of the previously outstanding number of shares. For that reason, despite the recognition that a share dividend is not a distribution of earnings, the accounting treatment of relatively insignificant share dividends (defined under US GAAP, for example, as being less than 20% to 25% of the outstanding shares prior to declaration) is consistent with its being a real dividend. Accordingly, retained earnings are debited for the fair market value of the shares to be paid as a dividend, and the share capital and additional contributed capital accounts are credited for the appropriate amounts based on the par or stated value of the shares, if any. A share dividend declared but not yet paid is classified as such in the shareholders' equity section of the statement of financial position. Since such a dividend never reduces assets, it cannot be a liability.

IFRS does not address share dividends, so this guidance is based on other national GAAP. This suggests that relatively small share dividends are accounted for as distributions of earnings, while large share dividends, which are commonly called share splits, are not so reported. The selection of 20 to 25% as the threshold for recognizing a share dividend as an earnings distribution is arbitrary, but it is based somewhat on the empirical evidence that small share dividends tend not to result in a reduced market price per share for outstanding shares. In theory, any share dividend should result in a reduction of the market value of outstanding shares in an inverse relationship to the size of the share dividend. The aggregate value of the outstanding shares should not change, but the greater number of shares outstanding after the share dividend should necessitate a lower per share price. As noted, however, the declaration of small share dividends tends not to have this impact, and this phenomenon supports the accounting treatment.

On the other hand, when share dividends are larger in magnitude, it is observed that per share market value declines after declaration of the dividend. In such situations it would not be valid to treat the share dividend as an earnings distribution. Rather, it should be accounted for as a split. The precise treatment depends on the legal requirements of the jurisdiction of incorporation and on whether the existing par value or stated value is reduced concurrent with the share split.

If the par value is not reduced for a large share dividend and if the law of the jurisdiction of incorporation requires that earnings be capitalized in an amount equal to the aggregate of the par value of the share dividend declared, the event should be described as a share split effected in the form of a dividend, with a charge to retained earnings and a credit to the ordinary share account for the aggregate par or stated value. When the par or stated value is reduced in recognition of the split and the pertinent laws do not require treatment as a dividend, there is no formal entry to record the split but merely a notation that the number of shares outstanding has increased and the per share par or stated value has decreased accordingly.

The concepts of small versus large share dividends are illustrated in the following examples:

Assume that shareholders' equity for the Wasabi Corp. on November 1, 2009, is as follows:

Ordinary shares €1 par, 100,000 shares outstanding	€ 100,000
Contributed capital in excess of par	1,100,000
Retained earnings	750,000

Small share dividend: On November 10, 2009, the directors of Wasabi Corp. declared a 15% share dividend, or a dividend of 1.5 ordinary shares for every 10 shares held. Before the share dividend, the share is selling for €23 per share. After the 15% share dividend, each original share worth €23 will become 1.15 shares, each with a value of €20 (€23/1.15). The share dividend is to be recorded at the market value of the new shares issued, or €300,000 (15,000 new shares at the postdividend price of €20). The entries to record the declaration of the dividend and the issuance of shares (on November 30) by Wasabi Corp. are as follows:

Nov. 10	Retained earnings		€300,000	
	Share dividends distributable			15,000
	Contributed capital in excess of par			285,000
Nov. 30	Share dividends distributable		15,000	
	Ordinary shares, €1 par			15,000

Large share dividend: In practice, US GAAP results in the par or stated value of the newly issued shares being transferred to the share capital account from either retained earnings or contributed capital in excess of par. To illustrate, assume that on November 10, 2009, Wasabi Corp. declares a 50% large share dividend, a dividend of one share for every two held. Legal requirements call for the transfer to share capital of an amount equal to the par value of the shares issued. Entries for the declaration on November 10 and the issuance of 50,000 new shares (=100,000 × .50) on November 30 are as follows:

Nov. 10	Retained earnings	50,000	
	Share dividends distributable		50,000
	OR		
	Contributed capital in excess of par	50,000	
	Share dividends distributable		50,000
Nov. 30	Share dividends distributable	50,000	
	Ordinary shares, €1 par		50,000

Liquidating dividends. Liquidating dividends are not distributions of earnings, but rather, a return of capital to the investing shareholders. A liquidating dividend is normally recorded by the declarer through charging additional contributed capital rather than retained earnings. The exact accounting for a liquidating dividend is affected by the laws where the business is incorporated, and these laws vary among jurisdictions. There will often be tax implications of liquidating dividend payments, as well.

Accounting for Treasury Share Transactions

The term treasury share refers to the entity's shares that were issued but subsequently reacquired and are being held ("in the company's treasury") without having been canceled. An entity may buy back its own shares, subject to laws of the jurisdiction of incorporation, for possibly many different and legitimate business purposes, such as to have on hand for later share-based payments to employees or vendors, or to decrease the "float" of shares outstanding—which may be done to provide upward pressure on the quoted price of the share or increase the earnings per share by decreasing the number of outstanding shares.

IFRS does not specifically address the accounting for treasury share transactions. As a general principle, however, "earnings" cannot be created by transactions in an entity's own shares, and thus the proper accounting would be to report these as capital transactions only. US GAAP, on the other hand, offers explicit guidance on the accounting for treasury share transactions, and this is the basis for the suggested approaches in the following paragraphs.

Treasury shares do not reduce the number of shares issued but do reduce the number of shares outstanding, as well as total shareholders' equity. These shares are not eligible to receive cash dividends. Treasury shares are not an asset, although in some circumstances, they may be presented as an asset if adequately disclosed. Reacquired shares that are awaiting delivery to satisfy a liability created by the firm's compensation plan or reacquired shares that are held in a profit-sharing trust is still considered outstanding and would not be considered treasury shares. In each case, the share would be presented as an asset with the accompanying footnote disclosure.

There are three approaches for the treatment of treasury shares under US GAAP: the cost, par value, and constructive retirement methods.

Cost method. Under the cost method, the gross cost of the shares reacquired is charged to a contra equity account (treasury shares). The equity accounts that were credited for the original share issuance (ordinary shares, contributed capital in excess of par, etc.) remain intact. When the treasury shares are reissued, proceeds in excess of cost are credited to a contributed capital account. Any deficiency is charged to retained earnings (unless contributed capital from previous treasury share transactions exists, in which case the deficiency is charged to that account, with any excess charged to retained earnings). If many treasury share purchases are made, a cost flow assumption (e.g., FIFO or specific identification) should be adopted to compute excesses and deficiencies on subsequent share reissuances. The advantage of the cost method is that it avoids identifying and accounting for amounts related to the original issuance of the shares, and is therefore the simpler more frequently used method. The cost method is most consistent with the one-transaction concept. This concept takes the view that the classification of shareholders' equity should not be affected simply because the corporation was the middle "person" in an exchange of shares from one shareholder to another. In substance, there is only a transfer of shares between two shareholders. Since the original balances in the equity accounts are left undisturbed, its use is most acceptable when the firm acquires its shares for reasons other than retirement, or when its ultimate disposition has not yet been decided.

Par value method. Under the second approach, the par value method, the treasury share account is charged only for the aggregate par (or stated) value of the shares reacquired. Other contributed capital accounts (excess over par value, etc.) are relieved in proportion to the amounts recognized on the original issuance of the shares. The treasury share acquisition is treated almost as a retirement. However, the ordinary (or preferred) share account continues at the original amount, thereby preserving the distinction between an actual retirement and a treasury share transaction.

When the treasury shares accounted for by the par value method are subsequently resold, the excess of the sale price over par value is credited to contributed capital. A reissuance for a price below par value does not create a contingent liability for the purchaser, as sale of shares at amounts below par may do under the laws of certain jurisdictions. It is generally only the original purchaser who risks this obligation to the entity's creditors.

Constructive retirement method. The constructive retirement method is similar to the par value method except that the aggregate par (or stated) value of the reacquired shares is charged to the share account rather than to the treasury share account. This method is superior when (1) it is management's intention not to reissue the shares within a reasonable time period, or (2) the jurisdiction of incorporation defines reacquired shares as having been retired.

The two-transaction concept is most consistent with the par value and constructive retirement methods. First, the reacquisition of the firm's shares is viewed as constituting a contraction of its capital structure. Second, the reissuance of the shares is the same as issuing new shares. There is little difference between the purchase and subsequent reissuance of treasury shares and the acquisition and retirement of previously issued shares and the issuance of new shares.

Treasury shares originally accounted for by the cost method can subsequently be restated to conform to the constructive retirement method. If shares were acquired with the intention that they would be reissued and it is later determined that such reissuance is unlikely, it is proper to restate the transaction.

Example of accounting for treasury share

1. 100 shares (€50 par value) that were sold originally for €60 per share are later reacquired for €70 each.
2. All 100 shares are subsequently resold for a total of €7,500.

To record the acquisition, the entry is

Cost method			*Par value method*			*Constructive retirement method*		
Treasury shares	7,000		Treasury shares	5,000		Ordinary shares	5,000	
Cash		7,000	Additional contributed			Additional contrib-		
			capital—ordinary share	1,000		uted capital—		
						ordinary share	1,000	
			Retained earnings	1,000		Retained earnings	1,000	
			Cash		7,000	Cash		7,000

To record the resale, the entry is

Cost method			*Par value method*			*Constructive retirement method*		
Cash	7,500		Cash	7,500		Cash	7,500	
Treasury shares		7,000	Treasury shares		5,000	Ordinary shares		5,000
Additional con-			Additional contributed			Additional contrib-		
tributed capital—			capital—ordinary			uted capital—		
treasury shares		500	shares		2,500	ordinary shares		2,500

If the shares had been resold for €6,500, the entry is

Cost method			*Par value method*			*Constructive retirement method*		
Cash	6,500		Cash	6,500		Cash	6,500	
*Retained earnings	500		Treasury shares		5,000	Ordinary shares		5,000
Treasury shares		7,000	Additional contributed			Additional contributed		
			capital—ordinary share		1,500	capital—ordinary share		1,500

* *"Additional contributed capital—treasury shares" or "Additional contributed capital—retired shares" of that issue would be debited first to the extent it exists.*

Alternatively, under the par or constructive retirement methods, any portion of or the entire deficiency on the treasury share acquisition may be debited to retained earnings without allocation to contributed capital. Any excesses would always be credited to an "Additional contributed capital—retired shares" account or its equivalent.

The laws of some jurisdictions govern the circumstances under which a corporation may acquire treasury share and they may prescribe the accounting for the share. For example, a charge to retained earnings may be required in an amount equal to the treasury share's total cost. In such cases, the accounting according to state law prevails. Also, some jurisdictions define excess purchase cost of reacquired (i.e., treasury) shares as distributions to shareholders that are no different in nature than dividends. In such cases, the financial statement presentation should adequately disclose the substance of these transactions (e.g., by presenting both dividends and excess reacquisition costs together in the retained earnings statement).

When a firm decides to retire the treasury share formally, the journal entry is dependent on the method used to account for the share. Using the original sale and reacquisition data from the illustration above, the following entry would be made:

Cost method			*Par value method*		
Ordinary shares	5,000		Ordinary shares	5,000	
Additional contributed capital—ordinary			Treasury shares		
shares	1,000				5,000
*Retained earnings	1,000				
Treasury shares		7,000			

* *"Additional contributed capital—treasury shares" may be debited to the extent that it exists.*

If the constructive retirement method were used to record the treasury share purchase, no additional entry would be necessary on formal retirement of the shares.

After the entry is made, the pro rata portion of all contributed capital existing for that issue (i.e., capital shares and additional contributed capital) will have been eliminated. If share is purchased for immediate retirement (i.e., not put into the treasury) the entry to record the retirement is the same as that made under the constructive retirement method.

In the case of donated treasury shares, the intentions of management are important. If the shares are to be retired, the capital share account is debited for the par or stated value of the shares, "Donated capital" is credited for the fair market value, and "Additional contributed capital—retired shares" is debited or credited for the difference. If the intention of management is to reissue the shares, three methods of accounting are available. The first two methods, cost and par value, are analogous to the aforementioned treasury share methods except that "Donated capital" is credited at the time of receipt and debited at the time of reissuance. Under the cost method, the current market value of the shares is recorded (an apparent contradiction), whereas under the par value method, the par or stated value is used. Under the last method, only a memorandum entry is made to indicate the number of shares received. No journal entry is made at the time of receipt. At the time of reissuance, the entire proceeds are credited to "Donated capital." The method actually used is generally dependent on the circumstances involving the donation and the preference of the reporting entity itself; any legal restrictions must also be considered in making this determination.

Accounting for Share-Based Payments

Prior to the IASB's issuance of IFRS 2, *Share-Based Payment,* there had been no guidance under IFRS to the accounting for employee share-based compensation or other share-based payment situations. This was an area seriously in need of attention—not merely under IFRS, which lacked any requirements, but also under most national GAAP, where (unlike in North America), the issuance of share options to employees had only recently become a common business practice. US GAAP had first (under APB 25) permitted ignoring the cost of options granted to employees under normal circumstances (where exercise prices at least equaled grant-date market prices), but belatedly had attempted to deal with this more substantively in the mid-1990s, but the resulting standard had become severely compromised due to strongly voiced opposition to full fair value accounting. Subsequent to the development and promulgation of IFRS 2, a revised US standard (FAS 123[R]) largely adopted the IFRS approach, under which expense equal to the fair value of share-based compensation must be given statement of comprehensive income recognition.

Overview. The IASB issued its final standard on share-based compensation in 2004, for application beginning January 1, 2005. The general principle is that all share-based payment transactions should be recognized in the financial statements, using fair value measurement, with expense recognized when the goods are received or services are rendered. Furthermore—and very importantly—the same recognition and measurement standards apply to both public and private companies. Given the added challenge of estimating fair value for nontraded shares, this was a major point of contention among those responding to the draft standard. Realistically, entities granting share-based compensation to executives and other employees almost always have a sense of the value being transferred, for otherwise these bargained transactions would not make business sense, nor would they satisfy the demands or expectations of the recipients.

In theory, transactions in which goods or services are received as consideration for equity instruments of the entity are to be measured at the fair value of the goods or services received by the reporting entity. However, if their value cannot be readily determined (as the standard suggests is the case for employee services in limited situations) they are to be measured with reference to the fair value of the equity instruments granted.

In the case of transactions with parties other than employees, there is a rebuttable presumption that the fair value of the goods or services received is more readily determinable than is the value of the shares granted. This follows logically from the fact that, in arm's-length transactions, it should be the case that management would be highly cognizant of the value it has received (whether merchandise, plant assets, personal services, etc.) and that such data would not pose any effort to gather and utilize. Arguments to the contrary raise basic questions about managerial performance and can rarely be given much credence.

IFRIC 2 provides additional guidance to transactions in which the entity cannot identify specifically some or all of the goods or services received. If the identifiable consideration received (if any) appears to be less than the fair value of the equity instruments granted or liability incurred, typically this situation indicates that other consideration (i.e., unidentifiable goods or services) has also been (or will be) received. The entity should measure the unidentifiable goods or services received (or to be received) at the grant date as the difference between the fair value of the share-based payment given or promised and the fair value of any identifiable goods or services received (or to be received).

Where payment is made or promised in the reporting entity's shares only, the value is determined using a fair value technique that computes the cost at the date of the transaction, which is not subsequently revised, absent revised terms which increase the amount of fair value to be transferred to the recipients. In contrast, for cash-settled transactions, the liability should be remeasured at each reporting date until it is settled.

For transactions measured at the fair value of the equity instruments granted (such as compensation transactions with employees), fair value is estimated at grant date. A point of contention here has often been whether grant date or exercise date is the more appropriate reference point, but the logic of the former is that the economic decision, and the employee's contractual commitment, were made as of the grant date, and the accidents of timing of subsequent exercise (or, in some cases, forfeiture) are not indicative of the bargained-for value of the transaction. The grant date is when the employee accepts the commitment, not when the offer is first made. Accordingly, IFRS 2 requires the use of grant date to ascertain the fair value to be associated with the transaction.

When share capital is issued immediately, measurement is not generally difficult. For example, if 100 shares having a fair (market) value of €33 per share are given outright to an employee, the compensation cost is simply computed as €3,300. Since the grant vests immediately (no future service is demanded from the recipient), the expense is immediately reported.

The more problematic situation is when employees (or others) are granted *options* to later acquire shares that permit exercise over a defined time horizon. The holders' ability to wait and later assess the desirability of exercising the options has value—and the lengthier the period until the options expire, the more likely the underlying shares will increase in value, and thus the greater is the value of the option. Even if the underlying shares are publicly traded, the value of the options will be subject to some debate. Only when the options themselves are traded (which is rarely the case with employee share options, which are restricted to the grantees themselves) will fair value be directly determinable by observation. If market options on the entity's shares do trade, the value will likely exceed that to be attributed to nontradable employee share options, even if having nominally similar terms (exercise dates, prices, etc.).

The standard holds that, to estimate the fair value of a share option in the likely instance where an observable market price for that option does not exist, an *option pricing model* should be used. IFRS 2 does not specify which particular model should be used. The entity must disclose the model used, the inputs to that model, and various other information bearing on how fair value was computed. In practice, these models are all fairly sophisticated and complicated (although commercially available software promises to ease the computational complexities) and a number of the variables have inherently subjective aspects.

One issue that has to be dealt with involves the tax treatment of options, which varies across jurisdictions. In most instances the tax treatment will not comply with the fair value measurement mandated under IFRS 2, and thus there will be a need for specific guidance as to the accounting for the tax effects of granting the options and of the ultimate exercise of those options, if they are not forfeited by the option holders. This is described later in this discussion.

The tax treatment of share-based payments prescribed under IFRS 2 differs from that under US GAAP standard, FAS 123(R). The *Basis for Conclusions* of IFRS 2 notes that in jurisdictions where a tax deduction is given, such as the US, the measurement of the tax deduction does not coincide with that of the accounting deduction. Where the tax deduction is in excess of the expense reported in the statement of comprehensive income, the excess is taken directly to equity.

Employee share options. For equity-settled transactions, the fundamental approach is to expense the value of share options granted over the period during which the employee is earning the option—that is, the period until the option vests (becomes unconditional). If the options vest (become exercisable) immediately, the employee receiving the grant cannot be compelled to perform future services, and accordingly the fair value of the options is compensation in the period of the grant. More commonly, however, there will be a period (several years, typically) of future services required before the options may be exercised; in those cases, compensation is to be recognized over that vesting period. There are two practical difficulties with this: (1) estimating the value of the share options granted (true even if vesting is immediate); and (2) allowing for the fact that not all options initially granted will ultimately vest or, if they vest, be exercised by the holders.

Measurement. IFRS 2 requires that where directly observable market prices are not available (which is virtually always the case for employee share options, since they cannot normally be sold), the entity must estimate fair value using a valuation technique that is "consistent with generally accepted valuation methodologies for pricing financial instruments, and shall incorporate all factors and assumptions that knowledgeable, willing market participants would consider in setting the price." No specific valuation method is endorsed by the standard, however.

Appendix B of the standard notes that all acceptable option pricing models take into account

- The exercise price of the option
- The current market price of the share
- The expected volatility of the share price
- The dividends expected to be paid on the shares
- The risk-free interest rate
- The life of the option

In essence, the grant date value of the share option is the current market price, less the present value of the exercise price, less the dividends that will not be received during the vesting period, adjusted for the expected volatility. The time value of money, as is well understood, arises because the holder of an option is not required to pay the exercise price until the exercise date. Instead, the holder of the option can invest his funds elsewhere, while waiting to exercise the option. According to IFRS 2, the time value of money component is determined by reference to the rate of return available on *risk-free* securities. If the share pays a *dividend,* or is expected to pay a dividend during the life of the option, the value to the holder of the option from delaying payment of the exercise price is only the excess (if any) of the return available on a risk-free security over the return available from exercising the option today and owning the shares. The time value of money component for a divided-paying share equals the discounted present value of the expected interest income that could be earned less the discounted present value of the expected dividends that will be forgone during the expected life of the option.

The time value associated with *volatility* represents the ability of the holder to profit from appreciation of the underlying shares while being exposed to the loss of only the option premium, and not the full current value of the shares. A more volatile share has a higher probability of big increases or decreases in price, compared with one having lower volatility. As a result, an option on a highly volatile share has a higher probability of a big payoff than an option on a less volatile share, and so has a higher value relating to volatility fair value component. The longer the option term, the more likely, for any given degree of volatility, that the share price will appreciate before option expiration, making exercise attractive. Greater volatility, and longer term, each contribute to the value of the option.

Volatility is the measure of the amount by which a share's price fluctuates during a period. It is expressed as a percentage because it relates share price fluctuations during a period to the share's price at the beginning of the period. Expected annualized volatility is the predicted amount that is the input to the option pricing model. This is calculated largely from the share's historical price fluctuations.

To illustrate this basic concept, assume that the present market price of the underlying shares is €20 per share, and the option plan grants the recipient the right to purchase shares at today's market price at any time during the next five years. If a risk-free rate, such as that available on US Treasury notes having maturities of five years is 5%, then the present value of the future payment of €20 is €15.67 $\{= [€20 \div (1.05)^5]\}$, which suggests that the option has a value of (€20 – €15.67 =) €4.33 per share before considering the value of lost dividends. If the shares are expected to pay a dividend of €.40 per share per year, the present value of the dividend stream that the option holder will forego until exercise five years hence is about €1.64, discounting again at 5%. Therefore, the *net* value of the option being granted, assuming it is expected to be held to the expiration date before being exercised, is (€4.33 – €1.64 =) €2.69 per share. (Although the foregoing computation was based on the full five-year life of the option, the actual requirement is to use the *expected term* of the option, which may be shorter.)

Commercial software is readily available to carry out these calculations. However, accountants must understand the theory underlying these matters so that the software can be appropriately employed and the results verified. Independent auditors, of course, have additional challenges in verifying the financial statement impacts of share-based compensation plans.

Estimating volatility does however, involve special problems for unlisted or newly listed companies, since the estimate is usually based on an observation of past market movements, which are not available for such entities. The *Basis for Conclusions* says that IASB decided that, nonetheless, an estimate of volatility should still be made. Appendix B of IFRS 2 states that newly listed entities should compute actual volatility for whatever period this information is available, and should also consider volatility in the prices of shares of other companies operating in the same industry. Unlisted entities should consider the volatility of prices of listed entities in the same industry, or, where valuing them on the basis of a model, such as net earnings, should use the volatility of the earnings.

IASB considered the effect of the *nontransferability* on the value of the option. The standard option pricing models (such as Black-Scholes) were developed to value traded options and do not take into account nontransferability. It came to the view that nontransferability generally led to the option being exercised early, and that this should be reflected in the expected term of the option, rather than by any explicit adjustment for nontransferability itself.

The likelihood of the option vesting is a function of the vesting conditions. IASB concluded that these conditions should not be factored into the value of the option, but should be reflected in calculating the number of options to be expensed. For example, if an entity granted options to 500 employees, the likelihood that only 350 would satisfy the vesting conditions should be used to determine the number of options expensed, and this should be subsequently adjusted in the light of actual experience as it unfolds.

Accounting for Employee Share Options under IFRS 2: Valuation Models

IFRS 2 fully imposes a fair value approach to measuring the effect of share options granted to employees. It recognizes that directly observable prices for employee options are not likely to exist, and thus that valuation models will have to be employee in most, or almost all, instances. The standard speaks to the relative strengths of two types of approaches: the venerable Black-Scholes (now called Black-Scholes-Merton) option pricing model, designed specifically to price publicly traded European-style options (exercisable only at the expiration date) and subject to criticism as to possible inapplicability to nonmarketable American-style options; and the mathematically more challenging but more flexible lattice models, such as the binomial. IFRS 2 does not dictate choice of model and acknowledges that the Black-Scholes model may be validly applied in many situations.

To provide a more detailed examination of these two major types of options valuation approaches, several examples will now be developed.

Both valuation models (hereinafter referred to as BSM and binomial) must take into account the following factors, at a minimum:

1. Exercise price of the option
2. Expected term of the option, taking into account several things including the contractual term of the option, vesting requirements, and postvesting employee termination behaviors
3. Current price of the underlying share
4. Expected volatility of the price of the underlying share
5. Expected dividends on the underlying share
6. Risk-free interest rate(s) for the expected term of the option

In practice, there are likely to be ranges of reasonable estimates for expected volatility, dividends, and option term. The closed form models, of which BSM is the most widely regarded, are predicated on a deterministic set of assumptions that remain invariant over the full term of the option. For example, the expected dividend on the shares on which options are issued must be a fixed amount each period over the full term of the option. In the real world, of course, the condition of invariability is almost never satisfied. For this reason, current thinking is that a lattice model, of which the binomial model is an example, would be preferred. Lattice models explicitly identify nodes, such as the anniversaries of the grant date, at each of which new parameter values can be specified (e.g., expected dividends can be independently defined each period).

Other features that may affect the value of the option include changes in the issuer's credit risk, if the value of the awards contains cash settlement features (i.e., if they are liability instruments). Also, contingent features that could cause either a loss of equity shares earned or reduced realized gains from sale of equity instruments earned, such as a "clawback" feature (for example, where an employee who terminates the employment relationship and begins to work for a competitor is required to transfer to the issuing entity shares granted and earned under a share-based payment arrangement.

Before presenting specific examples of accounting for share options, simple examples of calculating the fair value of options using both the BSM and the binomial methods are provided. First, an example of the BSM, closed-form model is provided.

BSM actually computes the theoretical value of a "European" call option, where exercise can occur only at the expiration date. "American" options, which describes most employee share options, can be exercised at any time until expiration. The value of an American-style option on dividend-paying shares is generally greater than a European-style option, since preexercise the holder does not have a right to receive dividends that are paid on the shares. (For non-dividend-paying shares, the values of American and European options will tend to converge.) BSM ignores dividends, but this is readily dealt with, as shown below, by deducting from the computed option value the present value of expected dividend stream over the option holding period.

BSM also is predicated on constant volatility over the option term, which available evidence suggests may not be a wholly accurate description of share price behavior. On the other hand, the reporting entity would find it very difficult, if not impossible, to compute differing volatilities for each node in the lattice model described later in this section, lacking a factual basis for presuming that volatility would increase or decrease in specific future periods.

The BSM model is

$$C = SN(d1) - Ke^{(-rt)}N(d2)$$

Where:

C	=	Theoretical call premium
S	=	Current share price
t	=	Time until option expiration
K	=	Option striking price
r	=	Risk-free interest rate
N	=	Cumulative standard normal distribution
e	=	Exponential term (2.7183)
d_1	=	$\dfrac{1n(S/K) + (r+s^2/2)^t}{svvt}$
d_2	=	$d_2 = d_1 - s$
s	=	Standard deviation of share returns
1n	=	Natural logarithm

The BSM valuation is illustrated with the following assumed facts; note that dividends are ignored in the initial calculation but will be addressed once the theoretical value is computed. Also note that volatility is defined in terms of the variability of the entity's share price, measured by the standard deviation of prices over the past three years, which is used as a surrogate for expected volatility over the next twelve months.

Example—Determining the fair value of options using the BSM model

BSM is a closed-form model, meaning that it solves for an option price from an equation. It computes a theoretical call price based on five parameters—the current share price, the option exercise price, the expected volatility of the share price, the time until option expiration, and the short-term risk-free interest rate. Of these, expected volatility is the most difficult to ascertain. Volatility is generally computed as the standard deviation of recent historical returns on the shares. In the following example, the shares are currently selling at €40 and the standard deviation of prices (daily closing prices can be used, among other possible choices) over the past several years was €6.50, thus yielding an estimated volatility of €6.50/€40 = 16.25%.

Assume the following facts:

S = €40
t = 2 years
K = €45
r = 3% annual rate
s = standard deviation of percentage returns = 16.25% (based on €6.50 standard deviation of share price compared to current €40 price)

From the foregoing data, all of which is known information (the volatility, s, is computed or assumed, as discussed above) the factors d_1 and d_2 can be computed. The cumulative standard normal variates (N) of these values must then be determined (using a table or formula), following which the BSM option value is calculated, *before the effect of dividends*. In this example, the computed amounts are

$N(d_1) = 0.2758$
$N(d_2) = 0.2048$

With these assumptions the value of the share options is approximately €2.35. This is derived from the BSM as follows:

$$
\begin{aligned}
C &= SN(d_1) - Ke^{(-rt)}N(d_2) \\
&= 40(.2758) - 45(.942)(.2048) \\
&= 11.032 - 8.679 \\
&= 2.35
\end{aligned}
$$

The foregone two-year stream of dividends, which in this example are projected to be €0.50 annually, have a present value of €0.96. Therefore, the net value of this option is €1.39 (= €2.35– .96).

Example—Determining the fair value of options using the binomial model

In contrast to the BSM, the binomial model is an open form, inductive model. It allows for multiple (theoretically, unlimited) branches of possible outcomes on a "tree" of possible price movements and induces the option's price. As compared to the BSM approach, this relaxes the constraint on exercise timing. It can be assumed that exercise occurs at any point in the option period, and past experience may guide the reporting entity to make certain such assumptions (e.g., that one-half the options will be exercised when the market price of the shares reach 150% of the strike price). It also allows for varying dividends from period to period.

It is assumed that the common (Cox, Ross, and Rubinstein) binomial model will be used in practice. To keep this preliminary example relatively simple in order to focus on the concepts involved, a single-step binomial model is provide here for illustrative purposes. Assume an option is granted of a €20 share that will expire in one year. The option exercise price equals the share price of €20. Also, assume there is a 50% chance that the price will jump 20% over the year and a 50% chance the shares will drop 20%, and that no other outcomes are possible. The risk-free interest rate is 4%. With these assumptions there are three basic calculations.

1. Plot the two possible future share prices.
2. Translate these share prices into future options values.
3. Discount these future values into a single present value.

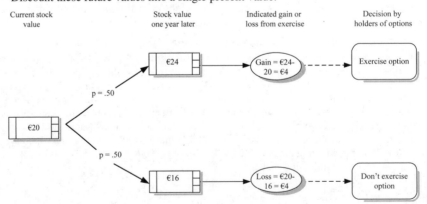

In this case, the option will only have value if the share price increases, and otherwise the option would expire worthless and unexercised. In this simplistic example, there is only a 50% chance of the option having a value of (€4 ÷ 1.04 =) €3.84, and therefore the option is worth (€3.84 × .50 =) €1.92 at grant date.

The foregoing was a simplistic single-period, two-outcome model. A more complicated and realistic binomial model extends this single-period model into a randomized walk of many steps or intervals. In theory, the time to expiration can be broken into a large number of ever-smaller time intervals, such as months, weeks, or days. The advantage is that the parameter values (volatility, etc.) can then be varied with greater precision from one period to the next (assuming, or course, that there is a factual basis upon which to base these estimates). Calculating the binomial model then involves the same three calculation steps. First, the possible future share prices are determined for each branch, using the volatility input and time to expiration (which grows shorter with each successive node in the model). This permits computation of terminal values for each branch of the tree. Second, future share prices are translated into option values at each node of the tree. Third, these future option values are discounted and added to produce a single present value of the option, taking into account the probabilities of each series of price moves in the model.

Example—Multiperiod option valuation using the binomial model

Consider the following example of a two-period binomial model. Again, certain simplifying assumptions will be made so that a manual calculation can be illustrated (in general, computer programs will be necessary to compute option values). Eager Corp. grants 10,000 options to its employees at a time when the market price of shares is €40. The options expire in two years; expected dividends on the shares will be €0.50 per year; and the risk-free rate is currently 3%, which is not expected to change over the two-year horizon. The option exercise price is €43.

The entity's past experience suggests that, after one year (of the two-year term) elapses, if the market price of the share exceeds the option exercise price, one-half of the options will be exercised by the holders. The other holders will wait another year to decide. If at the end of the second year—without regard to what the share value was at the end of the first year—the market value exceeds the exercise price, all the remaining options will be exercised. The workforce has been unusually stable and it is not anticipated that option holders will cease employment before the end of the option period.

The share price moves randomly from period to period. Based on recent experience, it is anticipated that in each period the shares may increase by €5, stay the same, or decrease by €5, with equal probability, versus the price at the period year-end. Thus since the price is €40 at grant date, one year hence it might be either €45, €40, or €35. The price at the end of the second year will follow the same pattern, based on the price when the first year ends.

Logically, holders will rather exercise their options than see them expire, as long as there is gain to be realized. Since dividends are not paid on options, holders have a motive to exercise earlier than the expiration date, which explains why historically one-half the options are exercised after one year elapses, as long as the market price exceeds the exercise price at that date, even though the exercising holders risk future market declines.

The binomial model formulation requires that each sequence of events and actions be explicated. This gives rise to the commonly seen decision tree representation. In this simple example, following the grant of the options, one of three possible events occur: either the share price rises €5 over the next year, or it remains constant, or it falls by €5. Since these outcomes have equal a priori probabilities, p=1/3 is assigned to each outcome of this first year event. If the price does rise, one-half the option holders will exercise at the end of the first year, to reap the economic gain and capture the second year's dividend. The other holders will forego this immediate gain and wait to see what the share price does in the second year before making an exercise decision.

If the share price in the first year either remains flat or falls by €5, no option holders are expected to exercise. However, there remains the opportunity to exercise after the second year elapses, if the share price recovers. Of course, holding the options for the second year means that no dividends will be received.

The cost of the options granted by Eager Corp., measured by fair value using the binomial model approach is computed by the sum of the probability-weighted outcomes, discounted to present value using the risk-free rate. In this example, the rate is expected to remain at 3% per year throughout the option period, but it could be independently specified for each period—another advantage the binomial model has over the more rigid BSM. The sum of these present value computations measures the cost of compensation incorporated in the option grant, regardless of what pattern of exercise ultimately is revealed, since at the grant date, using the available information about share price volatility, expected dividends, exercise behavior and the risk-free rate, this best measures the value of what was promised to the employees.

The following graphic offers a visual representation of the model, although in practice it is not necessary to prepare such a document. The actual calculations can be made by computer program, but to illustrate the application of the binomial model, the computation will be presented explicitly here. There are four possible scenarios under which, in this example, holders will exercise the options, and thus the options will have value. All other scenarios (combinations of share price movements over the two-year horizon) will cause the holders to allow the options to expire unexercised.

First, if the share price goes to €45 in the first year, one-half the holders will exercise at that point, paying the exercise price of €43 per share. This results in a gain of €2 (= €45 – €43) per share. However, having waited until the first year-end, they lost the opportunity to receive the €0.50 per share dividend, so the net economic gain is only €1.50 (= €2.00 – €0.50) per share. As this occurs after one year, the present value is only €1.50 × 1.03^{-1} = €1.46 per share. When this is weighted by the probability of this outcome obtaining (given that the share price rise to €45 in the first year has only a 1/3 probability of happening, and given further that only one-half the option holders would elect to exercise under such conditions), the actual expected value of this outcome is [(1/3)(1/2)(€1.46) =] €0.24. More formally,

$$[(1/3)(1/2)(€2.00 – €0.50)] × 1.03^{-1} = €0.2427$$

The second potentially favorable outcome to holders would be if the share price rises to €45 the first year and then either rises another €5 the second year or holds steady at €45 during the second year. In either event, the option holders who did not exercise after the first year's share price rise will all exercise at the end of the second year, before the options expire. If the price goes to €50 the second year, the holders will reap a gross gain of €7 (=€50 – €43) per share; if it remains constant at €45, the gross gain is only €2 per share. In either case, dividends in both years one and two will have been foregone. To calculate the compensation cost associated with these branches of the model, the first-year dividend lost must be discounted for one year, and the gross gain and the second-year dividend must be discounted for years. Also, the probabilities of the entire sequence of events must be used, taking into account the likelihood of the first year's share price rise, the proclivity of holders to wait for a second year to elapse, and the likelihood of a second-year price rise or price stability. These computations are shown below.

For the outcome if the share price rises again

$[(1/3)(1/2)(1/3)] \{[(€7.00) × 1.03^{-2}] – [(€0.50) × 1.03^{-1}] – [€0.50 × 1.03^{-2}]\} =$
$[0.05544] \{€6.59 – €0.48 – €0.47\} = €0.31276$

For the outcome if the share price remains stable

$[(1/3)(1/2)(1/3)] \{[(€2.00) × 1.03^{-2}] – [(€0.50) × 1.03^{-1}] – [€0.50 × 1.03^{-2}]\} =$
$[0.05544] \{€1.88 – €0.48 – €0.47\} = €0.05147$

The final favorable outcome for holders would occur if the share price holds constant at €40 the first year but rises to €45 the second year, making exercise the right decision. Note that none of the holders would exercise after the first year given that the price, €40, was below exercise price. The calculation for this sequence of events is as follows:

$[(1/3)(1/3)] \{[(€2.00) × 1.03^{-2}] – [(€0.50) × 1.03^{-1}] – [€0.50 × 1.03^{-2}]\} =$
$[0.1111] \{€1.88 – €0.48 – €0.47\} = €0.10295$

Summing these values yields €0.709879 (€0.2427 + €0.31276 + €0.05147 + €0.10295), which is the expected value per optional granted. When this per-unit value is then multiplied by the number of options granted, 10,000, the total compensation cost to be recognized, €7,098.79, is derived. This would be attributed over the required service period, which is illustrated later in this section. (In the facts of this example, no vesting requirements were specified; in such cases, the employees would not have to provide future service in order to earn the right to the options, and the entire cost would be recognized upon grant.)

A big advantage of the binomial model is that it can value an option that is exercisable before the end of its term (i.e., an American-style option). This is the form that employee share-based compensation arrangements normally take. IASB appears to recognize the virtues of the binomial type of model, because it can incorporate the unique features of employee share options. Two key features that should generally be incorporated into the binomial model are vesting restrictions and early exercise. Doing so, however, requires that the reporting entity will have had previous experience with employee behaviors (e.g., gained with past employee option programs) that would provide it with a basis for making estimates of future behavior. In some instances, there will be no obvious bases upon which such assumptions can be developed.

The binomial model permits the specification of more assumptions than does the BSM, which has generated the perception that the binomial will more readily be manipulated so as to result in lower option values, and hence lower compensation costs, when contrasted to the BSM. But, this is not necessarily the case: switching from BSM to the binomial model can increase, maintain, or decrease the option's value. Having the ability to specify additional parameters, however, does probably give management greater flexibility and, accordingly, will present additional challenges for the auditors who must attest to the financial statement effects of management's specification of these variables.

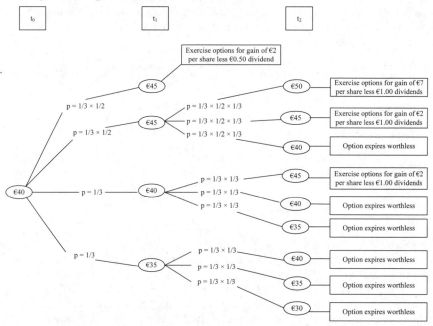

Accounting entries. Having calculated the fair value of the option at the grant date, this value then has to be expensed through the statement of comprehensive income by allocation over the financial years during which the option is vesting, since it is over that period that the grantee is presumably earning the related compensation. The corresponding credit is made to an equity account.

Suppose a company grants 1,000 share options with a vesting period of four years to 50 employees. The fair value of each option is determined to be €20, and the company expects, in light of past experience with employee turnover and other factors, that 75% of the options will vest. Ignore graded vesting features of these options. The expense (and credit to equity) in the first year will be (50,000 options × €20 × 0.75 × 0.25 =) €187,500.

At the end of the second year, the entity now considers that 80% of the options will probably vest. As with all changes in accounting estimates, the impact of this reassessment is allocated to current and future period, with no adjustment to already-concluded fiscal periods. The expense for the current (second) year is the cumulative cost based on the new parameter values, less the amount already expensed in the first year. The cumulative amount is (50,000 options × €20 × 0.80 × 0.5 =) €400,000. The year two expense therefore will be (€400,000 – €187,500 =) €212,500.

Assume that in year three there are no changes to the estimates, and the cumulative cost over the three-year period accordingly is (50,000 × €20 × 0.80 × 0.75 =) €600,000. The annual expense in year three therefore is (€600,000 – €400,000 =) €200,000.

At the end of the four-year vesting period, 41 (or 82%) of the original employees granted options are still with the company, and their options vest. The fourth year's expense (and credit to equity) takes into account the actual options vested. The cumulative cost is (50,000 × €20 × 0.82 =) €820,000 and the fourth year's expense is (€820,000 – €600,000 =) €220,000.

At some future date some or all of the options may be exercised by the remaining employees, but this will not necessarily occur. IFRS 2 takes the view that the amount credited to equity, arising from the issue of options, is *not* to be adjusted subsequently to take account of any failure to exercise the options (which is termed a forfeiture). This is consistent with the belief that the accounting for options should be a reflection of the bargain made when the option was originally agreed to. However, the entity is free to reclassify any of these amounts within equity, and where an option is exercised, the original amount recognized, plus the exercise amount, should become part of contributed capital.

The journal entries would be

	Debit	Credit	Memorandum cumulative equity item
Year 1			
Employee remuneration	187,500		
Share options		187,500	187,500
Year 2			
Employee remuneration	212,500		
Share options		212,500	400,000
Year 3			
Employee remuneration	200,000		
Share options		200,000	600,000
Year 4			
Employee remuneration	220,000		
Share options		220,000	820,000

If the entity subsequently modifies the conditions of the option, then this must be reflected in the accounting. The fair value at the original grant date remains the *minimum amount to be expensed.* If the modification increases the fair value—for example, by reducing the exercise price or increasing the number of shares—the additional fair value must be expensed in the period from the modification date to the new vesting date. If the vesting conditions are changed in a way that would likely increase the probability of vesting, then this will be reflected in the number of options expected to vest. If the modification reduces the fair value, then the original fair value continues to be the basis of expensing.

If the entity cancels the option or settles it before the end of the vesting period, this should be treated as an acceleration of the vesting period, and the original fair value at grant date should be expensed over the shorter period. If a payment is made to the employee in respect of the cancellation or settlement, this is treated as a repurchase of an equity interest, and is deducted from equity. In the event that the payment exceeds the value recognized in equity, the excess is reported as an expense. If the entity settles by issuing a new option, this is treated as a modification of the original scheme and accounted for accordingly. The current IFRS 2 specifies the accounting method when an entity cancels a grant of equity instruments but does not state how cancellations by a party other than the entity should be accounted for.

Amended definition of vesting conditions and treatment of cancellations. In February 2006, IASB issued Exposure Draft (ED), *Proposed Amendments to IFRS 2, Share-Based Payment: Vesting Conditions and Cancellations*, which proposed to restrict vesting conditions to service conditions and performance conditions; and require that cancellations by parties other than the entity (e.g., an employee, a shareholder, or any other party) be accounted in the same way as cancellations by the entity. In early 2008 these amendments were finalized, effective for periods beginning in 2009, with earlier application permitted.

The amendment provides that *vesting conditions* are defined as service conditions and performance conditions only; any other features of share-based payments are not vesting conditions. Other features that are not vesting conditions are to be included in the grant date fair value measurement, which also includes market-related vesting conditions.

The amendment also provides that *cancellations,* whether by action of the reporting entity or by other parties, are given the same accounting treatment, which involves acceleration of the vesting period. Per IFRS 2, any amounts not previously recognized as compensation expense are fully recognized as of the date of cancellation; payments made, if any, to the holder are treated as equity repurchases. The amendment eliminates any risk of differential treatment of cancellations precipitated by actions of the holder, the issuer, or third parties.

Recognition of compensation cost for share options with graded vesting characteristics and service conditions. Under IFRS 2, the compensation cost for share options with graded vesting characteristics and service conditions must be made on an accelerated attribution basis. Unlike US GAAP, IFRS does not permit the straight-line method for attribution of compensation cost of share options with service conditions and graded vesting characteristics. A graded vesting plan assigns the share options to the period in which they vest. This is because IFRS 2 views each tranche of vesting as a separate grant for which service has been provided since the date of the original grant.

The mandatory use of the accelerated amortization method for stock options with graded vesting features results in a higher compensation cost in the earlier years of the vesting period as shown in the example below.

1,000 share options are granted to 100 employees at a grant price of €10 per option which gives a total share option grant value of €1,000,000. The share option plan provides for a graded vesting of these 1,000 share options, in four equal tranches over a four year period (or 25%) at each anniversary of the grant. Ignore forfeiture rates for this example. Under the accelerated attribution method, the compensation cost for each of the four years is as follows:

	Year 1	*Year 2*	*Year 3*	*Year 4*
	€	€	€	€
First year vesting 25%	250,000			
Second year vesting 25%	125,000	125,000		
Third year vesting 25%	83,333	83,333	83,333	
Fourth year vesting 25%	62,500	62,500	62,500	62,500
Total Compensation Cost for each of the years	520,833	270,833	145,833	62,500

Accordingly, options which vest in Year 2 are deemed to have a two-year vesting period and the ones which vest in Year 3 have a three-year vesting period. The accelerated attribution method shows that the compensation cost for graded options is highly front loaded from the year of grant. The straight line method of attribution followed under US GAAP would have resulted in a share option compensation expense of only €250,000 in Year 1 compared to €520,833 under IFRS.

Nonemployee transactions. Share-based payments to nonemployees are fairly rare, and are perhaps encountered most frequently in connection with start-up entities, which are often cash-starved and thus willing to dilute ownership in return for the provision of vital services or goods by vendors willing to accept payment in entity shares. The basic principle of IFRS 2 is that such transactions are expensed as measured by the fair value of the goods received or the services rendered. For nonemployee transactions, there is a rebuttable presumption that the value of the goods or services can be measured reliably. That fair value is measured at the date the goods are received or the services are rendered. Per IFRS 2, only "in rare cases," if the entity concludes that it cannot measure these, should the expense be measured by reference to the fair value of the instruments granted.

It should be noted that this also has a bearing on revenue recognition by the counterparty (the entity providing the goods or services and receiving the shares). One of the abuses noted during the late 1990s "dot-com" market bubble was that the same parcel of shares, exchanged for professional services in connection with a start-up, was valued very modestly by the issuing company (for purposes of computing the expense to be recognized), but was simultaneously valued much more highly by the service provider (as revenue). If the transaction is accounted for at the fair value of the services provided, obviously that value should be exactly the same, seen from either party's perspective.

Cash-settled transactions. Sometimes employees will receive a variable amount of remuneration, which is based on the performance of the entity's shares, but resulting in an additional cash payment to the employee, rather than an equity instrument. This describes the issuance of the essential characteristic of various share, or share appreciation rights plans, or of shares that are redeemable by the company at the holder's election. The calculation of compensation expense is to be based on the underlying share option, in accordance with the above described method for equity-settled transactions, but the credit entry is to a liability account, not to equity. Another important distinction: the liability must be remeasured at each reporting date, unlike straight option grants, which are fixed in value at the date of issuance.

An entity may make an arrangement where the employee (or other counterparty) has a choice of cash or equity settlement. In this case, the entity should value the option as a compound financial instrument, and value the right to receive cash as debt, and the right to receive any additional amount as equity. IFRS 2 notes that in many cases the arrangement is structured so that the equity alternative has the same value as the cash alternative, in which case the whole amount is considered to be debt, since there is no extra value in the equity choice.

If the employee decides at the date of exercise to receive the equity alternative, the liability is transferred into equity. If the employee takes the cash alternative, the liability is extinguished. However, if a separate equity element had been established, this remains part of equity, as with other vested options that are not exercised.

In some cases the choice between cash settlement and equity settlement is in the hands of the employer. Here the standard relies on the present obligation notion similar to that used in IAS 37: where the company has a past history of making cash settlements or a stated policy of doing this (i.e., where there is a reasonable expectation of cash settlement), the transaction is considered to give rise to a liability. In the absence of such an obligation, the entity would account for the transaction as equity-settled. In the event that the entity ultimately decides to settle in cash, the cash payment is treated as a repurchase of equity.

IFRIC 11, *Group and Treasury Share Transactions,* addresses certain ambiguities found in IFRS 2 pertaining to situations where the reporting entity either is required to or chooses to acquire the shares needed to satisfy obligations to employees to deliver its shares (e.g., under an employee share option plan). While the entity will expend cash to make these treasury share purchases, IFRIC 11 holds that this does not serve to make such plans cash-settled for purposes of financial reporting. Thus, recording the obligation as a liability, and measuring it at fair value as of the reporting dates, is not prescribed. Instead, these arrangements are accounted for as equity-settled obligations, effectively bifurcating the commitment to the employees from the means to be utilized to obtain the shares needed.

This interpretation also holds that if the shares to be given to employees are provided by the entity's shareholders, the accounting is likewise for equity-settled obligations.

IFRIC 11 also addresses various circumstances whereby a parent entity's equity shares are granted to employees of its subsidiaries. One common situation occurs where the parent is publicly traded but its subsidiaries are not (e.g., where the subsidiaries are wholly owned by the parent company), and thus the parent company's shares are the only "currency" that can be used in share-based payments to employees. The interpretation holds that, provided that the arrangement is accounted for as equity-settled in the consolidated (group) financial statements of the parent company, the subsidiary is to measure the services under the equity-settled accounting requirements. A capital contribution by the parent is also recognized by the subsidiary in such situations.

Furthermore, if the employee transfers from one subsidiary to another, each is to measure compensation expense by reference to the fair value of the equity instruments at the date the rights were granted by the parent, allocated according to the relative portion of the vesting period the employee works for each subsidiary. There is no remeasurement associated with the transfer between entities. If a vesting condition other than a market condition (defined by IFRS 2, Appendix A) is not met and the share-based compensation is forfeited, each subsidiary adjusts previously recognized compensation cost to remove cumulative compensation cost from each of the subsidiaries.

On the other hand, if the subsidiary grants rights to its parent company's shares to the subsidiary's employees, that entity accounts for this as a cash-settled transaction. This means the obligation is reported as a liability, and adjusted to fair value at each reporting date.

Disclosures. IFRS 2 imposed extensive disclosure requirements, calling for an analysis of share-based payments made during the year, of their impact on earnings and financial position, and of the basis upon which fair values were measured.

Each type of share-based payment that existed during the year must be described, giving vesting requirements, the maximum term of the options, and the method of settlement (but entities that have several "substantially similar" schemes may aggregate this information). The movement (i.e., changes) within each scheme must be analyzed, including the number of share options and the weighted-average exercise price for the following:

- Outstanding at the beginning of the year
- Granted during the year
- Forfeited during the year
- Exercised during the year (plus the weighted-average share price at the time of exercise)
- Expired during the year
- Outstanding at the end of the period (plus the range of exercise prices and the weighted-average remaining contractual life).
- Exercisable at the end of the period

The entity must disclose the total expense recognized in the statement of comprehensive income arising from share-based payment transactions, and a subtotal of that part which was settled by the issue of equity. Where the entity has liabilities arising from share-based payment transactions, the total amount at the end of the period must be separately disclosed, as must be the total intrinsic value of those options that had vested.

The fair value methodology disclosures apply to new instruments issued during the reporting period, or old instruments modified in that time. Regarding share options, the entity must disclose the weighted-average fair value, plus details of how fair value was measured. These will include the option pricing model used, the weighted-average share price, the exercise price, expected volatility, option life, expected dividends, the risk-free interest rate and any other inputs. The measurement of expected volatility must be explained, as must be the manner in which any other features of the option were incorporated in the measurement.

Where a modification of an existing arrangement has taken place, the entity should provide an explanation of the modifications, and disclose the incremental fair value and the basis on which that was measured (as above).

Where a share-based payment was made to a nonemployee, such as a vendor, the entity should confirm that fair value was determined directly by reference to the market price for the goods or services.

If equity instruments *other than share options* were granted during the period, the number and weighted-average fair value of these should be disclosed together with the basis for measuring fair value, and if this was not market value, then how it was measured. The disclosure should cover how expected dividends were incorporated into the value and what other features were incorporated into the measurement.

Members' Shares in Cooperative Entities

Certain organizations are so-called membership organizations or cooperatives. These are often entities providing services to a group having common membership or interests, such as labor unions or university faculty and staff. Credit unions (a form of savings and loan association) are a common example of this form of organization. Other cooperatives may serve as marketing vehicles, as in the case of farmers' co-ops, or as buying organizations, as in co-ops formed by merchants in certain types of businesses, generally in order to gain economies of scale and market power in order to compete with larger merchant chains. Generally, these types of organizations will refund or rebate profits to the members in proportion to the amount of business transacted over a time period, such as a year.

Ownership in cooperatives is represented by shares. Members' shares in cooperative entities have some characteristics of equity, but also, often, characteristics of debt, since they are not permanent equity which cannot be withdrawn. Members' shares typically give the holder the right to request redemption for cash, although that right may be subject to certain limitations or restrictions, imposed by law or by the terms of the membership agreement. IFRIC 2 gives guidance on how those redemption terms should be evaluated in determining whether the shares should be classified as financial liabilities or as equity.

Under IFRIC 2, shares for which the member has the right to request redemption are normally liabilities. Even when the intent is to leave in the equity interest for a long period, such as until the member ceases business operations, this does not qualify as true equity as defined under the IASB *Framework*. However, the shares qualify as equity if

- The cooperative entity has an unconditional right to refuse redemption, or
- Local law, regulation, or the entity's governing charter imposes prohibitions on redemption.

However, the mere existence of law, regulation, or charter provisions that would prohibit redemption only if conditions (such as liquidity constraints) are met, or are not met, does not result in members' shares being treated as equity.

Financial Statement Presentation under IFRS

The following is an illustration of the treatment of equity that may be required in the financial statements.

Equity Section of Consolidated Statement of Financial Position

(in thousands of euros)	*2009*	*2008*
Ordinary shares		
Authorized: 10,000,000 Par value = €1		
Issued: 6,650,000	6,650	6,585
Share premium and reserves		
Share premium	12,320	12,110
Legal reserve	665	665
Share options granted	724	676
Translation adjustment	(1,854)	(2,266)
Treasury shares	(320)	(320)
	11,535	10,865
Retained earnings	4,230	3,898
Owners of the parent company	22,415	21,348
Noncontrolling interest	360	353
Total equity	22,775	21,701

Examples of Financial Statement Disclosures

Roche Group
Period Ending December 2007

28. Equity attributable to Roche shareholders

Share capital. As of December 31, 2007, the share capital of Roche Holding Ltd, which is the Group's parent company, consists of 160,000,000 shares with a nominal value of 1.00 Swiss franc each, as in the preceding year. The shares are bearer shares and the Group does not maintain a register of shareholders. Based on information supplied to the Group, a shareholder group with pooled voting rights owns 50.0125% (2005: 50.0125%) of the issued shares. This is further described in Note 33. Based on information supplied to the Group, Novartis International Ltd, Basel, and its affiliates own 33.3330% (participation below 33 1/3%) of the issued shares (2006: 33.3330%).

Nonvoting equity securities *(Gennussscheine).* As of December 31, 2007, 702,562,700 nonvoting equity securities were in issue as in the preceding year. Under Swiss company law these nonvoting equity securities have no nominal value, are not part of the share capital and cannot be issued against a contribution which would be shown as an asset in the balance sheet of Roche Holding Ltd. Each nonvoting equity security confers the same rights as any of the shares to participate in the net profit and any remaining proceeds from liquidation following repayment of the nominal value of the shares and, if any, participation certificates. In accordance with the law and the Articles of Incorporation of Roche Holding Ltd, the Company is entitled at all times to exchange all or some of the nonvoting equity securities into shares or participation certificates.

Dividends. On March 5, 2007, the shareholders approved the distribution of a dividend of CHF 3.40 per share and nonvoting equity security (2006: CHF 2.50) in respect of the 2006 business year. The distribution to holders of outstanding shares and nonvoting equity securities totaled 2,930 million Swiss francs (2006: 2,152 million Swiss francs) and has been recorded against retained earnings in 2007. The Board has proposed dividends for the 2007 business year of 4.60 Swiss francs per share and nonvoting equity security. This is subject to approval at the Annual General Meeting on March 4, 2008.

Own equity instruments.

Holdings of own equity instruments *in equivalent number of nonvoting equity securities*

	December 31, 2007 millions	December 31, 2006 millions
Nonvoting equity securities	0.4	0.2
Low exercise price options	1.9	6.8
Derivative instruments	9.3	8.2
Total own equity instruments	11.6	15.2

Own equity instruments are recorded within equity at original purchase cost. Details of own equity instruments held at December 31, 2007, are shown in the table below. Fair values are disclosed for information purposes.

Own equity instruments at December 31, 2006: supplementary information

	Equivalent number of nonvoting equity securities millions	Maturity	Strike price (CHF)	Market value (millions of CHF)
Nonvoting equity securities	0.4	n/a	n/a	70
Low exercise price options	1.9	Sept. 1, 2008	10.00	349
Derivative instruments	9.3	Feb. 2, 2010– Feb. 8, 2014	123.00–229.60	412
Total	11.6			831

Nonvoting equity securities and Low Exercise Price Options are mainly held for the potential conversion obligations that may arise from the Group's convertible debt instruments (see Note 30). Following from the conversion and redemption of the "LYONs V" US dollar exchangeable notes in 2007 (see Note 27), the Group reduced its holdings in its own equity instruments during the year. The Group's potential obligations to employees for the Roche Option Plan and Roche Stock-settled Stock Appreciation Rights (see Note 11) are covered by the remaining own equity instruments, which mainly consist of call options that are exercisable at any time up to their maturity. The net cash inflow from transactions in own equity instruments was 1,085 million Swiss francs (2006: net cash inflow of 1,367 million Swiss francs. These mainly arose from a reduction in own equity instrument holdings following the conversion and redemption of the "LYONs V" notes.

The Group holds none of its own shares.

Reserves.

Fair value reserve. The fair value reserve represents the cumulative net change in the fair value of available-for-sale financial assets until the asset is sold, impaired, or otherwise disposed of.

Hedging reserve. The hedging reserve represents the effective portion of the cumulative net change in the fair value of cash flow hedging instruments related to hedged transactions that have not yet occurred.

Translation reserve. The translation reserve represents the cumulative currency translation differences relating to the consolidation of Group companies that use functional currencies other than Swiss francs.

Nestlé S.A.
For the year ended December 31, 2007

25. Share capital of Nestlé S.A.

	2007	2006
Number of registered shares of nominal value CHF 1 each	393,072,500	400,735,700
In millions of CHF	393	401

At the Annual General Meeting on April 19, 2007, the shareholders approved the cancellation of 7,663,200 shares. The share capital includes the nominal value of treasury shares (refer Note 21).

26. Treasury shares

This item represents the treasury shares held in Nestlé S.A.

Number of shares	*2007*	*2006*
Purpose of holding		
Management options rights*	2,737,411	4,153,228
Restricted share units*	1,077,126	764,886
Freely available shares	1,116,441	1,601,764
Warrants on SWANS and Turbo bond issues of		
Nestlé Holdings Inc., USA	1,703,059	2,230,269
Share buy-back program	8,294,000	7,663,200
Trading	1,872,705	600,279
Total at December 31	16,800,742	17,013,626

> * The Group buys or transfers from existing treasury shares portfolios the number of shares necessary to satisfy all potential outstanding obligations under the Management Share Option Plan (MSOP) and the Restricted Share Unit Plan (RSUP) when the benefit is awarded and holds them until the maturity of the plan or the exercise of the rights/delivery of RSU.

In millions of CHF	*2007*	*2006*	*2005*
Book value at December 31	8,013	4,644	2,770
Market value at December 31	8,736	7,367	6,008

Novartis Group
Annual Report 2007

Notes to the Financial Statements

Accounting Policies

Equity-based compensation. The fair value of Novartis shares, Novartis American Depositary Shares (ADS) and related options granted to associates as compensation is recognized as an expense over the related vesting or service period. Novartis calculates the fair value of the options at the grant date using the trinomial valuation method, which is a variant of the lattice binomial approach. Shares and ADSs are valued using the market value on the grant date. The amount for shares and options are charged to income over the relevant vesting or service periods, adjusted to reflect actual and expected levels of vesting. The charge for equity-based compensation is included in the personnel expenses of the various functions where the associates are located.

Notes to the Financial Statements

17. Details of shares and share capital movements

		*Number of shares**			
	Dec. 31, 2005	*Movement in year*	*Dec. 31, 2006*	*Movement in year*	*Dec. 31, 2007*
Total Novartis shares	2,739,171,000	(10,200,000)	2,728,971,000		2,728,971,000
Treasury shares					
Shares reserved for share-based compensation of associates	40,291,620	(6,733,603)	33,558,017	(5,190,724)	28,367,293
Unreserved treasury shares	362,962,880	(15,781,356)	347,181,524	(88,968,851)	436,150,375
Total treasury shares	403,254,500	(22,514,959)	380,739,541	83,778,127	464,517,668
Total outstanding shares	2,335,916,500	12,314,959	2,348,231,459	(88,778,127)	2,264,453,332
	USD millions	*USD millions*	*USD millions*	*USD millions*	*USD millions*
Share capital	994	(4)	990		990
Treasury shares	(146)	6	(140)	(35)	(175)
Outstanding share capital	848	2	850	(35)	815

* *All shares are registered, authorized, issued, and fully paid. All are voting shares and, except for 272,741,016 treasury shares, are dividend bearing.*

There are outstanding written call options on Novartis shares of 23.4 million originally issued as part of the share-based compensation of associates. The market maker has acquired these options but they have not yet been exercised. The weighted-average exercise price of these options is USD 42.69 and they have remaining contractual lives of up to 8 years.

25. Changes in consolidated equity

25.1 At the 2007 Annual General Meeting a CHF 1.35 per share dividend was approved amounting to USD 2.6 billion which was paid in 2007 (2006: dividend payment was CHF 1.15 per share and amounted to USD 2 billion). The amount available for dividend distribution is based on the available distributable retained earnings of Novartis AG determined in accordance with the legal provisions of the Swiss Code of Obligation.

25.2 In 2007, 85.3 million shares were acquired under the fourth and fifth share buy-back programs on the SWX second trading line (2006: no shares). Overall in 2007, a total of 83.8 million shares, net have been purchased (2006: 8 million shares, net sold) for USD 4.7 billion (2006: USD 0.2 billion). These transactions include shares bought and sold on the first and second trading line, transactions with associates and the exercising of options related to equity-based compensation.

25.3 In 2007, no shares were cancelled. Pursuant to a resolution approved at the February 28, 2006 Annual General Meeting, 10.2 million shares were cancelled with a nominal value of USD 4 million.

25.4 Equity-settled share-based compensation is expensed in the income statement in accordance with the vesting or service period of the share-based compensation plans. The value for the shares and options granted including associated tax represents an increase in equity.

25.5 Transfers in 2006 and 2007 between components of equity are due to a net transfer of cumulative translation effects and actuarial losses between fair value adjustments from continuing operations and fair value adjustment related to Gerber and Medical Nutrition divestments. In 2006, share premium has been reduced USD 1 million to the permitted minimum under Swiss company law of 20% of the Novartis AG share capital and Group retained earnings were increased by this amount.

27. Share participation plans of associates

Associate and management equity-based participation plans can be separated into the Novartis equity plan "Select" and other equity-based plans ("the Plans"). The expense recorded in the income statement spreads the cost of each grant equally over the vesting period. Assumptions are made concerning the forfeiture rate which is adjusted during the vesting period so that at the end of the vesting period there is only a charge for vested amounts. As permitted by the transitional rules of the relevant accounting standard, grants prior to November 7, 2002, have not been included in the income statement. The expense for continuing operations related to all Novartis equity plans in the 2007 income statement was USD 689 million (2006: USD 640 million) resulting in a total carrying amount for liabilities arising from share-based payment transactions of USD 153 million (2006: USD 154 million). The total amount of cash used to settle awards in 2007 was USD 124 million (2006: USD 100 million). As of December 31, 2007, there was USD 551 million of total unrecognized compensation cost related to nonvested equity-based compensation arrangements granted under the Plans. That cost is expected to be recognized over a weighted-average period of 1.80 years. The amount of related income tax benefit recognized in the income statement was USD 186 million (2006: USD 169 million). In addition, due to its majority owned US quoted subsidiary Idenix Pharmaceuticals Inc., Novartis recognized an additional equity-based compensation expense of USD 9 million (2006: USD 9 million). Participants in the Novartis equity plans from discontinuing operations were granted 73,002 shares (2006: 97,388 shares) and 320,495 options (2006: 325,303 options). The expense recorded in the 2007 income statement from discontinued operations amounted to USD 22 million (2006: USD 13 million).

27.1 Novartis Equity Plan "Select"

Awards under this plan may be granted each year based on the associate's individual year-end performance rating, talent rating and Group or business area performance. If an associate receives a rating below a certain threshold, no awards are granted under the plan. Participants in this plan can elect to receive their incentive in the form of shares, share options, or a combination of both. Each share option is tradable, expires on its tenth anniversary and is exercisable to receive one share (1:1). The exercise price equals the market price of the underlying share at the grant date. If associates in North America choose to receive the Select incentive amount (or part of it) in tradable share options on American Depositary Shares, then the resulting number of share options is determined by dividing the respective Select incentive amount, by a value that equals 95% of the IFRS value of the options on American Depositary Shares. For associates in other countries, the divisor equals 90% of the IFRS value of options on Novartis shares. Shares and tradable share options have a vesting period of two years in Switzerland and three years in other countries. As a result, if a participant leaves Novartis, unvested shares or options are forfeited, unless determined otherwise by the Compensation Committee (for example, in connection with a reorganization or divestment). Participants in continuing operations for the Novartis equity plan "Select" were granted 1,062,684 shares (2006: 1,164,061 shares) for the Novartis Equity Plan "Select" outside North America and 1,685,533 ADS (2006: 2,047,530 ADS) for the Novartis Equity Plan "Select" for North America.

a. **Novartis Equity Plan "Select" outside North America.** Directors (through 2002), executives and other selected employees of Group companies (collectively, the "Participants") may receive equity awards. These equity awards are made both in recognition of past performance and as an incentive for future contributions by the Participants. They allow the Participants to benefit as the price of the shares increases over time, and so provide a long-term incentive for improvements in the Group's profitability and success. The share options are tradable; therefore they can be used to purchase the underlying Novartis share or they can be transferred to a market maker. In 2004, the vesting period for the plan was changed from a two-year vesting period to a three-year vesting period for most countries. Due to pending new tax legislation in Switzerland, it was decided not to implement the three-year vesting period in Switzerland. The current view is that the new law will not come into force before 2009, at the earliest, at which point the vesting period might be reviewed. The following table shows the assumptions on which the valuation of share options granted during the period was based:

	Novartis Equity Plan "Select" outside North America 2007	Novartis Equity Plan "Select" outside North America 2006
Valuation date	February 5, 2007	February 6, 2006
Expiration date	February 3, 2017	February 5, 2016
Closing share price on grant date	CHF 72.85	CHF 71.30
Exercise price	CHF 72.85	CHF 71.30
Volatility	14.75%	16%
Expected dividend yield	2.55%	2.05%
Interest rate	2.84%	2.50%
Market value of option at grant date	CHF 12.45	CHF 13.91

The expense recorded in the 2007 income statement amounted to USD 137 million (2006: USD 108 million). The weighted-average prices in the table below are translated from Swiss Francs into USD at historical rates for the granted, sold, and forfeited figures. The year-end prices are translated using the corresponding year-end rates.

	2007		2006	
	Options (millions)	Weighted-average exercise price (USD)	Options (millions)	Weighted-average exercise price (USD)
Options outstanding at January 1	16.9	46.6	16.3	43.6
Granted	7.4	58.4	4.4	54.0
Sold	(3.3)	44.4	(3.4)	41.6
Forfeited	(0.6)	56.9	(0.4)	50.1
Outstanding at December 31	20.4	51.0	16.9	46.6
Exercisable at December 31	9.3	44.0	5.9	40.2
Weighted-average fair value of options granted during the year (USD)	5.5		9.7	

All options were granted at an exercise price which, since 2004, was equal to the market price of the Group's shares at the grant date and between 2000 and 2003 was greater than the market price of the Group's shares at the grant date. The weighted-average exercise price during the period the options were sold in 2007 was USD 44.4, which led to the realization of a total intrinsic value of approximately USD 32 million. The weighted-average remaining contractual term for options outstanding at the year-end was 7.2 years and 5.5 years for options exercisable. Options outstanding had an aggregate intrinsic value of USD 45 million and USD 45 million for options exercisable.

The following table summarizes information about share options outstanding at December 31, 2007:

Range of exercise prices (USD)	Options outstanding			Options exercisable	
	Number outstanding (millions)	Average remaining contractual life (years)	Weighted-average exercise price (USD)	Number exercisable (millions)	Weighted-average exercise price (USD
30-34	1.5	3.8	34.6	1.5	34.6
35-39	0.9	3.1	36.9	0.9	36.9
40-44	0.4	2.2	42.7	0.4	42.7
45-49	6.5	6.4	47.3	6.5	47.3
50-54	4.0	8.1	54.0		
55-59	7.1	9.1	58.4		
Total	20.4	7.2	51.0	9.3	44.0

b. **Novartis Equity Plan "Select" for North America.** The plan provides for equity awards to North American based Directors (through 2002), executives and other selected associates, thus replacing the US Management ADS Appreciation Rights plan. The terms and conditions of the Novartis Equity Plan "Select" for North America are substantially equivalent to the Novartis Equity Plan "Select" outside North America. As of 2004, ADS options granted under the plan are tradable; therefore, they can be used to purchase the underlying Novartis share or they can be transferred to a market maker.

The following table shows the assumptions on which the valuation of share options granted during the period was based:

	Novartis Equity Plan "Select" for North America 2007	Novartis Equity Plan "Select" for North America 2006
Valuation date	February 5, 2007	February 6, 2006
Expiration date	February 3, 2017	February 5, 2016
Closing ADS price on grant date	USD 58.38	USD 54.70
Exercise price	USD 58.38	USD 54.70
Volatility	14.25%	15%
Expected dividend yield	2.90%	2.05%
Interest rate	5.23%	5.0%
Market value of option at grant date	USD 14.11	USD 15.67

The expense recorded in continuing operations in the 2007 income statement amounted to USD 231 million (2006: USD 205 million). Under the previous US Management ADS Appreciation Rights plan, Novartis associates on US employment contracts were entitled to cash compensation equivalent to the increase in the value of Novartis ADSs compared to the market price of the ADSs at the grant date. The income of US Management ADS Appreciation Rights Plan recorded in the 2007 income statement amounted to USD 6 million whereas in 2006 Novartis recorded an expense of USD 13 million.

	2007		2006	
Fair value comparison	ADS Options (millions)	Weighted-average exercise price (USD)	ADS Options (millions)	Weighted-average exercise price (USD)
Options outstanding at January 1	37.8	44.7	41.9	41.2
Granted	12.5	58.4	7.7	54.7
Sold or exercised	(5.6)	41.5	(10.1)	37.0

Fair value comparison	ADS Options *(millions)*	2007 Weighted-average exercise price *(USD)*	ADS Options *(millions)*	2006 Weighted-average exercise price *(USD)*
Forfeited	(1.8)	53.8	(1.7)	48.0
Outstanding at December 31	42.9	48.7	37.8	44.7
Exercisable at December 31	16.9	40.6	16.0	38.0
Weighted-average fair value of options granted during the year (USD)	9.7		15.6	

All share options were granted at an exercise price which was equal to the market price of the ADS at the grant date. The weighted-average exercise price during the period the share options were exercised in 2007 was USD 41.5, which led to the realization of a total intrinsic value of approximately USD 86 million. Participants paid a total of USD 232 million as exercise price. The actual tax benefit from share options exercised was USD 80.1 million. The weighted-average remaining contractual term for options outstanding at the year-end was 7.0 years and 5.0 years for options exercisable. Options outstanding had an aggregate intrinsic value of USD 290 million and USD 239 million for options exercisable.

The following table summarizes information about ADS options outstanding at December 31, 2007:

Range of exercise prices	ADS Options outstanding Number outstanding *(millions)*	Average remaining contractual life *(years)*	Weighted-average exercise price *(USD)*	ADS Options exercisable Number exercisable *(millions)*	Weighted-average exercise price *(USD)*
35-39	10.4	4.9	36.7	10.4	36.7
40-44	2.0	3.2	42.0	2.0	42.0
45-49	12.0	6.1	47.2	4.2	46.3
50-54	6.8	8.1	54.7	0.2	54.7
55-59	11.7	9.0	58.4	0.1	58.4
Total	42.9	7.0	48.7	16.9	40.6

27.2 Other long-term incentive plans

a. **Long-term performance plan.** The Novartis Long-Term Performance Plan rewards key executives who have a significant impact on the long-term success of the Group. Performance is measured against Economic Value Added targets (EVA, as defined in the Novartis accounting manual). Any actual awards will depend on the Group's overall accumulated performance over a three-year period. If the actual performance of the Group is below a threshold level or the participant leaves during the performance period for reasons other than retirement, disability, or death, then generally no shares are awarded. The Compensation Committee amended the Long-Term Performance Plan in 2005 to make Group EVA, as opposed to division or business unit EVA, the relevant criterion and to make the performance period three years. The first delivery of shares, if any, under the amended plan will take place in January 2009 for the performance period 2006 to 2008. For the performance period that ended December 31, 2007, approximately 125 key executives were granted performance shares. The expense recorded in continuing operations in the 2007 income statement amounted to USD 37 million (2006: USD 25 million). During 2007 a total of 539,762 shares (2006: 503,630 shares) were granted to executives.

b. **Leveraged share savings plans.** Associates in certain countries and certain key executives worldwide are encouraged to receive their bonus awards fully or partially in Novartis shares instead of cash. To that end, Novartis maintains several leveraged share savings plans under which Novartis matches investments in shares after a holding period. In principle, participating associates may only participate in one of these plans in any given year.

- Shares invested in the Swiss Employee Share Ownership Plan (ESOP), which is available in Switzerland to approximately 11,000 associates, have a three-year blocking period and are matched at the end of the blocking period with one share for every two shares invested. Approximately 5,800 associates chose to participate in this plan related to bonuses paid for performance in 2006.

- In the UK, associates can invest up to 5% of their monthly salary, up to a maximum of GBP 125, in shares and may also be invited to invest all or part of their net bonus in shares. Two invested shares are matched with one share, which will vest after three years.
- Approximately 25 key executives worldwide were invited to participate in a five-year Leveraged Share Savings Plan (LSSP) as part of compensation for performance in 2006. Shares are invested in this plan for five years. At the end of the investment period, Novartis matches the invested shares at a ratio of 1:1 (i.e. one share awarded for each invested share).

In general, no shares are matched under these plans if an associate leaves Novartis prior to expiration of the blocking period for reasons other than retirement, disability, or death. The expense recorded in continuing operations in the 2007 income statement amounted to USD 270 million (2006: USD 271 million). During 2007, 4,726,256 shares (2006: 3,527,635 shares) were granted to participants.

18 EARNINGS PER SHARE

PERSPECTIVE AND ISSUES

Many investors and other consumers of corporate financial information find comfort in identifying a "shorthand" means of measuring an entity's performance, notwithstanding oft-voiced concerns that any condensed gauge of earnings inevitably risks being incomplete, and even misleading, as a picture of the entity's results for the period. The accounting profession had long opposed publications of earnings per share data, because of the perceived peril of offering a single indicium of the entity's economic performance. Nonetheless, investors in particular are devoted users of earning per share data, which is taken by many to be the single best predictor of the entity's future performance. Ultimately, recognizing that such statistics were being computed in widely varying ways and then broadly disseminated, the accounting standard setters decided to at least impose uniform practices.

The IFRS governing the calculation and disclosure of earnings per share (EPS) is IAS 33. It requires that one measure—or two measures in the case of reporting entities having complex capital structures—be presented for each period for which a statement of comprehensive income is being reported. According to IAS 1, as revised in 2007, if an entity presents the components of profit or loss in a separate income statement, it presents basic and fully diluted earnings per share (or one earnings per share measure, if applicable) in that separate statement. The principal goal in these measures is to ensure that the number of shares used in the computation(s) fully reflects the impact of dilutive securities, including those which may not be outstanding during the period, but which, if they were to become outstanding, would impact the actual future earnings available for allocation to current shareholders.

When the entity's capital structure is uncomplicated, EPS is computed by simply dividing profit or loss by the average number of outstanding equity shares. The computation becomes more complicated with the existence of securities that, while not presently equity shares, have the potential of causing additional equity shares to be issued in future, thereby diluting each currently outstanding share's claim to future earnings. Examples of such dilutive securities include convertible preference shares and convertible debt, as well as various options and warrants. It was long recognized that if calculated earnings per share were to ignore these potentially dilutive securities, there would be a great risk of misleading current shareholders regarding their claim to future earnings of the reporting entity.

The IFRS on EPS computations was the result of a joint international effort to refine the EPS measurements then in common use. Revised IAS 33 largely presaged the latest iteration of the requirement under US GAAP, which is set forth in FAS 128. The purpose of IAS 33 is to prescribe the ground rules for the determination and presentation of earnings per share.

As the name of the measure indicates, EPS is derived by dividing a measure of earnings by a measure of number of common shares. The standard emphasizes the denominator of the earnings per share calculation and notes that even though EPS calculations have limitations—because different accounting policies typically can be used in the determination of earnings, which is in the numerator of the equation—a consistently determined denominator enhances the consistency and meaningfulness of financial reporting.

IAS 33 states that the standard's applicability is both to enterprises whose ordinary shares or potential ordinary shares are publicly traded, and those entities that are in the process of issuing ordinary shares or potential ordinary shares in public securities markets. While IAS 33 does not define the point in the share issuance process when these requirements become effective, in practice this ambiguity has not been a source of difficulty.

Some private entities wish to report a statistical measure of performance, and often choose to use EPS as the well-understood yardstick to employ. While these entities are not required to issue EPS data, when they elect to do so they must also comply with the requirements of IAS 33.

In situations when both parent company and consolidated financial statements are presented, IAS 33 stipulates that the information called for by this standard need only be presented for consolidated information. The reason for this rule is that users of financial statements of a parent company are interested in the results of operations of the group as a whole, as opposed to the parent company on a stand-alone basis. Of course, nothing prevents the enterprise from also presenting the parent-only information, including EPS, should it choose to do so. Again, the requirements of IAS 33 would have to be met by those making such an election.

Certain changes were made to IAS 33, effective in 2005. The objective was to reduce or eliminate alternatives, redundancies and conflicts within IFRS, to address certain convergence issues, and to make selective but minor improvements. The resulting revision to IAS 33 provides additional guidance and illustrative examples on selected complex matters, including the impact of contingently issuable shares; potential common shares of subsidiaries, joint ventures or associates; participating equity instruments; written put options; purchased put and call options; and mandatorily convertible instruments. The fundamental approach to the determination and presentation of earnings per share set forth by IAS 33 was not reexamined, however. These changes are discussed in this chapter.

Further, minor changes had been expected to occur as part of the FASB-IASB convergence efforts, and in mid-2008 an Exposure Draft was released to move EPS computations made under IFRS closer to what has long been standard practice under US GAAP. As of late 2008, the expectation is that these proposed changes, which are discussed later in this chapter, will be enacted by late 2009.

Sources of IFRS
IAS 23, 36, 38

DEFINITIONS OF TERMS

A number of terms used in a discussion of earnings per share have special meanings in that context. When used, they are intended to have the meanings given in the following definitions.

Antidilution. An increase in earnings per share or reduction in net loss per share, resulting from the inclusion of a potentially dilutive security, in EPS calculations.

Basic earnings per share. The amount of net profit or loss for the period that is attributable to each ordinary share that is outstanding during all or part of the period.

Call price. The amount at which a security may be redeemed by the issuer at the issuer's option.

Common share. A share that is subordinate to all other shares of the issuer. Also known as ordinary shares.

Common share equivalent. This expression is used under US GAAP to denote a security which, because of its terms or the circumstances under which it was issued, is in substance equivalent to a common share. There is no directly equivalent concept under IFRS.

Contingent issuance. A possible issuance of ordinary (equity) shares, for little or no consideration, that is dependent on the exercise of conversion rights, options, or warrants, and the satisfaction of certain conditions set forth in a contingent issuance, or similar arrangement.

Conversion price. The price that determines the number of ordinary (equity) shares into which a security is convertible. For example, €100 face value of debt convertible into five ordinary (equity) shares would be stated to have a conversion price of €20.

Conversion rate. The ratio of (1) the number of common shares issuable on conversion to (2) a unit of convertible security. For example, a preference share may be convertible at the rate of three ordinary shares for each preference share.

Conversion value. The current market value of the common shares obtainable on conversion of a convertible security, after deducting any cash payment required on conversion.

Diluted earnings per share. The amount of net profit for the period per share, reflecting the maximum dilutions that would have resulted from conversions, exercises, and other contingent issuances that individually would have decreased earnings per share and in the aggregate would have had a dilutive effect.

Dilution. A reduction in earnings per share or an increase in net loss per share, resulting from the assumption that convertible securities have been converted and/or that options and warrants have been exercised, or other contingent shares have been issued on the fulfillment of certain conditions. Securities that would cause such earnings dilution are referred to as dilutive securities.

Dual presentation. The presentation with equal prominence of two different earnings per share amounts in the statement of comprehensive income: One is basic earnings per share; the other is diluted earnings per share.

Earnings per share. The amount of earnings (profit or loss) for a period attributable to each ordinary (equity) share (common share). It should be used without qualifying language (e.g., diluted) only when no potentially dilutive convertible securities, options, warrants, or other agreements providing for contingent issuances of ordinary (equity) shares are outstanding.

Exercise price. The amount that must be paid for a ordinary (equity) share on exercise of a share option or warrant.

If-converted method. A method of computing earnings per share data that assumes conversion of convertible securities as of the beginning of the earliest period reported (or at time of issuance, if later). This method was mandated under US GAAP and can be analogized to IFRS when appropriate.

Option. The right to purchase ordinary (equity) shares in accordance with an agreement upon payment of a specified amount including, but not limited to, options granted to and share purchase agreements entered into with employees.

Ordinary shares. Those shares that are subordinate to all other shares of the issuer. Also known as common shares. Ordinary shares participate in profit for the period only after other types of shares such as preference shares have participated. An entity may have more than one class of ordinary shares; ordinary shares of the same class have the same rights to receive dividends.

Potential common (ordinary) shares. A financial instrument or other contract which could result in the issuance of common shares to the holder. Examples include convertible debt or preferred shares, warrants, options, and employee share purchase plans.

Put option. Contract which gives the holder the right to have the issuer (the reporting entity) repurchase shares held, at a specified price, usually for a limited stipulated time period.

Redemption price. The amount at which a security is required to be redeemed at maturity or under a sinking-fund arrangement.

Senior security. Any security having preferential rights and which is neither an ordinary (equity) share nor a common share equivalent (as defined above). A nonconvertible preference share is an example of a senior security.

Time of issuance. The time of issuance generally is the date when agreement as to terms has been reached and announced, even though such agreement is subject to certain further actions, such as directors' or shareholders' approval.

Treasury stock method. A method of recognizing the use of proceeds that would be obtained on exercise of options and warrants in computing earnings per share. It assumes that any proceeds would be used to purchase ordinary (equity) shares at current market prices.

Warrant. A security giving the holder the right to purchase shares of common stock in accordance with the terms of the instrument, usually on payment of a specified amount.

Weighted-average number of shares. The number of shares determined by relating (1) the portion of time within a reporting period that a particular number of shares of a certain security has been outstanding to (2) the total time in that period. For example, if 100 shares of a certain security were outstanding during the first quarter of a fiscal year and 300 shares were outstanding during the balance of the year, the weighted-average number of outstanding shares would be 250 [= $(100 \times 1/4) + (300 \times 3/4)$].

CONCEPTS, RULES, AND EXAMPLES

Simple Capital Structure

A simple capital structure may be said to exist either when the capital structure consists solely of common, or ordinary (equity), shares or when it includes no potential ordinary shares, which could be in the form of options, warrants, or other rights, that on conversion or exercise could, in the aggregate, dilute earnings per share. Dilutive securities are essentially those that exhibit the rights of debt or other senior security holders (including warrants and options) and which have the potential on their issuance to reduce the earnings per share.

Computational guidelines. In its simplest form, the EPS calculation is profit or loss divided by the weighted-average number of common, or ordinary, shares outstanding. The objective of the EPS calculation is to determine the amount of earnings attributable to each ordinary share. Complexities arise because profit or loss does not necessarily represent the earnings available to the ordinary shareholder, and a simple weighted-average of ordinary shares outstanding does not necessarily reflect the true nature of the situation. Adjustments can take the form of manipulations of the numerator or of the denominator of the formula used to compute EPS, as discussed in the following paragraphs.

Numerator. The profit or loss figure used as the numerator in any of the EPS computations must reflect any claims against it by holders of senior securities. The justification for this reduction is that the claims of the senior securities must be satisfied before any income is available to the common, or ordinary, shareholder. These senior securities are usually in the form of preference shares, and the deduction from income is the amount of the dividend declared during the year on the preference shares. If the preference shares are cumulative, the dividend is to be deducted from profit (or added to the loss), whether it is declared or not. If preference shares do not have a cumulative right to dividends and current period dividends have been omitted, such dividends should not be deducted in computing EPS. Cumulative dividends in arrears that are paid currently do not affect the calculation of EPS in the current period, since such dividends have already been considered in prior periods' EPS computations. However, the amount in arrears should be disclosed, as should all of the other effects of the rights given to senior securities on the EPS calculation.

Denominator. The weighted-average number of ordinary shares outstanding is used so that the effect of increases or decreases in outstanding shares on EPS data is related to the portion of the period during which the related consideration affected operations. The difficulty in computing the weighted-average exists because of the effect that various transactions have on the computation of ordinary shares outstanding. Although it is impossible to analyze all the possibilities, the following discussion presents some of the more common transactions affecting the number of ordinary shares outstanding. The theoretical construct set forth in these relatively simple examples can be followed in all other situations.

If a company reacquires its own shares (referred to as treasury shares) in countries where it is legally permissible to do so, the number of shares reacquired should be excluded from EPS calculations as of the date of acquisition. The same computational approach holds for the issuance of ordinary shares during the period. The number of shares newly issued is included in the computation only for the period after their issuance date. The logic for this treatment is that since the consideration for the shares was not available to the reporting entity, and hence could not contribute to the generation of earnings, until the shares were issued, the shares should not be included in the EPS computation prior to issuance. This same logic applies to the reacquired shares because the consideration expended in the repurchase of those shares was no longer available to generate earnings after the reacquisition date.

A share dividend (bonus issue) or a share split does not generate additional resources or consideration, but it does increase the number of shares outstanding. The increase in shares as a result of a share split or dividend, or the decrease in shares as a result of a reverse split, should be given retroactive recognition for all periods presented. Thus, even if a share dividend or split occurs at the end of the period, it is considered effective for the entire period of each (i.e., current and historical) period presented. The reasoning is that a share dividend or split has no effect on the ownership percentage of the common shareholder, and likewise has no impact on the resources available for productive investment by the reporting entity. As such, to show a dilution in the EPS in the period of the split or dividend would erroneously give the impression of a decline in profitability when in fact it was merely an increase in the shares outstanding due to the share dividend or split. Furthermore, financial statement users' frame of reference is the number of shares outstanding at the end of the reporting period, including shares resulting from the split or dividend, and using this in computing all periods' EPS serves to most effectively communicate to them.

IAS 33 carries this logic one step further by requiring the disclosure of pro forma (adjusted) amounts of basic and diluted earnings per share for the period in case of issue of shares with no corresponding change in resources (e.g., share dividends or splits) occurring *after* the end of the reporting period, *but before* the issuance of the financial statements. The reason given is that the nondisclosure of such transactions would affect the ability of the users of the financial statements to make proper evaluations and decisions. It is to be noted, however, that the EPS numbers as presented in the statement of comprehensive income are not required by IAS 33 to be retroactively adjusted, as is the case under US GAAP, because such transactions do not reflect the amount of capital used to produce the net profit or loss for the period.

Complications also arise when a business combination occurs during the period. In a combination accounted for as an acquisition (the only method allowable since IAS 3 eliminated the pooling of interests method), the shares issued in connection with a business combination are considered issued and outstanding as of the date of acquisition and the income of the acquired company is included only for the period after acquisition.

IAS 33 recognizes that in certain countries it is permissible for ordinary shares to be issued in partly paid form, and the standard accordingly stipulates that partly paid instruments should be included as ordinary share equivalents to the extent to which they carry rights (during the financial reporting year) to participate in dividends in the same manner as fully paid shares. Further, in the case of contingently issuable shares (i.e., ordinary shares issuable on fulfillment of certain conditions, such as achieving a certain level of profits or sales), IAS 33 requires that such shares be considered outstanding and included in the computation of basic earnings per share only when all the required conditions have been satisfied.

IAS 33 gives examples of situations where ordinary shares may be issued, or the number of shares outstanding may be reduced, without causing corresponding changes in resources of the corporation. Such examples include bonus issues, a bonus element in other issues such as a rights issue (to existing shareholders), a share split, a reverse share split, and a capital reduction without a corresponding refund of capital. In all such cases the number of ordinary shares outstanding before the event is adjusted, as if the event had occurred at the beginning of the earliest period reported. For instance, in a "5-for-4 bonus issue" the number of shares outstanding prior to the issue is multiplied by a factor of 1.25. These and other situations are summarized in the tabular list that follows.

Weighted-Average (W/A) Computation	
Transaction	*Effect on W/A computation*
Common shares outstanding at the beginning of the period	Increase number of shares outstanding by the number of shares
Issuance of common shares during the period	Increase number of shares outstanding by the number of shares issued weighted by the portion of the year the common shares are outstanding
Conversion into common shares	Increase number of shares outstanding by the number of shares converted weighted by the portion of the year shares are outstanding
Company reacquires its shares	Decrease number of shares outstanding by number of shares reacquired times portion of the year outstanding
Share dividend or split	Increase number of shares outstanding by number of shares issued or increased due to the split
Reverse split	Decrease number of shares outstanding by decrease in shares
Pooling of interest	Increase number of shares outstanding by number of shares issued
Purchase	Increase number of shares outstanding by number of shares issued weighted by the portion of year since the date of acquisition

Rights offerings are used to raise additional capital from existing shareholders. These involve the granting of rights in proportion to the number of shares owned by each shareholder (e.g., one right for each 100 shares held). The right gives the holder the opportunity to purchase a share at a discounted value, as an inducement to invest further in the entity, and in recognition of the fact that, generally, rights offerings are less costly as a means of floating more shares, versus open market transactions which involve fees to brokers. In the case of rights shares, the number of ordinary shares to be used in calculating basic EPS is the number of ordinary shares outstanding prior to the issue, multiplied by the following factor:

$$\frac{\text{Fair value immediately prior to the exercise of the rights}}{\text{Theoretical ex-rights fair value}}$$

There are several ways to compute the theoretical value of the shares on an ex-rights basis. IAS 33 suggests that this be derived by adding the aggregate fair value of the shares immediately prior to exercise of the rights to the proceeds from the exercise, and dividing the total by the number of shares outstanding after exercise.

To illustrate, consider that the entity currently has 10,000 shares outstanding, with a market value of €15 per share, when it offers each holder rights to acquire one new share at €10 for each four shares held. The theoretical value ex-rights would be given as follows:

$$\frac{(10,000 \times €15) + (2,500 \times €10)}{12,500} = \frac{€175,000}{12,500} = €14$$

Thus, the ex-rights value of the ordinary shares is €14 each.

The foregoing do not characterize all possible complexities arising in the EPS computation; however, most of the others occur under a complex structure which is considered in the following section of this chapter. The illustration below applies the foregoing concepts to a simple capital structure.

Example of EPS computation—Simple capital structure

Assume the following information:

Numerator information			*Denominator information*	
a.	Profit from continuing operations	€130,000	a. Common shares outstanding January 1, 2008	100,000
b.	Loss on discontinued operations	30,000	b. Shares issued for cash April 1, 2008	20,000
c.	Profit for the year	100,000	c. Shares issued in 10% share dividend declared in July 2008	12,000
d.	6% cumulative preference shares, €100 par, 1,000 shares issued and outstanding	100,000	d. Treasury shares purchased October 1, 2008	10,000

When calculating the numerator, the claims of senior securities (i.e., preference shares) should be deducted to arrive at the earnings attributable to ordinary (equity) shareholders. In this example the preference shares are cumulative. Thus, regardless of whether or not the board of directors declares a preference dividend, holders of the preference shares have a claim of €6,000 (1,000 shares × €100 × 6%) against 2007 earnings. Therefore, €6,000 must be deducted from the numerator to arrive at profit or loss attributable to the owners of ordinary (common) shares.

Note that any cumulative preference dividends in arrears are ignored in computing this period's EPS since they would have been incorporated into previous periods' EPS calculations. Also note that this €6,000 would have been deducted for noncumulative preferred only if a dividend of this amount had been declared during the period.

There may be various complications resulting from the existence, issuance, or redemption of preferred shares. Thus, if "increasing rate" preferred shares are outstanding—where contractually the dividend rate is lower in early years and higher in later years—the amount of preferred dividends in the early years must be adjusted in order to accrete the value of later, increased dividends, using an effective yield method akin to that used to amortize bond discount. If a premium is paid to preferred shareholders to retire the shares during the reporting period, this payment is treated as additional preferred dividends paid for purposes of EPS computations. Similarly, if a premium is paid (in cash or in terms of improved conversion terms) to encourage the conversion of convertible preferred shares, that payment (including the fair value of additional common shares granted as an inducement) is included in the preferred dividends paid in the reporting period, thereby reducing earnings allocable to common shares for EPS calculation purposes. Contrariwise, if preferred shares are redeemed at a value lower than carrying (book) amount—admittedly, not a very likely occurrence—that amount is used to reduce earnings available for common shareholders in the period, thereby increasing EPS.

In 2007 IASB issued a revised IAS 1, *Presentation of Financial Statements,* which replaced the income statement with a "statement of comprehensive income." All nonowner changes in equity (comprehensive income) are presented in either one or two statements of comprehensive income, separately from owner changes in equity. Profit or loss and other comprehensive income items should be presented in the statement of comprehensive income. An entity is allowed to present the components of profit or loss *either* in the statement of comprehensive income *or* in a separate income statement. A separate income statement forms part of a complete set of financial statements and is displayed immediately before the statement of comprehensive income. This revised IAS 1 amended IAS 33 to the effect that, if an entity presents the components of profit or loss in a separate income statement, it presents basic and diluted earnings per share (or one earnings per share measure, if applicable) in that separate statement (see Chapter 3).

The EPS calculations for the foregoing fact pattern follow.

Earnings per common share

On profit from continuing operations = (€130,000 – €6,000 preference dividends) ÷ Weighted number of ordinary shares outstanding (see below) = €1.00

On profit for the year = (€130,000 – €30,000 – €6,000) ÷ Weighted number of ordinary shares outstanding (see below) = €0.76

Only the EPS amounts relating to the parent company, in the case of consolidated (group) financial statements, must be provided.

The computation of the denominator is based on the weighted-average number of ordinary shares outstanding. Recall that use of a simple average (e.g., the sum of year-beginning and year-end outstanding shares, divided by two) is not considered appropriate because it fails to accurately give effect to various complexities. The table below illustrates one way of computing the weighted-average number of shares outstanding. Note that, had share issuances occurred mid-month, the weighted-average number of shares would have been based on the number of days elapsing between events.

Item	*Number of shares actually outstanding*	*Fraction of the year outstanding*	*Shares times fraction of the year*
Number of shares as of beginning of the year January 1, 2008	110,000 [100,000 + 10%(100,000)]	12/12	110,000
Shares issued April 1, 2008	22,000 [20,000 + 10%(20,000)]	9/12	16,500
Treasury shares purchased October 1, 2008	(10,000)	3/12	(2,500)
Weighted-average number of common shares outstanding			124,000

Recall that the share dividend declared in July is considered to be retroactive to the beginning of the year. Thus, for the period January 1, 2008 through April 1, 2008, 110,000 shares are considered to be outstanding. When shares are issued, they are included in the weighted-average beginning with the date of issuance. The share dividend applicable to these newly issued shares is also assumed to have existed for the same period. Thus, we can see that of the 12,000 share dividend, 10,000 shares relate to the beginning balance and 2,000 shares to the new issuance (10% of 100,000 and 20,000, respectively). The purchase of the treasury shares requires that these shares be excluded from the calculation for the remainder of the period after their acquisition date. The figure is subtracted from the calculation because the shares were purchased from those outstanding prior to acquisition. To complete the example, we divided the previously derived numerator by the weighted-average number of common shares outstanding to arrive at EPS, which is [(€100,000 − €6,000) ÷ 124,000 =] €0.76.

Reporting a €0.24 loss per share (€30,000 ÷ 124,000) due to the discontinued operations is optional. The numbers computed above for the EPS based on profit for the year are the only presentation required in the statement of comprehensive income or separate income statement presented.

Complex Capital Structure

The computation of EPS under a complex capital structure involves all of the complexities discussed under the simple structure and many more. By definition, a complex capital structure is one that has dilutive potential common, or ordinary, shares, which are those that have the potential to be exercised and thereby reduce EPS. The effects of any antidilutive potential ordinary shares (those that increase EPS) is not to be included in the computation of diluted earnings per share. Thus, diluted EPS can never provide a more favorable impression of financial performance than does the basic EPS.

Note that a complex structure requires dual presentation of both basic EPS and diluted EPS even when the basic earnings per share is a loss per share. Under the current standard, both basic and diluted EPS must be stated, unless diluted EPS would be antidilutive.

For the purposes of calculating diluted EPS, the net profit attributable to ordinary shareholders and the weighted-average number of shares outstanding should be adjusted for the effects of all the dilutive potential ordinary shares. That is, the dilutive securities are presumed to have been converted or exercised, with common (ordinary) shares outstanding for the entire period, and with statement of comprehensive income effects of the dilutive securities (e.g., interest or dividends) removed from earnings. In removing the effects of dilutive securities that in fact were outstanding during the period, the associated tax effects must also be eliminated, and all consequent changes—such as employee profit-sharing contributions that are based on reported net income—must similarly be adjusted.

According to IAS 33, the numerator, representing the net profit attributable to the ordinary shareholders for the period, should be adjusted by the after-tax effect, if any, of the following items:

1. Interest recognized in the period for the convertible debt which constitutes dilutive potential ordinary shares
2. Any dividends recognized in the period for the convertible preferred shares which constitute dilutive potential ordinary shares, where those dividends have been deducted in arriving at net profit attributable to ordinary shareholders
3. Any other, consequential changes in profit or loss that would result from the conversion of the dilutive potential ordinary shares

For example, the conversion of debentures into ordinary shares will reduce interest expense which in turn will cause an increase in the profit for the period. This will have a consequential effect on contributions based on the profit figure, for example, the employer's contribution to an employee profit-sharing plan. The effect of such consequential changes on profit or loss available for common (ordinary) shareholders should be considered in the computation of the numerator of the diluted EPS ratio.

The denominator, which has the weighted number of ordinary shares, should be adjusted (increased) by the weighted-average number of ordinary shares that would have been outstanding assuming the conversion of all dilutive potential ordinary shares.

Example

To illustrate, consider Mumbai Corporation, which has 100,000 shares of ordinary shares outstanding the entire period. It also has convertible debentures outstanding, on which interest of €30,000 was paid during the year. The debentures are convertible into 100,000 shares. Profit after tax (effective rate is 30%) amounts to €15,000, which is net of an employee profit-sharing contribution of €10,000, determined as 40% of after-tax income. Basic EPS is €15,000 ÷ 100,000 shares = €0.15. Diluted EPS assumes that the debentures were converted at the beginning of the year, thereby averting €30,000 of interest which, after tax effect, would add €21,000 to net results for the year. Conversion also would add 50,000 shares, for a total of 200,000 shares outstanding. Furthermore, had operating results been boosted by the €21,000 of avoided after-tax interest cost, the employee profit sharing would have increased by €21,000 × 40% = €8,400, producing net results for the year of €15,000 + €21,000 − €8,400 = €27,600. Diluted EPS is thus €27,600 ÷ 200,000 = €0.138. Since this is truly dilutive, IFRS requires display of this amount.

Determining Dilution Effects

In the foregoing example, the assumed conversion of the convertible debentures proved to be dilutive. If it had been *antidilutive,* display of the (more favorable) diluted EPS would not be permitted under IFRS. To ascertain whether the effect would be dilutive or anti-dilutive, each potential ordinary share issue (i.e., each convertible debenture, convertible preferred, or other issuance outstanding having distinct terms) must be evaluated separately from other potential ordinary share issuances. Since the interactions among potential ordinary share issues might cause diluted EPS to be moderated under certain circumstances, it is important that each issue be considered in the order of decreasing effect on dilution. In other words, the most dilutive of the potential ordinary share issues must be dealt with first, then the next-most dilutive, and so on.

Potential ordinary shares are generally deemed to have been outstanding common shares for the entire reporting period. However, if the potential shares were only first issued, or became expired or were otherwise cancelled during the reporting period, then the related ordinary shares are deemed to have been outstanding for only a portion of the reporting period. Similarly, if potential share are exercised during the period, then for that part of the year the actual shares outstanding are included for purposes of determining basic EPS, and the potential (i.e., unexercised) shares are used in the determination of diluted EPS by deeming these to have been exercised or converted for only that fraction of the year before the exercise occurred.

To determine the sequencing of the dilution analysis, it is necessary to use a "trial and error" approach. However, options and warrants should be dealt with first, since these will not affect the numerator of the EPS equation, and thus are most dilutive in their impact. Convertible securities are dealt with subsequently, and these issues will affect both numerator and denominator, with varying dilutive effects.

Options and warrants. The exercise of options and warrants results in proceeds being received by the reporting entity. If actual exercise occurs, of course, the entity has resources which it will, logically, put to productive use, thereby increasing earnings to be enjoyed by ordinary shareholders (both those previously existing and those resulting from exercising their options and warrants). However, the presumed exercise for purposes of diluted EPS computations does not invoke actual resources being received, and earnings are not enhanced as they might have been in the case of actual exercise. If this fact were not dealt with, diluted EPS would be unrealistically depressed since the number of assumed shares would be increased but earnings would reflect the lower, actual level of investment being utilized by the entity.

Without using the terminology of the corresponding US GAAP standard, IFRS prescribes the use of the "treasury stock method" set forth in greater detail by US GAAP to deal with the hypothetical proceeds from the presumed option and warrant exercises. This method assumes that the proceeds from the option and warrant exercises would have been used to repurchase outstanding shares, at the average prevailing market price during the reporting period. This assumed repurchase of shares eliminates the need to speculate as to what productive use the hypothetical proceeds from option and warrant exercise would be put, and also reduces the assumed number of outstanding shares for diluted EPS calculation.

Treasury Stock Method

Denominator must be increased by net dilution, as follows:

Net dilution = Shares issued – Shares repurchased

where

Shares issued = Proceeds received/Exercise price

Shares repurchased = Proceeds received/Average market price per share

---

IAS 33's "shortcut" way of expressing the required use of the "treasury stock method" is as follows: "The difference between the number of ordinary shares issued and the number of ordinary shares that would have been issued at the average market price of ordinary shares during the period shall be treated as an issue of ordinary shares for no consideration."

Example

Assume the reporting entity issued 1,000 common shares to option holders who exercised their rights and paid €15,000 to the entity. During the reporting period, the average price of ordinary shares was €25. Using the proceeds of €15,000 to acquire shares at a per share cost of €25 would have resulted in the purchase of 600 shares. Thus, a net of 400 additional shares would be assumed outstanding for the year, at no net consideration to or from the entity.

In all cases where the exercise price is lower than the market price, assumed exercise will be dilutive and some portion of the shares will be deemed issued for no consideration. If the exercise price is greater than the average market price, the exercise should not be assumed since the result of this would be antidilutive.

Convertible instruments. Convertible instruments are assumed to be converted when the effect is dilutive. Convertible preferred shares will be dilutive if the preferred dividend declared (or, if cumulative, accumulated) in the current period is lower than the computed basic EPS. If the contrary situation exists, the impact of assumed conversion would be antidilutive, which is not permitted by IFRS.

Similarly, convertible debt is dilutive, and thus assumed to have been converted, if the after-tax interest, including any discount or premium amortization, is lower than the computed basic EPS. If the contrary situation exists, the assumption of conversion would be antidilutive, and thus not to be taken into account for diluted EPS computations.

While the term used under US GAAP is not explicitly employed by IAS 33, the methodology to be employed is essentially identical to the US GAAP-defined "if-converted" method. The if-converted method is used for those securities that are currently sharing in the earnings of the company through the receipt of interest or dividends as senior securities but have the potential for sharing in the earnings as ordinary shares. The if-converted method logically recognizes that the convertible security can only share in the earnings of the company as one or the other, not as both. Thus, the dividends or interest less tax effects applicable to the convertible security as a senior security are not recognized in the profit or loss figure used to compute EPS, and the weighted-average number of shares is adjusted to reflect the conversion as of the beginning of the year (or date of issuance, if later). See the example of the if-converted method for illustration of treatment of convertible securities when they are issued during the period and therefore were not outstanding for the entire year.

Example of the if-converted method

Assume a net profit for the year of €50,000 and a weighted-average number of common shares outstanding of 10,000. The following information is provided regarding the capital structure.

1. 7% convertible debt, 200 bonds each convertible into 40 ordinary shares. The bonds were outstanding the entire year. The income tax rate is 40%. The bonds were issued at par (€1,000 per bond). No bonds were converted during the year.
2. 4% convertible, cumulative preferred shares, par €100, 1,000 shares issued and outstanding. Each preferred share is convertible into 2 common shares. The preferred shares were issued at par and were outstanding the entire year. No shares were converted during the year.

The first step is to compute the basic EPS, that is, assuming only the issued and outstanding ordinary shares. This figure is simply computed as €4.60 (€50,000 – €4,000 preferred dividends) ÷ (10,000 ordinary shares outstanding). The diluted EPS must be less than this amount for the capital structure to be considered complex and for a dual presentation of EPS to be necessary.

To determine the dilutive effect of the preferred shares an assumption (generally referred to as the if-converted method) is made that all of the preferred shares are converted at the earliest date that it could have been during the year. In this example, the date would be January 1. (If the preferred had been first issued during the year, the earliest date conversion could have occurred would have been the issuance date.) The effects of this assumption are twofold: (1) if the preferred is converted, there will be no preferred dividends of €4,000 for the year; and (2) there will be an additional 2,000 shares of common outstanding during the year (the conversion rate is 2 for 1 on 1,000 shares of preferred). Diluted EPS is computed, as follows, reflecting these two assumptions:

$$\frac{\text{Net profit for the year}}{\substack{\text{Weighted-average of common shares outstanding} \\ \text{+ Shares issued upon conversion of preferred}}} = \frac{€50,000}{12,000 \text{ shares}} = €4.17$$

The convertible preferred is dilutive because it reduced EPS from €4.60 to €4.17. Accordingly, a dual presentation of EPS is required.

In the example, the convertible bonds are also assumed to have been converted at the beginning of the year. Again, the effects of the assumption are twofold: (1) if the bonds are converted, there will be no interest expense of €14,000 (7% × €200,000 face value), and (2) there will be an additional 8,000 shares (200 bonds × 40 shares) of common shares outstanding during the year. One note of caution, however, must be mentioned; namely, the effect of not having €14,000 of interest expense will increase income, but it will also increase tax expense. Consequently, the net effect of not having interest expense of €14,000 is €8,400 [(1 – 0.40) × €14,000]. Diluted EPS is computed as follows, reflecting the dilutive preferred and the effects noted above for the convertible bonds.

$$\frac{\text{Net profit for the year + Interest expense (net of tax)}}{\substack{\text{Weighted-average of common shares outstanding + Shares} \\ \text{issued upon conversion of preferred and conversion of bonds}}} = \frac{€50,000 + €8,400}{20,000 \text{ shares}} = €2.92$$

The convertible debt is also dilutive, as it reduces EPS from €4.17 to €2.92. Together the convertible bonds and preferred reduced EPS from €4.60 to €2.92.

Contingent Issuances of Ordinary Shares

As for the computation of basic EPS, shares whose issuance is contingent on the occurrence of certain events are considered outstanding and included in the computation of diluted EPS only if the stipulated conditions have been met (i.e., the event has occurred). If at the end of the reporting period the triggering event has not occurred, issuance of the contingently issuable shares is not to be assumed.

Issuances that are dependent on certain conditions being met can be illustrated as follows. Assume that a condition or requirement exists in a contract to increase earnings over a period of time to a certain stipulated level and that, upon attainment of this targeted level of earnings, the issuance of shares is to take place. This is regarded as a contingent issuance of shares for purposes of applying IAS 33. If the condition is met at the end of the reporting period, the effect is included in basic EPS, even if the actual issuance takes place after year end (e.g., upon delivery of the audited financial statements, per terms of the contingency agreement).

If the condition must be met and then maintained for a subsequent period, such as for a two-year period, then the effect of the contingent issuance is excluded from basic EPS, but is included in diluted EPS. In other words, the contingent shares, which will not be issued until the defined condition is met for two consecutive years, are assumed to be met for diluted EPS computation if the condition is met at the end of the reporting period. Meeting the terms of the contingency for the current period forms the basis for the expectation that the terms may again be met in the subsequent period, which would trigger the issuance of the added shares, causing dilution of EPS.

In some instances the terms of the contingent issuance arrangement make reference to share prices over a period of time extending beyond the end of the reporting period. In such instances, if issuance is to be assumed for purposes of computing diluted EPS, only the prices or other data through the end of the reporting period should be deemed pertinent to the computation of diluted EPS. Basic EPS is not affected, of course, since the contingent condition is not met at the end of the reporting period.

IAS 33 identifies circumstances in which the issuance of contingent shares is dependent upon meeting both future earnings and future share price threshold levels. Reference must be made to both these conditions, as they exist at the end of the reporting period. If both threshold conditions are met, the effect of the contingently issuable shares is included in the computation of diluted EPS.

The standard also cites circumstances where the contingency does not pertain to market price of ordinary shares or to earnings of the reporting entity. One such example is the achievement of a defined business expansion goal, such as the opening of a targeted number of retail outlets; other examples could be the achievement of defined level of gross revenues, or development of a certain number of commercial contracts. For purposes of computing diluted EPS, the number of retail outlets, level of revenue, etc., at the end of the reporting period are to be presumed to remain constant until the expiration of the contingency period.

Example

Contingent shares will be issued at year-end 2010, with 1,000 shares issued for each retail outlet in excess of the number of outlets at the base date, year-end 2008. At year-end 2009, seven new outlets are open. Diluted EPS should include the assumed issuance of 7,000 additional shares. Basic EPS would not include this, since the contingency period has not ended and no new shares are yet required to be issued.

Contracts Which May Be Settled in Shares or for Cash

Increasingly complex financial instruments have been issued by entities in recent decades. Among these are obligations that can be settled in cash or by the issuance of shares, at the option of the debtor (the reporting entity). Thus, debt may be incurred and later settled, at the entity's option, by increasing the number of its ordinary shares outstanding, thereby diluting EPS but averting the need to disperse its resources for purposes of debt retirement.

Note that this situation differs from convertible debt, discussed above, inasmuch as it is the debtor, not the debt holder, which has the right to trigger the issuance of shares.

Per revised IAS 33, it is to be presumed that the debtor will elect to issue shares to retire this debt, if making that assumption results in a dilution of EPS. This is assumed for the calculation of diluted EPS, but is not included in basic EPS.

A similar result obtains when the reporting entity has written (i.e., issued) a call option to creditors, giving them the right to demand shares instead of cash in settlement of an obligation. Again, if dilutive, share issuance is to be presumed for diluted EPS computation purposes.

Written put options. The entity may also write put options giving shareholders the right to demand that the entity repurchase certain outstanding shares. Exercise is to be presumed if the effect is dilutive. According to IAS 33, the effect of this assumed exercise is to be calculated by assuming that the entity will issue enough new shares, at average market price, to raise the proceeds needed to honor the put option terms.

Example

If the entity is potentially required to buy back 25,000 of its currently outstanding shares at €40 each, it must assume that it will raise the required €1,000,000 cash by selling new ordinary shares into the market. If the average market price was €35 during the reporting period, it must be assumed that €1,000,000 ÷ €35 = 28,572 shares would be issued, for a net dilution of about 3,572 net ordinary shares, which is used to compute diluted EPS.

The foregoing guidance does not apply, however, to the situation where the reporting entity holds options, such as call options on its own shares, since it is presumed that the options would only be exercised under conditions where the impact would be antidilutive. That is, the entity only would choose to repurchase its optioned shares if the option price were below market price. Similarly, if the entity held a put contract (giving it the right to sell shares to the option writer) on its own shares, it would only exercise this option if the option price were above market price. In either instance, the effect of assumed exercise would likely be antidilutive.

Computations of Basic and Diluted Earnings Per Share

Using the data presented earlier in this chapter, the complete computation of basic and diluted EPS under IAS 33 is shown in the following table:

Items	EPS on outstanding common shares (the "benchmark" EPS) Numerator	Denominator	Basic Numerator	Denominator	Diluted Numerator	Denominator
Profit for the year	€50,000		€50,000		€50,000	
Preferred dividend	(4,000)					
Common shs. outstanding		10,000 shs.		10,000 shs.		10,000 shs.

Items	EPS on outstanding common share (the "benchmark" EPS) Numerator	Denominator	Basic Numerator	Denominator	Diluted Numerator	Denominator
Conversion of preferred				2,000		2,000
Conversion of bonds	_____	_____	_____	_____	8,400	8,000
Totals	€46,000	÷ 10,000 shs.	€50,000	÷ 12,000 shs.	€58,400	÷ 20,000 shs.
EPS		€4.60		€4.17		€2.92

The preceding example was simplified to the extent that none of the convertible securities were, in fact, converted during the year. In most real situations, some or all of the securities may have been converted, and thus actual reported earnings (and basic EPS) would already have reflected the fact that preferred dividends were paid for only part of the year and/or that interest on convertible debt was accrued for only part of the year. These factors would need to be taken into consideration in developing a time-weighted numerator and denominator for the EPS equations.

Furthermore, the sequence followed in testing the dilution effects of each of several series of convertible securities may affect the outcome, although this is not always true. It is best to perform the sequential procedures illustrated above by computing the impact of each issue of potential ordinary shares from the most dilutive to the least dilutive. This rule also applies if convertible securities (for which the if-converted method will be applied) and options (for which the treasury stock approach will be applied) are outstanding simultaneously.

Finally, if some potential ordinary shares are only issuable on the occurrence of a contingency, conversion should be assumed for EPS computation purposes only to the extent that the conditions were met by the end of the reporting period. In effect, the end of the reporting period should be treated as if it were also the end of the contingency period.

No antidilution. No assumptions of conversion should be made if the effect would be antidilutive. As in the discussion above, it may be that the sequence in which the different issues or series of convertible or other instruments that are potentially ordinary shares are considered will affect the ultimate computation. The goal in computing diluted EPS is to calculate the maximum dilutive effect. The individual issues of convertible securities, options, and other items should be dealt with from the most dilutive to the least dilutive to effect this result.

Disclosure Requirements under IAS 33

1. Entities should present both basic EPS and diluted EPS in the statement of comprehensive income or in the income statement, if presented separately, for each class of ordinary shares that has a different right to share in profit or loss for the period. Equal prominence should be given to both the basic EPS and diluted EPS figures for all periods presented.

2. Entities should present basic EPS and diluted EPS even if the amounts disclosed are negative. In other words, the standard mandates disclosure of not just *earnings per share,* but even *loss per share* figures.

3. Entities should disclose amounts used as the numerator in calculating basic EPS and diluted EPS along with a reconciliation of those amounts to profit or loss for the period. Disclosure is also required of the weighted-average number of ordinary shares used as the denominator in calculating basic EPS and diluted EPS along with a reconciliation of these denominators to each other.

4. a. In addition to the disclosure of the figures for basic EPS and diluted EPS, as required above, if an enterprise chooses to disclose per share amounts using a reported component of the separate income statement other than profit or loss for the period attributable to ordinary shareholders, such amounts should be calcu-

lated using the weighted-average number of ordinary shares determined in accordance with the requirements of IAS 33; this will ensure comparability of the per share amounts disclosed;

b. In cases where an enterprise chooses to disclose the above per share amounts using a reported component of the separate income statement, other than profit or loss for the year, a reconciliation is mandated by the standard, which should reconcile the difference between the reported component of profit or loss and profit or loss reported in the statement of comprehensive income or separate income statement presented; and

c. When additional disclosure is made by an enterprise of the above per share amounts, basic and diluted per share amounts should be disclosed with equal prominence (just as basic EPS and diluted EPS figures are given equal prominence).

5. Entities are encouraged to disclose the terms and conditions of financial instruments or contracts generating potential ordinary shares since such terms and conditions may determine whether or not any potential ordinary shares are dilutive and, if so, the effect on the weighted-average number of shares outstanding and any consequent adjustments to the net profit attributable to the ordinary shareholders.

6. If changes (resulting from a bonus issue or share split, etc.) in the number of ordinary or potential ordinary shares occur after the end of the reporting period but before issuance of the financial statements, and the per share calculations reflect such changes in the number of shares, such a fact should be disclosed.

7. Entities are also encouraged to disclose a description of ordinary share transactions or potential ordinary share transactions other than capitalization issues and share splits, occurring after the end of the reporting period that are of such importance that nondisclosure would affect the ability of the users of the financial statements to make proper evaluations and decisions.

Proposed Changes to IAS 33

IASB exposed changes to IAS 33 in August 2008, with the expectation that these will be finalized by late 2009. The objective is to converge IFRS with practice under US GAAP (FAS 128). The proposals in the EPS Exposure Draft would purportedly achieve convergence by establishing a principle to determine which instruments are included in the calculation of basic EPS; by clarifying the treatment of contracts that involve the entity receiving its own ordinary shares for cash or other financial assets; by clarifying that the principles for contracts to repurchase an entity's own shares for cash or other financial assets should also apply to mandatorily redeemable ordinary shares; and by amending the calculation of diluted EPS for participating instruments and two-class ordinary shares.

Regarding the first of these issues, IASB states that the principle to determine which instruments are to be included in the calculation of basic EPS would have the weighted-average number of ordinary shares include only those instruments that give (or are deemed to give) holders the right to share currently in profit or loss of the period. Accordingly, if ordinary shares issuable for little or no cash or other consideration, or mandatorily convertible instruments, do not meet this condition, they would no longer impact the computation of basic EPS.

As to the second of the matters to be addressed, the proposed revision to IAS 33 would require that contracts such as gross physically settled written put options and forward purchase contracts be treated as if the entity had already repurchased the shares. Therefore, the reporting entity would exclude those shares from the denominator of the EPS calculation, thereby increasing the calculated earnings per share. To calculate EPS, the reporting entity would allocate dividends on those shares to the financial liability relating to the present value of the redemption amount of the contract. The liability would therefore be handled as a participating instrument, and specific guidance in the proposed standard would apply to this instrument. It notes, however, that such contracts sometimes require the holder to remit back to the entity and dividends paid on the shares to be purchased; in such a case, the liability would not be deemed a participating instrument.

The amended calculation of diluted EPS for participating instruments and two-class ordinary shares would involve application of a test to determine whether a convertible financial instrument would have a more dilutive effect if conversion is assumed. The reporting entity would assume the more dilutive treatment for diluted EPS.

The proposed changes also include several simplifications to existing calculation rules. Thus, the proposal holds that if an instrument is measured at fair value through profit or loss, changes in its fair value would be said to fully reflect the economic effect of the instrument on current equity holders for the period. That is, the changes in fair value would reflect the benefits received, or detriments incurred, by the current equity holders during the period, and the numerator of the EPS calculation would already include those changes. Accordingly, for an instrument (or the derivative component of a compound financial instrument) that is measured at fair value through profit or loss, the proposal is that the reporting entity should not further adjust the numerator or denominator of the diluted EPS calculation.

To calculate diluted EPS for options, warrants, and their equivalents that are *not* measured at fair value through profit or loss, the reporting entity assumes the exercise of those instruments, if dilutive. In the existing versions of IAS 33 (and also of FAS 128), the calculation of diluted EPS assumes that the entity uses the proceeds to buy back its own ordinary shares at the *average* market price during the period. In order to simplify the calculation of diluted EPS, IASB has proposed that the ordinary shares should be regarded as issued at the *end-of-period* market price, rather than at their average market price during the period.

Under the proposed amendments to IAS 33, contracts to repurchase an entity's own shares and contracts that may be settled in ordinary shares or by cash would either be measured at fair value through profit or loss or the liability for the present value of the redemption amount would meet the definition of a participating instrument. For those instruments, no adjustments would be required in calculation diluted EPS or the application guidance on participating instruments and two-class ordinary shares would apply. Therefore, IASB has proposed to delete the calculation requirements for contracts that may be settled in ordinary shares or cash, and for contracts to repurchase an entity's own shares, currently found in IAS 33.

The amendments provide that the numerators used in the calculation of basic and diluted EPS must be reconciled to profit or loss attributable to the ordinary equity holders of the parent. Additionally, the denominators in the calculations of basic EPS and diluted EPS must be reconciled to each other.

Examples of Financial Statement Disclosures

Roche Group AG
Period Ending December 2007

9. Earnings per share and nonvoting equity security

Basic earnings per share and nonvoting equity security

For the calculation of basic earnings per share and nonvoting equity security, the number of shares and nonvoting equity securities is reduced by the weighted-average number of its own nonvoting equity securities held by the Group during the period.

	Continuing businesses		Group	
	2007	*2006*	*2007*	*2006*
Net income attributable to Roche shareholders (millions of CHF)	9,761	7,860	9,761	7,880
Number of shares (millions)	160	160	160	160
Number of nonvoting equity securities (millions)	703	703	703	703
Weighted-average number of own nonvoting equity securities held (millions)	(4)	(11)	(4)	(11)
Weighted-average number of shares and nonvoting equity securities in issue used to calculate basic earnings per share (millions)	859	852	859	852
Basic earnings per share and nonvoting equity security (CHF)	11.36	9.22	11.36	9.24

Diluted earnings per share and nonvoting equity security

For the calculation of diluted earnings per share and nonvoting equity security, the net income and weighted-average number of shares and nonvoting equity securities outstanding are adjusted for the effects of all dilutive potential shares and nonvoting equity securities.

Potential dilutive effects arise from the convertible debt instruments were to be converted, this would lead to a reduction in interest expense and an increase in the number of shares which may have a net dilutive effect on the earnings per share. The exercise of outstanding vested employee stock options would have a dilutive effect. The exercise of the outstanding vested Genentech employee stock options would have a dilutive effect if the net income of Genentech is positive. The diluted earnings per share and nonvoting equity security shows the potential impacts of these dilutive effects on the earnings per share figures.

	Continuing businesses		Group	
	2007	*2006*	*2007*	*2006*
Net income attributable to Roche shareholders (millions of CHF)	9,761	7,860	9,761	7,880
Elimination of interest expense, net of tax, of convertible debt instruments, where dilutive (millions of CHF)	4	25	4	25
Increase in minority share of Group net income, net of tax, assuming all outstanding Genentech stock options exercised (millions of CHF)	(141)	(100)	(141)	(100)
Net income used to calculate diluted earnings per share (millions of CHF)	9,624	7,785	9,624	7,805
Weighted-average number of shares and nonvoting equity securities in issue (millions)	859	852	859	852
Adjustment for assumed conversion of convertible debt instruments, where dilutive (millions)	1	7	1	7
Adjustment for assumed exercise of equity compensation plans, where dilutive (millions)	2	3	2	3
Weighted-average number of shares and nonvoting equity securities in issue used to calculate dilutive earnings per share (millions)	862	862	862	862
Diluted earnings per share and nonvoting equity security (CHF)	11.16	9.03	11.16	9.05

Nestlé S.A.
Period Ending December 2006

7. Earnings per share from continuing operations

	2007	*2006*
Basic earnings per share in CHF	27.81	23.71
Net profit from continuing operations (in millions of CHF)	10,649	9,123
Weighted-average number of shares outstanding	382,880,947	384,801,089
Fully diluted earnings per share in CHF	27.61	23.56
Net profit from continuing operations, net of effects of dilutive potential ordinary shares (in millions of CHF)	10,678	9,152
Weighted-average number of shares outstanding, net of effects of dilutive potential ordinary shares	386,787,626	388,509,548
Reconcilation of net profit from continuing operations (in millions of CHF)		
Net profit used to calculate basic earnings per share	10,649	9,123
Elimination of interest expense, net of taxes, related to the Turbo Zero Equity-Link issued with warrants on Nestlé S.A. shares	29	29
Net profit used to calculate diluted earnings per share	10,678	9,152
Reconciliation of weighted-average number of shares outstanding		
Weighted-average number of shares outstanding used to calculate basic earnings per share	382,880,947	384,801,089
Adjustment for assumed exercise of warrants, where dilutive	1,966,621	2,230,249
Adjustment for share-based payment schemes, where dilutive	1,940,058	1,478,210
Weighted-average number of shares outstanding used to calculate diluted earnings per share	386,787,626	388,509,548

19 INTERIM FINANCIAL REPORTING

PERSPECTIVE AND ISSUES

Interim financial reports are financial statements covering periods of less than a full fiscal year. Most commonly such reports will be for a period of three months (which are referred to as quarterly financial reports), although in some jurisdictions, tradition calls for semiannual financial reporting. The purpose of quarterly or other interim financial reports is to provide financial statement users with more timely information for making investment and credit decisions, based on the expectation that full-year results will be a reasonable extrapolation from interim performance. Additionally, interim reports can yield significant information concerning trends affecting the business and seasonality effects, both of which could be obscured in annual reports.

The basic objective of interim reporting is to provide frequent and timely assessments of an entity's performance. However, interim reporting has inherent limitations. As the reporting period is shortened, the effects of errors in estimation and allocation are magnified. The proper allocation of annual operating expenses to interim periods is also a significant concern. Because the progressive tax rates of most jurisdictions are applied to total annual income and various tax credits may arise, the accurate determination of interim period income tax expense is often difficult. Other annual operating expenses may be concentrated in one interim period, yet benefit the entire year's operations. Examples include advertising expenses and major repairs or maintenance of equipment, which may be seasonal in nature.

The effects of seasonal fluctuations and temporary market conditions further limit the reliability, comparability, and predictive value of interim reports. Because of this reporting environment, the issue of independent auditor association with interim financial reports remains problematic.

While some national standards had long existed regarding interim financial reporting—most notably in the United States, where the pertinent requirements were established in 1973—IFRS on this topic developed more recently. The international standard on interim financial reporting, IAS 34, was issued in February 1998.

Two distinct views of interim reporting have been advocated, particularly by US and UK standard setters, although some believe that this distinction is more apparent than real. The first view holds that the interim period is an integral part of the annual accounting period (the *integral* view), while the second views the interim period as a unique accounting period of its own (the *discrete* view). Depending on which view is accepted, expenses would either be recognized as incurred, or would be allocated to the interim periods based on forecasted annual activity levels such as sales volume. The integral approach would require more use of estimation, and forecasts of full-year performance would be necessary antecedents for the preparation of interim reports.

Sources of IFRS
IAS 1, 20, 32, 34   *IFRIC* 10
IASB's Framework for the Preparation and Presentation of Financial Statements

DEFINITIONS OF TERMS

Discrete view. An approach to measuring interim period income by viewing each interim period separately.

Estimated annual effective tax rate. An expected annual tax rate which reflects estimates of annual earnings, tax rates, tax credits, etc.

Integral view. An approach to measuring interim period income by viewing each interim period as an integral part of the annual period. Expenses are recognized in proportion to revenues earned through the use of special accruals and deferrals.

Interim financial report. An interim financial report refers to either a complete set of financial statements for an interim period (prepared in accordance with the requirements of IAS 1), or a set of condensed financial statements for an interim period (prepared in accordance with the requirements of IAS 34).

Interim period. A financial reporting period shorter than a full financial year (e.g., a period of three or six months).

Last-twelve-months reports. Financial reporting for the twelve-month period which ends on a given interim date.

Seasonality. The normal, expected occurrence of a major portion of revenues or costs in one or two interim periods.

Year-to-date reports. Financial reporting for the period which begins on the first day of the fiscal year and ends on a given interim date.

CONCEPTS, RULES, AND EXAMPLES

Alternative Concepts of Interim Reporting

The argument is often made that interim reporting is generically unlike financial reporting covering a full fiscal year. Two distinct views of interim reporting have developed, representing alternative philosophies of financial reporting. Under the first view, the interim period is considered to be an integral part of the annual accounting period. This view directs that annual operating expenses are to be estimated and then allocated to the interim periods based on forecasted annual activity levels, such as expected sales volume. When this approach is employed, the results of subsequent interim periods must be adjusted to reflect prior estimation errors.

Under the second view, each interim period is considered to be a discrete accounting period, with status equal to a fiscal year. Thus, no estimations or allocations that are different from those used for annual reporting are to be made for interim reporting purposes. The same expense recognition rules should apply as under annual reporting, and no special interim accruals or deferrals are to be permitted. Annual operating expenses are recognized in the interim period in which they are incurred, irrespective of the number of interim periods benefited, unless deferral or accrual would be called for in the annual financial statements.

Proponents of the integral view argue that the unique expense recognition procedures are necessary to avoid creating possibly misleading fluctuations in period-to-period results. Using the integral view results in interim earnings which are hopefully more indicative of annual earnings and, thus, useful for predictive and other decision-making purposes. Proponents of the discrete view, on the other hand, argue that the smoothing of interim results for purposes of forecasting annual earnings has undesirable effects. For example, a turning point in an earnings trend that occurred during the year may be obscured.

Yet others have noted that the distinction between the integral and the discrete approaches is arbitrary and, in fact, rather meaningless. These critics note that interim periods bear the same relationship to full years as fiscal years do to longer intervals in the life cycle of a business, and that all periodic financial reporting necessitates the making of estimates and allocations. Direct costs and revenues are best accounted for as incurred and earned, respectively, which equates a discrete approach in most instances, while many indirect costs are more likely to require that an allocation process be applied, which is suggestive of an integral approach. In short, a mix of methods will be necessary as dictated by the nature of the cost or revenue item being reported upon, and neither a pure integral nor a pure discrete approach could be utilized in practice. The IFRS on interim financial reporting, IAS 34, does, in fact, adopt a mix of the discrete and the integral views, as described more fully below.

Objectives of Interim Financial Reporting: The IASB's Perspective

The purpose of interim financial reporting is to provide information that will be useful in making economic decisions (as, of course, is the purpose of annual financial information). Furthermore, interim financial reporting is expected to provide information specifically about the financial position, performance, and change in financial position of an entity. The objective is general enough to embrace the preparation and presentation of either full financial statements or condensed information.

While accounting is often criticized for looking at an entity's performance through the rearview mirror, in fact it is well understood by standard setters that to be useful, such information must provide insights into future performance. As outlined in the objective of the IASB's standard on interim financial reporting, IAS 34, the primary, but not exclusive, purpose of timely interim period reporting is to provide interested parties (e.g., investors and creditors) with an understanding of the entity's earnings-generating capacity and its cash-flow-generating capacity, which are clearly future-oriented. Furthermore, the interim data is expected to give interested parties not only insights into such matters as seasonal volatility or irregularity, and provide timely notice about changes in patterns or trends, both as to income or cash-generating behavior, but also into such balance-sheet-based phenomena as liquidity.

In reaching the positions set forth in the standard, the International Accounting Standards Committee (IASC, predecessor of the IASB) had considered the importance of interim reporting in identifying the turning points in an entity's earnings or liquidity. It was concerned that the integral approach to interim reporting can mask these turning points and thereby prevent users of the financial statements from taking appropriate actions. If this observation is correct, this would be an important reason to endorse the discrete view. In fact, the extent to which application of an integral approach masks turning points is probably related to the extent of "smoothing" applied to revenue and expense data.

It seems quite reasonable that interim reporting in conformity with the integral view, if done sensitively, could reveal turning points as effectively as would reports prepared under the discrete approach. As support for this assertion, one can consider national economic statistics (e.g., gross national product, unemployment), which are most commonly reported on seasonally adjusted bases, which is analogous to the consequence of utilizing an integral approach to interim reporting of entity financial information. Such economic data is often quite effective at highlighting turning points and is accordingly employed far more typically than is unadjusted monthly data, which would be roughly comparable to reporting under the discrete approach.

While the objectives of interim reporting are highly consistent with those of annual financial reporting, there are further concerns. These involve matters of cost and timeliness, as well as questions of materiality and measurement accuracy. In general, the belief has been that to be truly useful, the information must be produced in a more timely fashion than is often the case with annual reports (although other research suggests that users' tolerance for delayed information is markedly declining in all arenas), and that some compromises in terms of accuracy may be warranted in order to achieve greater timeliness.

Basic Conclusions about Application of Accounting Principles to Interim Financial Reports

Although a cursory reading of the standard may give the impression that IAS 34 favors a pure discrete view, some of the examples given in Appendix 2 to IAS 34 (e.g., those explaining the accounting treatment of income taxes and employer payroll taxes, or the example which explains the application of the standard to the treatment of contingent lease payments) lead one to believe that, in fact, the IASC pursued an approach which was a combination of the discrete and the integral views.

Most noteworthy, however, is the fact that the approach adopted by IAS 34 is very different from the posture of certain leading national accounting standards, such as that imposed under US GAAP, which mandates the integral view. It is interesting to note, however, that neither standard's position is theoretically pure, in the sense that not all measures are consistent with the stated overall philosophy. Thus, the IASB's approach seems quite balanced. For example, while in IAS 34 the discrete view is endorsed for many purposes, the method of accounting for income taxes prescribed is clearly consistent with an integral view, not a discrete view.

There is no requirement under IFRS that entities prepare interim financial statements. Furthermore, even if annual financial statements are prepared in accordance with IFRS, the reporting entity is free to present interim financial statements on bases other than IFRS, as long as they are not misrepresented as being IFRS compliant.

If interim financial statements are IFRS-based, IAS 34 states that interim financial data should be prepared in conformity with accounting policies used in the most recent annual financial statements. The only exception noted is when a change in accounting principle has been adopted since the last year-end financial report was issued. The standard also stipulates that the definitions of assets, liabilities, income, and expenses for the interim period are to be identical to those applied in annual reporting situations.

While IAS 34, in many instances, is quite forthright about declaring its allegiance to the discrete view of interim financial reporting, it does incorporate a number of important exceptions to the principle. These matters are discussed in greater detail below.

Statements and Disclosures to Be Presented in Interim Financial Reports

Content of an interim financial report. Instead of repeating information previously presented in annual financial statements, interim financial reports should preferably focus on new activities, events, and circumstances that have occurred since the date of publication of the latest complete set of financial statements. IAS 34 recognizes the need to keep financial statement users informed about the latest financial condition of the reporting entity, and has thus moderated the presentation and disclosure requirements in the case of interim financial reports. Thus, in the interest of timeliness and with a sensitivity to cost considerations, and also to avoid repetition of information previously (and recently) reported, the standard allows an entity, at its option, to provide information relating to its financial position in a condensed format, in lieu of comprehensive information provided in a complete set of financial statements prepared in accordance with IAS 1. The minimum requirements as to the components of the interim financial statements to be presented (under this option) and their content are discussed later.

IAS 34 sets forth the following three important aspects of interim financial reporting:

- That the above concession (i.e., permitting presentation of condensed financial information) by the standard is not intended to either prohibit or discourage the reporting entity from presenting a complete set of interim financial statements, as defined by IAS 1;
- That even when the choice is made to present condensed interim financial statements, if an entity chooses to add line items or additional explanatory notes to the condensed financial statements, over and above the minimum prescribed by this standard, the standard does not, in any way, prohibit or discourage the addition of such extra information; and
- That the recognition and measurement guidance in IAS 34 applies equally to a complete set of interim financial statements as to condensed interim financial statements. Thus, a complete set of interim financial statements would include not only the disclosures specifically prescribed by this standard, but also disclosures required by other IFRS. For example, disclosures required by IFRS 7, such as those pertaining to interest rate risk or credit risk, would need to be incorporated in a complete set of interim financial statements, in addition to the selected footnote disclosures prescribed by IAS 34.

Minimum components of an interim financial report. IAS 34 sets forth minimum requirements in relation to condensed interim financial reports. The standard mandates that the following financial statements components be presented when an entity opts for the condensed format:

- A condensed statement of financial position
- A condensed statement of comprehensive income
- A condensed statement of cash flows
- A set of selected footnote disclosures

Form and content of interim financial statements.

1. IAS 34 mandates that if an entity chooses to present the "complete set of (interim) financial statements" instead of opting for the allowed method of presenting only "condensed" interim financial statements, then the form and content of those state-

ments should conform to the requirements set by IAS 1 for a complete set of financial statements.

2. However, if an entity opts for the condensed format approach to interim financial reporting, then IAS 34 requires that, at a minimum, those condensed financial statements include each of the headings and the subtotals that were included in the entity's most recent annual financial statements, along with selected explanatory notes, as prescribed by the standard.

    It is interesting to note that IAS 34 mandates expansiveness in certain cases. The standard notes that extra line items or notes may need to be added to the minimum disclosures prescribed above, if their omission would make the condensed interim financial statements misleading. This concept can be best explained through the following illustration:

    > At December 2008, an entity's comparative statement of financial position had trade receivables that were considered doubtful, and hence, were fully reserved as of that date. Thus, on the face of the statement of financial position as of December 31, 2008, the amount disclosed against trade receivables, net of provision, was a zero balance (and the comparative figure disclosed as of December 31, 2007, under the prior year column was a positive amount, since at that earlier point of time, that is, at the end of the previous year, a small portion of the receivable was still considered collectible). At December 31, 2008, the fact that the receivable (net of the provision) ended up being presented as a zero balance on the face of the statement of financial position was well explained in the notes to the annual financial statements (which clearly showed the provision being deducted from the gross amount of the receivable that caused the resulting figure to be a zero balance that was then carried forward to the statement of financial position). If at the end of the first quarter of the following year the trade receivables were still doubtful of collection, thereby necessitating creation of a 100% provision against the entire balance of trade receivables as of March 31, 2009, and the entity opted to present a condensed statement of financial position as part of the interim financial report, it would be misleading in this case to disclose the trade receivables as of March 31, 2009, as a zero balance, without adding a note to the condensed statement of financial position explaining this phenomenon.

3. IAS 34 requires disclosure of earnings per share (both basic EPS and diluted EPS) on the face of the interim statement of comprehensive income. This disclosure is mandatory whether condensed or complete interim financial statements are presented. However, since EPS is only required by (IAS 33) for publicly-held companies, it is likewise only mandated for interim financial statements of such reporting entities.

4. IAS 34 mandates that an entity should follow the same format in its interim statement showing changes in equity as it did in its most recent annual financial statements.

5. IAS 34 requires that an interim financial report be prepared on a consolidated basis if the entity's most recent annual financial statements were consolidated statements. Regarding presentation of separate interim financial statements of the parent company in addition to consolidated interim financial statements, if they were included in the most recent annual financial statements, this standard neither requires nor prohibits such inclusion in the interim financial report of the entity.

Selected explanatory notes. While a number of notes would potentially be required at an interim date, there could clearly be far less disclosure than is prescribed under other enacted IFRS. IAS 34 reiterates that it is superfluous to provide the same notes in the interim financial report that appeared in the most recent annual financial statements, since financial statement users are presumed to have access to those statements in all likelihood. To the contrary, at an interim date it would be meaningful to provide an explanation of events and transactions that are significant to an understanding of the changes in financial position and performance of the entity since the last annual reporting. In keeping with this line of thinking, it provides a list of minimum disclosures required to accompany the condensed interim financial statements, which are outlined below.

1. A statement that the same accounting policies and methods of computation are applied in the interim financial statements compared with the most recent annual financial statements, or if those policies or methods have changed, a description of the nature and effect of the change;
2. Explanatory comments about seasonality or cyclicality of interim operations;
3. The nature and magnitude of significant items affecting interim results that are unusual because of nature, size, or incidence;
4. Dividends paid, either in the aggregate or on a per share basis, presented separately for ordinary (common) shares and other classes of shares;
5. Revenue and operating result for business segments or geographical segments, whichever has been the entity's primary mode of segment reporting (profit or loss disclosure only if reviewed by chief operating decision maker);
6. Any significant events occurring subsequent to the end of the interim period;
7. Issuances, repurchases, and repayments of debt and equity securities;
8. The nature and quantum of changes in estimates of amounts reported in prior interim periods of the current financial year, or changes in estimates of amounts reported in prior financial years, if those changes have a material effect in the current interim period;
9. The effect of changes in the composition of the entity during the interim period, like business combinations, acquisitions, or disposal of subsidiaries, and long-term investments, restructuring, and discontinuing operations; and
10. The changes in contingent liabilities or contingent assets since the most recent annual financial statements.

IAS 34 provides examples of the disclosures that are required. For instance, an examples of unusual items are ". . .the write-down of inventories to net realizable value and the reversal of such a write-down."

Finally, in the case of a complete set of interim financial statements, the standard allows additional disclosures mandated by other IFRS. However, if the condensed format is used, then additional disclosures required by other IFRS are *not* required.

Comparative interim financial statements. IAS 34 endorses the concept of comparative reporting, which is generally acknowledged to be more useful than is the presentation of information about only a single period. This is consistent with the position that has been taken by the accounting profession around the globe for many decades (although comparative reports are not an absolute requirement in some jurisdictions, most notably in the US). IAS 34 furthermore mandates not only comparative (condensed or complete) interim statements of comprehensive income (e.g., the second quarter of 2009 presented together with the second quarter of 2008), but the inclusion of year-to-date information as well (e.g., the first half of 2009 and also the first half of 2008). Thus, an interim statement of comprehensive income would ideally be comprised of four columns of data. On the other hand, in the case of the remaining components of interim financial statements (i.e., statement of financial position, statement of cash flows, and statement of changes in stockholders' equity), the presentation of two columns of data would meet the requirements of IAS 34. Thus, the other components of the interim financial statements should present the following data for the two periods:

- The statement of financial position as of the end of the current interim period and a comparative statement of financial position as of the end of the immediately preceding fiscal year (*not* as of the comparable year-earlier date);
- The statement of cash flows cumulatively for the current financial year to date, with a comparative statement for the comparable year-to-date period of the immediately preceding financial year; and
- IAS 34 requires that the statement showing changes in equity cumulatively for the current financial year to date be presented, with a comparative statement for the comparable year-to-date period of the immediately preceding financial year.

The following illustration should amply explain the above-noted requirements of IAS 34.

XYZ Limited presents quarterly interim financial statements and its financial year ends on December 31 each year. For the second quarter of 2009, XYZ Limited should present the following financial statements (condensed or complete) as of June 30, 2009:

1. A statement of comprehensive income with four columns, presenting information for the three-month periods ended June 30, 2009, and June 30, 2008; and for the six-month periods ended June 30, 2009, and June 30, 2008
2. A statement of financial position with two columns, presenting information as of June 30, 2009, and as of December 31, 2008
3. A statement cash flows with two columns presenting information for the six-month periods ended June 30, 2009, and June 30, 2008
4. A statement of changes in equity with two columns presenting information for the six-month periods ended June 30, 2009, and June 30, 2008

IAS 34 recommends that, for highly seasonal businesses, the inclusion of additional statement of comprehensive income columns for the twelve months ending on the date of the most recent interim report (also referred to as rolling twelve-month statements) would be deemed very useful. The objective of recommending rolling twelve-month statements is that seasonality concerns would be thereby eliminated, since by definition each rolling period contains all the seasons of the year. (Rolling statements, however, cannot correct cyclicality that encompasses more than one year, such as that of secular business expansions and recessions.) Accordingly, IAS 34 encourages companies affected by seasonality to consider including these additional statements, which could result in an interim statement of comprehensive income comprising six or more columns of data.

Accounting Policies in Interim Periods

Consistency. The standard logically states that interim period financial statements should be prepared using the same accounting principles that had been employed in the most recent annual financial statements. This is consistent with the idea that the latest annual report provides the frame of reference that will be employed by users of the interim information. The fact that interim data is expected to be useful in making projections of the forthcoming full-year's reported results of operations makes consistency of accounting principles between the interim period and prior year important, since the projected results for the current year will undoubtedly be evaluated in the context of year-earlier performance. Unless the accounting principles applied in both periods are consistent, any such comparison is likely to be impeded.

The decision to require consistent application of accounting policies across interim periods and in comparison with the earlier fiscal year is a logical implication of the view of interim reporting as being largely a means of predicting the next fiscal year's results. It is also driven by the conclusion that interim reporting periods stand alone (rather than being merely an integral portion of the full year). To put it differently, when an interim period is seen as an integral part of the full year, it is easier to rationalize applying different accounting policies to the interim periods, if doing so will more meaningfully present the results of the portion of the full year within the boundaries of the annual reporting period. For example, deferral of certain costs at interim statement of financial position dates, notwithstanding the fact that such costs could not validly be deferred at year-end, might theoretically serve the purpose of providing a more accurate predictor of full-year results.

On the other hand, if each interim period is seen as a discrete unit to be reported upon without having to serve the higher goal of providing an accurate prediction of the full-year's expected outcome, then a decision to depart from previously applied accounting principles is less easily justified. Given the IAS 34's clear preference for the discrete view of interim financial reporting, its requirement regarding consistency of accounting principles is entirely logical.

Consolidated reporting requirement. The standard also requires that, if the entity's most recent annual financial statements were presented on a consolidated basis, then the interim financial reports in the immediate succeeding year should also be presented similarly. This is entirely in keeping with the notion of consistency of application of accounting policies. The rule does not, however, either preclude or require publishing additional "parent company only" interim reports, even if the most recent annual financial statements did include such additional financial statements.

Materiality As Applied to Interim Financial Statements

Materiality is one of the most fundamental concepts underlying financial reporting. At the same time, it has largely been resistant to attempts at precise definition. Some IFRS do require that items be disclosed if material or significant, or if of "such size" as would warrant separate disclosure. Guidelines for performing an arithmetical calculation of a threshold for materiality (in order to measure "such size") is not prescribed in IAS 1, or for that matter in any other IFRS. Rather, this determination is left to the devices of each individual charged with responsibility for financial reporting.

IAS 34 advanced the notion that materiality for interim reporting purposes may differ from that defined in the context of an annual period. This follows from the decision to endorse the discrete view of interim financial reporting, generally. Thus, for example, discontinuing operations would have to be evaluated for disclosure purposes against whatever benchmark, such as gross revenue, is deemed appropriate as that item is being reported in the interim financial statements—not as it was shown in the prior year's financial statements or is projected to be shown in the current full-year's results.

The effect of the foregoing would normally be to lower the threshold level for reporting such items. Thus, it is deemed likely that some items separately set forth in the interim financials may not be so presented in the subsequent full-year's annual report that includes that same interim period.

The objective is not to mislead the user of the information by failing to include a disclosure that might appear to be material within the context of the interim report, since that is the user's immediate frame of reference. If later the threshold is raised and items previously presented are no longer deemed worthy of such attention, this is not thought to create a risk of misleading the user, in contrast to a failure to disclose an item in the interim financial statements that measured against the performance parameters of the interim period might appear significant.

Example of interim period materiality consideration

To illustrate, assume that Xanadu Corp. has gross revenues of €2.8 million in the first fiscal quarter and will, in fact, go on to generate revenues of €12 million for the full year. Traditionally, for this company's financial reporting, materiality is defined as 5% of revenues. If in the first quarter income from discontinued operations amounting to €200,000 is earned, this should be separately set forth in the quarterly financial statements since it exceeds the defined 5% threshold for materiality. If there are no other discontinued operations results for the balance of the year, it might validly be concluded that disclosure in the year-end financials may be omitted, since the €200,000 income item is not material in the context of €12 million of full year revenues. Thus, Xanadu's first quarter report might detail the discontinued operations, but that is later subsumed in continuing operations.

Recognition Issues

General concepts. The definitions of assets, liabilities, income, and expense are to be the same for interim period reporting as at year-end. These items are defined in the IASB's *Framework*. The effect of stipulating that the same definitions apply to interim reporting is to further underscore the concept of interim periods being discrete units of time upon which the statements report. For example, given the definition of assets as resources generating future economic benefits for the entity, expenditures that could not be capitalized at year-end because of a failure to meet this definition could similarly not be deferred at interim dates. Thus, by applying the same definitions at interim dates, IAS 34 has mandated the same recognition rules as are applicable at the end of full annual reporting periods.

However, while the overall implication is that identical recognition and measurement rules are to be applied to interim financial statements, there are a number of exceptions and modifications to the general rule. Some of these are in simple acknowledgment of the limitations of certain measurement techniques, and the recognition that applying those definitions at interim dates might necessitate interpretations different from those useful for annual reporting. In other cases, the standard clearly departs from the discrete view, since such departures are not only wise, but probably fully necessary. These specific recognition and measurement issues are addressed below.

Recognition of annual costs incurred unevenly during the year. It is frequently observed that certain types of costs are incurred in uneven patterns over the course of a fiscal year, while not being driven strictly by variations in volume of sales activity. For example, major expenditures on advertising may be prepaid at the inception of the campaign; tooling for new product production will obviously be heavily weighted to the preproduction and early production stages. Certain discretionary costs, such as research and development, will not bear any predictable pattern or necessary relationship with other costs or revenues.

If an integral view approach had been designated by IAS 34, there would be potent arguments made in support of the accrual or deferral of certain costs. For instance, if a major expenditure for overhauling equipment is scheduled to occur during the final interim period, logic could well suggest that the expenditure should be anticipated in the earlier interim periods of the year, if those periods were seen as integral parts of the fiscal year. Under the discrete view adopted by the standard, however, such an accrual would be seen as an inappropriate attempt to smooth the operating results over all the interim periods constituting the full fiscal year. Accordingly, such anticipation of future expenses is prohibited, unless the future expenditure gives rise to a true liability in the current period, or meets the test of being a contingency which is probable and the magnitude of which is reasonably estimable.

For example, many business entities grant bonuses to managers only after the annual results are known; even if the relationship between the bonuses and the earnings performance is fairly predictable from past behavior, these remain discretionary in nature and need not be granted. Such a bonus arrangement would not give rise to a liability during earlier interim periods, inasmuch as the management has yet to declare that there is a commitment that will be honored. (Compare this with the situation where managers have contracts specifying a bonus plan, which clearly would give rise to a legal liability during the year, albeit one which might involve complicated estimation problems. Also, a bonus could be anticipated for interim reporting purposes if it could be considered a constructive obligation, for example, based upon past practice for which the entity has no realistic alternative, and assuming that a realistic estimate of that obligation can be made).

Another example involves contingent lease arrangements. Often in operating lease situations the lessee will agree to a certain minimum or base rent, plus an amount that is tied to a variable such as sales revenue. This is typical, for instance, in retail rental contracts, such as for space in shopping malls, since it encourages the landlord to maintain the facilities in an appealing fashion so that tenants will be successful in attracting customers. Only the base amount of the periodic rental is a true liability, unless and until the higher rent becomes payable as defined sales targets are actually achieved. If contingent rents are payable based on a sliding scale (e.g., 1% of sales volume up to €500,000, then 2% of amounts up to €1.5 million, etc.), the projected level of full-year sales should not be used to compute rental accruals in the early periods; rather, only the contingent rents payable on the actual sales levels already achieved should be so recorded.

The foregoing examples were clearly categories of costs that, while often fairly predictable, would not constitute a legal obligation of the reporting entity until the associated conditions were fully met. There are, however, other examples that are more ambiguous. Paid vacation time and holiday leave are often enforceable as legal commitments, and if this is so, provision for these costs should be made in the interim financial statements. In other cases, as when company policy is that accrued vacation time is lost if not used by the end of a defined reporting year, such costs might not be subject to accrual under the discrete view. The facts of each such situation would have to be carefully analyzed to make a proper determination.

Revenues received seasonally, cyclically, or occasionally. IAS 34 is clear in stipulating that revenues such as dividend income and interest earned cannot be anticipated or deferred at interim dates, unless such practice would be acceptable under IFRS at year-end. Thus, interest income is typically accrued, since it is well established that this represents a contractual commitment. Dividend income, on the other hand, is not recognized until declared, since even when highly predictable based on past experience, these are not obligations of the paying corporation until actually declared.

Furthermore, seasonality factors should not be smoothed out of the financial statements. For example, for many retail stores a high percentage of annual revenues occur during the holiday shopping period, and the quarterly or other interim financial statements should fully reflect such seasonality. That is, revenues should be recognized as they occur.

Income taxes. The fact that income taxes are assessed annually by the taxing authorities is the primary reason for reaching the conclusion that taxes are to be accrued based on the estimated average annual effective tax rate for the full fiscal year. Further, if rate changes have been enacted to take effect later in the fiscal year (while some rate changes take effect in midyear, more likely this would be an issue if the entity reports on a fiscal year and the new tax rates become effective at the start of a calendar year), the expected effective rate should take into account the rate changes as well as the anticipated pattern of earnings to be experienced over the course of the year. Thus, the rate to be applied to interim period earnings (or losses, as discussed further below) will take into account the expected level of earnings for the entire forthcoming year, as well as the effect of enacted (or substantially enacted) changes in the tax rates to become operative later in the fiscal year. In other words, and as the standard puts it, the estimated average annual rate would "reflect a blend of the progressive tax rate structure expected to be applicable to the full year's earnings including enacted or substantially enacted changes in the income tax rates scheduled to take effect later in the financial year."

IAS 34 addresses in detail the various computational aspects of an effective interim period tax rate which are summarized in the following paragraphs.

Multiplicity of taxing jurisdictions and different categories of income. Many entities are subject to a multiplicity of taxing jurisdictions, and in some instances the amount of income subject to tax will vary from one to the next, since different laws will include and exclude disparate items of income or expense from the tax base. For example, interest earned on government-issued bonds may be exempted from tax by the jurisdiction that issued them, but be defined as fully taxable by other tax jurisdictions the entity is subject to. To the extent feasible, the appropriate estimated average annual effective tax rate should be separately ascertained for each taxing jurisdiction and applied individually to the interim period pretax income of each jurisdiction, so that the most accurate estimate of income taxes can be developed at each interim reporting date. In general, an overall estimated effective tax rate will not be as satisfactory for this purpose as would a more carefully constructed set of estimated rates, since the pattern of taxable and deductible items will fluctuate from one period to the next.

Similarly, if the tax law prescribes different income tax rates for different categories of income (such as the tax rate on capital gains which usually differs from the tax rate applicable to business income in many countries), then to the extent practicable, a separate tax rate should be applied to each category of interim period pretax income. The standard, while mandating such detailed rules of computing and applying tax rates across jurisdictions or across categories of income, recognizes that in practice such a degree of precision may not be achievable in all cases. Thus, in all such cases, IAS 34 softens its stand and allows usage of a "weighted-average of rates across jurisdictions or across categories of income" provided "it is a reasonable approximation of the effect of using more specific rates."

Tax credits. In computing an expected effective tax rate for a given tax jurisdiction, all relevant features of the tax regulations should be taken into account. Jurisdictions may provide for tax credits based on new investment in plant and machinery, relocation of facilities to backward or underdeveloped areas, research and development expenditures, levels of export sales, and so forth, and the expected credits against the tax for the full year should be given consideration in the determination of an expected effective tax rate. Thus, the tax effect of new investment in plant and machinery, when the local taxing body offers an investment credit for qualifying investment in tangible productive assets, will be reflected in those interim periods of the fiscal year in which the new investment occurs (assuming it can be forecast to occur later in a given fiscal year), and not merely in the period in which the new investment occurs. This is consistent with the underlying concept that taxes are strictly an annual phenomenon, but it is at variance with the purely discrete view of interim financial reporting.

The interim reporting standard notes that, although tax credits and similar modifying elements are to be taken into account in developing the expected effective tax rate to apply to interim earnings, tax benefits which will relate to onetime events are to be reflected in the interim period when those events take place. This is perhaps most likely to be encountered in the context of capital gains taxes incurred in connection with occasional dispositions of investments and other capital assets; since it is not feasible to project the rate at which such transactions will occur over the course of a year, the tax effects should be recognized only as the underlying events transpire.

While in most cases tax credits are to be handled as suggested in the foregoing paragraphs, in some jurisdictions tax credits, particularly those that relate to export revenue or capital expenditures, are in effect government grants. The accounting for government grants is set forth in IAS 20; in brief, grants are recognized in income over the period necessary to properly match them to the costs which the grants are intended to offset or defray. Thus, compliance with both IAS 20 and IAS 34 would necessitate that tax credits be carefully analyzed to identify those which are, in substance, grants, and then accounting for the credit consistent with its true nature.

Tax loss tax credit carrybacks and carryforwards. When an interim period loss gives rise to a tax loss carryback, it should be fully reflected in that interim period. Similarly, if a loss in an interim period produces a tax loss carryforward, it should be recognized immediately, but only if the criteria set forth in IAS 12 are met. Specifically, it must be deemed probable that the benefits will be realizable before the loss benefits can be given formal recognition in the financial statements. In the case of interim period losses, it may be necessary to assess not only whether the entity will be profitable enough in future fiscal years to utilize the tax benefits associated with the loss, but, furthermore, whether interim periods later in the same year will provide earnings of sufficient magnitude to absorb the losses of the current period.

IAS 12 provides that changes in expectations regarding the realizability of benefits related to net operating loss carryforwards should be reflected currently in tax expense. Similarly, if a net operating loss carryforward benefit is not deemed probable of being realized until the interim (or annual) period when it in fact becomes realized, the tax effect will be included in tax expense of that period. Appropriate explanatory material must be included in the notes to the financial statements, even on an interim basis, to provide the user with an understanding of the unusual relationship between pretax accounting income and the provision for income taxes.

Volume rebates or other anticipated price changes in interim reporting periods. IAS 34 prescribes that where volume rebates or other contractual changes in the prices of goods and services are anticipated to occur over the annual reporting period, these should be anticipated in the interim financial statements for periods within that year. The logic is that the effective cost of materials, labor, or other inputs will be altered later in the year as a consequence of the volume of activity during earlier interim periods, among others, and it would be a distortion of the reported results of those earlier periods if this were not taken into account. Clearly this must be based on estimates, since the volume of purchases, etc., in later portions of the year may not materialize as anticipated. As with other estimates, however, as more accurate information becomes available this will be adjusted on a prospective basis, meaning that the results of earlier periods should not be revised or corrected. This is consistent with the accounting prescribed for contingent rentals and is furthermore consistent with IAS 37's guidance on provisions.

The requirement to take volume rebates and similar adjustments into effect in interim period financial reporting applies equally to vendors or providers, as well as to customers or consumers of the goods and services. In both instances, however, it must be deemed probable that such adjustments have been earned or will occur, before giving recognition to them in the financials. This high a threshold has been set because the definitions of assets and liabilities in the IASB's *Framework* require that they be recognized only when it is probable that the benefits will flow into or out from the entity. Thus, accrual would only be appropriate for contractual price adjustments and related matters. Discretionary rebates and other price adjustments, even if typically experienced in earlier periods, would not be given formal recognition in the interim financials.

Depreciation and amortization in interim periods. The rule regarding depreciation and amortization in interim periods is more consistent with the discrete view of interim reporting. Charges to be recognized in the interim periods are to be related to only those assets actually employed during the period; planned acquisitions for later periods of the fiscal year are not to be taken into account.

While this rule seems entirely logical, it can give rise to a problem that is not encountered in the context of most other types of revenue or expense items. This occurs when the tax laws or financial reporting conventions permit or require that special allocation formulas be used during the year of acquisition (and often disposition) of an asset. In such cases, depreciation or amortization will be an amount other than the amount that would be computed based purely on the fraction of the year the asset was in service. For example, assume that convention is that one-half year of depreciation is charged during the year the asset is acquired, irrespective of how many months it is in service. Further assume that a particular asset is acquired at the inception of the fourth quarter of the year. Under the requirements of IAS 34, the first three quarters would not be charged with any depreciation expense related to this asset (even if it was known in advance that the asset would be placed in service in the fourth quarter). However, this would then necessitate charging fourth quarter operations with one-half year's (i.e., two quarters') depreciation, which arguably would distort that final period's results of operations.

IAS 34 does address this problem area. It states that an adjustment should be made in the final interim period so that the sum of interim depreciation and amortization equals an independently computed annual charge for these items. However, since there is no requirement that financial statements be separately presented for a final interim period (and most entities, in fact, do not report for a final period), such an adjustment might be implicit in the annual financials, and presumably would be explained in the notes if material (the standard does not explicitly require this, however).

The alternative financial reporting strategy, that is, projecting annual depreciation, including the effect of asset dispositions and acquisitions planned for or reasonably anticipated to occur during the year, and then allocating this ratably to interim periods, has been rejected. Such an approach might have been rationalized in the same way that the use of the effective annual tax rate was in assigning tax expense or benefits to interim periods, but this has not been done.

Inventories. Inventories represent a major category for most manufacturing and merchandising entities, and some inventory costing methods pose unique problems for interim financial reporting. In general, however, the same inventory costing principles should be utilized for interim reporting as for annual reporting. However, the use of estimates in determining quantities, costs, and net realizable values at interim dates will be more pervasive.

Two particular difficulties are addressed in IAS 34. These are the matters of determining net realizable values at interim dates and the allocation of manufacturing variances.

Regarding net realizable value determination, the standard expresses the belief that the determination of NRV at interim dates should be based on selling prices and costs to complete at those dates. Projections should therefore not be made regarding conditions which possibly might exist at the time of the fiscal year-end. Furthermore, write-downs to NRV taken at interim reporting dates should be reversed in a subsequent interim reporting period only if it would be appropriate to do so at the end of the financial year.

The last of the special issues related to inventories that are addressed by IAS 34 concerns allocation of variances at interim dates. When standard costing methods are employed, the resulting variances are typically allocated to cost of sales and inventories in proportion to the dollar magnitude of those two captions, or according to some other rational system. IAS 34 requires that the price, efficiency, spending, and volume variances of a manufacturing entity are recognized in income at interim reporting dates to the extent those variances would be recognized at the end of the financial year. It should be noted that some standards have prescribed deferral of such variances to year-end based on the premise that some of the variances will tend to offset over the course of a full fiscal year, particularly if the result of volume fluctuations due to seasonal factors. When variance allocation is thus deferred, the full balance of the variances are placed onto the statement of financial position, typically as additions to or deductions from the inventory accounts. However, IAS 34 expresses a preference that these variances be disposed of at interim dates (instead of being deferred to year-end) since to not do so could result in reporting inventory at interim dates at more or less than actual cost.

Example of interim reporting of product costs

Dakar Corporation encounters the following product cost situations as part of its quarterly reporting:

- It only conducts inventory counts at the end of the second quarter and end of the fiscal year. Its typical gross profit is 30%. The actual gross profit at the end of the second quarter is determined to have been 32% for the first six months of the year. The actual gross profit at the end of the year is determined to have been 29% for the entire year.
- It determines that, at the end of the second quarter, due to peculiar market conditions, there is a net realizable value (NRV) adjustment to certain inventory required in the amount of €90,000. Dakar expects that this market anomaly will be corrected by year-end, which indeed does occur in late December.
- It suffers a decline of €65,000 in the market value of its inventory during the third quarter. This inventory value increases by €75,000 in the fourth quarter.
- It suffers a clearly temporary decline of €10,000 in the market value of a specific part of its inventory in the first quarter, which it recovers in the second quarter.

Dakar uses the following calculations to record these situations and determine quarterly cost of goods sold:

	Quarter 1	*Quarter 2*	*Quarter 3*	*Quarter 4*	*Full Year*
Sales	€10,000,000	€8,500,000	€7,200,000	€11,800,000	€37,500,000
(1-Gross profit percentage)	70%		70%		
Cost of goods, gross profit method	7,000,000		5,040,000		
Cost of goods, based on actual physical count		5,580,000[1]		8,255,000[2]	25,875,000
Temporary net realizable value decline in specific inventory [3]		90,000		(90,000)	0
Decline in inventory value with subsequent increase [4]			65,000	(65,000)	0
Temporary decline in inventory value [5]	10,000	(10,000)	0	0	0
Total cost of goods sold	€7,010,000	€5,660,000	€5,105,000	€8,100,000	€25,875,000

[1] Calculated as [€18,500,000 sales × (1– 32% gross margin)] – €7,000,000 (Quarter 1 cost of sales)
[2] Calculated as [€37,500,000 sales × (1 – 29% gross margin)] – €17,620,000 (Quarters 1-3 cost of sales)
[3] Even though anticipated to recover, the NRV decline must be recognized.
[4] Full recognition of market value decline, followed by recognition of market value increase, but only in the amount needed to offset the amount of the initial decline.
[5] No deferred recognition to temporary decline in value.

Example of interim reporting of other expenses

Dakar Corporation encounters the following expense situations as part of its quarterly reporting:

- Its largest customer, Festive Fabrics, has placed firm orders for the year that will result in sales of €1,500,000 in the first quarter, €2,000,000 in the second quarter, €750,000 in the third quarter, and €1,650,000 in the fourth quarter. Dakar gives Festive Fabrics a 5% rebate if Festive Fabrics buys at least €5 million of goods each year. Festive Fabrics exceeded the €5 million goal in the preceding year and was expected to do so again in the current year.

- It incurs €24,000 of trade show fees in the first quarter for a trade show that will occur in the third quarter.
- It pays €64,000 *in advance* in the second quarter for a series of advertisements that will run through the third and fourth quarters.
- It receives a €32,000 property tax bill in the second quarter that applies to the *following* twelve months.
- It incurs annual factory air filter replacement costs of €6,000 in the first quarter.
- Its management team is entitled to a year-end bonus of €120,000 if it meets a sales target of €40 million, prior to any sales rebates, with the bonus dropping by €10,000 for every million dollars of sales not achieved.

Dakar uses the following calculations to record these situations:

	Quarter 1	*Quarter 2*	*Quarter 3*	*Quarter 4*	*Full year*
Sales	€10,000,000	€8,500,000	€7,200,000	€11,800,000	€37,500,000
Deduction from sales	(75,000)[1]	(100,000)	(37,500)	(82,500)	(295,000)
Marketing expense			24,000[2]		24,000
Advertising expense			32,000[3]	32,000	64,000
Property tax expense		8,000[4]	8,000	8,000	24,000
Maintenance expense	1,500[5]	1,500	1,500	1,500	6,000
Bonus expense	30,000[6]	25,500	21,600	17,900	95,000

[1] *The sales rebate is based on 5% of the actual sales to the customer in the quarter when the sale is incurred. The actual payment back to the customer does not occur until the end of the year, when the €5 million goal is definitively reached. Since the firm orders for the full year exceed the threshold for rebates, the obligation is deemed probable and must be recorded.*

[2] *The €24,000 trade show payment is initially recorded as a prepaid expense and then charged to marketing expense when the trade show occurs.*

[3] *The €64,000 advertising payment is initially recorded as a prepaid expense and then charged to advertising expense when the advertisements run.*

[4] *The €32,000 property tax payment is initially recorded as a prepaid expense and then charged to property tax expense on a straight-line basis over the next four quarters.*

[5] *The €6,000 air filter replacement payment is initially recorded as a prepaid expense and then charged to maintenance expense over the one-year life of the air filters.*

[6] *The management bonus is recognized in proportion to the amount of revenue recognized in each quarter. Once it becomes apparent that the full sales target will not be reached, the bonus accrual should be adjusted downward. In this case, the downward adjustment is assumed to be in the fourth quarter, since past history and seasonality factors made nonachievement of the full goal unlikely until fourth quarter results were known. (Note: with other fact patterns, quarterly accruals may have differed.)*

Foreign Currency Translation Adjustments at Interim Dates

Given the IASC's embracing of the discrete view regarding interim reporting, it is not surprising that the same approach to translation gains or losses as is mandated at year-end would be adopted in IAS 34. IAS 21 prescribes rules for translating the financial statements for foreign operations into either the functional currency or the presentation currency and also includes guidelines for using historical, average, or closing foreign exchange rates. It also lays down rules for either including the resulting adjustments in income or in equity. IAS 34 requires that consistent with IAS 21, the actual average and closing rates for the interim period be used in translating financial statements of foreign operations at interim dates. In other words, the future changes to exchanges rates (in the current financial year) are not allowed to be anticipated by IAS 34.

Where IAS 21 provides for translation adjustments to be recognized in the statement of comprehensive income in the period it arises, IAS 34 stipulates that the same approach be applied during each interim period. If the adjustments are expected to reverse before the end of the financial year, IAS 34 requires that entities not defer some foreign currency translation adjustments at an interim date.

Adjustments to Previously Reported Interim Data

While year-to-date financial reporting is not required, although the standard does recommend it in addition to normal interim period reporting, the concept finds some expression in the standard's position that adjustments *not* be made to earlier interim periods' results. By measuring income and expense on a year-to-date basis, and then effectively backing into the most recent interim period's presentation by deducting that which was reported in earlier interim periods, the need for retrospective adjustment of information that was reported earlier is obviated. However, there may be the need for disclosure of the effects of such measurement strategies when this results effectively in including adjustments in the most current interim period's reported results.

Example of interim reporting of contingencies

Dakar Corporation is sued over its alleged violation of a patent in one of its products. Dakar settles the litigation in the fourth quarter. Under the settlement terms, Dakar must retroactively pay a 3% royalty on all sales of the product to which the patent applies. Sales of the product were €150,000 in the first quarter, €82,000 in the second quarter, €109,000 in the third quarter, and €57,000 in the fourth quarter. In addition, the cumulative total of all sales of the product in prior years is €1,280,000. Under provisions of IAS 34, Dakar cannot restate its previously issued quarterly financial results to include the following royalty expense, so instead will report the royalties expense, including that for earlier years, in the fourth quarter:

	Quarter 1	Quarter 2	Quarter 3	Quarter 4	Full year
Sales related to lawsuit	€150,000	€82,000	€109,000	€57,000	€398,000
Royalty expense	0	0	0	11,940	11,940
Royalty expense related to prior year sales	0			38,400	38,400

Accounting Changes in Interim Periods

A change in accounting policy other than one for which the transition is specified by a new standard should be reflected by restating the financial statements of prior interim periods of the current year and the comparable interim periods of the prior financial year.

One of the objectives of this requirement of IAS 34 is to ensure that a single accounting policy is applied to a particular class of transactions throughout the entire financial year. To allow differing accounting policies to be applied to the same class of transactions within a single financial year would be troublesome since it would result in "interim allocation difficulties, obscured operating results, and complicated analysis and understandability of interim period information."

Use of estimates in interim periods. IAS 34 recognizes that preparation of interim financial statements will require a greater use of estimates than annual financial statements. Appendix C to the standard provides examples of use of estimates to illustrate the application of this standard in this regard. The Appendix provides nine examples covering areas ranging from inventories to pensions. For instance, in the case of pensions, the Appendix states that for interim reporting purposes, reliable measurement is often obtainable by extrapolation of the latest actuarial valuation, as opposed to obtaining the same from a professionally qualified actuary, as would be expected at the end of a financial year. Readers are advised to read the other illustrations contained in Appendix C of IAS 34 for further guidance on the subject.

Impairment of assets in interim periods. IAS 34 stipulated that an entity was to apply the same impairment testing, recognition, and reversal criteria at an interim period as it would at the end of its financial year. The frequency of interim financial reporting, however, was not to affect the annual financial statements. This prescription created unanticipated conflicts, since certain impairments were not, according to other standards, subject to later reversals.

One apparent conflict between IAS 34's directives and the IAS 36 requirement is that an impairment loss recognized on goodwill cannot be later reversed. If, for example, an impairment of goodwill were indicated in the first fiscal quarter, but at year-end that impairment no longer existed, it would be impossible to comply with the proscription against having interim reporting affect annual results unless the impairment in the first quarter were reversed later in the year.

Another apparent conflict pertained to the IAS 39 mandate that impairments recognized on financial assets carried at cost (e.g., unquoted equity instruments) could not be reversed. Furthermore, IAS 39 also stipulated that losses on available-for-sale equity securities, if recognized in profit or loss (i.e., those losses deemed other than temporary in nature), could not later be reversed into income.

To resolve these specific conflicts (and no others), IFRIC Interpretation 10, *Interim Financial Reporting and Impairment*, directs that impairments of goodwill recognized in interim periods may not be later reversed, even if at year's end no impairment would otherwise have been reported. This interpretation therefore brings to an end the IAS 34-based mandate that the frequency of interim reporting cannot itself impact annual financial reporting.

IFRIC 10 also applies to losses recognized regarding equity securities classified as available for sale under IAS 39. That standard directs that, once written down as impaired by means of a charge against earnings, a subsequent increase in the fair value of available-for-sale equity securities, and for financial assets carried at cost (e.g., unquoted equity securities for which fair value cannot be reliably measured) cannot be recognized through income. For example, if an impairment is recognized in the second quarter of an entity's fiscal year, but the security's fair value has recovered by year's end, IAS 39 prohibits reporting the value increase in earnings. This conflicts with the IAS 34 prescription that frequency of interim reporting is not to affect annual results of operations. IFRIC 10 stipulates that an impairment loss recognized in connection with available-for-sale equity securities or financial instruments carried at cost cannot be reversed in subsequent interim periods. This is thus yet another mandate that conflicts with, and supersedes, the fundamental principle of IAS 34.

Interim financial reporting in hyperinflationary economies. IAS 34 requires that interim financial reports in hyperinflationary economies be prepared using the same principles as at the financial year-end. Thus, the provisions of IAS 29 would need to be complied with in this regard. IAS 34 stipulates that in presenting interim data in the measuring unit, entities should report the resulting gain or loss on the net monetary position in the interim period's statement of comprehensive income. IAS 34 also requires that entities do not need to annualize the recognition of the gain or loss or use estimated annual inflation rates in preparing interim period financial statements in a hyperinflationary economy.

Examples of Financial Statement Disclosures

Roche Group
For the half-year ended June 30, 2008

Roche Group Interim Consolidated Financial Statements

Roche Group consolidated income statement for the six months ended June 30, 2008 *in millions of CHF*

	Pharmaceuticals	*Diagnostics*	*Corporate*	*Group*
Sales[2]	17,257	4,747	--	22,004
Royalties and other operating income[2]	1,059	77	--	1,136
Cost of sales	(4,219)	(2,313)	--	(6,532)
Marketing and distribution	(3,164)	(1,207)	--	(4,371)
Research and development[2]	(3,670)	(437)	--	(4,107)
General and administration	(670)	(286)	(133)	(1,089)
Operating profit before exceptional items[2]	6,593	581	(133)	7,041
Major legal cases[9]	315	--	--	315
Operating profit[2]	6,908	581	(133)	7,356

Roche Group consolidated balance sheet *in millions of CHF*

	June 30, 2008	*December 31, 2007*
Noncurrent assets		
Property, plant, and equipment	17,560	17,832
Goodwill[7]	8,088	6,835
Intangible assets[8]	7,069	6,346
Investments in associated companies	9	9
Financial long-term assets	1,056	1,333
Other long-term assets	479	527
Deferred income tax assets	1,046	1,317
Postemployment benefit assets	1,173	1,332
Total noncurrent assets	36,480	35,531
Current assets		
Inventories	5,902	6,113
Accounts receivable	9,553	9,804
Current income tax assets	274	263
Other current assets	2,778	2,452
Marketable securities	11,648	20,447
Cash and cash equivalents	4,057	3,755
Total current assets	34,212	42,834
Total assets	70,692	78,365
Noncurrent liabilities		
Long-term debt	(3,682)	(3,834)
Deferred income tax liabilities	(1,621)	(1,527)
Postemployment benefit liabilities	(3,527)	(3,696)
Provisions[9]	(666)	(688)
Other noncurrent liabilities	(479)	(723)
Total noncurrent liabilities	(9,975)	(10,468)
Current liabilities		
Short-term debt	(1,908)	(3,032)
Current income tax liabilities	(1,760)	(2,215)
Provisions[9]	(579)	(1,517)
Accounts payable	(1,953)	(1,861)
Accrued and other current liabilities	(5,341)	(5,829)
Total current liabilities	(11,541)	(14,454)
Total liabilities	(21,516)	(24,922)
Total net assets	49,176	53,443

	June 30, 2008	December 31, 2007
Equity		
Capital and reserves attributable to Roche shareholders	41,617	45,483
Equity attributable to noncontrolling interests	7,559	7,960
Total equity	49,176	53,443

As disclosed in Note 1. Postemployment benefit assets, deferred tax liabilities and equity have been restated in the December 31, 2007 balance sheet following the adoption of IFRIC Interpretation 14 in 2008. A reconciliation to the previously published balance sheet is provided in Note 1.

Roche Group consolidated statement of recognized income and expense *in millions of CHF*

	Six months ended June 30	
	2008	2007
Available-for-sale investments		
Valuation gains (losses) taken to equity	(184)	23
Transferred to income statement on sale or impairment	1	(111)
Cash flow hedges		
Gains (losses) taken to equity	(114)	8
Transferred to income statement	49	--
Transferred to the initial balance sheet carrying value of hedged items	--	--
Exchange differences on translation of foreign operations	(3,475)	537
Defined benefit postemployment plans	--	--
Actuarial gains (losses)	(136)	777
Limit on asset recognition	(9)	(248)
Income taxes on items taken directly to or transferred from equity	99	(168)
Net income recognized directly in equity	(3,769)	818
Net income recognized in income statement	5,732	5,862
Total recognized income and expense	1,963	6,680
Attributable to	--	--
Roche shareholders	1,754	5,737
Noncontrolling interests	209	943
Total	1,963	6,680
Effect of changes in accounting policy attributable to	--	--
Roche shareholders	--	297
Noncontrolling interests	--	--
Total	--	297

As disclosed in Note 1. the entries for defined benefit postemployment plans have been restated in the statement of recognized income and expense for 2007 following the adoption of IFRIC Interpretation 14 in 2008. A reconciliation to the previously published statement of recognized income and expense is provided in Note 1.

Roche Group consolidated cash flow statement *in millions of CHF*

	Six months ended June 30	
	2008	2007
Cash flows from operating activities		
Cash generated from operations	8,764	9,328
(Increase) decrease in working capital	(903)	(1,101)
Payments made for defined benefit postemployment plans	(185)	(193)
Utilization of legal and environmental provisions	(507)	(262)
Utilization of restructuring and other	(272)	(190)
Other operating cash flows	3	--
Cash flows from operating activities, before income taxes paid	6,900	7,582
Income taxes paid	(2,122)	(2,728)
Total cash flows from operating activities	4,778	4,854
Cash flows from investing activities		
Purchase of property, plant, and equipment	(1,527)	(1,566)
Purchase of intangible assets	(207)	(221)
Disposal of property, plant, and equipment	41	91
Disposal of intangible assets	--	1

	Six months ended June 30	
	2008	*2007*
Disposal of products	284	68
Business combinations[6]	(2,657)	(977)
Divestments of subsidiaries	--	--
Interest and dividends received	333	516
Sales of marketable securities	11,618	7,900
Purchases of marketable securities	(4,099)	(5,306)
Other investing cash flows	(114)	(3)
Total cash flows from investing activities	3,672	593
Cash flows from financing activities		
Proceeds from issue of long-term debt instruments[10]	--	--
Repayment and redemption of long-term debt instruments[10]	(1,000)	(717)
Increase (decrease) in other long-term debt	1	6
Transactions in own equity instruments[11]	(88)	819
Change in ownership interest in subsidiaries	--	--
Chugai[4]	(934)	--
Ventana[6]	(1,285)	--
Increase (decrease) in short-term borrowings	(52)	(343)
Interest and dividends paid	(4,041)	(3,061)
Exercises of equity-settled equity compensation plans	129	279
Genentech and Chugai share repurchases[3,4]	(794)	(1,100)
Other financing cash flows	--	47
Total cash flows from financing activities	(8,064)	(4,070)
Net effect of currency translation on cash and cash equivalents	(84)	25
Increase (decrease) in cash and cash equivalents	302	1,402
Cash and cash equivalents at beginning of period	3,755	3,210
Cash and cash equivalents at end of period	4,057	4,612

Roche Group consolidated statement of changes in equity *in millions* **of CHF**

	Roche shareholders	*Noncontrolling interests*	*Total*
Six months ended June 30, 2007			
At January 1, 2007–as previously published	39,444	7,370	46,814
Changes in accounting policy	297	--	297
At January 1, 2007–restated	39,741	7,370	47,111
Net income recognized directly in equity	818	--	818
Net income recognized in income statement	4,919	943	5,862
Total recognized income and expense	5,737	943	6,680
Dividends paid	(2,930)	(56)	(2,986)
Transactions in own equity instruments	816	--	816
Equity compensation plans	357	280	637
Genentech and Chugai share repurchases[3,4]	(600)	(500)	(1,100)
Convertible debt instruments[10]	(244)	--	(244)
Changes in noncontrolling interests	15	(15)	--
At June 30, 2007	42,892	8,022	50,914
Six months ended June 30, 2008			
At January 1, 2008	45,483	7,960	53,443
Net income recognized directly in equity	(3,066)	(703)	(3,769)
Net income recognized in income statement	4,820	912	5,732
Total recognized income and expense	1,754	209	1,963
Ventana acquisition[6]	--	321	321
Dividends paid	(3,969)	(45)	(4,014)
Transactions in own equity instruments	(88)	--	(88)
Equity compensation plans	327	237	564
Genentech shares repurchases[3]	(445)	(349)	(794)
Changes in ownership interests in subsidiaries	--	--	--

	Roche shareholders	Noncontrolling interests	Total
Chugai[4]	(530)	(404)	(934)
Ventana[6]	(964)	(321)	(1,285)
Changes in noncontrolling interests	49	(49)	--
At June 30, 2008	41,617	7,559	49,176

As disclosed in Note 1. equity as at 1 January 2007 and the entries for defined benefit postemployment plans have been restated in the statement of recognized income and expense for 2007 following the adoption of IFRIC interpretation 14 in 2008. A reconciliation to the previously published statement of recognized income and expense is provided in Note 1.

1. Accounting policies

Basis of preparation of financial statements

These financial statements are the unaudited interim consolidated financial statement (hereafter "the Interim Financial Statements") of Roche Holding Ltd., a company registered in Switzerland, and its subsidiaries (hereafter "the Group") for the six-month period ending June 30, 2008 (hereafter "the interim period"). They are prepared in accordance with International Accounting Standard 34 (IAS 34), *Interim Financial Reporting.* These Interim Financial Statements should be read in conjunction with the Consolidated Financial Statements for the year ended December 31, 2006 (hereafter "the Annual Financial Statements"), as they provide an update of previously reported information. They were approved for issue by the Board of Directors on July 20, 2008

The Interim Financial Statements have been prepared in accordance with the accounting policies set out in the Annual Financial Statements, except for accounting policy changes made after the date of the Annual Financial Statements. The presentation of the Interim Financial Statements is consistent with the Annual Financial Statements, except where noted below. Where necessary, comparative information has been reclassified or expanded from the previously reported Interim Financial Statements to take into account any presentational changes made in the Annual Financial Statements or in these Interim Financial Statements.

The presentation of the Interim Financial Statements requires management to make estimates and assumptions that affect the reported amounts of revenues, expenses, assets, liabilities, and disclosure of contingent liabilities at the date of the Interim Financial Statements. If in the future such estimates and assumptions, which are based on management's best judgment at the date of the Interim Financial Statements, deviate from the actual circumstances, the original estimates and assumptions will be modified as appropriate in the period in which the circumstances change.

The Group operates in industries where significant seasonal or cyclical variations in total sales are not experienced during the financial year. Income tax expense is recognized based upon the best estimate of the weighted-average income tax rate expected for the full financial year.

Changes in accounting policies

In 2007 the Group early adopted IFRS 8, *Operating Segments,* and IAS 23 (revised), *Borrowing Costs,* which are required to be implemented from January 2009 at the latest. In 2008 the Group has early adopted the revised versions of IFRS 3, *Business Combinations,* and IAS 27, *Consolidated and Separate Financial Statements,* that were published in early 2008 and which are required to be implemented from January 1, 2010, at the latest. The Group has also adopted IFRIC Interpretation 14 which related to IAS 19, *Employee Benefits.* The Group is currently assessing the potential impacts of the other new and revised standards that will be effective from January 1, 2009, notably the revisions to IFRS 2, *Share-Based Payment.*

IFRS 3 (*revised*), *Business Combinations.* Amongst other matters, the revised standard requires that directly attributable transaction costs are expensed in the current period, rather than being included in the cost of acquisition as previously. The revised standard also requires that contingent consideration arrangements should be included in acquisition accounting at fair value and expands the disclosure requirements for business combinations. The Group has applied the revised standard prospectively for all business combinations since January 1, 2008, and transaction costs totaling 42 million Swiss francs have been expensed in 2008 that would have been included in the cost of acquisition under the previous accounting policy. Business combinations in 2007 and prior periods have not been restated. Had the new accounting policy been applied in

2007, the Group would have expensed an additional 5 million Swiss francs of transaction costs in the interim period of 2007 (15 million Swiss francs in the full year 2007) and goodwill would have been reduced by these amounts in the respective periods. This change has a negative impact of 0.05 Swiss francs on earnings per share and nonvoting equity security (basic and diluted) in 2008, and would have had a negative impact of 0.01 Swiss francs in the full year 2007) if the revised standard had been applied retrospectively.

IAS 27 (revised), Consolidated and Separate Financial Statements. Amongst other matters, the revised standard requires that changes in ownership interests in subsidiaries are accounted for as equity transactions if they occur after control has already been obtained and if they do not result in a loss of control. Additionally the revised standard renames minority interests as noncontrolling interests. The Group has applied the revised standard retrospectively. There were no transactions in 2007 that required restatement.

IFRIC Interpretation 14 to IAS 19, Employee Benefits. The interpretation adds to the existing requirements of IAS 19 regarding the interaction between the limits on recognition of assets from defined benefit postemployment plans and any minimum funding requirement of such plans. Some of the Group's plans do have a minimum funding requirement and the application of this Interpretation results in an increase in the assets recorded on the Group's balance sheet and a corresponding increase in the Group's equity. The Group has applied the revised standard retrospectively and the impacts on the previously published balance sheet and statement of recognized income and expense are shown in the tables below. The application of the Interpretation has no impact on net income and earnings per share.

Restated balance sheet (selected items) at December 31, 2007 *in millions of CHF*

	As originally published	Application of IFRIC 14	Group restated
Postemployment benefit assets	1,150	182	1,332
Deferred tax liabilities	(1,481)	(46)	(1,527)
Capital and reserves attributable to Roche shareholders	45,347	136	45,483

Restated statement of recognized income and expense for the six months ended June 30, 2007 *in millions of CHF*

	As originally published	Application of IFRIC 14	Group restated
Available-for-sale investments			
Valuation gains (losses) taken to equity	23	--	23
Transferred to income statement on sale or impairment	(111)	--	(111)
Cash flow hedges			
Gains (losses) taken to equity	8	--	8
Transferred to income statement	--	--	--
Transferred to the initial balance sheet carrying value of hedged items	--	--	--
Exchange differences on translation of foreign operations	537	--	537
Defined benefit postemployment plans			
Actuarial gains (losses)	777	--	777
Limit on asset recognition	(450)	202	(248)
Income taxes on items taken directly to or transferred from equity	(118)	(50)	(168)
Net income recognized directly in equity	666	152	818
Net income recognized in income statement	5,862	--	5,862
Total recognized income and expense	6,528	152	6,680
Attributable to			
Roche shareholders	5,585	152	5,737
Noncontrolling interests	943	--	943
Total	6,528	152	6,680

Presentation of operating results in the income statement. The income statement for the six months ended June 30, 2007, has been restated following the presentational changes adopted in the second half of 2007. The Group has made these presentational changes to more accurately reflect the underlying business, to further improve comparability of its results to those of other health-care companies and to allow readers to make a more accurate assessment of the sustainable earnings capacity of the Group. Total operating profit is unchanged, and the presentational changes have no effect on the nonoperating results, net income and earnings per share. These changes, which have been applied retrospectively, are listed below.

- Intangible assets: Amortization and impairment of intangible assets are no longer reported as a separate line, but are now reported as part of Cost of sales (for intangibles relating to marketed products) or as part of Research and development (for intangibles relating to technology and development, and including any impairment on intangibles that are not yet available for use).
- Alliance and royalty expenses: All royalties, alliance and collaboration expenses, including all collaboration profit-sharing arrangements are now reported as part of Cost of sales. Previously some of these were included in Marketing and distribution or General and administration depending upon the terms of the particular agreement. Additionally, royalty expenses payable on royalty income are now reported as part of Royalties and other operating income to more accurately reflect the substance of the underlying transactions. Previously these expenses were included in General and administration.
- Phase IV and similar costs: All such costs, which only arise in the Pharmaceuticals Division, are now reported as part of Research and development. Previously some of these costs were included in Marketing and distribution and General and administration depending on their nature.

Restated income statement for the six months ended June 30, 2007 *in millions of CHF*

	As originally published	*Intangible assets*	*Alliances/ royalties*	*Phase IV*	*Restated*
Group					
Sales	22,827	--	--	--	22,827
Royalties and other operating income	1,191	--	(33)	--	1,158
Cost of sales	(5,629)	(456)	(735)	--	(6,820)
Marketing and distribution	(5,552)	--	650	343	(4,559)
Research and development	(3,635)	(32)	--	(350)	(4,017)
General and administration	(1,237)	--	118	7	(1,112)
Amortization and impairment of intangible assets	(488)	488	--	--	--
Operating profit	7,477	--	--	--	7,477
Pharmaceuticals division					
Sales	18,268	--	--	--	18,268
Royalties and other operating income	1,100	--	(30)	--	1,070
Cost of sales	(3,715)	(300)	(813)	--	(4,828)
Marketing and distribution	(4,462)	--	650	343	(3,469)
Research and development	(3,276)	(31)	--	(350)	(3,657)
General and administration	(944)	--	193	7	(744)
Amortization and impairment of intangible assets	(331)	331	--	--	--
Operating profit	6,640	--	--	--	6,640
Diagnostics division					
Sales	4,559	--	--	--	4,559
Royalties and other operating income	91	--	(3)	--	88
Cost of sales	(1,914)	(156)	78	--	(1,992)
Marketing and distribution	(1,090)	--	--	--	(1,090)
Research and development	(359)	(1)	--	--	(360)
General and administration	(181)	--	(75)	--	(256)
Amortization and impairment of intangible assets	(157)	157	--	--	--
Operating profit	949	--	--	--	949

Unrealized internal profits on inventories that have been sold from one operating segment to another but which have not yet been sold on to external customers at the balance sheet date are eliminated as a consolidation entry. Previously this elimination was allocated to the originating operating segment. The segment results for the six months ended June 30, 2007, have been restated following this presentational change.

2. Operating segment information

Divisional Information *in millions of CHF*

Six months ended 30 June	Pharmaceuticals division		Diagnostics division		Corporate		Group	
	2008	*2007*	*2008*	*2007*	*2008*	*2007*	*2008*	*2007*
Revenues from external customers								
Sales	17,257	18,268	4,747	4,559	--	--	22,004	22,827
Royalties and other operating income	1059	1070	77	88	--	--	1136	1158
Total	18,316	19,338	4,824	4,647	--	--	23,140	23,985
Revenues from other operating segments								
Sales	3	3	5	2	--	--	8	5
Royalties and other operating income	--	--	--	--	--	--	--	--
Elimination of inter-divisional income	--	--	--	--	--	--	(8)	(5)
Total	3	3	5	2	--	--	--	--
Segment results								
Operating profit before exceptional items	6,593	6,640	581	949	(133)	(112)	7,041	7,477
Major legal cases	315	--	--	--	--	--	315	--
Operating profit	6,908	6,640	581	949	(133)	(112)	7,356	7,477
Capital expenditure								
Business combinations	203	75	3,234	871	--	--	3,437	946
Additions to property, plant, and equipment	1,000	1,185	539	398	1	1	1,540	1,584
Additions to intangible assets	205	423	2	6	--	--	207	429
Total capital expenditure	1,408	1,683	3,775	1,275	1	1	5,184	2,959
Research and development								
Research and development costs	3,670	3,657	437	360	--	--	4,107	4,014
Other segment information								
Depreciation of property, plant, and equipment	470	451	313	283	3	2	786	736
Amortization of intangible assets	249	315	223	157	--	--	472	472
Impairment of property, plant, and equipment	--	2	8	--	--	--	8	2
Impairment of goodwill	--	--	--	--	--	--	--	--
Impairment of intangible assets	30	16	--	--	--	--	30	16
Equity compensation plan expenses	266	297	19	11	8	7	293	315

Pharmaceuticals subdivisional information *in millions of CHF*

Six months ended 30 June	Roche Pharmaceuticals		Genentech		Chugai Pharmaceuticals Division		Group	
	2008	2007	2008	2007	2008	2007	2008	2007
Revenues from external customers								
Sales	10,938	11,367	4,867	5,227	1,452	1,674	17,257	18,268
Royalties and other operating income	495	473	556	548	8	49	1,059	1,070
Total	11,433	11,840	5,423	5,775	1,460	1,723	18,316	19,338
Revenues from other operating segments								
Sales	282	345	295	634	13	--	590	979
Royalties and other operating income	7	4	825	694	65	43	897	741
Elimination of inter-divisional income	--	--	--	--	--	--	(1,484)	(1,717)
Total	289	349	1,120	1,328	78	43	3	3
Segment results								
Operating profit before exceptional items	3,693	3,583	2,630	2,949	279	334	6,602	6,866
Elimination of inter-divisional profit	--	--	--	--	--	--	(9)	(226)
Subtotal	3,693	3,583	2,630	2,949	279	334	6,908	6,640
Major legal cases	--	--	315	--	--	--	315	--
Operating profit	3,693	3,583	2,945	2,949	279	334	6,908	6,640
Capital expenditure								
Business combinations	203	75	--	--	--	--	203	75
Additions to property, plant, and equipment	374	383	442	672	184	130	1,000	1,185
Additions to intangible assets	125	85	80	336	--	--	205	423
Total capital expenditure	702	543	522	1,010	184	130	1,408	1,683
Research and development								
Research and development costs	2,149	2,189	1,262	1,228	292	304	3,703	3,721
Elimination of costs within division							(33)	(64)
Total	2,149	2,189	1,262	1,228	292	304	3,670	3,657
Other segment information								
Depreciation of property, plant, and equipment	267	257	160	158	43	36	470	451
Amortization of intangible assets	124	200	92	81	33	34	249	315
Impairment of property, plant, and equipment	--	1	--	--	--	1	--	2
Impairment of goodwill	--	--	--	--	--	--	--	--
Impairment of intangible assets	30	16	--	--	--	--	30	16
Equity compensation plan expenses	56	52	209	244	1	1	266	297

3. Genentech

The common stock of Genentech is publicly traded and is listed on the New York Stock Exchange, under the symbol DNA. At June 30, 2008, the Group's interest in Genentech was 55.9% (December 31, 2007: 55.8%). Genentech prepares financial statements in conformity with accounting principles generally accepted in the United States (US GAAP). These are filed on a quarterly basis with the US Securities and Exchange Commission (SEC). Due to certain consolidation entries and differences in the requirements of International Financial Reporting Standards (IFRS) and US GAAP, there are differences between Genentech's stand-alone results on a US GAAP basis and the results of Genentech as consolidated by the Roche Group in accordance with IFRS. These are discussed in Note 3 of the Annual Financial Statements. The impacts on the interim results are reconciled in the table below.

Reconciliation of Genentech results

	Six months ended June 30, 2008		Six months ended June 30, 2007	
	USD millions	CHF millions[a]	USD millions	CHF millions[a]
Operating income (US GAAP basis)	2,748		2,183	
Redemption costs	78		52	
Equity compensation plan expenses (US GAAP basis)	208		203	
Special litigation items	(300)		26	
Operating income (non-US GAAP basis)	2,734		2,464	
Add (deduct) differences and consolidation entries				
Add back redemption costs	(78)		(52)	
Equity compensation plan expenses (IFRS basis)	(199)		(198)	
Capitalized in-process research and development	58		181	
Other differences and consolidation entries	(11)		7	
Operating profit before exceptional items (IFRS basis)	2,504	2,630	2,402	2,949
Add (deduct) exceptional items				
Major legal cases	310	315	--	--
Segment result/operating profit (IFRS basis)	2,814	2,945	2,402	2,949
Add (deduct) nonoperating items (IFRS basis)				
Financial income and financing costs		135		106
Income taxes		(1,257)		(1,201)
Net income (IFRS basis)		1,623		1,854
Noncontrolling interest calculation				
Noncontrolling interest (average during period)		44.1%		44.2%
Income applicable to noncontrolling interest (IFRS basis)		804		820

Translated at 1 USD = 1.05 CHF (2007: 1 USD = 1.23 CHF).

Genentech share repurchases and equity compensation plans

On April 15, 2008, Genentech's Board of Directors approved an extension of the existing stock repurchase programme authorizing Genentech to repurchase up to 150 million shares of Genentech's common stock for a total of 10 billion US dollars through June 30, 2009. Since the program's inception, Genentech has repurchased approximately 83 million shares for a total of approximately 6.0 billion US dollars.

Genentech prepaid share repurchase program. On May 8, 2008, Genentech entered into a prepaid share repurchase arrangement with a financial institution for 500 million US dollars under which Genentech's shares will be purchased in the open market by the financial institution from July 1, 2008, through September 25, 2008. The prepaid amount has been recorded against equity as at June 30, 2008. For the purposes of the Group's consolidation, noncontrolling interests are calculated assuming that an equivalent number of shares have been repurchased based on the amount of the prepayment and the Genentech share price at each month-end. Accordingly the Roche Group's ownership at June 30, 2008, is estimated at 56.3% for the purposes of the consolidation of the financial statements.

During the interim period the net cash outflow from repurchases of Genentech common stock including prepayments, was 794 million Swiss francs (2007: 818 million Swiss francs) and exercises from Genentech's equity compensation plans resulted in a cash inflow equivalent to 240 million Swiss francs (2007: 339 million Swiss francs).

4. Chugai

The common stock of Chugai is publicly traded and is listed on the Tokyo Stock Exchange under the stock code "TSE:4519." At 30 June 2008 the Group's interest in Chugai was 61.5% (31 December 2007: 51.5%). Chugai prepares financial statements in conformity with accounting principles generally accepted in Japan (JGAAP). These are filed on a quarterly basis with the Tokyo Stock Exchange. Due to certain consolidation entries and differences in the requirements of International Financial Reporting Standards (IFRS) and JGAAP, there are differences between Chugai's stand-alone results on a JGAAP basis and the results of Chugai as consolidated by the Roche Group in accordance with IFRS. These are discussed in Note 4 of the Annual Financial Statements.

Reconciliation of Chugai results

	Six months ended June 30		Six months ended June 30	
	JPY billions	*CHF millions*	*JPY billions*	*CHF millions*
Operating profit before acquisition accounting impacts (IFRS basis)	31.2	312	36.0	368
Depreciation of property, plant, and equipment	(0.3)	(3)	(0.3)	(3)
Amortization of intangible assets arising from business combinations	(3.0)	(30)	(3.1)	(31)
Operating profit (IFRS basis)	27.9	279	32.6	334
Add (deduct) nonoperating items (IFRS basis)				
Financial income and financing costs		12		5
Income taxes		(109)		(131)
Net income (IFRS basis)		182		208
Noncontrolling interest calculation				
Add back acquisition accounting impact on net income		20		20
Net income excluding acquisition accounting		202		228
Noncontrolling interest (average during interim period)		47.7%		48.9%
Income applicable to noncontrolling interest (IFRS basis)		97		112

Translated at 100 JPY = 1.00 CHF (2007: 100 JPY = 1.02 CHF).

Dividends

The dividends distributed to third parties holding Chugai shares during the interim period totaled 40 million Swiss francs (2007: 50 million Swiss francs) and have been recorded to equity. Dividends paid by Chugai to Roche are eliminated on consolidation as intercompany items.

Tender offer for Chugai shares

On 22 May 2008, the Group announced a tender offer to acquire additional common shares of Chugai to increase the Group's ownership of Chugai's issued shares from 50.1% to 59.9%. The tender offer was fully subscribed at the offer price of 1,730 Japanese yen per share and on June 24, 2008, the Group acquired 54.9 million common shares of Chugai for a cash consideration of 95.0 billion Japanese yen (912 million Swiss francs). Taking into account the shares that had previously been repurchased by Chugai but not retired, the Group's ownership in Chugai's outstanding shares increased to 61.5%. The total cash outflow of 934 million Swiss francs, including directly attributable costs of 22 million Swiss francs, has been recorded to equity as a change in ownership interest in subsidiaries.

Chugai share repurchases

There were no share repurchases in the interim period of 2008. During the interim period of 2007, Chugai repurchased 9.5 million of its common shares for a total consideration of 27.6

billion Japanese yen (282 million Swiss francs). As a result, the Group's ownership in Chugai increased to 51.5% at that time.

5. Financial income and financing costs

Financial income *in millions of CHF*

	Six months ended June 30 2008	Six months ended June 30 2007
Gains on sale of equity securities	95	155
(Losses) on sale of equity securities	--	(1)
Dividend income	1	1
Gains (losses) on equity derivatives, net	13	(1)
Write-downs and impairments of equity securities	(10)	(5)
Net income from equity securities	99	149
Interest income	390	520
Gains on sale of debt securities	7	65
(Losses) on sale of debt securities	(52)	(57)
Gains (losses) on debt security derivatives, net	(51)	--
Net gains (losses) on financial assets at fair-value-through-profit-or-loss	(6)	8
Write-downs and impairments of long-term loans	--	--
Net interest income and income from debt securities	288	536
Expected return on plan assets of defined benefit plans	339	335
Foreign exchange gains (losses), net	(82)	81
Gains (losses) on foreign currency derivatives, net	50	(108)
Net foreign exchange gains (losses)	(32)	(27)
Net other financial income (expense)	(10)	(14)
Total financial income	684	979

Financing costs *in millions of CHF*

	Six months ended June 30 2008	Six months ended June 30 2007
Interest expense	(106)	(144)
Amortization of discount on debt instruments	--	(6)
Gains (losses) on interest rate derivatives, net	(1)	--
Net gains (losses) on financial liabilities at fair-value-through-profit-or-loss	(1)	14
Time cost of provisions	(16)	(36)
Interest cost of defined benefit plans	(323)	(307)
Total financing costs	(447)	(479)

Net financial income *in millions of CHF*

	Six months ended June 30 2008	Six months ended June 30 2007
Financial income	684	979
Financial costs	(447)	(479)
Net financial income	237	500
Financial result from Treasury management	221	472
Financial result from Pension management	16	28
Net financial income	237	500

9. Provisions and contingent liabilities

Provisions *in millions of CHF*

	June 30, 2008	December 31, 2007
Legal provisions	101	985
Environmental provisions	177	203
Other provisions	147	193
Total provisions	1,245	2,205
Of which		
Current portion	579	1,517
Noncurrent portion	666	688
Total provisions	1,245	2,205

Payments in the interim period from previously recorded provisions totaled 780 million Swiss francs (2007: 452 million Swiss francs). Included in these amounts are 515 million Swiss francs (2007: 262 million Swiss francs) relating to legal provisions.

Major legal cases

Income (expense) from major legal cases is disclosed separately in the income statement due to the materiality of the amounts and in order to fairly present the Group's results. Income of 315 million Swiss francs was recorded in the interim period following the April 24, 2008 California Supreme Court decision in the City of Hope Litigation (see below).

Genentech legal cases

On June 10, 2002, Genentech announced that a Los Angeles County Superior Court jury voted to award the City of Hope National Medical Center (City of Hope) approximately 300 million US dollars in compensatory damages based on a finding of a breach of a 1976 agreement between Genentech and the City of Hope. On June 24, 2002, the jury voted to award the City of Hope 200 million US dollars in punitive damages in the same case. On September 13, 2002, Genentech filed a notice of appeal of the jury verdict and damages awards with the California Court of Appeal. On October 21, 2004, the Court of Appeal affirmed the verdict and damages awards in all respects. Also, on October 21, 2004, Genentech announced that it would seek review by the California Supreme Court, which has discretion over which cases it will review. On November 24, 2004, Genentech filed its petition for review by the California Supreme Court and on February 2, 2005, the California Supreme Court granted this petition. The appeal to the California Supreme Court was heard on February 5, 2008, and on April 24, 2008, overturned the award of 200 million US dollars in punitive damages to the City of Hope, but upheld the award of 300 million US dollars in compensatory damages. On May 9, 2008, Genentech paid 476 million US dollars to the City of Hope, reflecting the amount of compensatory damages awarded, plus interest thereon from the date of the original decision on June 10, 2002.

During the appeals process interest had accrued on the total amount of the damages at a simple annual rate of 10%. During the interim period interest of 11 million Swiss francs (2007: 31 millions Swiss francs) was recorded as the time cost of provisions within financing costs.

A full provision, totaling 776 million US dollars (875 million Swiss francs) as at December 31, 2007, had been recorded for these awards. As a result of the April 24, 2008, California Supreme Court decision, provisions totaling 310 million US dollars (315 million Swiss francs) were released to income as a favorable litigation settlement, of which 200 million US dollars (203 million Swiss francs) relates to the original award recorded in 2002 as an exceptional major legal case expense and 110 million US dollars (112 million Swiss francs) relates to interest accrued as a charge to financing costs in the interviewing periods.

On October 3, 2002, Genentech entered into an arrangement with third-party insurance companies to post a surely bond in connection with this judgment. As part of this arrangement Genentech had pledged 768 million US dollars in cash and investments to secure this bond. This amount, which was equivalent to 889 million Swiss francs at December 31, 2007, was recorded as restricted cash within other current assets in the Annual Financial Statements. In July 2008 Genentech received the court's final administrative order that the judgment was fully satisfied by Genentech's 476 million US dollars payment to the City of Hope. As a result, the entirety of the pledged 788 million US dollars will become unrestricted cash and available for use in Genentech's operations during the third quarter of 2008.

On October 4, 2004, Genentech received a subpoena from the United States Department of Justice, requesting documents related to the promotion of Rittuxan. Genentech is cooperating with the associated investigation, which is both civil and criminal in nature, and through counsel Genentech are having discussions with government representatives about the status of their investigation and Genentech's views on this matter, including potential resolution. The government has called, and may continue to call, former and current Genentech employees to appear before a grand jury in connection with this investigation. The outcome of this matter cannot be determined at this time.

On June 11, 2008, Genentech announced that it had settled its patent litigation with MedImmune, Inc. involving the Cabilly patent (US Patent No. 6,331,415) which is co-owned by Genentech and the City of Hope. Under the terms of the settlement agreement the litigation which was pending before the US District Court for the Central District of California has now been fully resolved and dismissed.

Genentech's annual report and quarterly SEC filings contain the detailed disclosures of litigation matters that are required by US GAAP. These include further details on the above matters, as well as including information on other litigation that is not currently as significant as the matter referred to above.

Other than the matters noted above, no significant changes in the Group's contingent liabilities have occurred since the approval of the Annual Financial Statements by the Board of Directors.

20 OPERATING SEGMENTS

PERSPECTIVE AND ISSUES

With the increasing complexity of business enterprises, and the growing popularity of the conglomerate form of business by the mid-1960s, it became clear that consolidated financial reporting, while obviously necessary, might alone not provide users with sufficient insights for the making of informed economic decisions. At first merely recommended, supplemental segment reporting became required under some national GAAP by the late 1970s. Segment reporting is the disclosure of disaggregated financial information about the reporting entity's operations in different industries or different geographic regions. Because of the perception that domestic and foreign operations constitute differing risks to the entity, segment disclosures also encompass information about the reporting entity's foreign operations and export sales, and—to address yet another aspect of risk—about its major customers.

Early proposals to require segment financial information were met with firm opposition by many preparers, who objected to the additional effort required of them, and more particularly expressed concern that providing disclosures of sensitive disaggregated data to competitors would expose them to strategic risks. These concerns were deemed by analysts and standard setters to be exaggerated, and in any event to not offset the important needs of users of financial information. The popular consensus was that, without the ability to understand which of an entity's major operations were making the most positive contributions to its results, users would be hindered in their ability to make intelligent investment decisions. Ultimately, the need to provide useful information to financial statement users was understood as being more important than the perceived competitive risks to the reporting entity, and segment disclosures of various types have been made mandatory under many financial reporting regimes, albeit often limited to publicly held reporting entities.

As was often the case, financial reporting under US GAAP set the pace for these requirements. The US Securities and Exchange Commission began requiring certain limited line-of-business information in registrants' annual filings in 1970, but in many instances this data was not included in the annual reports issued to stockholders. By 1974, the SEC required registrants to include some of this line-of-business information in their reports to stockholders. Later, FAS 14 was issued (in 1976), which established specific requirements under US GAAP for the disclosure of segment information in financial reports issued to stockholders, a set of requirements that initially applied to all reporting entities and to interim as well as annual financial statements. These requirements were later deleted for interim reports and for non–publicly held companies, due to complaints about cost of preparation.

Under FAS 14, a rather wide range of definitions of business segments was deemed to be acceptable, meaning that comparability across entities was not fully achieved, limiting the usefulness of the information.

The first international standard calling for segment reporting, IAS 14, was originally issued in 1981, and was closely modeled on the then-US GAAP standard. Thus, the range of acceptable definitions of business segments under IFRS was also fairly broad. Subsequently, this standard was significantly revised, effective in mid-1998, by changing the method of determining reportable segments to conform more closely to how the respective reporting entities were actually internally managed. Since the purpose of these disclosures was to put users in "the shoes of management," granting reporting entities this flexibility was seen as making financial reporting more useful to investors. This essentially mirrored the approach adopted under US GAAP (FAS 131).

Under the approach employed through 2008, the burden of preparing segment disclosures was lessened if the segment data captured by the entity's managerial reporting system corresponded with the standard's definitions of business and/or geographical segments. In other cases, it was still necessary for reporting entities to disaggregate and reaggregate data from the management information system in order to develop needed financial statement disclosures. Segment information, while recommended for all issuers of financial statements, is required only for those which have publicly traded debt or equity issues, or which are in the process of preparing a public offering. As of January 1, 2009, IAS 14 is superseded by IFRS 8, which substantially changes the requirements for segment determinations and largely conforms to current US GAAP. This chapter will only address the now-mandatory requirements under IFRS 8, but readers needing to apply or understand IAS 14 can find guidance in earlier (pre-2009) editions of this book.

Sources of IFRS
IFRS 8

DEFINITIONS OF TERMS

Accounting policies. Specific principles, bases, conventions, rules and practices adopted by an entity in preparing and presenting its financial statements.

Cash flows. Inflows and outflows of cash and cash equivalents.

Common costs. Operating expenses incurred by the enterprise for the benefit of more than one business segment.

Consolidated financial information. Aggregate (financial) information relating to an entity as a whole whether or not the entity has consolidated subsidiaries.

Corporate assets. Assets maintained for general corporate purposes and not used in the operations of any business segment.

Discontinued operation. Resulting from the sale or abandonment of an operation that represents a separate, major line of business of an entity; the assets, net profit or loss, and activities can be distinguished physically, operationally, and for financial reporting purposes.

Extraordinary items. Income or expenses that arise from events or transactions that are clearly distinct from the ordinary activities of the entity and, therefore, are not expected to recur frequently or regularly.

General corporate expenses. Expenses incurred for the benefit of the corporation as a whole, which cannot be reasonably allocated to any segment.

Identifiable assets. Those tangible and intangible assets used by a business segment, including those the segment uses exclusively, and an allocated portion of assets used jointly by more than one segment.

Intersegment sales. Transfers of products or services, similar to those sold to unaffiliated customers, between business segments or geographic areas of the entity.

Intrasegment sales. Transfers within a business segment or geographic area.

Minority interest. That part of the net results of operations and of net assets of a subsidiary attributable to interests which are not owned, directly or indirectly through subsidiaries, by the parent.

Operating activities. The principal revenue producing activities of an entity and other activities that are not investing or financing activities.

Operating profit or loss. A business segment's revenue minus all operating expenses, including an allocated portion of common costs.

Operating segment. A component of an entity

- That engages in business activities from which it may earn revenues and incur expenses (including revenues and expenses relating to transactions with other components of the same entity),
- Whose operating results are regularly reviewed by the entity's chief operating decision maker to make decisions about resources to be allocated to the segments and assess its performance, and
- For which discrete financial information is available.

Ordinary activities. Any activities which are undertaken by an entity as part of its business and such related activities in which the entity engages in furtherance of, incidental to or arising from, these activities.

Reportable segment. Operating segments that

- Have been identified in accordance to above or result from aggregating two or more of those segments in accordance with aggregation criteria, and
- Exceed the quantitative thresholds.

Revenue. The gross inflow of economic benefits during a period arising in the ordinary course of business activities from sales to unaffiliated customers and from intersegment sales or transfers, excluding inflows from equity participants.

Segment accounting policies. The policies adopted for reporting the consolidated financial statements of the entity, as well as for segment reporting.

Segment assets. Operating assets employed by a segment in operating activities, whether directly attributable or reasonably allocable to the segment; these should exclude those generating revenues or expenses which are excluded from the definitions of segment revenue and segment expense.

Segment expense. Expense that is directly attributable to a segment, or the relevant portion of expense that can be allocated on a reasonable basis to a segment; it excludes interest expense, losses on sales of investments or extinguishment of debt, equity method losses of associates and joint ventures, income taxes, and corporate expenses not identified with specific segments.

Segment revenue. Revenue that is directly attributable to a segment, or the relevant portion of revenue that can be allocated on a reasonable basis to a segment, and that is derived from transactions with parties outside the enterprise and from other segments of the same entity; it excludes extraordinary items, interest and dividend income, and gains on sales of investments or extinguishment of debt.

Transfer pricing. The pricing of products or services between business segments or geographic areas.

CONCEPTS, RULES, AND EXAMPLES

Conceptual Basis for Segmental Reporting

Business organizations grew in complexity over the years, and the conglomerate form of organization (where unrelated or dissimilar operations are united within one reporting entity, sometimes to provide the overall entity with benefits of countercyclicality among the constituent operations) became ever more popular, and it consequently became necessary to concede that financial statements which present the full scope of an entity's operations declined markedly in utility. While it is certainly possible to assess the overall financial health of the reporting entity using such financial reports, it is much more difficult to evaluate management's operating and financial strategies, particularly with regard to its emphases on specific lines of business or geographic spheres of operation. For example, the extent to which operating results for a given period are the consequence of the development of new products having greater potential for future growth, compared to more mature product lines which nonetheless still account for a majority of the entity's total sales, would tend to be masked in financial statements which did not present results by business segment.

The need for the inclusion of at least some disaggregated information in general-purpose financial reports became critical by the late 1960s, and several national accounting rule-making bodies accordingly began to address this topic around that time. In the US, for example, the need for segment information was one of the first agenda items identified upon the FASB's formation in 1973. The original and long operative US requirement, FAS 14, was promulgated in 1976. A revised standard, largely (but not entirely) embracing largely the same approach as does the current (revised) IAS 14, was adopted as FAS 131, effective in 1998. (A current IASB draft would converge with US GAAP, as discussed below.)

In the UK, the Companies Act of 1967 first mandated the disclosure of limited segment data; this requirement was expanded by later revisions of the Act, and disaggregated information was formally made part of the notes to the financial statements in 1981. A related professional accounting standard (SSAP 25) was adopted in 1990, with segments again defined either by class of business (similar to product or service areas) or by geographic location, with company management charged with the responsibility of determining which type of categorization would be most meaningful to financial statement users. As in the US, a threshold value of 10% is established for making the determination that a segment is material and thus needs to be reported on a disaggregated basis, and the criteria are virtually identical to the former US requirements under FAS 14. Information to be disclosed was also modeled on the US requirement—sales, operating results, and identifiable assets (called net assets under the UK standard, but not actually defined there).

As to IFRS, the relevant rules date from the original IAS 14 issued in 1983. The standard was reformatted, but not substantively altered, in 1995. In 1998 the IASC approved a significantly modified successor standard, revised IAS 14, which is the basis for the discussion in this chapter. A replacement for IAS 14 was exposed by IASB in early 2006 and adopted as IFRS 8 late that year, which was given a long phase-in and is only mandatorily effective for financial statements for years beginning in 2009. IFRS 8 essentially adopts the approach endorsed under US GAAP. This chapter discusses in detail only the new standard IFRS 8.

Segment Reporting Requirements under IFRS 8

The IASB and FASB jointly pursued a project to revise the segment financial information reporting requirements set forth under both sets of standards, as part of the convergence program first agreed to by these bodies in 2002 (the "Norwalk Agreement"). IASB issued ED 8, *Operating Segments*, in early 2006, and the final standard, IFRS 8, was promulgated later that year, with a mandatory effective date of 2009. The delayed effective date was responsive to IASB's publicly expressed intention to maintain the "stable platform" of standards until 2009, to facilitate adoption of IFRS by both the many EU-based publicly held entities affected by the mandate to begin reporting under IFRS, and for other reasons.

IFRS 8 differs substantially from the standard it replaced. It largely conforms to the requirements of the corresponding US GAAP standard, FAS 131, which had been issued in 1997, the same year that the final revised version of IAS 14 was released. IFRS 8 establishes how an entity is to report information about its operating segments in *annual* financial statements. Additionally, due to a consequential amendment made to IAS 34, entities are required to report selected information about their operating segments in *interim* financial reports. IFRS 8 also sets out requirements for related disclosures about products and services, geographical areas, and major customers.

IFRS 8 requires that an entity report financial and descriptive information about its *reportable segments.* Reportable segments are defined as *operating segments* or aggregations thereof that meet certain defined criteria. Operating segments are components of an entity about which separate financial information is available that is evaluated regularly by the chief operating decision maker in deciding how to allocate resources and in assessing performance. Generally, segment financial information is required to be reported on the same basis as is used internally for evaluating operating segment performance and deciding how to allocate resources to operating segments. This conforms to the objective of putting users in the "shoes of management" in their ability to evaluate management performance.

In the past, there had been debate over the value and validity of disclosing results of operations on a segmental basis. IFRS 8 requires an entity to report a measure of operating segment profit or loss and of segment assets. It also requires the reporting entity to report a measure of segment liabilities and particular income and expense items if such measures are regularly provided to the chief operating decision maker. It requires reconciliations of total reportable segment revenues, total profit or loss, total assets, liabilities and other amounts disclosed for reportable segments to corresponding amounts in the entity's financial statements.

The new standard also generally requires certain informational disclosures apart from any correspondence to information used in making management operating decisions. This includes information about the revenues derived from its products or services (or groups of similar products and services), about the countries in which it earns revenues and holds assets, and about major customers. However, information that is not prepared for internal use need not be reported if the necessary information is not available and the cost to develop it would be excessive.

Descriptive information about the way the operating segments were determined, the products and services provided by the segments, differences between the measurements used in reporting segment information and those used in the entity's financial statements, and changes in the measurement of segment amounts from period to period must also be provided in the notes to the financial statements. This information is necessary for users to meaningfully interpret the operating segment financial data, including making comparisons to prior periods.

Changes from predecessor standard IAS 14. The key changes from reporting under the immediate predecessor standard, revised IAS 14, are set forth in the following paragraphs.

1.   IFRS 8 applies to

   a.   The separate or individual financial statements of an entity

(1) Whose debt or equity instruments are traded in a public market (a domestic or foreign stock exchange or an over-the-counter market, including local and regional markets), or

(2) That files, or is in the process of filing, its financial statements with a securities commission or other regulatory organization for the purpose of issuing any class of instruments in a public market; and

b.   The consolidated financial statements of a group with a parent

(1) Whose debt or equity instruments are traded in a public market (a domestic or foreign stock exchange or an over-the-counter market, including local and regional markets), or

(2) That files, or is in the process of filing, the consolidated financial statements with a securities commission or other regulatory organization for the purpose of issuing any class of instruments in a public market.

2.   IFRS 8 imposes a "management approach" to the identification of operating segments, which is to be based on internal reports that are regularly reviewed by the entity's chief operating decision maker in order to allocate resources to the segment and assess its performance. This differs from the approach under IAS 14, which required that a primary and a secondary classification scheme be identified, with one being based on operations and the other on geographic areas. For purposes of the new standard, an operating segment is a component of an entity: (a) that engages in business activities from which it may earn revenues and incur expenses (including revenues and expenses relating to transactions with other components of the same entity), (b) whose operating results are regularly reviewed by the entity's chief operating decision maker to make decisions about resources to be allocated to the segment and assess its performance, and (c) for which discrete financial information is available. As under parallel US GAAP standard FAS 131, the "chief operating decision maker" designation does not necessarily refer to a single individual, but to a function within the reporting entity.

3.   IFRS 8 allows for the discrete reporting of a component of an entity that sells primarily or exclusively to other operating segments of the entity, if the entity is managed that way. Under IAS 14, only segments that sell exclusively or primarily to external customers could be deemed reportable segments.

4.   The new standard requires that the amount of each operating segment item (revenue, assets, etc.) that is reported be the same measure that is reported to the chief operating decision maker for the purposes of allocating resources to the segment and assessing its performance. IAS 14, on the other hand, required that segment information to be prepared in conformity with the accounting policies adopted for preparing and presenting the financial statements of the consolidated group or entity. This is a controversial change, since it may well be the case, for many reporting entities, that internal measures will diverge from IFRS-compliant ones. (Note that accounting standards, including IFRS and US GAAP, do not control management reporting practices, but only govern external reporting.)

5.   IFRS 8 requires reconciliations of total reportable segment revenues, total profit or loss, total assets, and other total amounts disclosed for reportable segments to corresponding amounts in the entity's financial statements. This was less of an issue under IAS 14 since amounts reported already conformed to external financial reporting.

6.   The standard requires an explanation of how segment profit or loss and segment assets are measured for each reportable segment. This is necessitated by the fact that the proposed standard does not define these terms in the abstract. IAS 14, on the other hand, does define each of these as being in full conformity with IFRS.

7.   It also requires that the entity report information about the revenues derived from its products or services (or groups of similar products and services), about the countries in which it earns revenues and holds assets, and about major customers, regardless of whether that information is used by management in making operating decisions. There was no such requirement under IAS 14.

8.   IFRS 8 requires the reporting entity to provide descriptive information about the way that the operating segments were determined, the products and services provided by the segments, differences between the measurements used in reporting segments information and those used in the entity's financial statements, and changes in the measurement of segment amounts from period to period.

9.   Finally, it requires the reporting entity to report interest revenue separately from interest expense for each reportable segment, unless (principally for financial institutions) a majority of the segment's revenues are from interest and the chief operating decision maker relies primarily on net interest revenue to assess the performance of the segment and to make decisions about resources to be allocated to the segment. IAS 14 does not require disclosure of interest income and expense.

IFRS 8 also expands disclosures of both segment and entity-wide information, which now must include the following:

1.   General information, which includes the factors used to identify the entity's operating segments, including the basis of organization and the types of products and services from which each reportable segment derives its revenues.

2.   Information about profit, including a measure (unspecified) of profit or loss and total assets or loss and assets for each reportable segment; a number of specified income statement headings for each reportable segment—if the amounts are included in the measure of segment profit or loss reviewed by the chief operating decision maker (or are otherwise regularly provided to the chief operating decision maker); and, for each reportable segment (if the amounts are included in the determination of segment assets, or otherwise are also reviewed by the chief operating decision maker), the amount of investment in associates and joint ventures accounted for by the equity method; and the total expenditures for additions to noncurrent assets other than financial instruments, deferred tax assets, postemployment benefit assets and rights arising under insurance contracts. Also to be disclosed would be all measurements of segment profit or loss and segment assets to be explained, including an explanation of the nature of any differences between amounts reported for segment purposes and those for the entity as a whole; the nature and effect of any changes from prior periods in the measurements used; and the nature and effect of any asymmetrical allocations to reportable segments.

3.   Reconciliations—with all material reconciling items separately identified and described—of the total of the reportable segments' revenues to the entity's revenue; of the total of the reportable segments' measures of profit or loss to the entity's profit or loss before income tax expense or income and discounted operations; of the total of the reportable segments' assets to the (continued) entity's assets; and of the total of the reportable segments' amounts for every other material item of information disclosed to the corresponding amount for the entity.

4. Entity-wide disclosures for all entities (including those having only a single reportable business segment), of information about its products and services, geographical areas and major customers. This requirement applies, regardless of the entity's organization, if the information is not included as part of the disclosures about segments.

IFRS 8 requires the expanded application of segment reporting requirements to interim financial statements. While previously this was seen as an onerous burden, the embrace of the "management approach" and the countenancing (at least implicitly) of non-IFRS measures in segment data, means that the burden would be lightened, making inclusion in interim reports more feasible. Of course, there is no absolute requirement under IFRS to publish interim reports, nor is there a requirement to have interim financial statements comply with IFRS. However, if such IFRS-compliant interim financial reports are prepared, they will now (for qualifying reporting entities) have to include certain operating segment information.

The new standard also calls for the recasting of comparative prior period information in the period of first reporting under the new rules. Again, since a "management approach" is prescribed, it is anticipated that such data will already exist and will have been employed internally by management during the earlier period(s). This requirement is waived if it is impracticable to accomplish, however.

Operating Segments and Reportable Segments

IFRS 8 defines reportable segments as being a subset of operating segments. In other words, there may be certain operating segments that fail to meet the threshold test for being reportable under this standard. Therefore, an understanding of these key concepts is vital to the proper application of the standard.

Operating segments. An operating segment is a component of an entity: (1) that engages in business activities from which it may earn revenues and incur expenses (including revenues and expenses relating to transactions with other components of the same entity), (2) whose operating results are regularly reviewed by the entity's chief operating decision maker to make decisions about resources to be allocated to the segment and assess its performance, and (3) for which discrete financial information is available.

Revenue generation is not an absolute threshold test for an operating segment. An operating segment may engage in business activities for which it has yet to earn revenues, for example, start-up operations may be operating segments before earning revenues.

By the same token, not every part of an entity is necessarily an operating segment or part of an operating segment. Thus, a corporate headquarters, as well as certain functional departments, may earn no revenues, or may generate revenues that are merely incidental to the activities of the entity as a whole. These would not be deemed to be operating segments under the definitions set forth under IFRS 8. For the purposes of the new standard, an entity's postemployment benefit plans are not operating segments, either.

For many entities, the three characteristics of operating segments set forth above will serve to clearly identify its operating segments. In other situations, an entity may produce reports in which its business activities are presented in a variety of ways (particularly in so-called "matrix organization" structures, where there are multiple and overlapping lines of reporting responsibilities. If the chief operating decision maker uses more than one set of segment information, other factors may be necessary to identify a single set of components as constituting an entity's operating segments, including the nature of the business activities of each component, the existence of managers responsible for them, and information presented to the board of directors. Of course, any such decision should be documented, and should be maintained over time, to the extent possible, in order to ensure comparability of disclosures. The chief operating decision maker should review segment definitions to ensure accuracy and consistency.

Reportable segments. Only reportable segments give rise to the financial statement disclosures set forth by IFRS 8. Reportable segments are operating segments as defined above, or *aggregations* of two or more such operating segments, that exceed the quantitative thresholds described below.

Operating segments often exhibit similar long-term financial performance if they have similar economic characteristics. For example, similar long-term average gross margins for two operating segments would be expected if their economic characteristics were similar. Two or more operating segments may *optionally* be aggregated into a single operating segment if aggregation is consistent with the core principle of IFRS 8, the segments have similar economic characteristics, and segments are similar in each of the following respects:

1. The nature of the products and services;
2. The nature of the production processes;
3. The type or class of customer for their products and services;
4. The methods used to distribute their products or provide their services; and
5. If applicable, the nature of the regulatory environment, for example, banking, insurance or public utilities.

An operating segment (or aggregation thereof) becomes a mandatorily reportable segment if one of the defined quantitative thresholds is met. These are that

1. The segment's reported revenue, including both sales to external customers and intersegment sales or transfers, is 10% or more of the combined revenue, internal and external, of all operating segments.
2. The absolute amount of its reported profit or loss is 10% or more of the greater, in absolute amount, of (1) the combined reported profit of all operating segments that did not report a loss and (2) the combined reported loss of all operating segments that reported a loss.
3. Its assets are 10% or more of the combined assets of all operating segments.

Note that the foregoing criteria are essentially identical to those formerly employed by predecessor segment reporting standards.

Furthermore, if the total external revenue reported by operating segments constitutes less than 75% of the entity's revenue, additional operating segments must be identified as reportable segments, even if they do not meet the criteria established under IFRS 8, until at least 75% of the entity's revenue is included in reportable segments.

A reporting entity may combine information about operating segments that do not meet the quantitative thresholds with information about other operating segments that do not meet the quantitative thresholds to produce a reportable segment only if the operating segments have similar economic characteristics and share a majority of the aggregation criteria set forth above. Thus, a catch-all ("all other segments") category should not be used, unless truly immaterial. The sources of the revenue included in the all other segments category must be described.

More segments may be optionally defined by management as being reportable, even if the foregoing criteria are not met. Operating segments that do not meet any of the quantitative thresholds may be considered reportable, and separately disclosed, if management believes that information about the segment would be useful to users of the financial statements.

This may be particularly relevant if, for various reasons, an operating segment traditionally meeting the test as a reportable segment falls below each threshold in the current year, but management expects the segment to regain its former prominence within a relatively brief time. To ensure interperiod comparability, it may be maintained as a reportable segment notwithstanding its current diminished significance. If management judges that an operating segment identified as a reportable segment in the immediately preceding periods is of continuing significance, information about that segment must, per IFRS 8, continue to be reported separately in the current period even if it no longer meets the criteria for reportability.

If an operating segment is identified as a reportable segment in the current period in accordance with the above-stated quantitative thresholds, segment data for a prior period presented for comparative purposes is to be restated to reflect the newly reportable segment as a separate segment, even if that segment did not satisfy the criteria for reportability in the prior period, unless the necessary information is not available and the cost to develop it would be excessive.

The standard notes that there may be a practical limit to the number of reportable segments that an entity separately discloses beyond which segment information may become too detailed (the so-called information overload situation). Although no precise limit has been determined, as the number of segments that are reportable increases above ten, the entity should consider whether a practical limit has been reached. There is no absolute requirement to limit the number of segments, however.

Disclosure Requirements under IFRS 8

A reporting entity is required to disclose information to enable users of its financial statements to evaluate the nature and financial effects of the business activities in which it engages and the economic environments in which it operates.

To operationalize this principle, the reporting entity is required to disclose the following *for each period for which a statement of comprehensive income* is presented:

1. *General information,* as follows:

    a. Factors used to identify the entity's reportable segments, including the basis of organization (for example, whether management has chosen to organize the entity around differences in products and services, geographical areas, regulatory environments, or a combination of factors and whether operating segments have been aggregated), *and*

    b. Types of products and services from which each reportable segment derives its revenues.

2. *Information about reported segment profit or loss,* including specified revenues and expenses included in reported segment profit or loss, *segment assets, segment liabilities* and the basis of measurement, as follows:

    a. The reporting entity is to report a measure of profit or loss and total assets for each reportable segment.

    b. It is to report a measure of liabilities for each reportable segment if such an amount is regularly provided to the chief operating decision maker.

    c. It also is to disclose the following about each reportable segment if the specified amounts are included in the measure of segment profit or loss reviewed by the chief operating decision maker, or are otherwise regularly provided to the chief operating decision maker, even if not included in that measure of segment profit or loss:

(1) Revenues from external customers;

(2) Revenues from transactions with other operating segments of the same entity;

(3) Interest revenue;

(4) Interest expense;

(5) Depreciation and amortization;

(6) Material items of income and expense disclosed in accordance with IAS 1;

(7) The entity's interest in the profit or loss of associates and joint ventures accounted for by the equity method;

(8) Income tax expense or income; and

(9) Material noncash items other than depreciation and amortization.

An entity is to report interest revenue separately from interest expense for each reportable segment unless a majority of the segment's revenues are from interest and the chief operating decision maker relies primarily on net interest revenue to assess the performance of the segment and make decisions about resources to be allocated to the segment. In that situation, an entity may report that segment's interest revenue net of its interest expense and disclose that it has done so.

d. The reporting entity is to disclose the following about each reportable segment if the specified amounts are included in the measure of segment assets reviewed by the chief operating decision maker or are otherwise regularly provided to the chief operating decision maker, even if not included in the measure of segment assets:

(1) The amount of investment in associates and joint ventures accounted for by the equity method, and

(2) The amounts of additions to noncurrent assets other than financial instruments, deferred tax assets, postemployment benefit assets and rights arising under insurance contracts. If the entity does not present a classified balance sheet, noncurrent assets are to be deemed those that include amounts expected to be recovered more than twelve months after the date of the statement of financial position.

(3) Reconciliations of the totals of segment revenues, reported segment profit or loss, segment assets, segment liabilities and other material segment items to corresponding entity amounts as follows:

(a) The total of the reportable segments' revenues to the entity's revenue.

(b) The total of the reportable segments' measures of profit or loss to the entity's profit or loss before tax expense (tax income) and discontinued operations. However, if an entity allocates to reportable segments items such as tax expense (tax income), the entity may reconcile the total of the segments' measures of profit or loss to the entity's profit or loss after those items.

(c) The total of the reportable segments' assets to the entity's assets.

(d) The total of the reportable segments' liabilities to the entity's liabilities if segment liabilities are reported to the entity's chief operating decision maker.

(e) The total of the reportable segments' amounts for every other material item of information disclosed to the corresponding amount for the entity.

IFRS 8 dictates that all material reconciling items are to be separately identified and described. For example, the amount of each material adjustment needed to reconcile reportable segment profit or loss to the entity's profit or loss arising from different accounting policies is required to be separately identified and described.

IFRS 8 also mandates that reconciliations of statements of financial position amounts for reportable segments to the entity's statement of financial position amounts be presented for *each date* at which a *statement of financial position* is presented. If, as is typical, comparative statements of financial position are presented, information for prior periods is to be restated.

If the reporting entity changes the structure of its internal organization in a manner that causes the composition of its reportable segments to change, the corresponding information for earlier periods, including interim periods, is to be restated, unless the information is not available and the cost to develop it would be excessive. The determination of whether the information is not available and the cost to develop it would be excessive must be made separately for each individual item of disclosure—thus a blanket conclusion regarding impracticability would normally not be appropriate. The standard demands that, following a change in the composition of its reportable segments, the entity disclose whether it has restated the corresponding items of segment information for earlier periods.

Furthermore, if the reporting entity has changed the structure of its internal organization in a manner that causes the composition of its reportable segments to change, and if segment information for earlier periods, including interim periods, is *not* restated to reflect the change, it must disclose in the year in which the change occurs segment information for the current period on both the old basis and the new basis of segmentation, unless the necessary information is not available and the cost to develop it would be excessive. This requirement is expected to discourage frequent changes in structure affecting segment reporting.

Entity-wide disclosure requirements. IFRS 8 also mandates disclosures of certain entity wide data. These disclosures are required regardless of whether the entity has reportable segment disclosures to be made under this standard. These disclosures need not be provided, however, if they are redundant with information contained in the reportable segment disclosures.

1. *Information about products and services.* Revenues from external customers for each product and service, or each group of similar products and services, are to be identified, unless the necessary information is not available and the cost to develop it would be excessive, in which case that fact shall disclosed. The amounts of revenues reported are to be based on the financial information used to produce the entity's financial statements.

2. *Information about geographical areas.* The reporting entity is to disclose the following geographical information, unless the necessary information is not available and the cost to develop it would be excessive:

   a. Revenues from external customers (1) attributed to the entity's country of domicile and (2) attributed to all foreign countries in total from which the entity derives revenues. If revenues from external customers attributed to an individual foreign country are material, those revenues are to be disclosed separately. An entity is required to disclose the basis for attributing revenues from external customers to individual countries.

   b. Noncurrent assets other than financial instruments, deferred tax assets, post-employment benefit assets, and rights arising under insurance contracts (1) located in the entity's country of domicile and (2) located in all foreign countries in total in which the entity holds assets. If assets in an individual foreign country are material, those assets shall be disclosed separately. If a classified statement of financial position is not presented (i.e., if liquidity ordering is utilized), noncurrent assets are to be defined as assets that include amounts expected to be recovered more than twelve months after the reporting date.

The amounts reported are to be based on the financial information that is used to produce the entity's financial statements. If the necessary information is not available and the cost to develop it would be excessive, that fact shall be disclosed. An entity may provide, in addition to the information required by this paragraph, subtotals of geographical information about groups of countries.

3. *Information about major customers.* Information about the extent of the reporting entity's reliance on its major customers must be provided. If revenues from transactions with a single external customer amount to 10% or more of the entity's revenues, it is to disclose that fact, the total amount of revenues from each such customer, and the identity of segment or segments reporting the revenues. The entity need not disclose the identity of a major customer or amount of revenues that each segment reports from that customer. For the purposes of this requirement under IFRS 8, a group of entities known to be under common control is to be considered a single customer, and a government (national, state, provincial, territorial, local or foreign) and entities known to be under the control of that government are to be considered a single customer.

Example of Financial Statement Disclosures under IFRS 8

Roche Group
Consolidated Financial Statements 2007

Notes to the Roche Group Consolidated Financial Statements

1. Summary of significant accounting policies

Segment reporting

IFRS 8, *Operating Segments*. The new standard, which replaces IAS 14, *Segment Reporting*, requires some changes to the methodology and format of segment reporting. The Group has determined that its reportable operating segments under the new standard are the same as the primary business segments under the old standard. The new standard requires additional disclosure for operating segments given in Note 2. Unrealized internal profits on inventories that have been sold from one operating segment to another but which have not yet been sold on to external customers at the balance sheet date are eliminated as a consolidation entry. Previously this elimination was allocated to the originating operating segment. The segment results for 2006 have been restated following this presentational change.

Restated Pharmaceuticals Divisional information for year ended December 31 2006

In millions of CHF	Roche Pharma	Genentech	Chugai	Pharma Division
As originally published				
Operating profit	6,025	3,951	569	10,545
–including unrealized profits on inventories	(114)	(51)	--	(165)
Restated				
Operating profit	6,139	4,002	569	10,710
Elimination of profit within division				(165)
Total				10,545

Future changes in IFRS. The Group has early adopted IRFS 8, *Operating Segments,* and IAS 23 (revised), *Borrowing Costs,* which are required to be implemented from January 1, 2009, at the latest. The Group does not expect that the new interpretations that will be effective from January 1, 2008, will have a significant effect on the Group's results and financial position. The

Group is currently assessing the potential impacts of the new and revised standards that will be effective from January 1, 2009, and beyond, which include further revisions to IAS 1, *Presentation of Financial Statements*; and revisions to IFRS 3, *Business Combinations*; IAS 27, *Consolidated and Separate Financial Statements*; and IFRS 2, *Share-Based Payment*.

2. Operating segment information

Divisional information

in millions of CHF	Pharmaceuticals Division 2007	Pharmaceuticals Division 2006	Diagnostics Division 2007	Diagnostics Division 2006	Corporate 2007	Corporate 2006	Group 2007	Group 2006
Revenues from external customers								
Sales	36,783	33,294	9,350	8,747	--	--	46,133	42,041
Royalties and other operating income	2,057	1,209	186	182	--	--	2,243	1,391
Total	38,840	34,503	9,536	8,929	--	--	48,376	43,432
Revenues from other operating segments								
Sales	8	23	5	6	--	--	13	29
Royalties and other operating income	--	--	--	--	--	--	--	--
Elimination of interdivisional profit	--	--	--	--	--	--	(13)	(29)
Total	8	23	5	6	--	--	--	--
Segment results								
Operating profit	13,042	10,545	1,648	1,422	(222)	(237)	14,468	11,730
Elimination of interdivisional profit							--	--
Total							14,468	11,730
Capital expenditure								
Business combinations	1,165	--	1,186	--	--	--	2,351	--
Additions to property, plant, and equipment	2,588	3,030	1,058	846	2	2	3,648	3,878
Additions to intangible assets	791	584	258	9	--	--	1,049	593
Total capital expenditure	4,544	3,614	2,502	855	2	2	7,048	4,471
Other segment information								
Depreciation of property, plant, and equipment	957	924	599	532	4	5	1,560	1,461
Amortization of intangible assets	645	646	331	331	--	--	976	977
Impairment of property, plant, and equipment	4	40	2	31	--	--	6	71
Impairment of goodwill	--	--	--	--	--	--	--	--
Impairment of intangible assets	58	13	--	184	--	--	58	197
Equity compensation plan expenses	568	632	26	44	14	14	608	690

Pharmaceuticals subdivisional information

in millions of CHF	Roche Pharmaceuticals 2007	Roche Pharmaceuticals 2006	Genentech 2007	Genentech 2006	Chugai 2007	Chugai 2006	Pharmaceuticals Division 2007	Pharmaceuticals Division 2006
Revenues from external customers								
Sales	22,970	20,666	10,414	9,125	3,399	3,503	36,783	33,294
Royalties and other operating income	900	391	1,078	797	79	21	2,057	1,209
Total	23,870	21,057	11,492	9,922	3,478	3,524	38,840	34,503
Revenues from other operating segments								
Sales	562	789	922	451	--	--	1,484	1,240
Royalties and other operating income	10	12	1,510	1,096	57	2	1,577	1,110
Elimination of revenue within division	--	--	--	--	--	--	(3,053)	(2,327)
Total	572	801	2,432	1,547	57	2	8	23
Segment results								
Operating profit	7,225	6,139	5,298	4,002	610	569	13,133	10,710
Elimination of profit within division							(91)	(165)
Total							13,042	10,545

in millions of CHF	Roche Pharmaceuticals		Genentech		Chugai		Pharmaceuticals Division	
	2007	*2006*	*2007*	*2006*	*2007*	*2006*	*2007*	*2006*
Capital expenditure								
Business combinations	94	--	1,071	--	--	--	1,165	--
Additions to property, plant, and equipment	1,045	1,091	1,327	1,749	216	190	2,588	3,030
Additions to intangible assets	501	416	282	168	8	--	791	584
Total capital expenditure	1,640	1,507	2,680	1,917	224	190	4,544	3,614
Other segment information								
Depreciation of property, plant, and equipment	530	544	337	298	90	82	957	924
Amortization of intangible assets	398	410	179	164	68	72	645	646
Impairment of property, plant, and equipment	2	38	--	--	2	2	4	40
Impairment of goodwill	--	--	--	--	--	--	--	--
Impairment of intangible assets	16	13	42	--	--	--	58	13
Equity compensation plan expenses	100	121	465	510	3	1	568	632

Net operating assets

in millions of CHF	Assets		Liabilities		Net Assets	
	2007	*2006*	*2007*	*2006*	*2007*	*2006*
Roche Pharmaceuticals	16,384	15,365	(3,228)	(3,789)	13,096	11,576
Genentech	12,993	11,358	(4,049)	(3,583)	8,944	7,775
Chugai	3,663	3,773	(561)	(636)	3,102	3,137
Elimination within division	(450)	(364)	--	--	(450)	(364)
Pharmaceuticals Division	32,590	30,132	(7,898)	(8,008)	24,692	22,124
Diagnostics Division	16,323	14,547	(2,263)	(2,134)	14,060	12,413
Corporate	232	192	(271)	(139)	(39)	53
Total operating	49,145	44,871	(10,432)	(10,281)	38,713	34,590
Nonoperating	29,038	29,543	(14,444)	(17,319)	14,594	12,224
Group	78,183	74,414	(24,876)	(27,600)	53,307	46,814

Information by geographical segment

in millions of CHF	Revenues from external customers		Noncurrent assets	
2007	Sales to third parties *(by destination)*	Royalties and other operating *income*	Property, plant, and *equipment*	Goodwill and intangible *assets*
Switzerland	489	430	2,404	2,354
European Union	15,465	127	5,096	2,755
– of which Germany	*3,277*	*117*	*3,437*	*2,699*
Rest of Europe	1,620	--	53	4
Europe	17,574	557	7,553	5,113
United States	17,069	1,598	7,949	7,446
Rest of North America	1,004	3	126	19
North America	18,073	1,601	8,075	7,465
Latin America	2,784	--	454	42
Japan	3,562	85	1,382	559
Rest of Asia	2,681	--	254	--
Asia	6,243	85	1,636	559
Africa, Australia and Oceania	1,459	--	114	2
Total	46,133	2,243	17,832	13,181

Information by geographical segment

in millions of CHF	Revenues from external customers		Noncurrent assets	
		Royalties and	*Property,*	*Goodwill and*
	Sales to third parties	*other operating*	*plant, and*	*intangible*
2006	*(by destination)*	*income*	*equipment*	*assets*
Switzerland	471	142	2,042	1,926
European Union	13,823	99	4,571	2,872
– of which Germany	*2,993*	*98*	*3,002*	*2,818*
Rest of Europe	1,307	1	200	4
Europe	15,601	242	6,813	4,802
United States	15,685	1,115	7,485	5,858
Rest of North America	985	6	100	33
North America	16,670	1,121	7,585	5,891
Latin America	2,539	7	391	55
Japan	3,713	21	1,299	633
Rest of Asia	2,384	--	217	--
Asia	6,097	21	1,516	633
Africa, Australia and Oceania	1,134	--	112	2
Total	42,041	1,391	16,417	11,383

Sales are allocated to geographical areas by destination according to the location of the customer. Royalties and other operating income are allocated according to the location of the Group company that receives the revenue.

European Union information is based on members of the EU as at December 31, 2007. The comparative information in 2006 has been restated to include Bulgaria and Romania within the "European Union" Segment.

Major customers. The US national wholesale distributor, AmerisourceBergen Corp., represented approximately 6 billion Swiss francs (2006: 5 billion Swiss francs) of the Group's revenues. Over 85% of these revenues were in the Genentech operating segment, with the residual in the Roche Pharmaceuticals and Diagnostics segments. The Group also reported substantial revenues from the US national wholesale distributors, Cardinal Health Inc. and McKesson Corp., and in total these three customers represented approximately a quarter of the Group's revenues, the majority of this being at Genentech.

21 ACCOUNTING POLICIES, CHANGES IN ACCOUNTING ESTIMATES, AND ERRORS

PERSPECTIVE AND ISSUES

It is axiomatic that a true picture of an entity's performance only emerges after a series of fiscal period's results have been reported and reviewed. The information set forth in an entity's financial statements over a period of years must, accordingly, be comparable if it is to be of value to users of those statements. Users of financial statements usually seek to identify trends in the entity's financial position, performance, and cash flows by studying and analyzing the information contained in those statements. Thus it is imperative that, to the maximum extent possible, the same accounting policies be applied from year to year in the preparation of financial statements, and that any necessary departures from this rule be clearly disclosed. This fundamental theorem explains why IFRS requires restatement of prior periods' financial statements for many changes in accounting principles and for corrections of accounting errors.

Financial statements are impacted by the choices made from among different, acceptable accounting principles and methodologies. Companies select those accounting principles and methods that they believe depict, in their financial statements, the economic reality of their financial position, results of operations, and changes in financial position. While IASB has made great progress in narrowing the range of acceptable alternative accounting for given economic events and transactions (e.g., elimination of LIFO inventory costing), there still remain choices (e.g., FIFO and weighted-average inventory costing) that can impair the ability to compare one entity's position and results with another.

Lack of comparability among entities and within a given entity over time can result because of changes in the assumptions and estimates underlying the application of the accounting principles and methods, from changes in the details in acceptable principles made by a promulgating authority, such as an accounting standard-setting body, for other reasons. While there is no preventing these various factors from causing changes to occur, it is important that changes be made only when they result in improved financial reporting, or when necessitated by imposition of new financial reporting requirements. Whatever the reason for introducing change, and hence the risk of noncomparability, to the financial reporting process, adequate disclosures must be made so that users of the financial statements are able to comprehend the effects and compensate for them in performing financial analyses.

IAS 8 deals with accounting changes (i.e., changes in accounting estimates and changes in accounting principles) and also addresses the accounting for the correction of errors. A principal objective of IAS 8—which was last revised in 2003, effective in 2005—is to prescribe accounting treatments and financial statement disclosures that will enhance comparability, both within an entity over a series of years, and with the financial statements of other entities.

Even though the correction of an error in financial statements issued previously is not considered an accounting change, it is discussed by IAS 8, and therefore is covered in this chapter.

In the preparation of financial statements there is an underlying presumption that an accounting policy, once adopted, should not be changed, but rather is to be uniformly applied in accounting for events and transactions of a similar type. This consistent application of accounting policies enhances the utility of the financial statements. The presumption that an entity should not change an accounting policy may be overcome only if the reporting entity justifies the use of an alternative acceptable accounting policy on the basis that it is preferable under the circumstances.

The IASB's *Improvements Project* resulted in significant changes being made to IAS 8. It now requires retrospective application of voluntary changes in accounting policies and retrospective restatement to correct prior period errors with the earliest reported retained earnings balance being adjusted for any effects of a correction of an error or of a voluntary change in accounting policy on earlier years. The only exception to this rule occurs when restatement would be impracticable to accomplish, and this is intentionally made a difficult criterion to satisfy. The revised standard removed the allowed alternative in the previous version of IAS 8 (1) to include in profit or loss for the current period the adjustment resulting from changing an accounting policy or correcting a prior period error and (2) to present unchanged comparative information from financial statements of prior periods.

The *Improvements Project* also resulted in some reorganization of materials in the standards, specifically relocating certain guidance between IAS 1 and IAS 8. As revised, certain presentational issues have been moved to IAS 1, while guidance on accounting policies, previously found in IAS 1, has been moved to IAS 8. In addition, included in revised IAS 8 is a newly established hierarchy of criteria to be applied in the selection of accounting policies.

As amended, IAS 8 incorporates the material formerly found in SIC 18, *Consistency— Alternative Methods*, which requires that an entity select and apply its accounting policies for a period consistently for similar transactions, other events and conditions, unless a standard or an interpretation specifically requires or permits categorization of items for which different policies may be appropriate, in which case an appropriate accounting policy shall be selected and applied consistently to each category. Simply stated, the expectation is that, absent changes in promulgated standards, or changes in the character of the transactions being accounted for, the reporting entity should continue to use accounting policies from one period to the next without change, and use them for all transactions and events within a given class or category without exception.

When IFRS are revised or new standards are developed, they often are promulgated a year or more prior to the date set for mandatory application. Disclosure of future changes in accounting policies must be made when the reporting entity has yet to implement a new standard that has been issued but that has not yet come into effect. In addition, disclosure is now required of the planned date of adoption, along with an estimate of the effect of the change on the entity's financial position, except if making such an estimate requires undue cost or effort.

Sources of IFRS
IAS 8

DEFINITIONS OF TERMS

Accounting policies.   Specific principles, bases, conventions, rules, and practices adopted by an entity in preparing and presenting financial statements. Management is required to adopt the accounting policies that result in a fair, full, and complete presentation of financial position, performance, and cash flows of the reporting entity.

Change in accounting estimate.   An adjustment of the carrying amount of an asset or liability, or related expense, resulting from reassessing the expected future benefits and obligations associated with that asset or liability. The use of reasonable estimates is an essential part of the financial statement preparation process and does not undermine their reliability.

Change in accounting estimate effected by a change in accounting policy.   A change in accounting estimate that is inseparable from the effect of a related change in accounting policy (for example, a change in depreciation method).

Change in accounting policy.   A change in accounting policy that either (1) is required by an IFRS or (2) is a change that results in the financial statements providing faithfully represented and more relevant information about the effects of transactions, other events or conditions on the entity's financial position, financial performance or cash flows.

Comparability.   An enhancing quality of financial reporting information that enables users to identify similarities in the differences between two sets of economic phenomena. Comparability should not be confused with uniformity. For information to be comparable, like things must look alike and different things must look different. Consistency refers to the use of the same accounting policies and procedures, either from period-to period within an entity or in a single period across entities. Comparability is the goal; consistency is a means to achieve it.

Consistency.   Consistency refers to use of the same accounting policies and procedures, either from period-to-period within an entity or in a single period across entities. Comparability is the goal; consistency is a means to achieve it. It enhances the usefulness of financial statements to users by facilitating analysis and understanding of comparative accounting data.

Cumulative catch-up.   A method used to reflect a change in accounting estimate whereby the results of the change are recognized in the statement of income of the period of the change.

Cumulative effect.   The difference between the beginning retained earnings balance of the year in which the change is reported and the beginning retained earnings balance that would have been reported if the new principle had been applied retrospectively for all prior periods that would have been affected.

Impracticable.   Applying a requirement is impracticable when the entity cannot apply it after making every reasonable effort to do so. For management to assert that it is impracticable to apply a change in an accounting policy retrospectively or to make a retrospective restatement to correct an error, one or more of the following conditions must be present: (1) after making every reasonable effort the effect of the retrospective application or restatement is not determinable; (2) the retrospective application or restatement requires assumptions regarding what management's intent would have been in that period; or (3) the retrospective application or restatement would require to make significant estimates of amounts for which it is impossible to develop objective information that would have been available at the time the original financial statements for the prior period (or periods) were authorized for issue to provide evidence of circumstances that existed at that time regarding the amounts to be measured, recognized, and/or disclosed by retrospective application.

International Financial Reporting Standards (IFRS). Standards and Interpretations adopted by the International Accounting Standards Board (IASB). They comprise International Financial Reporting Standards, International Accounting Standards (IAS), and Interpretations developed by the International Financial Reporting Interpretations Committee (IFRIC) or the former Standing Interpretations Committee (SIC).

Material. Omissions or misstatements of items are material if they could, individually or collectively, influence the economic decisions that users make on the basis of the financial statements. Materiality depends on the size and nature of the omission or misstatement judged in the surrounding circumstances.

Prior period errors. Omissions from, and misstatements in, the entity's financial statements for one or more prior periods arising from a failure to use, or misuse of, reliable information that (1) was available when financial statements for those periods were authorized for issue and (2) could reasonably be expected to have been obtained and taken into account in the preparation and presentation of those financial statements. Such errors include the effects of mathematical mistakes, mistakes in applying accounting principles, oversight or misuse of available facts, use of unacceptable GAAP, and fraud.

Pro forma information. Financial information that is prepared on an "as if" basis. The disclosure of required numbers computed on the assumption that certain events have transpired.

Prospective application. The method of reporting a change in accounting policy and of recognizing the effect of a change in an accounting estimate, respectively, by (1) applying the new accounting policy to transactions, other events, and conditions occurring after the date as at which the policy is changed and (2) recognizing and disclosing the effect of the change in the accounting estimate in the current and future periods affected by the change.

Retrospective application. Applying a new accounting policy to past transactions, other events and conditions as if that policy has always been applied.

Retrospective restatement. Correcting the recognition, measurement and disclosure of amounts of elements of financial statements as if a prior period error had never occurred.

CONCEPTS, RULES, AND EXAMPLES

Importance of Comparability and Consistency in Financial Reporting

Accounting principles—whether various IFRS or national GAAP—have long held that an important objective of financial reporting is to encourage comparability among financial statements produced by essentially similar entities. This is necessary to facilitate informed economic decision making by investors, creditors, regulatory agencies, vendors, customers, prospective employees, joint venturers, and others. While full comparability will not be achieved as long as alternative principles of accounting and reporting for like transactions and events remain acceptable, a driving force in developing new accounting standards has been to enhance comparability. The IASB's convergence objective is to remove alternatives both within IFRS and between IFRS and US GAAP, in order to arrive at a single set of international, high-quality, financial reporting rules, with few exceptions and alternatives other than those demanded by the vicissitudes among the underlying facts and circumstances of the items or transactions being accounted for.

Comparability is one of the key qualitative characteristics of financial reporting information identified in the IABS's *Framework*. It is similarly cited in the underlying foundational documents of various national GAAP, such as US GAAP *Statements of Financial Reporting Concepts*.

An important implication of comparability is that users be informed about the accounting policies that were employed in the preparation of the financial statements, any changes in those policies, and the effects of such changes. Disclosure of accounting policies, per se, was discussed in Chapters 2, 3, and 4. This chapter addresses the criteria for selecting and changing accounting policies, together with the accounting treatment and disclosure of changes in accounting policies, changes in accounting estimates, and corrections of errors in accordance with IAS 8.

Strict adherence to IFRS or any other set of standards obviously helps in achieving comparability, since a common accounting language is employed by all reporting parties. IFRS has the clear advantage, now, of being officially sanctioned as the "language of business" across the European Union, and momentum seemingly favors IFRS as more nations, from Australia to China to Russia, either converge to or simply adopt IFRS as the requirement for, at least, financial reporting by publicly held companies. While historically some accountants opposed the focus on comparability, on the grounds that uniformity of accounting removes the element of judgment needed to produce the most faithful representation of an individual entity's financial position and performance, others have expressed concern that overemphasis on comparability might be an impediment to the development of improved accounting methods. Increasingly, however, the paramount importance of comparability is being recognized, to which the current convergence efforts strongly attest.

As contrasted with comparability, consistency refers to a given reporting entity's uniform and unvarying adherence, from one period to the next, to a defined set of accounting policies and procedures. The quality of consistency enhances the utility of financial statements to users by facilitating analysis and the understanding of comparative accounting data.

According to IAS 1

The presentation and classification of items in the financial statements should be retained from one period to the next unless it is apparent that, following a significant change in the nature of the entity's operations or a review of its financial statements, that another presentation or classification would be more appropriate with regard to the criteria for the selection and application of accounting policies in IAS 8; or an IFRS requires a change in presentation.

It is, however, inappropriate for an entity to continue accounting for transactions in the same manner if the policies adopted lack qualitative characteristics of relevance and reliability. Thus, if more reliable and relevant accounting policy alternatives exist, it is better for the entity to change its methods of accounting for defined classes of transactions with, of course, adequate disclosure of both the nature of the change and of its effects.

Accounting Policies

In accordance with IAS 1, the reporting entity's management is responsible for selecting and applying accounting policies that

1. Present fairly financial position, results of operations, and cash flows or an entity, as required by IFRS
2. Provide information in a manner that provides relevant, reliable, comparable and understandable information
3. Present additional disclosures that enable users to understand the impact of particular transactions, other events, and conditions on the entity's financial position and performance.

Under IFRS, and in conformity with various national GAAP, management is required to disclose, in the notes to the financial statements, a description of all significant accounting policies of the reporting entity. In theory, if only one method of accounting for a type of transaction is acceptable, it is not necessary to explicitly cite it in the accounting policies note, although many entities do routinely identify all accounting policies affecting the major financial statement captions.

A listing of accounting policies commonly disclosed by reporting entities follows (the listing is not intended to be all-inclusive):

- Advertising costs and arrangements
- Cash equivalents
- Changes in accounting policies
- Combined financial statements, principles of combination
- Concentrations of credit risk, major customers and/or suppliers
- Consolidated financial statements, principles of consolidation
- Consolidated financial statements, special-purpose entities (SPEs)
- Deferred income taxes
- Derivatives and hedging activities
- Employee benefits
- Fair value elections, methods, assumptions, inputs used
- Financial instruments
- Fiscal year
- Foreign currency translation
- Goodwill
- Guarantees
- Impairment of long-lived assets, goodwill, other intangibles, investments, etc.
- Income taxes
- Intangibles, amortizable and/or nonamortizable
- Interest capitalization
- Internal-use software
- Inventories
- Investments
- Long-term contracts
- Nature and extent of risks arising from financial instruments
- Nature of operations
- Not-for-profits; restrictions that are satisfied in the year they originate
- Operating cycle
- Pension and other postemployment plans
- Property and equipment, depreciation and amortization
- Property and equipment, changes from held-and-used to held-for-sale
- Rebates
- Receivables, past due, interest and late charges, determination of allowance for bad debts
- Reclassifications
- Revenue recognition
- Share-based payment arrangements
- Shipping and handling costs
- Start-up costs
- Use of estimates
- Warranties

The "summary of significant accounting policies" is customarily, but not necessarily, the first note disclosure included in the financial statements. A more all-encompassing title such as "Nature of business and summary of significant accounting policies" is frequently used.

Selecting Accounting Policies

IAS 8 has established a hierarchy of accounting guidance for selecting accounting policies in accordance with IFRS. This is comparable to the "hierarchy of GAAP" established under US auditing standards many years ago (recently superseded by guidance in the FASB Accounting Standards Codification), and provides a logical ordering of authoritativeness for those instances when competing and possibly conflicting guidance exists. Given the relative paucity of authoritative guidance under IFRS (which is, of course, seen as a virtue by those who prefer "principles-based" standards, vis-à-vis the more "rules-based" standards arguably exemplified by US GAAP), heavy reliance is placed on reasoning by analogy from the existing standards and from materials found in various nonauthoritative sources.

According to IAS 8, when an IFRS standard, or an interpretation of a standard applies to an item in the financial statements, the accounting policy or policies applied to that item are to be determined by considering the following in descending order of authoritativeness:

1. The standard itself (including any appendices that form a part of it);
2. Any relevant Interpretations;
3. Appendices that do not form a part of the standard; and
4. Implementation guidance issued in respect of the standard.

IAS 8 provides guidance to which management refers when selecting accounting policies in the absence of Standards and Interpretations. When there is *not* any IFRS standard or Interpretation that specifically applies to a item in the financial statements, transaction, other event or condition, management must use judgment in developing and applying an accounting policy. This should result in information that is both

1. Relevant to the decision-making needs of users; and
2. Reliable in the sense that the resulting financial statements—

   a. Will represent faithfully the financial position, performance, and cash flows of the entity;
   b. Will reflect the economic substance of transactions, other events, and conditions, and not merely their legal form;
   c. Are neutral (i.e., free from bias);
   d. Are prudent; and
   e. Are complete in all material respects.

In making this judgment, management must give consideration to the following sources, listed in descending order of significance:

1. The requirements and guidance in IFRS and in interpretations dealing with similar and related issues, and appendices and implementation guidance issued in respect of those standards;
2. The definitions, recognition criteria and measurement concepts for assets, liabilities, income and expenses set out in the *Framework*; and
3. Pronouncements of other standard-setting bodies that use a similar conceptual framework to develop accounting standards (from discussions at IASB meetings, it seems likely that people anticipate that preparers would look to US GAAP next after IFRS).

4. Other accounting literature (e.g., textbooks, handbooks, scholarly articles), and accepted industry practices, to the extent (but only to the extent) that these are consistent with the promulgated standards and interpretations cited above.

Changes in Accounting Policies

A change in an accounting policy means that a reporting entity has exchanged one accounting principle for another. According to IAS 8, the term *accounting policy* includes the accounting principles, bases, conventions, rules and practices used. For example, a change in inventory costing from weighted-average to first-in, first-out would be a change in accounting policy, as would a change in accounting for borrowing costs from capitalization to immediate expensing.

Changes in accounting policy are permitted if

1. The change is required by a standard or an interpretation, or
2. The change in accounting principle will result in a more relevant and reliable presentation of events or transactions in the financial statements of the entity.

IAS 8 does not regard the following as changes in accounting policies:

1. The adoption of an accounting policy for events or transactions that differ in substance from previously occurring events or transactions; and
2. The adoption of a new accounting policy to account for events or transactions that did not occur previously or that were immaterial in prior periods

The provisions of IAS 8 are not applicable to the initial adoption of a policy to carry assets at revalued amounts, although such adoption is indeed a change in accounting policy. Rather, this is to be dealt with as a revaluation in accordance with IAS 16 or IAS 38, as appropriate under the circumstances.

Applying changes in accounting policies. Generally, IAS 8 provides that a change in an accounting policy should be reflected in financial statements by retrospective application to all prior periods presented as if that policy had always been applied, unless it is impracticable to do so. When a change in an accounting policy is made consequent to the enactment of a new IFRS, it is to be accounted for in accordance with the transitional provisions set forth in that standard.

An entity should account for a change in accounting policy as follows:

1. In general, initial application of an IFRS should be accounted for in accordance with the specific transitional provisions, if any, in that IFRS.
2. Initial application of an IFRS that does not include specific transitional provisions applying to that change, should be applied *retrospectively.*
3. Voluntary changes in accounting policy should be applied *retrospectively.*

Retrospective application. In accordance with IAS 8, retrospective application of a new accounting principle involves (1) adjusting the opening balance of each affected component of equity for the earliest prior period presented and (2) presenting other comparative amounts disclosed for each prior period as if the new accounting policy had always been applied.

Retrospective application to a prior period is required if it is practicable to determine the effect of the correction on the amounts in both the opening as well as closing statements of financial position for that period. Adjustments are made to the opening balance of each affected component of equity, usually to retained earnings.

For example, assume that a change is adopted in 2009 and comparative 2008 financial statements are to be presented with the 2009 financial statements. The change in accounting policy also affects previously reported 2006-2007 financial position and financial performance, but these are not to be presented in the current financial report. Therefore, since other components of equity are not affected, the cumulative adjustment (i.e., the cumulative amount of expense or income which would have been recognized in years prior to 2008) as of the beginning of 2008 is made to opening retained earnings in 2008.

Retrospective application is accomplished by the following steps:

At the beginning of the first period presented in the financial statements,

Step 1 -   Adjust the carrying amounts of assets and liabilities for the cumulative effect of changing to the new accounting principle on periods prior to those presented in the financial statements.

Step 2 -   Offset the effect of the adjustment in Step 1 (if any) by adjusting the opening balance of each affected component of equity (usually opening balance of retained earnings).

For each individual prior period that is presented in the financial statements,

Step 3 -   Adjust the financial statements for the effects of applying the new accounting principle to that specific period.

Example of retrospective application of a new accounting principle

In 1998, upon the incorporation of Belmont Corporation (BC), its management elected to recognize advertising costs as incurred. BC has been consistently following that policy in its financial statements. In 2009, BC's management reviewed its accounting policies and concluded that application of its current policy was resulting in substantial costs associated with the production of television advertising being recognized in financial reporting periods that preceded the periods in which the related revenues were earned. Consequently, management decided to change BC's policy to elect to expense advertising costs the first time the advertising takes place as permitted by SOP 93-7, *Reporting on Advertising Costs*. Additional assumptions follow:

- As has been its policy in the past, BC plans to issue comparative financial statements presenting two years, 2009 and 2008.
- Income tax rate of 40% was in effect for all relevant periods.
- Prior to the change in accounting principle, there were no temporary differences or loss carryforwards and, thus, there were no deferred income tax assets or liabilities.
- Advertising costs are deductible for income tax purposes when incurred and, therefore, upon adoption of the new accounting policy, BC will have a temporary difference between the book and income tax bases of its asset, deferred advertising costs. These advertising costs that are being recognized in the financial statements in the year after they are deducted on BC's income tax return represent a future taxable temporary difference that will give rise to a deferred income tax liability.
- The financial statements originally issued as of and for the years ended December 31, 2008 and 2007, prior to the adoption of the new accounting principle are presented below with advertising-related captions shown separately for illustrative purposes.

Belmont Corporation
Statements of Comprehensive Income and Retained Earnings
Prior to Change in Accounting Principle
Years Ended December 31, 2008 and 2007

	2008	*2007*
Sales	€ 2,300,000	€ 2,000,000
Cost of sales	(850,000)	(750,000)
Gross profit	1,450,000	1,250,000
Advertising expense	65,000	55,000
Other operating expenses	385,000	445,000
	450,000	500,000

	2008	2007
Income from operations	1,000,000	750,000
Other income (expense)	11,000	10,000
Income before income taxes	1,011,000	760,000
Income taxes	(404,000)	(304,000)
Profit or loss	607,000	456,000
Retained earnings, beginning of year	13,756,000	14,500,000
Dividends	(1,400,000)	(1,200,000)
Retained earnings, end of year	€12,963,000	€13,756,000

Belmont Corporation
Statements of Financial Position
Prior to Change in Accounting Principle
December 31, 2008 and 2007

	2008	2007
Assets		
Current assets		
Cash and cash equivalents	€ 2,200,000	€ 2,400,000
Deferred advertising cost	--	--
Prepaid expenses	125,000	120,000
Other current assets	22,000	20,000
Total current assets	2,347,000	2,540,000
Property and equipment	10,729,000	11,311,000
Total assets	€13,076,000	€13,851,000
Liabilities and Shareholders' Equity		
Deferred income taxes	€ --	€ --
Other current liabilities	35,000	12,000
Total current liabilities	35,000	12,000
Noncurrent liabilities	65,000	70,000
Total liabilities	100,000	82,000
Shareholders' equity		
Ordinary share	13,000	13,000
Retained earnings	12,963,00	13,756,000
Total shareholders' equity	12,976,000	13,769,000
Total liabilities and shareholders' equity	€13,076,000	€13,851,000

Belmont Corporation
Statements of Cash Flows
Prior to Change in Accounting Principle
Years Ended December 31, 2008 and 2007

	2008	2007
Operating activities		
Profit or loss	€ 607,000	€ 456,000
Depreciation	715,000	715,000
Deferred income taxes	--	--
Gain on sale of property and equipment	--	--
Changes in		
Deferred advertising costs	--	--
Prepaid expenses	(5,000)	1,000
Other current assets	(2,000)	1,500
Other current liabilities	23,000	900
Net cash provided by operating activities	1,338,000	1,174,400
Investing activities		
Property and equipment		
Acquisition	(133,000)	(120,000)
Proceeds from sale	--	--
Net cash used for investing activities	(133,000)	(120,000)
Financing activities		
Dividends paid to shareholders	(1,400,000)	(1,200,000)

	2008	*2007*
Long-term debt		
Borrowed	--	--
Repaid	(5,000)	(5,000)
Net cash used for financing activities	(1,405,000)	(1,205,000)
Decrease in cash and cash equivalents	(200,000)	(150,600)
Cash and cash equivalents, beginning of year	2,400,000	2,550,600
Cash and cash equivalents, end of year	€2,200,000	€2,400,000

Step 1 -   Adjust the carrying amounts of assets and liabilities at the beginning of the first period presented in the financial statements (January 1, 2008, in this example). for the cumulative effect of changing to the new accounting principle on periods prior to those presented in the financial statements.

In this example, the preparer refers to the previously issued 2007 financial statements presented above. Assume the following data regarding advertising costs at December 31, 2007/January 1, 2008:

Costs incurred during 2007 for advertising that will not take place for the first time until 2008	€25,000
Deferred income tax liability that would have been recognized at December 31, 2007, computed at 40% of the temporary difference	(10,000)
Net adjustment to beginning assets and liabilities	€15,000

Step 2 -   Offset the effect of the adjustment in Step 1 by adjusting the opening balance of retained earnings (or other components of equity, if affected).

The €15,000 net effect of the adjustment in Step 1 is presented in the statement of income and retained earnings as an adjustment to the January 1, 2008 retained earnings as previously reported at December 31, 2007.

Step 3 -   Adjust the financial statements of each individual prior period presented for the effects of applying the new accounting principle to that specific period.

In this case, the following adjustments are necessary to adjust the 2008 financial statements for the period-specific effects of the change in accounting principle:

Cost incurred in	*Year the advertising was first run*	
2007	2008	€ 25,000
2008	2009	(45,000)

Pretax, period-specific adjustment to advertising costs at 12/31/07	(20,000)
× 40% income tax effect	8,000
Effect on 2008 net income	€(12,000)

Adjustments to the 2008 financial statements for the period-specific effects of retrospective application of the new accounting principle are

Adjustments to 2008 financial statements

	Deferred advertising costs	Deferred income tax liability	Advertising expense	Income tax expense
Balance at 12/31/08 prior to adjustment	€ --	€ --	€65,000	€404,000
Adjustment to opening balances from retrospective application to 2008	25,000	10,000	--	--
Advertising costs incurred in 2007, first run in 2008	(25,000)	--	25,000	--
Advertising costs incurred in 2008, first run in 2009	45,000	--	(45,000) (20,000)	--
Income tax effect of net adjustment to 2008 advertising expense (40%)	--	8,000	--	8,000
Adjusted amounts for 2008 financial statements	€45,000	€18,000	€45,000	€412,000

The adjusted comparative financial statements, reflecting the retrospective application of the new accounting principle, follow.

Belmont Corporation
Statements of Comprehensive Income Retained Earnings
Reflecting Retrospective Application of Change in Accounting Principle
Years Ended December 31, 2009 and 2008

	2009	2008 as adjusted
Sales	€ 2,700,000	€ 2,300,000
Cost of sales	995,000	850,000
Gross profit	1,705,000	1,450,000
Advertising expense	66,000	45,000
Other selling, general, and administrative expenses	423,000	385,000
	489,000	430,000
Income from operations	1,216,000	1,020,000
Other income (expense)	9,000	11,000
Income before income taxes	1,225,000	1,031,000
Income taxes	490,400	412,000
Profit or loss	734,600	619,000
Retained earnings, beginning of year, as originally reported		13,756,000
Adjustment for retrospective application of new accounting principle (Note X)		15,000
Retained earnings, beginning of year, as adjusted	12,990,000	13,771,000
Dividends	1,600,000	1,400,000
Retained earnings, end of year	€12,124,600	€12,990,000

Belmont Corporation
Statements of Financial Position
Reflecting Retrospective Application of Change in Accounting Principle
Years Ended December 31, 2009 and 2008

	2009	2008 as adjusted
Assets		
Current assets		
Cash and cash equivalents	€ 2,382,000	€ 2,200,000
Deferred advertising costs	16,000	45,000
Prepaid expenses	123,000	125,000
Other current assets	21,000	22,000
Total current assets	2,542,000	2,392,000
Property and equipment	9,800,000	10,729,000
Total assets	12,342,000	13,121,000
Liabilities and shareholders' equity		
Deferred income taxes	€ 6,000	€ 18,000
Other current liabilities	36,000	35,000
Total current liabilities	42,400	53,000
Noncurrent liabilities	162,000	65,000
Total liabilities	204,400	118,000
Shareholders' equity		
Ordinary share	13,000	13,000
Retained earnings	12,124,600	12,990,000
Total shareholders' equity	12,137,600	13,003,000
Total liabilities and shareholders' equity	€12,342,000	€13,121,000

Belmont Corporation
Statements of Cash Flows
Reflecting Retrospective Application of Change in Accounting Principle
Years Ended December 31, 2009 and 2008

	2009	2008 as adjusted
Operating activities		
Profit or loss	€ 734,600	€ 619,000
Depreciation	725,000	715,000
Deferred income taxes	(11,600)	8,000
Gain on sale of property and equipment	(1,200,000)	--
Changes in		
Deferred advertising costs	29,000	(20,000)
Prepaid expenses	2,000	(5,000)
Other current assets	1,000	(2,000)
Other current liabilities	1,000	23,000
Net cash provided by operating activities	€ 281,000	€1,338,000
Investing activities		
Property and equipment		
Acquisition	(1,096,000)	(133,000)
Proceeds from sale	2,500,000	--
Net cash provided by (used for) investing activities	1,404,000	(133,000)
Financing activities		
Dividends paid to stockholders	(1,600,000)	(1,400,000)
Long-term debt		
Borrowed	105,000	--
Repaid	(8,000)	(5,000)
Net cash used for financing activities	(1,503,000)	(1,405,000)
Increase (decrease) in cash and cash equivalents	182,000	(200,000)
Cash and cash equivalents, beginning of year	2,200,000	2,400,000
Cash and cash equivalents, end of year	€2,382,000	€2,200,000

It is important to note that, in presenting the previously issued financial statements for 2008, the caption "as adjusted" is included in the column heading. Prior to the issuance of FAS 154, many preparers used the caption "as restated." FAS 154 explicitly defines a restatement as a revision to previously issued financial statements to correct an error. Therefore, to avoid misleading the financial statement reader, use of the terms restatement or restated are to be limited to prior period adjustments to correct errors as discussed later in this chapter.

Indirect effects. The example above only reflects the direct effects of the change in accounting principle, net of the effect of income taxes. Changing accounting principles sometimes results in indirect effects from legal or contractual obligations of the reporting entity, such as profit sharing or royalty arrangements that contain monetary formulas based on amounts in the financial statements. In the preceding example, if Belmont Corporation had an incentive compensation plan that required it to contribute 15% of its pretax income to a pool to be distributed to its employees, the adoption of the new accounting policy would potentially require BC to provide additional contributions to the pool computed as

	Pretax effect of retroactive application	Contractual rate	Indirect effect
Prior to 2008	€25,000	15%	€3,750
2008	(20,000)	15%	(3,000)
			€ 750

Contracts and agreements are often silent regarding how such a change might affect amounts that were computed (and distributed) in prior years. Management of Newburger

Company might have discretion over whether to make the additional contributions. Further, it would probably consider it undesirable to reduce the 2008 incentive compensation pool because of an accounting change of this nature, and it might thus decide for valid business reasons not to reduce the pool under these circumstances.

IAS 8 specifies that irrespective of whether the indirect effects arise from an explicit requirement in the agreement or are discretionary, if incurred they are to be recognized in the period in which the reporting entity makes the accounting change, which is 2009 in the example above.

Impracticability exception. Comparative information presented for a particular prior period need not be restated if doing so is *impracticable*. IAS 8 includes a definition of "impracticability" (see Definitions of Terms in this chapter) and guidance on its interpretation.

The standard states that applying a requirement is impracticable when the entity cannot apply it after making every reasonable effort to do so. In order for management to assert that it is impracticable to retrospectively apply the new accounting principle, one or more of the following conditions must be present:

1. Management has made every reasonable effort to determine the retrospective adjustment and is unable to do so because the effects of retrospective application are not determinable (e.g., where the information is not available because it was not captured at the time).
2. If it were to apply the new accounting principle retrospectively, management would be required to make assumptions regarding its intent in a prior period that would not be able to be independently substantiated.
3. If it were to apply the new accounting principle retrospectively, management would be required to make significant estimates of amounts for which it is impossible to develop objective information that would have been available at the time the original financial statements for the prior period (or periods) were issued to provide evidence of circumstances that existed at that time regarding the amounts to be measured, recognized, and/or disclosed by retrospective application.

Inability to determine period-specific effects. If management is able to determine the adjustment to the opening balance of each affected component of equity as at the beginning of the earliest period for which retrospective application is practicable, but is unable to determine the period-specific effects of the change on all of the prior periods presented in the financial statements, IAS 8 requires the following steps to adopt the new accounting principle:

1. Adjust the carrying amounts of the assets and liabilities for the cumulative effect of applying the new accounting principle at the beginning of the earliest period presented for which it is practicable to make the computation, which may be the current period.
2. Any offsetting adjustment required by applying step 1. is made to each affected component of equity (usually to beginning retained earnings) of that period.

Inability to determine effects on any prior periods. If it is impracticable to determine the effects of adoption of the new accounting principle on any prior periods, the new principle is applied prospectively as of the earliest date that it is practicable to do so. The most common example of this occurs when management of a reporting entity decides to change its inventory costing assumption from first-in, first-out (FIFO) to weighted-average (WA), as illustrated in the following example:

Example of change from FIFO to LIFO

During 2009 Waldorf Corporation (WC) decided to change the inventory costing formula from FIFO to weighted-average (WA). The inventory values are as listed below using both FIFO and WA methods. Sales for the year were €15,000,000 and the company's total purchases were €11,000,000. Other expenses were €1,200,000 for the year. The company had 1,000,000 ordinary shares outstanding throughout the year.

Inventory values

	FIFO	*WA*	*Difference*
12/31/08 Base year	€ 2,000,000	€2,000,000	€ --
12/31/09	4,000,000	1,800,000	2,200,000
Variation	€ 2,000,000	€(200,000)	€ 2,200,000

The computations for 2009 would be as follows:

	FIFO	*WA*	*Difference*
Sales	€15,000,000	€15,000,000	€ --
Cost of goods sold			
Beginning inventory	2,000,000	2,000,000	--
Purchases	11,000,000	11,000,000	--
Goods available for			
sale	13,000,000	13,000,000	--
Ending inventory	4,000,000	1,800,000	2,200,000
	9,000,000	11,200,000	(2,200,000)
Gross profit	6,000,000	3,800,000	2,200,000
Other expenses	1,200,000	1,200,000	--
Net income	€ 4,800,000	€ 2,600,000	€2,200,000

The following is an example of the required disclosure in this circumstance:

Note A: Change in Method of Accounting for Inventories

During 2009, management changed the company's method of accounting for all of its inventories from first-in, first-out (FIFO) to weighted-average (WA). The change was made because management believes that the WA method provides a better matching of costs and revenues. In addition, with the adoption of WA, the company's inventory pricing method is consistent with the method predominant in the industry. The change and its effect on net income (€000 omitted except for per share amounts) and earnings per share for 2009 are as follows:

	Profit or loss	*Earnings per share*
Profit or loss before the change	€4,800	€4.80
Reduction of net income due to the change	2,200	2.20
Profit or loss as adjusted	€2,600	€2.60

Management has not retrospectively applied this change to prior years' financial statements because beginning inventory on January 1, 2009, using WA is the same as the amount reported on a FIFO basis at December 31, 2008. As a result of this change, the current period's financial statements are not comparable with those of any prior periods. The FIFO cost of inventories exceeds the carrying amount valued using WA by €2,200,000 at December 31, 2009.

Changes in amortization method. Tangible or intangible long-lived assets are subject to depreciation or amortization, respectively, as set forth in IAS 16 and IAS 38. Changes in methods of amortization may be implemented in order to more appropriately recognize amortization or depreciation as an asset's future economic benefits are consumed. For example, the straight-line method of amortization may be susituted for an accelerated method when it becomes clear that the straight-line method more accurately reports the consumption of the asset's utility to the reporting entity.

While a change in amortization method would appear to be a change in accounting policy and thus subject to the requirements of IAS 8 as revised, in fact special accounting for this change is mandated by IAS 16 and IAS 38.

Under IAS 16 (as amended effective 2006), which governs accounting for property, plant, and equipment (long-lived tangible assets), a change in the depreciation method is a change in the technique used to apply the entity's accounting policy to recognize depreciation as an asset's future economic benefits are consumed. Therefore it is deemed to be a change in an accounting estimate, to be accounted for as described below. Similar guidance is found in IAS 38, pertaining to intangible assets. These standards are discussed in greater detail in Chapters 8 and 9.

The foregoing exception applies when a change is made to the method of amortizing or depreciating existing assets. A different result obtains when only newly acquired assets are to be affected by the new procedures.

When a company adopts a different method of amortization for newly acquired identifiable long-lived assets, and uses that method for all new assets of the same class without changing the method used previously for existing assets of the same class, this is to be accounted for as a change in accounting policy. No adjustment is required to comparative financial statements, nor is any cumulative adjustment to be made to retained earnings at the beginning of the current or any earlier period, since the change in principle is being applied prospectively only. In these cases, a description of the nature of the method changed and the effect on profit or loss and related per share amounts should be disclosed in the period of the change.

In the absence of any specific transitional provisions in a standard, a change in an accounting policy is to be applied retrospectively in accordance with the requirements set forth in IAS 8 for voluntary changes in accounting policy, as described below.

When applying the transitional provisions of a standard has an effect on the current period or any prior period presented, the reporting entity is required to disclose

1. The fact that the change in accounting policy has been made in accordance with the transitional provisions of the standard, with a description of those provisions;
2. The amount of the adjustment for the current period and for each prior period presented;
3. The amount of the adjustment relating to periods prior to those included in the comparative information; and
4. The fact that the comparative financial information has been restated, or that restatement for a particular prior period has not been made because it was impracticable.

If the application of the transitional provisions set forth in a standard may be expected to have an effect in future periods, the reporting entity is required to disclose the fact that the change in an accounting policy is made in accordance with the prescribed transitional provisions, with a description of those provisions affecting future periods.

Although the "impracticability" provision of revised IAS 8 may appear to suggest that restatement of prior periods' results could easily be avoided by preparers of financial statements, this is not an accurately drawn implication of these rules. The objective of IFRS in general, and of revised IAS 8 in particular, is to enhance the interperiod comparability of information, since doing such will assist users in making economic decisions, particularly by allowing the assessment of trends in financial information for predictive purposes. There is accordingly a general presumption that the benefits derived from restating comparative information will exceed the resulting cost or effort of doing so—and that the reporting entity would make every reasonable effort to restate comparative amounts for each prior period presented.

In circumstances where restatement is deemed impracticable, the reporting entity will disclose the reason for not restating the comparative amounts.

In certain circumstances, a new standard may be promulgated with a delayed effective date. This is done, for example, when the new requirements are complex and IASB wishes to give adequate time for preparers and auditors to master the new materials. (During the transition to IFRS of EU publicly held companies, there was an effort made to maintain a "stable platform" of reporting rules, and thus several new standards were given delayed effective dates.) If, as of a financial reporting date, the reporting entity has not elected early adoption of the standard, it must disclose (1) the nature of the future change or changes in accounting policy; (2) the date by which adoption of the standard is required; (3) the date as at which it plans to adopt the standard; and (4) either (a) an estimate of the effect that the change(s) will have on its financial position, or (b) if such an estimate cannot be made without undue cost or effort, a statement to that effect.

Example of disclosure of newly promulgated IFRS

Roche Group AG
Financial Statements 2007

Changes in accounting policies. The Group adopted certain new and revised International Financial Reporting Standards and Interpretations effective January 1, 2007. A description of those changes that are material to the Group and their effect on the consolidated financial statements is given below.

IFRS 7, *Financial Instruments: Disclosures*. The new standard, which replaces the disclosure requirements previously contained in IAS 32, *Financial Instruments: Presentation*, requires additional disclosure concerning the significance of the Group's financial instruments, the nature and extent of risks arising from these instruments, and the manner in which these risks are managed. The presentation requirements required by IAS 32 remain unchanged. The disclosure requirements in IFRS 7 include qualitative and quantitative information about risk exposure arising from financial instruments, in particular credit risk, liquidity risk, and market risk. The standard also requires qualitative disclosure about management's objectives, policies and processes for managing these risks, hence providing an overview of the Group's use of an exposure to financial instruments. These are given in Note 32.

As a result of the implementation of IFRS 7, the classification of two noncurrent asset balances has been changed and the balance sheet at December 31, 2006, has been restated. Total noncurrent assets are unchanged. Pension reimbursement rights are now classified as postemployment benefit assets and finance lease receivables are now classified as financial long-term assets.

Restated noncurrent assets in the balance sheet at December 31, 2006
(in millions of CHF)

	As originally published	Pension reimbursement rights	Finance lease receivables	Group restated
Financial long-tem assets	2152	--	51	2203
Other long-tem assets	794	(116)	(51)	627
Postemployment benefit assets	831	116	--	947

IFRS 8, *Operating Segments*. The new standard, which replaces IAS 14 Segment Reporting, requires some changes to the methodology and format of segment reporting. The Group has determined that its reportable operating segments under the new standard are the same as the primary business segments under the old standard. The new standard requires additional disclosure for operating segments given in Note 2. Unrealized internal profits on inventories that have been sold from one operating segment to another but which have not yet been sold to external customers at the balance sheet date are eliminated as a consolidation entry. Previously this elimination was allocated to the originating operating segment. The segment results for 2006 have been restated following this presentational change.

Restated Pharmaceuticals Divisional Information for year ended December 31, 2006
(in millions of CHF)

	Roche Pharma	Genentech	Chugai	Pharma Division
As originally published				
Operating profit	6,025	3,951	569	10,545
Including unrealized profits on inventories	(114)	(51)	--	(165)
Restated				
Operating profit	6,139	4,002	569	10,710
Elimination of profit within division				(165)
Total				10,545

IAS 1 (revised), *Presentation of Financial Statements: Capital Disclosures.* The revisions to IAS 1 require additional disclosure concerning the Group's objectives, policies, and processes for managing capital. These are given in Note 32.

IAS 23 (revised), *Borrowing Costs.* The revised standard requires that interest and other borrowing costs incurred with respect to qualifying assets are capitalized and included in the carrying value of the assets. Under the Group's previous accounting policy such costs were expensed as interest costs. The group has applied the new standard prospectively from January 1, 2007, and borrowing costs totaling 48 million Swiss francs using a rate of 4.79% were capitalized as property, plant and equipment in 2007 which would have been expensed under the previous accounting policy. The comparative results for 2006 have not been restated. Had the new accounting policy been applied in 2006, the Group would have capitalized an additional 32 million Swiss francs as property, plant, and equipment and financing costs would have been lower by this amount. This had a positive impact of 0.02 CHF on earnings per share and nonvoting equity security (basic and diluted) in 2007, and would have had a similar positive impact in 2006 if the revised standard had been applied retrospectively.

Presentation of operating results in the income statement. The income statement for the year ended December 31, 2006, has been restated following the presentational changes adopted in 2007. The Group has made these presentational changes to more accurately reflect the underlying business, to further improve comparability of its results to those of other healthcare companies and to allow readers to make a more accurate assessment of the sustainable earnings capacity of the Group. Total operating profit is unchanged, and the presentational changes have no effect on the nonoperating results, net income, and earnings per share. These changes, which have been applied retrospectively, are listed below.

- Intangible assets: Amortization and impairment of intangible assets are no longer reported as a separate line, but are now reported as part of "Cost of sales" (for intangibles relating to marketed products) or as part of "Research and Development" (for intangibles relating to technology and development, and including any impairment on intangibles that are not yet available for use).
- Alliance and royalty expenses: All royalties, alliance and collaboration expenses, including all collaboration profit-sharing arrangements are now reported as part of "Cost of sales." Previously some of these were included in "Marketing and distribution" or "General and administration" depending upon the terms of the particular agreement. Additionally, royalty expenses payable on royalty income are now reported as part of "Royalties and other operating income" to more accurately reflect the substance of the underlying transactions. Previously these expenses were included in "General and administration."
- Phase IV and similar costs: All such costs, which only arise in the Pharmaceuticals Division are now reported as part of "Research and development." Previously some of these costs were included in "Marketing and distribution" and "General and administration" depending on their nature.

Restated Income Statement for the Year Ended December 31, 2006
(in millions of CHF)

	As originally published	Intangible assets	Alliance royalties	Phase IV	Restated
Group					
Sales	42,041	--	--	--	42,041
Royalties and other operating income	1,466	--	(75)	--	1,391
Cost of sales	(10,616)	(1,059)	(1,610)	--	(13,285)
Marketing and distribution	(10,856)	--	1,260	642	(8,954)
Research and development	(6,589)	(115)	--	(661)	(7,365)
General and administration	(2,542)	--	425	19	(2,098)
Amortization and impairment of intangible assets	(1,174)	1,174	--	--	--
Operating profit	11,730	--	--	--	11,730
Pharmaceuticals Division					
Sales	33,294	--	--	--	33,294
Royalties and other operating income	1,277	--	(68)	--	1,209
Cost of sales	(6,868)	(619)	(1,545)	--	(9,032)
Marketing and distribution	(8,761)	--	1,260	642	(6,859)
Research and development	(5,889)	(40)	--	(661)	(6,590)
General and administration	(1,849)	--	353	19	(1,477)
Amortization and impairment of intangible assets	(659)	659	--	--	--
Operating profit	10,545	--	--	--	10,545
Diagnostics Division					
Sales	8,747	--	--	--	8,747
Royalties and other operating income	189	--	(7)	--	182
Cost of sales	(3,748)	(440)	(65)	--	(4,253)
Marketing and distribution	(2,095)	--	--	--	(2,095)
Research and development	(700)	(75)	--	--	(775)
General and administration	(456)	--	72	--	(384)
Amortization and impairment of intangible assets	(515)	515	--	--	--
Operating profit	1,422	--	--	--	1,422

Future changes in IFRS. The Group has early adopted IFRS 8, *Operating Segments,* and IAS 23 (revised), *Borrowing Costs,* which are required to be implemented from January 1, 2009, at the latest. The Group does not expect that the new interpretations that will be effective from January 1, 2008, will have a significant effect on the Group's results and financial position. The Group is currently assessing the potential impacts of the new and revised standards that will be effective from January 1, 2009, and beyond, which include further revisions to IAS 1, *Presentation of Financial Statements;* and revisions to IFRS 3, *Business Combinations;* IAS 27, *Consolidated and Separate Financial Statements;* and IFRS 2, *Share-Based Payment.*

Change in Accounting Estimates

The preparation of financial statements requires frequent use of estimates—for such items as asset service lives, residual values, fair values of financial assets or financial liabilities, likely collectability of accounts receivable, inventory obsolescence, accrual of warranty costs, provision for pension costs, and so on. These future conditions and events and their effects cannot be perceived with certainty; therefore, changes in estimates will be highly likely to occur as new information and more experience is obtained. IAS 8 requires that changes in estimates be *recognized prospectively* by "including it in a profit or loss in

1. The period of change if the change affects that period only; or
2. The period of change and future periods if the change affects both."

For example, on January 1, 2009, a machine purchased for €10,000 was originally estimated to have a ten-year useful life, and a salvage value of €1,000. On January 1, 2014 (five years later), the asset is expected to last another ten years and have a salvage value of €800. As a result, both the current period (this year ending December 1, 2009) and subsequent periods are affected by the change.   Annual depreciation expense over the estimated remaining useful life is computed as follows:

Original cost	€10,000
Less estimated salvage (residual) value	(1,000)
Depreciable amount	9,000
Accumulated depreciation, based original assumptions (10-year life)	
2009	900
2010	900
2011	900
2012	900
2013	900
	4,500
Carrying value at 1/1/2014	5,500
Revised estimate of salvage value	(800)
Depreciable amount	4,700
Remaining useful life at 1/1/2014	10 years
	€ 470 depreciation per year
Effect on 2014 net income	€ 470 − €900 = €430 increase

The annual depreciation charge over the remaining life would be computed as follows:

$$\frac{\text{Book value of asset} - \text{Residual value}}{\text{Remaining useful life}} = \frac{€5,500 - €800}{10 \text{ years}} = €470/\text{yr.}$$

An impairment affecting the cost recovery of an asset should not be handled as a change in accounting estimate but instead should be treated as a loss of the period. (See the discussions in Chapters 8 and 9.)

In some situations it may be difficult to distinguish between changes in accounting policy and changes in accounting estimates. For example, a company may change from deferring and amortizing a cost to recording it as an expense as incurred because the future benefits of the cost have become doubtful. In this instance, the company is changing its accounting principle (from deferral to immediate recognition) because of its change in the estimate of the future utility of a particular cost incurred currently.

According to IAS 8, when it is difficult to distinguish a change in an accounting policy from a change in an accounting estimate, the change is treated as a change in an accounting estimate. In the example in the preceding paragraph, the company is changing its accounting principle (from cost deferral to immediate recognition) because of its change in the estimate of the future value of a particular cost. The effect would be the same as that attributable to the current or future periods.

Because the two changes are indistinguishable, in the authors' opinion changes of this type should logically be considered changes in estimates and accounted for in accordance with IAS 8. However, the changes must be clearly indistinguishable to warrant being combined. The ability to compute each element independently would preclude combining them as a single change.

Correction of Errors

Although good internal control and the exercise of due care should serve to minimize the number of financial reporting errors that occur, these safeguards cannot be expected to completely eliminate errors in the financial statements. As a result, it was necessary for the accounting profession to promulgate standards that would ensure uniform treatment of accounting for error corrections.

IAS 8 deals with accounting for error corrections. Under earlier versions of this standard, so-called "fundamental errors" could be accounted for in accordance with either benchmark or allowed alternative approaches to effecting corrections. The IASB's *Improvements Project* resulted in the elimination of the concept of fundamental error, and also the elimination of what had formerly been the allowed alternative treatment. Under revised IAS 8, therefore, the only permitted treatment is "retrospective restatement" as a prior period adjustment (subject to an exception when doing so is impracticable, as described below). Prior periods must be restated to report financial position and financial performance as they would have been displayed had the error never taken place.

There is a clear distinction between errors and changes in accounting estimates. Estimates by their nature are approximations that may need revision as additional information becomes known. For example, when a gain or loss is ultimately recognized on the outcome of a contingency that previously could not be estimated reliably, this does not constitute the correction of an error and cannot be dealt with by restatement. However, if the estimated amount of the contingency had been miscomputed from data available when the financial statements were prepared, at least some portion of the variance between the accrual and the ultimate outcome might reasonably be deemed an error. An error requires that information available, which should have been taken into account, was ignored or misinterpreted.

Errors are defined by revised IAS 8 as omissions from and other misstatements of the entity's financial statements for one or more prior periods that are discovered in the current period and relate to reliable information that (1) was available when those prior period financial statements were prepared; and (2) could reasonably be expected to have been obtained and taken into account in the original preparation and presentation of those financial statements. Errors include the effects of mathematical mistakes, mistakes in applying accounting policies, oversights or misinterpretations of facts, and the effects of financial reporting fraud.

IAS 8 specifies that, when correcting an error in prior period financial statements, the term "restatement" is to be used. That term is exclusively reserved for this purpose so as to effectively communicate to users of the financial statements the reason for a particular change in previously issued financial statements.

An entity should correct material prior period error retrospectively in the first set of financial statements authorized for issue after their discovery by (1) "restating the comparative amounts for the prior periods presented in which the error occurred or (2) if the error occurred before the earliest prior period presented, restating the opening balances of assets, liabilities and equity for the earliest prior period presented."

Restatement consists of the following steps:

Step 1 - Adjust the carrying amounts of assets and liabilities at the beginning of the first period presented in the financial statements for the amount of the correction on periods prior to those presented in the financial statements.

Step 2 - Offset the amount of the adjustment in Step 1 (if any) by adjusting the opening balance of retained earnings (or other components of equity or net assets, as applicable to the reporting entity) for that period.

Step 3 - Adjust the financial statements of each individual prior period presented for the effects of correcting the error on that specific period (referred to as the period-specific effects of the error).

Example of prior period adjustment

Assume that Belmont Corporation (BC) had overstated its depreciation expense by €50,000 in 2007 and €40,000 in 2008, both due to mathematical mistakes. The errors affected both the financial statements and the income tax returns in 2007 and 2008 and are discovered in 2009.

BC's statements of financial position and statements of comprehensive income and retained earnings as of and for the year ended December 31, 2008, prior to the restatement were as follows:

Belmont Corporation
Statement of Comprehensive Income and Retained Earnings
Prior to Restatement
Year Ended December 31, 2008

	2008
Sales	€2,000,000
Cost of sales	
Depreciation	750,000
Other	390,000
	1,140,000
Gross profit	860,000
Selling, general, and administrative expenses	450,000
Income from operations	410,000
Other income (expense)	10,000
Income before income taxes	420,000
Income taxes	168,000
Profit or loss	252,000
Retained earnings, beginning of year	6,463,000
Dividends	(1,200,000)
Retained earnings, end of year	€5,515,000

Belmont Corporation
Statement of Financial Position
Prior to Restatement
December 31, 2008

	2008
Assets	
Current assets	€ ,540,000
Property and equipment	
Cost	3,500,000
Accumulated depreciation and amortization	(430,000)
	3,070,000
Total assets	€ 5,610,000
Liabilities and stockholders' equity	
Income taxes payable	€ --
Other current liabilities	12,000
Total current liabilities	12,000
Noncurrent liabilities	70,000
Total liabilities	82,000
Shareholders' equity	
Ordinary share	13,000
Retained earnings	5,515,000
Total shareholders' equity	5,528,000
Total liabilities and shareholders' equity	€ 5,610,000

The following steps are followed to restate BC's prior period financial statements:

Step 1 -   Adjust the carrying amounts of assets and liabilities at the beginning of the first period presented in the financial statements for the cumulative effect of correcting the error on periods prior to those presented in the financial statements.

        The first period presented in the financial statements is 2008. At the beginning of that year, €50,000 of the mistakes had been made and reflected on both the income tax return and financial statements. Assuming a flat 40% income tax rate and ignoring the effects of penalties and interest that would be assessed on the amended income tax returns, the following adjustment would be made to assets and liabilities at January 1, 2008:

Decrease in accumulated depreciation	€50,000
Increase in income taxes payable	(20,000)
	€30,000

Step 2 - Offset the effect of the adjustment in Step 1 by adjusting the opening balance of retained earnings (or other components of equity or net assets, as applicable to the reporting entity) for that period.

Retained earnings at the beginning of 2008 will increase by €30,000 as the offsetting entry resulting from Step 1.

Step 3 - Adjust the financial statements of each individual prior period presented for the effects of correcting the error on that specific period (referred to as the period-specific effects of the error).

The 2008 prior period financial statements will be corrected for the period-specific effects of the restatement as follows:

Decrease in depreciation expense and accumulated depreciation	€40,000
Increase in income tax expense and income taxes payable	(16,000)
Increase 2008 profit or loss	€24,000

The restated financial statements are presented below.

Belmont Corporation
Statements of Comprehensive Income Retained Earnings
As Restated
Years Ended December 31, 2009 and 2008

	2008 *restated*
Sales	€ 2,000,000
Cost of sales	
Depreciation	710,000
Other	390,000
	1,100,000
Gross profit	900,000
Selling, general, and administrative expenses	450,000
Income from operations	450,000
Other income (expense)	10,000
Income before income taxes	460,000
Income taxes	184,000
Profit or loss	276,000
Retained earnings, beginning of year, as originally reported	6,463,000
Restatement to reflect correction of depreciation (Note X)	30,000
Retained earnings, beginning of year, as restated	6,493,000
Dividends	(1,200,000)
Retained earnings, end of year	€ 5,569,000

Belmont Corporation
Statements of Comprehensive Income Retained Earnings
As Restated
Years Ended December 31, 2009 and 2008

	2008 *restated*
Assets	
Current assets	€ 2,540,000
Property and equipment	
Cost	3,500,000
Accumulated depreciation and amortization	(340,000)
	3,160,000
Total assets	€ 5,700,000

		2008 *restated*
Liabilities and shareholders' equity		
Income taxes payable	€	36,000
Other current liabilities		12,000
Total current liabilities		48,000
Noncurrent liabilities		70,000
Total liabilities		118,000
Shareholders' equity		
Ordinary share		13,000
Retained earnings		5,569,000
Total shareholders' equity		5,582,000
Total liabilities and shareholders' equity	€	5,700,000

When restating previously issued financial statements, management is to disclose

1. The fact that the financial statements have been restated
2. The nature of the error
3. The effect of the restatement on each line item in the financial statements
4. The cumulative effect of the restatement on retained earnings (or other applicable components of equity or net assets)

These disclosures need not be repeated in subsequent periods.

The correction of an error in the financial statements of a prior period discovered subsequent to their issuance is reported as a prior period adjustment in the financial statements of the subsequent period. In some cases, however, this situation necessitates the recall or withdrawal of the previously issued financial statements and their revision and reissuance.

Impracticability exception. Revised IAS 8 stipulates that the amount of the correction of an error is to be accounted for retrospectively. As with changes in accounting policies, comparative information presented for a particular period need not be restated, if restating the information is impracticable. As a result, when it is impracticable to determine the cumulative effect, at the beginning of the current period, of an error, on all prior periods, the entity changes the comparative information as if the error had been corrected, prospectively from the earliest date practicable.

However, because the value ascribed to truly comparable data is high, this exception is not to be viewed as an invitation to not restate comparable periods' financial statements to remove the effects of most errors. The standard sets out what constitutes impracticability, as discussed earlier in this chapter, and this should be strictly interpreted. When comparative information for a particular prior period is not restated, the opening balance of retained earnings for the next period must be restated for the amount of the correction before the beginning of that period.

In practice, the major criterion for determining whether or not to report the correction of the error is the materiality of the correction. There are many factors to be considered in determining the materiality of the error correction. Materiality should be considered for each correction individually as well as for all corrections in total. If the correction is determined to have a material effect on profit or loss, or the trend of earnings, it should be disclosed in accordance with the requirements set forth in the preceding paragraph.

The prior period adjustment should be presented in the financial statements as follows:

Retained earnings, January 1, 2007, as reported previously	€xxx
Correction of error (description) in prior period(s) (net of €xx tax)	xxx
Adjusted balance of retained earnings at January 1, 2007	xxx
Profit or loss for the year	xxx
Retained earnings December 31, 2007	€xxx

In comparative statements, prior period adjustments should also be shown as adjustments to the beginning balances in the retained earnings statements. The amount of the adjustment on the earliest statement shall be the amount of the correction on periods prior to the earliest period presented. The later retained earnings statements presented should also show a prior period adjustment for the amount of the correction as of the beginning of the period being reported on.

Because it is to be handled retrospectively, the correction of an error—which by definition relates to one or more prior periods—is excluded from the determination of profit or loss for the period in which the error is discovered. The financial statements are presented as if the error had never occurred, by correcting the error in the comparative information for the prior period(s) in which the error occurred, unless undue cost or effort exception is invoked. The amount of the correction relating to errors that occurred in periods prior to those presented in comparative information in the financial statements is adjusted against the opening balance of retained earnings of the earliest prior period presented. This treatment is entirely analogous to that now prescribed for changes in accounting policies.

Also, any other information presented with respect to prior periods, such as historical summaries of financial data, also is to be restated, again unless restatement would require undue cost or effort.

When an accounting error is being corrected, the reporting entity is to disclose the following:

1. The nature of the error;
2. The amount of the correction for each prior period presented;
3. The amount of the correction relating to periods prior to those presented in comparative information; and
4. That comparative information has been restated, or that the restatement for a particular prior period has not been made because it would require undue cost or effort.

22 FOREIGN CURRENCY

PERSPECTIVE AND ISSUES

International trade, always important, continues to become more prevalent, and "multi-national corporations" (MNC), now comprised not only of the international giants which are household names, but also many midtier companies, are the norm. Corporations worldwide are reaching beyond national boundaries and engaging in international trade. Global economic restructuring is rampant: signings of trade pacts such as GATT, NAFTA, and the World Trade Organization (WTO) have lent further impetus to the process of internationalization. International activity by most domestic corporations has increased significantly, which means that transactions are consummated not only with independent foreign entities but also with foreign subsidiaries.

Foreign subsidiaries, associates, and branches typically handle their accounts and prepare financial statements in the respective currencies of the countries in which they are located. Thus, it is more than likely that a MNC ends up receiving, at year-end, financial statements from various foreign subsidiaries expressed in a number of foreign currencies, such as dollars, euros, pounds, lira, dinars, won, rubles, and yen. However, for users of these financial statements to analyze the MNC's foreign involvement and overall financial position and results of operations properly, foreign-currency-denominated financial statements must first be expressed in terms that the users can understand. This means that the foreign currency financial statements of the various subsidiaries will have to be translated into the currency of the country where the MNC is registered or has its major operations.

IFRS governing the translation of foreign currency financial statements and the accounting for foreign currency transactions are found primarily in IAS 21, *The Effects of Changes in Foreign Exchange Rates*. IAS 21 applies to

1. Accounting for foreign currency transactions (e.g., exports, imports, and loans) which are denominated in other than the reporting entity's functional currency
2. Translation of foreign currency financial statements of branches, divisions, subsidiaries, and other investees that are incorporated in the financial statements of an entity by consolidation, proportionate consolidation, or the equity method of accounting

IAS 21 did not address hedge accounting for foreign currency items, other than the classification of exchange differences arising from a foreign currency liability accounted for as a hedge of a net investment in a foreign entity. IAS 39 subsequently established the accounting for hedges of a net investment in a foreign entity, which closely parallels that prescribed for cash flow hedging as set forth under that standard.

As part of the IASB's *Improvements Project*, a number of changes to IAS 21 have been made, and several previously issued SICs (interpretations) have been withdrawn. Besides relocating the guidance on most foreign currency derivatives to IAS 39 (without altering it, however), the major changes were to replace the current option of *reporting currency* with the twin concepts of *functional currency* (the currency of the primary economic environment in which the entity operates) and *presentation currency* (the currency in which the entity presents its financial statements). Additionally, the current freedom to choose a functional currency has been terminated; the current allowed alternative—to capitalize certain exchange differences—has been eliminated; unrestricted choice is now permitted to report in any currency; and new requirements have been imposed for the translation of comparative amounts. The revised IAS became effective in 2005.

IAS 21 requires that exchange differences arising on a monetary item that is, in substance, part of the reporting entity's net investment in a foreign operation, are initially to be recognized in other comprehensive income and reclassified from equity to profit or loss on disposal of net investment, regardless of the currency in which the item is denominated. The 2003 IAS 21 guidance required the monetary item to be denominated in the functional currency of either the reporting entity or the foreign operation for exchange differences on this item to be recognized in other comprehensive income. The amendments, published in December 2005, specify that this requirement applies irrespective of the currency of the monetary item and of whether the monetary item results from a transaction with the reporting entity and any of its subsidiaries (see discussion at the end of this chapter).

Sources of IFRS
IAS 21, 39   *SIC* 7

DEFINITIONS OF TERMS

Closing rate. This refers to the spot exchange rate (defined below) at the end of the reporting period.

Conversion. The exchange of one currency for another.

Exchange difference. The difference resulting from reporting the same number of units of a foreign currency in the presentation currency at different exchange rates.

Exchange rate. This refers to the ratio for exchange between two currencies.

Fair value. The amount for which an asset could be exchanged, or a liability could be settled, between knowledgeable willing parties in an arm's-length transaction.

Foreign currency. A currency other than the functional currency of the reporting entity (e.g., the Japanese yen is a foreign currency for a US reporting entity).

Foreign currency financial statements. Financial statements that employ as the unit of measure a foreign currency that is not the presentation currency of the entity.

Foreign currency transactions. Transactions whose terms are denominated in a foreign currency or require settlement in a foreign currency. Foreign currency transactions arise when an entity (1) buys or sells on credit goods or services whose prices are denominated in foreign currency, (2) borrows or lends funds and the amounts payable or receivable are denominated in foreign currency, (3) is a party to an unperformed foreign exchange contract, or (4) for other reasons acquires or disposes of assets or incurs or settles liabilities denominated in foreign currency.

Foreign currency translation. The process of expressing in the presentation currency of the entity amounts that are denominated or measured in a different currency.

Foreign entity. When the activities of a foreign operation are not an integral part of those of the reporting entity, such a foreign operation is referred to as a foreign entity.

Foreign operation. A foreign subsidiary, associate, joint venture, or branch of the reporting entity whose activities are based or conducted in a country other than the country where the reporting entity is domiciled.

Functional currency. The currency of the primary economic environment in which the entity operates, which thus is the currency in which the reporting entity measures the items in its financial statements, and which may differ from the presentation currency in some instances.

Group. A parent company and all of its subsidiaries.

Monetary items. Money held and assets and liabilities to be received or paid in fixed or determinable amounts of money.

Net investment in a foreign operation. The amount refers to the reporting entity's interest in the net assets of that operation.

Nonmonetary items. All items presented in the statement of financial position other than cash, claims to cash, and cash obligations.

Presentation currency. The currency in which the reporting entity's financial statements are presented. There is no limitation on the selection of a presentation currency by a reporting entity.

Reporting entity. An entity or group whose financial statements are being referred to. Under this standard, those financial statements reflect (1) the financial statements of one or more foreign operations by consolidation, proportionate consolidation, or equity accounting; (2) foreign currency transactions; or (3) both of the foregoing.

Spot exchange rate. The exchange rate for immediate delivery of currencies exchanged.

Transaction date. In the context of recognition of exchange differences from settlement of monetary items arising from foreign currency transactions, transaction date refers to the date at which a foreign currency transaction (e.g., a sale or purchase of merchandise or services the settlement for which will be in a foreign currency) occurs and is recorded in the accounting records.

CONCEPTS, RULES, AND EXAMPLES

Applicability of Translation Guidance Provided by Revised IAS 21

Increasingly entities carry on business transactions on a multinational, or even global, basis. Vendors and customers may be located in other nations, and transactions may be de-

nominated in foreign currencies (foreign currency transactions). Accounting for these transactions in the currency of the reporting entity (its functional currency, as defined later in this
discussion) is one of the matters addressed by IAS 21.

Furthermore, many entities have foreign operations—for example, manufacturing or
distribution activities conducted in foreign countries, organized as subsidiaries, joint ventures, investees, or simply as branches—and these operations will likely have a variety of
transactions with the parent and other affiliated entities (capital infusions, dividends, et al.).
This creates both the problem of accounting for foreign-currency-denominated transactions,
as mentioned in the preceding paragraph, but also the complex process of consolidating (if a
subsidiary) the foreign operation's financial statements with those of the reporting (parent)
entity, or of computing the reporting entity's share of the foreign operation's earnings if the
equity method is applicable.

Finally, entities may, without limitation, report their financial statements in foreign currencies (e.g., a German company can elect to report in UK pounds sterling—which presumably might be done if the reporting entity has a large analyst following or many shareholders
in the UK). This practice would necessitate that all balances be translated into the presentation currency, and for this to occur consistently and accurately there needs to be a set of
rules.

IAS 21 provides the needed guidance on how to include foreign currency transactions
and foreign operations in the financial statements of an entity and how to translate financial
statements into a presentation currency. Compared to the guidance under the predecessor
standard (adopted in 1993), the provisions of the revised standard are somewhat easier to
grasp, particularly since certain options previously available to financial statement preparers
have been eliminated. IAS 21 does not apply to the presentation, in the statement of cash
flows, of cash flows arising from transactions in a foreign currency, or to the translation of
cash flows of a foreign operation, which are within the scope of IAS 7, *Statement of Cash
Flows.*

Revised IAS 21 should be applied to accounting for transactions and balances in foreign
currencies, except for those derivative transactions and balances that are within the scope of
IAS 39, *Financial Instruments: Recognition and Measurement.* However, those foreign
currency derivatives that are not within the scope of IAS 39 (e.g., some foreign currency derivatives that are embedded in other contracts), and the translation of amounts relating to
derivatives from its functional currency to its presentation currency are within the scope of
this standard.

The revised IAS 21 changed the requirements for the determination of an entity's functional currency. The distinction between foreign operations that are integral to the operations
of the reporting entity ("integral foreign operations") and others that are not integral ("foreign entities") no longer directly affects the method of translating foreign currency financial
statements. An entity that was previously classified as an integral foreign operation has the
same functional currency as the reporting entity. Accordingly, only one translation method
is used for foreign subsidiaries—the method which previously only applied to foreign entities.

The distinction between an integral foreign operation and a foreign entity is now considered among the indicators useful in determining the reporting entity's functional currency,
but it alone is not determinative. Under the revised standard, each of the entities to be included in the reporting entity's financial statements are to ascertain their respective appropriate functional currencies, which then must be used to measure financial position and results
of operations. Greater emphasis is now to be given to the currency of the economy that determines the pricing of the entities' transactions, rather than to the currencies in which trans-

actions are denominated. The term "measurement currency" used by SIC 19 has been eliminated and SIC 19 has been withdrawn.

Functional Currency

The concept of *functional currency* is key to understanding translation of foreign currency financial statements. Functional currency is defined as being the currency of the primary economic environment in which an entity operates. This is normally, but not necessarily, the currency in which that entity principally generates and expends cash.

In determining the relevant functional currency, an entity would give primary consideration to the following factors:

1. The currency that mainly influences sales prices for goods and services, as well as the currency of the country whose competitive forces and regulations mainly determine the sales prices of the entity's goods and services, and
2. The currency that primarily influences labor, material, and other costs of providing those goods or services.

Note that the currency which influences selling prices is most often that currency in which sales prices are denominated and settled, while the currency that most influences the various input costs is normally that in which input costs are denominated and settled. There are many situations in which input costs and output prices will be denominated in or influenced by differing currencies (e.g., an entity which manufactures all of its goods in Mexico, using locally sourced labor and materials, but sells all or most of its output in Europe in euro-denominated transactions).

In addition to the foregoing, IAS 21 notes other factors which may commonly also provide evidence of an entity's functional currency. These may be deemed secondary considerations. These are

1. The currency in which funds from financing activities (i.e., from the issuance of debt and equity instruments) are generated, and
2. The currency in which receipts from operating activities are usually retained.

In making a determination of whether the functional currency of a foreign operation (e.g., a subsidiary, branch, associate, or joint venture) is the same as that of the reporting entity (parent, investor, etc.), certain additional considerations may also be relevant. These include

1. Whether the activities of the foreign operation are carried out as an extension of the reporting entity, rather than being executed more or less autonomously;
2. What proportion of the foreign operation's activities is comprised of transactions with the reporting entity;
3. Whether the foreign operation's cash flows directly impact upon the cash flows of the reporting entity, and are available for prompt remittance to the reporting entity; and
4. Whether the foreign operation is largely cash flow independent (i.e., if its own cash flows are sufficient to service its existing and reasonably anticipated debts without the injection of funds by the reporting entity).

Foreign operations are characterized as being adjuncts of the operations of the reporting entity when, for example, the foreign operation only serves to sell goods imported from the reporting entity and in turn remits all sales proceeds to the reporting entity. On the other hand, the foreign operation is seen as being essentially autonomous when it accumulates cash and other monetary items, incurs expenses, generates income and arranges borrowings, all done substantially in its local currency.

In practice, there are many gradations along the continuum between full autonomy and the state of being a mere adjunct to the reporting entity's operations. When there are mixed indications, and thus the identity of the functional currency is not obvious, judgment is required to make this determination. The selection of the functional currency should most faithfully represent the economic effects of the underlying transactions, events and conditions. According to IAS 21, however, priority attention is to be given to the identity of the currency (or currencies) that impact selling prices for outputs of goods and services, and inputs for labor and materials and other costs. The other factors noted above are to be referred to secondarily, when a clear conclusion is not apparent from considering the two primary factors.

Example

A US-based company, Majordomo, Inc., has a major subsidiary located in the UK, John Bull Co., which produces and sells goods to customers almost exclusively in EU member states. Transactions are effected primarily in euros, both for sales and, to a lesser extent, for raw materials purchases. The functional currency is determined to be euros in this instance, given the facts noted. Transactions are to be measured in euros, accordingly. For purposes of the John Bull Co.'s stand-alone financial reporting, euro-based financial data will be translated into pounds Sterling, using the translation rules set forth in revised IAS 21. For consolidation of the UK subsidiary into the financial statements of parent entity Majordomo, Inc., translation into US dollars will be required, again using the procedures defined in the standard.

In some cases the determination of functional currency can be complex and time-consuming. The process is difficult especially if the foreign operation acts as an investment company or holding company within a group and has few external transactions. Management must document the approach followed in the determination of the functional currency for each entity within a group—particularly when factors are mixed and judgment is required.

Once determined, an entity's functional currency will rarely be altered. However, since the entity's functional currency is expected to reflect its most significant underlying transactions, events and conditions, there obviously can be a change in functional currency if there are fundamental changes in those circumstances. For example, if the entity's manufacturing and sales operations are relocated to another country, and inputs are thereafter sourced from that new location, this may justify changing the functional currency for that operation. When there is a change in an entity's functional currency, the entity should apply the translation procedures applicable to the new functional currency *prospectively* from the date of the change.

If the functional currency is the currency of a hyperinflationary economy, as that term is defined under IAS 29, *Financial Reporting in Hyperinflationary Economies*, the entity's financial statements are restated in accordance with the provisions of that standard. Revised IAS 21 stresses that an entity cannot avert such restatement by employing tactics such as adopting an alternate functional currency, such as that of its parent entity. There are currently very few such economies in the world, but this situation of course may change in the future.

Monetary and Nonmonetary Items

For purposes of applying IAS 21, it is important to understand the distinction between monetary and nonmonetary items. Monetary items are those granting or imposing "a right to receive, or an obligation to deliver, a fixed or determinable number of units of currency." In contrast, nonmonetary items are those exhibiting "the absence of a right to receive, or an obligation to deliver, a fixed or determinable number of units of currency. Examples of monetary items include accounts and notes receivable; pensions and other employee benefits to be paid in cash; provisions that are to be settled in cash; and cash dividends that are properly recognized as a liability. Examples of nonmonetary items include inventories; amounts prepaid for goods and services (e.g., prepaid insurance); property, plant, and equipment; goodwill; other intangible assets; and provisions that are to be settled by the delivery of a nonmonetary asset.

Reporting Foreign Currency Transactions in the Functional Currency

Foreign currency transactions are those denominated in, or requiring settlement in, a foreign currency. These can include such common transactions as those arising from

1. The purchase or sale of goods or services in transactions where the price is denominated in a foreign currency.
2. The borrowing or lending of funds, where the amounts owed or to be received are denominated in a foreign currency; or
3. Other routine activities such as the acquisition or disposition of assets, or the incurring of settlement of liabilities, if denominated in a foreign currency.

Under the provisions of IAS 21, foreign currency transactions are to be initially recorded in the functional currency by applying to the foreign-currency-denominated amounts the spot exchange rate between the functional currency and the foreign currency at the date of the transaction. However, when there are numerous, relatively homogeneous transactions over the course of the reporting period (e.g., year), it is acceptable, and much more practical, to apply an appropriate average exchange rate. In the simplest scenario, the simple numerical average (i.e., the midpoint between the beginning and ending exchange rates) could be used. Care must be exercised to ensure that such a simplistic approach is actually meaningful, however.

If exchange rate movements do not smoothly occur throughout the reporting period, or if rates move alternately up and down over the reporting interval, rather than monotonically up or down, then a more carefully constructed, weighted-average exchange rate should be used. Also, if transactions occur in other than a smooth pattern over the period—as might be the case for products characterized by seasonal sales—then a weighted-average exchange rate might be needed if exchange rates have moved materially over the course of the reporting period. For example, if the bulk of revenues is generated in the fourth quarter, the annual average exchange rate would probably not result in an accurately translated statement of comprehensive income.

Example

Continuing the preceding example, the UK-based subsidiary, John Bull, which produces and sells goods to customers almost exclusively in EU member states, also had sizeable sales to a Swiss company in 2009, denominated in Swiss francs. These occurred primarily in the fourth quarter of the year, when the Swiss franc-euro exchange rate was atypically strong. In converting these sales to the functional currency (euros), the average exchange rate in the fourth quarter was deemed to be most relevant.

Subsequent to the date of the underlying transaction, there may be a continuing need to translate the foreign currency denominated event into the entity's functional currency. For example, a purchase or sale transaction may have given rise to an account payable or an account receivable, which remains unsettled at the next financial reporting date (e.g., the following month-end). According to IAS 21, at each end of the reporting period the foreign currency *monetary* items (such as payables and receivables) are to be translated using the closing rate (i.e., the exchange rate at the date of the statement of financial position).

Example

If John Bull Co. (from the preceding examples) acquires receivables denominated in a foreign currency, Swiss francs (CHF), in 2009, these are translated into the functional currency, euros, at the date of the transaction. If the CHF-denominated receivables are still outstanding at year-end, the company will translate those (ignoring any allowance for uncollectibles) into euros at the year-end exchange rate. If these remain outstanding at the end of 2010 (again ignoring collectibility concerns), these will be translated into euros using the *year-end 2010* exchange rate.

To the extent that exchange rates have changed since the transaction occurred (which will likely happen), exchange differences will have to be recognized by the reporting entity, since the amount due to or from a vendor or customer, denominated in a foreign currency, is now more or less valuable than when the transaction occurred.

Example

Assume now that John Bull Co. acquired the above-noted receivables denominated in Swiss francs in 2009, when the exchange rate of the Swiss franc versus the euro was CHF 1 = €.65. At year-end 2009, the rate is CHF 1 = €.61, and by year-end 2010, the euro has further strengthened to CHF 1 = €.58. Assume that John Bull acquired CHF 10,000 of receivables in mid-2009, and all remain outstanding at year-end 2010. (Again, for purposes of this example only, ignore collectibility concerns).

At the date of initial recognition, John Bull records accounts receivable denominated in CHF in the euro equivalent value of €6,500, since the euro is the functional currency (translation to British pounds or US dollars—a presentation currency—will be dealt with later). At year-end 2009 these receivables are the equivalent of only €6,100, and as a result a loss of €400, which must be recognized in the company's 2009 profit and loss statement. In effect, by holding CHF-denominated receivables while the Swiss franc declined in value against the euro, John Bull suffered a loss. The Swiss franc further weakens over 2010, so that by year-end the CHF 10,000 of receivables will be worth only €5,800, for a further loss of €300 in 2010, which again is to be recognized currently in John Bull's results of operations.

Nonmonetary items (such as property purchased for the company's foreign operation), on the other hand, are to be translated at historical exchange rates. The actual historical exchange rate to be used, however, depends on whether the nonmonetary item is being reported on the historical cost basis, or on a revalued basis, in those instances where the latter method of reporting is permitted under IFRS. If the nonmonetary items are measured in terms of historical cost in a foreign currency, then these are to be translated by using the exchange rate at the actual historical date of the transaction. If the item has been restated to a fair value measurement, then it must be translated into the functional currency by applying the exchange rate at the date when the fair value was determined.

Example—historical cost accounting employed by reporting entity

Assume that John Bull Co. acquired machinery from a Swiss manufacturer, in a transaction denominated in Swiss francs in 2009, when the CHF-euro exchange rate was CHF 1 = €.65. The price paid was CHF 250,000. For purposes of this example, ignore depreciation. At the transaction date, John Bull Co. records the machinery at €162,500. This same amount will be presented in the year-end 2009 and 2010 statements of financial position. The change in exchange rates subsequent to the transaction date will not be considered, since machinery is a nonmonetary asset.

Example—revaluation accounting employed by reporting entity

Assume again that John Bull Co. acquired machinery from a Swiss manufacturer, in a transaction denominated in Swiss francs in 2009, when the CHF-euro exchange rate was CHF 1 = €.65. The price paid was CHF 250,000. For purposes of this example, ignore depreciation. At year-end

2009, John Bull Co. elects to use the allowed alternative method of accounting under IAS 16, and determines that the fair value of the machinery is CHF 285,000. In the entity's year-end statement of financial position, this is reported at the euro equivalent of the revalued amount, using the exchange rate at the revaluation date, or €173,850 (= CHF 285,000 × €.61). This same amount will appear in the 2010 statement of financial position (assuming no further revaluation is undertaken post-2009).

If a nonmonetary asset was acquired in a foreign currency transaction by incurring debt which is to be repaid in the foreign currency (e.g., when a building for the foreign operation was financed locally by commercial debt), subsequent to the actual transaction date the translation of the asset and the related debt will be at differing exchange rates (unless rates remain unchanged, which is not likely to happen.) The result will be either a gain or a loss, which reflects the fact that a nonmonetary asset was purchased but the burden of the related obligation for future payment will vary as the exchange rates fluctuate over time, until the debt is ultimately settled—in other words, the reporting entity has assumed exchange rate risk. On the other hand, if the debt were obtained in the reporting (parent) entity's home country or were otherwise denominated in the buyer's functional currency, there would be no exchange rate risk and no subsequent gain or loss resulting from such an exposure.

Example

Assume now that John Bull Co. acquired machinery from a Swiss manufacturer, in a transaction denominated in Swiss francs in 2009, when the CHF-euro exchange rate was CHF 1 = €.65. The price paid was CHF 250,000. For purposes of this example, ignore depreciation. At the transaction date, John Bull Co. records the machinery at €162,500. This same amount will be presented in the year-end 2009 and 2010 statements of financial position. The change in exchange rates subsequent to the transaction date will not be considered, since machinery is a nonmonetary asset.

However, the purchase of the machinery was effected by signing a 5-year note, payable in Swiss francs. Assume for simplicity the note is not subject to amortization (i.e., due in full at maturity). The note is recorded, at transaction date, as a liability of €162,500. However, at year-end 2009, since the euro has strengthened, the obligation is the equivalent of €152,500. As a result an exchange gain of €10,000 is reported in profit or loss in the current period.

At year-end 2010, this obligation has the euro-equivalent value of €145,000, and thus a further gain of €7,500 is realized by John Bull Co. for financial reporting purposes.

Had the machinery been acquired for a euro-denominated obligation of €162,500, this valuation would remain in the financial statements until ultimately retired. In this case, the Swiss machinery manufacturer, not the British customer (whose functional currency is the euro), accepted exchange rate risk, and John Bull Co. will report no gain or loss arising from exchange differences.

Other complications can arise when accounting for transactions executed in a foreign currency. IAS 21 identifies circumstances where the carrying amount of an item is determined by comparing two or more amounts, for example when inventory is to be presented at the lower of cost or net realizable value, consistent with the requirements of IAS 2, *Inventories*. Another cited example pertains to long-lived assets, which must be reviewed for impairment, per IAS 36, *Impairments of Assets*. In situations such as these (i.e., where the asset is nonmonetary and is measured in a foreign currency) the carrying amount in terms of functional currency is determined by comparing

1. The cost or carrying amount, as appropriate, translated at the exchange rate at the date when that amount was determined (i.e., the rate at the date of the transaction for an item measured in terms of historical cost, or the date of revaluation if the item were restated under relevant IFRS); and

2. The net realizable value or recoverable amount, as appropriate, translated at the exchange rate at the date when *that* value was determined (which would normally be the closing rate at the end of the reporting period).

Note that by comparing translated amounts that are determined using exchange rate ratios as of differing dates, the actual effect of performing the translation will reflect two economic phenomena; namely, the IFRS-driven lower of cost or fair value comparison (or equivalent), and the changing exchange rates. The effect may be that an impairment loss is to be recognized in the functional currency when it would not have been recognized in the foreign currency, or the opposite relationship may hold (and, of course, there could be impairments in either case, albeit for differing amounts).

Example

John Bull Co. acquired raw materials inventory from a Swiss manufacturer, in a transaction denominated in Swiss francs in 2009, when the CHF-euro exchange rate was CHF 1 = €.65. The price paid was CHF 34,000. At year-end, when the exchange rate was CHF 1 = €.61, the net realizable value of the inventory, which was still on hand, was CHF 32,000. Applying the IAS 21 requirements, it is determined that (1) the purchase price in euros was €22,100 (= CHF 34,000 × €.65); and (2) NRV at the end of the reporting period is €19,520 (= CHF 32,000 × €.61). A lower of cost or realizable value impairment adjustment is reported equal to €2,580. (= €22,100 – €19,520).

See below for another example, where a NRV loss is called for even though NRV in the foreign currency is greater than cost, due to the interaction of exchange rate changes and NRV movements.

Translation of Foreign Operations and Foreign Entities

As noted, revised IAS 21, which became effective in 2005, diminishes the importance of distinguishing between *integral foreign operations* and *foreign entities,* which under earlier versions of the standard were central to determining how to translate foreign entity (e.g., subsidiary) financial statements. These requirements are now included among the secondary indicators to be used in determining an entity's functional currency.

As a consequence of this change, there is no longer a meaningful distinction between integral foreign operations and foreign entities. All entities that were previously classified as integral foreign operations now will have the same functional currency as their respective reporting entities (e.g., parent entities) have. For example, if a British subsidiary is integral to the operations of its US parent entity, the US dollar would be its functional currency.

Under the revised standard, only a single translation method can be used for foreign operations, and this is the same method that is applicable to foreign entities. Specifically, the reporting entity is required to translate the assets and liabilities of its foreign operations and foreign entities at the closing (end of the reporting period) rate, and required to translate income and expenses at the exchange rates at the dates of the transactions (or at the average rate for the period, if this offers a reasonable approximation of actual transaction date rates).

Furthermore, IAS 21 now permits the reporting entity to present its financial statements in any currency (or currencies) that it chooses to use. This guideline applies whether the reporting unit is a stand-alone entity, a parent preparing consolidated financial statements, or a parent company, an investor, or a venturer preparing separate financial statements, as permitted under IAS 27.

As noted previously, sometimes an adjustment may be required to reduce the carrying amount of an asset in the financial statements of the reporting entity even though such an adjustment was not necessary in the separate, foreign currency based financial statements of the foreign operation. This stipulation of IAS 21 can best be illustrated by the following case study.

Example

Inventory of merchandise owned by a foreign operation of the reporting entity is being carried by the foreign operation at 3,750,000 SR (Saudi riyals) in its statement of financial position. Suppose that the indirect exchange rate fluctuated from 3.75 SR = 1 US dollar at September 15, 2009, when the merchandise was bought, to 4.25 SR = 1 US dollar at December 31, 2009 (i.e., the end of the reporting period). The translation of this item into the functional currency will necessitate an adjustment to reduce the carrying amount of the inventory to its net realizable value if this value when translated into the functional currency is lower than the carrying amount translated at the rate prevailing on the date of purchase of the merchandise.

Although the net realizable value, which in terms of Saudi riyals is 4,000,000 (SR), is higher than the carrying amount in Saudi riyals (i.e., 3,750,000 SR) when translated into the functional currency (i.e., US dollars) at the end of the reporting period, the net realizable value is lower than the carrying amount (translated into the functional currency at the exchange rate prevailing on the date of acquisition of the merchandise). Thus, on the financial statements of the foreign operation the inventory would not have to be adjusted. However, when the net realizable value is translated at the closing rate (which is 4.25 SR = 1 US dollar) into the functional currency, it will require the following adjustment:

1. Carrying amount translated at the exchange rate on September 15, 2009 (i.e., the date of acquisition) = SR 3,750,000 ÷ 3.75 = $1,000,000
2. Net realizable value translated at the closing rate = SR 4,000,000 ÷ 4.25 = $941,176
3. Adjustment needed = $1,000,000 − $941,176 = $58,824

Conversely, IAS 21 further stipulates that an adjustment that already exists on the financial statements of the foreign operation may need to be reversed in the financial statements of the reporting entity. To illustrate this point, the facts of the example above are repeated, with some variation, below.

Example

All other factual details remaining the same as the preceding example; it is now assumed that the inventory, which is carried on the books of the foreign operation at Saudi riyals (SR) 3,750,000, instead has a net realizable value of SR 3,250,000 at year-end. Also assume that the indirect exchange rate fluctuated from SR 3.75 = 1 US dollar at the date of acquisition of the merchandise to SR 3.00 = 1 US dollar at the end of the reporting period.

Since in terms of Saudi riyals, the net realizable value at the end of the reporting period was lower than the carrying value of the inventory, an adjustment must have been made in the statement of financial position of the foreign operation (in Saudi riyals) to reduce the carrying amount to the lower of cost or net realizable value. In other words, a contra asset account (i.e., a lower of cost or market reserve) representing the difference between the carrying amount (SR 3,750,000) and the net realizable value (SR 3,250,000) must have been created on the books of the foreign operation.

On translating the financial statements of the foreign operation into the functional currency, however, it is noted that due to the fluctuation of the exchange rates the net realizable value when converted to the functional currency (SR 3,250,000 ÷ 3.00 = $1,083,333) is no longer lower than the translated carrying value which is to be converted at the exchange rate prevailing on the date of acquisition of the merchandise (SR 3,750,000 ÷ 3.75 = $1,000,000).

Thus, a reversal of the adjustment (for lower of cost or market) is required on the financial statements of the reporting entity, upon translation of the financial statements of the foreign operation.

IAS 21 Financial Statement Translation Method in Greater Detail

Over the years, various national and international accounting standard-setting regimes, subscribing to various philosophies, have attempted to deal with the task of translating the financial statements of foreign operations or entities. No one methodology has been fully satisfactory in accomplishing the objectives of financial reporting for the parent or other reporting entity, and there remains a good deal of confusion among users of the financial statements regarding these matters. IAS 21 embraced one (of four) popular approaches, a method that was commonly known as the *current rate* method under US GAAP, as its prescribed methodology.

Under revised IAS 21, which maintains the fundamental approach of its predecessor standard, there are two sets of translation requirements. The first of these deals with translation of foreign currency *transactions* by each individual entity, which may also be part of reporting group (e.g., consolidated parent and subsidiaries). This requires that all transactions and balances be translated into the individual entities' functional currencies. The second set of requirements is for the translation of entities' financial statements (e.g., those of subsidiaries) into the presentation currency (e.g., of the parent). These matters are addressed in the following paragraphs.

Conversion of foreign currency transactions and balances into functional currency. When an entity keeps its books and records in a currency other than its functional currency, conversion of foreign currency items presented in the statement of financial position into functional currency is driven by the distinction between monetary and nonmonetary items. Foreign currency monetary items are translated using the closing rate (the spot exchange rate at the end of the reporting period). Foreign currency nonmonetary items are translated using the historical exchange rates. There is a presumption that the effect of exchange rate changes on the foreign operation's net assets will directly affect the parent's cash flows, so the exchange rate adjustments are reported in the parent's profit or loss.

For example, branch sales offices or production facilities of a large, integrated operation (e.g., the European field operation of a US corporation, which is principally supplied by the home office but which occasionally also enters into local currency transactions) would qualify for this treatment. Since the US dollar influences sales prices, most (but not all) of its sales are US dollar denominated, and most of its costs, including merchandise, are the result of US transactions, the application of the previously mentioned criteria would conclude that the functional currency of the European sales office is the US dollar, and translation of foreign currency denominated assets and liabilities, and transactions would follow the monetary/nonmonetary distinction noted above with the effect of exchange rate differences reported in profit or loss.

In general, translation of nonmonetary items (inventory, plant assets, etc.) is done by applying the historical exchange rates. The historical rates usually are those in effect when the asset was acquired or (less often) when the nonmonetary liability was incurred, but if there was a subsequent revaluation, if this is permitted under IFRS, then using the exchange rate at the date when the fair value was determined.

When a gain or loss on a nonmonetary item is recognized in profit or loss (e.g., from applying lower of cost or realizable value for inventory), any exchange component of that gain or loss should be recognized in profit or loss. When, on the other hand, a gain or loss on a nonmonetary item is recognized under IFRS in other comprehensive income (e.g., from revaluation of plant assets, or from fair value adjustments made to available-for-sale-securities investments), any exchange component of that gain or loss should also be recognized in other comprehensive income.

As a result of conversion into functional currency, if a foreign unit is in a net monetary asset position (monetary assets in excess of monetary liabilities), an increase in the direct exchange rate causes a favorable result (gain) to be reported in profit or loss; if it is in a net monetary liability position (monetary liabilities in excess of monetary assets), it reports an unfavorable result (loss). If a foreign unit is in a net monetary asset position, a decrease in the direct exchange rate causes an unfavorable result (loss) to report, but if it is in a net monetary liability position, a favorable result (gain) is reported.

Net investment in foreign operation. A special rule applies to a net investment in a foreign operation. According to revised IAS 21, when the reporting entity has a monetary item that is receivable from or payable to a foreign operation for which settlement is neither planned nor likely to occur in the foreseeable future, this is, in substance, a part of the entity's net investment in its foreign operation. This item should be accounted for as follows:

1. Exchange differences arising from translation of monetary items forming part of the net investment in the foreign operations should be reflected in profit or loss in the *separate* financial statements of the reporting entity (investor/parent) and in the separate financial statements of the foreign operations, *but*
2. In the consolidated financial statements which include the investor/parent and the foreign operations, the exchange difference should be recognized initially in other comprehensive income and reclassified from equity to profit or loss upon disposition of the foreign operation.

Note that when a monetary item is a component of a reporting entity's net investment in a foreign operation and it is denominated in the functional currency of the reporting entity, an exchange difference arises only in the foreign operation's individual financial statements. Conversely, if the item is denominated in the functional currency of the foreign operation, an exchange difference arises only in the reporting entity's separate financial statements.

Translation of financial statements to the presentation currency. The other requirements and procedures under IAS 21 pertain to translating foreign currency denominated financial statements, rather than accounting for specific transactions executed in foreign currencies. The most commonly encountered need for this is when the parent entity is preparing consolidated financial statements, and one or more of the subsidiaries have reported in their respective currencies. The same need presents itself if an investee or joint venture's financial information is to be incorporated via the proportionate consolidation or the equity methods of accounting.

If an entity's presentation currency differs from the entity's functional currency, it needs to translate its financial statements into the presentation currency. In accordance with IAS 21, the method used for financial statement translation into the presentation currency is essentially what is commonly called the *current rate* method under US GAAP.

Under the translation to the presentation currency approach (which is also the primary method mandated under US GAAP), all assets and liabilities, both monetary and nonmonetary, are translated at the closing (end of the reporting period) rate, which simplifies the process compared to all other historically advocated methods. More importantly, this more closely corresponds to the viewpoint of financial statement users, who tend to relate to currency exchange rates in existence at the end of the reporting period (the date of the statement of financial position) rather than to the various specific exchange rates that may have applied in prior months or years.

However, financial statements of preceding years should be translated at the rate(s) appropriately applied when these translations were first performed, (i.e., these are *not* to be updated to current closing or average rates). This rule applies because it would cause great confusion to users of financial statements if amounts once reported (when current) were now all restated even though no changes were being made to the underlying data, and of course the underlying economic phenomena, now one or more years in the past, cannot have changes since initially reported upon.

The theoretical basis for this translation approach is the "net investment concept," wherein the foreign entity is viewed as a separate entity that the parent invested into, rather than being considered as part of the parent's operations. Information provided about the foreign entity retains the internal relationships and results created in the foreign environments (economic, legal, and political) in which the entity operates. This approach works best, of course, when foreign-denominated debt is used to purchase the assets that create foreign-denominated revenues; these assets thus serve as a hedge against the effects caused by changes in the exchange rate on the debt. Any excess (i.e., net) assets will be affected by this foreign exchange risk, and this is the effect that is recognized in the parent company's statement of financial position, as described below.

The following rules should be used in translating the financial statements of a foreign entity:

1. All assets and liabilities in the current year-end statement of financial position, whether monetary or nonmonetary, should be translated at the closing rate in effect at the date of that statement of financial position.

2. Income and expense items in each statement of comprehensive income should be translated at the exchange rates at the dates of the transactions, except when the foreign entity reports in a currency of a hyperinflationary economy (as defined in IAS 29), in which case they should be translated at the closing rates.

3. All resulting exchange differences should be recognized in other comprehensive income and reclassified from equity to profit or loss on the disposal of the net investment in a foreign entity.

4. All assets and liabilities in *prior period* statements of financial position, being presented currently (e.g., as comparative information) whether monetary or nonmonetary, are translated at the exchange rates (closing rates) in effect at the date of each of the statements of financial position.

5. Income and expense items in *prior period* statements of income, being presented currently (e.g., as comparative information), are translated at the exchange rates as of the dates of the original transactions (or averages, where appropriate).

Under the translation to the presentation currency approach, all assets and liabilities are valued (1) higher, as a result of a direct exchange rate increase, or (2) lower, as a result of a direct rate decrease. Since the liabilities offset a portion of the assets, constituting a natural hedge, only the subsidiary's net assets (assets in excess of liabilities) are exposed to the risk of fluctuations in the currency exchange rates. As a result, the effect of the exchange rate change can be calculated by multiplying the foreign entity's average net assets by the change in the exchange rate.

On the books of the parent, the foreign entity's net asset position is reflected in the parent's investment account. If the equity method is applied, the investment account should be adjusted upward or downward to reflect changes in the exchange rate; if a foreign entity is included in the consolidated financial statements, the investment account is eliminated.

Guidance Applicable to Special Situations

Noncontrolling interests. When a foreign entity is consolidated, but it is not wholly owned by the reporting entity, there will be noncontrolling interest reported in the consolidated statement of financial position. IAS 21 requires that the accumulated exchange differences resulting from translation and attributable to the noncontrolling interest be allocated to and reported as noncontrolling interest in net assets.

Goodwill and fair value adjustments. Any goodwill arising on the acquisition of a foreign entity and any fair value adjustments to the carrying amounts of assets and liabilities arising on the acquisition of that foreign operation should be treated as assets and liabilities of the foreign operation. Thus they should be expressed in the functional currency of the foreign operation and translated at the closing rate in accordance with IAS 21.

Exchange differences arising from elimination of intragroup balances. While incorporating the financial statements of a foreign entity into those of the reporting entity, normal consolidation procedures such as elimination of intragroup balances and transactions are undertaken as required by IAS 27 and IAS 31.

Different reporting dates. When reporting dates for the financial statements of a foreign entity and those of the reporting entity differ, the foreign entity normally switches and prepares financial statements with reporting dates coinciding with those of the reporting entity. However, sometimes this may not be practicable to do. Under such circumstances IAS 27 allows the use of financial statements prepared as of different dates, provided that the difference is no more than three months. In such a case, the assets and liabilities of the foreign entity should be translated at the exchange rates prevailing at the end of the reporting period of the foreign entity. Adjustments should be made for any significant movements in exchange rates between the end of the reporting period of the foreign entity and that of the reporting entity in accordance with the provisions of IAS 27 and IAS 28 relating to this matter.

Disposal of a foreign entity. Any cumulative exchange differences are to be recognized in other comprehensive income and accumulated in a separate component of equity until the disposal of the foreign entity. The standard prescribes the treatment of the cumulative exchange differences account on the disposal of the foreign entity. This balance, which has been deferred, should be reclassified from equity to profit or loss in the same period in which the gain or loss on disposal is recognized.

Disposal has been defined to include a sale, liquidation, repayment of share capital, or abandonment of all or part of the entity. Normally, payment of dividends would not constitute a repayment of capital. However, in rare circumstances, it does; for instance, when an entity pays dividends out of capital instead of accumulated profits, as defined in the companies' acts of certain countries, such as the United Kingdom, this would constitute repayment of capital. In such circumstances, obviously, dividends paid would constitute a disposal for the purposes of this standard.

IAS 21 further stipulates that in the case of a partial disposal of an interest in a foreign entity, only a proportionate share of the related accumulated exchange differences is recognized as a gain or a loss. A write-down of the carrying amount of the foreign entity does not constitute a partial disposal, and thus the deferred exchange differences carried forward as part of equity would not be affected by such a write-down.

Comprehensive example of the practical application of the translation into the presentation currency

Assume that a US company has a 100%-owned subsidiary in Germany that began operations in 2009. The subsidiary's operations consist of utilizing company-owned space in an office building. This building, which cost five million euros, was financed primarily by German banks, although the parent did invest two million euros in the German operation. All revenues and cash expenses are received and paid in euros. The subsidiary also maintains its books and records in euros.

The financial statements of the German subsidiary are to be translated for incorporation into the US parent's financial statements. The subsidiary's statement of financial position at December 31, 2009, and its combined statement of income and retained earnings for the year ended December 31, 2009, are presented below in euros.

German Company
Statement of Financial Position
December 31, 2009
(in thousands of €)

Assets		Liabilities and shareholders' equity	
Cash	€ 500	Accounts payable	€ 300
Note receivable	200	Unearned rent	100
Land	1,000	Mortgage payable	4,000
Building	5,000	Ordinary shares	400
Accumulated depreciation	(100)	Additional paid-in capital	1,600
		Retained earnings	200
		Total liabilities and	
Total assets	€6,600	shareholders' equity	€6,600

German Company
Combined Statement of Profit or Loss and Retained Earnings
For the Year Ended December 31, 2009
(in thousands of €)

Revenues	€2,000
Operating expenses (including depreciation expense of €100)	1,700
Profit for the year	300
Add retained earnings, January 1, 2009	--
Deduct dividends	(100)
Retained earnings, December 31, 2009	€ 200

Various *assumed* exchange rates for 2009 are as follows:

€1 = $0.90 at the beginning of 2009 (when the ordinary shares were issued and the land and building were financed through the mortgage)
€1 = $1.05 weighted-average for 2009
€1 = $1.10 at the date the dividends were declared and the unearned rent was received
€1 = $1.20 closing (December 31, 2009)

The German company's financial statements must be translated into US dollars in terms of the provisions of IAS 21 (i.e., by the current rate method). This translation process is illustrated below.

German Company
Statement of Financial Position Translation
December 31, 2009
(in thousands of €)

Assets	Euros	Exchange rates	US dollars
Cash	€ 500	1.20	$ 600
Accounts receivable	200	1.20	240
Land	1,000	1.20	1,200
Building (net)	4,900	1.20	5,880
Total assets	€6,600		$7,920
Liabilities and shareholders' equity			
Accounts payable	€ 300	1.20	$ 360
Unearned rent	100	1.20	120
Mortgage payable	4,000	1.20	4,800
Ordinary shares	400	0.90	360
Additional paid-in capital	1,600	0.90	1,440
		(see combined income and retained	
Retained earnings	200	earnings statement translation)	205
Cumulative exchange difference (translation adjustments)	--	--	635
Total liabilities and shareholders' equity	€6,600		$7,920

German Company
Combined Statement of Profit or Loss and Retained Earnings Translation
For the Year Ended December 31, 2009
(in thousands of €)

	Euros	Exchange rates	US dollars
Revenues	€2,000	1.05	$2,100
Expenses (including €100 depreciation expense)	1,700	1.05	1,785
Profit for the year	300		315
Add retained earnings, January 1	--	--	--
Deduct dividends	(100)	1.10	(110)
Retained earnings, December 31	€ 200		$ 205

German Company
Statement of Cash Flows Translation
For the Year Ended December 31, 2009
(in thousands of €)

	Euros	Exchange rates	US dollars
Operating activities			
Profit for the year	€ 300	1.05	$ 315
Adjustments to reconcile net income to net cash provided by operating activities:			
Depreciation	100	1.05	105
Increase in accounts receivable	(200)	1.05	(210)
Increase in accounts payable	300	1.05	315
Increase in unearned rent	100	1.10	110
Net cash provided by operating activities	600		635
Investing activities			
Purchase of land	(1,000)	0.90	(900)
Purchase of building	(5,000)	0.90	(4,500)
Net cash used by investing activities	(6,000)		(5,400)
Financing activities			
Ordinary shares issue	2,000	0.90	1,800
Mortgage payable	4,000	0.90	3,600
Dividends paid	(100)	1.10	(110)
Net cash provided by financing	5,900		5,290
Effect on exchange rate changes on cash	N/A		75
Increase in cash and equivalents	500		600
Cash at beginning of year	--		--
Cash at end of year	€ 500	1.20	$ 600

The following points should be noted concerning the translation into the presentation currency:

1. All assets and liabilities are translated using the closing rate at the end of the reporting period (€1 = $1.20). All revenues and expenses should be translated at the rates in effect when these items are recognized during the period. Due to practical considerations, however, weighted-average rates can be used to translate revenues and expenses (€1 = $1.05).

2. Shareholders' equity accounts are translated by using historical exchange rates. Ordinary shares were issued at the beginning of 2009 when the exchange rate was €1 = $0.90. The translated balance of retained earnings is the result of the weighted-average rate applied to revenues and expenses and the specific rate in effect when the dividends were declared (€1 = $1.10).

3. Cumulative exchange differences (translation adjustments) result from translating all assets and liabilities at the closing (current) rate, while shareholders' equity is translated by using historical and weighted-average rates. The adjustments have no direct effect

on cash flows; however, changes in exchange rate will have an indirect effect on sale or liquidation. Prior to this time, the effect is uncertain and remote. Also, the effect is due to the net investment rather than the subsidiary's operations. For these reasons the translation adjustments balance is reported as a separate component in the shareholders' equity section of the US company's consolidated statement of financial position. This balance essentially equates the total debits of the subsidiary (now expressed in US dollars) with the total credits (also in dollars). It may also be determined directly, as shown next, to verify the translation process.

4. The cumulative exchange differences (translation adjustments) credit of $635 is calculated as follows:

Net assets at the beginning of 2009 (after ordinary shares were issued and the land and building were acquired through mortgage financing)	€2,000 (1.20 – 0.90)	=	$600 credit
Profit for the year	€ 300 (1.20 – 1.05)	=	45 credit
Dividends	€ 100 (1.20 – 1.10)	=	10 debit
Exchange difference (translation adjustment)			$635 credit

5. Since the net exchange differences (translation adjustment) balance that appears as a separate component of shareholders' equity is cumulative in nature, the change in this balance during the year should be disclosed in the financial statements. In the illustration, this balance went from zero to $635 at the end of 2009. The analysis of this change was presented previously. The translation adjustment has a credit balance because the German entity was in a net asset position during the period (assets in excess of liabilities) and the spot exchange rate at the end of the period is higher than the exchange rate at the beginning of the period or the average for the period.

In addition to the foregoing transactions, assume that the following occurred during 2010:

German Company
Statement of Financial Position
December 31, 2010
(in thousands of €)

Assets	2010	2009	Increase/(decrease)
Cash	€1,000	€ 500	€500
Accounts receivable	--	200	(200)
Land	1,500	1,000	500
Building (net)	4,800	4,900	(100)
Total assets	€7,300	€6,600	€700
Liabilities and shareholders' equity			
Accounts payable	€ 500	€ 300	€200
Unearned rent	--	100	(100)
Mortgage payable	4,500	4,000	500
Ordinary shares	400	400	--
Additional paid-in capital	1,600	1,600	--
Retained earnings	300	200	100
Total liabilities and shareholders' equity	€7,300	€6,600	€700

German Company
Combined Statement of Profit or Loss and Retained Earnings
For the Year Ended December 31, 2010
(in thousands of €)

Revenues	€2,200
Operating expenses (including depreciation expense of €100)	1,700
Profit for the year	500
Add: Retained earnings, Jan. 1, 2010	200
Deduct dividends	(400)
Retained earnings, Dec. 31, 2010	€ 300

Exchange rates were:

€1 = $1.20 at the beginning of 2010
€1 = $1.16 weighted-average for 2010
€1 = $1.08 closing (December 31, 2010)
€1 = $1.10 when dividends were paid in 2010 and land bought by incurring mortgage

The translation process for 2010 is illustrated below.

German Company
Statement of Financial Position Translation
December 31, 2010
(in thousands of €)

Assets	Euros	Exchange rates	US dollars
Cash	€1,000	1.08	$1,080
Land	1,500	1.08	1,620
Building	4,800	1.08	5,184
Total assets	€7,300		$7,884
Liabilities and shareholders' equity			
Accounts payable	€ 500	1.08	$ 540
Mortgage payable	4,500	1.08	4,860
Ordinary shares	400	0.90	360
Addl. paid-in capital	1,600	0.90	1,440
		(see combined income and retained	
Retained earnings	300	earnings statement translation)	345
Cumulative translation adjustments	--		339
Total liabilities and shareholders' equity	€7,300		$7,884

German Company
Combined Statement of Profit or Loss and Retained Earnings Translation
For the Year Ended December 31, 2010
(in thousands of €)

	Euros	Exchange rates	US dollars
Revenues	€2,200	1.16	$2,552
Operating expenses (including depreciation of €100)	1,700	1.16	1,972
Profit for the year	500	1.16	580
Add: Retained earnings 1/1/10	200	--	205
Less: Dividends	(400)	1.10	(440)
Retained earnings 12/31/10	€ 300		$ 345

German Company
Statement of Cash Flows Translation
For the Year Ended December 31, 2010
(in thousands of €)

	Euros	Exchange rates	US dollars
Operating activities			
Profit for the year	€ 500	1.16	$ 580
Adjustments to reconcile net income to net cash provided by operating activities:			
Depreciation	100	1.16	116
Decrease in accounts receivable	200	1.16	232
Increase in accounts payable	200	1.16	232
Decrease in unearned rent	(100)	1.16	(116)
Net cash provided by operating activities	900		1,044
Investing activities			
Purchase of land	(500)	1.10	(550)
Net cash used by investing activities	(500)		(550)

	Euros	*Exchange rates*	*US dollars*
Financing activities			
Mortgage payable	500	1.10	550
Dividends	(400)	1.10	(440)
Net cash provided by financing activities	100		110
Effect of exchange rate changes on cash	N/A		(124)
Increase in cash and equivalents	500		480
Cash at beginning of year	500		600
Cash at end of year	€1,000	1.08	$1,080

Using the same mode of analysis that was presented before, the total exchange differences (translation adjustment) attributable to 2010 would be computed as follows:

Net assets at January 1, 2010	€2,200 (1.08 – 1.20) =	$264 credit
Net income for 2010	€500 (1.08 – 1.16) =	40 credit
Dividends for 2010	€400 (1.08 – 1.10) =	8 debit
Total		$296 credit

The balance in the net exchange differences (translation adjustment) account at the end of 2010 would be $339 ($635 from 2009 less $296 from 2010). The balance in this account decreased during 2010 since the German entity was in a net asset position during the period and the spot exchange rate at the end of the period (closing rate) is lower than the exchange rate at the beginning of the period or the average for the period.

6. Use of the equity method by the US company in accounting for the subsidiary would result in the following journal entries based on the information presented above:

	2009		2010	
Original investment				
Investment in German subsidiary	1,800*		--	
Cash		1,800		--

* *[$0.90 × common share of €400 plus additional paid-in capital of €1,600]*

	2009		2010	
Earnings pickup				
Investment in German subsidiary	315*		580**	
Equity in subsidiary income		315		580

* *[$1.05 × net income of €300]*
** *[$1.16 × net income of €500]*

	2009		2010	
Dividends received				
Cash	110*		440**	
Investment in German subsidiary		110		440

	2009		2010	
Exchange difference (translation adjustments)				
Investment in German subsidiary	635			
Translation adjustments		635		
Translation adjustments			296	
Investment in German subsidiary				296

* *[$1.10 × dividend of €100]*
** *[$1.10 × dividend of €400]*

Note that the shareholders' equity of the US company should be the same whether or not the German subsidiary is consolidated (per IAS 28). Since the subsidiary does not report the translation adjustments on its financial statements, care should be exercised so that it is not forgotten in application of the equity method.

7. If the US company disposes of its investment in the German subsidiary, the translation adjustments balance becomes part of the gain or loss that results from the transaction and must be eliminated. For example, assume that on January 2, 2010, the US company sells its entire investment for €3,000. The exchange rate at this date is €1 = $1.08. The balance in the investment account at December 31, 2010, is $2,484 as a result of the entries made previously.

Investment in German Subsidiary		
1/1/09	1,800	
	315	110
	635	
1/1/10	2,640	
	580	440
		296
12/31/10	2,484	

The following entries would be made to reflect the sale of the investment:

Cash (€3,000 × $1.08)	3,240	
Investment in German subsidiary		2,484
Gain from sale of subsidiary		756
Translation adjustments	339	
Gain from sale of subsidiary		339

If the US company had sold a portion of its investment in the German subsidiary, only a proportionate share of the translation adjustments balance (cumulative amount of exchange differences) would have become part of the gain or loss from the transaction. To illustrate, if 80% of the German subsidiary was sold for €2,500 on January 2, 2010, the following journal entries would be made:

Cash (€2,500 × $1.08)	2,700.00	
Investment in German subsidiary (0.8 × $2,484)		1,987.20
Gain from sale of subsidiary		712.80
Cumulative exchange difference (translation adjustments) (0.8 × $339)	271.20	
Gain from sale of subsidiary		271.20

Translation of Foreign Currency Transactions in Further Detail

According to IAS 21, a foreign currency transaction is a transaction that is "denominated in or requires settlement in a foreign currency." Denominated means that the amount to be received or paid is fixed in terms of the number of units of a particular foreign currency, regardless of changes in the exchange rate.

From the viewpoint of a US company, for instance, a foreign currency transaction results when it imports or exports goods or services to a foreign entity or makes a loan involving a foreign entity and agrees to settle the transaction in currency other than the US dollar (the presentation currency of the US company). In these situations, the US company has "crossed currencies" and directly assumes the risk of fluctuating exchange rates of the foreign currency in which the transaction is denominated. This risk may lead to recognition of foreign exchange differences in the profit or loss of the US company. Note that exchange differences can result only when the foreign currency transactions are denominated in a foreign currency.

When a US company imports or exports goods or services and the transaction is to be settled in US dollars, the US company will incur neither gain nor loss because it bears no risk due to exchange rate fluctuations. The following example illustrates the terminology and procedures applicable to the translation of foreign currency transactions.

Assume that a US company, an exporter, sells merchandise to a customer in Germany on December 1, 2009, for €10,000. Receipt is due on January 31, 2010, and the US company prepares financial statements on December 31, 2009. At the transaction date (December 1, 2009), the spot rate for immediate exchange of foreign currencies indicates that €1 is equivalent to $1.18.

To find the US dollar equivalent of this transaction, the foreign currency amount, €10,000, is multiplied by $1.18 to get $11,800. At December 1, 2009, the foreign currency transaction should be recorded by the US company in the following manner:

Accounts receivable—Germany	11,800	
Sales		11,800

The accounts receivable and sales are measured in US dollars at the transaction date using the spot rate at the time of the transaction. While the accounts receivable is measured and reported in US dollars, the receivable is denominated or fixed in euros.

Foreign exchange gains or losses may occur if the spot rate for euros changes between the transaction date and the date of settlement (January 31, 2010). If financial statements are prepared between the transaction date and the settlement date, all receivables and payables that are denominated in a currency different than that in which payment will ultimately be received or paid (the euro) must be restated to reflect the spot rates in existence at the end of the reporting period.

Assume that on December 31, 2009, the spot rate for euros is €1 = $1.20. This means that the €10,000 is now worth $12,000 and that the accounts receivable denominated in euros should be increased by $200. The following journal entry would be recorded as of December 31, 2009:

Accounts receivable—Germany	200	
Foreign currency exchange difference		200

Note that the sales account, which was credited on the transaction date for $11,800, is not affected by changes in the spot rate. This treatment exemplifies what may be called a two-transaction viewpoint. In other words, making the sale is the result of an operating decision, while bearing the risk of fluctuating spot rates is the result of a financing decision. Therefore, the amount determined as sales revenue at the transaction date should not be altered because of a financing decision to wait until January 31, 2010, for payment of the account.

The risk of a foreign exchange transaction loss can be avoided either by demanding immediate payment on December 1 or by entering into a forward exchange contract to hedge the exposed asset (accounts receivable). The fact that the US company in the example did not act in either of these two ways is reflected by requiring the recognition of foreign currency exchange differences (transaction gains or losses) in its profit or loss (reported as financial or nonoperating items) in the period during which the exchange rates changed.

This treatment has been criticized, however, because both the unrealized gain and/or loss are recognized in the financial statements, a practice that is at variance with traditional GAAP. Furthermore, earnings will fluctuate because of changes in exchange rates and not because of changes in the economic activities of the entity.

On the settlement date (January 31, 2010), assume that the spot rate is €1 = $1.17. The receipt of €10,000 and their conversion into US dollars would be journalized in the following manner:

Foreign currency	11,700	
Foreign currency transaction loss	300	
Accounts receivable—Germany		12,000
Cash	5,100	
Foreign currency		5,100

The net effect of this foreign currency transaction was to receive $11,700 from a sale that was measured originally at $11,800. This realized net foreign currency transaction loss of $100 is reported on two income statements: a $200 gain in 2009 and a $300 loss in 2010. The reporting of the gain or loss in two income statements causes a temporary difference between pretax accounting and taxable income. This results because the transaction loss of $100 is not deductible until 2010, the year the transaction was completed or settled. Accordingly, interperiod tax allocation is required for foreign currency transaction gains or losses.

Losses from Severe Currency Devaluation or Depreciation

IAS 21 requires recognition of exchange differences as income or expense in the period in which they arise, as illustrated in the foregoing example. Previously, there had been an allowed alternative treatment for certain losses incurred due to effects of exchange rate changes on foreign-denominated obligations associated with asset acquisition. This allowed alternative treatment resulted in capitalization of the loss. However, revised IAS 21 removed the limited option in the previous version of IAS 21 to capitalize exchange differences resulting from a severe devaluation or depreciation of a currency against which there is no means of hedging. Under the current standard, such exchange differences must be uniformly recognized in profit or loss.

Disclosure Requirements

A number of disclosure requirements have been prescribed by IAS 21. Primarily, disclosure is required of the amounts of exchange differences included in profit or loss for the period, exchange differences that are included in the carrying amount of an asset, and those that are recognized in other comprehensive income.

When there is a change in classification of a foreign operation, disclosure is required as to the nature of the change, reason for the change, and the impact of the change on the current and each of the prior years presented. When the presentation currency is different from the currency of the country of domicile, the reason for this should be disclosed, and in case of any subsequent change in the presentation currency, the reason for making this change should also be disclosed. An entity should also disclose the method selected to translate goodwill and fair value adjustments arising on the acquisition of a foreign entity. Disclosure is encouraged of an entity's foreign currency risk management policy.

The following additional disclosures are required:

- When the functional currency is different from the currency of the country in which the entity is domiciled, the reason for using a different currency;
- The reason for any change in functional currency or presentation currency;
- When financial statements are presented in a currency other than the entity's functional currency, the reason for using a different presentation currency, and a description of the method used in the translation process;
- When financial statements are presented in a currency other than the functional currency, an entity should state the fact that the functional currency reflects the economic substance of underlying events and circumstances;
- When financial statements are presented in a currency other than the functional currency, and the functional currency is the currency of a hyperinflationary economy, an entity should disclose the closing exchange rates between functional currency and presentation currency existing at the end of each reporting period presented;
- When additional information not required by IAS is displayed in financial statements and in a currency other than presentation currency, as a matter of convenience to certain users, an entity should

  - Clearly identify such information as supplementary information;
  - Disclose the functional currency used to prepare the financial statements and the method of translation used to determine the supplementary information displayed;
  - Disclose the fact that the functional currency reflects the economic substance of the underlying events and circumstances of the entity and the supplementary information is displayed in another currency for convenience purposes only; and
  - Disclose the currency in which supplementary information is displayed.

Hedging a Net Investment in a Foreign Entity or Specific Transactions

Hedging a net investment. While IAS 21 did not address hedge accounting for foreign currency items other than classification of exchange differences arising on a foreign currency liability accounted for as a hedge of a net investment in a foreign entity, IAS 39 has established accounting requirements which largely parallel those for cash flow hedges. (Cash flow hedging is discussed in Chapter 10.) Specifically, IAS 39 states that the portion of the gain or loss on the hedging instrument that is determined to be an effective hedge is to be recognized in other comprehensive income, whereas the ineffective portion of the hedge is to be either recognized immediately in results of operations if the hedging instrument is a derivative instrument, or else reported in other comprehensive income if the instrument is not a derivative.

The gain or loss associated with an effective hedge is reported in other comprehensive income, similar to foreign currency translation gain or loss. In fact, if the hedge is fully effective (which is rarely achieved in practice, however) the hedging gain or loss will be equal in amount and opposite in sign to the translation loss or gain.

In the examples set forth earlier in this chapter (see page 914), which illustrated the accounting for a foreign (German) operation of a US company, the cumulative translation gain as of year-end 2009 was reported as $635,000. If the US entity had been able to enter into a hedging transaction that was perfectly effective (which would most likely have involved a series of currency forward contracts), the net loss position as of that date would have been $635,000. If this were reported in other comprehensive income and accumulated in shareholders' equity, as required under IAS 39 and revised IAS 1, it would have served to exactly offset the cumulative translation gain at that point in time.

It should be noted that under the translation methodology prescribed by IAS 21 the ability to precisely hedge the net (accounting) investment in the German subsidiary would have been very remote, since the cumulative translation gain or loss is determined by both the changes in exchange rates since the common share issuances of the subsidiary (which occurred at discrete points in time and thus could conceivably have been hedged), as well as the changes in the various periodic increments or decrements to retained earnings (which having occurred throughout the years of past operations, would involve a complex array of exchange rates, making hedging very difficult to achieve). As a practical matter, hedging the net investment in a foreign subsidiary would serve a very limited economic purpose at best. Such hedging is more often done to avoid the potentially embarrassing impact of changing exchange rates on the reported results of operations and financial position of the parent company, which may be important to management, but rarely connotes real economic performance over a longer time horizon.

Notwithstanding the foregoing comments, it is possible for a foreign currency transaction to act as an economic hedge against a parent's net investment in a foreign entity if

1. The transaction is designated as a hedge.
2. It is effective as a hedge.

To illustrate, assume that a US parent has a wholly owned British subsidiary which has net assets of £2 million. The US parent can borrow £2 million to hedge its net investment in the British subsidiary. Assume further that the British pound is the functional currency and that the £2 million liability is denominated in pounds. Fluctuations in the exchange rate for pounds will have no net effect on the parent company's consolidated statement of financial position because increases (decreases) in the translation adjustments balance due to the translation of the net investment will be offset by decreases (increases) in this balance due to the adjustment of the liability denominated in pounds.

Hedging transactions. It may be more important for managers to hedge specific foreign currency denominated transactions, such as merchandise sales or purchases which involve exposure for the time horizon over which the foreign currency denominated receivable or payable remains outstanding. For example, consider the illustration set forth earlier in this chapter (see page 920), which discussed the sale of merchandise by a US entity to a German customer, denominated in euros, with the receivable being due sometime after the sale. During the period the receivable remains pending, the creditor is at risk for currency exchange rate changes that might occur, leading to exchange rate gains or losses, depending on the direction the rates move. The following discussion sets forth the possible approach that could have been taken (and the accounting therefor) to reduce or eliminate this risk.

In the example, the US company could have entered into a forward exchange contract on December 1, 2009, to sell €10,000 for a negotiated amount to a foreign exchange broker for future delivery on January 31, 2010. Such a forward contract would be a hedge against the exposed asset position created by having an account receivable denominated in euros. The negotiated rate referred to above is called a futures or forward rate. This instrument would qualify as a derivative under IAS 39.

In most cases, this futures rate is not identical to the spot rate at the date of the forward contract. The difference between the futures rate and the spot rate at the date of the forward contract is referred to as a discount or premium. Any discount or premium must be amortized over the term of the forward contract, generally on a straight-line basis. The amortization of discount or premium is reflected in a separate revenue or expense account, not as an addition or subtraction to the foreign currency transaction gain or loss amount. It is important to observe that under this treatment, no net foreign currency transaction gains or losses result if assets and liabilities denominated in foreign currency are completely hedged at the transaction date.

To illustrate a hedge of an exposed asset, consider the following additional information for the German transaction.

On December 1, 2009, the US company entered into a forward exchange contract to sell €10,000 on January 31, 2010, at $1.14 per euro. The spot rate on December 1 is $1.12 per euro. The journal entries that reflect the sale of goods and the forward exchange contract appear as follows:

Sale transaction entries			Forward exchange contract entries (futures rate €1 = $1.14)		
12/1/09 (spot rate €1 = $1.12)			Due from exchange broker ($)	11,400	
Accounts receivable (€)—Germany	11,200		Due to exchange broker (€)		11,200
Sales		11,200	Premium on forward contract		200
12/31/09 (spot rate €1 = $1.15)			Foreign currency transaction loss	300	
Accounts receivable (€)—Germany	300		Due to exchange broker (€)		300
Foreign currency transaction			Premium on forward contract	100	
gain		300	Financial revenue		
			($100 = $200/2 months)		100
1/31/10 (spot rate €1 = $1.17)					
Foreign currency	11,700		Due to exchange broker	11,500	
Accounts receivable (€)—			Foreign currency transaction loss	200	
Germany		11,500	Foreign currency		11,700
Foreign currency transaction gain		200			
			Cash	11,400	
			Due from exchange broker		11,400
			Premium on forward contract	100	
			Financial revenue		100

The following points should be noted from the entries above:

1. The net foreign currency transaction gain or loss is zero. The account "Due from exchange broker" is fixed in terms of US dollars, and this amount is not affected by changes in spot rates between the transaction and settlement dates. The account "Due to exchange broker" is fixed or denominated in euros. The US company owes the exchange broker €10,000, and these must be delivered on January 31, 2010. Because this liability is denominated in euros, its amount is determined by spot rates. Since spot rates change, this liability changes in amount equal to the changes in accounts receivable because both of the amounts are based on the same spot rates. These changes are reflected as foreign currency transaction gains and losses that net out to zero.

2. The premium on forward contract is fixed in terms of US dollars. This amount is amortized to a financial revenue account over the life of the forward contract on a straight-line basis.

3. The net effect of this transaction is that $11,400 was received on January 31, 2010, for a sale originally recorded at $11,200. The $200 difference was taken into income via amortization.

Interpretations on Currency Transactions as Derivatives

The IASC's IAS 39 Implementation Guidance Committee (IGC) has addressed a number of issues that pertain to translation of financial statements and foreign currency transactions. It has considered whether a currency swap that requires an exchange of different currencies of equal fair values at inception is a derivative, and has ruled that indeed it is. The IGC finds that the definition of a derivative instrument includes such currency swaps because the initial exchange of currencies of equal fair values does not result in an initial net investment in the contract, but instead, is an exchange of one form of cash for another form of cash of equal value. Such a contract has underlying variables (the foreign exchange rates) and will be settled at a future date. Thus, the criteria for being defined as a derivative financial instrument are all met.

The IGC offers an illustration similar to the following to demonstrate how such a swap works. Assume that Axis Corp. and Basic GmbH enter into a five-year fixed-for-fixed currency swap on euros and US dollars. The current spot exchange rate is 1 euro per dollar. The five-year interest rate in the United States is presently 8%, while the five-year interest rate in euro countries is 6%. At the initiation of the swap, Axis pays 20 million euros to Basic, which in return pays $20 million to Axis. During the life of the swap, Axis and Basic make periodic interest payments to each other gross (i.e., without netting). Basic pays 6% per year on the 20 million euros it has received (1.2 million euros per year), while Axis pays 8% per year on the 20 million dollars it has received ($1.6 million per year). At the termination of the swap, the two parties again exchange the original principal amounts.

The IGC has also noted that certain foreign currency denominated transactions can involve embedded derivative instruments. It illustrates this concept with an example of a supply contract that provides for payment in a currency other than (1) the currency of the primary economic environment of either party to the contract and (2) the currency in which the product is routinely priced in international commerce. This arrangement contains an implicit embedded derivative that should be separated under IAS 39.

In the IGC's example, a Norwegian company agrees to sell oil to a company in France. The oil contract is denominated in Swiss francs, although oil contracts are routinely denominated in US dollars in international commerce. Importantly, neither company carries out any significant activities in Swiss francs. In this case, the Norwegian company regards the supply contract as a host contract with an embedded foreign currency forward to purchase Swiss francs. The French company regards the supply contract as a host contract with an embedded foreign currency forward to sell Swiss francs. Each company includes fair value changes on the currency forward in net profit or loss unless the reporting entity designates it as a cash flow hedging instrument, if doing so would be appropriate under the circumstances.

Currency of Monetary Items Comprising Net Investment in Foreign Operations

Amendments made to IAS 21 in December 2005 clarified that monetary items (whether receivable or payable) between any subsidiary of the group and a foreign operation may form part of the group's investment in that foreign operation. Thus, these monetary items can be denominated in a currency other than the functional currency of either the parent or the foreign operation itself, for exchange differences on these monetary items to be recognized in other comprehensive income and accumulated in a separate component of equity until the disposal of the foreign operation.

The previous (2003) version of IAS 21 had stated that the exchange differences on monetary items that formed part of the reporting entity's net investment in a foreign operation could be recognized in other comprehensive income and accumulated in equity in the consolidated statements only if the monetary item was denominated in either the functional currency of the parent or of that foreign operation. Under this guidance, if the loan was made in the third currency, as shown in the example below, any exchange difference would be recognized in profit or loss.

Example

Assume the following group structure: Parent, a French company, Eiffel SARL (Group Eiffel), has a functional currency of the euro. Parent company has a 100% direct interest in a US investment company, Freedom, Inc., which has a functional currency of the US dollar. Freedom, in turn, owns a British subsidiary, Royal Ltd. (100% ownership), which has a functional currency of the pound sterling. Freedom lends $100,000 to Royal. The question is whether the loan can be accounted for as part of Group Eiffel's net investment in Royal with any exchange differences recognized in other comprehensive income.

Under provisions of the 2003 version of IAS 21, the $100,000 loan between Freedom and Royal could *not* be accounted for as part of Group Eiffel's net investment, since the loan was made in a third currency, and not in the functional currency of the parent (the euro) or of the foreign subsidiary (£). As a result, any exchange differences on this loan would be reported in the consolidated profit or loss statement of Group Eiffel.

The results obtained under the 2003 version of IAS 21 struck many as not being entirely logical, and these concerns were dealt with in the 2005 amendment. This allows that exchange differences on loans such as in the foregoing example, can be recognized in *other comprehensive income* and in equity in the consolidated statement of financial position of reporting entities such as Group Eiffel. This change in accounting requirements allows many more funding structures to be accounted for as net investments in foreign operations. Thus, the accounting will no longer be dependent upon which of the group's entities conducts a transaction with the foreign operation, nor will it be dependent upon the currency of the monetary items.

Hedges of a Net Investment in a Foreign Operation

In 2007 IFRIC issued Draft Interpretation D22, *Hedges of a Net Investment in a Foreign Operation,* which proposed guidance on accounting for the hedge of a net investment in a foreign operation, since IAS 39 contains only minimal guidance on this type of hedge transactions. In mid-2008 this was finalized as IFRIC 16, which is effective for annual periods beginning on or after October 1, 2008, with earlier application permitted.

IFRIC 16 holds that the hedged risk in a hedge of a net investment in a foreign operation is the foreign currency risk arising between the functional currency of the foreign operation and the functional currency of any parent (the immediate, intermediate or ultimate parent entity of that foreign operation). Consequently, hedge accounting cannot be applied to the foreign currency risk arising between the functional currency of the net investment and the presentation currency of the parent entity. This applies also to an entity with a net investment in foreign operation that is a joint venture, an associate or a branch.

IFRIC 16 also clarifies that an entity can hedge (the hedge item) up to 100% of the carrying amount of the net assets (net investment) of the foreign operation in the consolidated financial statements of the parent. In addition, as with other hedge relationships, an exposure to foreign currency risk cannot be hedged twice. This means that if the same foreign currency risk is nominally hedged by more than one parent entity within the group (a direct and an indirect parent entity), only one hedge relationship can qualify for hedge accounting.

IAS 39 does not require that the operating unit that is exposed to the risk being hedged hold the hedging instrument. IFRIC 16 clarifies that this requirement also applies to the hedge of the net investment in a foreign operation. The functional currency of the entity holding the instrument is irrelevant in determining effectiveness and any entity within the group, regardless of its functional currency, can hold the hedging instrument.

IFRIC 16 affects those entities that have hedged against the presentation currency of the ultimate parent entity, where the presentation currency differs from its functional currency. Those entities will not be able to continue to apply hedge accounting since this interpretation clarifies that the hedged risk can only arise between the functional currency of the foreign operation and the functional currency of the parent. Other entities may need to reexamine and redesignate hedge relationships as a result of this additional guidance.

Examples of Financial Statement Disclosures

Roche Group
Annual Report 2006

Notes to the consolidated financial statements

Foreign currency translation

Most Group companies use their local currency as their functional currency. Certain Group companies use other currencies (namely US dollars, Swiss francs or euros) as their functional currency where this is the currency of the primary economic environment in which the entity operates. Local transactions in other currencies are initially reported using the exchange rate at the date of the transaction. Gains and losses from the settlement of such transactions and gains and losses on translation of monetary assets and liabilities denominated in other currencies are included in income, except when they are qualifying cash flow hedges or arise on monetary items that, in substance, form part of the Group's net investment in a foreign entity, which are deferred into equity.

Upon consolidation, assets and liabilities of Group companies using functional currencies other than Swiss francs (foreign entities) are translated into Swiss francs using year-end rates of exchange. Sales, costs, expenses, net income and cash flows are translated at the average rates of exchange for the year. Translation differences due to the changes in exchange rates between the beginning and the end of the year and the difference between net income translated at the average and year-end exchange rates are taken directly to equity. On disposal of a foreign entity, the identified cumulative currency translation differences within equity relating to that foreign entity are recognized in income as part of the gain or loss on divestment.

Foreign exchange risk

The Group operates across the world and is exposed to movements in foreign currencies affecting the Group financial result and the value of the Group's equity. Foreign exchange risk arises because the amount of local currency paid or received for transactions denominated in foreign currencies may vary due to changes in exchange rates (transaction exposures) and because the foreign currency denominated financial statements of the Group's foreign subsidiaries may vary upon consolidation into the Swiss franc denominated Group Financial Statements (translation exposures).

The objective of the Group's foreign exchange risk management activities is to preserve the economic value of its current and future assets and to minimize the volatility of the Group's financial result. The primary focus of the Group's foreign exchange risk management activities is on hedging transaction exposures arising through foreign currency flows or monetary positions held in foreign currencies. The Group does not currently hedge translation exposures using financial instruments.

The Group monitors transaction exposures on a daily basis. The net foreign exchange result and the corresponding VaR parameters are reported on a monthly basis. The Group uses forward contracts, foreign exchange options and cross-currency swaps to hedge transaction exposures. Application of these instruments intends to continuously lock in favorable developments of foreign exchange rates, thereby reducing the exposure to potential future movements in such rates.

Nokia
Annual Report 2007

Notes to the consolidated financial statements

Foreign currency translation

Functional and presentation currency

The financial statements of all Group entities are measured using the currency of the primary economic environment in which the entity operates (functional currency). The consolidated financial statements are presented in euro, which is the functional and presentation currency of the Parent Company.

Transactions in foreign currencies

Transactions in foreign currencies are recorded at the rates of exchange prevailing at the dates of the individual transactions. For practical reasons, a rate that approximates the actual rate at the date of the transaction is often used. At the end of the accounting period, the unsettled balances on foreign currency receivables and liabilities are valued at the rates of exchange prevailing at the year-end. Foreign exchange gains and losses arising from balance sheet items, as well as fair value changes in the related hedging instruments, are reported as Financial Income and Expenses.

Foreign Group companies

In the consolidated accounts all income and expenses of foreign subsidiaries are translated into euro at the average foreign exchange rates for the accounting period. All assets and liabilities of foreign Group companies are translated into euro at the year-end foreign exchange rates with the exception of goodwill arising on the acquisition of foreign companies prior to the adoption of IAS 21 (revised 2004) on January 1, 2005, which is translated to euro at historical rates. Differences resulting from the translation of income and expenses at the average rate and assets and liabilities at the closing rate are treated as an adjustment affecting consolidated shareholders' equity. On the disposal of all or part of a foreign Group company by sale, liquidation, repayment of share capital or abandonment, the cumulative amount or proportionate share of the translation difference is recognized as income or as expense in the same period in which the gain or loss on disposal is recognized.

23 RELATED-PARTY DISCLOSURES

PERSPECTIVE AND ISSUES

Transactions between enterprises that are considered *related parties* (as defined by IAS 24) must be adequately disclosed in financial statements of the reporting entity. Such disclosures have long been a common feature of financial reporting, and most national accounting standard-setting bodies have imposed similar mandates. The rationale for compelling such disclosures is the concern that entities which are related to each other, whether by virtue of an ability to control or to exercise significant influence (both as defined under IFRS) usually have leverage in the setting of prices to be charged and on other transaction terms. If these events and transactions were simply mingled with transactions conducted with customers or vendors on normal arm's-length terms, the users of the financial statements would likely be impeded in their ability to project future earnings and cash flows for the reporting entity, given that related-party transaction terms could be arbitrarily altered at any time. Thus, in order to ensure transparency, reporting entities are required to disclose the nature, type, and components of transactions with related parties.

IAS 24 addresses the related-party issue and prescribes extensive disclosures. This standard became effective in 1986 and was revised effective 2005, as part of IASB's *Improvements Project.* In early 2007, an Exposure Draft of an amendment to IAS 24 was published, addressing issues pertaining to state-controlled entities as they could affect related-party disclosures. This would reduce the disclosure requirements for some entities that are related only in the sense that they are all controlled by the same governmental unit but that otherwise have no transactional relationship. The amendment would remove certain inconsistencies in the definition of related parties. Based on feedback received to the initial Exposure Draft, IASB held further deliberations and made additional changes to the draft, which it decided to reexpose in November 2008. Thus, the adoption of the now-revised amendments to IAS 24 will not occur at least until 2009.

Although IAS 24 states "related-party relationships are a normal feature of commerce and business," it nevertheless recognizes that a related-party relationship could have an effect on the financial position and operating results of the reporting entity, due to the possibility that transactions with related parties may not be effected at the same amounts as are those between unrelated parties. For that reason, extensive disclosure of such transactions is deemed necessary to convey a full picture of the entity's position and results of operations.

While IAS 24 has been operative for over two decades, it is commonly observed that related-party transactions are not being properly disclosed in all instances. This is due in part, perhaps, to the perceived sensitive nature of such disclosures. As a consequence, even when a note to financial statements that is captioned "related-party transactions" is presented, it is often fairly evident that the gamut of disclosures required by IAS 24 have not been included. There seems to be particular resistance to reporting certain types of related-party transactions, such as loans to directors, key management personnel, or close members of the executives' families. Presumably, these deficiencies will occur less frequently over time, and as independent auditors become more familiar with IFRS requirements.

One specific subset of related-party disclosure often omitted arises in connection with state-owned enterprises, which transact business with other state-owned companies, and which tend to not include details regarding same in the related-party transaction notes. This may occur simply due to the sheer volume of such transactions, but presumably this alone does not warrant such omissions. This issue is one of the narrowly defined questions being addressed by IASB in a currently ongoing project.

IAS 1 demands, as a prerequisite to asserting that financial statements have been prepared in conformity with IFRS, that there be *full compliance* with all IFRS. This requirement pertains to all recognition and measurement standards, and extends to the disclosures to be made as well. As a practical matter, it becomes incumbent upon the auditors to ascertain whether disclosures, including related-party disclosures, comply with IFRS when the financial statements represent such to be the case.

Interest in disclosures of related-party transactions and arrangements was heightened as a consequence of the many financial reporting frauds reported in the late 1990s and early 2000s, since many of these involved undisclosed related-party transactions. Related-party disclosures are prescribed by most national GAAP, including US GAAP. The US GAAP counterpart of IAS 24 is FAS 57, which was issued in 1982. While there are some differences between the US standard and IAS 24, in general these two standards could be considered similar to each other.

Sources of IFRS
IAS 1, 8, 24, 27, 28, 30

DEFINITIONS OF TERMS

Close members of the family of an individual. For the purpose of IAS 24, close members of the family of an individual are defined as "those that may be expected to influence, or be influenced by, that person in their dealings with the entity." The following may be considered close members of the family: an individual's domestic partner and children, children of the individual's domestic partner, and dependents of the individual or the individual's domestic partner.

Compensation. Compensation encompasses all employee benefits (as defined in IAS 19) and also includes share-based payments as envisaged in IFRS 2. Employee benefits include all forms of consideration paid in exchange for services rendered to the entity. It also includes such consideration paid on behalf of a parent of the entity in respect to activities of the entity. Compensation thus includes short-term employee benefits (such as wages, salaries, paid annual leave), postemployment benefits (such as pensions), other long-term benefits (such as long-term disability benefits), termination or end-of-service benefits, and share-based payments.

Control. An entity is considered to have the ability to control another entity if it has the power to govern the financial and operating policies of the other entity so as to obtain benefits from its activities.

Joint control. An entity is considered to be jointly in control with another entity if they contractually agree to share control over an economic activity.

Key management personnel. IAS 24 defines key management personnel as "those persons having authority and responsibility for planning, directing, and controlling the activities of the reporting entity, including directors (whether executive or otherwise) of the entity."

Related party. Entities are considered to be related parties when one of them either (1) has the ability to control the other entity, (2) can exercise significant influence over the other entity in making financial and operating decisions, (3) has joint control over the other, (4) is a joint venture in which the other entity is a joint venturer, (5) functions as key management personnel of the other entity, or (6) is a close family member of any individual having the ability to control or influence the entity or is a key management member thereof.

Related-party transactions. Related-party transactions are dealings between related parties involving transfer of resources or obligations between them, regardless of whether a price is charged for the transactions.

Significant influence. For the purposes of this standard, an entity is considered to possess the ability to exercise significant influence over another entity if it participates in, as opposed to controls, the financial and operating policy decisions of that other entity.

CONCEPTS, RULES, AND EXAMPLES

The Need for Related-Party Disclosures

For strategic or other reasons, entities sometimes will carry out certain aspects of their business activities through associates or subsidiaries. For example, in order to ensure that it has a guaranteed supply of raw materials, an entity may decide to purchase a portion of its requirements (of raw materials) through a subsidiary or, alternatively, will make a direct investment in its vendor, the better to assure continuity of supply. In this way, the entity might be able to control or exercise significant influence over the financial and operating decisions of its major supplier (the investee), including insuring a source of supply and, perhaps, affecting the prices charged. Such related-party relationships and transactions are thus a normal feature of commerce and business, and need not suggest any untoward behavior.

A related-party relationship could have an impact on the financial position and operating results of the reporting enterprise because

1. Related parties may enter into certain transactions with each other which unrelated parties may not normally want to enter into (e.g., uneconomic transactions).
2. Amounts charged for transactions between related parties may not be comparable to amounts charged for similar transactions between unrelated parties (either higher or lower prices than arm's-length).
3. The mere existence of the relationship may sometimes be sufficient to affect the dealings of the reporting entity with other (unrelated) parties. (For instance, an entity may cease purchasing from its former major supplier upon acquiring a subsidiary which is the other supplier's competitor.)
4. Transactions between entities would not have taken place if the related-party relationship had not existed. For example, a company sells its entire output to an associate at cost. The producing entity might not have survived but for these related-party sales to the associate, if it did not have enough business with arm's-length customers for the kind of goods it manufactures.
5. The existence of related-party relationships may result in certain transactions *not* taking place, which otherwise would have occurred. Thus, even absent actual transactions with related entities, the mere fact that these relationships exist could con-

stitute material information from the viewpoints of various users of financial statements, including current and potential vendors, customers, and employees. Related-party information is thus unique, in that even an absence of transactions might be deemed a material disclosure matter.

Because of peculiarities such as these, which often distinguish related-party transactions from those with unrelated entities, accounting standards (including IFRS) have almost universally mandated financial statement disclosure of such transactions. Disclosures of related-party transactions in financial statements is a means of conveying to users of financial statements the messages that certain related-party relationships exist as of the date of the financial statements, and that certain transactions were consummated with related parties during the period which the financial statements cover, together with the financial impacts of these related-party transactions have been incorporated in the financial statements being presented. Since related-party transactions could have an effect on the financial position and operating results of the reporting entity, disclosure of such transactions would be prudent based on the increasingly cited principle of transparency (in financial reporting). Only if such information is disclosed to the users of financial statements will they be able to make informed decisions.

Scope of the Standard

IAS 24 is to be applied in dealing with related parties and transactions between a reporting entity and its related parties. The requirements of this standard apply to the financial statements of each reporting entity. IAS 24 sets forth disclosure requirements only; it does not prescribe the accounting for related-party transactions, nor does it address the measurements to be applied in the instance of such transactions. Thus, related-party transactions are reported at the nominal values ascribed to them, and are not subject to further interpretation for financial reporting purposes, since there is generally no basis upon which to conclude, or even speculate, about the extent to which related-party transactions might approximate or vary from those between unrelated parties with regard to prices or other terms of sale.

IAS 24 is to be employed in determining the existence of related-party transactions and balances; identifying the ending balances between related parties; concluding on whether disclosures are required under the circumstances; and determining the content of such disclosures.

Related-party disclosures are required not only in the consolidated (group) financial statements, but also in the separate financial statements of the parent entity or a venturer or investor. In separate statements any intragroup transactions and balances must be disclosed in the related-party note, although these will be eliminated in consolidated financial reports.

In practice, it appears that some entities have been lax in disclosing transactions among subsidiaries and associates, where the effects of the intragroup transactions have been eliminated from the group financial statements via consolidation or the application of equity method accounting. That is, since there are no visible intragroup transactions or balances in the actual financial statements, many have either failed to make the required IAS 24 disclosures or have, upon deliberation, concluded these are unnecessary or potentially confusing to readers and would constitute "information overload." However, it is clear that IAS 24 does require disclosure of these transactions. As part of its current project, IASB is considering this issue.

Applicability

The requirements of the standard should be applied to related parties as set forth below. A party is related to an entity if

1. It controls (directly or indirectly through intermediaries) or is controlled by, or is under common control with the reporting entity. Examples include a parent company, subsidiaries, and fellow subsidiaries of a common parent.
2. It has an interest in the entity giving it significant influence.
3. It has joint control over the entity.
4. It is an associate of the reporting entity, as defined in IAS 28;
5. It is a party who is a member of key management personnel of the entity or its parent.
6. It is a close family member of those having control over the entity or those who are members of the key management team of the entity.
7. It is an entity that is controlled, jointly controlled or significantly influenced by, or for which significant voting power in such entity resides with (directly or otherwise) any individual who is a key management member or a close family member of those having control or serving in a key management role.
8. It is a postemployment benefit plan for the benefit of the employees of the entities, or of any entity that is a related-party of the reporting entity.

Close family members. IAS 24 defines these as persons who would be expected to be able to exert influence over, or be influenced by, the individual who has control over the reporting entity or serves in a key management capacity with the reporting entity. It includes domestic partners and children, children of the domestic partner, and dependants of the individual or his/her domestic partner. Transactions with any such persons would be subject to IAS 24 disclosure requirements.

Substance over Form

The standard clarifies that in applying the provisions of IAS 24 to each possible related-party relationship, consideration should be given to the substance of the relationship and not merely to its legal form. Thus, certain relationships might not rise to the level of related parties for purpose of necessitating disclosure under the provisions of IAS 24. Examples of such situations follow:

1. Two entities having only a common director or other key management personnel, notwithstanding the specific requirements of IAS 24 above.
2. Certain agencies, entities, or departments which play a role in the day-to-day business of the entity (even if they participate in its decision-making process). For example

    a. Providers of finance (e.g., banks and creditors)
    b. Trade unions
    c. Public utilities
    d. Government departments and agencies

3. Entities upon which the reporting entity may be economically dependent, due to the volume of business the entity transacts with them. For example

    a. A single customer;
    b. A major supplier;
    c. A franchisor;
    d. A distributor; or
    e. A general agent.

4. Two venturers, simply because they share joint control over a joint venture.

Significant Influence

The existence of the ability to exercise significant influence is an important concept in relation to this standard. It is one of the two criteria stipulated in the definition of a related-party, which when present would, for the purposes of this standard, make one party related to another. In other words, for the purposes of this standard, if one party is considered to have the ability to exercise significant influence over another, then the two parties are considered to be related.

The existence of the ability to exercise significant influence may be evidenced in one or more of the following ways:

1. By representation on the board of directors of the other enterprise;
2. By participation in the policy-making process of the other enterprise;
3. By having material intercompany transactions between two enterprises;
4. By interchange of managerial personnel between two enterprises; or
5. By dependence on another enterprise for technical information.

Significant influence may be gained through agreement, by statute, or by means of share ownership. Under the provisions of IAS 24, similar to the presumption of significant influence under IAS 28, an enterprise is deemed to possess the ability to exercise significant influence if it directly or indirectly through subsidiaries holds 20% or more of the voting power of another enterprise (unless it can be clearly demonstrated that despite holding such voting power the investor does not have the ability to exercise significant influence over the investee). Conversely, if an enterprise, directly or indirectly through subsidiaries, owns less than 20% of the voting power of another enterprise, it is presumed that the investor does not possess the ability to exercise significant influence (unless it can be clearly demonstrated that the investor does have such an ability despite holding less than 20% of the voting power). Further, while explaining the concept of significant influence, IAS 28 also clarifies that "a substantial or majority ownership by another investor does not *necessarily* preclude an investor from having significant influence" (emphasis added).

In the authors' opinion, by defining the term "related-party" to include the concepts of control and significant influence, and by further broadening the definition to cover not just direct related-party relationships, but even indirect ones such as those with "close members of the family of an individual," the IASB intended to cast a wide net, in order to cover related-party transactions which would sometimes not be considered such. This creates some ambiguity relative to disclosures made under this standard, and thus makes the related-party issue itself a more contentious one, since it lends itself to aggressive interpretations by the reporting entity. This obviously could have a significant bearing on the related-party disclosures flowing from these interpretations. Experience suggests this is often a matter of some contention between reporting entities and their independent auditors.

Financial Statement Disclosures

IAS 24 recognizes that in many countries certain related-party disclosures are prescribed by law. In particular, transactions with directors, because of the fiduciary nature of their relationship with the enterprise, are mandated financial statement disclosures in some jurisdictions. In fact, corporate legislation in some countries goes further and requires certain disclosures which are even more stringent than the disclosure requirements under IAS 24, or under most national GAAP.

For example, under one regulation, in addition to the usual disclosures pertaining to related-party transactions, companies are required to disclose not just year-end balances that are due to or due from directors or certain other related parties, but are also required to disclose the highest balances for the period (for which financial statements are presented) which were due to or due from them to the corporate entity. In the authors' opinion, such a requirement is appropriate, since absent this disclosure balances at year-end can be "cleaned up" (e.g., via short-term bank borrowings) and the artificially low amounts reported can provide a misleading picture to financial statement users regarding the real magnitude of such transactions and balances.

For example, a reporting entity which has advanced large sums of money to its directors could make arrangements for the directors to repay the loans to the enterprise a few days before the end of the reporting period, agreeing to reestablish the loans shortly after the first day of the new reporting period. This type of practice, which is often referred to as "window dressing," can cause the financial statements and associated notes to be somewhat misleading while nonetheless nominally compliant with the pertinent financial reporting requirements. Under IAS 24, it does not appear that the amounts of loans to directors outstanding *during* the year (despite being material) would need to be disclosed, since none were actually outstanding on the date of the statement of financial position. In such a situation, disclosure of not just outstanding balances at the end of the reporting period, but also the highest balance(s) due to or due from related parties during the period (or the time-weighted average balance), would improve the quality of information disclosed.

There is nothing in IAS 24 that prohibits supplemental disclosures such as those identified in the preceding paragraph. Commitment to a "substance over form" approach, with the goal of maximizing representational faithfulness and ensuring transparency of the financial reporting process would, indeed, make expanded disclosures such as this appear all but mandatory. While many do seek to satisfy the mere letter of the requirements under IFRS, the "principles-based" approach of these standards would, it could easily be argued, demand that preparers (and their auditors) undertake to comply with the spirit of the rules as well.

IAS 24 provides examples of situations where related-party transactions may lead to disclosures by a reporting entity in the period that they affect.

- Purchases or sales of goods (finished or unfinished, meaning work in progress)
- Purchases or sales of property and other assets
- Rendering or receiving of services
- Agency arrangements
- Leasing arrangement
- Transfer of research and development
- License agreements
- Finance (including loans and equity participation in cash or in kind)
- Guarantees and collaterals
- Settlement of liabilities on behalf of the entity or by the entity on behalf of another party.

The foregoing should not be considered an exhaustive list of situations requiring disclosure. As very clearly stated in the standard, these are only "examples of situations . . . which may lead to disclosures." In practice, many other situations are encountered which would warrant disclosure. For example, a contract for maintaining and servicing computers, entered into with a subsidiary company, would need to be disclosed by the reporting entity in parent company financial statements.

Disclosure of Parent-Subsidiary Relationships

IAS 24 requires disclosure of relationships between parent and subsidiaries irrespective of whether there have been transactions between the related parties. The name of the parent entity must be provided in the subsidiary's financial statement disclosures; if the ultimate controlling party is a different entity, its name must be disclosed. One reason for this requirement is to enable users of the reporting entity's financial statements to seek out the financial statements of the parent or ultimate controlling party for possible review. If neither of these produces financial statements, IAS 24 provides that the name of the "next most senior parent" that produces financial statements must be stated, in addition. These requirements are in addition to those set forth by IAS 27, IAS 28, and IAS 31.

To illustrate this point, consider the following example:

> Company A owns 25% of Company B, and by virtue of share ownership of more than 20% of the voting power, would be considered to possess the ability to exercise significant influence over Company B. During the year, Company A entered into an agency agreement with Company B; however, no transactions took place during the year between the two companies based on the agency contract. Since Company A is considered a related-party to Company B by virtue of the ability to exercise significant influence, rather than control (i.e., there is not a parent-subsidiary relationship), no disclosure of this related-party relationship would be needed under IAS 24. In case, however, Company A owned 51% or more of the voting power of Company B and thereby would be considered related to Company B on the basis of control, disclosure of this relationship would be needed, irrespective of whether any transactions actually took place between them.

Disclosures to Be Provided

Per IAS 24, if there have been transactions between related parties, the reporting entity should disclose

1. The nature of the related-party transaction, and
2. Information about transactions and outstanding balances necessary to understand the potential effect of the relationship on the financial statements. At a minimum the following disclosure shall be made:

   a. The amount of the transaction
   b. Amount of outstanding balances and their terms and conditions, including whether they are secured and details of any guarantees given or received;

3. Provision for doubtful debts related to the amount of the outstanding balances;
4. Any expense recognized during the period in respect of bad or doubtful debts due from the related parties.

The disclosures required are to be made *separately* for each of the following categories:

1. The parent;
2. Entities with joint control or significant influence over the entity;
3. Subsidiaries;
4. Associates
5. Joint venture in which the entity is a venturer;
6. Key management personnel of the entity or its parent; and
7. Other related parties.

Arm's-length transaction price assertions. The assertion that related-party transactions were made at terms that are normal or that the related-party transactions are at arm's-length can be made only if it can be supported. It is presumed that it would rarely be prudent to make such an assertion. The default presumption is that related-party transactions are not *necessarily* conducted on arm's-length terms, which is not taken to imply that transactions were conducted on other bases, either.

Thus, for example, when an entity purchases raw materials amounting to €5 million from an associated company, these are at normal commercial terms (which can be supported, e.g., by competitive bids), and these purchases account for 75% of its total purchases for the year, the following disclosures would seem appropriate:

> During the year, purchases amounting to €5 million were made from an associated company. These purchases were made at normal commercial terms, at prices equivalent to those offered by competitive unrelated vendors. At December 31, 2006, the balance remaining outstanding and owed to this associated company amounted to €2.3 million.

Note that the obtaining of sufficient competent evidence to support an assertion that terms, including prices, for related-party transactions were equivalent to those which would have prevailed for transactions with unrelated parties may be difficult. For example, if the reporting entity formerly purchased from multiple unrelated vendors but, after acquiring a captive source of supply, moves a large portion of its purchases to that vendor, even if prices are the same as had been formerly negotiated with the many unrelated suppliers, this might not warrant an assertion such as the above. The reason is that, with 75% of all purchases being made with this single, related-party supplier, it might not be valid to compare those prices with the process previously negotiated with multiple vendors each providing only a smaller fraction of the reporting entity's needs. Had a large (almost single-source) supply arrangement been executed with any one of the previous suppliers, it might have been possible to negotiate a lower schedule of prices, making comparison of former prices paid for small purchases inapplicable to support this assertion.

Aggregation of disclosures IAS 24 requires that items of a similar nature may be disclosed in the aggregate. However, when separate disclosure is necessary for an understanding of the effects of the related-party transactions on the financial statements of the reporting entity, aggregation would not be appropriate.

A good example of the foregoing is an aggregated disclosure of total sales made during the year to a number of associated companies, instead of separately disclosing sales made to each associated company. On the other hand, an example of separate disclosure (as opposed to aggregated disclosure) is the disclosure of year-end balances due from various related parties disclosed by category (e.g., advances to directors, associated companies, etc.). In the latter case, it makes sense to disclose separately by categories of related parties, instead of aggregating all balances from various related parties together and disclosing, say, the total amount due from all related parties as one amount, since the character of the transactions could well be at variance, as might be the likelihood of timely collection. In fact, separate disclosure in this case seems necessary for an understanding of the effects of related-party transactions on the financial statements of the reporting entity.

IAS 24 specifically cites other IAS which also establish requirements for disclosures of related-party transactions. These include

- IAS 27, which requires disclosure of a listing of significant subsidiaries
- IAS 28, which requires disclosure of a listing of significant associates
- IAS 8, which requires disclosure of exceptional items (i.e., those that are of such size, nature, or incidence that their disclosure is relevant to explain the performance of the enterprise) that arise in transactions with related parties

Compensation. A controversial topic is the disclosure of details regarding management compensation. In some nations, such disclosures (at least for the upper echelon of management) are required, but in other instances these are secrets closely kept by the reporting entities. As part of its deliberations resulting in the revision that became effective in 2005, the IASB considered deleting these disclosures, given privacy and other concerns, and the belief that other "approval processes" (i.e., internal controls) regulated these arrangements, which therefore would not be subject to frequent abuse. However, these disclosures were maintained in the revised standard because these are deemed relevant for decision making by statement users and are clearly related-party transactions.

The reporting entity is required to disclose key management personnel compensation in total and for each of the following categories:

- Short-term employee benefits,
- Postemployment benefits,
- Other long-term benefits,
- Terminal benefits, and
- Share-based payment.

Proposed Amendment to IAS 24

In early 2007, the IASB proposed an amendment to IAS 24 that, if adopted, would eliminate certain disclosures for some entities controlled or significantly influenced by a state in relation to transactions with other entities controlled or significantly influenced by that state. The proposal sets forth certain indicators that would guide the reporting entity in applying this exemption. Indicators that the exemption could *not* be applied include the presence of common board members; the existence of direction or compulsion by the state; the transacting of business by the related parties at nonmarket rates; related parties sharing resources; and related parties undertaking economically significant transactions.

The proposed amendment also will eliminates what have been viewed as inconsistencies by including relationships between subsidiaries and associates of the same entity (the investor/parent company) in the individual or separate financial statements of both the subsidiaries and associates. It would also eliminate from the definition of related parties those situations where one person has significant influence over one entity and a close member of the family of that person has significant influence over another entity. Finally, it would include as related parties where an entity is an investee of a member of key management and the other entity is managed by the key member.

Since the exposure of these draft amendments to IAS 24, the IASB has continued to deliberate these issues, and is (as of late 2008) planning to reexpose a revised draft, which would modify certain of the tentative conclusions in the original Exposure Draft issued in 2007. It is now anticipated, therefore, that a final amendment will not be promulgated until the second half of 2009.

Examples of Financial Statement Disclosures

Novartis AG
For the year ended December 31, 2006

28. Related Parties

Roche/Genentech

Novartis has two agreements with Genentech, Inc., USA, a subsidiary of Roche Holdings AG (Roche) which is indirectly included in the consolidated financial statements using equity accounting as Novartis holds 33.3% of the outstanding voting shares of Roche.

Novartis Ophthalmics, part of the Novartis Pharmaceuticals Division, has licensed the exclusive rights to develop and market *Lucentis* outside the US for indications related to diseases of the eye. As part of this agreement, Novartis paid an initial milestone and R&D reimbursement fee and shared the cost for the subsequent development by making additional milestone payments upon the achievement of certain development points and product approval. Novartis also pays royalties on the net sales of *Lucentis* products outside the US. *Lucentis* sales of USD 393 million (2006: USD 19 million) have been recognized by Novartis.

In February 2004, Novartis Pharma AG, Genentech, Inc., and Tanox, Inc., finalized a three-party collaboration to govern the development and commercialization of certain anti-IgE antibodies including *Xolair* and TNX-901. Under this agreement, all three parties have codeveloped *Xolair* in the US. On August 2, 2007, Genentech, Inc. completed its acquisition of Tanox, Inc. and has taken over its rights and obligations. The Novartis shares held in Tanox were sold to Genentech and realized a gain of USD 117 million. Novartis and Genentech are copromoting *Xolair* in the US where Genentech records all sales.

Novartis markets the product and records all sales and related costs in Europe as well as co-promotion costs in the US. Genentech and Novartis share the resulting profits from sales in the US, Europe, and some East Asia countries according to agreed profit-sharing percentages.

The net fund inflow out of the two agreements described above was USD 4 million in 2007 (2006: net cash inflow of USD 116 million). Novartis recognized total sales of *Xolair* of USD 140 million (2006: USD 102 million) including sales to Genentech for the US market.

Clariant International Ltd.
Period Ending December 2007

32. Related-Party Transactions

Clariant maintains business relationships with related parties. One group consists of the associates, where the most important ones are described in Note 6. The most important business with these companies is the purchase of services by Clariant (e.g., energy and rental of land and buildings) in Germany. In addition to this, Clariant exchanges services and goods with other parties which are associates (i.e., in which Clariant holds a stake of between 20% and 50%).

The second group of related parties is key management comprising the Board of Directors (nonexecutive members) and Board of Management. The information required by Art. 663b bis of the Swiss Code of Obligations regarding the emoluments for the members of the Board of Directors and the Board of Management is disclosed in the Statutory Accounts of Clariant Ltd on pages 160 and 161 of this report (not based on IFRS valuations). More information on the relationship with the Board of Directors is given in the chapter on Corporate Governance (nonaudited).

The third group of related parties are the pension plans of major subsidiaries. Clariant provides services to its pension plans in Switzerland, the UK, and the US. These services comprise mainly administrative and trustee services. The total cost of these services is CHF 1 million (2006: CHF 1 million), of which approximately half is charged back to the pension plans. The number of full-time employees corresponding to these are approximately 6 (2006: 6).

Transactions with associates

CHF (million)	2007	2006
Income from the sale of goods to related parties	37	41
Income from the rendering of services to related parties	4	7
Expenses from the purchase of goods from related parties	(27)	(8)
Expenses from services rendered by related parties	(255)	(272)

Payables, receivables, and loans with associates

CHF (millions)	12/31/2007	12/31/06
Receivables from related parties	8	8
Payables to related parties	45	19

Transactions with key management

CHF (millions)	2007	2006
Transactions with Board of Management		
Salaries and other short-term benefits	6	8
Termination benefits	4	--
Postemployment benefits	1	1
Share-based payments	1	1
Total	12	10

	12/31/2007	12/31/06
Number of granted shares for the reporting period	30,334	117,419

There were no outstanding loans by the Group to any members of the Board of Directors or Board of Management.

Nokia Group
Period ending December 2007

Nokia Pension Foundation is a separate legal entity that manages and holds in trust the assets for the Group's Finnish employee benefit plans. These assets do not include Nokia shares. The Group recorded net rental expense of EUR 0 million in 2007 (EUR 2 million in 2006 and EUR 2 million in 2005) pertaining to a sale-leaseback transaction with the Nokia Pension Foundation involving certain buildings and a lease of the underlying land.

At December 31, 2007, the Group had borrowings amounting to EUR 69 million (EUR 69 million in 2006) from Nokia Unterst-utzungskasse GmbH, the Group's German pension fund, which is a separate legal entity. The loan bears interest at 6% annum and its duration is pending until further notice by the loan counterparts who have the rights to terminate the loan with a 90-day notice period.

There were no loans granted to the members of the Group Executive Board and the Board of Directors at December 31, 2007, 2006, or 2005.

EURm	2007	2006	2005
Share of results of associated companies	44	28	10
Dividend income	12	1	1
Share of shareholders' equity of associated companies	158	61	33
Sales to associated companies	82	--	--
Purchases from associated companies	125	--	--
Receivables from associated companies	61	--	--
Liabilities to associated companies	69	14	14

Roche Group
Period ending December 2007

Controlling Shareholders

The share capital of Roche Holding Ltd., which is the Group's parent company, consists of 160,000,000 bearer shares. Based on information supplied by a shareholder group with pooled voting rights, comprising Ms. Vera Michalski-Hoffmann, Ms. Maja Hoffmann, Mr. André S. Hoffmann, Dr. Andreas Oeri, Ms. Sabine Duschmalé-Oeri, Ms. Catherine Oeri, Ms. Beatrice Oeri, and Ms. Maja Oeri, that group holds 80,020,000 shares as in the preceding year, which represents 50.0125% of the issued shares. This figure does not include any shares without pooled voting rights that are held outside this group by individual members of the group.

Mr. André S. Hoffmann and Dr. Andreas Oeri are members of the Board of Directors of Roche Holding Ltd. and in this capacity receive an annual remuneration of 300,000 Swiss francs. Since February 28, 2006, Mr. Hoffman is a Vice-Chairman of the Board, and in 2006 he received a further 83,333 Swiss francs in this capacity. Dr. Oeri is Chairman of the Corporate Governance and Sustainability Committee and in 2007 received 60,000 Swiss francs for his time and expenses in this capacity (2006: 10,000 Swiss francs).

There were no other transactions between the Group and the individual members of the above shareholders' group.

Subsidiary and Associated Companies

A listing of the major Group subsidiaries and associated companies is included in Note 37. Transactions between the parent company and its subsidiaries and between subsidiaries are eliminated on consolidation. There were no significant transactions between the Group and its associated companies.

24 SPECIALIZED INDUSTRY ACCOUNTING

BANKS AND SIMILAR FINANCIAL INSTITUTIONS

PERSPECTIVE AND ISSUES

Disclosure requirements relating to financial statements of banks and similar financial institutions had long been set forth by IAS 30. Commencing with years beginning on or after January 1, 2007, however, a new, unified financial instruments disclosure standard, IFRS 7, has superseded the former standard. IFRS 7 is addressed in detail in Chapter 5.

A broad definition of the term "bank" was set forth by IAS 30, and it covers all those entities (whether or not officially called a bank)

1. Which are financial institutions,
2. Whose principal activities are to accept deposits and borrow money for the purpose of lending and investing, and
3. Which are within the scope of banking and similar regulations.

Since banks' operations differ in many material respects from other commercial entities, with liquidity and solvency being of paramount importance, the financial reporting by these entities inevitably is somewhat specialized in nature. In recognition of their special needs, IAS 30 established a number of disclosure requirements. Some of these disclosures are unusual when compared to those of other commercial entities, and may even be perceived by users of the banks' financial statements as excessive or superfluous. However, these disclosures have been made mandatory for banks, based on the unique characteristics of banks' operations and the role banks play in maintaining public confidence in the monetary system of the country through their close relationship with regulatory authorities (such as the country's central bank) and the government. Further, a bank is exposed not only to liquidity risks but even risks arising from currency fluctuations, interest rate movements, changes in market prices, and counterparty failure. These risks arise not only in connection with assets and liabilities that are recognized on a bank's statement of financial position, but also due to various off–statement of financial position items. Thus, certain disclosure requirements as outlined by IAS 30 relate to off-statement of financial position items as well.

The development of IAS 30 took about ten years, an inordinate amount of time when contrasted to other standards produced by the former IASC. This was partly because of IASC's efforts to obtain input from bankers worldwide, and partly due to the regulated nature of the banking industry, which adds to the complexity of imposing uniform disclosure requirements across national boundaries. The development of its successor standard, IFRS 7, also involved a multiyear effort, including an Exposure Draft in mid-2004 and a final standard in mid-2005, with a delayed effective date to provide financial statement preparers time to adapt to the new requirements.

Although IAS 30 applied exclusively to financial statements of banks and similar financial institutions, it did not, of itself, define all the disclosures that were required by those entities. They were also required to conform to all other relevant disclosure requirements of standards such as IAS 24 (related parties), IAS 19 (segment reporting), IAS 32 and IAS 39 (the latter both dealing with financial instruments). Successor standard IAS 7, applicable to all reporting entities that purport to conform to IFRS requirements, incorporates special statement of cash flows provisions that are applicable to financial institutions, and its appendix illustrates the use of the direct method by financial institutions.

Sources of IFRS	
IAS 1, 7, 16, 18, 24, 32, 37, 39	*IFRS* 7

CONCEPTS, RULES, AND EXAMPLES

Financial Reporting by Banks

Under previous standard IAS 30, the accounting and disclosures by banks and other financial institutions was set forth with substantial specificity. Much of this guidance has been eliminated, since the replacement standard, IFRS 7 (which became effective in 2007), deals with financial instrument disclosures *in general*. The actual form of the financial statements to be presented by banks and other financial institutions (e.g., the captions of revenue and expense categories) is no longer explicitly addressed. (Revised IAS 1 is thus the source for such guidance.)

In the following abbreviated discussion, the authors offer certain of the guidance that had been provided under IAS 30. This should be understood as being only suggestions, and not actual requirements, in determining the form and content of financial institution financial statements.

IAS 1, most recently amended in 2007, applies to financial statements of all commercial, industrial, and business entities, including banks and similar financial institutions. It requires that disclosure be made of all significant accounting policies that were adopted in the preparation and presentation of an entity's financial statements. For financial institutions, appropriate disclosure of accounting policies would typically include the following:

1. The accounting policy setting forth the recognition of the principal types of income. An example of this disclosure follows:

    "Interest income and loan commitment fees are recognized on a time proportion basis[*] taking into account the principal outstanding and the rate applicable. Other fee income is recognized when due."

    [*] *IAS 18 specifically requires that interest income be recognized on a time proportion basis.*

2. Accounting policies relating to the valuation of investments and dealing securities. An illustration follows:

    Example of accounting policy relating to valuation of investments

    Trading investments. Trading investments are carried at fair values with any gain or loss arising from changes in fair values being taken to the Statement of Comprehensive Income.

3. Accounting policy explaining the distinction between transactions and events that result in the recognition of assets and liabilities on the statement of financial position versus those that give rise to contingencies and commitments, including off-balance-sheet items. An example follows:

    Example of accounting policy relating to off-balance-sheet items

    Commitments. Undrawn lending facilities, such as lines of credit extended to customers, that are irrevocable according to agreements with customers (and cannot be withdrawn at the discretion of the bank), are disclosed as commitments rather than as loans and advances to customers. If, and to the extent, the facilities are utilized by customers before year-end, these will be reported as actual loans and advances.

4. Accounting policy that outlines the basis for the determination of

    a. The provision for possible losses on loans and advances

    b. Write-off of uncollectible loans and advances

Example of accounting policies (adapted from published financial statements)

Impairment of loans and advances. Loans and advances are reviewed periodically at the date of each statement of financial position to determine whether there is objective evidence of impairment. If there is evidence of such impairment, it is to be estimated as set forth below.

  a. In case of "originated loans and advances" based on the present value of the expected cash flows discounted at the instrument's original effective interest rate.
  b. In case of other "loans and advances" specific allowances are provided against those loans and advances that are *identified as impaired* based on reviews of the outstanding balances and in case of *portfolios of similar loans and advances* the expected cash flows which are estimated based on previous experience taking into consideration the credit rating of the underlying customers and their payment history and are discounted at original effective interest rates.

In subsequent years if the impairment losses reverse the provision is written back through the statement of comprehensive income.

5. Accounting policy explaining the basis for determining and setting aside amounts toward general banking risks and the accounting treatment accorded to this reserve.

   Regulatory bodies, such as the central bank of the country in which the bank is incorporated, or local legislation may require or allow a bank to set aside amounts for general banking risks, including future losses or other unforeseeable risks or even reserves for contingencies over and above accruals required by IAS 37. It would not be proper to allow banks to charge these additional reserves to the statement of comprehensive income, as this would distort the true financial position of the bank. An example is

Note 1. Statutory Reserves

   As required by the Companies Commercial Code of Nation XYZ, and in accordance with the Bank's articles of association, 10% of the net income for the year is set aside as a statutory reserve annually. Such appropriations of net income are to continue until the balance in the statutory reserve equals 50% of the bank's paid-up capital.

The following suggestions have their origin in the requirements first set forth by IAS 30. These remain, in the authors' opinion, reasonable guidance for the preparation and presentation of the financial statements of banks:

1. The statement of comprehensive income of a bank should be presented in a manner that groups income and expenses by nature and discloses the amounts of the principal types of income and expenses.

   a. Disclosures in the statement of comprehensive income or in the footnotes should include, but are not limited to, the following items:

      (1) Interest and similar income
      (2) Interest expense and similar charges
      (3) Dividend income
      (4) Fee and commission income
      (5) Fee and commission expense
      (6) Gains less losses arising from dealing securities
      (7) Gains less losses arising from investment securities
      (8) Gains less losses arising from dealing in foreign currencies
      (9) Other operating income
      (10) Losses on loans and advances

(11) General and administrative expenses

(12) Other operating expenses

These disclosures, to be incorporated into the bank's statement of comprehensive income, are of course in addition to disclosure requirements of other international accounting standards.

b. Separate disclosure of the principal types of income and expenses, as above, is essential in order that users of the bank's financial statements can assess the performance of the bank.

c. The offsetting of income and expense items is prohibited, except those relating to hedges and to assets or liabilities wherein the legal right of setoff exists and the offsetting represents the expectation as to the realization or settlement of the asset or liability. If offsetting of items of income and expense had been allowed, it would prevent users from assessing the return on particular classes of assets; this, in a way, would restrict users of financial statements in their assessment of the performance of the bank.

d. The following statement of comprehensive income items are, however, allowed to be presented on a net basis:

(1) Gains or losses from dealings in foreign currencies

(2) Gains or losses from disposals of investment securities

(3) Gains or losses from disposals and changes in the carrying amount of dealing securities

Example of bank financial reporting

ABC Banking Corporation
Statement of Comprehensive Income
For the Years Ended December 31, 2009 and 2008

	2009	*2008*
Operating income		
Interest income	€400,000	€380,000
Interest expense	(205,000)	(200,000)
Net interest income	195,000	180,000
Net income from trading securities	2,000	2,000
Net gain from dealings in foreign currencies	14,000	10,000
Net gain from disposal of available-for-sale investments	20,000	13,000
Fees and commission	50,000	40,000
Other operating income	8,000	8,000
	289,000	253,000
Operating expenses		
Provision for losses on loans and advances	70,000	50,000
Provision for impairment of investments	1,000	1,000
	71,000	51,000
Profit from operations	218,000	202,000
Other income	9,000	8,000
	227,000	210,000
General and administration expenses	80,000	75,000
Depreciation on property and equipment	11,000	10,000
Provision for taxation	6,000	6,000
Net income for the year	130,000	119,000
Change in fair value of securities available for sale	20,000	(5,000)
Comprehensive income for the year	€150,000	€114,000

2. The statement of financial position of a bank should group assets and liabilities by nature and list them in the order of their respective liquidity. This is explained further as follows:

a. Disclosure of the grouping of assets and liabilities by their nature and listing them by their respective liquidity is made either on the face of the statement of financial position or in the footnotes.

Assets	*Liabilities*
Cash and balances with the central bank	Deposits from other banks
Treasury bills and other bills eligible for rediscounting with the central bank	Other money market deposits
	Amounts owed to other depositors
Government and other securities held for dealing purposes	Certificates of deposits
Placements with, and loans and advances to, other banks	Promissory notes and other liabilities evidenced by paper
	Other borrowed funds
Other money market placements	
Loans and advances to customers	
Investment securities	

These disclosures, to be incorporated into the bank's statement of comprehensive income, are of course in addition to disclosure requirements set forth by other international accounting standards.

b. Grouping the assets and liabilities by nature does not pose a problem and, in fact, is probably the most logical way of combining financial statement items for presentation on the bank's statement of financial position. For instance, deposits with other banks and loans/advances to other banks are combined and presented as a separate line item on the asset side of a bank's statement of financial position and referred to as placements with other banks. These items would, however, be presented differently on financial statements of other commercial entities since deposits with banks in those instances would be combined with other cash and bank balances, and loans to banks would probably be classified as investments. On the other hand, balances with other banks are not combined with balances with other parts of the money market, even though by nature they are placements with other financial institutions, since this gives a better understanding of the bank's relations with and dependency on other banks versus other constituents of the money market.

c. Listing of assets by liquidity could be considered synonymous with listing of liabilities by maturity, since maturity is a measure of liquidity in case of liabilities. For instance, certificates of deposits are liabilities of banks and have contractual maturities of perhaps, one month, three months, six months, and one year. Similarly, there are other bank liabilities, such as promissory notes, that may not be due, perhaps, for another three years from the date of the statement of financial position. Thus, a relative maturity analysis would suggest that the certificates of deposit be listed on the bank's statement of financial position before or above the promissory notes since they would mature earlier. Similarly, assets of a bank could be analyzed based on their relative liquidity, and those assets that are more liquid than others (i.e., will convert into cash faster than others) should be listed on the statement of financial position above the others. Thus, cash balances and balances with the central bank are usually listed above other assets on the statement of financial position of all banks, being relatively more liquid than other assets.

d. Offsetting of assets against liabilities, or vice versa, is generally not allowed unless a legal right of setoff exists and the offsetting represents the expectation as to the realization or settlement of the asset or liability. This is a requirement established by IAS 1, which applies to all entities reporting in accordance with IFRS, and was not intended only for financial institutions.

e. The since-superseded IAS 25 had previously provided that entities not normally distinguishing between current and long-term investments in their statements of financial position were nevertheless to make such a distinction for measurement purposes. Under IAS 39, the current versus long-term distinction is no longer important, but it will instead be necessary to assign all such investments to the trading, available-for-sale, or held-to-maturity portfolios. IAS 30 stipulates that banks must disclose the market value of investments in securities if different from the carrying values in the financial statements. Since both trading and available-for-sale securities are carried in the statement of financial position at fair value, this added disclosure requirement now only impacts held to maturity securities, which are maintained at amortized cost.

Example

ABC Banking Corporation
Statement of Financial Position
As at December 31, 2009 and 2008

	2009	*2008*
Assets		
Cash and balances with central bank	€ 480,000	€ 370,000
Placements with other banks	3,685,000	2,990,000
Portfolio held for trading	8,286,000	6,786,000
Nontrading investments	364,000	26,000
Loans and advances, net	40,000	28,000
Investment property	358,000	283,000
Property and equipment, net	90,000	89,000
Other assets	55,000	44,000
Total assets	€13,358,000	€10,616,000
Liabilities and Shareholders' Equity		
Liabilities:		
Due to banks	€ 2,187,000	€ 998,000
Customer deposits	8,040,000	6,536,000
Long-term loan from government	1,300,000	1,380,000
Other liabilities	108,000	96,000
Total liabilities	11,635,000	8,930,000
Shareholders' Equity:		
Share capital	1,250,000	1,250,000
Statutory reserve	73,000	60,000
Contingency reserve	29,000	12,000
General reserve	325,000	325,000
Retained earnings	46,000	39,000
Total shareholders' equity	1,723,000	1,686,000
Total liabilities and shareholders' equity	€13,358,000	€10,616,000
Commitments and contingent liabilities	€15,300,000	€12,100,000

Statement of Cash Flows for Banks and Other Financial Institutions

Statements of cash flows are an integral part of financial statements. Every entity is required to present a statement of cash flows in accordance with the provisions of IAS 7.

Although the general requirements of IAS 7 are common to all entities, the standard does contain special provisions that are applicable only to financial institutions. These specific provisions deal with reporting of certain cash flows on a "net basis." The following cash flows are to be reported on a net basis:

1. Cash receipts and payments on behalf of customers when the cash flows reflect the activities of the customer rather than those of the entity; the standard refers to "the accepting and repayment of demand deposits of a bank"

2. Cash receipts and payments for the acceptance and repayment of deposits with a fixed maturity date

3. The placement of deposits with and withdrawal of deposits from other financial institutions

4. Cash advances and loans made to customers and the repayment of those advances and loans

The appendix to IAS 7 (see the discussion below) illustrates the application of the standard to financial institutions preparing statements of cash flows under the direct method (for a more detailed discussion of statements cash flows, see Chapter 4).

Example of statement of cash flows for banks

Community Bank
Consolidated Statement of Cash Flows
For the Year Ended December 31, 2009
(€000)

Cash flows from operating activities:		
Interest and commission receipts	€28,447	
Interest payments	(23,463)	
Recoveries on loans previously written off	237	
Cash payments to employees and suppliers	(997)	
Operating profit before changes in operating assets	4,224	
(Increase) decrease in operating assets:		
Placements with other banks	(650)	
Deposits with Central bank for regulatory purposes	234	
Funds advanced to customers	(288)	
Net increase in credit card receivables	(360)	
Interest receivable	(120)	
Increase (decrease) in operating liabilities:		
Deposits from customers	600	
Balances due to other banks	(200)	
Net cash from operating activities before income tax	3,440	
Income taxes paid	(100)	
Net cash from operating activities		€3,340
Cash flows from investing activities:		
Proceeds from disposal of subsidiary Y	50	
Dividends received	200	
Interest received	300	
Proceeds from sales of nontrading securities	1,200	
Purchase of investment property	(600)	
Purchase of property, plant, and equipment	(500)	
Net cash from investing activities		650
Cash flows from financing activities:		
Issuance of equity capital	1,000	
Issue of preference shares by subsidiary undertaking	800	
Dividends paid	(1,600)	
Net cash from financing activities		200
Effects of exchange rate changes on cash and cash equivalents		600
Net increase in cash and cash equivalents		4,790
Cash and cash equivalents at beginning of period		4,050
Cash and cash equivalents at end of period		€8,840

Disclosures by Banks and Similar Institutions

With the supersession of IAS 30 by IFRS 7, there is no longer a discrete set of disclosure requirements set forth for financial institutions under IFRS. Nevertheless, the nature of such entities' operations suggests that certain disclosures are likely to be needed in the typical financial reporting situation. The following paragraphs discuss these matters in greater detail.

Contingencies and commitments including off–statement of financial position items. Contingent liabilities are *possible obligations* that arise from past events whose existence will be confirmed only by the ultimate outcome of one or more uncertain future events that are not wholly within the control of the entity. Contingent liabilities could also be *present obligations* that arise from past events but are not recognized either because it is not probable that an outflow of resources will be required or because the amount of the obligation cannot be measured reliably. Generally, the accounting for and disclosure of provisions and contingent liabilities has been addressed by IAS 37. Exceptions have been made in certain cases; for instance, liabilities of life insurance companies arising from insurance policies issued by them and other entities, such as retirement benefit plans, have been specifically excluded from the scope of IAS 37. Specific contingent liabilities relating to the banking industry (see list below) were previously required to be disclosed in accordance with the provisions of IAS 30, since provisions or contingent liabilities of banking or similar financial institutions were not specifically excluded from the purview of IAS 37.

The result was that the general principles of recognizing provisions or disclosing contingent liabilities, as set forth in IAS 37, differed for the banking industry compared to other commercial entities. This created some confusion, since the need for specific requirements under IAS 30 was not entirely clear, notwithstanding that IAS 30 stated

> *...This standard is of particular relevance to banks because banks often engaged in transactions that lead to contingent liabilities and commitments, some revocable and others irrevocable, which are frequently significant in amount and substantially larger than those of other commercial entities.*

Fortunately, this is no longer an issue. Financial institutions are subject to the same disclosures for contingencies and commitments as are all other entities purporting to comply with IFRS.

Disclosures that are likely to be needed in financial reporting by banks and other financial institutions include the following:

1. The nature and amount of commitments to extend credit that are irrevocable because they cannot be withdrawn at the discretion of the bank without incurring significant penalty or expenses
2. The nature and amount of contingencies and commitments arising from off-balance-sheet items, including those relating to

    a. Direct credit substitutes, which include general guarantees of indebtedness, bank acceptances, and standby letters of credit, which serve as financial backup for loans and securities

    b. Transaction-related contingencies, which include performance bonds, bid bonds, warranties, and standby letters of credit related to particular transactions

    c. Trade-related contingencies, which are self-liquidating and short-term trade-related contingencies arising from the movement of goods, such as documentary credit wherein the underlying goods are used as security for the bank credit (sometimes referred to as trust receipts, or simply as TR)

    d. Sales and repurchase agreements that are not reflected or recognized in the bank's statement of financial position

    e. Interest and foreign exchange rate related items, which include items such as options, futures, and swaps

    f. Other commitments, including other off–statement of financial position items such as revolving underwriting facilities and note issuance facilities

It is important for the users of the bank's financial statements to be cognizant about the contingencies and irrevocable commitments because these may have a future effect on the liquidity and solvency of the bank. For instance, undrawn borrowing facilities granted to customers, to which the bank is irrevocably committed, are indicative of what could happen to a bank's liquidity position if a majority of the customers utilize their lines at the same time—for example, if there were to be a sudden shortage of funds in the market, due to underlying economic causes or otherwise. Thus, disclosing such irrevocable commitments and contingencies, in the footnotes or elsewhere, is of paramount importance to the user of the bank's financial statements.

Also, off–statement of financial position items, such as letters of credit (LC), guarantees, acceptances, and so on, constitute an important part of the bank's business and thus should be disclosed in the financial statements, since without knowing about the magnitude of such items, a fair evaluation of the bank's financial position is not possible (mostly because it adds significantly to the level of business risk the bank is exposed to at any given point of time).

Certain items that are typically not included in the statement of financial position are commonly referred to as memoranda accounts, and less frequently are called contra items. These are often interrelated items that are both contingent assets and contingent liabilities, such as bills held for collection for customers, that if and when collected will in turn be remitted to the customer and not retained by the bank. The logic is that since the asset and liability both have contingent aspects, and since the bank is effectively only acting as an agent on behalf of a customer, it is valid to exclude both elements from the statement of financial condition. The *existence* of such items, however, generally must be disclosed even if not formally recognized in the body of the financial statements.

Example of disclosure of contingencies and commitments

	2009	2008
At December 31, 2009 and 2008, the contingent liabilities and commitments were the following (in thousands of euros):		
Letters of credit	€10,000	€ 9,000
Guarantees	11,000	8,000
Acceptances	12,000	11,000
Bills for collection	13,000	12,000
Commitments under undrawn lines of credit	15,000	12,000
	€61,000	€52,000

Illustrative Extracts from Published Financial Statements

UBS
December 31, 2007

Notes to the financial statements

Note 21. Provisions

CHF million	Operational[1]	Litigation[2]	Other[3]	December 31, 2007 Total	December 31, 2006 Total[3]
Balance at the beginning of the year	185	699	788	1,672	2,072
Additions from acquired companies	0	0	0	0	26
Increase in provisions recognized in the income statement	302	318	110	730	630
Release of provisions recognized in the income statement	(41)	(117)	(58)	(216)	5

CHF million

	Operational[1]	*Litigation*[2]	*Other*[3]	December 31, 2007 *Total*	December 31, 2006 *Total*[3]
Provisions used in conformity with designated purpose	(123)	(386)	(61)	(570)	(466)
Capitalized reinstatement costs	0	0	6	6	22
Disposal of subdiaries	0	0	(16)	(16)	(607)
Reclassifications	(6)	6	155	155	36
Foreign currency translation	(19)	(46)	(23)	(88)	(46)
Balance at the end of the year	298	474	901	1,673	1,672

[1]   *Includes provisions for litigation resulting from security risks and transaction processing risks.*

[2]   *Includes litigation resulting from legal, liability and compliance risks.*

[3]   *Other amounts include: In 2006, in connection with a strategy review of its business and a review of its office space planning, Wealth Management US decided not to use office space rented by UBS under a long-term contract in a new building in New Jersey. Senior management approved a proposal to enter into a 10-year sublease contract with an external party for the unused office space. Under the terms of this contract, the sublease income is not sufficient to cover the rent UBS pays under its original contract and costs incurred for arranging the sublease. UBS recorded a provision to cover the shortfall of this onerous lease contract which amounted to CHF 105 million on December 31, 2007, and CHF 185 million on December 31, 2006.*

Litigation. UBS Group operates in a legal and regulatory environment that exposes it to potentially significant litigation risks. As a result, UBS is involved in various disputes and legal proceedings, including litigation, arbitration, and regulatory and criminal investigations. Such cases are subject to many uncertainties, and their outcome is often difficult to predict, particularly in the earlier stages of a case. In certain circumstances, to avoid the expense and distraction of legal proceedings, UBS may, based on a cost-benefit analysis, enter a settlement even though UBS denies any wrongdoing. The Group makes provisions for cases brought against it only when after seeking legal advice, in the opinion of management, it is probable that a liability exists, and the amount can be reasonably estimated (see table above). No provision is made for claims asserted against the Group that in the opinion of management are without merit and where it is not likely that UBS will be found liable.

Currently, UBS is responding to a number of regulatory inquiries and investigations, and is involved in a number of litigations and disputes, related to the subprime crisis, subprime securities, and structured transactions involving subprime securities. These matters concern, among other things, UBS's valuations, disclosures, write-downs, underwriting, and contractual obligations.

At December 31, 2007, UBS is involved in the following legal proceedings which could be material to the Group in a given reporting period:

a.   Tax Shelter: In connection with a criminal investigation of tax shelters, the United States Attorney's Office for the Southern District of New York ("US Attorney's Office") is examining UBS's conduct in relation to certain tax-oriented transactions in which UBS and others engaged during the years 1996-2000. Some of these transactions were the subject of the Deferred Prosecution Agreement which the accounting firm KPMG LLP entered into with the US Attorney's Office in August 2005, and are at issue in United States v. Stein, S1 05 Cr. 888 (LAK). USB is cooperating in the government's investigation.

b.   Municipal Bonds: In November 2006, UBS and others received subpoenas from the US Department of Justice, Antitrust Division, and the SEC relating to derivative transactions entered into with municipal bond issuers and to the investment of proceeds of municipal bond issuances. Both investigations are ongoing, and UBS is cooperating. In the SEC investigation, on February 4, 2008, UBS received a "Wells notice" advising that the SEC staff is considering recommending that the SEC bring a civil action against UBS AG in connection with the bidding of carious financial instruments associated with municipal securities. Under the SEC's Wells process, UBS will have the opportunity to set forth reasons of law, policy or fact why such an action should not be brought.

c. HealthSouth: UBS is defending itself in two purported securities class actions brought in the US District Court of the Northern District of Alabama by holders of stock and bonds in HealthSouth Corp. UBS also is a defendant in HealthSouth derivative litigation in Alabama State Court and has responded to an SEC investigation relating to UBS's role as a banker for HealthSouth.

d. Parmalat: UBS is involved in a number of proceedings in Italy related to the bankruptcy of Parmalat. These proceedings include, inter alia, clawback proceedings against UBS Limited in connection with a structured finance transaction. Further, UBS is a defendant in two civil damages claims brought by Parmalat, one of which relates to the same structured finance transaction against UBS Limited, while the other against UBS AG relates to certain derivative transactions. In addition, UBS Limited and one current and one former UBS employee are the subject of criminal proceedings in Milan. UBS AG and UBS Limited are defendants in civil actions brought by Parmalat investors in parallel with the criminal proceedings in Milan. Furthermore, four current or former UBS employees are defendants in relation to criminal proceedings in Parma. Civil claims have also been recently filed in parallel with the criminal proceedings by Parmalat against the individuals and UBS Limited and also by Parmalat investors against the individuals, UBS AG and UBS Limited. UBS AG and UBS Limited deny the allegations made against them and against the individuals in these matters and are vigorously defending themselves in these proceedings.

e. Insight One: In early July 2007, UBS agreed to a settlement of the Insight One case after the New York State Attorney General filed a civil complaint regarding UBS's fee-based brokerage program for private clients in the United States in December 2006. UBS denied that the program was part of a scheme to disadvantage clients, but chose to settle to bring the proceedings to an end. Under the settlement, UBS paid a total of USD 23.3 million, of which USD 21.3 million was paid to certain current and former Insight One customers pursuant to an agreed-upon remediation plan, and USD 2 million was paid in penalties. In 2006, UBS established provisions sufficient to cover the settlement, and therefore the settlement did not impact UBS's Net profit in 2007.

f. Bankruptcy Estate of Enron: In June 2007, UBS and Enron settled adversarial proceedings in the US Bankruptcy Court for the Southern District of New York brought by Enron to avoid and recover payments made prior to filing for bankruptcy in connection with equity forward and swap transactions. UBS believed it had valid defenses to all of Enron's claims, but chose to settle to eliminate the uncertainty created by the proceeding. Under the terms of the settlement, UBS paid Enron USD 115 million and waived a proof of claim for approximately USD 5.5 million that UBS filed in Enron's bankruptcy case. In 2006, UBS recognized a provision for more than half of the settlement amount, with the difference recognized in 2007. Therefore, the settlement did not materially impact UBS's Net profit in 2007.

Maturities of Assets and Liabilities

Information about maturities of assets and liabilities is among the most important disclosures expected of banks, since it gives users a concise picture of the bank's liquidity. Well-managed banks typically exhibit closely aligned maturities of assets, such as loans and investments, and liabilities, such as time deposits. To the extent these are mismatched, it not only raises a liquidity (or even solvency) question, but also in periods of changing interest rates it places the bank at risk of having its normal "spread" (the difference between interest earned and interest paid) become diminished or turn negative.   Since even an otherwise healthy institution, having positive net worth, can have mismatches in some of the maturities, potential problems are identified through the schedule of asset and liability maturities which would not otherwise be apparent from the financial statements.

Maturity groupings applied to assets and liabilities differ from bank to bank. A typical classification scheme is as follows:

1. Up to one month
2. From one month to three months
3. From three months to one year
4. From one year to five years
5. From five years and above

While the typology used is not firmly prescribed, it is imperative that the maturity periods adopted by a bank be the same for assets and liabilities. This ensures that the maturities are matched and brings to light dependency, if any, on other sources of liquidity.

Maturities could be expressed in more than one way—for instance, by remaining period to the repayment date or by the original period to the repayment date. Under IAS 30, it had been recommended that the maturity analysis of assets and liabilities be by the remaining period to the repayment date, as it was thought that this provided the best basis upon which to evaluate the liquidity of the bank.

In some countries time deposits may be withdrawn even on demand, and advances given by the bank may become repayable on demand. In such cases, maturities according to the contractual dates should be used for the purposes of this analysis since it reflects the liquidity risks attaching to the bank's assets and liabilities.

Certain assets do not have a contractual maturity date. In all such cases the period in which these assets are assumed to mature is usually taken to be the expected date on which the assets will be realized. For instance, in the case of fixed assets that have no maturity date as such, the authors are of the opinion that their remaining useful lives as of the date of the statement of financial position could be used as a measure of the maturity profile of these assets.

Example of disclosure of maturities of assets and liabilities

The maturity profile of assets and liabilities at December 31, 2008, was as follows:

	(€ in thousands)			
	Up to 3 months	*3 months to 1 year*	*1 year to 5 years*	*Over 5 years*
Assets				
Cash and short-term funds	€ 10,157	€ --	€ --	€ --
Deposits with banks	298,771	--	--	--
Investments—available-for-sale	101,013	--	--	--
Trading investments	113,109	76,173	--	--
Investments—held-to-maturity	--	--	--	284,281
Accrued interest and other assets	9,919	18,681	2,150	--
Investment property	--	--	366,259	--
Fixed assets	--	--	--	57,997
Total assets	€532,969	€ 94,854	€368,409	€ 342,278
Liabilities				
Deposits from banks	€105,492	€ 18,400	€ --	€ --
Customer deposits	36,062	1,033	130,127	--
Accrued interest and other payable	38,882	9,952	30,865	--
Medium-term facilities	--	250,000	330,000	--
Total liabilities	€180,436	€279,385	€490,992	€ --

Concentration of Assets, Liabilities and Off–Statement of Financial Position Items

Banks should disclose any significant concentrations of assets, liabilities, and off-balance-sheet items. Such disclosures are a means of identification of potential risks, if any, that are inherent in the realization of the assets and liabilities (the funds available) to the bank.

Concentration of assets, liabilities, and off-balance-sheet items could be disclosed in the following ways:

1. By geographical areas such as individual countries, group of countries, or regions within a country
2. By customer groups such as governments, public authorities, and commercial entities
3. By industry sectors such as real estate, manufacturing, retail, and financial
4. Other concentrations of risk appropriate in the circumstances of the bank

Example of disclosure of concentration of assets, liabilities, and off-balance-sheet items

(€ in thousands)

	2008			2007		
	Assets	*Liabilities*	*Off-balance-sheet*	*Assets*	*Liabilities*	*Off-balance-sheet*
Geographical region						
North America	€ 679,829	€ 26,103	€ 57,479	€ 681,958	€ 86,267	€ 146,099
Europe	662,259	778,470	621,316	574,699	662,690	1,117,110
Middle East	93,003	184,485	114,984	71,328	216,486	98,236
Other	279	--	--	10,525	370	198,138
Total	€1,395,370	€989,058	€793,779	€1,338,510	€965,813	€1,559,583
Industry sector						
Banking and finance	€ 314,563	€866,483	€715,141	€ 482,874	€846,513	€1,484,248
Food processing	40,535	--		40,777	--	--
Luxury merchandise	336,966	3,797	11,811	224,829	--	1,649
Retail	356,879	--	--	315,554	--	--
Real estate	96,743	--	63,871	68,744	--	72,947
Manufacturing and services	153,151	--	--	124,366	--	--
Other	96,533	118,779	2,956	81,366	119,300	739
Total	€1,395,370	€989,058	€793,779	€1,338,510	€965,813	€1,559,583

Losses on Loans and Advances

Loans and advances to customers may sometimes become uncollectible, and in those circumstances the bank would have to suffer losses on loans, advances, and other credit facilities. The amount of losses that are specifically identified and the potential losses not specifically identified should both be recognized as expenses and deducted from the carrying amount of the loans and advances. The assessment of these losses is dependent on management judgment and it is essential that it should be applied consistently from one period to another. Any amounts are set aside in excess of the foregoing provision for losses on loans and advances, if required by local circumstances or legislation, should be treated as an appropriation of retained earnings and are not to be included in the determination of net profit or loss for the period. Similarly, any credits resulting in the reduction of such amounts are to be credited to retained earnings.

Disclosures that were initially prescribed by IAS 30 are summarized below.

1. The accounting policy describing the basis on which uncollectible loans and advances are recognized as an expense and written off.
2. Details of movements in the provision for losses on loans and advances during the period: These details should include the amount recognized as an expense in the period on account of losses on loans and advances, the amount charged in the period for loans and advances written off, and the amount credited in the period resulting from the recovery of the amounts previously written off.
3. The aggregate amount of the provision for losses on loans and advances at the date of the statement of financial position.

Example of disclosure of loans and advances

	2008	2007
Balance, beginning of the year	€500,000	€400,000
Provision during the year—against specific advances	50,000	50,000
Written off during the year	(10,000)	(20,000)
Balance, end of the year	€540,000	€430,000

Illustrative Extracts from Published Financial Statements

UBS
December 31, 2007

Notes to the financial statements

Note 10a. Due from banks and loans (held at amortized cost)

By type of exposure

CHF million	*12/31/07*	*12/31/06*
Banks[1]	60,935	50,456
Allowance for credit losses	(28)	(30)
Net due from banks	60,907	50,426
Loans[1]		
Residential mortgages	122,435	124,548
Commercial mortgages	21,058	19,989
Other loans	193,374	154,531
Subtotal	336,867	299,068
Allowance for credit losses	(1,003)	(1,226)
Net loans	335,864	297,842
Net due from banks, loans (held at amortized cost)	396,771	348,268

[1]   *Includes Due from banks and loans from industrial holdings in the amount of CHF 27 million and CHF 93 million for 2007 and 2006, respectively.*

Additional information about due from banks, loans (held at amortized cost) and loans designated at fair value

CHF million	*12/31/07*	*12/31/06*
Net due from banks and loans (held at amortized cost)	396,771	348,268
Loans designated at fair value[2]	4,116	2,252
Total	400,887	350,520

[2]   *Equals the sum of Loans and Structured loans in Note 12.*

By geographical region (based on the location of the borrower)

CHF million	*12/31/07*	*12/31/06*
Switzerland	166,435	163,090
Rest of Europe/Middle East/Africa	79,322	67,584
Americas	128,318	102,768
Asia/Pacific	27,843	18,334
Subtotal	401,918	351,776
Allowance for credit losses	(1,031)	(1,256)
Net due from banks, loans (held at amortized cost) and loans designated at fair value	400,887	350,520

UBS
December 31, 2007

Notes to the financial statements

Note 9b. Allowances and provisions for credit losses

CHF million	Specific allowances and provisions	Collective loan loss allowances and provisions	Total 12/31/07	Total 12/31/06
Balance at the beginning of the year	1,294	38	1,332	1,776
Write-offs	(321)	0	(321)	(363)
Recoveries	55	0	55	62
Increase/(decrease) in credit loss allowance and provisions	242	(4)	238	(156)
Disposals	(131)	0	(131)	0
Foreign currency translation and other adjustments	(9)	0	(9)	13
Balance at the end of the year[1]	1,130	34	1,164	1,332[1]

[1] During 2006, all country provisions were released.

CHF million	Specific allowances and provisions	Collective loan loss allowances and provisions	Total 12/31/07	Total 12/31/06
As a reduction of due from banks	28	0	28	30
As a reduction of loans	969	34	1,003	1,226
As a reduction of other balance sheet positions	70	0	70	0
Subtotal	1,067	34	1,101	1,256
Included in other liabilities related to provisions for contingent claims	63	0	63	76
Total allowances and provisions for credit losses	1,130	34	1,164	1,332

UBS
December 31, 2007

Notes to the financial statements

Note 9c. Impaired due from banks and loans

CHF million	12/31/07	12/31/06
Total gross impaired due from banks and loans[1]	2,392	2,628
Allowance for impaired due from banks	28	30
Allowance for impaired loans	969	1,188
Total allowances for credit losses related to impaired due from banks and loans	997	1,218
Average total gross impaired due from bank and loans[2]	2,483	3,003

[1] All impaired due from banks and loans have a specific allowance for credit losses.

[2] Average balances are calculated from quarterly data.

CHF million	12/31/07	12/31/06
Total gross impaired due from banks and loans	2,392	2,628
Estimated liquidation proceeds of collateral	(1,104)	(1,059)
Net impaired due from banks and loans	1,288	1,569
Total allowances for credit losses related to impaired due from banks and loans	997	1,218

UBS
December 31, 2007

Notes to the financial statements

Note 9d. Nonperforming due from banks and loans

A loan (included in Due from banks or loans) is classified as nonperforming (1) when the payment of interest, principal, or fees is overdue by more than 90 days and there is no firm evidence that it will be made good by later payments or the liquidation of collateral; or (2) when insolvency proceedings have commenced; or (3) when obligations have been restructured on concessionary terms.

CHF million	12/31/07	12/31/06
Total gross nonperforming due from banks and loans	1,481	1,918
Total allowances for credit losses related to nonperforming due from banks and loans	873	1,112
Average total gross nonperforming due from banks and loans[1]	1,820	2,135

[1] *Average balances are calculated from quarterly data.*

CHF million	12/31/07	12/31/06
Nonperforming due from banks and loans at the beginning of the year	1,918	2,363
Net additions/(reductions)	(165)	(157)
Write-offs and disposals	(272)	(288)
Nonperforming due from banks and loans at the end of the year	1,481	1,918

By type of exposure

CHF million	12/31/07	12/31/06
Banks	26	29
Loans		
Secured by real estate	428	561
Other	1,027	1,328
Total loans	1,455	1,889
Total nonperforming due from banks and loans	1,481	1,918

By geographical region (based on the location of borrower)

CHF million	12/31/07	12/31/06
Switzerland	1,349	1,744
Rest of Europe/ Middle East/Africa	78	106
Americas	51	62
Asia/Pacific	3	6
Total nonperforming due from banks and loans	1,481	1,918

Related-Party Transactions

Parties are considered to be related if one has the ability to control the other or exercise significant influence over the other in making financial and operating decisions. IAS 24 requires that related-party transactions be disclosed. When a bank has entered into transactions with related parties, the nature of the relationship (e.g., director, shareholder, etc.), as well as information about the transactions and the outstanding balances should be disclosed. The disclosures to be made include the bank's lending policy to related parties and, in respect of related-party transactions, the amount included in or the proportion of

1. Each of loans and advances, deposits and acceptances, and promissory notes; disclosures may include the aggregate amounts outstanding at the beginning and end of the year as well as changes in these accounts during the year
2. Each of the principal types of income, interest expense, and commissions paid
3. The amount of the expense recognized in the period for the losses on loans and advances and the amount of the provision at the date of the statement of financial position

4.   Irrevocable commitments and contingencies and commitments from off-balance-sheet items

Example of related-party disclosures

Note 5. Related-party transactions

The bank has entered into transactions in the ordinary course of business with certain related parties, such as shareholders holding more than 20% equity interest in the bank and with certain directors of the bank.

At December 31, 2008 and 2007, the following balances were outstanding in the aggregate in relation to those related-party transactions:

	2008	*2007*
Loans and advances	€2,000,000	€1,800,000
Customer deposits	750,000	600,000
Guarantees	3,000,000	1,500,000

For the years ended December 31, 2008 and 2007, the following income and expense items are included in the aggregate amounts arising from the above-related transactions:

	2008	*2007*
Interest income	€300,000	€270,000
Interest expense	40,000	35,000
Commissions	60,000	30,000

Illustrative Extracts from Published Financial Statements

UBS
December 31, 2007

Notes to the financial statements

Note 31. Related parties

    a.   Remuneration of key management personnel
    b.   Equity holdings
    c.   Loans, advances and mortgages to key management personnel
    d.   Associated companies
    e.   Other related-party transactions
    f.   Additional information

The Group defines related parties as associated companies, postemployment benefit plans for the benefit of UBS employees, key management personnel, close family members of key management personnel, and enterprises which are, directly or indirectly, controlled by, jointly controlled by, or significantly influenced by, or in which significant voting power resides with key management personnel or their close family members. Key management personnel is defined as members of the Board of Directors (BoD) and Group Executive Board (GEB). This definition is based on the requirements of IAS 24, *Related-Party Disclosures.*

    a.   **Remuneration of key management personnel**
          The executive members of the BoD have top-management employment contracts and receive pension benefits upon retirement. Total remuneration of the executive members of the BoD and GEB including those who stepped down during 2007 is as follows:

	For the year ended		
CHF million	*12/31/07*	*12/31/06*	*12/31/05*
Base salaries and other cash payments	14	16	15
Incentive awards—cash	38	107	90
Employer's contributions to retirement benefit plans	2	1	1
Benefits in kind, fringe benefits (at market value)	2	2	3
Equity compensation benefits[1]	22	1,132	121[2]
Total	78	239	230

[1] *Expense for shares and options granted in measured at grant date and allocated over the vesting period, generally 3 years for options and 5 years for shares.*

[2] *In line with the "accrual principle" outlined by the SWX in September 2007, UBS has this year amended its reporting of both basic and matching stock option grants to align them with the performance year for which they were earned, rather than the year in which they were granted. This has resulted in a restatement of the 2005 and 2006 stock option, and 2005 and 2006 total compensation figures for members of the GEB and executive members of the Board of Directors.*

Peter Wuffli relinquished his position as Group CEO on July 6, 2007, Clive Standish retired on September 30, 2007, and Huw Jenkins stepped down from the GEB on September 30, 2007: all three executives are contractually entitled to receive base salary, pro rata incentive, and certain employment benefits until the expiry of their 12-month notice period. Huw Jenkins is retained in a consultancy position with UBS until September 30, 2008. The total amount due under all three contacts—CHF 15.3 million payable in 2008 and CHF 45.3 million payable in 2009—has been fully accrued in 2007 and reflected in the 2007 income statement. The nonexecutive members of the BoD do not have employment or service contracts with UBS, and thus are not entitled to benefits upon termination of their service on the BoD. Payments to these individuals for their services as external board members amounted to CHF 5.7 million in 2007, CHF 5.9 million in 2006, and CHF 6.1 million in 2005.

b. **Equity holdings**

	As at		
	12/31/07	*12/31/06*	*12/31/05*
Number of stock options from equity participation plans held by executive members of the BoD and the GEB[1]	6,828,152	10,886,798	10,862,250
Number of shares held by members of the BoD, GEB and parties closely linked to them	6,693,012	7,974,724	8,713,984

[1] *Further information about UNS's equity participation plans can be found in Note 30.*

Of the share totals above, at December 31, 2007, December 31, 2006, and December 31, 2005, 4,852 shares, and 7,146 shares, and 6,538 shares, respectively were held by close family members of key management personnel and 2,200,000 shares, and 2,200,000 shares, and 2,486,060 shares, respectively, were held by enterprises which are directly or indirectly controlled by, jointly controlled by or significantly influenced by or in which significant voting power resides with key management personnel or their close family members. Further information about UBS's equity participation plans can be found in Note 30. No member of the BoD or GEB is the beneficial owner of more than 1% of the Group's shares at December 31, 2007.

c. **Loans, advances, and mortgages to key management personnel**

Executive members of the BoD and GEB members have been granted loans, fixed advances and mortgages on the same terms and conditions that are available to other employees, based on terms and conditions granted to third parties adjusted for reduced credit risk. Nonexecutive BoD members are granted loans and mortgages at general market conditions.

Movements in the loan, advances, and mortgage balances are as follows:

CHF million	12/31/07	12/31/06
Balance at the beginning of the year	19	21
Additions	0	1
Reductions	(4)	(3)
Balance at the end of the year	15	19

No unsecured loans were granted to key management personnel as at December 31, 2007 and December 31, 2006.

d. **Associated companies**

Movements in loans to associated companies are as follows:

CHF million	12/31/07	12/31/06
Balance at the beginning of the year	375	321
Additions	60	116
Reductions	(215)	(48)
Credit loss (expense)/recovery	0	1
Foreign currency translation	0	(15)
Balance at the end of the year	220	375
Thereof unsecured loans	56	177
Thereof allowances for credit losses	4	5

All loans to associated companies are transacted at arm's length.

Other transactions with associated companies transacted at arm's length are as follows:

	For the year ended or as at		
CHF million	12/31/07	12/31/06	12/31/05
Payments to associates for goods and services received	87	58	397
Fees received for services provided to associates	20	79	258
Commitments and contingent liabilities to associates	33	32	0

Note 33 provides a list of significant associates.

e. **Other related-party transactions**

During 2007 and 2006, UBS entered into transactions at arm's length with enterprises which are directly or indirectly controlled by, jointly controlled by or significantly influenced by or in which significant voting power resides with key management personnel or their close family members. In 2007 and 2006, these companies included Aebi and Co. AG (Switzerland), Bertarelli Family (Switzerland), BMW Group (Germany), DKSH Holding AG (Switzerland), Kedge Capital Funds Ltd. (Jersey), Kedge Capital Selected Funds Ltd. (Jersey), Lista AG (Switzerland), Löwenfeld AG (Switzerland), Martown Trading Ltd. (Isle of Man), Royal Dutch Shell plc (UK), Seromer Biotech SA (Switzerland, previously Bertarelli Biotech SA), Serono Group (Switzerland), Stadler Rail Group (Switzerland), Team Alinghi (Switzerland), Team Alinghi (Spain), and Unisys Corporation (USA). Related parties in 2007 also included Bertarelli Investment Ltd. (Jersey), Flat Group (Italy), Levy Kaufmann-Kohler (Switzerland), Limonares Ltd. (Jersey), Omega Fund I Ltd. (Jersey), Omega Fund II Ltd. (Jersey), Omega Fund III Ltd. (Jersey), Omega Fund IV Ltd. (Jersey), SGS Societe Fenerale de Survelliance SA (Switzerland) and Walo Group (Switzerland).

Movements in loans to other related parties are as follows:

CHF million	12/31/07	12/31/06
Balance at the beginning of the year	872	919
Additions	301	34
Reductions	485	81
Balance at the end of the year[1]	688	872

[1] *In 2007, includes loans, guarantees and contingent liabilities of CHF 270 million and unused committed facilities of CHF 418 million but excludes unused uncommitted working capital facilities and unused guarantees of CHF 205 million. In 2006, includes loans, guarantees, and contingent liabilities of CHF 128 million and unused committed facilities of CHF 744 million but excludes unused uncommitted working capital facilities and unused guarantees of CHF 173 million.*

Other transactions with these related parties include

CHF million	For the year ended		
	12/31/07	*12/31/06*	*12/31/05*
Goods sold and services provided to UBS	8	8	15
Fees received for services provided by UBS	16	8	1

As part of its sponsorship of Team Alinghi, defender for the "America's Cup 2007," UBS paid CHF 8.9 million (EUR 5.4 million) as a sponsoring fee for 2007. Team Alinghi's controlling shareholder is UBS board member Ernesto Bertarelli.

f. **Additional information**

UBS also engages in trading and risk management activities (e.g., swaps, options, forwards) with various related parties mentioned in previous sections. These transactions may give rise to credit risk either for UBS or for a related party towards UBS. As part of its normal course of business, UBS is also a market maker in equity and debt instruments and at times may hold positions in instruments of related parties.

Disclosure of General Banking Risks

Based on local legislation or circumstances, a bank may need to set aside a certain amount each year for general banking risks, including future losses or other unforeseeable risks, in addition to the provision for losses on loans and advances explained earlier. The bank may also be required to earmark a certain amount each year as a contingency reserve, over and above the amounts accrued under IAS 10. All such amounts set aside should be treated as appropriations of retained earnings, and any credits resulting from the reduction of such amounts should be returned directly to retained earnings and not included in determination of net income or loss for the year.

Disclosure of Assets Pledged as Security

If the bank is required by law or national custom to pledge assets as security to support certain deposits or other liabilities, the bank should then disclose the aggregate amount of secured liabilities and the nature and carrying amount of the assets pledged as security.

Illustrative Extracts from Published Financial Statements

UBS
December 31, 2007

Notes to the financial statements

Note 27. Pledged assets and transferred financial assets which do not qualify for derecognition

Financial assets are pledged in securities borrowing and lending transactions, in repurchase and reverse repurchase transactions, under collateralized credit lines with central banks, against loans from mortgage institutions and for security deposits relating to stock exchange and clearinghouse memberships.

Pledged assets

CHF million	Carrying amount *12/31/07*	Related liability *12/31/06*
Financial assets pledged:		
Financial assets pledged to third parties for liabilities with and without the right of rehypothecation	232,948	366,866
Thereof: Financial assets pledged to third parties with right of rehypothecation	164,311	251,478
Mortgage loans	200	81
Total financial assets pledged	233,148	366,947
Other assets pledged		
Precious metals and other commodities	8,628	5,432

The following table presents details of financial assets which have been sold or otherwise transferred, but which do not qualify for derecognition. Criteria for derecognition are discussed in (Note 1a4).

Transfer of financial assets which do not qualify for derecognition

CHF million	*Continued asset recognition in full——Total assets*	
	12/31/07	*12/31/06*
Nature of transaction		
Securities lending agreements	87.7	98.9
Repurchase agreements	73.5	146.5
Other financial asset transfers	75.9	69.8
Total	237.1	315.2

The transactions are mostly conducted under standard agreements employed by financial market participants and are undertaken with counterparties subject to UBS's normal credit risk control processes. The resulting credit exposures are controlled by daily monitoring and collateralization of the positions. The financial assets which continue to be recognized are typically transferred in exchange for cash or other financial assets. The associated liabilities can therefore be assumed to be approximately the carrying amount of the transferred financial assets.

UBS retains substantially all risks and rewards of the transferred assets in each situation of continued recognition in full. These include credit risk, settlement risk, country risk, and market risk.

Repurchase agreements and securities lending agreements are discussed in Notes 1a12 and 1a13. Other financial asset transfers include sales of financial assets while concurrently entering into a total rate of return swap with the same counterparty and sales of financial assets involving guarantees.

Transferred financial assets which are subject to partial continued recognition were immaterial in 2007 and 2006. The carrying amounts of the partially recognized transferred financial assets are included in the table.

Disclosure of Trust Activities

If a bank is holding in trust, or in any other fiduciary capacity, assets belonging to others, those assets should not be included on the bank's financial statements since they are being held on behalf of third parties such as trusts and retirement funds. If a bank is engaged in significant trust activities, this deserves disclosure of the fact and an indication of the extent of those trust activities. Such disclosure will take care of any potential liability in case the bank fails in its fiduciary capacity. The safe custody services that banks offer are not part of these trust activities.

Illustrative Extracts from Published Financial Statements

UBS
December 31, 2007

Notes to the financial statements

Off-balance-sheet and other information

Fiduciary transactions

CHF million	*12/31/07*	*12/31/06*
Deposits:		
With other banks	46,074	41,075
With Group Banks	2,186	1,650
Total	48,260	42,725

Unified Financial Instruments Disclosure Requirements: IFRS 7

When IAS 30 was promulgated, many of the now-extant standards (most importantly, those addressing accounting for financial instruments, IAS 32 and IAS 39) had yet to be issued, and banking, as an important highly regulated industry with worldwide impact, was perhaps uniquely in need of standardized financial reporting guidance. However, by the late 1990s, many began to note that IAS 30 was in need of an overhaul, since there were growing instances of redundancies with other later standards, and in some particulars, a need for new or expanded coverage. Also, fundamental changes had been taking place in the financial services industries, and in the way in which financial institutions were managing their activities and their risk exposures.

The IASC added a project to its agenda to revise IAS 30 in 1999, and in 2000 appointed a steering committee for that purpose, including representatives of financial institutions, auditors, and bank and securities regulators. IASB, after its creation, endorsed that undertaking and continued to use that steering committee, which has been expanded to include analysts and nonfinancial institutions, as an advisory group. It subsequently became clear that the project should also consider disclosure and presentation issues that arise for all types of entities that engage in deposit taking, lending, or securities activities, whether or not regulated and supervised as banks. This was because, since IAS 30 was first released, there had been widespread dismantling of regulatory barriers in many countries, and increasing competition between banks and nonbank financial services firms and conglomerates in providing the same types of financial services. This, in turn, made it inappropriate to limit the scope of this project to banks and similar financial institutions.

At the inception of this project it was expected that three types of changes to the existing requirements of IAS 30 would be considered. The first would be to eliminate apparent redundancies between IAS 30 and other, mostly subsequent, standards. For example, the guidance in IAS 30 on the offsetting of assets and liabilities was duplicative of that subsequently incorporated into IAS 1 and IAS 32. The disclosures about fair values were later addressed globally by IAS 32, as were matters pertaining to the disclosure of maturities of assets and liabilities. Related-parties disclosures are set forth by IAS 24, and information regarding concentrations of credit risk is required by IAS 32. Finally, the guidance on loan loss recognition in IAS 30 may have been made superfluous due to later issuance of IAS 39.

A second category of revisions were to be made in order to bring the existing requirement under IAS 30 up to date. According to IASB, financial services industry representatives had been positive about the guidance in IAS 30 relative to statement of financial position and statement of comprehensive income presentation, but believed that further guidance would eliminate remaining differences across countries in reporting formats which result in costs for financial institutions operating in several jurisdictions and difficulties for users in comparing financial statements across countries. Thus, some saw the need for further detailed guidance, which could reduce or eliminate remaining variations.

Finally, a third category of changes to IAS 30 were to be undertaken to enhance the quality of disclosures. Two key areas cited were

1. Disclosures supplementing the statement of financial position and statement of comprehensive income, and
2. Risk exposure information

The IASB decided that it was impracticable to incorporate the above proposals into IAS 32 for completion in time for the important 2005 transition to IFRS by EU member state publicly held companies, and instead opted to develop a separate Exposure Draft that would replace the financial disclosure requirements in both IAS 32 and IAS 30. This effort was brought to fruition with the promulgation of IFRS 7, which became mandatorily effective in 2007. Earlier application has been encouraged.

IFRS 7 Requirements in Detail

IFRS 7 superseded the disclosure requirements formerly found in IAS 32 and replaces IAS 30 in its entirety. IFRS 7 is covered in detail in Chapter 5. In October 2008, the IASB published amendments to IAS 39 and IFRS 7 to allow reclassification of certain financial instruments from held for trading to either held maturity, loans, and receivables, or available-for-sale categories under certain circumstances. The amendments are discussed in Chapter 10.

APPENDIX A

EXAMPLE BANK SIGNIFICANT ACCOUNTING POLICIES

UBS
December 31, 2007

Notes to the financial statements

Note 1. Summary of significant accounting policies

1. **Basis of accounting**

    UBS AG and subsidiaries ("UBS" or the "Group") provide a broad range of financial services including advisory services, underwriting, financing, market making, asset management and brokerage on a global level, and retail banking in Switzerland. The Group was formed on June 29, 1998, when Swiss Bank Corporation and Union Bank of Switzerland merged. The merger was accounted for using the uniting of interests method of accounting.

    The consolidated financial statements of UBS (the "financial statements") are prepared in accordance with International Financial Reporting Standards (IFRS), issued by the International Accounting Standards Board (IASB), and stated in Swiss francs (CHF), the currency of the country in which UBS AG is incorporated. On March 8, 2007, the Board of Directors approved them for issue.

2. **Use of estimates in the preparation of financial statements**

    In preparing the financial statements, management is required to make estimates and assumptions that affect reported income, expenses, assets, liabilities, and disclosure of contingent assets and liabilities. Use of available information and application of judgment are inherent in the formation of estimates. Actual results in the future could differ from such estimates, and the differences may be material to the financial statements.

3. **Subsidiaries and associates**

    The Financial Statements comprise those of the parent company (UBS AG) and its subsidiaries including certain special-purpose entities, presented as a single economic entity. The effects of intragroup transactions are eliminated in preparing the financial statements. Subsidiaries including special-purpose entities that are directly or indirectly controlled by the Group are consolidated. UBS controls an entity if it has the power to govern the financial and operating policies so as to obtain benefits from the entity's activities. Subsidiaries acquired are consolidated from the date control is transferred to the Group. Subsidiaries to be divested are consolidated up to the date of disposal (i.e., loss of control).

    Equity attributable to minority interests is presented in the consolidated balance sheet within equity, separately from equity attributable to UBS shareholders. Net income attributable to minority interest is shown separately in the income statement.

    The Group sponsors the formation of entities, which may or may not be directly or indirectly owned subsidiaries, for the purpose of asset securitization transactions and structured debt issuance, and to accomplish certain narrow and well-defined objectives. These companies may acquire assets directly or indirectly from UBS or its affiliates. Some of these companies are bankruptcy-remote entities whose assets are not available to satisfy the claims of creditors of the Group or any of its subsidiaries. Such companies are consolidated in the Group's financial statements when the substance of the relationship between the Group and the company indicates that the company is controlled by the Group.

    Investments in associates in which UBS has a significant influence are accounted for under the equity method of accounting. Significant influence is normally evidenced when UBS owns 20% or more of a company's voting rights. Investments in associates are initially recorded at cost, and the carrying amount is increased or decreased to recognize the Group's share of the investee's net profit or loss (including net profit or loss recognized directly in equity) after the date of acquisition.

Interests in jointly controlled entities, in which UBS and one or more third parties have joint control, are accounted for under the equity method. A jointly controlled entity is subject to a contractual agreement between UBS and one or more third parties, which establishes joint control over its economic activities. Interests in such entities are reflected under investments in associates on the balance sheet and the related disclosures are included in the disclosures for associates. UBS holds certain interests in jointly controlled real estate entities.

Assets and liabilities of subsidiaries and investments in associates are classified as "held for sale" if UBS has entered into an agreement for their disposal within a period of 12 months. Major lines of business and subsidiaries that were acquired exclusively with the intent for resale are presented as discontinued operations in the income statement in the period where the sale occurred or it becomes clear that a sale will occur within 12 months. Discontinued operations are presented in the income statement as profit from discontinued operations before tax, comprising the total of profit or loss before tax from operations and net gain or loss on sale before tax, as well as discontinued operations tax expense.

4. **Recognition and derecognition of financial instruments**

UBS recognizes financial instruments on its balance sheet when, and only when, the Group becomes a party to the contractual provisions of the instrument. UBS enters into transactions where it transfers financial assets recognized on its balance sheet but retains either all risks and rewards of the transferred financial assets or a portion of them. If all or substantially all risks and rewards are retained, the transferred financial assets are not derecognized from the balance sheet. Transfers of financial assets with retention of all or substantially all risks and rewards include, for example, securities lending and repurchase transactions described in this Note under parts 12. and 13. They further include transactions where financial assets are sold to a third party with a concurrent total rate of return swap on the transferred assets to retain all their risks and rewards. These types of transactions are accounted for as secured financing transactions.

In transactions where substantially all of the risks and rewards of ownership of a financial asset are neither retained nor transferred, UBS derecognizes the financial asset if control over the asset is lost. The rights and obligations retained in the transfer are recognized separately as assets and liabilities as appropriate. In transfers where control over the financial asset is retained, the Group continues to recognize the asset to the extent of its continuing involvement, determined by the extent to which it is exposed to changes in the value of the transferred asset. Examples of such transactions are transfers of financial assets involving guarantees, writing put options, acquiring call options, or specific types of swaps linked to the performance of the asset.

UBS removes a financial liability from its balance sheet when, and only when, it is extinguished (i.e., when the obligation specified in the contract is discharged or cancelled or expires).

Assets held in an agency or fiduciary capacity are not assets of the Group and are not reported in the financial statements, provided the recognition criteria of IFRS are not satisfied.

5. **Determination of fair value**

For an overview of financial assets and financial liabilities accounted for at fair value, refer to the IAS 39 measurement categories presented in Note 28: financial assets and financial liabilities held for trading, financial assets and financial liabilities designated at fair value through profit or loss, and financial investments available-for-sale. For details on the determination of fair value, including those on fair value measurements for instruments linked to the US residential mortgage market, refer to Note 26.

For financial instruments traded in active markets, the determination of fair values of financial assets and financial liabilities is based on quoted market prices or dealer price quotations. For all other financial instruments, fair value is determined using valuation techniques. Valuation techniques include net present value techniques, the discounted cash flow method, comparison to similar instruments for which market observable prices exist and valuation models. UBS uses widely recognized valuation models for determining fair values of common and more simple financial instruments like options or interest rate and currency swaps. For these financial instruments, inputs into models are market observable.

For more complex instruments, UBS uses internally developed models, which are usually based on valuation methods and techniques generally recognized as standard within the industry. Some of the inputs to these models may not be market-observable and are therefore estimated based on assumptions. The impact on Net profit of financial instrument valuations reflecting nonmarket observable inputs is disclosed in Note 26d. When entering into a transaction where model inputs are unobservable, the financial instrument is initially recognized at the transaction price, which is generally the best indicator of fair value. This may differ from the value obtained from the valuation model. The timing of the recognition in income of this initial difference in fair value ("Deferred day 1 profit or loss") depends on the individual facts and circumstances of each transaction but is never later than when the market data becomes observable. Refer to Note 26e, for details on deferred day 1 profit or loss.

The output of a model is always an estimate or approximation of a value that cannot be determined with certainty, and valuation techniques employed may not fully reflect all factors relevant to the positions UBS holds. Valuations are therefore adjusted, where appropriate, to allow for additional factors including model risks, liquidity risk, and counterparty credit risk. Based on the established fair value and model governance policies and related controls and procedures applied, management believes that these valuation adjustments are necessary and appropriate to fairly state financial instruments carried at fair value on the balance sheet.

A breakdown of fair values of financial instruments measured on the basis of quoted market prices in active markets (level 1), valuation techniques reflecting market observable inputs (level 2), and valuation techniques reflecting significant nonmarket observable inputs (level 3) is provided in Note 26b.

6. **Trading portfolio assets and liabilities**

Trading portfolio assets consist of money market paper, other debt instruments, including traded loans, equity instruments, precious metals, and other commodities owned by the Group ("long" positions). Trading portfolio liabilities consist of obligations to deliver financial instruments such as money market paper, other debt instruments and equity instruments which the Group has sold to third parties but does not own ("short" positions).

The trading portfolio is carried at fair value. Gains and losses realized on disposal or redemption and unrealized gains and losses from changes in the fair value of trading portfolio assets and liabilities are reported as net trading income. Interest and dividend income and expense on trading portfolio assets or liabilities are included in interest and dividend income or interest and dividend expense.

The Group uses settlement date accounting when recording trading financial asset transactions. From the date the transaction is entered into (trade date), UBS recognizes any unrealized profits and losses arising from revaluing that contract to fair value in net trading income. The corresponding receivable or payable is presented on the balance sheet as a positive or negative replacement value. When the transaction is consummated (settlement date), a resulting financial asset is recognized on or derecognized from the balance sheet at the fair value of the consideration given or received plus or minus the change in fair value of the contract since the trade date. When the Group becomes party to a sales contract of a financial asset classified in its trading portfolio, it derecognizes the asset on the day of its transfer (settlement date).

Trading portfolio assets transferred to external parties that do not qualify for derecognition (see part 4) are reclassified on UBS's balance sheet from trading portfolio assets to trading portfolio assets pledged as collateral, if the transferee has received the right to sell or repledge them.

7. **Financial assets and financial liabilities designated at fair value through profit or loss ("Fair Value Option")**

    A financial instrument may only be designated at fair value through profit or loss at inception and this designation cannot subsequently be changed. Financial assets and financial liabilities designated at fair value are presented in separate lines on the face of the balance sheet.

    The conditions for applying the fair value option are met on the basis that

    a. They are hybrid instruments which consist of a debt host and an embedded derivative component, or
    b. They are items that are part of a portfolio which is risk managed on a fair value basis and reported to senior management on that basis, or
    c. The application of the fair value option reduces or eliminates an accounting mismatch that would otherwise arise.

    Hybrid instruments which fall under criterion (a) above include

    (1) Bonds and compound debt liabilities issued,
    (2) Compound debt liabilities–OTC, and
    (3) Hybrid financial assets from reverse repurchase agreements. Bonds and compound debt liabilities issued and OTC generally include embedded derivative components which refer to an underlying (e.g., equity price, interest rate, commodities price or index). UBS has designated almost all of its issued hybrid debt instruments as financial liabilities designated at fair value through profit or loss.

    Besides hybrid instruments, the fair value option is also applied to certain loans and loan commitments which are substantially hedged with credit derivatives. The application of the fair value option to these instruments reduces an accounting mismatch, as loans would have been otherwise accounted for at amortized cost or as financial investments available-for-sale (refer to part 8), whereas the hedging credit protection is accounted for as a derivative instrument at fair value through profit or loss. Loan commitments other than onerous loan commitments are only recognized on balance sheet if the fair value option has been applied.

    UBS has also applied the fair value option to a hedge fund investment which is part of a portfolio managed on a fair value basis. Fair value changes related to financial instruments designated at fair value through profit or loss are recognized in net trading income.

    Interest and dividend income and interest expense on financial assets and liabilities designated at fair value through profit or loss are included in interest income or interest expense. UBS applies the same recognition and derecognition principles to financial instruments designated at fair value as for financial instruments held for trading (refer to part 4. and 6.).

8. **Financial investments available-for-sale**

    Financial investments available-for-sale are nonderivative financial assets that are not classified as held for trading, designated at fair value through profit or loss, or loans and receivables. They are recognized on a settlement date basis. Financial investments available-for-sale are instruments that, in management's opinion, may be sold in response to or in anticipation of needs for liquidity or changes in interest rates, foreign exchange rates or equity prices. Financial investments available-for-sale consist mainly of equity instruments, including certain private equity investments. In addition, certain debt instruments are classified as financial investments available-for-sale.

    Financial investments available-for-sale are carried at fair value. Lock-in periods for equity investments are considered when determining fair value. Unrealized gains or losses are reported in equity, net of applicable income taxes, until such investments are sold, collected or otherwise disposed of, or until any such investment is determined to be impaired. On disposal of an investment, the accumulated unrealized gain or loss included in equity is transferred to net profit and loss for the period and reported in other income. Gains and losses on disposal are determined using the average cost method.

Interest and dividend income on financial investments available-for-sale are included in interest and dividend income from financial investments available-for-sale.

If a financial investment available-for-sale is determined to be impaired, the cumulative unrealized loss previously recognized in equity is included in net profit for the period and reported in other income. UBS assesses at each balance sheet date whether there is objective evidence that a financial investment available-for-sale is impaired. In case of such evidence, it is considered impaired if its cost exceeds the recoverable amount. For a quoted financial investment available-for-sale, the recoverable amount is determined by reference to the market price. It is considered impaired if objective evidence indicates that the decline in market price has reached such a level that recovery of the cost value cannot be reasonably expected within the foreseeable future. For nonquoted financial instruments (debt and equity instruments), the recoverable amount is determined by applying recognized valuation techniques. The standard method applied for nonquoted equity investments available-for-sale is based on the multiple of earnings observed in the market for comparable companies. Management may adjust valuations determined in this way based on its judgment. For nonquoted debt instruments, UBS typically determines the recoverable amount by applying the discounted cash flow method.

After the recognition of impairment on a financial investment available-for-sale, (a) increases in fair value of equity instruments are reported in equity and (b) increases in fair value of debt instruments up to original cost are recognized in other income, provided the fair value increase has been triggered by a specific event (as defined by IFRS).

9. **Loans and receivables**

For an overview of financial assets and financial liabilities accounted for as loans and receivables, refer to the IAS 39 measurement categories presented in Note 28.

Loans include loans originated by the Group where money is provided directly to the borrower, participation in a loan from another lender, and purchased loans that are not quoted in an active market and for which no intention of immediate or short-term resale exists. Originated and purchased loans that are intended to be sold in the short term are generally recorded as trading portfolio assets. Certain purchased nonperforming loans are recognized as financial investments available-for-sale.

Loans are recognized when cash is advanced to borrowers. They are initially recorded at fair value, which is the cash given to originate the loan, plus any transaction costs, and are subsequently measured at amortized cost using the effective interest rate method.

Interest on loans is included in interest earned on loans and advances and is recognized on an accrual basis. Fees and direct costs relating to loan origination, refinancing or restructuring, and to loan commitments are deferred and amortized to interest earned on loans and advances over the life of the loan using the straight-line method which approximates the effective interest rate method. Fees received for commitments that are not expected to result in a loan are included in credit-related fees and commissions over the commitment period. Loan syndication fees where UBS does not retain a portion of the syndicated loan are credited to commission income.

Commitments. Letters of credit, guarantees and similar instruments commit UBS to make payments on behalf of third parties under specific circumstances. These instruments, as well as undrawn irrevocable credit facilities, carry credit risk and are included in the exposure to credit risk table, in the audited "Credit risk" section of *Risk, Treasury and Capital Management 2007,* with their gross maximum exposure to credit risk.

10. **Allowance and provision for credit losses**

An allowance or provision for credit losses is established if there is objective evidence that the Group will be unable to collect all amounts due on a claim according to the original contractual terms or the equivalent value. A "claim" means a loan carried at amortized cost, a commitment such as a letter of credit, a guarantee, a commitment to extend credit, or other credit products.

An allowance for credit losses is reported as a reduction of the carrying value of a claim on the balance sheet. For an off-balance-sheet item such as a commitment, a provision for credit loss is reported in other liabilities. Additions to allowances and provisions for credit losses are made through credit loss expense.

Allowances and provisions for credit losses are evaluated at a counterparty-specific level and collectively based on the following principles:

Counterparty-specific: A claim is considered impaired when management determines that it is probable that the Group will not be able to collect all amounts due according to the original contractual terms or the equivalent value. Individual credit exposures are evaluated based upon the borrower's character, overall financial condition, resources, and payment record; the prospects for support from any financially responsible guarantors; and, where applicable, the realizable value of any collateral.

The estimated recoverable amount is the present value, using the loan's original effective interest rate, of expected future cash flows, including amounts that may result from restructuring or the liquidation of collateral. Impairment is measured and allowances for credit losses are established for the difference between the carrying amount and the estimated recoverable amount.

Upon impairment, the accrual of interest income based on the original terms of the claim is discontinued, but the increase of the present value of impaired claims due to the passage of time is reported as interest income. All impaired claims are reviewed and analyzed at least annually. Any subsequent changes to the amounts and timing of the expected future cash flows compared with the prior estimates result in a change in the allowance for credit losses and are charged or credited to credit loss expense. An allowance for impairment is reversed only when the credit quality has improved to such an extent that there is reasonable assurance of timely collection of principal and interest in accordance with the original contractual terms of the claim or equivalent value.

A write-off is made when all or part of a claim is deemed uncollectible or forgiven. Write-offs are charged against previously established allowances for credit losses or directly to credit loss expense and reduce the principle amount of a claim. Recoveries in part or in full of amounts previously written off are credited to credit loss expense.

A loan is classified as nonperforming when the payment of interest, principal or fees is overdue by more than 90 days and there is no firm evidence that it will be made good by later payments or the liquidation of collateral, or when insolvency proceedings have commenced, or when obligations have been restructured on concessionary terms.

Collectively: All loans for which no impairment is identified on a counterparty-specific level are grouped into subportfolios with similar credit risk characteristics to collectively assess whether impairment exists within a portfolio. Allowances from collective assessment of impairment are recognized as credit loss expense and result in an offset to the aggregated loan position. As the allowance cannot be allocated to individual loans, the loans are not considered to be impaired and interest is accrued on each loan according to contractual terms.

11. **Securitizations**

UBS securitizes financial assets, which generally results in the sale of these assets to special-purpose entities, which in turn issue securities to investors. UBS applies the policies set out in part 4 in determining whether the respective special purpose entity must be consolidated, and those set out in part 3 in determining whether derecognition of transferred financial assets is appropriate. The following statements mainly apply to financial asset transfers which are considered true sales to nonconsolidated entities.

Interests in the securitized financial assets may be retained in the form of senior or subordinated tranches, interest-only strips, or other residual interests ("retained interests"). Retained interests are primarily recorded in trading portfolio assets and carried at fair value. Gains or losses on securitization are recorded in net trading income, which is generally when the derecognition criteria are satisfied.

Typically, the Group seeks to exit its risk in retained interests shortly after close of the securitization. The Group is also an active market maker in these securities and may therefore subsequently reacquire interests in the assets it securitizes. Financial assets purchased with the intention of securitizing them in the future, often referred to as warehousing assets or loans, are generally reflected in trading portfolio assets, with changes in fair value recognized in net trading income. Synthetic securitization structures typically involve derivative financial instruments for which the principles set out in part 14 apply. Purchased asset-backed securities (MBS), originated by third parties are recognized as financial assets held-for-trading, or in a minority of cases, as financial investments available-for-sale.

UBS securitizes residential and commercial mortgage and other assets, acting as lead or co-manager. In addition, UBS acts as warehouse agent, structurer and placement agent in various collateralized debt obligation (CDO) and collateralized loan obligation (CLO), MBS and other ABS securitizations. In such capacity, UBS may purchase collateral on its own behalf or on behalf of customers during the period prior to securitization. UBS typically sells the collateral into designated trusts at the close of the securitization and underwrites the offerings to investors. UBS earns fees for its placement and structuring services. For residential mortgage loan and other securitizations, the investors and the securitization vehicle generally have no recourse to UBS's other assets for failure of loan holders to pay when due.

Consistent with the valuation of similar inventory, fair value of retained tranches or warehousing assets is initially and subsequently determined using market price quotations where available or internal pricing models that utilize variables such as yield curves, prepayment speeds, default rates, loss severity, interest rate volatilities and spreads. The assumptions used for pricing are based on observable transactions in similar securities and are verified by external pricing sources, where available.

12. **Securities borrowing and lending**

Securities borrowing and securities lending transactions are generally entered into on a collateralized basis. In such transactions, USB typically lends or borrows securities in exchange for securities or cash collateral. Additionally, UBS borrows securities from its clients' custody accounts in exchange for a fee. The majority of securities lending and borrowing agreements involve shares, and the remainder typically involve bonds and notes. The transactions are conducted under standard agreements employed by financial market participants and are undertaken with counterparties subject to UBS's normal credit risk control processes. UBS monitors the market value of the securities received or delivered on a daily basis and requests or provides additional collateral or returns or recalls surplus collateral in accordance with the underlying agreements.

The securities which have been transferred, whether in a borrowing/lending transaction or as collateral, are not recognized on or derecognized from the balance sheet unless the risks and rewards of ownership are also transferred. In such transactions where UBS transfers owned securities and where the borrower is granted the right to sell or re-pledge them, the securities are reclassified on the balance sheet from Trading portfolio to Trading portfolio assets pledged as collateral. Cash collateral received is recognized with a corresponding obligation to return it (cash collateral on securities lent). Cash collateral delivered is derecognized with a corresponding receivable reflecting UBS's right to receive it back (Cash collateral on securities borrowed). Securities received in a lending or borrowing transaction are disclosed as off-balance-sheet items if UBS has the right to resell or re-pledge them, with securities that UBS has actually resold or repledged also disclosed separately (see Note 24). Additionally, the sale of securities received in a borrowing or lending transaction triggers the recognition of a trading liability (short sale).

Consideration exchanged (i.e., interest received or paid) is recognized on an accrual basis and recorded as interest income or interest expense.

13. **Repurchase and reverse repurchase transactions**

Securities purchased under agreements to resell (reverse repurchase agreements) and securities sold under agreements to repurchase (repurchase agreements) are generally treated as collateralized financing transactions. Nearly all repurchase and reverse repurchase agreements involve debt instruments, such as bonds, notes or money market paper. The transactions are conducted under standard agreements employed by financial market participants and are undertaken with counterparties subject to UBS's normal credit risk control processes. UBS monitors the market value of the securities received or delivered on a daily basis and requests or provides additional collateral or returns or recalls surplus collateral in accordance with the underlying agreements. In reverse repurchase agreements, the cash delivered is derecognized and a corresponding receivable, including accrued interest, is recorded under the balance sheet line reverse repurchase agreements, recognizing UBS's right to receive it back. In repurchase agreements, the cash received, including accrued interest, is recognized on the balance sheet with a corresponding obligation to return it (repurchase agreements). Securities received under reverse repurchase agreements and securities delivered under repurchase agreements are not recognized on or derecognized from the balance sheet, unless the risks and rewards of ownership are obtained or relinquished. In repurchase agreements where UBS transfers owned securities and where the recipient is granted the right to resell or repledge them, the securities are reclassified in the balance sheet from trading portfolio assets to trading portfolio assets pledged as collateral. Securities received in a reverse repurchase agreement are disclosed as off-balance-sheet items if UBS has the right to resell or repledge them, with securities that UBS has actually resold or repledged also disclosed separately (see Note 24). Additionally, the sale of securities received in reverse repurchase transactions triggers the recognition of a trading liability (short sale).

Interest earned on reverse repurchase agreements and interest incurred on repurchase agreements is recognized as interest income or interest expense over the life of each agreement. The Group offsets reverse repurchase agreements and repurchase agreements with the same counterparty, maturity, currency and Central Securities Depository (CSD) for transactions covered by legally enforceable master netting agreements when net or simultaneous settlement is intended.

14. **Derivative instruments and hedge accounting**

All derivative instruments are carried at fair value on the balance sheet and are reported as positive replacement values or negative replacement values. Where the Group enters into derivatives for trading purposes, realized and unrealized gains and losses are recognized in net trading income.

Credit losses incurred on over-the-counter (OTC) derivatives are also reported in net trading income.

Hedge accounting. The Group also uses derivative instruments as part of its asset and liability management activities to manage exposures to interest rate, foreign currency, and credit risks, including exposures arising from forecast transactions. The Group applies either fair value or cash flow hedge accounting when transactions meet the specified criteria to obtain hedge accounting treatment.

At the time a financial instrument is designated as a hedge, the Group formally documents the relationship between the hedging instruments(s) and hedged item(s) including the risk management objectives and strategy in undertaking the hedge transaction, together with the methods that will be used to assess the effectiveness of the hedging relationship. Accordingly, the Group assesses, both at the inception of the hedge and on an ongoing basis, whether the hedging derivatives have been "highly effective" in offsetting changes in the fair value or cash flows of the hedged items. UBS regards a hedge as highly effective only if the following criteria are met: (1) at inception of the hedge and throughout its life, the hedge is expected to be 93% highly effective in achieving offsetting changes in fair value or cash flows attributable to the hedged risk and (2) actual results of the hedge are within a range of 80% to 125%. In the case of hedging a forecast transaction, the transaction must have a high probability of occurring and must present an exposure to variations in cash flows that could ultimately affect the reported net profit or loss. The Group discontinues hedge accounting when it determines that a derivative is not, or has ceased to be, highly effective as a hedge; when the derivative expires, or is sold, terminated, or exercised; when the hedged item matures, is sold or repaid; or when a forecast transaction is no longer deemed highly probable.

Hedge ineffectiveness represents the amount by which the changes in the fair value of the hedging derivative differ from changes in the fair value of the hedged item or the amount by which changes in the present value of cash flows of the hedging derivative differ from changes (or expected changes) in the present value cash flow of the hedged item. Such ineffectiveness is recorded in current period earnings in net trading income, as are gains and losses on components of a hedging derivative that are excluded from assessing hedge effectiveness.

Fair value hedges. For qualifying fair value hedges, the change in fair value of the hedging derivative is recognized in the income statement.

Those changes in fair value of the hedged item that are attributable to the risks hedged with the derivative instrument are reflected in an adjustment to the carrying value of the hedged item, which is also recognized in the income statement. The fair value change of the hedged item in a portfolio hedge of interest rate risks is reported separately from the hedged portfolio in other assets or other liabilities as appropriate. If the hedge relationship is terminated for reasons other than the derecognition of the hedged item, the difference between the carrying value of the hedged item at that point and the value at which it would have been carried had the hedge never existed (the "unamortized fair value adjustment"), is, in the case of interest-bearing instruments, amortized to the income statement over the remaining term of the original hedge, while for noninterest bearing instruments that amount is immediately recognized in earnings. If the hedged instrument is derecognized, (e.g., due to sale or repayment), the unamortized fair value adjustment is recognized immediately in the income statement.

Cash flow hedges. A fair value gain or loss associated with the effective portion of a derivative designated as a cash flow hedge is recognized initially in equity. When the cash flows that the derivative is hedging materialize, resulting in income or expense, then the associated gain or loss on the hedging derivative is simultaneously transferred from equity to the corresponding income or expense line item.

If a cash flow hedge for a forecast transaction is deemed to be no longer effective, or if the hedge relationship is terminated, the cumulative gain or loss on the hedging derivative previously reported in equity remains there until the committed or forecast transaction occurs or is no longer expected to occur, at which point it is transferred to the income statement.

Economic hedges which do not qualify for hedge accounting. Derivative instruments which are transacted as economic hedges but do not qualify for hedge accounting are treated in the same way as derivative instruments used for trading purposes, (i.e., realized and unrealized gains and losses are recognized in net trading income), except that, in certain cases, the forward points on short-duration foreign exchange contracts are presented in net interest income. In particular, the Group has entered into economic hedges of credit risk within the loan portfolio using credit default swaps to which it cannot apply hedge accounting. In the event that the Group recognizes an impairment on a loan that is economically hedged in this way, the impairment is recognized in credit loss expense, whereas any gain on the credit default swap is recorded in net trading income. See Note 23 for additional information. Where UBS designates an economically hedged item at fair value through profit or loss, all fair value changes, including impairments, on both the hedged item and the hedging instrument are reflected in net trading income (refer to part 7). Credit losses incurred on over-the-counter (OTC) derivatives are reported in net trading income.

Embedded derivatives. A derivative may be embedded in a "host contract." Such combinations are known as hybrid instruments and arise predominantly from the issuance of certain structured debt instruments. If the host contract is not carried at fair value with changes in fair value reported in the income statement, the embedded derivative is generally required to be separated from the host contract and accounted for as a stand-alone derivative instrument at fair value if the economic characteristics and risks of the embedded derivative are not closely related to the economic characteristics and risks of the host contract and the embedded derivative actually meets the definition of a derivative. Bifurcated embedded derivatives are presented on the same balance sheet line as the host contract, and are shown in Note 28 in the "held-for-trading" category, reflecting the measurement and recognition principles applied.

Typically, UBS applies the fair value option to hybrid instruments (see part 7), so that bifurcation of an embedded derivative component is not required.

15. **Cash and cash equivalents**

Cash and cash equivalents consist of cash and balances with central banks, balances included in due from banks with original maturity of less than three months, and money market paper included in trading portfolio assets and financial investments available-for-sale.

16. **Physical commodities**

Physical commodities (precious metals, base metals, energy and other commodities) held by UBS as a result of its broker-trader activities are accounted for at fair value less costs to sell and presented within the trading portfolio. Changes in fair value less costs to sell are reflected in net trading income.

17. **Property and equipment**

Property and equipment includes own-used properties, investment properties, leasehold improvements, IT, software and communication, plant and manufacturing equipment, and other machines and equipment.

With the exception of investment properties, Property and equipment is carried at cost less accumulated depreciation and accumulated impairment losses, and is periodically reviewed for impairment. The useful life of property and equipment is estimated on the basis of the economic utilization of the asset.

Classification of own-used property. Own-used property is defined as property held by the Group for use in the supply of services or for administrative purposes, whereas investment property is defined as property held to earn rental income and/or for capital appreciation. If a property of the Group includes a portion that is own-used and another portion that is held to earn rental income or for capital appreciation, the classification is based on whether or not these portions can be sold separately. If the portions of the property can be sold separately, they are separately accounted for as own-used property and investment property. If the portions cannot be sold separately, the whole property is classified as own-used property unless the portion used by the Group is minor. The classification of property is reviewed on a regular basis to account for major changes in its usage.

Leasehold improvements. Leasehold improvements are investments made to customize buildings and offices occupied under operating lease contracts to make them suitable for the intended purpose. The present value of estimated reinstatement costs to bring a leased property into its original condition at the end of the lease, if required, is capitalized as part of the total leasehold improvements costs. At the same time, a corresponding liability is recognized to reflect the obligation incurred. Reinstatement costs are recognized in profit and loss through depreciation of the capitalized leasehold improvements over their estimated useful life.

Software. Software development costs are capitalized when they meet certain criteria relating to identifiability, it is probable that future economic benefits will flow to the enterprise, and the cost can be measured reliably. Internally developed software meeting these criteria and purchased software are classified within IT, software and communication.

With the exception of investment properties, property and equipment is carried at cost less accumulated depreciation and accumulated impairment losses and is periodically reviewed for impairment. The useful life of property and equipment is estimated on the basis of the economic utilization of the asset. Property and equipment is depreciated on a straight-line basis over its estimated useful life as follows

Properties, excluding land	Not exceeding 50 years
Leasehold improvements	Residual lease term, but not exceeding 10 years
Other machines and equipment	Not exceeding 10 years
IT, software and communication	Not exceeding 5 years

Property held for sale. Property formerly own-used or leased to third parties under an operating lease and equipment the Group has decided to sell are classified as assets held for sale and recorded in other assets. Upon classification as held for sale, they are no longer depreciated and are carried at the lower of book value or fair value less costs to sell. Foreclosed properties are included in properties held for resale and recorded in other assets. They are carried at the lower of cost and net realizable value.

Investment property. Investment property is carried at fair value with changes in fair value recognized in the income statement in the period of change. UBS employs internal real estate experts to determine the fair value of investment property by applying recognized valuation techniques. In cases where prices of recent market transactions of comparable properties are available, fair value is determined by reference to these transactions.

18. **Goodwill and other intangible assets**

Goodwill represents the excess of the cost of an acquisition over the fair value of the Group's share of net identifiable assets of the acquired entity at the date of acquisition. Goodwill is not amortized: it is tested yearly for impairment, and, additionally, when a reasonable indication of impairment exists. The impairment test is conducted at the segment level as reported in Note 2a. The segment has been determined as the cash generating unit for impairment testing purposes as this is the level at which the performance of investments is reviewed and assessed by management. Refer to Note 16 for details.

Intangible assets comprise separately identifiable intangible items arising from acquisitions and certain purchased trademarks and similar items. Intangible assets acquired in business combinations are recognized on the balance sheet with their fair value at the date of acquisition and, if they have a definite useful life, are amortized using the straight-line method over their estimated useful economic life, generally not exceeding 20 years. Almost all identified intangible assets of UBS have a definite useful life. At each balance sheet date, intangible assets are reviewed for indications of impairment or changes in estimated future benefits. If such indications exist, the intangible assets are analyzed to assess whether their carrying amount is fully recoverable.

Intangible assets are classified into two categories: (1) infrastructure, and (2) customer relationships, contractual rights and other. Infrastructure consists of an intangible asset recognized in connection with the acquisition of PaineWebber Group, Inc. Customer relationships, contractual rights and other includes mainly intangible assets for client relationships, non-compete agreements, favorable contracts, proprietary software, trademarks and trade names acquired in business combinations.

19. **Income taxes**

Income tax payable on profits is recognized as an expense based on the applicable tax laws in each jurisdiction in the period in which profits arise. The tax effects of income tax losses available for carryforward are recognized as a deferred tax asset if it is probable that future taxable profit will be available against which those losses can be utilized.

Deferred tax liabilities are recognized for temporary differences between the carrying amounts of assets and liabilities in the balance sheet and their amounts as measured for tax purposes, which will result in taxable amounts in future periods. Deferred tax assets are recognized for temporary differences that will result in deductible amounts in future periods, but only to the extent it is probable that sufficient taxable profits will be available against which these differences can be utilized.

Deferred tax assets and liabilities are measured at the tax rates that are expected to apply in the period in which the asset will be realized or the liability will be settled based on enacted rates.

Tax assets and liabilities of the same type (current or deferred) are offset when they arise from the same tax reporting group, they relate to the same tax authority, the legal right to offset exists, and they are intended to be settled net or realized simultaneously.

Current and deferred taxes are recognized as income tax benefit or expense except for current and deferred taxes recognized (1) upon the acquisition of a subsidiary, (2) unrealized gains or losses on financial investments available-for-sale, for changes in fair value of derivative instruments designated as cash flow hedges, for certain foreign currency translations of foreign operations, (3) for certain tax benefits on deferred compensation awards, and (4) for gains and losses on the sale of treasury shares. Deferred taxes recognized in a business combination (item [1]) are considered when determining goodwill. Items (2), (3), and (4) are recorded in net income recognized directly in equity.

20. **Debt issued**

Debt issued is initially measured at fair value, which is the consideration received, net of transaction costs incurred. Subsequent measurement is at amortized cost, using the effective interest rate method to amortize cost at inception to the redemption value over the life of the debt. Refer to Note 28.

Hybrid debt instruments that are related to non-UBS AG equity instruments, foreign exchange, credit instruments or indices are considered structured instruments. If such instruments have not been designated at fair value through profit and loss, the embedded derivative is separated from the host contract and accounted for as a stand-alone derivative if the criteria for separation are met. The host contract is subsequently measured at amortized cost. UBS has designated most of its structured debt instruments at fair value through profit and loss–see Part 7. The fair value option is not applied to certain hybrid instruments which contain bifurcatable embedded derivatives with references to foreign exchange rates and precious metal prices and which are not hedged by derivative instruments. Those hybrids are still bifurcation of the embedded derivative.

Debt instruments with embedded derivatives that are related to UBS AG shares or to a derivative instrument that has UBS AG shares as its underlying are separated into a liability and an equity component at issue date if they require physical settlement. When the hybrid debt instrument is issued, a portion of the net proceeds is allocated to the debt component based on its fair value. The determination of fair value is generally based on quoted market prices for UBS debt instruments with comparable terms. The debt component is subsequently measured at amortized cost. The remaining amount of the net proceeds is allocated to the equity component and reported in Share premium. Subsequent changes in fair value of the separated equity component are not recognized. However, if the hybrid instrument or the embedded derivative related to UBS AG shares is to be cash settled or if it contains a settlement alternative, then the separated derivative is accounted for as a trading instruments with changes in fair value recorded in net trading income unless the entire hybrid debt instrument is designated at fair value through profit or loss with changes in fair value of the entire hybrid instrument also reflected in net trading income (see Part 7).

It is the Group's policy to hedge the fixed interest rate risk on debt issues (except for certain subordinated long-term note issues), and to apply fair value hedge accounting, if the fair value option is not applied to such financial instruments (see part 7). When hedge accounting is applied to fixed-rate debt instruments, the carrying values of debt issues are adjusted for changes in fair value related to the hedged exposure rather than carried at amortized cost–refer to part 14, for further discussion. Bonds issued by UBS held as a result of market making activities or deliberate purchases in the market are treated as a redemption of debt. A gain or loss on redemption is recorded depending on whether the repurchase price of the bond is lower or higher than its carrying value. A subsequent sale of own bonds in the market is treated as a reissuance of debt. Interest expense on debt instruments is included in interest on debt issued.

21. **Retirement benefits**

UBS sponsors a number of retirement benefit plans for its employees worldwide. These plans include both defined benefit and defined contribution plans and various other retirement benefits such as postemployment medical benefits. Contributions to defined contribution plans are expensed when employees have rendered services in exchange for such contributions, generally in the year of contribution.

The Group uses the projected unit credit actuarial method to determine the present value of its defined benefit plans and the related service cost and, where applicable, past service cost.

The principal actuarial assumptions used by the actuary are set out in Note 31.

The Group recognizes a portion of its actuarial gains and losses as income or expense if the net cumulative unrecognized actuarial gains and losses at the end of the previous reporting period are outside the corridor defined as the greater of

1. 10% of present value of the defined benefit obligation at that date (before deducting plan assets); and
2. 10% of the fair value of any plan assets at that date.

The unrecognized actuarial gains and losses exceeding the greater of these two values are recognized in the income statement over the expected average remaining working lives of the employees participating in the plans. If an excess of the fair value of the plan assets over the present value of the defined benefit obligation cannot be recovered fully through refunds or reductions in future contributions, no gain is recognized solely as a result of deferral of an actuarial loss or past service cost in the current period, and no loss is recognized solely as a result of deferral of an actuarial gain in the current period.

22. **Equity participation plans**

UBS provides various equity participation plans in the form of share plans and share option plans. UBS recognizes the fair value of share and share option awards determined at the date of grant as compensation expense over the required service period, which generally is equal to the vesting period. The fair value of share awards is equal to the market price at the date of grant. For share options, fair value is determined using a Monte Carlo valuation model that takes into account the specific terms and conditions under which the share options are granted. Equity-settled awards are classified as equity instruments and are not remeasured subsequent to the grant date, unless an award is modified such that its fair value immediately after modification exceeds its fair value immediately prior to modification. Any increase in fair value resulting from a modification is recognized as compensation expense, either over the remaining service period or immediately for vested awards.

Cash-settled awards are classified as liabilities and remeasured to fair value at each balance sheet date as long as they are outstanding. Decreases in fair value reduce compensation expense and no compensation expense, on a cumulative basis, is recognized for awards that expire worthless or remain unexercised.

23. **Amounts due under unit-linked investment contracts**

UBS Global Asset Management's financial liabilities from unit-linked contracts are presented as Other Liabilities (refer to Note 20) on the balance sheet. These contracts allow investors to invest in a pool of assets through investment units issued by a UBS subsidiary. The unit holders receive all rewards and bear all risks associated with the reference asset pool The financial liability represents the amount due to unit holders and is equal to the fair value of the reference asset pool.

24. **Provisions**

Provisions are recognized when UBS has a present obligation (legal or constructive) as a result of a past event, and it is probable that an outflow of resources embodying economic benefits will be required to settle the obligation and a reliable estimate can be made of the amount of the obligation. Provisions are reflected under other liabilities on the balance sheet. Refer to Note 21.

The majority of UBS's provisions relate to operational risks, including litigation. When a provision is recognized its amount needs to be estimated as the exact amount of the obligation is generally unknown. The estimate is based on all available information and reflects the amount that has the highest probability of being paid. UBS revises existing provisions up or down as soon as it is able to quantify the amounts more accurately.

25. **Equity, treasury shares and contracts on UBS shares**

UBS AG shares held. UBS AG shares held by the Group are classified in equity as treasury shares and accounted for at weighted-average cost. The difference between the proceeds from sales of Treasury shares and their costs (net of tax, if any) is classified as share premium.

Contracts with gross physical settlement. Contracts that require gross physical settlement in UBS AG shares are classified as equity and reported as share premium. Upon settlement of such contracts the proceeds received—less cost (net of tax, if any)—are reported as share premium.

Contracts with net cash settlement or settlement option for counterparty. Contracts on UBS AG shares that require net cash settlement or provide the counterparty with a choice of settlement are classified as trading instruments, with changes in fair value reported in the income statement. An exception to this treatment is physically settled written put options and forward share purchase contracts, including contracts where physical settlement is a settlement alternative. In both cases the present value of the obligation to purchase own shares in exchange for cash is transferred out of equity and recognized as a liability at inception of a contract. The liability is subsequently accreted, using the effective interest rate method, over the life of the contract to the nominal purchase obligation by recognizing interest expense. Upon settlement of a contract, the liability is derecognized, and the amount of equity originally transferred to liability is reclassified within equity to Treasury shares. The premium received for writing put options is recognized directly in share premium.

Minority interests. Net profit and equity are presented including minority interests. Net profit is split into net profit attributable to UBS shareholders and net profit attributable to minority interests.

Trust preferred securities issued. UBS has issued trust preferred securities through consolidated preferred funding trusts, which hold debt issued by UBS. UBS AG has fully and unconditionally guaranteed all of these securities. UBS's obligations under these guarantees are subordinated to the prior payment in full of the deposit liabilities of UBS and all other liabilities of UBS. The trust preferred securities represent equity instruments which are owned by third parties. They are presented as minority interests in UBS's consolidated financial statements with dividends paid also reported under equity attributable to minority interests. UBS bonds held by preferred funding trusts are eliminated in consolidation.

26. **Discontinued operations and noncurrent assets held for sale**

UBS classifies noncurrent nonfinancial assets (or disposal groups) as held for sale (e.g., properties, if their carrying amount will be recovered principally through a sale transaction rather than through continuing use—see part 17). Such assets (or disposal groups) are available for immediate sale in their present condition subject to terms that are usual and customary for sale of such assets (or disposal groups) and their sale is considered highly probable. These assets are measured at the lower of their carrying amount and fair value less costs to sell.

UBS presents discontinued operations under a separate line in the income statement if an entity or a component of an entity has been disposed of or is classified as held for sale and (1) represents a separate major line of business or geographical area of operations, or (2) is a subsidiary acquired exclusively with a view to resale (e.g., certain private equity investments). Net profit from discontinued operations includes the total of operating profit from discontinued operations and the gain or loss recognized on sale or measurement to fair value less costs to sell of the net assets constituting the discontinued operation. A component of an entity comprises operations and cash flows that can be clearly distinguished, operationally and for financial reporting purposes, from the rest of UBS's operations and cash flows. If an entity or a component of an entity is classified as a discontinued operation, UBS restates prior periods in the income statement–see part 3. Refer to Note 36 for details.

27. **Leasing**

UBS enters into lease contracts, predominately of premises and equipment, as a lessor as well as a lessee. The terms and conditions of these contracts are assessed and the leases are classified as operating leases or finance leases according to their economic substance. When making such an assessment, the Group focuses on the following aspects:

1. Transfer of ownership of the asset to the lessee by the end of the lease term
2. Existence of a bargain purchase option held by the lessee
3. Whether the lease term for the major part of the economic life of the asset
4. Whether the present value of the minimum lease payments amount to at least substantially all of the fair value of the leased asset at inception of the lease term

If one or more of these conditions is met, the lease is generally classified as a finance lease, while the nonexistence of such conditions normally leads to a classification as an operating lease.

Lease contracts classified as operating leases where UBS is the lessee are disclosed in Note 25, Operating Lease Commitments. These contracts include noncancelable long-term leases of office buildings in most UBS locations. Lease contracts classsified as an operating lease. Lease contracts classified as operating leases where UBS is the lessee are disclosed in Note 27, Operating Lease Commitments. These contracts include noncancelable long-term leases of office buildings in most UBS locations. Lease contracts classified as operating leases where UBS is the lessor, and finance lease contracts where UBS is the lessor or the lessee, are not material. Contractual agreements which are not considered leases in their entirety but which include lease elements are not material to UBS.

28. **Fee income**

UBS earns fee income from a diverse range of services it provides to its customers. Fee income can be divided into two broad categories: Income earned from services that are provided over a certain period of time, for which customers are generally billed on an annual or semiannual basis, and income earned from providing transaction-type services. Fees earned from services that are provided over a certain period of time are recognized ratably over the service period. Fees earned from providing transaction-type services are recognized when the service has been completed. Performance linked fees or fee components are recognized when the performance criteria are fulfilled.

The following fee income is predominantly earned from services that are provided over a period of time: investment fund fees, fiduciary fees, custodian fees, portfolio and other management and advisory fees, insurance-related fees, credit-related fees, and commission income. Fees predominantly earned from providing transaction-type services include underwriting fees, corporate finance fees, and brokerage fees.

29. **Foreign currency translation**

Foreign currency transactions are recorded at the rate of exchange on the date of the transaction. At the balance sheet date, monetary assets and liabilities denominated in foreign currencies are reported using the closing exchange rate. Exchange differences arising on the settlement of transactions at rates different from those at the date of the transaction, as well as unrealized foreign exchange differences on unsettled foreign currency monetary assets and liabilities, are recognized in the income statement.

Unrealized exchange differences on nonmonetary financial assets (investments in equity instruments) are a component of the change in their entire fair value. For a nonmonetary financial asset held for trading and for nonmonetary financial assets designated at fair value through profit or loss, unrealized exchange differences are recognized in the income statement. For nonmonetary financial investments available-for-sale, unrealized exchange differences are recorded directly in equity until the asset is sold or becomes impaired.

When preparing consolidated financial statements, assets and liabilities of foreign entities are translated at the exchange rates at the balance sheet date, while income and expense items are translated at weighted-average rates for the period. Differences resulting from the use of closing and weighted-average exchange rates and from revaluing a foreign entity's net asset balance at the closing rate are recognized directly in foreign currency translation within equity.

30. **Earnings per share (EPS)**

Basic earnings per share are calculated by dividing the net profit and loss for the period attributable to ordinary shareholders by the weighted-average number of ordinary shares outstanding during the period. Diluted earnings per share are calculated using the same method as for basic EPS, but the determinants are adjusted to reflect the potential dilution that could occur if options, warrants, convertible debt securities or other contracts to issue ordinary shares were converted or exercised into ordinary shares.

31. **Segment reporting**

UBS's financial businesses are organized on a worldwide basis into three Business Groups and the Corporate Center. Global Wealth Management & Business Banking consists of three segments: Wealth Management International & Switzerland, Wealth Management US, and Business Banking Switzerland. The Business Groups Investment Bank and Global Asset Management constitute one segment each. The Industrial Holdings segment holds all industrial operations controlled by the Group. In total, UBS reports six business segments in 2007. Corporate Center includes all corporate functions and elimination items, and is not considered a business segment.

Segment income, segment expenses, and segment performance include transfers between business segments and between geographical segments. Such transfers are conducted either at internally agreed transfer prices or, where possible, at arm's length.

32. **Revenues from industrial holdings and goods and materials purchased**

Revenues from industrial holdings include sale of goods and services from three consolidated entities and are derived from various businesses. Revenue is generally recognized upon customer acceptance of goods delivered and when services have been rendered. Expenses from goods and materials purchased include costs for raw materials, parts and finished goods purchased from third-party suppliers to produce the goods and services sold.

APPENDIX B
EXAMPLE BANK FINANCIAL STATEMENTS
UBS Group Financial Statements
December 31, 2007

Income Statement

CHF million, except per share data	*Note*	*For the year ended*			*% change from*
		12/31/07	*12/31/06*	*12/31/05*	*12/31/06*
Continuing operations					
Interest income	3	109,112	87,401	59,286	25
Interest expense	3	(103,775)	(80,880)	(49,758)	28
Net interest income	3	5,337	6,521	9,528	(18)
Credit loss (expense)/recovery		(238)	156	375	
Net interest income after credit loss expense		5,099	6,677	9,903	(24)
Net fee and commission income	4	30,634	25,456	21,184	20
Net trading income	3	(8,353)	13,743	8,248	
Other income	5	4,332	1,598	1,127	171
Revenues from industrial holdings		268	262	229	2
Total operating income		31,980	47,736	40,691	(33)
Personnel expenses	6	24,798	23,591	20,057	5
General and administrative expenses	7	8,465	7,980	6,504	6
Depreciation of property and equipment	15	1,251	1,252	1,247	0
Amortization of intangible assets	16	282	153	133	84
Goods and materials purchased		119	116	97	3
Total operating expenses		34,915	33,092	28,048	6
Operating profit from continuing operations before tax		(2,935)	14,644	12,643	
Tax expense	22	1,311	2,785	2,465	(53)
Net profit from continuing operations		(4,246)	11,859	10,178	
Discontinued operations					
Operating profit from discontinued operations before tax	36	135	879	5,094	(85)
Tax expense	22	(266)	(12)	582	0
Net profit from discontinued operations		401	891	4,512	(55)
Net profit		(3,845)	12,750	14,690	
Net profit attributable to minority interests		539	493	661	9
From continuing operations		539	390	430	38
From discontinued operations		0	103	231	(100)
Net profit attributable to UBS shareholders		(4,384)	12,257	14,029	
From continuing operations		(4,785)	11,469	9,748	
From discontinued operations		401	788	4,281	(49)
Earnings per share					
Basic earnings per share (CHF)	8	(2.28)	6.20	6.97	
From continuing operations		(2.49)	5.80	4.84	
From discontinued operations		0.21	0.40	2.13	(48)
Diluted earnings per share (CHF)	8	(2.28)	5.95	6.68	
From continuing operations		(2.49)	5.57	4.65	
From discontinued operations		0.21	0.38	2.03	(45)

Balance Sheet

CHF million	*Note*	*12/31/07*	*12/31/06*	*% change from 12/31/06*
Assets				
Cash and balances with central banks		18,793	3,495	438
Due from banks	9	60,907	50,426	21
Cash collateral on securities borrowed	10	207,063	351,590	(41)
Reverse repurchase agreements	10	376,928	405,834	(7)
Trading portfolio assets	11	610,061	627,036	(3)

CHF million	Note	12/31/07	12/31/06	% change from 12/31/06
Assets				
Trading portfolio assets pledged as collateral	11	164,311	251,478	(35)
Positive replacement values	23	428,217	292,975	46
Financial assets designated at fair value	12	11,765	5,930	98
Loans	9	335,864	297,842	13
Financial investments available-for-sale	13	4,966	8,937	(44)
Accrued income and prepaid expenses		11,953	10,361	15
Investments in associates	14	1,979	1,523	30
Property and equipment	15	7,234	6,913	5
Goodwill and intangible assets	16	14,538	14,773	(2)
Other assets	17, 22	18,000	17,249	4
Total assets		2,272,579	2,346,362	(3)
Liabilities				
Due to banks	18	145,762	203,689	(28)
Cash collateral on securities lent	10	31,621	63,088	(50)
Repurchase agreements	10	305,887	545,480	(44)
Trading portfolio liabilities	11	164,788	204,773	(20)
Negative replacement values	23	443,539	297,063	49
Financial liabilities designated at fair value	19	191,853	145,687	32
Due to customers	18	641,892	555,886	15
Accrued expenses and deferred income		21,848	21,527	1
Debt issued	19	222,077	190,143	17
Other liabilities	20,21,22	60,776	63,251	(4)
Total liabilities		2,230,043	2,290,587	(3)
Equity				
Share capital		207	211	(2)
Share premium		8,884	9,870	(10)
Net income recognized directly in equity, net of tax		(1,188)	815	
Revaluation reserve from step acquisitions, net of tax		38	38	0
Retained earnings		38,081	49,151	(23)
Equity classified as obligation to purchase own shares		(74)	(185)	60
Treasury shares		(10,363)	(10,214)	(1)
Equity attributable to UBS shareholders		35,585	49,686	(28)
Equity attributable to minority interests		6,951	6,089	14
Total equity		42,536	55,775	(24)
Total liabilities and equity		2,272,579	2,346,362	(3)

Statement of Changes in Equity

CHF million	For the year ended		
	12/31/07	12/31/06	12/31/05
Share capital			
Balance at the beginning of the year	211	871	901
Issue of share capital	0	1	2
Capital repayment by par value reduction	0	(631)	0
Cancellation of second trading line treasury shares	(4)	(30)	(32)
Balance at the end of the year attributable to UBS shareholders	207	211	871
Share premium			
Balance at the beginning of the year	9,870	9,992	9,231
Premium on shares issued and warrants exercised	12	46	36
Net premium/(discount) on treasury share and own equity derivative activity	(560)	(271)	(309)
Employee share and share option plans	139	(508)	768
Tax benefits from deferred compensation awards	(577)	611	266
Balance at the end of the year attributable to UBS shareholders	8,884	9,870	9,992
Balance at the end of the year attributable to minority interests	556	461	2,415
Subtotal–balance at the end of the year	9,440	10,331	12,407

CHF million	For the year ended		
	12/31/07	*12/31/06*	*12/31/05*
Net income recognized directly in equity, net of tax			
Foreign currency translation			
Balance at the beginning of the year	(1,618)	(432)	(2,520)
Movements during the year	(1,009)	(1,186)	2,088
Subtotal—balance at the end of the year attributable to UBS shareholders[1]	(2,627)	(1,618)	(432)
Balance at the end of the year attributable to minority interests	(480)	(208)	(26)
Subtotal–balance at the end of the year	(3,107)	(1,826)	(458)
Net unrealized gains/(losses) on financial investments available-for-sale, net of tax			
Balance at the beginning of the year	2,876	931	761
Net unrealized gains/(losses) on financial investments available-for-sale	1,213	2,574	463
Impairment charges reclassified to the income statement	14	19	96
Realized gains reclassified to the income statement	(2,638)	(649)	(396)
Realized losses reclassified to the income statement	6	1	7
Subtotal—balance at the end of the year attributable to UBS shareholders	1,471	2,876	931
Balance at the end of the year attributable to minority interests	32	30	21
Subtotal—balance at the end of the year	1,503	2,906	952
Change in fair value of derivative instruments designated as cash flow hedges, net of tax			
Balance at the beginning of the year	(443)	(681)	(322)
Net unrealized gains/(losses) on the revaluation of cash flow hedges	239	1	(474)
Net unrealized (gains)/losses reclassified to the income statement	172	237	115
Subtotal—balance at the end of the year attributable to UBS shareholders	(32)	(443)	(681)
Balance at the end of the year attributable to minority interests	0	0	0
Subtotal—balance at the end of the year	(32)	(443)	(681)
Net income recognized directly in equity, net of tax—attributable to UBS shareholders	(1,888)	815	(182)
Net income recognized directly in equity—attributable to minority interests	(448)	(178)	(5)
Balance at the end of the year	(1,636)	637	(187)
Revaluation reserve from step acquisitions, net of taxes			
Balance at the beginning of the year	38	101	90
Movements during the year	0	(63)	11
Balance at the end of the year attributable to UBS shareholders	38	38	101
Retained earnings			
Balance at the beginning of the year	49,151	44,105	36,692
Net profit attributable to UBS shareholders for the year	(4,384)	12,257	14,029
Dividends paid[2]	(4,275)	(3,214)	(3,105)
Cancellation of second trading line treasury shares	(2,411)	(3,997)	(3,511)
Balance at the end of the year attributable to UBS shareholders	38,081	49,151	44,105
Balance at the end of the year attributable to minority interests	16	(25)	170
Balance at the end of the year	38,097	49,126	44,275
Equity classified as obligation to purchase own shares			
Balance at the beginning of the year	(185)	(133)	(96)
Movements during the year	111	(52)	(37)
Balance at the end of the year attributable to UBS shareholders	(74)	(185)	(133)
Treasury shares			
Balance at the beginning of the year	(10,214)	(10,739)	(11,105)
Acquisitions	(7,169)	(8,314)	(8,375)
Disposals	4,605	4,812	5,198
Cancellation of second trading line treasury shares	2,415	4,027	3,543
Balance at the end of the year attributable to UBS shareholders	(10,363)	(10,214)	(10,739)

CHF million		*For the year ended*	
	12/31/07	*12/31/06*	*12/31/05*
Minority interest—preferred securities	6,827	5,831	5,039
Total equity attributable to UBS shareholders	35,585	49,686	44,015
Total equity attributable to minority interests	6,951	6,089	7,619
Total equity	42,536	55,775	51,634

[1]   *Net of CHF 83 million, CHF (292) million and CHF 236 million of related taxes for the years ended 2006, 2005, and 2004, respectively.*

[2]   *Dividends of CHF 1.60 per share, CHF 1.50 per share and CHF 1.30 per share were paid on April 24, 2006, April 26, 2005, and April 20, 2004, respectively.*

CHF million		*For the year ended*	
	12/31/07	*12/31/06*	*12/31/05*
Balance at the beginning of the year	6,089	7,619	5,426
Issuance of preferred securities	996	1,219	1,539
Other increases	101	131	44
Decreases and dividend payments	(502)	(3,191)	(595)
Foreign currency translation	(272)	(182)	544
Minority interest in net profit	539	493	661
Balance at the end of the year	6,951	6,089	7,619

Shares issued

		For the year ended		*% change from*
Number of shares	*12/31/07*	*12/31/06*	*12/31/05*	*12/31/06*
Balance at the beginning of the year	2,105,273,286	2,177,265,044	2,253,716,354	(3)
Issuance of share capital	1,294,058	2,208,242	3,418,878	(41)
Cancellation of second trading line treasury shares	(33,020,000)	(74,200,000)	(79,870,188)	55
Balance at the end of the year	2,073,547,344	2,105,273,286	2,177,265,044	(2)

Treasury shares

Number of shares				
Balance at the beginning of the year	164,475,699	208,519,748	249,326,620	(21)
Acquisitions	102,074,942	117,160,339	156,436,070	(13)
Disposals	(75,425,117)	(87,004,388)	(117,372,754)	13
Cancellation of second trading line treasury shares	(33,020,000)	(74,200,000)	(79,870,188)	55
Balance at the end of the year	158,105,524	164,475,699	208,519,748	(41)

During the year a total of 33,020,000 shares acquired under the second trading line buyback program 2006 were cancelled. The 36,400,000 shares purchased under the buyback program 2007 (CHF 2,599 million) previously intended for cancellation have been rededicated for further use.

On December 31, 2007, a maximum of 144,338 shares could be issued against the future exercise of options from former PaineWebber employee option plans. These shares are shown as conditional share capital in the UBS AG (Parent Bank) disclosure. In addition, during 2006, shareholders approved the creation of conditional capital of up to a maximum of 150 million shares to fund UBS's employee share option programs. As of December 31, 2007 and December 31, 2006, 5,704 shares and zero shares, respectively, have been issued under this program.

All issued shares are fully paid.

Statement of Recognized Income and Expense

For the year ended	12/31/07 *Attributable to*			12/31/06 *Attributable to*			12/31/05 *Attributable to*		
CHF million	*UBS share-holders*	*Minority interests*	*Total*	*UBS share-holders*	*Minority interests*	*Total*	*UBS share-holders*	*Minority interests*	*Total*
Net unrealized gains/ (losses) on financial investments available-for-sale, before tax	(1,825)	2	(1,823)	2,610	9	2,619	152	(58)	94
Change in fair value of derivative instruments designated as cash flow hedges, before tax	541	0	541	332	0	332	(479)	0	(479)
Foreign currency translation	(1,009)	(272)	(1,281)	1,186	(182)	(1,368)	2,088	544	2,632
Tax on items transferred to/(from) equity	290	0	290	(759)	0	(759)	138	0	138
Net income recognized directly in equity	(2,003)	(270)	(2,273)	997	(173)	824	1,899	486	2,385
Net income recognized in the income statement	(4,384)	539	(3,845)	12,257	493	12,750	14,029	661	14,690
Total recognized income and expense	(6,387)	269	(6,118)	13,254	320	13,574	15,928	1,147	17,075

Statement of Cash Flows

CHF million		*For the year ended*	
	12/31/07	12/31/06	12/31/05
Cash flow from/(used in) operating activities			
Net profit	(3,845)	12,750	14,690
Adjustments to reconcile net profit to cash flow from/(used in) operating activities			
Noncash items included in net profit and other adjustments:			
Depreciation of property and equipment	1,253	1,325	1,556
Amortization of goodwill and other intangible assets	282	196	340
Credit loss expense/(recovery)	238	(156)	(374)
Equity in income of associates	(120)	(117)	(152)
Deferred tax expense/(benefit)	(437)	(517)	(382)
Net loss/(gain) from investing activities	(4,085)	(2,092)	(5,062)
Net loss/(gain) from financing activities	3,779	3,659	4,025
Net (increase)/decrease in operating assets:			
Net due from/to banks	(60,762)	80,269	(1,690)
Reverse repurchase agreements and cash collateral on securities borrowed	173,433	(61,382)	(125,097)
Trading portfolio, net replacement values, and financial assets designated at fair value	60,729	(177,087)	(74,799)
Loans/due to customers	47,955	64,029	47,265
Accrued income, prepaid expenses, and other assets	(2,467)	(4,536)	(1,227)
Net increase/(decrease) in operating liabilities:			
Repurchase agreements and cash collateral on securities lent	(271,060)	66,370	64,558
Accrued expenses and other liabilities	7,494	14,975	15,536
Income taxes paid	(3,663)	(2,607)	(2,394)
Net cash flow from/(used in) operating activities	(51,276)	(4,921)	(63,207)

CHF million

	For the year ended		
	12/31/07	*12/31/06*	*12/31/05*
Cash flow from/(used in) investing activities			
Investments in subsidiaries and associates	(2,337)	2,856)	(1,540)
Disposal of subsidiaries and associates	885	1,154	3,240
Purchase of property and equipment	(1,910)	(1,793)	(1,892)
Disposal of property and equipment	134	499	270
Net (investment in)/divestment of financial investments available for sale	5,981	1,723	(2,487)
Net cash flow from/(used in) investing activities	2,753	4,439	(2,409)
Cash flow from/(used in) financing activities			
Net money market paper issued/(repaid)	32,672	16,921	23,221
Net movements in treasury shares and own equity derivative activity	(3,550)	(3,624)	(2,416)
Capital issuance	0	1	2
Capital repayment by par value reduction	0	(631)	0
Dividends paid	(4,275)	(3,214)	(3,105)
Issuance of long-term debt, including financial liabilities designated at fair value	110,874	97,675	76,307
Repayment of long-term debt, including financial liabilities designated at fair value	(62,407)	(59,740)	(30,457)
Increase in minority interests[1]	1,094	1,331	1,572
Dividend payments to/purchase from minority interests	(619)	(1,072)	(575)
Net cash flow from/(used in) financing activities	73,789	47,647	64,549
Effects of exchange rate differences	(12,251)	(2,117)	5,018
Net increase/(decrease) in cash and cash equivalents	13,015	45,048	3,951
Cash and cash equivalents, beginning of the year	136,090	91,042	87,091
Cash and cash equivalents, end of the year	149,105	136,090	91,042
Cash and cash equivalents comprise:			
Cash and balances with central banks	18,793	3,495	5,359
Money market paper[2]	77,215	87,144	57,826
Due from banks with original maturity in less than three months	53,097	45,451	27,857
Total	149,105	136,090	91,042

[1] *Includes issuance of preferred securities of CHF 996 million and CHF 1,219 and CHF 1,539 million for the years ended December 31, 2007 and December 31, 2006 and December 31, 2005 respectively.*

[2] *Money market paper is included in the balance sheet under Trading portfolio assets and Financial investments available for sale. CHF 3,364 million, CHF 7,183 million, and CHF 4,744 million were pledged at December 31, 2007, December 31, 2006, and December 31, 2005, respectively.*

APPENDIX C

EXAMPLE BANK FINANCIAL INSTRUMENTS DISCLOSURES

UBS
Financial Statements
December 31, 2007

Notes to the financial statements

Note 10. Securities borrowing, securities lending, repurchase and reverse repurchase agreements

The Group enters into collateralized reverse repurchase and repurchase agreements and securities borrowing and securities lending transactions that may result in credit exposure in the event that the counterparty to the transaction is unable to fulfill its contractual obligations. The Group controls credit risk associated with these activities by monitoring counterparty credit exposure and collateral values on a daily basis and requiring additional collateral to be deposited with or returned to the Group when deemed necessary.

Balance sheet assets

CHF million	Cash collateral on securities borrowed 12/31/07	Reverse repurchase agreements 12/31/07	Cash collateral on securities borrowed 12/31/06	Reverse repurchase agreements 12/31/06
By counterparty				
Banks	48,480	221,575	53,538	209,606
Customers	158,583	155,353	298,052	196,228
Total	207,063	376,928	351,590	405,834

Balance sheet liabilities

CHF million	Cash collateral on securities lent 12/31/07	Repurchase agreements 12/31/07	Cash collateral on securities lent 12/31/06	Repurchase agreements 12/31/06
By counterparty				
Banks	29,512	139,156	44,118	274,910
Customers	2,109	166,731	18,970	270,570
Total	31,621	305,887	63,088	545,480

Note 11. Trading portfolio

The Group trades in debt instruments (including money market paper and tradable loans), equity instruments, precious metals, commodities and derivatives to meet the financial needs of its customers and to generate revenue. Note 23 provides a description of the various classes of derivatives instruments.

CHF million	12/31/07	12/31/06
Trading portfolio assets		
Money market paper	76,866	86,790
Thereof pledged as collateral with central banks	198	20,053
Thereof pledged as collateral (excluding central banks)	35,604	45,356
Thereof pledged as collateral and can be repledged or resold by counterparty	32,239	38,173
Debt instruments		
Swiss government and government agencies	304	340
US Treasury and government agencies	75,137	114,714
Other government agencies	57,864	71,170
Corporate listed	127,990	214,129
Other—unlisted	152,669	111,001
Total	413,964	511,354
Thereof pledged as collateral	170,276	244,697
Thereof can be repledged or resold by counterparty	106,747	158,549

CHF million	12/31/07	12/31/06
Equity instruments		
Listed	181,034	183,731
Unlisted	25,968	27,938
Total	207,002	211,669
Thereof pledged as collateral[1]	26,870	56,760
Thereof can be repledged or resold by counterparty	25,325	54,756
Traded loans	47,122	47,630
Precious metals and other commodities[1]	29,418	21,071
Total trading portfolio assets	774,372	878,514
Trading portfolio liabilities		
Debt instruments		
Swiss government and government agencies	85	129
US Treasury and government agencies	50,187	81,385
Other government agencies	40,610	58,538
Corporate listed	24,722	21,788
Other unlisted	4,822	2,101
Total	120,426	163,941
Equity instruments	44,362	40,832
Total trading portfolio liabilities	164,788	204,733

[1] *Other commodities predominantly consist of energy.*

Note 12. Financial investments available for sale

CHF million	12/31/07	12/31/06
Money market paper	349	354
Other debt instruments		
Listed	317	260
Unlisted	717	261
Total	1,034	521
Equity investments		
Listed	1,865	5,880
Unlisted	1,718	2,182
Total	3,583	8,062
Total financial investments for sale	4,966	8,937
Net unrealized gains/(losses)–before tax	1,900	3,723
Net unrealized gains/(losses)–after tax	1,503	2,906

Note 23. Derivative instruments and hedge accounting

A derivative is a financial instrument, the value of which is derived from the value of another ("underlying") financial instrument, an index or some other variable. Typically, the underlying is a share, commodity or bond price, an index value or an exchange or interest rate.

The majority of derivative contracts are negotiated as to amount ("notional"), tenor and price between UBS and its counterparties, whether other professionals or customers (over-the-counter or OTC contracts).

The rest are standardized in terms of their amounts and settlement dates and are bought and sold on organized markets (exchange-traded contracts).

The notional amount of a derivative is generally the quantity of the underlying instrument on which the derivative contract is based and is the basis upon which changes in the value of the contract are measured. It provides an indication of the underlying volume of business transacted by the Group but does not provide any measure of risk.

Derivative instruments are carried at fair value, shown in the balance sheet as separate totals of positive replacement values (assets) and negative replacement values (liabilities). Positive replacement values represent the cost to the Group of replacing all transactions with a fair value in the Group's favor if all the relevant counterparties of the Group were to default at the same time, assuming transactions could be replaced instantaneously. Negative replacement values represent the cost to the Group's counterparties of replacing all their transactions with the Group with a fair value in their favor if the Group were to default. Positive and negative replacement values on different transactions are only netted if the transactions are with the same counterparty and the cash flows will be settled on a net basis. Changes in replacement values of derivative instruments are recognized in the income statement unless they meet the criteria for certain hedge accounting relationships as explained in Note 1a14, Derivative instruments and hedge accounting.

Types of derivative instruments. The Group uses the following derivative financial instruments for both trading and hedging purposes:

Forwards and futures are contractual obligations to buy or sell financial instruments or commodities on a future date at a specified price. Forward contracts are tailor-made agreements that are transacted between counterparties on the OTC market, whereas futures are standardized contracts transacted on regulated exchanges.

Swaps are transactions in which two parties exchange cash flows on a specified notional amount for a predetermined period. Most swaps are traded OTC. The major types of swap transactions undertaken by the Group are as follows:

- Interest rate swap contracts generally entail the contractual exchange of fixed-rate and floating-rate interest payments in a single currency, based on a notional amount and a reference interest rate, (e.g., LIBOR).
- Cross-currency swaps involve the exchange of interest payments based on two different currency principal balances and reference interest rates and generally also entail exchange of principal amounts at the start and/or end of the contract.
- Credit default swaps (CDSs) are the most common form of credit derivative, under which the party buying protection makes one or more payments to the party selling protection in exchange for an undertaking by the seller to make a payment to the buyer following a credit event (as defined in the contract) with respect to a third-party credit entity (as defined in the contract). Settlement following a credit event may be a net cash amount or cash in return for physical delivery of one or more obligations of the credit entity and is made regardless of whether the protection buyer has actually suffered a loss. After a credit event and settlement, the contract is terminated.
- Total rate of return swaps give the total return receiver exposure to all of the cash flows and economic benefits and risks of an underlying asset, without having to own the asset, in exchange for a series of payments, often based on a reference interest rate, (e.g., LIBOR). The total return payer has an equal and opposite position.
- Options are contractual agreements under which, typically, the seller (writer) grants the purchaser the right, but not the obligation, either to buy (call option) or to sell (put option) by or at a set date, a specified quantity of a financial instrument or commodity at a predetermined price. The purchaser pays a premium to the seller for this right. Options involving more complex payment structures are also transacted. Options may be traded OTC or on a regulated exchange and may be traded in the form of a security (warrant).

Derivatives transacted for trading purposes. Most of the Group's derivative transactions relate to sales and trading activities. Sales activities include the structuring and marketing of derivative products to customers to enable them to take, transfer, modify or reduce current or expected risks. Trading includes market making, positioning and arbitrage activities. Market making involves quoting bid and offer prices to other market participants with the intention of generating revenues based on spread and volume. Positioning means managing market risk positions with the expectation of profiting from favorable movements in prices, rates, or indices. Arbitrage activities involve identifying and profiting from price differentials between the same product in different markets or the same economic factor in different products.

Derivatives transacted for hedging purposes. The Group enters into derivative transactions for the purposes of hedging assets, liabilities, forecast transactions, cash flows and credit exposures. The accounting treatment of hedge transactions varies according to the nature of the instrument hedged and whether the hedge qualifies as such for accounting purposes.

Derivative transactions may qualify as hedges for accounting purposes. These are described under the corresponding headings in this note. The Group's accounting policies for derivatives designated and accounted for as hedging instruments are explained in Note 1a14, Derivative instruments and hedge accounting, where terms used in the following sections are explained.

The Group has also enters into CDSs that provide economic hedges for credit risk exposures in the loan and traded product portfolios but do not meet the requirements for hedge accounting treatment.

The Group has also entered into a limited volume of interest rate swaps and other interest rate derivatives (e.g., futures) for day-to-day economic interest rate risk management purposes, but without applying hedge accounting. The fair value changes of such swaps are booked to Net trading income.

Fair value hedges. The Group's fair value hedges principally consist of interest rate swaps that are used to protect against changes in the fair value of fixed-rate instruments due to movements in market interest rates. The fair values of outstanding interest rate derivatives designated as fair value hedges were a CHF 125 million net positive replacement value at December 31, 2007, and a CHF 222 million net positive replacement value at December 31, 2006.

Fair value hedges of interest rate risk

CHF billion	12/31/07	12/31/06
Gains/(losses) on hedging instruments	15	(28)
Gains/(losses) on hedging items attributable to the hedged risk	(11)	(11)
Net gains/(losses) representing ineffective portions of fair value hedges	4	(17)

In addition, the Group has entered into a fair value hedge accounting relationship using foreign exchange derivatives to protect a certain portion of equity investments available-for-sale from foreign currency exposure. The time value associated with the FX derivatives is excluded from the evaluation of hedge ineffectiveness. The fair value of outstanding FX derivates designated as fair value hedges was a CHF 0 million at December 2007 and CHF 1 million net positive replacement value at December 31, 2006.

Fair value hedges of foreign exchange risk

CHF *billion*	12/31/07	12/31/06
Gains/(losses) on hedging instruments	42	49
Gains/(losses) on hedging items attributable to the hedged risk	(44)	(44)
Net gains/(losses) representing ineffective portions of fair value hedges	(2)	5

Fair value hedge of portfolio interest rate risk. The Group also applies fair value hedge accounting of portfolio interest rate risk. The change in fair value of the hedged items is recorded separately from the hedged item on the balance sheet. The fair value of derivatives designated for this hedge method at December 31, 2007, was a CHF 58 million net positive replacement value and at December 31, 2006, was a CHF 21 million net positive replacement value.

CHF billion	12/31/07	12/31/06
Gains/(losses) on hedging instruments	37	15
Gains/(losses) on hedging items attributable to the hedged risk	(30)	(23)
Net gains/(losses) representing ineffective portions of fair value hedges	7	(8)

Cash flow hedges of forecast transactions. The Group is exposed to variability in future interest cash flows on nontrading assets and liabilities that bear interest at variable rates or are expected to be refunded or reinvested in the future. The amounts and timing of future cash flows, representing both principal and interest flows, are projected for each portfolio of financial assets and liabilities, based on contractual terms and other relevant factors, including estimates of prepayments and defaults. The aggregate principal balances and interest cash flows across all portfolios over time form the basis for identifying the nontrading interest rate risk of the Group, which is hedged with interest rate swaps, the maximum maturity of which is 22 years.

The schedule of forecast principal balances on which the expected interest cash flows arise as at December 31, 2007, is shown below.

Forecast cash flows

CHF billion	≤1 year	1–3 years	3–5 years	5–10 years	Over 10 years
Cash inflows (assets)	218	395	285	273	15
Cash outflows (liabilities)	84	147	106	102	2
Net cash flows	134	248	179	171	13

Gains and losses on the effective portions of derivatives designated as cash flow hedges of forecast transactions are initially recorded in equity as net income recognized directly in equity and are transferred to current period earnings when the forecast cash flows affect net profit or loss. The gains and losses on ineffective portions of such derivatives are recognized immediately in the income statement. A CHF 443 million gain, a CHF 36 million loss and a CHF 35 million gain, were recognized 2007, 2006, and 2005, respectively, due to hedge ineffectiveness.

As at December 31, 2007 and 2006, the fair values of outstanding derivatives designated as cash flow hedges of forecast transactions were a CHF 99 million net positive replacement value and a CHF 462 million net negative replacement value, respectively. No Swiss franc hedging interest rate swaps terminated during 2007 and 2006. At the end of 2007 and 2006, unrecognized income of CHF 135 million and CHF 214 million associated with terminated swaps remained deferred in Equity. It will be removed from Equity when the hedged cash flows have an impact on net profit or loss. Amounts reclassified from Net income recognized directly in equity to current period earnings due to discontinuation of hedge accounting were a CHF 79 million net gain in 2007, a CHF 132 million net gain in 2006 and a CHF 243 million net gain in 2005. These amounts were recorded in net interest income.

Risks of derivative instruments. Derivative instruments are transacted in many trading portfolios, which generally include several types of instruments, not just derivatives. The market risk of derivatives is managed and controlled as an integral part of the market risk of these portfolios. The Group's approach to market risk is described in audited "Market risk" section in Risk, Treasury and Capital Management 2007.

Derivative instruments are transacted with many different counterparties, most of whom are also counterparties for other types of business. The credit risk of derivatives is managed and controlled in the context of the Group's overall credit exposure to each counterparty. The Group's approach to credit risk is described in the audited "Credit risk" section in Risk, Treasury and Capital Management 2007. It should be noted that, although, the positive replacement values shown on the balance sheet can be an important component of the Group's credit exposure, the positive replacement values for a counterparty are rarely an adequate reflection of the Group's credit exposure on its derivatives business with that counterparty. This is because, on the one hand, replacement values can increase over time ("potential future exposure"), while on the other hand, exposure may be mitigated by entering into master netting agreements and bilateral collateral arrangements with counterparties. Both the exposure measures used by the Group internally to control credit risk and the capital requirements imposed by regulators reflect these additional factors. There are additional capital requirements show in the Risk-weighted assets (BIS) table in the "Capital management" section in Risk, Treasury and Capital Management 2007 under Off-balance-sheet exposures as forward and swap contracts and purchased options, which reflect the additional potential future exposure.

In the audited Exposure to credit risk table in the "Credit risk" section in Risk, Treasury and Capital Management 2007, and in the Risk-weighted assets (BIS) table in the "Capital management" section in Risk, Treasury and Capital Management 2007, the replacement are lower than those shown in the balance sheet because they reflect close-out netting arrangements accepted by the Swiss Federal Banking Commission (SFBC) as being enforceable in insolvency. The impact of such netting agreements on the gross replacement values shown in the tables on the next two pages is to reduce both positive and negative replacement values by CHF 292,371 million and CHF 219,820 million at December 31, 2007 and 2006, respectively. As a result, positive replacement values after netting for UBS Group were CHF 135,846 million at December 31, 2007, and CHF 73,155 million at December 31, 2006. These figures differ from those shown in the sections mentioned above in Risk, Treasury and Capital Management 2007 because they cover the whole UBS Group, whereas the relevant tables in Risk, Treasury and Capital Management 2007 cover only those entities which are subject to consolidation for regulatory capital purposes.

CHF million	Within 3 months PRV[2]	Within 3 months NRV[3]	3 – 12 months PRV	3 – 12 months NRV	1 – 5 years PRV	1 – 5 years NRV	Over 5 years PRV	Over 5 years NRV	Total PRV	Total NRV	Total notional CHF bn
Interest rate contracts											
Over-the-counter (OTC) contracts											
Forward contracts	686	760	129	131	31	48			846	939	1,534.8
Swaps	4,852	5,351	7,864	8,137	52,447	55,061	77,270	69,027	142,433	137,576	28,363.5
Options	410	289	204	622	3,416	4,753	15,770	17,280	19,800	22,944	1,405.0
Exchange-traded contracts[4]											
Futures											2,072.7
Options	568	622	265	263	28	27			861	912	89.9
Total	6,516	7,022	8,462	9,153	55,922	59,889	93,040	86,307	163,940	162,371	33,465.9
Credit derivative contracts											
Over-the-counter (OTC) contracts											
Credit default swaps	207	248	6,471	5,951	60,864	62,495	26,822	30,905	94,364	99,599	5,172.3
Total rate of return swaps	412	313	143	243	2,457	2,814	7,922	3,235	10,934	6,605	188.3
Total	619	561	6,614	6,194	63,321	65,309	34,744	34,140	105,298	106,204	5,360.6
Foreign exchange contracts											
Over-the-counter (OTC) contracts											
Forward contracts	8,248	8,792	2,554	2,867	888	623	14	33	11,704	12,315	1,322.2
Interest and currency swaps	26,887	28,169	15,780	13,616	19,412	21,934	12,467	11,605	74,546	75,324	4,871.9
Options	4,807	4,396	5,887	5,519	1,316	1,313	52	76	12,062	11,304	1,506.9
Exchange-traded contracts[4]											
Futures											12.0
Options	66	57	9	9					75	66	4.5
Total	40,008	41,414	24,230	22,011	21,616	23,870	12,533	11,714	98,387	99,009	7,717.5
Equity/index contracts											
Over-the-counter (OTC) contracts											
Forward contracts	2,384	2,006	1,736	1,047	550	738	87	63	4,757	3,854	175.8
Options	3,134	4,163	4,689	9,103	5,412	12,054	1,216	3,548	14,451	28,868	291.4
Exchange-traded contracts[4]											
Futures											55.6
Options	6,114	6,193	7,909	8,727	6,520	7,173	221	315	20,764	22,408	325.5
Total	11,632	12,362	14,334	18,877	12,482	19,965	1,524	3,926	39,972	55,130	848.3
Precious metals contracts											
Over-the-counter (OTC) contracts											
Forward contracts	463	993	864	659	1,007	489	47	71	2,381	2,212	39.9
Options	488	1,020	1,107	1,116	1,842	1,691	170	130	3,607	3,957	79.1

Note 23. Derivative Instruments and Hedge Accounting[1] (continued)

As at December 31, 2007

CHF million	Within 3 months PRV[2]	NRV[3]	3 – 12 months PRV	NRV	1 – 5 years PRV	NRV	Over 5 years PRV	NRV	Total PRV	Total NRV	Total notional CHF bn
Exchange-traded contracts[4]											
Futures											0.2
Options	145	127	226	233	43	41	217	201	414	401	28.0
Total	1,096	2,140	2,197	2,008	2,892	2,221			6,402	6,570	147.2
Commodity contracts, excluding precious metals contracts											
Over-the-counter (OTC) contracts											
Forward contracts	2,421	2,425	1,580	1,567	1,886	1,751	1,065	1,157	6,952	6,900	111.5
Options	469	459	896	1,187	878	1,048	117	134	2,360	2,828	24.9
Exchange-traded contracts[4]											
Futures											170.3
Options	1,606	1,453	2,284	2,342	1,016	732	1,182	1,291	4,906	4,527	181.3
Total	4,496	4,337	4,760	5,096	3,780	3,531			14,218	14,255	488.0
Total derivative instruments	64,367	67,836	60,597	63,339	160,013	174,785	143,240	137,579	428,217[5]	443,539[6]	

[1] Bifurcated embedded derivatives are presented in the same balance sheet line as the host contract and are excluded from the table. Payables and receivables resulting from the valuation of regular-way purchases and sales of financial assets between trade and settlement date are recognized as replacement values and therefore included in the table.
[2] PRV: Positive Replacement Value.
[3] NRV: Negative Replacement Value.
[4] Exchange-traded products include own account trades only.
[5] The impact of netting agreements accepted by the Swiss Federal Banking Commission (SFBC) for capital adequacy calculations is to reduce positive replacement values to CHF 135,846 million.
[6] The impact of netting agreements accepted by the SFBC for capital adequacy calculations is to reduce negative replacement values to CHF 151,168 million.

As at December 31, 2006

CHF million	Within 3 months PRV[2]	NRV[3]	3 – 12 months PRV	NRV	1 – 5 years PRV	NRV	Over 5 years PRV	NRV	Total PRV	Total NRV	Total notional CHF bn
Interest rate contracts											
Over-the-counter (OTC) contracts											
Forward contracts	1,001	764	172	177	38	34			1,211	975	1,848.0
Swaps	5,629	4,784	9,891	10,134	46,690	47,128	51,609	46,429	113,819	108,295	22,643.4
Options	273	308	127	440	2,252	3,563	13,529	15,148	16,181	19,459	1,432.5
Exchange-traded contracts.[4]											
Futures											2,904.4
Options	406	438	474	485	96	96			976	1,019	34.7
Total	7,309	6,294	10,664	11,236	49,076	50,821	65,138	61,397	132,187	129,748	28,863.0

Note 23. Derivative Instruments and Hedge Accounting[1] (continued)
As at December 31, 2006

	Term to maturity										
	Within 3 months		3 – 12 months		1 – 5 years		Over 5 years		Total	Total	Total notional
CHF million	PRV[2]	NRV[3]	PRV	NRV	PRV	NRV	PRV	NRV	PRV	NRV	CHF bn
Credit derivative contracts											
Over-the-counter (OTC) contracts											
Credit default swaps	35	54	363	673	12,874	14,035	7,425	7,953	20,697	22,715	2,536.6
Total rate of return swaps	54	63	100	74	583	1,606	4,284	3,512	5,021	5,255	103.0
Total	89	117	463	747	13,457	15,641	11,709	11,465	25,718	27,970	2,639.6
Foreign exchange contracts											
Over the counter (OTC) contracts											
Forward contracts	4,565	4,322	1,765	1,968	827	531	17	103	7,174	6,924	784.0
Interest and currency swaps	24,724	22,977	10,363	10,599	14,641	12,366	12,821	11,831	62,549	57,773	4,064.6
Options	2,877	2,624	2,987	3,042	828	1,041	51	49	6,743	6,756	1,276.2
Exchange-traded contracts[4]											
Futures											20.8
Options	12	16	2	2					14	18	0.1
Total	32,178	29,939	15,117	15,611	16,296	13,938	12,889	11,983	76,480	71,471	6,145.7
Equity/index contracts											
Over-the-counter (OTC) contracts											
Forward contracts	1,179	1,464	386	1,217	506	8	14	103	2,085	2,792	107.8
Options	1,073	3,485	3,702	5,655	6,121	8,821	1,605	2,795	12,501	20,756	258.0
Exchange-traded contracts[4]											
Futures											72.4
Options	4,277	4,602	8,238	8,396	9,978	10,458			22,946	23,889	270.7
Total	6,529	9,551	12,326	15,268	16,605	19,287	2,072	3,331	37,532	47,437	708.9
Precious metals contracts											
Over-the-counter (OTC) contracts											
Forward contracts	348	339	573	355	757	371	37	48	1,715	1,113	25.6
Options	293	580	676	784	1,554	1,281	118	68	2,641	2,713	70.6
Exchange-traded contracts[4]											
Futures											1.0
Options	75	142	242	196	332	369			649	707	23.9
Total	716	1,061	1,491	1,335	2,643	2,021	155	116	5,005	4,533	121.1
Commodity contracts, excluding precious metals contracts											
Over-the-counter (OTC) contracts											
Forward contracts	3,254	3,223	2,894	3,155	1,724	1,579	766	840	8,638	8,797	86.3
Options	221	236	447	368	595	654	1	27	1,264	1,285	13.0

Note 23. Derivative Instruments and Hedge Accounting[1] (continued)

As at December 31, 2006

CHF million	Term to maturity										
	Within 3 months		3 – 12 months		1 – 5 years		Over 5 years		Total	Total	Total notional
	PRV[2]	NRV[3]	PRV	NRV	PRV	NRV	PRV	NRV	PRV	NRV	CHF bn
Exchange-traded contracts[4]											
Futures											236.7
Options	1,884	1,895	2,349	2,152	1,918	1,775	767	867	6,151	5,822	67.1
Total	5,359	5,354	5,690	5,675	4,237	4,008			16,053	15,904	403.1
Total derivative instruments	52,180	52,316	45,751	49,872	102,314	105,716	92,730	89,159	292,975[5]	297,063[6]	

[1] Bifurcated embedded derivatives are presented in the same balance sheet line as the host contract and are excluded from the table. Payables and receivables resulting from the valuation of regular-way purchases and sales of financial assets between trade and settlement date are recognized as replacement values and therefore included in the table.

[2] PRV: Positive Replacement Value.

[3] NRV: Negative Replacement Value.

[4] Exchange-traded products include own account trades only.

[5] The impact of netting agreements accepted by the Swiss Federal Banking Commission (SFBC) for capital adequacy calculations is to reduce positive replacement values to CHF 73,155 million.

[6] The impact of netting agreements accepted by the SFBC for capital adequacy calculations is to reduce negative replacement values to CHF 77,243 million.

Note 30. Fair value of financial instruments

26a. Fair value of financial instruments

Fair value is the amount for which an asset could be exchanged, or a liability settled, between knowledgeable, willing parties in an arm's-length transaction. For financial instruments carried at fair value, market prices or rates are used to determine fair value where an active market exists (such as a recognized stock exchange), as it is the best evidence of the fair value of a financial instrument (level 1). Refer to note 1a5 for an overview on the determination of fair value.

Market prices and rates are not, however, available for certain financial assets and liabilities held and issued by UBS. In these cases, fair values are estimated using present value or other valuation techniques, using inputs based on market conditions existing at balance sheet dates. If available, market observable inputs are applied to valuation models. Fair value measurements are considered level 2 if all significant inputs are market observable. Where one or more significant input is not market observable, valuations are considered level 3, and the nonmarket observable valuation parameters are estimated based on appropriate assumptions.

Valuation techniques are generally applied to OTC derivatives and unlisted financial investments and liabilities held for trading and designated at fair value. The most frequently applied pricing models and valuation techniques include forward pricing and swap models using present value calculations, option models such as the Black-Scholes model or generalizations of it, and credit models such as default rate models or credit spread models.

The values derived from applying these techniques are significantly affected by the choice of valuation model and the underlying assumptions made concerning factors such as the amounts and timing of future cash flows, discount rates, volatility, and credit risk.

The fair values of Loans and Debt issued measured at amortized cost are CHF 332.9 billion and CHF 222.8 billion at December 31, 2007, and CHF 296.6 billion and CHF 191.1 billion at December 31, 2006. For all other balance sheet lines including financial instruments, the fair value represents the carrying amount, or the deviation between fair value and carrying amount is negligible.

The following methods and significant assumptions have been applied in determining the fair values of financial instruments:

a. Trading portfolio assets and liabilities, trading portfolio assets pledged as collateral, financial assets and liabilities designated at fair value through profit or loss, derivatives, credit commitments held for trading and designated at fair value, and other transactions undertaken for trading purposes are measured at fair value by reference to quoted market prices when available. If quoted market prices are not available, then fair values are estimated on the basis of pricing models, or other recognized valuation techniques. Accrued interest is recognized as part of the fair value of such instruments.

    The Group's own credit risk is included in the determination of fair value of financial liabilities accounted for at fair value, including derivative liabilities, in cases where market participants would consider it relevant to pricing. It was calculated based on a yield curve generated from observed external pricing for funding associated with new senior debt issued by the Group. For fully collateralized transactions and other instruments for which market participants do not include an entity-specific adjustment for own credit, no adjustment for own credit changes is made. For the deferral and recognition of day 1 profit or loss, refer to note 26e.

    Fair value is equal to the carrying amount for these items. For financial instruments linked to the US residential mortgage market, refer to the section on the next page.

b. Financial investments available-for-sale are measured at fair value by reference to quoted market prices when available. If quoted market prices are not available, then fair values are estimated on the basis of pricing models or other recognized valuation techniques. Lock-in periods for equity investments are considered when determining fair value. Fair value is equal to the carrying amount for these items, and unrealized gains and losses, excluding impairment write-downs, are recorded in equity until an asset is sold, collected or otherwise disposed of.

c. The fair value of demand deposits and savings accounts with no specific maturity is assumed to be the amount payable on demand at the balance sheet date;

d. The fair value of variable-rate financial instruments accounted for at amortized cost is assumed to be approximated by their carrying amounts and, in the case of loans, does not reflect changes in their credit quality, as the impact of impairment is recognized separately by deducting any allowances for credit losses from the carrying values.

e. The fair value of fixed-rate loans and mortgages carried at amortized cost is estimated by comparing market interest rates when the loans were granted with current market rates offered on similar loans. Changes in the credit quality of loans within the portfolio are not taken into account in determining gross fair values, as the impact of impairment is recognized separately by deducting any allowances for credit losses from the carrying values.

These valuation techniques and assumptions provide a measurement of fair value for UBS's assets and liabilities as shown in the table. However, because other institutions may use different methods and assumptions when estimating fair value using a valuation technique, and when estimating the fair value of financial instruments not carried at fair value, such fair value disclosures cannot necessarily be compared from one financial institution to another.

UBS's undrawn credit commitments are at variable rates, except certain commitments with fixed credit spreads which are classified as held for trading or accounted for under the fair value option. Accordingly, UBS has no significant exposure to fair value fluctuations resulting from interest rate movements related to commitments which are recognized with their fair value on balance sheet.

The fair values of UBS's fixed-rate loans, long- and medium-term notes and bonds issued are predominantly hedged by derivative instruments, mainly interest rate swaps, as explained in Note 23. The interest rate risk inherent in balance sheet positions with no specific maturity may also be hedged with derivative instruments based on management's view of their average cash flow and repricing behavior.

Derivative instruments used for hedging are carried on the balance sheet at fair values, which are included in the positive or negative replacement values. When the interest rate risk on a fixed-rate financial instrument is hedged with a derivative in a fair value hedge, the fixed-rate financial instrument (or hedged portion thereof) is measured at fair value only in relation to the interest rate risk, not the credit risk, as explained in (e). Fair value changes are recorded in net profit. The treatment of derivatives designated as cash flow hedges is explained in Note 1a14. The amount shown in the table as Derivative instruments designated as cash flow hedges is the net change in fair values on such derivatives that is recorded in equity and not yet transferred to income or expense.

Positions related to the US residential mortgage market

Where possible, holdings are marked at the quoted market price in an active market. In the current market environment, such price information is typically not available for instruments linked to the US subprime residential mortgage market, and UBS applies valuation techniques to measure such instrument. Valuation techniques use "market observable inputs," where available, derived from similar assets in similar and active markets, from recent transaction prices for comparable items or from other observable market data. For positions where observable reference data is not available, UBS uses valuation models with nonmarket observable inputs.

For the year ended December 31, 2007, UBS used valuation models primarily for super senior RMBS CDO tranches referenced to subprime RMBSs. The model used to value these positions projects losses on the underlying mortgage pools and applies the implications of these projected lifetime losses through to the RMBS securities and then to the CDO structure. The primary inputs to the model are monthly remittance data that describe the current performance of the underlying mortgage pools. These are received near the end of each month and relate to the preceding month's cash flows on the mortgages underlying the relevant mortgage-backed securities. Since this valuation model was adopted in third quarter 2007, UBS has sought to calibrate the model to market information and to review the assumptions of the model on a regular basis. In fourth quarter 2007, UBS calibrated its loss projection estimates to ensure the super senior RMBS

CDO valuation model would value relevant market indices (for example, ABX indices) consistently with their observed levels in the market. Despite the various limitations in the comparability of these indices to UBS's own positions, it was felt that adopting this approach would be best in view of the further deterioration in liquidity and resultant lack of observed transactions to which the model could be calibrated. The valuation model also considers the impact of variability in projected lifetime loss levels and applies a discount rate for expected cash flows derived from relevant market index prices (for example, ABX indices). The external ratings of the RMBSs underlying the CDO tranches or the CDO tranches themselves are inputs to the valuation model only to the extent that they impact the timing of potential "events of default." The valuation model incorporates the potential timing and impact of such default events based on an analysis of the contractual rights of various parties to the transaction and the estimated performance of the underlying collateral. There is no single market standard for valuation models in this area and such models have inherent limitations, and different assumptions and inputs would generate different results. The super senior RMBS CDO valuation model is used to value transactions where UBS is net long the super senior RMBS CDO exposure and transactions where UBS holds a gross long position hedged one-to-one with an offsetting short position provided by a monoline insurer. The valuation model therefore provides an estimate of the current credit exposure to monoline insurers via such transactions. The fair value of these positions also takes the counterparty credit risk of the monocline insurers into account. Where valuation techniques based on observable inputs are used to value RMBS positions, a consistent approach is used to value related hedge positions with monocline insurers.

Adverse fair value changes of instruments related to the US residential mortgage market are reflected in net trading income. The related trading positions are recognized on UBS's balance sheet as trading portfolio instruments or positive and negative replacement values. Financial instruments related to the US subprime and Alt-A market include collateralized debt obligations (CDOs), mortgage-backed securities, mortgage loans and derivatives linked to the US mortgage market. Such instruments are either purchased in transactions with third parties or retained in structures such as securitizations originated by UBS. The parameters to measure such instruments generally include expected credit default rates, weighted-average life, prepayment speed and discount rates. Information about the risks and exposures of such items is included in the "Risk concentrations" section in *Risk, Treasury and Capital Management 2007*.

30b. Determination of fair values from quoted market prices or valuation techniques

For trading portfolio assets and liabilities, financial assets and liabilities designated at fair value and financial investments available-for-sale which are listed or otherwise traded in an active market, for exchange-traded derivatives, and for other financial instruments for which quoted prices in an active market are available, fair value is determined directly from those quoted market prices (level 1).

For financial instruments which do not have quoted market prices directly available from an active market, fair values are estimated using valuation techniques or models, based wherever possible on assumptions supported by observable market prices or rates prevailing at the balance sheet date (level 2). This is the case for the majority of OTC derivatives, and for many unlisted instruments and other items which are not traded in active markets.

For some types of financial instruments, fair values cannot be obtained directly from quoted market prices, or indirectly using valuation techniques or models supported by observable market prices or rates. This is generally the case for private equity investments in unlisted securities, and for certain complex or structured financial instruments. In these cases fair value is estimated indirectly using valuation techniques or models for which the inputs are reasonable assumptions, based on market conditions (level 3). The illiquidity of a broad range of financial instruments linked to the US residential mortgage market required an extended use of valuations based on partially or fully nonmarket observable market inputs in the second half of 2007.

The following table presents the valuation methods used to determine fair values of financial instruments carried at fair value:

		12/31/07				12/31/06		
CHF billion	*Quoted market price*	*Valuation techniques— market observable inputs*	*Valuation techniques— nonmarket observable inputs*	*Total*	*Quoted market price*	*Valuation techniques— market observable inputs*	*Valuation techniques— nonmarket observable inputs*	*Total*
Trading portfolio assets	249.3	323.4	37.3	610.0	215.1	411.8	0.1	627.0
Trading portfolio assets pledged as collateral	85.3	55.8	23.2	164.3	243.5	8.0	0.0	251.5
Positive replacement values	6.8	407.4	14.0	428.2	31.3	250.2	11.5	293.0
Financial assets designated at fair value	1.8	10.0	0.0	11.8	0.0	5.1	0.8	5.9
Financial investments available-for-sale	1.2	2.4	1.4	5.0	2.5	4.6	1.8	8.9
Total assets	344.4	799.0	75.9	1,219.3	492.4	679.7	14.2	1,186.3
Trading portfolio liabilities	119.9	44.9	0.0	164.8	169.9	34.9	0.0	204.8
Negative replacement values	6.6	420.1	16.8	443.5	32.7	255.2	9.2	297.1
Financial liabilities designated at fair value	0.0	149.5	42.4	191.9	0.0	113.0	32.7	145.7
Total liabilities	126.5	614.5	59.2	800.2	202.6	403.1	41.9	647.6

30c. Sensitivity of fair values to changing significant assumptions to reasonably possible alternatives

Included in the fair value of financial instruments carried at fair value on the balance sheet are those estimated in full or in part using valuation techniques based on assumptions that are not supported by market observable prices or rates (level 3).

There may be uncertainty about a valuation, resulting from the choice of model used, the assumptions embedded in those models, the extent to which inputs are not market observable, or as a result of other elements affecting the valuation technique. Valuation adjustments, including model reserves, are applied to reflect such uncertainties and are deducted from the fair values produced by the models or other valuation techniques.

All models used for valuation undergo an internal validation process before they are approved for use.

Based on UBS's established fair value and model governance policies and the related controls and procedural safeguards the Group employs, management believes the resulting estimated fair values recorded in the balance sheet and the changes in fair values recorded in the income statement are reasonable and are the most appropriate at the balance sheet date.

Uncertainties associated with the use of model-based valuations (both level 2 and level 3) are predominantly addressed through the use of model reserves. These reserves reflect the amounts the UBS estimates are appropriate to deduct from the valuations produced directly by the models to reflect uncertainties in the relevant modeling assumptions and inputs used. In arriving at these estimates, UBS considers the range of market practice and how it believes other market participants would assess these uncertainties. Model reserves are periodically reassessed in light of information from market transactions, pricing utilities, and other relevant sources. The level of these model reserves is, nevertheless, to a large extent judgmental.

To estimate the potential effect on the financial statements from the use of alternative valuation techniques or assumptions, UBS makes use of the model reserve amounts described above, by scaling the level of the model reserves higher and lower, to assess the impact on valuation of increasing or decreasing the amount of model-related uncertainty considered.

The potential effect of using reasonably possible alternative assumptions has been quantified as follows:

- Scaling the model reserve amounts upward in line with less favorable assumptions would reduce fair value by approximately CHF 2,710 million at December 31, 2007; by approximately CHF 1,038 million at December 31, 2006, and approximately CHF 1,094 million at December 31, 2005.
- Scaling the model reserve amounts downward in line with more favorable assumptions would increase fair value by approximately CHF 2,160 million at December 31, 2007, approximately CHF 955 million at December 31, 2006, and approximately CHF 1,176 million at December 31, 2005.

30d. Changes in fair value recognized in profit or loss during the period which were estimated using valuation techniques with nonmarket observable inputs

Total net trading income/(loss) for the years ended December 31, 2007, December 31, 2006, and December 31, 2005, was CHF (8,353) million, CHF 13,743 million and CHF 8,248 million, respectively, which represents the net result from a range of products traded across different business activities, including the effect of foreign currency translation of monetary assets and liabilities and including both realized and unrealized income. Unrealized income is determined from changes in fair values, using quoted prices in active markets when available, and otherwise estimated using valuation techniques with market observable and/or nonmarket observable inputs.

Net trading income includes net losses of CHF 11,580 million, net gains of CHF 354 million and net losses of CHF 468 million from unrealized fair value changes of financial instruments for which fair value is calculated on the basis of valuation techniques with significant nonmarket observable inputs (level 3) for the years ended December 31, 2007, 2006, and 2005.

Such valuation techniques reflecting significant nonmarket observable inputs (level 3) include mainly models for more complex financial instruments and for financial instruments for which markets were illiquid at the balance sheet date. They require the use of reasonable assumptions and estimates based on market conditions at balance sheet date.

Net trading income is often generated from transactions involving several financial instruments or subject to hedging or other risk management techniques. This may result in different portions of the transaction being priced using different methods. In many cases, the amounts estimated using valuation techniques with nonmarket observable inputs were offset or partially offset by changes in fair value of other financial instruments or transactions, for which quoted market prices or rates were available, or on which the gain or loss has been realized. Consequently, the changes in fair value which were estimated using valuation techniques with nonmarket observable inputs and have been recognized in profit or loss during the period represent only a portion of net trading income.

30e. Deferred day 1 profit or loss

The table reflects financial instruments for which fair value is determined using valuation models where not all inputs are market observable. Such financial instruments are initially recognized at their transaction price although the values obtained from the relevant valuation model on day 1 may differ. The table shows the aggregate difference yet to be recognized in profit or loss at the beginning and end of the period and a reconciliation of changes in the balance of this difference (movement of deferred day 1 profit or loss).

	12/31/07	*12/31/06*
CHF billion		
Balance at the beginning of the year	951	1,343
Deferred profit/(loss) on new transactions	1,259	890
Recognized (profit)/loss in the income statement	(1,383)	(1,200)
Revision to fair value estimates	(224)	--
Foreign currency translation	(53)	(82)
Balance at the end of the year	550	951

ACCOUNTING AND REPORTING BY RETIREMENT BENEFIT PLANS

PERSPECTIVE AND ISSUES

IAS 26 sets out the form and content of the general-purpose financial reports of retirement benefit plans. This standard deals with accounting and reporting to all participants of a plan as a group, and not with reports which might be made to individuals about their particular retirement benefits. The standard applies to

- Defined contribution plans where benefits are determined by contributions to the plan together with investment earnings thereon; and
- Defined benefit plans where benefits are determined by a formula based on employees' earnings and/or years of service.

IAS 26 may be compared to IAS 19. The former addresses the financial reporting considerations for the benefit plan itself, as the reporting entity, while the latter deals with employers' accounting for the cost of such benefits as they are earned by the employees. While these standards are thus somewhat related, there will not be any direct interrelationship between amounts reported in benefit plan financial statements and amounts reported under IAS 19 by employers.

IAS 26 became effective for financial statements of retirement benefit plans in 1988. While IAS 19 has been revised twice, IAS 26 has never been revised by the IASC. It was, however, reformatted in 1994 to bring it in line with the current IASC practice. There are no current plans to address this topic again.

Sources of IFRS
IAS 26

DEFINITIONS OF TERMS

Actuarial present value of promised retirement benefits. The present value of the expected future payments by a retirement benefit plan to existing and past employees, attributable to the service already rendered.

Defined benefit plans. Retirement benefit plans whereby retirement benefits to be paid to plan participants are determined by reference to a formula usually based on employees' earnings and/or years of service.

Defined contribution plans. Retirement benefit plans whereby retirement benefits to be paid to plan participants are determined by contributions to a fund together with investment earnings thereon.

Funding. The transfer of assets to a separate entity (distinct from the employer's entity), the "fund," to meet future obligations for the payment of retirement benefits.

Net assets available for benefits. The assets of a retirement benefit plan less its liabilities other than the actuarial present value of promised retirement benefits.

Participants. The members of a retirement benefit plan and others who are entitled to benefits under the plan.

Retirement benefit plans. Formal or informal arrangements based upon which an entity provides benefits for its employees on or after termination of service, which are usually referred to as "termination benefits." These could take the form of annual pension payments or lump-sum payments. Such benefits, or the employer's contributions towards them, should however be determinable or possible of estimation in advance of retirement, from the provisions of a document (i.e., based on a formal arrangement) or from the entity's practices (which is referred to as an informal arrangement).

Vested benefits. Entitlements, the rights to which, under the terms of a retirement benefit plan, are not conditional on continued employment.

CONCEPTS, RULES, AND EXAMPLES

Scope

IAS 26 should be applied in accounting and reporting by retirement benefit plans. The terms of a retirement plan may require that the plan present an annual report; in some jurisdictions this may be a statutory requirement. IAS 26 does not establish a mandate for the publication of such reports by retirement plans. However, if such reports are prepared by a retirement plan, then the requirements of this standard should be applied to them.

IAS 26 regards a retirement benefit plan as a separate entity, distinct from the employer of the plan's participants. It is noteworthy that this standard also applies to retirement benefit plans that have sponsors other than employer (e.g., trade associations or groups of employers). Furthermore, this standard deals with accounting and reporting by retirement benefit plans to all participants as a group; it does not deal with reports to individual participants with respect to their retirement benefit entitlements.

The standard applies the same basis of accounting and reporting to informal retirement benefit arrangements as it applies to formal retirement benefit plans. It is also worthy of mention that this standard applies whether or not a separate fund is created and regardless of whether there are trustees. The requirements of this standard also apply to retirement benefit plans with assets invested with an insurance company, unless the contract with the insurance company is in the name of a specified participant or a group of participants and the responsibility is solely of the insurance company.

Defined Contribution Plans

Retirement benefit plans are usually described as being either defined contribution or defined benefit plans. When the quantum of the future benefits payable to the retirement benefit plan participants is determined by the contributions paid by the participants' employer, the participants, or both, together with investment earnings thereon, such plans are defined contribution plans. Defined benefit plans, by contrast, promise certain benefits, often determined by formulae which involve factors such as years of service and salary level at the time of retirement, without regard to whether the plan has sufficient assets; thus the ultimate responsibility for payment (which may be guaranteed by an insurance company, the government or some other entity, depending on local law and custom) remains with the employer. In rare circumstances, a retirement benefit plan may contain characteristics of both defined contribution and defined benefit plans; such a hybrid plan is deemed to be a defined benefit plan for the purposes of this standard.

IAS 26 requires that the report of a defined contribution plan contain a statement of the net assets available for benefits and a description of the funding policy. In preparing the statement of the net assets available for benefits, the plan investments should be carried at fair value, which for marketable securities would be market value. In case an estimate of fair value is not possible, disclosure is required of the reason as to why fair value has not been used. As a practical matter, most plan assets will have determinable market values, since the plans' trustees' discharge of their fiduciary responsibilities will generally mandate that only marketable investments be held.

An example of a statement of net assets available for plan benefits, for a defined contribution plan, is set forth below.

XYZ Defined Contribution Plan
Statement of Net Assets Available for Benefits
December 31, 2008
(€000)

Assets	
Investments at fair value	
US government securities	€ 5,000
US municipal bonds	3,000
US equity securities	3,000
Non-US equity securities	3,000
US debt securities	2,000
Non-US corporate bonds	2,000
Others	1,000
Total investments	19,000
Receivables	
Amounts due from stockbrokers on sale of securities	15,000
Accrued interest	5,000
Dividends receivable	2,000
Total receivables	22,000
Cash	5,000
Total assets	€46,000
Liabilities	
Accounts payable	
Amounts due to stockbrokers on purchase of securities	€10,000
Benefits payable to participants—due and unpaid	11,000
Total accounts payable	21,000
Accrued expenses	11,000
Total liabilities	€32,000
Net assets available for benefits	€14,000

Defined benefit plans. When amounts to be paid as retirement benefits are determined by reference to a formula, usually based on employees' earnings and/or years of service, such retirement benefit plans are defined benefit plans. The key factor is that the benefits are fixed or determinable, without regard to the adequacy of assets which may have been set aside for payment of the benefits. This contrasts to the defined contribution plans approach, which is to provide the workers, upon retirement, with the amounts which have been set aside, plus or minus investment earnings or losses which have been accumulated thereon, however great or small that amount may be.

The standard requires that the report of a defined benefit plan should contain *either*

1. A statement that shows

    a. The net assets available for benefits;
    b. The actuarial present value of promised retirement benefits, distinguishing between vested and nonvested benefits; and
    c. The resulting excess or deficit;

or

2. A statement of net assets available for benefits including *either*

    a. A note disclosing the actuarial present value of promised retirement benefits, distinguishing between vested and nonvested benefits; or
    b. A reference to this information in an accompanying actuarial report.

IAS 26 recommends, but does not mandate, that in each of the three formats described above, a trustees' report in the nature of a management or directors' report and an investment report may also accompany the statements.

The standard does not make it incumbent upon the plan to obtain annual actuarial valuations. If an actuarial valuation has not been prepared on the date of the report, the most recent valuation should be used as the basis for preparing the financial statement. The date of the valuation used should be disclosed. Actuarial present values of promised benefits should be based either on current or projected salary levels; whichever basis is used should be disclosed. The effect of any changes in actuarial assumptions that had a material impact on the actuarial present value of promised retirement benefits should also be disclosed. The report should explain the relationship between actuarial present values of promised benefits, the net assets available for benefits and the policy for funding the promised benefits.

As in the case of defined contribution plans, investments of a defined benefit plan should be carried at fair value, which for marketable securities, would be market value.

The following are examples of the alternative types of reports prescribed for a defined benefit plan:

ABC Defined Benefit Plan
Statement of Net Assets Available for Benefits, Actuarial Present Value of Accumulated
Retirement Benefits and Plan Excess or Deficit
December 31, 2008
(€000)

1. Statement of net assets available for benefits

Assets	
Investments at fair value	
US government securities	€ 50,000
US municipal bonds	30,000
US equity securities	30,000
Non-US equity securities	30,000
US debt securities	20,000
Non-US corporate bonds	20,000
Others	10,000
Total investments	€190,000
Receivables	
Amounts due from stockbrokers on sale of securities	150,000
Accrued interest	50,000
Dividends receivable	20,000
Total receivables	220,000
Cash	50,000
Total assets	460,000
Liabilities	
Accounts payable	
Amounts due to stockbrokers on purchase of securities	100,000
Benefits payable to participants–due and unpaid	110,000
Total accounts payable	210,000
Accrued expenses	110,000
Total liabilities	320,000
Net assets available for benefits	€140,000

2. Actuarial present value of accumulated plan benefits

Vested benefits	€100,000
Nonvested benefits	20,000
Total	€120,000

3. Excess of net assets available for benefits over actuarial present value of accumulated plan benefits   € 20,000

ABC Defined Benefit Plan
Statement of Changes in Net Assets Available for Benefits
December 31, 2008
(€000)

Investment income	
Interest income	€ 40,000
Dividend income	10,000
Net appreciation (unrealized gain) in fair value of investments	10,000
Total investment income	60,000
Plan contributions	
Employer contributions	50,000
Employee contributions	50,000
Total plan contributions	100,000
Total additions to net asset value	160,000
Plan benefit payments	
Pensions (annual)	30,000
Lump sum payments on retirement	30,000
Severance pay	10,000
Commutation of superannuation benefits	15,000
Total plan benefit payments	85,000
Total deductions from net asset value	85,000
Net increase in asset value	75,000
Net assets available for benefits	
Beginning of year	65,000
End of year	€140,000

Additional Disclosures

IAS 26 requires that the reports of a retirement benefit plan, both defined benefit plans and defined contribution plans, should also contain the following information:

1. A statement of changes in net assets available for benefits;
2. A summary of significant accounting policies; and
3. A description of the plan and the effect of any changes in the plan during the period.

Reports provided by retirement benefits plans may include the following, if applicable:

1. A statement of net assets available for benefits disclosing

    a. Assets at the end of the period suitably classified;
    b. The basis of valuation of assets;
    c. Details of any single investment exceeding either 5% of the net assets available for benefits or 5% of any class or type of security;
    d. Details of any investment in the employer; and
    e. Liabilities other than the actuarial present value of promised retirement benefits;

2. A statement of changes in net assets available for benefits showing the following:

    a. Employer contributions;
    b. Employee contributions;

   c. Investment income such as interest and dividends;
   d. Other income;
   e. Benefits paid or payable (analyzed, for example, as retirement, death and disability benefits, and lump-sum payments);
   f. Administrative expenses;
   g. Other expenses;
   h. Taxes on income;
   i. Profits and losses on disposal of investments and changes in value of investments; and
   j. Transfers from and to other plans;

  3. A description of the funding policy;
  4. For defined benefit plans, the actuarial present value of promised retirement benefits (which may distinguish between vested benefits and nonvested benefits) based on the benefits promised under the terms of the plan, on service rendered to date and using either current salary levels or projected salary levels. This information may be included in an accompanying actuarial report to be read in conjunction with the related information; and
  5. For defined benefit plans, a description of the significant actuarial assumptions made and the method used to calculate the actuarial present value of promised retirement benefits.

According to the standard, since the report of a retirement benefit plan contains a description of the plan, either as part of the financial information or in a separate report, it may contain the following:

  1. The names of the employers and the employee groups covered;
  2. The number of participants receiving benefits and the number of other participants, classified as appropriate;
  3. The type of plan—defined contribution or defined benefit;
  4. A note as to whether participants contribute to the plan;
  5. A description of the retirement benefits promised to participants;
  6. A description of any plan termination terms; and
  7. Changes in items 1. through 6. during the period covered by the report.

Furthermore, it is not uncommon to refer to other documents that are readily available to users and in which the plan is described, and to include only information on subsequent changes in the report.

AGRICULTURE

PERSPECTIVE AND ISSUES

Over most of its existence, the former IASC was focused on the task of developing or endorsing existing standards that are pertinent to general-purpose financial reporting. In the latter years of its existence, completion of the core set of standards, which too was oriented toward general-purpose financial statement needs, was of paramount importance, in order to gain IOSCO endorsement and wider acceptance. The special needs of individual industries, of necessity, received very little attention during this period.

However, the IASC was able, before restructuring (described in Chapter 1) took place and IASB became the international accounting standard-setting body, to complete its project on accounting for agricultural activities. This was a major undertaking, having widespread implications, particularly for those many nations that rely heavily on the agricultural sectors of their economies.

Agriculture, the first set of specialized financial reporting issues to be given a comprehensive financial reporting model (banking was given only expanded disclosure rules, subsequently subsumed in expanded in the financial instrument disclosure requirements of IFRS 7), received a great deal of attention from IASC. When the IASC's draft statement of position was issued, it marked the first real attention paid to one of the world's most prominent economic activities by any of the various accounting rule-making bodies. For developing nations, agriculture is indeed disproportionately significant, and given the IASC's role in establishing financial reporting standards for those nations, this focus on agriculture was perhaps to be expected.

Sources of IFRS
IAS 41

DEFINITIONS OF TERMS

Active market. Market for which all these conditions exist: the items traded within the market are homogeneous; willing buyers and sellers can normally be found at any time; and prices are available to the public.

Agricultural activity. Managed biological transformation of biological assets into agricultural produce for sale, consumption, further processing, or into other biological assets.

Agricultural land. Land used directly to support and sustain biological assets in agricultural activity; the land itself is not a biological asset, however.

Agricultural produce. The harvested product of the entity's biological assets awaiting sale, processing, or consumption.

Bearer biological assets. Those which bear agricultural produce for harvest. The biological assets themselves are not the primary agricultural produce, but rather are self-regenerating (such as sheep raised for wool production; fruit trees).

Biological assets. Living plants and animals controlled by the entity as a result of past events. Control may be through ownership or through another type of legal arrangement.

Biological transformation. The processes of growth, degeneration, production and procreation, which cause qualitative and quantitative changes in living organisms and the generation of new assets in the form of agricultural produce or additional biological assets of the same class.

Carrying amount. Amount at which an asset is recognized in the statement of financial position after deducting any accumulated depreciation or amortization and accumulated impairment losses thereon.

Consumable biological assets. Those which are to be harvested as the primary agricultural produce, such as livestock intended for meat production, annual crops, and trees to be felled for pulp.

Fair value. The amount for which an asset could be exchanged or a liability settled between knowledgeable, willing parties in an arm's-length transaction.

Group of biological assets. A herd, flock, etc., that is managed jointly to ensure that the group is sustainable on an ongoing basis, and is homogeneous as to both type of animal or plant and activity for which the group is deployed.

Harvest. The detachment of agricultural produce from the biological asset, the removal of a living plant from agricultural land for sale and replanting, or the cessation of a biological asset's life processes.

Immature biological assets. Those that are not yet harvestable or able to sustain regular harvests.

Mature biological assets. Those that are harvestable or able to sustain regular harvest. Consumable biological assets are mature when they have attained harvestable specifications; bearer biological assets are mature when they are able to sustain regular harvests.

Net realizable value. Estimated selling price in the ordinary course of business, less the estimated costs of completion and the estimated costs necessary to make the sale.

CONCEPTS, RULES, AND EXAMPLES

Background

Historically, agricultural activities received scant, if any, attention from the world's accounting standard setters. This may have been due to the fact that the major national and international accounting standard setters have been those of the US and the UK, whose economies are far less dependent upon agriculture than those of many lesser-developed nations of the world. The IASC, in seeking to become the world's preeminent accounting standard setter, has until very recently had its greatest impact on the financial reporting standards of the developing nations, many of which have adopted IAS as a whole, and many more of which have based their respective national standards on the IAS. Perhaps because of the IASC's sensitivity to this constituency, its agriculture project, begun some five years ago, received a good deal of serious attention. The culmination of this lengthy project, the newly issued standard IAS 41, is by far the most comprehensive addressing of this financial reporting topic ever undertaken.

The earlier exclusion of agriculture from most established accounting and financial reporting rules can best be understood in the context of certain unique features of the industry. These include biological transformations (growth, procreation, production, degeneration) which alter the very substance of the biological assets; the wide variety of characteristics of the living assets which challenge traditional classification schemes; the nature of management functions in the industry; and the predominance of small, closely held ownership. On the other hand, since in many nations agriculture is a major industry, in some cases accounting for over 50% of gross national product, logic would suggest that comprehensive systems of financial reporting for business entities cannot be deemed complete while excluding so large a segment of the economy.

In the past, the general lack of urgency in dealing with this subject has been abetted by the fact that much of agriculture is controlled by closely held or family held businesses, with few, if any, outside owners who might have demanded formal financial statements prepared in accordance with agreed-upon accounting principles. Also, grantors of farm credit have historically looked to the character of the borrower, usually a longtime resident with deep roots in the community, rather than to financial statements. While some of these factors continue to be valid, the IASC concluded that the time had long since arrived to give financial reporting concerns their due attention.

In the realm of previously established international accounting standards, most of the rules which logically could have addressed agricultural issues (IAS 2 on inventories; IAS 16 on plant, property, and equipment; and IAS 18 on revenue recognition) deliberately excluded most or all agriculture-related applications. A review of published financial statements for agriculture-related entities would have revealed the consequences of this neglect: a wide range of methods and principles have been applied to such businesses as forest products, livestock, and grain production.

For example, some forest products companies have accounted for timberlands at original cost, charging depreciation only to the extent of net harvesting, with reforestation costs charged to expense as incurred. Others in the same industry capitalized reforestation costs and even carrying costs, and charged depletion on a units-of-production basis. Still others have been valuing forest lands at the net present value of expected future cash flows. This wide disparity obviously has impaired users' ability to gauge the relative performance of entities operating within a single industry group, hindering investment and other decision making by them.

For this reason, the IASC concluded in the mid-1990s that excluding agriculture from the scope of IAS was no longer appropriate. At the same time, it also accepted the need for a relatively simple, uniform, and coherent set of principles applicable to this industry group because of the preponderance of small, less sophisticated businesses. The IASC concluded that embracing fair value in addition to, or instead of, the historical cost model, which had already been applied by existing IAS (e.g., to plant and equipment and to investments), offered the best solution to this problem. The new standard will apply only to biological assets, as those are the aspects of agriculture that have unique characteristics; the accounting for assets such as inventories and plant and equipment will be guided by such existing standards as IAS 2 and 16. In other words, once the biological transformation process is complete (e.g., when grain is harvested, animals are slaughtered, or trees are cut down), the specialized accounting principles imposed on agriculture will cease to apply.

Defining Agriculture

Agriculture is to be defined as essentially the management of the biological transformation of plants and animals to yield produce for consumption or further processing. The term agriculture encompasses livestock, forestry, annual and perennial cropping, orchards, plantations, and aquiculture. Agriculture is distinguished from "pure exploitation," where resources are simply removed from the environment (e.g., by fishing or deforestation) without management initiatives such as operation of hatcheries, reforestation, or other attempts to manage their regeneration. IAS 41 does not apply to pure exploitation activities, nor does it apply to agricultural produce, which is harvested and is thus a nonliving product of the biological assets. The standard furthermore does not govern accounting for agriculture produce which is incorporated in further processing, as occurs in integrated agribusiness entities that involve activities which are not unique to agriculture.

IAS 41 sets forth a three-part test or set of criteria for agricultural activities. First, the plants or animals which are the object of the activities must be alive and capable of transformation. Second, the change must be managed, which implies a range of activities (e.g., fertilizing the soil and weeding in the case of crop growing; feeding and providing health care in the instance of animal husbandry; etc.). Third, there must be a basis for the measurement of change, such as the ripeness of vegetables, the weight of animals, circumference of trees, and so forth. If these three criteria are all satisfied, the activity will be impacted by the financial reporting requirements imposed by IAS 41.

Biological assets are the principal assets of agricultural activities, and they are held for their transformative potential. This results in two major types of outcomes: the first may involve asset changes—as through growth or quality improvement, degeneration, or procreation. The second involves the creation of separable products initially qualifying as agricultural produce. The management of the biological transformation process is the distinguishing characteristic of agricultural activities.

Biological assets often are managed in groups, as exemplified by herds of animals, groves of trees, and fields of crops. To be considered a group, however, the components must be homogeneous in nature and there must further be homogeneity in the activity for which the group is deployed. For example, cherry trees maintained for their production of fruit are not in the same group as cherry trees grown for lumber.

IAS 41 applies to forests and similar regenerative resources excluded from IAS 16; producers' inventories of livestock, agriculture, and forest products, including those excluded from IAS 2, to the extent they are to be measured at net realizable value; and natural increases in herds and agricultural and forest products excluded from IAS 18. It also addresses financial statement presentation and disclosure (which is the primary province of IAS 1). Furthermore, it establishes that, unless explicit exclusions are provided, all international accounting standards are meant to apply equally to agriculture.

Basic Principles of IAS 41: Fair Value Accounting Is Necessary

IAS 41 applies to all entities which undertake agricultural activities. Animals or plants are to be recognized as assets when it is probable that the future economic benefits associated with the asset will flow to the reporting entity, and when the cost or value to the entity can be measured reliably. There is a strong presumption that any entity entering into agricultural activities on a for-profit basis will have an ability to measure cost and/or fair value. The new standard also governs the initial measurement of agricultural produce, which is the end product of the biological transformation process; it furthermore guides the accounting for government grants pertaining to agricultural assets.

The most important feature of the new standard is the requirement that biological assets are to be measured at their respective fair values as of each date of the statements of financial position. This departure from historical cost is the most significant facet of IAS 41, and is one which has generated a good deal of debate during the drafting and exposure draft stages. The imperative to deploy fair value accounting springs from the fact that there are long production periods for many crops (an extreme being forests under management for as long as thirty years before being harvested) and, even more typically, for livestock. In the absence of fair value accounting with changes in value being reported in operating results, the entire earnings of a long-term production process might only be reported at lengthy intervals, which would not faithfully represent the underlying economic activities being carried out. This is entirely analogous to long-term construction projects, for which percentage-of-completion accounting is commonly prescribed, for very similar reasons.

Historical cost based accounting, with revenue to be recognized only upon ultimate sale of the assets, would often result in a gross distortion of reported results of operations, with little or no earnings being reflected in some periods, or even losses being reported to the extent that production expenses are not inventoried. Other periods—when trees are harvested, for example—would reflect substantial reported profits. Thus, the use of historical costs based on completed transactions is no longer deemed meaningful in the case of agricultural activities.

Not only are such periodic distortions seen as being misleading, but it also has been concluded that each stage of the biological transformation process has significance. Each stage (growth, degeneration, procreation, and production) is now seen as contributing to the expected economic benefits to be derived from the biological assets. Unless a fair value model were employed for financial reporting, there would be a lack of explicit recognition (in effect, no matching) of the benefits associated with each of these discrete events. Furthermore, this recognition underlines the need to apply the same measurement concept to each stage in the life cycle of the biological assets; for example, for live weight change, fleece weight change, aging, deaths, lambs born, and wool shorn, in the case of a flock of sheep.

The obvious argument in favor of historical cost based measures derives from the superior reliability of that mode of measurement. With completed transactions, there is no imprecision due to the inherently subjective process of making or obtaining fair value assessments. By contrast, superior relevance is the strongest argument for current value measurement schemes. The IASC evaluated various measures, including current cost and net realizable value, as well as market value, as alternatives to historical cost, but ultimately identified fair value (ironically, the one approach not addressed in the IASC's seminal document, the *Framework for the Preparation and Presentation of Financial Statements)* as having the best combination of attributes for the determination of agriculture-related earnings. The IASC was particularly influenced by the market context in which agriculture takes place and the transformative characteristics of biological assets, and it concluded that fair value would offer the best balance of relevance, reliability, comparability, and understandability.

The IASC also concluded that annual determinations of fair value would be necessary to properly portray the combined impact of nature and financial transactions for any given reporting period. Less frequent measurements were rejected because of the continuous nature of biological transformations, the lack of direct correlation between financial transactions and the different outcomes arising from biological transformation (thus, the former could not serve as surrogate indicators of the latter during off periods), the volatilities which often characterize natural and market environments affecting agriculture, and the fact that market-based measures are in fact readily available.

The idea of maintaining historical cost as an allowed alternative was rejected, essentially because historical cost is not viewed as meaningful in the context of biological assets, but also due to concerns about the extreme lack of comparability that would result from permitting two so disparate methodologies to coexist. Notwithstanding the fact that historical cost is rejected as being meaningful in this context, the IASC agreed that an exception should exist for those circumstances when fair value cannot be reliably estimated. In such instances, historical costs will continue to be employed instead.

Determining Fair Values

The primary determinant of fair value is market value, just as it is for financial instruments having active markets (as defined in IAS 32, discussed at length in Chapter 5). The required use of "farm gate" market prices will reflect both the "as is" and "where is" attributes of the biological assets. That is, the value is meant to pertain to the assets as they exist, where they are located, in the condition they are in as of the measurement (statement of financial position) date. They are not hypothetical values, as for instance hogs when delivered to the slaughterhouse. Where these "farm gate" prices are not available, market values will have to be reduced by transaction costs, including transport, to arrive at net market values which would equate to fair values as intended by IAS 41.

In the case of products for which market values might not be readily available, other approaches to fair value determination will have to be employed. This is most likely to become an issue where market values exist but, due to market imperfections, are not deemed to be useful. For example, when access to markets is restricted or unduly influenced by temporary monopoly or monopsony conditions, or when no market actually exists as of the date of the statement of financial position, alternative measures will be called for. In such circumstances, it might be necessary to refer to such indicators as the most recent market prices for the class of asset at issue, market prices for similar assets (e.g., different varieties of the same crop), sector benchmarks (e.g., relating value of a dairy farm to the kilograms of milk solids or fat produced), net present value of expected future cash flows discounted at a risk-class rate, or net realizable values for short-cycle products for which most growth has already occurred. Last and probably least useful would be historical costs, which might be particularly suited to biological assets that have thus far experienced little transformation.

One practical problem arises when an indirect method of valuation implicitly values both the crop and the land itself, taken together as a whole. IAS 41 indicates that such valuations must be allocated to the different assets to give a better indication of the future economic benefits each will confer. If a combined market price, for example, can be obtained for the land plus the immature growing crops situated thereon, and a quotation for the land alone can also be obtained, this will permit a fair value assessment of the immature growing crops (while the land itself will generally be presented on the statement of financial position at cost, not fair value, under IAS 16). Another technique would involve the subdivision of the assets into classes based on age, quality, or other traits, and the valuation of each subgroup by reference to market prices. While these methods may involve added effort, IAS 41 concludes that the usefulness of the resulting financial statements will be materially enhanced if this is done.

Increases in fair value due to the growth of the biological asset is only one-half of the accounting equation, of course, since there will normally have been cost inputs incurred to foster the growth (e.g., applications of fertilizer to the fields, etc.). Under the provisions of IAS 41, costs of producing and harvesting biological assets are to be charged to expense as incurred. This is necessary, since if costs were added to the assets' carrying value (analogous to interest on borrowings in connection with long-term construction projects) and the assets were then also adjusted to fair value, there would be risk of double-counting cost or value increases. As mandated, however, value increases due to either price changes or growth, or both, will be taken into current income, where costs of production will be appropriately matched against them, resulting in a meaningful measure of the net result of periodic operations.

Recognition of Changes in Biological Assets

When the IASC's agriculture project was undertaken, the presumption was that changes resulting from fluctuations in fair value were generically distinct from physical changes due to growth and other natural phenomena. Accordingly, the 1996 DSOP proposed that the change in carrying amounts for a group of biological assets would be so allocated. The original intent was to have changes in value, which corresponds to revaluations of plant and equipment assets under the alternative treatment permitted by IAS 16, reported directly in equity, while changes due to growth would be included in current period operating results. However, even if this bifurcation strategy had been conceptually sound, the practical difficulties of allocating such value changes soon became obvious.

By 1999, when the Exposure Draft was issued, the IASC's position had shifted to the inclusion of both of these value changes in current period results of operations. The draft did urge separate disclosure of the fair value changes and the effects of growth, either on the face of the statement of comprehensive income or in the notes thereto; this was not to be made an actual requirement. The final standard, IAS 41, has dropped this suggestion entirely, probably because it would have proven to be unpopular and therefore rarely complied with.

The actual recognition and measurement requirements of IAS 41 are as follows:

1. Biological assets are to be measured at their fair value, less estimated costs to sell, except where fair value cannot be measured reliably. In the latter instance, historical cost is to be used.
2. Agricultural produce harvested from an entity's biological assets should be measured at fair value less estimated costs to sell at the point of harvest. That amount effectively becomes the cost basis, to which further processing costs may be added, as the conditions warrant, with accounting thereafter guided by IAS 2, *Inventories,* or other applicable standard.
3. The presumption is that fair value can be measured reliably for a biological asset. That presumption can be rebutted, only at the time of initial recognition, for a bio-

logical asset for which market-determined prices or values are not available and for which alternative estimates of fair value are determined to be clearly unreliable. Once the fair value of such a biological asset becomes reliably measurable, it must be measured at its fair value less estimated costs to sell.

4. If an active market exists for a biological asset or for agricultural produce, the quoted price in that market is the appropriate basis for determining the fair value of that asset. If an active market does not exist, however, the reporting entity should use market-determined prices or values, such as the most recent market transaction price, when available.

5. Under certain circumstances, market-determined prices or values may not be available for an asset, as it exists in its current condition. In these circumstances, the entity should use the present value of expected net cash flows from the asset discounted at a current market-determined pretax rate, in determining fair value.

6. The gain or loss which is reported upon initial recognition of biological assets, and also those arising from changes in fair value less estimated point-of-sales costs, should be included in net profit or loss for the period in which the gain or loss arises. That is, these are reported in current period results of operations, and not taken directly into equity.

7. The gain or loss arising from the initial recognition of agricultural produce should be included in net profit or loss for the period in which it arises.

8. Land is to be accounted for under IAS 16, *Property, Plant, and Equipment,* or IAS 40, *Investment Property,* as is appropriate under the circumstances. Biological assets that are physically attached to land are recognized and measured at their fair value less estimated point-of-sales costs, separately from the land.

9. If the entity receives an unconditional government grant related to a biological asset measured at its fair value less estimated point-of-sales costs, the grant should be recognized as income when it first becomes receivable. If the grant related to a biological asset measured at its fair value less estimated costs to sell is conditional, including grants which require an entity not to engage in specified agricultural activity, the grant should be recognized in income when the conditions attaching to it are first met.

10. For government grants pertaining to biological assets which are measured at cost less accumulated depreciation and any accumulated impairment losses, IAS 20, *Accounting for Government Grants and Disclosure of Government Assistance,* should be applied. (See Chapter 26.)

11. Some contracts for the sale of biological assets or agricultural produce are not within the scope of IAS 39, *Financial Instruments: Recognition and Measurement,* because the reporting entity expects to deliver the commodity, rather than settle up in cash. Under IAS 41, such contracts are to be measured at fair value until the biological assets are sold or the produce is harvested.

Agricultural Produce

Agricultural produce is distinguished from biological assets and is not to be measured at fair value other than at the point of harvest, which is the point where biological assets become agricultural produce. For example, when crops are harvested they become agricultural produce and are initially valued at the fair value as of the date of harvest, at the location of harvest (i.e., the value of harvested crops at a remote point of delivery would not be a pertinent measure). If there has been a time interval between the last valuation and the harvest, the value as of the harvest date should be determined or estimated; any increase or decrease since the last valuation would be taken into earnings.

Financial Statement Presentation

Statement of financial position. Official thinking about the level of detail required when the reporting entity has biological assets has evolved since the DSOP first issued. At that time, it was suggested that biological assets should be set forth as a distinct class of assets, being part of neither current nor noncurrent assets. By the time the Exposure Draft was issued, inclusion of biological assets in current and noncurrent assets, as appropriate, either in the aggregate or by major groups of biological assets, was proposed. The ED furthermore encouraged that biological assets be categorized according to class of animal or plant, nature of activities (e.g., being maintained for harvesting or as breeding stock), and the maturity or immaturity for the intended purpose. It suggested that if the plant or animal is being maintained for consumption (to be harvested, etc.), maturity would be gauged by attainment of harvestable specifications. If the plant or animal is for bearing purposes, the maturity criterion would be the attainment of sufficient maturity to sustain economic harvests.

When IAS 41 was promulgated, however, it only established a requirement that the carrying amount of biological assets be presented separately on the face of the statement of financial position (i.e., not included with other, nonbiological assets). Preparers were encouraged to describe the nature and stage of production of each group of biological assets in narrative format in the notes to the financial statements, optionally quantified. Consumable biological assets are to be differentiated from bearer assets, with further subdivisions into mature and immature subgroups for each of these broad categories. The purpose of these disclosures is to give the users of the financial statements some insight into the timing of future cash flows, since the mature subgroups will presumably be realized through market transactions in the near future, and the pattern of cash flows resulting from bearer assets differs from those deriving from consumables.

Statement of comprehensive income. The changes in fair value should be presented on the face of the statement of comprehensive income, ideally broken down between groups of biological assets. However, group level detail may be reserved to the notes to the financial statements.

Also, while separate disclosure of the components of fair value change (i.e., that due to growth and that due to price changes) had been encouraged in the exposure draft, this is no longer being promoted, while of course not being prohibited either. Clearly, the change in fair value which is a consequence of price changes (whether general inflation or specific changes in the market prices of given commodities, such as wheat, due to factors such as the expectations regarding the harvest) is generically distinct from the growth which has occurred during the period being reported on. Distinguishing between these two factors would be important in making the financial reporting process more meaningful, and several examples of how this dichotomizing of fair value changes can be accomplished and presented in the financial statements was included in the Exposure Draft preceding IAS 41's issuance.

IAS 1 permits the presentation of expenses in accordance with either a natural classification (e.g., materials purchases, depreciation, etc.) or a functional basis (cost of sales, administrative, selling, etc.). The draft statement on agriculture had urged that the natural classification of income and expenses be adopted for the statement of comprehensive income. Sufficient detail is to be included in the face of the statement of comprehensive income to support an analysis of operating performance. However, these are recommendations, not strict requirements.

Disclosures. IAS 41 establishes new disclosure requirements for biological assets measured at cost less any accumulated depreciation and any accumulated impairment losses (i.e., for those exceptional biological assets which are **not** being carried at fair value). The new disclosures are as follows:

1. A separate reconciliation of changes in the carrying amount of those biological assets,
2. A description of those biological assets,
3. An explanation of why fair value cannot be measured reliably,
4. A statement of the range of estimates within which fair value is highly likely to lie (if this is possible to give),
5. The amount of any gain or loss recognized on disposal of the biological assets,
6. The depreciation method used,
7. The useful lives or the depreciation rates used, and
8. The gross carrying amount and the accumulated depreciation at the beginning and end of the reporting period.

In addition to the foregoing, these disclosures are required

1. If the fair value of biological assets previously measured at cost less any accumulated depreciation and any accumulated impairment losses subsequently becomes reliably measurable, the reporting entity must disclose a description of the biological assets, and explanation of how fair value has become reliably measurable, and the effect of the change in accounting method; and
2. Information about any significant decreases in the expected level of government grants related to agricultural activity covered by IAS 41.

The normally anticipated disclosures regarding the nature of operations, which are necessary to comply with IAS 1, also apply to entities engaging in biological and agricultural operations. These disclosures could incorporate, either in narrative form or as quantified terms, information about the groups of biological assets, the nature of activities regarding each of these groups, the maturity or immaturity for intended purposes of each group, the relative significance of different groups by reference to nonmonetary amounts (e.g., numbers of animals, acres of trees) dedicated to each, and nonfinancial measures or estimates of the physical quantities of each group of assets at the date of the statement of financial position and the output of agricultural produce during the reporting period.

Good practice, necessary to make the financial statements meaningful for users, would dictate that disclosures be made of the measurement bases used to derive fair values; whether an independent appraiser was utilized; where relevant, the discount rate employed to compute net present values, along with the number of years' future cash flows assumed; additional details about the changes in fair value from the prior period, where needed; any restrictions on title and any pledging of biological assets as security for liabilities; commitments for further development or acquisitions of biological assets; specifics about risk management strategies employed by the entity (note that the use of hedging is widespread; the futures market, now heavily employed to control financial risks, was developed originally for agricultural commodities); and activities which are unsustainable, along with estimated dates of cessation of those activities. Other possible disclosures include the carrying amount of agricultural land (at either historical cost or revalued amount) and of agricultural produce (governed by IAS 2, and subject to separate classification in the statement of financial position).

Agricultural Land

Agricultural land is not deemed a biological asset; thus, the principles espoused in IAS 41 for biological and agricultural assets do not apply to land. The requirements of IAS 16, which are applicable to other categories of plant, property, and equipment, apply equally to agricultural land. The use of the allowed alternative method (i.e., revaluation), particularly for land-based systems such as orchards, plantations, and forests, where the fair value of the biological asset was determined from net realizable values which included the underlying land, would be logical and advisable, but is not actually a requirement. It would also enhance the usefulness of the financial statements if land held by entities engaged in agricultural activities is further classified in the statement of financial position according to specific uses. Alternatively, this information can be conveyed in the notes to the financial statements.

Intangible Assets Related to Agriculture

Under IAS 38, intangible assets may be carried at cost (the benchmark treatment) or at revalued amounts (the allowed alternative treatment), but only to the extent that active markets exist for the intangibles. In general, it is not expected that such markets will exist for commonly encountered classes of intangible assets. On the other hand, agricultural activities are expected to frequently involve intangibles such as water rights, production quotas, and pollution rights, and it is anticipated that for these intangibles active markets may in fact exist.

To enhance the internal consistency of financial statements of entities engaged in biological and agriculture operations, if intangibles which pertain to the entity's agricultural activities have active markets, these should be presented in the statement of financial position at their fair values. This is not, however, an actual requirement.

Government Grants

IAS 20 addresses the accounting for government grants, whether received with conditions attached or not, and whether received in cash or otherwise. As noted above, IAS 41 effectively amends this in the case of reporting by entities an unconditional government grant related to a biological asset measured at its fair value less estimated costs to sell. It also provides that, for grants which are conditional, recognition in income will occur when there is reasonable assurance that the conditions have been met. If conditional grants are received before the conditions have been met, the grant should be recognized as a liability, not as revenue. For grants received in the form of nonmonetary assets, fair value is to be assessed in order to account for the grant. IASB intends to replace or amend IAS 20 (see discussion in Chapter 26).

EXTRACTIVE INDUSTRIES

Another key industry segment that was targeted for establishment of financial reporting standards by the former IASC was that involved in exploration for and extraction of mineral resources. An Issues Paper was released in late 2000, prior to the restructuring that resulted in the creation of IASB. The many complex issues that needed to be addressed, and other matters that required priority attention for IASC/IASB, caused this project to be delayed for several years, but in late 2004 IASB promulgated a standard, IFRS 6, which dealt with the accounting for exploration for, and evaluation of, mineral resources. This became effective January 1, 2006.

IFRS 6 deals with somewhat limited issues, and IASB, assisted by a task force consisting of national standard setters, has continued to examine other related matters. As of late 2007, a Discussion Paper is expected in the latter half of 2008, and there remains the possibility that further standards on this topic area may ultimately be developed.

Sources of IFRS
IFRS 6

DEFINITIONS OF TERMS

Exploration and evaluation assets. Exploration and evaluation expenditures recognized as assets in accordance with the reporting entity's accounting policy.

Exploration and evaluation expenditures. Expenditures incurred by a reporting entity in connection with the exploration for and evaluation of mineral resources, before the technical feasibility and commercial viability of extracting a mineral resource have been demonstrated.

Exploration for and evaluation of mineral resources. The search for mineral resources, including minerals, oil, natural gas, and similar nonregenerative resources after the entity has obtained legal rights to explore in a specific area, as well as the determination of the technical feasibility and commercial viability of extracting the mineral resource.

CONCEPTS, RULES AND EXAMPLES

Background. Before its demise, the IASC had begun to direct a good deal of attention to the financial reporting needs of specialized industries. Among those deemed worthy of such attention were certain extractive industries, which were seen as having significant financial accounting and reporting issues, and as being disproportionately relevant to the economies of the lesser-developed nations, with which IFRS has historically had the greatest influence. In particular, it had focused on those industries most often operating internationally, thereby exerting significant economic influence worldwide. The accounting and reporting practices by companies in those industries were seen as being unusually diverse, and often varying significantly from those of entities in other types of industries. It was perceived that these conditions would make within-industry and across-industry comparisons difficult for users of the financial statements.

This effort yielded a major Issues Paper in 2000, with the expectation that definitive standards would be promulgated as early as 2002. When the IASB was established as the successor to IASC, however, this project received reduced attention, with the Improvements Project (which subsequently resulted in over a dozen new or amended standards at year-end 2003) and the Convergence Projects being of greater immediate concern.

In mid-2001 IASB signaled that this project would not take priority on its technical agenda, and by late 2002 it was stated that it would not be feasible to timely complete a comprehensive project for the mass adoption of IFRS by the EU in 2005. Subsequently, in early 2004, IASB asked a group of staff from the national standard setters in Australia, Canada, Norway, and South Africa (each of which have important mining industries) to undertake research that would build on the results of the Issues Paper and the responses that it had generated. The goal is to develop proposals for standard-setting projects.

The ongoing research is considering all issues associated with accounting for "upstream" extractive activities. Specifically, this is intended to address the treatment of

1. Reserves/resources—which will include determining whether

    a. Reserves/resources can or should be recognized as assets on the statement of financial position;

    b. Predevelopment costs incurred following the discovery of reserves/resources should be capitalized or expensed if reserves/resources are not recognized;

    c. Predevelopment costs incurred prior to the discovery of reserves/resources should be capitalized or expensed; and

    d. Reserves/resources information should be disclosed—and if so, what information.

2. Other issues identified in the Issues Paper and implementation issues arising from the application of IFRS by entities conducting extractive activities.

The work plan is for the project team to produce a discussion document, incorporating the IASB's preliminary views regarding accounting for extractive activities, which is now expected to be published in late 2008.

Meanwhile, in early 2004, IASB issued ED 6, which proposed an interim solution, designed to facilitate compliance with IFRS by entities reporting exploration and evaluation assets, without making substantial changes to existing accounting practices. In this regard, ED 6 was similar to IFRS 4, *Insurance Contracts*, discussed later in this chapter. In mid-2005, this culminated with the issuance of IFRS 6, *Exploration for and Evaluation of Mineral Resources*, detailed below.

The reasons cited by IASB for the development of an interim standard addressing exploration for and evaluation of mineral resources were as follows:

1. There were no extant IFRS that specifically addressed the exploration for and evaluation of mineral resources, which had been excluded from the scope of IAS 38. Furthermore, mineral rights and mineral resources such as oil, natural gas and similar nonregenerative resources were excluded from the scope of IAS 16. Accordingly, a reporting entity having such assets and activities is required to determine accounting policies for such expenditures in accordance with IAS 8.
2. There were alternative views on how the exploration for and evaluation of mineral resources and, particularly, the recognition of exploration and evaluation assets, were required to be accounted for under IFRS.
3. Accounting practices for exploration and evaluation expenditures under various national GAAP standards were quite diverse, and often differed from practices in other sectors for items that could have been considered similar (e.g., the accounting practices for research costs under IAS 38).
4. Exploration and evaluation expenditures represented a significant cost to entities engaged in extractive activities.
5. While relatively few entities incurring exploration and evaluation expenditures were reporting under IFRS at the time (circa 2005), many more are expected to do so, particularly given the EU mandate for publicly listed entities to report consolidated results in conformity with IFRS, which became effective in 2005.

IFRS 6 in Greater Detail

IFRS 6 sets forth a set of generalized principles that define the main issues for reporting entities that have activities involving the exploration for and evaluation of mineral resources. These principles are as follows:

1. IFRS fully applies to these entities, except when they are specifically excluded from the scope of a given standard.
2. Reporting entities may continue employing their existing accounting policies to account for exploration and evaluation assets, but any change in accounting will have to qualify under the criteria set forth by IAS 8.
3. A reporting entity that recognizes exploration and evaluation assets must assess those assets for impairment annually, in accordance with IAS 36. However, the entity may conduct the assessment at the level of "a cash-generating unit for exploration and evaluation assets," rather than at the level otherwise required by IAS 36. As set forth by IFRS 6, this is a higher level of aggregation than would have been the case under a strict application of the criteria in IAS 36.

Thus, according to IFRS 6, entities that have assets used for exploration and evaluation of mineral resources are to report under IFRS, but certain assets may be subject to alternative measurement requirements. The adoption of new, specialized requirements will be optional, at least at this time. The next phase of the extractive industries project may result in new requirements, but is unlikely before sometime in 2009, at the earliest.

Cash-generating units for exploration and evaluation assets. The most significant aspect of IFRS 6 concerns its establishment of a unique definition of *cash-generating units* for impairment testing. It created a different level of aggregation for mineral exploration and evaluation assets, when compared to all other assets subject to impairment considerations under IAS 36. The reason for this distinction is that IASB was concerned that requiring entities to use the standard definition of a cash-generating unit, as set forth by IAS 36, when assessing exploration and evaluation assets for impairment might have negated the effects of the other aspects of the proposal, thereby resulting in the inappropriate recognition of impairment losses under certain circumstances. Specifically, IASB was of the opinion that the standard definition of a cash-generating unit could cause there to be uncertainty about whether the reporting entity's existing accounting policies were consistent with IFRS, because exploration and evaluation assets would often not be expected to

1. Be the subject of future cash inflow and outflow projections relating to the development of the project, on a reasonable and consistent basis, without being heavily discounted because of uncertainty and lead times;
2. Have a determinable net selling price; or
3. Be readily identifiable with other assets that generate cash inflows as a specific cash-generating unit.

In IASB's view, the implications of the foregoing matters were that an exploration and evaluation asset would often be deemed to be impaired, inappropriately, if the IAS 36 definition of a cash-generating unit was applied without at least the potential for modification.

Given the foregoing concern, in the draft standard IASB had proposed a unique definition of a cash-generating unit for exploration and evaluation assets. The cash-generating unit for exploration and evaluation assets was to be the cash-generating unit that represents the smallest identifiable group of assets that, together with exploration and evaluation assets, generates cash inflows from continuing use to which impairment tests were applied by the entity under the accounting policies applied for its most recent annual financial statements. The entity would be permitted to elect, under the proposed rules, to apply either the IAS 36 definition of a cash-generating unit, or the special definition above. The election would have to be made when the proposed IFRS was first applied. Beyond the choice of definition of the cash-generating unit, the mechanics of the impairment test itself would be as set forth at IAS 36.

During the development of IFRS 6, IASB expressed concern that the availability of a choice in defining cash-generating units might impair the reliability and relevance of financial statements. To limit this risk, it proposed that a cash-generating unit for exploration and evaluation assets could be no larger than a segment, as defined by then-extant standard IAS 14.

As adopted, IFRS 6 mandates the proposed approach to impairment testing. Specifically, the standard provides that the reporting entity is to determine an accounting policy for allocating exploration and evaluation assets to cash-generating units or groups of cash-generating units for the purpose of assessing those assets for impairment as that need arises. Accordingly, each cash-generating unit or group of units to which an exploration and evaluation asset is allocated is not to be larger than a segment based on either the entity's primary or secondary reporting format, determined in accordance with IAS 14. The level identified by the entity for the purposes of testing exploration and evaluation assets for impairment can comprise one or more cash-generating units. (Note that IFRS 8 has since been promulgated, and it replaces IAS 14 effective 2009. See discussion of IFRS 8 in Chapter 20.)

IFRS 6 provides that exploration and evaluation assets are to be assessed for impairment when facts and circumstances suggest that the carrying amount of an exploration and evaluation asset might exceed the recoverable amount, as with other impairment testing prescribed by IAS 36. When facts and circumstances indicate that the carrying amount might exceed the respective recoverable amount, the reporting entity is required to measure, present, and disclose any resulting impairment loss in accordance with IAS 36, with the exception that the extent of aggregation may be greater than for other assets.

In addition to the criteria set forth in IAS 36, IFRS 6 identifies certain indications that impairment may have occurred regarding the exploration and evaluation assets. It states that one or more of the following facts and circumstances indicate that the reporting entity should test exploration and evaluation assets for impairment:

1. The period for which the entity has the right to explore in the specific area has expired during the period or will expire in the near future, and is not expected to be renewed.
2. Substantive expenditure by the entity on further exploration for and evaluation of mineral resources in the specific area is neither budgeted nor planned.
3. Exploration for and evaluation of mineral resources in the specific area have not resulted in the discovery of commercially viable quantities of mineral resources, and accordingly the reporting entity decided to discontinue such activities in the specific area.
4. Sufficient data exist to suggest that, although a development in the specific area is likely to proceed, the carrying amount of the exploration and evaluation asset is unlikely to be recovered in full from successful development or by sale.

If testing identifies impairment, the consequent adjustment of carrying amounts to the lower, impaired value results in a charge to current operating results, just as described by IAS 36 (discussed in Chapter 8).

Assets subject to IFRS 6 categorization. IFRS 6 provides a listing of assets that would fall within the definition of exploration and evaluation expenditures. These assets are those that are related to the following activities:

1. Acquisition of rights to explore;
2. Topographical, geological, geochemical, and geophysical studies;
3. Exploratory drilling;
4. Trenching;
5. Sampling; and
6. Activities in relation to evaluating technical feasibility and commercial viability of extracting a mineral resource.

The qualifying expenditures notably *exclude* those that are incurred in connection with the development of a mineral resource once technical feasibility and commercial viability of extracting a mineral resource have been established. Additionally, any administration and other general overhead costs are explicitly excluded from the definition of qualifying expenditures.

Availability of cost or revaluation models. Consistent with IAS 16, IFRS 6 requires initial recognition of exploration and evaluation assets based on actual cost, but subsequent recognition can be effected under either the historical cost model or the revaluation model.

The standard does not offer guidance regarding accounting procedures, but it is presumed that those set forth under IAS 16 would be applied (e.g., regarding recognition of impairment and recoveries of previously recognized impairments). (See discussion in Chapter 8.)

Financial statement classification. IFRS 6 provides that the reporting entity is to classify exploration and evaluation assets as tangible or intangible according to the nature of the assets acquired, and apply the classification consistently. It notes that certain exploration and evaluation assets, such as drilling rights, have traditionally been considered intangible assets, while other assets have historically been identified as tangible (such as vehicles and drilling rigs). The standard states that, to the extent that a tangible asset is consumed in developing an intangible asset, the amount reflecting that consumption (that would otherwise be reported as depreciation) becomes part of the cost of the intangible asset. Using a tangible asset to develop an intangible asset, however, does not warrant classifying the tangible asset as an intangible asset.

In the statement of financial position, exploration and evaluation assets are to be set forth as a separate class of long-lived assets.

IFRS 6 only addresses exploration and evaluation. It holds that once the technical feasibility and commercial viability of extracting a mineral resource has been demonstrated, exploration and evaluation assets are no longer to be classified as such. At that point, the exploration and evaluation assets are to be assessed for impairment, and any impairment loss recognized, before reclassification of any remainder as operating or other asset classes.

Disclosure requirements under IFRS 6. A reporting entity is required to disclose information that identifies and explains the amounts recognized in its financial statements that pertain to the exploration for and evaluation of mineral resources. This could be accomplished by disclosing

1. Its accounting policies for exploration and evaluation expenditures, including the recognition of exploration and evaluation assets.
2. The amounts of assets, liabilities, income, and expense (and, if a statement of cash flows using the direct method is presented, cash flows) arising from the exploration for and evaluation of mineral resources.

The Exposure Draft preceding IFRS 6 had proposed that the mandatory disclosures identify the level at which the entity assesses exploration and evaluation assets for impairment. While this is not set forth in IFRS 6, it is obviously a good practice, and is therefore strongly recommended by the authors.

The IASC Issues Paper

As discussed, IFRS 6 addressed only a limited range of issues arising in the accounting for entities involved in mineral production. The full scope of the issues to be ultimately addressed can be appreciated from a review of the various preliminary documents produced by IASC/IASB dealing with this important group of financial reporting matters.

IASC's 2000 Issues Paper directed attention to the upstream activities of mining and petroleum producers, defined as consisting of exploration and production. These excluded "downstream" activities such as refining, marketing, and transportation, which would continue to be governed by other relevant international standards, such as IAS 2 and IAS 16.

It set forth in vast detail the accounting practices found in the mining and petroleum industries, discussing the strengths and weaknesses of each of the alternative methods.

Key issues. The Issues Paper identified a number of key financial reporting issues that must be resolved. These include the following items:

1. Which costs of finding, acquiring, and developing mineral reserves should be capitalized;
2. How capitalized costs should be depreciated (amortized);
3. The extent to which quantities and values of mineral reserves, rather than costs, should impact upon recognition, measurement, and disclosure; and
4. How to define, classify, and measure mineral reserves.

With regard to cost recognition, the two most popular methods, "full costing" and "successful efforts," are seen as representing the two ends of a continuum. Under full cost accounting, all costs incurred in searching for, acquiring, and developing mineral reserves in a large cost center, such as a country or continent, are capitalized as part of the cost of whatever reserves have been found, even though a specific cost was incurred in a failed effort. The underlying theory is that entities in such industries know that many "dry holes" must be drilled (to use the oil exploration industry as an example) to find one producing well, and accordingly are cognizant of the fact that all such costs are actually the necessary costs of developing successful wells. Full cost accounting is used by many midsize to small petroleum entities, but rarely has been employed by mining entities.

On the other hand, under successful efforts accounting (which is used by most large oil and gas companies and by some mining entities), costs that lead directly to finding mineral reserves are capitalized, while costs that do not lead directly to mineral reserves are charged to expense. The concept here is not so much that costs associated with unsuccessful efforts are rightfully charged to current expense, but rather, from a practical perspective, given that many projects are ongoing at any time (which is particularly true for the larger entities), essentially the same result will occur with less complicated accounting, if only costs associated with successful ventures are capitalized and amortized. In other words, the matching objective is met equally well, in these situations, by use of the less burdensome successful efforts method of accounting.

According to the IASC paper, many mining entities use an accounting method which lies between the extremes of the full costing and successful efforts methods. Other entities use various hybrid methods, adding to the difficulty of establishing a taxonomy of accounting methods. Imposing a uniform methodology is thus seen as being a pressing need.

A third major approach to cost capitalization is the "area-of-interest" method. According to the IASC paper, some view the area-of-interest concept (sometimes also referred to as the "project method") as a variation on the successful efforts method of accounting, while others see it as a version of full cost accounting applied on an area-of-interest basis. Under the area-of-interest approach, all costs that relate directly to an area of interest or that can be logically allocated to the area of interest are recorded as belonging to that area. That is, prospecting costs, mineral acquisition costs, exploration costs, appraisal costs, and development costs are associated with an individual geological area that has features that are conducive to a coordinated, unified search program and that has been identified as being a favorable environment for the presence of, or known to contain, a mineral deposit. These costs would be accumulated and deferred for each area of interest, to be depreciated as the reserves from that area of interest are produced.

The area-of-interest approach is believed to be fairly commonly employed in the mining industry, although the precise extent of its usage remains under debate. Some studies cited by IASC suggest that this method is the most commonly used way to account for costs—more so than either the successful efforts or full cost methods. Thus, while the area-of-interest approach is not one which is set forth in most textbooks (which typically only cite the successful efforts and full costing approaches), it may have great currency in actual usage.

Probably the other issue which is most important and central to this project is whether financial reporting is to be based on traditional historical costs, or on a fair value approach, driven by estimates of actual mineral reserves on hand and expected final selling prices therefore. The latter approach has been advocated for decades (in the US, the SEC's proposed "reserve recognition accounting," which was ultimately not adopted, was one such attempt). While many coherent arguments can be made for fair value accounting for mineral reserves, persistent questions about reliability (both of quantity estimates and of selling price projections) have ultimately prevented abandonment of historical cost-based methods. However, fair value data has been widely incorporated into supplemental disclosures (such as those required under SEC rules in the US).

Steering Committee's views. The Steering Committee developed tentative views on many of the major issues set out in the Issues Paper. In some cases, these address only the basic issues and do not extend to the subissues associated with a given basic issue. These views are tentative and will be revisited in light of comment letters received, and thus may change markedly as the research continues.

The Steering Committee's tentative views have been summarized as follows in the Issues Paper:

1. An International Financial Reporting Standard on financial reporting in the extractive industries is needed.
2. IASB should develop a single IFRS with common standards for both the mining and petroleum industries, but with separate requirements or guidance for mining or petroleum, as necessary, to address industry-specific issues.
3. The IFRS should be restricted to upstream activities (exploration for, and development and production of, minerals).
4. Information about reserve quantities and values, and changes in them, is a key indicator of the performance of an extractive industries entity.
5. The primary financial statements of an extractive industries entity should be based on historical costs, not on estimated reserve values.
6. Information about reserve quantities and values, and changes in them, should be disclosed as supplemental information.
7. The Steering Committee favored adoption of a method of accounting more consistent with the successful efforts concept than with other concepts (such as full costing or area-of-interest accounting).
8. All preacquisition prospecting and exploration costs should be charged to expense when incurred, and not deferred to future periods, analogous to the accounting for research expenditures.
9. All direct and incidental property acquisition costs should be initially recognized as an asset.
10. All postacquisition exploration and appraisal costs should be initially recognized as an asset, pending the determination of whether commercially recoverable reserves have been found.
11. Some limit should be imposed if postacquisition exploration and appraisal costs are deferred, pending determination of whether commercially recoverable reserves have been found.
12. All development costs should be recognized as an asset.
13. Construction costs that relate to a single mineral cost center should be capitalized as part of the capitalized costs of that cost center (normally to be depreciated on a unit-of-production basis if the life of the assets is coincident with the life of the mineral reserves, or on a straight-line basis if the economic life is less than the life of the re-

serves). Construction costs that relate to more than one mineral cost center should be accounted for in the same way as other property, plant, and equipment under IAS 16, (normally depreciated on a time basis).

14. Postproduction exploration and development costs should be treated in the same way as any other exploration or development costs.

15. Both the benchmark (immediate expensing) and allowed alternative (capitalization and amortization) treatments of borrowing costs contained in IAS 23 should be permitted. (Note that, since the Issues Paper was published, IAS 23 has been amended to conform to US GAAP, so that immediate expensing of qualifying financing costs is no longer to be permitted.)

16. Overhead cost should be attributed to the relevant phase of operations (prospecting, acquisition, exploration, valuation, development, and construction) and further identified with a specific prospect, property, or area of interest. The overhead cost should be capitalized if, and only if, the indirect costs of that phase of operations are capitalized for that specific prospect, property, or area of interest.

17. The Steering Committee did not favor cost reinstatement (reversing a prior period expense recognition in a subsequent period in which information becomes available that commercially recoverable reserves have been discovered).

18. Costs should be accumulated by area of interest or geological units smaller than an area of interest (e.g., the field or the mine).

19. Use unit-of-production depreciation for all capitalized preproduction costs with two exceptions

    a. Use straight-line depreciation for capitalized construction costs that serve a single mineral cost center, if the economic life of the asset is less than the life of the reserves, and

    b. Follow IAS 16 for capitalized construction costs that serve two or more cost centers (sometimes called service assets).

20. Changes in reserve estimates should be reflected prospectively; that is, included in the determination of net profit or loss in the period of the change and future periods, consistent with the requirements of IAS 8.

21. IAS 37 should be applied without modification to the recognition of removal and restoration costs and obligations in the extractive industries.

22. If the amount of a provision is part of the cost of acquiring the asset, it is recognized as such and is included in the depreciable amount of the asset.

23. The cost relating to a provision necessitated by production activities after an asset is installed should be capitalized as an additional cost of acquiring the asset, if the cost provides incremental future economic benefits.

24. If the cost associated with a provision was initially capitalized, changes in the estimated amount of the provision should be recognized is subsequent periods as an adjustment to the carrying amount of the asset.

25. IAS 36 should be applied without modification to account for impairments of assets in the extractive industries.

26. Impairment of capitalized preproduction costs should be assessed based on proved and probable reserves.

27. An impairment test cannot be applied to deferred preproduction costs whose outcome is unknown. The Steering Committee favors some type of limit if preproduction costs are deferred, pending determination of whether commercially recoverable reserves are found.

28. The general provisions of IAS 18 should apply to entities in the extractive industries, and IAS 18 should be amended to eliminate the scope exclusion.

29. Revenue received prior to the production phase should be recognized as revenue to other income, not as a reduction of capitalizable costs.

30. Royalties paid in cash, royalties paid in kind, and severance taxes should all be included in the producer's gross revenue and deducted as an expense.

31. Inventories of minerals should be measured at historical cost, even if those minerals have quoted market prices in active markets with a short time between production and sale and insignificant costs to be incurred beyond the point of production, and the entity intends to sell those minerals in that market.

32. All members of the Steering Committee favored disclosure of reserve quantities. The Steering Committee was divided regarding disclosure of reserve values, however.

33. Proved and probable reserves should be disclosed separately, and within proved reserves disclosure should be made separately of proved developed and proved undeveloped reserves.

ACCOUNTING FOR INSURANCE CONTRACTS

Background

Before the IASC ceased existence, it undertook a major project to address the accounting for insurance contracts, a subject that has proven to be challenging for many of the national accounting standard setters as well. The objective of this project was to address only accounting for insurance contracts rather than all the various complex aspects of accounting by insurance companies. The process involved the development of an extensive Issues Paper, which was published in late 1999, a Draft Statement of Principles published in 2001, and the draft pronouncement, ED 5, in mid-2003. The final standard on the portions of the project (what came to be referred to as Phase I) covered in ED 5 was issued in early 2004 as IFRS 4, *Insurance Contracts,* which became effective for periods beginning in 2005, when European adoption of IFRS (by publicly held companies) was first required.

Subsequent to the promulgation of IFRS 4, the IASB continued to address insurance-related accounting concerns in its *Insurance Contracts Phase II* project. A working group was formed in late 2004, to consider accounting by insurers. The intent is to develop guidance for measurement, the applicability of discounting, risk or service adjustments, gain or loss on initial measurement or liability recognition, acquisition costs, participating contracts, and various other relevant topics. In May 2007 IASB published a Discussion Paper, *Preliminary Views on Insurance Contracts*, and expects to impose a new standard by 2010. This paper proposes that an insurer should measure its insurance liabilities using three building blocks. These are discussed later in this section.

IFRS 4 addresses only the financial reporting for insurance contracts by any entity that issues these contracts—which is not limited merely to insurance companies. It applies to insurance contracts issued, reinsurance contracts held, and financial instruments issued with a discretionary participation feature. The matter of the actual accounting for insurance contracts is not addressed in this standard, but it is discussed in the recently published Discussion Paper and will be the subject of a planned new standard.

Sources of IFRS
IFRS 4

Insurance Contracts

An insurance contract is an arrangement under which one party (the insurer) accepts significant insurance risk by agreeing with another party (the policyholder) to compensate the policyholder or other beneficiary if a specified uncertain future event (the insured event) adversely affects the policyholder or other beneficiary (other than an event that is only a change in one or more of a specified interest rate, security price, commodity price, foreign exchange rate, index of prices or rates, a credit rating or credit index, or similar variable—which would continue to be accounted for under IAS 39 as derivative contracts). A contract creates sufficient insurance risk to qualify as an insurance contract only if there is a reasonable possibility that an event affecting the policyholder or other beneficiary will cause a significant change in the present value of the insurer's net cash flows arising from that contract. In considering whether there is a reasonable possibility of such significant change, it is necessary to consider the probability of the event and the magnitude of its effect. Also, a contract that qualifies as an insurance contract at inception or later remains an insurance contract until all rights and obligations are extinguished or expire. If a contract did not qualify as an insurance contract at inception, it should be subsequently reclassified as an insurance contract if, and only if, a significant change in the present value of the insurer's net cash flows becomes a reasonable possibility.

A range of other arrangements, which share certain characteristics with insurance contracts, would be excluded from any imposed insurance contracts accounting standard, since they are dealt with under other IAS. These include financial guarantees (including credit insurance) measured at fair value; product warranties issued directly by a manufacturer, dealer or retailer; employers' assets and liabilities under employee benefit plans (including equity compensation plans); retirement benefit obligations reported by defined benefit retirement plans; contingent consideration payable or receivable in a business combination; and contractual rights or contractual obligations that are contingent on the future use of, or right to use, a nonfinancial item (for example, certain license fees, royalties, lease payments, and similar items).

IFRS 4 applies to all insurance contracts, including reinsurance. Thus, the standard does not relate only to insurance companies, strictly defined. However, it does not apply to other assets and liabilities of issuers of insurance contracts, although other IFRS do apply. Insurance assets and liabilities will be subject to recognition when contractual rights and obligations, respectively, are created under the terms of the contract. When these no longer exist, derecognition will take place.

IFRS 4 does not apply to product warranties issued directly by a manufacturer, dealer or retailer; employers' assets and liabilities under employee benefit plans and retirement benefit obligations reported by defined benefit retirement plans; contractual rights or obligations that are contingent on the future use of or right to use a nonfinancial item, as well as lessee's residual value guarantees on finance leases; financial guarantees entered into or retained on transferring financial assets or financial liabilities within the scope of IAS 39; contingent consideration payable or receivable in a business combination; or direct insurance contracts that an entity holds as a policyholder.

Recognition and Measurement of Insurance Liabilities under IFRS 4

Insurance risk. IFRS 4 sets forth the accounting and financial reporting requirements which will now be applicable to all insurance contracts (including reinsurance contracts) that are issued by the reporting entity, and to reinsurance contracts that the reporting entity holds, except for specified contracts which are covered by other standards. IFRS 4 does not apply to other assets and liabilities of an insurer (e.g., financial assets and financial liabilities which are addressed by IAS 39), nor does it address accounting or financial reporting by policy-holders. The standard uses the term "insurer" to denote the party accepting liability as an insurer, whether or not the entity is legally or statutorily an insurance company.

IFRS 4 replaces what had been an indirect definition of an insurance contract under IAS 32 with a positive definition based on the transfer of significant insurance risk from the policyholder to the insurer. This definition covers most motor, travel, life, annuity, medical, property, reinsurance, and professional indemnity contracts. Some catastrophe bonds and weather derivatives would also qualify, as long as payments are linked to a specific climatic or other insured future event that would adversely affect the policyholder. On the other hand, policies that transfer no significant insurance risk—such as some savings and pensions plans—will be deemed financial instruments, addressed by IAS 39, regardless of their legal form. IAS 39 also applies to contracts that principally transfer financial risk, such as credit derivatives and some forms of financial reinsurance.

There may be some difficulty in classifying the more complex products (including certain hybrids). To facilitate this process, IASB has explained that insurance risk will be deemed *significant* only if an insured event could cause an insurer to pay significant additional benefits in *any* scenario, apart from a scenario that lacks commercial substance (which in the Exposure Draft preceding IFRS 4 was denoted as a "plausible" event). As a practical matter, reporting entities should compare the cash flows from (1) the occurrence of the insured event against (2) all other events. If the cash flows under the former are significantly larger than under the latter, significant insurance risk is present.

For example, when the insurance benefits payable upon death are significantly larger than the benefits payable upon surrender or maturity, there is significant insurance risk. The significance of the additional benefits is to be measured irrespective of the probability of the insured event, if the scenario has commercial substance. Reporting entities have to develop internal quantitative guidance to ensure the definition is applied consistently throughout the entity. To qualify as significant, the insurance risk also needs to reflect a *preexisting* risk for the policyholder, rather than having arisen from the terms of the contract.

This requirement would specifically exclude from the cash flow comparison features such as waivers of early redemption penalties within investment plans or mortgages in the event of death. Since it is the contract itself that brought the charges into place, the waiver does not represent an additional benefit received for the transfer of a preexisting insurance risk.

The application of this IFRS 4 definition may result in the redesignation of a significant fraction of existing insurance contracts as investment contracts. In other situations, the impact could be the opposite. For example, a requirement to pay benefits earlier if an insured event occurs could make a contract insurance; this means that many pure endowment contracts are likely to meet the definition of insurance. All told, insuring entities will need to set clear, consistent, and justifiable contract classification criteria and rigorously apply these.

Adequacy of insurance liabilities. IFRS 4 imposes a *liability adequacy test*, which requires that at each reporting (i.e., statement of financial position) date the "insurer" must assess whether its recognized insurance liabilities are adequate, using then-current estimates of future cash flows under the outstanding insurance contracts. If as a result of that assessment it is determined that the carrying (i.e., book) amount of insurance liabilities (less related deferred acquisition costs and related intangible assets, if appropriate—see discussion below) is insufficient given the estimated future cash flows, the full amount of such deficiency must be reported currently in earnings.

The standard defines minimum requirements for the adequacy test that is to be applied to the liability account. These minimum requirements are that

1. The test considers the current estimates of all contractual cash flows, and of such related cash flows as claims handling costs, as well as cash flows that will result from embedded options and guarantees.
2. If the test shows that the liability is inadequate, the entire deficiency is recognized in profit or loss.

In situations where the insuring entity's accounting policies do not require a liability adequacy test, or provides for a test that does not meet the minimum requirements noted above, then the entity is required under IFRS 4 to

1. Determine the carrying amount of the relevant insurance liabilities, less the carrying amount of

    a. Any related deferred acquisition costs; and
    b. Any related intangible assets, such as those acquired in a business combination or portfolio transfer.

2. Determine whether the carrying amount of the relevant net insurance liabilities is less than the carrying amount that would be required if the relevant insurance liabilities were within the scope of IAS 37.

The IAS 37-based amount is the required minimum liability to be presented. Therefore, if the current carrying amount is less, the insuring entity must recognize the entire shortfall in current period earnings. The corresponding credit to this loss recognition will either decrease the carrying amount of the related deferred acquisition costs or related intangible assets or increase the carrying amount of the relevant insurance liabilities, or both, dependent upon the facts and circumstances.

In applying the foregoing procedures, any related reinsurance assets are not considered, because an insuring entity accounts for these separately, as noted later in this discussion.

If an insuring entity's liability adequacy test meets the minimum requirements set forth above, this test is applied at the level of aggregation specified above. On the other hand, if the liability adequacy test does not meet the stipulated minimum requirements, the comparison must instead be made at the level of a portfolio of contracts that are subject to broadly similar risks and which are managed together as a single portfolio.

For purposes of comparing the recorded liability to the amount required under IAS 37, it is acceptable to reflect future investment margins only if the carrying (i.e., book) amount of the liability also reflects those same margins. Future investment margins are defined under IFRS 4 as being employed if the discount rate used reflects the estimated return on the insuring entity's assets, or if the returns on those assets are projected at an estimated rate of return, and discounted at a different rate, with the result included in the measurement of the liability. There is a rebuttable presumption that future investment margins should not be used, however, although exceptions (see below) can exist.

Impairment testing of reinsurance assets. When an insuring entity obtains reinsurance (making it the *cedant*), an asset is created in its financial statements. As with other assets, the reporting entity must consider whether an impairment has occurred as of the reporting (statement of financial position) date. Under IFRS 4, a reinsurance asset is impaired only when there is objective evidence that the cedant may not receive all amounts due to it under the terms of the contract, as a consequence of an event that occurred after initial recognition of the reinsurance asset, and furthermore the impact of that event is reliably measurable in terms of the amounts that the cedant will receive from the reinsurer.

When the reinsurance asset is found to be impaired, the carrying value is adjusted downward and a loss is recognized in current period earnings for the full amount.

Selection of accounting principles. IFRS requires certain accounting practices to be adopted with regard to insurance contracts, but also allows other, existing procedures to remain in place under defined conditions. An insuring entity may, under provisions of IFRS 4, change accounting policies for insurance contracts only if such change makes the financial statements more relevant to the economic decision-making needs of users and no less reliable, or more reliable and no less relevant to those needs. Relevance and reliability are to be assessed by applying the criteria set forth in IAS 8.

To justify changing its accounting policies for insurance contracts, an insuring entity must demonstrate that the change brings its financial statements nearer to satisfying the criteria of IAS 8, but the change does not necessarily have to achieve full compliance with those criteria. The standard addresses changes in accounting policies in the context of current interest rates; continuation of existing reporting practices; prudence; future investment margins; and "shadow accounting." These are discussed in the following paragraphs.

Regarding interest rates, IFRS 4 provides that an insuring entity is permitted, although it is not required, to change its accounting policies such that it remeasures designated insurance liabilities to reflect current market interest rates, and recognizes changes in those liabilities in current period earnings. It may also adopt accounting policies that require other current estimates and assumptions for the designated liabilities. IFRS 4 permits an insuring entity to change its accounting policies for designated liabilities, without consistently applying those policies to all similar liabilities, as the requirements under IAS 8 would suggest. If the insuring entity designates liabilities for this policy choice, it must continue to apply current market interest rates consistently in all periods to all these liabilities until they are later eliminated.

An unusual feature of IFRS 4 is that it offers affected reporting entities the option to continue with their existing accounting policies. Specifically, an insuring entity is allowed to continue the following practices if in place prior to the effective date of IFRS 4:

1. Measuring insurance liabilities on an *undiscounted* basis.
2. Measuring contractual rights to future investment management fees at an amount that exceeds their fair value as implied by a comparison with current fees charged by other market participants for similar services. It is likely that the fair value at inception of those contractual rights equals the origination costs paid, unless future investment management fees and related costs are out of line with market comparables.
3. Employing nonuniform accounting policies for the insurance contracts (and related deferred acquisition costs and intangible assets, if any) of subsidiaries, except as permitted by the above-noted interest provision. If those accounting policies are not uniform, the insuring entity may change them if the change does not make the accounting policies more diverse, and also satisfies the other requirements of the standard.

The concept of *prudence*, as set forth in IFRS 4, is meant to excuse an insuring entity from a need to change its accounting policies for insurance contracts in order to eliminate excessive prudence (i.e., conservatism). However, if the insuring entity already measures its insurance contracts with sufficient prudence, it is not permitted to introduce additional prudence following adoption of IFRS 4.

The matter of *future investment margins* requires some explanation. Under IFRS 4 it is clearly preferred that the measurement of insurance contracts should not reflect future investment margins, but the standard does not require reporting entities to change accounting policies for insurance contracts to eliminate future investment margins. On the other hand, adopting a policy that would reflect this is presumed to be improper (the standard states that there is a rebuttable presumption that the financial statements would become less relevant and reliable if an accounting policy that reflects future investment margins in the measurement of insurance contracts is adopted, unless those margins affect the contractual payments). The standard offers two examples of accounting policies that reflect those margins. The first is using a discount rate that reflects the estimated return on the insurer's assets, while the second is projecting the returns on those assets at an estimated rate of return, discounting those projected returns at a different rate and including the result in the measurement of the liability.

IFRS 4 states that the insuring entity could possibly overcome this rebuttable presumption if the other components of a change in accounting policies increase the relevance and reliability of its financial statements sufficiently to outweigh the decrease in relevance and reliability caused by the inclusion of future investment margins. As an example, it cites the situation where the existing accounting policies for insurance contracts involve excessively prudent (i.e., conservative) assumptions set at inception, and a statutory discount rate not directly referenced to market conditions, and ignore some embedded options and guarantees. This entity might make its financial statements more relevant and no less reliable by switching to a comprehensive investor-oriented basis of accounting that is widely used and involves current estimates and assumptions; a reasonable (but not excessively prudent) adjustment to reflect risk and uncertainty; measurements that reflect both the intrinsic value and time value of embedded options and guarantees; and a current market discount rate, even if that discount rate reflects the estimated return on the insuring entity's assets.

The actual ability to overcome IFRS 4's rebuttable presumption is fact dependent. Thus, in some measurement approaches, the discount rate is used to determine the present value of a future profit margin, which is then attributed to different periods using a formula. In such approaches, the discount rate affects the measurement of the liability only indirectly, and the use of a less appropriate discount rate has a limited or no effect on the measurement of the liability at inception. In yet other approaches, the discount rate determines the measurement of the liability directly, and because the introduction of an asset-based discount rate has a more significant effect, it is highly unlikely that an insurer could overcome the rebuttable presumption noted above.

Finally, there is the matter of *shadow accounting*. According to IFRS 4, an insurer is permitted, but not required, to change its accounting policies so that a recognized but unrealized gain or loss on an asset affects those measurements in the same way that a realized gain or loss does. This is because, under some accounting models, realized gains or losses on an insurer's assets have a direct effect on the measurement of some or all of (1) its insurance liabilities, (2) related deferred acquisition costs, and (3) related intangible assets. IFRS 4 provides that the related adjustment to the insurance liability (or deferred acquisition costs or intangible assets) may be recognized in equity if, and only if, the unrealized gains or losses are recognized directly in equity.

Unbundling. Specific requirements pertain to *unbundling* of elements of insurance contracts, and dealing with embedded derivatives, options and guarantees.

Unbundling refers to the accounting for components of a contract as if they were separate contracts. Some insurance contracts consist of an insurance component and a deposit component. IFRS 4 in some cases requires the reporting entity to unbundle those components, and in other fact situations provides the entity with the option of unbundled accounting. Specifically, unbundling is *required* if both the following conditions are met:

1. The insuring entity can measure the deposit component (inclusive of any embedded surrender options) separately, *and*

2. The insuring entity's accounting policies do not otherwise require it to recognize all obligations and rights arising from the deposit component.

On the other hand, unbundling is permitted, but not required, if the insuring entity can measure the deposit component separately but its accounting policies require it to recognize all obligations and rights arising from the deposit component, regardless of the basis used to measure those rights and obligations.

Unbundling is actually prohibited if an insuring entity cannot measure the deposit component separately.

If unbundling is applied to a contract, the insuring entity applies IFRS 4 to the insurance component of the contract, while using IAS 39 to account for the deposit component of that contract.

Recognition and measurement. IFRS 4 prohibits the recognition of a liability for any provisions for possible future claims, if those claims arise under insurance contracts that are not in existence at the reporting date. Catastrophe and equalization provisions are thus prohibited, because they do not reflect loss events that have already occurred and, therefore, recognition would be inconsistent with IAS 37. Loss recognition testing is required for losses already incurred at each date of the statement of financial position, as described above. An insurance liability (or a part of an insurance liability) is to be removed from the statement of financial position only when it is extinguished (i.e., when the obligation specified in the contract is discharged or canceled or expires).

In terms of display, offsetting of reinsurance assets against the related insurance liabilities is prohibited, as is offsetting of income or expense from reinsurance contracts against the expense or income from the related insurance contracts.

Discretionary participation features in insurance contracts. Insurance contracts sometimes contain a discretionary participation feature, as well as a guaranteed element. (That is, some portion of the return to be accrued to policyholders is at the discretion of the insuring entity.) Under the provisions of IFRS 4, the issuer of such a contract may, but is not required to, recognize the guaranteed element separately from the discretionary participation feature. If the issuer does not recognize them separately, it must classify the entire contract as a liability. If, on the other hand, the issuer classifies them separately, it will classify the guaranteed element as a liability. If the entity recognizes the discretionary participation feature separately from the guaranteed element, the discretionary participation feature can be classified either as a liability or as a separate component of equity; the standard does not specify how the decision should be reached. In fact, the issuer may even split that feature into liability and equity components, if a consistent accounting policy is used to determine that split.

When there is a discretionary participation feature which is reported in equity, the reporting entity is permitted to recognize all premiums received as revenue, without separating any portion that relates to the equity component. Changes in the guaranteed element and in the portion of the discretionary participation feature classified as a liability are to be reported in earnings, while changes in the part of the discretionary participation feature classified as equity are to be accounted for as an allocation of earnings, similar to how minority interest is reported.

If the contract contains an embedded derivative within the scope of IAS 39, that standard must be applied to that embedded derivative.

Disclosure. Under the provisions of IFRS 4, insuring entities must disclose information that identifies and explains the amounts in its financial statements arising from insurance contracts. This is accomplished by disclosure of accounting policies for insurance contracts and related assets, liabilities, income and expense; of recognized assets, liabilities, income and expense (and, if it presents its statement of cash flows using the direct method, cash flows) arising from insurance contracts. Additionally, if the insuring entity is a cedant, it must also disclose gains and losses recognized in profit or loss on buying reinsurance; and, if the cedant defers and amortizes gains and losses arising on buying reinsurance, the amortization for the period and the amounts remaining unamortized at the beginning and end of the period.

Disclosure is also required of the process used to determine the assumptions that have the greatest effect on the measurement of the recognized amounts described above. When practicable, quantified disclosure of those assumptions is to be presented as well. The effect of changes in assumptions used to measure insurance assets and insurance liabilities is required, reporting separately the effect of each change that has a material effect on the financial statements.

Finally, reconciliation of changes in insurance liabilities, reinsurance assets and, if any, related deferred acquisition costs are mandated by IFRS 4.

Regarding the amount, timing and uncertainty of cash flows, the entity is required to disclose information that helps users to understand these matters as they result from insurance contracts. This is accomplished if the insuring entity discloses its objectives in managing risks arising from insurance contracts and its policies for mitigating those risks.

Phase II of the IASB Insurance Project

The bulk of the materials contained in the DSOP on insurance, which was issued by the IASC in 2001, will, if endorsed by IASB, become part of the standard(s) that is being developed in Phase II of the Insurance Project. IASB issued a Discussion Paper in May 2007; the timing of an Exposure Draft has not been determined. The lengthy deliberations suggest the complexity of the issues and the controversy anticipated to follow any firm decisions IASB will make. The US standard setter, FASB, is also considering releasing this Discussion Paper and then, possibly, joining with IASB to produce a final standard.

IASB unveiled its discussion paper, *Preliminary Views on Insurance Contracts*, in May 2007. This is the product of the second phase of IASB's project on insurance; the first phase culminated in the issuance of IFRS 4 in 2004, which mandated enhanced disclosures and made relatively minor improvements in certain recognition and measurement procedures. The Preliminary Views document addresses insurance liabilities (the insurer's obligations under an insurance contract) and insurance assets (the insurer's rights under an insurance contract). It does not discuss accounting by policyholders for insurance contracts, a topic that will be dealt with in a later phase of the IASB Insurance Project.

According to IFRS 4, an insurance contract is a "contract under which one party (the insurer) accepts significant insurance risk from another party (the policyholder) by agreeing to compensate the policyholder if a specified uncertain future event (the insured event) adversely affects the policyholder." This definition is not challenged by the Preliminary Views. The views set forth by IASB do apply to all types of insurance contracts: life and nonlife, direct insurance and reinsurance, and would apply throughout the life of a contract, to both the preclaims period (i.e., the coverage period when the insurer is standing ready to meet valid claims) as well as to the claims period (when the insured events have occurred but the ultimate payment is still uncertain).

Regarding recognition and derecognition, the Discussion Paper states that the insurer should recognize rights and obligations created by an insurance contract when the insurer becomes a party to the contract. An insurer should derecognize an insurance liability (or a part of an insurance liability) when it is extinguished (i.e., when the obligation specified in the contracts is discharged, cancelled, or expires). Derecognition of financial assets (including insurance assets) is the subject of another project, and is therefore not addressed in this document.

Concerning measurement, IASB's Discussion Paper view is that an insurer should measure all its insurance liabilities using what it describes as three building blocks: (1) the explicit, unbiased, market-consistent, probability-weighted and current estimates of the contractual cash flows; (2) current market discount rates that adjust the estimated future cash flows for the time value of money; and (3) an explicit and unbiased estimate of the margin that market participants require for bearing risk (a *risk margin*) and for providing other services, if any (a *service margin*).

The matter of margin has been subject to some debate. Some believe that margin should be calibrated to the observed price for the transaction with the policyholder, which would have the consequence that an insurer would never recognize a profit at inception. Others (a majority) believe that the observed price for the transaction with the policyholder, although a reasonableness check on the initial measurement of the insurance liability, should not override an unbiased estimate of the margin another party would require if it took over the insurer's contract rights and obligations.

IASB has concluded that a measurement using the three building blocks would provide several benefits to users of the financial statements. These perceived advantages include

1. Relevant information about the amount, timing and uncertainty of future cash flows arising from existing insurance contracts;
2. Explicit and more robust estimates of cash flows and margins;
3. A consistent approach to changes in estimates;
4. An appropriate and consistent approach for all types of insurance (and reinsurance) contracts.

Having this information would

1. Provide a coherent framework to deal with more complex contracts (such as multi-year, multiline or stop loss contracts) and to resolve emerging issues without resorting to unprincipled distinctions and arbitrary new rules;
2. Limit the need for arbitrary rules on such matters as embedded derivatives, financial reinsurance, and amendments to existing contracts.

Furthermore, a measurement approach using the aforenoted building blocks would

1. Enhance consistency with other IFRSs that require current estimates of future cash flows in measuring financial and nonfinancial liabilities;
2. Provide clearer reporting of economic mismatches between insurance liabilities and related assets, and a reduction in accounting mismatches; and
3. Improve consistency with observable current market prices, to the extent available.

These prices would provide an understandable and credible benchmark for users, even though market prices are not available to support all inputs used in measuring insurance liabilities. The measurement that uses the three building blocks has been denoted by IASB as current exit value. The Discussion Paper defines *current exit value* as the amount the insurer would expect to pay at the reporting date to immediately transfer its remaining contractual rights and obligations to another entity.

A measurement at current exit value is not intended to imply that an insurer can, will, or should transfer its insurance liabilities to a third party immediately. Generally, insurers cannot transfer the liabilities to a third party and would not wish to do so. Rather, the purpose of specifying this measurement objective is to provide information useful for making economic decisions.

According to the preliminary views document, an insurer has an asset relating to its ability to derive net economic benefits from future premiums that the policyholder must pay to retain guaranteed insurability. Guaranteed insurability is a right that permits continued coverage without reconfirmation of the policyholder's risk profile and at a price that is contractually constrained. The insurer should recognize that asset, and measure it in the same way as the related insurance liability (i.e., at current exit value). That asset is part of a customer relationship, not a contractual asset. Nevertheless, the insurer should present that asset as part of the related insurance liability. The insurer need not separate that asset from the liability for recognition, measurement, or presentation. Thus, measurement of the insurance liability would be based on estimated cash flows from both that asset and the liability.

The immediate observations were not unanimously endorsed by IASB. Some believe that an insurer should not recognize net economic benefits expected from future premiums if the policyholder cannot be compelled to pay the premiums. Others believe that the criterion of guaranteed insurability is open to inconsistent application and abuse, and accordingly the recognition of a profit at the inception of an insurance contract should be prohibited, but that a customer relationship intangible could be recognized if shown to be recoverable. Yet others believe that an insurer should always present the recognized part of a customer relationship separately from an insurance liability.

The recommendation is that an insurer recognize acquisition costs as an expense when incurred. If the insurer expects to recover acquisition costs from future premiums that policyholders must pay to retain guaranteed insurability, those premiums reduce the measurement of the liability because the insurer includes them in the recognized part of the customer relationship. If the insurer recovers acquisition costs from premiums already received, receiving that part of those premiums would not increase the measurement of the liability.

Risk margin refers to the component that reflects the difference between a liability having a series of fixed cash flows (such as bank debt) and one having uncertain cash flows (insurance). Whether seen as a "reserve" (the Discussion Paper uses the term "shock absorber") or as additional compensation received for bearing risk impacts the accounting to be applied. Currently, IASB favors the compensation interpretation. Risk margins should be determined for a portfolio of insurance contracts that are subject to broadly similar risks and are managed together as a single portfolio. Risk margins should not reflect the benefits of diversification between portfolios and negative correlation between portfolios.

A cedant in a reinsurance arrangement would be required to measure reinsurance assets at current exit value. For risks associated with the underlying insurance contract, a risk margin typically increase the measurement of the reinsurance asset and equals the risk margin for the corresponding part of the underlying insurance contract. The current exit value of reinsurance assets incorporates a reduction for the expected (probability-weighted) present value of losses from default or disputes, with a further reduction for the margin that market participants would require for bearing the risk that defaults or disputes exceed the expected value.

Since some insurance contracts contain both an insurance component and a deposit component, the Discussion Paper suggests that an insurer should treat these contracts as follows:

1. If the components are so interdependent that the components can be measured only on an arbitrary basis, the phase II standard on insurance contracts should apply to the whole contract;
2. If the components are not interdependent, the phase II standard should apply to the insurance component and IAS 39 should apply to the deposit component; and
3. If the components are interdependent but can be measured separately on a basis that is not arbitrary, IAS 39 should apply to the deposit component.

The whole contract would be measured by applying the phase II standard. Consequently, the insurance component would be measured as the difference between the measurement of the whole contract and the measurement of the deposit component.

The current exit value of a liability is the price for a transfer that neither improves nor impairs its credit characteristics. An insurer should disclose the effect of such credit characteristics at inception and subsequent changes, if any, in their effect. In practice, such effects are normally small.

Many insurers and reinsurers issue both insurance contracts and contracts that do not transfer significant insurance risk (which thus are investment contracts). Investment contracts are within the scope of IAS 39 and, in some cases, IAS 18, *Revenue*. There are differences between existing requirements in IAS 39 and IAS 18 and the IASB's preliminary views on insurance contracts.

One building block to be used in measuring an insurance liability is estimates of the cash flows in each scenario. To the extent that a legal or constructive obligation exists at the reporting date, the estimated cash flows for each scenario should include an unbiased estimate of the policyholder dividends resulting from that obligation. An insurer would need to consider the guidance in IAS 37, *Provisions, Contingent Liabilities and Contingent Assets*, to determine whether such an obligation exists. Such an obligation may arise when the insurer becomes a party to the participating contract, but that will depend on the facts of each case. A revised version of IAS 37 is expected in 2008.

In measuring a participating liability at current exit value, an insurer would be required to measure asset-dependent cash flows on a basis consistent with the measurement of the underlying assets. The insurer should use option pricing techniques that capture, on a market-consistent basis, both the intrinsic value and time value of the asymmetric pay-offs resulting from the participation feature. The preliminary views apply equally to participating insurance contracts and participating investment contracts. They apply to participating contracts issued by both shareholder-owned insurers and mutuals.

Regarding universal life contracts, estimates of crediting rates in each scenario would have to reflect the rate that the insurer estimates it would pay in that scenario to satisfy a legal or constructive obligation that exists at the reporting date.

For unit-linked contracts, benefits depend partly on the fair value of a designated pool of assets. Accounting mismatches could arise if those assets are not measured at fair value through profit or loss but the related liability is measured at current exit value. IASB would prefer to eliminate those mismatches, but has not yet formed a preliminary view on whether this is appropriate. Nor has it yet formed a preliminary view on the recognition and presentation of those assets.

For index-linked contracts, the insurer is not compelled to hold the underlying assets, and it could transfer the liability without a simultaneous transfer of the assets. Existing requirements in IFRSs thus remain appropriate for assets held to back index-linked contracts.

Profit or loss is expected to include all changes in the carrying amount of insurance liabilities. In developing an exposure draft, IASB will consider whether an insurer should present premiums as revenue or as deposit receipts, and whether the face of an insurer's income statement should present separately specified components of the changes in the carrying amount of insurance liabilities. IASB has not yet formed a preliminary view on these topics.

25 INFLATION AND HYPERINFLATION

PERSPECTIVE AND ISSUES

While the use of fair value as a measurement attribute for purposes of financial statement display has become increasingly popular in recent years, accounting principles—both most national GAAP and IFRS—still remain substantially grounded in historical costing. Notwithstanding that under US GAAP a major pronouncement has established a hierarchy of fair value measurement techniques—and that a forthcoming IFRS standard is likely to do likewise, probably replicating the US GAAP standard—few or no new mandates to apply fair value accounting have been issued.

In periods of price stability, the use of historical cost information does not do much of a disservice to understanding the reporting entity's financial position and results of operations. However, in times of price instability—or, in the case of long-lived assets, even in periods of modest changes in prices over long stretches of time—financial reporting can be distorted. Over many decades, a wide variety of solutions to this problem have been proposed, and, in certain periods of rampant inflation, some of these have even been put into practice.

The now-withdrawn international standard, IAS 15, was one such attempt to neutralize the effects of changing prices on the financial statements. It was promulgated (effective in 1983, superseding an earlier standard, IAS 6) to stipulate the disclosures needed to communicate the impact of changing prices on reporting entities' results of operations and financial positions. It granted preparers the option of applying general price level adjustments or using current costs (i.e., current replacement costs for the service potential represented by the assets in place).

The persistent inflation experienced by many industrialized nations during the 1960s, 1970s, and early 1980s caused there to be a reexamination of the long-held and widespread commitment to historical cost as the principal basis for financial reporting. (An exception had been those nations, such as many in Latin America, where inflation had been endemic for many decades, and where price-level adjusted financial reporting was commonly employed.) Popular interest in alternative techniques of inflation accounting (as the various methods are all called) declined markedly once price stability was restored, by the mid-1980s. Most of the financial reporting standards adopted (including those under US and UK GAAP, and under IFRS) have either been revoked, made optional, or fallen into disuse during this time. (IAS 15 was made optional in 1989.) As part of the IASB's *Improvements Project*, IAS 15, the standard on inflation accounting, was withdrawn in 2005.

While the standard has been withdrawn, it does remain as a matter of record as one highly evolved set of guidance that entities can still utilize, should the decision be made to present supplementary financial statements on a basis which removes the effects of cost changes. For reporting entities electing to present inflation adjusted financial statements, this will continue to be instructive, together with selected literature published by US and UK standard setters and other bodies such as the US Securities and Exchange Commission. Thus, although presentation of inflation-adjusted financial statements is no longer required, for entities choosing to present such financial data, this guidance continues to be pertinent.

IAS 29, which has *not* been withdrawn, addresses financial reporting in *hyperinflationary* economies. While, in general, this applies the same principles as are employed when using general price level accounting, the objective is to convert the financial statements of entities operating under conditions that render unadjusted financial statement of little or no value into meaningful measures of financial position and performance. Fortunately, over recent years there have been very few nations suffering from hyperinflation (certain African nations are the major exceptions), but as with more moderate inflationary cycles, these have hardly disappeared from the economic horizon, and of course the possibility for renewed inflation in the future remains. Since there is some current need for this guidance, and the possibility of more need over time, this will also be explained in some detail in the present chapter. It should be noted that the withdrawal of IAS 15 had no bearing on the status of IAS 29.

Sources of IFRS
IAS 29　　　　　*IFRIC* 7

DEFINITIONS OF TERMS

Common dollar reporting. Synonymous with general price level or constant dollar financial reporting.

Constant dollar accounting. An accounting model that treats dollars of varying degrees of purchasing power essentially in the manner that foreign currencies are treated; dollars are translated into current purchasing power units and presented in restated financial statements. Constant dollar accounting converts all nonmonetary assets and equities from historical to current dollars by applying an index of general purchasing power. Specific value changes are ignored, and thus there are no holding gains or losses recognized. Monetary items are brought forward without adjustment, and these accounts (cash, claims to fixed amounts of cash, and obligations to pay fixed amounts of cash) therefore do give rise to purchasing power gains or losses. Constant dollar accounting does not attempt to address value changes.

Current cost accounting. An accounting model that attempts to measure economic values and changes therein, whether or not realized in the traditional accounting sense. In current cost accounting financial statements, nonmonetary items are reflected at current value amounts, measured variously by replacement cost, exit value, fair market value, net present value, or by other methodologies. Current cost based statements of earnings will report as operating income the amount of resources that are available for distribution (to shareholders and others) without impairing the entity's ability to replace assets as they are sold or consumed in the operation of the business. Holding gains may or may not also be reportable as a component of income, although these are never deemed to be distributable unless the entity is liquidating itself. In a pure current cost accounting system, no purchasing power gains or losses are given recognition, but hybrid models have been proposed under US GAAP and IAS, which do recognize these as well as specific price changes.

Distributable (replicatable) earnings. The amount of resources that could be distributed (e.g., by dividends to shareholders) from the current period's earnings without impairing the entity's operating capacity vs. its level at the beginning of the period. This parallels the classic definition of economic income. It is generally conceded that current cost would provide the best measure of distributable earnings. Traditional historical cost based financial reporting, on the other hand, does not attempt to measure economic income, but rather, seeks to match actual costs incurred against revenues generated; the result in many cases is that this measure of income will exceed real economic earnings.

Economic value. The ideal measure of current value/current cost; also known as deprival value. In practice, surrogate measures are often used instead.

Excess of specific price changes over general price level increase. A measure first introduced by the US GAAP standard on inflation accounting (FAS 33, similarly demoted to optional status by FAS 89) and usable under IAS 15 as well. This is the amount of increase in current cost of inventories and plant assets, in excess of the increase that would have occurred during the period had the change in values been at the rate of change of a broadbased market basket of goods and services.

Exit value. Also known as net realizable value, this is the measure of the resources that could be obtained by disposing of a specified asset, often for scrap or salvage value. Valuing assets at exit value is not generally valid as a measure of current cost, since value in use usually exceeds exit value, and most assets held by the enterprise will not be disposed of; however, for assets that are not to be replaced in the normal course of business, exit value may be a meaningful measure.

Fair value. Fair market value, or market value. For certain specialized properties, such as natural resources, this may be the most meaningful measure of current cost.

Fair value accounting. A now obsolete term which implies current cost or current value financial reporting.

Gains/losses on net monetary items. Synonymous with general purchasing power gains and losses.

Gearing adjustment. A term used in the proposed British inflation accounting standard, which reflects the conclusion that if an entity is financed externally (i.e., by debt), it may not need to retain resources in an amount equal to the replacement cost of goods sold and of depreciation in order to maintain existing productive capacity; sufficient borrowed funds must, however, continue to be available so that the existing degree of financial leverage (gearing) can be maintained in the future. This adjustment was not addressed by IAS 15.

Holding gains/losses. In general, the increase or decrease in the current cost of non-monetary assets (plant assets and inventories, for the most part) during a period. Notwithstanding the gain/loss terminology, such items are not generally recognized as part of income but rather as part of stockholders' equity, although practice varies. Holding gains are not distributable to shareholders without impairing operating capacity. In some models, only the excess of specific price changes over general price level changes are deemed to be holding gains/losses.

Hyperinflation. The condition in an economy in which there is such extreme inflation that historical cost financial statements become meaningless; characterized by a general aversion of the population to holding monetary assets, the conducting of business in ways that provide some protection against inflation, such as denominating transactions in a stable foreign currency or indexing to compensate for price changes, and a cumulative inflation rate over three years approaching 100%.

Inventory profits. The overstatement of income resulting from charging cost of sales at historical levels instead of at replacement costs; during periods of rapid inflation, historical cost based income will exceed real, economic earnings (distributable or replicatable earnings); this is partly the result of inventory profits. Not all entities are affected similarly. Those using LIFO costing will be less severely affected, and entities having faster inventory turnover will also have less inventory profits.

Monetary items. Claims to, or obligations to pay, fixed sums of cash or its equivalent. Examples are accounts receivable and accounts payable. If constant dollar accounting is employed, net monetary assets or liabilities will create purchasing power gains or losses in periods of changing general prices, since such fixed claims to cash or obligations to pay cash gain or lose value as the general purchasing power of the currency grows or shrinks.

Net present value. The future cash flows that will be generated by operation of an asset, discounted by a relevant factor such as the opportunity cost of capital, to an equivalent present value amount. This is a surrogate measure for economic value (deprival value) that is useful in certain circumstances (e.g., determining the future net cash flow of income producing real estate). For other assets, such as machinery, this is difficult to compute because future cash flows are difficult to forecast and because the assets are part of integrated processes generating cash flows that cannot be attributed to each component.

Net realizable value. Generally used in accounting to denote the amount that could be realized from an immediate disposition of an asset; also known as exit value. Net realizable value is sometimes used for current costing purposes if the asset in question is not intended to be held beyond a brief period.

Nonmonetary items. Items that are neither claims to, nor obligations to pay, fixed sums of cash or its equivalent. Examples are inventories and plant assets. When constant dollar accounting is employed, all nonmonetary items are adjusted to current dollar equivalents by application of a general measure of purchasing power changes. If current cost accounting is employed, nonmonetary items are recorded at current economic values (measured by replacement cost, deprival value, etc.); nonmonetary equity accounts may be explicitly adjusted or the necessary balancing amounts can be imputed. Holding gains and losses result from applying current cost measures to nonmonetary items.

Price level accounting. See constant dollar accounting.

Purchasing power accounting. See constant dollar accounting.

Purchasing power gains/losses. The economic benefit or detriment that results when an entity has claims to fixed amounts of cash (monetary assets) or has obligations to pay fixed sums (monetary liabilities) during periods when the general purchasing power of the monetary unit is changing. An excess of monetary assets over monetary liabilities coupled with rising prices results in a purchasing power loss; an excess of monetary liabilities results in a gain. These are reversed if prices are declining.

Realized holding gains/losses. Holding gains/losses can be realized or unrealized. If an appreciated item of inventory is sold, the holding gain is realized; if unsold at period end, it is unrealized. Historical cost based accounting does not recognize unrealized holding gains/losses (with some exceptions), and realized holding gains/losses are merged with other operating income and not given separate recognition. Use of the term holding gain/loss was prohibited by the US GAAP inflation accounting standard and was not addressed by the now-withdrawn IAS 15.

Recoverable amount. The amount that could be obtained either from the continued use of an asset (the net present value of future cash flows) or from its disposal (exit or net realizable value).

Replacement cost. The lowest cost that would be incurred to replace the service potential of an asset in the normal course of the business.

Replicatable earnings. See distributable earnings.

Reproduction cost. The cost of acquiring an asset identical to the one presently in use. The distinction between reproduction cost and replacement cost is that operating efficiencies and technological changes may have occurred and the nominally identical asset would have a different productive capacity. Typically, replacement costs are lower than reproduction costs, and use of the latter would tend to overstate the effects of inflation.

Unrealized holding gains/losses. Holding gains or losses that have yet to be realized through an arm's-length transaction.

Value in use. Also known as value to the business, this is defined as the lesser of current cost or net recoverable amount.

INFLATION-ADJUSTED FINANCIAL REPORTING

CONCEPTS, RULES, AND EXAMPLES

Historical Review of Inflation Accounting

Accounting practice today, on virtually a worldwide basis, relies heavily on the historical cost measurement strategy, whereby resources and obligations are given recognition as assets and liabilities, respectively, at the original (dollar, yen, etc.) amount of the transaction from which they arose. Once recorded, these amounts are not altered to reflect changes in value, except to the limited extent that various national GAAP standards or IFRS require recognition of impairments (e.g., lower of cost or fair value for inventories, etc.). Most long-lived assets such as buildings are amortized against earnings on a rational basis over their estimated useful lives, while short-lived assets are expensed as physically consumed. Liabilities are maintained at cost until paid off or otherwise discharged.

It is useful to recall that before the historical cost model of financial reporting achieved nearly universal adoption, various alternative recognition and measurement approaches were experimented with. Fair value accounting was in fact widely employed in the nineteenth and early twentieth centuries, and for some regulatory purposes (especially in setting utility service prices, where regulated by governmental agencies) remained in vogue until somewhat more recently. The retreat from fair value accounting was, in fact, due less to any inherent attractiveness of the historical cost model than to negative reaction to abuses in fair value reporting. This came to a climax during the 1920s in much of the industrialized world, when prosperity and inflation encouraged overly optimistic reflections of values, much of which were reversed after the onset of the worldwide Great Depression.

Most of what are known as generally accepted accounting principles (GAAP) were developed after the crash of 1929. The more important of the basic postulates, which underlie most of the historical cost accounting principles, include the realization concept, the stable currency assumption, the matching concept, conservatism (or prudence), and historical costing. Realization means that earnings are not recognized until a definitive event, involving an arm's-length transaction in most instances, has occurred. Stable currency refers to the presumption that a €1,000 machine purchased today is about the same as a €1,000 machine purchased twenty years ago, in terms of real productive capacity. The matching concept has come to suggest a quasi-mechanical relationship between costs incurred in prior periods and the revenues generated currently as a result; the net of these is deemed to define earnings. Conservatism, among other things, implies that all losses be provided for but that gains not be anticipated, and is often used as an argument against fair value accounting. Finally, the historical costing convention was adopted as the most objectively verifiable means of reporting economic events.

The confluence of these underlying postulates has served to make historical cost based accounting, as it has been practiced for the past sixty years, widely supported. Even periods of rampant inflation, as the Western industrialized nations experienced during the 1970s, has not seriously diminished enthusiasm for this model, despite much academic research and the fairly sophisticated and complete alternative financial reporting approaches proposed in the United Kingdom and the United States and a later international accounting standard that built on those two recommendations. All of these failed to generate wide support and have largely been abandoned, being relegated to suggested supplementary information status, with which very few reporting enterprises comply.

What should accounting measure? Accounting was invented to measure economic activity in order to facilitate it. It is an information system, the product of which is used by one or more groups of decision makers: managers, lenders, investors, even current and prospective employees. In common with other types of decision-relevant data, financial statements can be evaluated along a number of dimensions, of which relevance and objectivity are frequently noted as being the most valuable. Information measured or reported by accounting systems should be, on the one hand, objective in the sense that independent observers will closely agree that the information is correct, and on the other hand, the information should be computed and reported in such as way that its utility for decision makers is enhanced.

Objectivity has become what one critic called an occupational distortion of the accounting profession. While objectivity connotes a basic attitude of unprejudiced fairness that should be highly prized, it has also come to denote an excessive reliance on completed cash transactions as a basis for recording economic phenomena. However, objectivity at the cost of diminished relevance may not be a valid goal. It has been noted that "relevance is the more basic of the virtues; while a relevant valuation may sometimes be wrong, an irrelevant one can never be of use, no matter how objectively it is reached." Both the FASB in the United States and the IASB in the international arena have published conceptual framework documents which support the notion that more relevant information, even if necessitating a departure from the historical costing tradition, could be more valuable to users of financial statements.

Why inflation undermines historical cost financial reporting. Actual and would-be investors and creditors, as well as entity managers and others, desire accounting information to support their decision-making needs. Financial statements that ignore the effects of general price level changes as well as changes in specific prices are inadequate for several reasons.

1. Reported profits often exceed the earnings that could be distributed to shareholders without impairing the entity's ability to maintain the present level of operations, because inventory profits are included in earnings and because depreciation charges are not adequate to provide for asset replacements.
2. Statements of financial position fail to reflect the economic value of the business, because plant assets and inventories, especially, are recorded at historical values that may be lower than current fair values or replacement costs.
3. Future earnings prospects are not easily projected from historical cost based earnings reports.
4. The impact of changes in the general price level on monetary assets and liabilities is not revealed, yet can be severe.
5. Because of the foregoing deficiencies, future capital needs are difficult to forecast, and in fact may contribute to the growing leveraging (borrowing) by many enterprises, which adds to their riskiness.
6. Distortions of real economic performance lead to social and political consequences ranging from suboptimal capital allocations to ill-conceived tax policies and public perceptions of corporate behavior.

Example

A business starts with one unit of inventory, which cost €2 and which at the end of the period is sold for €10 at a time when it would cost €7 to replace that very same unit on the display shelf. Traditional accounting would measure the earnings of the entity at €10 – €2 = €8, although clearly the business is only €3 "better off" at the end of the period than at the beginning, since real economic resources have only grown by €3 (after replacing the unit sold there is only that amount of extra resource available). The illusion that there was profit of €8 could readily destroy the entity if, for example, dividends of more than €3 were withdrawn or if fiscal policy led to taxes of more than €3 on the €8 profit.

On the other hand, if the financial report showed only €3 profit for the period, there could be several salutary effects. Owners' expectations for dividends would be tempered, the entity's real capital would more likely be preserved, and projections of future performance would be more accurate, although projections must always be fine-tuned since the past will never be replicated precisely.

The failure of the historical cost statement of financial position to reflect values is yet another major deficiency of traditional financial reporting. True, accounting was never intended to report values per se, but the excess of assets over liabilities has always been denoted as net worth, and to many that clearly connotes value. Similarly, the alternative titles for the statement of financial position, balance sheet, and statement of financial condition, strongly suggest value to the lay reader. The confusion largely stems from a failure to distinguish *realized* from *unrealized* value changes; if this distinction were carefully maintained, the statement of financial position could be made more useful while remaining true to its traditions.

Evolving use of the financial statements. The traditional statement of financial position was the primary, even the only, financial statement presented during much of accounting's history. However, beginning during the 1960s, what is currently known as the statement of comprehensive income achieved greater importance, partly because users came to realize that the statement of financial position had become the repository for unamortized costs, deferred debits and credits, and other items that bore no relationship to real economic assets and obligations. In the aggressive and high-growth 1960s and early 1970s, the focus was largely on summary measures of enterprise performance, such as earnings per share, which derived from the statement of comprehensive income. During this era, the matching concept became the key underlying postulate that drove new accounting rules.

Following a series of unpleasant economic events, including numerous liquidity crises and recessions in the 1970s and 1980s, the focus substantially shifted back to the statement of financial position. Partly in response, the major accounting standard-setting bodies developed conceptual standards that urged the elimination of some of the items previously found on statements of financial position that were not really either assets or liabilities. Some of these were the leftovers from double entry bookkeeping, which was oriented toward achieving statement of comprehensive income goals (e.g., the optimal matching of revenues and expenses); an example is the interperiod tax allocations that resulted in the reporting of ever-growing deferred tax liabilities that were never going to be paid. While the tension between achieving a meaningful statement of financial position and an accurate statement of comprehensive income is inherent in the double-entry accounting model in use for almost 500 years, accountants are learning that improvements in both can be achieved. Inflation adjusted accounting can contribute to this effort, as will be demonstrated.

General vs. specific price changes. An important distinction to be understood is that between general and specific price changes, and how the effects of each can be meaningfully reported on in financial statements. Changes in specific prices, as with the inventory example above, should not be confused with changes in the general level of prices, which give rise to what are often referred to as purchasing power gains or losses, and result from holding net monetary assets or liabilities during periods of changing general prices. As most consumers are well aware, during periods of general price inflation, holding net monetary assets typically results in experiencing a loss in purchasing power, while a net liability position leads to a gain, as obligations are repaid with "cheaper" dollars. Among other effects, prolonged periods of general price inflation motivates entities to become more leveraged (more indebted to others) because of these purchasing power gains, although in reality creditors are aware of this and adjust interest rates to compensate.

Specific prices may change in ways that are notably different from the trend in overall prices, and they may even move in opposite directions. This is particularly true of basic commodities such as agricultural products and minerals, but may also be true of manufactured goods, especially if technological changes have great influence. For example, even during the years of rampant inflation during the 1970s some commodities, such as copper, were dropping in price, and certain goods, such as computer memory chips, were also declining even in nominal prices. For entities dealing in either of these items, holding inventories of these *nonmonetary* goods (usually a hedge against price inflation) would have produced large economic losses during this time. Thus, not only the changes in general prices, but also the changes in specific prices, and very important, the interactions between these can have major effects on an enterprise's real wealth. Measurement of these phenomena should be within the province of accounting.

Experiments and proposals for inflation accounting. Over the past fifty years there have been a number of proposals for pure price level accounting, financial reporting that would be sensitive to changes in specific prices, and combinations of these. There have been proposals (academic proposals) for comprehensive financial statements that would be adjusted for inflation, as well as for supplemental disclosures that would isolate the major inflation effects without abandoning primary historical cost based statements (generally, the professional proposals and regulatory requirements were of this type). To place the former requirements of the now-withdrawn standard IAS 15 in context, a number of its more prominent predecessors will be reviewed in brief.

Price level accounting concepts and proposals. At its simplest, price level accounting views any given currency at different points in time as being analogous to different currencies at the same point in time. That is, 1955 US dollars have the same relationship to 2009 dollars as 2009 Swiss francs have to 2009 dollars or euros. They are "apples and oranges" and cannot be added or subtracted without first being converted to a common measuring unit. Thus, "pure" price level accounting is held to be within the mainstream historical cost tradition and is merely a translation of one currency into another for comparative purposes. A broadly based measure of all prices in the economy should be used in accomplishing this (often, a consumer price index of some sort is employed).

Consider a simple example. Assume that the index of general prices was as follows:

January 1, 1987	65
January 1, 1999	100
January 1, 2009	182
December 31, 2009	188

Also assume the following items selected from the December 31, 2009 statement of financial position:

	Historical cost	*Price level adjusted cost*
Cash	€ 50,000	€ 50,000
Inventories (purchased 1/1/08)	350,000	
× 188/182		361,538
Land (acquired 1/1/87)	500,000	
× 188/65		1,446,154
Machinery (purchased 1/1/99)	300,000	
× 188/100		564,000
Accumulated depreciation	(200,000)	
× 188/100		(376,000)
Book value of assets	1,000,000	2,045,692
Less monetary liabilities	(500,000)	(500,000)
Net assets	€ 500,000	€1,545,692

In the foregoing, all nonmonetary items were adjusted to "current dollars" using the same index of general prices. This is not based on the notion that items such as inventory and machinery actually experienced price changes of that magnitude, but on the idea that converting these to current dollars is a process akin to converting foreign currency denominated financial statements. The implication is that the historical cost statement of financial position, showing net assets of €500,000, is equivalent to a statement of financial position that reports some items in British pounds sterling, some in US dollars, some in Mexican pesos, and so on. The price level adjusted statement of financial position, by contrast, is deemed to be equivalent to a statement of financial position in which all items have been translated into euros.

This analogy is a weak one, however. Not only are such statements essentially meaningless, they can also be misleading from a policy viewpoint. For example, during a period of rising prices, an entity holding more monetary assets than monetary liabilities will report an economic loss due to the decline in the purchasing power of its net monetary assets. Nonmonetary assets, of course, are adjusted for price changes and thus appear to be immune from purchasing power gains or losses. The implication is that holding nonmonetary assets is somehow preferable to holding monetary assets.

In the foregoing example, the net monetary liabilities at year-end are €500,000 – €50,000 = €450,000. Assuming the same net monetary liability position at the beginning of 2009, the gain experienced by the entity (due to owning monetary debt during a period of depreciating currency) would be given as

$$(€450,000 \times 188/182) - €450,000 = €14,835$$

This suggests that the entity has experienced a gain, at the obvious expense of its creditors, which have incurred a corresponding loss, in the amount of €14,835. This fails entirely to recognize that creditors may have demanded an inflation adjusted rate of return based on actual past and anticipated future inflationary behavior of the economy; if this were addressed in tandem with the computed purchasing power gain, a truer picture would be given of the real wisdom of the entity's financial strategy.

Furthermore, the actual price level protection afforded by holding investments in nonmonetary assets is a function of the changes in their specific values. If the replacement value of the inventory had declined, for example, during 2009, having held this inventory during the year would have been an economically unwise maneuver. Land that cost €500,000 might, due to its strategic location, now be worth €2.5 million, not the indicated €1.4 million, and the machinery might be obsolete due to technological changes, and not worth the approximately €190,000 suggested by the price level adjusted book value. In fairness, of course, the advocates of price level accounting do not claim that these adjusted amounts represent *values*. However, the utility of these adjusted captions from the statement of financial position for decision makers is difficult to fathom and the potential for misunderstanding is great.

US and UK proposals. A number of proposals have been offered over the years for either replacing traditional financial statements with price level adjusted statements, or for including supplementary price level statements in the annual report to shareholders. In the United States, the predecessor of the current accounting standard setter, the Accounting Principles Board, proposed supplementary reporting in 1969; no major publicly held corporation complied with this request, however. The FASB made a similar proposal in 1974 and might have succeeded in imposing this standard had not the US securities market watchdog, the SEC, suggested instead that a current value approach be developed. (Later the SEC did impose a replacement costing requirement on large companies, and the FASB followed with its own version a few years thereafter.)

In the United Kingdom a similar course of events occurred. After an early postwar recommendation (not implemented) that there be earnings set aside for asset replacements, a late-1960s proposal for supplementary price level adjusted reporting was made, followed a few years later by a more comprehensive constant dollar recommendation. As happened in the United States at about the same time, what appeared to be a private sector juggernaut favoring price level adjustments was derailed by governmental intervention. A Royal Commission, established in 1973, eventually produced the Sandilands report, supporting current value accounting and not addressing the reporting of purchasing power gains or losses at all. This marked the end of British enthusiasm for general price level adjusted financial statements. Even a fairly complex later proposal (ED 18) made in 1977 did not incorporate any measure of purchasing power gains or losses, although it did add some novel embellishments to what basically was a current value model.

Other European nations have never been disposed favorably toward general price level accounting, with the exception of France. However, Latin American nations, having dealt with virtually runaway inflation for decades, have generally welcomed this type of financial reporting and in some cases have required it, even for some tax purposes. While price level adjustments are no more logical in Brazil, for example, than in the United States, since specific prices are changing, often at widely disparate rates, the role of accounting in those nations, serving as much more of an adjunct to the countries' respective tax collection and macroeconomic policy efforts than in European or other Western nations, has tended to encourage support for this approach to accounting for changing prices.

Current value models and proposals. By whatever name it is referred to, current value (replacement cost, current cost) accounting is really based on a wholly different concept than is price level (constant dollar) accounting. Current value financial reporting is far more closely tied to the original intent of the accounting model, which is to measure enterprise economic wealth and the changes therein from period to period. This suggests essentially a "statement of financial position orientation" to income measurement, with the difference between net worth (as measured by current values) at year beginning and year-end being, after adjustment for capital transactions, the measure of income or loss for the intervening period. How this is further analyzed and presented in the statement of comprehensive income (as realized and unrealized gains and losses) or even whether some of these changes even belong in the statement of comprehensive income (or instead, are reported in a separate statement of movements in equity, or are taken directly into equity) is a rather minor bookkeeping concern.

Although the proliferation of terminology of the many competing proposals can be confusing, four candidates as measures of current value can readily be identified: economic value, net present value, net realizable value (also known as exit value), and replacement cost (which is a measure of entry value). A brief explanation will facilitate the discussion of the IAS requirements later in this chapter.

Economic value is usually understood to mean the equilibrium fair market value of an asset. However, apart from items traded in auction markets, typically only securities and raw commodities, direct observation of economic value is not possible.

Net present value is often suggested as the ideal surrogate for economic value, since in a perfect market values are driven by the present value of future cash flows to be generated by the assets. Certain types of assets, such as rental properties, have predictable cash flows and in fact are often priced in this manner. On the other hand, for assets such as machinery, particularly those that are part of a complex integrated production process, determining cash flows is difficult.

Net realizable values (NRV) are more familiar to most accountants, since even under existing US, UK, and international accounting standards, there are numerous instances when references to NRV must be made to ascertain whether asset write-downs are to be required. NRV is a measure of "exit values" since these are the amounts that the organization would realize on asset disposition, net of all costs; from this perspective, this is a conservative measure (exit values are lower than entry values in almost all cases, since transactions are not costless), but also is subject to criticism since under the going concern assumption it is not anticipated that the enterprise will dispose of all its productive assets at current market prices, indeed, not at any prices, since these assets will be retained for use in the business.

The biggest failing of this measure, however, is that it does not assist in measuring economic income, since that metric is intended to reveal how much income an entity can distribute to its owners, and so on, while retaining the ability to replace its productive capacity as needed. In general, an income measure based on exit values would overstate earnings (since depreciation and cost of sales would be based on lower exit values for plant assets and inventory) when compared with an income measure based on entry values. Thus, while NRV is a familiar concept to many accountants, this is not the ideal candidate for a current value model.

Replacement cost is intended as a measure of entry value and hence of the earnings reinvestment needed to maintain real economic productive capacity. Actually, competing proposals have engaged in much hairsplitting over alternative concepts of entry value, and this deserves some attention here. The simplest concept of replacement value is the cost of replacing a specific machine, building, and so on, and in some industries it is indeed possible to determine these prices, at least in the short run, before technology changes occur. However, in many more instances (and in the long run, in all cases) exact physical replacements are not available, and even nominally identical replacements offer varying levels of productivity enhancements that make simplistic comparisons distortive.

As a very basic example, consider a machine with a cost of €40,000 that can produce 100 widgets per hour. The current price of the replacement machine is €50,000, that superficially suggests a specific price increase of 25% has occurred. However, on closer examination, it is determined that while nominally the same machine, some manufacturing enhancements have been made (e.g., the machine will require less maintenance, will require fewer labor inputs, runs at a higher speed, etc.) which have altered its effective capacity (considering reduced downtime, etc.) to 110 widgets per hour. Clearly, a naive adjustment for what is sometimes called "reproduction cost" would overstate the machine's value on the statement of financial position and overstate periodic depreciation charges, thereby understating earnings. A truer measure of the replacement cost of the service potential of the asset, not the physical asset itself, would be given as

$$€40,000 \times (50,000/40,000) \times 100/110 = €45,454$$

That is, the service potential represented by the asset in use has a current replacement cost of €45,454, considering that a new machine costs 25% more but is 10% more productive.

Consider another example: An integrated production process uses machines A and B, which have reproduction costs today of €40,000 and €45,000, respectively. However, management plans to acquire a new type of machine, C, which at a cost of €78,000 will replace both machines A and B and will produce the same output as its predecessors. The combined reproduction cost of €85,000 clearly overstates the replacement cost of the service potential of the existing machines in this case, even if there had been no technological changes affecting machines A and B.

Some, but not all, proposals that have been made in academia over the past sixty years, and by standards setters and regulatory authorities over the past twenty-five years, have understood the foregoing distinctions. For example, the US SEC requirements of the mid-1970s called for measures of the replacement cost of productive capacity, which clearly implied that productivity changes had to be factored in. The subsequent private sector rules issued by FASB seemed to redefine what the SEC had mandated to highlight its own current cost requirement; in essence, the FASB's current costs were nothing other than the SEC's replacement costs. Other proposals have been more ambiguous, however. Furthermore, measuring the impact of technological change adds vastly to the complexity of applying replacement cost measures, since raw replacement costs (known as reproduction costs) are often easily obtained (from catalog prices, etc.), but productivity adjustments must be ascertained by carefully evaluating advertising claims, engineering studies, and other sources of information, which can be a complex and costly process.

Limitations on replacement cost. While entry value is clearly the most logical of the alternative measures discussed thus far, under certain circumstances one of the other candidates would be preferable as a measure to use in current cost financial reporting. For example, consider a situation in which the value in use (economic value or net present value of future cash flows) is lower than replacement cost, due to changing market conditions affecting pricing of the entity's output. In such a circumstance, although the enterprise may continue to use the machines on hand and to sell the output profitably, it would not contemplate replacement of the asset, instead viewing it as a "cash cow." If current cost financial statements were to be developed that incorporated depreciation based on the replacement cost of the machine, earnings would be understated, since actual replacement is not to be provided for. A number of other hypothetical circumstances could also be presented; the end result is that a series of decision rules can be developed to guide the selection of the best measure of current cost. These are summarized in the following table, where NRC stands for net replacement cost, which is synonymous with current cost; NRV is net realizable value or exit value; and EV is the same as net present value.

Conditions	_Value to the business_
EV > NRC > NRV	NRC
NRC > EV > NRV	EV
NRC > NRV > EV	NRV
EV > NRV > NRC	NRC
NRV > EV > NRC	NRC
NRV > NRC > EV	NRC

Measuring Income under the Replacement Cost Approach

There are two reasons to employ replacement cost accounting: (1) to compute a measure of earnings that can probably be replicated on an ongoing basis by the enterprise and approximates real economic wealth creation, and (2) to present a statement of financial position that presents the economic condition of the entity at a point in time. Of these, the first is by far the more important objective, since decision makers' use of financial statements is largely oriented toward the future operations of the business, in which they are lenders, owners, managers, or employees.

Given the foregoing, the principal use of replacement cost information will be to assist in computing current period earnings on a true economic basis. The statement of comprehensive income items which on the historical cost basis are most distortive, in most cases, are depreciation and cost of sales. Historical cost depreciation can be based on asset prices that are ten to forty years old, during which time even modest price changes can compound to very sizable misrepresentations. Cost of sales will not typically suffer from compounding over such a long period, since turnover for most businesses will be in a matter of months (although this can be greatly distorted if low LIFO inventory costs are released into cost of sales), but since cost of sales will account for a much larger part of the entity's total costs than does depreciation, it can still have a major impact.

Thus, current cost/replacement cost/current value earnings are typically computed by adjusting historical cost income by an allowance for replacement cost depreciation and cost of sales. Typically, these two adjustments will effectively derive a modified earnings amount that closely approximates economic earnings. This modified amount can be paid out as dividends or otherwise disbursed, while leaving the enterprise with the ability to replace its productive capacity and continue to operate at the same level as it had been. (This does not, however, address the matter of purchasing power that may have been gained or lost by holding net monetary assets or liabilities during the period, which requires yet another computation.)

Determining current costs. In practice, replacement costs are developed by applying one or more of four principal techniques: indexation, direct pricing, unit pricing, and functional pricing. Each has advantages and disadvantages, and no single technique will be applicable to all fact situations and all types of assets. The following are useful in determining current costs of plant assets.

Indexation is accomplished by applying appropriate indices to the historical cost of the assets. Assuming that the assets in use were acquired in the usual manner (bargain purchases and other such means of acquisition will thwart this effort, since any index when applied to a nonstandard base will result in a meaningless adjusted number) and that an appropriate index can be obtained or developed (which incorporates productivity changes as well as price variations), this will be the most efficient approach to employ. For many categories of manufactured goods, such as machinery and equipment, this technique has been widely used with excellent results. One concern is that many published indices actually address only reproduction costs, and if not adjusted further, the likely outcome will be that costs are overstated and adjusted earnings will be artificially depressed.

Direct pricing, as the name suggests, relies on information provided by vendors and others having data about the selling prices of replacement assets. To the extent that these are list prices that do not reflect actual market transactions, these must be adjusted, and the same concern with productivity enhancements mentioned with reference to indexation must also be addressed. Since many enterprises are in constant, close contact with their vendors, obtaining such information is often straightforward, particularly with regard to machinery and other equipment.

Unit pricing is the least commonly employed method but can be useful when estimating the replacement cost of buildings. This is the bricks-and-mortar approach, which relies on statistical data about the per-unit cost of constructing various types of buildings and other assets. For example, construction cost data may suggest that single-story light industrial buildings in cold climates (e.g., Europe) with certain other defined attributes may have a current cost of €47 per square foot, or that a first-class high-rise urban hotel in England has a construction cost of €125,000 per room. By expanding these per-unit costs to the scale of the enterprise's facilities, a fairly accurate replacement cost can be derived. There are complications; for example, costs are not linearly related to size of facility due to the presence of fixed costs, but these are widely understood and readily dealt with. Unit pricing is typically not meaningful for machinery or equipment, however.

Functional pricing is the most difficult of the four principal techniques and is best reserved for highly integrated production processes, such as refineries and chemical plants, where attempts to price individual components would be exceptionally difficult. For example, a plant capable of producing 400,000 tons of polyethylene annually could be priced as a unit by having an engineering estimate made of the cost to construct similar capacity in the current environment. Clearly, this is not a merely mechanical effort, as indexation in particular is likely to be, but demands the services of a skilled estimator. Technological issues are neatly avoided since the focus is on creating a new plant with defined output capacity, using whatever mix of components would be most cost-effective. This technique has been widely employed in actual practice.

Inventory costing problems. For a merchandising concern, direct pricing is likely to be an effective technique to assist in developing cost of sales on a current cost basis. Manufacturing firms, on the other hand, will need to build up replacement cost basis cost of goods manufactured and sold by separately analyzing the cost behavior of each major cost element (e.g., labor contracts, overhead expenses, and raw materials prices). It is unlikely that these will have experienced the same price movements, and therefore an averaging approach would not be sufficiently accurate. Also, as product mix changes over time, the entity may be subject to varying influences from one period to the next. Finally, the inventory costing method used (e.g., weighted–average vs. FIFO) will affect the extent of adjustment to be made, with (assuming that costs trend upward over time) relatively greater adjustments made to cost of sales determined on the FIFO basis, since relatively older costs are included in the GAAP statement of comprehensive income. Note that the now-banned LIFO method would have had an even more dramatically distorting effect on the statement of financial position.

Whatever assortment of methods is used, the end product is a restated inventory of plant assets, depreciation on which must then be computed. For the current cost earnings data to be comparable with the historical cost financial statements, it is usually recommended that no other decisions be superimposed. For example, no changes in asset useful lives should be made, for to do so would exacerbate or ameliorate the impact of the replacement cost depreciation and make interpretation very difficult for anyone not intimately familiar with the company. Some ancillary costs may need to be adjusted in computing cost of sales and depreciation on the revised basis. For example, if the only replacement machines available will reduce the need for skilled labor, the (higher) replacement cost depreciation should be reduced by related cost savings, if accurately predictable. There are literally scores of similar issues to be addressed, and indeed entire volumes have been written providing detailed guidance on how to apply current cost measures.

Examples of current costing adjustments to depreciation and cost of sales

Example 1

Hapsburg Corp. is a wholesale distributor for a single product. For 2009, the company reports sales of €35,000,000, representing sales of 600,000 units of its single product. The traditional statement of comprehensive income reports cost of sales as follows:

	(000 omitted)
Beginning inventory	€ 8.8
Purchases, net	25.7
Ending inventory	(6.5)
Cost of goods sold	€28.0

Reference to purchase orders reveals the fact that product cost early in 2009 was €42 per unit and was €55 per unit late in December of that year. The company employs FIFO accounting.

Since there is no evidence presented to the effect that net realizable value of the product is below current replacement cost, current cost can be used without modification.

Beginning current cost	€42.0
Ending current cost	€55.0
Average	€48.5

Total cost of sales for the period, on a replacement cost basis, is therefore €48.5 × 600,000 units = €29,100,000.

Example 2

In the following example, deprival value is, for one product line, better measured by net realizable value than by replacement cost. The company, St. Ignatz Mfg. Co., manufactures and sells two products, A and B. Product A has been a declining item for several years, and management now believes that it must close this line due to the shrinking market share, which will not support higher costs. St. Ignatz will continue to produce Product B and may possibly expand into new products in the future.

Company records show the following results in 2009:

	(000,000 omitted)		
	Product A	*Product B*	*Total*
Sales	€19.5	€40.5	€60.0
Cost of sales			
Beginning inventory	12.5	6.8	
Purchases	8.7	20.0	
Ending inventory	(3.0)	(5.4)	
Cost of sales	18.2	21.4	39.6
Gross profit	€ 1.3	€19.1	20.4
All other expenses			(18.8)
Net income			€ 1.6

The company's manufacturing records show the following data:

Current costs, beginning of year	€52.0	€75.0
Current costs, ending of year	63.0	79.0
Current costs, average	57.5	77.0

Sales in 2009 comprised 390,000 units of Product A and 540,000 units of Product B. Management believes that the market for Product A cannot support further price increases, and thus the remaining inventory will probably be sold at a loss. Selling expenses are estimated at €6 per unit.

Product A has a recoverable value lower than current manufacturing costs. The net recoverable amount is given by the selling price per unit less selling expenses: €50 − €6 = €44 per unit.

Current cost of sales is €44 × €390,000 = €17,160,000. Note that recoverable amount, not replacement cost, is used.

Product B has an average current cost of €77 per unit, so 2009 cost of sales on a current cost basis is €77 × €540,000 = €41,580,000.

Total cost of sales on the current cost basis is therefore €17,160,000 + €41,580,000 = €58,740,000.

Example 3

Jacquet Corp. reports depreciation of €16,510 for 2009 in its historical cost based financial statements prepared on the basis of IFRS. A summary of plant assets reveals the following:

Asset class	Total depreciable cost*	Useful life (yr.)	Depreciation rate (%)**
A	€24,000	8	12 1/2
B	50,000	10	10
C	45,000	12	8 1/3
D	60,000	15	6 2/3
E	19,000	25	4

* *Depreciable cost is historical cost less salvage value.*
** *Depreciation rate is 1/useful life.*

Management employs appraisals and other methods, including information from vendors and indices, to develop current cost data as shown below.

Asset class	1/1/09	Current costs 12/31/09	Average
A	€28,000	€31,000	€29,500
B	56,000	60,000	58,000
C	55,000	60,000	57,500
D	62,000	68,000	65,000
E	30,000	33,000	31,500

From this information the current cost depreciation for the year 2009 can be computed as follows:

Asset class	Depreciation rate (%)	Average current cost	Depreciation
A	12 1/2	€29,500	€ 3,687.50
B	10	58,000	5,800.00
C	8 1/3	57,500	4,792.00
D	6 2/3	65,000	4,333.00
E	4	31,500	1,260.00
			€19,872.50

Note that the replacement cost basis depreciation for the year is €3,362.50 greater than was the historical cost depreciation.

Purchasing power gains or losses in the context of current cost accounting. Thus far, general price level (or purchasing power or constant dollar) accounting has been viewed as a reporting concept totally separate from current value (or current cost or replacement cost) accounting. As noted, advocates of price level adjustments have argued that these are not attempts to measure value, as current cost accounting is, but merely to "translate" old dollars into current dollars. For their part, advocates of current value accounting have generally been more focused on deriving a measure of the "replicatable" economic earnings of the enterprise, usually with no mention of the fact that changing specific prices of productive assets exist against a backdrop of changing general price levels.

In fact, the FASB requirements imposed in the late 1970s (and made optional in the mid-1980s because of lack of interest) attempted to measure both general and specific price changes. That standard included a requirement for reporting purchasing power gains or losses, as well as for stating the amount of adjustment for current cost depreciation and cost of sales. The IASC (predecessor of IASB) had imposed a somewhat similar requirement in the former IAS 15, albeit with less specificity. Although IAS 15 has been withdrawn, any entity that reports on an IAS-compliant basis and desires to report the effects of changing prices would be well-served to apply procedures set forth in IAS 15, supplemented as necessary by guidance under US GAAP.

Requirements under Former IAS 15

The experience of the international accounting standard that was designed to reveal the effects of inflation is very similar to the experiences in the United States and the United Kingdom. That is, while there was a great clamor, primarily from the financial analyst community, in favor of this supplementary financial reporting model, once it was mandated there was a noticeable decline in interest. It would appear that analysts much prefer to develop their own estimates of the impact of inflation on the companies they follow and may have an inherent distrust of management-supplied data. As for management, it generally argued that such information was useless before the standard was imposed, which at the time seemed to be self-serving posturing in the hope that an expensive new mandate could be averted.

As in the United States, after a few years of mandatory presentation of supplementary inflation adjusted information (IAS 15 was imposed in 1981), the IASC announced in 1989 that presentation would no longer be required to comply with the standard, although it would still be encouraged. This status continued until the Improvements Project determined to eliminate the guidance entirely.

Alternative approaches permitted. The standard was intended to require certain supplementary current value and constant dollar information. A great deal of latitude was given to entities, which could choose from among a range of supportable methods to accomplish this directive. As the standard notes, the two main methods are intended to (1) recognize income after the general purchasing power of shareholders' equity has been maintained (price level accounting), and (2) recognize income after the operating capacity of the enterprise is maintained (current value accounting, which may or may not also include adjustments related to the general price level).

General purchasing power approach. IAS 15 did not stipulate what index was to be used to measure the change in the general level of prices but did identify depreciation and cost of sales as being subject to adjustment. It also noted the need to measure the effect of changing prices on net monetary items held.

Current cost approach. IAS 15 acknowledged the existence of various methods, with replacement cost being identified as the principal measurement strategy, subject to the caveat that when replacement cost was found to be higher than both net realizable value and present value, replacement value was not to be used. Instead, the higher of net realizable value and present value would denote current value, as explained earlier in this chapter. Replacement costs were said to be found in information about current acquisitions of new or used assets of similar productive capacities or service potentials. Specific price indices were also favorably noted as sources of current cost data. Briefly stated, net realizable value is generally a representation of net current selling price (i.e., exit value), while present value is the discounted amount of future receipts attributable to the asset.

IAS 15 had discussed, at some length, the need to determine an adjustment for the effects of changing prices on net monetary items, including long-term debt, but suggested that some current cost methods (which were not named) may not need to address this separately. In particular, the discussion in IAS 15 alluded to the argument (made explicitly in the British proposal of the 1970s but not otherwise enacted in any standards) that since depreciable assets in particular are often acquired at least in part in exchange for monetary debt, the gross replacement cost adjustment exaggerates the negative effect on earnings and that this is moderated to the extent leveraging is used.

In fact, one can make this argument, but as noted earlier in the chapter, to do so assumes that added borrowing in periods of rising prices is "costless" in the sense that no premium is added by lenders to compensate for either (1) the borrowers' greater riskiness as they become more leveraged, or (2) for the loss to be incurred on repayment of the debt in devalued currency. It is not likely that in the long run lenders will go uncompensated for either of these, and therefore to offset the higher charges for depreciation and cost of sales by the fraction to be borne by the lenders may be imprudent.

Minimum disclosures that had been required by IAS 15. The disclosures which were first required, then later made optional, under now-withdrawn IAS 15 included the following:

1. The amount of adjustment to, or the adjusted amount of, depreciation of property, plant, and equipment
2. The amount of adjustment to, or the adjusted amount of, cost of sales
3. The adjustments relating to monetary items, the effect of borrowing, or equity interests when such adjustments have been taken into account in determining income under the (inflation) accounting method adopted
4. The overall effect on results of the adjustments described above, as well as any other items reflecting the effects of changing prices
5. If a current cost method is used, the current cost of property, plant, and equipment and of inventories should be disclosed.
6. There should be a description of the methods used to compute the foregoing items.

Example of disclosure consistent with IAS 15

DeKalb Thermodynamics Inc.
Statements of Income from Continuing Operations
Year Ended December 31, 2009

	As reported in primary statements	Adjusted for general inflation	Adjusted for changes in specific prices (current costs)
Net sales and other revenue	€253,000	€253,000	€253,000
Cost of goods sold	197,000	204,384	205,408
Depreciation and amortization	10,000	14,130	19,500
Other operating expense	20,835	20,835	20,835
Interest expense	7,165	7,165	7,165
Provision for income taxes	9,000	9,000	9,000
	244,000	255,514	261,908
Income (loss) from continuing operations	€ 9,000	€ (2,514)	€ (8,908)
Gain from decline in purchasing power of net amounts owed		€ 7,729	€ 7,729
Increase in specific prices (current costs) of inventories and property, plant, and equipment held during the year			€ 24,608
Effect of general price level increase			18,959
Excess of increase in specific prices over increase in general price level			€ 5,649

NOTE: Current costs are determined by consulting current prices posted for plant assets, net of applicable discounts, and by reference to indexed or replacement costs adjusted for productivity increases. The gain on purchasing power change is determined by reference to the consumer price index for all urban consumers.

The *Improvements Project* concluded that IAS 15 was no longer needed and should be withdrawn. The IASB stated that, "...the Board does not believe that entities should be required to disclose information that reflects the effects of changing prices in the current economic environment." In the authors' view, for those (few) entities which believe that inflation adjusted financial reporting continues to serve a useful purpose, the guidance in IAS 15 and in the foregoing discussion of this chapter continues to be germane.

FINANCIAL REPORTING IN HYPERINFLATIONARY ECONOMIES
CONCEPTS, RULES, AND EXAMPLES

Hyperinflation and Financial Reporting

Hyperinflation is a condition that is difficult to define precisely, as there is not a clear demarcation between merely rampant inflation and true hyperinflation. However, in any given economic system, when the general population has so lost faith in the stability of the local economy that business transactions are commonly either denominated in a stable reference currency of another country, or are structured to incorporate an indexing feature intended to compensate for the distortive effects of inflation, this condition may be present. As a benchmark, when cumulative inflation over three years approaches or exceeds 100%, it must be conceded that the economy is suffering from hyperinflation.

Hyperinflation is obviously a major problem for any economy, as it creates severe distortions and, left unaddressed, results in uncontrolled acceleration of the rate of price changes, ending in inevitable collapse as was witnessed in post–World War I Germany. From a financial reporting perspective, there are also major problems, since even over a brief interval such as a year or even a quarter, the statement of comprehensive income will contain transactions with such a variety of purchasing power units that aggregation becomes meaningless, as would adding dollars, francs, and marks. This is precisely the problem discussed earlier in this chapter, but raised to an exponential level.

In a truly hyperinflationary economy, users of financial statements are unable to make meaningful use of such statements unless they have been recast into currency units having purchasing power defined by prices at or near the date of the statements. Unless this common denominator is employed, the financial statements are too difficult to interpret for purposes of making management, investing, and credit decisions. Although some sophisticated users, particularly in those countries where hyperinflation has been endemic, such as some of the South American nations, including Brazil and Argentina, and for certain periods nations such as Israel, are able to apply rules of thumb to cope with this problem, in general modifications must be made to general-purpose financial statements if they are to have any value.

Under international accounting standards, if hyperinflation is deemed to characterize the economy, a form of price level accounting must be applied to the financial statements to conform to generally accepted accounting principles. IAS 29 requires that all the financial statements be adjusted to reflect year-end general price levels, which entails applying a broad-based index to all nonmonetary items on the statement of financial position and to all transactions reported in the statement of comprehensive income and the statement of cash flows.

Restating Historical Cost Financial Statements under Hyperinflation Conditions

The precise adjustments to be made depend on whether the financial reporting system is based on historical costs or on current costs, as those terms were described in the now-withdrawn IAS 15 and explained earlier in this chapter. Although in both cases the goal is to restate the financial statements into the measuring unit that exists at the date of the statement of financial position, the mechanics will vary to some extent.

If the financial reporting system is based on historical costing, the process used to adjust the statement of financial position can be summarized as follows:

1. Monetary assets and liabilities are already presented in units of year-end purchasing power and receive no further adjustment. (See the appendix for a categorization of different assets and liabilities as to their status as monetary or nonmonetary.)

2. Monetary assets and liabilities that are linked to price changes, such as indexed debt securities, are adjusted according to the terms of the contractual arrangement. This does not change the characterization of these items as monetary, but it does serve to reduce or even eliminate the purchasing power gain or loss that would have otherwise been experienced as a result of holding these items during periods of changing general prices.

3. Nonmonetary items are adjusted by applying a ratio of indices, the numerator of which is the general price level index at the date of the statement of financial position and the denominator of which is the index as of the acquisition or inception date of the item in question. For some items, such as plant assets, this is a straightforward process, while for others, such as work in process inventories, this can be more complex.

4. Certain assets cannot be adjusted as described above, because even in nominally historical cost financial statements these items have been revised to some other basis, such as fair value or net realizable amounts. For example, under the allowed alternative method of IAS 16, plant, property, and equipment can be adjusted to fair value. In such a case, no further adjustment would be warranted, assuming that the adjustment to fair value was made as of the latest date of the statement of financial position (although IAS 16 only demands that this be done at least every three years). If the latest revaluation was as of an earlier date, the carrying amounts should be further adjusted to compensate for changes in the general price level from that date to the date of the statement of financial position, using the indexing technique noted above.

5. Consistent with the established principles of historical cost accounting, if the restated amounts of nonmonetary assets exceed the recoverable amounts, these must be reduced appropriately. This can easily occur, since (as discussed earlier in this chapter) specific prices of goods will vary by differing amounts, even in a hyperinflationary environment, and in fact some may decline in terms of current cost even in such cases, particularly when technological change occurs rapidly. Since the application of price level accounting, whether for ordinary inflation or for hyperinflation, does not imply an abandonment of historical costing, being a mere translation into more timely and relevant purchasing power units, the rules of that mode of financial reporting still apply. Generally accepted accounting principles require that assets not be stated at amounts in excess of realizable amounts, and this constraint applies even when price level adjustments are reflected.

6. Equity accounts must also be restated to compensate for changing prices. Paid-in capital accounts are indexed by reference to the dates when the capital was contributed, which are usually a discrete number of identifiable transactions over the life of the enterprise. Revaluation accounts, if any, are eliminated entirely, as these will be subsumed in restated retained earnings. The retained earnings account itself is the most complex to analyze and in practice is often treated as a balancing figure after all other statement of financial position accounts have been restated. However, it is

possible to compute the adjustment to this account directly, and that is the recommended course of action, lest other errors go undetected. To adjust retained earnings, each year's earnings should be adjusted by a ratio of indices, the numerator being the general price level as of the date of the statement of financial position, and the denominator being the price level as of the end of the year for which the earnings were reported. Reductions of retained earnings for dividends paid should be adjusted similarly.

7. IAS 29 addresses a few other special problem areas. For example, the standard notes that borrowing costs typically already reflect the impact of inflation (more accurately, interest rates reflect inflationary expectations), and thus it would represent a form of double counting to fully index capital asset costs for price level changes when part of the cost of the asset was capitalized interest, as defined in IAS 23 as an allowed alternative method (which under revised IAS 23, effective 2009, is the only permitted method). As a practical matter, interest costs are often not a material component of recorded asset amounts, and the inflation-related component would only be a fraction of interest costs capitalized. However, the general rule is to delete that fraction of the capitalized borrowing costs which represents inflationary compensation, since the entire cost of the asset will be indexed to current purchasing units.

To restate the current period's statement of comprehensive income, a reasonably accurate result can be obtained if revenue and expense accounts are multiplied by the ratio of end-of-period prices to average prices for the period. Where price changes were not relatively constant throughout the period, or when transactions did not occur ratably, as when there was a distinct seasonal pattern to sales activity, a more precise measurement effort might be needed. This can be particularly important when a devaluation of the currency took place during the year.

While IAS 29 addresses the statement of cash flows only perfunctorily (its issuance was prior to the revision of IAS 7), this financial statement must also be modified to report all items in terms of year-end purchasing power units. For example, changes in working capital accounts, used to convert net income into cash flow from operating activities, will be altered to reflect the real (i.e., inflation-adjusted) changes.

To illustrate, if beginning accounts receivable were €500,000 and ending receivables were €650,000, but prices rose by 40% during the year, the apparent €150,000 increase in receivables (which would be a use of cash) is really a €50,000 decrease [(€500,000 × 1.4 = €700,000) – €650,000], which in cash flow terms is a source of cash. Other items must be handled similarly. Investing and financing activities should be adjusted on an item-by-item basis, since these are normally discrete events that do not occur ratably throughout the year.

In addition to the foregoing, the adjusted statement of comprehensive income will report a gain or loss on net monetary items held. As an approximation, this will be computed by applying the change in general prices for the year to the average net monetary assets (or liabilities) outstanding during the year. If net monetary items changed materially at one or more times during the year, a more detailed computation would be warranted. In the statement of comprehensive income, the gain or loss on net monetary items should be associated with the adjustment relating to items that are linked to price level changes (indexed debt, etc.) as well as with interest income and expense and foreign exchange adjustments, since theoretically at least, all these items contain a component that reflects inflationary behavior.

Restating Current Cost Financial Statements under Hyperinflation Conditions

If the financial reporting system is based on current costing (as described earlier in the chapter), the process used to adjust the statement of financial position can be summarized as follows:

1. Monetary assets and liabilities are already presented in units of year-end purchasing power and receive no further adjustment. (See the appendix for a categorization of different assets and liabilities as to their status as monetary or nonmonetary.)

2. Monetary assets and liabilities that are linked to price changes, such as indexed debt securities, are adjusted according to the terms of the contractual arrangement. This does not change the characterization of these items as monetary, but it does serve to reduce or even eliminate the purchasing power gain or loss that would have otherwise been experienced as a result of holding these items during periods of changing general prices.

3. Nonmonetary items are already stated at year-end current values or replacement costs and need no further adjustments. Issues related to recoverable amounts and other complications associated with price level adjusted historical costs should not normally arise.

4. Equity accounts must also be restated to compensate for changing prices. Paid-in capital accounts are indexed by reference to the dates when the capital was contributed, which are usually a discrete number of identifiable transactions over the life of the enterprise. Revaluation accounts are eliminated entirely, as these will be subsumed in restated retained earnings. The retained earnings account itself will typically be a "balancing account" under this scenario, since detailed analysis would be very difficult, although certainly not impossible, to accomplish.

The current cost statement of comprehensive income, absent the price level component, will reflect transactions at current costs as of the transaction dates. For example, cost of sales will be comprised of the costs as of each transaction date (usually approximated on an average basis). To report these as of the date of the statement of financial position, these costs will have to be further inflated to year-end purchasing power units, by means of the ratio of general price level indices, as suggested above.

In addition to the foregoing, the adjusted statement of comprehensive income will report a gain or loss on net monetary items held. This will be similar to that discussed under the historical cost reporting above. However, current cost statements of comprehensive income, if prepared, already will include the net gain or loss on monetary items held, which need not be computed again.

To the extent that restated earnings differ from earnings on which income taxes are computed, there will be a need to provide more or less tax accrual, which will be a deferred tax obligation or asset, depending on the circumstances.

Comparative Financial Statements

Consistent with the underlying concept of reporting in hyperinflationary economies, all prior-year financial statement amounts must be updated to purchasing power units as of the most recent date of the statement of financial position. This will be a relatively simple process of applying a ratio of indices of the current year-end price level to the year earlier price level.

Other Disclosure Issues

IAS 29 requires that when the standard is applied, the fact that hyperinflation adjustments have been made be noted. Furthermore, the underlying basis of accounting, historical cost or current cost, should be stipulated, as should the price level index that was utilized in making the adjustments.

Economies Which Cease Being Hyperinflationary

When application of IAS 29 is discontinued, the amounts reported in the last statement of financial position that had been adjusted become, effectively, the new cost basis. That is, previously applied adjustments are not reversed, since an end to a period of hyperinflation generally means only that prices have reached a plateau, not that they have deflated to earlier levels.

Revisions to IAS 29

Certain consequential amendments were made to IAS 29 due to the withdrawal of IAS 15. The most important of these was to conform to the new requirements incorporated into revised IAS 21. This stipulates that the results of operations and financial position of an entity whose functional currency is the currency of a hyperinflationary economy is to be translated into a different presentation currency using the following procedures:

1. All amounts (i.e., assets, liabilities, equity items, income items and expense items, including comparatives) are to be translated at the closing rate at the date of the most recent statement of financial position, except that
2. When amounts are being translated into the currency of a nonhyperinflationary economy, comparative amounts shall be those that were presented as current year amounts in the relevant prior year financial statements (i.e., not adjusted for either subsequent changes in the price level or subsequent changes in exchange rates).

Revised IAS 21 further requires that, when the functional currency of an entity is the currency of a hyperinflationary economy, its financial statements are to be restated under IAS 29, before the translation method set out in IAS 21 is applied, except for comparative amounts that are being translated into a currency of a nonhyperinflationary economy. When the economy ceases to be hyperinflationary and the entity no longer restates its financial statements in accordance with IAS 29, the financial statements will use the amounts restated to the price level at the date the entity ceased restating its financial statements as the historical costs for translation into the presentation currency.

Guidance on Applying the Restatement Approach

IFRIC has issued an Interpretation of IAS 29 (IFRIC 7, *Applying the Restatement Approach*) that addresses the matter of differentiating between monetary and nonmonetary items. IAS 29 requires that when the reporting entity identifies the existence of hyperinflation in the economy of its functional currency, it must restate its financial statements for the effects of inflation. The restatement approach distinguishes between monetary and nonmonetary items, but in practice it has been noted there is uncertainty about how to restate the financial statements for the first time, particularly with regard to deferred tax balances, and concerning comparative information for prior periods. IFRIC 7 addresses these matters.

Under IFRIC 7, which became effective for annual periods beginning on or after March 1, 2006, it is required that, in the first year that an entity identifies the existence of hyperinflation, it would start applying IAS 29 as if it had always applied that standard—that is, as if the economy had always been hyperinflationary. Therefore, it must recreate an opening statement of financial position at the beginning of the earliest annual accounting period presented in the restated financial statements, for the first year it applies IAS 29.

The implication of this Interpretation is that restatements of nonmonetary items that are carried at historical cost are effected as of the dates of first recognition (e.g., acquisition). The restatements cannot be effected merely from the opening date of the statement of financial position (which would commonly be at the beginning of the comparative financial statement year). For example, if the year-end 2007 statement of financial position is the first one under IAS 29, with two-year comparative reporting employed, but various plant assets acquired, say, in 2002, the application of IFRIC 7 would require restatements for price level changes from 2002 to year-end 2007.

Nonmonetary assets that are not reported at historical costs (e.g., plant assets revalued for IFRS-basis financial reporting, per IAS 16) require a different mode of adjustment. In this situation, the restatements are applied only for the period of time elapsed since the latest revaluation dates (which should, per IAS 16, be recent dates in most instances). For example, if revaluation was performed at year-end 2006, then only the period from year-end 2006 to year-end 2007 would be subject to adjustment, as the year-end 2006 revaluation already served to address hyperinflation occurring to that date.

IFRIC 7 provides that if detailed records of the acquisition dates for items of property, plant, and equipment are not available or are not capable of estimation, the reporting entity should use an independent professional assessment of the fair value of the items as the basis for restatement. Likewise, if a general price index is not available, it may be necessary to use an estimate based on the changes in the exchange rate between the functional currency and a relatively stable foreign currency, for example, when the entity restates its financial statements.

IFRIC 7 also provides specific guidance on the difficult topic of deferred tax balances in the *opening* statement of financial position of the entity subject to IAS 29 restatement. A two-step computational procedure is required to effect the restatement of deferred tax assets and liabilities. First, deferred tax items are remeasured in accordance with IAS 12, *after* having restated the nominal carrying amounts of all other nonmonetary items in the opening statement of financial position as of that (opening statement of financial position) date. Second, the remeasured deferred tax assets and/or liabilities are restated for hyperinflation's effects from the opening date of the statement of financial position to the reporting date (the most recent date of the statement of financial position).

After restatement of the financial statements has been accomplished, the corresponding amounts (i.e., comparatives) in any later statements of financial position are restated by applying changes in the measuring unit only to the restated amounts in the immediately preceding statement of financial position.

APPENDIX

MONETARY VS. NONMONETARY ITEMS

Item	Monetary	Nonmonetary	Requires analysis
Cash on hand, demand deposits, and time deposits	x		
Foreign currency and claims to foreign currency	x		
Securities			
Common stock (passive investment)		x	
Preferred stock (convertible or participating) and convertible bonds			x
Other preferred stock or bonds	x		
Accounts and notes receivable and allowance for doubtful accounts	x		
Mortgage loan receivables	x		
Inventories		x	
Loans made to employees	x		
Prepaid expenses			x
Long-term receivables	x		
Refundable deposits	x		
Advances to unconsolidated subsidiaries	x		
Equity in unconsolidated subsidiaries		x	
Pension and other funds			x
Property, plant, and equipment and accumulated depreciation		x	
Cash surrender value of life insurance	x		
Purchase commitments (portion paid on fixed-price contracts)		x	
Advances to suppliers (not on fixed-price contracts)	x		
Deferred income tax charges	x		
Patents, trademarks, goodwill, and other intangible assets		x	
Deferred life insurance policy acquisition costs	x		
Deferred property and casualty insurance policy acquisition costs		x	
Accounts payable and accrued expenses	x		
Accrued vacation pay			x
Cash dividends payable	x		
Obligations payable in foreign currency	x		
Sales commitments (portion collected on fixed-price contracts)		x	
Advances from customers (not on fixed-price contracts)	x		
Accrued losses on purchase commitments	x		
Deferred revenue			x
Refundable deposits	x		
Bonds payable, other long-term debt, and related discount or premium	x		
Accrued pension obligations			x
Obligations under product warranties		x	
Deferred income tax obligations	x		
Deferred investment tax credits		x	
Life or property and casualty insurance policy reserves	x		
Unearned insurance premiums		x	
Deposit liabilities of financial institutions	x		

26 GOVERNMENT GRANTS

PERSPECTIVE AND ISSUES

Government grants or other types of assistance, where provided, are usually intended to encourage entities to embark on activities that they would not have otherwise undertaken. An existing standard, IAS 20, addresses selected accounting and reporting issues arising in connection with such grants. Government *assistance*, according to this standard, is action by the government aimed at providing economic benefits to some constituency by subsidizing entities that will provide them with jobs, services, or goods that might not otherwise be available, either at all or at the desired cost. A government *grant*, on the other hand, is government assistance that entails the transfer of resources in return for compliance, either past or future, with certain conditions relating to the enterprise's operating activities, such as for remediating an environmentally compromised plant site. However, there is a wide range of government interventions and interactions with business, beyond narrowly construed assistance and grants, and this is an area of accounting where the IASB is expected to expand its literature significantly in the near term.

IAS 20 was promulgated in 1982 and has remained intact since inception. Although accepted by IOSCO as a "core standard" in its present form, it has been subject to wide criticism, including in Australia, where accountants believe that its national GAAP is superior on this topic. However, as Australian GAAP was replaced by IASB in 2005, the asserted benefits of the superior standard have been foregone, pending possible revision to IAS 20.

Accounting for grants as a deferred credit is considered to be inconsistent with the IASB's *Framework,* and reducing the carrying value of assets by a grant is not accepted by some. The Board had taken the view that it should await finalization of a general standard on revenue recognition before undertaking an overhaul of IAS 20. However, the perceived need to deal with the grant of emission rights (which led to the promulgation of IFRIC 3, subsequently withdrawn) at first persuaded the Board to seek to make a short-term change by harmonizing IAS 20 with the government grant rules in IAS 41, but inadequacies of that approach were soon identified. An initial undertaking, as part of the IASB-FASB convergence program, has been superseded by a stand-alone project to revise, which effort would incorporate emission rights as well as other types of grants. In mid-2006, however, this project was placed on hold, pending decisions on amending IAS 37 (dealing with contingencies), which as of late 2008 has still not been finalized, although it has been deliberated upon and discussed many times by IASB. Finalization of this amendment in 2009 is anticipated.

As originally issued, IAS 20 held that below-market interest on government loans was not government assistance, per se. As part of the 2007 Improvements Project, IASB has issued (in early 2008) an amendment to IAS 20, under which (effective 2009) the economic effect of below-market interest rates on government loans is to be measured and reported as a government grant. The economic effect is gauged by the difference between the face amount of the loan and the present value of the future payments discounted by a relevant (market) interest rate, as illustrated in this chapter.

A former gap in the literature, addressing the accounting for service concessions, which occur relatively frequently in Europe, where government assets may be operated by commercial entities, has recently been dealt with by the issuance of IFRIC 12, *Service Concession Arrangements,* which resolved a related series of three draft interpretations IFRIC 12 is discussed later in this chapter.

Until it is revised, however, IAS 20 provides authoritative guidance on financial statement presentation for all entities enjoying government assistance, with additional guidance to be found in IAS 41, which is, however, at this time restricted to agriculture situations. IAS 20 deals with the accounting treatment and disclosure of government grants and the disclosure requirements of government assistance. Depending on the nature of the assistance given and the associated conditions, government assistance could be of many types, including grants, forgivable loans, and indirect or nonmonetary forms of assistance, such as technical advice.

Sources of IFRS
IAS 20, 41   *SIC* 10, 29, *IFRIC* 12

DEFINITIONS OF TERMS

Fair value. The amount for which an asset could be exchanged between a knowledgeable, willing buyer and a knowledgeable, willing seller in an arm's-length transaction.

Forgivable loans. Those loans which the lender undertakes to waive repayment of under certain prescribed conditions.

Government. For the purposes of IAS 20, the term government refers not only to a government (of a country), as is generally understood, but also to government agencies and similar bodies whether local, national, or international.

Government assistance. Government assistance is action by government aimed at providing an economic benefit to an enterprise or group of enterprises qualifying under certain criteria. It includes a government grant and also includes other kinds of nonmonetary government assistance such as providing, at no cost, legal advice to an entrepreneur for setting up a business in a free trade zone. It excludes benefits provided indirectly through action affecting trading conditions in general; for example, laying roads that connect the industrial area in which an enterprise operates to the nearest city or imposing trade constraints on foreign companies in order to protect domestic entrepreneurs in general.

Government grants. A government grant is a form of a government assistance that involves the transfer of resources to an enterprise in return for past or future compliance (by the enterprise) of certain conditions relating to its operating activities. It excludes

- Those forms of government assistance that cannot reasonably be valued, and

- Transactions with governments that cannot be distinguished from the normal trading transactions of the enterprise.

Grants related to assets. Those government grants whose primary condition is that an enterprise qualifying for them should acquire (either purchase or construct) a long-term asset or assets are referred to as "grants related to assets." Subsidiary conditions may also be attached to such a grant. Examples of subsidiary conditions include specifying the type of long-term assets, location of long-term assets, or periods during which the long-term assets are to be acquired or held.

Grants related to income. Government grants, other than those related to assets, are grants related to income.

CONCEPTS, RULES AND EXAMPLES

Scope

IAS 20 deals with the accounting treatment and disclosure requirements of grants received by enterprises from a government. It also mandates disclosure requirements of other forms of government assistance.

The standard specifies certain exclusions. In addition to the four exclusions contained within the definitions of the terms "government grant" and "government assistance," IAS 20 *excludes* the following from the purview of the standard:

1. Special problems arising in reflecting the effects of changing prices on financial statements or similar supplementary information;
2. Government assistance provided in the form of tax benefits (including income tax holidays, investment tax credits, accelerated depreciation allowances and concessions in tax rates);
3. Government participation in the ownership of the enterprise; and
4. Government grants covered by IAS 41.

The rationale behind excluding items 1. and 2. above seems fairly obvious, as they are covered by other international accounting standards: IAS 29 addresses accounting in hyperinflationary conditions, while tax benefits are dealt with by IAS 12. The reason for excluding item 3. above, however, has been the subject of some controversy and conjecture.

Authorities on the subject have offered different opinions as plausible reasons for specifically excluding "government participation in the ownership of the enterprise" from the scope of IAS 20. According to one school of thought, participation in ownership of an enterprise is normally made in anticipation of a return on the investment, while government assistance is provided with a different economic objective in mind, for example, the public interest or public policy. Thus, when the government invests in the equity of an enterprise (with the intention, for example, of encouraging the enterprise to undertake a line of business that it would normally not have embarked upon), such government participation in ownership of the enterprise would *not qualify* as a government grant under this standard.

Government Grants

Government grants are assistance provided by government by means of a transfer of resources (either monetary or nonmonetary) to business or other types of entities. In order to qualify as a government grant, in strict technical terms, it is a prerequisite that the grant should be provided by the government to an enterprise in return for past or future compliance with conditions relating to the operating activities of the enterprise.

For years, it was unclear whether the provisions of IAS 20 would apply even to government assistance aimed at encouraging or supporting business activities in certain regions or industry sectors, since related conditions may not specifically relate to the operating activities of the enterprise. Examples of such grants are: government grants which involve transfer of resources to enterprises to operate in a particular area (e.g., an economically less developed area) or a particular industry (e.g., one that due to low profitability may not otherwise be attractive to entrepreneurs). SIC 10 clarified that "the general requirement to operate in certain regions or industry sectors in order to qualify for the government assistance constitutes such a condition in accordance with IAS 20." This has put to rest the confusion as to whether or not such government assistance does fall within the definition of government grants, and thus the requirements of IAS 20 apply to them as well.

Recognition of Government Grants

Criteria for recognition. Government grants are provided in return for past or future compliance with certain defined conditions. Thus grants should not be recognized until there is *reasonable assurance* that both

1. The enterprise will comply with the conditions attaching to the grant; and
2. The grant(s) will be received.

Certain concerns affecting the application of IAS 20, relating to recognition and treatment of government grants, are addressed in the following paragraphs.

Firstly, the mere receipt of the grant does not provide any assurance that, in fact, the conditions attaching to the grant have been or will be complied with by the enterprise. Both of these conditions are equally important, and the reporting entity should have reasonable assurance with respect to these two conditions before a grant is to be recognized.

Secondly, the term "reasonable assurance" has not been defined by this standard. However, one of the recognition criteria for income under the IASC's *Framework* is the existence of "sufficient degree of certainty." Furthermore, under IAS 18, revenue is recognized only when it is *probable* that economic benefits will flow to the reporting entity. Thus, the criterion of reasonable assurance could possibly be interpreted as *probable*. Comparing this with the criterion for the recognition of contingent gains under IAS 37, it appears that in that setting the criterion has been made more stringent than in the circumstance of recognition of a government grant. In the case of recognition of a government grant, it seems the criterion has been relaxed to a degree lower than virtual certainty—it has been pegged instead at the reasonable assurance level. By contrast, under IAS 37 contingent gains could be recognized if, and only if, realization was virtually certain.

Thirdly, under IAS 20 a forgivable loan from a government is treated as a government grant when there is *reasonable assurance* that the enterprise will meet the terms of forgiveness set forth in the loan. Thus, upon receiving a forgivable loan from a government and furthermore upon fulfilling the criterion of reasonable assurance with respect to meeting the terms of forgiveness of the loan, an enterprise would normally recognize the receipt of a government grant, rather than a loan. Some have suggested that the grant should be recognized when the loan is forgiven, not when the forgivable loan is received. Under IAS 20, however, it is quite apparent that delayed recognition is not prescribed, but that "a forgivable loan from the government is treated as a grant when there is reasonable assurance that the enterprise will meet the terms for forgiveness of the loan." In the authors' opinion, this unambiguously directs that the recognition of the grant is to be made at the point of time when the forgivable loan is granted, as opposed to the point of time when it is actually forgiven.

Once a grant has been recognized, IAS 20 clarifies that any related contingency would be accounted for in accordance with IAS 37. Contingent assets and liabilities, as these are defined under IFRS, are not subject to formal recognition, although disclosure is acceptable and often useful.

Recognition period. Two broad approaches with respect to the accounting treatment of government grants have been discussed by the standard: the "capital approach" and the "income approach." IAS 20 clearly does *not* support the capital approach, which advocates crediting a grant directly to shareholders' equity. Endorsing the income approach, the standard sets forth the rule for recognition of government grants as follows: Government grants should be recognized as income, on a systematic and rational basis, over the periods necessary to match them with the related costs. As a corollary, and by way of abundant precaution, the standard reiterates that government grants should *not* be credited directly to shareholders' interests.

The standard established rules for recognition of grants under different conditions. These are explained through numerical examples as follows:

1. Grants in recognition of specific costs are recognized as income over the same period as the relevant expense.

To illustrate this rule, let us consider the following example:

An enterprise receives a grant of €30 million to defray environmental costs over a period of five years. Environmental costs will be incurred by the enterprise as follows:

Year	Costs
1	€1 million
2	€2 million
3	€3 million
4	€4 million
5	€5 million

Total environment costs will equal €15 million, whereas the grant received is €30 million.

Applying the principle outlined in the standard for recognition of the grant, that is, recognizing the grant as income "over the period which matches the costs" and using a "systematic and rational basis" (in this case, a reverse sum-of-the-years' digits amortization), the total grant would be recognized as follows:

Year	Grant recognized
1	€30 * (1/15) = € 2 million
2	€30 * (2/15) = € 4 million
3	€30 * (3/15) = € 6 million
4	€30 * (4/15) = € 8 million
5	€30 * (5/15) = €10 million

2. Grants related to depreciable assets are usually recognized as income over the periods and in the proportions in which depreciation on those assets is charged.

The following example will illustrate the above rule:

An enterprise receives a grant of €100 million to purchase a refinery in an economically backward area. The enterprise has estimated that such a refinery would cost €200 million. The secondary condition attached to the grant is that the enterprise should hire labor locally (i.e., from the economically backward area where the refinery is located) instead of employing workers from other parts of the country. It should maintain a ratio of 1:1 (local workers : workers from outside) in its labor force for the next five years. The refinery is to be depreciated using the straight-line method over a period of ten years.

The grant will be recognized over a period of ten years. In each of the ten years, the grant will be recognized in proportion to the annual depreciation on the refinery. Thus, €10 million will be recognized as income in each of the ten years. With regard to the secondary condition of maintenance of the ratio of 1:1 in the labor force, this contingency would need to be disclosed in the footnotes to the financial statements for the next five years (during which period the condition is in force) in accordance with disclosure requirements of IAS 37.

3. Grants related to nondepreciable assets may also require the fulfillment of certain obligations and would then be recognized as income over periods which bear the cost of meeting the obligations.

To understand this rule, let us consider the following case study:

> ABN Inc. was granted 1000 acres of land, on the outskirts of the city, by a local government authority. The condition attached to this grant was that ABN Inc. should clean up this land and lay roads by employing laborers from the village in which the land is located. The government has fixed the minimum wage payable to the workers. The entire operation will take three years and is estimated to cost €60 million. This amount will be spent as follows: €10 million each in the first and second years and €40 million in the third year. The fair value of this land is presently €120 million.
>
> ABN Inc. would need to recognize the fair value of the grant over the period of three years in proportion to the cost of meeting the obligation. Thus, €120 million will be recognized as follows:

Year	Grant recognized
1	€120 * (10/60) = €20 million
2	€120 * (10/60) = €20 million
3	€120 * (40/60) = €80 million

4. Grants are sometimes received as part of a package of financial or fiscal aids to which a number of conditions are attached.

When different conditions attach to different components of the grant, the terms of the grant would have to be evaluated in order to determine how the various elements of the grant would be earned by the enterprise. Based on that assessment, the total grant amount would then be apportioned.

For example, an enterprise receives a consolidated grant of €120 million. Two-thirds of the grant is to be utilized to purchase a college building for students from third-world or developing countries. The balance of the grant is for subsidizing the tuition costs of those students for four years from the date of the grant.

The grant would first be apportioned as follows:

Grant related to assets (2/3) = €80 million, and
Grant related to income (1/3) = €40 million

The grant related to assets would be recognized in income over the useful life of the college building, for example, ten years, using a systematic and rational basis. Assuming the college building is depreciated using the straight-line method, this portion of the grant (i.e., €80 million) would be recognized as income over a period of ten years at €8 million per year.

The grant related to income would be recognized over a period of four years. Assuming that the tuition subsidy will be offered evenly over the period of four years, this portion of the grant (i.e., €40 million) would be taken to income over a period of four years at €10 million per year.

5. A government grant that becomes receivable as compensation for expenses or losses already incurred or for the purpose of giving immediate financial support to the enterprise with no future related costs should be recognized as income of the period in which it becomes receivable.

Sometimes grants are awarded for the purposes of giving immediate financial support to an enterprise, for example, to revive a commercial insolvent business (referred to as "sick unit" in some less-developed countries). Such grants are not given as incentives to invest funds in specified areas or for a specified purpose from which the benefits will be derived over a period of time in the future. Instead such grants are awarded to compensate an enterprise for losses incurred in the past. Thus, they should be recognized as income in the period in which the enterprise becomes eligible to receive such grants.

A grant may be awarded to an enterprise to compensate it for losses incurred in the past for operating out of an economically backward area that has been hit by an earthquake recently. During the period the enterprise operated in that area, the area experienced an earthquake and thus the enterprise incurred massive losses. Such a grant received by the enterprise should be recognized as income in the year in which the grant becomes receivable. Under IAS 20, when losses suffered were extraordinary in nature, the grant would potentially need to be presented as an extraordinary item in the financial statements. However, extraordinary item classification has been eliminated by revised IAS 1 and may no longer be employed.

Nonmonetary Grants

A government grant may not always be given in cash or cash equivalents. Sometimes a government grant may take the form of a transfer of a nonmonetary asset, such as grant of a plot of land or a building in a remote area. In these circumstances the standard prescribes the following optional accounting treatments:

1. To account for both the grant and the asset at the fair value of the nonmonetary asset, or
2. To record both the asset and the grant at a "nominal amount."

Presentation of Grants Related to Assets

Presentation on the statement of financial position. Government grants related to assets, including nonmonetary grants at fair value, should be presented in the statement of financial position in either of the two ways:

1. By setting up the grant as deferred income, or
2. By deducting the grant in arriving at the carrying amount of the asset.

To understand this better, let us consider the following case study:

Natraj Corp. received a grant related to a factory building which it bought in 2008. The total amount of the grant was €3 million. Natraj Corp. purchased the building from an industrialist identified by the government. The factory building was located in the slums of the city and was to be repossessed by a government agency from the industrialist, in case Natraj Corp. had not purchased it from him. The factory building was purchased for €9 million by Natraj Corp. The useful life of the building is not considered to be more than three years mainly because it was not properly maintained by the industrialist.

Under Option 1: Set up the grant as deferred income.

- The grant of €3 million would be set up initially as deferred income in 2008.
- At the end of 2008, €1 million would be recognized as income and the balance of €2 million would be carried forward in the statement of financial position.
- At the end of 2009, €1 million would be taken to income and the balance of €1 million would be carried forward in the statement of financial position.
- At the end of 2010, €1 million would be taken to income.

Under Option 2: The grant will be deducted from carrying value.

The grant of €3 million is deducted from the gross book value of the asset to arrive at the carrying value of €6 million. The useful life being three years, annual depreciation of €2 million per year is charged to the income statement for the years 2008, 2009 and 2010.

The effect on the operating results is the same whether the first or the second option is chosen.

Under the second option, the grant is indirectly recognized in income through the reduced depreciation charge of €1 million per year, whereas under the first option, it is taken to income directly.

Presentation in the statement of cash flows. When grants related to assets are received in cash, there is an inflow of cash to be shown under the investing activities section of the statement of cash flows. Furthermore, there would also be an outflow resulting from the purchase of the asset. IAS 20 specifically requires that both these movements should be shown separately and not be netted. The standard further clarifies that such movements should be shown separately regardless of whether or not the grant is deducted from the related asset for the purposes of the statement of financial position presentation.

Presentation of Grants Related to Comprehensive Income

The standard allows a free choice between two presentations.

Option 1: Grant presented as a credit in the statement of comprehensive income, either separately or under a general heading other income
Option 2: Grant deducted in reporting the related expense

The standard does not show any bias towards any one option. It acknowledges the reasoning given in support of each approach by its supporters. The standard considers both methods as acceptable. However, it does recommend disclosure of the grant for a proper understanding of the financial statements. The standard recognizes that the disclosure of the effect of the grants on any item of income or expense may be appropriate.

Repayment of Government Grants

When a government grant becomes repayable—for example, due to nonfulfillment of a condition attaching to it—it should be treated as a change in estimate, under IAS 8, and accounted for prospectively (as opposed to retrospectively).

Repayment of a grant related to income should

1. First be applied against any unamortized deferred income (credit) set up in respect of the grant, and
2. To the extent the repayment exceeds any such deferred income (credit), or in case no deferred credit exists, the repayment should be recognized immediately as an expense.

Repayment of a grant related to an asset should be

1. Recorded by increasing the carrying amount of the asset or reducing the deferred income balance by the amount repayable, and
2. The cumulative additional depreciation that would have been recognized to date as an expense in the absence of the grant should be recognized immediately as an expense.

When a grant related to an asset becomes repayable, it would become incumbent upon the enterprise to assess whether any impairment in value of the asset (to which the repayable grant relates) has resulted. For example, a bridge is being constructed through funding from a government grant and during the construction period, because of nonfulfillment of the terms of the grant, the grant became repayable. Since the grant was provided to assist in the construction, it is possible that the enterprise may not be in a position to arrange funds to complete the project. In such a circumstance, the asset is impaired and may need to be written down to its recoverable value, in accordance with IAS 36.

Government Assistance

Government assistance includes government grants. IAS 20 deals with both accounting and disclosure of government grants and disclosure of government assistance. Thus government assistance comprises government grants and other forms of government assistance (i.e. those not involving transfer of resources).

Excluded from the government assistance are certain forms of government benefits that cannot reasonably have a value placed on them, such as free technical or other professional advice. Also excluded from government assistance are government benefits that cannot be distinguished from the normal trading transactions of the enterprise. The reason for the second exclusion is obvious: although the benefit cannot be disputed, any attempt to segregate it would necessarily be arbitrary.

Loans at zero or low interest are a form of government assistance. They should not have a value attributed to them in the financial statements, since the benefit could only be quantified by imputing interest costs, which is arbitrary. Thus, an enterprise that is currently benefiting from such assistance (e.g., in the form of low interest), but is likely to borrow funds in the near future at commercial rates of interest, would need to disclose when the full interest is going to commence.

Disclosures

The following disclosures are prescribed:

1. The accounting policy adopted for government grants, including the methods of presentation adopted in the financial statements;
2. The nature and extent of government grants recognized in the financial statements and an indication of other forms of government assistance from which the enterprise has directly benefited; and
3. Unfulfilled conditions and other contingencies attaching to government assistance that has been recognized.

Anticipated Changes to IAS 20

As noted, general and widespread dissatisfaction with IAS 20 has been voiced for many years. The IASB decided in 2004 that IAS 20 was to be amended by replacing its rules with those set forth in IAS 41, *Agriculture,* notwithstanding a staff recommendation that IAS 20 be withdrawn as inconsistent with the *Framework.* The agriculture standard embraced the basic concept that government grants are income (neither a capital contribution nor a reduction of the cost of acquiring an asset).

IAS 41 distinguishes between unconditional and conditional grants, with the former to be taken directly to income when received or receivable, and the latter taken to income only when the conditions have been met. The conditions might relate to operating in a particular location for a specific period, in which case the grant is income at the end of the period, unless it becomes unconditional on a proportional or other basis. A condition is a stipulation that entitles government to the return of the granted resources if a specified future event that is not presently regarded as remote either occurs or does not occur. IASB determined that the definition should refer to the condition having commercial substance (i.e., in order to exclude routine or normal trading transactions).

IASB staff recommended that an entity should recognize a government grant as an asset at the *earlier* of having an unconditional right to receive the government grant without conditions attached to its retention, or actually receiving the government grant.

While this tentative solution was not the preferred solution of some IASB members, it was nonetheless agreed that further development was outside the scope of a short-term convergence project. IASB agreed not to provide guidance on whether an asset and liability would be recognized when a repayment clause is attached to a condition, or whether no asset should be recognized at all until the grant is fully nonrepayable.

It is expected that revised IAS 20 will hold that an asset acquired in connection with a government grant should be tested for impairment on initial recognition. Any liability recognized in relation to the grant is to be considered part of the cash-generating unit.

A conflict between IAS 20 and IAS 39 has been resolved by the issuance of an amendment to IAS 20 effected by the 2007 Improvements Project. Previously, IAS 20 previously did not take account of low-interest or interest-free loans, or of the effect of government guarantees, while IAS 39 states that liabilities should be measured at fair value, which implies recognition of market rates of interest. The IAS 20 exclusion has now been removed, and the principle set forth by IAS 39 will apply beginning in 2009.

Example of application of amendment to IAS 20 for below-market loans

Maytag Corp. is encouraged to relocate to Springville Township on July 1, 2009, by an economic stimulus package that includes a €3,000,000 loan due in equal annual installments (inclusive of interest) through 2019. The local government provides this loan at a below-market rate of 3%, which differs markedly from Maytag's own marginal borrowing rate of 6.5%. The present value of the annual payments ($351,000 each), discounted at 6.5%, is only $2,528,251. Accordingly, the receipt of the loan on July 1, 2009, is recorded by the following journal entry:

Cash	3,000,000	
Discount on loans payable	471,749	
Loan payable		3,000,000
Income—government grants		471,749

The discount on the loan payable is amortized ratably over the ten year term, such that an effective rate of 6.5% on the loan balance will be reported as interest expense in Maytag's income statements. If the grant was unconditional, it would be taken into income immediately, as suggested by the above journal entry. However, if Maytag has ongoing obligations (such as to remain as an employer in the community throughout the term of the loan), then it should be amortized to income ratably (straight-line) over the term of the obligation.

Emission Rights

Beginning in 2005, a number of countries have proposed implementing emission reduction incentives. These proposals are generally based on the notion that an enterprise will be given pollution allowances up to its current levels. It can either reduce pollution and sell its surplus allowances or, if it increases the pollution it produces, it must buy further allowances in the market. Each year the entity will have to surrender allowances appropriate to the volume of its polluting emissions.

IFRIC issued a Draft Interpretation (DI Emission Rights) in 2003, which proposed that the pollution allowance should be recognized as an intangible asset at fair value. Any difference between fair value and the amount paid would be treated as a government grant. An entity that made emissions that would require it to give up allowances should create a provision as the emissions are made. Comment letters pointed out that the changes in fair value of the allowance would flow to equity, while the changes in the provision amount would flow through the income statement. As a consequence, IFRIC proposed to the IASB that IAS 38, *Intangible Assets*, should be amended to permit pollution allowances to be treated as akin to a currency, with fair value changes recognized in income. The IASB agreed with this proposed solution, but IFRIC decided not to proceed at the time.

IFRIC did later issue an interpretation, IFRIC 3, *Emission Rights*, in late 2004, to have become effective in early 2005. However, in June 2005 this interpretation was withdrawn.

The now-withdrawn IFRIC 3 dealt with the required accounting by participants in "cap and trade schemes" that are already operational. It concluded that a cap and trade scheme gives rise to: (1) an asset for allowances held; (2) a government grant; and (3) a liability for the obligation to deliver allowances equal to emissions that have been made. These were to be recorded individually, not presented as a net asset or liability.

IFRIC 3 also held that allowances, whether issued by government or purchases, were to be treated as intangible assets, in accordance with IAS 38. It stated that allowances that were issued for less than fair value were to be measured initially at fair value. If issued for less than fair value, the difference between the amount paid and fair value was to be accounted for as a government grant, within the scope of IAS 20.

IFRIC 3 stipulated that, initially, the grant was to have been recognized as deferred income in the statement of financial position, and then taken into income on a systematic basis over the compliance period for which the allowances had been issued, regardless of whether the allowances were held or sold.

Furthermore, it stated that, as emissions would later be made, a liability was to be recognized for the obligation to deliver allowances equal to emissions made. This liability was to have been treated as a provision in accordance with IAS 37, measured at the best estimate of the expenditure required to settle the present obligation at the date of the statement of financial position. This would usually be the present market price of the number of allowances required to cover emissions made up to the date of the statement of financial position.

The existence or requirements of an emission rights scheme could cause a reduction in the cash flows expected to be generated by certain assets. In such instances, IFRIC 3 would have directed that such a reduction be understood as an indication that those assets may be impaired and thus trigger a test for impairment under IAS 36.

Following the withdrawal of IFRIC 3, IASB concluded that emission rights are a form of government grant. In December 2007 IASB added a project on emissions trading schemes to its technical agenda, which does not include fundamental revisions to IAS 20. This project is to address whether tradable permits under allowances and credits schemes are assets, and if so, how these permits should be accounted for if received from the government at less than fair value and how changes in value should be reported in income. This project is in the early stages of discussion, but is thought likely to eventually result in an amendment to either IAS 38 (intangible assets) or IAS 39 (financial instruments), as well as to IAS 20 (government grants).

Service Concessions

Government involvement directly with business is much more common in Europe and elsewhere than in North America, and European adoption of IFRS has created a need to expand the IFRS literature to address a number of such circumstances. The *service concession*, particularly common in France, typically occurs when a commercial entity operates a commercial asset which is owned by, or has to be transferred to, a local, regional, or national government organization. More generally, these arrangements exist when the public is provided with access to major economic or social facilities. The most famous example of this is perhaps the Channel Tunnel, linking England and France. This was built by a commercial entity which has a concession to operate it for a period of years, at the end of which time the asset reverts to the British and French governments. A more mundane example would be companies that erect bus shelters free of charge in municipalities, in return for the right to advertise on them for a period of time.

SIC 29, issued in 2001 as an interpretation of IAS 1, addressed only disclosures to be made for service concession arrangements. Under SIC 29, both the concession operator and the concession provider are directed to make certain disclosures in the notes to financial statements that purport to conform with IFRS. These disclosures include

1. A description of the arrangement
2. The significant terms of the arrangement that might affect the nature, timing, or amounts of future cash flows, which could include terms and repricing dates and formulae.
3. The nature and the extent of rights to use specified assets; obligations to provide (or rights to expect) services; obligations to acquire or build property or equipment; options to deliver (or rights to receive) specific assets at the conclusion of the concession period; renewal and termination options; and other rights and obligations, such as for major overhauls of equipment.
4. Changes to the concession arrangement occurring during the reporting period.

Beginning in 2003, IFRIC was working on the actual accounting for service concession, which involved the issuance of three draft interpretations, which culminated with the issuance of IFRIC 12 in late 2006. IFRIC 12 sets forth a typology of service concession arrangements, two accounting models, and stipulates how revenue is to be recognized.

Service concession arrangements. Service concession arrangements are those whereby a government or other body grants contracts for the supply of public services (e.g., roads, energy distribution, prisons or hospitals) to private operators. The Interpretation draws a distinction between two types of service concession arrangements. In one, the operator receives a *financial asset,* specifically an unconditional contractual right to receive cash or another financial asset from the government in return for constructing or upgrading the public sector asset. In the other, the operator receives an *intangible asset*—a right to charge for use of the public sector asset that it constructs or upgrades. The right to charge users is not an unconditional right to receive cash, because the amounts that might be received are contingent on the extent to which the public uses the service.

IFRC 12 allows for the possibility that both types of arrangement may exist within a single contract: to the extent that the government has given an unconditional guarantee of payment for the construction of the public sector asset, the operator has a financial asset; to the extent that the operator has to rely on the public using the service in order to obtain payment, the operator has an intangible asset. The accounting to be applied is governed by the extent to which one or both types of assets are received.

Accounting under the financial asset model. The operator recognizes a financial asset to the extent that it has an *unconditional* contractual right to receive cash or another financial asset from, or at the direction of, the grantor for the construction services. The operator has an unconditional right to receive cash if the grantor contractually guarantees to pay the operator

- Specified or determinable amounts or
- The shortfall, if any, between amounts received from users of the public service and specified or determinable amounts, even if payment is contingent on the operator ensuring that the infrastructure meets specified quality or efficiency requirements.

Under the provisions of IFRIC 12, the operator measures the financial asset at fair value.

Accounting under the intangible asset model. The operator recognizes an intangible asset to the extent that it receives a right (a license) to charge users of the public service. A right to charge users of the public service is not an unconditional right to receive cash because the amounts are contingent on the extent that the public uses the service.

Under the provisions of IFRIC 12, the operator measures the intangible asset at fair value.

Operating revenue. The operator of a service concession arrangement recognizes and measures revenue in accordance with IASs 11 and 18 for the services it performs. No special revenue recognition principles are to be applied. Thus, the financial asset model would require the use of percentage of completion revenue recognition in most instances, while the intangible asset model would suggest that revenue be recognized as services are performed.

Accounting by the government (grantor). IFRIC 12 does not deal with the accounting to be applied by the government unit that grants service concession arrangements. That is because IFRSs are not designed to apply to not-for-profit activities in the private sector or the public sector. However, another standard-setting body, the International Public Sector Accounting Standard Board (IPSASB), has started its own project on service concession arrangements, which will give serious consideration to accounting by grantors. The principles applied in IFRIC 12 will be considered as part of the project.

IFRIC 12 is effective for annual periods beginning on or after January 1, 2008.

27 FIRST-TIME ADOPTION OF INTERNATIONAL FINANCIAL REPORTING STANDARDS

PERSPECTIVE AND ISSUES

While IFRS had been gaining adherents on a slow but steady pace for many years, 2005 was a true watershed in that over 7,000 publicly traded companies in nations of the European Union were required to begin reporting group (consolidated) financial statements using IFRS, vastly increasing the total number of companies worldwide employing international standards. Other nations have, in recent years, either embraced IFRS, announced plans to do so, or are endeavoring to "converge" their national GAAP with IFRS. The US standard-setting body, FASB, agreed on a program to converge with IFRS in 2002, and in the years since that pact (the "Norwalk Agreement") was signed, a number of US GAAP standards have been modified to conform to their IFRS equivalents (and, true to the spirit of convergence, several international standards have been modified to converge to US GAAP equivalents). In 2007, the US securities regulatory authority, the SEC, agreed to begin accepting filings by foreign private issuers (i.e., foreign registrants in the US) having financial statements prepared in conformity with IFRS. This was followed in 2008 by SEC action to permit voluntary adoption for financial reporting purposes by registrants meeting strict market size criteria, and the publication of a so-called roadmap which outlines the path to complete supercession of US GAAP by IFRS by 2016, if defined milestones are first met.

With these developments and the expectation of future events in mind, IASB issued a comprehensive standard on "first-time adoption," IFRS 1, in mid-2003

When a reporting entity undertakes to prepare its financial statements in accordance with international accounting standards for the first time, a number of implementation questions must be addressed and resolved. IASB's predecessor standard setter, IASC, had provided only limited guidance on this matter, which was set forth in interpretive rule SIC 8. This was later replaced by the more comprehensive current standard, IFRS 1, *First-Time Adoption of IFRS*. IFRS 1 differed in several important respects from SIC 8.

The worldwide trend toward universal adoption of IFRS has continued since the EU action of 2005. Several nations have since announced plans to drop existing national GAAP in favor of IFRS. Canada will converge to or adopt IFRS by 2011 (Canadian GAAP is currently very similar to US GAAP), China began converging to IFRS in 2007, and even Japan appears to be accelerating its IFRS converging efforts. Many more countries in Eastern Europe, South Asia, and the Far East are planning to be included in the growing list of new converts to IFRS. It is within this context that IASB decided to promulgate a standard on this subject as its maiden pronouncement, notwithstanding the existing guidance already extant as SIC 8.

IASB endeavored to provide a "stable platform" of standards, with few revisions and no new standards having near-term effective dates, in order to facilitate the transition process by EU-based public companies. IASB announced that any new standards to be issued in the near term would likely have implementation dates of 2009 or later, and indeed subsequent pronouncements (e.g., revised IAS 1, IFRS 8) were given 2009 mandatory effective dates, although earlier application was permitted. This was intended to provide a respite from the challenges of dealing with constantly evolving standards during what was expected to be a challenging transition phase.

IFRS 1 became effective in 2004, and was amended slightly in 2005 (to exempt entities adopting IFRS and IFRS 6 for the first time before 2006 from certain comparative disclosure requirements and from certain recognition and measurement requirements) and in 2008 (to permit entities to use "deemed cost" of fair value or carrying value under prior GAAP as the surrogate initial cost of investments in subsidiaries, associates, and jointly controlled entities in separate financial statements). A further proposed amendment to IFRS 1, which would expand the exemptions available to first-time adopters of IFRS, was issued in September 2008 and is promised for finalization in the latter part of 2009.

Sources of IFRS

IFRS 1
IASB Framework for the Preparation and Presentation of Financial Statements

---

DEFINITIONS OF TERMS

Date of transition to IFRS. This refers to the beginning of the earliest period for which an entity presents full comparative information under IFRS in its "first IFRS financial statements" (defined below).

Deemed cost. An amount substituted for "cost" or "depreciated cost" at a given date. In subsequent periods, this value is used as the basis for depreciation or amortization.

Fair value. The amount for which an asset could be exchanged, or a liability settled, between knowledgeable, willing parties in an arm's-length transaction.

First IFRS financial statements. The first annual financial statements in which an entity adopts IFRS by making an explicit and unreserved statement of compliance with IFRS.

First-time adopter (of IFRS). An entity is referred to as a first-time adopter in the period in which it presents its first IFRS financial statements.

International financial reporting standards (IFRS). The standards issued by the International Accounting Standards Board (IASB). More generally, the term connotes the currently outstanding standards (IFRS), the interpretations issued by the International Financial Reporting Interpretations Committee (IFRIC), as well as all still-effective previous standards

(IAS) issued by the predecessor International Accounting Standards Committee (IASC), and the interpretations issued by the IASC's Standards Interpretations Committee (SIC).

Opening IFRS statement of financial position. The statement of financial position prepared in accordance with the requirements of IFRS 1 as of the "date of transition to IFRS." IFRS 1 only requires that a first-time adopter *prepare* an opening statement of financial position; the entity is not required to actually *present* an opening statement of financial position. Thus, whether or not this statement of financial position is *published* along with the "first IFRS financial statements," this would still be considered to be the entity's opening IFRS statement of financial position.

Previous GAAP. This refers to the basis of accounting (e.g., national standards) a first-time adopter used immediately prior to IFRS adoption.

Reporting date. The end of the latest period covered by financial statements or by an interim financial report.

CONCEPTS, RULES AND EXAMPLES

Background

IFRS 1 was issued by the IASB in June 2003, superseding SIC 8. Certain aspects of SIC 8 reportedly had been considered difficult to implement by first-time adopters (of IFRS). The principal concerns were

1. The requirement that all standards be applied by the first-time adopter with full retrospective application, and
2. The rule that a first-time adopter was expected to apply different versions of IFRS in those instances where new versions of a standard had been introduced during the periods covered by the first set of financial statements prepared under IFRS.

The main differences between the requirements of IFRS 1 and the provisions of SIC 8 may be summarized as follows:

- While SIC 8 mandated full retrospective application, IFRS 1 requires retrospective application in a majority of instances, with *targeted exemptions* in certain cases and *prohibitions* against retrospective application in certain other instances;
- IFRS 1 clarified certain issues that SIC 8 had either not categorically addressed or had failed to explain in adequate detail. For instance, SIC 8 had not explicitly stated whether a first-time adopter was expected to use hindsight in the retrospective application of the various standards (IFRS), and also whether the "transitional provisions" of the individual IAS were to be considered as well. These matters have been resolved by IFRS 1; and
- IFRS 1 mandated new disclosures that were not required under SIC 8.

Scope and applicability of the standard. IFRS 1 applies to an entity that presents its first IFRS financial statements. It specifies the requirements that an entity must follow when it first adopts IFRS as the basis for preparing its general-purpose financial statements. IFRS 1 refers to these entities as *first-time adopters.* Since specific requirements apply to the financial statements of first-time adopters, the narrowly delimited definition of *first IFRS financial statements* must be carefully reviewed.

Per IFRS 1, an entity must apply the standard in its first IFRS financial statements and in *each interim financial report* it presents under IAS 34 for a part of the period covered by its first IFRS financial statements. For example, if 2009 is the first annual period for which IFRS financial statements are being prepared, the quarterly or semiannual statements for 2009, if presented, must also comply with IFRS.

According to the standard, an entity's first IFRS financial statements refer to the first annual financial statements in which the entity adopts IFRS by making an *explicit and unreserved statement* (in the financial statements) of compliance with IFRS. IFRS-compliant financial statements presented in the current year would qualify as first IFRS financial statements if the reporting entity presented its most recent previous financial statements

- Under national GAAP or standards that were inconsistent with IFRS in all respects;
- In conformity with IFRS in all respects, but without an explicit and unreserved statement to that effect;
- With a categorical statement that the financial statements complied with certain IFRS, but not with all applicable standards;
- Under national GAAP or standards that differ from IFRS but using some individual IFRS to account for items which were not addressed by its national GAAP or other standards;
- Under national GAAP or standards, but with a reconciliation of selected items to amounts determined under IFRS.

Other examples of situations where an entity's current year's financial statements would qualify as its first IFRS financial statements are

- Where the entity prepared financial statements in the previous period under IFRS but the financial statements had been identified as being "for internal use only" and had not been made available to the entity's owners or any other external users;
- Where IFRS-compliant financial reporting had been produced in earlier years, with explicit and unreserved statement of this fact, but national GAAP, not IFRS, was used in the period immediately preceding the preparation of the current year's first IFRS financial statements;
- Where the entity prepared a reporting package in the previous period under IFRS for consolidation purposes without preparing a complete set of financial statements as mandated by IAS 1; and
- Where the entity did not present financial statements for the previous periods at all.

The following example would help illustrate the implications of this requirement of the standard.

Excellent Inc., incorporated in Mysteryland, is a progressive multinational corporation that has always presented its financial statements under the national GAAP of the country of incorporation, with additional disclosures made in its footnotes. The supplementary data included value-added statements and a reconciliation of major items on its statement of financial position to International Financial Reporting Standards (IFRS). Excellent Inc. has significant borrowings from international financial institutions, and these have certain restrictive financial covenants—such as a defined upper limit on the ratio of external debt to equity, and minimum annual return on investments. In order to monitor compliance with these covenants, Excellent Inc. also prepared a separate set of financial statements in accordance with IFRS, but these were never made available to the international financial institutions or to the shareholders of Excellent Inc.

With the growing global acceptance that IFRS had been receiving in recent years, the finance minister of Mysteryland attempted to have the country adopt IFRS as its national GAAP, but this was vetoed by the nation's accounting standard setters. Mysteryland's accession to membership in the WTO is being planned for 2009, and the country is taking steps to gain recognition as a global economic player. Mysteryland was invited to participate in the World Economic Forum, and to publicize his country's commitment to globalization, the finance minister announces at this event that his country would adopt IFRS as its national GAAP beginning in 2009. This announcement was subsequently ratified by Mysteryland's parliament (and later by its national standard-setting body) and thus it was publicly announced that IFRS would be adopted as the country's national GAAP from 2009.

Excellent Inc. had always presented its financial statements under its national GAAP but had also voluntarily provided a reconciliation of major items on its statement of financial position to IFRS in its footnotes, and "for internal purposes" had also prepared a separate set of financial statements under IFRS. Despite these previous overtures towards IFRS compliance, in the year 2009—when Excellent Inc. moves to IFRS as its national GAAP and presents its financial statements to the outside world under IFRS, with an explicit and unreserved statement that these financial statements comply with IFRS—it will nonetheless be considered a first-time adopter and will have to comply with the requirements of IFRS 1.

Exceptions to the "first-time adopter" rule. If the reporting entity's financial statements in the previous year contained an explicit and unreserved statement of compliance with IFRS, but in fact did not fully comply with all aspects of IFRS, such an entity would *not* be considered a first-time adopter for the purposes of IFRS 1 in the current year. The disclosed or undisclosed departures from IFRS in previous year's financial statements of this entity would be treated as an "error" under IFRS 1, which warrants correction made in the manner prescribed by IAS 8. IFRS 1 identifies three situations in which IFRS 1 would *not* apply. These exceptions are as follows:

1. When an entity presented its financial statements in the previous year that contained an explicit and unreserved statement of compliance with IFRS, and its auditors qualified their report on those financial statements;
2. When an entity in the previous year presented its financial statements under national requirements (i.e., its national GAAP) along with another set of financial statements that contained an explicit or unreserved statement of compliance with IFRS, and in the current year it discontinues this practice of presenting under its national GAAP and presents only under IFRS; and
3. When an entity in the previous year presented its financial statements under national requirements (its national GAAP) and those financial statements contained (improperly) an explicit and unreserved statement of IFRS compliance.

Opening IFRS statement of financial position. At the *date of transition to IFRS,* the reporting entity is required to prepare an opening IFRS statement of financial position. This opening IFRS statement of financial position serves as the starting point for the entity's accounting under IFRS. The requirement under IFRS 1 is to *prepare* an opening statement of financial position, which does not mean that the opening IFRS statement of financial position must also be *presented* in the entity's first IFRS financial statements. In fact, it is likely that most entities will not make such a presentation, although some selected elements might be incorporated into various footnote explanations.

For example, if a reporting entity adopts IFRS effective at year-end 2009, and plans to present comparative financial statements for the current year and its immediate predecessor, it will apply IFRS as these exist at year-end 2009 in the preparation of a January 1, 2008 statement of financial position, and in the preparation of 2008 and 2009 financial statements. The January 1, 2008 statement of financial position may or may not be presented, as there is currently no requirement to do so (although this is required by revised IAS 1, which becomes mandatorily effective in 2009).

As defined in Appendix A to IFRS 1, therefore, *date of transition to IFRS* refers to *the beginning of the earliest period for which an entity presents full comparative information under IFRS as part of its first IFRS financial statements.* Thus the date of transition to IFRS depends on two factors: first, the date of adoption of IFRS and second, the number of years of comparative information that the entity decides to present along with the financial information of the year of adoption. The following illustration will clarify this point:

Adaptability Inc. presented its financial statements, under its previous GAAP, on a calendar year basis. The most recent such financial statements it presented were as of December 31, 2008. Adaptability Inc. decided to adopt IFRS as at December 31, 2009, and to present comparative information for the year 2008. Thus, the beginning of the earliest period for which the entity should present full comparative information would be January 1, 2008. Accordingly, the opening IFRS statement of financial position for purposes of compliance with IFRS 1 would be that as of January 1, 2008 (equivalent to the year-end 2007 statement of financial position).

Alternatively, if Adaptability Inc. decided (or was required, e.g., by the stock listing authorities) to present three-year comparative information (i.e., for both 2008 and 2007), as well as for the current year 2009, then the beginning of the earliest period for which the entity would present full comparative information would be January 1, 2007 (equivalent to the year-end 2004 statement of financial position). Accordingly, the opening IFRS statement of financial position for purposes of compliance with IFRS 1 would be that as of January 1, 2007, under these circumstances.

Adjustments required in preparing the opening IFRS statement of financial position (or in transition from previous GAAP to IFRS as of the first-time adoption). In preparing the opening IFRS statement of financial position, an entity should apply the following four rules, except in cases where IFRS 1 grants targeted exemptions and prohibits retrospective application:

1. *Recognize* all assets and liabilities whose recognition is required under IFRS;

    It is expected that many companies will recognize additional assets and liabilities under IFRS reporting, when compared with the national GAAP formerly employed. Areas which may result in this effect include

    - Defined benefit pension plans
    - Deferred taxation
    - Assets and liabilities under finance leases
    - Provisions where there is a legal or construction obligation
    - Derivative financial instruments
    - Acquired intangible assets
    - Share-based payments (per IFRS 2)

2. *Derecognize* items as assets or liabilities if IFRS do not permit such recognition;

    Some assets and liabilities recognized under a company's previous (national) GAAP will have to be derecognized. For example

    - Provisions where there is no legal or constructive obligation (e.g., general reserves)
    - Internally generated intangible assets
    - Deferred tax assets where recovery is not probable

3. *Reclassify* items that it recognized under previous GAAP as one type of asset, liability, or component of equity, but are a different type of asset, liability, or component of equity under IFRS. Assets and liabilities that might be reclassified to conform to IFRS include

    - Investments accounted for in accordance with IAS 39
    - Certain financial instruments previously classified as equity
    - Any assets and liabilities that have been offset where the criteria for offsetting in IRS are not met—for example, the offset of an insurance recovery against a provision
    - Noncurrent assets held-for-sale (per IFRS 5)

4. *Measure* all recognized assets and liabilities according to principles set forth in IFRS. Assets and liabilities that might have to be measured differently include

- Receivables (IAS 18)
- Employee benefit obligations (IAS 19)
- Deferred taxation (IAS 12)
- Financial instruments (IAS 39)
- Provisions (IAS 37)
- Impairments of property, plant, and equipment, and intangible assets (IAS 36)
- Assets held for disposal (under IFRS 5)
- Share-based payments (per IFRS 2)

The following comprehensive example illustrates the practical application of the four rules outlined above:

Situation

ABC Corp. presented its most recent financial statements under the national GAAP of XYZ country through 2008. It adopted IFRS from 2009 and is required to prepare an opening IFRS statement of financial position as at January 1, 2008. In preparing the IFRS opening statement of financial position, ABC Corp. noted the following:

Under its previous GAAP, ABC Corp. had deferred training costs of $250,000 and had classified proposed dividends of $400,000 as a current liability. Furthermore, it had not made a provision for warranty of $100,000 in the financial statements since the concept of "constructive obligation" was not recognized under its previous GAAP. Finally, in arriving at the amount to be capitalized as part of costs necessary to bring an asset to its working condition, ABC Corp. had not included professional fees of $50,000 paid to architects at the time when the building it presently occupies as its home office was being constructed.

Solution

In order to prepare the opening IFRS statement of financial position at January 1, 2008, ABC Corp. would need to make the following adjustments to its statement of financial position at December 31, 2007, presented under its previous GAAP:

1. IAS 38 does not allow training costs to be deferred whereas ABC Corp.'s previous GAAP allowed this treatment. Thus, $250,000 of such deferred costs should be *derecognized* (expensed) under IFRS;
2. IAS 37 requires recognition of a provision for warranty but ABC Corp.'s previous GAAP did not allow a similar treatment. Thus, a provision for warranty of $100,000 should be *recognized* under IFRS;
3. IAS 10 does not allow proposed dividends to be recognized as a liability, instead they are to be included in footnotes. ABC Corp.'s previous GAAP allowed proposed dividends to be treated as a current liability. Therefore, proposed dividends of $400,000 should be *eliminated* from current liability and just disclosed in footnotes; and
4. IAS 16 requires all directly attributable costs of bringing an asset to its working condition for its intended use to be capitalized as part of the carrying cost of property, plant, and equipment. Thus $50,000 of architects' fees should be capitalized as part of (i.e., used in the *measurement* of) property, plant, and equipment under IFRS.

Accounting policies. IFRS 1 stipulates that in preparing an opening IFRS statement of financial position the first-time adopter is to use the same accounting policies as it has used throughout all periods presented in its first IFRS financial statements. Furthermore, the standard requires that those accounting policies must comply with each IFRS effective at the "reporting date" (as explained below) for its first IFRS financial statements, except under certain defined circumstances wherein the entity claims targeted exemptions from retrospective application of IFRS, or is prohibited by IFRS from applying IFRS retrospectively (both concepts are discussed below). In other words, a first-time adopter should consistently apply the same accounting policies throughout the periods presented in its first IFRS financial statements and these accounting policies should be based on "latest version of the IFRS" effective at the reporting date. (The rationale for this is discussed later in this section.)

If a new IFRS has been issued on the reporting date, but application is not yet mandatory, although reporting entities have been encouraged to apply it before the effective date, the first-time adopter is permitted, but not required, to apply it as well.

Reporting period. "Reporting date" for an entity's first IFRS financial statements refers to the end of the latest period covered by the annual financial statements or interim financial statements, if any, that the entity presents under IAS 34 for the period covered by its first IFRS financial statements. This is illustrated in the following examples:

> **Example 1:** Xodus Corp. presents its first annual financial statements under IFRS for the calendar year 2009, which include an explicit and unreserved statement of compliance with IFRS. It also presents full comparative financial information for the calendar year 2008. In this case, the latest period covered by these annual financial statements would end on December 31, 2009, and the *reporting date* for the purposes of IFRS 1 is December 31, 2009 (presuming the entity does not present financial statements under IAS 34 for interim periods within calendar year 2009).

> **Example 2:** Alternatively, if Xodus Corp. decides to present its first IFRS interim financial statements for the six months ended June 30, 2009, in addition to the first IFRS annual financial statements for the year ended December 31, 2009, the *reporting date* may no longer be December 31, 2009; it is dependent upon how the interim financial statements are prepared. If the interim financial statements for the six months ended June 30, 2009 were prepared in accordance with IAS 34, then the reporting period would be June 30, 2009 (instead of December 31, 2009). If however, the interim financial statements for the six months ended June 30, 2009, were not prepared in accordance with IAS 34, then the reporting date would continue to be December 31, 2009 (and not June 30, 2009).

Rationale for using the "current version of IFRS." With the passage of time, IFRS have been revised or amended several times and in some instances the current version of IFRS is vastly different from the earlier versions that were either superseded or amended. In a very important decision, IFRS 1 requires a first-time adopter to use the current version of IFRS, without considering the superseded or amended versions. This obviates the need to identify varying iterations of the standards that would have guided the preparation of the entity's financial statements at each prior reporting date, which would have been a very time-consuming and problematic task. This means that the comparative financial statements accompanying the first IFRS compliant reporting may differ—perhaps materially—from what would have been presented in those earlier periods had the entity commenced reporting consistent with IFRS at an earlier point in time.

IASB's original thinking was to grant the first-time adopter an option to elect application of IFRS *as if it had always applied IFRS* (i.e., from the entity's inception). To actualize this, the first-time adopter would have had to consider the various iterations of IFRS that had historically existed over the period of time culminating with its actual adoption of IFRS. Upon reflection, this would have created not merely great practical difficulties for preparers, but would have negatively impacted comparability among reporting entities. Thus, IFRS 1 as promulgated offers no such option.

Transitional provisions contained in other IFRS. Certain IFRS set forth transitional provisions that are meant to facilitate transition to those particular new standards. These transitional provisions, in some cases, permit entities adopting a new standard to deviate from the provisions of other existing standards to an extent, usually in cases when retrospective application of those standards would make it cumbersome to apply the new standard.

IFRS 1 concluded that the transitional provisions in other IFRS were intended to apply to situations where changes in accounting policies were being made by an entity that already reported under IFRS, and thus those standards provide the transitional provisions that were not specifically designed to apply to first-time adopters. IFRS 1 therefore does not permit first-time adopters to invoke transition provisions in other IFRS (although IFRS 1 itself does create certain exceptions, explained below). If this clarification had not been provided in IFRS 1, there could have been confusion in applying certain IFRS that have transitional provisions, as to whether the first-time adopters would need to apply those provisions as well.

Targeted exemptions from other IFRS. IFRS 1 allows a first-time adopter to elect to use one or more targeted exemptions.

Under IFRS 1, a first-time adopter of IFRS may elect to use exemptions from the general measurement and restatement principles in one or more of the following instances:

- Business combinations that occurred before the date of transition to IFRS;
- Assets (property, plant, and equipment, intangible assets, and investment property) measured at fair value or revalued under previous GAAP;
- Employee benefits;
- Cumulative translation differences;
- Compound financial instruments; and
- Assets and liabilities of subsidiaries, associates, and joint ventures at the date of transition to IFRS.

The application of these targeted exemptions is explained in detail below.

Business combinations. IFRS 1 exempts the first-time adopter from mandatory retrospective application in the case of business combinations that occurred before the date of transition to IFRS. That is, requirements under IAS 22 (the standard in effect when IFRS 1 was promulgated) can be applied in accounting for combinations that occurred before the first reporting under IFRS, but this *need not be done.* Thus, under IFRS 1, an entity may elect to use previous national GAAP accounting relating to such business combinations. The IASB provided this exemption because, if retrospective application of IAS 22 had been made obligatory, it could have forced entities to estimate (or make educated guesses) about conditions that presumably prevailed at the respective dates of past business combinations. This would have been particularly challenging where data from past business combinations had not been preserved. The use of such estimates could have adversely affected the relevance and reliability of the financial statements, and was thus seen as a situation to be avoided.

In evaluating responses to the draft of its standard on first-time adoption of IFRS, the IASB concluded that notwithstanding the fact that restatement of past business combinations to conform with IFRS was conceptually preferable, a pragmatic assessment of cost versus benefit weighed in favor of *permitting* but *not requiring* such restatement. However, the IASB did place an important limitation on this election: if a first-time adopter having multiple acquisition transactions restates *any* business combination, it must restate *all* business combinations that took place subsequent to the date of that restated combination transaction. First-time adopters thus cannot "cherry pick" among past business combinations to apply IFRS opportunistically to certain of them.

> For instance, if BBB Inc., a first-time adopter, did not seek this exemption, instead opted to apply IFRS 3 (which replaced the former standard, IAS 22, in 2004) retrospectively, and restated a major business combination that took place three years ago, then, under this requirement of IFRS 1, BBB Inc. is required to restate all business combinations that took place subsequent to the date of this major business combination to which it applied IFRS 3 retrospectively. Earlier combinations would *not* have to be restated, however.

If the entity employs the exemption under IFRS 1 and does not apply IFRS 3 retrospectively to a past business combination, it must observe these rules.

1. The first-time adopter should preserve the same classification (an *acquisition* or a *uniting of interests*) as was applied in its previous GAAP financial statements.

2. The first-time adopter should recognize all assets and liabilities at the date of transition to IFRS that were acquired or assumed in a past business combination, except

   a. Certain financial assets and financial liabilities that were derecognized under its previous GAAP; and

   b. Assets (including goodwill) and liabilities that were not recognized in the acquirer's consolidated statement of financial position under previous GAAP and also would not qualify for recognition under IFRS in the separate statement of financial position of the acquiree.

   Any resulting change should be recognized by the first-time adopter in retained earnings (or another component of equity, if appropriate) unless the change results from the recognition of an intangible asset that was previously incorporated within goodwill.

3. The first-time adopter should derecognize (i.e., exclude) from its opening IFRS statement of financial position any item recognized under previous GAAP that does not qualify for recognition, either as an asset or liability, under IFRS. The resulting change from this derecognition should be accounted by the first-time adopter as follows: first, if the first-time adopter had classified a past business combination as an acquisition and recognized as an intangible asset an item that does not qualify for recognition as an asset under IAS 38, it should reclassify that item (and any related deferred tax and minority interests) as part of goodwill (unless it deducted goodwill from equity, instead of presenting it as an asset, under its previous GAAP); and second, the first-time adopter should recognize all other resulting changes in retained earnings.

4. In cases where IFRS require subsequent measurement of some assets and liabilities on a basis other than original cost, such as fair value, the first-time adopter should measure these assets and liabilities on that basis in its opening IFRS statement of financial position, even if these assets and liabilities were acquired or assumed in a past business combination. Any resulting change in the carrying amount should be recognized by the first-time adopter in retained earnings (or another component of equity, if appropriate), instead of as an adjustment to goodwill.

5. Subsequent to the business combination, the carrying amount under previous GAAP of assets acquired and liabilities assumed in the business combination should be treated as their *deemed cost* under IFRS at that date. If IFRS require a cost-based measurement of those assets and liabilities at a later date, deemed cost should be used instead (e.g., as the basis for cost-based depreciation or amortization from the date of the business combination).

6. If assets acquired or liabilities assumed were not recognized in a past business combination under the previous GAAP, the first-time adopter should recognize and measure them in its consolidated statement of financial position on the basis that IFRS would require in the separate statement of financial position of the acquiree.

7. The carrying amount of goodwill in the opening IFRS statement of financial position should be its carrying amount under previous GAAP at the date of transition to IFRS, after the following adjustments:

a. The carrying amount of goodwill should be increased due to a reclassification that would be needed for an intangible asset recognized under previous GAAP but which does not qualify as an intangible asset under IAS 38. Similarly, the carrying amount of goodwill should be decreased due to inclusion of an intangible asset as part goodwill under previous GAAP but which requires separate recognition under IFRS.

b. If the purchase consideration of a past business combination was based on a contingency which was resolved prior to the date of transition to IFRS, and a reliable estimate of the adjustment relating to the contingency can be made and it is probable that a payment will be made, the first-time adopter should adjust the carrying amount of goodwill by that amount. Similarly, if a previously recognized contingency can no longer be measured reliably, or its payment is no longer probable, the first-time adopter should adjust the carrying amount of goodwill accordingly.

c. Whether or not there is evidence of impairment of goodwill, the first-time adopter should apply IAS 36 in testing goodwill for impairment, if any, and should recognize the resulting impairment loss in retained earnings (or, if so required by IAS 36, in revaluation surplus).

The impairment test should be based on conditions at the date of transition to IFRS.

8. No other adjustments are permitted by IFRS 1 to the carrying amount of goodwill at the date of transition to IFRS. Thus, adjustments such as the following *cannot* be made:

a. Excluding in-process research and development acquired in that business combination,

b. Adjusting previous amortization of goodwill, or

c. Reversing adjustments to goodwill that IFRS 3 would not permit but which were appropriately made under previous GAAP.

9. If under its previous GAAP a first-time adopter did not consolidate a subsidiary acquired in a business combination (i.e., because the parent did not treat it as a subsidiary under previous GAAP), the first-time adopter should adjust the carrying amounts of the subsidiary's assets and liabilities to the amounts that IFRS would require in the subsidiary's separate statement of financial position. The deemed cost of goodwill would be equal to the difference at the date of transition to IFRS between the parent's interest in those adjusted carrying amounts and the cost in the parent's separate financial statements of its investment in the subsidiary.

10. The above adjustments to recognized assets and liabilities should also flow through to minority interests and deferred assets.

IFRS 1 states that these exemptions for past business combinations also apply to past acquisitions of investments in associates and in joint ventures. Furthermore, the date chosen for electing to apply IFRS 3 retrospectively to past business combinations applies equally to all such investments.

Fair value or revaluation as deemed cost. An entity may elect to measure an item of property, plant, and equipment at fair value at the date of its transition to IFRS and use the fair value as its deemed cost at that date. A first-time adopter may elect to use a previous GAAP revaluation of a item of property, plant, and equipment at, or before, the date of transition to IFRS as deemed costs at the date of revaluation if the revaluation amount, when determined, was broadly comparable to either fair value or cost (or depreciated cost under IFRS adjusted for changes in general or specific price index).

These elections are equally available for investment property measured under the cost model and intangible assets that meet the recognition criteria and the criteria for revaluation (including the existence of an active market).

If a first-time adopter has established a deemed cost under the previous GAAP for any of its assets or liabilities by measuring them at their fair values at a particular date because of the occurrence of an event such as privatization or an initial public offering (IPO), it is allowed to use such an event-driven fair value as deemed cost for IFRS at the date of that measurement.

Employee benefits. Under IAS 19 an entity may have unrecognized actuarial gains or losses when it uses the corridor approach defined under that standard. Prior GAAP may not have provided similar treatment, however. Retrospective application of IAS 19 would necessitate splitting the cumulative gains and losses, from inception of the plan until the date of transition to IFRS, into a recognized and an unrecognized portion. This would necessitate an enormously complicated analysis in some situations.

IFRS 1 allows a first-time adopter to elect to recognize all cumulative actuarial gains and losses at the date of transition to IFRS, even if it uses the corridor approach for subsequent actuarial gains or losses. IFRS 1 does mandate, however, that if an election is made for one employee benefit plan, it should apply to all other employee plans of that reporting entity.

Cumulative translation differences. IAS 21 requires an entity to classify certain translation differences as a separate component of equity, and upon disposal of the foreign operation to transfer the cumulative translation difference relating to the foreign operation to the statement of comprehensive income as part of the gain or loss on disposal.

A first-time adopter is exempted from a transfer of the cumulative translation adjustment that existed on the date of transition to IFRS. If it elects this exemption, the cumulative translation adjustment for all foreign operations would be deemed to be zero at the date of transition to IFRS. The gain or loss on subsequent disposal of any foreign operation should exclude translation differences that arose before the date of transition to IFRS, but would include all subsequent translation adjustments.

Compound financial instruments. If an entity has issued a compound financial instrument, such as a convertible debenture, IAS 32 requires that at inception, it should split and separate the liability component of the compound financial instrument from equity. If the liability portion no longer is outstanding at the date of adoption of IFRS, a retrospective and literal application of IAS 32 would require separating two portions of equity. The first portion, which is in retained earnings, represents the cumulative interest accreted on the liability component. The other portion represents the original equity component of the instrument, and would be in paid-in capital.

IFRS 1 exempts a first-time adopter from this split accounting if the former liability component is no longer outstanding at the date of transition to IFRS.

Assets and liabilities of subsidiaries, associates, and joint ventures. IFRS 1 discusses exemptions under two circumstances.

1. If a subsidiary becomes a first-time adopter later than its parent, the subsidiary must, in its separate (stand-alone) financial statements, measure its assets and liabilities at either

   a. The carrying amounts that would be included in its parent's consolidated financial statements, based on its parent's date of transition to IFRS (if no adjustments were made for consolidation procedures and for the effect of the business combination in which the parent acquired the subsidiary), or

b.   The carrying amounts required by the other provisions of IFRS 1, based on subsidiary's date of transition to IFRS.

2.   If a reporting entity becomes a first-time adopter after its subsidiary (or associate or joint venture) does, the entity is required, in its consolidated financial statements, to measure the assets and liabilities of the subsidiary (or associate or joint venture) at the same carrying amounts as in the separate (stand-alone) financial statements of the subsidiary (or associate or joint venture), after adjusting for consolidation and equity accounting adjustments and for effects of the business combination in which an entity acquired the subsidiary.   In a similar manner, if a parent becomes a first-time adopter for its separate financial statements earlier or later than for its consolidated financial statements, it shall measure its assets and liabilities at the same amounts in both financial statements, except for consolidation adjustments.

Exceptions to retrospective application of other IFRS.   IFRS 1 *prohibits* retrospective application of certain aspects of other IFRS.   These relate to

1.   **Derecognition of financial assets and financial liabilities.**   If a first-time adopter derecognized financial assets or financial liabilities under its previous GAAP in a financial year prior to January 1, 2001, it should not rerecognize those assets and liabilities under IFRS.

However, a first-time adopter should recognize all derivatives and other interests retained after derecognition and still existing, and consolidate all special-purpose entities (SPE) that it controls at the date of transition to IFRS (even if the SPE existed before the date of transition to IFRS or hold financial assets or financial liabilities that were derecognized under previous GAAP).

2.   **Hedge accounting.**   A first-time adopter is required, at the date of transition to IFRS, to measure all derivatives at fair value and eliminate all deferred losses and gains on derivatives that were reported under its previous GAAP.

However, a first-time adopter is not permitted to reflect a hedging relationship in its opening IFRS statement of financial position if it does not qualify for hedge accounting under IAS 39.   But if an entity designated a net position as a hedged item under its previous GAAP, it may designate an individual item within that net position as a hedged item under IFRS, provided it does so prior to the date of transition to IFRS.   Transitional provisions of IAS 39 apply to hedging relationships of a first-time adopter at the date of transition to IFRS.

3.   **Estimates.**   An entity's estimates under IFRS at the date of transition to IFRS should be consistent with estimates made for the same date under its previous GAAP, unless there is objective evidence that those estimates were in error, as that term is defined under IFRS.

Any information an entity receives after the date of transition to IFRS about estimates it made under previous GAAP should be treated by it as a *nonadjusting* event after the date of the statement of financial position, and accorded the treatment prescribed by IAS 10 (i.e., by making disclosure in footnotes as opposed to actual adjustment of items in the financial statements).

Presentation and disclosure.

1.   A first-time adopter should present at least one year of comparative financial statement information.   If an entity also presents historical summaries of selected data for periods prior to the first period that it presents full comparative information under IFRS, and IFRS does not require the summary data to be in compliance with IFRS, such data should be labeled prominently as not being in compliance with

IFRS and also disclose the nature of the adjustment that would make that data IFRS-compliant.

2. A first-time adopter should explain how the transition to IFRS affected its reported financial position, financial performance, and cash flows. In order to comply with the above requirement, reconciliation of equity and profit and loss as reported under previous GAAP to IFRS should be included in the entity's first IFRS financial statements.

3. If an entity uses fair values in its opening IFRS statement of financial position as deemed cost for an item of property, plant, and equipment, an investment property or an intangible asset, then disclosure is required for each line item in the opening IFRS statement of financial position of the aggregate of those fair values and of the aggregate adjustments made to the carrying amounts reported under previous GAAP.

4. If an entity presents an interim financial report under IAS 34 for a part of the period covered by its first IFRS financial statements, in addition to disclosures made under IAS 34 the first-time adopter should present a reconciliation of the equity and profit and loss under previous GAAP for the comparable interim period to its equity and profit and loss under IFRS.

It is anticipated, and recommended, that transition-period disclosures be presented as a complete package, covering

- A full set of restated financial statements (statements of financial position, statements of comprehensive income, statements of cash flows and statements of changes in shareholders' equity);
- Notes explaining the restatement, including reconciliations from previously reported amounts to restated amounts under IFRS; and
- Notes on the accounting policies to be applied under IFRS and applied at transition

Additional footnote detail in the annual financial statements for the first year IFRS is applied may also be useful. At a minimum, however, to provide a thorough understanding of the transition, it will be advisable to identify all the relevant factors considered by the preparer (the reporting entity) in converting to IFRS, in the transition disclosure package itself.

Options with and within accounting standards. An entity adopting IFRS for the first time may have a choice among accounting standards as well as accounting policies as a result of: (1) Options with accounting standards (newly issued IFRS), and (2) Options within accounting standards.

In conformity with IFRS 1, an entity should adopt IFRS issued and effective at the reporting date of the entity's first IFRS financial statements. Some IFRS may not be issued as of the date of an entity's transition to IFRS but will be effective at the reporting date. It is also possible to adopt a standard whose application is not yet mandatory for the reporting period but whose early adoption is permitted. The IASB has a number of projects currently on its agenda where standards are expected to be finalized in the near future with application dates beyond that date, including those dealing with such matters as derecognition, liabilities, fair value measurement and accounting for income taxes.

On first-time adoption of IFRS, an entity must choose which accounting policies will be adopted. IFRS require an entity to measure some assets and liabilities at fair value, and some others (for example, pension liabilities) at net realizable value or other forms of current value that reflect explicit current projections of future cash flows. An entity will have a choice between different options of accounting policies within accounting standards that may be applied in preparing its first IFRS financial statements. Examples of areas where options within IFRS exist include cost versus revaluation basis of accounting for property, plant, and equipment and intangible assets (IAS 16, IAS 38); cost versus fair value basis of accounting for investment property (IAS 40); and proportionate consolidation versus equity accounting of jointly controlled entities (IAS 31). There are several other areas where there is a choice of accounting policies under IFRS which may have a significant impact on an entity's future results. Once an accounting policy is adopted, opportunities to change may be restricted to justified situations where the change would result in a more appropriate presentation.

In many respect, entities are given a "fresh start" and are required to redetermine their accounting policies under IFRS, fully restating past comparative information. The limited optional exceptions also present some opportunities for entities to determine optimal outcomes.

Consequential amendments to other IFRS. IFRS 1 amended IAS 39 with respect to recognition of derivatives or other retained interests (such as servicing rights or liabilities) and special-purpose entities (SPE) controlled by the transferor. Specifically, the first-time adopter is required to

1. Recognize all derivatives and other interests, such as servicing rights or servicing liabilities, retained after the derecognition transaction and still existing at the date of transition to IFRS; and

2. Consolidate all special-purpose entities (SPE) that it controls at the date of transition to IFRS, even if the SPE existed before the date of transition to IFRS or hold financial assets or financial liabilities that were derecognized under previous GAAP.

Proposed amendments to IFRS 1. In September 2008, the IASB published an Exposure Draft (ED) proposing amendments to IFRS 1, *First-Time Adoption of International Financial Reporting Standards*. The proposed amendments provide more exemptions from the full retrospective application of IFRS, with regard to the measurement of assets in the oil and gas sector and regulated industries, as well as accounting for leases.

It is common in some countries to use the "full cost accounting" to measure exploration and evaluation assets and assets in the development and production phases. Since this approach is not allowed under IFRS, the process of remeasuring the assets on the first-time adoption of IFRS would likely be tedious and expensive. The proposed amendment would allow an entity that used full cost accounting under its previous GAAP to measure exploration and evaluation assets, as well as oil and gas assets in the development or production phases, at the date of transition to IFRS, at the amount determined under the entity's previous GAAP. The amount determined under the entity's previous GAAP is than allocated pro rata to the underlying assets, using reserve volumes or reserve values, as of the date of transition. Additionally, the ED proposes that these assets should be tested for impairment at the date of transition to IFRS, to ensure that assets are not reported at more than their recoverable amount.

The ED proposes an exemption for entities that provide products or services that are subject to rate regulation, where prices are established by legislation or an independent regulator, to recover the cost of operations and earn a predetermined return on investment. Such entities often include in the cost of property, plant, and equipment amounts that do not qualify for capitalization under IAS 16, *Property, Plant, and Equipment* and IAS 23, *Borrowing Costs* (e.g., an imputed cost of equity financing). Proposed amendments allow entities to use the carrying amount of items of property, plant, and equipment held, or previously held, for use in such operations as their deemed cost at the date of transition to IFRSs if both retrospective restatement and using fair value as deemed cost are impracticable.

The ED proposes that if a first-time adopter made, under previous GAAP, the same determination as that required by IFRIC 4, *Determining Whether an Arrangement Contains a*

Lease, but that assessment was at a date other than that required by IFRIC 4, the first-time adopter need not reassess that determination when it adopts IFRS.

The proposed amendments to IFRS 1 should benefit first-time adopters, by reducing the cost of implementing IFRS. Entities should evaluate potential impacts of electing to use the proposed exemptions, including implications for information systems, taxes, and results.

Areas of likely differences from predecessor national GAAP. While the extent to which first-time IFRS-compliant financial statements will differ from the former presentation under national GAAP depends entirely on which national GAAP was previously applied (since IFRS is most similar to US GAAP and UK GAAP, and was dissimilar from certain other national standards, including many EU nations' prior GAAP), the following summarizes what, in the authors' opinion, are likely to be the more complex areas.

1. The use of revaluation for fixed assets, intangibles, and investment property under IFRS differs from that permitted under the various national GAAP. In fact, a strict historical cost requirement is more commonly found, so that revaluation of fixed assets is not permitted. The fair value approach to investment property, imposed by revised IAS 40, is new for even those previously familiar with IAS, and at variance with national GAAP, in the main.

2. The "fair value" override permitted under IFRS (and also under UK GAAP), is intended to place the ultimate objective of financial reporting above any specific measurement rules imposed under the standards, thus offering preparers (and their auditors) the right to contravene specific IFRS requirements when necessary in order to better reflect the truth in the financial statements. While a somewhat similar option exists for US reporting (found in US professional ethical standards, however, not in US GAAP), this is very rarely invoked (and not generally permitted by the SEC, notwithstanding the profession's endorsement), and is also very rare under European GAAP. Where used, it generally has been achieved by variations in the informative disclosures, and not by applying alternative measures to transactions and balances. It is too early to predict if, and to what extent, preparers and their auditors may seek to draw upon this permission to depart from strict application of IFRS.

3. The requirements for first-time adoption, under IFRS 1, make conversion a process that will require full retrospective application of current IFRS standards. This undertaking will be arduous, which creates some risk of misapplication, etc. For example, for standards which have been revised over the past several years, there will be confusion about whether the requirements should be the current ones or those in effect historically from time to time.

4. The reporting of extraordinary items is now barred under IFRS, but still receives varying treatment under different national GAAP (e.g., elimination of negative goodwill is extraordinary item under US GAAP). Depending on past experience, preparers may have greater or lesser difficulties in finding the appropriate "home" for charges and credits that would otherwise have been deemed extraordinary.

5. Statements of cash flows prepared in compliance with IFRS offer certain alternatives, for reporting items such as dividends and interest, that are not permitted under US GAAP and may vary from some or all European national GAAP. The election among alternatives should be communicated to users, if the impact is material.

6. Changes in accounting policies require the restatement of comparative financial statements, while some national GAAP, including that of the US, require reporting in the current period a cumulative charge or credit for the change, perhaps with required pro forma disclosures for the prior comparative periods.

7.   Special-purpose entities (now called variable interest entities in the US) now face strict consolidation rules under US GAAP, with somewhat less strict rules under IFRS, and yet less strict requirements under some national GAAP and no rules at all, in some cases). Adopters of IFRS will have to determine which previously non-consolidated SPEs might now have to be consolidated in the beneficiary's financial statements, and this might be accomplished with varying degrees of precision.

8.   Consolidation rules are strict under US GAAP, and similarly strict under IFRS (i.e., very few exceptions to mandatory consolidation of majority owned subsidiaries), but under some national GAAP there were less stringent requirements which permitted the nonconsolidation of nonhomogeneous subsidiaries.

9.   Reporting the currency effects of the consolidation of foreign subsidiaries varies. Both IFRS and US GAAP require (in almost all instances) that statement of financial position translation be at the current rate, statement of comprehensive income generally at transaction date rates, and the effect of net translation be reported in the equity section of the statement of financial position. Other national GAAP use various methods, some of which reported translation in the statement of comprehensive income.

10. Some business combinations are still being accounted for as unitings (poolings) of interest under national GAAP, while this method is banned under US GAAP and now also under IFRS. Poolings subsequent to elimination of this method under IFRS will have to be restated as purchases.

11. National GAAP treatment of goodwill (that is, whether to amortize, and over what period) varies; IFRS now largely conforms to US GAAP requirement that no amortization be recognized, but that impairment testing be done every year. Restatement to IFRS will thus have to adjust for prior purchase business combinations.

12. National GAAP treatment of negative goodwill varies, but some still permit deferred recognition in income, while under IFRS (which has been largely conformed to US GAAP), net negative goodwill receives statement of comprehensive income recognition at the acquisition date.

13. Long-term construction contract accounting varies under national GAAP, and some do not permit percentage-of-completion method to be used in any circumstances. IFRS requires percentage-of-completion method (US GAAP generally does also, with some exceptions).

14. Pension accounting requirements vary considerably among the European nations. Besides the diversity of requirements, this is a complex area, making transition to IFRS quite challenging. US GAAP and IFRS are similar to each other, and both are more strict (in terms of reporting pension obligations on employers' financial statements) than some national GAAP.

15. Similar to pension accounting is the area of other postemployment benefits. OPEB reporting rules are similar under US GAAP and IFRS, but other national GAAP rules are vague, meaning that there are many variations in interpretation of the expense accrual requirements. Upon adopting IFRS, it is likely that additional liabilities may have to be reported by these entities.

16. The rules governing accounting for internally developed assets vary considerably. IFRS requires expensing of research expenses, but requires capitalization of development expenditures. In contrast, US GAAP requires expensing of both research and development expense as incurred. National GAAP do vary, but in some cases even internally constructed tangible assets must be expensed, in addition to research and development costs.

17. Capital lease accounting by lessee and lessor varies across national GAAP, while under US GAAP and IFRS the financial reporting considerations are similar. Entities first adopting IFRS will have to determine if leased assets need to be capitalized, with the associated debt obligation shown as liabilities.

18. Impairment of long-lived assets is accounted for under various methodologies across national GAAP. Reversals of previously recognized write-downs are permitted by IFRS under certain circumstances, while this is not necessarily permitted under other GAAP. (US GAAP does not permit this.)

19. Interest capitalization on long-term construction projects varies across national GAAP. This is merely optional under IFRS (but is required under US GAAP).

20. The fair value option for accounting for investment property can be applied under IFRS, but under national GAAP use of depreciated historical cost is more likely required. (US GAAP also requires cost-based accounting for nonsecurities investments.) Entities adopting fair value reporting upon conversion to IFRS will have some issues in making determinations of fair values at historical dates.

21. Agricultural (biological) activities are accounted for by fair value method under IFRS, whereas national GAAP generally requires application of historical cost-based methods, as is also true under US GAAP.

22. Accounting for derivatives and hedging activities are very similar under current US GAAP and IFRS, but most national GAAP have not yet adapted fair value accounting for derivatives, so much of this had been "off the books" under prior standards. Conversion to IFRS reporting will force these derivatives onto the statements of financial position of the reporting entities.

23. Recognition of restructuring obligations varies across national GAAP. Under US GAAP, which is strictest now that liability definition must be met, relatively less of these accruals can be made.

24. Deferred tax provisions may be based on the older, statement of comprehensive income–oriented matching concept, under some national GAAP standards. This contrasts with the more modern, statement of financial position–oriented IFRS and US GAAP liability method approach to deferred tax accounting. There may also be differences from the IFRS comprehensive allocation method (UK GAAP, until recently, used the partial allocation approach).

25. Classification of financial instruments as debt or equity varies across national GAAP. Recent US GAAP has expanded need to consider some nominal equity instruments as debt, and IFRS has been consistently strict on this matter. Other national GAAP still permit equity classification for instruments having certain features of debt. Upon conversion to IFRS, these statement of financial position may show reduction in equity, increase in debt, as a consequence.

26. Requirements concerning the reporting of discontinued operations vary. Some standards have no requirements for this at all, in contrast to US GAAP and IFRS requirements. Adoption of IFRS may necessitate reclassification of these items within the preparer's statement of comprehensive income.

APPENDIX A

DISCLOSURE CHECKLIST

This checklist provides a reference to the disclosures common to the financial statements of entities that are complying with International Financial Reporting Standards (IFRS), including those set forth by the International Accounting Standards (IAS) promulgated by the IASC earlier. These disclosures are set forth by IFRS/IAS and IFRIC/SIC and are effective for periods beginning after December 31, 2007. Certain changes have been mandated but will not become mandatorily effective until years beginning in 2009, and are identified as such. Changes which have been proposed but which have not been promulgated are not incorporated in this checklist. Superseded disclosures have been excluded.

DISCLOSURE CHECKLIST INDEX

General

Statement of Financial Position

Statement of Comprehensive Income

   D.   Extraordinary Items

   E.   Noncurrent Assets Held for Sale and Discontinued Operations

   F.   Segment Data

   G.   Construction Contracts

   H.   Foreign Currency Translation

   I.   Business Combinations

   J.   Earnings Per Share

   K.   Dividends Per Share

   L.   Impairments of Assets

   M.   Financial Instruments

Statement of Cash Flows

   A.   Basis of Presentation

   B.   Format

   C.   Additional Recommended Disclosures

Statement of Changes in Equity

   A.   Statement of Changes in Equity

Notes to the Financial Statements

   A.   Structure of the Notes

   B.   Accounting Policies

   C.   Service Concession Arrangements

Interim Financial Statements

   A.   Minimum Components of an Interim Financial Report

   B.   Form and Content of Interim Financial Statements

   C.   Selected Explanatory Notes

Insurance Contracts

Agriculture

   A.   General

   B.   Additional Disclosure for Biological Assets Where Fair Value Cannot Be Measured Reliably

   C.   Government Grants

Exploration for and Evaluation of Mineral Resources

GENERAL

A.   Identification of Financial Statements and Basis of Reporting

   1.   The financial statements should be identified clearly and distinguished from other information in the same published document. In addition, the following information shall be displayed prominently, and repeated when it is necessary for a proper understanding of the information presentation:

      a.   Name of the entity whose financial statements are being presented, or other means of identification, and any change in that information from the preceding balance sheet;

      b.   Disclosure whether the financial statements cover the individual entity or a group of entities;

      c.   The accounting policies, including measurement bases and other policies necessary to an understanding of the financial statements;

      d.   Presentation currency as defined in IAS 21;

      e.   When presentation currency differs from functional currency, state this fact, disclose the functional currency and the reason for using a different presentation currency;

      f.   Level of rounding used in presentation of the figures in the financial statements;

g. Balance sheet date or the period covered by the financial statements, whichever is appropriate to that component of financial statement.

h. Identify each component of the financial statements.

(IAS 1, Paras 49, 51 & 112; IAS 21, Para 53)

2. An entity shall disclose the following, if not disclosed elsewhere in information published in the financial statements:

a. Entity's country of incorporation, domicile and legal form;

b. Address of its registered office or principal place of business if different from the registered office;

c. Name of the reporting entity's parent and the ultimate parent of the group;

d. Description of the nature of the entity's operations and its principal activities;

(IAS 1, Para 126)

3. An entity shall disclose the following relating to the company's management of capital:

a. Qualitative information regarding its objectives, policies and processes to manage capital;

b. A summary of the quantitative data concerning what the company manages as capital;

c. Whether externally imposed capital requirements have been complied with during the period or the consequences for not having complied;

(IAS 1, Paras 135 a,b,c)

B. Compliance with International Financial Reporting Standards

1. Financial statements shall present fairly the financial position, financial performance and the cash flows of the entity. Fair presentation requires the faithful presentation of the transactions, other events, and condition in accordance with the definitions and recognition criteria for assets, liabilities, income and expenses set out in the framework. The application of IFRS, with additional disclosure when necessary, is presented to result in financial statements that achieve a fair presentation.

(IAS 1, Para 15)

2. An entity whose financial statements comply with IFRS shall make an explicit and unreserved statement of such compliance in the notes. Financial statements shall not be described as complying with IFRS unless they comply with all the requirements of IFRS.

(IAS 1, Para 16)

3. In extremely rare circumstances in which management concludes that compliance with a requirement in a Standard or an Interpretation would be so misleading that it would conflict with the objective of financial statements set out in the Framework, the entity shall depart from that requirement in the manner set out in IAS 1, paragraph 20 (see below) if the relevant regulatory framework requires, or otherwise does not prohibit, such a departure.

(IAS 1, Para 19)

4. When an entity departs from a requirement of a Standard or an Interpretation in accordance with IAS 1, paragraph 17, it shall disclose

a. That management has concluded that the financial statements present fairly the entity's financial position, financial performance and cash flows;

b. That it had complied with applicable Standards and Interpretations, except that it had departed from a particular requirement to achieve a fair presentation;

c. The title of the Standard or Interpretation from which the entity has departed, the nature of the departure, including the treatment that the Standard or Interpretation would require, the reason why the treatment would be so misleading in the circumstances that it would conflict with the objective of financial statements set out in the Framework, and the treatment adopted; and

    d.   For each period presented, the financial impact of the departure on each item in the financial statements that would have been reported in complying with the requirement.

(IAS 1, Para 20)

5.   When an entity has departed from a requirement of an IFRS in a prior period, and that departure affects the amounts recognized in the financial statements for the current period, it shall make the disclosures set out in IAS 1, Paras 20(c) and (d).

(IAS 1, Para 20)

6.   When in extremely rare circumstances in which management concludes that compliance with a requirement of the Standard or Interpretation would be misleading and that it would conflict with the objective of the financial statements set out in the Framework, but the regulatory framework prohibits departure from the requirement, the entity shall, to the maximum extent possible, reduce the perceived misleading aspects of compliance by disclosing the following:

    a.   The title of the Standard of Interpretation in question, the nature of the requirement, and the reason why the management has concluded that complying with the requirement is so misleading in the circumstances that it conflicts with the objective of the financial statement se out in the Framework; and

    b.   For each period presented, the adjustment to each item of the financial statements that the management has concluded would be necessary to achieve a fair presentation.

(IAS 1, Para 19)

C.   Changes in Accounting Policies, Changes in Accounting Estimates and Errors

1.   When initial application of a Standard or an Interpretation has an effect on the current period or any prior period, would have such an effect except that is impracticable to determine the amount of the adjustment, or might have an effect on future periods, an entity shall disclose

    a.   The title of the Standard or Interpretation;

    b.   When applicable, that the change in accounting policy is made in accordance with its transitional provisions;

    c.   The nature of change in accounting policy;

    d.   When applicable, a description of the transitional provisions;

    e.   When applicable, the transitional provisions that might have an effect on future periods;

    f.   For current period and each prior period presented, to the extent practicable, the amount of the adjustment

        (1)   For each financial statement line item affected; and

        (2)   If IAS 33, *Earnings per Share,* applies to the entity, for basic and diluted earnings per share;

    g.   The amount of the adjustment relating to periods before those presented, to the extent practicable; and

    h.   If retrospective application required by IAS 8, paragraph 19(a) or (b) is impracticable for a particular prior period, or for periods before those presented, the circumstances that led to the existence of that condition and a description of how and from when the change in accounting policy has been applied.

(Financial statements of subsequent periods need not repeat these disclosures.)

(IAS 8, Para 28)

2.   When a voluntary change in accounting policy has an effect on the current period or any prior period, would have an effect on that period except that it is impracticable to determine the amount of the adjustment, or might have an effect on future periods, an entity shall disclose

    a.   The nature of change in accounting policy;

    b.   The reasons why applying the new accounting policy provides reliable and more relevant information;

    c.   For the current period and each prior period presented, to the extent practicable, the amount of the adjustment

       (1) For each financial statement line item affected; and
       (2) If IAS 33 applies to the entity, for basic and diluted earning per share;

    d.   The amount of the adjustment relating to periods before those presented, the circumstances that led to the existence of that condition and description of how and from when the change in accounting policy has been applied.

    e.   If retrospective application is impracticable for a particular prior period, or for periods before those presented, the circumstances that led to the existence of that condition and a description of how and from when the change in accounting policy has been applied.

(Financial statements of subsequent periods need not repeat these disclosures.)

(IAS 8, Para 29)

3.   When an entity has applied a new Standard or Interpretation that has been issued but is not yet effective, the entity shall disclose

    a.   This fact; and
    b.   Known or reasonably estimable information relevant to assessing the possible impact that application of the new Standard or Interpretation will have on entity's financial statements in the period of application.

(IAS 8, Para 30)

4.   An entity shall disclose the nature and amount of a change in an accounting estimate that has an effect in the current period or is expected to have an effect in future periods when it is impracticable to estimate that effect.

(IAS 8, Para 39)

5.   If the amount of the effect in future periods is not disclosed because estimating it is impracticable, an entity shall disclose the fact.

(IAS 8, Para 40)

6.   In correcting material prior period errors, as outlined in IAS 1, paragraph 42, an entity shall disclose the following:

    a.   The nature of the prior period error;
    b.   For each prior period presented, to the extent practicable, the amount of correction;

       (1) For each financial statement line item affected;
       (2) If IAS 33 applies to the entity, for basic and diluted earnings per share;

    c.   The amount of correction at the beginning of the earliest prior period presented; and
    d.   If retrospective restatement is impracticable for a particular prior period, the circumstances that led to the existence of that condition and description of how and from when the error has been corrected.

(Financial statements of the subsequent periods need not repeat these disclosures.)

(IAS 8, Para 49)

7.   A prior period error shall be corrected by retrospective restatement except to the extent that it is impractical to determine either the period-specific effects or the cumulative effect of the error.

(IAS 8, Para 43)

8.   When it is impracticable to determine the period-specific effects of an error on comparative information for one or more prior periods presented, the entity shall restate the opening balances of assets, liabilities and equity for the earliest period for which retrospective restatement is practical.

(IAS 8, Para 44)

9. When it is impracticable to determine the cumulative effect, at the beginning of the current period, of an error on all prior periods, the entity shall restate the comparative information to correct the error prospectively from the earliest date practicable.

(IAS 8, Para 45)

D. Related-Party Disclosures

1. Relationships between parents and subsidiaries shall be disclosed irrespective of whether there have been transactions between those related parties. An entity shall disclose the name of the entity's parent and, if different, the ultimate controlling party. If neither the entity's parent nor the ultimate controlling party produces financial statements available for public use, the name of the next most senior parent that does so shall also be disclosed.

(IAS 24, Para 12)

2. If there have been transactions between related parties, an entity shall disclose the nature of the related-party relationship as well as the information about the transactions and out-standing balances necessary for an understanding of the potential effect of the relationship on the financial statements. These disclosure requirements are in addition to the requirements in IAS 24, paragraph 16 to disclose key management personnel compensation. At a minimum, disclosure shall include

   a. The amount of the transactions;
   b. The amount of outstanding balances; and
      (1) Their terms and conditions, including whether they are secured, and the nature of the consideration to be provided in settlement; and
      (2) Details of any guarantees given or received;
   c. Provisions for doubtful debt related to the amount of outstanding balances; and
   d. The expense recognized during the period in respect of bad or doubtful debts due from related parties.
      The disclosure required by above paragraph shall be made separately for each of the following categories:
      (1) The parent;
      (2) Entities with joint control or significant influence over the entity;
      (3) Subsidiaries;
      (4) Associates;
      (5) Joint ventures in which the entity is a venturer;
      (6) Key management personnel of the entity or its parent; and
      (7) Other related parties.

(IAS 24, Paras 17 & 18)

3. Aggregation of items of similar nature is permitted, unless separate disclosure is needed for an understanding of the effects of the related-party transactions on the financial statements of the reporting entity.

(IAS 24, Para 22)

4. An entity shall disclose key management personnel compensation in total and for each of the following categories:

   a. Short-term employee benefits;
   b. Postemployment benefits;
   c. Other long-term benefits;
   d. Termination benefits; and
   e. Share-based payments

(IAS 24, Para 16)

E. Contingent Liabilities and Contingent Assets

1. An entity should disclose for each class of contingent liability, unless the possibility of any outflow in settlement is remote, a brief description of the nature of the contingent liability. If practicable, an entity should also disclose an estimate of its financial effects, an indication of the uncertainties relating to the amount or timing of the outflow, and the possibility of any reimbursement.

(IAS 37, Para 86)

2. An entity should show a brief description of the nature of the contingent assets at the balance sheet date, where an inflow of economic benefits is probable. Where practical, an estimate of the financial effect should be disclosed.

(IAS 37, Para 89)

3. Where an entity does not disclose any information required by IAS 37, para 86, and IAS 37, para 89, because it is not practical to do so, that fact should be disclosed.

(IAS 37, Para 91)

   a. When provisions and contingent liabilities arise from a single event, the relationship between the provision and the contingent liability should be made clear.

(IAS 37, Para 88)

   b. Disclose contingencies arising from postemployment benefit obligations and termination benefits.

(IAS 19, Paras 125 & 141)

4. In extremely rare circumstances, if disclosures of some or all of the information required by IAS 37, para 89, would prejudice seriously the position of the entity in a dispute with other parties, on the subject matter of the contingent liability or contingent asset, an entity need not disclose such information. Instead, in such cases it should disclose the general nature of the dispute, along with the fact that, and reason why, the information has not been disclosed by the entity.

(IAS 37, Para 92)

F. Events After the Balance Sheet Date

1. When nonadjusting events after the balance sheet date are so significant that nondisclosure would affect the ability of the users of the financial statements to make proper evaluations and decisions, an entity should disclose the nature of the event and an estimate of its financial effect. Such disclosure is required for each significant category of nonadjusting post-balance-sheet event. If such an estimate is not possible, a statement to that effect should be made.

(IAS 10, Para 21)

2. The date when the financial statements were authorized for issue and who gave the authorization should be disclosed by an entity. If the entity's owners or others have the power to amend the financial statements after issuance, the entity should disclose that fact.

(IAS 10, Para 17)

3. If an entity receives information after the balance sheet date that existed at the balance sheet date, the entity should update the disclosures that relate to these conditions, based on the new information received.

(IAS 10, Para 19)

4. In respect of loans classified as current liabilities, if the following events occur between the balance sheet date and the date financial statements are authorized for issue, those events qualify for disclosures of nonadjusting events in accordance with IAS 10:

      a.   Refinancing on a long-term basis;

      b.   Rectification of a breach of a long-term loan agreement; and

      c.   The receipt from the lender of a period of grace to rectify a breach of a long-term loan agreement ending at least twelve months after the balance sheet date.

(IAS 1, Para 67)

5.   Disclose income tax consequences of dividends proposed or declared after the balance sheet date; if payable at a rate different than normal due to being paid out as dividends, disclose nature of income tax effects and estimated amount.

(IAS 12, Paras 81 & 82)

G. Comparative Information

1.   In the case of provisions, comparative information is not required for the reconciliation of carrying amount at the beginning and end of the period.

(IAS 37, Para 84)

2.   Except when a Standard or an Interpretation permits or requires otherwise, comparative information shall be disclosed in respect of the previous period for all amounts reported in the financial statements. Comparative information shall be included for narrative and descriptive information when it is relevant to an understanding of the current period's financial statements.

(IAS 1, Para 36)

3.   When the presentation and classification of items in the financial statements is amended, comparative amounts should be reclassified unless the reclassification is impracticable. When comparative amounts are reclassified, an entity shall disclose

      a.   The nature of the reclassification;

      b.   The amount of each item or class of items that is reclassified; and

      c.   The reason for the reclassification.

(IAS 1, Para 38)

4.   When it is impracticable to reclassify comparative amounts, an entity shall disclose

      a.   The reason for nonreclassifying the amounts; and

      b.   The nature of the adjustment that would have been made if the amounts had been reclassified.

(IAS 1, Para 39)

H. Going Concern

1.   When management is aware in making its assessment of material uncertainties related to events or conditions which may cast significant doubt upon the entity's ability to continue as a going concern, those uncertainties should be disclosed. When the financial statements are not prepared on a going concern basis, that fact should be disclosed, together with the basis on which the financial statements are prepared and the reason why the entity is not considered to be a going concern.

(IAS 1, Para 23)

I. Current/Noncurrent Distinction

1.   An entity shall present current and noncurrent assets, and current and noncurrent liabilities, as separate classifications on the face of the balance sheet except when a presentation based on liquidity provides information that is reliable and more relevant. When that exception applies, all assets and liabilities shall be presented broadly in order of liquidity.

(IAS 1, Para 51)

2. Whether an entity chooses a classified presentation of the balance sheet with current/ noncurrent distinction, or it presents an unclassified balance sheet, it should disclose, for each asset and liability item that combines amounts expected to be recovered or settled both before and after twelve months from the balance sheet date, the amount expected to be recovered or settled after more than twelve months.

(IAS 1, Para 52)

3. For some entities, such as financial institutions, a presentation of assets and liabilities in increasing or decreasing order of liquidity provides information that is reliable and more relevant than a current/noncurrent presentation because the entity does not supply goods or services within a clearly identifiable operating cycle.

(IAS 1, Para 54)

4. If an entity declares dividends to equity shareholders after the balance date, the entity shall not recognize those dividends as a liability at the balance sheet date.

(IAS 10, Para 12)

J. Uncertainties

1. Entities are encouraged to disclose, outside the financial statements, a financial review by management, setting forth information about the principal uncertainties they face. Such a report may provide a review of

   a. The main factors that influence and determine financial performance, including changes in environment in which the entity operates, the entity's response to those changes and their effect;
   b. The entity's sources of funding and its target ratio of liabilities to equity;
   c. The entity's resources not recognized in the statement of financial position in accordance with IFRS.

(IAS 1, Para 13)

K. Judgments and Estimations

1. An entity shall disclose, in the summary of significant accounting policies or other notes, the judgments, apart from those involving estimations, management has made in the process of applying the entity's accounting policies that have the most significant effect on the amounts recognized in the financial statements.

(IAS 1, Para 113)

2. An entity shall disclose in the notes information about the key assumptions concerning the future, and other key sources of estimation uncertainty at the balance sheet date, that have a significant risk of causing a material adjustment to the carrying amounts of assets and liabilities within the next financial year. In respect of those assets and liabilities, the notes shall include details of their nature and their carrying amount as at the balance sheet date.

(IAS 1, Para 116)

L. First-Time Adoption of IFRS

1. IFRS 1 does not exempt a first-time adopter from the presentation and disclosure requirements of other IFRS—thus a first-time adopter should provide all disclosures required by other IFRS.

(IFRS 1, Para 35)

2. An entity's first IFRS financial statements shall include at least one year of comparative information under IFRS.

(IFRS 1, Para 36)

3. If an entity presents historical summaries of selected data for periods before the first period for which it presents full comparative information under IFRS, or if it presents comparative

information under previous GAAP as well as comparative information required by IFRS 1, then it shall

    a.   Label the previous GAAP information prominently as not being prepared under IFRS; and

    b.   Disclose the nature of the main adjustments that would be required to make it comply with IFRS (quantifying those adjustments is not required).

(IFRS 1, Para 37)

4.   A first-time adopter shall present reconciliation (of equity and profit or loss presented under previous GAAP to corresponding amounts presented under IFRS) to explain how the transition from previous GAAP to IFRS affected its reported financial position, financial performance and cash flows.

(IFRS 1, Para 38)

    a.   First-time IFRS financial statements should include reconciliations of equity under prior GAAP and IFRS as of date of transition and end of most recently presented financial statements under prior GAAP.

    b.   First-time IFRS financial statements should include reconciliations of results of operations under prior GAAP and IFRS for the most recently presented financial statements under prior GAAP.

    c.   If any impairment losses were recognized or reversed for first time in preparing opening IFRS balance sheet, the IAS 36 disclosures that would have been required if these would have been recognized in the period beginning with the transition date should be disclosed.

(IFRS 1, Para 39)

5.   If an entity did not present financial statements for previous periods, its first IFRS financial statements shall disclose that fact.

(IFRS 1, Para 43)

6.   If an entity uses fair values in its opening IFRS balance sheet as deemed costs for items of property, plant, and equipment, investment property or intangible assets, then its opening IFRS balance sheet shall disclose, for each line item (in the opening balance sheet)

    a.   The aggregate of those fair values; and

    b.   The aggregate adjustment to the carrying amounts reported under previous GAAP.

(IFRS 1, Para 44)

7.   If a first-time adopter presents interim financial reports under IAS 34 for part of the period covered by its first IFRS financial statements, it shall

    a.   Present reconciliation of equity and profit or loss under previous GAAP at the end of an interim period to corresponding amounts under IFRS at a comparable date (this reconciliation is in addition to the reconciliation required to be presented in 4. above)

(IFRS 1, Para 45)

    b.   If a first-time adopter in its most recent annual financial statements under previous GAAP did not disclose information material to an understanding of the current interim period, its interim financial report shall disclose that information or include a cross-reference to another published document that includes it.

(IFRS 1, Para 46)

M. Share-Based Payment

1.   An entity shall disclose information that enables users of the financial statements to understand the nature and extent of share-based payment arrangements that existed during the period.

(IFRS 2, Para 44)

2.   The entity shall disclose at least the following:

    a.   A description of each type of share-based payment arrangement at any time during the period, including the general terms and condition of each arrangement, such as vesting requirement, the maximum term of options granted, and the method of settlement. An entity having similar type of share-based payment arrangements shall aggregate this information unless separate disclosure is required to satisfy the principle in IFRS 2, paragraph 44.

    b.   The number and weighted-average exercise prices of share options for each of the following group of options:

        (1) Outstanding at the beginning of the period;
        (2) Granted during the period;
        (3) Forfeited during the period;
        (4) Exercised during the period;
        (5) Expired during the period;
        (6) Outstanding at the end of the period; and
        (7) Exercisable at the end of the period.

    c.   If share options exercised during the period, the weighted-average prices at the date of exercise. If share options exercised regularly during the period, than the entity may disclose weighted-average share price during the period.

    d.   For share options outstanding at the end of the period, the range of the prices and weighted-average remaining contractual life. If the range of the prices is wide, the outstanding options shall be divided into ranges that are meaningful for assessing the number and timing of additional shares that may be issued and the cash that may be received upon exercise of those options.

(IFRS 2, Para 45)

3.   An entity shall disclose information that enables users of the financial statements to understand how the fair value of the goods and services received, or the fair value of the equity instruments granted, during the period was determined.

(IFRS 2, Para 46)

4.   If the entity has measured the fair value of goods or services received as consideration for equity instruments of the entity indirectly, by reference to the fair value of the equity instruments granted, to give to the principle in IFRS 2, paragraph 46, the entity shall disclose at least the following:

    a.   For share options granted during the period, the fair value at the measurement date and how that fair value was measured, including

        (1) The option pricing model used and the inputs to that model, including the weighted average share price, exercise price, expected volatility, option life, expected dividend and risk-free interest rate and any other inputs to the model, including the method used and assumptions made to incorporate the effects of expected early exercise;
        (2) How expected volatility was determined, including an explanation of the extent to which expected volatility was based on historical volatility; and
        (3) Whether and how any other features of the option grant were incorporated into the measurement of fair value, such as market condition.

    b.   For other equity instruments granted during the period, the number and the weighted-average fair value of those equity instruments at the measurement, and information on how that fair value was measured, including

        (1) If fair value was not measured on the basis of an observable market price, how it was determined;
        (2) Whether and how expected dividends were incorporated into the measurement of fair value; and

(3) Whether and how any other features of the equity instruments granted were incorporated into the measurement of fair value.

   c.   For share-based payment arrangements that were modified during the period

      (1) An explanation of those modifications;

      (2) The incremental fair value granted (as a result of those modifications); and

      (3) Information on how the incremental fair value granted was measured, consistently with the requirements set out in a. and b. above, where applicable.

(IFRS 2, Para 47)

5. If the entity has directly measured the fair value of the goods and services received during the period, the entity shall disclose how that fair value was determined.

(IFRS 2, Para 48)

   a.   If the assumption that fair value of goods or services exchanged for shares, other than employee services, can be measured has been rebutted, this must be stated together with an explanation.

(IFRS 2, Para 49)

6. An entity shall disclose information that enables users of the financial statements to understand the effect of share-based payment transaction on the entity's profit or loss of the period and on its financial position.

(IFRS 2, Para 50)

7. To give effect to IFRS 2, paragraph 50, the entity shall disclose at least the following:

   a.   The total expenses recognized for the period arising from share-based payment transactions in which goods or services received did not qualify for recognition as assets and hence were recognized immediately as an expense, including separate disclosure of that portion of the total expense that arises from transactions accounted for as equity-settled share-based payment transaction;

   b.   For liabilities arising from share-based payment transaction

      (1) The total carrying amount at end of the period; and

      (2) The total intrinsic value at the end of the period of liabilities for which the counterparty's right to cash or other assets had vested by the end of the period.

(IFRS 2, Para 51)

8. If the information required to be disclosed by this IFRS does not satisfy the principles in IFRS 2, paragraphs 44, 46, and 50, the entity shall disclose such additional information as is necessary to satisfy them.

(IFRS 2, Para 52)

N. **Insurance Contracts**

1. An insurer shall disclose information that identifies and explains the amount in its financial statements arising from insurance contracts.

(IFRS 4, Para 36)

2. To comply with IFRS 4, paragraph 36, an insurer shall disclose

   a.   Its accounting policies for insurance contracts and related assets and liabilities, income and expense;

   b.   The recognized assets, liabilities, income and expense (and, if it presents its cash flow statement using the direct method, cash flows) arising from insurance contracts. Furthermore, if the insurer is a cedant, it shall disclose

      (1) Gains and losses recognized in profit or loss on buying reinsurance;

    (2) If the cedant differs and amortizes gains and losses arising on buying reinsurance, the amortization for the period and the amounts remaining unamortized at the beginning and at the end of the period.

  c. The process used to determine the assumptions that have the greatest effect on the measurement of the recognized amounts described in b. When practicable, an insurer shall also give quantified disclosures of those assumptions.

  d. The effect of changes in assumption used to measure insurance assets and insurance liabilities, showing separately the effect of each change that has a material effect on the financial statements.

  e. Reconciliation of changes in insurance liabilities, reinsurance assets and if any, related deferred acquisition costs.

(IFRS 4, Para 37)

3. An insurer shall give the information to understand the amount, timing and uncertainty of future cash flows from insurance contracts.

(IFRS 4, Para 38)

4. To comply with IFRS 4, paragraph 38, an insurer shall disclose

  a. Its objectives in managing risks arising from insurance contracts and its policies for mitigating those risks.

  b. Those terms and conditions of insurance contracts that have a material effect on the amount, timing, and uncertainty of the insurer's future cash flows.

  c. Information about insurance risk (both before and after risk mitigation by reinsurance), including information about

    (1) The sensitivity of profit or loss and equity to changes in variables that have material effect on them;

    (2) Concentrations of insurance risk;

    (3) Actual claims compared with previous estimates (i.e., claim development). The disclosure about claims development shall go back to the period when the earliest material claim arose for which there is still uncertainty about the amount and timing of the claims payment, but need not go back more than ten years. An insurer need not disclose this information for claims for which uncertainty about the amount and timing of claims payments is typically resolved within one year.

  d. The information about interest rate risk and credit risk that IAS 32 would require if the insurance contracts were within the scope of IAS 32.

  e. Information about exposures to interest rate risk or market risk under embedded derivatives contained in a host insurance contract if the insurer is not required to, and does not, measure the embedded derivatives at fair value.

(IFRS 4, Para 39)

5. An entity need not apply the disclosure requirements in this IFRS to comparative information that relates to the annual period beginning before January 1, 2005, except for the disclosure required by IFRS 4, paragraph 37(a) and (b) about accounting policies, and recognized assets, liabilities, income and expense (and cash flow if direct method is used).

(IFRS 4, Para 42)

6. If it is impracticable to apply a particular requirement to comparative information that relates to annual periods beginning January 1, 2005, an entity shall disclose that fact. Applying the liability adequacy test to such comparative information might sometimes be impracticable, but it is highly unlikely to be impracticable to apply other requirements to such comparative information.

(IFRS 4, Para 43)

7. When an entity first applies this IFRS and if it is impracticable to prepare information about claim development that occurred before the beginning of the earliest period for which an entity presents full comparative information that complies with this IFRS, the entity shall disclose this fact.

(IFRS 4, Para 44)

STATEMENT OF FINANCIAL POSITION

A. Minimum Disclosures on the Face of the Statement of Financial Position

1. The face of the balance sheet should include, as a minimum, the following categories:

    a. Property, plant, and equipment;
    b. Investment property;
    c. Intangible assets;
    d. Financial assets (excluding amounts shown under e., h., and i.);
    e. Investments accounted for using the equity method;
    f. Biological assets;
    g. Inventories;
    h. Trade and other receivables;
    i. Cash and cash equivalents;
    j. Trade and other payables;
    k. Provisions;
    l. Financial liabilities (excluding amounts shown under j.);
    m. Liabilities and assets for current tax, as defined in IAS 12, *Income Taxes;*
    n. Deferred tax liabilities and deferred tax assets, as defined in IAS 12;
    o. Minority interest, and presented within equity
    p. Issued capital and reserves attributable to owners of the parent.

(IAS 1, Para 68)

B. Additional Line Items on the Face of the Balance Sheet

1. Additional line items, headings and subtotals should be presented on the face of the balance sheet when an IFRS requires it, or when such presentation is necessary to present fairly the entity's financial position.

(IAS 1, Para 69)

C. Further Subclassifications of Line Items Presented

1. An entity shall disclose either on the face of the balance sheet or in the notes further subclassifications of the line items presented, classified in a manner appropriate to the entity's operations. The detail provided in subclassifications depends on the requirement of IFRS and on the size, nature, and function of the amounts involved.

(IAS 1, Para 75)

D. Inventories

1. The accounting policies and the cost formula used in inventory valuation.

(IAS 2, Para 36[a])

2. Total carrying amount and the breakdown of the carrying amount by appropriate subclassifications, such as merchandise, production supplies, work in progress, and finished goods.

(IAS 2, Paras 36[b] & 37)

3. Carrying amount of inventories at fair value less cost to sell.

(IAS 2, Para 36[c])

4. Carrying amount of inventories pledged as securities.

(IAS 2, Para 36[h])

5. The amount of any reversal of any write-down that is recognized as a reduction in the amount of inventories recognized as expense in the period in accordance with paragraph 34.

(IAS 2, Para 36 [f])

6. The financial statement shall disclose

   a. The amount of inventories recognized as an expense during the period.

(IAS 2, Para 36(d))

7. When inventories are sold, the carrying amount of those inventories shall be recognized as an expense in the period in which the related revenue is recognized. The amount of any write-down of inventories to net realizable value and all losses of inventories shall be recognized as an expense in the period the write-down or loss occurs. The amount of any reversal of any write-down of inventories arising from an increase in net realizable value shall be recognized as a reduction in the amount of inventories recognized as an expense in the period in which the reversal occurs.

(IAS 2, Para 34)

8. The financial statement shall disclose

   a. The amount of any write-down of inventories recognized as an expense in the period in accordance with paragraph 34;
   b. The circumstances or events that led to the reversal of a write-down of inventories in accordance with paragraph 34.

(IAS 2, Paras 36[e] & [g])

E. Property, Plant, and Equipment (PP&E)

1. In respect of each class (i.e., groupings of assets of a similar nature and use) of PP&E, the following disclosures are required:

   a. Measurement basis/bases used for the determination of the gross carrying amount; if more than one basis has been employed, then also the gross carrying amount determined in accordance with that basis in each category;
   b. The depreciation method(s) used;
   c. Either the useful lives or the depreciation rates used;
   d. The gross carrying amount and the accumulated depreciation at the beginning and the end of the period;
   e. A reconciliation of the carrying amount at the beginning and the end of the period disclosing

      (1) Additions;
      (2) Assets classified as held-for-sale or included in a disposal group classified as held-for-sale in accordance with IFRS 5, *Noncurrent Assets Held-for-Sale and Discontinued Operations,* and other disposals;
      (3) Acquisitions by means of business combinations;
      (4) Increases/decreases resulting from revaluations and from impairment losses recognized or reversed directly in equity (if any);
      (5) Impairment losses recognized in profit or loss (if any);
      (6) Impairment losses reversed in profit or loss (if any);
      (7) Depreciation;
      (8) Net exchange differences arising from translation of financial statements of a foreign entity (in accordance with IAS 21); and
      (9) Other changes, if any.

(IAS 16, Para 73)

2. Additional disclosures to be made include the following:

   a. The existence and amount of restrictions on title, and PP&E pledged as security for liabilities;

   b. If it is not disclosed separately on the face of the income statement, the amount of compensation from third parties for items of P&PE that were impaired, lost or given up that is included in profit or loss;

   c. The amount of expenditures in respect of PP&E in the course of construction; and

   d. The amount of outstanding commitments for acquisition of PP&E.

   (IAS 16, Para 74)

3. In case items of PP&E are stated at revalued amounts, disclose the following information:

   a. The effective date of revaluation;

   b. Whether an independent party prepared the valuation;

   c. The methods and significant assumptions applied in estimating the item's fair value;

   d. The extent to which the item's fair value was determined directly by reference to observable prices in an active market or in a recent market transaction at arm's length or were estimated using other valuation techniques;

   e. The carrying amount of each class of PP&E that would have been included in the financial statements had the assets been carried under the benchmark treatment; and

   f. The revaluation surplus, including the movement for the period in that account and disclosure of any restrictions on the distribution of the balance in the revaluation surplus account to shareholders.

   (IAS 16, Para 77)

4. An entity should disclose information on impaired property, plant, and equipment under IAS 36 in addition to information required under IAS 16, para 73[e] (iv to vi)

   (IAS 16, Para 78)

5. Other recommended disclosures

   a. The carrying amount of temporarily idle PP&E;

   b. The gross carrying amount of fully depreciated PP&E still in use;

   c. The carrying amount of PP&E retired from active use and not classified as held-for-sale; and

   d. In cases where items of PP&E are carried at cost model the fair value of PP&E if it is materially different from the carrying amount.

   (IAS 16, Para 79)

F. Intangible Assets

1. In the case of each class of intangible assets, distinguishing between internally generated intangible assets and other intangible assets, the financial statements should disclose

   a. The useful lives of the amortization rates used;

   b. The amortization methods used;

   c. The gross carrying amount and the accumulated amortization (aggregated with accumulated impairment) at the beginning and at the end;

   d. The line item(s) of the income statement in which the amortization of intangible assets is included;

   e. A reconciliation of the carrying amount at the beginning and the end of the period showing:

      (1) Additions, indicating separately those from internal development, those acquired separately, and through business combinations;

      (2) Assets classified as held-for-sale or included in a disposal group classified as held-for-sale in accordance with IFRS 5, and other disposals;

(3) Increases or decreases resulting from revaluations and from impairment losses recognized or reversed directly in equity (if any);

(4) Impairment losses recognized in profit or loss (if any);

(5) Impairment losses reversed in profit or loss (if any);

(6) Amortization recognized;

(7) Net exchange differences arising on translation of financial statements of a foreign entity; and

(8) Other changes in carrying amount.

(IAS 38, Para 118)

2. Additional disclosures with respect to intangibles are the following:

  a. An intangible asset assessed as having an indefinite useful life, the carrying amount of that asset and the reasons supporting the assessment of an indefinite useful life. In giving these reasons, the entity shall describe the factor(s) that play a significant role in determining that the asset has an indefinite useful life.

  b. In the case of an individual intangible asset that is material to the financial statements as a whole, a description, the carrying amount, and the remaining amortization period;

  c. In the case of intangible assets acquired by way of a government grant and initially recognized at fair value: the fair value initially recognized for these assets, their carrying amounts, and whether they are carried under the benchmark treatment or the allowed alternative treatment for subsequent measurements;

  d. The existence and the carrying amount of intangible assets pledged as security for liabilities; and

  e. The amount of commitments for the acquisition of intangible assets.

(IAS 38, Para 122)

3. In the case of intangible assets carried under the allowed alternative method (i.e., at revalued amounts), the following disclosures are prescribed:

  a. By class of intangible assets: the effective date of the revaluation, the carrying amount of revalued intangible assets carried under the benchmark treatment (i.e., at cost less accumulated amortization); and

  b. The quantum of revaluation surplus that relates to intangible assets at the beginning and the end of the period, indicating the changes during the period and any restrictions on the distributions of the balance to shareholders.

  c. The methods and significant assumptions applied in estimating the assets' fair values.

(IAS 38, Para 124)

4. The financial statements should disclose the aggregate amount of research and development expenditure recognized as an expense during the period.

(IAS 38, Para 126)

5. Provide a reconciliation of goodwill carrying value, showing gross carrying amount and any impairment loss, as of beginning of period; any additions; any adjustments arising from recognition of deferred taxes subsequent to acquisition date; disposals; impairment losses during period; net exchange differences during period; other changes in the carrying amount; and gross amount and accumulated impairment loss as of end of period.

(IFRS 3, Para 75)

G. Other Long-Term Assets (Consolidated Financial Statement and Investment in Subsidiaries)

1. The following items should be disclosed separately:

  a. The reasons why the ownership, directly or indirectly through subsidiaries, of more than one-half of the voting, or potential voting power of an investee, does not constitute control.

(IAS 27, Para 40[d])

2. A parent need not present consolidated financial statements if and only if

   a. The parent is itself a wholly owned subsidiary, or is a partially owned subsidiary of another entity and its other owners, including those not otherwise entitled to vote, have been informed about, and do not object to, the parent not presenting consolidated financial statement;

   b. The parent's debt or equity instrument is not traded in a public market (a domestic or foreign exchange or an over the counter market, including local and regional markets);

   c. The parent did not file, nor is it in the process of filing, its financial statements with a securities commission or other regulatory organization for purpose of issuing any class of instruments in a public market; and

   d. The ultimate or any intermediate parent of the parent produces consolidated financial statement available for public use that comply with IFRS.

   (IAS 27, Para 10)

3. Consolidated financial statements are to be prepared using uniform accounting policies for like transactions and other events in similar circumstances.

   (IAS 27, Para 28)

4. The following disclosures shall be made in consolidated financial statements:

   a. The nature of the relationship between the parent and the subsidiary, when the parent does not own, directly or indirectly through subsidiaries, more than one-half of the voting power;

   b. The reasons why the ownership, of more than half of the voting power of an investee does not constitute control;

   c. The reporting date of the financial statements of a subsidiary when such financial statements are used to prepare consolidated financial statements and are of a reporting date of for a period that is different from that of the parent, and the reason for using the different reporting date or period.

   d. The nature and extent of any significant restrictions (e.g., resulting from borrowing arrangements or regulatory requirements) on the ability of subsidiaries to transfer funds to the parent in the form of cash dividends or to repay loans or advances.

   (IAS 27, Para 40)

5. When separate financial statements are prepared for a parent that, in accordance with IAS 27, paragraph 10, elects not to prepare consolidated financial statements, those separate financial statements shall disclose

   a. The fact that the financial statements are separate financial statements; that the exemption from consolidation has been used; the name and country of incorporation or residence of the entity whose consolidated financial statements that comply with International Financial Reporting Standards have been produced for public use; and the address where those consolidated financial statements are obtainable;

   b. A list of significant investments in subsidiaries; jointly controlled entities and associates, including the name, country or incorporation or residence, proportion of ownership interest, and, if different, proportion of voting power held; and

   c. A description of the method used to account for the investments listed under b.

   (IAS 27, Para 41)

6. When a parent (other than a parent covered by paragraph 41), venturer with an interest in a jointly controlled entity or an investor in an associate prepares separate financial statements, those separate financial statements shall disclose

   a. The fact that the statements are separate financial statements and the reasons why those statements are prepared if not required by law;

b. A list of significant investments in subsidiaries, jointly controlled entities and associates, including the name, country of incorporation or residence, proportion of ownership interest and, if different, proportion of voting power held;

c. A description of a method used to account for the investments listed under b.; and shall identify the financial statements prepared in accordance with IAS 27, paragraph 9, IAS 28 and IAS 31, to which they relate.

(IAS 27, Para 42)

H. Investments in Associates

1. Investments in associates accounted for using the equity method should be classified as noncurrent assets and separately set forth in the balance sheet. The investor's share of profit or losses of such investments should be disclosed as separate item in the income statement. The carrying amount of those investments and the investor's share of any discontinued operations of such associates should be disclosed.

(IAS 28, Para 38)

2. The fact that the investor's share of investee's carrying value includes amount analogous to goodwill, and any accumulated impairment, should be stated.

(IAS 28, Para 23)

3. The following disclosures shall be made:

a. The fair value of investments in associates for which there are published price quotations;

b. Summarized financial information of associates, including the aggregated amounts of assets, liabilities, revenues, and profit or loss;

c. The reasons why the presumption that an investor does not have significant influence is overcome if the investor holds, directly or indirectly though subsidiaries, less than 20% of the voting or potential voting power of the investee but concludes that it has significant influence;

d. The reasons why the presumption that an investor has significant influence is overcome if the investor holds, directly or indirectly through subsidiaries, 20% or more of the voting or potential voting power of the investee but concludes that it does not have significant influence;

e. The reporting date of the financial statements of an associate, when such financial statements are used in applying the equity method and are as of a reporting date or for a period that is different from that of the investor, and the reason for using different reporting date or different period;

f. The nature and extent of any significant restrictions on the ability of associates to transfer funds to the investor in the form of cash dividends, or repayments of loans or advances;

g. The unrecognized share of losses of an associate, both for the period and cumulatively, if an investor has discontinued recognition of its share of losses of an associate;

h. The fact that an associate is not accounted for using the equity method;

i. Summarized financial information of associates, either individually or in groups, that are not accounted for using the equity method, including the amounts of total assets, total liabilities, revenues and profit or loss.

(IAS 28, Para 37)

4. The investor's share of changes recognized directly in the associate's equity shall be recognized directly by the investor and disclosed in the statement of changes in equity.

(IAS 28, Para 39)

5. In accordance with 37, *Provisions, Contingent Liabilities, and Contingent Assets*, the investor shall disclose

a. Its share of the contingent liabilities of an associate incurred jointly with other investors; and

    b.   Those contingent liabilities that arise because that investor is severally liable for all or part of the liabilities of the associate.

(IAS 28, Para 40)

I. Investments in Joint Ventures

1.   The venturer is to disclose a listing and description of interests in significant joint ventures and proportions held in each, and aggregate current assets, noncurrent assets, current liabilities, noncurrent liabilities, income and expense related to interests in joint ventures.

(IAS 31, Para 56)

2.   Separately from other contingent liabilities, disclose contingent liabilities arising from interest in joint ventures and share in each incurred jointly with other venturers; shares in contingent liabilities of the joint ventures themselves for which there are contingent obligations; and contingent liabilities arising in connection with contingent liability for obligations of the other venturers.

(IAS 31, Para 54)

3.   Separately from other commitments, disclose capital commitments arising in connection with joint obligations with other venturers, and share of capital commitments of the joint ventures themselves.

(IAS 31, Para 55)

4.   The venturer shall disclose the method used to recognize its interests in jointly controlled entities.

(IAS 31, Para 57)

J. Investment Property

1.   In certain cases investment property will be property that is owned by the reporting entity and leased to others under operating-type lease arrangements. The disclosure requirement set forth in IAS 17 continue unaltered by IAS 40. (In addition IAS 40 stipulates a number of new disclosure requirements set out below.)

(IAS 40, Para 74)

2.   An entity shall disclose

    a.   Whether it applies the fair value model or cost model.

    b.   If it applies fair value model, whether and in what circumstances the property held under operating leases are classified and accounted for as investment property.

    c.   When classification is difficult, an entity that holds an investment property will need to disclose the criteria used to distinguish investment property from owner-occupied property and from property held for sale in the ordinary course of business.

    d.   The method and any significant assumptions that were used in ascertaining the fair values of the investment properties are to be disclosed as well. Such disclosure should also include a statement about whether the determination of fair value was supported by market evidence or it relied heavily on other factors (which the entity needs to disclose as well) due to the nature of the property and the absence of comparable market data;

    e.   If investment property has been revalued by an independent valuer having recognized and relevant qualifications and who has recent experience with properties having similar characteristics of location and type, the extent to which the fair value of investment property is based on valuation by such an independent valuer, if there is no such valuation, the fact should be disclosed as well;

    f.   The amounts recognized in profit or loss for

        (1)   Rental income from investment property;

        (2)   Direct operating expenses including repairs and maintenance arising from investment property that generated rental income during the period;

(3) Direct operating expenses including repairs and maintenance arising from investment property that did not generate rental income during the period; and

(4) The cumulative change in fair value recognized in profit or loss on a sale of investment property from a pool of assets in which the cost model is used.

g. The existence and the amount of any restrictions which may potentially affect the reliability of investment property or the remittance of income and proceeds from disposal to be received; and

h. Material contractual obligations to purchase or build investment property or for repairs, maintenance, or improvements thereto.

(IAS 40, Para 75)

3. Disclosure applicable to investment property measured using the fair value model

a. In addition to the disclosures outlined in IAS 40, para 75, the standard requires that an entity that uses the fair value model should also disclose a reconciliation to be presented of the carrying amount of investment property, from business combinations, and those derived from capitalized expenditures. It will also identify assets classified as held for sale or included in a disposal group classified as held-for-sale in accordance with IFRS 5 and other disposals, gains, or losses from fair value adjustment, the net exchange differences, if any, arising from the translation of the financial statements of a foreign entity, transfers to and from inventories and owner-occupied properties and any other movements. *(It will not be required that comparative reconciliation data be presented for prior periods.)*

b. Under exceptional circumstances, due to lack of reliable fair value, when an entity measures investment property using the cost model under IAS 16, the above reconciliation should disclose amounts separately for that investment property from amounts relating to other investment property. In addition, an entity should also disclose

(1) A reconciliation—relating to that investment property separately—of the carrying amount at the beginning and end of the period.

(2) A description of such a property,

(3) An explanation of why fair value cannot be reliably measured,

(4) If possible, the range of estimates within which fair value is highly likely to lie, and

(5) On disposal of such an investment property, the fact that the entity has disposed of investment property not carried at fair value along with its carrying amount at the time of disposal and the amount of gain or loss recognized.

(IAS 40, Paras 76 & 78)

4. Disclosures applicable to investment property measured using the cost model

a. In addition to the disclosure requirements outlined in IAS 40, para 75, the standard requires that an entity that applies the cost model should also disclose: the depreciation methods used, the useful lives or the depreciation rates used, and the gross carrying amount and the accumulated depreciation (aggregated with accumulated impairment losses) at the beginning and end of the period. It should also disclose a reconciliation of the carrying amount of investment property at the beginning and the end of the period showing the following details: additions resulting from acquisitions, those resulting from business combinations, and those deriving from capitalized expenditures subsequent to the property's initial recognition. It should also disclose disposals, depreciation, impairment losses recognized and reversed, the net exchange differences, if any, arising from the translation of the financial statements of a foreign entity, transfers to and from inventories and owner-occupied properties, and any other movements.

b. The fair value of investment property carried under the cost model should also be disclosed. In exceptional cases, when the fair value of the investment property cannot be reliably estimated, the entity should also disclose

(1) A description of such property,

(2) An explanation of why fair value cannot be reliably measured, and

(3) If possible, the range of estimates within which fair value is highly likely to lie.

(IAS 40, Para 79)

K. Financial Instruments

1. When IFRS 7 requires disclosures by class of instrument, the entity shall group financial instruments into classes that are appropriate to the nature of the information disclosed and that take into account the characteristics of those financial instruments. Sufficient information must be provided to permit reconciliation to the line items presented in the balance sheet.

(IFRS 7, Para 6)

2. An entity shall disclose information that enables users of its financial statements to evaluate the significance of financial instruments for its financial position and performance.

(IFRS 7, Para 7)

3. The carrying amounts of each of the following categories, as defined in IAS 39, is to be disclosed either on the face of the balance sheet or in the notes:

   a. Financial assets reported at fair value through profit or loss, showing separately

      (1) Those designated as such upon initial recognition; and
      (2) Those classified as held-for-trading in accordance with IAS 39.

   b. Held-to-maturity investments.
   c. Loans and receivables.
   d. Available-for-sale financial assets.
   e. Financial liabilities reported at fair value through the income statement, showing separately

      (1) Those designated for such accounting upon acquisition under the fair value option; and
      (2) Those classified as held for trading purposes.

   f. Financial liabilities measured at amortized cost.

(IFRS 7, Para 8)

4. For financial assets or liabilities carried at fair value and identified as a loan or receivable (or groups of loans or receivables)

   a. The maximum exposure to credit risk of the loan or receivable (or group of loans or receivables) at the reporting date.
   b. The amount by which any related credit derivatives or similar instruments mitigate that maximum exposure to credit risk.
   c. The amount of change, during the period and cumulatively, in the fair value of the loan or receivable (or group of loans or receivables) that is attributable to changes in the credit risk of the financial asset determined either

      (1) As the amount of change in its fair value that is not attributable to changes in market conditions that give rise to market risk, or
      (2) Using an alternative method the entity believes more faithfully represents the amount of change in its fair value that is attributable to changes in the credit risk of the asset.

   d. The amount of the change in the fair value of any related credit derivatives or similar instruments that has occurred during the period and cumulatively since the loan or receivable was designated at fair value to be reported through profit or loss.

(IFRS 7, Para 9)

5. If the entity has designated a financial liability to be reported at fair value through profit or loss in accordance with paragraph 9 of IAS 39, it is to disclose

a. The amount of change, during the reporting period and cumulatively, in the fair value of the financial liability that is attributable to changes in the credit risk of that liability determined either

   (1) As the amount of change in its fair value that is not attributable to changes in market conditions that give rise to market risk; or

   (2) Using an alternative method the entity believes more faithfully represents that amount of change in its fair value that is attributable to changes in the credit risk of the liability.

b. The difference between the financial liability's carrying amount and the amount the entity would be contractually required to pay at maturity to the holder of the obligation.

(IFRS 7, Para 10)

6. Disclosure is to be made of

   a. The methods used to determine the amount of change that is attributable to changes in credit risk in compliance with the requirements of IFRS 7, paragraphs 9(c) and 10(a), and

   b. If it is believed that the disclosure given to comply with the requirements of IFRS 7 paragraphs 9(c) or 10(a) does not faithfully represent the change in the fair value of the financial asset or financial liability attributable to changes in its credit risk, the reasons for reaching this conclusion and the factors believed to be relevant.

(IFRS 7, Para 11)

7. Disclosure is to be made of reclassifications of financial assets measured at cost or amortized cost; or at fair value.

(IFRS 7, Para 12)

8. Disclosure is to be made, for each class of financial asset that has been transferred in a way that does not permit derecognition (or complete derecognition), of

   a. The nature of the assets not derecognized.
   b. The nature of the risks and rewards of ownership to which the entity remains exposed.
   c. When the entity continues to recognize all of the assets, the carrying amounts of the assets and of the associated liabilities.
   d. When the entity continues to recognize the assets to the extent of its continuing involvement, the total carrying amount of the original assets, the amount of the assets that the entity continues to recognize, and the carrying amount of the associated liabilities.

(IFRS 7, Para 13)

9. When collateral has been put up by the entity, disclosure is required of

   a. The carrying amount of financial assets the entity has pledged as collateral for either liabilities or contingent liabilities, including amounts that have been reclassified in the balance sheet separately from other assets because the transferee has the right to sell or repledge, in accordance with IAS 39, paragraph 37(a).
   b. The terms and conditions relating to the pledge.

(IFRS 7, Para 14)

10. When collateral has been received by the entity, disclosure is required of

    a. The fair value of collateral held.
    b. The fair value of any such collateral sold or repledged, and whether the entity has an obligation to return it.
    c. The terms and conditions associated with the entity's use of the collateral.

(IFRS 7, Para 15)

11. When financial assets are impaired by credit losses and the entity records the impairment in a separate account (e.g., an allowance account used to record individual impairments or a

similar account used to record a collective impairment of assets) rather than directly reducing the carrying amount of the asset, it shall disclose a reconciliation of changes in that account during the period for each class of financial assets.

(IFRS 7, Para 16)

12. If the reporting entity has issued a compound financial instrument (i.e., an instrument that contains both a liability and an equity component), *and* the instrument has multiple embedded derivatives whose values are interdependent (e.g., a callable convertible debt instrument), it is to disclose the existence of those features.

(IFRS 7, Para 17)

13. For loans payable recognized at the reporting date, the entity is to disclose

    a. Details of any defaults occurring during the period as to principal, interest, sinking fund, or redemption terms of those loans payable.
    b. The carrying amount of the loans payable in default at the reporting date.
    c. Whether the default was remedied, or whether the terms of the loans payable were renegotiated, before the financial statements were authorized for issuance.

(IFRS 7, Para 18)

14. If, during the period, there were breaches of loan agreement terms other than those described in IFRS 7, paragraph 18, disclosure is to be made of the same information as required by paragraph 18, if those breaches permitted the lender to demand accelerated repayment (unless the breaches were remedied, or the terms of the loan were renegotiated, on or before the reporting date).

(IFRS 7, Para 18)

15. For each class of financial assets and financial liabilities, the entity is to disclose the fair value of that class of assets and liabilities in a way that permits it to be compared with its carrying amount. It is to disclose

    a. The methods and, when a valuation technique is used, the assumptions applied in determining fair values of each class of financial assets or financial liabilities.
    b. Whether fair values have been determined, in whole or in part, directly by reference to published price quotations in an active market or are estimated using a valuation technique.
    c. Whether the fair values recognized or disclosed in the financial statements have been determined in whole or in part using a valuation technique based on assumptions that are not supported by prices from observable current market transactions in the same instrument and not based on available observable market data. Also, in such circumstances, disclose whether changing one or more of the assumptions to reasonably possible alternative assumptions would change fair value significantly, and disclose the effect of those changes.
    d. If the immediately preceding condition applies, the total amount of the change in fair value estimated using such a valuation technique that was recognized in profit or loss during the period.

(IFRS 7, Para 27)

16. If a difference exists between the fair value at initial recognition and the amount that would be determined at that date using a valuation technique, disclosure must be made, by class of financial instrument, of

    a. The entity's accounting policy for recognizing that difference in profit or loss to reflect a change in factors (including time) that market participants would consider in setting a price.
    b. The aggregate difference yet to be recognized in profit or loss at the beginning and end of the period, together with a reconciliation of changes in the balance of this difference.

(IFRS 7, Para 28)

17. For an investment in equity instruments that do not have a quoted market price in an active market, or derivatives linked to such equity instruments, that is measured at cost because its fair value cannot be measured reliably, or for a contract continuing a discretionary participation feature, if the fair value of that feature cannot be measured reliably, the entity is to disclose information to help users of the financial statements make their own judgments about the extent of possible differences between the carrying amount of those financial assets or financial liabilities and their fair value, including

    a. The fact that fair value information has not been disclosed for these instruments because their fair value cannot be measured reliably.
    b. A description of the financial instruments, their carrying amount, and an explanation of why fair value cannot be measured reliably.
    c. Information about the market for the instruments.
    d. Information about whether and how the entity intends to dispose of the financial instruments.
    e. If financial instruments whose fair value previously could not be reliably measured are derecognized, that fact, their carrying amount at the time of derecognition, and the amount of gain or loss recognized.

    (IFRS 7, Para 30)

18. The reporting entity is to disclose qualitative and quantitative information that enables users of its financial statements to evaluate the nature and extent of risks arising from financial instruments to which the entity is exposed at the reporting date.

    (IFRS 7, Para 31)

19. For each type of risk arising from financial instruments, the entity shall disclose the following qualitative matters:

    a. The exposures to that risk and how they arise.
    b. The entity's objectives, policies and processes for managing the risk and the methods used to measure the risk.
    c. Any changes in these items from what was reported in the previous period.

    (IFRS 7, Para 33)

20. For each type of risk arising from financial instruments, the entity shall disclose the following quantitative matters:

    a. Summary quantitative data about the reporting entity's exposure to that risk at the reporting date. This disclosure is to be based on the information provided internally to key management personnel of the entity (e.g., the entity's board of directors or chief executive officer).
    b. Additional disclosures (see below), to the extent not provided in accordance with the preceding paragraph, unless the risk is not material.
    c. Concentrations of risk if not apparent from the preceding disclosures, which should include

        (1) A description of how management determines concentrations.
        (2) A description of the shared characteristics that identifies each concentration (e.g., counterparty, geographical area, currency or market).
        (3) The amount of the risk exposure associated with all financial instruments sharing that characteristic.

    (IFRS 7, Para 34)

21. If the quantitative data disclosed as at the reporting date are unrepresentative of an entity's exposure to risk during the period, an entity shall provide further information that is representative.

    (IFRS 7, Para 35)

22. Regarding *credit risk*, the entity is to disclose, by class of financial instrument, the following:

    a. The amount that best represents its maximum exposure to credit risk at the reporting date, without taking account of collateral held or other credit enhancements.
    b. Regarding the preceding amount, a description of collateral held as security and other credit enhancements.
    c. Information about the credit quality of financial assets that are neither past due nor impaired.
    d. The carrying amount of financial assets that would otherwise be past due or impaired, but whose terms have been renegotiated.

    (IFRS 7, Para 36)

23. By class of financial asset, the following must be disclosed:

    a. An analysis of the age of financial assets that are past due as of the reporting date, but which are not impaired.
    b. An analysis of financial assets that are individually determined to be impaired as of the reporting date, including the factors that were considered in determining the condition of impairment.
    c. For the amounts disclosed in the preceding items, a description of collateral held by the entity as security and other credit enhancements and, unless impracticable, an estimate of the fair value of such items.

    (IFRS 7, Para 37)

24. When the reporting entity obtains financial or nonfinancial assets during the period by taking possession of collateral it holds as security, or by calling on other credit enhancements (e.g., guarantees), and such assets meet the recognition criteria of IFRS, the entity is to disclose

    a. The nature and carrying amount of the assets obtained.
    b. When the assets are not readily convertible into cash, the entity's policies for disposing of such assets, or for using them in its operations.

    (IFRS 7, Para 38)

25. Regarding *liquidity risk*, the entity is to disclose, by class of financial instrument, the following:

    a. A maturity analysis for financial liabilities that shows the remaining contractual maturities.
    b. A description of how it manages the liquidity risk inherent in the foregoing item.

    (IFRS 7, Para 39)

26. Regarding *market (interest rate)* risk, the entity is to disclose, by class of financial instrument, the following (unless a sensitivity analysis is presented, as discussed below, that reports on interdependencies among risk variables):

    a. A sensitivity analysis for *each* type of market risk to which the entity is exposed at the reporting date, showing how profit or loss and equity would have been affected by changes in the relevant risk variable that were reasonably possible at that date.
    b. The methods and assumptions used in preparing the sensitivity analysis.
    c. Changes from the previous period in the methods and assumptions used, and the reasons for such changes.

    (IFRS 7, Para 40)

27. A sensitivity analysis, such as value-at-risk, that reflects interdependencies between risk variables (e.g., between interest rates and exchange rates) if used to manage financial risks, may be used in place of the analysis specified in item 26, above. In such instance, disclosure must be made of

    a. An explanation of the method used in preparing the sensitivity analysis, and of the main parameters and assumptions underlying the data provided.

b.　An explanation of the objective of the method used and of limitations that may result in the information not fully reflecting the fair value of the assets and liabilities involved.

(IFRS 7, Para 41)

28.　When the sensitivity analyses employed (either approaches noted in the foregoing) are unrepresentative of a risk inherent in a financial instrument, disclosure must be made of that fact and the reason the sensitivity analyses are deemed to be unrepresentative.

(IFRS 7, Para 42)

L.　Provisions

1.　For each class of provision, for the current year only (comparative presentation not required)

a.　The carrying amount at the beginning and end of the period;
b.　Exchange differences from translation of foreign entities' financial statements;
c.　Additional provisions made during the current period, including increases to existing provisions;
d.　Amounts utilized (i.e., incurred and charged against the provision) during the period;
e.　Unused amounts reversed during the period; and
f.　The increase during the period in the discounted amount resulting from the passage of time and the effect of any change in discount rate.

(IAS 37, Para 84)

2.　For each class of provision an entity should disclose the following:

a.　A brief description of the nature of the obligation and the expected timing of resulting outflows of economic benefits;
b.　An indication of any uncertainties about the amount or timing of those outflows. Where necessary, disclosure of major assumptions made concerning future events; and
c.　The amount of any expected reimbursement, disclosing any asset that has been recognized for that expected reimbursement.

(IAS 37, Para 85)

3.　Unless the possibility of any outflow in settlement is remote, an entity shall disclose for each class of contingent liability at the balance sheet date a brief description of the nature of contingent liability and, where practicable

a.　An estimate of its financial effect;
b.　An indication of the uncertainties relating to the amount or timing of any outflow; and
c.　The possibility of any reimbursement.

(IAS 37, Para 86)

4.　Where an inflow of economic benefits is probable, an entity shall disclose a brief description of the nature of the contingent assets at the balance sheet date, and where practicable, an estimate of their financial effect, measured using the principles set out in IAS 37, paragraphs 36-52.

(IAS 37, Para 89)

5.　In *extremely rare circumstances,* if some or all disclosures as outlined in IAS 37, paragraphs 84 and 85, are expected to prejudice seriously the position of the entity in a dispute with other parties, an entity need not disclose such information. Instead, it should disclose the general nature of the dispute, along with the fact that, and reason why, the information has not been disclosed.

(IAS 37, Para 92)

M.　Deferred Tax Liabilities and Assets

1.　The following shall be disclosed separately:

a. The aggregate current and deferred tax relating to items that are charged or credited to equity;

b. An explanation of the relationship between tax expense (income) and accounting profit in either or both of the following forms:

(1) A numerical reconciliation between tax expense (income) and accounting profit multiplied by the applicable tax rate(s) is (are) computed; or

(2) A numerical reconciliation between average effective tax rate and the applicable tax rate, disclosing also the basis on which the applicable tax rate is computed;

c. An explanation of changes in the applicable tax rate(s) compared to the previous accounting period;

d. The amount (and expiration date, in any) of deductible temporary differences, unused tax losses, and unused tax credits for which no deferred tax asset is recognized in the balance sheet;

e. The aggregate amount of temporary differences associated with investments in subsidiaries, branches and associates and interests in joint ventures, for which deferred tax liabilities have not been recognized.

f. In respect of each temporary difference, and in respect of each type of unused tax credits

(1) The amount of deferred tax assets and liabilities recognized in the balance sheet for each period presented;

(2) The amount of deferred tax income or expense recognized in the income statement, if this is not apparent from changes in the amounts recognized in the balance sheet for each period presented;

(3) In respect of discontinued operations, the tax expense relating to

(a) The gain or loss on discontinuance; and

(b) The profit or loss from the ordinary activities of the discontinued operation for the period, together with the corresponding amounts for each prior period presented; and

g. The amount of income tax consequences of dividends to shareholders of the entity that were proposed or declared before the financial statements were authorized for issue, but are not recognized as a liability in the financial statements.

(IAS 12, Para 81)

2. An entity shall disclose the amount of deferred tax asset and the nature of the evidence supporting its recognition, when

a. The utilization of the deferred tax asset is dependent on future taxable profits in excess of the profits arising from the reversal of existing taxable temporary differences; and

b. The entity has suffered a loss in either the current or preceding period in the jurisdiction to which the deferred tax relates.

(IAS 12, Para 82)

3. In the circumstances described in paragraph set out below, an entity shall disclose the nature of the potential income tax consequences that would result from the payment of dividends to its shareholders. In addition, the entity shall disclose the amounts of the potential income tax consequences not practically determinable. In some jurisdictions, income taxes are payable at a higher or lower rate if part or all of the net profit or retained earnings is paid out as a dividend to shareholders of the entity. In these circumstances, current and deferred tax assets and liabilities are measured at the tax rate applicable to undistributed profits.

(IAS 12, Paras 82A & 52A)

4. Current tax assets and tax liabilities should not be offset unless there is a legally enforceable right of offset and the entity intends to settle on a net basis, or to realize the asset and settle the liability simultaneously.

(IAS 12, Para 71)

5. Deferred tax assets and tax liabilities relating to different jurisdictions should be presented separately.

    (IAS 12, Para 74)

6. Deferred tax assets and tax liabilities relating to different entities in a group which are taxed separately by the taxation authorities should not be offset unless there is a legally enforceable right of offset.

    (IAS 12, Para 74)

7. When utilization of the deferred tax asset is dependent upon future taxable profits in excess of amounts arising from the reversal of existing taxable temporary differences, and the entity has incurred losses in either the current or preceding period in the tax jurisdiction to which the deferred tax asset relates, the amount of deferred tax asset should be disclosed together with the nature of any evidence supporting its recognition.

    (IAS 12, Para 82)

N.   Employee Benefits—Defined Benefit Pension and Other Postretirement Benefit Programs

1. The entity's accounting policy for recognizing actuarial gains and losses.
2. A general description of the type of plan.
3. A reconciliation of opening and closing balances of the present value of the defined benefit obligation, showing separately, as applicable, the effects during the period attributable to each of the following:

    a. The current service cost;
    b. The interest cost;
    c. Contributions by plan participants;
    d. Actuarial gains and losses;
    e. Foreign currency exchange rate changes on plans measured in a currency different from the entity's presentation currency;
    f. The benefits paid;
    g. The past service cost;
    h. The effect of business combinations;
    i. The effect of any curtailments; and
    j. The effect of any settlements.

4. An analysis of the defined benefit obligation into amounts arising from plans that are wholly unfunded and those amounts arising from plans that are wholly or partly funded.
5. A reconciliation of the opening and closing balances of the fair value of plan assets and of the opening and closing balances of any reimbursement right recognized as an asset in accordance with paragraph 104A showing separately, if applicable, the effects during the period attributable to each of the following:

    a. The expected return on plan assets;
    b. The actuarial gains and losses;
    c. The effect of foreign currency exchange rate changes on plans measured in a currency different from the entity's presentation currency;
    d. Contributions by the employer;
    e. Contributions by plan participants;
    f. Any benefits paid;
    g. The effect of any business combinations; and
    h. Any settlements.

6. A reconciliation of the present value of the defined benefit obligation in (3) and the fair value of the plan assets in (5) to the assets and liabilities recognized in the balance sheet, showing at least

    a. The net actuarial gains or losses not recognized in the balance sheet (see IAS 19, paragraph 92);

    b.   The past service cost not recognized in the balance sheet (see IAS 19, paragraph 92);

    c.   Any amount not recognized as an asset, because of the limit in IAS 19, paragraph 58(b);

    d.   The fair value at the balance sheet date of any reimbursement right recognized as an asset in accordance with IAS 19, paragraph 104A (with a brief description of the link between the reimbursement right and the related obligation); and.

    e.   Any other amounts recognized in the balance sheet.

7.   The total expense recognized in profit or loss for each of the following, and the line item(s) in which they are included:

    a.   Current service cost;

    b.   Interest cost;

    c.   Expected return on plan assets;

    d.   Expected return on any reimbursement right recognized as an asset in accordance with IAS 19, paragraph 104A;

    e.   Actuarial gains and losses;

    f.   Past service cost;

    g.   The effect of any curtailment or settlement; and

    h.   The effect of the limit in IAS 19, paragraph 58(b).

8.   The total amount recognized in the statement of recognized income and expense for each of the following:

    a.   Actuarial gains and losses; and

    b.   The effect of the limit set forth at IAS 19, paragraph 58(b).

9.   For entities that recognize actuarial gains and losses in the statement of recognized income and expense in accordance with IAS 19, paragraph 93A, the cumulative amount of actuarial gains and losses recognized in the statement of recognized income and expense.

10.   For each major category of plan assets, to include, but not be limited to, equity instruments, debt instruments, property, and all other assets, the percentage or amount that each major category constitutes of the fair value of the total plan assets.

11.   The amounts included in the fair value of plan assets for

    a.   Each category of the entity's own financial instruments; and

    b.   Any property occupied by, or other assets used by, the entity.

12.   A narrative description of the basis used to determine the overall expected rate of return on assets, including the effect of the major categories of plan assets.

13.   The actual return on plan assets, as well as the actual return on any reimbursement right recognized as an asset in accordance with IAS 19, paragraph 104A.

14.   The principal actuarial assumptions used as at the balance sheet date, including, when applicable

    a.   The discount rates;

    b.   The expected rates of return on any plan assets for the periods presented in the financial statements;

    c.   The expected rates of return for the periods presented in the financial statements on any reimbursement right recognized as an asset in accordance with IAS 19, paragraph 104A;

    d.   The expected rates of salary increases (and of changes in an index or other variable specified in the formal or constructive terms of a plan as the basis for future benefit increases);

    e.   Medical cost trend rates; and

    f.   Any other material actuarial assumptions used.

An entity is also to disclose each actuarial assumption in absolute terms (for example, as an absolute percentage), and not just as a margin between different percentages or other variables.

15.   The effect of an increase of one percentage point and the effect of a decrease of one percentage point in the assumed medical cost trend rates on

    a.   The aggregate of the current service cost and interest cost components of net periodic postemployment medical costs; and

    b.   The accumulated postemployment benefit obligation for medical costs.

For the purposes of this disclosure, all other assumptions are to be held constant. For plans operating in a high-inflation environment, the disclosure shall be the effect of a percentage increase or decrease in the assumed medical cost trend rate of a significance similar to one percentage point in a low-inflation environment.

16.   The amounts for the current annual period and previous four annual periods of

    a.   The present value of the defined benefit obligation, the fair value of the plan assets and the surplus or deficit in the plan; and

    b.   The experience adjustments arising on

        (1)   The plan liabilities expressed either as

            (a)   An amount or

            (b)   A percentage of the plan liabilities at the balance sheet date, and

        (2)   The plan assets expressed either as

            (a)   An amount or

            (b)   A percentage of the plan assets at the balance sheet date.

17.   The employer's best estimate, as soon as it can reasonably be determined, of contributions expected to be paid to the plan during the annual period beginning after the balance sheet date.

(IAS 19, Para 120A)

O.   Employee Benefits—Other Benefit Plans

1.   For defined contribution pension plans and similar arrangements, the amount recognized as expense for the period being reported upon must be disclosed.

(IAS 19, Para 46)

2.   For long-term compensated absences, long-term disability plans, profit sharing or bonus arrangements or deferred compensation plans payable more than twelve months after the end of the period in which benefits are earned, and similar types of benefit plans, any disclosures which would be mandated by other international standards, such as IAS 1, IAS 8, and IAS 24 (there being no specific disclosures required by IAS 19).

(IAS 19, Para 131)

3.   If there is uncertainty regarding the number of employees who will accept an offer of termination benefits, the entity is to disclose information about the resulting contingent liability, unless the possibility of an outflow in settlement is remote. If material, the nature and amount of the expense arising from termination benefits is to be disclosed. Termination benefits for key management personnel, as required by IAS 24, should also be disclosed.

(IAS 19, Paras 141-143)

4.   For short-term employee benefits, such as short-term compensated absences and profit sharing or bonus arrangements to be paid within twelve months after the end of the period in which the employees render the related services, any disclosures which would be required by other international accounting standards, such as IAS 24, must be made.

(IAS 19, Para 23)

P.   Leases—from the Standpoint of a Lessee

1.   For finance leases

    In addition to requirements of IAS 32, the revised IAS 17, para 23, mandates the following disclosures for lessees under finance leases:

a. For each class of asset, the net carrying amount at balance sheet date;

b. A reconciliation between the total of minimum lease payments at the balance sheet date, and their present value. In addition, an entity should disclose the total of the minimum lease payments at the balance sheet date, their present value, for each of the following periods:

    (1) Due in one year or less,

    (2) Due in more than one but no more than five years, and

    (3) Due in more than five years.

c. Contingent rents recognized as expense for the period.

d. The total of minimum sublease payments to be received in the future under noncancelable subleases as of the balance sheet date.

e. A general description of the lessee's significant leasing arrangements including, but not necessarily limited to the following:

    (1) The basis for determining contingent rentals;

    (2) The existence and terms of renewal or purchase options and escalation clauses; and

    (3) Restrictions imposed by lease arrangements such as on dividends or assumptions of further debt or further leasing.

(IAS 17, Para 31)

2. For operating leases, including those arising from sale-leaseback transactions

Lessees should, in addition to the requirements of IAS 32, make the following disclosures for operating leases:

a. Total of the future minimum lease payments under noncancelable operating leases for each of the following periods:

    (1) Due in one year or less;

    (2) Due in more than one year but no more than five years; and

    (3) Due in more than five years.

b. The total of future minimum sublease payments expected to be received under noncancelable subleases at the balance sheet date;

c. Lease and sublease payments included in profit or loss for the period, with separate amounts of minimum lease payments, contingent rents, and sublease payments;

d. A general description of the lessee's significant leasing arrangements including, but not necessarily limited to the following:

    (1) The basis for determining contingent rentals,

    (2) The existence and terms of renewal or purchase options and escalation clauses, and

    (3) Restrictions imposed by lease arrangements such as on dividends or assumption of further debt or on further leasing.

(IAS 17, Para 35)

Q. Leases—from the Standpoint of a Lessor

1. For finance leases

Lessors under finance leases are required to disclose, in addition to disclosures under IAS 32, the following:

a. A reconciliation between the total gross investment in the lease at the balance sheet date, and the present value of minimum lease payments receivable as of the balance sheet date, categorized into

    (1) Those due in one year or less;

    (2) Those due in more than one year but not more than five years; and

    (3) Those due beyond five years.

b. Unearned finance income.

c. The accumulated allowance for uncollectible minimum lease payments receivable.

    d.   Total contingent rentals included in income.

    e.   A general description of the lessor's significant leasing arrangements.

(IAS 17, Para 47)

2.   For operating leases

    For lessors under operating leases the following expanded disclosures are prescribed:

    a.   Future minimum lease payments under noncancelable operating leases, in the aggregate and classified into

        (1)   Those due in no more than one year;

        (2)   Those due in more than one but not more than five years; and

        (3)   Those due in more than five years.

    b.   Total contingent rentals included in income for the period.

    c.   A general description of leasing arrangements to which it is a party.

(IAS 17, Para 56)

R.   Lease—Substance of the Transaction Involving the Legal Form

1.   All aspects of an arrangement that does not, in substance, involve a lease under IAS 17 should be considered in determining the appropriate disclosures that are necessary to understand the arrangement and the accounting treatment adopted. An entity should disclose the following in *each period* that an arrangement exists:

    a.   A description of the arrangement including

        (1)   The underlying asset and any restrictions on its use;

        (2)   The life and other significant terms of the arrangement;

        (3)   The transactions that are linked together, including any options; and

    b.   The accounting treatment applied to any fee received;

    c.   The amount of fees recognized as income in the period; and

    d.   The line item of the income statement in which the fee income is included.

(SIC 27, Para 10)

2.   The disclosures required in accordance with SIC 27, paragraph 10, above, should be provided individually for each arrangement or in aggregate for each class of arrangement. (A "class" is a grouping of arrangements with underlying assets of a similar nature [e.g., power plants]).

(SIC 27, Para 11)

S.   Stockholders' Equity

1.   The following disclosures should be made by an entity either on the face of the balance sheet or in the notes:

    a.   For each class of share capital

        (1)   The number of shares authorized;

        (2)   The number of shares issued and fully paid, and issued but not fully paid;

        (3)   Par value per share, or the fact that the shares have no par value;

        (4)   A reconciliation of the number of shares outstanding at the beginning of the year to the number of shares outstanding at the end of the year;

        (5)   The rights, preferences and restrictions attaching to each class of shares, including restrictions on the distribution of dividends and the repayment of capital;

        (6)   Shares held by the entity itself or by subsidiaries or associates of the entity; and

        (7)   Shares reserved for future issuance under options and sales contracts, including terms and amounts.

    b.   For reserves within the owners' equity, a description, nature, and purpose of each reserve;

(IAS 1, Para 76)

2. An entity without share capital, such as a partnership, should disclose information equivalent to that required above, showing movements during the year in each category of equity interest and the rights, preferences, and restrictions attaching to each category of equity interest.

(IAS 1, Para 77)

3. Treasury shares require the following disclosures:

    a. The amount of reductions to equity for treasury shares should be disclosed separately. This disclosure could be either on the face of the balance sheet or in the notes to the financial statements.
    b. Where the entity, or its subsidiary, reacquires its own shares from parties able to control or exercise significant influence over the entity, this should be disclosed as a related-party transaction under IAS 24.

(IAS 32, Para 34)

4. Transaction costs of issuing equity instruments or of acquiring them should be accounted for as a deduction from equity and separately disclosed. The related income taxes recognized directly in equity should also be included in the disclosure of the aggregate amount of current and deferred income tax credited or charged to equity.

(IAS 32, Para 35)

STATEMENT OF COMPREHENSIVE INCOME

A. Minimum Disclosures on the Face of the Income Statement

1. Minimum disclosures on the face of the income statement should include the following:

    a. Revenue;
    b. Finance costs;
    c. Share of profits and losses of associates and joint ventures accounted for using the equity method;
    d. Tax expense;
    e. A single amount which will include (1) post-tax profit/loss of discontinued operation and post-tax gain or loss recognized on the measurement to fair value less costs to sell or on the disposal of the assets or disposal groups constituting the discontinued operation;
    f. Profit or loss;

(IAS 1, Para 81)

2. The following items shall be disclosed on the face of the statement of comprehensive income as allocations of the profit or loss for the period:

    a. Profit or loss attributable to minority interest; and
    b. Profit or loss attributable to owners of the parent.

(IAS 1, Para 82)

3. Additional line items, headings and subtotals should be presented on the face of the income statement when required by an IAS or when such a presentation is necessary in order to fairly present the entity's financial performance.

(IAS 1, Para 83)

4. All items of income and expense in a period are to be included in profit or loss unless an IFRS requires or permits otherwise.

(IAS 1, Para 85)

5. The amount of income tax relating to each component of other comprehensive income, including reclassification adjustments, are to be disclosed either in the statement of comprehensive income or in the notes.

(IAS 1, Para 90 and IAS 12, Para 81)

6. Reclassification adjustments relating to components of other comprehensive income are to be disclosed.

(IAS 1, Para 92)

B. Investment Property

1. General disclosures:

    a. Which accounting model (fair value or cost) has been applied;
    b. If the fair value model, disclose, whether and in what circumstances property interest held under operating leases are classified and accounted for as investment property;
    c. When classification was problematic, the criteria used to distinguish investment property from owner-occupied property and from property held for sale in the ordinary course of business;
    d. The methods and significant assumptions applied in determining the fair value of investment property, including a statement whether the determination of fair value was supported by market evidence or was more heavily based on other factors (which are to be disclosed) because of the nature of the property and lack of comparable market data;.
    e. If fair value is based on a valuation by an independent party having appropriate credentials and experience, this fact is to be disclosed. If there has been no such valuation, that fact must also be disclosed.

(IAS 40, Para 75)

2. Amounts included in income statement for

    a. Rental income from investment property;
    b. Direct operating expense (including repairs and maintenance) arising from investment property that is the source of the rental income during the period; and
    c. Direct operating expenses (including repairs and maintenance) arising from investment property that did not generate rental income for the period.
    d. Cumulative change in fair value recognized in profit or loss on sale of investment property from pool of assets in which the cost model is used into a pool in which fair value model is used.

(IAS 40, Para 75f)

3. In the case of investment property carried under the fair value model, as part of the reconciliation of the carrying amount of the investment at the beginning and the end of the period, the entity should disclose the following:

    a. Additions, comprising additions from acquisitions and from subsequent expenditure recognized in the carrying amount of an asset;
    b. Additions following from acquisitions through business combination;
    c. Assets held for sale or included in a disposal group held for sale in accordance with IFRS 5 and any other disposal;
    d. Net profit or losses incurred from fair value adjustment;
    e. Exchange differences arising on the translation of financial statements into a different presentation currency of the reporting entity;
    f. Transfers to and from inventories and owner-occupied property; and
    g. Any other changes.

(IAS 40, Para 76)

4. In the case of investment property carried under the cost model, as part of the reconciliation of the carrying amount of the investment at the beginning and at the end of the period, the depreciation, the amount of impairment losses recognized and reversed and the net exchange differences arising from the translation of the financial statements of a foreign entity and any additions resulting from acquisitions and from subsequent expenditure recognized as an asset and from acquisitions through business combinations and assets classified as held-for-sale or

included in a disposal group classified as held-for-sale in accordance with IAS 36, transfers to and from inventories and owner-occupied property and other changes.

(IAS 40, Para 79d)

C. Income Taxes

1. Tax expense related to profit or loss from ordinary activities should be presented on the face of the income statement.

(IAS 12, Para 77)

2. The major components of tax expense should be presented separately. These commonly would include the following:

   a. Current tax expense;
   b. Any adjustments recognized in the period for current tax of prior periods;
   c. The amount of deferred tax expense relating to the origination and the reversal of timing differences;
   d. The amount of deferred tax expense relating to changes in tax rates or the imposition of new taxes;
   e. The amount of deferred tax expense or benefit relating to changes in tax rates or the imposition of new taxes;
   f. The amount of the benefit arising from a previously unrecognized tax loss, tax credit, or temporary difference of a prior period that is used to reduce current taxes;
   g. The amount of a benefit from a previously unrecognized tax loss, tax credit, or temporary difference of a prior period that is used to reduce deferred taxes;
   h. Deferred tax expense related to a write-down of a deferred tax asset or the reversal of a write-down; and
   i. The amount of tax expense relating to changes in accounting policies and correction of fundamental errors, accounted for consistent with the allowed alternative method under IAS 8.

(IAS 12, Paras 79 & 80)

3. The following items also require separate disclosure:

   a. Tax expense relating to items which are charged or credited to equity;
   b. Tax expense relating to extraordinary items;
   c. An explanation of the relationship between tax expense or benefit and accounting profit or loss either (or both) as

      (1) A numerical reconciliation between tax expense or benefit and the product of accounting profit or loss times the applicable tax rate(s), with disclosure of how the rate(s) was determined; or
      (2) A numerical reconciliation between the average effective tax rate and the applicable rate, also with disclosure of how the applicable rate was determined.

   d. An explanation of changes in the applicable tax rates vs. the prior period;
   e. The amount and expiration date of deductible temporary differences, and unused tax losses and tax credits for which no deferred tax asset has been recognized;
   f. Aggregate temporary differences associated with investments in subsidiaries, branches, and associates, and interests in joint ventures, for which deferred tax liabilities have not been recognized;
   g. For each type of temporary difference, and for each type of unused tax loss or unused credit, the amount of deferred tax asset and liability recognized in the balance sheet and the amount of deferred tax expense or benefit recognized in the income statement, unless otherwise apparent from changes in the balance sheet accounts; and
   h. With regard to discontinued operations, the tax expense relating to the gain or loss on discontinuance and the tax expense on the profit or loss from ordinary activities of the discontinued operation.

   i.   Amount of income tax on dividend that was declared or proposed before the financial statements are authorized for issue but are not recognized as a liability in the financial statements.

(IAS 12, Para 81)

D.   Extraordinary Items

1.   An entity shall not designate any item of income and expense as being an extraordinary item, either on the face of the income statement or in the notes.

(IAS 1, Para 85)

E.   Noncurrent Assets Held for Sale and Discontinued Operations

1.   An entity shall present and disclose information that enables users of the financial statements to evaluate the financial effects of discontinued operations and disposals of noncurrent assets (or disposal groups).

(IFRS 5, Para 30)

2.   An entity shall disclose

   a.   A single amount on the face of the income statement comprising the total of

   (1)   The posttax profit or loss of discontinuing operations; and;

   (2)   The posttax gain or loss recognized on the measurement to fair value less costs to sell or on the disposal of the assets or disposal group(s) constituting the discontinued operation.

   b.   An analysis of the single amount in a. into

   (1)   The revenue, expenses and pretax profit or loss of discontinued operations;

   (2)   The related income tax expense as required by IAS 12, paragraph 81(h);

   (3)   The gain or loss recognized on the measurement to fair value less costs to sell or on the disposal of the assets or disposal group(s) constituting the discontinued operation; and

   (4)   The related income tax expense as required by IAS 12, paragraph 81(h). The analysis may be presented in the notes or on the face of the income statement. If it is presented on the face of the income statement it shall be presented in a section identified as relating to discontinued operations (i.e., separately from continuing operations). The analysis is not required for disposal groups that are newly acquired subsidiaries that meet the criteria to be classified as held-for-sale on acquisition.

   c.   The net cash flows attributable to the operating, investing, and financing activities of discontinued operations. These disclosures may be presented either in the notes or on the face of the financial statements. These disclosures are not required for disposal groups that are newly acquired subsidiaries that meet the criteria to be classified as held-for-sale on acquisition.

(IFRS 5, Para 33)

3.   An entity shall re-present the disclosures in IFRS 5, paragraph 33 for prior period presented in the financial statements so that the disclosures relate to all operations that have been discontinued by the balance sheet date for the latest period presented.

(IFRS 5, Para 34)

4.   An entity shall present a noncurrent asset classified as held-for-sale and the assets of a disposal group classified as held-for-sale separately from other assets in the balance sheet. The liabilities of the disposal group classified as held-for-sale shall be presented separately from other liabilities in the balance sheet. Those assets and liabilities shall not be offset and presented as a single amount. The major classes of assets and liabilities classified as held-for-sale shall be separately disclosed either on the face of the balance sheet or in the notes. An

entity shall present separately any cumulative income or expense recognized directly as equity relating to a noncurrent asset classified as held-for-sale.

(IFRS 5, Para 38)

5. If the disposal group is a newly acquired subsidiary that meets the criteria to be classified as held-for-sale on acquisition, disclosure of the major classes of assets and liabilities is not required.

(IFRS 5, Para 39)

6. An entity shall not reclassify or re-present amounts presented for noncurrent assets or for the assets and liabilities of disposal groups classified as held-for-sale in the balance sheet for prior periods to reflect the classification in the balance sheet for the latest period presented.

(IAS 5, Para 40)

7. An entity shall disclose the following information in the notes in the period in which a noncurrent asset (disposal group) has been either classified as held-for-sale or sold:

    a. A description of the noncurrent asset (or disposal group);
    b. A description of the facts and circumstances of the sale, or leading to the expected disposal, the expected manner and timing of that disposal;
    c. The impairment gain or loss recognized in accordance with IFRS 5, and if not separately presented on the face of the income statement, the caption in the income statement that includes that gain or loss;
    d. If applicable, the segment in which the noncurrent asset (or disposal group) is presented in accordance with IAS 14, *Reporting Financial Information by Segment.*

(IFRS 5, Para 41)

8. If, as per IFRS 5, an entity changes to the plan of sale, it shall disclose, in the period of the decision to change the plan to sell the noncurrent asset (or disposal group), a description of the facts and circumstances leading to the decision and the effect of the decision on the results of operations for the period and any prior periods presented.

(IFRS 5, Para 42)

F. Segment Data

1. General information about segments

    a. Factors used to identify the entity's reportable segments, including the basis of organization (for example, whether management has chosen to organize the entity around differences in products and services, geographical areas, regulatory environments, or a combination of factors and whether operating segments have been aggregated),
    b. Types of products and services from which each reportable segment derives its revenues

(IFRS 8, Para 22)

2. Information about profit or loss, assets and liabilities

    a. The reporting entity is to report a measure of profit or loss and total assets for each reportable segment.
    b. It is to report a measure of liabilities for each reportable segment if such an amount is regularly provided to the chief operating decision maker.
    c. It also is to disclose the following about each reportable segment if the specified amounts are included in the measure of segment profit or loss reviewed by the chief operating decision maker, or are otherwise regularly provided to the chief operating decision maker, even if not included in that measure of segment profit or loss:

        (1) Revenues from external customers;
        (2) Revenues from transactions with other operating segments of the same entity;
        (3) Interest revenue;
        (4) Interest expense;

    (5)   Depreciation and amortization;

    (6)   Material items of income and expense disclosed in accordance with IAS 1;

    (7)   The entity's interest in the profit or loss of associates and joint ventures accounted for by the equity method;

    (8)   Income tax expense or income; and

    (9)   Material noncash items other than depreciation and amortization.

d.   An entity is to report interest revenue separately from interest expense for each reportable segment unless a majority of the segment's revenues are from interest and the chief operating decision maker relies primarily on net interest revenue to assess the performance of the segment and make decisions about resources to be allocated to the segment. In that situation, an entity may report that segment's interest revenue net of its interest expense and disclose that it has done so.

(IFRS 8, Para 23)

e.   The reporting entity is to disclose the following about each reportable segment if the specified amounts are included in the measure of segment assets reviewed by the chief operating decision maker or are otherwise regularly provided to the chief operating decision maker, even if not included in the measure of segment assets:

    (1)   The amount of investment in associates and joint ventures accounted for by the equity method, and

    (2)   The amounts of additions to noncurrent assets other than financial instruments, deferred tax assets, postemployment benefit assets and rights arising under insurance contracts. If the entity does not present a classified balance sheet, noncurrent assets are to be deemed those that include amounts expected to be recovered more than twelve months after the balance sheet date.

(IFRS 8, Para 24)

3.   Reconciliations of the totals of segment revenues, reported segment profit or loss, segment assets, segment liabilities and other material segment items to corresponding entity amounts as follows:

a.   The total of the reportable segments' revenues to the entity's revenue.

b.   The total of the reportable segments' measures of profit or loss to the entity's profit or loss before tax expense (tax income) and discontinued operations. However, if an entity allocates to reportable segments items such as tax expense (tax income), the entity may reconcile the total of the segments' measures of profit or loss to the entity's profit or loss after those items.

c.   The total of the reportable segments assets to the entity's assets.

d.   The total of the reportable segments liabilities to the entity's liabilities if segment liabilities are reported in accordance with paragraph 23.

e.   The total of the reportable segments amounts for every other material item of information disclosed to the corresponding amount for the entity.

(IFRS 8, Para 28)

4.   Entity-wide disclosures:

a.   Information about products and services. Revenues from external customers for each product and service, or each group of similar products and services, are to be identified, unless the necessary information is not available and the cost to develop it would be excessive, in which case that fact shall be disclosed. The amounts of revenues reported are to be based on the financial information used to produce the entity's financial statements.

(IFRS 8, Para 32)

b.   Information about geographic areas. The reporting entity is to disclose the following geographical information, unless the necessary information is not available and the cost to develop it would be excessive:

(1) Revenues from external customers (a) attributed to the entity's country of domicile and (b) attributed to all foreign countries in total from which the entity derives revenues. If revenues from external customers attributed to an individual foreign country are material, those revenues are to be disclosed separately. An entity is required to disclose the basis for attributing revenues from external customers to individual countries.

(2) Noncurrent assets other than financial instruments, deferred tax assets, post-employment benefit assets, and rights arising under insurance contracts (a) located in the entity's country of domicile and (b) located in all foreign countries in total in which the entity holds assets. If assets in an individual foreign country are material, those assets shall be disclosed separately. If a classified statement of financial position is not presented (i.e., if liquidity ordering is utilized), noncurrent assets are to be defined as assets that include amounts expected to be recovered more than twelve months after the reporting date.

(IFRS 8, Para 33)

c. Information about major customers. Information about the extent of the reporting entity's reliance on its major customers must be provided. If revenues from transactions with a single external customer amount to 10% or more of the entity's revenues, it is to disclose that fact, the total amount of revenues from each such customer, and the identity of the segment or segments reporting the revenues. The entity need not disclose the identity of a major customer or the amount of revenues that each segment reports from that customer. For the purposes of this requirement under IFRS 8, a group of entities known to be under common control is to be considered a single customer, and a government (national, state, provincial, territorial, local or foreign) and entities known to be under the control of that government are to be considered a single customer.

(IFRS 8, Para 34)

G. Construction Contracts

1. An entity which accounts for construction contracts in accordance with IAS 11 should disclose the following in its financial statements:

   a. The amount of contract revenue recognized as revenue in the period;
   b. The methods used to determine the contract revenue recognized in the period; and
   c. The methods used to determine the stage of completion for contracts in progress.

(IAS 11, Para 39)

2. Each of the following should be disclosed for the contracts in progress:

   a. The aggregate amount of costs incurred and recognized profits (net of any recognized losses) to date;
   b. The amount of advances received; and
   c. The amount of retentions.

(IAS 11, Para 40)

3. On the balance sheet, present gross amounts due from customers as an asset, and gross amounts due to customers for contract work as a liability.

(IAS 11, Para 42)

H. Foreign Currency Translation

1. Disclosure is required of the following:

   a. The amount of exchange differences included in net profit or loss for the period;
   b. Net exchange differences classified as a separate component of equity, and a reconciliation of the amount of such exchange differences at the beginning and the end of the period.

(IAS 21, Para 52)

2. If the reporting currency is different from the currency of the country in which the entity is domiciled, disclosure is required of the following:

   a. The reason for using a different currency; and
   b. The reason for any change in the reporting currency.

   (IAS 21, Para 53)

3. When there is a change in classification of a significant foreign operation, the following disclosures are required:

   a. The nature of the change; and
   b. The reason for the change;

   (IAS 21, Para 54)

4. When an entity presents its financial statements in a currency that is different from its functional currency, it shall describe the financial statements as complying with IFRS only if they comply with all the requirements of each applicable Standard and each applicable Interpretation of those Standards including the translation method.

   (IAS 21, Para 55)

5. When an entity displays its financial statements or other financial information in a currency that is different from either its functional currency or its presentation currency and the requirements of IAS 21, paragraph 21 are not met, it shall

   a. Clearly identify the information as supplementary information to distinguish it from the information that complies with IFRS;
   b. Disclose the currency in which the supplementary information is displayed; and
   c. Disclose the entity's functional currency and the method of translation used to determine the supplementary information.

   (IAS 21, Para 57)

I. Business Combinations

1. An acquirer shall disclose information that enables users of its financial statements to evaluate the nature and financial effect of business combinations that were effected

   a. During the period;
   b. After the balance sheet date but before the financial statements are authorized for issue.

   (IFRS 3, Para 66)

2. The acquirer shall disclose the following information for each business combination that was effected during the period:

   a. The names and descriptions of the combining entities or businesses;
   b. The acquisition date;
   c. The percentage of voting equity acquired;
   d. The cost of combination and a description of the components of that cost, including any costs directly attributable to combination. When equity instruments are issued or issuable as part of the cost, the following shall be disclosed:

      (1) The number of equity instruments issued or issuable; and;
      (2) The fair value of those instruments and the basis for determining the fair value; if a published price does not exist for the instruments at the date of the exchange, the significant assumptions used to determine fair value shall be disclosed. If a published price exists at a date of exchange but was not used as the basis for determining the cost of combination, that fact shall be disclosed together with: the reasons the published price was not used; the method and significant assumptions used to attribute a value to the equity instruments; and the aggregate amount of the difference between the value attributed to, and the published price of, the equity instruments.

    e.   Details of any operations the entity has decided to dispose of as a result of the combination.

    f.   The amounts recognized at the acquisition date for each class of the acquiree's assets, liabilities and contingent liabilities and, unless disclosure should be impracticable, the carrying amounts of each of these classes, determined in accordance with IFRS, immediately before the combination. If such disclosure would be impracticable, that fact should be disclosed, together with an explanation of why this is the case.

    g.   The amount of any excess recognized in profit or loss in accordance with IFRS 3, paragraph 56, and the line item in the income statement in which the excess is recognized.

    h.   A description of the factors that contributed to a cost that results in the recognition of goodwill, a description of each intangible asset that was not recognized separately from goodwill and an explanation of why the intangible asset's fair value could not be measured reliably, or a description of the nature of any excess recognized in profit or loss in accordance with IFRS 3.

    i.   The amount of the acquiree's profit or loss since the acquisition date included in the acquirer's profit or loss of the period, unless disclosure would be impracticable, that fact shall be disclosed, together with an explanation of why this is the case.

(IFRS 3, Para 67)

3.   The information required to be disclosed by IFRS 3, paragraph 67, shall be disclosed in aggregate for business combinations effected during the reporting period that are individually immaterial.

(IFRS 3, Para 68)

4.   If the initial accounting for a business combination that was effected during the period was determined only provisionally described in IFRS 3, paragraph 62, the fact should be also disclosed together with an explanation of why this is the case.

(IFRS 3, Para 69)

5.   To give effect to the principle in IFRS 3, paragraph 66(a), the acquirer shall disclose the following information, unless such disclosure should be impracticable:

    a.   The revenues of the combined entity for the period as though the acquisition date for all business combinations effected during the period had been the beginning of that period.

    b.   The profit or loss of the current entity for the period as though the acquisition date for all business combinations effected during the period had been the beginning of the period. If disclosure of this information is impracticable, the fact shall be disclosed, together with an explanation of why this is the case.

(IFRS 3, Para 70)

6.   To give effect to the principle in IFRS 3, paragraph 66(b), the acquirer shall disclose the information required by IFRS 3, paragraph 67, for each business combination effected after the balance sheet date but before the financial statements are authorized, for issue, unless such disclosure would be impracticable. If disclosure of any of this information would be impracticable, the fact shall be disclosed together with an explanation of why this is the case.

(IFRS 3, Para 71)

7.   An acquirer shall disclose information that enables its users to evaluate the financial effects of gains, losses, error corrections, and other adjustments recognized in the current period that relate to business combinations that were effected in the current or in previous periods.

(IFRS 3, Para 72)

8.   To give effect to the principle in IFRS 3, paragraph 72, the acquirer shall disclose the following information:

    a.   The amount and an explanation of any gain or loss recognized in the current period that

     (1) Relates to the identifiable assets acquired or liabilities or contingent liabilities assumed in a business combination that was effected in the current or the previous period; and

     (2) Is of such size and nature or incidence that disclosure is relevant to an understanding of the combined entity's financial performance.

  b. If the initial accounting for a business combination that was effected in the immediately preceding period was determined only provisionally at the end of that period, the amounts and explanations of the adjustments to the provisional values recognized during the current period.

  c. The information about error corrections required to be disclosed by IAS 8 for any of the acquiree's identifiable assets, liabilities or contingent liabilities, or changes in the values assigned to those items, that acquirer recognizes during the current period in accordance with IFRS 3, paragraphs 63 and 64.

(IFRS 3, Para 73)

9. An entity shall disclose information to evaluate the changes in the carrying amount of goodwill during the period.

(IFRS 3, Para 74)

10. To give effect to the principle in IFRS 3, paragraph 74, the entity shall disclose a reconciliation of the carrying amount of goodwill at the beginning and the end of the period, showing separately

  a. The gross amount and accumulated impairment losses at the beginning of the period;

  b. Additional goodwill recognized during the period except goodwill included in a disposal group that, on acquisition, meets the criteria to be classified as held for sale in accordance with IFRS 5;

  c. Adjustments resulting from the subsequent recognition of deferred tax assets during the period in accordance with IFRS 3, paragraph 65;

  d. Goodwill included in disposal group classified as held for sale in accordance with IFRS 5 and goodwill derecognized during the period without having been previously included in a disposal group classified for sale;

  e. Impairment losses recognized during the period in accordance with IAS 36;

  f. Net exchange differences arising during the period in accordance with IAS 21, *The Effects of Changes in Foreign Exchange Rates*;

  g. Any other changes in the carrying amount during the period.

  h. The gross amount and accumulated impairment losses at the end of the period.

(IFRS 3, Para 75)

11. An entity shall disclose information about the recoverable amount and impairment of goodwill in accordance with IAS 36 in addition to the information required to be disclosed by IFRS 3, paragraph 75(5).

(IFRS 3, Para 76)

12. An entity shall disclose such additional information as is necessary to satisfy the objectives set out in IFRS 3, paragraphs 66, 72, and 74 if it is not able to satisfy these objectives under any situation.

(IFRS 3, Para 77)

13. An acquirer shall disclose information that enables users of its financial statements to evaluate the nature and financial effect of business combinations that were effected during the period and after the balance sheet date, but before the financial statements were authorized for issuance.

(IFRS 3, Para 66)

14. Business disposals during the period require disclosure of total consideration; the portion of total consideration received in cash or equivalents; the amount of cash or equivalents that was in the disposed-of operation; and the amount of assets and liabilities other than cash or equivalents, summarized by major categories.

(IAS 7, Para 40)

J. Earnings Per Share

1. Entities should present both basic EPS and diluted EPS on the face of the income statement for each class of ordinary shares that has a different right to share in the net profit for the period. Equal prominence should be given to both the basic EPS and diluted EPS figures for all periods presented.

(IAS 33, Para 66)

2. Entities should present basic EPS and diluted EPS even if the amounts disclosed are negative.

(IAS 33, Para 69)

3. Where relevant, EPS from continuing operations should be presented also.

(IAS 33, Para 66)

4. Entities should disclose amounts used as the numerator in calculating basic EPS and diluted EPS along with a reconciliation of those amounts to the net profit or loss for the period. Disclosure is also required of the weighted-average number of ordinary shares used as the denominator in calculating basic EPS and diluted EPS along with a reconciliation of these denominators to each other.

(IAS 33, Paras 70[a] & 70[b])

5. a. In addition to the disclosure of the figures for basic EPS and diluted EPS, as required above, if an entity *chooses to disclose* per share amounts using a reported component of net profit, other than net profit or loss for the period attributable to ordinary shareholders, such amounts should be calculated using weighted-average number of ordinary shares determined in accordance with the requirements of IAS 33; this will ensure comparability of the per share amounts disclosed;

   b. In cases where an entity chooses to disclose the above per share amounts using a component of net profit not reported as a line item in the income statement, a reconciliation is mandated by the standard, which should reconcile the difference between the component of net income used with a line item reported in the income statement; and

   c. When additional disclosure is made by an entity of the above per share amounts, basic and diluted per share amounts should be disclosed with equal prominence (just as basic EPS and diluted EPS figures are given equal prominence).

(IAS 33, Para 73)

6. Entities are encouraged to disclose the terms and conditions of financial instruments or contracts generating potential ordinary shares, since such terms and conditions may determine whether or not any potential ordinary shares are dilutive and, if so, the effect on the weighted-average number of shares outstanding and any consequent adjustments to the net profit attributable to the ordinary shareholders.

(IAS 33, Para 72)

7. If changes (resulting from bonus issue or share split etc.) in the number of ordinary or potential ordinary shares occur, after the balance sheet date but before issuance of the financial statements, and the per share calculations reflect such changes in the number of shares, such a fact should be disclosed.

(IAS 33, Para 70[d])

8. An entity shall disclose the instruments (including contingently issuable shares) that could potentially dilute basic earnings per share in the future, but were not included in the calculation of diluted earnings per share because they are antidilutive for the period(s) presented.

(IAS 33, Para 70[c])

K. Impairments of Assets

1. For each class of assets, the financial statements should disclose

    a. The amount of impairment losses recognized in the income statement during the period and the line item(s) of the income statements in which those impairment losses are included;

    b. The amount of reversals of impairment losses recognized in the income statement during the period and the line item(s) of the income statement in which those impairment losses are reversed;

    c. The amount of impairment losses recognized directly in equity during the period; and

    d. The amount of reversals of impairment losses recognized directly in equity during the period.

    (IAS 36, Para 126)

2. If impairment loss for an asset or a cash-generating unit is recognized or reversed during the period and is **material** to the financial statements as a whole, an entity should disclose

    a. Events and circumstances that led to the recognition or reversal of the impairment loss;

    b. Amount of the impairment loss recognized or reversed;

    c. For an individual asset, its nature and the primary reportable segment to which it belongs, based on the entity's primary format (as defined in IAS 14, if that IAS applies to the entity);

    d. For a cash-generating unit, a description of the cash-generating unit, the amount of the impairment loss recognized or reversed by the class of assets and by the reportable segment based on the entity's primary format (as defined by IAS 14, if that IAS applies to the entity) and if the aggregation of assets for identifying the cash-generating unit has changed since the previous estimate of the cash-generating unit's recoverable amount (if any), the entity should describe the current and former manner of aggregating assets and the reasons for the change;

    e. Whether the recoverable amount of the asset (cash-generating unit) is its net selling price or its value in use;

    f. The basis used to determine net selling price (such as with reference to an active market or any other manner) in case the recoverable amount is net selling price; and

    g. If recoverable amount is value in use, the discount rate(s) used in the current estimate and previous estimate (if any) of value in use.

    (IAS 36, Para 130)

3. If impairment losses recognized (reversed) during the period are **material** in aggregate to the financial statements of the entity as a whole, an entity should disclose a brief description of the following:

    a. The main classes of assets affected by impairment losses and reversals of impairment losses; and

    b. The main events and circumstances that led to the recognition (reversal) of these impairment losses.

    (IAS 36, Para 131)

4. If any portion of goodwill acquired in a business combination effected during the current period was not allocated to a cash-generating unit at the balance sheet date, per IAS 36, para 84, the amount of the unallocated goodwill is to be disclosed, with an explanation of why it remains unallocated.

    (IAS 36, Para 133)

5.   For each cash-generating unit with material amounts of indefinite-life intangibles or goodwill

    a.   Disclose the carrying amount of goodwill; the carrying amount of indefinite life intangibles; the basis on which recoverable amounts were determined.

    b.   If the recoverable amounts were based on value in use, describe key assumptions made by management affecting the cash flow projections, management's approach to value determination for each key assumption, the period over which cash flows were projected with an explanation, as necessary, for projections over greater than five years, and the growth rate used to project cash flows, with explanations for any that exceed the entity's historical long-term growth rate.

    c.   If the recoverable amounts were based on fair value less costs to sell, disclose methodology used to determine such amounts where not based on observable market data; describe each key assumption and management's approach to determining values assigned to key assumptions.

    d.   When a reasonably possible change in a key assumption could cause the carrying value of the cash-generating unit to exceed its recoverable amount, disclose the amount by which the aggregate recoverable amounts exceed carrying values, the value(s) assigned to key assumption(s), and the amount by which the value assigned to assumption(s) would need to change to cause the recoverable amounts to equal the carrying amounts.

(IAS 36, Para 134)

6.   If not disclosed separately in the statement of comprehensive income, compensation from third parties for items of property, plant, and equipment that were impaired, lost, or given up that is included in profit or loss should be disclosed.

(IAS 16, Para 74)

L.   Financial Instruments

1.   The entity is to disclose the following items of income, expense, gains or losses either on the face of the financial statements or in the notes:

    a.   Net gains or net losses on

        (1)   Financial assets or financial liabilities reported at fair value with changes recognized through profit or loss, showing separately those on financial assets or financial liabilities designated as such upon initial recognition, and those on financial assets or financial liabilities that are classified as held for trading.

        (2)   Available-for-sale financial assets, showing separately the amount of gain or loss recognized directly in equity during the period and the amount removed from equity and recognized in profit or loss for the period.

        (3)   Held-to-maturity investments.

        (4)   Loans and receivables.

        (5)   Financial liabilities measured at amortized cost.

    b.   The total interest income and total interest expense (calculated by means of the effective interest method) for financial assets or financial liabilities that are not carried at fair value with changes reported currently through profit or loss.

    c.   Fee income and expense (other than amounts included in determining the effective interest rate) arising from

        (1)   Financial assets or financial liabilities that are not carried at fair value with changes recognized currently through profit or loss.

        (2)   Trust and other fiduciary activities that result in the holding or investing of assets on behalf of individuals, trusts, retirement benefit plans, and other institutions.

    d.   Interest income on impaired financial assets accrued in accordance with IAS 39.

    e.   The amount of any impairment loss for each class of financial asset.

(IFRS 7, Para 20)

STATEMENT OF CASH FLOWS

A. Basis of Presentation

1. A statement of cash flows should be prepared in accordance with IAS 7 and presented as an integral part of an entity's financial statements for each period for which the financial statements are presented.

(IAS 7, Para 1)

2. The statement of cash flows should report cash flows during the period, classified by

    a. Operating activities;
    b. Investing activities; and
    c. Financing activities.

(IAS 7, Para 10)

B. Format

1. Cash flows from operating activities should be reported using either

    a. The direct method, under which major classes of gross cash receipts and gross cash payments are disclosed; **or**
    b. The indirect method, wherein net profit or loss for the period is adjusted for the following:

        (1) The effects of noncash transactions;
        (2) Any deferrals or accruals of past or future operating cash receipts or payments; and
        (3) Items of income or expense related to investing or financing cash flows.

(IAS 7, Para 18)

2. An entity should generally report (separately) major gross cash receipts and payments from investing and financing activities.

(IAS 7, Para 21)

3. Under the following circumstances, however, an entity's[1] cash flows arising from operating, investing, or financing activities may be reported on a net basis:

    a. Cash receipts and payments on behalf of customers when the cash flows reflect the activities of the customer rather than those of the entity; and
    b. Cash receipts and payments for items in which the turnover is quick, the amounts are large, and maturities are short.

(IAS 7, Para 22)

4. Cash flows arising from extraordinary items should be classified as either

    a. Operating activities;
    b. Investing activities; or
    c. Financing activities.

    Each of these items should be disclosed separately.

(IAS 7, Para 29)

5. Cash flows from interest received and dividends received and dividends paid should be classified consistently (from period to period) as either

    a. Operating activities;

---

[1] *Cash flows of financial institutions may be reported on a net basis under the following cases:*
1. *Cash flows from the acceptance and repayment of deposits with fixed maturity dates;*
2. *Placement of deposits with and withdrawal of deposits from other financial institutions; and*
3. *Cash advances and loans made to customers and the repayment of those advances and loans.*

(IAS 7, Para 24)

b. Investing activities; or
c. Financing activities.

Each of these items should be disclosed separately.

(IAS 7, Para 31)

6. In relation to cash and cash equivalents, a cash flow statement should

a. Disclose the policy which it adopts in determining the components;
b. Disclose the components; and
c. Present a reconciliation of the amounts in its statement of cash flows with similar items reported in the balance sheet.

(IAS 7, Paras 45 & 46)

7. The effect of exchange rate changes on cash and cash equivalents held or due in foreign currency should be presented separately from cash flows from operating, investing, and financing activities.

(IAS 7, Para 28)

8. Noncash transactions arising from investing and financing activities should be excluded from the statement of cash flows. Such transactions do not require the use of cash and cash equivalents and thus should be disclosed elsewhere in the financial statements by way of a note that provides all the relevant information about these activities.

(IAS 7, Para 43)

9. Cash payments and receipts relating to taxes on income should be separately disclosed and classified as cash flows from operating activities unless they could specifically be identified with financing and/or investing activities.

(IAS 7, Para 35)

10. In relation to acquisitions or disposals of subsidiaries or other business units which should be presented separately and classified as investing activities, an entity should disclose the following:

a. The total purchase or sale price;
b. Portion of the consideration discharged by cash and cash equivalents;
c. Amount of cash and cash equivalents acquired or disposed; and
d. Amount of assets and liabilities (other than cash or cash equivalents) summarized by major category.

(IAS 7, Para 40)

11. Significant cash and cash equivalent balances held by the entity which are not available for use by the group should be disclosed by the entity along with a commentary by management.

(IAS 7, Para 48)

C. Additional Recommended Disclosures

Additional disclosures which may be relevant to financial statement users in understanding an entity's financial position and liquidity have been encouraged by IAS 7 and include the following:

1. The amount of undrawn borrowing facilities including disclosure of restrictions, if any, as to their use;
2. The aggregate amount of cash flows related to interests in joint ventures reported using the proportionate consolidation;
3. The aggregate amount of cash flows that represent increases in operating capacity separately from those cash flows that are required to maintain the operating capacity; and

4. Disclosure of segmental cash flow information in order to provide financial statement users better information about the relationship of cash flows of the business as a whole vis-à-vis cash flows from its segments.

(IAS 7, Para 50)

STATEMENT OF CHANGES IN EQUITY

A. Statement of Changes in Equity

1. As a separate component of its financial statements, an entity should present a statement showing the following items:

    a. Total comprehensive income for the period, showing separately the total amounts attributable to owners of the parent and to minority interest;
    b. For each component of equity, the effects of retrospective application or retrospective restatement recognized in accordance with IAS 8;
    c. The amounts of transactions with owners in their capacity as owners, showing separately contributions by and distributions to owners: and
    d. For each component of equity, a reconciliation between the carrying amount at the beginning and the end of the period, separately disclosing each change.

(IAS 1, Para 106)

2. Either in the statement of changes in equity or in the notes, the amount of dividends recognized as distributions to owners during the period, and the related per share amounts.

(IAS 1, Para 107)

NOTES TO THE FINANCIAL STATEMENTS

A. Structure of the Notes

1. The notes to the financial statements should

    a. Present information regarding the basis of preparation of the financial statements and the specific accounting policies selected and applied for significant transactions and events;
    b. Disclose information required by IAS which is not presented elsewhere in the financial statements; and
    c. Provide additional information which is not presented on the face of the financial statements but which is necessary for a fair presentation.

(IAS 1, Para 112)

2. The notes to the financial statements should be presented in a systematic manner. Each item on the face of the balance sheet, income statement and cash flow statement should be cross-referenced to any related information in the notes to the financial statements.

(IAS 1, Para 113)

3. The following order of presentation of the notes is normally adopted which assists users of financial statements in understanding them and comparing them with those of other entities:

    a. Statement of compliance with IFRS;
    b. Summary of significant accounting policies applied;
    c. Supporting information for items presented in the statements of financial position and of comprehensive income, in the separate income statement (if presented), and in the statements of changes in equity and of cash flows, in the order in which each statement and each line item is presented; and
    d. Other disclosures, including

        (1) Contingencies and commitments and other financial disclosures; and
        (2) Nonfinancial disclosures.

(IAS 1, Para 114)

4. An entity shall disclose in the notes

    a. The amount of dividends proposed or declared before the financial statements were authorized for issue but not recognized as a distribution to equity holders during the period, and the related amount per share; and

    b. The amount of any cumulative preference share not recognized.

(IAS 1, Para 137)

B. Accounting Policies

1. The accounting policies section of the notes to the financial statements should describe the following:

    a. The measurement basis/bases used in preparing the financial statements; and

    b. Other accounting policies used that are relevant to an understanding of the financial statements.

(IAS 1, Para 117)

2. Examples of accounting policies that an entity may consider presenting include, but are not restricted to, the following:

    a. Revenue recognition;

    b. Basis of consolidation of subsidiaries and method of accounting for investments in associates;

    c. Business combinations;

    d. Joint ventures;

    e. Recognition and depreciation/amortization of tangible and intangible assets;

    f. Capitalization of borrowing costs and other expenditures;

    g. Construction contracts;

    h. Investment properties;

    i. Financial instruments and investments;

    j. Hedge accounting;

    k. Leases;

    l. Research and development costs;

    m. Inventories;

    n. Taxes, including deferred taxes;

    o. Provisions;

    p. Employee benefit costs;

    q. Foreign currency translation and hedging;

    r. Definition of business and geographical segments and the basis for allocation of costs between segments;

    s. Definition of cash and cash equivalents;

    t. Inflation accounting; and

    u. Government grants.

C. Service Concession Arrangements

1. All aspects of a service concession arrangement should be taken into account in determining the appropriate disclosures in the notes. Both a concession operator and a concession provider should disclose the following *in each period:*

    a. A description of the service concession arrangement;

    b. Significant terms of the arrangement that may affect the amount, timing, and certainty of future cash flows (e.g., period of concession, repricing dates, and the basis upon which the repricing or renegotiation is determined);

    c. The nature and extent (e.g., the quantity, time period, or amount as appropriate) of

        (1) Rights to use specified assets;

        (2) Obligations to provide or rights to expect provision of services;

        (3) Obligations to acquire or build items of property, plant, and equipment;

(4) Obligations to deliver or rights to receive specified assets at the end of the concession period;

(5) Renewal and termination options; and

(6) Other rights and obligations (e.g., major overhauls); and

    d.   Changes in the arrangement taking place during the period.

2.   The above-mentioned disclosures should be provided individually for each service concession arrangement or in aggregate for each class of service concession arrangements. A "class" is a grouping of service concession arrangements involving services of a similar nature (e.g., toll collections, telecommunications, and water treatment services).

(SIC 29, Paras 6 & 7)

INTERIM FINANCIAL STATEMENTS

A. Minimum Components of an Interim Financial Report

1.   An interim financial report should include, at a minimum, the following components:

    a.   A condensed balance sheet;

    b.   A condensed income statement;

    c.   A condensed statement showing **either** all changes in equity **or** changes in equity other than those arising from capital transactions with owners and distributions to owners;

    d.   A condensed cash flow statement; and

    e.   Selected set of footnote disclosures.

(IAS 34, Para 8)

B. Form and Content of Interim Financial Statements

1.   If an entity chooses the "complete set of (interim) financial statements" route, instead of opting for the shortcut method of presenting only "condensed" interim financial statements, then the form and content of those statements should conform to the requirements of IAS 1 for a complete set of financial statements.

(IAS 34, Para 9)

2.   However, if an entity opts for the condensed format of interim financial reporting, then IAS 34, paragraph 10, requires that, at a minimum, those condensed financial statements should include

    a.   Each of the headings, and

    b.   Subtotals that were included in the entity's most recent annual financial statements, along with selected explanatory notes, prescribed by the Standard.

(Additional line items or notes should be included if their omission would make the condensed interim financial statements misleading.)

(IAS 34, Para 10)

3.   Basic and diluted earnings per share should be presented on the face of an income statement, complete or condensed, for an interim period.

(IAS 34, Para 11)

4.   An interim financial report should be prepared on a consolidated basis if the entity's most recent annual financial statements were consolidated statements. As regards presentation of separate interim financial statements of the parent company in addition to consolidated interim financial statements, if they were included in the most recent annual financial statements, this Standard neither requires nor prohibits such inclusion in the interim financial report of the entity.

(IAS 34, Para 14)

C. Selected Explanatory Notes

1. The minimum disclosures required to accompany the condensed interim financial statements are the following:

    a. A statement that the same accounting policies and methods of computation are applied in the interim financial statements compared with the most recent annual financial statements or if those policies or methods have changed, a description of the nature and effect of the change;

    b. Explanatory comments about seasonality or cyclicality of interim operations;

    c. The nature and magnitude of significant items affecting interim results that are unusual because of nature, size, or incidence;

    d. Dividends paid, either in the aggregate or on a per share basis, presented separately for ordinary (common) shares and other classes of shares;

    e. Revenue and operating result for business segments or geographical segments, whichever has been the entity's primary mode of segment reporting;

    f. Any significant events occurring subsequent to the end of the interim period;

    g. Issuances, repurchases, and repayments of debt and equity securities;

    h. The nature and quantum of changes in estimates of amounts reported in prior interim periods of the current financial year or changes in estimates of amounts reported in prior financial years, if those changes have a material effect in the current interim period;

    i. The effect of changes in the composition of the entity during the interim period like business combinations, acquisitions or disposal of subsidiaries and long-term investments, restructuring, and discontinuing operations; and

    j. The changes in contingent liabilities or contingent assets since the most recent annual report.

    (IAS 34, Para 16)

2. Disclose any other events or transactions material to understanding of current interim period.

    (IAS 34, Para 16)

INSURANCE CONTRACTS

1. An insurer shall disclose information that identifies and explains the amount in its financial statements arising from insurance contracts.

    (IFRS 4, Para 36)

2. To comply with IFRS 4, paragraph 36, an insurer shall disclose

    a. Its accounting policies for insurance contracts and related assets and liabilities, income, and expense;

    b. The recognized assets, liabilities, income, and expense (and, if it presents its cash flow statement using the direct method, cash flows) arising from insurance contracts. Furthermore, if the insurer is a cedant, it shall disclose

        (1) Gains and losses recognized in profit or loss on buying reinsurance;

        (2) If the cedant differs and amortizes gains and losses arising on buying reinsurance, the amortization for the period and the amounts remaining unamortized at the beginning and at the end of the period.

    c. The process used to determine the assumptions that have the greatest effect on the measurement of the recognized amounts described in b. When practicable, an insurer shall also give quantified disclosures of those assumptions.

    d. The effect of changes in assumption used to measure insurance assets and insurance liabilities, showing separately the effect of each change that has a material effect on the financial statements.

    e. Reconciliation of changes in insurance liabilities, reinsurance assets and if any, related deferred acquisition costs.

    (IFRS 4, Para 37)

3. An insurer shall give the information to understand the amount, timing, and uncertainty of future cash flows from insurance contracts.

(IFRS 4, Para 38)

4. To comply with IFRS 4, paragraph 38, an insurer shall disclose

   a. Its objectives in managing risks arising from insurance contracts and its policies for mitigating those risks.
   b. Those terms and conditions of insurance contracts that have a material effect on the amount, timing, and uncertainty of the insurer's future cash flows.
   c. Information about insurance risk (both before and after risk mitigation by reinsurance), including information about

      (1) The sensitivity of profit or loss and equity to changes in variables that have material effect on them;
      (2) Concentrations of insurance risk;
      (3) Actual claims compared with previous estimates (i.e., claim development). The disclosure about claims development shall go back to the period when the earliest material claim arose for which there is still uncertainty about the amount and timing of the claims payment, but need not go back more than ten years. An insurer need not disclose this information for claims for which uncertainty about the amount and timing of claims payments is typically resolved within one year.

   d. The information about interest rate risk and credit risk that IAS 32 would require if the insurance contracts were within the scope of IAS 32.
   e. Information about exposures to interest rate risk or market risk under embedded derivatives contained in a host insurance contract. If the insurer is not required to, and does not, measure the embedded derivatives at fair value.

(IFRS 4, Para 39)

5. An entity need not apply the disclosure requirements in this IFRS to comparative information that relates to the annual period beginning before January 1, 2005, except for the disclosure required by IFRS 4, paragraph 37(a) and (b) about accounting policies, and recognized assets, liabilities, income and expense (and cash flow if direct method is used).

(IFRS 4, Para 42)

6. If it is impracticable to apply a particular requirement to comparative information that relates to annual periods beginning January 1, 2005, an entity shall disclose that fact. Applying the liability adequacy test to such comparative information might sometimes be impracticable, but it is highly unlikely to be impracticable to apply other requirements to such comparative information.

(IFRS 4, Para 43)

7. When an entity first applies this IFRS and if it is impracticable to prepare information about claim development that occurred before the beginning of the earliest period for which an entity presents full comparative information that complies with this IFRS, the entity shall disclose this fact.

(IFRS 4, Para 44)

AGRICULTURE

A. General

1. An entity should present the carrying amount of its biological assets separately on the face of its balance sheet.
2. An entity should disclose the aggregate gain or loss arising during the current period on initial recognition of biological assets and agricultural produce and from the change in fair value less estimated point-of-sale costs of biological assets.

(IAS 41, Paras 39 & 40)

3. An entity should provide a description of each group of biological assets disclosed by the entity.

    (IAS 41, Para 41)

4. If not disclosed elsewhere in information published with the financial statements, an entity should describe

    a. The nature of its activities involving each group of biological assets; and
    b. Nonfinancial measures or estimates of the physical quantities of

        (1) Each group of the entity's biological assets at the end of the period; and
        (2) Output of agricultural produce during the period.

    (IAS 41, Para 46)

5. An entity should disclose the methods and significant assumptions applied in determining the fair value of each group of agricultural produce at the point of harvest and each group of biological assets.

    (IAS 41, Para 47)

6. An entity should disclose the fair value less estimated point-of-sale costs of agricultural produce harvested during the period, determined at the point of harvest.

    (IAS 41, Para 48)

7. An entity should disclose

    a. The existence and carrying amounts of biological assets whose title is restricted, and the carrying amounts of biological assets pledged as security for liabilities;
    b. The amount of commitments for the development or acquisition of biological assets; and
    c. Financial risk management strategies related to agricultural activity.

    (IAS 41, Para 49)

8. An entity should present a reconciliation of changes in the carrying amount of biological assets between the beginning and the end of the current period. Comparative information is not required. The reconciliation should include

    a. The gain or loss arising from changes in fair value less estimated point-of-sale costs;
    b. Increases due to purchases;
    c. Decreases due to sales;
    d. Decreases due to harvest;
    e. Increases resulting from business combinations;
    f. Net exchange differences arising on the translation of financial statements of a foreign entity; and
    g. Other changes.

    (IAS 41, Para 50)

9. Disclose (grouped or otherwise) the amount of change in fair value less estimated point of sale costs included in net profit or loss due to physical changes and price changes.

    (IAS 41, Para 51)

B. Additional Disclosure for Biological Assets Where Fair Value Cannot Be Measured Reliably

1. If an entity measures biological assets at their cost less any accumulated depreciation and any accumulated impairment losses at the end of the period, the entity should disclose for such biological assets

    a. A description of the biological assets;
    b. An explanation of why fair value cannot be measured reliably;
    c. If possible, the range of estimates within which fair value is highly likely to lie;
    d. The depreciation method used;
    e. The useful lives or the depreciation rates used; and
    f. The gross carrying amount and the accumulated depreciation (aggregated with accumulated impairment losses) at the beginning and end of the period.

    (IAS 41, Para 54)

2. If, during the current period, an entity measures biological assets at their cost less any accumulated depreciation and any accumulated impairment losses, an entity should disclose any gain or loss recognized on disposal of such biological assets and the reconciliation required by IAS 41, para 50, should disclose amounts related to such biological assets separately. In addition, the reconciliation should include the following amounts included in net profit or loss related to those biological assets:

    a. Impairment losses;
    b. Reversals of impairment losses; and
    c. Depreciation.

(IAS 41, Para 55)

3. If the fair value of biological assets previously measured at their cost, less any accumulated depreciation and any accumulated impairment losses, becomes reliably measurable during the current period, an entity should disclose for those biological assets

    a. A description of the biological assets;
    b. An explanation of why fair value has become reliably measurable; and
    c. The effect of the change.

(IAS 41, Para 56)

C. Government Grants

1. An entity should disclose the following related to agricultural activity covered by this Standard:

    a. The nature and extent of government grants recognized in the financial statements;
    b. Unfulfilled conditions and other contingencies attaching to government grants; and
    c. Significant decreases expected in the level of government grants.

(IAS 41, Para 57)

EXPLORATION FOR AND EVALUATION OF MINERAL RESOURCES

1. An entity shall disclose information that identifies and explains the amounts recognized in its financial statements arising from the exploration for and evaluation of mineral resources.

(IFRS 6, Para 23)

2. To comply with paragraph 23, IFRS 6, an entity shall disclose

    a. Its accounting policies for explorations and evaluation of expenditures including the recognition of exploration and evaluation assets.
    b. The amounts of assets, liabilities, income and expense, and operating and investing cash flows arising from the exploration for and evaluation of mineral resources.

(IFRS 6, Para 24)

3. An entity shall treat exploration and evaluation assets as a separate class of assets and make the disclosures required by either IAS 16 or IAS 38 consistent with how the assets are classified.

(IFRS 6, Para 25)

4. If an entity applies IFRS 6, *Exploration for and Evaluation of Mineral Resources,* for a period beginning before January 1, 2006, it shall disclose the fact.

(IFRS 6, Para 26)

5. Exploration and evaluation assets shall be assessed for impairment when facts and circumstances suggest that the carrying amount of an exploration and evaluation asset may exceeds its recoverable amount. When facts and circumstances suggest that the carrying amount exceeds the recoverable amount, an entity shall measure, present, and disclose any resulting impairment loss in accordance with IAS 36.

(IFRS 6, Para 18)

ILLUSTRATIVE FINANCIAL STATEMENTS PRESENTED UNDER IFRS

This appendix contains the complete set of comparative financial statements of Clariant Group for the years 2007 and 2006, presented in accordance with international accounting standards. In the authors' view, this set of financial statements offers a useful benchmark for the presentation and disclosures to be made by a major, international, diversified business enterprise.

It is not the intent to suggest that this example set of financial statements is all-inclusive of either industry practices or the reporting and disclosure standards under IFRS. Rather, this is merely illustrative of common practices at this time, from which readers may construct disclosures apropos to their individual needs and circumstances.

Consolidated financial statements of the Clariant Group

Consolidated Balance Sheets
at December 31, 2007 and 2006

	Notes[1]	12/31/2007 CHF mn	%	12/31/2006 CHF mn	%
Assets					
Noncurrent assets					
Property, plant, and equipment	4	2,401		2,422	
Intangible assets	5	339		335	
Investments in associates	6	294		288	
Financial assets	7	17		63	
Prepaid pension assets	15	122		90	
Deferred income tax assets	8	113		89	
Total noncurrent assets		**3,286**	45.1	**3,287**	45.7
Current assets					
Inventories	9	1,477		1,513	
Trade receivables	10	1,449		1,446	
Other current assets	11	535		378	
Cash and cash equivalents	12	509		443	
Current income tax receivables		29		24	
Total current assets		3,999	54.9	3,804	52.9
Noncurrent assets held for sale	22	--		97	1.4
Total assets		**7,285**	100.0	**7,188**	100.0
Equity					
Share capital	13, 28	978		1,035	
Treasury shares (par value)	13, 28	(16)		(16)	
Other reserves	28	642		648	
Retained earnings	28	709		706	
Total capital and reserves attributable to Clariant shareholders		**2,313**		**2,373**	
Minority interests	28	59		60	
Total equity	28	**2,372**	32.6	**2,433**	33.8
Liabilities					
Noncurrent liabilities					
Financial debts	14	1,267		1,376	
Deferred income tax liabilities	8	179		183	
Retirement benefit obligations	15	515		495	
Provisions for noncurrent liabilities	16	231		244	
Total noncurrent liabilities		**2,192**	30.0	**2,298**	32.0

	Notes[1]	12/31/2007 CHF mn	%	12/31/2006 CHF mn	%
Current liabilities					
Trade payables	17	1,321		1,207	
Financial debts	18	728		623	
Current income tax liabilities		244		215	
Provision for current liabilities	19	428		351	
Total current liabilities		**2,721**	37.4	**2,396**	33.3
Liabilities directly associated with					
noncurrent assets held for sale	22	--	0.0	61	0.9
Total liabilities		**4,913**	67.4	**4,755**	66.2
Total equity and liabilities		**7,285**	100.0	**7,188**	100.0

[1] *The notes form an integral part of the consolidated financial statements.*

Consolidated Income Statements
For the years ended December 31, 2007 and 2006

	Notes[1]	2007 CHF mn	%	2006 CHF mn	%
Sales	20, 21	8,533	100.0	8,100	100.0
Costs of goods sold		(6,045)		(5,614)	
Gross profit		**2,488**	29.2	**2,486**	30.7
Marketing and distribution		(1,384)		(1,328)	
Administration and general overhead costs		(391)		(394)	
Research and development		(211)		(207)	
Income from associates	6	37		35	
Gain from the disposal of activities not qualifying as discontinued operations	23	1		4	
Restructuring and impairment	27	(262)		(211)	
Operating income		**278**	3.3	**385**	4.8
Finance income	25	31		33	
Finance costs	25	(102)		(143)	
Income before taxes		**207**		**275**	
Taxes	8	(99)		(144)	
Net income from continuing operations		**108**	1.3	**131**	1.6
Discontinued operations:					
Income from discontinued operations	22	(103)	0.1	(209)	
Net income/loss		**5**	0.1	**(78)**	(1.0)
Attributable to:					
Shareholders of Clariant Ltd		(2)		(85)	
Minority interests		7		7	
Net income/loss		**5**	0.1	**(78)**	(1.0)
Basic earnings per share attributable to the shareholders of Clariant Ltd (CHF/share):					
Continuing operations	26	0.44		0.55	
Discontinued operations	26	(0.45)		(0.92)	
Total		**(0.01)**		**(0.37)**	
Diluted earnings per share attributable to the shareholders of Clariant Ltd (CHF/share):					
Continuing operations	26	0.44		0.54	
Discontinued operations	26	(0.45)		(0.92)	
Total		**(0.01)**		**(0.38)**	

[1] *The notes form an integral part of the consolidated financial statements.*

Consolidated Statements of Cash Flows
For the years ended December 31, 2007 and 2006

	Notes[1]	2007 CHF mn	2006[2] CHF mn
Net income		5	(78)
Adjustment for:			
Depreciation of property, plant, and equipment (PPE)	4	264	269
Impairment		84	231
Amortization of intangible assets	5	9	7
Impairment of working capital		53	57
Income from associates	6	(37)	(35)
Tax expense		99	117
Net financial income and costs		94	99
Gain from the disposal of activities not qualifying as discontinued operations	23	(1)	(4)
Loss on disposal of discontinued operations	22	70	101
Other noncash items		(20)	28
Total reversal of noncash items		**615**	**870**
Dividends received from associates	6	30	22
Interest paid		(86)	(69)
Interest received		29	22
Income taxes paid		(88)	(75)
Cash flow before changes in working capital		**505**	**692**
Changes in inventories		(39)	(156)
Changes in trade receivables		20	(48)
Changes in trade payables		76	(45)
Changes in other current assets and liabilities		(69)	(56)
Changes in provisions		47	(59)
Cash flow from operating activities		**540**	**328**
Investments in PPE	4	(312)	(358)
Investments in financial assets and associates		(15)	(4)
Investments in other intangible assets	5	(8)	(4)
Changes in current financial assets[3]		(116)	5
Sale of PPE and intangible assets		18	25
Acquisition of companies, businesses and participations	24	(8)	(45)
Proceeds from the disposal of discontinued operations	22	25	46
Proceeds from the disposal of subsidiaries and associates	23	23	33
Cash flow from investing activities		**(393)**	**(302)**
Reduction of share capital to shareholders of Clariant Ltd	28	(57)	(58)
Treasury share transactions		(8)	(4)
Proceeds from financial debts		308	1,130
Repayments of financial debts		(317)	(867)
Dividends paid to minority shareholders	28	(9)	(7)
Cash flow from financing activities		**(83)**	**194**
Currency translation effect on cash and cash equivalents		2	
Net change in cash and cash equivalents		**66**	**220**
Cash and cash equivalents at the beginning of the period	12	**443**	**223**
Cash and cash equivalents at the end of the period	12	**509**	**443**

[1] *The notes form an integral part of the consolidated financial statements.*
[2] *Restated (see Note 1.07).*
[3] *This item concerns the investment of cash and cash equivalents earmarked for the bond repayment in March 2008 in short-term deposits over ninety days.*

Consolidated Statements of Recognized Income and Expense
For the years ended December 31, 2007 and 2006

	Notes[1]	2007 CHF mn	2006 CHF mn
Net investment hedge	29	(31)	(16)
Currency translation differences		26	1
Tax on items taken directly to or transferred from equity		(3)	
Net income recognized directly in equity		**(8)**	**(15)**
Net income/loss		5	(78)
Total recognized income and expense for the period	**28**	**(3)**	**(93)**
Attributable to			
Shareholders of Clariant Ltd	28	(11)	(100)
Minority interests	28	8	7

This statement shows only changes in equity other than those arising from capital transactions with owners and distributions to owners. For a comprehensive presentation of equity, see note 28.

[1] *The notes form an integral part of the consolidated financial statements.*

Changes in fair value of financial assets classified as available-for-sale amount to less than CHF 1 million in 2006 and 2007

Notes to the Consolidated Financial Statements

1. Accounting policies
1.01 General information

Clariant Ltd (the "Company") and its consolidated subsidiaries (together the "Group") are a global leader in the field of specialty chemicals. The Group develops, manufactures, distributes and sells a broad range of specialty chemicals which play a key role in its customers' manufacturing and treatment processes or add value to their end products. The Group has manufacturing plants around the world and sells mainly in countries within Europe, the Americas and Asia.

The company is a limited liability company incorporated and domiciled in Switzerland. The address of its registered office is Rothausstrasse 61, CH-4132 Muttenz, Switzerland. The Company is listed on the Swiss Stock Exchange (SWX).

The Board of Directors has approved the consolidated financial statements for issue on February 12, 2008. They will be subject to approval by the Annual General Meeting of Shareholders scheduled for April 10, 2008.

1.02 Basis of preparation

The consolidated financial statements of the Clariant Group have been prepared in accordance with International Financial Reporting Standards (IFRS) and with the following significant accounting policies. The consolidated financial statements have been prepared under the historical cost convention as modified by the revaluation of financial assets and liabilities (including derivative instruments at fair value through profit or loss).

The preparation of financial statements in conformity with IFRS requires the use of estimates and assumptions. These affect the reported amounts of assets and liabilities and the disclosure of contingent assets and liabilities at the date of the financial statements and the reported amounts of revenues and expenses during the reporting period. Although these estimates are based on management's best knowledge of current events and circumstances, actual results may ultimately differ from those estimates. The areas involving a higher degree of judgment or complexity, or areas where assumptions and estimates are significant to the consolidated financial statements, are disclosed under note 3.

1.03 International financial reporting standards effective in 2007

In 2005 the IASB issued IFRS 7, *Financial Instruments*: disclosures, and the complementary amendment to IAS 1, *Presentation of Financial Statements—Capital Disclosures,* which became effective as of January 1, 2007. This standard introduces new disclosures to improve the information about financial instruments. It requires the disclosure of qualitative and quantitative information about exposure to risk arising from financial instruments, including specified minimum disclosures about credit risk, liquidity risk and market risk, including sensitivity analysis to market risk. It replaces the disclosure requirements in IAS 32, *Financial Instruments: Disclosure and Presentation.* It is applicable to all entities that report under IFRS. The standard was adopted as of January 1, 2007, and comparable information was restated. As it covers disclosure requirements only, it did not have any impact on the classification and valuation of the Group's financial instruments.

In 2005 the IASB issued IFRIC 7, *Applying the Restatement Approach under IAS 29, Financial Reporting in Hyperinflationary Economies,* which became effective as of March 2006. This interpretation provides guidance on how to apply the requirements of IAS 29 in a reporting period in which an entity identifies the existence of hyperinflation economy of its functional currency, when the economy was not hyperinflationary in the prior period. As none of the group entities has a currency of a hyperinflationary economy as its functional currency, this interpretation did not have any impact on the Group's accounts.

In 2006 the IASB issued IFRIC 8, *Scope of IFRS 2,* which became effective as of May 1, 2006. This interpretation requires consideration of transactions involving the issuance of equity instruments, where the identifiable consideration received is less than the fair value of the equity instruments issued, to establish whether or not they fall within the scope of IFRS 2. The Group has applied this interpretation from January 1, 2007, but it did not have any impact on the Group's accounts.

In 2006 the IASB issued IFRIC 9, *Reassessment of Embedded Derivatives,* which became effective as of June 1, 2006. This interpretation requires an entity to assess whether an embedded derivative is required to be separated from the host contract and accounted for as a derivative when the entity first becomes a party to the contract. Subsequent reassessment is prohibited unless there is a change in the terms of the contract that significantly modifies the cash flows that otherwise would be required under the contract, in which case reassessment is required. The Group has applied this interpretation since January 1, 2007, but it did not have any impact on the Group's accounts.

In 2006 the IASB issued IFRIC 10, *Interim Financial Reporting and Impairment,* which became effective as of November 1, 2006. This interpretation prohibits the reversal of impairment losses recognized in an interim period on goodwill, investments in equity instruments and investments in financial assets carried at cost, at a subsequent balance sheet date. The Group has applied this interpretation since January 1, 2007, but it did not have any impact on the Group's accounts.

1.04 International financial reporting standards not yet effective

Certain new standards, amendments and interpretations to existing standards have been published that are mandatory for the Group's accounting periods beginning on or after January 1, 2008, or later periods but which the Group has not early adopted, as follows:

IFRS 8, Operating Segments (effective for annual periods beginning on or after January 1, 2009). IFRS 8 replaces IAS 14, *Segment Reporting.* This standard requires entities to define operating segments and segment performance in the financial statements based on information used by the chief operating decision maker. This new requirement could have an impact on the segments presented, the items reported and their respective measurement. The Group has not undergone a thorough analysis and therefore no final assessment of the impact can presently be made. The group will apply this standard from January 1, 2009.

IAS 23 (revised), Borrowing Costs (effective for annual periods beginning on or after January 1, 2009). This revised standard requires that all borrowing costs that are directly attributable to the acquisition, construction or production of a qualifying asset be capitalized as part of the cost of that asset. The Group estimates that this new accounting treatment of borrowing costs will reduce its finance costs and increase depreciation.

IAS 1 (revised), Presentation of Financial Statements (effective for annual periods beginning on or after January 1, 2009). This revised standard requires the presentation in a statement of changes in equity, all owner changes in equity. All nonowner changes in equity are required to be presented in one statement of comprehensive income or in two statements (a separate income statement and a statement of comprehensive income).

The revised standard also requires the presentation of a statement of financial position as at the beginning of the earliest comparative period in a complete set of financial statements when an accounting policy is applied retrospectively or a retrospective restatement is made as defined in IAS 8, or when items are reclassified in the financial statements.

Further, the standard requires the disclosure of reclassification adjustments and income tax relating to each component of other comprehensive income and the presentation of dividends recognized as distributions to owners and related amounts per share in the statement of changes in equity or in the notes. The Group will apply the revised standard from January 1, 2009. As the new requirements concern disclosures only, they will not impact the Group's accounting policies.

IFRS 2 (amended) (effective for accounting periods beginning on or after January 1, 2009) deals with two matters. It clarifies that vesting conditions can be service conditions and performance conditions only. Other features of share-based payment are not vesting conditions. It also specifies that all cancellations, whether by the entity or by other parties, should receive the same accounting treatment. Whether this new requirement will impact the Group's accounting policies is currently under investigation.

IFRS 3 (revised), Business Combinations, requires significant changes in the application of the acquisition method to business combinations. All payments to purchase a business are to be recorded at fair value at the acquisition date, with some contingent payments subsequently remeasured at fair value through profit or loss. Goodwill may be calculated based on the parent's share of net assets or it may also include goodwill related to the minority interest. All transaction costs will be expensed. The standard is applicable to business combinations occurring in accounting periods beginning on or after July 1, 2009, with earlier application permitted. These new requirements may impact significantly the Group's accounting policies for future business combinations.

IAS 27 (amended) (effective for accounting periods beginning on or after July 1, 2009) requires the effects of all transactions with noncontrolling interests to be recorded in equity if there is no change in control. They will no longer result in goodwill or gains and losses. The standard also specifies the accounting when control is lost. Any remaining interest in the entity is remeasured to fair value and a gain or loss is recognized in profit or loss. In addition, total comprehensive income must be attributed to the owners of the parent and to the noncontrolling interests even if this results in the noncontrolling interests having a deficit balance. These new requirements could impact the accounting for future transactions with noncontrolling interest (formerly minority interest).

IFRIC 11, IFRS 2, Group and Treasury Share Transactions (effective for annual periods beginning on or after March 1, 2007). This interpretation requires a share-based payment arrangement in which an entity receives goods or services as consideration for its own equity instruments to be accounted for as an equity-settled payment transaction, regardless of how the equity instruments are obtained. The Group will apply this interpretation from January 1, 2008, but it is not expected to have any impact on the Group's accounts.

IFRIC 12, Service Concession Arrangements (effective for annual periods beginning on or after January 1, 2008). This interpretation addresses how service operators should apply existing IFRSs to account for the obligations they undertake and rights they receive in service concession arrangements. This interpretation is not expected to have any impact on the Group's accounts.

IFRIC 13, Customer Loyalty Programs (effective for annual periods beginning on or after July 1, 2008). IFRIC 13 clarifies that where goods or services are sold together with a customer loyalty incentive (for example, loyalty points of free products), the arrangement is a multiple-element arrangement and the consideration receivable from the customer is allocated between the components of the arrangement using fair values. This interpretation is not expected to have any impact on the Group's accounts.

IFRIC 14, IAS 19. The limit on a defined benefit asset, minimum funding requirements and their interaction (effective for annual periods beginning on or after January 1, 2008). IFRIC 13 provides guidance on assessing the limit in IAS 19 on the amount of the surplus that can be recognized as an asset. It also explains how the pension asset or liability may be affected by a statutory or contractual minimum funding requirement. Clariant is currently assessing the impact of this interpretation on the Group's accounts.

The above mentioned standards and interpretations will be adopted as they become effective.

1.05 Scope of consolidation

Subsidiaries. Subsidiaries are those entities in which the Group has an interest of more than one half of the voting rights or otherwise has the power to govern the financial and operating policies. These entities are consolidated. The existence and effect of potential voting rights that are presently exercisable or presently convertible are considered when assessing whether the Group controls another entity. Subsidiaries are consolidated from the date on which control is transferred to the Group and cease to be consolidated from the date control is terminated.

The Group uses the purchase method of accounting to account for the acquisition of subsidiaries. The cost of an acquisition is measured at the fair value of the assets given, equity instruments issued and liabilities incurred or assumed at the date of exchange, plus costs directly attributable to the acquisition. Identifiable assets acquired and liabilities and contingent liabilities assumed in a business combination are measured initially at their fair values at the acquisition date, irrespective of the extent of a minority interest. The excess of the cost of acquisition over the fair value of the Group's share of the identifiable net assets acquired is recorded as goodwill. If the costs of acquisition are less than the fair value of the net assets of the subsidiary acquired, the difference is recognized directly in the income statement.

Transactions with minority interests. The Group applies a policy of treating transactions with minority interests as transactions with parties external to the Group. Disposals to minority interests result in gains and losses for the Group that are recorded in the income statement. Purchases from minority interests results in goodwill, being the difference between any consideration paid and the relevant share acquired of the carrying value of net assets of the subsidiary.

Investments in associates. Associates are entities where the Group has between 20% and 50% of the voting rights, or over which the Group has significant influence, but which it does not control. Investments in associates are accounted for by the equity method of accounting and are initially recognized at cost. The Group's investments in associates include goodwill (net of any accumulated impairment loss) identified on acquisition.

The company's share of the postacquisition profits or losses of associates is recognized in the income statement and its share of postacquisition movements in reserves is recognized in reserves. The cumulative postacquisition movements are adjusted against the cost of the investment. When the Group's share of losses in an associate equals or exceeds its interest in the associate, including any other unsecured receivables, the Group does not recognize further losses, unless it has incurred obligations or made payments on behalf of the associate.

All associates use the same set of accounting policies (IFRS) that are applied to the consolidated accounts of the Group.

1.06 Principles and methods of consolidation

The annual closing date of the individual financial statements is December 31. The consolidated financial statements are prepared in accordance with the historical cost convention except for the revaluation to market value of certain financial assets and liabilities and applying uniform presentation and valuation principles.

Intercompany income and expenses, including unrealized gross profits from internal Group transactions and intercompany receivables and payables, are eliminated. The results of minority interests are separately disclosed in the income statement and balance sheet.

1.07 Reclassification

The presentation of the cash flow statement was changed to provide more relevant information. Comparative information was reclassified accordingly. In the new cash flow statement presentation, all noncash expenses are added back to the net result, including interest and tax expenses. The receipts and payments of interest and payments of taxes are reported separately in operating activities. Dividends received from associates are classified as cash flows from operating activities, as investments in associates are of a strictly operating nature. In the prior version of the cash flow statement dividends received were classified cash flows from investing activities.

1.08 Revenue recognition

Sales of goods are recognized when the significant risks and rewards of ownership of the assets have been transferred to a third party and are reported net of sales taxes and rebates. Provisions for rebates to customers are recognized in the same period that the related sales are recorded, based on the contract terms.

Interest income is recognized on a time proportion basis, taking into account the principal outstanding and the effective rate over the period to maturity when it is determined that such income will accrue to the Group. Dividends are recognized when the right to receive payment is established.

1.09 Exchange rate differences

Functional currency. Items included in the financial statements of each entity are measured using the currency of the primary economic environment in which the entity operates (the functional currency). The consolidated financial statements are presented in Swiss francs, which is the functional and presentation currency of the parent.

Transactions and balances. Foreign currency transactions are translated into the functional currency using the exchange rates prevailing at the dates of the transactions. Foreign exchange gains and losses resulting from the settlement of such transactions and from the translation of monetary assets and liabilities denominated in foreign currencies, are recognized in the income statement, except when deferred in equity as qualifying cash flow hedges and net investment hedges. Translation differences on debt securities and other monetary financial assets measured at fair value are included in foreign exchange gains and losses.

Group companies. Income statements and cash flows of foreign entities are translated into the Group's presentation currency at sales weighted average exchange rates for the year and their balance sheets are translated at the exchange rates prevailing on December 31. Exchange rate differences arising on the translation of the net investment in foreign entities and of borrowings and other currency instruments designated as hedges of such investments, are taken to shareholders' equity. Net investments also include loans for which settlement is neither planned nor likely to occur in the foreseeable future. When a foreign entity is sold, such exchange rate differences are recognized in the income statement as part of the gain or loss on sale.

Goodwill and fair value adjustments arising on the acquisition of foreign entities after March 31, 2004, are treated as assets and liabilities of the foreign entity and translated at the closing rate.

1.10 Property, plant, and equipment

Property, plant, and equipment are valued at historical acquisition or production costs and depreciated on a straight-line basis to the income statement, using the following maximum estimated useful lives in accordance with Group guidelines:

Buildings	40 years
Machinery and equipment	16 years
Furniture, vehicles, computer hardware	5 to 10 years
Land is not depreciated	

Financing costs associated with the construction of property, plant, and equipment are not capitalized.

Subsequent costs are included in the asset's carrying amount or recognized as a separate asset, as appropriate, only when it is probable that future economic benefits associated with the item will flow to the Group and the costs of the item can be measured reliability. All repairs and maintenance are charged to the income statement during the financial period in which they are incurred.

Gains and losses on disposals are determined by comparing proceeds with the carrying amount. These are included in the income statement.

1.11 Intangible assets

Goodwill represents the excess of the cost of an acquisition over the fair value of the Group's share of the net identifiable assets of the acquired subsidiary/associate at the date of acquisition. Goodwill on acquisitions of associates is included in investments in associates. Goodwill is tested annually for impairment and carried at cost less accumulated impairment losses. Gains and losses on the disposal of an entity include the carrying amount of goodwill relating to the entity sold.

Goodwill is allocated to cash-generating units for the purpose of impairment testing.

Trademarks and licenses are capitalized at historical costs and amortized on a straight-line basis to the income statement over their estimated useful lives, with a maximum of ten years.

Acquired computer software licenses are capitalized on the basis of the costs incurred to acquire and bring to use the specific software. These are amortized on a straight-line basis to the income statement over their estimated useful lives (three to five years). Costs associated with developing and maintaining computer software programs are recognized as an expense when incurred. Cost that are directly associated with the production of identifiable and unique software products controlled by the Group, and that will probably generate economic benefits beyond one year, are recognized as intangible assets. Direct costs include the software development employee costs and an appropriate portion of relevant overheads.

1.12 Impairment of assets

Property, plant, and equipment and other noncurrent assets, including goodwill and other intangible assets, are reviewed for impairment losses whenever events or changes in circumstances indicate that the carrying amount may not be recoverable. An impairment loss is recognized for the amount by which the carrying amount of the asset exceeds its recoverable amount, which is the higher of an asset's fair value less costs to sell or value in use. For the purpose of assessing impairment, assets are grouped at the lowest level for which there are separately identifiable cash flows (cash-generating unit).

An impairment loss is recognized as an expense in the income statement and is first allocated to the goodwill associated with the cash-generating unit and then to the other assets of the cash-generating unit. An impairment loss may be reversed, for assets excluding goodwill, in subsequent periods if only if there is a change in the estimates used to determine the asset's recoverable amount.

1.13 Inventories

Purchased goods are valued at acquisition costs, while self-manufactured products are valued at manufacturing costs including related production overhead costs. Borrowing costs are excluded. Inventory held at the balance sheet date is primarily valued at standard cost, which approximates actual costs on a weighted-average basis. The valuation method is also used for valuing the cost of goods sold in the income statement. Adjustments are made for inventories with a lower net realizable value. Unsaleable inventories are fully written off. These adjustments are recorded as provisions, which are deducted directly from the inventory value in the balance sheet. The provisions are reversed when the inventories concerned are either sold or destroyed and as a consequence are removed from the balance sheet.

1.14 Trade receivables

Trade receivables are recognized initially at fair value and subsequently measured at amortized cost, less impairment of trade receivables. A provision for the impairment of trade receivables is established when there is objective evidence that the Group will not be able to collect all amounts due according to the original terms of receivables. The amount of the provision is the difference between the carrying amount and the recoverable amount, being the present value of expected cash flows, discounted at the market rate of interest for similar borrowers. The amount of the provision is recognized in the income statement.

1.15 Cash and cash equivalents

Cash and cash equivalents comprise cash on hand, deposits and calls with banks, as well as short-term investment instruments with an initial lifetime of 90 days or less. Bank overdrafts are shown within financial debt in current liabilities on the balance sheet.

1.16 Derivative financial instruments and hedging

Under IAS 39, derivative financial instruments are initially recognized at fair value on the date a derivative contract is entered into and are subsequently remeasured at their fair value. Depending on the type of the derivative financial instrument, fair value calculation techniques include, but are not limited to, quoted market value, present value of estimated future cash flows (e.g., interest rate swaps) or corresponding exchange rates at balance sheet date (e.g., forward foreign exchange contracts). The method of recognizing the resulting gain or loss is dependent on whether the derivative contract is designated to hedge a specific risk and qualifies for hedge accounting.

On the date a derivative contract is entered into, Clariant designates certain derivatives as either (a) a hedge of the fair value of a recognized asset or liability (fair value hedge), (b) a hedge of a forecast transaction (cash flow hedge) or firm commitment, or (c) a hedge of a net investment in a foreign entity.

Changes in the fair value of derivatives in fair value hedges that are highly effective are recognized in the income statement, along with any changes in the fair value of the hedged asset or liability that is attributable to the hedged risk. Changes in the fair value of derivatives in cash flow hedges are recognized as a hedging reserve in shareholders' equity. Where the forecast transaction results in the recognition of a nonfinancial asset or nonfinancial liability, the gains and losses previously included in equity are included in the initial measurement of the asset or liability. Otherwise, amounts recorded in equity are transferred to the income statement and classified as income or expense in the same period in which the forecast transaction affects the income statement. The gain or loss relating to the ineffective portion is recognized immediately in the income statement.

Hedges of net investments in foreign entities are accounted for similar to cash flows hedges. Clariant hedges certain net investments in foreign entities with foreign currency borrowings and cross-currency swaps. All foreign exchange gains and losses on the effective portion of the hedge are recognized in equity and included in cumulative translation differences. Any gains or losses relating to an ineffective portion are recognized immediately in the income statement. Gains and losses accumulated in equity are included in the income statement when the foreign operation is disposed of.

When a hedging instrument expires or is sold, or when a hedge no longer meets the criteria for hedge accounting, any cumulative gain or loss existing in equity at that time remains in equity and is recognized in the income statement when the committed or forecast transaction is ultimately recognized in the income statement. However, if a forecast or committed transaction is no longer expected to occur, the cumulative gain or loss that was recognized in equity is immediately transferred to the income statement.

Certain derivative instruments, while providing effective economic hedges under Clariant policies, do not qualify for hedge accounting. Changes in the fair value of any derivative instruments that do not qualify for cash flow hedge accounting under IAS 39 are recognized immediately in the income statement.

Financial instruments are used in the normal course of business to reduce risk arising from currency translation and interest rate or price movements. Clariant manages and records centrally its cover of various positions arising from existing assets and liabilities as well as future business transactions. To minimize counterparty risk, Clariant enters into financial instruments only with reputable international banks. The result of using financial instruments in Clariant's risk management program is permanently monitored, checked and communicated to Group management.

1.17 Leases

Leases under which the Clariant Group assumes substantially all of the risks and benefits of ownership are classified as finance leases. At the inception of the lease, the leased asset and a lease liability are recognized at the lower of the fair value of the leased property or the present value of the minimum lease payments. In subsequent periods the leased asset is depreciated on a straight-line basis, like other property, plant, and equipment, over the shorter of its estimated useful life or the lease term. The depreciation amount of the asset and the interest amount on the finance lease liability are charged to the income statement.

A lease is classified as an operating lease if the substance of the transaction does not meet any of the requirements of a finance lease. Lease payments under an operating lease are charged to the income statement on a straight-line basis over the term of the lease.

1.18 Current income tax

The taxable profit (loss) of Group companies, on which the reporting period's income tax payable (recoverable) is calculated using applicable local tax rates, is determined in accordance with the rules established by the taxation authorities of the countries in which they operate. Current income taxes for current and prior periods, to the extent they are unpaid, are recognized as liabilities. In case income taxes already paid in respect of current and prior periods exceed the income tax liability amount of those periods, the exceeding amounts are recognized as assets. Current income tax receivables and current income tax liabilities are offset if there is a legally enforceable right to set off the recognized amounts and if there is the intention to settle on a net basis or to realize the asset and settle the liability simultaneously.

1.19 Deferred income tax

Deferred income tax is calculated using the comprehensive liability method. This method calculates a deferred tax asset or liability on the temporary differences that arise between the recognition of items in the balance sheets of Group companies used for tax purposes and the one prepared for consolidation purposes. An exception is that no deferred income tax is calculated for the temporary differences in investments in Group companies and associates, provided that the investor (parent company) is able to control the timing of the reversal of the temporary difference and it is probable that the temporary difference will not reverse in the forseeable future. Furthermore, withholding taxes or other taxes on the eventual distribution of retained earnings of Group companies are only taken into account when a dividend has been planned, since generally the retained earnings are reinvested.

Deferred taxes, calculated using applicable local tax rates, are included in noncurrent assets and noncurrent liabilities, with any changes during the year recorded in the income statement. Changes in deferred taxes on items that are recognized in equity are recorded in equity.

Deferred income tax is determined using tax rates (and laws) that have been enacted or substantially enacted by the balance sheet date and are expected to apply when the related deferred income tax asset is realized or the deferred income tax liability is settled.

Deferred income tax assets are recognized to the extent that it is probable that future taxable profit will be available against which the temporary differences or the tax losses carried forward can be utilized.

1.20 Equity compensation benefits

In 2005 Clariant replaced its two equity compensation plans, the Clariant Executive Stock Option Plan (CESOP) and the Management Stock Incentive Plan (MSIP), with the Clariant Executive Bonus Plan (CEBP). Under this new plan, specific groups of executives and managers are granted a certain number of registered shares in Clariant Ltd. The options and shares granted under the old plans up to February 2005 continue to vest. The fair value of the employee services received in exchange for the grant of the shares and options is recognized as an expense. The total amount to be expensed over the vesting and measurement periods is determined by the reference to the fair value of shares and options granted. An adjustment is made for dividends not distributed during the vesting period. Nonmarket vesting conditions are included in assumptions about the number of shares and options that are expected to become exercisable. At each balance sheet date, the entity revises its estimates of the number of shares and options expected to vest. It recognizes the impact of the revision of original estimates, if any, in the income statement, and a corresponding adjustment to equity over the remaining vesting period.

1.21 Obligations for pensions and similar employee benefits

Group companies operate various pension schemes. The Group has both defined benefit and defined contribution plans. A defined benefit plan is a pension plan that defines an amount of pension benefit that an employee will receive on retirement, usually dependent on one or more factors such as age, years of service and compensation. A defined contribution plan is a pension plan under which the Group pays fixed contributions into a separate entity. The Group has no legal or constructive obligations to pay further contributions if the fund does not hold sufficient assets to pay all employees the benefits relating to employee service in the current and prior periods.

For **defined contribution plans,** the Group pays contributions to publicly or privately administered pension insurance plans on a mandatory, contractual or voluntary basis. The Group has no further payment obligations once the contributions have been paid. Contributions to defined contribution plans are recorded in the income statement in the period to which they relate.

For **defined benefits plans,** the amount to be recognized in the provision is determined using the Projected Unit Credit Method, according to which each period of employee service gives rise to an additional unit of benefit entitlement and each unit is measured separately to build up the final obligation. Actuarial valuation techniques that take into consideration the demographic and financial assumptions are used to determine the carrying value of the net postemployment liability. Independent actuaries perform these valuations on a regular basis, at least every three years.

The portion of the actuarial gains and losses to be recognized as income or expense is the excess of the net cumulative unrecognized actuarial gains and losses at the end of the previous reporting year over the greater of 10% of the present value of the defined benefit obligation at that date and 10% of the fair value of any plan assets at that date, divided by the expected average remaining working lives of the employees participating in the plan.

Some Group companies provide **postretirement health care benefits** to their retirees. The entitlement to these benefits is usually conditional on the employee remaining in service up to retirement age and the completion of a minimum service period. The expected costs of these benefits are accrued over the period of employment using an accounting methodology similar to that for defined benefit pension plans. Actuarial gains and losses arising from experience adjustments and changes in actuarial assumptions are charged or credited to the income statement over the expected average remaining working lives of the related employees. These obligations are valued annually by independent qualified actuaries.

Termination benefits are provided for in accordance with the legal requirements of certain countries. Termination benefits are payable when employment is terminated before the normal retirement date, or whenever an employee accepts voluntary redundancy in exchange for these benefits. The Group recognizes termination benefits when it is demonstrably committed to either terminating the employment of current employees according to a detailed formal plan without possibility of withdrawal, or providing termination benefits as a result of an offer made to encourage voluntary redundancy. Benefits failing due more than twelve months after balance sheet date are discounted to present value. The charges for defined benefit plans, defined contribution plans and termination benefits are included in personnel expenses and reported in the income statement under the corresponding functions of the related employees and in expenses for restructuring and impairment.

Other **long-term employee benefits** are employee benefits (other than postemployment benefits and termination benefits) which do not fall due wholly within twelve months after the end of the period in which the employees render the related services. These include long-term compensated absences such as long-service or sabbatical leave and jubilee or other long-service benefits. The accounting policy for other long-term employee benefits is equal to that for postemployment benefits, with the exception that actuarial gains and losses and past service costs are recognized immediately in the income statement.

Short-term employee benefits are employee benefits (other than termination benefits) which fall due wholly within twelve months after the end of the period in which the employees render the related service. Accounting for short-term employee benefits is straightforward and they are measured on an undiscounted basis.

1.22 Provisions

Provisions are recognized when the Group has a binding present obligation. This may be either legal because it derives from a contract, legislation or other operation of law, or constructive because the Group created valid expectations on the part of third parties by accepting certain responsibilities. To record such an obligation it must be probable that an outflow of resources embodying economic benefits will be required to settle the obligation and a reliable estimate can be made for the amount of the obligation. The amount recognized as a provision is the best estimate (most probable outcome) of the expenditure required to settle the present obligation at the balance sheet date. The noncurrent provisions are discounted if the impact is material.

1.23 Research and development

Research and development expenses are capitalized to the extent that the recognition criteria according to IAS 38 are met. The Group considers that regulatory and other uncertainties inherent in the development of key new products preclude it from capitalizing development costs. At the balance sheet date, no research and development projects met the recognition criteria. Laboratory buildings and equipment included in property, plant, and equipment are depreciated over the estimated useful lives. The reason for this practice is the structure of research and development in the industries that Clariant engages in, making it difficult to demonstrate how singular intangible assets will generate probable future economic benefits.

1.24 Segment reporting

Clariant is divided operationally on a worldwide basis into the following four divisions, which are at the same time the Group's reportable business segments:

- Textile, Leather & Paper Chemicals
- Pigments & Additives
- Masterbatches
- Functional Chemicals

These divisions, which are based on internal management structures, are best described as follows:

The **Textile, Leather & Paper Chemicals Division** is a supplier of specialty chemicals and dyes for the textile, leather and paper industries. Textile dyes include dispersion, reactive, acid, metal complex and sulfur dyes. The Textile Business encompasses special chemicals for pretreatment, dyeing, printing and finishing of textiles. Optical brighteners and chemicals for functional treatment are also part of the range. The Leather Business produces chemicals and colorants for retanning, tanning, dyeing and finishing. Its offering includes wet-end dyes and auxiliaries, wet-end chemicals and finishing chemicals. The Paper Business supplies paper dyes, optical brighteners and process and pulping chemicals.

The **Pigments & Additives Division** develops and produces colorants for paints and coatings, for plastics and for special applications. The product range includes high-performance pigments, pigment preparations and dyes to meet the specific demands of, for example the automotive and electronics industries. Printing pigments are supplied to the printing ink industry and increasingly for nonimpact printing, ink-jet and laser printing. The core business also includes additives to improve light and weather resistance as well as heat resistant properties in plastics and coating. Nonhalogenated flame retardants are used in protective coatings, resins, thermoplastics and polyester fibers. The division's portfolio also includes high-quality waxes based on various materials.

The **Functional Chemicals Division's** products are based on surfactants and polymers. The Detergents Business, which offers anionic and cationic surfactants, as well as bleach activators, is a partner to the detergent industry. Performance Chemicals supplies such different industries as personal care products, crop protection, paints, lacquers, and plastics. The Process Chemicals Business markets products for the production and refining of oil and natural gas and for metalworking, mining and the aerospace and automotive industry. Since January 1, 2007, the division also comprises the activities of Specialty Fine Chemicals which were formerly a part of the Life

Science Chemicals Division. That division was dissolved at the end of 2006 when the biggest part of its activities were sold. Comparable information was restated.

The **Masterbatches Division** supplies color and additive concentrates and special mixtures of these components used by manufacturers of plastic goods. These products are supported by value-added services that help customers deal with such issues as complex local and international regulations, multicontinent manufacturing, speed-to-market, pricing pressures and the demands of progressively more sophisticated consumers.

Corporate. Income and expenses relating to Corporate include the costs of the Group headquarters and those of corporate coordination functions in major countries. In addition, Corporate includes certain items of income and expense, which are not directly attributable to specific divisions.

The Group's divisions are business segments that offer different products. These business segments are managed separately because they manufacture, distribute and sell distinct products, which require differing technologies and marketing strategies. These products are also subject to risks and returns that are different from those of other business segments. Geographical segments provide products within a particular economic environment that are subject to risks and returns that are different from those operating in other economic environments. The Group designates business segments as its primary reportable segments and geographical segments as its secondary reportable segments.

Segment revenue is revenue reported in the company's income statement that is directly attributable to a segment and the relevant portion of the company income that can be allocated on a reasonable basis to a segment, whether from sales to external customers or from transactions with other segments.

Segment expense is an expense resulting from the operating activities of a segment that is directly attributable to the segment and the relevant portion of an expense that can be allocated on a reasonable basis, including expenses relating to sales to external customers and expenses relating to transactions with other segments.

Intersegment sales are determined on an arm's-length basis.

Division and business net operating assets consist primarily of property, plant and equipment, intangible assets, inventories, and receivables less operating liabilities. Corporate assets and liabilities principally consist of net liquidity (cash, cash equivalents and other current financial assets less financial debts) and deferred and current taxes.

1.25 Treasury shares

Treasury shares are deducted from equity at their par value of CHF 4.25 per share. Differences between this amount and the amount paid for acquiring, or received for disposing of treasury shares are recorded in retained earnings.

1.26 Dividend distribution

Dividend distribution to the Company's shareholders is recognized as a liability in the Group's financial statements in the period in which the dividends are approved by the Company's shareholders.

1.27 Noncurrent assets (or disposal groups) held for sale

Noncurrent assets (or disposal groups) are classified as assets held for sale and stated at the lower of carrying amount and fair value less costs to sell if their carrying amount is to be recovered principally through a sale transaction rather than through continuing use. In noncurrent assets held for sale Clariant reports assets and associated liabilities of the Custom Manufacturing activities for 2006.

1.28 Share capital

All issued shares are ordinary shares and as such are classified as equity. Incremental costs directly attributable to the issue of new shares or options are shown in equity as a deduction, net of tax, from the proceeds.

Where any Group company purchases the Company's equity share capital (treasury shares), the consideration paid, including any directly attributable incremental costs (net of income taxes) is deducted from equity attributable to the Company's equity holders until the shares are cancelled, reissued or disposed of. Where such shares are subsequently sold or reissued, any consideration received, net of any directly attributable incremental transaction costs and the related income tax effects, is included in equity attributable to the Company's equity holders.

1.29 Financial debt

Financial debt is recognized initially at fair value, net of transaction costs incurred. Financial debt is subsequently stated at amortized cost. Any difference between the proceeds (net of transaction costs) and the redemption value, is recognized in the income statement over the period of the financial debt.

Financial debt is classified as a current liability where it is due within twelve months from the balance sheet date. This includes the portion of noncurrent debt that is due within twelve months. Financial debt is classified as a noncurrent liability where Group has an unconditional right to defer settlement of the liability for at least twelve months after the balance sheet date.

1.30 Investments

The Group classifies its investments in the following categories: financial assets at fair value through profit or loss, loans and receivables, held-to-maturity investments and available-for-sale financial assets. The classification depends on the purpose for which the investments were acquired. Management determines the classification of its investments on initial recognition and reevaluates this designation at every reporting date.

Financial assets at fair value through profit or loss. This category has two subcategories: financial assets held for trading and those designated at fair value through profit or loss at inception. A financial asset is classified in this category if acquired principally for the purpose of selling in the short-term or if so designated by management. Derivatives are also categorized as held-for-trading unless they are designated as hedges. Assets in this category are classified as current assets if they are either held for trading or are expected to be realized within twelve months of the balance sheet date.

Loans and receivables. Loans and receivables are nonderivative financial assets with fixed or determinable payments that are not quoted in an active market. They arise when the Group provides money and goods directly to a debtor with no intention of trading the receivable. They are included in current assets in the balance sheet.

Held-to-maturity investments. Held-to-maturity investments are nonderivative financial assets with fixed or determinable payments and fixed maturities that the Group's management has the positive intention and ability to hold to maturity.

Available-for-sale financial assets. Available-for-sale financial assets are nonderivatives that are either designated to that category or not classified to any of the other categories. They are included in noncurrent assets unless management intends to dispose of the investment within twelve months of the balance sheet date.

Purchases and sales of investments are recognized on settlement date, which is the date on which the Group receives or delivers the asset. Investments are initially recognized at fair value plus transaction costs for all financial assets not carried at fair value through profit or loss. Investments are derecognized when the rights to receive cash flows from the investments have expired or have been transferred and the Group has transferred substantially all risks and rewards of ownership. Available-for-sale financial assets and financial assets at fair value through profit or loss are subsequently carried at fair value. Loans and receivables and held-to-maturity investments are carried at amortized cost using the effective interest rate method. Realized and unrealized gains and losses arising from changes in the fair value of the "financial assets at fair value through profit or loss" category are included in the income statement in the period in which they arise. Changes in the fair value of monetary securities denominated in a foreign currency and classified as available-for-sale are analyzed between translation differences resulting from changes in amortized cost of the security and other changes in the carrying amount of the security. The translation differences on monetary securities are recognized in profit or loss; translation differences on nonmonetary securities are recognized in equity. Changes in the fair value of monetary and nonmonetary securities classified as available-for-sale are recognized in equity.

When securities classified as available-for-sale are sold or impaired, the accumulated fair value adjustments are included in the income statement as gains and losses from investment securities.

The fair values of quoted investments are based on current bid prices. If the market for a financial asset is not active (and for unlisted securities), the Group establishes fair value by using valuation techniques. These include the use of recent arm's-length transactions, reference to other instruments that are substantially the same, discounted cash flow analysis and option pricing models refined to reflect the issuer's specific circumstances.

The Group assesses at each balance sheet date whether there is objective evidence that a financial asset or a group of financial assets is impaired. In the case of equity securities classified as available-for-sale, a significant or prolonged decline in the fair value of the security below its cost is considered in determining whether the securities are impaired. If any such evidence exists for available-for-sale financial assets, the cumulative loss, measured as the difference between the acquisition cost and the current fair value, less any impairment loss on that financial asset previously recognized in profit or loss, is removed from equity and recognized in the income statement. Impairment losses recognized in the income statement on equity instruments are not reversed through the income statement.

1.31 Emission rights

In 2005 the European Union started a system whereby companies are granted certain amounts of rights to emit carbon dioxide. These rights are initially granted free of charge and can be exchanged with other companies. At present the accounting for such emission rights is not clearly regulated by IFRS. Clariant accounts for these rights as follows:

At the time of the Group receives emission rights from the governments, these are recognized as intangible assets at fair value (usually represented by the market price). The difference between the amount paid which is usually nil, since the rights are assigned by the governments free of charge, and the fair value of the emission right, is recognized as a liability.

When the rights are used in operating activities, this is recognized by recording an expense based on the actual emission in the income statement and a liability in the balance sheet. At the same time, the liability recorded on initial recognition of the emission right is released proportionally to the income statement. At the end of the reporting period the liability recorded as a result of the use of the emission rights and the asset initially recognized for emission rights are offset against each other. If any emission rights are purchased from third parties, they are recorded at historical cost which is usually fair value.

The carrying values of emission rights and the corresponding liability are not revalued due to the subsequent fluctuations in market price. When emission rights are sold, the respective amount recognized as an intangible asset and the respective amount recognized as a liability in the balance sheet are derecognized. The difference between the sale price obtained in the disposal and the net amount of the intangible asset and the liability derecognized is recorded as an income or an expense in the income statement.

2. Financial risk management
2.1 Financial risk factors

The Group's activities expose it to a variety of financial risks: market risk (including currency rate risk, cash flow risk, interest rate risk and price risk), credit risk, liquidity risk and settlement risk. The Group's overall risk management program focuses on the unpredictability of financial markets and seeks to reduce potential adverse effects on the Group's financial performance at reasonable hedging costs. The Group uses derivative financial instruments to hedge certain risk exposures.

Financial risk management is carried out by a central treasury department (Group Treasury) under policies approved by Management and the Board of Directors. Group Treasury identifies, evaluates and hedges financial risks in close cooperation with the Group's operating units. Written principles for overall foreign exchange risk, credit risk, use of derivative financial instruments, nonderivative financial instruments and investing excess liquidity (counterparty risk) are in place.

Market risk
Foreign exchange risk

Exposure to foreign exchange risk. The Group operates internationally and is exposed to foreign exchange risks arising from various currency exposures, primarily with respect to the Euro and the US dollar. Foreign exchange risk arises from future commercial transactions, recognized assets and liabilities and net investments in foreign operations, when they are denominated in a currency that is not the respective subsidiary's functional currency.

Foreign exchange risk management. To manage foreign exchange risk arising from future commercial transactions and recognized assets and liabilities, entities in the Group use forward contracts and FX options, according to the Group's foreign exchange risk policy. Group Treasury is responsible, in close coordination with the Group's operating units, for managing the net position in each foreign currency by performing appropriate hedging actions.

The Group's foreign exchange risk management policy is to selectively hedge net transaction foreign exchange exposures in each major currency according to defined hedging ratios.

Currency exposures arising from the net assets of the Group's foreign operations are managed primarily through borrowings denominated in the relevant foreign currency.

As per December 2007, a bond denominated in euro with a notional amount of EUR 600 million was designated as a hedge of a net investment. As per December 31, 2007, the unrealized foreign exchange loss, resulting from the translation of the bond into Swiss francs, amounted to CHF 31 million (2006: CHF 16 million) and was recognized in the cumulative translation reserves in the shareholders' equity.

The purpose of this hedge is to offset part of the foreign exchange risk lying with the Group's European subsidiaries and resulting from movements in the exchange rate euro/Swiss francs.

Foreign exchange risk sensitivity. The estimated percentage change of the following foreign exchange rates used in this calculation is based on the foreign exchange rate volatility for a term of 360 days observed at December 28, 2007.

At December 31, 2007, if the euro had strengthened/weakened by 4% against the Swiss franc with all other variables held constant, pretax profit for the year would have been CHF 2 million higher/lower (2006: CHF 3 million if the euro had varied by 3%), mainly as a result of foreign exchange gains/losses on translation of euro-denominated intragroup financing and trade receivables (2006: mainly as a result of foreign exchange gains/losses on translation of euro denominated cash and cash equivalents, as well as intercompany and trade receivables).

Equity would have been CHF 40 million lower/higher (2006: CHF 29 million), arising from foreign exchange gains/losses on translation of the euro financing.

At December 31, 2007, if the US dollar had strengthened/weakened by 7% against the Swiss franc with all other variables held constant, pretax profit for the year would have been CHF 8 million higher/lower (2006: CHF 12 million changes if the US dollar had varied by 9%), mainly as a result of foreign exchange gains/losses on translation of US dollar denominated trade receivables.

Interest rate risk

Exposure to interest rate risk. Financial debt issued at variable rates as well as cash and cash equivalents expose the Group to cash flow interest rate risk: the net exposure as per December 31, 2007, was not significant. Financial debt issued at fixed rates does not expose the Group to fair value interest rate risk because it is recorded at amortized cost. At the end of 2007 year-end, 91% of the net financial debt was at fixed rates (2006: 86%).

Interest rate risk management. It is the Group's policy to manage the cost of interest using fixed and variable rate debt and interest-related derivative. Group Treasury monitors the net debt fix-to-float mix on an ongoing basis.

Interest rate risk sensitivity. To calculate the impact of a potential interest rate shift on profit and loss, a weighted-average interest rate change was determined, based on the terms of the financial debt issued at variable rates, cash and cash equivalents and the movements of the corresponding interest rates (interest rates comparison between end of 2007 and end of 2006).

At December 31, 2007, if the CHF interest rates on net current financial debt issued at variable interest rates had been 34 basis points higher/lower with all other variables held constant, pretax profit for the year would have been CHF 1.3 million lower/higher (2006: CHF 1.4 million for a CHF interest rate shift of 128 basis points).

At December 31, 2007, if USD interest rates on net current financial debt issued at variable interest rates had been 72 basis points higher/lower with all other variables held constant, pretax profit for the year would have been CHF 0.7 million lower/higher (2006: CHF 1.0 million shift for a US dollar interest rate change of 93 basis points).

Other price risk. With regard to the financial statements the Group was not exposed to other price risk in the sense of IFRS 7, *Financial Instruments: Disclosures,* as per December 31, 2007.

Credit risk

Exposures to credit risk. Credit risk arises from cash and cash equivalents, derivative financial instruments and deposits with banks and financial institutions, as well as credit exposures to wholesale and retail customers, including outstanding receivables and committed transactions. As per December 31, 2007, the Group had no significant concentration of credit risk regarding customers due to diversity.

Credit risk management. The Group has a Group credit risk policy in place to ensure that sales of products are made to customers only after an appropriate credit limit allocation process.

Financial instruments contain an element of risk that the counterparty may be unable to either issue securities or to fulfill the settlement terms of a contract. Clariant therefore only cooperates with counterparties or issuers that are least A-rated. The cumulative exposure to these counterparties is constantly monitored by the Group management, therefore there is no expectation of a material loss due to counterparty risk in the future.

The Group maintains a cash pooling structure with a leading European bank, over which most European subsidiaries execute their cash transactions denominated in Euro. As a result of this cash pool the Group at certain times has substantial current financial assets and at other times substantial current financial liabilities. In view of the bank being rated AA by the most important rating agencies Clariant does not consider this to pose any particular counterparty risk.

Liquidity risk

Liquidity risk management. The Group aims to maintain sufficient, but not excessive, cash and marketable securities, the availability of funding through an adequate amount of committed credit facilities and the ability to close out market positions. Due to the dynamic nature of the underlying business, Group Treasury aims to maintain flexibility in funding by keeping reasonable amounts of committed credit lines available.

As per December 31, 2007, the Group faced the below described maturity profile. The amounts disclosed are the contractual undiscounted cash flows. In 2008 an amount of CHF 1,760 million (CHF 1,570 million in 2007) will become due whereof the main part are the trade and other accounts payable for around CHF 952 million (CHF 856 million in 2007). The other CHF million are mainly due for the repayment of a CHF 384 million bond in March 2008 (CHF 175 million bond was repaid in August 2007) and various current financial debts from legal entities with an amount of CHF 250 million (CHF 350 million in 2007). The remaining amount includes positions such as drawn securitization, interest payments on the bonds and warranties. For the three years between 2009 and 2011 an annual amount, mainly interest, of CHF 50–60 million will fall due and is already known. In 2012 the outstanding debt position of around CHF 300 million is driven by a repayment of a CHF 250 million bond due in April and interest payments about CHF 50 million during the year. The repayment of the EUR 600 million bond including the linked interest payments will become due in 2013.

The Group covers its liabilities out of operational cash flow generated, liquidity reserves in form of cash and cash equivalents (December 31, 2007: CHF 509 million vs. December 31, 2006: CHF 443 million), nonutilized, available asset-backed-security lines (December 31, 2007: CHF 158 million vs. December 2006: CHF 146 million), committed open credit lines (December 31, 2007: CHF 750 million vs. December 2006 unchanged), uncommitted open cash pool limits (December 2007: CHF 200 million vs. December 31, 2006 unchanged) and through the selected issuance of capital market instruments.

2.2 Fair value estimation

The fair value of financial instruments traded in active markets (such as derivatives and securities) is based on quoted market prices at the balance sheet date. The quoted market price used for the valuation of financial assets held by the Group is the current bid price; the appropriate quoted market price for the valuation of financial liabilities is the current ask price.

The fair value of financial instruments that are not traded in an active market (for example, over-the-counter derivatives) is determined by using valuation techniques. The Group uses a variety of methods and makes assumptions that are based on market conditions existing at each balance sheet date. Quoted market prices or dealer quotes for similar instruments are used for noncurrent debt. Other techniques, such as discounted cash flows, are used to determine fair value for the remaining financial instruments. The fair value of interest rate swaps is calculated as the pres-ent value of the future cash flows according to the appropriate interest curves. The fair value of forward foreign exchange contracts is determined using forward exchange market rates at the balance sheet date.

2.3 Capital risk management

The Group's objectives when managing capital are to safeguard the Group's ability to continue as a going concern in order to provide returns for shareholders and benefits for other stakeholders and to maintain an optimal capital structure to minimize the cost of capital.

In order to maintain or adjust the capital structure, the Group may adjust the amount of dividends paid to shareholders, return capital to shareholders, issue new shares or sell assets to reduce debt.

The Group monitors capital on the basis of invested capital as part of the return on invested capital concept. Invested capital is calculated as the sum of total equity as reported in the consolidated balance sheet plus current and noncurrent financial liabilities as reported in the consolidated balance sheet plus estimated liabilities from operating leases, less cash and cash equivalents not needed for operating purposes, less net assets held for sale as reported in the consolidated balance sheet. The Group is not subject to externally imposed capital requirements.

Invested capital was as follows on December 31, 2007 and 2006 respectively:

CHF mn	2007	2006
Total equity	2,372	2,433
Total current and noncurrent financial liabilities	1,995	1,999
Estimated operating lease liabilities	625	662
Less cash and cash equivalents	(509)	(443)
Cash needed for operating purposes	171	162
Less assets held for sale	--	(36)
Invested capital	**4,654**	**4,777**

3. Critical accounting estimates and judgments

Estimates and judgments are continually evaluated and are based on historical experience and other factors, including expectations of future events that are believed to be reasonable under the circumstances.

The Group makes estimates and assumptions concerning the future. The resulting accounting estimates will, by definition, seldom equal the related actual results. The estimates and assumptions that have a significant risk of causing a material adjustment to the carrying amounts of assets and liabilities within the next financial year are discussed below.

1. **Estimated impairment of goodwill and property, plant, and equipment.** The Group tests annually whether goodwill has suffered any impairment, in accordance with the accounting policy stated above in notes 1.11 and 1.12. The recoverable amounts of cash-generating units have been determined based on value-in-use calculations. In the same procedure, the recoverable value of property, plant, and equipment is also assessed according to the same rules. These calculations require the use of estimates, in particular in relation to the expected growth of sales, discount rates, the development of raw material prices and the success of restructuring measures implemented (see notes 5 and 27).

2. **Environmental liabilities.** The Group is exposed to environmental regulations in numerous jurisdictions. Significant judgment is required in determining the worldwide provision for environmental remediation. The Group constantly monitors its sites to ensure compliance with legislative requirements and to assess the liability arising from the need to adapt to changing legal demands. The Group recognizes liabilities for environmental remediation based on the latest assessment of the environmental situation of the individual sites and the most recent requirements of the respective legislation. Where the final remediation results in expenses that differ from the amounts that were previously recorded, such differences will impact the income statement in the period in which such determination was made (see notes 16, 19 and 33).

3. **Income and other taxes.** The Group is subject to income and other taxes in numerous jurisdictions. Significant judgment is required in determining the worldwide provision for income and other taxes. There are many transactions and calculations for which the ultimate tax determination is uncertain at the time a liability must be recorded. The Group recognizes liabilities for anticipated tax audit issues based on estimates of whether additional taxes will be due. Where the final tax outcome of these matters is different from the amounts that were initially recorded, such differences impact the income tax and deferred tax provisions in the period in which such determination is made.

    Some subsidiaries operate in a way that leads to tax losses, which can be used to offset taxable gains of subsequent periods. The Group constantly monitors the development of such tax loss situations. Based on the business plans for the subsidiaries concerned the recoverability of such tax losses is determined. In the case that a tax loss is deemed to be recoverable the capitalization of a deferred tax asset for such tax losses is then decided. The time horizon for such a calculation is in line with the midterm planning scope of the Group.

4. **Estimates for the accounting for employee benefits.** IAS 19, *Employee Benefits*, requires that certain assumptions are made in order to determine the amount to be recorded for retirement benefit obligations and pension plan assets, in particular for defined benefit plans. These mainly actuarial assumptions such as expected inflation rates, long-term increase in health care costs, employee turnover, expected return on plan assets and discount rates. Substantial changes in the assumed development of any one of these variables may significantly change the Group's retirement benefit obligation and pension plan assets (see note 15).

4. Property, plant, and equipment

CHF mn	Land	Buildings	Machinery and equipment	Furniture, vehicles, computer hardware	Plant under construction	Total	Insured value at December 31
At January 1, 2006							
Cost	619	2,480	5,088	526	215	8,928	--
Accumulated depreciation	(156)	(1,652)	(4,067)	(448)	--	(6,323)	--
Net book value	**463**	**828**	**1,021**	**78**	**215**	**2,605**	--
Additions	1	29	110	17	201	358	--
Acquisitions	1	6	8	1	1	17	--
Reclassifications	9	35	213	13	(270)	--	--
Reclassified to held-for sale	--	--	(1)	--	--	(1)	--
Disposals	(28)	(63)	(53)	(4)	(28)	(176)	--
Depreciation	--	(60)	(180)	(29)	--	(269)	--
Impairment	(50)	(9)	(59)	(1)	(8)	(127)	--
Exchange rate differences	1	1	8	--	5	15	--
At December 31, 2006	**397**	**767**	**1,867**	**75**	**116**	**2,422**	--
Cost	564	2,357	5,020	501	124	8,566	--
Accumulated depreciation	(167)	(1,590)	(3,953)	(426)	(8)	(6,144)	--
Net book value	**397**	**767**	**1,067**	**75**	**116**	**2,422**	**9,571**

CHF mn	Land	Buildings	Machinery and equipment	Furniture, vehicles, computer hardware	Plant under construction	Total	Insured value at December 31
Additions	--	23	82	13	194	312	--
Acquisitions	--	--	2	--	--	2	--
Reclassifications	--	34	122	10	(166)	--	--
Reclassified to held for sale	--	--	--	--	(5)	(5)	--
Disposals	(6)	(12)	(9)	(1)	(1)	(29)	--
Depreciation	--	(60)	(178)	(26)		(264)	--
Impairment	(10)	(25)	(39)	(1)	(3)	(78)	--
Reversal of impairment	--	--	1	--	--	1	
Exchange rate differences	11	15	13	1	--	40	--
At December 31, 2007	**392**	**742**	**1,061**	**71**	**135**	**2,401**	**--**
Cost	570	2,429	4,789	494	151	8,433	--
Accumulated depreciation	(178)	(1,687)	(3,728)	(423)	(16)	(6,032)	--
Net book value	**392**	**742**	**1,061**	**71**	**135**	**2,401**	**9,237**

As at December 31, 2007, commitments for the purchase of PPE totaled CHF 51 million (2006: CHF 59 million).

Land, buildings, furniture and machinery and equipment include the following amounts where the Group is a lessee under a finance lease:

CHF mn	2007	2006
Cost—capitalized finance leases	22	28
Accumulated depreciation	(6)	(11)
Net book value	**16**	**17**

Finance lease liability—minimum lease payments:

CHF mn	2007	2006
No later than 1 year	3	3
Later than 1 year but no later than 5 years	10	11
Later than 5 years	19	19
Total minimum lease payments	**32**	**33**
Future finance charge on finance leases	(16)	(16)
Present value of finance lease liabilities	**16**	**17**

The present value of finance lease liabilities is as follows:

CHF mn	2007	2006
No later than 1 year	2	3
Later than 1 year but no later than 5 years	7	7
Later than 5 years	7	7
Total minimum lease payments	**16**	**17**

The corresponding liability related to finance lease contracts is disclosed in note 14.

5. Intangible assets

CHF mn	Goodwill	Other	Total
At January 1, 2006			
Cost	403	122	525
Accumulated amortization		(107)	(107)
Net book value	**403**	**15**	**418**
Additions	5	4	9
Acquisitions		18	18
Disposals		(1)	(1)
Amortization		(7)	(7)
Impairment	(100)	--	(100)
Exchange rate differences	(2)	--	(2)
At December 31, 2006	**306**	**29**	**335**

CHF mn	Goodwill	Other	Total
Cost	406	136	542
Accumulated amortization	(100)	(107)	(207)
Net book value	**306**	**29**	**335**
Additions		8	8
Acquisitions		5	5
Amortization		(9)	(9)
At December 31, 2007	**306**	**33**	**339**
Cost	406	146	552
Accumulated amortization	(100)	(113)	(213)
Net book value	**306**	**33**	**339**

The amount reported as goodwill is the result of a number of acquisitions in various divisions. All goodwill is tested annually for impairment. Other intangibles comprise patents, trademarks and software etc. Clariant does not have any internally generated intangible assets. Amortization of intangibles is recorded in Administration and general overhead costs in the income statement.

Addition to the carrying amount of goodwill in 2006 mainly include CHF 3 million arising from the purchase of the Masterbatch activities from Ciba Specialty Chemicals. The remaining addition of CHF 2 million arose from smaller acquisitions in France, the United States and India.

Impairment test for goodwill

Goodwill is allocated to the Group's cash-generating units (CGU). Cash-generating units consist of either Business segments in accordance with the Group's segment reporting or, in the case where independent cash flows can be identified, of parts of the respective Business units.

Goodwill is allocated to the following CGUs:

CHF mn	12/31/07	12/31/06
Textiles	6	6
Leather	231	231
Pigments & Additives	27	27
Masterbatches	35	35
Functional Chemicals	7	7
Net book value	**306**	**306**

The recoverable amount of a CGU is determined based on value-in-use calculations. These calculations use cash flow projections based on financial budgets approved by Management covering a four-year period. No further growth is assumed beyond this four-year period. The main assumption used for cash flow projections were EBITDA in percent of sales and sales growth. The assumptions regarding these two variables are based on Management's past experience and future expectations of business performance. The pretax discount rates used are based on the Group's weighted-average cost of capital adjusted for specific country risks associated with the cash flow projections. The assumed discount rate was 10% for all cash-generating units (2006: 9.0%).

The most important part of goodwill is the amount of CHF 231 million (2006: CHF 231 million) remaining from the BTP acquisition in 2000. This goodwill is allocated to the CGU Leather. For the impairment testing procedure the planning assumptions were critically reviewed. These comprise radical measures to improve the CGU's performance in the coming years. It is planned to streamline the CGU's product portfolio, to close unprofitable production sites and generally reduce overhead costs. In the business plan it is assumed that these measures will lead to a substantial improvement in the CGU's topline growth, but also raise profitability over its current level. Based on these assumptions the recoverable amount of the CGU Leather on a value-in-use basis exceeds its carrying amount. The recoverable amount would be equal to the carrying amount if the assumed annual sales growth rate were reduced by 0.3%, or alternatively, if the operating margin were reduced by 0.4% of sales.

If the assumed growth rate were reduced by two percentage points the carrying amount would exceed the recoverable amount of the CGU's net asset by CHF 98 million. If raw material costs were assumed to be two percentage point of sales higher the carrying amount of the net assets would exceed the recoverable amount by CHF 72 million. In 2006, the goodwill of Leather was already revalued for impairment in the amount of CHF 100 million.

The CGU Textiles holds goodwill in the amount of CHF 6 million. The net assets of this CGU were also tested for impairment and deemed recoverable. The recoverable amount would be equal to the carrying amount if the assumed annual sales growth rate were reduced by 0.7%, or alternatively, if the operating margin were reduced by 0.6% of sales. If the assumed annual growth rate were reduced by one percentage point the carrying amount would exceed the recoverable amount of the CGU's net assets by CHF 45 million. If raw material costs were assumed to be one percentage point of sales higher the carrying amount of the net assets would exceed the recoverable amount by CHF 52 million.

The CGU Pigments & Additives holds goodwill in the amount of CHF 27 million, the CGU Masterbatches holds goodwill in the amount of CHF 35 million and the CGU Functional Chemicals holds goodwill in the amount of CHF 7 million. For all these CGUs it was assumed that they achieve sales growth above market growth. It was also assumed that the EBITDA in percent of sales will improve over present performance as a result of the restructuring measures implemented. For all these CGUs it was determined that the net present value of their expected cash flows exceeds the carrying amount of the net assets allocated on a value-in-use basis.

6. Investments in associates

CHF mn	2007	2006
Beginning of the year	**288**	**282**
Acquisitions	3	1
Disposals	(13)	(6)
Share of profit	37	35
Dividends received	(30)	(22)
Exchange rate differences	9	(2)
End of the year	**294**	**288**

The key financial data of the Group's principal associates are as follows:

CHF mn	Country of incorporation	Assets	Liabilities	Revenue	Profit/(loss)	% Interest held
2006						
Infraserv GmbH & Co. Höchst KG	Germany	1,229	705	1,324	56	32
Infraserv GmbH & Co. Gendorf KG	Germany	197	97	355	11	50
Infraserv GmbH & Co. Knapsack KG	Germany	173	73	239	(1)	21
Others		102	44	179	--	--
Total		**1,701**	**919**	**2,097**	**66**	--
2007						
Infraserv GmbH & Co. Höchst KG	Germany	1,457	874	1,473	58	32
Infraserv GmbH & Co. Gendorf KG	Germany	221	120	404	12	50
Infraserv GmbH & Co. Knapsack KG	Germany	195	87	304	10	21
Others		166	60	242	17	
Total		**2,039**	**1,141**	**2,423**	**97**	

There were no unrecognized losses in the years 2007 and 2006. No accumulated unrecognized losses existed as at the balance sheet date.

The Infraserv companies were set up by the former Hoechst group to cater to the infrastructure needs of its subsidiaries prior to 1997. The shareholdings in associates summarized under "Other" concern mainly companies specializing in selling Clariant products. Due to the specialized nature of these companies there is no active market in which these shareholdings could be traded, hence no fair value is indicated. However, there is no evidence that the recoverable amount would be lower than the carrying amount.

7. Financial assets

CHF mn	2007	2006
Beginning of the year	63	47
Exchange rate differences	1	
Accrued interest		4
Additions	11	12
Repayments and disposals	(58)	
End of the year	**17**	**63**

Financial assets include the following:

CHF mn	12/31/2007	12/31/2006
Vendor loan note		48
Other investments	17	15
Total	**17**	**63**

Financial assets are denominated in the following currencies:

CHF mn	12/31/2007	12/31/2006
EUR	13	7
USD	1	--
CHF	2	56
Other	1	--
Total	**17**	**63**

The carrying amounts of these assets are classified as follows:

CHF mn	12/31/2007	12/31/2006
Held to maturity	--	58
Designated as available-for-sale	17	5
Total	**17**	**63**

The value reported for the assets held to maturity is approximately fair value.

The fair value of the vendor loan note which was classified as "held to maturity" was determined based on discounted cash flows at a discount rate of 8%. Other investments are valued in the same manner at discount rates as applicable in the respective country or at their quoted market prices. During 2006 and 2007 there were no impairments on financial assets held to maturity or held for sale. The maximum exposure to credit risk of financial assets at the reporting date is their fair value.

8. Taxes

CHF mn	2007	2006
Current income taxes	(126)	(164)
Deferred income taxes	27	20
Total	**(99)**	**(144)**

The main elements contributing to the difference between the Group's overall expected tax expense/rate and the effective tax expense/rate for continuing operations are

	2007 CHF mn	%	2006 CHF mn	%
Income before tax	**207**		**275**	
Expected tax expense/rate[1]	**(57)**	27.5	**(74)**	26.9
Effect of taxes on items not tax-deductible	(47)	22.7	(57)	20.7
Effect of utilization and changes in recognition of tax losses and tax credits	33	(15.9)	(11)	4.0
Effect of tax losses and tax credit of current year not recognized	(32)	15.5	(8)	2.9
Effect of adjustments to current taxes due to prior periods	(8)	3.9	6	(2.2)
Effect of tax-exempt income	8	(3.9)	6	(2.2)
Effect of other items	4	(1.9)	(6)	2.2
Effective tax expense/rate	**(99)**	47.8	**(144)**	52.4

[1] *Calculated based on the income before tax of each subsidiary (weighted-average).*

Compared to 2006 the expected tax rate was higher in 2007 due to a part of the profit in countries with higher tax rates.

The movement of the net deferred tax balance is as follows:

CHF mn	2007	2006
Beginning of the year	(94)	(140)
Effect of acquisitions	--	(1)
Effect of disposals	--	(4)
Effect of discontinued operations	--	24
Tax on disposal result of discontinued operations	--	20
Reclassified to held-for-sale	--	(6)
Tax on vested equity share-based payments reversed to equity	(3)	(4)
Income statement charge	27	20
Exchange rate differences	4	(3)
End of the year	**(66)**	**(94)**

Deferred income tax assets and liabilities are offset when there is a legally enforceable right to offset current tax assets against current tax liabilities and when the deferred income taxes relate to the same taxation authority.

CHF mn	12/31/2007	12/31/2006
Deferred tax liabilities on:		
PPE and intangible assets	264	286
Prepaid pensions, other accruals and provisions	35	11
Total deferred tax liabilities	**299**	**297**
Thereof offset with deferred tax assets within the same jurisdiction	120	114
Net deferred tax liabilities	**179**	**183**

CHF mn	12/31/2007	12/31/2006
Deferred tax assets on:		
PPE and intangible assets	41	50
Retirement benefit obligations	57	80
Tax losses carried forward and tax credits	82	40
Other accruals and provisions	53	33
Total deferred tax assets	**233**	**203**
Thereof offset with deferred tax liabilities within the same jurisdiction	120	114
Net deferred tax assets	**113**	**89**
Net deferred tax balance	**(66)**	**(94)**

Of the deferred tax assets capitalized CHF 20 million refer to tax losses of the French subsidiaries (2006: CHF 20 million) and CHF 13 million to tax losses of the Italian subsidiaries (2006: CHF 20 million) and CHF 20 million to tax losses of the US subsidiaries (2006: CHF 0 million). Clariant considers it probable that these tax losses can be recovered as a result of the efforts made both in the restructuring program and in the implementation of the new principal structure.

The total of temporary differences on investments in subsidiaries, for which no deferred taxes were calculated, was CHF 376 million at December 31, 2007 (CHF 725 million at December 31, 2006).

The tax losses on which no deferred tax assets are recognized are reviewed for recoverability at each balance sheet date. The largest part of these tax losses arose in Switzerland and is not deemed to be recoverable before they expire.

Tax losses on which no deferred tax assets were calculated are as follows:

CHF mn	*12/31/2007*	*12/31/2006*
Expiry by:		
2007	--	128
2008	372	129
2009	709	642
2010	10	46
2011	102	
After 2011 (2006: after 2010)	872	883
Total	**2,065**	**1,828**
Unrecognized tax credits	**48**	**8**

The tax credits expire between 2008 and 2013.

9. Inventories

CHF mn	*12/31/2007*	*12/31/2006*
Raw material, consumables, work in progress	551	559
Finished products	926	954
Total	**1,477**	**1,513**
Movements in write-downs of inventories		
Beginning of the year	52	75
Additions	45	45
Reversals	(50)	(52)
Effect of disposals	--	(12)
Reclassified to held-for-sale	--	(4)
End of the year	**47**	**52**

As at December 31, 2007, inventories in the amount of CHF 21 million were pledged as collateral for liabilities (2006: CHF 57 million).

The cost for raw materials and consumables recognized as an expense and included in "Costs of goods sold" amounted to CHF 3,987 million (2006: CHF 3,667 million).

10. Trade receivables

CHF mn	*12/31/2007*	*12/31/2006*
Gross accounts receivable—trade	1,490	1,503
Gross accounts receivable—associates	8	8
Less: provision for impairment of accounts receivable	(49)	(65)
Total trade receivables—net	**1449**	**1,446**

The following summarizes the movement in the provision for doubtful accounts receivable:

CHF mn	*2007*	*2006*
At January 1	(65)	(67)
Charged to the income statement	(18)	(29)
Amounts used	15	12
Acquisitions		(1)
Unused amounts reversed	19	18
Exchange rate differences		2
At December 31	**(49)**	**(65)**

Of the provision for impairment the following amounts concerned trade receivables that were individually impaired:

CHF mn	*12/31/2007*	*12/31/2006*
Trade receivables aged up to six months	(7)	(19)
Trade receivables aged over six months	(34)	(40)
Total trade receivables—net	**(41)**	**(59)**

There is no concentration of credit risk with respect to trade receivables, as the Group has a large number of internationally dispersed customers.

The Group recognizes impairment of trade receivables in "Marketing and distribution" in the income statement.

The amount recognized in the books for trade receivables is equal to their fair value.

The maximum credit risk on trade receivables is equal to their fair value. Collaterals are only taken in rare cases (2007: CHF 5 million, 2006: CHF 5 million).

The carrying amounts of the Group's trade receivables are denominated in the following currencies:

CHF mn	2007	2006
Currency		
EUR	644	640
USD	288	291
GBP	37	40
JPY	70	72
CHF	7	(1)
Other	403	404
Total trade receivables—net	**1,449**	**1,446**

As of December 31, 2007, trade receivables in the amount of CHF 214 million (2006: CHF 223 million) were past due, but not impaired. These relate to a number of customers for whom there is no recent history of default. The ageing analysis of these trade receivables is as follows:

CHF mn	2007	2006
Up to 3 months past due, but not impaired	200	197
3 to 6 months past due, but not impaired	12	14
More than 6 months past due, but not impaired	2	12
Total trade receivables—net	214	223

11. Other current assets

Other current assets include the following:

CHF mn	2007	2006
Other receivables	314	270
Current financial assets	167	42
Prepaid expenses and accrued income	54	66
Total	**535**	**378**

Other receivables include staff loans, advances, advance payments, VAT, and sales tax receivables.

Current financial assets include deposits with an original maturity exceeding 90 days, securities and loans to third parties and are classified as available-for-sale. The amount recognized in the books for other current assets is equal to their fair value.

The maximum exposure to credit risk of other current assets at the reporting date is their fair value. There was no impairment of current financial assets in 2007 and 2006.

Other receivables are denominated in the following currencies:

CHF mn	12/31/2007	12/31/2006
EUR	182	121
USD	19	15
GBP	11	4
JPY	2	2
CHF	10	39
Other	90	89
Total	**314**	**270**

Current financial assets are denominated in the following currencies:

CHF mn	12/31/2007	12/31/2006
EUR	29	1
USD	1	--
CHF	131	30
Other	6	11
Total	**167**	**42**

12. Cash and cash equivalents

CHF mn	12/31/2007	12/31/2006
Cash at bank and on hand	241	328
Short-term bank deposits	268	115
Total	**509**	**443**

The effective interest rate on short-term bank deposits in Swiss francs was 2.40% (2006: 1.60%); these deposits have an average maturity of 56 days (2006: 26 days).

There were no major short-term bank deposits denominated in currencies other than Swiss francs.

The maximum exposure to credit risk on cash and cash equivalents is equal to their book value.

13. Changes in share capital and treasury shares

Registered shares each with a par value of CHF 4.25 (2006: CHF 4.50)	Number of shares 2007	Par value 2007 CHF mn	Number of shares 2006	Par value 2006 CHF mn
At January 1	230,160,000	978	230,160,000	1,035
At December 31	**230,160,000**	**978**	**230,160,000**	**1,035**
Treasury shares	(3,792,691)	(16)	(3,511,698)	(16)
Outstanding capital at December 31	**226,367,309**	**962**	**226,648,302**	**1,019**

Treasury shares (number of shares)	2007	2006
Holdings at January 1	3,511,698	3,867,293
Shares purchased at fair market value	1,470,000	
Shares purchased on exercise of put options		750,000
Shares sold at fair market value	(880,000)	(500,000)
Shares transferred to employees	(309,007)	(605,595)
Holdings at December 31	**3,792,691**	**3,511,698**

All shares are duly authorized and fully paid in.

Dividends are paid out as and when declared and are paid out equally on all shares, including treasury shares.

In accordance with Article 5 of the Company's Articles of Incorporation, no limitations exist with regard to the registration of shares which are acquired in one's own name and on one's own account. Special rules exist for nominees.

In accordance with Article 12 of the Company's Articles of Incorporation, each share has the right to one vote. A shareholder can only vote for his own shares and for represented shares, up to a maximum of 10% of the total share capital.

Based on the information available at the time of this report, Bestinver Gestion S.A. SGIIC held 7.56% of the Clariant shares at December 31, 2007 (December 2006: less than 5%).

14. Noncurrent financial debts

CHF mn	Interest rate in %	Term	Notional amount	Net amount 12/31/2007	Net amount 12/31/2006
Straight bonds	3.750	1997-2007	200 CHF mn	--	175
Straight bonds	4.250	2000-2008	500 CHF mn	384	384
Straight bonds	3.125	2007-2012	250 CHF mn	250	--
Straight bonds	4.375	2006-2013	600 EUR mn	994	961
Total straight bonds				**1,628**	**1,520**
Liabilities to banks and other financial institutions[1]				**9**	**21**
Obligations under finance leases				**14**	**14**
Subtotal				**1,651**	**1,555**
Less current portion				**(384)**	**(179)**
Total				**1,267**	**1,376**

CHF mn	Interest rate in %	Term	Notional amount	Net amount 12/31/2007	Net amount 12/31/2006
Breakdown by maturity			2008	--	392
			2009	7	8
			2010	2	--
			2011	--	--
			2012	251	--
			thereafter	1,007	976
Total				**1,267**	**1,376**
Breakdown by currency			CHF	251	384
			EUR	1,007	977
			Other	9	15
Total				**1,267**	**1,376**
Fair value comparison (including current portion)					
Straight bonds				1,549	1,509
Others				23	35
Total				**1,572**	**1,544**
Total net book value of assets pledged as collateral for financial debts				**33**	**114**
Total collaterized financial debts				18	17

[1] *Average interest rate in 2007: 4.5% (2006: 4.6%).*

In April 2007, a CHF 250 million bond was issued (2006: EUR 600 million) and bonds in the amount of CHF 175 million were paid back on expiry (August 2007; 2006: CHF 159 million). The net effect from bond transactions in 2007 was CHF 75 million (2006: CHF 802 million).

Valuation. Noncurrent financial debt is recognized initially at fair value, net of transaction costs incurred. Financial debt is subsequently stated at amortized cost. There are no long-term financial liabilities valued at fair value through profit and loss.

The fair values reported for the bonds are quoted market prices as of the balance sheet date. The fair values of the other noncurrent financial debts, which are equal to their book value, are determined on a discounted cash flow basis.

Covenants. Clairant Ltd is borrowing and guaranteeing all obligations under one syndicated bank facility. The facility ranks pari passu with all other unsubordinated third-party debt.

The facility contains customary covenants that restrict the sale of assets, mergers, lines, sale-leaseback transactions and acquisitions, and requires the Group to maintain specified interest cover ratios. These ratios are tested at the end of each financial half-year. The facility does not affect the ability of the Group to utilize its accounts receivable securitization program. The Group is in compliance with all covenants.

Exposure to the Group's borrowings to interest rate changes

- Bonds: The interest rates of all bonds are fixed.
- Liabilities to banks and other financial institutions: Mostly consisting of syndicated bank loans with variable interest rates (LIBOR plus applicable margin according to a defined pricing grid based on the Group's performance).
- Other financial debts: Mostly current debt at variable interest rates.

Collateral. Certain Asian subsidiaries pledge trade receivables and inventories as a security for bank overdraft facilities. In case the subsidiaries default on their obligations the borrowers have the right to take possession of these assets and receive the cash flows resulting from them.

The assets are pledged at the usual market conditions.

15. Retirement benefit obligations

Apart from the legally required social security schemes, the Group has numerous independent pension plans. The assets are principally held externally. For certain Group companies however, no independent assets exist for the pension and other noncurrent employee benefit obligations. In these cases the related liability is included in the balance sheet.

Defined benefit postemployment plans. Defined benefit pensions and termination plans cover the majority of the Group's employees. Future obligations and the corresponding assets of those plans considered as defined benefit plans under IAS 19 are reappraised annually and reassessed at least every three years by independent actuaries. Assets are valued at fair values. US employees transferred to Clariant with the Hoechst Specialty Chemicals business remain insured with Hoechst for their pension claims incurred prior to June 30, 1997.

Postemployment medical benefits. The Group operates a number of postemployment medical benefit schemes in the USA, Canada, and France. The method of accounting for the liabilities associated with these plans is similar to the one used for defined benefit pension schemes. These plans are not externally funded, but are covered by provisions in the balance sheets of the Group companies concerned.

Expenses for net benefits are recorded in the same line and function in which the personnel costs are recorded.

Changes in the present value of defined benefit obligations:

	Pension plans (funded and unfunded)		Postemployment medical benefits (unfunded)	
CHF mn	2007	2006	2007	2006
Beginning of the year	2080	2,097	95	113
Change in the scope of consolidation	--	1	--	--
Current service cost	58	72	2	2
Interest costs on obligation	91	84	5	5
Contributions to plan by employees	13	12	--	--
Benefits paid out to personnel in reporting period	(96)	(82)	(4)	(4)
Actuarial loss (gain) of reporting period	(110)	(54)	(7)	(9)
Past service costs (gain) of reporting period	--	1	--	--
Termination benefits	--	2	--	--
Effect of curtailments	--	(22)	2	(6)
Effect of settlements	6	--	--	--
Reduction in obligations due to divestitures	--	(15)	--	--
Reclassified to held-for-sale	--	(30)	--	--
Exchange rate differences	(30)	14	(5)	(6)
End of the year	**2,012**	**2,080**	**88**	**95**

Changes in the fair value of plan assets:

CHF mn	2007	2006
Beginning of the year	1,698	1,567
Expected return on plan assets	96	85
Contributions to plan by employees	13	12
Contributions to plan by employer	79	59
Benefits paid out to personnel in reporting period	(71)	(58)
Actuarial gain (loss) of reporting period	(24)	48
Effect of settlements	(2)	
Reclassified to held-for-sale	--	(18)
Exchange rate differences	(46)	3
End of the year	**1,743**	**1,698**

The Group expects to contribute CHF 60 million to its defined benefit pension plans in 2008. As of December 31, 2007, the pension plan assets included no registered shares issued by the company (2006: nil).

The amounts recognized in the balance sheet are as follows:

CHF mn	Defined benefit pension plans		Postemployment medical benefits		Total	
	12/31/07	*12/31/06*	*12/31/07*	*12/31/06*	*12/31/07*	*12/31/06*
Present value of funded obligations	(1,604)	(1,667)	--	--	(1,604)	(1,667)
Fair value of plan assets	1743	1,698	--	--	1743	1,698
Surplus/(Deficit)	**139**	**31**	**--**	**--**	**139**	**31**
Present value of unfunded obligations	(408)	(413)	(88)	(95)	(496)	(508)
Unrecognized actuarial losses (gains)	50	142	--	7	50	149
Unrecognized past service costs (gains)	1	1	(11)	(15)	(10)	(14)
Limitation on recognition of assets	(49)	(29)	--	--	(49)	(29)
Net liabilities in the balance sheet	**(267)**	**(268)**	**(99)**	**(103)**	**(366)**	**(371)**

Thereof recognized in

CHF mn	Defined benefit pension plans		Postemployment medical benefits		Total	
	12/31/07	*12/31/06*	*12/31/07*	*12/31/06*	*12/31/07*	*12/31/06*
Retirement benefit obligation	(389)	(358)	(99)	(103)	(488)	(461)
Prepaid pension assets	122	98	--	--	122	90
Net liabilities in the balance sheet for defined benefit plans	**(267)**	**(268)**	**(99)**	**(103)**	**(366)**	**(371)**

The amounts recognized in the income statement are as follows:

CHF mn	2007	2006	2007	2006	2007	2006
Current service cost	(58)	(72)	(2)	(2)	(60)	(74)
Interest cost	(91)	(84)	(5)	(5)	(96)	(89)
Expected return on plan assets	96	85	--	--	96	85
Net actuarial losses recognized in the current year	(8)	(11)	--	--	(8)	(11)
Past service costs recognized in the current year	(1)	(1)	3	4	2	3
Termination benefits	--	(2)	--	--	--	(2)
Effect of curtailments	1	22	--	5	1	27
Limitation on recognition of assets	(5)	(29)	--	--	(5)	(29)
Total expenses	**(66)**	**(92)**	**(4)**	**2**	**(70)**	**(90)**

Thereof the amount of CHF 1 million (20056 CHF 1 million) is reported under discontinued operations.

CHF mn	2007	2006	2007	2006	2007	2006
Actual return on plan assets	72	133	--	--	72	133

Reconciliation to prepaid pension asset and retirement benefit obligations reported in the balance sheet:

CHF mn	12/31/2007	12/31/2006
Defined benefit obligation	(488)	(461)
Defined contribution obligation	(27)	(34)
Retirement benefit obligation	**(515)**	**(495)**
Prepaid pension plan asset	**122**	**90**
Net retirement benefit obligation recognized	**(393)**	**(405)**

The major categories of plan assets as a percentage of total plan assets:

	12/31/2007	12/31/2006
	%	%
Equities	39	47
Bonds	35	31
Cash	9	6
Property	12	12
Alternative investments	5	4

Principal actuarial assumptions at the balance sheet date in % weighted-average:

	2007	2006
	%	%
Discount rate	4.9	4.4
Expected return on plan assets	5.4	5.6
Expected inflation rate	1.8	2.0
Future salary increases	2.5	2.6
Long-term increase in health care costs	9.6	10.1

The weighted-average expected long-term rate of return on plan assets represents the average rate of return expected to be earned on plan assets over the period the benefits included in the benefit obligation are to be paid. In developing the expected rate of return, the Company considers long-term compound annualized returns of historical market data for each asset category, as well as historical actual returns on the Company's plan assets. Using this reference information, the Company develops for each pension plan a weighted-average expected long-term rate of return.

A one-percentage point change in health care cost trend rates would have the following effects on the obligations for postemployment medical benefits:

CHF mn	One percentage point increase	One percentage point decrease
Effect on the aggregate of the service cost and interest cost	1	(1)
Effect on defined benefit obligation	9	(7)

Amounts for current and previous periods

CHF mn	2007	2006	2005
Defined benefit pension plans			
Defined benefit obligation for pension plans, funded and unfunded	(2,012)	(2,080)	(2,097)
Fair value of plan assets	1,743	1,698	1,567
Deficit	**(269)**	**(382)**	**(530)**
Experience adjustments on plan liabilities	(23)	3	(23)
Experience adjustments on plan assets	(24)	48	123
Postemployment medical benefits			
Defined benefit obligation for postemployment medical plans	(88)	(95)	(113)
Experience adjustment on plan liabilities	(2)	(2)	(3)

Defined contribution postemployment plans. In 2007, CHF 34 million were charged to the income statements of the Group companies as contributions to defined contribution plans (2006: CHF 32 million).

In Germany approximately 6,600 Clariant employees are insured in a Defined Benefit Plan which is a multiemployer plan and as such is accounted for as a Defined Contribution Plan. The reason for this accounting practice is that the plan exposes the participating Clariant companies to actuarial risks associated with the current and former employees of other companies, which are members of the same pension plan. There is no consistent or reliable basis for allocating the obligation, plan assets and cost to individual companies participating in the plan.

Based on the statutory actuarial calculation of 2006, the pension fund's obligations are fully funded. Also for 2007 it is anticipated that the pension plan liabilities are covered by the respective assets.

In case the multiemployer plan faces a situation where the pension plan liabilities exceed the assets, this can be remedied either by increasing the employers' contributions to the pension plan or by reducing the benefits which are paid out to the entitled parties. In the case of a reduction of the benefits it has to be verified whether this triggers the requirement for additional funding by the employer. The decision is at the discretion of the board of the pension fund, which is constituted by representatives of the companies participating in the multiemployer plan and their employee representatives..

Clariant contributions to this pension plan amounted to CHF 18 million in 2007 (CHF 16 million in 2006).

The multiemployer plan originates in the pension plan scheme of the German companies of the former Hoechst Group, to which a part of the activities of Clariant pertained until 1997. Several of the companies which were formerly part of the Hoechst Group continue to participate in this multiemployer plan.

16. Movements in provisions for noncurrent liabilities

CHF mn	Environmental provisions	Personnel provisions	Restructuring provisions	Other provisions	Total provisions for noncurrent liabilities 2007	Total provisions for noncurrent liabilities 2006
At January 1	134	41	1	68	244	289
Additions	16	10	3	21	50	57
Effect of acquisitions	--	--	--	--	--	1
Effect of disposals	--	--	--	--	--	(23)
Reclassifications	(25)	(10)	(1)	--	(36)	(25)
Reclassified to held-for-sale	--	--	--	--	--	(4)
Amounts used	(1)	(6)	--	(7)	(14)	(16)
Unused amounts reversed	(6)	(1)	--	(14)	(21)	(35)
Changes due to the passage of time and changes in discount rates	1	--	--	2	3	1
Exchange rate differences	--	2	--	3	5	(1)
At December 31	**119**	**36**	**3**	**73**	**231**	**244**
Debts falling due						
Between 1 and 3 years	55	6	3	29	93	69
Between 3 and 5 years	33	12	--	7	52	38
Over 5 years	31	18	--	37	86	137
At December 31	**119**	**36**	**3**	**73**	**231**	**244**

Environmental provisions. Environmental provisions for environmental liabilities are made when there is a legal or constructive obligation for the Group which will result in an outflow of economic resources. It is difficult to estimate the action required by Clariant in the future to correct the effects on the environment of prior disposal or release of chemical substances by Clariant or other parties and the associated costs, pursuant to environmental laws and regulations. The material components of the environmental provisions consist of the costs to fully clean and refurbish contaminated sites and to treat and contain contamination at sites where the environmental exposure is less severe. The Group's future remediation expenses are affected by a number of uncertainties which include, but are not limited to, the method and extent of remediation and the percentage of material attributable to Clariant at the remediation sites relative to that attributable to other parties.

The environmental provisions reported in the balance sheet concern a number of different obligations, mainly in Switzerland, the United States, Germany, the United Kingdom, Brazil and Italy.

Provisions are made for remedial work where there is an obligation to remedy environmental damage, as well as for containment work where required by environmental regulations. All provisions relate to environmental liabilities arising in connection with activities that occurred prior to the date when Clariant took control of the relevant site. At each balance sheet date Clariant critically reviews all provisions and makes adjustment where required.

Personnel provisions. Personnel provisions include compensated long-term absences such as sabbatical leave, jubilee or other long-service benefits, noncurrent disability benefits, profit sharing and bonuses payable twelve months or more after the end of the period in which they were earned.

Restructuring provisions. Restructuring provisions are established where there is a legal or constructive obligation for the Group that will result in the outflow of economic resources and which is expected to occur twelve months or more after the end of the reporting period. The term restructuring refers to the activities that have as a consequence, staff redundancies and the shutdown of production lines or entire sites. However, expenses for termination benefits which are borne by the pension and termination plans are included in pension plan liabilities (see note 15).

Other provisions. Other provisions include provisions for obligations relating to tax and legal cases in various countries where settlement is expected after twelve months or more.

All noncurrent provisions are discounted to reflect the time value of money where material. Discount rates reflect current market assessments of the time value of money and the risk specific to the provisions in the respective countries.

17. Trade payables

CHF mn	12/31/2007	12/31/2006
Trade payables	705	650
Payables to associates	45	19
Accruals	369	351
Other payables	202	187
Total	1,321	1,207

The amount recognized in the books for trade payables is equal to their fair value.

18. Current financial debts

CHF mn	12/31/2007	12/31/2006
Banks and other financial institutions (including employee's accounts)	344	444
Current portion of noncurrent financial debts	384	179
Total	**728**	**623**

Current financial debt is recognized initially at fair value, net of transaction costs incurred. Financial debt is subsequently stated at amortized cost. There are no current financial liabilities valued at fair value through profit or loss.

The fair value of current financial debt, other than the current portion of noncurrent financial debt, approximates its carrying amount due to the short-term nature of these instruments.

19. Movements in provisions for current liabilities

CHF mn	Environmental provisions	Restructuring provisions	Personnel provisions	Other provisions	Total provisions for current liabilities 2007	Total provisions for current liabilities 2006
At January 1	19	54	152	126	351	431
Additions and reclassifications	27	114	152	103	396	305
Effect of disposals					--	(5)
Reclassified to held-for-sale				5	5	(19)
Amounts used	(16)	(30)	(166)	(74)	(286)	(319)
Unused amounts reversed	(3)	(4)	(11)	(21)	(39)	(43)
Exchange rate differences	--	(3)	2	2	1	1
At December 31	27	131	129	141	428	351

Environmental provisions. Environmental provisions for environmental liabilities are made when there is a legal or constructive obligation for the Group which will result in an outflow of economic resources. It is difficult to estimate the action required by Clariant in the future to correct the effects on the environment of prior disposal or release of chemical substances by Clariant or other parties and the associated costs, pursuant to environmental laws and regulations. The material components of the environmental provisions consist of the costs to fully clean and refurbish contaminated sites and to treat and contain contamination at sites where the environmental exposure is less severe. The Group's future remediation expenses are affected by a number of uncertainties which include, but are not limited to, the method and extent of remediation and the percentage of material attributable to Clariant at the remediation sites relative to that attributable to other parties.

The environmental provisions reported in the balance sheet concern a number of different obligations, mainly in Switzerland, the United States, Germany, the United Kingdom and Brazil.

Provisions are made for remedial work where there is an obligation to remedy environmental damage, as well as for containment work where required by environmental regulations. All provisions relate to environmental liabilities arising in connection with activities that occurred prior to the date when Clariant took control of the relevant site.

Restructuring provisions. Restructuring provisions are established where there is a legal or constructive obligation for the Group that will result in the outflow of economic resources and which is expected to occur within the next twelve months. The term restructuring refers to the activities that have as a consequence, staff redundancies and the shutdown of production lines or entire sites. However, expenses for termination benefits which are borne by the pension and termination plans are included in pension plan liabilities (see note 15).

Personnel provisions. Personnel provisions include holiday entitlements, compensated absences such as annual leave, profit sharing and bonuses payable within twelve months. Such provisions are provided for in proportion to the services rendered by the employee concerned.

Other provisions. Other provisions are recorded for liabilities (comprising tax, legal, and other items in various countries) falling due within the twelve months, for which no invoice has been received at the reporting date and/or for which the amount can only be reliably estimated.

20. Regional breakdown of key figures 2007 and 2006

Region	Sales[1]		Operating income[2]		Number of employees at December 31	
CHF mn	*2007*	*2006*	*2007*	*2006*	*2007*	*2006*
Continuing operations						
Europe	4,155	3,939	21	85	10,749	11,174
Thereof in Germany	1,252	1,173	111	100	4,962	5,154
Thereof in Switzerland	147	140	(161)	40	1,642	1,610
The Americas	2,364	2,292	158	195	4,879	4,925
Thereof in the US	995	1,031	15	65	1,652	1,733
Thereof in Brazil	589	521	52	38	1,648	1,695
Asia/Africa/Australia	2,014	1,869	99	105	5.303	5,649
Total continuing operations	**8,533**	**8,100**	**278**	**385**	**20,931**	**21,748**

Region	Investments in PPE and intangibles		Depreciation of PPE and intangibles		Net operating assets at December 31[3]	
CHF mn	*2007*	*2006*	*2007*	*2006*	*2007*	*2006*
Continuing operations						
Europe	188	208	258	332	2,204	2,339
Thereof in Germany	93	104	106	137	428	523
Thereof in Switzerland	15	20	34	36	690	620
The Americas	78	75	53	48	758	829
Thereof in the US	32	34	25	23	219	280
Thereof in Brazil	24	24	20	18	264	255
Asia/Africa/Australia	48	46	39	33	771	821
Total continuing operations	**314**	**329**	**350**	**413**	**3,733**	**3,989**

[1] *Allocated by region of third-party sale's destination.*
[2] *Allocated by region of production and selling entity.*
[3] *Noncurrent and current assets (excluding cash and short-term deposits) less noninterest-bearing liabilities.*

21. Divisional breakdown of key figures 2007 and 2006

Intersegment transactions are entered into under the normal circumstances and terms and condition that would also be available to unrelated third parties.

Segment assets consist of property, plant, and equipment, goodwill, inventories, receivables, and investments in associates. They exclude deferred tax assets, financial assets, and operating cash. Segment liabilities comprise trade payables. They exclude items such as taxation, provisions for liabilities and corporate borrowings.

Divisions
CHF mn

	Textile, leather & paper chemicals (TLP)		Pigments & additives (PA)		Masterbatches (MB)		Functional chemicals (FUN)		Total divisions continuing operations[3]		Corporate[3]		Total group[3]	
	2007	2006	2007	2006	2007	2006	2007	2006	2007	2006	2007	2006	2007	2006
Divisional sales	2339	2310	2137	2031	1381	1255	2803	2615	8660	8211	--	--	8660	8211
Sales to other divisions	(7)	(7)	(61)	(50)	(1)	(1)	(58)	(53)	(127)	(111)	--	--	(127)	(111)
Total sales	**2332**	**2303**	**2076**	**1981**	**1380**	**1254**	**2745**	**2562**	**8533**	**8100**	--	--	**8533**	**8100**
Operating expenses	(2187)	(2143)	(1904)	(1784)	(1259)	(1135)	(2558)	(2339)	(7908)	(7401)	(123)	(142)	(8031)	(7543)
Income from associates	--	1	20	19	3	1	7	9	30	30	7	5	37	35
Gain from the disposal of subsidiaries and associates	--	--	--	--	--	--	--	--	--	--	1	4	1	4
Restructuring and impairment	(105)	(111)	(115)	(5)	(22)	(9)	--	(35)	(242)	(160)	(20)	(51)	(262)	(211)
Operating income	**40**	**50**	**77**	**211**	**102**	**111**	**194**	**197**	**413**	**569**	**(135)**	**(184)**	**278**	**385**
Finance income													31	33
Finance costs													(102)	(143)
Income before taxes													**207**	**275**
Taxes													(99)	(144)
Net income from continuing operations													**108**	**131**
Discontinued operations:														
Income from discontinued operations													(103)	(209)
Net income													**5**	**(78)**
Total assets	1767	1905	1779	1804	728	707	1515	1435	5789	5851	1496	1337	7285	7188
Liabilities	(172)	(155)	(174)	(150)	(111)	(107)	(197)	(169)	(654)	(581)	(4259)	(4174)	(4913)	(4755)
Total equity and minority interests	**1595**	**1750**	**1605**	**1654**	**617**	**600**	**1318**	**1266**	**5135**	**5270**	**(2763)**	**(2837)**	**2372**	**2433**
Net debts[4]											1361	1556	1361	1556
Total net operating assets[1]	**1595**	**1750**	**1605**	**1654**	**617**	**600**	**1318**	**1266**	**5135**	**5270**	**(1402)**	**(1281)**	**3733**	**3989**
Thereof:														
Investments in PPE and intangibles for the period[5]	71	74	71	79	64	51	85	114	291	318	23	11	314	329
Investments in associates	3	13	143	190	5	4	139	77	290	284	4	4	294	288
Operating income	40	50	77	211	102	111	194	197	413	569	(135)	(184)	278	385
Add: Systematic depreciation of PPE[5]	72	71	84	76	29	31	68	64	253	242	11	14	264	256
Add: Impairment loss on PPE and goodwill	55	103	17	--	5	1	(1)	4	76	107	1	43	77	150
Add: Amortization of other intangibles	--	--	2	1	1	--	2	--	2	2	7	5	9	7
EBITDA[2]	**167**	**224**	**180**	**288**	**136**	**143**	**261**	**265**	**744**	**920**	**(116)**	**(122)**	**628**	**798**
Add: Restructuring and impairment	105	111	115	5	22	9	--	35	242	160	20	51	262	211
Less: Impairment loss on PPE and goodwill (Reported under restructuring and impairment)	(55)	(103)	(17)	--	(5)	--	1	(4)	(76)	(107)	(1)	(43)	(77)	(150)
Less: Gain from the disposal of subsidiaries and associates	--	--	--	--	--	--	--	--	--	--	(1)	(4)	(1)	(4)
EBITDA before restructuring and disposals	**217**	**232**	**278**	**293**	**153**	**152**	**262**	**296**	**910**	**973**	**(98)**	**(118)**	**812**	**855**

Divisions CHF mn	Textile, leather & paper chemicals (TLP)		Pigments & additives (PA)		Masterbatches (MB)		Functional chemicals (FUN)		Total divisions continuing operations[3]		Corporate[3]		Total group[3]	
	2007	2006	**2007**	2006	**2007**	2006	**2007**	2006	**2007**	2006	**2007**	2006	**2007**	2006
Operating income	40	50	77	211	102	111	194	197	413	569	(135)	(184)	278	385
Add: Restructuring and impairment	105	111	115	5	22	9	–	35	242	160	20	51	262	211
Less: Gain from the disposal of subsidiaries and associates	–	–	–	–	–	–	–	–	–	–	(1)	(4)	(1)	(4)
Operating income before restructuring, impairment and disposals	**145**	**161**	**192**	**216**	**124**	**120**	**194**	**232**	**655**	**729**	**(116)**	**(137)**	**539**	**592**

[1] *Within net operating assets, PPE including infrastructure, inventory, trade payables, receivables and goodwill were allocated to each division. All other balance sheet positions generally included in the calculation of net operating assets were allocated to Corporate.*

[2] *EBITDA is earning before interest, tax, depreciation and amortization*

[3] *Restated (see Note 1.24)*

[4] **Calculation of net debt**
CHF mn

	12/31/2007	12/31/2006
Non-current financial debt	1267	1376
Add: Current financial debt	728	623
Less: Cash and cash equivalents	(509)	(443)
Less: Current deposits 90 to 365 days	(125)	–
Net debt	**1361**	**1556**

[5] **Discountinued operations**
CHF mn

	2007	2006
Investment in PPE and intangibles	6	33
Systematic depreciation	–	13

22. Discontinued operations and assets held for sale

Custom Manufacturing. In September 2006 Clariant launched a project to sell its Custom Manufacturing Business pertaining to the Division Life Science Chemicals. On June 29, 2007, the business, comprising sites in Germany and the United States, was transferred to International Chemical Investors Group (ICIG). As a result, these activities are reported as discontinued operations in accordance with IFRS 5, *Noncurrent Assets Held for Sale and Discontinued Operations*. The related assets and liabilities were reclassified to assets held for sale and associated liabilities in the balance sheet in 2006. Based on the sale price expected to be realized on the disposal of this business, the assets were depreciated for impairment by an amount of CHF 81 million in 2006.

The result of discontinued operations is as follows:

CHF mn	2007[1] (6 months)	2006
Sales	82	211
Restructuring	3	(11)
Impairment	(7)	(81)
Operating expenses	(111)	(248)
Operating loss	**(33)**	**(129)**
Financial result	--	(1)
Loss from discontinued operations before taxes	**(33)**	**(130)**
Taxes	--	24
Loss from discontinued operations after taxes	**(33)**	**(106)**
Loss on the disposal of the discontinued operation	(72)	--
Taxes (current and deferred)	7	--
Loss from discontinued operations after taxes	**(98)**	**(106)**
Cash flow from discontinued operations		
Operating cash flows	(18)	(65)
Investing cash flows	(7)	(17)
Financing cash flows	(15)	2
Total cash flow	**(40)**	**(80)**
Net assets held for sale		
Property, plant and equipment	--	1
Deferred tax assets	--	6
Inventories	53	48
Trade receivables	22	40
Other current assets	1	1
Cash and cash equivalents	5	1
Total assets held for sale	**81**	**97**
Trade payables	28	21
Income tax provisions	--	2
Provisions	21	38
Total liabilities associated with assets held for sale	**49**	**61**
Number of employees of the disposal group	458	486
Net income and cash flow from the disposal of discontinued operations		
Total proceeds received in 2007	23	--
Consideration for sale	**23**	**--**
Net assets sold including disposal-related expenses and liabilities incurred	(95)	--
Loss on disposals before tax expense	**(72)**	**--**
Taxes (current and deferred)	7	--
After tax loss on disposal	**(65)**	**--**
The net cash flow from sale is determined as follows:		
Proceeds received in 2007	23	--
Payments made in 2007	(30)	--
Less: Cash and cash equivalents in subsidiary sold	(5)	--
Net cash flow from sale	**(12)**	**--**

[1] *Net assets transferred at the date of the disposal*

Pharmaceutical fine chemicals. On June 30, 2006, Clariant sold its Pharmaceutical Fine Chemicals Business, belonging to the Life Science Chemicals Division, to TowerBrook Capital Partners. As a result, these activities are reported as discontinued operations in accordance with IFRS 5, *Noncurrent Assets Held for Sale and Discontinued Operations.*

The transaction comprised the sale of activities in Germany, France, the UK, and the US and Italy.

The result of discontinued operations is as follows:

CHF mn	2007	2006 (6 months)
Sales		114
Restructuring		(2)
Operating expenses		(113)
Operating loss	**--**	**(1)**
Financial result		(4)
Loss from discontinued operations before taxes	**--**	**(5)**
Taxes		3
Loss from discontinued operations after taxes	**--**	**(2)**
Loss on the disposal of the discontinued operation	(5)	(121)
Deferred tax on tax loss generated		20
Loss from discontinued operations	**(5)**	**(103)**
Cash flow from discontinued operations		
Operating cash flows	--	3
Investing cash flows	--	(17)
Financing cash flows	--	14
Total cash flow		--
Net assets of disposal group		
Property, plant and equipment	--	115
Deferred tax assets	--	5
Inventories	--	75
Trade receivables	--	40
Other current assets	--	5
Cash and cash equivalents	--	7
Trade payables	--	(41)
Financial debt	--	(8)
Provisions	--	(37)
Income tax liabilities	--	(3)
Total net assets of disposal group		**158**
Number of employees of the disposal group		760
Net income and cash flow from the disposal of discontinued operations		
Total proceeds received in 2006		53
Less: Payment to be made to buyer in 2007		(8)
Plus: Payment to be received from buyer in 2008		9
Consideration for sale		**54**
Net assets sold including disposal-related expenses	(5)	(174)
Loss on disposals before tax expense	**(5)**	**(120)**
Taxes (current and deferred)	--	19
After tax loss on disposal	**(5)**	**(101)**
The net cash flow from sale is determined as follows:		
Proceeds received in 2006	--	53
Payments made to buyer in 2007	(3)	
Less: Cash and cash equivalents in subsidiary sold	--	(7)
Net cash flow from sale	**(3)**	**46**

CHF mn	2007	2006 (6 months)
Total cash flow from the disposal of discontinued operations and assets held for sale		
Net cash flow from sale of Custom Manufacturing	(12)	--
Net cash flow from sale of Pharmaceutical Fine Chemicals	(3)	46
Net cash flow from repayment of vendor loan note	40	--
Net cash flow	**25**	**46**

Reconciliation of loss from discontinued operations as reported in the income statement

CHF mn	Pharmaceutical Fine Chemicals	Custom Manufacturing	Total 2006
2006			
Sales	114	211	325
Restructuring	(2)	(11)	(13)
Impairment	--	(81)	(81)
Operating expenses	(113)	(248)	(361)
Operating loss	**(1)**	**(129)**	**(130)**
Financial result	(4)	(1)	(5)
Loss from discontinued operations before taxes	**(5)**	**(130)**	**(135)**
Taxes	3	24	27
Loss from discontinued operations after taxes	**(2)**	**(106)**	**(108)**
Loss on the disposal of the discontinued operation	(121)	--	(121)
Deferred tax on tax loss generated	20	--	20
Loss from discontinued operations	**(103)**	**(106)**	**(209)**
Thereof loss on disposal of discontinued operations and assets held for sale	*(101)*	*--*	*(101)*
2007			
Sales	--	82	82
Restructuring	--	3	3
Impairment	--	(7)	(7)
Operating expenses	--	(111)	(111)
Operating loss	**--**	**(33)**	**(33)**
Financial result	--	--	--
Loss from discontinued operations before taxes	**--**	**(33)**	**(33)**
Taxes	--	--	--
Loss from discontinued operations after taxes	**--**	**(33)**	**(33)**
Loss on the disposal of the discontinued operation	(5)	(72)	(77)
Taxes (current and deferred)	--	7	7
Loss from discontinued operations	**(5)**	**(98)**	**(103)**
Thereof loss on disposal of discontinued operations and assets held for sale	*(5)*	*(65)*	*(70)*

23. Disposal of activities not qualifying as discontinued operations

In this section are reported disposals of subsidiaries, associates and activities that do not qualify as discontinued operations in the sense of IFRS 5.

On May 7, 2007, Clariant sold associate Abieta Chemie GmbH, Germany. Clariant Australia sold its Masterbatch activities on May 1, 2007, and its Textile, Leather and Paper activities on October 1, 2007.

On reclassification to noncurrent assets held for sale these balance sheet itmes were revalued to the lower of book value or fair value less costs to sell. This revaluation caused an impairment devaluation of CHF 3 million relating to Australian Masterbatch activities and 2 million relating to its Textile, Leather and Paper activities, which is reported in the income statement line "Restructuring and impairment."

On September 30, 2006, Clariant sold the activities of Site Services, Energy Supply, ESHA Services and Enterprise Functions of the subsidiary Industriepark Gersthofen Servicegesellschaft.

On reclassification to noncurrent assets held for sale in the second quarter of 2006 the net assets of this company were revalued to the lower of their carrying amount and fair value less costs to sell. This revaluation caused an impairment charge of CHF 43 million, which is reported in the income statement line "Restructuring and impairment."

CHF mn	Total 2006	Total 2005
Net income and cash flow from the disposal of activities		
Consideration for sale received	17	33
Consideration for sale receivable	3	--
Total consideration for sale	**20**	**33**
Net assets sold including disposal-related expenses	(19)	(29)
Gain on disposals	**1**	**4**
Net cash flow	**23**	**33**

24. Business Combinations

Toschem. On October 1, 2007, Clariant acquired the Colombian company Toschem de Colombia Ltda, a leading supplier of chemicals and services to the oil and gas and industrial water treatment markets in Colombia for the amount of CHF 5 million. The acquired business contributed sales of CHF 2 million and net profit of less than CHF 1 million to the Group for the period from October 1, 2007, to December 31, 2007. If the acquisition had occurred on January 1, 2007, group sales would have increased by CHF 8 million and net income would have increased by less than CHF 1 million. These amounts have been calculated using the Group's accounting policies and by adjusting the results of the subsidiaries to reflect the additional depreciation and amortization that would have been charged assuming the fair value adjustment to intangibles had applied from January 1, 2007, together with the consequential tax effects.

Details of net assets acquired and goodwill are as follows:

Purchase consideration:	
CHF mn	
Cash paid	3
Cash payable	1
Total purchase consideration	**4**
Fair value of net assets acquired	(4)
Goodwill	**--**

The assets and liabilities as of October 1, 2007 arising from the acquisition are as follows:

Purchase consideration:	Preacquisition	Fair value adjustments	Recognized carrying amounts
CHF mn			
Inventories	1	--	1
Property, plant and equipment	1	--	1
Intangibles	--	2	2
Net assets acquired	**2**	**2**	**4**
Purchase consideration settled in cash	--	--	(3)
Cash flow on acquisition	**--**	**--**	**(3)**

Masterandino. On November 1, 2007, Clariant acquired the Colombian company Masterandino, a Masterbatch producer in Colombia for the amount of CHF 5 million. The acquired business contributed sales of CHF 1 million and net profit of less than CHF 1 million to the Group for the period from November 1, 2007, to December 31, 2007. If the acquisition had occurred on January 1, 2007, Group sales would have increased by CHF 6 million and net income would have increased by CHF 1 million. These amounts have been calculated using the Group's accounting policies and by adjusting the results of the subsidiaries to reflect the additional depreciation and amortization that would have been charged assuming the fair value adjustment to intangibles had applied from January 1, 2007, together with the consequential tax effects.

Details of net assets acquired and goodwill are follows:

Purchase consideration:	
CHF mn	
Cash paid	5
Total purchase consideration	**5**
Fair value of net assets acquired	(5)
Goodwill	**--**

The assets and liabilities as of November 2007 arising from the acquisition are as follows:

Purchase consideration:	*Preacquisition*	*Fair value adjustments*	*Recognized carrying amounts*
CHF mn			
Inventories	1	--	1
Property, plant and equipment	1	--	1
Intangibles	--	3	3
Net assets acquired	**2**	**3**	**5**
Purchase consideration settled in cash	--	--	(5)
Cash flow on acquisition	**--**	**--**	**(5)**

KiON. On February 14, 2006, the Group acquired all of the shares in KiON Corporation, located in the USA, at an amount of CHF 16 million. The acquired business contributed sales of CHF 1 million and net loss of less than CHF 1 million to the Group for the period from February 14, 2006, to December 31, 2006. If the acquisition had occurred on January 1, 2006, Group sales would have increased and net income would have decreased by less than CHF 1 million. These amounts have been calculated using the Group's accounting policies and by adjusting the results of the subsidiaries to reflect the additional depreciation and amortization that would have been charged assuming the fair value adjustment to intangibles had applied from January 1, 2006, together with the consequential tax effects.

Details of net assets acquired and goodwill are as follows:

Purchase consideration:	
CHF mn	
Cash paid	16
Total purchase consideration	**16**
Fair value of net assets acquired	(16)
Goodwill	**--**

The assets and liabilities as of February 14, 2006, arising from the acquisition are as follows:

Purchase consideration:	*Preacquisition*	*Fair value adjustments*	*Recognized carrying amounts*
CHF mn			
Property, plant and equipment	1	--	1
Intangibles	--	15	15
Net assets acquired	**1**	**15**	**16**
Purchase consideration settled in cash	--	--	16
Cash flow on acquisition	**--**	**--**	**16**

Ciba Masterbatches. On December 1, 2006, the Group acquired the Ciba Specialty Chemicals' Masterbatches business at an amount of CHF 30 million. This transaction comprised share deals in France and Saudi Arabia and an asset deal in Malaysia. All the shares were acquired in France and 93% of the shares in Saudi Arabia. The acquired business contributed sales of CHF 5 million and net loss of less than CHF 1 million to the Group for the period from December 1, 2006 to December 2006.

If the acquisition had occurred on January 1, 2006, Group sales would have increased by CHF 76 million and net income would have increased by CHF 3 million. These amounts have been calculated using the Group's accounting policies and by adjusting the results of the subsidiaries to reflect the additional depreciation and amortization that would have been charged assuming the fair value adjustment to property, plant, and equipment and intangibles had applied from January 1, 2006, together with the consequential tax effects.

Details of net assets acquired and goodwill are as follows:

Purchase consideration:	
CHF mn	
Cash paid	30
Direct costs relating to the acquisition	1
Total purchase consideration	**31**
Fair value of net assets acquired	(28)
Goodwill	**3**

The goodwill recognized on the acquisition is justified due to the expected synergies from the transaction and the assembled workforce.

The assets and liabilities as of December 1, 2006, arising from the acquisition are as follows.

Purchase consideration:	*Preacquisition*	*Fair value adjustments*	*Recognized carrying amounts*
CHF mn			
Cash and cash equivalents	2	--	2
Trade receivables	20	(1)	19
Inventories	16	(1)	15
Property, plant and equipment	24	(8)	16
Intangibles	--	3	3
Current liabilities	(21)	--	(21)
Noncurrent liabilities	(4)	(1)	(5)
Deferred tax liabilities	(1)	1	--
Net assets	36	(7)	29
Minorities	(1)	--	(1)
Net assets acquired	**35**	**(7)**	**28**
Purchased consideration settled in cash	--	--	(31)
Cash and cash equivalents	--	--	2
Cash flow on acquisition	**--**	**--**	**(29)**

25. Finance income and costs

CHF mn	*2007*	*2006*
Finance income		
Interest income	26	30
Thereof interest on loans and receivables	24	19
Thereof income from financial assets held to maturity	1	1
Other financial income	5	3
Thereof gains on the valuation of fair value hedges	1	2
Total finance income	**31**	**33**
Finance costs		
Interest expense	(107)	(112)
Other financial expenses	(18)	(20)
Currency result, net	23	(11)
Total finance costs	**(102)**	**(143)**

Other financial income mainly consists of market valuation gains due to engagement in interest rate swaps and other investments. Other financial expenses included losses on the sale of securities, bank charges and miscellaneous finance expenses.

In 2007 and 2006 no gains or losses on fair value hedges or cash flow hedges transferred from equity, no ineffective parts of cash flow hedges or hedges of a net investment were recorded in the income statement.

26. Earnings per share (EPS)

Earnings per share are calculated by dividing the Group net income by the average number of outstanding shares (issued shares less treasury shares).

CHF mn	2007	2006
Net income attributable to shareholders of Clariant Ltd		
Continuing operations	101	124
Discontinued operations	(103)	(209)
Total	**(2)**	**(85)**
Diluted net income attributable to shareholders of Clariant Ltd		
Continuing operations	101	124
Discontinued operations	(103)	(209)
Total	**(2)**	**(85)**
Shares		
Holdings on January 1	226,648,302	226,292,707
Effect of the issuance of share capital and transactions with treasury shares on weighted-average number of shares outstanding	505,534	474,547
Weighted-average number of shares outstanding	**227,153,836**	**226,767,254**
Adjustment for granted Clariant shares	1,181,689	1,059,753
Adjustment for dilutive share options	31,872	43,761
Weighted-average diluted number of shares outstanding	**228,367,397**	**227,870,768**
Basic earnings per share attributable to shareholders of Clariant Ltd (CHF/share)		
Continuing operations	0.44	0.55
Discontinued operations	(0.45)	(0.92)
Total	**(0.01)**	**(0.37)**
Diluted earnings per share attributable to shareholders of Clariant Ltd (CHF/share)		
Continuing operations	0.44	0.54
Discontinued operations	(0.45)	(0.92)
Total	**(0.01)**	**(0.38)**

Diluted earnings per share are calculated adjusting the weighted-average number of ordinary shares outstanding to assume conversion of all dilutive potential ordinary shares.

The dilution effect is triggered by two different items. One is the effect of Clariant shares granted as part of the share-based payment plan, which have not yet vested. To calculate this dilutive potential it is assumed that they had vested on January 1 of the respective period. The other item is the effect of options granted as part of the share-based payment plan, which have not yet vested. To calculate this dilutive potential it is assumed that all options which were in the money at the end of the respective period had been exercised on January 1 of the same period.

27. Restructuring and Impairment

In order to increase profitability over a sustained period, Clariant implements deep-going measures designed to improve the Group's performance. The aim of these efforts is to increase the Group's operating result and reduce net working capital. The changes that are being made to the processes and structures in order to achieve these aims result in a substantial loss of jobs across the Group.

Restructuring. In 2007 Clariant recorded expenses for restructuring in the amount of CHF 185 million in continuing operations for projects mainly in Germany, the United Kingdom, and the United States, where several sites are closed and the headcount is being further reduced. In September 2007 Clariant announced the closure of its production site in Selby, UK pertaining to the division Textile, Leather, Paper in the course of 2008. The closure will result in a substantial headcount reduction entailing restructuring costs in the amount of CHF 28 million. Additionally property, plant, and equipment in the amount of CHF 50 million was impaired based on value-in-use calculation. In October 2007 Clariant announced the closure of its production site in Coventry, USA by December 2008. The closure will result in a substantial headcount reduction entailing restructuring costs in the amount of CHF 41 million. Additionally the useful life of the assets of the site concerned was reassessed and brought in line with the timing of the plant closure. This lead to additional depreciation in the amount o f CHF 20 million to be charged to the income statement in the fourth quarter of 2007 and the year 2008. This charge would have been reported in subsequent periods, had it not been decided to close the plant. As this depreciation charge is clearly distinct from the depreciation charged in the regular course of business excluding any site closures, it is posted to the line "Restructuring and impairment" in the income statement. The amount charged to the income statement for the accelerated depreciation of the assets of the Coventry site amounts to CHF 4 million in 2007. The expenses concern the Pigments & Additives division. In 2006 the Clariant Group recorded expenses for restructuring in the amount of CHF 61 million in Continuing Operations for projects mainly in Germany, the United Kingdom and the United States.

Impairment. As a result of the permanent endeavors to improve the company's performance, PPE are regularly reviewed for their cash-generating potential. In numerous cases it was evident that such assets were impaired, as they would no longer be utilized and as a consequence they were written off. Clariant also assessed the recoverability of the carrying amount of noncurrent assets of several cash-generating units (CGU) in 2006 and 2007. For this purpose, assets were grouped at the lowest levels for which there are separately identifiable cash flows. An impairment loss was recognized as an expense in the income statement in the amount by which the carrying amount of the assets exceeded the recoverable amount, which is the higher of an asset's fair value less costs to sell and value in use. In May 2006 Clariant decided to sell its subsidiary Industriepark Gertsthofen Servicegesellschaft in Germany, pertaining to Site Services, Energy Supply, ESHA Services and Enterprise Functions. On reclassification to noncurrent assets held for sale the balance sheet items concerned were revalued to fair value less costs to sell. This revaluation caused an impairment charge of CHF 43 million, which is reported in the column "Corporate." On September 30, 2006, the company was sold (see note 23). In 2006 goodwill in the amount of CHF 100 million pertaining to the Leather business was written off for impairment. This is also described in note 5.

CHF mn	TLP 2007	TLP 2006	PA 2007	PA 2006	MB 2007	MB 2006	FUN 2007	FUN 2006	Total divisions 2007	Total divisions 2006	Corporate 2007	Corporate 2006	Total group 2007	Total group 2006¹
Cash out expenses for restructuring	20	6	7	9	13	3	18	14	58	32	21	6	79	38
Noncash expenses for														
Leaving indemnity	17	3	47	(1)	3	4	(6)	4	61	10	(1)	2	60	12
Others	13	(1)	44	(3)	1	2	(11)	13	47	11	(1)	--	48	11
Total noncash expenses for restructuring	**30**	**2**	**91**	**(4)**	**4**	**6**	**(17)**	**17**	**108**	**21**	**(2)**	**2**	**106**	**23**
Total restructuring expenses	**50**	**8**	**98**	**5**	**17**	**9**	**1**	**31**	**166**	**53**	**19**	**8**	**185**	**61**
Impairment of PPE														
Land and buildings	12	2	6	--	--	--	--	--	18	2	1	43	19	45
Machinery and equipment	43	1	11	--	5	--	--	4	59	5	--	--	59	5
Total impairment of PPE	**55**	**3**	**17**	**--**	**5**	**--**	**--**	**4**	**77**	**7**	**1**	**43**	**78**	**50**
Impairment of goodwill	--	100	--	--	--	--	--	--	--	100	--	--	--	100
Total impairment	**55**	**103**	**17**	**--**	**5**	**--**	**--**	**4**	**77**	**107**	**1**	**43**	**78**	**150**
Reversal of impairment and reversal of PPE	--	--	--	--	--	--	(1)	--	(1)	--	--	--	(1)	--
Total impairment and reversal of impairment	**55**	**103**	**17**	**--**	**5**	**--**	**(1)**	**4**	**76**	**107**	**1**	**43**	**77**	**150**
Total restructuring and impairment	**105**	**111**	**115**	**5**	**22**	**9**	**--**	**35**	**242**	**160**	**20**	**51**	**262**	**211**
Thereof noncash expenses	**85**	**105**	**108**	**(4)**	**9**	**6**	**(18)**	**21**	**184**	**128**	**(1)**	**45**	**183**	**173**

¹ Restated due to the integration of the Division Life Science Chemicals (LSC) into the Division Functional Chemicals (FUN).

28. Consolidated statement of changes in equity at December 31, 2007 and 2006

CHF mn	Total share capital	Treasury shares (par value)	Share premium reserves	Other reserves			Retained earnings	Total attributable to equity holders	Minority interests	Total equity
				Hedging reserves	Cumulative translation reserves	Total other reserves				
Balance December 31, 2005	1,093	(18)	767	--	(104)	663	793	2,531	60	2,591
Total recognized income and expense for the period					(15)	(15)	(85)	(100)	7	(93)
Dividends to third parties								--	(7)	(7)
Share capital reduction	(58)							(58)		(58)
Employee share and option scheme:										
Effect of employee services						--	(3)	(3)		(3)
Equity share options issued							(4)	(4)		(4)
Treasury share transactions		2					5	7		7
Balance December 31, 2006	**1,035**	**(16)**	**767**	**--**	**(119)**	**648**	**706**	**2,373**	**60**	**2,433**
Total recognized income and expense for the period					(6)	(6)	(5)	(11)	8	(3)
Dividends to third parties								--	(9)	(9)
Share capital reduction	(57)							(57)		(57)
Employee share and option scheme:										
Effect of employee services						--	7	7		7
Equity share options issued							4	4		4
Treasury share transactions							(3)	(3)		(3)
Balance December 31, 2007	**978**	**(16)**	**767**	**--**	**(125)**	**642**	**709**	**2,313**	**59**	**2,372**

During 2006 and 2007, Clariant reduced its share capital by CHF 0.25 per share resulting in a payout of CHF 57.5 million in each year.

In 2006 Clariant Ltd sold 1,000,000 put options on its own shares of which 250,000 were outstanding on December 31, 2006. The put options had a strike price of CHF 18.00 and expired in June 2007 without having been exercised.

29. Financial instruments

Risk management (hedging) instruments and off-balance-sheet risks. Clariant uses forward foreign exchange rate and option contracts, interest rate and currency swaps and other derivative instruments to hedge the Group's risk exposure to volatility in interest rates and currencies and to manage the return on cash and cash equivalents. Risk exposures from existing assets and liabilities as well as anticipated transactions are managed centrally.

Interest rate management. It is the Group's policy to manage the cost of interest using fixed and variable rate debt and interest-related derivatives.

Foreign exchange management. To manage the exposure to the fluctuations in foreign currency exchange rates, the Group follows a strategy of hedging both balance sheet and revenue risk, partially through the use of forward contracts and currency swaps in various currencies. In order to minimize financial expenses, the Group does not hedge the entire exposure.

The following tables show the contract or underlying principal amounts and the respective fair value of financial instruments by type at year-end.

The contract or underlying principal amounts indicate the volume of business outstanding at the balance sheet date and do not represent the amount at risk. The fair values represent market value or standard pricing models at December 31, 2007 and 2006, respectively.

Financial instruments CHF mn	Contract or underlying principal amount		Positive fair values		Negative fair values	
	12/31/2007	*12/31/2006*	*12/31/2007*	*12/31/2006*	*12/31/2007*	*12/31/2006*
Currency-related instruments						
Forward foreign exchange rate contracts	102	111	1	1	--	(2)
Total financial instruments	**102**	**111**	**1**	**1**	**--**	**(2)**

The fair value of these financial instruments is recorded in the position Other current assets in the balance sheet in the case of a positive value or as an accrual in the position Trade payable in the case of a negative value.

Financial instruments by currency	*12/31/2007*	*12/31/2006*
Forward foreign exchange rate contracts		
CHF mn		
USD	72	75
EUR	1	2
BRL	29	34
Total financial instruments	**102**	**111**

Financial instruments effective for hedge-accounting purposes	*2007*	*2006*
CHF mn		
Fair value of cash flow hedges:		
Contracts with positive fair values	--	--
Contracts with negative fair values		
Cross-currency swaps	--	--
Fair value of hedges of net investments in foreign entities:		
Contracts with positive fair values	--	--
Contracts with negative fair values		
Borrowings denominated in foreign currencies	(961)	--

On April 6, 2006, Clariant issued a bond in the amount of EUR 600 million, denominated in euros (see note 14). The bond was designated as a hedge of a net investment in some of Clariant's European subsidiaries. The unrealized foreign exchange loss at December 31, 2007, in the amount of CHF 31 million (2006: CHF 16 million) resulting from the translation of the bond into Swiss francs was recognized in the cumulative translation reserves in shareholders' equity.

Clariant engaged in two interest rate swaps in order to hedge the interest rate risk arising on this bond and accounted for these as fair value hedges. The interest rate swaps had a notional amount of EUR 100 million each and were entered into in May and June 2007 respectively. Both interest swaps were closed in August 2007.

CHF mn

Volumes of securitization of trade receivables	*12/31/2007*	*12/31/2006*
Trade receivables denominated in US dollars	73	88
Total	**73**	**88**
Related liability in the balance sheet denominated in US dollars	73	88
Total	**73**	**88**

Securitization. For a number of years Clariant has been using securitization as a means of financing. Trade receivables from certain companies are sold in asset backed securities (ABS) programs. Clariant retains the credit risk of the trade receivable and the interest rate risk liability incurred. Therefore the trade receivables are not derecognized from the balance sheet until payments from the customers are obtained and a current financial liability is recorded for the amount borrowed under the security of the trade receivables.

30. Employee participation plans

During 2005, the former Clariant Executive Stock Option Plan (CESOP) and Management Stock Incentive Plan (MSIP) were replaced by a new incentive plan called the Clariant Executive Bonus Plan (CEBP).

The number of shares to be granted under CEBP depends both on the performance of the Group and the performance of the Division/Function in which incentive plan members work.

The granted registered shares of Clariant Ltd become vested and are exercisable after three years. No options are granted under the CEBP.

The options granted under the former CESOP entitle the holder to acquire registered shares in Clariant Ltd (1 share per option) at a predetermined strike price. They become vested and are exercisable after three years and expire after ten years.

The expense recorded in the income statement spreads the costs of each grant equally over the measurement period of one year and the vesting period of three years. Assumptions are made concerning the forfeiture rate which is adjusted during the vesting period so that at the end of the vesting period there is only a charge for the vested amounts. As permitted by the transitional rules of IFRS 2, grants of options and shares prior to November 7, 2002, have not been restated.

During 2007 CHF 7 million (2006: CHF 9 million) for equity-settled share-based payments and CHF 1 million (2006: CHF 1 million) for cash-settled share-based payments were charged to the income statement.

As of December 31, 2007, the total carrying value of liabilities arising from share-based payments is CHF 19 million (2006: CHF 20 million). Thereof CHF 18 million (2006: CHF 19 million) was recognized in equity for equity-settled share-based payments and CHF 1 million (2006: CHF 1 million) in noncurrent liabilities for cash-settled share-based payments.

Options for Board of Directors (nonexecutive members)[1]

Base year	*Granted*	*Exercisable from*	*Expiry date*	*Exercise price*	*Share price at grant date*	**Number 12/31/2007**	*Number 12/31/2006*
1998	1998	2001	2008	53.80	56.76	10,137	10,137
1999	1999	2002	2009	61.80	60.76	10,418	10,418
2000	2000	2003	2010	48.00	47.97	6,229	6,229
Total						**26,784**	**26,784**

Options for senior members of Management[1]

Base year	Granted	Exercisable from	Expiry date	Exercise price	Share price at grant date	**Number 12/31/2007**	Number 12/31/2006
1997	1998	2001	2008	25.50	68.97	127,783	127,783
1997	1998	2001	2008	37.50	73.06	167,001	167,001
1998	1999	2002	2009	61.80	62.09	358,789	358,789
1999	2000	2003	2010	48.00	47.97	106,191	106,191
2000	2001	2004	2011	41.80	42.02	7,229	7,229
2001	2002	2005	2012	27.20	26.87	166,354	166,354
2002	2003	2006	2013	14.80	14.88	87,352	124,568
2003	2004	2007	2014	12.00	18.74	49,326	49,326
2003	2004	2007	2014	16.30	18.74	53,479	60,391
2004	2005	2008	2015	19.85	19.85	146,237	146,237
Total						**1,269,741**	**1,313,869**

[1] *Past and current members.*

As per December 31, 2007, the weighted-average remaining contractual life of the share options was 3.6 years.

Shares for Board of Directors (nonexecutive members)

Base year	Granted	Vesting in	Share price at grant date	**Number 12/31/2007**	Number 12/31/2006
2004	2004	2007	18.74	--	5,522
2005	2005	2008	19.85	10,077	10,077
2006	2006	2009	19.60	16,158	16,158
2007	2007	2010	19.15	22,192	
Total				**48,427**	**31,757**

Shares for members of Management

Base year	Granted	Vesting in	Share price at grant date	**Number 12/31/2007**	Number 12/31/2006
2003	2004	2007	18.74	--	282,271
2004	2005	2008	19.85	393,397	433,121
2005	2006	2009	19.60	285,555	312,604
2006	2007	2010	19.15	454,310	--
Total				**678,952**	**1,027,996**

All shares granted and shares for all options granted are held as treasury shares.

	Weighted-average exercise price	Options 2007	Shares 2007	Weighted-average exercise price	Options 2006	Shares 2006
Shares/options outstanding at January 1	37.07	1,340,743	1,059,753	44.90	1,369,918	1,454,678
Granted (incl. adjustment due to rights issue)			491,903			347,826
Exercised/distributed	15.03	(44,218)	(351,241)	14.80	(29,175)	(719,731)
Cancelled			(18,726)		--	(23,020)
Outstanding at December 31	**37.61**	**1,296,525**	**1,181,689**	**37.07**	**1,340,743**	**1,059,753**
Exercisable at December 31	39.87	1,150,288		41.44	1,084,699	--
Fair value of shares/options outstanding in CHF		1,279,331	12,443,145		3,159,820	19,340,492

The fair value of shares granted during 2007 is CHF 9 million (2006: CHF 6 million) calculated based on market value of shares at grant date.

31. Personnel expenses

CHF mn	*2007*	*2006*
Wages and salaries	(1,475)	(1,462)
Social welfare costs	(374)	(323)
Shares and options granted to directors and employees	(7)	(10)
Pension costs—defined contribution plans	(34)	(32)
Pension costs—defined benefit plans	(66)	(92)
Other postemployment benefits	(4)	2
Total	**(1,960)**	**(1,917)**

Thereof the amount of CHF 30 million (2006: CHF 100 million) is reported under discontinued operations.

32. Related-party transactions

Clariant maintains business relationships with related parties. One group consists of the associates, where the most important ones are described in note 6. The most important business with these companies is the purchase of services by Clariant (e.g., energy and rental of land and buildings) in Germany. In addition to this, Clariant exchanges services and goods with other parties which are associates (.e.g., in which Clariant holds a stake of between 20% and 50%).

The second group of related parties is key management comprising the Board of Directors (nonexecutive members) and the Board of Management. The information required by Art. 663b bis of the Swiss Code of Obligations regarding the emoluments for the members of the Board of Directors and the Board of Management is disclosed in the Statutory Accounts of Clariant Ltd on pages 160 and 161 of this report (not based on IFRS valuations). More information on the relationship with the Board of Directors is given in the chapter Corporate governance (nonaudited).

The third group of related parties are the pension plans of major subsidiaries. Clariant provides services to its pension plans in Switzerland, the United Kingdom and the United States. These services comprise mainly administrative and trustee services. The total cost of these services is CHF 1 million (2006: CHF 1 million), of which approximately half is charged back to the pension plans. The number of full-time employees corresponding to these are approximately 6 (2006: 6).

CHF mn		
Transactions with associates	*2007*	*2006*
Income from the sale of goods to related parties	37	41
Income from the rendering of services to related parties	4	7
Expenses from the purchase of goods from related parties	(27)	(8)
Expenses from services rendered by related parties	(255)	(272)
Payables and receivables with associates	*12/31/2007*	*12/31/2006*
Receivables from related parties	8	8
Payables to related parties	45	19
Transactions with key management	*2007*	*2006*
Salaries and other short-term benefits	6	8
Termination benefits	4	--
Postemployment benefits	1	1
Share-based payments	1	1
Total	**12**	**10**
Number of granted shares for the reporting period	130,334	117,419

There are no outstanding loans by the Group to any members of the Board of Directors or Board of Management.

33. Commitments and contingencies

Leasing commitments. The Group leases various land, buildings, machinery and equipment, furniture and vehicles under fixed-term agreements. The leases have varying terms, escalation clauses and renewal rights.

Commitments arising from fixed-term operating leases mainly concern buildings in Switzerland and Germany. The most important partners for operating leases of buildings in Germany are the Infraserv companies.

CHF mn	12/31/2007	12/31/2006
2007		70
2008	66	54
2009	48	39
2010	24	21
2011	16	13
2012	13	
Thereafter	37	20
Total	**204**	**217**
Guarantees in favor of third parties	63	53

Expenses for operating leases were CHF 86 million 2007 and CHF 87 million in 2006.

Purchase commitments. In the regular course of business, Clariant enters into relationships with suppliers whereby the Group commits itself to purchase certain minimum quantities of materials in order to benefit from better pricing conditions. These commitments are not in excess of current market prices and reflect normal business operations. At present, the purchase commitments on such contracts amount to about CHF 106 million (2006: CHF 176 million).

Contingencies. Clariant operates in countries where political, economic, social, legal and regulatory developments can have an impact on the operational activities. The effects of such risks on the Company's results, which arise during the normal course of business, are not foreseeable and are therefore not included in the accompanying financial statements.

In 2006, Clariant sold its Pharmaceutical Fine Chemicals business to Archimica, a company pertaining to Towerbrook Capital Partners. On October 25, 2007, Archimica Group Holdings B.V. filed a request for arbitration against Clariant before the Zurich Chamber of Commerce, raising various claims under the purchase agreement in an amount of EUR 42 million. Clariant fully contests such claims. Based on the situation no liability has been booked for these claims.

In the ordinary course of business, Clariant is involved in lawsuits, claims, investigations and proceedings, including product liability, intellectual property, commercial, environmental and health and safety matters. Although the outcome of any legal proceedings can not be predicted with certainty, management is of the opinion that apart from the case mentioned above there are no such matters pending which would be likely to have any material adverse effect in relation to its business, financial position or results of operations.

Environmental risk. Clariant is exposed to environmental liabilities and risks relating to its past operations, principally in respect of remediation costs. Provisions for nonrecurring remediation costs are made when there is a legal or constructive obligation and the cost can be reliably estimated. It is difficult to estimate the action required by Clariant in the future to correct the effects on the environment of prior disposal or release of chemical substances by Clariant or other parties, and the associated costs, pursuant to environmental laws and regulations. The material components of the environmental provisions consist of costs to fully clean and refurbish contaminated sites and to treat and contain contamination at sites where the environmental exposure is less severe.

The Group's future remediation expenses are affected by a number of uncertainties which include, but are not limited to, the method and extent of remediation and the percentage of material attributable to Clariant at the remediation sites relative to that attributable to other parties. The Group permanently monitors the various sites identified at risk for environmental exposure. Clariant believes that its provisions are adequate based upon currently available information; however given the inherent difficulties in estimating liabilities in this area, there is no guarantee that additional costs will not be incurred.

34. Exchange rates of principal currencies

Rates used to translate the consolidated balance sheets (closing rate):

	12/31/2007	*12/31/2006*
1 USD	1.13	1.22
1 GBP	2.25	2.39
100 JPY	1.01	1.02
1 EUR	1.66	1.61

Average sales-weighted rates used to translate the consolidated income statements and consolidated statements of cash flows:

	2007	*2006*
1 USD	1.20	1.26
1 GBP	2.40	2.31
100 JPY	1.02	1.08
1 EUR	1.64	1.57

APPENDIX C

Comparison of IFRS and US GAAP

IFRS 2009 chapter	Topic	US GAAP treatment	IFRS treatment
1	Introduction to International Financial Reporting Standards	No comprehensive guide to statement presentation is offered; however, certain standards require specific presentation of certain items. Publicly traded companies subject to SEC rules and regulations are required to present specific line items in accordance with the detailed requirements in Regulation S-X; GAAP departures when necessary are audit reporting issue.	Comprehensive guidance on presentation of financial statements provided; minimum line items identified for all financial statements (but less prescriptive than the requirements in SEC's Regulation S-X); fair presentation goal may necessitate IFRS departures.
		FASB's *Conceptual Framework* is similar to IASB's *Framework for the Preparation and Presentation of Financial Statements*; convergence with IFRS is promised.	FASB's *Conceptual Framework* is similar to IASB's *Framework for the Preparation and Presentation of Financial Statements*; latter is less detailed; convergence with US GAAP expected to occur.
		Comparative financials urged, but not required (required for SEC filings); greater specificity as to location of disclosures in body of statements or in notes.	Comparative financials (one year at a minimum) are required, including footnote data; disclosure can often be optional in financials or in notes.
		Formal GAAP hierarchy defined under US auditing literature (to be superseded shortly by FASB Codification).	No hierarchy established beyond IFRS, but implied by language of IAS 8.
		Justification for GAAP departure found in auditing literature (GAAS Rule 203) but very rarely invoked (may be eliminated under proposed new GAAP hierarchy, however).	"True and fair" override of IFRS permitted in "extremely rare" circumstances to achieve a fair presentation; adequate disclosures required.
2	Statement of Financial Position	Limited guidance on offsetting of assets and liabilities; classified balance sheet not required, but definition of current/ noncurrent differs from IFRS somewhat.	Specific guidance on offsetting of assets and liabilities; classified statement of financial position required (except when a liquidity presentation is used), some difference from GAAP definitions of current/noncurrent.
			Liquidity presentation permitted in lieu of current/noncurrent classification under limited circumstances.
		Debt being refinanced classified as noncurrent if refinancing is completed before the date of issuance of the financial statements.	Debt being refinanced classified as noncurrent if refinancing completed before the end of the reporting period.
		An entity elect to offset fair value amounts for certain assets and liabilities subject to master netting agreements (e.g., financial instruments).	Some offsetting of assets and liabilities with different counterparties permitted, for example, when legal provision exists (e.g., supplier's warranty agreement), or required, when offset criteria are met (financial instruments).

IFRS 2009 chapter	Topic	US GAAP treatment	IFRS treatment
3	Statements of Income, Comprehensive Income, and Changes in Equity	Expenses classified according to function (e.g., cost of sales, selling and administrative) only.	Expenses classified according to function (e.g., cost of sales, selling and administrative) or by nature (e.g., salaries, changes in inventories of finished goods and work in progress).
		IFRS 5 converged with SFAS 144 except for limited differences in scope, definition, measurement on initial classification (exchange differences recognized in equity are included in the carrying amount of the asset or disposal group under US GAAP but not under IFRS 5), subsequent measurement, and presentation of a discontinued operation.	Some differences in scope of IFRS 5 and SFAS 144 arise from other differences between IFRS and US GAAP. Subsequent measurement of a discontinued operation converged on the principles, but some differences arise from different requirements on reversals of previous impairments.
		Restructuring costs recognized when there is little discretion to avoid costs; most costs recognized when later incurred.	Restructuring costs recognized when announced or commenced, which is earlier than under US GAAP.
		Display of comprehensive income is mandatory, but three alternative modes of presentation are permitted (e.g., presentation of other comprehensive items directly in equity is permitted.)	Separate statement of comprehensive income is required, but two alternatives are permitted: presentation of all components of "profit or loss" and "other comprehensive income" in a single statement, or alternatively, in a two-statement format, with separate income statement and statement of comprehensive income; separate statement of changes in equity, is required (IAS 1).
		Other comprehensive income items can be presented in separate statement, combined with income statement, or in changes in stockholders' equity statement.	Other comprehensive income items are presented in separate statement of comprehensive income, and cannot be relegated to statement of changes in equity.
		Estimated operating results of discontinuing operation are included in the measurement for the expected gain or loss on disposal; timing of segregation of discontinuing operations from continuing operations may differ from that under IFRS; direct continuing cash flows or involvement in operations preclude discontinuing operations display.	Actual operating results of a discontinuing operation are reported as incurred; timing of recognition of gain or loss in discontinuance and income or loss from activities of the discontinuing operation may differ from US GAAP.
		Broader definition of discontinued operations than under IFRS, either a reportable business or geographical segment, or reporting unit, subsidiary, or asset group.	More general definition of discontinued operations as being a major line of business or geographical area of operations or major component thereof.

IFRS 2009 chapter	Topic	US GAAP treatment	IFRS treatment
3	Statements of Income, Comprehensive Income, and Changes in Equity	Restructuring costs recognized when there is little discretion to avoid costs; most costs recognized when later incurred.	Restructuring costs recognized when announced or commenced, which is earlier than under US GAAP.
		Extraordinary items classification (net-of-tax) permitted under limited circumstances will be revised to mirror IFRS.	Extraordinary item classification no longer permitted, but unusual items can be segregated.
4	Statement of Cash Flows	Interest paid and received and dividends received are classified as operating cash flows; dividends paid are classified as financing cash flows.	Choice allowed in classifying 1. Dividends and interest paid as operating or financing cash flows; or 2. Interest or dividends received as operating, investing, or financing cash flows.
		Overdrafts cannot be included in cash (show as financing source of cash).	Overdrafts can be included in cash under defined conditions.
		Separate disclosure of cash flows relating to discontinued operations is not required.	Separate disclosure of cash flows relating to discontinued operation is required either in the statement or in the notes.
		Presentation of cash flow per share is prohibited.	Presentation of cash flow per share is not prohibited.
5	Cash, Receivables, and Financial Instruments	No specific guidance offered under US GAAP or IFRS.	No specific guidance offered under either set of standards.
		Derecognition of financial assets based on loss of control, which requires isolation from transferor, transferee ability to pledge or sell, and absence of repurchase obligation by transferor.	Derecognition of financial assets based primarily on risks and rewards criterion; also, on loss of control, as a secondary test.
		Basis adjustment arising from firm commitments and forecasted transactions not in initial measurement of hedged item; hedging gains and losses on cash flow hedges recorded in other comprehensive income when they occur, reclassified to profit or loss when hedged item affects profit or loss.	Hedging gains and losses from cash flow hedges of firm commitments and of forecasted transactions can be included as part of the initial measurement of the cost basis of the related hedged item (basis adjustment).
		Hedging for part of term of hedged item not permitted.	Hedging for part of term of hedged item permitted if effectiveness can be shown.
		Hedging of portion of cash flows of hedged item not permitted.	Hedging of portion of cash flows of hedged item is permitted.
		Hedging effectiveness can be assumed in limited circumstances (using "shortcut method").	Hedging effectiveness must be demonstrable.
		Fair value option has been adopted, mirroring IFRS.	Option to designate any financial asset or liability for measurement at fair value through profit or loss.

IFRS 2009 chapter	Topic	US GAAP treatment	IFRS treatment
5	Cash, Receivables, and Financial Instruments	"Macrohedging" not permitted.	"Macrohedging" is permitted.
		Reclassifications to "trading" category required under certain conditions, but reclassification from trading not permitted.	Disclosure requirement applicable to all financial instruments, including those held by financial institutions, set forth in IFRS 7; limited reclassifications from treading category permitted.
		Nonderivative instruments can be used to hedge currency risk associated with net investment in foreign entity or a fair value hedge of unrecognized firm commitment.	Nonderivative instruments can be used to hedge foreign currency risk.
6	Inventory	Recognition in interim periods of inventory losses from market declines that reasonably can be expected to be restored in the fiscal year not required.	Recognition in interim periods of inventory losses from market declines that reasonably can be expected to be restored in the fiscal year is required; guidance in the areas of disclosure and accounting for inventories of service providers offered.
		Allowable methods include FIFO, average cost, and LIFO.	LIFO costing prohibited under IFRS.
		Presentation at lower of cost or market required.	Presentation at lower of cost or net realizable value required.
		Recent rule change so that certain costs (idle capacity, spoilage) cannot be added to overhead charge in inventory cost, conforming to IFRS rule.	Certain costs (idle capacity, spoilage) cannot be added to overhead charge in inventory cost.
		Lower of cost or market adjustments cannot be reversed.	Lower of cost or market adjustments must be reversed under defined conditions.
		Only in rare instances (mining of gold, etc.) are presentation at fair value in excess of cost permitted.	Certain defined situations, including agricultural products, permit reporting at fair value in excess of actual cost.
7	Revenue Recognition, Including Construction Contracts	No comprehensive standard on revenue recognition in general, but SEC requirements offer guidance.	Comprehensive standard on revenue recognition IAS 18 exists.
		Revenue is recognized when it is (1) earned and (2) either realized or realizable (SFAC 5).	Revenue is recognized when (1) it is probable that future economic benefits will flow to the entity and (2) these benefits can be measured reliably (IAS 18).
		Revenue recognition deferred on delivered part of multi-element contract if refund would be triggered by failure to deliver remaining elements.	Revenue recognized on delivered part of multielement contract even if refund triggered by failure to deliver remaining elements, if delivery is probable.
		Use of completed contract method for construction projects under certain circumstances is required; revenue-cost and gross-profit approaches to percentage-of-completion both allowed.	If percentage cannot be reliably estimated, use of cost recovery method required; "revenue-cost" approach to percentage of completion mandatory for construction projects.
		Estimated 200-plus individual revenue recognition provisions offered for specific industries or arrangements.	Specific guidance on revenue recognition principles for selected industries.

IFRS 2009 chapter	Topic	US GAAP treatment	IFRS treatment
7	Revenue Recognition, Including Construction Contracts	Joint project with IASB may result in completely new conceptual foundation for revenue recognition based on "asset and liability recognition" approach.	Joint project with FASB may result in completely new conceptual foundation for revenue recognition based on "asset and liability recognition" approach.
8	Property, Plant, and Equipment	Basis of measurement at cost; revaluations are prohibited	Basis of measurement is either cost or revalued amount. Revalued amount is fair value at date of revaluation less accumulated depreciation and impairment losses.
		Costs of major overhauls generally expensed as incurred (other treatments allowed).	Costs of major overhauls generally added to asset cost.
		Component depreciation for components of an asset with differing patterns of benefits is permitted but not required.	Component depreciation for components of an asset with differing patterns of benefits is required.
		Impairment suggested when book value exceeds gross expected future cash flows; second step to measure impairment uses discounted present value of cash flows.	Impairment suggested when the asset's book value exceeds its recoverable amount (greater of value in use discounted cash flows and fair value less cost to sell).
		Impairments recognized in current income.	If cost method used, impairments are recognized in profit or loss; if revaluation employed, impairment treated as reversal of revaluation unless it exceeds former write-up, in which case excess impairment taken to current profit or loss.
		Impairments once recognized cannot be reversed.	Impairments can be reversed under defined conditions.
		Investment property must be carried at depreciated cost.	Investment property can be carried at depreciated cost or fair value.
		Decommissioning (asset retirement) obligations not recomputed after initial computation, generally.	Decommissioning (asset retirement) obligations recomputed at current risk-adjusted rate at the end of each reporting date.
		Mandatory capitalization of construction period interest costs, only interest (i.e., no ancillary) costs subject to capitalization.	Mandatory capitalization of construction period interest costs; ancillary costs also can be capitalized.
9	Intangible Assets	Development costs are expensed (except for certain Web site development and internally generated software costs); related cash flows reported in "operating" section.	Development costs are capitalized if specific criteria are met and amortized; cash flows reported as "investing" activity.
		Cost basis required for intangibles.	Revaluation of intangibles traded in active markets permitted.
		Impairment implied when book value is greater than undiscounted cash flows to be derived from use of asset.	Impairment implied when book value is greater than recoverable amount (higher of value in use or fair value less costs to sell).
		Measurement of impairment conducted with reference to fair value (often operationalized using discounted cash flows).	Measurement of impairment conducted with reference to higher of value in use or fair value less costs to sell.

IFRS 2009 chapter	Topic	US GAAP treatment	IFRS treatment
9	Intangible Assets	Measurement of goodwill impairment uses 2-step approach, requires first comparing fair value of reporting unit to its carrying amount (book value including goodwill), then comparing implied goodwill to its carrying value; measured at level of reporting unit (business segment or one level below).	Measurement of goodwill impairments similar to other long-lived assets, requires only single-step computation; measured at lowest level goodwill can be assigned (cash-generating unit).
		No reversals of previously recognized impairments.	Impairments can be reversed, under defined conditions, except for goodwill.
10	Interests in Financial Instruments, Associates, Joint Ventures, and Investment Property	Derecognition of financial assets when transferor has surrendered control over the assets (legal isolation is required); partial derecognition prohibited; Qualifying SPEs permitted.	Derecognition of financial assets based on risks-and-rewards and control analyses; partial derecognition permitted if specific criteria are met; no concept of QSPE exists under IFRS.
		Option to designate any financial asset or financial liability to be measured at fair value through profit or loss allowed at initial recognition as well as certain subsequent dates; criteria in IAS 39 do not apply.	Option to designate any financial asset or financial liability to be measured at fair value through profit or loss allowed at initial recognition if one of three criteria in IAS 39 is met.
		Exit price is presumptively fair value of debt and equity securities at initial recognition, with certain exceptions.	Entry price is presumptively fair value of debt and equity instruments at initial recognition unless fair value must be determined using other observable market transactions or valuation techniques.
		Impairment of debt and equity securities is only recognized when the decline in fair value is considered other-than-temporary.	Impairment of debt and equity instruments is recognized when "loss events" provide objective evidence of impairment.
		Reversals of impairment losses prohibited for HTM and AFS securities. Reversals of impairment losses on loans recognized in income.	Reversals of impairment losses required for loans and receivables, HTM and AFS debt instruments if specific criteria are met.
		If held-to-maturity securities are sold, use of this category is prohibited thereafter.	If held-to-maturity securities are sold, use of this category is prohibited for next two years.
		Investments in debt and equity securities valued at cost less "other-than-temporary" impairments, if any.	Investments in debt and equity instruments valued at fair value or at cost, if fair value cannot be reliably measurable.
		Investments in unlisted securities valued at cost.	Investments in unlisted securities can be valued at fair value, if reliable measure available.
		Equity-method investments held for sale are measured at the lower of its fair value less cost to sell or carrying amount as of the date the investment is classified as held for sale.	Investor applies the equity method of accounting until significant influence is lost.

IFRS 2009 chapter	Topic	US GAAP treatment	IFRS treatment
10	Interests in Financial Instruments, Associates, Joint Ventures, and Investment Property	Investor should continue to recognize losses in excess of an investor's interest.	Investor should generally discontinue recognizing losses in excess of an investor's interest as long as the investor does not have legal or constructive obligation or made payments on behalf of the associate.
		Joint ventures generally accounted for by equity method, but select industries (e.g., construction) use proportional consolidation.	Joint ventures accounted for by equity method or proportional consolidation.
		No need to conform investor and investee accounting policies.	Need to conform investor and investee accounting policies.
		Investment property must be accounted for by cost (and depreciation) method.	Investment property can be accounted for by cost (and depreciation) method, or by fair value method with changes taken to income.
11	Business Combinations and Consolidated Financial Statements	Assets and liabilities arising from contingencies are recognized at acquisition at fair value if arise from *contractual contingencies*; all other contingencies (*noncontractual contingencies*) recognized if it is more likely than not that contingency gives rise to an asset or a liability.	Acquirer is required to recognize a contingent liability assumed in a business combination if it is a present obligation that arises from past events and its fair value can be measured reliably.
		Noncontrolling interest measured at fair value.	Noncontrolling interest measured either: (1) at fair value, or (2) as a proportionate share of identifiable net assets acquired; choice made on an acquisition-by-acquisition basis.
		Fair value is defined as the price that would be received to sell an asset or paid to transfer a liability in an orderly transaction between market participants at the measurement date (SFAS 157).	Fair value is defined as the amount for which an asset could be exchanged, or a liability settled, between knowledgeable, willing parties in an arm's-length transaction (IFRS 3).
		Acquirer (lessor) measures the acquisition-date fair value of as asset subject to an operating lease separately from the lease contract and recognizes a separate asset or liability if the terms of an operating lease are favorable or unfavorable compared with market terms.	Acquirer (lessor) is not required to recognize a separate asset or liability if the terms of an operating lease are favorable or unfavorable compared with market terms.
		Goodwill not amortized, tested for impairment.	Similar to US GAAP, but different impairment testing procedures.
		Consolidation rules for voting interests generally based on majority voting rights; for variable interest entities (VIE) rules are based on risks and rewards model.	Consolidation rules based on control criterion in IAS 27 (based on governance and risks and benefits); special consolidation requirements apply to special-purpose entities (SPEs).

IFRS 2009 chapter	Topic	US GAAP treatment	IFRS treatment
11	Business Combinations and Consolidated Financial Statements	"Qualifying" SPEs to be consolidated if QSPE exceptions not satisfied.	Special-purpose entities to be consolidated if controlled (generally the same approach as for commercial entities).
		Potential voting rights are generally not considered when determining whether control is present.	Potential voting rights that are currently exercisable must be considered when determining whether control is present.
		Not necessary to control parent and subsidiary accounting policies (if in accordance with US GAAP).	Need to conform parent and subsidiary accounting policies.
		Reporting date difference should not be more than three months (adjustment needed for any significant intervening transactions).	Reporting date difference cannot be more than three months (adjustment needed for any significant intervening transactions)
12	Current Liabilities, Provisions, Contingencies, and Events After the Reporting Period	Different recognition threshold for timing of recognition of liabilities associated with a restructuring than under IFRS; recognize under GAAP only if event occurs making this a present obligation.	A variety of recognition criteria for different items that may enter into the measurement of a provision are identified, missing under US GAAP; recognize when formal plan is announced.
		Short-term borrowings refinanced before statement issuance date can often be shown as noncurrent.	Short-term borrowings refinanced before the end of the reporting period can be shown as noncurrent, but if later (before issuance of financials) only disclosure may be affected).
		Provisions (estimated liabilities) measured by reference to low end of range of amounts needed to settle, sometimes but not always discounted to present value.	Provisions measured by reference to best estimate to settle, discounted to present value.
		Fair value of guarantee obligations must be recognized apart from contingent aspect.	Fair value of guarantee obligations must be recognized apart from contingent aspect.
		Specific rules for certain provisions (e.g., for environmental liabilities).	Only general guidance provided under IFRS.
		Contingent gains are not recognized.	IFRS provides for some recognition of contingent gains, if probable of realization.
13	Financial Instruments—Long-Term Debt	Convertible debt classified as liability.	Convertible debt assigned to both debt and equity, based on fair values of liability portion and residual amount allocated to equity.
		Noncurrent presentation of defaulted debt if waiver granted before statement issuance date.	Noncurrent presentation of defaulted debt if waiver granted before the end of the reporting period only.

IFRS 2009 chapter	Topic	US GAAP treatment	IFRS treatment
13	Financial Instruments—Long-Term Debt	Entities should reassess at the end of each reporting period whether an embedded derivative should be separated.	Entities should reassess at the end of each reporting period whether an embedded derivative should be separated only if there is a change in the terms that significantly modifies the cash flows.
14	Leases	The classification of a lease depends whether the lease meets certain specific criteria.	The classification of a lease depends on the substance of the lease transaction.
		Capital lease accounting is required if one of four defined conditions are met; otherwise, operating lease.	Finance lease treatment if risks and rewards are transferred to lessee; also if property is special purpose for lessee use.
		Gain or loss recognized on sale-leasebacks depends on the seller's retained interest in the asset.	Deferral (and amortization) of gain or loss on sale/leasebacks classified as finance lease is permitted.
		Leases of land and buildings are accounted for as a single unit unless land represents more than 25% value of the property.	Separation of land and building components of lease is now mandatory unless the land element is not material.
		Third-party guarantees cannot be included in minimum lease payments to determine whether capital lease criteria are met.	Third-party guarantees must be included in minimum lease payments to determine whether capital lease criteria are met.
		Lessors must use implicit rate and lessees generally would use incremental borrowing rate to calculate present value of minimum lease payments.	Generally, present value of minimum lease payments computed using implicit rate.
		Output contracts are leases.	Output contracts are not leases.
		Leasehold interest in land accounted for as prepayment.	Leasehold interest in land can be accounted for as investment property, valued at fair value with changes in current earnings; or else as prepayment.
		Lease obligations disclosures more extensive than under IFRS.	Lease obligations disclosures less extensive than under US GAAP.
15	Income Taxes	Deferred tax assets and liabilities are classified as current or noncurrent based on related asset or liability.	Deferred tax assets and liabilities are always noncurrent.
		Benefit of uncertain tax positions can only be recognized to the extent that there is at least a 50% likelihood of being sustained on exam.	No specific guidance on uncertain tax positions (apply general approach for contingent losses); based on management expectations.
		Recognize effect of rate changes when enacted.	Recognize effects of rate changes when "substantively enacted" which may precede US GAAP recognition.
		Prohibits recognition of effects of temporary differences related to 1. Foreign currency nonmonetary assets when the reporting currency is the functional currency, and 2. Intercompany transfers of inventory or other assets remaining within the company.	

IFRS 2009 chapter	Topic	US GAAP treatment	IFRS treatment
15	Income Taxes	Deferred tax is recognized on all undistributed earnings of domestic subsidiaries and joint ventures (since 1992); exceptions exist on undistributed earnings of foreign subsidiaries and corporate joint ventures.	Deferred tax is recognized on undistributed earnings of any form of the investee, except when (1) investor is able to control the timing and reversal of temporary differences, (2) it is probable that temporary differences will not reverse.
		Deferred tax on undistributed earnings measured using the higher of the distributed and undistributed profit rates.	Deferred tax on undistributed earnings measured using the rate applicable to undistributed profits.
		Several specific exemptions to general requirement to provide deferred tax on all temporary differences are set forth.	No exceptions to general principle that all temporary differences in carrying amount of assets and liabilities require deferred taxes.
		Recognize deferred tax asset in full and then reduce by a valuation allowance for the nonprobable portion.	Recognize deferred tax asset when realization is probable, which means "more likely than not" per IFRS 3.
		Rate reconciliation based on domestic federal rate times pretax profit from continuing operations only.	Rate reconciliation based on applicable rates times accounting profit.
		Tax effect of intragroup transactions recognized at seller entity's tax rate.	Tax effect of intragroup transactions recognized at buyer entity's tax rate.
16	Employee Benefits	Defined benefit plans; use of projected unit credit method required to match expense to periods of service; smoothing is accomplished by deferred recognition of actuarial gains and losses, amortization of prior service costs, et al.	Methodology very similar to that under US GAAP, with deferred recognition of actuarial gains or losses. However, past service costs on plan adoption or amendment are recognized immediately, not deferred.
		Past service costs amortized over service period or life expectancy of workers.	Past service costs expensed immediately.
		Actuarial gains and losses cannot be recognized in equity; are to be deferred and amortized to pension expense over expected term of plan participants to the extent that defined "corridor" is exceeded.	Actuarial gains and losses optionally can be recognized in equity under amendment to IAS 19 effective in 2006; if in earnings, either immediate recognition or amortization similar to US GAAP is permissible.
		Recognition of a minimum liability on the balance sheet to at least the unfunded accumulated pension benefit obligation.	No minimum liability to be reported in the statement of financial position.
		No limitation on recognition of pension assets.	Limitation on recognition of pension assets.
		Curtailment gains recognized only when employees terminate or plan suspension is adopted, computed differently than under IFRS.	Curtailment gains or losses recognized when announced; computed differently than US GAAP.
		Anticipating changes in the law that would affect variables such as state medical or social security benefits expressly prohibited.	Anticipate changes in future postemployment benefits based on its expectations in the law.

IFRS 2009 chapter	Topic	US GAAP treatment	IFRS treatment
16	Employee Benefits	Termination benefits expensed when employees accept and amount can be estimated, recognize contractual benefits when it is probable that employees will accept.	Termination benefits expensed when employer is committed to pay these.
17	Shareholders' Equity	Share-based payment awards granted by a subsidiary to its employees and to be settled by parent's equity instruments are classified as equity in the subsidiary's separate financial statements.	Share-based payment awards granted by a subsidiary to its employees and to be settled by parent's equity instruments are classified as liabilities in the subsidiary's separate financial statements.
		Accounting policy choice permitted for share-based payments with graded vesting features and with a service condition only: (1) amortize charges on a straight basis over the longest vesting period; or (2) on accelerated basis (as IFRS 2).	Recognition of charges for share-based payments with graded vesting features on an accelerated basis, reflecting vesting as it occurs.
		Accounting policy choice allowed for measurement of share-based payments with graded vesting features as either a single award (single grant-date fair value for the award); or, in substance, as multiple awards (as IFRS 2).	Measurement of charges for share-based payments with graded vesting features as, in substance, multiple awards, with a separate grant-date fair value for each vesting portion calculated.
		Option to capitalize compensation cost permitted based on other requirements under US GAAP (may differ from IFRS).	Option to capitalize compensation cost permitted subject to other requirements of IFRS (may differ from US GAAP).
		Fair value measurement of goods and services acquired for share from nonemployees using earlier of counterparty's commitment to perform or actual performance date.	Fair value measurement of goods and services acquired for share is the date the entity obtains the goods or the date counterparty renders service.
		Income tax benefits related to share-based payment (measured by spread between current fair value and exercise price) credited to equity; any payroll taxes recognized in expense at time of exercise.	Tax benefits related to share-based payments credited to equity only if in excess of compensation expense; any payroll taxes recognized in expense over same period as recognition of option plan cost (vesting period).
		Tax benefits related to share-based payments based on GAAP expense, later adjusted when actual tax effects are realized.	Tax benefits related to share-based payments based on expected applicable tax deduction.
		Modifications of awards require new measurement based on date of modification.	Modifications do not trigger new measurement of fair value.
18	Earnings Per Share	Very similar to IFRS, but with more detailed guidance on calculations.	Similar to US GAAP.
		Two-class method to participating securities applies irrespective of whether they are debt or equity instruments.	Two-class method to participating securities applies only to equity instruments; not required for debt instruments.
		Report basic and diluted EPS from continuing operations, discontinued operations, extraordinary items, cumulative effect of change in accounting policy, and net income.	Report basic and diluted EPS from continuing operations and net profit or loss share.

IFRS 2009 chapter	Topic	US GAAP treatment	IFRS treatment
18	Earnings Per Share	EPS data presented in the income statement.	EPS data presented in the statement of comprehensive income, unless separate income statement is prepared.
		For interim reporting, average the interim periods' incremental shares to compute EPS.	For interim reporting, use treasury stock method on year-to-date stock results, unlike US GAAP approach; calculation of year-to-date EPS (versus previously reported interim data) varies from US GAAP.
19	Interim Financial Reporting	Basic principle is that interim period is integral to full year, but actual requirements depart from this in many instances.	Basic principle is that interim period is discrete period, but actual requirements depart from this in many instances.
		Some timing differences in recognition of interim revenues and expenses vs. IFRS.	Some timing differences in recognition of interim revenues and expenses vs. US GAAP.
20	Segment Reporting	Noncurrent assets attributable to segments exclude intangible assets.	Noncurrent assets attributable to segments include intangible assets.
		No requirement for liabilities disclosure by segments.	Liabilities segment disclosure are required if such a measure is provided to the chief operating decision maker.
		Operating segments are identified based on products and services; no segment result definition given.	Operating segments are identified based on the core principle in IFRS 8; segment results defined; entity-wide and some geographic analyses are also required.
21	Changes in Accounting Policies and Estimates, and Corrections of Errors	Retrospective restatement for corrections of errors is required.	Retrospective restatement for corrections of errors is required, unless impracticable.
		Only entities subject to SEC rules and regulations are required to disclose the effect of new pronouncements not yet effective.	All entities are required to disclose the effect of new IFRS in issue but not yet effective.
22	Foreign Currency	Selection of functional currency is open to judgment, but in practice there is a greater emphasis on cash flows than on currency that influences pricing of output.	In selecting functional currency greater emphasis is given to currency of economy that influences and determines sales prices for goods and services.
		Equity accounts are translated at historical rates.	Translation of equity accounts not specified under IFRS.
		In highly inflationary economy (having cumulative three year price change of 100%), parent's currency (US dollar) must be used as functional currency.	In hyperinflationary economy, entity cannot avoid restatement under IAS 29 by adopting a stable currency (such as currency of its parent) as its functional currency.
		If the functional currency is the currency of a hyperinflationary economy, an entity must adopt a stable currency (such as the functional currency of its parent) as its functional currency.	If the functional currency is the currency of a hyperinflationary economy, the financial statements of subsidiaries must be adjusted to reflect changes in general price levels before translation.

IFRS 2009 chapter	Topic	US GAAP treatment	IFRS treatment
22	Foreign Currency	Highly inflationary economy is one that has cumulative inflation of approximately 100% or more over a 3-year period.	Hyperinflation is indicated by characteristics of the economic environment of a country, which include the general population's attitude towards the local currency, prices linked to a price index, and the cumulative inflation rate over three years is approaching or exceeds 100%.
23	Related-Party Disclosures	Similar to IFRS, but there is no requirements for the disclosures to be grouped into categories of related parties; disclosures of relationships in absence of transactions are often missing.	Comprehensive disclosures required under IFRS for each category of related party relationship, including those about control relationships even in the absence of actual transactions.
24	Specialized Industry Accounting	No primary guidance for government grants, agriculture, mineral exploration. Specialized guidance on inventories related to the motion picture, software, and agricultural industries, and others, found in "secondary" GAAP sources such as AICPA Guides, SOP, etc.	Guidance provided for government grants, agriculture, reporting by banks, insurance contracts, mineral exploration, and benefit plans. No guidance offered on range of industries covered by AICPA's Audit and Accounting Guides and Statements of Position; there is no "secondary" source for IFRS guidance.
25	Inflation and Hyperinflation	Does not generally permit inflation-adjusted financial statements; SEC rules allow foreign issuers reporting under IFRS (IAS 21, 29) to omit disclosure of any differences that would have resulted from application of SFAS 52.	In hyperinflationary economy, financials must be presented based on end of the reporting period date measuring unit, with comparative (prior period) statements restated on same basis.
26	Government Grants	No rules promulgated under US GAAP, but IFRS-like approach would be acceptable.	Government grants received as compensation for expenses already incurred are recognized as income once conditions are met; revenue-based grants deferred and matched as expense incurred; capital grants amortized as depreciation recognized.